A Standard History

of

Kansas and Kansans

—

WRITTEN AND COMPILED BY

WILLIAM E. CONNELLEY

Secretary of the Kansas State Historical Society, Topeka

—

ILLUSTRATED

—

VOLUME IV

—

LEWIS PUBLISHING COMPANY

CHICAGO   NEW YORK

1918

Archie W Baird

ARCHIE MARKLAND BAIRD. One of the additions to the manufacturing interests of Topeka, Archie Markland Baird has for many years been known in railroad circles of the state, and has been connected with numerous movements national in their character. His present business is the manufacture of pneumatic labor-saving devices. His knowledge of the business, his wide connections, and his executive capacity have brought his enterprise to a foremost and commanding position.

Mr. Baird was born at Kilmarnock, near Glasgow, Scotland, in 1857, and is a son of William and Janet (Markland) Baird, and a grandson of Archibald Baird, also a native of that place. Archibald Baird had a family of twelve sons and one daughter, all of whom grew to maturity, and it is a remarkable fact that all of these sons learned the blacksmith trade from their father, and some of them later came to the United States and became officials in the mechanical departments of several railroads. The children of Archibald Baird were: Andrew I., David, John, William, Thomas, Hugh, James, Elisha, Robert, Adam, Joseph and Andrew II, and one daughter, Jean. Of these, Andrew I died in young manhood; David came to America in 1857, took employment with the New York & New Haven Railroad at Hartford, Connecticut, and was foreman of the blacksmith shops for forty-five years; John was employed by the same railroad company; Thomas remained in Scotland and became a prominent manufacturer of cotton spindles; and Andrew II became general foreman of the Illinois Central Railroad shops and served that company for forty-five years.

William Baird, the father of Archie M. Baird, was born in 1810, and when a young man married Janet Markland, of Stewarton, near Kilmarnock, Scotland. They had five children born to them: Janey, Belle, Sarah, Jessie and Archie, of whom the two latter survive, Jessie now being the wife of James Thompson, who was for thirty years master mechanic of the Chicago & Northwestern Railroad.

Archie Baird was eight years old when brought to the United States, the family settling at Chicago, Illinois, where the youth attended school until he was fourteen. He was more interested in mechanical things than in learning facts from books, and his father, recognizing this fact, apprenticed him to become a patternmaker, but a little later the youth decided to become a boilermaker and sheet iron worker and followed that trade for about six years. He was then offered a position at the Green Point Navy Yard, but a little later was called to Vincennes, Indiana, by the Ohio & Mississippi Railroad, and, although but nineteen years old, accepted a big contract to reconstruct the boiler equipment of the road so as to be suitable for a standard gauge road. This line, having been reduced from a broad gauge of 60 inches to the standard gauge of 56½ inches, began operations under the new conditions after a period of six months. Mr. Baird states that on one Sabbath day 480 miles of the road was changed in this way.

Immediately after the completion of this contract, Mr. Baird was called to Cedar Rapids, Iowa, by the Burlington, Cedar Rapids & Northern Railroad to take charge of the new and expensive boiler shops of the company, and held this position for four years. In 1882 Mr. Baird went to the Wabash Railroad to take charge of the office of superintendent of the boiler shops, and after holding this post for two years was offered and accepted the position of assistant to J. W. Williams, who had been made superintendent of the Union Iron and Steel Mills, at Chicago. This large plant was equipped for wire, plate, rails, merchant bars, and a full line of blast furnaces in which ore was melted and never reheated until it came out as railroad steel. This is what is known as direct process. There was also the very latest machinery which disposed of the hand hook process, all being handled by hydraulics and live rollers. Mr. Baird and his superior were two years in building this wonderful mill. In 1886 Mr. Baird was called to the shops of the Wisconsin Central & Northern Pacific, at Waukesha, Wisconsin, where he held the position of general foreman boilermaker for four years, and then, in 1890, was called to Topeka by John Player, who was superintendent of motive power of the Atchison, Topeka & Santa Fe Railroad, and became general foreman of the shop. This position he held during a period of sixteen years. In 1906 he began to handle pneumatic hydraulic static devices, and in 1909 was sent by the company to Cotesville, Pennsylvania, to superintend the building of the new patented firebox, known as the Jacob Shupert box. He built 200 of these appliances and spent three months in testing and comparing them with the standard firebox. There were a number of university professors who assisted in the testing, and the box was finally accepted. Returning to Topeka, Mr. Baird took the position of safety boiler inspector of the whole Santa Fe system, instructing the different shop foremen so that these men would be able to fill the requirements of the new Federal laws. He then returned to his old position as general foreman boilermaker of the Santa Fe system, with headquarters at Topeka, and a little later was made assistant superintendent of the locomotive shops at Topeka, a capacity in which he acted until 1915. In that year he embarked in the manufacture of a full line of pneumatic labor-saving devices, and the business has grown to such an extent that its products now fill a fifty-page catalogue.

Mr. Baird was united in marriage, in 1877, with Miss Mary J. Lyons, of Chicago, Illinois, a daughter of Patrick Lyons of that city. Of the seven children born to them, the following are living: Mamie, who is the wife of I. S. Sheets, who is identified with the clerical department of the shops of the Atchison, Topeka & Santa Fe Railroad, at Topeka; Sadie, who is the wife of Fred J. Partridge, who is an an employe of the state in the office of Hon. Tom Bodkin, secretary of state of Kansas; and Mildred, a stenographer in the office of State Labor Commissioner McBride, and living at home with her parents. Mamie is a graduate of Saint Xavier College, Chicago; and Mildred and Sadie are graduates of Saint Mary's Academy, at Leavenworth, Kansas.

Mr. Baird has taken no active part in public affairs, but like all good business men has accepted his share of the responsibilities of citizenship and is always eager to assist in the advancement of movements making for the general welfare, for the advancement of education or for the betterment of civic conditions. He is a thirty-second degree Mason and a Knight Templar and Shriner and has filled most of the chairs, and is also a member of organizations of railroad men. His family belongs to the Catholic Church, while Mr. Baird favors Presbyterian doctrines.

JEPTHA D. VAWTER. In the task of giving credit to the men who made Kansas, it would be difficult to single out one who was more deserving of a place among those makers and builders than the late Jeptha D. Vawter of Shawnee County. He had much to do with the early history of that county, and what he accomplished, the ideals he lived for, and the influences that emanated from his life, are still vital and quickening.

His was a long as well as a useful life. He was born in Todd County, Kentucky, July 18, 1809. By character and early training he was moulded after the manner of the pioneers, being courageous, industrious and optimistic.

About 1847 he moved to Tazewell County, Illinois, and from there in the spring of 1868 came to Kansas, establishing a home on the southwest quarter of section 33, which is in the southwest corner of Williamsport Township of Shawnee County. It was in that immediate locality that the rest of his years were spent. Mr. Vawter became an extensive dealer in cattle, and in that capacity his name was not known alone in Shawnee County, but in other counties and in other states. He prospered as a result of good judgment and foresight, and at one time owned many hundreds of acres of Kansas' best land.

He was twice married. His first wife, Sarah M. Foster, bore him thirteen children, and the ten who reached maturity are: John W.; Benjamin F.; Henry C.; Lucinda C., who married Walter Hinman; Louisa E., who married Jesse McColm; Martha C., who married John Simpson; James E.; Harriet E., who married Lewis Mead; Sabrina C., who married Mahlon F. Stout; and William J. The mother of these children died December 18, 1883. For his second wife Mr. Vawter married Louisa K. Miller, by whom he became the father of one son named Clarence D.

For years Jeptha D. Vawter was a prominent and forceful character of his community. While he toiled and prospered he was not forgetful of the duties he owed to his home, the locality in which he lived, his state or his country. He lived to see his children established in homes of their own, happy and respected, and this fact afforded him much contentment when the evening shadows of his life were merging into the darkness of eternal earthly sleep. He was a devout Christian, and politically his actions were in accord with the republican party. At the time of his death on October 13, 1894, Jeptha D. Vawter had rounded out a career of a little more than eighty-five years.

THURMAN HILL, who is serving as county attorney, has identified himself with the community of Independence and Montgomery County as a rising young lawyer and as a public spirited citizen whose influence has already been displayed effectively as a campaign manager and through association with various public and business enterprises.

His family has been identified with Kansas for more than forty years. His grandparents, John and Mary Hill, came from England to New York State about 1850. His grandfather, John Hill, was born in 1825, was a ship contractor, but in 1874 moved to Kansas and took up a homestead and followed farming the rest of his active career. He died in Independence in 1901.

George Hill, father of the young attorney at Independence, has long been one of the respected and esteemed citizens of Montgomery County and is the head of a fine family. He was born in New York State in 1854, and was reared partly in Louisiana, but came to Kansas when a young man. That was in 1874, and his operations as a farmer and in various business and public capacities have been largely centered around Independence, where he still resides, owning an attractive residence at 903 West Myrtle Street. He owns land in Oklahoma, and has built up a large business in real estate at Independence. As a democrat he has participated in public life for many years. During Cleveland's administration he was postmaster of Independence, served five years as deputy county treasurer of Montgomery County, and has been a member of the school board and city council. Religiously he is a member of the Episcopal Church and fraternally is affiliated with Lodge No. 1, Woodmen of the World, and Independence Lodge No. 780, Benevolent and Protective Order of Elks.

The maiden name of his wife was Anna O. Young, who was born in New Jersey in 1850. They and all their twelve children are still living. A brief record of the children, who have reflected credit upon their parents, is as follows: Blanche is the wife of R. R. Wharton, who has charge of the packing department of the Coffeyville Mercantile Company at Coffeyville; Sylvia is the wife of R. O. Bolman, president and principal owner of the Coffeyville Mercantile Company, a large wholesale grocery house; H. N. is a freight conductor for the Santa Fe, with headquarters at Clovis, New Mexico; Nina is the wife of J. D. Sturgis, an agent of the Santa Fe at Longton, Kansas; Charles T. is a traveling salesman for the Coffeyville Mercantile Company and resides at Coffeyville; Mira, twin sister of Charles, is still at home with her parents; the seventh in order of birth is Thurman; Raymond is assistant cashier of the National Supply Company at Independence; Vernon is connected with the producing department of the Roxana Petroleum Company at Tulsa, Oklahoma; Anna is a graduate of Montgomery County High School, and is a teacher; Elda is in the freshman class of the high school; and Beatrice, the youngest, is now in the sixth grade.

Thurman Hill was born at Independence, Kansas, September 10, 1890. His early education was acquired in the local public schools, and he graduated from the Montgomery County High School in 1909 and took his LL. B. degree from the law department of the Kansas State University in 1912. In that year he was admitted to practice and at once began building up a reputation as a lawyer, and now has a good business both in civil and criminal branches of practice. His offices are in the Citizens Bank Building.

He is a stanch democrat politically. In the 1914 county campaign he was defeated by only thirty-seven votes in his candidacy for county attorney. He has shown much ability in politics, and recently was manager of the campaign for R. R. Bittman, who was elected mayor of Independence. He has appeared in various county and state conventions of his party and was secretary of the Democratic City Club in 1912, and in 1916 was secretary of the county convention. In 1916, having been nominated without opposition for the office of county attorney, he was elected by a majority of 1,702 votes.

In a business way, besides his law practice, he is secretary and treasurer of the Americus Oil Company, secretary and treasurer of the LeJune Oil Company and associated with other oil interests. He and his brother, Charles, own forty acres of farming land in Montgomery County. Mr. Hill is unmarried. He is a member of the Methodist Episcopal Church, being chairman of the publicity committee of the Business Men's Bible Class, is affiliated with Fortitude Lodge No. 107, Ancient Free and Accepted Masons, at Independence; Lodge No. 69, Independent Order of Odd Fellows, of Independence; the Order of Moose; is a member of the Montgomery County Bar Association, and belongs to the Phi Alpha Delta Greek letter law fraternity. While in university he was honored by his class with offices, and in 1911 played the position of catcher on the Kansas University baseball team. He is interested in all outdoor sports, and is a member of the Independence Tennis Club. He is president of the Montgomery County High School Alumni Association. He also belongs to the Independence Commercial Club.

WALTER ASHTON SMITH. Among the able and successful business men of Topeka, Walter Ashton Smith occupies a foremost place, for years being financially and officially connected with large enterprises in Shawnee and Decatur counties. As the vice president and treasurer of the Farm Mortgage Company, Mr. Smith is interested and influential in one of the largest corporations of its kind in the state.

Walter Ashton Smith was born at Monroeville, Huron County, Ohio, February 16, 1864, and is a son of Welding E. and Charlotte (Ashton) Smith. Welding E. Smith was born at Harrisburg, Pennsylvania, in which city he attended the public schools until eighteen years of age when he became an apprentice to the machinist's trade. He was a natural mechanic and possessed inventive genius and after removal to Ohio went into the business of manufacturing farm implements, having secured patents on a number of his inventions. When the Civil war broke out he gave financial aid to the Union but was prevented from becoming a soldier because of the loss of his left eye, the sight of which had been destroyed by a fragment of flying steel in his foundry. He continued in the manufacturing business until his death although during his later years confined himself to the manufacture of felloes for use on the rims of wagon and buggy wheels. He was an industrious, temperate, moral man, respected and esteemed by all who knew him. He married Charlotte Ashton, of English ancestry. She was born in Ohio, September 19, 1837, and still resides near the old homestead of her father, Thomas Ashton, who was one of the pioneers of Huron County. By trade he was a stone mason and built one of the first brick houses in that section of Ohio.

Walter Ashton Smith was educated in the public schools and after completing the high school course at Monroeville, taught school for one year in Huron County, in the meanwhile making plans for the future that included the securing of western lands through Government grants. He was scarcely twenty years of age when he joined his older brother, Frank D. Smith, and proceeded to Nebraska, June 4, 1884. After considerable looking around they decided no land in that section suited their purposes and came then to Kansas and located in Decatur County. There Frank D. Smith pre-empted a claim and Walter Ashton Smith entered the contest for a quarter section. After that preliminary he returned to Nebraska and taught school for six months at Hastings.

Returning to Decatur County he taught school for a year when he was able to prove up on his pre-empted claim, June, 1886, afterwards locating at Oberlin, Kansas, the county seat, where he remained for a quarter of a century.

At Oberlin Mr. Smith made a good impression and soon secured a position in the office of the registrar of deeds utilizing his salary to pay for a course in the normal school. Subsequently he was made deputy registrar of deeds for Decatur County, an office he filled for three years. During this time a set of abstract books was compiled and later a half interest in the books and business was bought by Otis L. Benton, a banker of Oberlin. In 1902 the Decatur County Abstract Company was organized and incorporated with Otis Benton as president and Walter Ashton Smith as vice president and manager. They continued to conduct this with success until it was absorbed and replaced by the Benton & Smith Investment Company, with a capital of $50,000, controlling the only complete set of abstract books in the county, and enlarging the farm loan and investment business. This investment company continued in business until about 1908, the capital stock was increased to $100,000 by the actual earnings of the concern, the entire interests of the same being the sole property of Mr. Benton and Mr. Smith. In 1910 Mr. Smith sold his interest in the company, which, at that time had a surplus of $40,000. He did not remain out of active business very long, however, for in April, 1912, in partnership with J. P. Slaughter, he organized the Farm Mortgage Company, with a capital of $100,000, Mr. Slaughter being president and Mr. Smith vice president and treasurer. Since its inception this enterprise has been prosperous.

On May 10, 1893, Mr. Smith was married to Miss Julia E. McGrew, of Eureka, Kansas, and they have three children, a son, Marion Ashton, who was born January 27, 1897, is a student in the State Agricultural College at Manhattan, Kansas; and two daughters, Lucile Evelyn and Corinne Alice, both of whom are at school. In March, 1911, Mr. Smith moved to Topeka and bought a residence in Potwin. This removal because of Topeka's excellent educational and church advantages, and was in the interests of his children. The family is interested in church affairs and many phases of the pleasant social life of the capital and a wide circle of congenial friends has been found. A short time prior to his departure from Oberlin, Mr. Smith built and gave to the Episcopal Society there a very beautiful church edifice—made of Coffeyville vitrified paving blocks —as a memento to his mother (a stanch Episcopalian) and as a thank offering to a benevolent Providence.

MATTHEW B. VAN PETTEN. The success which has attended the enterprise operating at Topeka under the name of the Pioneer Mortgage Company attests the foresight, sagacity and financial skill of its members, whose watchful care and fidelity have combined to build up and perpetuate their fortunes. The life of the financier is less conspicuous before the world than that of a member of a learned calling, or of one who mingles in public affairs, but is none the less one of arduous labor and thorough engrossment, requiring a high order of organizing talent, watchfulness of the trend of affairs and financial skill. The strictest fidelity, the utmost watchfulness, good judgment and experience are needed to counteract the effects of contraction in monetary credits, the casualties of poor crops and unprofitable business, as well as a multitude of other influences which have their effect upon monetary affairs. In few other callings of life is success so sure a gauge of uncommon ability.

Mr. Van Petten was born on a farm in Peoria County, Illinois, May 4, 1854, and has been a resident of Kansas since February, 1880. He is one of eight children born to M. B. and Ruby (Emery) Van Petten, the former a native of New York and the latter of New Hampshire, is a grandson on the paternal side of natives of Holland, and is related to many of the name who have taken a part in the wars of the United States. M. B. Van Petten the elder was a physician in Illinois, but later turned his attention to farming, became a prominent and influential citizen of his day and community, and served for a number of years as a member of the board of supervisors of Peoria County, Illinois, being chairman of the board at the time of his death in January, 1870.

Matthew B. Van Petten received his early education in the district schools of Peoria County, Illinois, after which he entered the Northwestern University, Chicago, but while at that institution contracted typhoid fever and was unable to complete his course. Instead, at the age of eighteen years, he returned to the home farm and worked for his mother, his father having died when he was sixteen years of age. While still living in Illinois, Mr. Van Petten was married, August 18, 1875, to Miss Mary Jane Buchanan, a native of Pennsylvania. who was living near Trivoli, Peor'a County. To this union there were born two children: Alfred Emery, who is president of the Pioneer Mortgage Company and Mary Eva, who is the wife of Harold Snoddy, who is carrying on agricultural operations near Auburn, Kansas.

In February, 1880, having heard reports of the great opportunities for advancement in Kansas, Mr. Van Petten came with his family to this state and first settled in the vicinity of Burlingame, Osage County, because of the plenteousness of coal and wood to be found in the locality. There he continued to be engaged in farming with marked success until 1893, when he moved to Burlingame and carried on farming. In 1909 he moved to Topeka, and was one of the original organizers of the Pioneer State Bank, in company with John P. Slaughter, of Topeka, and Charles G. Taylor, of Los Angeles, California. Mr. Van Petten was a member of the board and directors and the bank started with a capital of $5,000, but such an excellent business was that it was soon forced to increase its capitalization, and by subsequent advancements it reached $25,000. Later the controlling interest was sold and the Pioneer Mortgage Company was organized, August 29, 1907, with $100,000 capital. At that time J. P. Slaughter was president; A. E. Van Petten, vice president; and L. P. Robinson, secretary and treasurer, while M. B. Van Petten continued as a member of the board of directors and was active in its work. In 1913, there came a change in the personnel of the officials, A. E. Van Petten becoming president; M. B. Van Petten, first vice president; L. P. Robinson, second vice president; and Archie M. Catlin, secretary and treasurer. Each year this business has increased its business and widened its scope, and its surplus has grown proportionately. The concern operates in both Kansas and Oklahoma, having a branch office at Lawton in the latter state. Mr. Van Petten is a member of the Independent Order of Odd Fellows and of the Modern Woodmen of America, at Burlingame. In politics he is a republican, but not an office seeker, and while he has taken some interest in local affairs of a public character, it has been merely as a booster for his friends and his party. He is a member of the First

Methodist Church and is a class leader therein, but as his business keeps him away from the city a great deal of the time he is not able to be as active in religious work as he would prefer.

Mrs. Van Petten, whose death occurred July 12, 1914, was an untiring worker in all the ladies' branches of the First Methodist Church. A woman of broad sympathies and great heart, she was especially interested in the welfare of the children, was a member of both the Home and Foreign Missionary Societies, to the work of which she gave a great deal of her time and much of her energy and strength, and in her death the deserving poor lost one who had ever been their generous friend and kind adviser.

Roy Pitts is chief of the fire department at Independence. During his two years in that office he has developed the service to a high point of efficiency, partly by organization and partly by the introduction of modern apparatus, so that Independence today can boast of as perfect an equipment for fighting fire as any city of its size in Kansas.

When Mr. Pitts took charge of the department the apparatus consisted of a chief's car and a horse-drawn hose wagon. Since then he has taken the lead in giving the city a better apparatus. The city now has three motor propelled cars, one pump and hose car and the other a hose car, and both of these engines were designed by Chief Pitts. The first was built by the South Bend Motor Car Works at South Bend, Indiana. It is in itself a complete engine for prompt and efficient fire fighting. It carries 1,200 feet of hose, besides ladders, deluge, searchlight and all necessary tools, and can pump 750 gallons a minute. The other hose car, also designed by Mr. Pitts, was built by himself and the other firemen of the city on a Buick chassis. It carries an equipment of 1,000 feet of hose, ladders, chemicals, pyreenes, searchlight, etc. The chief's car, which was built by the Anderson Fire Coupling and Supply Company of Kansas City, Kansas, also carries a large amount of fire fighting equipment, including two forty-gallon chemicals, one hand chemical, two pyreenes, etc.

When he first took charge of the chief's office Mr. Pitts was called upon with his horse-drawn equipment to fight two large fires. Since the introduction of modern apparatus Independence has not had a fire of any importance, every blaze being checked almost at its incipiency, though a delay of two or three minutes, which would have been inevitable with the earlier apparatus, would have meant the destruction of much property.

Mr. Pitts is a member of the Kansas State Firemen's Association and the International Chiefs' Association, and attended the National Firemen's Convention of 1915 at Cincinnati and of 1916 at Providence, Rhode Island. He is also president and secretary of the Firemen's Relief Fund of Independence.

Roy Pitts is a Kansas man, and a few years ago came off his father's farm with all the rugged strength and vigor of such environment, and has proved himself the man for the place. He was born near Cherryvale, Kansas, May 16, 1888, and comes of a family of Irish descent but long a resident of the State of Indiana. His father, John W. Pitts, was born in Indiana in 1863, was reared there, and came to Montgomery County, Kansas, in 1884. Since then he has lived on his farm thirteen miles southwest of Independence. He is a successful diversified farmer and has a well improved and valuable place of 160 acres. He served three terms on the school board, and has been road supervisor in his district. He is independent in politics and a member of the Methodist Episcopal Church.

John W. Pitts married Emma Yates, who was born in Illinois in 1866. Their children are: Pearl, wife of Fred Furnace, and they have a good farm of 120 acres situated 1½ miles from their father's place; Roy; Olin, who for the past two years has been a member of the Independence Fire Department under his brother Roy; Lola, who died March 17, 1914, at the age of twenty-one; Maude, living at home; and Ernest, now in the eighth grade of the public schools.

Roy Pitts received his early education in Montgomery County public schools, and spent the first twenty-two years of his life on his father's farm. On January 28, 1910, he became a member of the Independence fire department, and served under Chief Foster until March 26, 1914, when he was appointed chief by Mayor C. H. Kerr. His office and headquarters for himself and men are in the City Building, and he has five regular firemen under him, with Earl Adams as assistant chief.

Politically Mr. Pitts is independent. He is affiliated with the Woodmen of the World at Independence, and with Independence Camp No. 648, Loyal Order of Moose, and is insured in the Travelers Insurance Company. On April 21, 1914, at Independence, he married Miss Essie Babb, daughter of Mrs. Carrie Babb of Independence.

REV. PATRICK McINERNEY is pastor of the Assumption Catholic Church of Topeka. Reared and trained for the duties of the priesthood abroad, he has been in the ministry of the church in America for the past eighteen years, and all that time has been spent in Kansas. He is an able priest, devoted to the cause, and has an important record of constructive work in the various parishes where he has served.

One of the eleven children of Patrick and Bridget (Purcell) McInerney, he was born in Ireland March 6, 1876. He attended the local schools of Ireland and the college at Ennis, County Clare, and afterwards pursued his studies in Belgium. He was ordained to the priesthood by Archbishop Langevin of St. Boniface, Canada, and in October, 1898, came to Kansas to serve as assistant priest at the Cathedral in Leavenworth. In February, 1900, he was sent to Olathe, Kansas, as pastor of St. Paul's Church, and remained there until October, 1907. He afterwards was pastor of Blessed Sacrament Church at Kansas' City, Kansas, and was at St. Peter's Church in that city from 1909 to June, 1911. He was at St. Thomas, Kansas, for three years, and in October, 1914, assumed his present duties as pastor of the Assumption Church at Topeka. Father McInerney has one assistant clergyman under him, and the parochial schools of the Assumption parish are directed by ten teachers.

DAVID BOWIE. The important and solid business enterprises of Topeka today are largely concerns that have been developed slowly and carefully, the integrity of character of their founders and the foresight and intelligent management of their officials resulting in expansion and prosperity. A well known concern of this kind, the Thomas Page Milling Company, of which David Bowie is vice president and treasurer, is a business carried on with abundant capital.

David Bowie was born in Stirling, Scotland, July 26, 1869, one of four children born to his parents, Thomas and Margaret (McLintock) Bowie. In 1875, when David Bowie was six years old his parents moved to Alloa, Scotland. His father there became a man of affairs and as a lawyer held commissions under the late Queen Victoria, to serve in certain offices. He was commissioner of the poor and filled other positions of responsibility until the time of his death in 1909.

David Bowie attended school in his native land until he qualified as a teacher, after which, for two years he taught school preparatory to entering upon an apprenticeship in the Clydesdale Bank of Scotland (Limited), where he continued for three years. In 1892, when Mr. Bowie came to Kansas it was in answer to the solicitations of his uncle, Thomas Page, who was in the milling business at Topeka. Mr. Bowie became a partner in the Thomas Page Milling Company here and as manager of the merchandise department and of the financial department, he has been largely instrumental in bringing about the great prosperity that attends this important enterprise. In 1915 the company was incorporated with a paid up capital of $100,000, with Thomas Page as president, David Bowie as vice president and treasurer and David G. Page as secretary. Additionally Mr. Bowie has large bank interests. He devoted a great deal of time and helped to make a success of the Shawnee State Bank, which was organized in 1902 with a capital of $60,000, with Thomas Page as president, D. J. Hathaway as vice president and David Bowie as secretary. He is a director of the Bank of Topeka, also of the Prudential Trust Company, is secretary and treasurer of the Mills Building Company, and treasurer of the Pelletier Stores Company, which he helped to organize.

Mr. Bowie has no political tastes nor ambitions but votes as an independent republican. He was reared in the Presbyterian faith and is a member and a trustee of the First Presbyterian Church of Topeka. His name is found as a member of numerous charitable organizations and his practical generosity has been evidenced on many occasions since he has been an honored resident of Topeka. Although he has no immediate family circle, as he is unmarried, his sound conception of business principles, his conscientious acceptance of a capitalist's responsibilities, and his genial personality, make him a welcome guest at any fireside.

CHARLES A. KARLAN. Though comparatively a newcomer in Kansas, Mr. Karlan in a few years has made a record of practical accomplishment and a reputation for himself such as few who have spent their entire lives within the state's borders have been able to attain.

He is an artist in furniture. The making of high grade furniture has been a specialty of his for many years, and it was in 1905 that he came to Topeka and set up his establishment in that line. It is no disparagement to other similar concerns to state that his is the largest and best equipped furniture factory and retail establishment in Kansas. Karlan-made furniture has a special significance among those who demand and appreciate artistic merit. It was from his original designs that the present furniture in the Memorial Building, the home of the State Historical Society, was made, and this alone has made his work familiar to thousands.

Charles A. Karlan was born in Detroit, Michigan, July 29, 1874, being one of the three surviving children out of the five born to Frederick and Wilhelmina Karlan. His parents spent their early years in Germany, where they married, and came to the United States in 1872. Charles A. Karlan grew up in Detroit, graduated from the high school there in 1892, and for three years was a student in the University of Michigan at Ann Arbor, until failing health compelled him to relinquish his studies, when he moved West. From boyhood he had a special knack at handling tools and has developed a mechanical trade into an artistic profession. He was first engaged in furniture manufacturing at Cedar Rapids, Iowa, and was there at the outbreak of the Spanish-American war in 1898. He at once left his work and became a member of Company F of the Eighth United States Infantry. At Daequira he had the distinction of being the second American soldier to put foot on Cuban soil in the time of war. In the campaign that followed for the subjugation of Cuba he was in seven distinct engagements, including Daequira, Siboney, El Caney and the siege and bombardment of Santiago. It was at Santiago that Mr. Karlan received a gunshot wound in the left leg. At the close of the Cuban campaign he received an honorable discharge as sergeant-major, and after recuperating resumed manufacturing at Cedar Rapids, Iowa. From there he moved to Topeka in 1905.

Mr. Karlan is a thirty-second degree Scottish Rite Mason, and is affiliated with the Benevolent and Protective Order of Elks and the Woodmen of the World; is a member of the Rotary Club, the Topeka Commercial Club, the Spanish-American War Veterans, and is active in the First Methodist Episcopal Church of Topeka.

In 1907 he married Miss Louise E. Biebel of St. Paul, Minnesota. Their two children are Charles B. and Frances Louise.

CHARLES L. MITCHELL is secretary and sales manager of Crane & Company of Topeka. As every one knows in that city and the state this is one of the largest publishing and stationery houses in Kansas. It may be said with propriety that Mr. Mitchell has deserved success because he has earned it. He was born at Kenosha, Wisconsin, February 12, 1873, a son of John C. and Sallie Ann (Connell) Mitchell. His father saw four years of active service in the Civil war and died in 1898, while the mother is still residing in Wisconsin. John C. Mitchell was a native of Scotland, being brought to America at the age of five years. The family spent five weeks on board the sailing vessel that brought them to the New World. The Mitchells took up a homestead in southwest Wisconsin, at what was then known as Southport, now Kenosha. While digging a well on this place the grandfather was asphyxiated by foul air, and this threw upon John C. Mitchell unusually heavy burdens and responsibilities in assisting to support his mother and the household. He and his sisters worked hard to prove up the homestead, and that land is still owned by members of the family. John C. Mitchell was always a hard working man and while he did his best to contribute the comforts to his family, his children were reared in comparatively humble circumstances and became inured at an early age to hard work and some privations.

These were the early circumstances of Charles L. Mitchell's career. He grew up in Kenosha, and received his education in the public schools and at Kenosha College. There was an element of willingness and energy in his makeup which undoubtedly accounts for his success in life. He paid his own way both through school and college. His earnings were the result of cutting lawns, caring for horses, washing buggies, and he also had the distinction of being one of the first two newsboys in Kenosha. From the age of fourteen he has depended upon his own exertions. When a boy he frequently drove horses for doctors, and from this experience he came to know every farmer in a radius of thirty miles around Kenosha. The physicians did much of their driving at night, and whenever they could employed

young Mitchell. The postmaster would also entrust him with a delivery of mail to farmers. That was long before the days of rural free delivery or even of telephones, and there was no remuneration connected with free mail delivery. At holiday time, however, the boy was remembered by scores of people for his obliging services.

While he was still getting his education an attack of typhoid developed tubercular conditions, and in February, 1892, he went to Denver as a suitable climate in which to overcome this threatened disease. Two weeks after his arrival he became messenger boy in the office of the purchasing agent of the Denver & Rio Grande Railroad. During the first six months of that employment he attended a night school and mastered shorthand. He was then promoted to the stenographic department of the railway office and his salary advanced from $25 to $60 a month. After four days of work as stenographer, owing to a reorganization of the clerical staff, he was made stationer of the company on a six-months' trial. That office gave him the responsibilities of buying stationery supplies for the entire system. He made good and held the position until 1899.

While thus employed Mr. Mitchell met Miss Edna Crane, daughter of George W. Crane of Topeka, who was then visiting in Denver. Being unable to see any further advancement in railway service, Mr. Mitchell soon afterward made application for the position of purchasing agent of the Detroit Copper Mining Company at Morenci, Arizona. His application was accepted, and he thus entered upon a position which soon brought increasing responsibilities. After two years in Arizona Mr. Mitchell came to Topeka and in 1902 married Miss Edna Crane as the culmination of an acquaintance begun several years before in Denver.

Returning with his wife to Morenci, he was soon happily settled in his home and with splendid prospects of business advancement. Besides having charge of the stock of the Copper Company and nine large warehouses, he also conducted a livery stable for saddle horses and that netted him more profits than his salary. He was also in partnership with a Kansas boy in the laundry business, and they shipped an average of over 1,000 pounds of laundry every week to El Paso.

In 1904 Mr. George Crane prevailed upon his son-in-law to sell out his interests in Arizona and come to Topeka to assist in the operation of the extensive establishment of Crane & Company. Mr. Mitchell agreed to do this, but on the eve of his departure, after his household goods had been shipped, his wife fell ill and a few days later occurred the death of both herself and her new born baby. This was a calamity which unsettled the purposes and activities of Mr. Mitchell for some time. He spent some time traveling, but finally settled in Topeka and became secretary and superintendent of Crane & Company. In 1907 he married Ethel Morton, daughter of William A. and Flora (Smith) Morton.

Upon the death of George Crane the company was reorganized, and Mr. Mitchell was relieved of the duties of superintendent and was made sales manager in charge of all the buying and selling. This position he has since continued to fill.

Mr. Mitchell is well known in social as well as business circles. He is past exalted ruler of the local lodge of the Benevolent and Protective Order of Elks; a member of Siloam Lodge No. 225, Ancient Free and Accepted Masons, Topeka Chapter No. 5, Royal Arch Masons; both the subordinate and encampment degrees of Odd Fellowship; the Ancient

Order of United Workmen; of the United Commercial Travelers; the Country Club; the Shawnee Golf Club, of which he is a director; the Topeka Commercial Club, the Topeka Rotary Club, the Lake View Fishing and Shooting Club and the Sons of Veterans. Mr. Mitchell is a republican of the standpat kind.

FRANK F. FLETCHER is the only architect practicing the profession exclusively at Independence. He has a long and successful record as a builder and was active as a contractor until an unfortunate injury obliged him to desist. He has since followed the profession of architect and has built up a very large clientele.

He was born in Louisiana, Missouri, September 19, 1870. His maternal grandfather was William Kling, who was born in Holland in 1800 and was a horticulturist. On coming to America he settled in Louisiana, Missouri, in 1818. Peter R. Fletcher, father of Frank F., was born in Hull, England, in 1827. As a young man he served two years in the British army. When about twenty years of age he came to the United States and located at Louisiana, Missouri. As a building contractor he erected courthouses and other public buildings in Missouri, Illinois, Kentucky, Tennessee and Texas. It was while engaged in the building of a courthouse at Denton, Texas, that he was killed in a railroad accident. He died at Dallas, Texas, in 1874. He was a republican, a Mason, and a member of the Cumberland Presbyterian Church. Peter R. Fletcher married Margaret Kling, who was born at Louisiana, Missouri, in 1835, and died there in 1870. Her children were: William, who is a contractor and builder at Corpus Christi, Texas; Annie, wife of John Beal, who has a printing and newspaper business at Mexico, Missouri; Henry, who was an invalid most of his life and died in 1899 at Louisiana, Missouri; Mollie, wife of J. W. Bell, a tailor at Los Angeles, California; and Frank F.

Reared and educated in Louisiana, Missouri, Frank F. Fletcher started out to make his own way when fourteen years of age. He learned the trade of brick mason, and followed that both as a journeyman and as a contractor until he was thirty-four years of age. He worked at St. Louis, Kansas City, Denver, New Orleans, Corpus Christi and in fact in all the larger cities and towns of the Mississippi Valley.

In the course of his work he arrived at Independence, Kansas, in 1904. There, on July 18, 1904, while working on the tower of the Presbyterian Church he was accidentally knocked off and received injuries which resulted in the permanent disablement of his right arm. He then took up architecture as a profession, and has offices at 112½ East Myrtle Street.

Among the many buildings he has designed in the past ten or twelve years should be mentioned especially the following: Residences of Judge T. J. Flanelley, R. W. Morrison, William Scott, W. R. Murrow, Frank Louy, Albert Jones, Thomas Wharton, Bert Stevens, Milton Cook, the Stevens & Robinson Building, the Robinson Veterinary Hospital and many others in and about Independence.

Mr. Fletcher owns three residences and two pieces of unimproved city property in Independence, and is secretary of the Hope Oil, Gas and Mineral Company. Since 1907 he has served as building and plumbing inspector for Independence. He is unmarried. Politically he is an independent republican, a member of the Cumberland Presbyterian Church and is affiliated with Independence Lodge No. 17, Ancient Order of United Workmen. He is one of the popular and highly esteemed citizens of Independence.

OLIVER FRANKLIN WINNER. The excellent business standing of Oliver Franklin Winner rests upon many years of connection with agricultural affairs in Shawnee County, where he is still the owner of a large and valuable property. Particularly is he known as an authority upon the subject of alfalfa growing, to which he has devoted many years of study and investigation. Mr. Winner is an Illinoisan by nativity, and was born at Belvidere, Boone County, in 1859, being a son of Martin W. Winner.

Martin W. Winner was born in New York, from which state he emigrated as a young man to Bremer County, Iowa, being a resident of Waverly at the time of the Civil war. He was a stanch Union man and endeavored to enlist in the army of the North, but owing to a slight physical disability was rejected. For twelve years he was engaged in the harness business, but eventually turned his attention to farming, in which vocation he continued to be engaged until his death, in 1901. Mr. Winner was married in 1858 to Miss Nancy Farr, of Boone County, Illinois, and they became the parents of two daughters and five sons: Oliver Franklin, of this review; Ida, who died in 1891; Clarence, who is traveling in the South; Albert, who is a farmer at Janesville, Iowa; Millie, who died in 1891; and Walter Harvey and Melvin, who are both engaged in the barber business in Iowa. Martin W. Winner was a man who led an exemplary life, free from bad habits of any kind, and especially strong in his aversion to the taking of alcoholic beverages. He was a firm believer in efficiency, and was himself able to carry to a successful conclusion any venture which he undertook. As a father, he had the confidence and affection of his children, and in his community he held the respect and regard of all who knew him. In his death his community lost one of its good and public-spirited citizens.

Oliver Franklin Winner was two years when taken by his parents to Iowa, and there he grew to manhood on the home farm and received his educational training in the public schools. He was twenty years of age when he left the parental roof to seek his fortunes in an independent career, and at that time took up his residence at Holton, Jackson County, Kansas, where he commenced farming. In 1904 he came to Shawnee County, where he purchased the 320-acre farm known as the John Wilkerson place. Within three years, so energetically and efficiently did he labor, he had it cleared and in a salable condition and disposed of it at an advance of $4,000 over its purchase price. When he sold that property Mr. Winner came to his present place, at North Topeka, and here continues to engage successfully in farming, with particular attention paid to alfalfa growing. He is known in this latter connection all over this part of the state as an authority, is frequently called upon for advice, gives occasional lectures before farmers' institutes, and contributes articles on the subject to leading farm papers, as he does also upon various other agricultural subjects. He has a wide audience and his opinions are respected and bear much weight among men who know. He is a citizen who has done his share in developing Shawnee County in an agricultural way, an exponent of good roads, a friend of education and a supporter of progress in regard to civic betterment.

In 1884 Mr. Winner was married to Miss Hattie Parmenter, daughter of Walter Parmenter, a Vermonter who migrated to Jackson County, Kansas, prior to the Civil war, and, as an ardent Free State man, joined one of the fighting Kansas regiments during that struggle and was at the front for three years. Mr. Parmenter was, as he still is, a bosom friend of W. A. Blossom, and both now reside at Holton, Kansas. To Mr. and Mrs. Winner there have been born five sons and three daughters: Ray, who was deputy county clerk of Shawnee County for four years and is now engaged in farming; Guy, who was formerly principal of schools at Wamego, Kansas, and for the past three years principal at Hoyt; Irene, a graduate of the musical department of Washburn College, now residing at home and teaching music; Benjamin, who is engaged in farming in partnership with his brother, Guy; Viva, who is the wife of Lester Pollum and lives at Wamego, Kansas; Howard, who divides his time between farming and attending school; and Zella and Zera, who are both pupils at the Topeka High School.

JOHN SAYRE DOWNES. The City of Topeka is the home of the largest organization of its kind in the United States, the Aetna Building and Loan Association, which maintains about 600 agencies in Kansas and Oklahoma. The growth and development of this institution during the quarter of a century in which it has been in existence is a commentary upon the success to be attained by enterprises in the Sunflower State when their policies are directed by men of substantial ability, strict integrity and business foresight. At the head of the Aetna Building and Loan Association today, in the office of president, is found John Sayre Downes, a business man of sterling capacity, who during the twenty years of his connection with the company has been appreciative of the value of fair treatment for policy holders and the results occuring therefrom. President Downes is a self-made man, whose own experience should serve as an encouraging example to those starting life in modest circumstances, as well as being illustrative of the desirable results attainable through thrift and wise investment.

John Sayre Downes was born on a farm in Oneida County, New York, August 31, 1855, and has been a resident of Kansas since 1878. He is one of six children born to Thomas and Mary (Sparrow) Downes, natives of England, who were brought as small children from that country to the United States by their respective parents in a sailing vessel in 1833, and in the absence of other transportation, they traveled from New York City to their Oneida County homes by way of the Erie Canal. Thomas Downes passed his life in farming in the Empire State, and being a man of industry and good judgment managed to accumulate a comfortable property, so that at the time of his death, in 1880, he was accounted a substantial citizen of his community.

John Sayre Downes was given a country school education by his parents, but as he was ambitious and enterprising he desired a better training and earned the money therefor by teaching in the schools of his native vicinity and clerking in a general store. Thus he was enabled to take courses in the Whitesboro and Cazenovia seminaries, and after his graduation from the latter, at the age of twenty years, came to Kansas and located in Marion County, where it was his intention to devote his career to raising stock. This he followed with some success for three years, but the possibilities offered by the rapidly advancing real estate values were too tempting to be put aside, and he entered the ranks of dealers in realty, a line for which he soon developed a remarkable aptitude. Opening an office at Marion, he began handling city real estate and dealing in farm loans, and during the thirteen years that he was so engaged placed himself in a position where he was ready to advance still further in the business world.

In 1896 Mr. Downes received an attractive offer from Byron Roberts, of Topeka, the first president of the Aetna Building and Loan Association, an institution which had been established several years before, and which already gave promise of becoming an important enterprise. Mr. Downes, disposing of his Marion holdings, came to Topeka, and, in order to learn the business from the ground up, took a clerkship. After three years he was promoted to the position of examiner, and remained in that capacity for twelve years, when he was elected to the presidency. Some idea of the growth of the Aetna may be seen in the rapid development of the association's assets, as follows: January 1, 1894, $49,210.10; 1896, $118,738.86; 1898, $316,972.77; 1900, $496,347.93; 1902, $854,840.92; 1904, $1,189,-775.04; 1906, $1,642,981.76; 1908, $2,170,948.16; 1910, $2,496,664.07; 1912, $3,415,671.58; 1914, $4,067,466.91; 1915, $4,576,502.20; 1916, $5,062,900.78. While the Aetna, the largest general building and loan association in the country, has agencies only in Kansas and Oklahoma, its stockholders, numbering more than 18,000, represent practically every state in the Union, and are to be found in Canada, Mexico and the Philippine Islands, from the trenches of Europe to the gold-fields of Alaska. The security upon which Aetna money is invested consists of first mortgages on real estate up to fifty per cent of its value, or of Aetna stock up to ninety per cent of its cash value, and the State Banking Departments of Kansas and Oklahoma maintain the same strict supervision over this association for the safeguarding of the stockholders' interests that is maintained over banks. The Aetna is of the mutual type of building and loan associations, as there are no preferred stockholders, but all members share equally in the results. The authorized capital of the concern is $20,000,000, and the association belongs to the Topeka Commercial Club and to the American Bankers' Association.

Mr. Downes' business career in Topeka dates only since 1896, but during this time he has achieved such a success as most men would regard as a triumph if accomplished through a half century of patient effort. Coming here at a time when the keenness of business competition, particularly in the matter of loans and investments, rendered success impossible unless through the exercise of sound judgment, allied to a certain degree of venturesome determination, he has achieved a reputation and acquired wealth through developing one of the country's great institutions. While Mr. Downes is a supporter of republican principles, he is not a politician, for his business affairs have been of such scope and importance that he has not had time to enter public life. However, he takes a keen interest in affairs which affect his community, and is always found allied with other public-spirited men in the advancement of movements for the civic welfare. Fraternally, he is affiliated with the Modern Woodmen of America. He and Mrs. Downes are members of the Episcopalian and Methodist churches, and Mrs. Downes takes an active part in church work and in the advancement of charitable enterprises.

Mr. Downes was married in June, 1883, to Miss Liza W. Carter, of Kentucky, at Florence, Kansas. To this union a son and a daughter have been born: Roy H., who is maintenance clerk in the office of the general manager of the Santa Fe Railroad; and Mrs. Marie Mize, of Topeka.

JOSEPH W. COCHRAN. Of the agriculturists of Shawnee County who have been the architects of their own fortunes, and who, from small beginnings, have worked their way to independence and position, Joseph W. Cochran is a leading representative. He began his career without advantages of any kind, and his early struggles to gain a foothold necessitated the use of all his energies, but his present fine farm of 107 acres, in Menoken Township, illustrates what may be gained through the exercise of industry and well directed effort.

Mr. Cochran was born on a farm near Lewistown, Mifflin County, Pennsylvania, May 16, 1865, and was the fourth of a family of eight children born to Joseph H. and Susanna (Myers) Cochran, natives of Pennsylvania. Joseph H. Cochran had charge of a large gang of construction and bridge workers on the Pennsylvania Railroad and also conducted a small farm until the Civil war, when he enlisted in Company E, Thirty-fifth Regiment, Pennsylvania Volunteer Infantry, with which he served for one and one-half years. Later he was connected with the United States Rolling Stock Company, of Urbana, Ohio, but as he felt that he was not progressing as he ought, in 1877 he decided to do as many other poor people were at the time, and seek his fortunes in the West. Accordingly, he bought five tickets and took his family of ten to Salina, arriving at that point after many experiences with the conductors on the various lines. Leaving his family at the immigration home at Salina, with but 75 cents, he walked thirty-five miles to the home of a friend, in Lincoln County, and during his absence the mother and children were sorely in need of food. The father finally returned, however, with a wagon, and the little party was taken to Mr. Cochran's friend's house, where they lived for ten days. Mr. Cochran then rented a "dug-out," which was the home for one year, while Mr. Cochran worked a rented farm. He then took a homestead and timber claim, but his troubles were not yet over, for his first crop was a failure, and for six months the family was compelled to exist upon corn bread. Later, the father built a shack of siding, 18x20, but it proved only a poor protection against the elements, and when it rained the rain poured in between the boards and drenched everything, even the bedding. In 1879 came the tornado, which tore off the roof and three sides of the shack, but nothing inside was touched. Another freak of the storm was that the hogs, in the direct path of the storm, were lifted and carried 1½ miles and there dropped, but none were killed, and all found their way back to the Cochran home unscathed. The family remained in the same community for ten years, and as their fortunes improved took an active part in the upbuilding of the community. They helped to build churches, and the children at first attended a subscription school which had been supported by their father and two other public-spirited citizens. Mr. Cochran, through his persistent and indefatigable industry and courage, gradually accumulated a competence, and at the time of his death, in 1905, was one of the substantial and most highly respected men of his community. He was a member of the Independent Order of Odd Fellows.

Joseph W. Cochran attended school in Lincoln County, and in 1889, 1890 and 1891 taught school in the Shawnee County district schools of Elmont, Union and Pleasant Ridge. On July 6, 1890, he was married to Miss Eva Godwin, and to this union there have been born six children: Floyd, of Oakland, Kansas; and Vernon, Elsie, Lola, Joseph and Raymond. At the time of his marriage, after he had paid the preacher and bought some furniture to furnish two rooms on the installment plan, Mr. Cochran was possessed of $2.50, but he had his health, and was ambitious and persevering. He secured a position in the shops of the Santa Fe Railroad, at Topeka, and by 1897 was able to make a first payment on a tract of eighty acres at Kiro, Kansas. There he continued to farm until 1912, when he sold this property and bought seventy-two acres in Menoken Township, Shawnee County, which he improved. Recently he has added thirty-five acres to his original purchase, and now operates the entire property, devoting himself to general farming. Mr. Cochran has been a witness to the great development that has been effected in this part of the state. A companion of the wilderness of the early days, when he shot deer, antelope and prairie chicken by the score and was near the Indian troubles in Russell County in 1878, he has also been a sharer in the great prosperity that has blessed the Sunflower State, and can truthfully say that he has done his share in bringing about the present desirable conditions.

Mr. Cochran has always been identified with the democratic party since the time he attained his majority, and has on several occasions been elected to fill public office, having been township trustee for five terms and a member of the school board for years, in addition to which he has rendered helpful service in promoting public-spirited enterprises. He is fraternally affiliated with Topeka Lodge No. 1243, Modern Woodmen of America. Mr. and Mrs. Cochran are members of the Presbyterian Church, and Mr. Cochran for some years was superintendent of the Sunday school.

WILLIAM P. BOWEN. For thirty years or more the name Bowen has been extensively associated with milling industries in Southern Kansas. William P. Bowen owns the only flour and feed milling enterprise at Independence, and this was established by himself and his father a great many years ago in connection with several other mills of the same kind located in other parts of the state. Mr. Bowen is not only a business man but a citizen well known throughout Montgomery County. He has filled the post of mayor of his home city, and has done much to advance community welfare.

He is descended from Welsh ancestors. Three brothers of the name came from Wales to the United States prior to the Revolutionary war. The one from whom he is descended located in Ohio after that war, and the other two located, according to the best information, in Virginia, and one in New York State.

William P. Bowen was born at Ottumwa, Iowa, August 31, 1855. His father was the late George W. Bowen, who died at Independence, Kansas, in 1912. He was born in Ohio in 1829, was reared largely in Indiana, and became an early settler at Ottumwa, Iowa, where he married the mother of William P. Bowen. While still a resident of Ottumwa he made his first business undertaking in Kansas in 1869, establishing a mill at Pleasanton in Lynn County. In 1870-71 he erected another mill at Chetopa, in Labette County, which at that time was just being settled up. In 1876 he erected still another mill at Labette City in the county of that name. In 1882 George W. Bowen brought his family to Kansas and established a home at Independence, with which city he was identified the rest of his life. He was a practical miller and made that industry his chief occupation. He operated both flour and feed mills and made his business turn to the benefit of the various communities in which he lived. Politically he was a republican and was especially active in the Methodist Episcopal Church. He filled a place on the official board of his home church many years, and in 1896 was a lay delegate to the general conference. He was also a member of the Masonic fraternity. George W. Bowen married Ellen Hackworth, who was born in Ohio in 1835 and died at Ottumwa, Iowa, in 1861. William P. Bowen was the oldest of her three children. The two daughters are: Clara E., wife of Christopher Haw, a wholesale hardware merchant at Ottumwa; and Emma A., wife of Rogers W. Berry, an attorney at Great Falls, Montana. For his second wife George W. Bowen married Angeline S. Miller, who is still living at Independence. Their one child is George M., engaged in the milling and oil business and living in his mother's home.

Until he was grown William P. Bowen lived at Ottumwa, Iowa, where he acquired a high school education and was also a student in Northwestern University. Leaving college in 1875, he became associated with his father, in the milling business, and during 1876 and a part of 1877 had charge of the mill at Labette City, Kansas. While living at Labette City he cast his first vote. In 1877 he returned to Ottumwa and was with his father in the milling business until the latter moved out to Independence in 1882. Thereafter father and son were together in milling until the former retired in 1903. Since then William P. Bowen has been owner and manager of the mill at Independence. His plant, which is a large and well equipped one and furnishes feed supplies to a large surrounding territory, is located on the Santa Fe Railroad track at the corner of Ninth and Railroad streets.

Mr. Bowen has had the honor of serving Independence as its mayor for three terms, and each of those terms was a progressive administration of municipal affairs. He has also been a member of the city council two terms and was on the board of education three terms. He is a republican. He has acquired many interests which identify him with this section of Kansas. He owns farm lands in Montgomery and Chautauqua counties and has an attractive residence at 712 North Ninth Street in Independence.

He belongs to the Commercial Club, is past master of Fortitude Lodge No. 107, Ancient, Free and Accepted Masons; a member of Keystone Chapter No. 22, Royal Arch Masons; is past eminent commander of St. Bernard Commandery No. 10, Knights Templar, all of Independence, and is affiliated with Abdallah Temple of the Nobles of the Mystic Shrine at Leavenworth. He also belongs to Lodge No. 17, Ancient Order of United Workmen, at Independence, and to the Woodmen of the World at Independence.

At Ottumwa, Iowa, January 17, 1878, Mr. Bowen married Miss Hester A. Purnell, daughter of William and Rebecca Purnell, both now deceased. Her father was a farmer and business man. To Mr. and Mrs. Bowen have been born four children: Louis H., who is in the flour and feed business at Little Rock, Arkansas; Mary A., whose home is at 4550 Walnut Street, Kansas City, Missouri, and she is the wife of R. M. Snyder, Jr., who is connected with the Kansas Natural

Gas Company; Charles E., assisting his father; and Bertha H., a teacher in the public schools of Independence.

ARCHIBALD STEEL JOHNSON, a resident of Kansas nearly forty years, has one of the very interesting places historically considered. It is located a few miles from North Topeka on rural route No. 6 in Shawnee County, and is a farm of eighty acres which he bought in 1907. The history of this farm is especially interesting. The site comprises the old historic Town of Indianola. This town was established when the Territory of Kansas was new. It was the home of a large number of abolitionists, though there were two or three pro-slavery families in the same community. When this was written in 1916 Mr. Johnson was storing a large crop of alfalfa hay into the building which had formerly been the Indianola Hotel. That hotel is sixty-two years old, stands out weatherbeaten and inconspicuous, though many of its timbers are as sound as when it was built. It has associations with many prominent men and events of early Kansas. It was the meeting place of the abolitionists and the builders of the hotel and the founders of the town expected that the capital of the state would be put there. Not far from the hotel were the homes of some of the first settlers including the Readers, Owens, Rameys, McNowns and others.

Born in Belmont County in Eastern Ohio in 1864, Archibald S. Johnson is a son of Alexander Johnson, who was born in the same county of Ohio in 1822. Alexander was a farmer all his active career. In 1877 he brought his family out to Kansas locating in Pottawatomie County on the Vermilion River, but soon afterward moving down toward St. Mary. In 1895 he moved to Menoken, where he spent his last years as a farmer. In 1863 Alexander Johnson married Sarah McMullen of Belmont County, Ohio. Their seven sons and one daughter were named Archibald, George, Larkin, William, Frank, Charles, Mack and Cicely. Alexander Johnson was a man of good habits, strictly temperate, an honorable, upright and hard-working citizen, and was entitled to the respect and esteem which he always enjoyed.

Archibald S. Johnson was about fifteen years of age when his parents moved out to Kansas. In the meantime he had attended school in Ohio, and in Kansas found ample employment for his energies on his father's farm. In 1890 he began independent farming at St. Mary's and in 1907 he bought the eighty acres including the old site of the historic Town of Indianola, and is farming that land very successfully and profitably.

In 1890 he married Clara McCleery of Pottawatomie County, Kansas. Of their three children two are living, Leota and Jennie. Jennie is still at home, while Leota is the wife of Joseph Bimbarner.

EDWIN SCOTTON. Precisely speaking there is no new country and pioneers and pioneer life no longer exist. An absorbing and fascinating condition has passed into history, and its lessons and inspiration live principally in the lives of those who endured the hardships and contributed by various services and diversified gifts to the upbuilding of the present. Shawnee County has as noble a roll call of early settlers as any part of Kansas, and among those inseparably associated with the Fulton County records, none are more deserving of perpetuation in its annals than is the late Edwin Scotton.

Peter Heil

Susan Heil

Mr. Scotton was born at Manchester, England, May 8, 1827, one of twelve children of his parents, a member of an old and honorable English family, and the son of an English manufacturer who owned large brickyards at Manchester. When he was seven years of age, in 1834, Edwin Scotton accompanied his parents to America, and after eight weeks arrived at Buffalo, New York, having come by way of Canada. The family lived at Buffalo until 1846, when they disposed of their property and went to a 160-acre farm near Huntington, Indiana, in an ox cart. Mr. Scotton, who had received his education in the schools of Buffalo, was married December 29, 1852, to Mary Price, who died November 27, 1856, leaving three children: John F., born October 14, 1853; one who died in infancy; and George C., born November 18, 1856. John F. and George C. Scotton are both now residents of Portland, Oregon. On October 21, 1857, Edwin Scotton was married to Marian Patterson, who died June 22, 1859, leaving one child: Mary A., born November 7, 1858, who is now Mrs. Ed Schooley and lives on the home farm in Menoken Township, Shawnee County. On December 22, 1860, Mr. Scotton was married a third time, being united with Mary Ratcliff. She was born in England, the daughter of a wealthy weaver, who brought his family to the United States but returned to his native land, leaving his daughter in a New Jersey woolen mill, where she supported herself until her marriage to Mr. Scotton.

On his 160-acre farm, Mr. Scotton built a log cabin of 1½ stories, and in this he and his wife lived for one year, when a sawmill was established near their farm and Mr. Scotton had lumber made from the native timber on his land, from which he built a comfortable frame house, the carpets for which were woven by hand by Mrs. Scotton. She also assisted him in the clearing and cultivation of his land, and the farm was highly improved and valuable, but Mr. Scotton thought that he could find better opportunities in the West, and traded his Indiana farm for 640 acres in Wabaunsee County, Kansas, and a small farm in Illinois. He arrived in 1869, but soon found his investment an unprofitable one, as the land was practically worthless for farming purposes, and he traded his Kansas farm for a team of horses and his Illinois land he sold for $320. Somewhat disheartened by this experience he bought twenty acres of land in Shawnee County, then on the edge of the infant Town of Topeka, but now all included in North Topeka. After residing on this property for two years he bought eighty acres in the Kaw River bottom, near Menoken, and for five years lived in a log house, until he erected a large frame residence which is still standing on the home place. From time to time he continued to add to his holdings until at the time of his death, which occurred November 25, 1912, he was the owner of 520 acres of fine land. He devoted himself to general farming and the raising of draught horses, and his operations were uniformly successful, due to his industry and well directed management. Mr. Scotton had a number of discouraging experiences in Kansas, passing through the grasshopper plague and several droughts, but the most severe trial he was called upon to bear was the flood of 1903, when he lost a large part of his property. Then followed the flood of 1908, which was also disastrous to his interests, but not as destructive as the 1903 flood.

Mr. Scotton was long a member of the Grange and took an active part in its work. He was a democrat in his political views, and while he never cared for public office, served six years as justice of the peace in his community, where he was known as a man of absolute honesty and integrity. He was a charter member of the North Topeka Baptist Church and trustee, and always took an active interest in its work, as he did also in education and the general betterment of civic conditions. In 1909 he retired from active affairs and removed to Topeka, where his last years were passed in quiet and comfort. Mrs. Scotton, who was active in church and charitable work, a friend of the poor and a comforter of the unfortunate, passed to her final reward August 11, 1908. There were three children in the family: W. E., born December 10, 1861; Emma Jane, who is now Mrs. Frank Luce, born August 15, 1867; and C. W., who died in infancy.

W. E. Scotton was born in Indiana and was six years of age when he accompanied his parents to Kansas, where the greater part of his education was secured in the public schools of North Topeka. The first built at that place was a small, two-room structure, with planks and board benches, but later his father assisted in the building of a more commodious school in the Menoken Township District, so that the children could have better opportunities. W. E. Scotton remained on the home farm, of which he was given charge when he was twenty-three years of age, and continued as its manager until his marriage to Vietta Betz, of Ohio, a daughter of L. C. and Elizabeth (Bird) Betz, both natives of the Buckeye State. L. C. Betz was injured so that he could not serve in the army during the Civil war, but one of his brothers, Fred Betz, saw active service throughout the struggle as a member of the Tenth Ohio Cavalry. There were four children in the Betz family: Mrs. Scotton; Daisy, who is the wife of T. N. Davis; Bessie, who is Mrs. P. B. Koontz, of Topeka; and Orville, a resident of California. Mr. and Mrs. Scotton have two children: Edwin Betz and Dorothy Frances, both at home.

At the time of his marriage, Mr. Scotton bought 160 acres of land in Menoken Township, which now forms a part of his well-improved farm of 205 acres, in addition to which he has a great deal of town property. He was extensively engaged in general farming and raising hogs and horses, but in 1906 came to Topeka and engaged in the coal and feed business. Ill health caused his retirement from this latter line, and he now lives quietly, looking after his large realty interests. Mr. Scotton is a democrat, and while living in Menoken Township served for four years as township trustee and as a member of the school board for two years. He is treasurer of Eugene Lodge No. 79, of Odd Fellows, an office which he has held for six years. He has also been prominent in church work, he and Mrs. Scotton being members of the North Topeka Baptist Church, of which he has been a deacon for three years and a trustee for a great many years, and in addition is treasurer of the Crittenden Home Society. He has always been a stanch supporter of any movement that has made for better educational or religious methods, for better morals or for better citizenship.

PETER HEIL, now living retired at Topeka, was born in Jefferson County, New York, December 9, 1840. When sixteen years of age he moved with his father, John Peter Heil, to Buchanan County, Iowa. His mother's maiden name was Louisa Bueling, and she died when her son Peter was six years old. His parents were natives of Germany, and came to the United States separately as young people, being married in New York State. When in his native state, Peter Heil attended district school for a few months, but after the removal of his people to the West his help was required to operate the home place and he had little chance for schooling thereafter.

In 1859 Mr. Heil accompanied the family in a covered wagon across Iowa and Missouri into the State of Kansas, the team driven by him consisting of six cows. On the way the little party met many of the disgusted returning argonauts from "Pike's Peak," who had flocked to Colorado at the report of the discovery of gold. The Heil family located on the prairie of Tecumseh Township, Shawnee County, where they bought out a claim consisting of some 172 acres, of which twelve were timberland on East Deer Creek. With the exception of a log cabin, about 16x20 feet, with a "shake roof," and some three or four acres of land broken, all the land was virgin as from the fashioning hand of the Creator. Here they arrived too late to commence operations that year, but in 1860 broke ground and put out crops, which, owing to the drouth, proved an absolute failure.

Peter Heil, in 1860, in consideration of having assisted his father in the building of a stone house, was "given his time." He at once came to Topeka, where for a short period he worked at the baker's trade, but this vocation did not prove congenial and he soon sought other means of making a livelihood. He finally secured a position driving cattle out to the Delaware Indian Reservation, near Lecompton, and there he was engaged in herding until the holidays of 1861. Early in that year he returned to Topeka, where he started to learn the brick and stone mason's trade under the tutorship of John Elliott, but the Civil war came on at that time to interrupt his activities in that direction. On July 16, 1861, he enlisted as a private in Company A, Fifth Kansas Cavalry, a command which fought its first engagement without uniforms, at Morristown, Missouri. This was followed by guard duty in guarding a supply train for the army of Gen. N. Lyon, and at Fort Scott they heard of the battle of Wilson's Creek, after which they were for a time employed in reorganizing the scattered units of the Federal army. Later Mr. Heil's command participated in the battle of Osceola, where it destroyed a great amount of supplies intended for the Confederate army, and subsequently, with 600 or 700 other Federals, Mr. Heil took part in an engagement with a large force of the enemy at Dry Wood, near Fort Scott. In 1861 and 1862 the Fifth Kansas wintered near Barnesville, and in the spring of the latter year went to Springfield with the intention of joining General Curtis. The command was delayed by an engagement at Carthage, and did not reach Curtis' command until after the battle of Pea Ridge had been fought. At Springfield the Fifth Kansas was engaged in guarding supply trains coming to General Curtis' army, and while thus engaged was intercepted by a detachment of Texas cavalry while crossing Black River. After a stirring half hour, the Texans were routed. The command then went on and joined General Curtis' army at Helena, Arkansas, where it was used in scouting and in raids, in which it participated in a number of minor engagements. Under General Washburn the Fifth was on a raid across the Mississippi River, in January, 1863, harassing the rear of the enemy at the time of General Grant's endeavor to go from Memphis to the rear of Vicksburg. During the siege of that city the command

was stationed in the rear of the beleagured city, to keep communication open, and took part in the engagement of July 4th, in which the Federal troops, although greatly outnumbered, killed, wounded and captured enough of the enemy to equal their entire force. The retreating Confederates were then followed to Little Rock, which place was captured, and the command then went to Pine Bluff, where the battle was fought November 25th against the forces of General Marmaduke. The command remained at Pine Bluff until its term of enlistment had expired. Here Mr. Heil, with others, went out to reinforce an empty supply train, and, encountering a large force of the enemy at Mark's Mill, Mr. Heil was captured. He was taken to Camp Ford, near Tyler, Texas, where he was confined ten months, when he was exchanged and sent to New Orleans, and from that city to St. Louis. He was given a thirty-day furlough and ordered to report at Leavenworth, Kansas, where, April 24, 1865, he received his honorable discharge.

On his return from the war, the young soldier resumed his trade, but the hardships of army life had so undermined his health and strength that he was compelled to seek a vocation in which he could again build up. Accordingly, he bought a tract of land in Mission Township, where he continued to be engaged in its successful agricultural pursuits until the fall of 1895, and since that time has resided at Topeka. On first coming to this city Mr. Heil established himself in the seed and supply business, but two years ago retired from active pursuits. In his political views Mr. Heil is a progressive republican and on a number of occasions has served in positions of public trust. He is a Methodist in his religious belief, and is a trustee and was on the building committee of the Lowman Memorial Methodist Episcopal Church. He is a member and post commander of Lincoln Post No. 1, G. A. R. During a long and active career, as soldier, farmer, business man and citizen, Mr. Heil has been true to every trust reposed in him, and is eminently deserving of the esteem and confidence in which he is held.

On December 26, 1865, Mr. Heil was united in marriage with Miss Susan Cox, daughter of Samuel Cox, and to this union seven children have been born, namely: Mary, who died in infancy; Ernest K.; Louis P.; Sheridan and Sherman, twins, both of whom died in infancy; Mabel L., and Roy Harrison.

PHILANDER HAMILTON ADAMS. Ever since the year 1871, members of the Adams family have contributed to the good citizenship, progress and development of Shawnee County, their activities having invaded the fields of agriculture, merchandising, consulting engineering, education, religion, and public service. The founder of the family in this state was the late Jacob Clendenin Adams, and at present it is worthily represented at Topeka by Philander Hamilton Adams, who at this time is the owner of the original homestead, in addition to being a well known business man of the capital city.

Jacob Clendenin Adams was born in 1823 at Ossian, New York, and when a young man left the Empire State and turned his face toward the setting sun. His destination was near Richmond, Indiana, which he reached after a long and tedious journey; and there he was engaged in teaching in the early subscription schools for several years. In 1849, he was united in marriage with Miss Nancy McCoy Hamilton, of Decatur County, Indiana, a daughter of James Edward and Jane McCoy Hamilton, who were large land owners. Not long after that event, he turned his attention to farming, in which he continued to be successfully engaged in Indiana until 1871, which year saw his advent in Kansas. By this time, Mr. Adams was a settled farmer, and when he came to Shawnee County he had no other idea than to engage in his adopted calling. That, however, was one of the worst years in the agricultural history of Kansas, with a state-wide drouth, a financial panic, and a grasshopper plague, and Mr. Adams concluded that he could wait until conditions were more favorable. By 1875, matters were again running smoothly, with good crops and prices booming, and Mr. Adams accordingly purchased 160 acres of fine Kaw River bottom lands, three miles west of North Topeka, on the lower Silver Lake road, which property, with the exception of a small tract, has since remained in the family possession, and now belongs to Philander Hamilton Adams, of Topeka. When Jacob Clendenin Adams came to Kansas, he still retained his property in Indiana, and to this he returned after a short stay in Kansas. He died in 1881. He was the father of eight children, to whom he gave the advantage of college education. They are as follows: Florence, the wife of George C. Merrill, professor of mathematics in Andover College, Massachusetts, and later of Washburn College, Kansas. Philander Hamilton, the subject of this sketch. Mary, who married Robert B. Steele, of 1634 College Avenue, Topeka, son of Rev. John A. Steele, first Presbyterian minister in Topeka. Lillian, the wife of W. W. Mills, a well known dry goods merchant of Topeka. Luella, who is the wife of Charles W. Emery, of Philadelphia, who is a descendant of a New England family. Arthur Lincoln, consulting hydraulic engineer, an acknowledged authority, and otherwise prominent, now deceased; a graduate of the University of Kansas, who married Mary Gemmell, of a distinguished Kansas family. Anna Laurie, an exceptionally brilliant woman, twin of Arthur L., who married Rev. William Baird; went to Korea as a missionary with her husband, and there died, June 9, 1916, leaving three sons who are attending school in America. James Edward, a graduate of Washburn College and Johns Hopkins University, now a missionary in Korea, who married for his first wife Nellie Dick, daughter of a Kansas pioneer doctor; she died in Korea, the mother of three sons and one daughter. In 1912, he was married to Caroline Babcock, daughter of a family of prominence and wealth of Neenah, Wisconsin. To this union, there have been born two children, a son and a daughter.

Philander Hamilton Adams was born in Decatur County, Indiana, in 1852, and there received his early education; later, he attended college in Michigan. He left Indiana, with his parents, in 1871, and after attending school for one year in Kansas, began his career as a stock dealer, but one year later returned to Indiana with his parents. In 1875, he again came to Kansas, this time to reside permanently, and began farming on the 160-acre farm which had been purchased by his father and on which he continued to carry on operations for a quarter of a century. At the end of that time, he left his family in their home at Topeka, and went to New Mexico, where for three years he was engaged in the cattle business. In 1904 he returned to Topeka, where he has since been identified with the dry goods firm operating under the style of the Mills Company. Mr. Adams has had a successful career, as shown in the prosperity he has gained, as farmer, cattleman, and merchant. He is a man of strong character and sound judgment, and likewise known as a good and public-spirited citizen, and a supporter of beneficial civic movements. Mr.

Adams was married first to Ada Metsker, of Shawnee County, a daughter of Judge D. C. Metsker, a pioneer of Kansas. Mrs. Adams died two years later, and in 1885 he was married to Nellie Quinton, of Denmark, Iowa, a singer of some note and daughter of Royal Bellows and Sarah Hornby Quinton, a most distinguished New England family of good old Revolutionary stock and fame. To this latter union there was born one son, Quinton, who is consulting electrical engineer for the Westinghouse Electric & Manufacturing Company, at New York and San Francisco. He has "made good" and is held in the highest esteem, being known as a young man of good morals, high ideals and aspirations, of unusual ability, backed by unlimited energy, and is of great promise.

R. W. LEWIS is now serving his second term as sheriff of Montgomery County. He is a native of Montgomery County, and for many years has had a reputation as a man who does things in a large and efficient way. That is true of his official career as also of his business record. Mr. Lewis has some extensive interests as a merchant in Independence, owns a large amount of property, and is one of the leading oil producers in that section of the state.

He is an American to the core, and represents a family that came from England to Virginia prior to the Revolution. His grandfather spent his life in Virginia as a planter.

R. W. Lewis was born in Montgomery County, Kansas, January 1, 1875. His father is E. T. Lewis, who was born in Virginia in 1844, and is now living practically retired on a small farm a mile north of Independence. He is a veteran of the Confederate army, having enlisted from his native state in 1862 and serving until the close of the war. He was in the Shenandoah Valley campaign and also in many of the battles around Richmond with Lee's army. He was twice wounded, and once taken a prisoner, but managed to make his escape. After the war he came West, lived in Jasper County, Missouri, for several years, and in 1871 homesteaded a quarter section in Montgomery County, Kansas. After locating his claim he returned to Missouri, where he was married, and at once brought his bride to the land where he spent many years in clearing and improving. This farm still belongs in the family, and for a number of years has been in the oil belt, and as late as February, 1916, two more successful wells were drilled there. E. T. Lewis is a deacon in the Baptist Church and is a member of Independence Lodge, No. 17, Ancient Order United Workmen. He was married to Miss Kate Wright, who was born in Kentucky in 1851. Their children are: Ida M., wife of Ray Spradling, a resident of Independence; and R. W. Lewis.

Sheriff Lewis grew up in Montgomery County, had the usual training of a farm boy, and besides the country schools attended high school at Independence. His years were spent quietly and somewhat uneventfully on his father's farm until 1898. In May of that year he enlisted in the famous Twentieth Kansas Regiment of Volunteers for service in the Spanish-American war. He went with the regiment to the Philippines under General Fred Funston, and was with his command in all its engagements in those islands for a year. He returned with the regiment and was mustered out and given his honorable discharge in October, 1899.

After this service which made him one of the honored veterans of the Philippine war, he spent two years on the home farm, but since 1901 his operations and activities have made him a resident of Independence. In that year he engaged in the grocery business, and still has interests in that line, owning the grocery store near the Western States Cement Plant, a mile southeast of Independence and also a grocery store and a residence on Sycamore Street. For three years he was also in the wholesale meat business, but then sold out. Mr. Lewis is vice president of the Legune Oil Company, and for a number of years has been one of the principal independent producers in this section. His property interests are extensive and widely distributed. He owns eighty acres of farm lands a mile southwest of Independence, has large holdings in a plantation in Louisiana, and has a resident property on East Main Street in Independence.

His political affiliations have always been with the democratic party. In the fall of 1912 he was elected for his first term as sheriff, taking office in January, 1913, and was re-elected in 1914 for the term beginning in January, 1915. His offices are in the courthouse and he has his home in the building especially constructed by the county for a sheriff's residence. Mr. Lewis is a member of the Sheriffs' National Association, and other affiliations are with Independence Lodge, No. 780, Benevolent and Protective Order of Elks, Lodge No. 69, Independent Order of Odd Fellows, and Independence Camp of the Modern Woodmen of America.

In March, 1904, Mr. Lewis married at Caney, Kansas, Miss Catherine Ellis, daughter of Alexander and Mary Ellis. Her parents now reside at Mr. Lewis' home near the Western States Cement Plant, and her father has charge of Mr. Lewis' grocery store there. To their marriage have been born three children: Robert Jr., born in 1906 and a student in the public schools; Thomas, born in 1911; and Mary Beth, born in 1914.

SAMUEL HUMMER, by his early settlement and his wide interests as a land owner and business man, is one of the sterling pioneers of Kansas whose names should receive the credit of some record in this publication.

He was born near Gettysburg and not far from the battlefield of that name in Adams County, Pennsylvania, in 1811. His father, P. H. Hummer, served as a soldier in the Revolutionary war. Samuel Hummer grew up in Pennsylvania, followed farming there for a number of years, and in 1868 brought his family out to Kansas. On the 16th of December of that year he ate his first meal in the state at the old Gordon Hotel on East Fourth Street in Topeka. He then settled on his farm and from the first gave particular attention to the raising of good grades of livestock. He was one of the successful men of his time, and lived a long and useful life, which came to its close in 1891 at the age of eighty.

In 1835 in Pennsylvania he married Anna Heller. To their marriage were born five daughters and four sons, and those who grew to maturity were Lewis, Hiram, Isabel, June, Clayton, Ann and Samuel Jr.

The late Samuel Hummer was a man of deep religious convictions, and for years was identified with the Dunkard Church, doing much to maintain that organization in the early days of Kansas. In disposition he was jovial and happy, possessed high moral character, never used liquor nor tobacco and was upright and square in all his dealings. He enjoyed the love and respect of his own family, though he always maintained strict discipline in the household.

Clayton W. Hummer, a son of this pioneer, was born in Adams County, Pennsylvania, in 1851, and

accompanied the family to Kansas. For many years he has been a successful farmer, though he started his career with practically nothing. Since then by hard work and good judgment he has acquired 1,500 acres of land, of which 1,000 acres is under cultivation, and all of it within ten miles of Topeka. He is one of the largest stock raisers in Shawnee County, raising the Durham, Shorthorn and Hereford cattle. His home is on rural route No. 3 out of North Topeka.

In 1896 Clayton W. Hummer married Catherine Copeland and they had two children, Harry Clayton, who is living, and Anna L., who died in infancy. In politics Mr. Hummer is a republican.

SEWARD ALLEN JONES. One of the finest printing establishments of the State of Kansas is that conducted at Topeka by Seward A. Jones and A. D. Birch, who have been its proprietors since 1915. Mr. Jones is a practical printer of experience, having gained his training in this direction in the difficult school of newspaper life, and from the time he reached the age of sixteen years has been identified with type and presses. In his present business he is demonstrating the fact that he is a thorough master of every department of printing.

Seward Allen Jones was born March 25, 1869, in Randolph County, Illinois, and is a son of Alexander G. Jones, and a member of a family which came to America about the time of the American Revolution and has always been noted for its patriotism and for the men of prominence which it has given to the trades and the professions. His grandfather, Gabriel Jones, was a native of Virginia, who removed from the Old Dominion to Illinois in 1830, settling in Randolph County, and subsequently becoming a man of importance and known wide and favorably throughout Southern Illinois. Eight uncles of Seward Allen Jones (his mother's maiden name was also Jones) fought in the Civil war, and three lost their lives while in the service. Alexander G. Jones began business with Gabriel Jones, who later became his father-in-law, at the age of fourteen years, and continued as a merchant until 1912, in which year his wife died and he retired somewhat from active affairs, now making his home with his son, Seward A. In spite of the fact that he is nearly seventy-two years of age, he is as active, both in mind and body, as most men twenty years his junior, and still acts as a secretary of the Young Men's Christian Association, in the work of which he has always taken a helpful part.

At the age of sixteen years, after receiving a public school education, Seward Allen Jones took up the printing business, which he followed until 1885, at that time coming to Mitchell County, Kansas, and establishing the Scottsville News. A short time later he went to Beloit and bought the Beloit Weekly Call, which he changed to a daily, and made it the first daily in Mitchell County as well as the first in the Sixth Congressional District of Kansas. This he continued to publish with increasing success, developing its advertising and subscription list to large proportions, until 1904, when he sold out to advantage and went to Concordia, there becoming the founder of the Concordia Daily Blade. This publication he conducted for five years, at the end of which time he came to Topeka, where, upon the death of Mr. M. O. Frost, he bought the printing plant of his estate and soon built up a business which necessitated his securing larger quarters. Accordingly, in 1915, in partnership with Mr. A. D. Birch, he purchased a new plant and established a business at No. 923 Kansas Avenue, one of the best in the state. The proprietors have installed modern printing machinery of every kind, and are prepared to handle the best grade of work in any line in printing.

Mr. Jones is one of the business men of Topeka who realizes that civic prosperity assists greatly in business progress, and therefore is always willing to help his community in beneficial enterprises. In business circles he bears the reputation of being an honorable and straightforward business man, while in the printing trade he is recognized as a master of the craft.

JACOB E. MAUS. One of the early settlers of Shawnee County as well as one of its prosperous farmers is Jacob E. Maus, who has additional claims to consideration, for he is a veteran of the great Civil war, a survivor of a struggle that brought peace and prosperity, almost uninterrupted for a half century.

Jacob E. Maus was born in Carroll County, Maryland, June 11, 1844. His parents were John and Louisa (Erb) Maus; his grandfather was Jacob Maus, and his great-grandfather was George Maus, who was a soldier in the Revolutionary war. John Maus followed the family avocation of farming and spent his entire life near the Village of Silver Run, Maryland, where he died in 1882. Of his family of children, Jacob E. was the only one to reach maturity.

Jacob E. Maus was afforded far better educational opportunities than many of his young comrades, attending the Silver Run High School after completing his course in the district schools, and after satisfactorily passing examination for a teacher's certificate, taught school acceptably for some time. In search of a wider field of effort, in 1863 Mr. Maus went to LaFayette, Indiana, and in that city, on January 15, 1864, enlisted for service in the Union army, becoming a member of Company L, Fifth Indiana Cavalry, which numerically became the Ninetieth. Mr. Maus' regiment reached the front in time to join General Sherman's army on its campaign to Atlanta, the first battle in which he participated being Resaca, following which he was almost continually under fire until the fall of Atlanta. After the capture of that city his command was ordered back to Nashville, under Gen. George H. Thomas, and from that time until his discharge Mr. Maus was engaged in what may be called constabulary duty—suppressing lawlessness and arresting guerillas. His honorable discharge and mustering out took place September 25, 1865, at Indianapolis, Indiana.

After his military life was over, Mr. Maus returned to his old home in Maryland and resided there until April, 1869, when he came to Kansas. He bought a small place containing thirty acres, in Mission Township, Shawnee County, on which he built a stone dwelling and a barn and lived there with his family until 1885, when he purchased his present place in Mission Township and has continued here ever since. He has prospered during the many years that he has been a resident of the county and has done his part in assisting in the substantial development of this section.

In Maryland, August 30, 1868, Mr. Maus was united in marriage with Emma E. Clark, who died in 1883. They became the parents of the following children: Cora, Frank, James, Charles, George, William, John and Chester Arthur, of whom Cora and George are now deceased.

In politics Mr. Maus is a republican but the earlier generations were democrats. One of his uncles, Jacob

Maus, was a slaveowner. He lost his life through accident, in 1860. Although Mr. Maus has never been a seeker for political honors, he has accepted the responsibilities of office when his fellow citizens have called upon him and has served in many local positions with efficiency and good results. He has always been willing to co-operate with his neighbors in the furthering of practical local improvements and personally has been a generous and benevolent man. He has long been a member of the Methodist Episcopal Church.

When Mr. Maus first came to Shawnee County, the whole country was one vast prairie, an oasis here and there indicating where a courageous pioneer like himself had made a settlement.

MARVIN FREDERICK TRUBY is one of the younger men who are supplying their enterprise in the fields of oil production at Independence.

Independence is his native birthplace, where he was born February 19, 1891. He attended the public schools there and the Montgomery County High School, and completed the sophomore year in the Kansas State University. Leaving college in 1910, he has since been in the oil business and has producing wells both in Kansas and in Oklahoma. He resides at 217 North Second Street. Mr. Truby is a member of the Episcopal Church and politically is an independent democrat. Fraternally he is a member of the Phi Gamma Delta Greek letter fraternity, and of Independent Lodge, No. 780, Benevolent and Protective Order of Elks. He is also a member of the Independence Country Club.

His parents are Marvin L. and Minnie M. (Bishop) Truby, who live in their attractive home at 217 North Second Street in Independence. The senior Mr. Truby is an oil and gas producer and is a member of several companies operating in the Kansas and Oklahoma fields. He also conducts a jewelry establishment at 106 North Penn Avenue.

ANDREY ABRAHAM POTTER. Genius knows no race nor land. Watered by opportunity it flowers in any clime and under all conditions. Among the notably efficient men who make up the faculty of the Kansas State Agricultural College, at Manhattan, particular attention may be directed to Prof. Andrey Abraham Potter because of the achievements which already crown his comparatively short life. As dean of the division of engineering and director of the engineering experiment station, of the Kansas State Agricultural College, he qualifies as an expert in his profession, his recognized standing in which has been signally pronounced upon by his appointment on important national boards and committees.

Andrey Abraham Potter was born at Vilna, Russia, August 5, 1882, and is a son of Gregor and Rivza (Pelonsky) Potter. At the age of fifteen years he came to the United States and in this country secured all his technical training. From the Massachusetts Institute of Technology he received his degree of S. B., in 1903, and in the summer session of 1908 he took a post graduate course in Columbia University. From 1903 to 1905 his activities gave him practical experience in steam turbine construction while in the employ of the General Electric Company at Schenectady, New York. Further practical engineering experience was gained with the General Electric Company at Lynn, and in consulting work in connection with the gas and natural oil fields, oil engines, power plant economies, municipal and private steam-electric and gas-electric power plants, continuing from 1905 to 1915. Additionally, from 1905 to 1910, Professor Potter was assistant professor in mechanical engineering and from 1910 to 1913 professor of mechanical engineering in the Kansas State Agricultural College, after which, until April, 1914, he was acting dean of the division of engineering and acting director of the engineering experiment station, since then he has been dean of the engineering division, director of the engineering experiment station and professor of steam and gas engineering. Hence, for eleven years he has been identified with this institution, working faithfully for its progress and rejoicing in every advance made.

Professor Potter is a man of versatile talent. His studies have been mainly directed along the line which natural talents indicated but he is thoroughly educated in other directions than the one he has found most congenial. As an author in the line of his profession, he has to his credit some fifty signed articles which have been published in such standard journals as Power, the Electrical World and the Coal Age, and other published articles on such subjects as: fuels, gas producers, steam and gas engines, steam turbines, power plant auxiliaries and power plant economies. He is responsible for about twelve bulletins on various phases of engineering research, all these papers being seasonable and scientific and demonstrating the thoroughness of his knowledge and the enthusiasm with which he has grappled with this difficult subject. Mr. Potter is also the author of a book, "Form Motors," which deals in the main with heat engines, concerning which it is a liberal education. On many occasions he has read and presented papers at meetings of the Land Grant College Engineering Association, the Society for the Promotion of Engineering Education (of which organization he is a member of the council, being secretary also of the former), the National Association of Stationary Engineers (of which he is an honorary member), the Kansas Local Engineering and Scientific Societies (of which he is a member), the American Society of Mechanical Engineers and other professional and scientific organizations. He has issued a valuable bulletin on boiler room economics in connection with Kansas State Agricultural College Engineering Experiment Station. These bulletins, scientific as they are, are invaluable to the profession and add much to the sum of general knowledge. Thirty-four years seems a very short period in which to have accumulated the positive knowledge that these and other writings of Professor Potter make manifest.

In 1906 Mr. Potter was united in marriage with Miss Eva Burtner, who was born in Kansas, and they have two children: James Gregor and Helen, aged respectively nine and five years. Mr. Potter is identified with the Masonic fraternity and belongs to several college honorary fraternities, including the Sigma Tau Engineering fraternity and the Phi Kappa Phi.

JOHN M. LEEPER. One of the very successful contractors at Topeka is John M. Leeper, who when a young man learned the trade of brick mason, and on that trade as a foundation has built up a large business in brick contracting and the services of his organization has entered into the construction of several of the most conspicuous public buildings in the state. He is a native of Kansas and was born in Lyon County, September 6, 1872, when that section of the state was still well out on the fron-

tier. His parents were Samuel S. and Elizabeth C. (Morey) Leeper. His father was born in Ohio, came to Kansas in 1870, settling in Lyon County, homesteaded a quarter section of land, and lived there as a farmer until his death, which resulted from his being thrown from a horse. His widow, who is now living at Topeka, was born in Iowa, the daughter of Benjamin M. Morey.

John M. Leeper received his early education in the district schools of Lyon County. While there he learned the trade of brick layer, followed it as a journeyman for a time, and then began taking contracts as an independent builder. For a number of years his home and business interests has been in Topeka. To mention only a few of the important contracts he has handled, he put in the brick work for the Memorial Building, for the state printing plant, for the Warren M. Crosby Dry Goods Building, for the Young Men's Christian Association Building, the Palace Clothing Company Building, and the Mrs. Warren M. Crosby Office Building, all of which are conspicuous structures in the business district of Topeka. He also had the contract for the Manual Training School at Pittsburg, Kansas, and the State Science Building at Emporia, besides a number of structures he has erected for the Wells Fargo Company Express and the Santa Fe Railway Company. Another important branch of his business activities is handling automobiles, automobile repair and supplies. This plant is located at 1113-19 West Sixth Street and is known as the Palace Auto Company. He has a thoroughly equipped establishment, and handles the Paige, Hupmobile and Chevrolet cars. His own attractive residence is at 601 Clay Street.

On October 1, 1894, at Topeka, Mr. Leeper married Miss Jestine Brown, who was born in Shawnee County, Kansas. They are the parents of five children: Mildred J., who was born at Topeka, August 22, 1895, and is the wife of Lowell Hoatson, a bookkeeper at Topeka; Dorothy B., born at Topeka June 4, 1897; Helen E., born December 4, 1901; Mary R., born at Topeka June 21, 1903; and John Milton, Jr., the youngest of the family, born January 7, 1913. Mr. Leeper is a thirty-second degree Scottish Rite and Knight Templar York Rite Mason, is also affiliated with the Mystic Shrine, and is a member of the Topeka Commercial Club.

AARON B. PERINE. One of the few remaining of the old pioneers of Kansas, Aaron B. Perine, of Topeka, came to this state sixty-three years ago, and has been a permanent resident of Kansas since 1854, except for the two years he was out of the state. In the early days he was engaged in work among the Indians for the Government, later turned his attention to the blacksmithing trade, and for many years now has been at the head of the successful Perine Plow Works. He was born at Dansville, Livingston County, New York, May 4, 1836, and is a son of John W. and Mariett (Ingalls) Perine.

Daniel Perrin (as the name was then spelled) was one of the Huguenots who fled from persecution from France, finally seeking refuge in America. On shipboard he met Maria Thorel, who later became his wife, and Aaron B. Perine is a direct descendant of these immigrants. His grandfather, William Perine, served eight years under Gen. George Washington in the Revolutionary war and attained the rank of captain. His father, John W. Perine, was a tanner by trade (then called the tan currier trade), and for the most

A B Perine

part he and his wife passed their lives in Livingston County, New York.

Aaron B. Perine passed his boyhood and youth in several counties of New York and received but a limited education as a lad, his father having died when he was but ten years old. His youthful energies were devoted to learning the blacksmith's trade, which he followed for a time in New York, and in October, 1854, when eighteen years old, came to Kansas for a short stay and for nine months was a resident of Lawrence. In order to encourage settlement, the authorities of Lawrence offered a city lot to anyone remaining in the town through the winter, and thus young Perine came into possession of a piece of town property. However, at that time he did not desire to remain in the new and sparsely settled community, and he therefore sold his title to his lot and in June, 1855, with the small amount of money thus secured and what he had been able to accumulate through helping to lay out the City of Lawrence, he returned to New York. Not long thereafter he again left the Empire State and went to Rockford, Illinois, then to Rochester, Minnesota, later to Joliet, Illinois, and then to Janesville, Wisconsin, finally settling at Iowa City, Iowa. From the latter place, in July, 1857, he again came to Kansas. He first located in Topeka, working at his trade in a shop located where Second and Jackson streets are now situated, and subsequently having a shop of his own at No. 426 Jackson Street. He then entered the employ of the United States Government as a mechanic under William Ross for the Pottawatomie Indians, and later under C. C. Hutchinson for the Saes and Foxes. In this capacity he made many smoking tomahawks, shoed ponies and did other work connected with his trade. His third shop was on Kansas Avenue, Topeka, where the Warren M. Crosby store is now located, and in this venture had as a partner Charles O. Knowles, to whom he later sold his interest in the business. When again ready to embark in business on his own account, he opened a shop where now stands the "Hip" Theatre, on Eighth Street, and it was at this time that he began manufacturing plows, a business in which he has since been engaged with ever-increasing success. The last-named establishment was sold to Dwight Thatcher, who was state printer at that time, and since then Mr. Perine has been located at his present place of business, 809 Quincy Street. His associates in business are his two sons, and the firm has an excellent reputation in commercial and industrial circles of Topeka. Mr. Perine is a citizen who has not failed in discharging his responsibilities, and who still takes an active interest in civic matters. Although he has reached an age where most men are willing to retire, he still has an energetic body and a clear mind which will not allow him to transfer wholly the duties of the business to younger shoulders and intellects.

Mr. Perine was married May 6, 1862, to Miss Mary E. Bodwell, and they have had nine children, namely: Emma G., who is deceased; Frederick James, a printer of Seattle, Washington; Clara Naomi, who is now Mrs. Samuel P. Erwin; Fannie, who is deceased; Loring Lewis; Louise, who is deceased; Raymond Charles; John William; and Sherman Bodwell. Mrs. Perine is a daughter of Anson G. Bodwell and Elizabeth (Ives) Bodwell, who were among the earliest settlers of Kansas and prominent in the work of the Underground Railroad during the border warfare period that preceded the Civil war.

Mr. Perine has been an interested reader of the Scriptures for many years and believes the present war is the beginning of the great time of trouble as foretold by the ancient Prophet Daniel. He thinks this will result in the complete overthrow of the present order of things throughout the world, and then Christ's Kingdom will be established upon earth and cover the whole world as the waters does the sea and it will be an Everlasting Kingdom and the Joy of all People.

Then the human race that have gone down in death will be raised again and with those still living will be given knowledge and ability to comply with all the conditions necessary to come back to perfection of being as Adam was before the fall and they will become lords of the earth as he was and have eternal life in the earthly phase of God's Kingdom where His will will be done the same as it is done in Heaven. Those refusing to comply with these conditions will die the second death, which means they will become as though they never had been.

Anson Green Bodwell, father of Mrs. Perine, was born at Simsbury, Connecticut, June 3, 1801, a son of James and Susannah (Humphrey) Bodwell, and a grandson of Benjamin and Mary (Woodbridge) Bodwell. Mr. Bodwell married Miss Elizabeth Ives, October 1, 1826, who died at Topeka, Kansas, February 13, 1885, Mr. Bodwell surviving until April 4, 1892, when he died in New York, he having reached the remarkable age of nearly ninety-one years. Both were their final resting place at Farmington, Connecticut. They were the parents of ten children, of whom eight grew to maturity, but of whom but two, Mrs. Perine and Mrs. Emeline Stagg, also of Topeka, are now living. Mr. Bodwell, who was a furniture maker by vocation, came to Kansas in 1857, his family following him in the following year, except his two sons, Lewis and Sherman (the latter a soldier of the Union during the Civil war), who came to this state in 1856. There was nothing especially noteworthy in the career of Mr. Bodwell beyond the fact that he was eminently honest, consistently industrious and greatly respected because of the possession of sterling qualities of mind and heart. In later years, Mr. Bodwell was a man of venerable appearance, and his memory is yet kept green in the minds of the few remaining old settlers who live at and about Topeka and who shared with him the privileges of assisting the city in its early and later years of development.

JAMES WILLIAM BELL, a resident of Topeka for more than thirty years, has built up a business and reputation as a buyer and dealer in horses which is by no means confined to the State of Kansas. His operations extend practically over the entire country. He has been a prominent exporter to foreign markets.

James William Bell was born in Greenbrier County in what is now West Virginia but was then Virginia, December 18, 1854. The Bell family goes back to Scotch-Irish antecedents and the first of the name came to Virginia in colonial times. David Henderson Bell, father of James William Bell, was born at Rockbridge, Virginia, in 1818, and when a young man removed to Greenbrier County in what was then the western part of the Old Dominion. Acquiring a large tract of land in that rugged region, he farmed and raised stock on an extensive scale.

For the pursuits of his mature years James William Bell had the equivalent of a liberal literary training. Most of his education was acquired in a school and under a prominent educator. This educator was Doctor Macalhaney and the school was known as Louisburg Academy. Outside of school his other experiences as a young man comprised much work on the home farm, and he also entered a store belonging to his uncle. After several years of clerical experience he removed to Richmond, Kentucky, where he was identified for several years with a large mercantile house, and then established a mercantile business of his own. During his career as a merchant Mr. Bell acquired solid and substantial success.

It was for reasons of ill health due to the confining nature of his business that he finally sold his interests in Kentucky and in 1885 sought recuperation in Topeka. His health was quickly restored in this invigorating atmosphere, and in the meantime he had become so fond of the city that he concluded to remain there permanently. Here he met and married the lady of his choice, a Mrs. Annie Belle Murray. At first he was in the real estate, loan and insurance business, but at the same time became interested as a dealer in horses and mules. This latter branch of the business was the basis of the activities which have constituted his real success in Kansas.

Mr. Bell soon confined himself to the buying of high class coach, driving and harness horses. These horses he shipped to all parts of the United States, Mexico and Canada, and also bought extensively for export. After the automobile came into general use and displaced to a large degree the great demand for coach horses, he turned his attention to draft and express horses. He has also bought extensively all classes of war horses for artillery, cavalry and other branches of the service. He is a recognized authority on every phase of the horse business and has had during his thirty years of experience some unusual incidents and achievements. He and Mr. W. A. Gilchrist as his partner bought a span of dappled gray draft horses who at the age of five years weighed 2,860. In a few months they increased the weight of these animals to 4,140. While the purchase price was $200 each, the pair were soon afterwards sold at auction for $2,050.

C. L. BLOOM. One of the most picturesque careers in the mid-continent oil and gas fields has been that of Camden L. Bloom of Independence. By an unusual capacity for hard labor and by a foresight seasoned by long and active experience he made one large fortune, which was swept away in the panic of 1907. With a few dollars realized by mortgaging his home, he made a new start, and today his operations and holdings would constitute another modest fortune at least.

His life began in Clearfield County, Pennsylvania, March 14, 1868. His people, the Blooms, came from Germany to Pennsylvania about the time of the Revolution. His father was A. W. Bloom, who was long and prominently known in Kansas and died at Independence August 24, 1909. He was born in Clearfield County, Pennsylvania, in 1837, and in that state he followed farming, though his chief business for a number of years centered in the rafting of extensive quantities of hemlock and white pine down the Susquehanna River. In 1877 he moved his family to Fulton County, Indiana, and three years later to Bollinger County, Missouri. In 1884 he made his next step toward the West, settling in Linn County, Kansas, and thereafter confining his attention entirely to farming. From Linn County he moved to Miami County, Kansas, and from there to Independence, where he lived retired until his death. He was a democrat in politics. A. W. Bloom married Rebecca MacCracken, who was born in Clearfield County, Pennsylvania, in 1843, and is now living in Independence in the home her son has provided. Their children were: Enoch, who died in in-

fancy; Minta, who died in Kansas City, Kansas, at the age of fifty-two, the wife of A. P. Stevens, who has charge of the car building department of the Frisco Railroad shops at Kansas City, Kansas; Harry, a farmer in Anderson County, Kansas; Camden L.; Retta, wife of J. E. Goens, of Independence, who is field manager for the Consolidated Gas, Oil & Manufacturing Company and who acquired all his knowledge of the oil business and has profited well by the instruction gained from Mr. C. L. Bloom; Grace, who lives at home with her mother; Maud, wife of H. P. Rouse, a merchant at Fredonia, Kansas; Lum P., an oil well driller at Wayside, Kansas; Dossa, at home with his mother.

No doubt a considerable part of Mr. Bloom's success can be ascribed to the fact that he is a thoroughly practical man in all phases of the oil business, and knew the industry in a technical and many sided way before he reached a position where he commanded the operations and activities of large capital and many men. In his sixteenth year he began for himself as a tool dresser. While thus employed he first became familiar with the methods and requirements of deep well boring. About that time he became acquainted with one of the officers of the Western Security Company, which at that time had its headquarters in Ottawa, Kansas. This company sent him to take charge of a ranch in Linn County, Kansas, known as the Blue Grass Farm, where some very fine blooded horses and cattle were raised. He acquitted himself accreditably during the three years he managed that, and then on account of ill health he resigned and traveling on horseback took a bunch of cattle to the Ozark Mountains, and made a living by trading for a number of months until his health was fully restored.

In 1887 Mr. Bloom formed a copartnership with A. P. McBride under the firm name of McBride & Bloom. Mr. Bloom was still under age, but both he and his partner had the physical stamina and the resourcefulness which prompted them to take contracts involving very heavy responsibilities. They were the pioneer contractors in the development work in the natural gas field of Miami County, Kansas, where the first natural gas agitation in the state was begun. With few exceptions they drilled in all the wells there, and Mr. Bloom had complete charge of the field work of the firm. In the early '90s, the firm drilled in the first two wells in the Neodesha section. That started the development of a very profitable oil and gas field.

The firm's corporations were then extended to Coffeyville, where they accepted a proposition to supply that city with natural gas. They constructed a plant, piped the town and made a success of that as practically every other of their important undertakings. In 1893 the attention of Mr. Bloom and his partner was attracted to the City of Independence, and he took a prominent part in the Independence Oil and Gas Company. It was here that his abilities as an organizer had their first real opportunity. He began developing and obtaining control of great holdings of gas and oil lands that eventually brought their company to a position among the strongest financial institutions of the state. Not only did the firm place the Independence Gas Company on a high plane of efficiency so far as production was concerned, but they also led in the movement to secure to Independence the proper fruit of these great natural resources by attracting great industrial establishments for the utilization of the great volume of gas produced there. In this campaign for industrial building Mr. Bloom's broad minded judgment and public spirit contributed an inestimable value to the city, and his services have always been highly appreciated by those who really understand the foundation upon which the prosperity of Independence rests. The firm of McBride & Bloom was chiefly responsible for the great oil development surrounding Independence, and though Mr. Bloom's interests have been widely diversified he has always been especially loyal to the city of his choice.

For fifteen years he was president of the Consolidated Gas, Oil & Manufacturing Company, was second vice president of the Commercial National Bank of Independence and a director and stockholder in a number of corporations. The partnership of McBride & Bloom existed for sixteen years. Among other operations they drilled wells throughout Kansas, Indian Territory, Missouri and Texas.

Though easily one of the wealthiest men of the state, Mr. Bloom always kept his wealth tied up in a multitude of enterprises and investments, and thus it was when the panic of 1907 swept over the country he was unable to realize quickly enough and soon found his fortune swept away, leaving him in debt to the extent of about $125,000. He was at that time forty years of age. He spent little time in lamenting what could not be helped and was quickly in the harness seeking to retrieve his losses. Throughout that period of depression Mr. Bloom credits much to the sustaining influence and devotion of his wife. They mortgaged their little home, raised $500, and with that he made a new start, and already he has not only cleared up all his indebtedness but is making rapid progress for the second fortune. As a contractor he is now running five strings of tools, four of them in Montgomery County and one in Uvalde County, Texas. In that section of Southwestern Texas he has taken leases on 50,000 acres, and only recently brought in the first well with a good production. For a year he had two men prospecting over Texas, and finally began operations in Uvalde County, where the prospects favor the development of a very extensive field. The Uvalde oil is of a twenty-four gravity.

At one time Mr. Bloom owned very extensive holdings in farm lands in southern Kansas, but has sold all that property. He owns a fine residence at 500 Maple Street and has other residence property in the Aggienette Addition to Independence. Another piece of property owned by him is an entire city square at the corner of First and Poplar streets, one of the most desirable locations in Independence. While helping himself he has always endeavored to help others. Several years ago he laid out an eighty-acre addition known as the Bloom Addition, which he sold on the easy payment plan to clerks and salaried people to furnish them opportunity to own homes of their own.

Mr. Bloom is associated with the Roth-Truby-Guernsey Company, a copartnership, and he has himself taken all the leases which constitute the holdings of that company. Under these auspices he developed and made a success of a gas field which had previously been given up by the Kansas Natural Gas Company. He has been manager since the inception of the Helen Oil Company, which owns holdings in Nowata County, Oklahoma, and the company was named in honor of his daughter. He is manager of the Bloom Oil and Gas Company, which has its holdings in Labette and Montgomery counties, Kansas, and this company has already progressed to the point of shipping oil. He is manager of a number of other concerns, and in every sense of the term is a man of large affairs. It was Mr. Bloom who approximated and closed the deal with R. M. Snyder for 75,000 acres of gas rights, which were the nucleus of the great holdings afterwards acquired by the Kansas Natural Gas Company. That

company started operations with these leases negotiated by Mr. Bloom, and through the subsequent development the Montgomery County field produced more gas than any other field in the mid-continent.

Mr. Bloom is an honored member of the Independence Commercial Club, and is affiliated with the following orders: Lodge No. 780, Protective and Benevolent Order of Elks; Lodge No. 1, Woodmen of the World; Camp No. 649, Modern Woodmen of America; Lodge No. 17, Ancient Order United Workmen; the United Commercial Travelers; the Knights of the Maccabees. Politically he is independent.

For his first wife Mr. Bloom married in Bollinger County, Missouri, Miss Rosa B. Vance. Her father, A. J. Vance, was an attorney and also was extensively engaged in mercantile business. His daughter Rosa thus grew up in a home of comfort, was given a liberal education and was a highly cultured woman. Mr. Bloom himself started life with very little schooling, and he has always confessed a great debt to the influence of his first wife, to whose finely developed mind and character he owes not a little of his own education. He also educated himself by constant association with the best people since his business undertakings have brought him in contact with the leaders of business all over the country. Mrs. Bloom died in 1892. On October 10, 1895, in Kansas City, Missouri, Mr. Bloom married Mrs. Anna Belle (Spaulding) Steele. Her father, A. T. Spaulding, is a retired farmer now living with Mr. and Mrs. Bloom. Mr. Bloom showed not less wisdom in the choice of his second wife, who stood by him loyally in his time of adversity, and by advice and practical assistance has enabled him to establish his financial standing. Mr. and Mrs. Bloom have one child, Helen, who was born October 6, 1899, and is now a sophomore in the Montgomery County High School.

ALBERT DICKENS. For seventeen years Albert Dickens has been connected with the Department of Instruction in the Kansas State Agricultural College at Manhattan, and as professor of horticulture is a recognized authority in that field, not only in Kansas but throughout the Middle West.

Though not born in Kansas, Mr. Dickens has lived in the state for the past forty years and is thoroughly familiar with its general agricultural conditions and its people. He was born at Anoka, Anoka County, Minnesota, October 24, 1867. When he was nine years of age his parents came to Kansas and in 1876 settled on a farm near Sterling, Rice County, where they were pioneers. William and Sarah (Ridge) Dickens, his parents, were natives of England. They came when young with their respective parents to the United States. They were identified during their early married life with the northwestern frontier in Minnesota and afterwards were industrious and capable farmers in Rice County, Kansas.

Reared on a farm, Albert Dickens had to make the best of his advantages, limited as they were. An older sister gave him much encouragement and assistance in his studies as a boy, and he also attended the country schools. After an examination he entered the Kansas State Agricultural College in January, 1890, and was graduated Bachelor of Science in 1893. Mr. Dickens has been connected with some form of educational work for nearly a quarter of a century. He taught in the public schools and at the same time carried on graduate studies in the Kansas State Agricultural College. In 1901 that institution awarded him the degree Master of Science.

In 1899 he was made an instructor in the Kansas State Agricultural College, being assistant in horticulture. Since 1901 he has held the chair of horticulture and has been head of the department in the college. He is widely known among the fruit men of this state, and has made his department a valuable co-operating factor to the individual fruit growers.

He is a member of the American Pomological Society, the Society of Horticultural Science, and the Kansas State Horticultural Society. He belongs to the fraternities Phi Kappa Phi and Alpha Zeta, and is active as a Mason, being past master of his lodge and also a member of the Royal Arch. In 1898 he married Bertha Kimball, who is also a graduate of the Kansas State Agricultural College. Their children are: Elizabeth, William, Richard K. and John B. Dickens.

EDWIN H. LUPTON. Ever since its arrival in America, some 250 years ago, the Lupton family has been identified with the opening up of new sections of this country. The earliest American progenitor was a pioneer of New England; later members were early settlers of Ohio, Michigan and Iowa, and the present representative of the family, Edwin H. Lupton, has been one of the foremost factors in encouraging settlement and development in certain parts of Kansas, particularly in Sheridan County, where he has large interests. In addition to being an extensive property owner, Mr. Lupton is president of the Bank Savings Life Insurance Company of Topeka, Kansas, is one of the leading real estate dealers of Hoxie and has been the medium through which some large transactions have been consummated.

Edwin H. Lupton was born in Muscatine County, Iowa, in 1858, and came to Kansas in 1886 from Nebraska, where he had located in 1880. He is a son of William C. Lupton, a native of Ohio, and a grandson of Gideon Lupton, who was born in Virginia. The family is of Quaker descent, and its members have always conformed to the beliefs of that creed. Gideon Lupton was one of the very early settlers of Ohio, and subsequently became a pioneer of Michigan, where he spent the last years of his life in agricultural pursuits and died. His son, William Carr Lupton, was born in Ohio, and in 1854 located in Muscatine County, Iowa, when that part of the country was still new. Later he bought considerable property in Benton County, in the same state, and moved to this land in 1859, there passing the rest of his life in farming ventures. As an illustration of the increase in land values, it may be noted that this property was bought by Mr. Lupton at $1.25 per acre, and is now worth $200 an acre. Mr. Lupton was a man of high moral character, whose word could always be relied upon, and who, in his daily life, exemplified the teachings of the Society of Friends. He was a good citizen, supporting all public-spirited movements, and was held in the highest esteem in his community. He married Miss Emma Walker, daughter of John Walker, an Englishman, and they became the parents of eight children, of whom three are now living: Gideon, who is a ranchman near Sheridan, Wyoming; May, who is Mrs. C. H. Brown, and also lives near Sheridan, Wyoming; and Edwin H.

Edwin H. Lupton was educated in the public schools of Iowa, and was twenty-two years of age when he went to Western Nebraska. There he was employed at various occupations, seeking one in which he could get a real start in life, his principal vocation being that of freighter between the most important towns of the locality at that time, viz.: St. Paul, Kearney, Grand Island and Loup City. When he gave up freighting, Mr. Lupton entered the employ of C. J. Burke, a hardware dealer of Kearney, and after spending several years as a clerk was admitted to partnership when he bought a half interest on credit. He remained in this line for two years and three months, and in 1886 disposed of his interests and came to Kansas, locating at Hoxie, the county seat of Sheridan County. With his small capital, laboriously accumulated during his years as clerk and hardware merchant, he began business as a banker and loan agent, but soon disposed of that business to enter in the more promising, and, as it turned out, more profitable one of real estate and insurance, for which Mr. Lupton seemed to have a veritable genius. During a period of thirty years in which he has been engaged in this business he has accumulated 7,000 acres of fine Western Kansas land, but it is his well taken contention that he is not only an accumulator, but a producer and developer as well. He is one of the most extensive farmers in Western Kansas, where he had 1,200 acres in wheat, 800 acres in grain, and other large tracts devoted to produce, and has the greatest faith in his part of the state, believing that any man with good health and the spirit of industry can make a success. That he is a skilled farmer is shown in the fact that on his special farm of forty acres, located at Hoxie, he sowed wheat in 1914, 1915 and 1916, and secured a yield of ninety-seven bushels per acre, or above thirty-two bushels per acre per year. He has had some remarkable earnings from some of his Sheridan County lands, an illustration of which statement is found in the fact that he has received 6 per cent on a value of $250 per acre on land that cost him $4.07 per acre. One of the things that he has the greatest faith in is the value of irrigation, and recently he negotiated a loan of $40,000 for an irrigation plant at Scott City. Mr. Lupton inherits many of the sterling qualities of his Quaker forebears, comes of a strictly temperance family, and is himself a total abstainer, having never touched a drink of alcoholic beverage in his life. His reputation in business circles of both Sheridan County and Topeka is an excellent one, and as a citizen he has done much to aid in the development, material and civic, of the state of his adoption.

Mr. Lupton was married in 1895 to Miss Clara B. Lytle, of Wadsworth, Ohio, a member of a family well and favorably known at that place. To this union there have been born two sons and two daughters: Margaret, Edwin H., Jr., and Claribel, who are graduates of the State University; and Elmer, who entered high school in 1916 at Topeka.

DAVID O. CRANE. Of the men who have served Topeka in official capacities of importance and responsibility, few have won more fairly a reputation for fidelity than has David O. Crane, since 1884 superintendent of the Topeka Cemetery. In the thirty-two years that he has been the incumbent of this office he has labored efficiently and conscientiously to discharge its duties in a reverent and honorable way, and the mere fact that he has held his office during such a long period should be sufficient evidence of the quality of his ability and the worth of his service.

Mr. Crane was born at Easton, Pennsylvania, February 12, 1842, and is a son of Franklin L. and Mary Elizabeth (Howell) Crane. His father was born at East Windsor, Connecticut, January 10, 1808, and was a veteran of the Civil war, through which struggle he fought as a private of Company E., Eleventh Regiment, Kansas Volunteer Infantry. Franklin L. Crane, Jr., a brother of David O. Crane, was a private in that same war, being identified with Company G., Second Regiment, Kansas Volunteer Infantry. Doubtless father and son who fought for the Union inherited their patriotic military tendency, for David Crane, the grandfather of David O., was a soldier of the Continental line during the War of the American Revolution.

David Orville Crane received his educational training in the public schools of Easton, Pennsylvania, and Dobbs Ferry, New York, at which latter place he resided for four years. The year 1858 saw his advent in Topeka, where he attended school during that winter, and then started to prepare himself for his career as an apprentice to the printer's trade, under the teaching of J. F. Cummings, at that time proprietor of the Topeka Tribune. He was so engaged when men's minds were turned from their personal affairs to the great issues that were affecting the country, and May 14, 1861, enlisted from Shawnee County, in the three months' service, as a musician, in Company A, Second Regiment, Kansas Volunteer Infantry, under Capt. Leonard W. Horne and Col. Robert B. Mitchell. The Second was recruited during May and was rendezvoused at Lawrence, was mustered into the United States service at Kansas City, Missouri, June 20th, and joined the brigade commanded by Major Sturgis, at Clinton, Missouri, which was attached to the division of Brigadier-General Lyon, near the Osage River, at St. Clair, Missouri.

The company of which Mr. Crane was a member was established in camp near Springfield, Missouri, where drilling commenced, and, after being put under the command of General Dietzler, the First and Second regiments had their baptism of fire at Forsythe, Missouri, July 22d. Subsequently, they moved south under General Lyon, and, on August 2d, engaged and defeated the enemy at Dug Springs, pursuing him to McCulloch's Ranch. The enemy fell back to concentrate his columns into a unit, and the Second Kansas retired to Springfield; where a large and heavy supply train awaited it, this train having been so large and unwieldy as to preclude the idea of rapid movement without its abandonment. General Lyon determined then to attack at daylight, August 10th, and accordingly Colonel Sigel's artillery opened the engagement of Wilson's Creek, with the Second Kansas supporting Totter's Battery on the extreme left of the Union line. During the first part of the battle, which was fought in a cornfield, the regular infantry fell back, but the Second Kansas covered the retreat with the aid of the battery mentioned and drove the enemy beyond the field. Colonel Mitchell fell, wounded, and General Lyon, himself twice shot, answered the call of Mitchell to lead the regiment. He had just turned to fulfill the order, with the words: "Come on, brave men!" when he fell, mortally wounded by a bullet in the breast. Lieutenant-Colonel Blair at once assumed command, and, after six hours of severe fighting, received orders to withdraw his troops. Feeling it impossible to retire at such a crucial moment, he held his ground for another hour and one-half, by which time the enemy's fire had been completely silenced and he withdrew. The Second Kansas was the only regiment to maintain its line during this battle from first to last, but it was at the cost of one-third of its number. At the close of this engagement, the command returned to Springfield, and then went by way of Rolla and St. Louis to Leavenworth, Kansas, where it received orders to reorganize. Mr. Crane received his honorable discharge October 31, 1861, and re-enlisted March 17, 1862, for three years' service, as a private in Company A, Fifth Regiment, Kansas Volunteer Cavalry, under Capt. William F. Creits and Col. Powell Clayton. This regiment participated in the engagement at Drywood, September 2, 1861; at Morristown, Missouri, September 17th, where Col. Hampton P. Johnson fell; at Osceola, where they attacked the rear of Price's army and routed the enemy. Lieutenant-Colonel Clayton assumed command of the regiment in February, 1862, and in May of that year, the hard-fighting Fifth drove the guerilla hordes of Coleman out of that section of the country. On July 6th it routed an Arkansas cavalry regiment at Salem, Arkansas, and in the following winter engaged in several skirmishes with the Confederate cavalry near Helena, Arkansas. On May 7, 1863, the regiment joined the expedition of Colonel Clayton through the country to the west and south of Helena, destroying supplies, etc., and August 15th joined Colonel Steele's Arkansas expedition. On September 10th it engaged the enemy at Little Rock, and October 25th was attacked at Pine Bluff by General Marmaduke, with 3,000 men and twelve pieces of artillery. Colonel Clayton had but 600 men to oppose this attack and nine pieces of artillery. After six hours of action the lines of the Gray were defeated at all points, the Confederates leaving the field in possession of Colonel Clayton and his brave men. Not long after this battle, Mr. Crane was transferred to Company H, Fifth Regiment, Kansas Volunteer Cavalry, with which he served throughout the remainder of the war. He was honorably discharged at Fort Leavenworth, Kansas, July 19, 1865, and returned to his Topeka home.

David O. Crane had charge of the Topeka Cemetery from 1868 until 1871 under the direction of his father, who had for some years served as its superintendent. In the spring of 1871 the younger man removed to Osage City, Kansas, where he held the office of city clerk for eight years and that of justice of the peace for two years, and continued to live in the same city until the death of his father, November 17, 1884, since which time he has lived at Topeka and has had charge of the cemetery. Prior to November, 1884, there had been 3,857 interments, and at the present time the number aggregates 15,659.

On March 3, 1869, Mr. Crane was joined in wedlock with Anna S. Kay, of Topeka, whose brother, James T. Kay, had served in Company C, Eighty-third Regiment, Indiana Volunteer Infantry, and was killed in battle during the Civil war. To this union there have been born four children, of whom three are living: Mrs. Mary E. Radcliff, Miss Anna S., and Franklin L.

Fraternally, Mr. Crane is affiliated with the Masons, in which he has taken all the degrees up to and including the thirty-second; the Independent Order of Odd Fellows; the Knights of Pythias; the Ancient Order of United Workmen; the Modern Woodmen of America, and the Fraternal Aid Society. He belongs also to Lincoln Post No. 1, Department of Kansas, Grand Army of the Republic. Mrs. Crane holds membership in Lincoln Circle No. 1, Ladies of the Grand Army of the Republic, and she and her daughters are members of Naomi Rebekah Lodge No. 95 and of the Order of the Eastern Star. Mr. Crane is a republican in politics and a man of high moral and religious principles. He was vice president of the Crane & Company, Printers, of Topeka, for a number of years, but owing to a continued illness, following a stroke of paralysis, resigned his office and since then has continued to give his entire attention, assisted by his wife and daughter, to the care of the Topeka Cemetery.

HERSCHEL C. PORTERFIELD. Thirty-five years in the oil fields and thirty years as a contractor and producer constitute the record of this veteran of an industry which has brought Kansas untold wealth. Like hundreds of men of this class, he has found Independence as the most satisfactory city for residence and business headquarters.

In another respect he is typical of perhaps a majority of the oil men of the country—his native state is Pennsylvania. Born in Butler County, August 10, 1856, he was one of several brothers to become identified with the oil industry in one way or another. Up to the age of eighteen he lived at home and attended the public schools of his native county. Then after six years more spent assisting in the work of his father's farm, he began regular employment as a worker in the oil district, first in Butler, then in Venango County, afterwards in Cattaraugus County, New York, Washington County and Toledo, Ohio, and from the East came to Kansas on April 1, 1903. He spent a time in Chanute, then went to Peru, but since 1904 has had his home and headquarters in Independence.

It was in Venango County, Pennsylvania, in 1886, that Mr. Porterfield did his first contracting. He bought a string of tools, and since then has worn out many sets and is now interested in five strings, which in recent years he has had at work in the oil districts of Kansas and Oklahoma.

He and M. D. Mitchell are the constituent members of the Amherst Oil Company, which has sixty-five producing oil and two gas wells, he being manager, foreman and director of the company. He is manager and has a fourth interest, besides what his sons own, in the Skinner Oil Company, that has seven producing oil wells. Nearly a half interest is owned by Mr. Porterfield in the Argue-Porterfield Company with its eight producing wells.

In the twelve years since he came to Independence Mr. Porterfield and family have resided at 1114 West Main Street. In politics he is independent with strong leanings toward prohibition, and is a member of the Methodist Church.

He comes of excellent family stock, largely Irish and Scotch, and has good reason to be proud of his own children. His Grandfather William Porterfield, of Irish descent, was born in Pennsylvania in 1784, was a farmer, and died in Butler County in 1864. He married Jane Lowry, who was of Scotch family, and she was born in 1791 and died in Butler County in 1866. The Lowrys were very prominent in Pennsylvania early affairs, and her two brothers, Mathew and Walter, were especially men of note.

Mr. Porterfield's father, Pliny F. Porterfield, was born in Butler County in 1826, spent nearly all his life there, and died in 1908 in the house where his son Herschel was born and on the place which has been in the family since the pioneers drove back the Indians and took possession of the land. Though a farmer, he was well educated, had taught school, and studied to be a physician. He was elected and served a long time as justice of the peace, and was a loyal worker and trustee of the Presbyterian Church. He was a repub-

lican, and a member of the Ancient Order of United Workmen. The maiden name of his wife was Amy A. Boomer, who was of Irish descent. She was born in 1833, and died at MacDonald, Pennsylvania, in 1912. This is a brief record of their children: Amelia Jane married Jonathan Hartman, and they reside at Lima, Ohio, Mr. Hartman having been connected with the Standard Oil Company until he was retired on a pension; Herschel C. is the second in age; Pliny Fisk died at the age of twelve; Carrie May, residing in Butler County, is the widow of Harry Gates, who was an oil producer; Amy Luella, deceased, married U. S. Rhodabarger, now an oil producer in Cleveland, Oklahoma; Harry B., resident of MacDonald, Pennsylvania, among other business interests is an assistant superintendent of the Standard Oil Company; William K. is an oil contractor and producer at Emlenton, Pennsylvania; P. F. is a foreman for the Standard Oil Company and lives in Pittsburg, Pennsylvania; Mary J. married Joseph McQuiston, of MacDonald, Pennsylvania, who has been a foreman for the Standard Oil; and B. L. is a foreman for the Standard Oil at Oakdale, Pennsylvania.

Most of Mr. Porterfield's own children are grown and established in business or homes of their own. In Venango County, Pennsylvania, in 1880, he married Miss Lydia A. Ogden, a daughter of J. N. and Priscilla Ogden. Her father is still living, a retired farmer and music teacher, at Oil City, Pennsylvania. Five children were born to Mr. and Mrs. Porterfield: Garnette Luella is the wife of Frank McKenna, a boiler maker by trade and a resident of Marietta, Ohio; H. M. is an oil producer and oil worker and lives at Wayside, Kansas; C. E. has followed in the same line as his father and brother and lives at Sedan, Kansas; Twila Annetta, living with her parents, is stenographer with Tomlinson & Shukers, attorneys; Virgil Lowry died December 2, 1915, at the age of eight years.

ARTHUR BOURNE SMITH, PH. B., B. L. S. The degree following Mr. Smith's name means Bachelor of Library Science. He is librarian for the Kansas State Agricultural College at Manhattan. That position he has held since 1911 and is a librarian of wide experience and has done much to make the library at Manhattan accessible and useful not only to the students of the Agricultural College but to all who use it for reference purposes.

Mr. Smith was born at Elizabeth City, North Carolina, August 2, 1873. He is a son of Charles Wesley Smith, now deceased, and Hester (Bourne) Smith, who now resides with her youngest son at Seattle, Washington. The father, who was born in Pennsylvania of German lineage, at the age of seventeen enlisted in a Pennsylvania regiment in defense of the Union. He gave four of the best years of his early life to that cause. After the war he located at Elizabeth City, North Carolina, and became head of a lumber and mercantile corporation which he had helped organize. It was a very successful business but ill health compelled him to resign his place there, and on leaving the South he removed to Elmira, New York, where he was a merchant until his death at the early age of thirty-five. He left a widow and four children. The children are Walter L.; Winnogene; Arthur B. and Charles Wesley Smith. Their mother was born in Pennsylvania, and comes of an old New England family of English lineage.

Soon after the father's death the widowed mother and her children moved to a farm in Tioga County, New York. That was the scene of Arthur B. Smith's early experiences. At the age of sixteen he was able

to obtain a teacher's license, and then began his work in the rural schools of New York. In 1895 he graduated from the Genesee Wesleyan Seminary at Lima, New York. In the meantime from 1892 to 1895 he was librarian in charge of the seminary. That experience gave the permanent bent to his subsequent career. In 1895-96 he was principal of the public school of Smithboro, New York. During 1896-1900 he was library assistant in the Wesleyan University at Middletown, Connecticut, and was graduated Ph. B. from that university in 1900. During 1900-02 he was assistant in the University of Illinois library, and there continued his studies in library science and was given the degree B. L. S. in 1902.

From June to September, 1902, Mr. Smith assisted in editing the Cumulative Book Index, United States Catalogue and Reader's Guide to Periodical Literature. In 1903 he became lecturer on bibliography in the University of California, and in that institution was head of the order department of the library from 1902 to 1911, head of accession division of the library during July and August, 1911, and instructor in summer schools in 1906 and 1907. In 1911 Mr. Smith came to Kansas and became librarian of the Kansas State Agricultural College at Manhattan. He is a member of the Kansas, the California and the American Library associations, and is treasurer of the Kansas Library Association. He is also a member of the Kansas State Teachers Association and belongs to the Delta Tau Delta, Greek letter fraternity. He is a Methodist. In 1902 he married Miss Mary Read of Delavan, New York.

WILLIAM BOAST. Nearly forty-five years ago the Boast family came to Shawnee County, Kansas. Mr. William Boast, who now lives retired in Topeka, had a long and active career in general farming and stock raising, and by industry and good foresight he accumulated 480 acres in Menoken Township of Shawnee County. He retired from active farm work in 1901, and later sold his old homestead and reinvested in a quarter section of land six miles north of North Topeka on the Rochester Road. He also owns 270 acres of fine Missouri land six miles north of Kansas City.

Mr. Boast is a member of an English-Canadian family. He was born in Richmond County of the Province of Quebec in 1854. His grandfather, Joseph Boast, was born in Yorkshire, England, and came to Canada in very early days. William Boast, Sr., who was born in Montreal, Canada, in 1821, brought his family to Kansas in 1872 and located in Shawnee County. For many years he was a prominent resident of Menoken Township, where he died in 1899 at the age of seventy-eight years, six months. He was a man of more than ordinary ability, and his public spirited citizenship was on a par with his success as a business man. William Boast, Sr., married Anna Scott of the Province of Quebec. Her father, George Scott, was a successful farmer. To their marriage were born ten children, five sons and five daughters. Those now living are William, Jr., Anna and Edward. The daughter Anna is Mrs. Clinton Antrim and lives at 1269 North Kansas Avenue in Topeka. The son Edward is a farmer and lives near Elmont.

William Boast, Jr., was eighteen years of age when the family came to Shawnee County, Kansas. In the meantime he had received a substantial education and was ready to take up the serious responsibilities of life. He lived with his father in

Menoken Township ten miles north of Topeka and afterwards went on a farm of his own, and with what success his activities as a farmer were carried on has already been noted.

In 1880 Mr. Boast married Miss Lulabell Coleman. Her father, A. M. Coleman, came from Indiana to Kansas in 1871 and was one of the early farmers of Menoken Township. Mr. and Mrs. Boast are the parents of three sons and one daughter, C. W., R. A., G. A. and Hazel Ann. The son C. W. is now a mail carrier in Topeka and lives in Highland Park. R. A. resides with his father at 909 North Jackson Street. G. A. is proprietor of a feed yard in Kansas City, Missouri. Hazel Ann recently completed her studies in the Topeka High School.

WILLIAM HENRY WILSON is one of the oldest of Topeka's merchants. He is an honored veteran of the Civil war, and has been a resident of Topeka since December 17, 1877. Along with success in business he has given his time unselfishly and conscientiously to the betterment of his city, and he should be long remembered for his efficient service while on the city school board. He has also attained the highest honors in Masonry.

His parents, Orrin and Sarah T. (Wilson) Wilson, had six children named Helen Jane, William Henry, George W., Clarence E., Mary E. and Louise. William Henry was born at South Granville, New York, April 16, 1842. His great-grandfather in the maternal line, William Park, was a sergeant and later quartermaster in Col. Elias Wood's Massachusetts Infantry during the Revolutionary war. His grandfather, William Wilson, who married Susan Bothwell, fought as an American soldier in the War of 1812, and participated in the campaign around Lake Champlain. After the war he returned to his farm in Washington County, New York, where he lived until death. Orrin Wilson was born July 4, 1803, was reared and educated in Western New York and spent all his life as a farmer.

It was in the district schools of New York State that William H. Wilson acquired his early training. However, at the age of fifteen he left school to begin an apprenticeship at the marble cutter's trade at Scoharie, New York. He was working at his trade until August 5, 1862, when he answered the call of patriotism and enlisted in Company C of the One Hundred and Thirty-fourth New York Infantry. In a few days he was made sergeant of the company, and was mustered in with his comrades September 22, 1862. Going to Fairfax Courthouse, Virginia, they were brigaded under Col. Orland Smith. They arrived two days after the first great battle of Fredericksburg, Virginia, having been delayed by the heavy roads. They then fell back three miles north of Falmouth, where they remained in camp until the second battle of Fredericksburg in January, 1863. After that the One Hundred and Thirty-fourth Regiment did fatigue duty, drilled, and guarded supply trains and forage at Aquia Creek Landing. After a few weeks they were started to participate in the Chancellorsville campaign, where they engaged the enemy on May 1st and 2d. On the second day of the fighting owing to Major-General Hooker losing control of himself their regiment was forced to withdraw as far as Stratford Courthouse, where the regiment was in camp until June, 1863. It then took part in the Gettysburg campaign. From June 29th until the 1st of July they were in camp at Emmettsburgh, Maryland, and then left in the early morning for Gettysburg, arriving on the field at 1 o'clock in the afternoon of the first day of fighting. They went through the town and were soon in the midst of the heaviest part of the engagement. That morning the regiment had mustered in 430 strong and they came out with only 178 men. In that battle, perhaps the greatest of the war, Mr. Wilson sustained a wound in the leg which kept him in Saterlee Hospital in West Philadelphia for a year and a half. While convalescing he had charge of his ward in the hospital, and used his leisure time to study and acquire a knowledge of drugs. He also applied himself to the study of military tactics and technique for seven weeks, and passed an examination before a board and was qualified to fill the position of first lieutenant of the United States Colored Troops, though the appointment never came. On being dismissed from the hospital he rejoined his regiment in North Carolina near Raleigh on April 25, 1865. Shortly afterwards Gen. Joseph Johnston surrendered to Gen. William T. Sherman, and that closed the war. His army division arrived in Washington City May 19, 1865, and on the 24th of that month he was in the grand review of Sherman's troops. He was mustered out at Bladensburg, Maryland, June 10, 1865, and received his honorable discharge at Albany, New York, June 22, 1865.

In the meantime his mother had died and after this loss Mr. Wilson had some real journeyman experience as a marble cutter, traveling about the country. He also lived in Monroeville, Ohio; then went to Fremont, Ohio, in 1866, and worked for a time as clerk in his cousin's store. In January, 1871, he engaged in the marble business at Decatur, Illinois. He was soon overtaken by the mining fever, and had a brief experience of two months in the mines of Utah, but after a visit to California returned to Decatur, Illinois, where he remained until moving to Topeka.

His first work in Topeka was as an under clerk for J. C. Wilson, clerk of the United States District Court at the time. He soon found more congenial employment as clerk in the Jones Brothers drug store. He was given this position because of the knowledge he had acquired at the hospital during the war. After two years with Jones Brothers he formed a partnership with Mr. Roe, and engaged in the drug business for himself at the corner of Fourth and Madison, under the firm name of Roe & Wilson. His store was there for four years, and he then sold his interest and set up a drug business of his own. He was the first and only tenant of the building he now occupies at 414 East Fourth Street, and has been there continuously for twenty-seven years.

Mr. Wilson's service on the Topeka Board of Education if described in detail would prove an important chapter in the history of local education. He held his membership on the board for sixteen years, was its vice president four years, and president two years. He was a member of the building committee fifteen years, and chairman of that committee eight years. In that time he was instrumental in building the most modern schoolhouses of the city, and remodeled the older buildings so as to better serve the purposes and the comfort of both teachers and pupils. It is characteristic of Mr. Wilson that he does well whatever he undertakes, and he applied himself with characteristic energy to the tasks involved while he was on the school board. He was chairman of the building committee when the manual training high school was erected. His services on the board were greatly appreciated by his fellow members and consequently his recommendations were always received with due respect and with almost complete confidence in the value of his judgment. Some of the most prominent men of Topeka were associated with him on the board of education, including P. I. Bonebrake and Edward Wilder. It is noteworthy that while a stanch republican Mr. Wilson has never been a politician, and his public services have been rendered without any expectation of material reward.

His Masonic record is one of especial interest. On the 1st of January, 1916, he was given a life membership in the Scottish Rite body of the Masonic order at Topeka as a reward for his faithful associations and work of half a century. He took his first degree at Monroeville, Ohio, November 27, 1865, soon after leaving the army. The second degree came December 28, 1865, and the third degree on January 10, 1866. In 1867 he was made a Royal Arch Mason at Fremont, Ohio, and in October, 1873, took the Knight Templar order in Beaumanoir Commandery No. 9 at Decatur, Illinois. In February, 1890, he took the degrees in Cryptic Masonry in Yabud Council No. 4, Royal and Select Masters, at Topeka. In November, 1894, he was given the degrees of Scottish Rite from the fourth to the thirty-second inclusive in Topeka Consistory No. 1. In October, 1895, he received the degrees of the Royal Order of Scotland at Washington, D. C., and in October, 1899, was given the supreme and honorary thirty-third degree at Washington. In May, 1903, during the session of the Imperial Council in Topeka he was made a Knight of the Red Cross of Constantine.

For many years Mr. Wilson has likewise been prominent in Grand Army circles and is a member of Lincoln Post No. 1 of Topeka. His friends have long appreciated the fact that Mr. Wilson has accomplished a great deal in the world and much more than many men whose early advantages were greater. He had a meager education in school and it was by continued night study and his work in the hospital while in the army that brought him a practical education and a more than ordinary knowledge of current history and affairs. Although now seventy-four years of age, he is still active in business, and is thoroughly in love with his work in all its branches.

While he was living at Decatur, Illinois, he was married October 16, 1875, to Miss Jennie Newell. Mrs. Wilson died October 31, 1880. Of her three children one died in infancy, Kate is also deceased, and the only survivor is William H., Jr., of Topeka. On May 26, 1886, Mr. Wilson married Kate W. Rudolph, who was born in Kansas. Three children have also blessed this union: Arthur R., Florence R. and Ruth Jeannette. The son is a resident of Akron, Ohio, while the daughters are still at home. Mrs. Wilson was born near Vinewood Park, in Topeka, and for years has been prominent in social life, as a member of Lincoln Circle and of the Eastern Star, of which she was worthy matron. While devoted to her home and children, she gave of her time and enthusiasm to do good in the community. The daughter Florence has also taken a prominent part in church and charitable work, and is very active in the First Congregational Church of Topeka.

WILLIAM E. CORBETT. One of the forceful characters of the middle period of Shawnee County history was the late William E. Corbett. During his thirty-eight years in this section his many sterling traits of character made him honored, respected and esteemed.

William E. Corbett was born in Maine and lost both parents by death before he was ten years old. For some eight years he made his home with his paternal grandfather and during this time was fortunate in one way, being sent to school and thus securing a practical education, which was helpful through his subsequent life. When nineteen years old, being robust as well as adventurous, he decided to start out for himself, the great western country particularly attracting him. He found employment in the harvest fields before reaching Minnesota, in which state he worked in logging camps for a few years, and as he received fair wages and was prudent enough to save them, he was able to accumulate some capital. He then returned to Maine, but was not satisfied with conditions there after his wider vision of the world, and in 1869 again came west and located in Kansas, buying 340 acres of Santa Fe Railroad land in Mission Township, Shawnee County, paying as much cash as he could spare at that time, going in debt for the balance. In his journey from Maine to Kansas he traveled by railroad as far as Quincy, Illinois. There he bought a span of mules and covered the rest of the distance riding one and using the other as a pack animal, and later they were very valuable adjuncts on the farm. While farming was his principal occupation, a large source of income was his livestock business, raising horses, cattle and hogs in great numbers, and in the course of time he accumulated a comfortable store of worldly goods. Like many others, however, Mr. Corbett worked too hard and doubtless thereby shortened his life. His death occurred April 14, 1907. Notable among his characteristics were his love of work, his upright, wholesome, sturdy manhood, his honesty and his generosity. Owing to the latter trait, coupled with a tender heart, he was often imposed upon by the unscrupulous.

After coming to Shawnee County Mr. Corbett was married to Leah Hampe, who died March 17, 1901. Four children were born to this union: Zella (Mrs. George Pratt), Hannah, William and Margaret (Mrs. Clarence Read).

William Corbett, the only son, was born on the old home place, October 22, 1886, and has lived here all his life. His fine farm of 184 acres is a part of his father's homestead, and under his intelligent and careful management it is yearly increased in value, its yields conclusively demonstrating that Shawnee County is not far behind the richest sections of this or other states. Many of the early settlers seem to have had remarkable foresight when they chose their land.

William Corbett was united in marriage with Miss Blanche Read, who is a daughter of Rev. A. C. Read, one of the old-time preachers in Kansas. They have had three children: William E., Edna and Gertrude, the last named dying when nineteen months old.

Mr. Corbett belongs to the progressive younger element of Shawnee County, advocating road improvement, educational advantages, cultural opportunities, and he is hearty in his support of these and other measures for the public good.

JOHN H. TOLE. While it is certainly true that a live and growing community such as Liberty offers many and widely diversified opportunities for advancement along every line of personal endeavor, yet it is just as true that only a certain percentage achieve distinction, and a large number fail of even attaining a competency. It takes something more than mere opportunity to elevate a man from the common level of every-day accomplishments. Unless he has within him that divine spark of genius for his life work, he will continue to belong to the great majority of mediocre humanity, instead of climbing up the ladder of endeavor until he is able to command a view of affairs that will give him that grasp on the rounds of events that nothing can loosen. In reviewing the career and achievements of John H. Tole, of the Liberty Lumber Company and vice president and director of the Liberty State Bank, the above facts are given prominence for he has proven their truth.

Mr. Tole was born at Pleasant Hill, Pike County, Illinois, April 29, 1858, and is a son of James H. and Harriet (Richards) Tole. The family was of Scotch-Irish origin and at an early day in the pioneer history of Kentucky located in the Blue Grass State. There, in 1810, was born Winslow Parker Tole, the grandfather of John H. Tole. He was reared in Kentucky, and there educated, but as a young man moved to Missouri, where he became a pioneer farmer and a buyer and seller of livestock, occupations in which he continued to be engaged throughout the remainder of his life, his death occurring in Pike County on his farm in 1880. The grandfather was a man of substance, who occupied a prominent place in his community and had the respect of his community as a citizen and a man. He was a devout member of the Christian Church. Mr. Tole was married first to Miss Bradley, and they became the parents of the following children: Jonathan, who went to California in 1860 and who probably spent the rest of his life there, as nothing more was heard from him; James H., the father of John H.; John, twin of James H., who also went to California in 1860 and of whom all track was lost; Milton, who died as a young man; and Elizabeth, of whom trace has been lost by the family. Grandfather Tole was married second to Miss Hughes, and they had four children: William, postmaster at Arrol, Missouri, who enlisted in a Missouri regiment during the Civil war because the Illinois quota was filled, and fought throughout the four years of that struggle, being twice wounded in the right arm; and Luke, Olive and another daughter, of whom all trace has been lost. The grandfather was married a third time to Miss Hall, and they had two children: Parker, who resides near Mexico, Missouri, on a farm; and a daughter Lydea of whom nothing is known.

James H. Tole, father of John H. Tole, was born in 1835, in Pike County, Missouri, and was there reared to manhood on his father's farm. As a young man he went to Pike County, Illinois, where he was reared and made his home in the vicinity of Pleasant Hill until 1873, in which year he came to Montgomery County, Kansas, and bought 160 acres of land in Liberty Township, one mile west of the Town of Liberty, from Harry Dodd, a property on which he resided until 1890. At that time, feeling that he had performed his share of duty, he turned the active work over to younger shoulders and retired to his home at Liberty, where he died in 1898. Mr. Tole was an industrious farmer, who used modern methods in his work and whose farm was one model in every respect. In business circles his word was as good as his bond and his citizenship was always of the highest order, although he never aspired to public office. Politically, he was a Douglas democrat, and his religious faith was that of the Christian Church. Mr. Tole married Miss Harriet Richards, who was born near Lafayette, Indiana, in 1836, of Scotch descent and a daughter of Grant Richards. Mr. Richards, who was a pioneer into Indiana and spent his life in farming, in later years went to Pleasant Hill, Illinois, where his death occurred in 1862. Mrs. Tole passed away on the Liberty Township farm in 1874, having been the mother of the following children: Josephine, who died at the age of three years; John Henry, of this review; W. W., who was engaged in farming near Liberty, died November 15, 1916; Lillie J., the wife of Allen Presler, an extensive traveler, who has visited Alaska as a surveyor and many other out-of-the-way places in the country and is now a resident of Reno, Nevada; Mary F., who died on a farm in Drum Creek Township, as the wife of Charles Swartz, a railroad engineer of Harrisonville, Texas; Minnie M., who is the wife of W. J. Reardon, living on the home farm one mile west of Liberty; and M. L. B., town marshal and a street commissioner of Eskridge, Kansas.

John Henry Tole attended the public schools of Pike County, Illinois, and Montgomery County, Kansas, and was reared on his father's farm, on which he resided until reaching the age of twenty-one years. For the two following school terms he taught in the country schools of Montgomery County, and then resumed farming as his regular vocation, being engaged therein until 1886. After serving in the capacity of township trustee of Liberty for one year, Mr. Tole entered the employ of S. A. Brown & Company in the grain and lumber business, thus securing his introduction to an industry which he was destined to make his life work. He remained in the employ of this firm at Liberty until 1891, when the business failed, and Mr. Tole turned his attention to wheat-buying, which he continued for two years, being identified with the George A. Adams Grain Company. In 1893 Mr. Tole founded the John H. Tole Lumber Company, a business which he conducted with a full measure of success until 1912, in which year he sold out to the W. D. Riley Lumber Company and turned his attention to his other business matters. In 1914, however, he again became the directing head of this industry when, with G. W. Ashley, he bought the yards, stock and equipment of this enterprise and changed the name to the Liberty Lumber Company, under which style it has since been conducted. While he still maintains his interests at Liberty, Mr. Tole is now a resident of Independence, whence he removed in 1913, and where his fine home is located at 210 North Eleventh Street. He also is the owner of eighty acres of good farming land, situated two miles northeast of Liberty, and owns property at Coffeyville, at 416 Elm Street. Mr. Tole has various other interests to claim his time and attention, being vice president and a director of the Liberty State Bank and a stockholder in the Cole-Trueman Ice and Cold Storage Company, as well as the owner of the third interest of the building of the general store establishment of David Heckman, at Liberty. Politically he is an independent democrat, and his fraternal connections are with Liberty Lodge, No. 123, Ancient Free and Accepted Masons; Odd Fellows Lodge No. 105, Liberty; the A. H. T. A., and Liberty Chapter of the Order of the Eastern Star. In each of his numerous fields of endeavor, Mr. Tole has displayed the same straightforwardness, the same honorable dealing that have placed his name so high in the estimation of his associates in business circles.

On January 21, 1901, Mr. Tole was united in marriage at Liberty, Kansas, with Mrs. Carrie M. (Goble) Kelso, widow of the late Samuel Kelso, for some years a farmer of Montgomery County, and daughter of Thomas J. Goble, an agriculturist living retired at Shawnee, Oklahoma. To Mr. and Mrs. Tole there have been born two children: John Hollis, who has just completed his grammar school at Independence; and Eunice Eugenia, who is still attending the graded school.

LELAND EVERETT CALL is professor of agronomy in the Kansas State Agricultural College at Manhattan. Though still a young man he has gone far in the science of agriculture, is already a recognized

authority in several special lines, and since coming to Kansas ten years ago has done much to uphold the prestige of the splendid school at Manhattan.

He was born at Kent, Ohio, February 9, 1881, the oldest of the four children of Charles A. and Olive (Prior) Call. Both his parents are natives of Ohio, and are still living in that state. His father is a farmer and it was on a farm that Professor Call and his brothers and sisters were reared and received their early training. His paternal grandfather, Moses Call, went to Ohio about 1840, was born in New Hampshire and represented an old New England family. He married a Miss Starr, whose father, Josiah Starr, removed to Ohio as early as 1812. The Starr family was identified with New England practically from the beginning of colonization. Professor Call's maternal grandfather was Samuel Prior, and that family went out of Connecticut into the Western Reserve of Ohio in the early days. Samuel Prior himself was born in Ohio and he married a Miss Everett, whose people also came from Connecticut.

Leland Everett Call as a boy attended the rural schools. He graduated from the high school at Hudson, Ohio, and in 1899 from the Western Reserve Academy of Hudson in 1902. He received every encouragement and advantage and wisely improved his opportunities not only to secure an education but make the best use of it. In 1906 he graduated from the Ohio State University with his bachelor's degree in agriculture. Six years later he returned to the University and after post-graduate work was granted the degree of Master of Science.

When Mr. Call came to the Kansas State Agricultural College on January 1, 1907, he began his duties as assistant in agronomy. He became associate professor in 1911 and since 1913 has held the chair of agronomy.

He is a member of the American Society of Agronomy and the Association for the Advancement of Science. He is an associate editor of the Journal of the American Society of Agronomy, and is a joint author of two books, the Call and Schafer work entitled "A Laboratory Manual of Agriculture," and the Call and Kent text book "Agriculture for the Kansas Common Schools." He belongs to the honorary scientific fraternity Sigma Xi, to the Alpha Zeta and Phi Kappa Phi, and is a member of the Congregational Church. In 1910 Mr. Call married Miss Clara Willis of New Bedford, Massachusetts. They are the parents of one child, Marjorie.

HON. ANSON S. COOKE. A resident of Kansas during a period of forty-five years, a pioneer of the prairies of Mitchell County, and for twelve years a member of the State Senate, Hon. Anson S. Cooke is well and favorably known in various parts of the commonwealth, and particularly so at Topeka where he now is living in retirement. During his long and useful career he has risen from poverty to affluence and from obscurity to prominence, and while engaged steadfastly and successfully in the promotion of his personal interests has also contributed to the welfare of the state which has so long been his home.

Senator Cooke was born August 13, 1849, in Lake County, Illinois, a son of Daniel G. Cooke. The family is of Quaker stock, with all the sterling characteristics of that creed, and originated in this country in New England, from whence came David Cooke, the grandfather of Anson S. David Cooke was an early settler of Oneida County, New York, arriving there at a time when the country was still new and wild game abundant, the bears being so numerous that it was almost impossible to raise livestock with any degree of success. Senator Cooke says that he has frequently heard his grandfather tell of driving them out of his hog pen. Daniel G. Cooke, father of the senator, was born in 1822, in Oneida County, New York, and was married in 1845 to Miss Mary Lavina Simonds, a daughter of D. J. Simonds. Mr. Simonds was for some years a well-known farmer of Lake County, Illinois, but later moved to Wisconsin, after having been the original owner of the land on which now stands the City of Zion City, Illinois. In 1860 Daniel G. Cooke moved to Eastern Iowa, where he lived during the Civil war period, and in 1865 took his family to near Maitland, Holt County, Missouri, where he passed the remaining years of his life and died in 1875. He and his wife were the parents of five children, namely: Anson S.; Albert, who is farming near Beloit, Mitchell County, Kansas; Franklin, who is living at Shelley, Idaho; Walter, who is also a farmer in Mitchell County, Kansas; Edwin John, who is in the mercantile business at Palo Alto, California; and Mary, who is Mrs. William Hunter, of Maitland, Missouri.

Anson S. Cooke received his education in the schools of Lake County, Illinois, in Eastern Iowa, and in Holt County, Missouri, and was reared as a farmer. He came to Kansas in 1872 and settled near Beloit, Mitchell County, locating a homestead on the southeast quarter of section 25, township 8 south, range 8 west, in Center Township, and there experienced the many vicissitudes that are part of the life of the pioneer, but through hard work and perseverance accumulated 600 acres of land and in doing so always maintained a reputation as an honorable citizen and straightforward man of business. He retired from farming in 1910 and moved to Topeka, where he bought a handsome and modern home at 1912 Lincoln Street. The people of Jewell and Mitchell counties recognized his worth and general qualifications, as well as his sterling integrity, and after sending him to fill many minor offices, elected him a member of the State Senate, in which he served for twelve years, there being an intermission of four years in his service in that body. Senator Cooke was known as one -of the hard-working members of the Upper House, did much for his constituents as well as his counties and the state during the time he belonged to the Legislature, and for many years had the friendship and respect of many of the leading public men of Kansas. He still takes a keen interest in public affairs and is a helpful factor in the promotion of public-spirited movements. He was elected to the Legislature as a populist but at the present time is a democrat. He is a member of the Methodist Episcopal Church, and was one of the very early and active prohibitionists of the state.

Mr. Cooke was married to Miss Catherine E. McMillan, a daughter of Michael McMillan, who brought his family to Mitchell County, Kansas, in pioneer days from Pennsylvania. Michael McMillan was of Scotch-Irish antecedents and became a well known and respected farmer and esteemed citizen in Mitchell County. Mr. and Mrs. Cooke became the parents of five children, namely: Clarence, whose death occurred in 1906; Louis, who is engaged in merchandising; Wilbur W., who is engaged in farming in Center Township, Mitchell County; Edgar R., who is connected with the Western Elec-

tric Company, at Chicago; and Esther Marla, who married Nelson Logan.

JOAB MULVANE. The spirit of enterprise which brings about progress is not the possession of every man, but it is the needful factor in accomplishing practical results in the life of an individual as well as a community. It includes foresight, courage and daring, and when caution is added, great things, often seemingly impossible things, may be brought about. Among the truly enterprising men who came to Kansas forty years ago and have achieved so well that their names are known and honored over the state at present is Joab Mulvane, of Topeka, ex-member of a State Legislature and the moving spirit in many lines of useful activity.

Joab Mulvane was born at Newcomerstown, Ohio, November 19, 1837, and he is one of the six survivors of the seven children born to his parents, David and Mary (Ross) Mulvane, the others being: John R., David A., William P., George W., Mary Jane, now Mrs. M. J. Dent, and Rebecca, the last named being deceased.

The pioneer of the Mulvane family in Ohio was John Mulvane, who was a soldier in the War of 1812 and afterward received a Government warrant for his services and settled in Tuscarawas County, Ohio, then a comparative wilderness. He cleared his land and improved it, and there he remained until his death. On this pioneer farm his son, David Mulvane, was born and grew to manhood. He had but meager educational opportunities, but possessed natural abilities that led him aright in business, public life and neighborhood affairs without the aid of much book learning. He assisted in the building of the Ohio Canal, a wonderful engineering feat at that time, working on the section between Cleveland and Marietta. When the canal was completed he returned to Newcomerstown and for a time operated a ferry over the Tuscarawas River and in the winter time did odd jobs as a cobbler, a trade he had learned without any apprenticeship and a very important one at that time. Afterward he started a small store in the town and bought, sold and took in trade almost everything the country roundabout produced. The tobacco and wool that he bought he shipped by way of the Ohio Canal to Cleveland, thence via Erie Canal and Hudson River to New York and Baltimore. Twice a year he made a trip to the eastern markets, traveling on horseback over the National Turnpike as far as Pittsburgh, Pennsylvania, thence by rail to the foot of the Allegheny Mountains. As the railroad did not climb the mountain passes and over the peaks, the passengers often made that part of their journey on foot. Provision was made for a stationary engine to draw each railway coach (empty) separately over the mountain and there ordinary traffic was resumed and the passengers dispatched on their way at a rate of speed that then seemed marvelous. Mr. Mulvane acquired a competency and was able to give his children many advantages. He married Mary Ross, a daughter of William Ross, who was a missionary to the Indians in Ohio. His wife bore the maiden name of Whitaker and her father was the founder of one of the largest steel and iron mills in the country, situated at Philadelphia.

Joab Mulvane was his parents' second son. He assisted his father in the store and attended the village schools and then entered an institution for collegiate advantages. His health broke down and his educational ambitions had to be abandoned. In the hope of becoming more robust he decided to journey to what was then the Far West, and as he had an uncle living in Bureau County, Illinois, he made that his objective point. The home of his uncle was near the home of Owen Lovejoy, who suffered death in 1837 from the hands of a pro-slavery mob.

When Mr. Mulvane came to Bureau County, both the Rock Island and the Chicago, Burlington & Quincy railroads were new concerns and had but few buildings for freight at stations, consequently much grain and other products ready for shipping had to be left on the ground to await trains. After a few months Mr. Mulvane returned to his Ohio home, where more comfortable methods of living prevailed than in Illinois, but he found the West had made an uneradicable impression and latent enterprise stirred within him so that but a few months later he was found once more on Illinois soil. In farm work near Princeton for a few years he regained his health and when his older brother, John R. Mulvane, joined him they went into a general mercantile business at Princeton, and Mr. Mulvane continued until 1876, when he sold his interest to his brother and came to Kansas. He had grown to importance in Bureau County, and in 1872 and 1873 was elected to the State Legislature. He was useful as a member of an important committee interested in reporting a bill creating a board of commissioners empowered to classify railways and issue schedules of maximum rates. It became the law determining the power of the state to regulate charges permissible by railroads.

During this period of his life he became interested in a hardware and farm implement business at Princeton which he conducted for some years and then joined his brother at Topeka and invested in realty and other interests and also bought and sold stock to some extent. In his various transactions several tracts of valuable land came into his possession which he still owns.

Mr. Mulvane's first identification with railroad affairs in Kansas may date from the time that William B. Strong, then general manager and later president of the Atchison, Topeka and Santa Fe Railroad Company, prevailed on Mr. Mulvane to go among the people of the State of Kansas to urge them to aid in the construction of several badly needed branch roads. In this undertaking Mr. Mulvane was quite successful and the first line was from Florence, Kansas, to McPherson.

During this time Mr. Mulvane organized and built the horse street car line at Topeka and for a number of years was president of the company operating it. The line then ran through the heart of the city and the present city system conformed to it in building. Edward Wilder, treasurer of the Atchison, Topeka & Santa Fe Railroad, was secretary and treasurer of the company. Mr. Mulvane's enterprising spirit was particularly displayed when, in association with John R. Mulvane, S. A. Walker and a man named Smith, organized and conducted the first telephone system in Topeka, continuing several years and then selling to the Missouri and Kansas Telephone Company. Some years after the organization of the Edison Electric Light and Power Company, Mr. Mulvane was influenced by Mr. Wilder to consent to become its president and remained in this office until it was sold to the present owners. During this time he also became president of the Topeka Water Company, which he later purchased, improved and then sold to eastern capitalists. He is a member of the board of directors of the Bank of Topeka, formerly the Topeka Bank and Savings Institution.

In 1885, at the request of President Strong, Mr.

Mulvane accepted the presidency of the numerous branch roads to be built in the state by the Santa Fe in connection with it, and a number of charters were taken out but later they were all covered by a charter known as the Chicago, Kansas & Western Railroad Company, under which between 900 and 1,000 miles of railroad were constructed. Localities through which these lines passed voted county and township aid in the sum of $4,000 per mile and received $4,000 per mile in stock in the railroad company so aided. Somewhat prior to this Mr. Mulvane had been engaged by the Santa Fe in extending lines from Wichita to Winfield and Arkansas City, and to Wellington and Caldwell in the counties of Sumner and Cowley. The flourishing Town of Mulvane in the last named county was so designated in honor of Joab Mulvane.

As an investment, Mr. Mulvane with others acquired some 2,000 acres on the Santa Fe line near Kansas City, Morris Station being located on this land. As president of the Kansas Town Company he acquired for that corporation a large acreage at Argentine, Kansas, primarily for the use of the Santa Fe road. The portion not so used was platted and sold and now comprises the greater part of Argentine. Other large enterprises interested Mr. Mulvane. With his brother, John R. Mulvane and the Bank of Topeka, he acquired the property of the Kansas Salt Company at Hutchinson, Kansas, was president of the company and operated and managed its affairs successfully for a number of years, when, through his business acumen a consolidation was brought about with the Hutchinson & Kansas Salt Company, in which Jay Gould owned a controlling interest. The consolidated company was subsequently sold to the National Salt Company of New York. Mr. Mulvane then became interested in the Chickasha Oil Company, located at Chickasha, Oklahoma, of which he is vice president and treasurer and a member of the executive board. He is also vice president and a member of the executive committee of the American Cement Plaster Company, of Lawrence, Kansas, a director and executive member of the Western States Portland Cement Company, of Independence, Kansas, and was president of the Shawnee Fire Insurance Company until it sold out to the National Fire Insurance Company.

At Princeton, Illinois, in 1859, Joab Mulvane was married to Sarah A. Ross, who died at Topeka, January 18, 1910. To this union were born six children: David W.; Zenia A., now Mrs. Speed Hughes, of Topeka; William J.; Margaret A., now Mrs. H. S. Morgan, of Topeka; John J. and Harriet M. Three are deceased: Harriet M., who is interred at Princeton, Illinois; and William J. and John J., who are interred by the side of their mother in the Topeka cemetery.

In politics Mr. Mulvane has ever been an outspoken republican and an effective party worker on many occasions. He has furthered in many ways the cause of education in Kansas and is a member of the board of trustees of Baker College at Baldwin. His attitude in relation to religion is well known. He is a member of the board of stewards of the First Methodist Episcopal Church at Topeka.

ARTHUR DEVORE is one of the able merchants of Southern Kansas. For a quarter of a century he has been manager of the Ulmer Furniture Company at Independence, one of the largest furniture and general household supply houses in the state. While his exceptional ability has gone into the making of this large establishment, he has not withheld his influence and work from any local affairs of importance, and is regarded as one of Independence's most progressive and public spirited men.

He has spent most of his life in Kansas, but was born at Wapakoneta, Ohio, April 23, 1862. His ancestors were French people, Huguenots, and during the persecution of that sect were expelled from France and settled in Maryland. His Grandfather Arthur DeVore was born in Pennsylvania, and went to Ohio as a pioneer, living on a farm in that state until his death. B. F. DeVore, father of the Independence merchant, was born in Pennsylvania in 1828. He was a pioneer of Independence, Kansas, having moved to that frontier town in 1870. He was reared in Pennsylvania, studied law at Cincinnati, was admitted to the bar, and was married at Wapakoneta, Ohio, where he practiced for a number of years. Later he moved to Hartford City, Indiana, and after coming to Independence was engaged in the mercantile business and later as a democrat was appointed postmaster, serving during Cleveland's administration. He was one of the most popular men in this section of the state. Evidence of this is found in the fact that at one time he was elected a member of the Legislature. His rival for that office was Hon. L. U. Humphrey, who later became governor of Kansas. He was elected over Mr. Humphrey in a county normally republican. He was also a past noble grand of Independence Lodge, No. 69, Independent Order Odd Fellows, and was identified with both the Encampment and Rebekah degrees of that order. His death occurred in Independence February 15, 1908, and such was his career that he is still held in grateful memory by local citizens. B. F. DeVore married Sarah J. Craig, who was born in Ohio in 1838 and is still living in Independence. Her children are: Arthur; Bessie, who resides at Colorado Springs, Colorado, the widow of Thomas A. May, who was in the railroad service; Frank M., cashier and credit man for the Ulmer Furniture Company at Independence.

Arthur DeVore was eight years old when his father moved to Independence, and he acquired his education in the local schools. When about sixteen he left school to take up a business career, and has applied his energies continuously to the line of merchandising. In 1888 he was made manager of the Ulmer Furniture Company, which had been established by the late Mr. Samuel H. Ulmer in 1870. It was the pioneer store of the kind in Independence, and has had a record of forty-seven years' successful merchandising. The store is one of the landmarks in the shopping center of Independence, located at 212-216 North Penn Avenue. Its stock comprises furniture, carpets, pianos, talking machines, and its trade is by no means limited to the city or the county but extends in a radius of a hundred miles about Independence, and many customers even live in Oklahoma and western Kansas.

Mr. DeVore in politics maintains an independent attitude. He is affiliated with Fortitude Lodge, No. 107, Ancient Free and Accepted Masons, Keystone Chapter, No. 22, Royal Arch Masons, Lodge No. 69, Independent Order of Odd Fellows, and is a charter member and was one of the first officers of Lodge No. 780, Benevolent and Protective Order of Elks. He is also affiliated with Camp No. 649, Modern Woodmen of America at Independence. As a business man he has been closely identified with business organizations at Independence for many years. He belongs to the Commercial Club, and an honor of which he is properly proud is that he is a charter member and a director of the Rotary Club. He assisted materially in developing the extensive business of the Independence Building and Loan Association, of which he is still a member, and at one time was its president.

In 1885 at Independence Mr. DeVore married Miss Carrie Ulmer. Her. father was the late Samuel H. Ulmer, founder of the Ulmer Furniture Company, and one of the pioneer merchants of Kansas. He died in 1888. He was in Kansas during the early days of the Civil war and a member of the Kansas Home Guard. During the war while making a business trip to Lawrence he was seized and barely escaped hanging on the ground that he was a member of the Quantrell band of raiders. That was a little after Quantrell had made his famous raid on Lawrence. He was identified by an acquaintance, who proved that not only he was unconnected with the gang of outlaws but was one of the vigilant defenders of Kansas as a member of the Volunteer Infantry. Later he was active in Grand Army circles. Mr. and Mrs. DeVore have one child, Hubert, who was born at Independence August 30, 1889, was educated in the high school, and is now in the Ulmer Furniture Company's store.

JOHN M. WINTER. Among the respected citizens of Manhattan, Kansas, no one stands higher than John Winter, a reliable business man and since May, 1914, postmaster of this city. He was born at Volkartshain Province Oberhessen, Grosherzogtum Hessen-Darmstadt, Germany, February 27, 1854, and is a son of John B. and Elizabeth (Greb) Winter. His father belonged to the working class and, although industrious, had accumulated little means, so that, when John had completed his public school training, his future lay almost entirely in his own hands. As soon as possible he began to learn the carpenter trade, in the meanwhile finding employment as a worker in the great timber lands in his native country, in which he was engaged both before and after his marriage.

The first break in the old German home circle was when Mr. Winter's father and other members of the family, and relatives also of his wife, sailed for America and from the United States sent back reports of better business opportunities in their new home. It was then that Mr. Winter began to seriously entertain thoughts of also crossing the Atlantic. When his mind was about made up as to the advantages of such a course, his employers promoted him to a more remunerative position, evidently with the object of retaining his services. In some perplexity Mr. Winter turned to his estimable wife for the settlement of what was really a very important matter, no doubt previously having had proof of her good judgment. She decided favorably as to emigration and in 1884, Mr. Winter and his family and accompanied by his mother, landed at New York, the date being the 14th of June. From that city Mr. Winter went first to Philadelphia, but by August of the same year was established and employed at the carpenter trade, in the City of Manhattan, Kansas, which has been his chosen home ever since. For some years he confined himself to carpentering but gradually branched out into affiliated lines and in the course of time became a building contractor. As such he has built up a reputation for honesty and efficiency that he may well be proud of.

Mr. Winter was married in 1879 to Miss Catherine Doebert. who was born in Germany, and they have four children: Catherine, who is the wife of Charles E. Hawks. of Chanute, Kansas; Henry B.. who is a prosperous architect at Manhattan; Caroline M., who is general delivery clerk in the postoffice at Manhattan; and Amelia Margaret, who is the wife of W. J. King, who is assistant highway engineer with the Kansas State Agricultural College.

Mr. Winter belongs to that class of men who in every community display public spirit and encourage progress. He has always been active, since locating here, in the affairs of the democratic party and in 1897 he was elected on the democratic ticket the first marshal of Manhattan, overcoming the normal republican majority because of his personal popularity. He rendered acceptable service during one year but declined to be a candidate for re-election. Subsequently he served for two years as a member of the city council, during which he was chairman of the finance and waterworks committees. His party loyalty, together with his high standing as a citizen exerted strong influence toward his appointment as postmaster of Manhattan, to which office he was appointed by President Wilson in May, 1914. It is universally admitted that Mr. Winter has fulfilled every demand as a public official. Under his administration of the affairs of the Manhattan postoffice, the service has been greatly improved and the business so increased that on July 1, 1916, Manhattan was placed among first class postoffices by Postmaster General Burleson.

Mr. Winter is a member of the Evangelical Lutheran Church. He belongs to the Knights of Pythias and also to the Ancient Order of United Workmen, in the latter organization several times representing his lodge in the grand lodge of the state. He has secured financial independence by means of industry, calm judgment and wholesome living and is not only a representative citizen himself, but is at the head of one of Manhattan's most respected families.

REV. WILLIAM BAKER was a well known figure in Kansas, and had a career of remarkable experience in foreign lands before taking up his residence in the Sunflower State. He lived and developed a fine farm in Wabaunsee County, but spent his last years in Topeka, where members of his family still reside.

He was born in London, England, July 6, 1838. His father, William Baker, Sr., was a basket manufacturer and also a native of London. The country home of the family was at Plaistow in Essex County.

Reared in the Episcopal or Established Church of England, Rev. William Baker was for a number of years identified with the educational activities of that church. In early manhood he went to teach the English language among the natives of South Africa in Basutoland. Altogether he spent five years as a teacher there under the auspices of the French Missionary Society. For a time he was a companion of the distinguished French missionary Coilliard. At the request of President Oom Paul Kruger in the Orange Free State these missionaries went to South Africa, and when the missionaries requested Oom Paul to call in the natives for worship, Oom asked if he should also call in the dogs. That question illustrated the typical Boer attitude toward all efforts for civilization and christianization in South Africa.

In 1878 Rev. Mr. Baker returned to England and married Miss Clara R. Williams of London. Her father, Alfred W. Williams, was a corn merchant and died early in life as the result of an accident.

In 1881 Mr. Baker received a letter from the governor of Kansas, John P. St. John, describing to him the prohibition amendment to the constitution of the state. Rev. Mr. and Mrs. Baker were so impressed by this letter that they determined to make their home in a state that was devoted to prohibition. In that year therefore they brought their little household to Kansas and located near Maple Hill in Wabaunsee County. Mr. Baker secured land on Mill Creek and there began general farming and stock raising. He was possessed of the English virtues of thrift and industry, and eventually accumulated a fine farm of 240 acres, which he named the Woodlands.

In 1901 Mr. Baker moved with his family to Topeka and bought a residence at 306 Harrison Street. In that home he spent his last days and passed away July 1, 1906, honored and widely respected for his many virtues. He was a man of the highest moral character, a splendid citizen and a good father. Though reared and many years identified with the Episcopal Church, he was afterwards a Congregationalist. After coming to Kansas he frequently lectured on temperance and also filled numerous pulpits.

Both he and his wife were people of very liberal education, and they reared their daughters with the best advantages at home and these daughters have been guided by high ideals to render themselves capable of worthy and self sacrificing public service. Four of the daughters have life diplomas as teachers and all expect to obtain degrees within a year or so. Florence, the oldest, is a teacher in Western Kansas. Lillian is a teacher in the Southwestern Texas State Normal School at San Marcos. May is the manager of the cafeteria in the Topeka High School. Violet is teacher of history in the Junior High School in North Topeka. Rose is a senior student in the agricultural college at Manhattan. Mr. Baker had two daughters by a former marriage, Ellen and Kate, both of whom have homes in distant states.

VERNON H. BRANCH of Wichita has had a successful career as a banker in Kansas covering a period of more than thirty-five years. In that time he has been officially identified with a number of important banks in different parts of the state, but is now concentrating all his efforts along the line of investment banking, and is one of the reliable investment bankers of Kansas.

He came to Kansas when a youth. His birth occurred at Milwaukee, Wisconsin, February 3, 1863, but when he was two years of age his parents removed to Orwell, Vermont, his father's childhood home. In that part of New England he spent his early childhood and youth until he was eighteen, and acquired a substantial common school training.

In December, 1881, Mr. Branch arrived at Concordia, Kansas, and became bookkeeper for the Cloud County Bank. Two years later he became its cashier, but resigned in 1886 to become secretary of the Security Investment Company at Cawker City in Mitchell County. From there moving to Beloit in the spring of 1900, he was a hardware merchant of Beloit a year, and then became a stockholder, director and cashier of the First National Bank of Beloit.

Since the summer of 1903 Mr. Branch has been a resident of Wichita. Acquiring stock in the National Bank of Wichita, he was made its vice president and a director, and when that bank and the Fourth National Bank were consolidated in 1908, he continued as a stockholder and director and also as cashier in the Fourth National. In the spring of 1911, Mr. Branch, having sold his interests in the Fourth National, resigned the post of cashier and opened offices as an investment banker on the ground floor of

the Beacon Building. During the panic of 1907 he served as secretary of the Wichita Clearing House Association and as a member and secretary of the Clearing House Committee.

On October 20, 1885, Mr. Branch married Luella Brown of Concordia, Kansas, daughter of Judge Daniel L. Brown. Mrs. Branch is very active in club affairs at Wichita, being secretary of the State Federation of Women's Clubs. Her heart and hand have always been liberally extended in charitable and philanthropic work, and her home is one of 'the centers of cultured influence in Wichita. There is one daughter, Hazel E., now one of the most highly educated young women of the state.. She holds her Master's degree from the Kansas State University, where she specialized in entomology, and now has entire charge of the curriculum at Bethany College in Topeka.

JAMES ARCHIBALD CAMPBELL. The Campbell family have been residents of Kansas thirty-five years, and the name is especially well known and prominent in connection with the civic life of Topeka and Shawnee County. James A. Campbell has long been a business man of that city, and his two sons, James A., Jr., and Edwin A. Campbell give a distinction to the family by the fact that at the same time they hold two of the county offices of Shawnee County. James A., Jr., is the present county surveyor, while Edwin A. is the present county treasurer.

Before James A. Campbell came to Kansas he was identified with the family interests in Scotland. He belongs to one of the oldest branches of the Argyll family, tracing an unbroken descent from Dugal Campbell, A. D. 1160, younger son of the third Knight of Lochow. The Campbells have been prominent in that country for generations, and particularly in military affairs. It is a matter of special interest that Mr. Campbell's great-uncle, Maj.-Gen. Sir Archibald Campbell, K. B., was in the British army during the American Revolution, fought for the mother country, was taken prisoner in Boston harbor and on May 3, 1778, was exchanged for Ethan Allen, the hero of Ticonderoga. Afterwards he was governor of Jamaica and later of Madras and is buried in Westminster Abbey, London. The old family estates of ''Inverneill'' and Ross in Scotland are now owned by Mr. Campbell's brother, Col. Duncan Campbell, of the British army.

James A. Campbell was born at Inverneill, Argyleshire, Scotland, November 30, 1843, and grew to manhood in his native country. His father, after whom he was named, was a captain in the British army and was in the military service of Great Britain until he retired. At that time he inherited the estates of Inverneill and Ross, and he lived there until his death in 1878 at the age of seventy-nine. Captain Campbell married Anne Bowdon, who died in 1845, when her son James A. was a child.

James A. Campbell received a liberal education and a thorough training for business. He attended a boarding school at Liverpool, England, and also Madras College at St. Andrews, Scotland. At Manchester, England, he learned mechanical engineering, but most of his early business experience was in handling mill supplies at Glasgow, and during that time he also acted as factor for his father's estates.

Giving up these connections and interests he came to America in 1880. His first home in this country was in Kansas, and his first experience was in farming in Chase County. A little later he became a draftsman in the building department of the Santa Fe

Vol. IV—3

Railway, and removing to Topeka about 1881 has lived in that city ever since. In 1884 he became bookkeeper for the Inter-Ocean mills and in 1898 transferred his services to the Mid-Continent mills. Since the fall of 1914 he has held a clerical position in the office of the surveyor of Shawnee County. On June 23, 1881, after coming to Kansas, Mr. Campbell married Euphemia Morison, a daughter of James Morison, of Rossie, Dunning, Perthshire, Scotland. Mr. and Mrs. Campbell have two sons and a daughter: Jessie A., wife of Edwin Davis, of Leavenworth, Kansas; James A.; and Edwin A. Both Mr. and Mrs. Campbell are members of the Episcopal Church.

James A. Campbell, Jr., present surveyor of Shawnee County, was born at Topeka, May 7, 1887, grew up in his home town and had his education in the public schools. He early found opportunity to make his own way in the world, and for four years was in the engineering department of the Santa Fe Railway, and after that for several years was employed by the Sanitary Drainage District of Chicago. Returning to Topeka, in 1910 he was elected surveyor of Shawnee County, and by re-election has held that office to the present time. He is a capable engineer, and his public record has been highly creditable. Mr. Campbell is a member of the Kansas Engineering Society, is a republican and a member of the Masonic Order. On September 3, 1913, he married Bertha Hull. They have one daughter, Jean.

Edwin A. Campbell, the second son of James A. Campbell, and now filling the office of treasurer of Shawnee County, was born at Topeka, March 1, 1889, and for a young man has had a career of noteworthy accomplishment. Reared in Topeka, he attended the public schools, but at the age of fifteen found employment for himself in the maintenance and construction department of the Santa Fe Railway. During the next 3½ years he gained very competent knowledge of engineering. He was then with the Shawnee Fire Insurance Company for eighteen months, and for a short time in 1910 was a clerk in the office of county assessor. Following that came about a year as deputy county clerk, and in May, 1911, became deputy county treasurer. The votes of the people elevated him from deputy to county treasurer in November, 1914, and he has filled that office with credit and distinction since October 12, 1915. He is also a republican and is affiliated with the Masonic and Elks fraternity. On June 30, 1913, he married Miss Dorothy Porter. They have two children: Diana and Edwin A., Jr.

VICTOR A. HAYS is an example of the successful American who began as a telegraph operator and has reached a commanding position in industrial affairs. He is president of the Kansas Natural Gas Company and has spent the greater part of his active career in the oil and gas fields of the East and Southwest.

Like many other successful men in the oil and gas industry Victor A. Hays is a native of Venango County, Pennsylvania, and of Irish ancestry. He was born near Oil City on April 27, 1863. He was educated in the public and Normal schools and began his independent career in 1880 by learning telegraphy. He was employed in that work until 1886, when he engaged in the natural gas business, entering the service of the Oil City Fuel Supply Company as bookkeeper, and has since been continuously in that business.

Mr. Hays has been identified with the Kansas Natural Gas Company since 1905, beginning as general auditor and holding that position until he was elected president in December, 1914. His home has been at

Independence since 1910. He is also president of the subsidiary companies of Kansas Natural Gas Company, including the Marnet Mining Company, the Edgar Oil Company, and the California Oil and Gas Company.

Mr. Hays resides at 216 South Fifth Street. He is a democrat, a member of the Presbyterian Church, is affiliated with Ionic Lodge, No. 525, Ancient·Free and Accepted Masons, at Pittsburgh, Pennsylvania, Duquesne Chapter, No. 193, Royal Arch Masons, at Pittsburgh, is now serving as eminent commander of St. Bernard Commandery, No. 10, Knights Templar of Independence, belongs to Wichita Consistory No. 2 of the thirty-second degree Scottish Rite, and to Mirza Temple of the Nobles of the Mystic Shrine at Pittsburg, Kansas. He is also a member of the Independence Country Club.

In 1904 Mr. Hays was married to Susan D. Thompson, of Allegheny City, Pennsylvania.

EDWIN J. MOFFITT, M. D. A physician and surgeon of Manhattan for the past fifteen years, Doctor Moffitt is highly esteemed professionally and also as a citizen. He is a man of wide experience and thorough professional qualifications, yet is unostentatious and allows his merits and abilities to speak for themselves.

He was born at Jesup, Iowa, May 23, 1872, a son of William and Alice (Muncey) Moffitt. William Moffitt, who was born at Cadiz, Ohio, of Scotch parents, was a Union soldier in the Civil war, as was also his father. Grandfather Moffitt attained the post of provost marshal, and died from wounds received while in the discharge of duty. A shoemaker by trade, William Moffitt soon after the close of the Civil war moved to Jesup, Iowa, where for many years he conducted the only exclusive boot and shoe house of that town. His death occurred in 1895 at the age of forty-eight. Doctor Moffitt's mother was of English parentage. Her father, Doctor Muncey, was a graduate of Rush Medical College of Chicago and practiced with splendid success and eminent service in Jesup, Iowa, from pioneer days until his death in 1913 at the advanced age of eighty-two.

Reared at Jesup, Iowa, to the age of sixteen, and spending the next five years at Waterloo, Iowa, Doctor Moffitt received a sound educational foundation for his professional career. It was both taste and natural gift that led him to the study of medicine. In 1896 he received his M. D. degree from Drake University at Des Moines, Iowa. Since then he has taken post-graduate courses in Chicago and elsewhere and is today, as he was twenty years ago, a constant student of medicine and surgery.

He began practice at Jesup, Iowa, with his maternal grandfather, Doctor Muncey, an association that continued very agreeably for five years. In 1898 Doctor Moffitt married Miss May Murphey, the only daughter and child of Mr. George S. Murphey, a prominent banker and citizen of Manhattan, Kansas. Three years later, in 1901, Doctor Moffitt and his wife came to Manhattan, and since then he has been identified with a large and increasing practice. He is district surgeon for the Union Pacific and Rock Island railroads, is a member of the hospital staff of physicians and surgeons for the Park View Hospital at Manhattan and is physician to the State Rebekah-Odd Fellows Home at Manhattan. His professional associations are with the Riley County Medical Society, the Kansas State

Medical Society, the American Medical Association and the Golden Belt Medical Society.

Fraternally he is affiliated with the Independent Order of Odd Fellows, the Benevolent and Protective Order of Elks, the Knights of Pythias and the Chapter Degree of Masonry. Religiously he is a Presbyterian.

Doctor and Mrs. Moffitt have three children, named Harriet Alice, Georgia May and Roberta Mary.

WALTER J. ARNOLD. The county engineer of Shawnee County, Walter J. Arnold has led an active and diversified career, and although not yet forty-one years of age has crowded into his life more experiences than the ordinary man sees in an entire lifetime. From gold mining in Colorado to chasing the insurgents in the Philippines is a long call, but unlike many men whose activities have led them to out-of-the-way-places, Mr. Arnold has been constantly advancing, and each new experience, each new employment, has brought him a little bit further ahead toward the goal of success. In his present capacity, which he has filled for some five years, he is one of the most efficient and popular officials in the state.

Mr. Arnold is a native of Saxony, born in the City of Dresden, in 1877, a son of Gustave and Ernestine (Zeuner) Arnold. In the old country the family belonged to the social democrats, and Friedrich Arnold, the grandfather of Mr. Arnold, was one of its pioneer leaders during the party's early struggle for recognition of its principles of more liberal government. Gustave Arnold was also born in Saxony, where he was married, and there became agent for an immigration company, in which capacity he came to the United States with his family in 1882, bringing with him a colony of his fellow-countrymen for settlement. Locating first near Pine Bluff, Arkansas, he remained at that place for about three years, then moved to Kansas City, where he remained for another year, and finally, in 1886, came to Topeka, where he spent the remaining years of his active life. Shortly after his arrival at the Kansas capital, he secured employment with the Crane Publishing Company, and for a quarter of a century remained in the service of this concern, his fidelity and industry winning him repeated promotions. Gustave Arnold was united in marriage with Ernestine Zeuner, also a native of Saxony, and they had eleven children born to them, of whom seven are living, as follows: Harry, who is connected with the United States Government Printing Office at Washington, District of Columbia; Walter J., of this review; Fred, who is employed at the Kansas State Printing Plant at Topeka; Herman, who is connected with the Gem Grocery Company, at Topeka; Gustave, who is with the Hall Lithographing Company, also of this city; Leonora, who is the wife of H. P. Irons, who is employed at the state printing plant; and Anna, who is the wife of William Tyson, who is a foreman in the Atchison, Topeka & Santa Fe storehouse at Topeka, Kansas.

Walter J. Arnold was about four years old when he was brought to America and four years older when he came with his parents to Kansas. He received his education in the public schools of Little Rock, Arkansas; Kansas City, Missouri; and Topeka, Kansas, and his first employment was as office boy in the office of the Western Union Telegraph Company, in the last-named city. A little later he entered the service of the Harvey Eating House

Company, then spent three years learning the blacksmith trade at Topeka, and then went to Denver and Cripple Creek, Colorado, as a blacksmith and remained at the latter place as a prospector during the gold excitement. Returning to his home at Topeka, in 1898 Mr. Arnold joined the Twentieth Kansas Volunteers for service in the Philippines. With his regiment he went to the Islands, where he subsequently saw much active service with this famous organization, returning with an excellent record after two years. His company had particularly thrilling experiences during the Filipino uprising, on the 4th, 5th and 6th of February, 1899, and was in the very important engagement of Caloocan, February 10th. The regiment of which Mr. Arnold was a member was active in repelling assaults during this time, and subsequently was sent on a four months' campaign in pursuit of the insurrectionists northward through the province of Luzon and going as far as San Fernandos, where Mr. Arnold was stricken with malarial fever. His general officer in this campaign was Col. Fred Funston, but on several occasions he was detailed to General Bell, who was chief of scouts.

When he returned to Kansas with his regiment from the Philippines, Mr. Arnold secured employment in the wheel shop of the Atchison, Topeka and Santa Fe Railroad, his knowledge of blacksmithing fitting him for this work. He was not, however, satisfied to remain a mere workman, and with an idea of bettering his condition took a course of study in the International Correspondence School, of Scranton, Pennsylvania. His course in architecture prepared him for a position offered to him as draftsman in the office of the city engineer, in 1902, and he continued in that capacity for four years, gaining much experience. He was then made assistant city engineer under John Rogers for two years, but resigned and went to St. Joseph, Missouri, as assistant engineer on construction work for the Independent Telephone Company, supervising the field work and preparing records from his field data of the underground cable conduits and supervised the construction of two new telephone exchange buildings. After completing these plans and records he returned to Topeka in 1910, and became a candidate, with twenty-one others, for the office of city commissioner, but failed of election. In 1911 he was again a candidate for the same office and although receiving a majority of the male votes was defeated by the women voters who through ignorance of his qualifications for the office preferred to vote for his opponent with whom they were personally acquainted through fraternal organizations. Previous to the election he had accepted the position of assistant engineer to V. R. Parkhurst, who had charge of the South Side Levee Drainage District work. In the following year, upon the resignation of J. A. C. Campbell, he was appointed county engineer by the county commissioners of Shawnee County, and since has continued to fill that position with ability. Since his appointment as county engineer he has prepared plans and specifications for over $100,000 worth of modern and up-to-date bridges and has supervised their construction. He is an energetic, intelligent and hard-working official, who deserves the success that has come to him, and who may be expected to go far in the future.

Mr. Arnold was married in 1907 to Miss Mae E. Thomas, daughter of Joseph W. and Sarah E. Thomas, of Topeka, and they are the parents of two children: Wanda Valeria, aged six years; and Ferdinand Waldemar, who is four years old.

JOHN A. POTTORF. When a man reaches the seventy-fourth milestone of his life's journey it may be taken for granted that he has had a wealth of experience which, if properly written out, would fill a volume. In the case of John A. Pottorf, who has already passed his seventy-fourth birthday, long life means more than length of years. He was not born with a silver spoon in his mouth and even when he came to Kansas a little over thirty years ago he had to begin as a farm renter. The overcoming of obstacles to success has been a vital part of his experience. The honors due him are not solely on account of his success as a farmer, but also because of his service in the Union army during the Civil war and the influence he has radiated from his character and the worthy children who have grown up under his roof.

He was born November 25, 1842, in Pike County, Illinois. His parents, Andrew and Lavina (Umbaugh) Pottorf, were both natives of Carroll County, Ohio, where their respective families were among the pioneers. In ancestry both father and mother were of the so-called Pennsylvania Dutch. Grandfather Pottorf was a native of Pennsylvania. In 1841, soon after their marriage, Andrew Pottorf and wife removed to Pike County, Illinois, and there, when their first son and child was born, they gave him the name John A. Three other children were born, but all were daughters. John A. was eight years of age when his mother died, and his father then returned with the motherless children to Ohio and placed them in the homes of relatives.

John A. Pottorf grew up in the home of his father's brother, whose wife was his mother's sister—in other words, each of these worthy people was related to him in the degree of uncle or aunt. His uncle being a farmer, Mr. Pottorf grew up amid the scenes of an Ohio farm. He acquired valuable lessons of industry and perseverance, and those have stood him in good stead in his later career. He also had the advantages of the common schools.

Reaching the age of eighteen he went out to his old birthplace in Illinois. He was there when the war broke out, and on September 1, 1862, he enlisted as a private in Company E of the Seventy-eighth Illinois Infantry. He was in service nearly three years, and was granted an honorable discharge as corporal on June 7, 1865. As a soldier he followed the fortunes of his regiment, and was never wounded severely and spent less than two weeks in hospital because of illness. Many of the great battles concerning which every American schoolboy is familiar formed part of the military experience of Mr. Pottorf. He fought at Chickamauga, and then was in the many days of continuous fighting up to Atlanta and after that in the march of Sherman's troops to the sea. He was in the last battle of the war, at Bentonville, South Carolina. Following that he participated in the grand review at Washington. Early in its organization Mr. Pottorf became a member of the Grand Army of the Republic, and through that organization has kept in touch with his old army comrades.

He made the transition from soldier to civilian very quickly. Becoming a farmer in Adams County, Illinois, he lived there until 1884, when he came out and settled in Riley County, Kansas. After renting land for a time he was able to purchase a small tract in section 12 in the northwestern part of Ogden Township. That has been his home ever since. He started with exceedingly limited capital, but his industry and ambition more than made up for lack of money. With the aid of his devoted wife he has come into the possession of more than 600 acres of farm lands, and has utilized these resources so that he well deserves a rank among the most successful farmers and stock raisers of Riley County. For many years his specialty has been the raising of hogs, and without any disparagement of others he might be well referred to as an authority on that branch of animal husbandry. At the same time he has brought his farm to a maximum state of productiveness, and has from time to time improved his lands with substantial buildings.

There is an interesting contrast on his home place today. Like many Kansas farmers he is the owner of an automobile. His garage is a building that was converted from its original purposes, as his first and humble home in Kansas, and Mr. and Mrs. Pottorf have many of their most precious memories centering around what is now the garage. In 1889 they moved out of the first house into a large and more convenient one, and that is their home of today. Mr. Pottorf has not been a silent witness of the remarkable changes that have occurred in Kansas during the past thirty years, but has done his part in bringing such changes about.

Even today he is busy and there has never been a time in his long life when he could not turn his hand to something useful. When he was sixty-five years of age he made a violin from timber taken from maple and apple trees which he had planted on his farm, and it is an instrument of excellent tone and Mr. Pottorf can play upon it skillfully. In matters of politics he has never aspired to office. He has preferred the quiet life of the farmer citizen, though he is a stanch republican, and belongs to that party by choice and principle, since his father before him was a democrat.

September 3, 1866, a little over a year after he left the army, Mr. Pottorf married Miss Martha Lawson. They were married in Adams County, Illinois, where Mrs. Pottorf was born August 23, 1848, and where her parents, Francis Miller and Emily Clark (Powell) Lawson, were early settlers. Her father was born in Washington County, Pennsylvania, of Scotch-Irish lineage, and her mother was a native of Tennessee.

·Four children have been born into the home of Mr. and Mrs. Pottorf: Clara married Lemuel Carpenter and they live in Canada; Mary is the wife of George Cutter of Riley County; Frank Miller, who lives on a farm in Riley County, married Pearl Wills; Andrew J., who graduated from the Kansas State Agricultural College in 1899, is a farmer in conjunction with his father, and married Lucy Maria Cottrell, who is a graduate of the same college with the class of 1898.

Mr. and Mrs. Pottorf are active members of the Methodist Church. They have journeyed together as husband and wife for fully half a century, sharing with fidelity each other's sorrows as well as joys, and now in their declining years are enjoying the fruits of industry, frugality and exemplary conduct. They have reared a respected family and have gained the esteem and confidence of all who have been so fortunate as to be their neighbors and friends.

WILLIAM R. MURROW. Kansas, with splendid natural resources and true western energy and progressiveness, has afforded to her native sons the best of opportunities, and it is gratifying to note that the greater percentage of the younger generation representative of pioneer families has had the good judgment to pay unfaltering allegiance to the Sunflower commonwealth and to aid in the furtherance of the civic and material progress and prosperity of the state. In the thriving City of Independence, Montgomery County, such a native son is he whose name initiates this paragraph, and his prominence and influence in the business affairs of this section of the state is indicated fully by his incumbency of the responsible position of the manager of the Kansas Gas & Electric Company.

William Rollins Murrow was born at Ellinwood, Barton County, Kansas, on May 16, 1878, and is a son of William D. D. and Ploma Elizabeth (Lawrence) Murrow, the former of whom was born on Prince Edward Island, Canada, in 1845, and the latter of whom was born on the shore of the Bay of Fundy, in Nova Scotia, Canada, in 1854. The father passed the closing years of his life at Ellinwood, Kansas, where he died in 1880, and the widowed mother was a resident of Kansas City, Missouri, at the time of her death, in 1895. The subject of this sketch is the only child of this sterling pioneer couple of Kansas. As a youth William D. D. Murrow lived in the City of Boston, Massachusetts, where he found employment in an establishment devoted to the manufacturing of machinery. He was a resident of that city at the outbreak of the Civil war and though he was but sixteen years of age at the time he promptly tendered his services in defense of the Union, by enlisting in the First Massachusetts Cavalry. With this valiant command he continued in service three years and seven months, and he participated in many of the important engagements that marked the progress of the great conflict. After the close of the war and the reception of his honorable discharge, this gallant young veteran returned to Boston, and there he continued his residence until 1877, when he came to Kansas and established his residence at Ellinwood, where he became the owner and manager of a hotel, the same having been conducted by him until his death. He was a republican in his political proclivities, was a man of sterling character and always commanded the confidence and good will of his fellow men, both he and his wife having been active members of the Baptist Church.

William R. Murrow was but two years of age at the time of his father's death and his mother later became the wife of Dudley Rhoads. The family removed to Hutchinson, Kansas, and later Mr. Rhoads opened and was proprietor of the Midland Hotel, at Hutchinson, a house that under his able management gained a high reputation and became one of the leading hotels of the West. He is now venerable in years and is living retired in the City of Chicago. The one child of the second marriage is Anna, who is the wife of Ned Roberts, who is a traveling salesman for a wholesale paper house at Columbus, Ohio, and who resides at Granville, that state.

In the public schools of Hutchinson, Kansas, William R. Murrow gained his early education, and after the removal of the family to Kansas City he continued his studies in the high school. In 1893, when about sixteen years of age, he went to the City of Chicago, where he found employment in the electrical operating department of the World's Columbian Exposition. After the close of the great exposition he was for eight months in the employ of the Edison Illuminating Company of St. Louis, Missouri. He then returned to Kansas City, where for a number of years he was employed as telegraph operator for the board of trade, he having learned the art of telegraphy in St. Louis. Finally he engaged in the electrical construction business in an independent way, with offices in the American Bank Building, Kansas City. He continued to be thus engaged for a period of three years, and in 1903 he returned to Kansas and at Peru, Chautauqua County, erected an electrical power house for the pumping of oil wells, this being the first plant of the kind built for that purpose in the entire United States. After the decline in the price of oil Mr. Murrow sold his power plant and obtained a franchise for an electric-light plant at Cherryvale, Montgomery County. In partnership with H. E. West he completed the construction of this plant, and after they had operated the same eighteen months they sold the plant and business to capitalists residing in Colorado Springs, Colorado. While still operating the electric plant at Cherryvale Mr. Murrow formed a partnership alliance with A. C. Stich, of Independence, and secured a franchise for the installing in this city of an electric-light and power plant. In the enterprise H. E. West and J. Barzen, of Kansas City, became associated, and in 1905 operations were instituted under the corporate title of the Independence Electric Company. The enterprise developed to substantial proportions and in 1911 the controlling company sold the property and business to the Kansas Gas & Electric Company, by which Mr. Murrow has since been retained as general manager of the plants at both Independence and Cherryvale, the latter plant having been purchased after that at Independence had been taken over by the present company. The Kansas Gas & Electric Company has the distinction of being the first in this section of Kansas to employ wireless telegraphy as a commercial agency and its wireless system touches the cities of Independence, Wichita and Pittsburg, Kansas. The official corps of the company is as here noted: President, H. P. Wright, of Kansas City, Missouri; vice president, L. O. Ripley, of Wichita; and secretary and treasurer, Charles E. Smyth, of Wichita. The local offices of the company at Independence are located at 113 South Sixth Street. Mr. Murrow has identified himself fully and loyally with the civic and business life of Independence and is the owner of his attractive home property, at 400 East Locust Street.

In politics Mr. Murrow gives his allegiance to the republican party, and in his home city he is affiliated with the Benevolent and Protective Order of Elks, the Rotary Club, the Commercial Club and the Country Club. He is also a member of the American Society of Electrical Engineers and of the national electrical organization known as the Jovian Order. In addition to his activities as manager of the Kansas Gas & Electric Company Mr. Murrow is vice president of the Elgin Oil & Gas Company, and one-half owner of the substantial business conducted under the title of the M. & M. Manufacturing Company, this name being given from the surname initials of the two interested principals, Mr. Murrow and Mr. Mark D. Mitchell. This company manufactures oil-well specialties and is also actively concerned in natural gas production.

On the 14th of January, 1905, was solemnized the marriage of Mr. Murrow to Miss Tillie N. Barzen, daughter of Jacob Barzen, a well known capitalist of Kansas City and one originally concerned in the organization of the Independence Electric Company, as previously noted. Mr. and Mrs. Murrow have two children: William Templer, who was born January 29, 1909, and Richard Barzen, who was born December 16, 1912.

The genealogy of the Murrow family traces back to stanch English origin and the first American representatives settled in the Dominion of Canada, whence the parents of the subject of this sketch removed to Boston, Massachusetts, when young, their marriage having been solemnized in that city.

MARY PIERCE VAN ZILE. A very important member of the faculty of the Kansas State Agricultural College is Mrs. Mary Pierce Van Zile, dean of women and dean of the division of home economics. Her name is a household word in many widely separated homes, for each year Mrs. Van Zile has under her immediate care and instruction from 800 to 900 girls. They come from many environments and are mostly in the most receptive period of their lives, and the influence exerted by Dean Van Zile largely moulds their future.

Mary Pierce Van Zile was born on her father's homestead, near Solomon, in Dickinson County, Kansas, February 7, 1873, and is a daughter of Lyman B. and Lea A. (Bandy) Pierce. The father was a native of Vermont and came of sterling New England stock. The mother was born in Indiana of equally excellent people and pioneer settlers. Lyman B. Pierce served as a soldier during the Civil war, in the Union army, for four years and three months, and shortly after its close pre-empted a homestead in Dickinson County, Kansas. After proving upon that land he removed to Henry County, Iowa, settling at Winfield, where he has since resided, devoting his active years largely to the manufacture of tiling, brick and sewer piping. He can look back over eighty years of a well-spent life.

At Winfield, Iowa, Mary Pierce spent her childhood and young womanhood. Her early education was received in the public schools of Winfield, and the years of 1889-91 were spent as a student in the Kansas State Agricultural College although she did not remain to graduate, for in December, 1892, she became the wife of Gilbert J. Van Zile. He was a graduate of the college in the class of 1890 and was a student of law and was admitted to the bar. During the six years of their married life, Mr. and Mrs. Van Zile resided at Carthage, Illinois, where he had built up a lucrative practice when illness fell upon him and a brilliant career was terminated by his death, in January, 1899. He left two sons, Ralph Pierce and Loren Gilbert. Mrs. Van Zile, unaided, has reared these sons to honorable manhood, giving them exceptional educational advantages. She has had the proud satisfaction of seeing the elder son a graduate of the Kansas State Agricultural College in the class of 1916, the younger son being a student here.

Soon after the death of her husband, Mrs. Van Zile returned to Iowa. Ambitious to be busy, useful and independent, she decided to enter the Iowa State College, at Ames, to pursue a course of study that would prepare her for the work she had in mind, and in 1904 she was graduated from this college in home economics. This field of trained work was, in many sections, entirely new, but in the City of Chicago she found her services acceptable and appreciated and for four years taught home economics in the public schools there. In the fall of 1908 she came to the Kansas State Agricultural College as professor of domestic science, and in 1909 was made dean of women, and in 1913 dean of the division of home economics. In her work in the college she has evinced exceptional ability, rendering skilled services which have made her division second to none in the completeness of its training in any similar institution.

Dean Van Zile is a member of the Presbyterian Church, of which church her venerable father has been a ruling elder for more than a half century. She has membership in several Greek letter college fraternities including Phi Kappa Phi and Omicron Nu. Mention has been made of the salutary influence she exerts over the hundreds of girls who annually come under her care and supervision. A womanly woman she is able to secure the confidence of her charges and her unfailing patience and sympathy arouse willing obedience, entire respect and warm affection. In a way, Dean Van Zile may be called a type of new woman—in her successful struggle for recognition as an efficient factor in the world's work, strong because of her high type of womanliness and because of her technical training that has made her equal to the tasks she has assumed.

GILBERT LeROY JORDAN. Through persistent aspiration and unceasing labor, Gilbert LeRoy Jordan has won his way to the most satisfying and stable compensation of business life. Still a young man, with his best years before him, he is at the head of one of Topeka's prominent business establishments, the College Hill Bakery, located at 1509 Lane Street, an enterprise which he has built up solely through his own efforts. Mr. Jordan commenced his business career without the aiding influences afforded by the possession of financial resources and has been the builder of his own fortune. He has kept persistently at what he started out to do, and has not allowed himself to be diverted from the attainment of his goal.

Gilbert L. Jordan was born on a farm in the vicinity of Victor, Iowa County, Iowa, September 24, 1880, but has been a resident of Kansas since 1895. He is one of four children born to the marriage of R. W. and Caroline (Watson) Jordan, natives of Ohio. R. W. Jordan was reared and educated in his native state, and in 1875 removed to Iowa, where he was for some years engaged in farming at different points. This he continued until coming to Kansas, in 1895, since which time he has given up his agricultural activities and has engaged in various business ventures in different towns and cities. At the present time he is the proprietor of the Palisade Hotel, at Peabody, Kansas, and is one of that city's prominent and influential citizens.

Gilbert L. Jordan received his early education in the country schools of Iowa, dividing his boyhood between attending the district schools in the winter months and assisting his father in the work of the farm during the summer seasons. He also attended school for a time at La Cygne, Kansas, but at the age of sixteen years gave up his studies and commenced devoting his entire time to work. Mr. Jordan passed two years on the farm before he became convinced that farm life was not congenial to him. He had always had a liking for the bakery business, and when he was eighteen years of age left home and went to Kansas City, Missouri, where he secured employment with F. L. Burk, who conducted one of the largest bakeries of that city. There Mr. Jordan learned his trade and learned it well. He remained with Mr. Burk from 1899 until 1907, in which latter year he went to Horton, Kansas, and established himself in business. During the four years that he remained at Horton, he gained confidence and found that he could make the business pay. He found, however, that he needed a larger field for his activities, and accordingly, in 1911, came to Topeka and purchased the bakery at No. 1411 West Fifteenth Street. Under the impetus of his hard work and the excellence of his products, the business grew by leaps and bounds,

and he was forced to seek larger quarters, eventually settling at 1509 Lane Street, where he installed modern machinery and implements. His trade here has grown to such proportions that recently he was compelled to add another story and install another oven, thus increasing the capacity of his output by 50 per cent. All this has been accomplished by Mr. Jordan within a space of five years at Topeka, and he is now the owner of one of the largest bakeries in the State of Kansas. His bakery is conducted in a sanitary manner, thus insuring its patrons of absolute cleanliness and purity, and as only the best of materials are used his patrons are assured of receiving a superior article of bakery goods. In business circles Mr. Jordan is accounted a shrewd but thoroughly honest man, capable of realizing his opportunities and able to make the most of them.

On October 8, 1902, Mr. Jordan was united in marriage with Miss Ethel Baughn, of Kansas, and to this union there have been born two sons: Norman and Lester. Mr. Jordan is not a politician, but generally gives his vote to the democratic party, although as a strong man of broad views on all subjects, he is liable to be independent in his choice of a candidate. He is prominent in Masonry, belonging to all the Topeka York Rite bodies and Orient Lodge No. 51, Ancient Free and Accepted Masons and Abdallah Shrine of Leavenworth. Mrs. Jordan is a member of the Euclid Methodist Church and takes some interest in its movements. She is also well known in fraternal circles, being a member of the Eastern Star Lodge of Topeka.

JAMES CLAUDE WILHOIT, M. D. This is the name of a prominent young physician and surgeon at Manhattan, but a man who in spite of his years has attained an enviable prominence in the professional and business life of his home state. Doctor Wilhoit has those natural gifts which together with thorough training make the proficient surgeon. His work is now largely surgery and diagnosis.

He was born at Westmoreland in Pottawatomie County, Kansas, July 14, 1885, a son of Dr. John W. and Jennie (Armstrong) Wilhoit. His parents were natives of Kentucky, where they married, and they came to Kansas in 1884 and since 1885 Dr. John W. Wilhoit has practiced medicine with success at St. George, Kansas, and in that vicinity. He is one of the well known men of his county, and has won an enviable reputation in his profession.

The early youth of Dr. J. C. Wilhoit was spent in the community of St. George. He attended the public schools there and later the State Normal School at Emporia. In 1907 he graduated M. D. from the University of Louisville, Kentucky. His first practical experience was at St. George, but after a year he located at Manhattan, where he has gained a large and lucrative practice.

Doctor Wilhoit is a member of the Riley County and the Kansas State Medical societies and the American Medical Association, and in 1915 was elected president of the county society and also president of the Golden Belt Medical Society. Ever since graduating he has taken every opportunity to associate with the leaders of the profession in America and secure the benefit of further study and observation. He spent some time in the Post-Graduate School of Medicine at New York City and has attended the clinics of the famous Mayo brothers at Rochester, Minnesota, and also the clinics of Chicago's foremost

J. C. Wilhoit

surgeon, John B. Murphy. He is a member of the American Clinical Surgical Congress.

Doctor Wilhoit is interested in a number of business affairs and is a member of the board of directors for the Kansas Life Insurance Company. He is well known in fraternal circles, being a Knight Templar Mason and Mystic Shriner and a member of the Benevolent and Protective Order of Elks. In 1908 he married Ethel J. Peck of St. Joseph, Missouri.

ROBERT LAWRENCE MITCHELL. Menoken Township, Shawnee County, in 1870 was mainly raw prairie land and the hardy pioneers who came here as homeseekers had weary tasks before them. Agricultural riches lay beneath the sod but it was toilsome labor to break up this sod, to plough and seed the land and then await the harvest. In the above year many of the eastern states contributed to the citizenship of Kansas and among those who came from Ohio was George J. Mitchell. He was a prosperous and intelligent farmer in Ohio. After sending his three sons to Oberlin College he thought to still further advance them in life and in 1870 bought 640 acres of wild land in Shawnee County, the ranch which has been the family property ever since, now increased to 800 acres, all in Menoken Township.

Robert Lawrence Mitchell, now deceased, was one of the sons who settled in Kansas, coming to this farm in 1872. He was born near Bridgeville, in Guernsey County, Ohio, February 7, 1848. His parents were George J. and Elmira Mitchell. As above mentioned Robert Lawrence Mitchell came to Menoken Township in 1872, accompanied by his brother-in-law, A. M. Bates, now a resident of Colorado. This farm had been Indian land and on one part of it they found an old Indian burial ground and many other evidences of occupation although no attempt had been made in the way of cultivation. Mr. Mitchell and Mr. Bates had a difficult proposition to face during the first two years, the great grasshopper scourge rendering useless their labor in 1874. In the next year Mr. Bates left the uplands and took land on the Kaw River bottoms, on which he remained until 1900 when he and his son moved to Colorado. After 1874 Mr. Mitchell gradually made progress and in the course of time became one of the leading men in the stock business in this township. He was a man of fine character, public spirited and free handed and was ever ready to assist laudable enterprises designed for the betterment of the community. He gave liberally to the Baptist Church, to which he and wife belonged, and was particularly interested in the founding of schools.

Mr. Mitchell was married to a Miss Keats and they had a family of six children: John, George, Harry, Bert, Nellie, now Mrs. Paul Priddy, and Grace. Harry and Bert conduct the farm ranch, carrying on general farming and stock raising. All the children were given educational advantages and Bert, prior to settling down on the farm, spent one year in the agricultural college at Manhattan. He was married to Miss Wilma Joy Antrim, October 18, 1905, and they have two children: Thelma and Helen. As was his late father, Mr. Mitchell is a republican but the family has never been very active in a political way and have sought no offices. It is a representative family in its good citizenship, however, and no other in this section is more widely or favorably known.

THE INDEPENDENCE TRIBUNE is one of the oldest papers in Kansas, with a record of continuous issue in one locality for forty-six years, and it is even older than that since the same plant had been used for publishing a paper in Missouri for several years before its removal to Independence, when that town was located on the frontier and at the very beginning of its growth and development. The Tribune ever since its establishment has been under the control of two veteran newspaper men, both brothers, W. T. Yoe, who is editor, and Charles Yoe, who is president of The Tribune Printing Company. The manager of the publication is Charles Albert Connelly, who grew up in the Tribune establishment and has himself been identified with that journal for more than thirty years.

The record of the Yoe brothers in connection with The Tribune is one of special interest to Kansans. W. T. Yoe was born at Port Republic, Calvert County, Maryland, March 26, 1845. The Yoes were an old Maryland family, having come from England with Lord Baltimore and most of the descendants of the first emigrants still live in Maryland. Walter Yoe, father of the Yoe brothers, was born in Maryland in 1800 and died at Rushville, Illinois, in 1867. He was reared and married in Maryland, and in 1848 moved to Rushville, Illinois. He followed his trade as carpenter and builder, was a republican in politics, served a time as a member of the Illinois militia. His wife was Elizabeth William Harris, who was born in Virginia in 1818 and died at Rushville, Illinois, in 1859. Her family came from the North of Ireland, and her brother, Rev. William Harris, was a Baptist minister, served as a colonel in the Confederate army, and died in Shelbville, Kentucky, in 1870. Walter Yoe and wife had three sons: W. T., Charles and Franklin F. Franklin is a druggist at Independence, Kansas, and thus all three of the brothers are identified with that city.

W. T. Yoe grew up in Rushville, Illinois, and most of his schooling came before he was thirteen years of age, having attended only six months after that time. His real education was acquired in a printing office, and a better university for training young men does not exist. At the age of thirteen he was at the office of the Citizen at Rushville, and later in the office of the Times, and made himself useful while accepting such opportunities as were presented to learn the printing trade and all there was to know about the newspaper business as conducted in a small town. Later for a time he clerked in a dry goods store, but in 1864, at the age of nineteen enlisted in Company K of the One Hundred and Thirty-seventh Illinois Regiment of Infantry and served nine months until the close of the war. After getting his honorable discharge, he returned to Rushville, but in 1866 moved to Shelbyville, Missouri, and was in the hardware business for a time.

The real beginning of the Independence Tribune came in 1868, when he and his brother Charles, having located at Shelbina, Shelby County, Missouri, and together with A. M. York and John W. Shaffer, became owners of the Shelby County Herald. Three years later, in 1871, the Yoe brothers and L. U. Humphrey and A. M. York moved the plant from Missouri to Independence, Kansas, which was then just starting as a more or less promising village of Montgomery County. When the plant was in readiness it began issuing the South Kansas Tribune, and in 1874 the Yoe brothers purchased all other interests and controlled the paper entirely until Mr. Connelly was made a partner in 1898.

The Tribune Printing Company now has as its proprietors W. T. and Charles Yoe and C. A. Connelly. It is a remarkable record, when the vicissitudes of newspaper experience are considered, that the Tribune has never missed an issue since it was established, although the office was destroyed by fire in 1883. The Tribune is a stanch old line standpat republican paper, is issued weekly, circulating in Montgomery and surrounding counties, and its prestige and influence are second to none among the papers in that section of the state. The company owns the building and plant at 109 South Penn Avenue. This is the pioneer paper of Montgomery County, and only two other papers in Kansas are older, considered from the standpoint of continuous existence and surviving to the present time. For forty-five years W. T. Yoe has directed the editorial management of the paper, while Charles Yoe has been president and business executive, with Mr. Connelly now as business manager.

W. T. Yoe is a republican of the old school, a member of the Methodist Church, and is affiliated with the Independent Order of Odd Fellows, the Woodmen of the World, the Modern Woodmen of America, the Knights and Ladies of Security and the Sons and Daughters of Justice. A number of years ago he was appointed postmaster at Independence by President Chester A. Arthur, and served three years, resigning before the expiration of his term. Governor Humphrey also appointed him a member of the state board of charities and for a time he was one of the board of regents of the State Agricultural College at Manhattan. He married Jennie E. Weatherby, a daughter of Warren W. and Harriet Weatherby, both of whom are now deceased. Her father was at one time postmaster at Shelbina, Missouri. Their children are seven: Harriet, living at home with her parents; Roy, on a farm in Southern Montgomery County; Edna May, wife of A. L. Bryan, who lives near Los Angeles, California, and is in the automobile supply business; Earl, foreman in the Tribune printing office at Independence; Ruth, wife of Guy Arey of Independence, Mr. Arey being in the oil business; Warren W., with the Petroleum Products Company; and George, in the engineering department for the Kansas Natural Gas Company, employed in the Oklahoma fields.

Charles Yoe, the younger of these veteran publishers, and the president of the company, was born at Rushville, Schuyler County, Illinois, September 22, 1849, the year following the removal of his parents to that locality. Gaining his education in the public schools there, at the early age of sixteen he started for himself and found employment at various seasons as a farmer, in sawing wood, peddling ice and in printing offices. For a time he was office boy for the Rushville Citizen, and was paper carrier. For about five months he was with John Nicholson on the Illinoisan at Beardstown, Illinois, and in 1868, as already stated, became associated with his brother and others in the management of the Shelby County Herald at Shelbina, Missouri, and from there accompanied the plant and paper to Independence, Kansas.

Mr. Charles Yoe is a republican, and served on the State Board of Charities under Governor Stanley and in 1910 was supervisor of the census. He is a member of the Methodist Episcopal Church. Among other business interests he is president of the Independence Building & Loan Association.

On August 8, 1880, in Montgomery County, he married Miss Agnes Overfield, a daughter of Thomas and Margaret Overfield. Her father was a farmer and is now deceased, and her mother resides in the home of Mr. and Mrs. Charles Yoe, and is eighty-five years of age. The Overfield family came to Kansas from Massachusetts in 1854, and were among the pioneers of the territory and had their part in the struggle for the free state movement.

CHARLES ALBERT CONNELLY, whose long and able connection with the Independence Tribune has already been noted, has been one of the live and progressive citizens of Independence and has accepted many opportunities to serve the community in addition to his work as a newspaper man.

He was born in Parke County, Indiana, August 12, 1869. His father, Charles T. Connelly, who was born in Parke County, Indiana, in 1845, is especially deserving of note in a history of Kansas. He was reared and married in Indiana and in 1885 moved to Garden City, Kansas, and proved up a claim there. In 1887 he came to Independence, and resumed his earlier profession as a teacher. In the meantime he had made an honorable record as a soldier of the Union during the Civil war. He enlisted in 1862 at the age of seventeen and served 3½ years until the close of the struggle, being a member of the Ninth Indiana Battery. From Independence he moved to Coffeyville, and served as principal of schools there, and during the summer vacations filled the post of city marshal. It was while in the performance of his duty that he was killed in 1892, when the Dalton gang of outlaws raided Coffeyville. He was a republican, a member of the Methodist Episcopal Church, was affiliated with the Independent Order of Odd Fellows and was clerk of the camp of the Modern Woodmen of America at the time of his death. Charles T. Connelly married Mary McCord, who was born in Parke County, Indiana, in 1846 and died there in 1873. The two children of that union were Charles Albert and Grace. The latter, who died in 1908, at the age of thirty-eight, was the wife of William N. Cox, county assessor of Parke County, Indiana. Charles T. Connelly married for his second wife Sarah Alexander, who died in 1896, survived by one daughter, Jessie May, now wife of Harry W. Lang, a druggist at Coffeyville, Kansas. This branch of the Connelly family came from Ireland to North Carolina in colonial times, and subsequent generations moved to Kentucky and from there into Indiana.

Charles A. Connelly, best known among his friends and business associates in Independence as Bert Connelly, spent the first sixteen years of his life in his native Parke County, Indiana, attended the public schools there and the Bloomingdale Academy of Indiana, and after coming to Independence was a pupil in the high school until 1888. However, in the meanwhile, in 1885, he had entered the office of the Tribune Printing Company. He made himself a master of its various details, and is an expert printer and newspaper man. In 1898 he was made a partner, and for a number of years has been business manager of the Tribune.

Mr. Connelly has served as director of the Independence Building and Loan Association; is a member and served as director of the Independence Commercial Club, belongs to the Rotary Club, served six years as treasurer of the school board, during which time four new modern school buildings were erected, and for two years was a member of the city council. President Taft appointed him postmaster of Independence, but his appointment was not confirmed on account of the closely following election of President Wilson. Mr. Connelly is a republican, is a trustee of the Methodist Episcopal Church, is affiliated with Fortitude Lodge No. 107, Ancient, Free and Accepted Masons, and a Royal Arch Mason at Independence; with Independence camp of the Modern Woodmen of America, of which he was banker four years, and his name is usually closely associated with any enterprise for the public good of his home city.

In 1894, at Independence, he married Miss Olive

May Stout, daughter of E. W. and Margaret Stout. Miss Stout is a member of the Daughters of the American Revolution and Eastern Star lodge. Her mother is still living at Independence, and her father, now deceased, was a grocery merchant of that city, member of the school board and stood high in the community. Mr. and Mrs. Connelly have two children, Glenn, born November 28, 1897, a graduate of Montgomery County High School, and now attending Baker University, and Margaret, born November 14, 1901, now a sophomore in the Montgomery County High School.

NELSON ANTRIM CRAWFORD is professor of industrial journalism and superintendent of printing with the Kansas State Agricultural College. For several years he was instructor in English in the Agricultural College but has been head of the journalism work since April, 1914.

In his special department he has done important work for the Agricultural College. For several years of his early life he was a newspaper reporter and was thus no stranger to the practical phases of journalism when he came to his present position. He has in the past two years increased the work of the department threefold. By virtue of being professor of industrial journalism he is also editor of The Kansas Industrialist, the organ of the Kansas State Agricultural College, and has charge of the college advertising and publicity. He is also editor of The Kansas Churchman, the official paper of the Episcopal Diocese of Kansas.

He was born at Miller, South Dakota, but was reared at Council Bluffs, Iowa, where for many years his father practiced law. His father, Nelson Antrim Crawford, Sr., was born in Ohio of Scotch lineage, the Crawfords being an old Pennsylvania family. The senior Crawford married Fannie Vandercook, who was born in Wisconsin of Holland Dutch origin. She is directly descended from New York Knickerbocker ancestry, and one of her forefathers was Simon Vandercook, an officer in the American Revolution. The presence of this ancestor in his family tree gives Professor Crawford memberships in the Sons of the Revolution.

Both Mr. Crawford's parents were teachers in Dakota Territory, and while there they met and married. Subsequently they moved to Council Bluffs, Iowa, and many years later to Lincoln, Nebraska, where they now reside. They had two sons, the younger of whom is Robert Platt Crawford, a practical newspaper man and journalist.

After graduating from the Council Bluffs High School, Nelson A. Crawford spent several years in newspaper work, and then entered the State University of Iowa, where he was graduated B. A. in 1910. In the fall of that year he came to the Kansas State Agricultural College to become instructor in English. Later he was assistant professor of English, and resigned that position in July, 1914, to accept his present post. While teaching English at Manhattan he was also a student in the University of Kansas, and in 1914 received his Master of Arts degree.

Mr. Crawford is a member of the American Association of Teachers of Journalism; is vice president of the American Association of Agricultural College Editors; is a member of the American Dialect Society; of the Society of the Quill; of the Kansas Editorial Association; of the Kansas Authors' Club. He is a former president of the Kansas Association of Teachers of English. He is now president of the Manhattan Press Club, and an associate member of the Topeka Press Club. Many articles from his pen that have been published in magazines attest his individual literary talents.

Mr. Crawford belongs to Phi Kappa Phi, scholarship society, and to Sigma Delta Chi, honorary journalism fraternity, and is also a Knight Templar. He is very prominent in the Episcopal Church, being a vestryman of the church at Manhattan, and in 1917 was a delegate to the Synod of the Province of the Southwest.

WILLIAM GIBSON DICKIE. Though he began his career on a Kansas farm with very few advantages in the way of schooling and has had to work for his own support and for that of others since boyhood, William G. Dickie has acquired a very honorable position in business affairs at Topeka, and has a record embodying many useful years spent in public office, in manufacturing lines, and in connection with several Kansas corporations.

A native of Kansas, he was born six miles west of Olathe, Johnson County, January 21, 1870. His parents, William Holmes and Charity (Gibson) Dickie, had moved to their farm in Johnson County only a short time before his birth. William Holmes Dickie, as was his wife, was a native of Pennsylvania. He gained his education in district schools while working on his father's farm, afterwards acquired a place of his own, was married, and in 1856 brought his family to Illinois. There at the outbreak of the war he enlisted in Company E of the One Hundred and Second Illinois Infantry, going in as a musician and immediately being assigned to the hospital corps, with which he served through the war. Released from the army he rejoined his family in Illinois, and they soon afterwards decided to move to Kansas, locating first on the farm in Johnson County above mentioned. Here they had the usual vicissitudes attending Kansas agriculture in those days. The first crops were entirely destroyed by grasshoppers. However, they were better off the second year, and in the course of time by the labors of all members of the household they were making a comfortable living.

On account of his military service William H. Dickie was never in robust health after the war, and the burden involved in the support of eight children had to be shared proportionately by all the younger members of the household as strength permitted. Thus William G. Dickie began to feel the serious responsibilities of life when only a child. He was ambitious to secure an education, but he had to study as opportunity presented itself in the intervals of work, and some time after leaving off from attendance at the district schools he was able to complete a course in the Spaulding Commercial College at Kansas City, Missouri.

His first position after leaving this school was as bookkeeper with the Farmers' Co-operative Shipping Association at Beloit, Kansas. This was an organization of the farmers of Mitchell County. In the meantime the Dickie family had moved to Mitchell County. The association of which Mr. Dickie was bookkeeper was one of the first of its kind and was the forerunner of the Farmers' Union. After two years he was offered and accepted the place of deputy county treasurer of Mitchell County, and was engaged in the creditable performance of the duties of that office for three years. He then resigned to become assistant cashier of the Beloit State Bank, a post he also held three years. His next promotion was as manager of the state printing establishment under John S. Parks, state printer. That called him to Topeka, with which city he has since been identified. He was with the state printing office six years, two years under Mr. Parks and four years under W. Y. Morgan, now lieutenant-governor of Kansas.

In the meantime on June 19, 1902, Mr. Dickie and Miss Bertha Morris of Lancaster, Wisconsin, were married. To their union was born one child named Margaret.

In 1903 Mr. Dickie organized and became president of the Jensen Manufacturing Company, manufacturers of creamery supplies. The plant of this company was built at East Eighth and the Santa Fe Railroad tracks, and is now occupied by the Pierson Transmitter Company of Topeka. Mr. Dickie's associates in that enterprise were W. F. Jensen, J. S. Parks and A. Jensen, and later George A. Clark. In 1912, after having operated successfully for nine years, the business of the company was purchased by the J. G. Cherry Company of Cedar Rapids, Iowa. Mr. Dickie then removed to Cedar Rapids to become supervisor in the manufacture of articles formerly made at Topeka. He lived at Cedar Rapids two years. While there, in October, 1912, he suffered a great loss in the death of his wife. She was laid to rest in Lancaster, Wisconsin, her former home.

On February 1, 1914, Mr. Dickie returned to Topeka and became president of the Kaw Paving Company. This is one of the large industries of Topeka, and his other associates in the executive management are H. A. Kingsley, vice president; H. L. Shire, secretary and treasurer; and Miss Cora Green, assistant secretary.

Mr. Dickie is one of the organizers and the vice president of the Kansas State Employers' Association. This association has relations with all lines of interest and industry in the state, and its purpose is to promote proper legislation indiscriminately for the good of employer and employe alike, and it has already accomplished a large amount of wholesome good. Mr. Dickie is on the board of directors of the Topeka Title and Bonding Company, is a member of the Commercial Club, is a Mason, and politically is independent in local matters, though a republican when it comes to national issues.

JAMES C. HOLLAND. The public architecture of Kansas, especially in the capital city, is largely a record of the skill and experience of one man, James C. Holland. Mr. Holland by all the standards that can be applied is a great architect. He has gained a well deserved prominence in this profession. His experience in Kansas covers more than thirty years. At one time he held the office of state architect, but throughout his business has largely been in connection with the designing and the superintending of construction of buildings which serve a public or quasi-public purpose.

A few years ago a signal recognition of his standing as an architect was given when he was one of the eight architects outside the city invited by the New York Society of Architects to membership in that body. When it is considered that this is the greatest organization of its kind in America, and when only men of recognized standing and ability are admitted to its membership, the invitation can be appraised at its real worth, and even Mr. Holland, who has never looked for praise or honors beyond a conscientious performance that would satisfy himself, had reason to be pleased with this invitation.

Both as to his family and himself a great deal might be said and the following sketch has a most appropriate place in any history of Kansas. James C. Holland was born at Lima, Ohio, in a log cabin April 2, 1853. The original spelling of the name was Howland. John Howland was the progenitor of the American family and came as a follower of Lord Baltimore during the early colonization of the present State of Maryland. What branch of the family adopted the spelling Holland is not now ascertainable. Mr. Holland's family, however, has spelled the name in that form for many generations. For many years the home of Mr. Holland's ancestors was around Plymouth Rock, Massachusetts. His father's cousin was the noted American author, whose writings were so widely read a generation ago and are still highly prized, John G. Holland.

Thomas Holland, grandfather of James C., was a pioneer in the State of Ohio, locating near Washington Court House in Fayette County, about 1803. There he endured all the hardships of pioneering, developed a good homestead, and by his marriage to Lorena Cahill reared a large family of children.

Barton Andrew Holland, the youngest child of Thomas and Lorena, and the father of James C. Holland, was a prominent man in Northwestern Ohio. All of the name in Ohio were substantial men, ranked above the average in point of citizenship, and fearlessly did their duty in whatever circumstance of life they were placed. Barton A. Holland in early life was a builder, and was quite widely known in that line. Early in the Civil war he was made a recruiting officer at Lima. He recruited the Ninety-ninth, One Hundred and Eighteenth and One Hundred and Eightieth Ohio Volunteer Regiments of Infantry. He himself went to the front as first lieutenant and later captain of a company in the One Hundred and Eighteenth, afterwards was made ranking captain in the One Hundred and Eightieth regiment, and still later became major of that regiment. With that rank he served until the close of the war. One of his sons, Thomas B., now one of Ohio's successful criminal lawyers, living at Paulding, was first lieutenant in the One Hundred and Eighteenth Regiment. For many years the Holland family lived in the vicinity of Lima, and another family in the same locality was the Osmons. Barton A. Holland married Lydia Osmon, a daughter of Thomas and Rachel (Osborn) Osmon.

When Major Holland returned from the war his health was shattered, and he was unable to continue actively his building business. He served as sheriff and deputy sheriff of Allen County, Ohio, and subsequently practiced law at Lima. While he was never a student in a law college he had the basic qualifications of the real lawyer. He possessed an analytical mind, was almost infallible in the matter of figures and measurements, and his reasoning powers and sound logic gave him high rank as a lawyer. He was also a power in Ohio politics, and was campaign manager of Calvin S. Brice when that Ohio statesman was elected United States senator by one vote. Barton A. Holland died in 1907. Much of the attribute which James C. Holland has shown for the profession of architecture he credits to inheritance from his father. He was especially influenced to take up the building business by a brother-in-law, James M. McKinney, then a prominent builder at Lima. Mr. Holland had a sound educational training, though perhaps measured by modern standards it did not include as wide a range of subjects as are found in a university curriculum. He attended the public schools of Lima, and afterwards removed with his parents to Ada, Ohio, and there helped to build and afterwards attended from the age of eleven years the noted normal school founded by Prof. H. S. Lehr, which afterwards was known as the Ohio Normal University and now the Ohio Northern University.

Mr. Holland spent about a year in the office of Rumbaugh & Bacon, architects, at Toledo. In 1879 he returned to Ada and resumed his business as a builder and designer. In 1880 he took a special course at Cornell University. On his return he was given the chair of architecture in his alma mater at Ada.

James C. Holland arrived at Topeka in 1885 with $110 of borrowed money. While at Ada he had met with a severe accident that not only kept him under a doctor's care for many months but left him penniless. Thus when he began his practice as an architect in Kansas he was practically insolvent. Because of his previous experience, his thorough technical qualifications, business gradually came to him at Topeka, and many years ago he took his place at the head of the profession.

In 1895 Mr. Holland was elected state architect. He filled that office three years, resigning to accept the position of special architect for the Santa Fe Railway Company. As state architect he really discharged three functions, as state house architect for finishing up the capitol building, as state architect, an office created by the board of public works, and as architect for the State Board of Charities. During the three years he spent in office he supervised the expenditure of nearly $750,000 in public buildings in Kansas. It is noteworthy that he completed all the central wing of the capitol building except the central dome, and even for that he had all the plans and specifications drawn, still the actual work of construction was finished by his successor.

On leaving the office of state architect he continued with the Santa Fe Railway until 1899, and since then has been in individual practice, and is now head of the firm of J. C. Holland & Son, with offices at 734 Kansas Avenue. For about twelve years Mr. Holland's services were largely employed by the Wells Fargo Express Company in designing their buildings over a widely extended territory.

As stated previously, Mr. Holland's work has been largely confined to the designing and superintendence of the construction of public buildings. There have been no local limitations to his practice. A few years ago the municipal government of Cohoes, New York, awarded him the contract for the city hall over twenty-eight competitors. That is only one of a long list of public buildings erected or supervised by Mr. Holland. He has designed nearly all the prominent public buildings of the City of Topeka, including the Shawnee County Courthouse, the high school and manual training school, the Journal Building, the Capper Building, the Mills Building, the Topeka Auditorium, the Topeka Young Men's Christian Association, the Presbyterian and Central Congregational churches, the Daily Capital Building and numerous others. He has constructed sixteen courthouses in different counties of Kansas, and a large number of schools, Young Men's Christian Association buildings, churches, jails and business buildings in this and other states.

Mr. Holland is a prominent Mason, a Knight Templar, a thirty-second degree Scottish Rite and a

Shriner. He is also an Elk, a member of the Toltecs, belongs to the Topeka Commercial and Rotary clubs, and in politics is a republican.

September 14, 1882, at Ada, Ohio, he married Miss Lizzie Braker. Mrs. Holland came with him to Kansas, and has loyally aided him in his business success and at the same time has devoted herself most unselfishly to her home and children. There are three children: Barton Andrew, Franklin Osmon and Lydia Lucile. The two sons are now associated with their father in business, while Lucile is the wife of R. H. Sowers of Topeka.

THOMAS JEFFERSON BOOTH, of Independence, is a native of Illinois, in Adams County, of which state he was born January 4, 1856. He was but eight years of age when his parents removed to Iowa and settled in Des Moines County, where they resided until 1869, in which year they settled in Montgomery County, Kansas, where the father took up a claim and resided until his death in 1878. Thomas J. Booth is a son of Milton and Agatha (Adams) Booth. His father was born in Virginia in 1808, and was a son of John Booth, an Englishman, who came to the United States as one of three brothers, he settling in Virginia. Agatha (Adams) Booth was born in Kentucky and was of German lineage. She bore her husband seven children, four of whom are deceased. All of them grew to womanhood and manhood. She died while the family was living in Iowa, and was but forty years of age at the time of her death. Thomas J. Booth was thirteen years of age when his father came to Montgomery County, Kansas, in 1869, and since then he has continued to reside in this county. He was reared on his father's farms in Illinois, Iowa and Kansas. He obtained a fair common school education in the public schools of Iowa and Kansas, and also taught several terms in the district or country schools. He aided his father on the farm, breaking prairie sod, herding cattle and doing other work common to the farm life of a youth. Mr. Booth married at the age of twenty-three, and he began the battle of life for himself as a farmer in Montgomery County. He continued strictly at farming until 1884, in which year he engaged in buying, feeding and shipping cattle. For ten consecutive years he was successfully engaged in the business. In 1894 Mr. Booth removed from the farm into the City of Independence, where he has since resided. In that year he became the organizer of the Union Implement & Hardware Company, of Independence, in which business concern he has continued to hold considerable stock, and for ten years he was secretary, treasurer and manager of the company. In 1904 Mr. Booth engaged in the oil business as a producer, and is still interested rather extensively in the oil industry. In 1916 he became president of the First National Bank of Independence. In this form of business he has met with that gratifying success that has attended all of his business undertakings. He is the owner of several business blocks and other real estate in Independence, of which city he has truly been a builder. Among the buildings he has erected in Independence is the Hotel Booth of which he is owner and proprietor. This he erected in 1911. The building is 91 by 111 feet, and five stories above the basement. It is said to be the only strictly fireproof hotel in Kansas, is modern throughout and is thoroughly sanitary in equipment.

Mr. Booth is independent in politics, but he has never sought political honors, preferring to give his time and attention to business affairs. Fraternally he is a Knight Templar Mason, a Scottish Rite Mason in the thirty-second degree and a member of the

Ancient Arabic Order Nobles of the Mystic Shrine. He is also a member of the Benevolent and Protective Order of Elks.

Mr. Booth has been twice married. In 1879 he married Amanda Peebler, a daughter of William and Elizabeth Peebler, who came to Montgomery County, Kansas, in 1870 from Iowa, in Jefferson County of which state their daughter was born. Mrs. Booth died in 1900, leaving three children, as follows: Clyde E. Booth, who died in 1903 at the age of nineteen years; Nellie B. became the wife of E. J. Lambert, a well known and successful lawyer and oil producer of Tulsa, Oklahoma, by whom she is the mother of a son and daughter, Thomas Benjamin and Mary Frances Lambert; and Ethel E., who became the wife of R. W. Kellough, one of the most prominent and able lawyers of Tulsa, Oklahoma, by whom she is the mother of two children, namely, Helen Virginia and Thomas Booth Kellough. Mr. Booth is very fond of his grandchildren, taking as much interest in them as if they were his own children. In 1904 Mr. Booth married a second time, Laura Bradley becoming his wife. She is a daughter of Milton and Emma Bradley, and was about eight years of age when her parents came to Independence, where she was reared. Mrs. Booth is refined and cultured, and presides with dignity in their home, which is at the Hotel Booth, where they have very elaborate apartments.

Mr. Booth is unassuming, and is highly esteemed in Independence. In all of his business transactions he has dealt with his fellow man fairly, and for probity of character no man of his resident city is more highly respected than he. He began his business career on limited capital, but success has attended his business endeavors.

EDWARD CARL JOHNSON. Identified with the Kansas State Agricultural College at Manhattan since the fall of 1912, Edward Carl Johnson is now dean of the division of college extension and is also superintendent of farmers' institutes and state leader of county agent work. At first his work was that of superintendent of institutes and demonstration in the division of college extension. Since September, 1915, his duties have been as just described.

Mr. Johnson is an expert in several departments affecting the broad science of agriculture. His authorship of a number of bulletins and monographs prove this. But his work has not been confined to a laboratory. He is a man of much enthusiasm and a successful worker in the co-operative movement between the agricultural school and the practical farmer.

Since coming to Kansas he has given special attention to extension work, increasing the number of farm bureau and county agents in Kansas from one to seventeen; by July 1, 1916, and organizing extension schools for both men and women. In that way the usefulness of the splendid college at Manhattan has been broadly extended to those persons who most need its advice and co-operation.

Dean Johnson is a Minnesota man by birth, and was born in Waseca County, April 18, 1880. His parents, August and Josephine (Peterson) Johnson, were born in Sweden, were married in the United States, and after their marriage located on a farm in Waseca County, Minnesota, where the son, Edward C., spent his youth. While on the farm he gained something of that practical knowledge which is at the basis of all successful farming. He attended the country schools and in 1901 completed the high school course at Waseca. After a year as a teacher in a district school near the old home, he entered the University of Minnesota in the liberal arts department, and was graduated A. B. in 1906. During his senior year in the university he was assistant instructor in botany, a subject in which he specialized and which became the basis for his later work. During 1906-07 he was instructor in botany at the University of Minnesota, and during the same year continued his post-graduate work. In the spring of 1907 he received his Master of Arts degree.

From the University of Minnesota he went direct to Washington, District of Columbia, and there became assistant plant pathologist in the Department of Agriculture. In 1908 he was made plant pathologist in charge of the cereal diseases work of the department. This was the field of his study and research until he came to the Kansas State Agricultural College four years ago.

During the winter of 1910-11 he took graduate work in the George Washington University at Washington, District of Columbia. He is a Fellow of the American Association for the Advancement of Science, a member of the American Association of Farmers' Institute Workers, a member of the Botanical Society of America, of the American Phyto Pathological Society and of the National Geographic Society. He also belongs to the national honorary fraternities of Phi Beta Kappa, Sigma Xi, Alpha Zeta and Phi Kappa Phi. Mr. Johnson is a member of the Congregational Church. In 1911 he married Miss Ruth Daniels of West Medway, Massachusetts. Their two children are named Carola and Josephine.

In addition to the routine of his duties which bring him in practical contact with the farmers of the great State of Kansas, Mr. Johnson has a growing reputation as an author, and besides numerous articles that he has contributed to farm journals and newspapers, he is author of a number of technical treatises. A brief description of these is as follows: "The Rusts of Grains in the United States," United States Department of Agriculture B. P. I. Bulletin No. 216, 1911, Mr. Johnson being a co-author with E. M. Freeman; "The Loose Smuts of Barley and Wheat," United States Department of Agriculture B. P. I. Bulletin No. 152, 1909, also co-author with E. M. Freeman; "Timothy Rust in the United States," United States Department of Agriculture B. P. I. Bulletin No. 224, 1911; "Methods in Breeding Cereals for Rust Resistance," Proceedings of the American Society of Agronomy, Vol. 2, pages 76-80, 1910; "Floret Sterility of Wheats in the Southwest," Phytopathology, Vol. 1, No. 1, 1911; "The Smuts of Wheat, Oats, Barley and Corn," United States Department of Agriculture Farmers' Bulletin No. 507, 1912; "A Study of Some Imperfect Fungi Isolated from Wheat, Oat and Barley Plants," United States Department of Agriculture Journal of Agricultural Research, Vol. 1, No. 6, pages 475-492, 1914; "Farmers' Institutes in Kansas; A Handbook for Institute Officers," Agricultural Education, Vol. 1, No. 22, Kansas State Agricultural College, 1913; "The Smuts of Kafir, Other Sorghums and Broom Corn," Agricultural Education, Vol. 6, No. 4, Kansas State Agricultural College, 1914; "Contour Farming in Kansas," Division of College Extension, Circular No. 7, Kansas State Agricultural College, 1914; "The Agricultural Agent and Farm Bureau Movement in Kansas,"

Joseph F. Johnson and Mrs. Lewis H. Johnson

Extension Bulletin No. 2, Kansas State Agricultural College.

LEVI F. JOHNSON. As it was only about sixty years ago that the first permanent settlements were made in Kansas, there are a number of the real pioneers still alive, men who can recount their experiences when the plains were covered with buffaloes, when Indians made camp along the creeks, when the prairie fires raged across the high grass, and when the woods were filled with game, the creeks with fish, and when everything was new and primitive.

Now living retired at a comfortable home in Winfield Levi F. Johnson had his share in the early making of Kansas, particularly of Cowley County. He made his first trip to Kansas in 1860 when he bought eighty acres of wild land near Frankfort, Marshall County. The unsettled conditions of the frontier made a permanent residence at that time undesirable, and it was not until after the war in which he fought bravely and gallantly as a Union soldier that he returned to Kansas, then a state, and entered upon his real work as a builder and home-maker. Mr. Johnson recalls many trips which he made years ago with parties to hunt buffalo, which could be still found in large herds. He had many exciting experiences on such expeditions, and he is one of the comparatively few men who can recall the actual taste of buffalo steak and the methods of hunting an animal which is now all but extinct.

Levi F. Johnson was born in Harrison County, Ohio, October 28, 1837, and has lived almost fourscore years. His parents were Aaron and Hannah (Feaster) Johnson. His father was born in Harrison County, Ohio, and died at Marion, Kansas, at the age of sixty-three. The mother's parents were Pennsylvania Dutch people. Levi F. Johnson was one of five children, the others being Rhoda, Daniel, Samuel and Mary. Of these Samuel and Levi are the only survivors. All the sons served in the Civil war. Daniel was killed at the battle of Chickamauga while fighting with the Fifty-first Ohio. Samuel was a member of the Forty-first Ohio Regiment.

Reared and educated in his native county, Levi F. Johnson after his first trip to Kansas and his return to his native state, was aroused by the news of the disaster at Bull Run, and hastened to enlist to defend the Union. He became a member of the Seventy-eighth Ohio Volunteer Infantry, and his early service was under General Grant. He participated in the capture of Fort Donelson, in the battle of Shiloh, at Corinth, and was in many of those battles leading up to the siege and capture of Vicksburg. He fought at Jackson, Champion Hill, and spent many days in the slow and steady approach to the Mississippi stronghold. Mr. Johnson says that during the siege of Vicksburg and contrary to the orders of the officers he and his Union comrades frequently visited with the rebels and traded tobacco and other supplies, and however bitterly they fought when time for battle arrived they were friends during the lulls of fighting. About the time Vicksburg fell Mr. Johnson was detailed to service in the Freedman's Bureau. He was placed in charge of a camp of refugee negroes at the Joe Davis plantation twenty-eight miles below Vicksburg. There efforts were made to render the negroes self-supporting. They were trained to grow cotton, and Mr. Johnson had the task of allotting lands, maintaining a general supervision over the former slaves, and distributing rations and mules supplied by the bureau. While in that work he received a discharge from the army, but was kept in his position until after the close of the war. During part of the time he had the management of about 2,000 negroes.

For three years after the war he remained in the South and was engaged in cotton growing. In a short time the price of cotton fell so that the growing of the staple became unprofitable, and after realizing only a few hundred dollars from his venture he returned to Kansas in 1868.

The next three years he spent on his eighty acres of land in Marshall County. Selling that to advantage in the spring of 1871 he sought what was reported as government land on the Osage Indian strip in what is now Cowley County. He paid the regular government price of $1.25 per acre and received his deed from President Grant. His purchase was in Beaver Township, west of the Arkansas River and six miles south and six miles west of Winfield. It was mostly bottom lands. Mr. Johnson had driven a span of horses and at once set to work to break up the ground, which he planted in corn. After the planting was made his crop received no further cultivation, but such was the fertility of the soil and the excellence of the season that the land produced one of the best crops of corn he ever saw. It also proved wonderfully productive of melons, potatoes and other crops. For his first dwelling there Mr. Johnson had a log cabin with a dirt floor.

In the meantime on June 12, 1870, in Marshall County he married Miss Dora Biggs, who was then a young lady of nineteen. She entered heartily into the pioneer spirit of living and helping, and a great share of the credit for the success which he has accomplished is due to this sensible and practical woman, who was not only a wife and mother but also a partner and sharer in all his undertakings.

Not far from their pioneer home was a little saw mill owned by a neighbor, and that produced the lumber needed for building purposes. Along the river grew many large trees, principally cottonwood and walnut, and the logs from these were worked up into the lumber which went into the early buildings in that section of Cowley County. In 1873 a larger mill was started and that mill sawed the timbers for the residence which Mr. Johnson still has on his farm. He also showed foresight and was not content merely with the crops raised from the virgin soil. He set out fifteen acres to fruit, and in a few years had an abundance of plums and apples not only for his own use and to supply his neighbors but also for the general market. He frequently sold as high as $180 worth of apples.

Besides general farming Mr. Johnson gave his attention to stock raising and by working on this diversified plan he got ahead rapidly and was able to buy other land when values were low. At the present time his ownership extends to 1,500 acres in that vicinity. Besides the old homestead he has 640 acres in a body five miles southeast of Winfield. He paid less than $8 an acre for that section of land and some of his land was bought at $13 an acre. He has also bought some valuable pieces of centrally located business property in Winfield, and that has proved a wise investment and insures a permanent income. Mr. Johnson is a director in the First National Bank of Winfield.

While he has always voted the republican ticket he has never been an office seeker. His public spirited efforts have been directed in a practical fashion to the improvement of his home locality. A number of years ago a bridge was badly needed over the Arkansas River. Appropriations for that purpose had twice been voted down, and he then personally assumed the risk and let the contract on his own responsibility for $2,800. The law then permitted commissioners to make appropriations in such cases if they saw fit, and in this instance he was reimbursed to the extent of $2,000. He also contracted for and built the first schoolhouse in District No. 61. This schoolhouse became the center of all neighborhood religious and social gatherings, a church and Sunday school having been started in a year or two after the house was put up. Mrs. Johnson was largely instrumental in these movements, and was one of the first Sunday school teachers in this neighborhood.

In November, 1910, Mr. and Mrs. Johnson removed to Winfield, the operation of the old homestead having been turned over to their son Robert C. The other children are: Minnie, wife of the Winfield hardware merchant, Thomas Backus; Eva, widow of Ed Sidel, living with her parents; and Rhoda, who has proven herself a very capable assistant to her father in general oversight of his extensive interests. Mr. Johnson is an active member of the local post of the Grand Army of the Republic.

HENRY CLINTON KIBBEE. Among the representative business men of Topeka, Henry Clinton Kibbee occupies a foremost place and is well known in financial circles not only in Kansas but over a wide territory. He came to this great state in 1887 and, with the whole world as his field of choice, has never found a more desirable section in which to live. His business concerns for thirty consecutive years have caused him to travel the country over, hence this is a proof of some value that Kansas can offer many attractions in the way of comfortable living and preservation of health.

Henry Clinton Kibbee was born at Port Huron, Michigan, May 24, 1859, and he is a son of Doctor Jared and Fanny E. (Gillingham) Kibbee. Dr. Jared Kibbee was a graduate of the old Cleveland Medical College, entering that institution after preparatory reading and study in his native state, Vermont. He practiced in Mount Clemens, Michigan, and was its first postmaster. Thence he went to Detroit and finally to Port Huron, Michigan. He returned to Cleveland and graduated in dentistry and continued during his active years to practice in that profession.

In the public schools of Port Huron, Henry C. Kibbee completed his educational course and had his health been robust, would probably have learned some trade as his natural inclination was in the directions of mechanics. In 1880 he left Michigan for Colorado and for three years he was engaged there in mercantile pursuits, mainly at Denver. In 1883, desiring an outdoor life, he went to Dakota Territory, now the State of South Dakota, and preempted land in Hand County with the expectation of making ranching his future business. Circumstances caused him to look further after two seasons, and he went then to Miller, the county seat, and accepted a position as clerk in a store as a temporary occupation.

In 1886 Mr. Kibbee became general agent and examiner of securities for the Mortgage Trust Company of Pennsylvania and has been identified with this corporation ever since. In its interest he has traveled all over the Middle West and with the officials and their patrons he is alike held in great respect. A confidential position held for thirty years is a testimonial to fidelity and efficiency of service that cannot be questioned. In 1887 he moved

to Hutchinson, Kansas, where he resided until 1900 when he removed to Topeka, which city has been his home for the past sixteen years. He has been active as a good citizen, in encouraging and assisting in many admirable public movements, but he has never been unduly active politically, limiting his efforts to casting his vote for the candidates of the democratic party.

Mr. Kibbee was united in marriage on October 4, 1889, to Miss Louise Halbig, who was a daughter of Christian and Louise Halbig, residents of Miller, South Dakota, at that time. Mr. and Mrs. Kibbee are members of the Episcopal Church. He is prominent in Masonry, has attained the thirty-second degree of Scottish Rite Masonry, and belongs to the Mystic Shrine.

HIRAM B. MILLER. Kansas wheat and corn and other farm products have been so much emphasized as partly to obscure the fact that the great basic industry of the state up to twenty-five or thirty years ago was live stock. Older residents of the state, now a little past their prime, will recall that the leading industry of their youth, except perhaps in the few counties along the eastern border, was the raising of live stock on the great ranges. Of the men who stood pre-eminent in that industry special mention should be made of the late Hiram B. Miller, who, however, was more than a cattle man and stock farmer. He impressed his influence on the legislation and civic well-being of Kansas and was one of the state's most honored citizens when he died at his home in Topeka, October 23, 1912.

In fact he was a historic character. He might fittingly be described as a product of the great West, for it was in the West that the greater part of his life was passed. He was a representative of that class whose virility, steadfastness of character and forcefulness leveled the waste places of the West and converted them into fertile fields and thriving cities.

Born in Cuyahoga County, Ohio, February 2, 1848, he spent his early youth in the vicinity of the present great City of Cleveland, had a common school education, and when a boy of sixteen enlisted for the defense of the Union in Company E of the Second Ohio Cavalry. He served in General Custer's Division of General Sheridan's Corps until peace was declared. Returning to his home state, for the succeeding four years he combined farming with teaching of district schools.

It was in 1869 Mr. Miller came out to Kansas. The Union Pacific Railroad had been completed only a year or so and very little of the country west of the Missouri was intersected with railroads. Kansas was still on the frontier, and one might travel for miles across its plains without meeting the obstruction of a fence. At first Mr. Miller was a teacher at Topeka, but in 1872 he moved to Osage City, which city will always honor his name and long residence. He set up a store at Osage, but being gifted with more than the average degree of intelligence and education it was but natural that his superabundant vitality would cause him to be identified with public as well as private affairs. He early saw the possibilities of Kansas as a live-stock producing community, and with the passing of time became extensively interested in the raising and handling of live stock. This interest he retained during the balance of his life, and he was always a leader in the industry. At one time associated with his brother, William W., he operated over 10,000 acres of land, and their herds were numbered by the thousand.

In 1896 he became one of the organizers and a director of the Osage County Bank. At the time of his death he was vice president of the Miller Live Stock Investment Company at Topeka, in which city he resided for the last three years. He was always a zealous republican, but his good citizenship transcended partisanship. He served at one time as mayor of Osage City and was twice elected state senator from Osage County. Not content with merely holding the office, he proved a legislator in the best sense of the term, and whether in such an office or in the management of his private affairs he exerted himself always for the good of Kansas. He was particularly active in progressive railroad legislation. His work and wisdom as a legislator led to his name being brought forward in 1892 for the governorship of Kansas, but he failed by a narrow majority in securing the nomination. In 1910 he was prominently mentioned for the same office, but he declined to enter the campaign. Mr. Miller was well known in Grand Army of the Republic circles and was always affiliated with the Masonic Order and the Knights of Pythias.

In 1873 he married Miss Eva L. Lapham. They had two sons: Clyde W., who lives at Miller, Kansas; and Ardie L., who died in 1890.

Successful from a material standpoint in the opinion of his fellow man, the late Mr. Miller was much more than that. He was honest, free-hearted, sociable, respected for his many sterling qualities, and among men was always considered a man. He left an impress for good, and his memory is to be revered because of what he accomplished and also for his love of home, country and his unblemished American citizenship.

FREDERIC M. WILHELM. When a boy in his early teens Frederic M. Wilhelm began working for himself and has risen from the position of an office employe to secretary of the Prairie Pipe Line Company of Independence. He has been closely identified with the present company and the Prairie State Oil and Gas Company at Independence for the past twelve years.

Thirty-three years of age, Mr. Wilhelm was born at Decatur, Indiana, January 6, 1883. His father, George Wilhelm, was born in Germany in 1854, and when ten years of age ran away from home and soon afterwards found his way to the United States, and located in Decatur, Indiana. On reaching manhood he became a farmer and later a merchant, and in 1884 moved to Lima, Ohio, where he died in 1897. He was a republican and a member of the Catholic Church. George Wilhelm married Elizabeth Mueller, who was born of German parentage in Ohio and is still living at Lima. Their children are: John C., who is connected with a pipe line and lives in Bartlesville, Oklahoma; Mary, wife of L. A. Feltz, secretary of the Citizens Savings and Building Association of Lima, Ohio, a very important institution with assets of $2,500,000; Catherine, at home with her mother; Frederic M.; Henry M., who was private secretary to the assistant general manager of the Prairie Oil & Gas Company when he died in Independence in January, 1914.

Frederic M. Wilhelm had a brief schooling in Lima, Ohio, but at the early age of fourteen left school to begin work in an office in Lima and was soon filling a position as stenographer. He continued there until 1904, when he came to Kansas and was made private secretary to the superintendent of the Prairie Oil and Gas Company at Neodesha. In August of the same year he came to Independence and by faithful performance of his duties and by a capacity for responsibility has been advanced until he is now secretary of the Prairie Pipe Line Company. The offices of this company are in the newly erected Prairie Oil and Gas Company Building on West Myrtle Street, probably one of the finest and most completely equipped office buildings of the state.

Mr. Wilhelm also owns his residence at 608 East Main Street. He is secretary and treasurer of the Independence Country Club, is a director of the Independence Building and Loan Association, and secretary and treasurer of the Sunflower Cigar Company. Politically he is a standpat republican and a member of the County Central Committee. His social affiliations are with Fortitude Lodge No. 107, Ancient, Free and Accepted Masons, and Lodge No. 780, Benevolent and Protective Order of Elks, both at Independence.

On June 15, 1908, at Neodesha, Kansas, he married Miss Helen Bauman, a daughter of August and Mary Bauman, of Neodesha. Her father is a grain merchant. They have two children, Virginia and Frederic B., the daughter being now a student in the public schools.

JOHN V. CORTELYOU, who took the chair of German at the Kansas State Agricultural College in 1904, was at that time only recently returned from Germany. Professor Cortelyou holds his Doctor of Philosophy degree from Heidelberg University, though he is an American by birth and training, and represents a long and interesting lineage of some of the old Dutch families of New Jersey.

He was born on a farm near Harlingen in Somerset County, New Jersey, September 19, 1874. He is a son of John G. and Mary (Van Zandt) Cortelyou, both natives of New Jersey and in both lines descended from old families of this country.

The paternal ancestry goes back to Jaques Cortelyou, who was a native of Utrecht, Holland, and of both French and Dutch lineage. The name Cortelyou is French. Jaques Cortelyou who came to America in 1652 settled at New Amsterdam, now New York City. His descendants afterwards became numerous in the states of New York, New Jersey and also on Long Island, and they are now represented in many parts of the Union. Professor Cortelyou is in the tenth generation from the original Jaques. Jaques had a son, Jaques Jr.; the heads of the next four successive generations bore the given name Hendrick. Then came an Abraham Cortelyou, and following him James G. Cortelyou, grandfather of Professor Cortelyou. James G. Cortelyou married Cornelia Polhemus. That is one of the most familiar family names in New Jersey genealogy. Cornelia was born in New Jersey, and was directly descended from Dr. Johannis Theodorus Polhemus, the first of that family in America. He came from Holland as a missionary to Brazil in 1635. About 1654 he accepted the pastorate of three churches on Long Island. One of them was at Brooklyn.

Professor Cortelyou's mother was also of Holland Dutch stock, the Van Zandts having come to America prior to the Revolutionary war.

John G. Cortelyou, his father, was a farmer in New Jersey, but in 1884, removing to the State of Nebraska he engaged in banking, at first in Ewing, but from 1890 until his death in 1904 at Omaha.

John V. Cortelyou was ten years of age when his parents removed to Nebraska. He completed his high school course at Omaha, and in 1897 graduated B. A. from the University of Nebraska. The following two years were spent in teaching at Humboldt, Nebraska, and he then resumed his studies in the State University, and gained his Master of Arts degree in 1901. The following three years he spent abroad at the University of Heidelberg. He is one of the ablest scholars and men of broadest culture connected with the State Agricultural School at Manhattan. He is a member of the Phi Beta Kappa, the Phi Kappa Phi and the Alpha Theta Chi.

Doctor Cortelyou was married in 1904 to Miss Grace Rushton, daughter of J. H. Rushton of Omaha, Nebraska. They are the parents of four children: Rushton Gardner, Helen Van Zandt, Mary Josephine and Dorothy Margaret.

ARTHUR H. BENNETT. Few men have contributed more practical encouragement to grain and stock raisers in Kansas than has Arthur H. Bennett, of Topeka, president of the Bennett Commission Company, whose business has been one of the chief commercial factors in its line in the city during the past decade. He was born May 9, 1869, on what was known as the "Old Thompson Farm," located near Marengo, McHenry County, Illinois, the only son of Fayette Henry and Mary Eliza (Merriman) Bennett.

The Bennett family is of Puritan stock, the progenitors of the family having come to America on the Mayflower. Fayette Henry Bennett was born July 4, 1838, in Chautauqua County, New York, the eldest son of Ashley C. and Charlotte S. (Wheeler) Bennett, grandson of Zebulon and Sarah (Cooper) Bennett and great-grandson of Zebulon Bennett. Fayette H. Bennett served for a time as a soldier in the Civil war, being a member of Company A, Ninety-fifth Regiment, Illinois Volunteer Infantry, and at the close of the war returned to Illinois and resumed his agricultural operations. He remained in that state until 1878, when he removed with his family to Kansas, settling at Clifton, Clay County, but in his declining years took up his residence at Topeka, where his death occurred July 12, 1910. Mr. Bennett was a devout Methodist in religion, and a strong temperance man, being active in the movements which eventuated in making Kansas a prohibition state. His religion was a part of his nature, inherited, no doubt, from his Puritan forbears. Prior to his death he had, at his own expense, supported a native missionary in China. In business circles he was known as a man of the highest integrity, in private life his every action was characterized by the strictest probity, and as a citizen he was foremost in promoting good movements for the betterment of education, religion and civic affairs.

Arthur H. Bennett was nine years of age when he accompanied his parents to Clifton, Kansas, and there he attended the public schools until 1886. In the latter year, and the year 1887, he was a student at Lawrence College, and in 1888 he began his business career in the employ of Isaac H. French, a grain merchant of Clay Center, Kansas. Here he received his introduction to the business in which he has since spent his activities. After several years at Clay Center, Mr. Bennett went with Mr. French to Kansas City, Missouri, to work in the grain exchange located in that city. While living there Mr. Bennett was married, July 15, 1891, to Miss Allicia Sophia McIlravy, of Lawrence, Kansas, a daughter of John William and Sophia (Van Buskirk) McIlravy, and their first home was at No. 27 East Thirty-second Street, Kansas City. In 1892 they moved to Clay Center, Kansas, and in the scene of his earliest activities Mr. Bennett embarked in business with a partner. This venture, although started modestly, was progressing well and promised to grow into a prosperous enterprise, but just at a time when its prospects seemed brightest the panic came on, and this was followed by the dishonesty of a trusted friend. The double blow swept away all of Mr. Bennett's savings, for he had invested his entire capital in the business, and he awoke not only to find himself bankrupt, but several thousand dollars in debt. Such a discouragement would have disheartened a less persevering man, but he possessed the qualities that do not admit of defeat, and he at once set about to recuperate his lost fortunes. For several years following he was again employed in the Grain Exchange of Kansas City, working energetically to clear off his indebtedness. His fidelity, energy and evident ability soon gained their reward, for he was placed in charge of the domestic business of the Greenleaf-Baker Grain Company, a large concern of Atchison, Kansas, in which city his first son was born: Arthur Harry, May 23, 1897. In 1898 Mr. Bennett came to Topeka, where his experience and abilities had gained him an important position with the Capital Elevator, of which, in 1900, he became the owner of a one-third interest. He subsequently disposed of his holding advantageously, and immediately thereafter founded the business of which he is now the head, the Bennett Commission Company, which deals almost exclusively in the now famous "Kansas Turkey" wheat, which has gained a reputation all over the country.

Mr. Bennett is a firm believer in organization, and for many years has been an active and official member of the Kansas Grain Dealers' Association and the National Grain Dealers' Associations. He stands high in the trade, and has been repeatedly honored by his associates, having served as a director in the national organization and as president and vice president of the state body. He is also keenly alive to the value of improvement along the line of live stock conditions in Kansas, and is himself a breeder of pure-bred horses, cattle, sheep and hogs. In this connection he is a leading and active member of the Duroc-Jersey Association, the American Shropshire Association, the Kansas Pure-Bred Horse Breeders' Association and the Kansas Improved Live Stock Breeders' Association.

For many years Mr. Bennett has been greatly interested in historical and genealogical research, and is a life member of the Kansas State Historical Society and a member of the Sons of the American Revolution, nine of his ancestors having served the American colonies in their struggle for independence from the rule of Great Britain. His ancestors came to America in the Mayflower and by virtue of this fact Mr. Bennett organized the Kansas Society Mayflower Descendants, of which society for several years he held the office of governor. In his religious belief he is a Methodist and has taken an active part in church movements. Their younger son, Fayette Ashley, was born at Topeka, March 14, 1900.

ZOLO A. EMERSON. Through the business ability and courtesy of its owner the general merchandise store of Zolo A. Emerson in a comparatively short time has become an important source of supply to the people of Auburn and the surrounding vicinity. In addition to rendering this service to his fellow citizens, Mr. Emerson has a further claim to their esteem in the manner in which he is discharging the duties of postmaster, which office he has efficiently filled since his appointment in 1908.

Mr. Emerson is a native of Holmes County, Ohio, born at Millersburg, September 24, 1873, one of the eight children of Albert B. and Betsy L. (Doughty) Emerson. The father was born in Ohio, while the mother, a native of Nottinghamshire, England, came to the United States when twelve years of age with her parents, who located at Pittsburgh, Pennsylvania. He was a miller by trade. Mr. Doughty came to Kansas, in 1872, and ran a mill on the Cottonwood River, which is still dependent upon water power for its operation. Albert B. Emerson received his educational advantages in Keene, Ohio. In his youth he mastered the shoemaker and harnessmaker's trades, which he followed until the outbreak of the Civil war, when he enlisted in Company I, Ninety-seventh Regiment, Ohio Volunteer Infantry, and served bravely and faithfully through three years of the war. He participated in fourteen battles of that struggle, including Missionary Ridge and Stone River. He was wounded at Kennesaw Mountain. He endured the starvation rations and hardships of army life cheerfully and patiently. His army record was an excellent one. Mrs. Emerson, who had been partly educated in her native land, was a remarkable woman in many ways. She was a skilled penwoman and was nurse in Hospital No. 1 at Chattanooga for four months. She contributed great and helpful services to the Union cause in writing out discharge papers and by making out statements for doctors to send to Washington of gangrene cases for soldiers in hospital unable for duty, and making clothing for soldiers at Steubenville, Ohio. She was the only woman in the war to make out all her husband's discharge papers ready for officers' signatures.

After the close of the war Albert B. Emerson bought a star mail route between Millersburg and Coshocton, Ohio. He came to Kansas in 1878, and with his family located at Cedar Point, Chase County, where Mr. Doughty, his father-in-law, had preceded him. There for a time he worked at his trade, later operated a general store, and after he had sold it was appointed postmaster, an office in which he served for eight years. He held various township offices and became somewhat of an influence in republican politics in his locality. Mr. Emerson was an honest, God-fearing man, who, by his straightforward living commanded the respect of all who knew him. His friends were legion, and he had in particular the love of children, especially of his own, who adored him. He was always a supporter of laudable enterprises, and his hand was ever extended to help those who had been less fortunate than he. When his death occurred, March 4, 1904, his community lost one of its best citizens. Fraternally he was connected with Florence Lodge of Odd Fellows, of which he was noble grand for many years, and also with the Ancient Order of United Workmen. He was a devout Christian, did much to assist the cause of religion and contributed to the building of churches and schools, and as a member of the Presbyterian Church served as superintendent of the Sunday schools at Florence and Cedar Point for many years, and was a life elder. He was a great reader and lover of refined literature. Mrs. Emerson, who survives her husband and resides at Florence, was her husband's constant aid and advisor. She always made the clothes for her own children, and has still found time to be a student, and for a number of years was a member of the school board at Cedar Point. Like her husband she commands the love and esteem of all who know her, and her advice is eagerly

Vol. IV—4

sought and freely given on many subjects. She belongs to the Literary Club and the Order of the Eastern Star. She has lived to see her children grow up about her and to assume honorable positions in life, a credit to themselves and to their careful rearing. The children are as follows: Minnie L., who is now Mrs. F. W. Byram, of Cedar Point, Kansas; Hugh W., who died in 1894; Xenia, now Mrs. W. G. Marlin, of Monee, Illinois; Albert V., district manager of the Southwest Telephone Company of Kansas, with headquarters at Great Bend; Lutie V., who is now Mrs. C. F. Ward, of Cottonwood Falls, Kansas; Zola A., of this review; William D., traffic manager of the Bell Telephone Company at Denver, Colorado; and Cadiz G., now Mrs. L. E. Cress, of Cedar Point, Kansas.

Zolo A. Emerson attended the public schools of Cedar Point and Florence High School, and, like his brothers, learned telegraphy and became an operator. He began his telegraph career with the Atchison, Topeka and Santa Fe Railroad and in 1896 entered the employ of the Postal Telegraph & Cable Co. at Lamar, Colorado, as manager. He was transferred to Flagstaff, Arizona; Newton, Kansas; Emporia, Kansas, and Topeka, Kansas. In 1908, desiring to be at the head of a business of his own, he bought his present establishment and started in a small way to deal in general merchandise, and since that time has built up a trade that has far exceeded his expectations. Mr. Emerson entertains a commendable interest in public affairs, is a firm believer in good schools and general civilizing agencies, and supports by his vote the republican party. In 1908 he was appointed postmaster by President Taft, and has continued to hold this office to the present time, giving his fellow-townsmen excellent mail service. As a fraternalist he has been through the chairs of Auburn Blue Lodge No. 32, Ancient, Free and Accepted Masons, and belongs to Topeka Chapter and Commandery, and is a Mason of the York Rite. He likewise holds membership in Auburn Lodge No. 556 of the Odd Fellows, in which he has been through the chairs. Mr. and Mrs. Emerson are members of the First Christian Church of Topeka, and have taken an active interest in its work.

On September 4, 1900, Mr. Emerson was married to an old schoolmate, Miss Nellie B. Williams, of Cedar Point, Kansas, and they have one child, Zonella Alice, who was born at Topeka, August 18, 1912.

PHARES ROOT, one of the well known business men of Independence, has spent nearly all his life in Kansas, his parents having moved to Elk County and taken their share of hardships and responsibilities as pioneers. Mr. Root has developed a prosperous business in the handling of automobile supplies and in operating a first class garage.

He was born in Indiana, September 26, 1869. His ancestors came from Germany in the early days and settled in Pennsylvania. His father, Joseph Root, was born in Ohio in 1844, but was reared and married in Starke County, Indiana. He is a tinner by trade, and in 1871 moved his family to Elk County, Kansas, and is still a resident and active business man of Elk Falls. Politically he is a republican. Joseph Root, though a young man at the time, made a creditable record as a soldier in the Union army. In 1861 he enlisted in the Indiana Infantry, and was in service until the close of the war. He married Amelia Nowlin, who was born in Indiana in 1839 and died at Elk Falls, Kansas, in 1911. They had two sons, and the older is William M., a painter living at Topeka.

Phares Root acquired his early education in the

schools of Elk County. Since the age of sixteen he has been dependent upon his own energies. For about three years he was clerk in a grocery store at Elk Falls. Then at Weir, Kansas, he put in a number of years weighing coal and in other employment at the mines, and fortified with this experience came to Elk Falls, and after clerking in a hardware store three years bought the stock and business and successfully conducted it for the next ten years. Selling out his business at Elk Falls, Mr. Root came to Independence in the fall of 1912, and bought Lew Ernest's automobile supply house, then situated on West Main Street. In December of that year he removed his quarters to 301-303 Main Street, and now has a well equipped garage in addition to his shop for the handling of automobile supplies. His business occupies a two-story building, 50 by 140 feet. He is local agent for the Ford automobile, and does an extensive business in repairing and painting and upholstering automobiles.

Mr. Root is interested in two oil companies, and is almost sole owner and stockholder in the Bull Moose Oil Company. He is active in the Commercial Club and the Rotary Club at Independence, is a republican, and in Odd Fellowship is past noble grand of the subordinate lodge at Elk Falls, a member of the Rebekahs at the same place, and is affiliated with the encampment at Independence. His home is at 615 East Maple Street. In 1891, at Fort Scott, Kansas, he married Miss Jessie Smith, daughter of Mr. and Mrs. Jacob Smith. Her father was a farmer, now deceased, and her mother resides at Danville, Illinois. To their marriage have been born four children: Stanley, who is manager of his father's business; Zora, a teacher in the Montgomery County High School; Leonard, in the freshman class of the high school; and Walter.

FREEMAN E. NIPPS is one of the veteran railroad men of Kansas. Like many who have found success in that army of industrial workers, he began at a country station and as a telegraph operator. For more than a quarter of a century he has been the agent of the Missouri Pacific Railway at Topeka. Unlike many railway men, he has at the same time identified himself closely with local affairs, and at the present time his name is familiarly known throughout Shawnee County as chairman of the board of commissioners.

Though most of his life has been spent within the borders of Kansas, Mr. Nipps was born at Muscatine, Iowa, July 14, 1865. A few years later his parents removed to Boone, Iowa. There he attended the public schools until he was fourteen, and at that time he accompanied his parents to Kansas. Mr. Nipps is a son of Jacob and Josephine (Pfeifer) Nipps. His father was a man of considerable prominence in Phillips County, Kansas. Before coming to this state he had enlisted in an Ohio regiment during the Civil War, but continued illness prevented his taking an active part for any length of time in the struggle to preserve the Union. By trade he was a mechanic, but the greater part of his career was devoted to agriculture. In order to better provide for his growing family of children he came to Kansas in 1879. That was a comparatively early year in the settlement of Northwestern Kansas, and unlike many who homesteaded at that time his prosperity enabled him to move his property by railroad to within some thirty or forty miles of his destination. The rest of the way to Phillips County was covered by wagon. As was the case of many Western Kansas settlers at the time his family at first lived in a sod

house on the prairie in Phillips County. The county was very sparsely populated and it was not unprecedented for a buffalo or an Indian to be seen on the open range. Jacob Nipps acquired title to 320 acres of land, and later added to this 320 acres more, and also owned good residence property in Phillipsburg. For a man of no extensive literary training, he was well posted on current topics and possessed an unusual fund of good, practical sense. He was an eager supporter of the cause of education and made many sacrifices that his children might have proper scholastic training. The citizens of Phillips County recognized his worth by making him the recipient of various local positions, and for two terms he was treasurer of that county. In religion he was a Methodist and in politics a republican. As long as he lived he commanded the greatest of respect for his many admirable qualities of mind and heart. His widow still survives and lives with a daughter at Muskogee, Oklahoma.

Freeman E. Nipps is one of four surviving children out of the seven born to his parents. After coming to Kansas he spent two terms in a district school and one term at a small college at Harlan. When only sixteen he passed an examination and secured a teacher's license, following which a district school had his services as a teacher for two terms.

His career as a railroad man began more than thirty years ago. At eighteen he took up the study of telegraphy at Kirwin, Kansas, and completed this apprenticeship at Jamestown, Kansas, where he was employed as station helper at $35 a month. His first important position in railroad work was as an operator at Atchison, following which he was stationed at various points for a number of years, chiefly at Bigelow and Logan. For two years he was clerk in the Kansas City office of the Missouri Pacific Railway, but since February, 1888, has been this company's agent at Topeka. This is one of the most responsible local positions along the road in Kansas.

His good citizenship has been dignified by important service rendered his home city. For four years he served as a councilman under the old form of city government. In 1912 he was elected a member of the board of commissioners for Shawnee County, and has held that office ever since. Upon the reorganization of the board in January, 1916, he was elected its chairman, a position he had declined a year previously, as the minutes of the board disclosed. Mr. Nipps is a republican, and is one of the most progressive of the younger generation of Topeka business men. He is a thirty-second degree Scottish Rite Mason, an Elk and an active member of the Topeka Commercial Club.

Mr. Nipps married Miss Mary Smith. She is a daughter of the late Hon. James Smith, a prominent Kansan, who served three terms as secretary of state from January, 1879, to January, 1885, and who died May 28, 1914.

HON. DAVID WINFIELD MULVANE. For years one of the prominent characters of Kansas who have helped to influence and direct national life has been David W. Mulvane of Topeka. In his home state Mr. Mulvane is best known as a lawyer and his power in republican politics has not been exercised through office but through his chieftainship in the party itself. For many years he has been identified with the state organization, and also with the national

Raymond C. Clapp, M.D.

party organization, and was one of the national party committee for a dozen years.

He was born in Princeton, Illinois, January 4, 1863, but has had his home in Kansas since early boyhood. His parents were Joab and Sarah Ann (Ross) Mulvane. In 1876 the family moved to Topeka and David W. Mulvane finished his education in the common schools of that city and afterwards attended Washburn College. From Washburn College he entered Yale University, where he was graduated A. B. with the class of 1885. Thus Mr. Mulvane is a man of eastern university training and has fused the culture of one of the oldest eastern colleges with the practical idealism of the Central West.

After leaving college he found employment with a railroad construction outfit, and though his father was one of Topeka's leading business men and financiers he was by no means disposed to a life of leisure. He early took up the study of law under the direction of Gen. A. L. Williams, one of Topeka's leading lawyers, and was admitted to the bar in 1890. During a quarter of a century of practice in Topeka he has long enjoyed almost a pre-eminence in the local bar, and is now senior member of the firm of Mulvane and Gault, with offices in the Mulvane Building at Topeka. His junior associate is Charles Gault.

Much of his time and attention have been diverted to banking and business affairs. In 1900 he was one of the chief organizers and incorporators of the Bank Savings National Life Insurance Company. He is also a director in the American Cement and Plaster Company, with headquarters at Lawrence, Kansas, is a director of the M. K. & T. Railroad Company, a director of the Capital Vitrified Brick Company, and a director of the Chickasha Cotton Seed Oil Company in Oklahoma.

Almost from the time of casting his first vote during the '80s he has exercised an increasing influence in republican party circles. In 1898 he became a member of the Republican State Central Committee, and served ten years. He was a member of the Republican National Committee from 1900 to 1912 and in 1904 was selected a member of its executive committee. For many years he has been one of the familiar figures in republican national conventions and has wielded a great influence in that party.

Mr. Mulvane is a member of the Shawnee County, the Kansas State and the American Bar associations, belongs to the Commercial Club and the Country Club of Topeka, is a thirty-second degree Scottish Rite Mason and Knight Templar, also a Mystic Shriner, and is a member of the Elks Club at Topeka. His church is the Methodist.

Mr. Mulvane married Helen M. Drexel of New York City in 1906.

RAYMOND C. CLAPP, M. D. A young man who availed himself of the best of modern facilities and scientific advantages in preparing himself for his exacting profession, Doctor Clapp has won assured status as one of the representative physicians and surgeons engaged in practice in the City of Wichita, where his success has been on a parity with his unqualified personal popularity.

Doctor Clapp was born at Lebanon, Virginia, on the 26th of September, 1880, and in the schools of his native place he continued his studies until his graduation in the high school. He then had the privilege of entering the historic old University of Virginia, at Charlottesville, in which institution he was graduated in 1903, with the degree of Bachelor of Arts. In preparation for his chosen profession he was next matriculated in the medical department of the University of Louisville, and in this excellent institution of the Kentucky metropolis he was graduated as a member of the class of 1907 and with the well earned degree of Doctor of Medicine.

In initiating the active work of his profession Doctor Clapp came to Kansas and established himself in practice at Coldwater, the judicial center of Comanche County, where he remained about one year. He then found a broader field of professional endeavor by removing, in 1909, to the City of Wichita, where he has since remained and where he has built up a substantial and representative practice in which he specialized in the treatment of genito-urinary diseases. His attractively appointed offices, at 420 East Douglas Avenue, are equipped with the latest approved appliances demanded in scientific practice of medicine and surgery, and the doctor is affiliated with the Sedgwick County Medical Society, the Kansas State Medical Society and the American Medical Association, as is he also with the time-honored Masonic fraternity. His father, Dr. Luther H. Clapp, served with distinction as a surgeon with a Confederate regiment in the war between the states, and after the close of the great conflict he was for a few years engaged in the practice of his profession at Lebanon, Virginia. He then removed to Pennington, that state, where he and his wife still maintain their home and where he continues to be actively engaged in the practice of his profession.

In 1907 was solemnized the marriage of Dr. Raymond C. Clapp to Miss Jessie Bunger, of Louisville, Kentucky, and their two children are Elizabeth and Raymond.

HENRY KNIGHT BROOKS of Topeka is a Kansas man by adoption, and is as loyal to the state as any native citizen. The state may properly congratulate itself that Mr. Brooks has found a congenial home here. As an inventor, manufacturer and practical all around mechanic he has a genius which has made his name familiar in industrial circles, not alone in Kansas but in many parts of the United States. For one thing he deserves credit for building up and developing the Capital Iron Works at Topeka, one of the cornerstones of that city's industrial prosperity. However, that has been only one phase of his busy career.

He was born in Kettering, Northamptonshire, England, January 8, 1869. His father, William Weston Brooks, was a college man and for many years was superintendent of public schools at Kettering in Northamptonshire, and later at Wisbech, Cambridgeshire. His mother was Eliza Knight, whose ancestors were Huguenot fugitives that found refuge in England from their persecutors in France. Mr. Brooks' maternal grandfather, Joseph J. Knight, was president of Albion College, South Hackney, and became a noted man in the East End of London, where much of his life was devoted to work among the slums and poorer classes. He advocated temperance when such a virtue was almost considered a crime, and he was caricatured as Anthony Hum in the Pickwick papers by Charles Dickens. He was a close friend and co-worker with Gen. William Booth of the Salvation Army.

As a boy Henry Knight Brooks attended private school, finished a common school education at Wisbech, Cambridgeshire, and from there went to London. For about a year he worked in a printing machinery plant. He moved to Leicester, and while there took a technical course given under the auspices of the University Extension, extending evening classes after working hours. He left the engineering firm in Leicester to take a better position with the Midland Railway Company. Becoming a student of the American form of government he soon decided to come to this country. For a time he was a resident on Long Island, New York, came west, was in Chicago for a time, and then continued until he reached Kansas.

In this state his first work was with the Santa Fe Company at Wellington, and he was there during the days of the cattle rush from Oklahoma, prior to the opening of the territory. Later he was with the Southern Kansas Railway Company at Ottawa, Kansas, but left there to go to Arizona, and was with the Southern Pacific Railroad Company at Tucson for about two years. Later he spent a short time at Los Angeles and San Francisco, and then determined to take a European trip, sailing from New York to England. Six months in Europe convinced him that he would not be contented there, and he was soon back in New York and again in Kansas, where he took a position with the Southern Kansas Railway Company.

His next position was as machinist for the Santa Fe Railway Company at Topeka. The superintendent of motive power and machine shops, Mr. J. Player, was asked by the Kansas State Agricultural College to recommend a man for the position of superintendent of the college iron shops and foundry. The choice fell on Mr. Brooks. At the time this position required a person able to teach the various mechanical trades. Mr. Brooks was at the college at Manhattan about a year, and during that time he married the present Mrs. Brooks, who was Edith B. Harrison, daughter of Col. J. Harrison of Ottawa, Kansas.

While in Manhattan one day he was asked over the telephone if he would accept a position then open as manager of the Capital Iron Works Company at Topeka. Taking the train, he looked the situation over and decided to accept. In a short time he discovered this company was in bad shape mechanically and financially, the management being scarcely able to pay his salary. That did not daunt him and he stuck to his position. It should be mentioned that this was just after the boom period in Kansas, and the Capital Iron Works were owned by the receivers of the Kansas National Bank. Judge Slonecker had charge of the bank's affairs, and Mr. Brooks has always considered him one of his best friends. The judge made a proposition to Mr. Brooks to purchase the property, and though the young mechanic's assets at that time were practically nothing and he was getting no salary, Judge Slonecker had such confidence in his capability that he took Mr. Brooks' notes for the property. A brother, G. W. Brooks, was made shop foreman, and they both put on their overalls and personally worked at the bench and in the foundry until such time as the business began to improve. There he spent several years of the hardest work of his career, and laid a foundation and system in the foundry, machine and structural iron shops that lasts to the present day.

About this time the National Light, Heat and Power Company of New York asked Mr. Brooks to assist them in some experimental work they were conducting on the passenger cars of the Santa Fe Railway Company. This work was the equipping of the Pullman and day coaches with an apparatus for the generation of electric light from the axle of the cars. Up to that time such experiments had not been

successful. His former experience in railway work stood Mr. Brooks in good stead, and he was soon prevailed upon to accept the position of mechanical engineer with the company with headquarters in Topeka. This took up most of his time and required a very considerable mechanical and electrical knowledge to make the system of lighting a success. Several other large concerns were also working out apparatus for lighting railway cars by electricity, since the use of compressed gas as then commonly used had proved very dangerous, especially in wrecks, and at best it was a very unsatisfactory method of car lighting. To begin with the electric apparatus was very crude, but after many improvements had been inaugurated by Mr. Brooks it was regarded as so satisfactory that a large purchase of the apparatus was made by the railway company, the contract running into a quarter of a million dollars. Such was the starting point of electric car lighting on the Santa Fe system, and today the equipment of that one company for electric lighting of passenger and Pullman cars is valued at above $1,000,000. This is one among the many benefits Mr. Brooks has conferred upon the world of invention and Kansans might properly give him credit for an important share in the excellent method of lighting railway cars at the present time.

In the meantime the business of the Capital Iron Works had progressed steadily, new buildings were being put up and modern machinery installed, and its general condition was so satisfactory that when the Railway Electric Light and Equipment Company made Mr. Brooks an offer of the position of assistant chief engineer, he concluded to accept the place for a time, especially in view of the very flattering salary offered him. He also was moved to accept by the opportunity given for following up several lines of mechanical and electrical work he had in mind. This took him out of Kansas and to New York City, where he was given charge of a new factory starting there for the manufacture of electric lighting apparatus. In a few months the factory outgrew its capacity. Mr. Brooks was then entrusted with the complete equipment of an additional factory located at Derby, Connecticut. This factory was no more built than it had to be operated night and day in order to supply the demand for the apparatus for electric lighting. This experience gave Mr. Brooks a further opportunity of working out a number of special features and improvements which had occurred to him, but in time he found it necessary to resign in order to work out these features on a larger scale.

He then associated himself with one of the most successful inventors of electrical apparatus in the country, Morris Moskowitz, and together they invented an apparatus which was without question one of the most perfect for electric lighting of trains ever produced. Patents on the apparatus were obtained and a company of New York capitalists formed to begin the manufacture. In the American company were such men as Chauncey Depew, Joseph Leiter, W. J. Arkell and other men of national reputation, while in the foreign company were the Earl of Kintore, Laycock of Sheffield, England, and many others. The later Edwin Hawley was president of the company, which was closely connected with the New York Air Brake Company of New York through Mr. C. A. Starbuck, its president. Almost from the start an enormous business was done, and Mr. Brooks was chief engineer of the company for six years, during which time he lived in New York City. He had direct supervision of the installation of lighting systems on over thirty of the leading railways of the country, and a large number of cars equipped with this company's apparatus are operating in Europe at this time. Mr. Brooks naturally feels somewhat proud of the fact that he helped name the company, which is called the United States Light & Heating Company. It is capitalized at $16,000,000, and the principal factory is now located at Niagara Falls. It covers over sixteen acres of ground, and is one of the most modern plans of its kind in the world, manufacturing complete electric car lighting systems, storage batteries, automobile starters and other apparatus. Its products are now sold in every important city in the United States and foreign countries.

After six years as chief engineer of this company Mr. Brooks again heard the call of Kansas, and so far as he knows and hopes Kansas is his permanent home. For the last eight years he has again been active head of the Topeka institution, The Capital Iron Works Company, during which time several new departments have been opened, and machinery installed and new buildings erected to meet increased demands. There is scarcely a building of any importance around Topeka or through the state which does not contain some work turned out by this firm, which has built up a reputation for "quality first," while the engineering staff maintained in connection with the works contains some of the most practical and expert technical men in the state.

As a matter of history it should be noted that a new industry has been developed in the West called the Steel Fixture Manufacturing Company, and this, though a large business in itself, is really a branch of the Capital Iron Works Company. Many of the courthouses, banks and public buildings are now equipped with furniture turned out by the Steel Fixture Company. Their products are installed in courthouses, banks and public buildings in many states, and only recently a large amount was placed in the New York custom house, and New San Francisco postoffice, showing that Kansas products are by no means limited to use in the Middle West. Many thousands of Kansans are familiar with some of the output of this company in the ornamental steel work found in the splendid Kansas State Memorial Building, especially the stairs, elevator grills, book stacks and counters. It is a distinction of which Kansas is proud and reflects credit upon Mr. Brooks' firm that no other industry of this character has a plant within 800 miles of Topeka.

Naturally enough Mr. Brooks has associations with many of the leading industrial and technical organizations in the country. He is a member of the American Society of Mechanical Engineers of New York, and has several times been invited to read papers on various subjects before that body. He is a member of the New York Railway Club, a charter member of the Kansas Society of New York, belongs to the Masonic fraternity, the Topeka Commercial Club, the Young Men's Christian Association, and always identifies himself with other progressive industrial and civic movements in his adopted state. He is also secretary and treasurer of the Kansas Employers Association. The purpose of this association is to promote the mutual interest of its members in industry and commerce, to endorse constructive legislation, to further all legitimate measures and principles which will work for the common good and industrial advancement and efficiency of our state.

WILLIAM ALEXANDER HOOD brought his extensive experience as a manufacturer, mining operator and oil and gas producer to Independence about three years ago, and is now rated as one of the leading producers in that field and also conducts a large business as a general contractor.

He is of old Southern stock, and his Scotch-Irish ancestors came from England to North Carolina in colonial times. William Alexander Hood was born in Birmingham, Alabama, October 6, 1876. His family connections in that great industrial center of the South have long been prominent in manufacturing and commercial affairs. His father, William Hood, a resident of Birmingham, was born in Mississippi in 1851, and afterwards moved to Birmingham, Alabama, where he married. While a merchant he has become extensively interested as a producer in the oil fields of both Kansas and Texas. He is a democrat and a chairman of the board of directors and board of stewards in his Methodist Church, and is also a member of the Masonic fraternity. William Hood married Vilanta Yielding, who was born in Alabama. Their children are: William Alexander; Ira, a merchant at Birmingham; Robert H., associated with his brother Ira at Birmingham; Nina, wife of G. T. Brazelton, who is in the real estate business at Birmingham; Walter H., a graduate with the degree LL. B. from Washington and Lee University and now a practicing attorney at Birmingham; Jennie Catherine, wife of Russell Hunt, cashier of the Sloss Steel and Iron Company at Birmingham; Norma, wife of Dr. B. S. Lester, one of the leading physicians and surgeons at Birmingham; Lucien, a hardware merchant at Birmingham.

In the public schools of Birmingham William A. Hood acquired his early training, graduating from the high school in 1895, and in 1897 received the Bachelor of Science degree from the Alabama Polytechnic Institute at Auburn. Then followed a very active business career which has been continued now for almost twenty years. For two years he was associated in the mercantile business with his father; was in the ice business three years, then entered the mining industry in Alabama for two years, and in Colorado for five years. In Colorado Mr. Hood owned one of the largest concentrating mills in the state, located at Silver Plume, and concentrating lead and zinc ores for the principal output of silver.

His interests also extended in the meanwhile to the oil fields around Electra in Northern Texas, and in 1913 he moved his home to Independence and in the fall of that year began operations as a contractor and oil producer at Wayside. He still operates both in Texas and Kansas. Mr. Hood now has a total of forty-nine oil wells, divided among various leases in the following numbers, twenty-seven, thirteen, six, two and one, and he also has fifteen producing gas wells in Kansas. His partner in these various operations is E. S. Riley. As a contractor he operates three separate strings of tools.

Politically Mr. Hood is a democrat, is a member of the Rotary Club at Independence and of the Sigma Alpha Epsilon college fraternity. An active worker in the Methodist Church, he is now president of the church choir.

In 1903, at Anniston, Alabama, Mr. Hood married Rosa Lela Weller, daughter of William H. and Erin Weller, who now reside at Demopolis, Alabama. William H. Weller is a prominent iron manufacturer, has coal mines, rolling mills and other interests in Alabama and also a large plantation in the southern part of that state. Mr. and Mrs. Hood have two children: Matilda Dale, born November 5, 1905; and William A., Jr., born November 24, 1908. Mr. Hood and family reside at 505 North Eighth Street, Independence. He also owns five residence properties in Birmingham, but has sold out his other real estate holdings.

HENRY BENNETT, of Topeka, has been a resident of Kansas over forty years. Before coming to Kansas he made an enviable record as a gallant soldier in the Union army, having served with the famous Chicago Board of Trade Battery. He has lived three-quarters of a century, but still retains his youth and the optimism of virile and aggressive manhood. No individual record could be more worthy of a place in Kansas history than that of Henry Bennett.

He was one of the two sons of William and Rachel (Ludby) Bennett, and was born at Chicago, Illinois, June 15, 1841. His people became identified with Chicago at the very beginning of municipal growth. In that city he was reared, and gained his education in the public schools. When he was fifteen years old he undertook a three years' apprenticeship at the carpenter's trade. During the latter part of that period he did almost a man's work, and yet his wages were only fifty cents a day, out of which he had to board and lodge himself. He then worked as a journeyman until 1861, and was paid $1.00 a day while his foreman received $1.25 per day. Thus through his individual career it is possible to understand the remarkable changes that have occurred during the past half century in the matter of wages paid to workmen. For the work he performed as a carpenter before the war, mechanics at the present time would receive four or five times the wages.

When President Lincoln issued his first call for 75,000 volunteers to put down the rebellion, Henry Bennett was one of those who enlisted for ninety days in Battery A, Chicago Light Artillery. Three days after the enrollment he was sent to Cairo but saw little active service. At the expiration of his enlistment he was sick with chills and fever, and did not have the opportunity to re-enlist with his former comrades. He returned to Chicago and recuperated so that he was ready for another enlistment in the summer of 1862. On July 21st of that year there occurred an enthusiastic meeting of the members of the Chicago Board of Trade, in which it was resolved to recruit and equip a company of light artillery for the war. This became the famous Chicago Board of Trade Battery. Mr. Bennett was one of the first to enroll, and owing to his previous military experience he was elected one of the two second lieutenants. Within forty-eight hours after the meeting a telegram was sent to the President offering the battery to the war department, and with almost equal celerity the board of trade raised three regiments of infantry. A few days later James H. Stokes was elected captain of the company by acclamation. He was a veteran artillerist, having received a commission from General Jackson and was captain of a company several years in the Florida war, and had also been an instructor at West Point. On September 9th the battery left Chicago for Louisville, Kentucky, where it was placed under the orders of General Christopher, chief of artillery of General Buell's command. It fought at Salvisa and in a part of the Perryville engagement. Later the battery went into camp at Bowling Green and subsequently to Nashville. In the meantime General Rosecrans succeeded General Buell in command, and

the battery was attached to the Pioneer Brigade of the Army of the Cumberland. The battery took an important part in the battle of Stone River at Murfreesboro in December, 1862. After the battle of Stone River it was converted into horse artillery, and attached to the Second Cavalry Division, Army of the Cumberland, and participated in a minor engagement on Duck River, and was stationed on the highest point in the battlefield. After the engagement of Duck River the command went through what was known as the Tullahoma campaign. In the spring of 1864, with his command, the battery took for Chattanooga, but at Bridgeport crossed the Tennessee River and entered upon the campaign which culminated in the battle of Chickamauga. In this historic engagement the Chicago Board of Trade Battery had the honor of firing the first round on the extreme left which brought on the engagement, and likewise two sections of the battery on the extreme right, at Crawfish Springs, fired the last round. Returning to Chattanooga, Lieutenant Bennett was detailed with his command to guard the fords to prevent the crossing of General Wheeler's Cavalry, but failing to do so pursued that energetic commander to Farmington, where a severe engagement ensued.

The next winter was spent near Huntsville, Alabama, and in the spring of 1864 joined Sherman's advance upon Atlanta. In the meantime Lieutenant Bennett had been detailed to return to Chicago to recruit members for their depleted ranks. The next important engagement in which he bore a part was at Resaca, and later at a little town on the Chattahoochie River where three cotton mills were busy night and day supplying the rebels with cloth. Upon orders, these mills were burned. He was next in the battle of Peachtree Creek, and in the general siege of Atlanta. The headquarters of the battery were at Decatur on the extreme right. A portion of the battery participated in the famous Kilpatrick's raid around the entire Confederate army. During July some desperate fighting occurred at Decatur between the opposing forces and the Union troops narrowly escaped destruction. One account of the fighting at this point says that during the Federal advance across Flint River the Confederate guns were silenced by Lieutenant Bennett's section of the battery. His men then rushed to the bank of the river and dislodged the sharpshooters from the opposite bank, when the column crossed and advanced to Jonesboro. He was also in the battle of Lovejoy's Station where the Federal losses were about 700.

After the reduction of Atlanta Lieutenant Bennett with his command joined the army of General Thomas at Nashville and took part in the tremendous fighting before that city on December 15-16th. He subsequently was with the forces in pursuit of General Hood, and spent the winter at Waterloo. In the spring of 1865, taking advantage of the general order which permitted soldiers having served two or more years to resign, Lieutenant Bennett resigned on February 18, 1865. He had received his lieutenant's commission on July 31, 1862, and was thus a gallant officer of the Army of the Cumberland for nearly 2½ years. He was once offered the captaincy of another battery, and once a majorship in a regiment of cavalry, but he declined these honors in order that he might remain among the comrades with whom he had so long been associated in times of danger and strife.

On his return to Chicago Mr. Bennett engaged in

the general contracting business as a member of the firm of Grannis & Bennett. Their office was on Twenty-second Street, between Michigan and Indiana avenues. After two years of partnership he was in business for himself, and from 1865 to 1876 superintended the construction of many large buildings in Chicago. His work was especially heavy after the fire of 1871, and at the time of the panic of 1873 he was employing 250 workmen. Among many other buildings he constructed the Grocers' Block at the corner of Wabash and Lake Street, a building which has very recently been torn down in order to make room for skyscraper construction.

In 1876 Mr. Bennett came to Kansas. His first undertaking here was as a stockraiser, and he bought a place sixteen miles from Topeka near Silver Lake, where his family lived while he attended to some contracting. A year later he put up a building for the insane asylum at Ossawatomie. Since the completion of that task his home has been in Topeka, but from that city his business activities have extended over a large portion of the state. During the past forty years Mr. Bennett has constructed many of the state buildings in whole or in part, and the record of his work includes churches, banks, business blocks and many of the important structures for the Santa Fe Railway.

In 1878 he went to Manhattan and put up the north wing of the Central Building of the Kansas State Agricultural College. He has since contracted for the building of several other structures for the state at Manhattan, including the auditorium, the mechanical engineering building, the veterinary building and the original creamery building. Just thirty years ago he took the contract for remodeling the east wing of the State House as a senate chamber and altogether has put in between $250,000 and $300,000 of interior finish work on the central part of the building.

Some of the more conspicuous of his operations in Topeka alone have been the Governor Crawford Block, the Columbia, the Masonic Block, the Independent Telephone Building, the original Central National Bank Building, the National Hotel, the old Copeland Hotel which was destroyed by fire and the present fireproof building on the old site. He built the governor's mansion, the Topeka Library Building, and the Edison office building. After he had passed his seventieth birthday his organization undertook the new Santa Fe office building, the Grace Cathedral, and the Sunday School building of the First Methodist Church, which has been completed.

In 1891 Mr. Bennett went to Mexico and for a year or so was engaged in constructing the general offices, a depot and a hotel for the Gulf & Monterey railroad, and also built a number of stations between Monterey and Mexico City for the Mexican National Railway. He also had several contracts for construction work on the World's Fair grounds at Chicago, and put up the Territorial Building for the territories of Oklahoma, Arizona, New Mexico and Alaska. After that he added two more buildings, the State Hospital for the Insane at Ossawatomie, and in 1896 erected the National Hotel at Cripple Creek, Colorado, and also the administration building of the hospital at Ossawatomie. It was during the construction of a hotel at Hutchinson, Kansas, in 1908 that Mr. Bennett's health received its first serious setback, when he was overcome by the heat, but he is still in the harness and has no intention of retiring. In the past twenty years his organiza-

tion has erected many buildings for the Santa Fe Railway Company all over the Southwest. These include the freight depot at Hutchinson, depots at Santa Fe and Lamy, New Mexico, a Harvey eating house at Las Vegas, and a thirty-five-stall roundhouse at Albuquerque, New Mexico. When Oklahoma was open to settlement he had a contract with the Rock Island Railroad for building every station on that company's line in Oklahoma. That was one of his largest years and besides all his work he put up the roundhouse and other buildings for the Rock Island at Blue Island, Illinois.

Two or three years ago Mr. Bennett's two sons took a large share of the responsibility and became active partners in the business, and more and more he is throwing the burden of hard work upon their shoulders.

Mr. Bennett is a member of the First Methodist Episcopal Church in Topeka, is an independent republican in politics, and is a Knight Templar Mason. He has always been interested in old army comrades, and is a past commander of the Loyal Legion in the State of Kansas. He also belongs to the Rotary and the Topeka Commercial Clubs.

On December 13, 1866, Mr. Bennett married Mary F. Vreeland, whose father Henry Vreeland was an old time contractor in Chicago. Four children have been born to their union: Belle B., widow of Dr. William Swan; Mary, wife of George B. Harrison and the mother of three children; Henry Jr. and J. Albert. The sons are married, have families, and are progressive representative business men of Topeka.

JAMES D. SULLIVAN is proprietor of the Art Store at 122-124 West Eighth Street and 728-730 Jackson Street in Topeka. During his residence in Topeka he has developed a large business, and this is due to his thorough training in the profession and his own sense of artistic values which have enabled him to render a valuable service to his large patronage.

James D. Sullivan was born in Norwich, Connecticut, January 11, 1861, a son of James and Mary (Bridgeman) Sullivan. He received a public school education, and also took a business course in a business college at Chicago. His best training for his profession came at Chicago, where he was long in the employ of the W. Scott Thurber Art Gallery, as a foreman, these galleries having a wide reputation over the Central West not only as dealers in some of the most notable art works of the world, but also as creative artists and decorators. He spent about nineteen years in the Thurber galleries and for three years was with the firm of Bowen & Lee in the same line.

In November, 1897, Mr. Sullivan came to Topeka and has directed his business as an art dealer and restorer of painting, and has always made artistic framing a specialty. One painting which Mr. Sullivan restored in which he takes the greatest pride is the painting of ''The Immaculate Conception,'' by Boneto. It hangs in the Parish Church of the Immaculate Conception at St. Marys, Kansas. This painting is over 160 years old and was sent to St. Marys over sixty years ago by Pope Pius IX in recognition of the work done among the Indians when St. Marys was only an Indian mission.

In politics he is a republican, is a member of the Commercial Club, is affiliated with the Knights of Columbus and the Knights and Ladies of Security, and belongs to the Catholic Church. In 1898 he married Miss Margaret Delahoyde of Chicago. They reside at 1135 Garfield Avenue, Topeka.

FRANCIS M. SPENCER. During more than a quarter century's identification with the building and contracting business in Kansas, with headquarters at Topeka, Mr. Spencer has established a reputation for responsible financial management and systematic and accurate execution of every contract which he undertakes, even down to the last detail.

Few men in the business in the entire state can exhibit a finer record in buildings actually completed and now conspicuous in various cities as Mr. Spencer. While a complete list would be impossible, the more notable of his contracts are the following: Topeka Manual Training School, the Capper Building, the New England Building, the Young Men's Christian Association Building, the Washburn College Observatory, the Washburn College Gymnasium, all of Topeka; the Santa Fe Railway Hospital at Mulvane, Kansas; the State Normal School Building at Emporia; the Central Park, Washington and Van Buren schools in Topeka; the Santa Fe Railway Motive Power Office Building at Topeka; St. Francis Hospital in Topeka, and has recently completed Ursuline Academy at Paola, Kansas, and the Kansas Masonic Grand Lodge Building of Topeka. His firm, F. M. Spencer & Son, contractors, is now engaged in erecting a Santa Fe depot and office building at Marceline, Missouri, and a union depot at Salina, Kansas.

Francis M. Spencer was born near Wilmington in Clinton County, Ohio, May 11, 1856, a son of John F. and Sarah (Shield) Spencer. His father was born in Clinton County, Ohio, April 14, 1828, was a farmer and moved to Kansas in 1873. In 1895 he retired from active work as a farmer, and his death occurred in Topeka, December 11, 1915. He was a republican, and his wife were Methodists, and on December 4, 1863, he was initiated in Lodge No. 312, Ancient Free and Accepted Masons, at Harveysburg, Ohio, and took his third degree there February 27, 1864. He was a loyal member of the order for more than half a century. His wife was born in Ohio February 19, 1823, and died in Kansas in 1893. Both belonged to pioneer Ohio families.

Reared on an Ohio farm until he was seventeen years of age Francis M. Spencer had a district school education, and when quite young began his apprenticeship at the carpenter's trade, which he mastered thoroughly. His home has been at Topeka since March 16, 1883. He worked at his trade as a journeyman until 1888, and then engaged in the business of building contractor, with what conspicuous success has already been shown. For a number of years his offices were at 627 Kansas Avenue, but for the past six years have been at 215 Mulvane Building. Mr. Spencer also owns some land in Texas and other western states, and his long business career has brought him a thoroughly deserved prosperity.

He is a member of the Co-operative Club in Topeka, and is a prominent Mason. His affiliations are with Orient Lodge No. 51, Ancient Free and Accepted Masons at Topeka; Topeka Chapter No. 5 Royal Arch Masons; Topeka Commandery No. 5 Knights Templar; Topeka Consistory No. 1 of the Scottish Rite; and Abdallah Temple of the Mystic Shrine at Leavenworth. For thirty-five years he has been identified with Odd Fellowship, and is a member of Lodge No. 40 at Topeka. He is a republican, and a member of the Central Congrega-

tional Church, in which his wife is a very active worker, having for many years taught a class of the Sunday school. She is a graduate of the Bible school under Mrs. Doctor Memminger.

For the past eighteen years Mr. Spencer and family have resided in their handsome home at 1352 Garfield Avenue. January 18, 1883, at Urbana, Ohio, he married Catherine M. Miller, who was born at Urbana, a daughter of Cornelius and Myra (Cunningham) Miller. Her father was a native of Maryland and her mother of Ohio. Mrs. Spencer is a member of the Federation of Women's Clubs in Kansas. They are the parents of three children. Nora A. is the widow of H. L. Adams, who was an auditor for the Santa Fe Railway Company and died at Topeka in 1910. Earl M. was born in Topeka and is associated with his father in the firm of F. M. Spencer & Sons. George, born at Topeka, is also an employe of this firm. Mr. and Mrs. Spencer's only grandchild is Margaret Spencer Adams, who was born October 19, 1907.

HON. F. DUMONT SMITH. During his thirty years of membership in the Kansas bar, F. Dumont Smith has attained such distinction as to make him a well known figure in the life and activities of the state. Noted as an exceptionally well trained lawyer, he has also been prominent as a public speaker, editor and writer and has wielded an influence proportionate to his versatile abilities. For many years his home was in Kinsley, but he is now at Hutchinson.

He is a man of fortunate endowment and of fine American ancestry. He was born on a farm near Kewanee, Illinois, January 31, 1861, a son of Samuel M. and Elizabeth (Rose) Anderson Smith. His first American ancestor was Nathaniel Smith who came from Yorkshire, England, in 1640, and settled in the valley of the Connecticut near New London. The maternal grandfather Samuel Bowles Anderson, a native of Vermont, was the first surveyor-general of Michigan. He married Maria Willard, who was descended from Major Josiah Willard, who came from Bristol, England, and established the Willard family in America in 1631.

Samuel M. Smith, father of the Hutchinson lawyer, was born in Connecticut, while his wife was a native of New York. They were married in Michigan, moved from there to Illinois, and about 1877 settled in the State of Virginia in the valley of the Potomac below Mount Vernon. In 1884 they established their home at Washington, District of Columbia, and in 1888 went south to Florida, where Samuel M. Smith died in 1892. His widow passed away at the home of her son in Kansas in 1890. Samuel M. Smith was a farmer by occupation and was a man of unusual energy and ability. He was an eloquent speaker, and in the early politics of Illinois was at the head of the Grangers organization. His wife was also noted for her strong character and her ability as a writer of charming verse, much of which was set to music.

Thus it was in the atmosphere of books, culture, and high ideals that F. Dumont Smith was reared. After a high school education he entered the National University Law School at Washington, where he was graduated LL. B. in 1886. In June of that year he was admitted to the bar in the Supreme Court of the District of Columbia, and in the fall of that year, October, came out and identified himself permanently with the State of Kansas. He soon had a large and profitable practice at Kinsley, which was his home until 1908, when he removed to Hutchinson.

In 1893 Mr. Smith was mayor of Kinsley, and in 1900 was elected on the republican ticket to the State Senate and was re-elected in 1904. He was sent to the Senate by the Thirty-ninth Senatorial District, embracing sixteen counties. Senator Smith is a Knight Templar Mason, a member of the Mystic Shrine, the Independent Order of Odd Fellows, the Knights of Pythias, the Ancient Order of United Workmen and the Woodmen of the World. He was reared in the faith of the Episcopal Church.

In May, 1888, at Washington, District of Columbia, after he had become established in practice in Kansas, he married Miss Florence Eustace, who was born at Dixon, Illinois. They have one son Eustace Dumont Smith, who graduated LL. B. in 1911 from the law school of the National University at Washington, District of Columbia, and is now his father's partner in law practice at Hutchinson.

Mr. Smith has traveled extensively in his own country and abroad, is familiar with various European countries, China and Japan, and many of his observations of men, manners and affairs have been translated into charming prose. His best literary effort is considered "Blue Waters and Green."

WILLIAM E. GRAVES, D. V. M. Among the men skilled in the practice of veterinary medicine and surgery in Kansas, one who has enjoyed a long and successful career, is Dr. William E. Graves. A graduate of a leading St. Louis institution, he began practice about the time that he attained manhood, came to Kansas in 1896 and carried on his vocation in Franklin County for ten years, and in 1906 changed his field of operation to Topeka, where he now has his home.

Doctor Graves was born on a farm in Pike County, Illinois, in 1852, a son of William and Susan (Noble) Graves. His father was born at Monticello, Kentucky, and was there married to the daughter of Adam Noble, a member of an old and honored family of Kentucky, and himself a pioneer of that state, as well as an early and noted circuit-rider of the Methodist Church. Almost immediately after their marriage, Mr. and Mrs. Graves, mounted on horse-back, started for their new home in Pike County, Illinois, a long and dangerous journey. Seated in back of Mrs. Graves was a young negro girl, who had been given them as a wedding present by Reverend Noble. Upon their arrival at their destination they found not over six families in the community, and it was a number of years before the county became even sparsely settled, but the families were all hospitable and friendly, sharing each others joys and sorrows and occasionally all gathering at one house, on some special occasion, such as Christmas, when a great feast would be laid and the festivities would continue for several days. On these occasions one of the principal dainties of the table would be a great jar of honey, invariably supplied by William Graves, who was known as a noted hunter of bee trees and could always be depended upon to find the delectable article in large quantities. Mrs. Graves always remembered this period as the happiest in her life. Mr. Graves was a man of the highest moral character and had none of the vices so general among the pioneers of that part of Illinois, and never touched liquor in any form. He was a sober, industrious and energetic workman, but in spite of his solidity and substantiality the spirit of adventure was in his blood and this eventually caused his death. The discovery of gold in California, in 1849, had caused many hardy and courageous men to undertake the long and perilous trip across the plains, and as the trails came to be more definitely located, it was considered that the journey was becoming less dangerous. In 1851 William Graves joined a party of gold-seekers in the great desert trip. In his young manhood he had learned the trade of wagonmaker, and it was considered that in addition to his other qualities his knowledge of this vocation should be of great assistance to the party. One menace had not been taken into consideration, however, and that was the awful scourge of cholera, which had insinuated itself not only into the mining camps, but all along the trail. Of the brave little party of a dozen or more who left Illinois, but one returned, this a man named Stotts, who brought word of the almost incredible hardships undergone by the party and the final extermination of the emigrants by cholera. Thus William Graves never returned to his Illinois home. He and his wife were the parents of five children, namely: Lucy, deceased; Elizabeth, deceased; Montroville, deceased; Eleanor, who is now Mrs. Horback, of Ottawa, Kansas; and William E.

William E. Graves never saw his father, as he died before the son's birth. Left with five children, the widowed mother had a hard time making both ends meet, but managed to keep her little brood together and give them a number of advantages that helped them to become useful men and women. William E. Graves received the usual public school education granted at that time in Pike County, and in his youth evidenced a love for animals that pointed out the road for him to follow in the choice of a life vocation. When eighteen years of age he went to St. Louis, where he entered the St. Louis Veterinary College, from which he was duly graduated at the age of twenty-one years. He at once entered upon the practice of his calling in Illinois, and after being located in a number of places came to Kansas in 1896 and established himself in business in Franklin County. There for ten years he succeeded in building up a large and profitable practice, particularly in the farming communities, and in 1906 came to Topeka, where he has since been located, his offices being situated at Twenty-first and Oakley streets.

Doctor Graves was married in 1875 to Miss Anna Brown, and three daughters have been born to them: Elsie, who is the wife of R. B. Nelson, bookkeeper for the Hall Lithographic Company; Catherine, a graduate of Washburn College, and now teaching vocal music in the Honey Grove (Texas) High School; and Izora, who is the wife of Earl Laxman, of Buffalo, New York. Mr. Laxman has had an unusual career. He was early left in charge of a widowed mother and proved himself a good and faithful son, well worthy the interest and friendship of all who knew him. He has made rapid progress in the business world, and although now only twenty-four years of age is superintendent of a large printing plant at Buffalo, at a salary of $3,000 per year.

JACOB SMITH, of Topeka, was one of the notable pioneers of Kansas. He lived in this state half a century. During this time he distinguished himself by a large degree of constructive enterprise in various business affairs. He was a pioneer merchant at Topeka, was also one of the early county officials, was a banker, was interested in the building of railroads and was throughout noted as a man of unusual sound judgment, of great foresight and discernment, and of absolute integrity. The record of his life as given in the following paragraphs is essentially a part of Kansas history.

He was born in Berks County, Pennsylvania, near

Reading, June 24, 1829, and died at his home in Topeka, November 30, 1908. His parents and grandparents were natives of Pennsylvania, their families having come to this country from Leipsic, Germany, at a very early date.

When he was two years old in 1831 his father, John Smith, and mother, Hannah Darsham, moved to Somerset, Perry County, Ohio. He received a good education in the country schools and one item of his early experience was clerking in the Boyden Store, where one of his classmates, Phil Sheridan, was also employed. Phil Sheridan later became the dashing cavalry leader and one of the most distinguished generals of the Civil war.

In April, 1852, Jacob Smith married Jane K. Von Cannon, at Tiffin, Ohio. Their wedding journey was to Bluffton, Indiana, where they were to make their home, and there Mr. Smith set up in the mercantile business. His daughter, Ida, was born there in 1855.

In 1857 Jacob Smith decided to come to Kansas. He left on March 5th for St. Louis, where on March 10th he took passage on the steamer Morning Star for Westport Landing, now Kansas City. The Morning Star and other steamers of its class were well appointed large boats and did a rushing business in passengers and freight between St. Louis and Kansas City. After six days he arrived at Westport, a small town of about 500 population, containing a two-story hotel and a few small stores. He remained there all night and the next morning arranged with a man named Green to take him to Lawrence. The stage at that time made only one trip a week. He crossed into Kansas and soon came to the Methodist Mission in charge of Rev. Thomas Johnson. There he met Rev. Mr. Johnson's son, Col. A. S. Johnson and a friendship began which lasted a lifetime. After arriving in Lawrence he determined to proceed to Topeka, and spent the night at a Mrs. Allen's near Big Springs. Mrs. Allen furnished bed and meals to travelers. On arriving at Topeka he stopped at the Garvey House at the corner of Kansas Avenue and Fifth Street.

Purchasing a claim west of Tecumseh on the river, Mr. Smith lived on it three months and then sold out at a good profit for $600, that money constituting his real capital for the beginning of a business career in Kansas. Returning to Topeka from his claim he engaged in the tinware business at 195 Kansas Avenue. In August of the same year he went back to Bluffton and brought his wife and baby West to their new home in Kansas. He was in St. Louis long enough to purchase a stock of hardware for a new store. This stock was freighted by steamer to Westport and wagon to Topeka. It required from six to eight days to make the round trip according to the condition of the roads.

According to an advertisement found in the Topeka State Record of January 14, 1860, Jacob Smith carried "a full line of stoves, iron steel hardware, window glass and agricultural implements, offering them at low rates wholesale and retail—largest assortment of cook, parlor and box stoves in the territory." J. Cole had charge of the tin shop connected with the store. Later his partners were E. H. Blake and George D. Hale. In 1879 Mr. Smith sold to Mr. Hale. Some years later the W. A. L. Thompson Hardware Company was formed, and Mr. Smith was given the honorary position of president of that firm, an office he held until his death.

In 1867 Jacob Smith bought three lots on the corner of Harrison and Fifth streets, and there built the house and planted the trees on the grounds where his family still reside. These were the lots on which the first schoolhouse of Topeka was built in 1857. The lots had been set apart by the Town Association in 1856, and the Emigrant Aid Society was to build the schoolhouse in consideration of other lots which were given to it by the town company. The society did not erect a building until 1857, when a brick structure 18 by 24 feet, two stories in height, was put on the back of the lot facing north on Fifth and Harrison. This was the first schoolhouse in the city and James Cowles was the first principal. When Mr. Smith bought the lots the schoolhouse was torn down, and the bricks and windows were used in the stable which still stands on the grounds, and after fifty-nine years they are in good condition.

For many years Mr. Smith also owned a large stock farm east of Topeka and across the river from the claim he first purchased. As the town grew the Bank of Topeka was started, of which he was one of the organizers and incorporators, and he was elected director and vice president on December 30, 1868, and for seven years served as president, from 1870 to 1877. Jacob Smith was also one of the first directors and stockholders of the Midland Railroad running from Topeka to Kansas City, now a part of the Santa Fe System. For a time he was also president of the De Soto and Pleasant Hill Railroad.

During the last twenty-five or thirty years of his life Mr. Smith was practically retired from business. He was a great traveler, and no one enjoyed traveling more. By his wide intercourse with men and affairs he had gained a large fund of information, and was also a great reader, a close observer and had a splendid memory. In the early days he was quite active in politics. He served as treasurer of Shawnee County from 1861 to 1866, during the Civil war period. During the war he took part in the Battle of the Blue on Colonel Vaele's staff, and on October 22, 1864, was commissioned sergeant of the Second Kansas State Militia. He was a member of Lincoln Post No. 1, G. A. R. In 1867 he was elected a councilman. Socially he was a member of the Ananias and Topeka clubs, and was affiliated with Masonic Lodge No. 17, at Topeka.

His first wife died February 18, 1859, leaving two daughters: Ida and Jessie. Jessie died in 1879, soon after her graduation from Bethany College. In 1866 Jacob Smith married Sarah Y. Linderman of Kansas City. She died in 1889. The only surviving child of this pioneer Kansan is Ida, who was married June 7, 1876, to W. A. L. Thompson of Topeka. They have two children, Helen, who married Harry W. Donaldson, and Roy T., who married Cornelia Gleed and has a son, Gleed Thompson.

ROSWELL L. COFRAN, a prominent Topeka business man and former mayor of the city, has the faculty of growing old gracefully, and is still vigorous and useful though past the age of three score and ten. His has been a long and varied career. He served as a soldier in the Civil war. For forty years he has been proprietor of one of the largest foundries and machine shops in the State of Kansas, and is still active in attending to his business affairs.

Born in the Green Mountain State of Vermont at Wheelock, Caledonia County, February 3, 1842, he is a son of John and Nancy (Hoyt) Cofran, both of whom spent all their lives in the same state. His mother died in 1879 and his father in 1889.

With his early education supplied by the grade schools of Wheelock, Roswell L. Cofran also attended the Orleans Academy in Orleans County, and then followed farming until September, 1861. He was then a youth of nineteen, and enlisted at Wheelock in Company E of the Sixth Vermont Infantry as a private soldier. He was later promoted to corporal, and was in service continually until February, 1863, when he was mustered out at Fort Hamilton, New York. He took part in the Peninsula campaign under General McClellan and manfully did his part in helping to preserve the Union.

After the war Mr. Cofran learned the trade of founder and machinist and followed it as a journeyman for a number of years. His home has been in Topeka since July, 1870. He was employed in the Topeka Foundry and Machine Works until 1876, at which time the business was reorganized as the Western Foundry and Machine Works, and he soon became its owner and proprietor. He has operated that plant now for fully forty years. The company does all kinds of machine and foundry work and turns out all classes of brass, bronze and aluminum castings. The plant is located at 201 Jefferson Street. It is one of the important industrial establishments of the Capital City.

To a great many people the name of Roswell L. Cofran suggests a vigorous and effective municipal policy in Topeka. He has had much to do in making Topeka municipally a first class city. He was a member of the city council and while still a member was elected mayor on the democratic ticket in 1885. He served one term from 1885 to 1887, and in 1889 was again elected for another two-year term. He was re-elected in 1891 and nearly twenty years later, in 1913, was elected for his fourth term as mayor, this time as an independent or people's candidate, serving from 1913 to 1915. Thus his administrations as mayor covered portions of three decades of growth and development. When he was first elected mayor Topeka had a great many wooden sidewalks. These had replaced by brick and that improvement indicates what he stood for in the way of general municipal improvement. He has always sought, whether as an official or a private citizen, to make Topeka a metropolitan city worthy to be the capital of the great State of Kansas.

On March 5, 1882, at Topeka, he married Caroline Fritsche, who was born in Chicago, Illinois, a daughter of Frederick Fritsche, a native of Germany. To their marriage have been born three children: Grace, born at Topeka, is the wife of Eli Bishoff, a grocer at Kansas City, Missouri; Maud, born at Topeka, is the wife of Clyde Lutz, a traveling salesman with his home at Des Moines, Iowa; Roswell L., Jr., was born at Topeka and is still at home.

Mr. Cofran is a Scottish and York Rite Mason, affiliating with Orient Lodge No. 51, Ancient Free and Accepted Masons, at Topeka; the Royal Arch Chapter; the Commandery No. 5 of the Knights Templar; with Abdallah Temple of the Mystic Shrine at Leavenworth; and is also a member of Shawnee Lodge No. 1 and Shawnee Encampment of the Independent Order of Odd Fellows, and of Lodge No. 38 of the Knights of Pythias. He and his family attend the Congregational Church. They all reside in a fine old home at 1263 Topeka Avenue.

JAMES J. BULGER has been a resident of Kansas since his boyhood and through recourse to the best of educational institutions in the Sunflower State he prepared himself for the legal profession, which he has dignified by his character and achievement and through the medium of which he advanced to judicial position, his service having been on the bench of the District Court of Cherokee County. Since 1912 he has been engaged in the general practice of his profession in the City of Wichita, where he has built up a large and important law business and retains a representative clientage.

Judge Bulger was born in Christian County, Illinois, on the 9th of November, 1875, and thus he was about ten years of age when, in 1886, his parents removed to Kansas and established their home near Baxter Springs. After completing the curriculum of the public schools Judge Bulger entered the Fort Scott Normal College, and in this institution he was graduated as a member of the class of 1895. With well formulated plans for his future career, he was soon afterward matriculated in the law department of the University of Kansas, in which he completed the prescribed course and in which he was graduated in 1898, with the degree of Bachelor of Laws. He was forthwith admitted to the bar and soon afterward he entered upon his professional novitiate, at Weir City, Cherokee County. There he remained a few months and he then consulted personal and professional expediency by establishing his residence at Columbus, the judicial center of the same county, and forming a professional alliance with the late Richard Blue, with whom he continued to be associated in the control of a successful general practice until 1906, when he was appointed to a responsible legal position in the claim department of the Union Pacific Railroad, with headquarters in the City of Omaha, Nebraska. Of this position he continued the incumbent until the death of his former law partner, Mr. Blue, in 1907, when he returned to Baxter Springs, to adjust some matters pertaining to their former law business, and while there he was appointed district judge, to complete the unexpired term of Judge C. A. McNeil. On the bench Judge Bulger continued his effective administration until the expiration of the term, and in 1912 he removed to Wichita, where he has since been engaged in practice in an individual way and where he has admirable standing both as a versatile trial lawyer and a counselor of broad and exact knowledge of the science of jurisprudence. Judge Bulger is a staunch and effective advocate of the principles of the republican party, is affiliated with the time-honored Masonic fraternity, and also holds membership in the Wichita Lodge of the Benevolent and Protective Order of Elks. In 1912 was solemnized his marriage to Miss Eulah Sawyer, of Galena, Kansas.

HENRY H. MILLER, M. D. Although the well directed labor of Dr. Henry H. Miller belongs to the past rather than present of Rossville, innumerable evidences abound of his sojourn in the community, and particularly of his diligence in protecting and preserving the health and sanitation of his adopted place. For forty-four years he was a prominent resident of Rossville, and during that time won his way into the confidence and respect of the people not alone as a medical adviser and kind friend, but as a contributor to all that made for their welfare and a supporter of the things that combined to advance religion, education and high citizenship.

Doctor Miller was born in Ashtabula County, Ohio,

May 4, 1850, the sixth son of Rev. John and Sarah (Shaffer) Miller, natives of New York and Switzerland, respectively. Rev. John Miller was a Methodist minister and circuit rider, moving from one small congregation to another and administering the gospel over a wide stretch of territory, in addition to which he carried on farming. He gave his children better educational advantages than were usual in those days. Henry H. was sent to college to complete his training for the profession which he had decided upon as his life work. He first attended the common schools of Alliance, Ohio, and after teaching school for several years, entered Mount Union College, after leaving which he went to the University of Pennsylvania. There he worked his way partly through college and secured his coveted degree of Doctor of Medicine. His older brothers had, in the meantime, come to Kansas, and immediately after his graduation the young physician came to this place, arriving June 25, 1872. From that time until his death, May 1, 1916, he continued in the practice of his profession. When he first arrived at Rossville, the population consisted of not more than 100 souls, and during the early days of his practice he rode on horseback all over the surrounding country, no hour being too late or any weather too severe for him to hasten to the bedside of some suffering human. He became honored and respected throughout the county, and his friendships extended over a wide area. A man of honesty and of upright living, he readily won the confidence of his fellow-citizens, and was entrusted with many offices of importance in the community, being clerk of the township school board for eighteen years, councilman for one term, and mayor of Rossville for one year. Politically, he was a republican. Doctor Miller assisted in every laudable enterprise launched in his community, was identified with the building of various churches and school buildings at Rossville, and at the same time gave his children good educational advantages. He was a Presbyterian and acted as elder in the church, in the work of which he took an active part. Fraternally, he was a thirty-second degree Scottish Rite Mason, a Shriner and a Knight Templar, was master of the Rossville lodge for thirteen years, and belonged to the first class to take the Consistory degrees at Topeka. He was the last living charter member of the Rossville lodge of the Ancient Order of United Workmen. For years he was president of the Annuity Union. Doctor Miller was one of the organizers of the Peoples State Bank and Rossville State Bank. He accumulated farm lands and town property, and was the owner, with his son, of eighty acres in Shawnee County.

About four years after his arrival at Rossville, April 13, 1876, Doctor Miller was married to Miss Ella M. Wyatt, of this place, and they had three children: Emma, who is now Mrs. J. S. Majors, of Topeka; Earl D., who is engaged in mercantile pursuits at Manhken, Kansas; and Dr. Henry B., of Rossville. Mrs. Miller, who was a Baptist and active in the work of her church, died September 30, 1894. On September 9, 1898, Doctor Miller was married to Miss Gertrude Partello, of Rossville, who survives him and lives at that place.

Dr. Henry B. Miller, son of Dr. Henry H. Miller, and one of the leading physicians of this part of Shawnee County, was born at Rossville, January 1, 1881. His early education was secured in the public schools, following which he took an academic course of two years at Bethany Academy, Lindsborg, Kansas, and enrolled as a student at Baker College, Baldwin. There he remained for 1½ years, when family

reverses caused him to give up, for the time being, his college career, and subsequently he studied shorthand and secured a position with the Santa Fe Railroad, at Topeka. Thus he was enabled to work his way through Baker College, from which he duly received the degree of Bachelor of Arts. Next, he taught school for one year at Overbrook, and following this secured an appointment to the position of assistant instructor in the chemical laboratory at Kansas University. He held this post one year and then did two years of post-graduate work, and in 1906 received his master's degree. At that time he went to the University of Pennsylvania. In 1908 he received his degree of Doctor of Medicine. To still further prepare himself, Doctor Miller then took a year of interne work at the University Hospital, at the Methodist Hospital and the Municipal Hospital, and September 1, 1909, returned to Rossville, where he became associated in practice with his father. Doctor Miller now has the largest practice in this part of the county, and is recognized as one of the most thorough, learned and skillful practitioners of the community.

Doctor Miller belongs to the various organizations of his profession, and is well known in fraternal circles, belonging to the Masons, the Knights Templar, the Red Men, and the Kappa Sigma and the Alpha Mu Phi Omega of the University of Pennsylvania. In his senior year at that institution he was elected an honorary member of the exclusive Sigma Xi fraternity. He is a staunch republican, but has not desired public office. Doctor Miller has always been a generous contributor to schools and churches as well as to all enterprises worthy of support for the betterment of his community and its people.

ALBERT ARTHUR HURD. The professional intimates of the late Albert Arthur Hurd unhesitatingly place him among the most able corporation lawyers who ever graced the Topeka bar. The reputation of men who gain eminence in this branch of the law is not made in a day. Such a reputation requires not only natural talent, but the most thorough preparation and strenuous, continuous and intense application and industry. That he became recognized as one of the best railroad lawyers in the United States was due to the possession of exceptional ability and character, and also to the fact that he was continuously identified with the Santa Fe Railway Company for a period of forty years. He entered the service of the company in 1875, in 1905 was made special counsel, and that appointment and the duties connected therewith were a splendid recognition of the strength and breadth of his influence upon the general progress of the corporation.

Albert Arthur Hurd was born at Lafayette, Illinois, September 27, 1849, a son of Theodore F. and Catherine (Driscoll) Hurd. He belonged to a family which was entitled to use a crest. His first paternal ancestor in America was John Hurd, a native of Somersetshire, England, who came to America before the year 1640 and settled at Windsor, Connecticut. From him the line of descent is traced down through his second son, Adam Hurd, and his wife, Hannah Hurd; John Hurd and Johanna Judson; Ebenezer Hurd and Sarah Pickett Lane; Josiah Hurd and Phebe Buell; Josiah Hurd and Hannah Brown; Dan Hurd and Phoebe Conger; Stephen Hurd and Nancy Hinchman, and Theodore F. Hurd and Catherine Martha Driscoll. Two brothers, Josiah and Dan Hurd, fought as soldiers of the Continental line during the war for American independence, and their descendants are thus entitled

to membership in the Sons and Daughters of the American Revolution. The father of Albert Arthur Hurd was a prominent and influential citizen of his day in Stark County, Illinois, and represented that county in the Illinois State Legislature in 1860.

The late Mr. Hurd was educated in the public schools of Galva, Illinois, later was a student at Northwestern University, and following his graduation there entered the law department of the Iowa State University. He was graduated with his degree in 1870, and in the same year was admitted to the bar of Kansas at Junction City. He soon afterwards settled at what was then the great center for the cattle trade of the entire Southwest—Abilene. Here he soon had all the legal business he could attend to, and enjoyed the confidence as well as the patronage of some of the prominent early time citizens. The young lawyer was elected the first city clerk of Abilene. Two other men prominent in history were connected with the city administration at the same time. One of them was Joseph G. McCoy as mayor, and the other was William Hickok, better known as "Wild Bill," who was marshal.

From Abilene Mr. Hurd removed to Newton, and there had his first experience in railroad work. Soon afterward he went to Great Bend and was there in time to become the first mayor of the city, a position which he filled with distinction. He continued in general practice until 1875, in which year he came to Topeka and was made assistant attorney with the Santa Fe Railway Company. Six years later he was advanced to the office of solicitor for the State of Kansas, and that was his position until 1905, when he was made special counsel, the post which he held at the time of his death.

Executive ability was one of the chief causes for his continuous advancement. He had the power to manage varied and complicated interests successfully, without friction and without confusion. The task of special counsel of a railway is one of great delicacy and of harassing difficulties. For handling the various and unending negotiations which arose, Mr. Hurd possessed the experience, mental poise and skill in an admirable harmony. He was a glove of velvet covering the railway's hand of iron; not only covering it, but guiding it; restraining its grasp within reasonable bounds. As is naturally the case with an able "specialist," he knew about all the other side had to say, yet he listened and weighed all that was offered, and having made up his mind what was best to be done, he had the needful weight to make his pertinacious and resolute client acquiesce in his views.

In politics Mr. Hurd was a republican, but never a politician. He was a supporter of everything that promised to be good for Topeka, and his strong character and broad mindedness lent force to each enterprise with which he was identified. Although not what is known as a "mixer," he attracted men to him, and the friendships he made were sincere and lasting. A lifelong student, he was fond of literature and was a great leader both in and outside his profession. While not a church member, he was a believer in religion of a practical sort, and his charities were many, though they were often hidden from the general view. Mr. Hurd was not a fraternalist, but belonged to a number of social organizations, including the Country Club and the Topeka Club, and, of course, he was a valued member of the various organizations of his calling, including the Kansas State and American Bar associations. As a business man he was remarkably successful and accumulated a large amount of property in and around Topeka. One of his valuable estates is Sommerheim Farm, a tract of 250 acres in Shawnee

County, the improvements on which made it an ideal country home. The amusements in which a man engages are a gauge of his temper and character. Some tread the weary rounds of business or professional endeavor with ceaseless devotion, never realizing that there lies about them in field and forest, in woodland stream, in shimmering lake, a store of wholesome and refreshing recreation which would take from the round of care many of its burdens, and, while invigorating the physical powers, infuse into the spirit the sweet and elevating influence which come from contact with nature in her wild and rustic beauty. Mr. Hurd was never insensible to these rural pleasures; he always loved to get away from the city's noise and competition and be among his plants and flowers, and he made of horticulture something more than a hobby.

After suffering from bronchitis two weeks Mr. Hurd died at his home, 1134 Tyler Street, Topeka, December 20, 1915. In speaking of Mr. Hurd the officiating minister, Dr. Benjamin F. Young, said in part as follows: "The numbers of friends that are here today are evidence of the respect and love with which Mr. Hurd was regarded in his community. He was a man of usefulness in his day, serving faithfully in the office he held, keeping before him a lofty ideal of devotion to duty. That sense of duty and that lofty ideal were taught him early by his parents, who were devoutly religious people. He was intensely devoted to his home and found it always the loveliest place in the world. The mysteries of life and death appall us, when we see a man in the midst of the duties of a useful life cut off from the world, but we refuse to believe that a mound of earth on the hilltop is the end of this man of affairs, this man of wide sweeping intellect, of firm grasp on problems of the time, of generosity and ability."

December 22, 1885, Mr. Hurd was married to Miss Theodosia E. Woosley of Erie, Kansas, daughter of Alexander Jones and Mary Elizabeth (Sturdivant) Woosley. Mrs. Hurd survives her husband, as does also his brother, G. W. Hurd, an attorney of Abilene, Kansas.

JULIUS WEISS. Recently the Topeka Daily Capital had an illustration on one of its pages showing a banquet table surrounded by a group of some of the best known and most prominent veteran business men of Topeka. Underneath was a text explaining the occasion.

A part of this reads as follows: "Fifty years at the old stand, forty-seven years at the same number and still an active business man. That is something of a distinction. March 1, 1866, Julius Weiss, a young captain of calvary who had served all through the Civil war in an Illinois regiment, opened a grocery store on Kansas Avenue. Wednesday evening, March 1, just fifty years to the day, a group of Mr. Weiss' friends gathered at his home, 421 Tyler, to celebrate the anniversary with him. Everybody there felt it was a great event, and it was.

"A likeness of Mr. Weiss taken fifty years ago, with bushy hair and long moustache, so fashionable in the early '60s, judging by all Civil war photographs, was shown on the place cards. It didn't look much like the kindly man with closely cropped gray VanDyke and high forehead who sat smiling at the head of the table. It was a unique dinner party and a jolly one. Several of Mr. Weiss' fifty-year customers were there. Nowadays we call them patrons. In the group were pre-staters, early-staters and a few recent comers like E. H. Crosby and F. M.

Pelletier. Mr. Crosby didn't come to Topeka until 1880, and was called a tenderfoot when he made the fact known.''

Some interesting individual history is revealed in the career of this veteran Topeka merchant. He was born at Magdeburg, Prussia, January 25, 1838, being the only survivor of three children. His parents were Theodore and Henrietta Weiss. His father was the manager of one of the first beet sugar refineries in the Kingdom of Wuertemberg, the king of that country being a stockholder in the concern. A man of splendid education, who had studied both in his own country and in Paris, he had unusual abilities and was a splendid representative of that fine German stock which came to America about 1848. He brought with him his family in that year, landing at New Orleans, and thence going up the river in the steamboat which carried General Scott after his victorious campaign in Mexico. Establishing his home in St. Louis, for some years he followed his profession as a metallurgist and assayer. Naturally he traveled a great deal, and was one of the first to go to the lead and zinc fields of Joplin, though a permanent boom in metals in that southwest Missouri country did not come until some years later. He finally moved to Topeka, where he died. His wife passed away at St. Louis.

Julius Weiss was ten years old when he came with the family to America, and later in the same year his mother died and the family soon moved to Bond County, Illinois, where he grew up on a farm. He attended the district schools and afterwards took a course in Bryant & Stratton's Business College at Chicago.

His first experience in business came after he was eighteen years of age and in a general store at Greenville, Illinois. He was clerking in that store when the war broke out in 1861. In July of that year he enlisted in the Third Illinois Cavalry, Company B, as a private, but was later made commissary of the regiment in 1862 with the rank of first lieutenant. In 1864 he was promoted to captain of Company H in the same regiment, and continued with that command and in that rank until mustered out in October, 1865.

He saw a great deal of hard fighting and campaigning during the war. His first service was in the Southwest Missouri campaign under General Curtis, and he participated in the battle of Pea Ridge. His command was then sent to Helena, Arkansas, and from there to Vicksburg under General McClernand. He was in the battle of Haines Bluff, then crossed the river, was ordered back to Memphis, and was on duty there and at Corinth guarding the Memphis and Charleston Railway. He was in the cavalry raids in Tennessee, Mississippi and Alabama as far as West Point, where the Federals had to retreat before General Forrest. Prior to this they had made a raid to Holly Springs, where they destroyed scores of locomotives and other Confederate supplies. His term of enlistment having expired and a reorganization of the regiment being effected at Memphis, Mr. Weiss accompanied the command to Paducah, Kentucky, where he was on guard duty, and afterwards his regiment as dismounted cavalry participated in the last battle of Nashville. Captain Weiss was not present at Nashville, since he had been ordered to St. Louis to procure supplies. He rejoined his command at Cross Hollows, Tennessee, afterwards was sent to Eastport, Mississippi, where the regiment was recruited to full strength of twelve companies. It

was stationed there during the great floods of the Mississippi River in the spring of 1865. On being sent back to St. Louis the regiment was again remounted, rearmed and reequipped and was ordered to the northwestern frontier at St. Paul, Minnesota. As Captain Weiss said at his fiftieth anniversary banquet he and his comrades went out to fight Indians, but much to their disgust they saw no Indians, at least in a hostile attitude. The regiment made camp at Minnehaha Falls, and from that point went to Devils Lake, Dakota, thence to Fort Berthold on the Missouri River, back to Devils Lake, then to Red Wing, to St. Paul, and finally to Springfield, Illinois, where he was mustered out with his command in October, 1865.

After this long and interesting career as a soldier, Captain Weiss returned to Greenville, Illinois, and resumed work in a store. From there in time claimed a population of 2,500. It was really nothing more than a frontier village with scarcely any municipal improvements. Here he engaged in the crockery and grocery business, and that line he has continued ever since, though the crockery department was discontinued a number of years ago. At first the firm name was McLean & Company, but six years later became Whitton & Weiss. In 1882, owing to the death of Mr. Whitton, a change was made to J. Weiss & Company, and that title has been significant of high class business in Topeka for the past thirty-five years.

Mr. Weiss is a Presbyterian, and is a democrat in politics. In 1872 he married Miss Ella Whitton, a sister of his former business partner. To their marriage were born two daughters, Margaret and Grace. Grace married Harry Chandler, and died leaving a daughter named Margaret.

Captain Weiss' father during his professional career acquired a fine selection of minerals, which he had carefully classified. This collection descended to Julius Weiss, and in the summer of 1915 he presented it to Washburn College, and it is the most valued part of the mineralogical exhibit in that institution.

PERRY E. COOK has for more than twenty years been one of the principal carpenter contractors and builders of Topeka. His work and skill have been particularly exemplified in some of the finer residences of the city, and a large clientage have always felt a peculiar degree of assurance when any contract was entrusted to the firm of Cook & Son. The firm has also handled a great deal of the better class of repair and remodeling contracts.

A resident of Kansas for thirty years, Perry E. Cook was born in Boone County, Indiana, December 12, 1859, a son of Oscar and Charity (Wiley) Cook. His father, who was a native of Cayuga County, New York, was a farmer. After living for many years in Boone County, Indiana, he moved to Appanoose County, Iowa, in October, 1877, but after three years returned to Indiana and established his home in Hendricks County where he lived until his death on March 1, 1912. He was a republican and a member of the Independent Order of Odd Fellows. His wife, who was born in Russellville, Kentucky, died in Indianapolis in August, 1915. She was a member of the Christian Church.

Reared on a farm, Perry E. Cook acquired his knowledge of books and literary learning through the district schools of Boone County, Indiana, and the grade schools of Royalton, Indiana. With an inclination for the handling of tools, he early turned his attention to the trade of carpenter and followed it as a master workman in various places in Iowa for seven years. In June, 1886, just thirty years ago, Mr. Cook arrived in Topeka, and worked at his trade as a journeyman until October, 1889. He then entered the Santa Fe Railway shops, where he remained about five years, and from that took up the business of contracting, the business he has followed ever since. His offices since 1906 has been at 110 West Sixth Avenue, and prior to that time they were at 117 West Fifth Street.

Mr. Cook owns a substantial home at 911 Highland Avenue, where he has resided for twelve years. He is a member of the Independent Order of Odd Fellows and in politics an independent republican. He has a fine family, and some of his sons are now associated with him in business. On December 25, 1884, at Marshalltown, Iowa, he married Aranda Conger, who was born in Peoria County, Illinois, October 31, 1861. When she was about nine years of age her parents, W. P. and Mary Hann Conger, who were natives respectively of Virginia and Illinois, moved from Peoria County to Marshalltown, Iowa, where the father still resides. He has always been a farmer, and is a veteran of the Union army during the Civil war. He is a republican and his wife a Methodist. Mr. and Mrs. Cook's four children were all born in Topeka: Wilbur O., a carpenter and associated with his father; Blanche M., wife of R. A. Showers, a carpenter; Perry E., now deceased; and Herbert W., who is in the insurance business.

EDWARD C. KASSEBAUM. On the highest point of bottom land between Kansas City, Missouri, and Manhattan, Kansas, is located the forty acre farm belonging to Edward C. Kassebaum, who carries on general farming, but who, perhaps, is more widely known as a grower of water melons, and in which he has attained something more than a local reputation. This farm is situated in Menoken Township, Shawnee County, and has been brought to a high state of cultivation under the practical and intelligent efforts of Mr. Kassebaum, who has been a resident of this locality all his life and who is accounted one of the most progressive agriculturists of his township.

Mr. Kassebaum was born on a farm near Rossville, Shawnee County, February 24, 1872, the fifth of the eight children of Henry Augustus and Mary L. (Probst) Kassebaum, who were both of German parentage. Henry Augustus Kassebaum came with his parents from Bremen, Germany, when he was seven years of age and located at Cincinnati, Ohio, where the family resided for a time, and where they became friends of the Probst family. Mrs. Kassebaum was born at Cincinnati. Later the two families moved to Indianapolis, Indiana, and the children there were reared, attending first a local school and later a German school at Cincinnati. They were married in 1859 and moved to Dillsburg, Indiana, where Mr. Kassebaum operated a general merchandise store and through good business ability acquired a modest capital. Having the interests of his children at heart, and desiring to rear them in the free air of the country, Mr. Kassebaum sold his store in 1871, and, coming to Kansas, purchased 840 acres of land on the hills of Shawnee County, where he became a successful stock raiser and wheat grower. Later, he added to this land until he had 1,400 acres, which property was divided among his children in 1912. As others were forced to do, he passed through the plague of the grasshoppers and the drought, but

was a man of perseverance and persistence, and did not allow himself to be discouraged or to be turned back from his goal. His children attended school 1½ miles from the homestead, walking to and from the school in all kinds of weather, and during the summer terms assisted their father in the work of the home place. Mr. Kassebaum was a republican, but never desired to hold public office. He was a booster of his community's interests and a hard worker in all uplift matters, and was a popular member of the Rossville Lodge of the Ancient Order of United Workmen. When he died, March 6, 1914, his community lost a good and helpful citizen.

Edward C. Kassebaum received his education in the public schools and was brought up as a farmer, receiving excellent instruction from his father in all branches of agricultural work. He was married March 17, 1897, to Miss Chettie James, daughter of Squire E. T. James, a sketch of whose career will be found on another page of this work. They have one daughter, Beatrice, who is a student in the schools of Topeka.

At the time of his marriage, Mr. Kassebaum purchased eighty acres of good land not far from his father's place, and resided thereon until he moved to his present forty-acre property, located not far from Menoken, in one of the most fertile spots in Northwest Shawnee County. While general farming has occupied his attention to a large degree, he has, of late years, been particularly interested in watermelon culture, a subject of which he has made an exhaustive study, and in this direction is one of the leaders of his county. His farm has been improved with handsome and substantial buildings, and its equipment is modern in every respect. In politics Mr. Kassebaum is a democrat. He has always been public-spirited, assisting in all matters that have promised to benefit his community, and while he has never sought nor cared for office has served as a member of the school board of Silver Lake Township. Fraternally, Mr. Kassebaum is a well known Mason, belonging to Silver Lake Blue Lodge, and the York Rite and Shrine at Topeka. He and Mrs. Kassebaum are members of the Rossville Presbyterian Church, in the work of which they have taken an active part.

JAMES EDWARD CONROY. One of the largest landowners and most successful farmers and stock raisers in Riley County is James Edward Conroy, whose entire life has been devoted to agricultural activities. Mr. Conroy is progressive and enterprising, believes in thoroughbred stock and in modern methods of farming and keeps himself well informed on these subjects and thereby prospers.

James Edward Conroy was born February 24, 1862 in Pottawatomie County, Kansas. He is a son of James and Mary (Dempsey) Conroy, both of whom were born in Queen's County, Ireland. They came to the United States and were married in the State of New York. In 1856 they came to Pottawatomie County, Kansas, and there James Conroy developed a fine farm of 400 acres. He died there in 1902, at the age of seventy-nine years. His widow survived until 1906, passing away when aged eighty-three years. They were faithful members of the Roman Catholic Church. They reared two sons, Martin and James E.

James E. Conroy was reared in his native county and attended the public schools. Farming and stockraising have occupied his attention from early manhood until the present. He remained in Pottawatomie County until 1902, when he sold his farm there and removed to Riley County and settled on lands he had purchased in Ogden Township and here he has since resided. All told, Mr. Conroy owns 1,073 acres of land. The main tract is situated on the Golden Belt road, which is the most traveled highway between Manhattan and Junction City, and some distance in front of his handsome and attractively surrounded residence is a station on the interurban railway between the two cities. Such a favorable location has many advantages in the way of business and opportunities for a wider social life than a farm usually affords. A part of Mr. Conroy's large acreage is ridge land which he uses for grazing purposes. He breeds thoroughbred Hereford cattle and other high grade stock. His land is in better condition and more substantially improved than any other estate in Riley County.

In 1887 Mr. Conroy was married to Miss Catherine Glenn and they have had eleven children, eight of whom survive. In church relationship the family are Roman Catholics. In addition to being a thrifty and up-to-date farmer, Mr. Conroy is an honorable and useful citizen and a highly esteemed neighbor in Ogden Township.

CHARLES G. CARLSON. While the earlier activities of this old Topeka resident from the time he identified himself with the State of Kansas in 1886 may not be widely known, his membership in the firm of Lundgren & Carlson, contractors and builders, has been productive of work of the highest class and exemplified, particularly along the lines of the Santa Fe Railway, in several states.

The partnership of Lundgren & Carlson was formed in 1901, the senior member being Mr. A. J. Lundgren. As builders their ability is now known far and wide throughout the State of Kansas. Their first important work in Topeka was done for J. W. Gleed and they built the Devon flats and also the flat at the northeast corner of Sixth and Topeka Avenue. This firm also erected the Lafayette and McKinley schools of Topeka. For several years they were almost exclusively employed by the Santa Fe Railroad Company in constructing depots, roundhouses, hotels and stations. They put up buildings at Peabody, Mulvane, Norman, Oklahoma, Stillwater, Oklahoma, Perry, Oklahoma, and did remodeling of Harvey eating houses to the value of $85,000. They built the depot at Lexington Junction in Missouri, the station at Richmond, Missouri, and, to mention one of their most recent contracts, they put up in 1916 a large freight office at Raton, New Mexico. They also have in process of construction a station at Chillicothe, Illinois, and one at Carrollton, Missouri. The large addition to the Topeka High School in 1915 was made by Lundgren & Carlson. The firm operates in Topeka one of the city's largest planing mills. Their mill is equipped for all kinds of mill work, and a large part of its output is bank fixtures, special design work, and they fulfill all classes of contracts for plate glass work.

Charles G. Carlson was born in Warmeland, Sweden, in 1867, and was about nineteen years of age when he came to Kansas. His father N. N. Carlson, who spent his life in Sweden, was a man of considerable distinction as a landscape gardener and a special authority on various branches of agriculture. For a number of years he had charge of the grounds of several large estates, but in the later years of his life he followed farming as a regular occupation, and lived on a farm until he came to

America in 1907. He and his wife were the parents of seven children, five of whom are still living. Their names were Christine, Charlotte, Fred, Charles G., Emil, Sophia and Axel.

Mr. Carlson had more than an ordinary training before he left his native land and came to America. Besides the public schools of his native province he was for one year in a preparatory school. At the age of seventeen he found work as a fireman or stoker on board ocean going vessels and it was after some experience and several voyages in that line that he became an American resident and arrived in Topeka.

His first employment in this city was with the bridge and building department of the Santa Fe Railway Company. After one year he took up regular work in the trade of carpenter and was in the employ of some of the well known Topeka contractors, including Mr. Council and Mr. Fellows, and he was also with the Frampton Planing Mill and the Horne Planing Mill. For two years he was a pattern maker for the Capital Iron Works and then joined Mr. Lundgren in the partnership which has now been in successful and prosperous existence for fifteen years.

On August 15, 1890, Mr. Carlson married Miss Matilda Johnson. She was also born in Warmeland, Sweden, a daughter of Jonas Johnson, who came to America in 1885, but in 1898 returned to his old home in Sweden and died there April 26, 1912. He was the father of seven children, all of whom came to Kansas, their names being Hadda, Adolph, Fred, Matilda, Alfred, Ida and Sophia.

WILLIAM OWEN. Much of the pioneer history of Kansas might be written around the names Owen and Packard. The late William Owen was one of the men who came from the East in the days of the '50s for the purpose of assisting in the movement to make a free state out of Kansas. His father-in-law, Cyrus Packard, was also a prominent leader in the free state movement.

Born in Rhode Island in 1827, William Owen came to Shawnee County, Kansas, in 1856, about the time the first territorial government was organized. As a young man in Rhode Island he learned and followed the trade of carpenter, and for a time was in the same vocation in Kansas. Later he conducted a sawmill, his being one of the first mills in the territory. He also was a merchant and kept a store at Rochester. After the war he was a farmer and carpenter, but in 1880 concentrated all his efforts upon farming and continued in that work for eighteen years, when he retired from business and moved to Topeka.

Mrs. William Owen before her marriage was Olive Packard, and the Packard and Owen families lived close neighbors after coming to Kansas. Her father, Cyrus Packard, who was born in the State of Maine June 5, 1796, served as a soldier in the War of 1812. He was a man of deep religious convictions, an active supporter of the Congregational Church and carried his religious beliefs and his social principles into practical action on every occasion. At the time of the abolition movement in Maine Cyrus Packard and one other man were the only ones in their community who had the courage to speak and advocate the cause openly. Cyrus Packard was nearly sixty years of age when the Kansas-Nebraska bill was passed and precipitated the conflict for a free state in Kansas. It was his

ardent belief in abolition that caused him to abandon his comfortable home and come out to help make Kansas free.

William Owen was likewise zealously identified with the free state movement. At one time he was captured by the slave faction in Kansas and was taken to Lecompton and put in prison. A few days later the governor of the territory arrived at Lecompton, dined with the prisoner, and in a few days secured his release. Mrs. William Owen herself has many interesting anecdotes to relate concerning early days in Kansas. She recalls the fact that John Brown stopped one night at the Owen house with sixteen negroes, and Brown was not an infrequent visitor at the Owen or Packard homes. In fact everyone associated with the old underground railroad knew the Owen and Packard families. General W. T. Sherman when a young man managing the Thomas Ewing ranch boarded with the Owen family and the general with Mr. Owen's assistance built what was known for many years as the Sherman cabin.

Mr. and Mrs. Owen had fourteen children, six sons and eight daughters. Ten of these children are still living.

F. C. HOYT. As a banker in Oklahoma and Southern Kansas F. C. Hoyt is widely known and his financial ability united with his conservative judgment has placed him in the front rank of bankers in the two states. He is now a resident of Wichita and president of the Union State Bank of that city.

Though born in Keokuk County, Iowa, in 1873, Mr. Hoyt was brought by his parents in 1876 to Portis, Osborne County, Kansas, and thus grew up to imbibe the spirit and atmosphere of Kansas life. His education came partly from public schools and partly from Stockton College, and as a youth he learned the printer's trade. As a journeyman printer he worked in a number of cities throughout the country and had the usual interesting experiences of one who follows that trade.

He was among the early settlers of Oklahoma Territory, and for one year conducted a weekly paper at Taloga in Dewey County. In the same county in 1898 he engaged in the drug business at Seiling, and gave four years to that enterprise. It was at Seiling that he first entered banking, establishing the First National Bank, of which he became president, and he is still at head of that institution, which, however, is only one of the various banks with which his name is identified. In 1902 he organized the First Bank of Cestos, Oklahoma, and was its active manager twelve years. He organized the Bank of Vici at Vici, Oklahoma, of which he is now president, and he is also president of the Exchange State Bank of Burns, Kansas, and is interested in the Neal State Bank of Neal, Kansas, and the Union Stock Yards Bank of Wichita.

In June, 1914, Mr. Hoyt removed from Cestos, Oklahoma, to Wichita, and has since been president of the Union State Bank. Politically he is a republican, and while in Oklahoma was very active in that party and did much toward getting passed the Free Homes and Statehood bills. At various times he was tendered nominations for important state offices, but always refused.

ZACHARIAH RESER. Among the comfortably situated residents of Rossville, Kansas, is Zachariah Reser, one of the substantial and well known retired farmers of Shawnee County. He has been a resident of Kansas for a half century and has large possessions here acquired through his own industry.

Zachariah Reser was born in Kentucky, March 13, 1848. His parents were Wyatt and Nancy Reser, natives of Kentucky and of their thirteen children seven survive and live in Kansas, representatives of a sturdy stock from which class came many pioneers hither. When Wyatt Reser and wife packed their household goods and children in the wagon that was to carry them out of their native state, they headed for Indiana and on reaching that state located on a farm near Rising Sun. There they lived until 1866 when they were attracted to Kansas and again a long journey was made and land was secured near Topeka and on that place the parents of Zachariah Reser died in advanced age.

Zachariah Reser was eighteen years old when he accompanied his parents to this state. He had not been given many educational advantages as he was an older member of the large family and from boyhood had been obliged to work hard for his own support and to help others. He was a good son and did his duty. In the course of time he secured a homestead in Pottawatomie County and later sold it and came to Shawnee County and bought sixty acres to which he has added until he now owns 400 acres of fine land. With his wife he lives retired at Rossville.

In 1868 Mr. Reser returned to Indiana and was married there to Lizzie Meyers, who died three years later. On January 17, 1883, Mr. Reser was married to Miss Mary Alice Lemon, who was born in Ohio, and is a daughter of Henry and Sarah (Braton) Lemon. They were pioneers of an early date in Kansas, coming into the state in a covered prairie wagon in 1855. Relatives had previously settled at Holton and there they stopped and later Mr. Lemon hauled merchandise for three years between Leavenworth and Atchison. He then rented and later bought a farm and on that place he died in 1904 and his wife in 1913. Mr. and Mrs. Reser have two children: Edith, who is the wife of U. G. Stewart; and George, a young man of twenty-four years, who carries on farming on the home place.

Mr. Reser has always been a good citizen but has kept free from party ties, voting independently but intelligently and has never accepted any political office, although, as a man of keen judgment and honest and upright living, he would have made an honest record. He and wife are Christian people, members of the Methodist Church and active in forwarding its good work. Both are members of the fraternal order of Knights and Ladies of Security.

CHARLES WESLEY PETER. A valuable, well conducted farm is that owned by Charles Wesley Peter, one of the substantial and respected citizens of Jackson Township, Riley County, a property largely developed through his own efforts and handsomely improved. Mr. Peter has been a resident of Kansas for forty-four years.

Charles Wesley Peter was born November 16, 1850, in Jackson County, Indiana. His parents were Jonas and Barbara (Bruenner) Peter, who were born in Switzerland. They were married in the United States and then settled in Jackson County, Indiana, where the mother died after the birth of four children: Susan, Mary, Charles Wesley and William F., the only survivor being Charles Wesley. Jonas Peter contracted a second marriage, with Barbara Rachel Littican, and they had three children: Eliza, Emma and George, the first named being deceased.

Jonas Peter was a successful farmer in Jackson County, Indiana, where he died in 1868, at the age of fifty-three years. In 1859 he had visited Kansas and bought 500 acres of land in Fancy Creek Valley, a part of which is included in the present farm of Charles Wesley Peter.

Ten years after his father had purchased the Riley County land, the late William F. Peter, of whom a biography appears in this work, came to Kansas and located on the property, and in 1872 Charles Wesley followed. The two brothers united in developing the lands and lived together in a primitive cabin until 1879, when Charles Wesley erected his comfortable frame residence.

In 1880 Charles Wesley Peter was married to Miss Amelia Knostman, who is a daughter of William Knostman. William Knostman was born in Hanover, Germany, September 7, 1830. When six years old he was brought to America by his parents and grew to manhood at Brownstown, Indiana. In Cincinnati, Ohio, he gained his first mercantile experience, and from 1857 to 1867 was in business at Catlettsburg, Kentucky. In the latter year he came to Manhattan, Kansas, where, until 1895, when he retired, he was active in the mercantile business, in which he was succeeded by his son, E. L. Knostman.

Mr. and Mrs. Peter have one son, Charles F., who is now engaged in farming in Fancy Creek Valley, where his father owns 360 well improved acres. General farming and stockraising is carried on with satisfactory results. Mr. and Mrs. Peter and their son are all members of the Methodist Episcopal Church. In politics Mr. Peter supports the men and measures of the republican party but merely as a good citizen desirous of stable government for he has no political ambition for himself. He has been identified with the Masonic fraternity for many years and as a Master Mason stands well in his lodge.

JOHN FRANKLIN HASKELL is the Topeka and Kansas representative of the greatest creamery organization in America. He is general manager and vice president of the Beatrice Creamery Company, consolidated, with headquarters in Topeka.

Both he and his brother George Everett have long been prominently identified with this business. His brother George E., who is president of the Beatrice Creamery Company, lives in Chicago. George was the founder of the industry at Beatrice, Nebraska, about 1890. He pushed the enterprise with so much success that it soon outgrew the limits of its home city, but the company still bears the name of that Nebraska town. The headquarters were removed to Lincoln, and since 1913 the main offices have been in Chicago. It was the first centralized creamery business and is today the largest institution of its kind in the United States.

John Franklin Haskell was born in Mitchell County, Iowa, October 12, 1862, and four years later his father died. The fact of his father's death is mentioned at this point because John F. Haskell soon had to shift for himself, and his business success and prominence has been due to his own efforts rather than the training and environment of early youth. His father was Josiah Haskell, a native of Michigan, where he was born in 1836, and an early settler in the State of Iowa. Josiah and his brothers Thomas and John were soldiers in the Civil war, Josiah serving four years in Company K of the Twenty-seventh Iowa Volunteer Infantry. He himself became a permanent invalid as a result of his service, while his brother John was killed in battle. The brother Thomas went through the war and returned home, but had at least one narrow escape from death. That makes an interesting incident. Thomas Haskell with four other Union soldiers were detached as guards for the Confederate prisoners. Along with the Confederates they also had under arrest one Union man who was being kept for a misdemeanor. While they were guarding their prisoners a colored woman came along selling pies. The guards bought some of the pies, ate generously of them, and in a few minutes they were all taken violently ill. Though it was not so diagnosed at the time, it was undoubtedly a case of ptomaine poisoning. All the guards died within a few hours except Thomas, who survived the painful ordeal. He and his comrades were somewhat isolated from the rest of the Union troops, and had it not been for the instinctive loyalty displayed by the Union soldier who was also under arrest the prisoners might easily have overpowered the stricken guards and made their escape. This Union soldier, taking in the situation, at once picked up a musket and stood guard over the Confederates until relief came.

Josiah Haskell married Miss Lodica Prince. She was born in New York, and a short time before the Civil war her father removed to Missouri. He was a Union man in a state where the predominant opinion was strongly hostile to his belief, and he found it convenient to leave Missouri and move to Iowa. Josiah Haskell and wife were the parents of four children, two sons and two daughters: The daughters were Ida May and Nellie, the former of whom died in 1887 and the latter in 1908. Reference has already been made to the older son George Everett, president of the Beatrice Creamery Company.

John Franklin Haskell had to content himself with a brief schooling. He left home and began earning his own way at the age of thirteen. At first he was employed on a farm and afterward found a job in a flour and feed mill. In 1880 he went to Wisconsin and began taking contracts to supply fuel for the tow-boats on the Mississippi River. These boats were engaged in towing logs and lumber rafts and that old phase of the lumber traffic is something that has long since disappeared. Giving up that line of business in 1888 Mr. Haskell entered a general store at Lynxville, Wisconsin, and for three years was engaged in buying and selling eggs.

In 1892 he went out to Beatrice, Nebraska, and found employment with the Haskell and Bosworth Creamery Company, which was the nucleus of the present great enterprise of the Beatrice Creamery Company. After a short time he was sent to Cuba, Kansas, and given charge of a branch house of the company for two years, and then was located at Herington, Kansas, taking charge of the large branch house there and being given full charge of the entire Kansas business. In 1904 Mr. Haskell removed to Topeka and became manager of the produce department of the Continental Creamery Company, which not long afterward was reorganized as the Beatrice Creamery Company. During 1914 he was president of the Topeka Commercial Club and was president of the Topeka Traffic Bureau from the spring of 1914 until the spring of 1916.

In 1882 Mr. Haskell married Miss Helen Lorraine Peck of Lynxville, Wisconsin. Mr. Haskell has some children of whom he may well be proud. The seven children born to their marriage were: Leona Violet, Clinton Howard, Helen Lorraine, Frankie Delphine, Everett Erskine, Willard Vernon, and Gladys, who died in childhood. Leona lives at home with her parents. Clinton, who married Miss Ethel Miller of Topeka, has charge of the office force of the Beatrice Creamery Company in Denver. Helen, who lives at home, was graduated from Washburn College in 1915. Frankie also graduated at Washburn in 1915 and is now pursuing post-graduate studies in the Columbia University. Everett is a merchant at Lyndon, Osage County. Willard is a student in the Topeka High School.

ROBERT M. BAKER was a pioneer Kansan. Nearly fifty years ago he identified himself with the frontier in Phillips County and helped to develop that wild prairie section into one of the finest agricultural districts of the state. In the year 1900 he moved his home to Topeka, where he lived in retirement until his death.

He was born at Mount Vernon, Ohio, in 1839. His father James Baker had a specially adventuresome and interesting career. James was born in the historic town of Battle, forty miles from London, England. As a young man a romantic experience caused him to run away from his home in England and come to America. Here his first employment was in assisting the troops of General Andrew Jackson to erect the breastworks of sand bags and cotton bales at New Orleans to repel the British invasion. A little later he went into Ohio, and there married the young lady on whose account he left England. The late Robert M. Baker grew up in Ohio, received his education there, and during the Civil war he and his brother Wilson did hazardous duty as bridge builder in Sherman's army, being attached to the pioneer corps. His brothers Isaac and Thomas were privates in the Union army. In 1868 Mr. Baker joined the Missouri Conference of the Methodist Church at Chillicothe, having early in life devoted himself to the cause of the ministry. He finally moved out to Kansas and located eight miles southwest of Phillipsburg, and three miles west of Glade on the Solomon River bottoms. He lived in Phillips until in 1900 removed to Topeka, where his death occurred in 1910 at the age of seventy-two.

Mr. Baker married Lucina Lawrence. Her father Jonathan H. Lawrence was a native of Morgan County, Ohio. Her grandfather Lawrence lived in a cabin on the coast of Maine during the War of 1812. When a British man-of-war attempted to land a small boat filled with sailors there, he as a sharpshooter wounded several and the sailors were glad to get back to their vessel. Subsequently he was promoted to the rank of lieutenant, and commanded an American ship which captured a British treasure vessel, and he was paid $4,000 as his share of the prize money. The British government subsequently offered $1,000 reward for his capture dead or alive. The Lawrence family came to America before the Revolution, and four brothers of the name served as patriot soldiers in that war. Mrs. Baker's brother Zacharia Lawrence was also a soldier in the Civil war and gave his life for his country, dying at Bridgeport, Alabama, when only sixteen years of age. He was a member of Company H in the Fourth Iowa Volunteer Infantry.

To the marriage of Mr. and Mrs. Robert Baker were born thirteen children, twelve sons and one daughter. Nine of the sons are still living named Warren, Harvey, Charles, Lewis, Benjamin, Arthur, Grant, Clarence and George. Clarence and George are members of the Kansas National Guard, in Battery A of Topeka, and are now doing service along the Mexican border. Warren is in the oil fields of California. Harvey was managing a greenhouse at Kansas City, Kansas. Charles is fireman at the city waterworks in Topeka. Lewis is in the Santa Fe shops at Topeka. Benjamin is a landscape gardener at the Children's Tuberculosis Hospital at Alamogordo, New Mexico. Arthur is employed by the Santa Fe and Grant is a foreman for the Topeka Street Railway Company. The son Harvey Baker was a member of Company D in the Twenty-first Kansas Infantry during the Spanish-American war. The daughter, Ella, died when two years of age.

WYLIE WHITE COOK. During a period of more than thirty years, Hon. Wylie White Cook has been almost constantly before the people of Kansas as the incumbent of public positions, and that he still retains in marked degree the confidence and respect of Kansans is evidence of his worth, fidelity and integrity, for the duties of the various offices which he has held have in nearly every case directly affected the welfare of the community. In Mr. Cook's case it has almost invariably been a case of the office seeking the man, for with but one exception in his long career his election or appointment has come to him without solicitation on his part, a fact which makes his record all the more remarkable. Mr. Cook, who has been a resident of Kansas since July 1, 1881, and is now living at Topeka, was one of three children of Levi and Margaret (White) Cook, and was born at Noblesville, Hamilton County, Indiana, July 1, 1859.

The family of which Mr. Cook is a member originated in Scotland, from which country the progenitors came to America in 1640. On the journey to this country, the father died and was buried at sea, and the mother, with several children, established the family in the East, from whence it scattered to Pennsylvania and North Carolina. It is from the latter branch that Wylie W. Cook is descended. His grandfather, Isaac Cook, was born, reared and married in North Carolina, and although of good old Quaker stock and a disbeliever in war was a member of a patrol regiment in the American army during the War of 1812. In 1826, Isaac Cook struck out for the untamed West, his children riding in the wagon, while he and his wife walked the entire distance to Indiana. Long before they had reached the Western Reserve they found the country sparsely settled, and as they came further and further toward the setting sun they were more and more frequently harassed by Indians and endangered by wild beasts. However, they eventually reached their new home in Henry County, Indiana, where they built a rude log cabin in the wilderness, cleared a farm after years of hard labor, and rounded out lives of usefulness which were characterized by honest labor and helpfulness to their neighbors that won them the respect and esteem of their community.

Levi Cook, father of Wylie W. Cook, was born in 1832, in Henry County, Indiana, six years after his parents' arrival. Although other settlers had commenced to arrive, the country was still wild and unpromising, and his boyhood was passed in helping his father to put the land in readiness for planting. His education was limited to attendance at the district schools, the primitive ones of his day, but in after years he became a man of broad general information, and of prominence in his community. For a number of years he served as county commissioner by popular vote of the people, was county assessor for a long period, and also acted as justice of the peace for many years. His home was at Noblesville, the county seat of Hamilton County, and there his death occurred. Mr. Cook was highly respected in his community as a man of sterling qualities and strength of character, a devout Christian, and an active worker in the movements founded by the Methodist Church.

Wylie White Cook received his education in the district schools of Hamilton County, Indiana, which he attended for three months each winter, the greater part of the remainder of the year being given to assisting his father in the cultivation of the home farm. He was thus engaged until he was sixteen years of age, when he received his teacher's certificate, and took charge of the school which he had himself attended. After two years spent as an educator, he turned his attention to mercantile lines, becoming a clerk in a dry goods store at Noblesville, and while there was married February 19, 1879, to Miss Mary L. Sanders, a native of Indiana. They became the parents of five children, of whom four are living: Minnie, who is the wife of R. S. Holding, of Cuba; Alberta L., of Honduras, auditor of the United Fruit Company; Lois M., wife of F. N. Moseley, connected with the United Fruit Company, at Port Antonio, Jamaica; and Edith, the wife of George L. Maltby, of Trenton, Missouri.

In July, 1881, Mr. and Mrs. Cook moved to Kansas and located in Labette County on a farm, where they remained until 1884, in which year Mr. Cook was appointed by the county commissioners to the office of assistant county clerk. In the following year he was elected county clerk by vote of the people and held that office for two years, following which he was again nominated but met with defeat at the hands of the Farmers Alliance Party. During this time he was located at Oswego, and at the expiration of his term of office he became outside representative for the Deming Investment Company, a capacity in which he acted for two years. From that time forward until 1895 he acted either as deputy county clerk or deputy county treasurer, and in January of the year mentioned was appointed by the late Hon. George E. Cole to the post of assistant state auditor, with headquarters at Topeka. After two years in this capacity he returned to his Labette County farm (which he still owns), and remained there until his reappointment to the office just mentioned, January 1, 1899, by Mr. Cole. He remained in that office until 1901, when he became interested in the purchase and sale of bonds, and in 1902 helped to organize and was elected treasurer of the Banking Trust Company, of Kansas City, Missouri, one of his associates being John W. Breidenthal. Mr. Cook was treasurer of this, the pioneer trust company of the state, until 1907, when he retired to become a special accountant, being engaged in this work until he was appointed, in 1909, to the post of chief of police of Kansas City, Kansas, by Mayor Guyer, under whose administration he served. Two years after retiring from that post, he was appointed commissioner of elections for Kansas City, by Governor Stubbs, and held this office until January 1, 1913, when he resigned to accept the position of assistant state treasurer under Earl Akers. He is now state treasurer. Mr. Cook is pardonably proud of the fact that aside from the office of county

treasurer in Labette County, his various official positions have been tendered him, and he has never on any occasion with this exception sought office. His services in his various positions have been singularly free from criticism, even by members of opposing parties, and his record will bear the closest inspection.

Mr. Cook is a member of the Blue Lodge, Chapter and Commandery of the Masonic order; of the Modern Woodmen of America and the Ancient Order of United Workmen, of Oswego; of the Loyal Order of Moose, of Topeka; and of the Improved Order of Red Men, of Kansas City. He has always been a loyal adherent of republican principles. He belongs to the First Methodist Church, as does Mrs. Cook, who takes an active and prominent part in religious and charitable work.

HENRY SHELLENBAUM was one of the most prominent pioneers of Riley County. He and others of his relationship were among the first to occupy and develop that beautiful tract of Kansas known as the Fancy Creek Valley. His energy helped transform a portion of the virgin landscape into fertile fields, but even more important than his material success was the sterling character of his manhood, and he passed on many of his virtues to his children and other descendants who are now active in the present generation of Kansas.

Henry Shellenbaum was born at Zurich, Canton Winterthur, Switzerland, October 1, 1833. He came to the United States with his parents and brothers and sisters at the age of twenty-one. His father died and was buried at sea. The widowed mother and her children located at Seymour, Indiana.

In 1856 Henry Shellenbaum with two other natives of Switzerland, Edward and Solomon Secrist, journeyed from Jackson County, Indiana to Kansas. Kansas was a territory and a hotbed of the critical troubles growing out of the free state movement. In November of that year the trio in quest of land joined a band of Indians on a hunting expedition through East and Central Kansas. Their purpose in joining the Indians was the better to explore and discover a suitable and favorable location. Thus as it happened they came upon the beautiful valley of Fancy Creek. After viewing it they were not long in making up their minds to establish permanent homes.

Henry Shellenbaum acquired a homestead in the Fancy Creek Valley. In connection with this homestead there is an interesting story told. The first white settlement had been made in Riley County in 1853. Arriving about three years later Henry Shellenbaum and his companions were thus among the very early pioneers. In the preceding year Gardiner Randolph and his grown up family of sons, daughters and sons-in-law had located near the mouth of Fancy Creek and had preempted and claimed much or nearly all of the fertile valley. Henry Shellenbaum sought as his claim a homestead that had been entered in the name of a minor son of Randolph. Then arose one of those family land disputes of the early days. The contention was carried before the land agent at Junction City. That official proposed to settle the matter in favor of the claimant who first succeeded in laying upon the disputed tract a foundation for a residence. Young Randolph had a horse, but Shellenbaum had to depend only upon his sturdy legs. Randolph was therefore the hare of the familiar fable, while Shellenbaum was the tortoise. With a fleet steed at his command Randolph decided that he would await until the next morning. Shellenbaum, taking time by the forelock, set out from Junction City immediately after the decision had been rendered by the agent, and under the cover of night walked across hills and valleys, encountering numerous obstacles, put proceeding directly and indefatigably to his destination. At daybreak he was on the scene, and without pausing began the work of laying the foundation of a log cabin. Early the next day young Randolph arrived on the scene. With much chagrin he had to witness the excavation and the foundation laid by his rival, and he withdrew leaving Henry Shellenbaum in possession of his original homestead in Riley County.

With that homestead as the scene of his original enterprise, Henry Shellenbaum lived out his long and useful life in Fancy Creek Valley.

April 24, 1861, he married Elizabeth Siebecker. The Siebecker home was not far from the Shellenbaum place. Wedding journeys in that early day of Kansas were always more or less primitive affairs. This one was probably distinctive in the form of vehicle if in nothing else. The carriage which the young couple used consisted of the trunk and crotch of a fallen tree. Some boards were nailed on the timbers forming the crotch, while the trunk of the tree served as the tongue, on each side of which was a vigorous young ox. Seated on this rude fabrication the young bride rode rejoicing to her future home, while her young husband walked alongside and drove the oxen. Their wedding supper was also a meal which their descendants may well remember. It consisted of "specht," a German word then current in that section of Kansas and meaning sidemeat bacon. With this meat was corn bread and coffee made of parched corn.

Henry Shellenbaum and wife became the parents of seven children. Five are still living: Anna M., Frank H. and Ida, all in the Riley community of Riley County; Edward, editor and owner of the Manhattan Nationalist; and Mrs. Sophia E. Vawter of Blue Rapids, Kansas. The deceased children were John J., who died in 1885, and Mrs. Louisa C. Vawter, who died in 1908. Mrs. Henry Shellenbaum was called to her reward in 1906, and her husband passed away September 24, 1914, when almost eighty-one years of age.

The first home of the family was a rude hut of unhewn logs. This primitive cabin later gave way to a more substantial one. Henry Shellenbaum combined a great deal of intelligence and thrift with the faculty of hard labor, and it is not strange that he prospered. In time the family home was built of the stone which entered into the fabric of so many early dwellings in the Fancy Creek Valley. There through years of hard work, in sunshine and storm, drought and plenty, Henry Shellenbaum continued his peaceful progress and was long accounted one of the most substantial citizens in the northern part of Riley County. He was equally a factor for good citizenship and for those things that count in the welfare and progress of a community.

One of his sons is Mr. Frank H. Shellenbaum, who has tried to live worthily of the standards set by his honored father, and is one of the leading farmers and stock raisers of Riley County. He was born on the old homestead near Randolph and was reared and educated there, being well trained for the vocation which he has followed. Besides his interests as a farmer and stock raiser he is president of the Citizens State Bank of Randolph.

ORRIN ELLIOTT WALKER. A definite and conspicuous place should be given the name of Orrin Elliott Walker on the list of men of Kansas who have not alone helped their own great state to grow but who have also been factors in the movements which have assisted in the development of other commonwealths. Coming to Kansas in 1879 and to Topeka in 1887, Mr. Walker left the Sunflower state in 1893, when he went to officiate in the opening of the Cherokee Strip, in Oklahoma, and in the community he made his home until 1898, when he returned to Topeka, where he now lives in retirement.

Mr. Walker is a native of New York, having been born at the small town of Deposit, in Delaware County, September 22, 1847, a son of Aaron S. and Elizabeth (Hamblet) Walker. On the maternal side, his great-grandfather was Aaron Stiles, who was a soldier of the Continental line during the Revolutionary war, after the close of which he became a Baptist clergyman. One of the five children of his parents, Mr. Walker lost his mother when he was but ten years of age, and was given only a meagre education in the country schools. His father married again, removed in 1870 to Warren, Pennsylvania, and engaged in the business of a building contractor, and it was at that place that Orrin E. Walker learned the stone mason's trade, serving a three-year apprenticeship. This vocation, however, did not appeal to him and he accepted the position of chief clerk in a general merchandise store at Sheffield, Pennsylvania, where he remained three years, then returning to his old home in the Empire state. He was now prepared to enter business on his own account, and accordingly began buying and shipping stock, gradually increasing the scope of his operations as he added to his capital. In 1879 he shipped to Wabaunsee County, Kansas, 300 head of Short Horn calves, and the success of this venture led to his coming to Kansas. In 1887 he located at Topeka, where he was identified with various lines of enterprise until 1893, the year in which the Cherokee Strip was opened. Mr. Walker, William P. Leach, now of Sulphur Springs, Texas, and I. V. Ladd, who is now a resident of Detroit, Michigan, were appointed by Secretary of the Interior Hoke Smith, under President Grover Cleveland, as the board of townsite trustees, September 16, 1893, to prove up the townsite of Newkirk, Oklahoma. No one was to be allotted a claim if it was proved that they had ever been on the Strip previous to the opening. Going on to the Strip on a handcar, the trustees passed the border line, where a great concourse of people had gathered to make the race for lands and townsites, which eventually proved a veritable Marathon. Mr. Walker satisfactorily and efficiently discharged the duties of trustee for two years and was chairman of the board. At the end of this time the office was abolished. He then took up a claim of a quarter-section of land outside the town of Newkirk, on which he proved up, and, after improving, sold in 1898. He then returned to Topeka and purchased the farm which he now owns, in Mission Township, Shawnee County, and established himself as a dairyman. He was successful in this venture and continued to be similarly occupied until 1915, when he rented the farm to his manager and retired from active participation in business affairs. His farm is located at Gage Park. Mr. Walker has taken a great interest in the development of Gage Park and it was largely through him the animals in the park were secured, and many of the animals he himself bought.

Mr. Walker was married January 19, 1873, at Deposit, New York, to Miss Loretta Whitaker. Mr. Walker is a member of the Blue Lodge, Chapter, Thirty-second Degree, Scottish Rite, York Rite and Shrine of Masonry, and he and Mrs. Walker belong to the First Presbyterian Church, in the work of which Mrs. Walker takes an active part, being a member of the various organizations connected with the church. One of Mr. Walker's greatest friends was the late John Sargent, Sr., and it is his belief that he posesses the last letter written by him before his tragic death, which occurred at Topeka.

JOHN CLARE. The name of John Clare recalls one of the very early territorial pioneers of Kansas. This family, of Irish origin, settled in Eastern Kansas about the time the original Kansas-Nebraska bill was being considered by Congress, and from that time to the present members of the family have shared their fortunes with the fortunes of the Sunflower State, have been worthy members of various communities and have done their share in carrying forward the work of advancement and progress.

The late John Clare was born in Queens County, Ireland, in 1836. His father Michael Clare first brought his family to America about 1840. In the City of Boston he taught school for several years, but then returned to the old country. In 1851 he came a second time to America, and located in Washington, D. C. In 1854, before the first territorial government of Kansas was organized, he located in Leavenworth. He lived there for eleven years, and in 1865 moved to Atchison County, establishing his home on a claim seven miles south of the city of Atchison. Thenceforward he took a very prominent part in the community of Mount Pleasant, where he organized the first public school and became its teacher. Michael Clare was born in Ireland in 1800 and died in 1875 on the homestead that he had improved at Mount Pleasant.

John Clare was eighteen years of age when the family came to Kansas in 1854. Thenceforward he was actively identified with those movements which eventually made Kansas a free state. He and his brother subsequently were employed by the government in the freighting service. Both became wagon masters, and conducted a number of government trains between Fort Leavenworth and Fort Laramie, Wyoming. They were engaged in that hazardous occupation for four years, and their children recall many thrilling experiences they would relate of their life on the plains.

After the war John Clare settled down to farming at Mount Pleasant in Atchison County. In 1869 he married Miss Margaret D'Arcy, a native of County Wishlaw, Ireland. She had also come to Kansas in the very early days. To their union were born nine children, five daughters and four sons: Michael, John, William, Charles, Ella, Maud L., Margaret, Frances and Agnes. Michael, John and William all own farms in Jefferson County, Kansas. The son Charles is a member of the Topeka fire department, at Station No. 4. Margaret is Mrs. Krall of Atchison. Maud L., Frances and Agnes still live at home in Topeka. The last years of his life John Clare spent in Jefferson County. He was quietly pursuing his vocation as a farmer when death came to him as the result of an accident. In 1910, following his death, Mrs. Clare moved to Topeka and bought the home at 700 Lane Street, where she died in 1914. That home is still occupied by their daughters.

ROBERT E. LAWRENCE was one of the pioneers and one of the important upbuilders of the City of Wichita. The land he pre-empted from the Government and used for farming and stock raising purposes many years is now included within the city limits, and much of it is built over with residences, business houses and institutions. By strenuous effort and much self denial in early days, he acquired a liberal prosperity, but dispensed it liberally and left his impress on much of the city's progress.

He was of New England birth and ancestry, and was born at Canaan, Connecticut, December 17, 1847. He died at Wichita January 28, 1911, after a long and useful career. He grew up on a farm, graduated from a boarding school in Southwestern Massachusetts, and at the age of twenty-two, in 1869, started for the West. He left Massachusetts with only $2.50 in money.

He possessed some of the Yankee ingenuity and commercial faculties which enabled him to get along in all conditions and among all sorts of people and earn a respectable livelihood. He paid his way as far as Neponset, Illinois, by selling stencils. During the winter spent at Neponset he taught school, and saved enough of his earnings to buy a pair of horses. These horses he drove through to Wichita and arrived in that frontier village in May, 1870. He at once pre-empted 160 acres and made that the scene of his first undertaking as a Kansas farmer. That 160 acres now surrounds the Kansas State Masonic Home, and the home and grounds occupy a portion of his original quarter section. The team of horses he drove through was stolen in the early fall of his arrival and in the fall of 1870 he returned to Illinois and taught school, but came back to Kansas in 1871 and began breaking the prairie soil with a yoke of wild Texas steers. By hard work and good judgment and foresight he kept adding to his holdings until at one time he owned nearly a section of land, all of which is now included within the city limits of Wichita. In the early days he was also in business as a freighter from Wichita to Emporia, until the railroad reached Wichita in 1872.

He was largely successful as a cattle breeder and dealer, and he imported a number of Polled Angus cattle from Scotland, and for many years made a specialty of that breed. His interests also extended into Oklahoma Territory, and from 1894 for about ten years he operated a farm in Kay County, where he continued his operations as a cattle breeder and raiser.

In Wichita, as that city developed, he erected and owned a number of buildings, both for business and residence, and for several years conducted a real estate office. He built the main part of the Masonic Home for a residence, and later sold the property to the Masons. He was also active in securing the Garfield University at Wichita, and donated the land on which its buildings stand. Garfield University is now Friends University.

It was due to his prominence in business affairs that political honors came to him as a matter of course. At one time he represented his district in the State Legislature, and for years was a member of the school board and also held other county and city offices. He was an elder in the First Presbyterian Church from the time it was organized until his death. On September 2, 1873, Robert E. Lawrence married

R. E. Lawrence

Laura Smith of Sandisfield, Massachusetts. Mrs. Lawrence now occupies the old home at 1011 North Topeka Street. Six children were born to them, and the four now living are Charles S., Harry A., Harriet A. and Ruth L.

Harry A. Lawrence, who for a number of years has been a factor in the business life of Wichita and in other parts of the Southwest, was born at Wichita December 5, 1884. He attended the city schools and in 1903 graduated from Lewis Academy of Wichita, and in 1906 finished the course at Hanover College in Indiana.

On leaving college he entered the employ of Davidson & Case Lumber Company as auditor for their Oklahoma business. In May, 1913, Mr. Lawrence and his brother Charles S. bought the Orient Lumber Company, immediately reorganizing it as the King-Lawrence Lumber Company, which they now conduct with Harry A. as secretary and treasurer. This company now has seven lumber yards in Kansas and Oklahoma, and it is one of the leading concerns of the kind in the two states. Harry A. Lawrence is also a director in the Farmers & Bankers Life Insurance Company and the Citizens Building & Loan Association.

On December 31, 1913, he married Bertha Hartwell, daughter of Senator James H. Stewart of Wichita. They have one daughter, Margaret Alden, born January 19, 1915.

GEORGE W. SOUTHERN has been a resident of Manhattan over thirty years and is one of the prominent business men of that city. He is the type of man who never waits for opportunity but goes out and finds it. Everything he has undertaken he has done well, and therefore stands deservedly high in the esteem of his many old-time acquaintances and friends in Riley County.

A native of the City of New York, where he was born March 16, 1866, he is a son of James and Louise (Bridger) Southern. His father was a native of England and of English stock. His mother was born in New York State and her mother was a Rockefeller.

Reared in New York, George W. Southern learned the trade of carriage trimmer. He was still engaged in that line of work when he arrived at Manhattan, Kansas, March 28, 1885. That city has ever since been the scene of his business and home associations. He soon gave up his trade to engage in the oil business, and for six years operated an oil wagon. His next enterprise was the opening of a furniture stock, handling both new and second-hand furniture. In 1898 he and D. C. Hults formed a co-partnership in the furniture and undertaking business. Four years later, on the death of Mr. Hults, Fred Wall bought his interest and became the partner of Mr. Southern. This was a mutually agreeable partnership until 1908, when it was dissolved, Mr. Wall taking the furniture department and Mr. Southern devoting himself thereafter exclusively to undertaking. He is now one of the leading funeral directors in Kansas, and his business has been conducted with gratifying success. He has made it a point to secure the most modern equipment and carries complete stock, and in addition the personal skill and care which he exercises over his business has been perhaps the chief cause of his success. Mr. Southern is generous almost to a fault, is kind and courteous to everyone, and is thorough in his profession and in all business affairs.

For eight years he served on the Kansas State Examining Board for Undertakers, and in 1915 was president of the Kansas State Funeral Directors'

Association. Politically he is a democrat, and though reared in the faith of the Episcopal Church now attends with his wife the Christian Science denomination. He is widely known in fraternal circles. He is a Knight Templar Mason, a member of the Mystic Shrine and has attained the eighteenth degree in the Scottish rite. He has also had a prominent part in the Independent Order of Odd Fellows, the Knights of Pythias, the Modern Woodmen of America and the Benevolent and Protective Order of Elks. Mr. Southern took the initiative in procuring a charter for the Elks Lodge at Manhattan and is its past exalted ruler.

He has been three times married. His first wife was Emma Hope, who died leaving one daughter Alice. Gertrude Tennant, his second wife, died leaving a daughter Ruth. For his present wife Mr. Southern married Cora Berkey. They are the parents of one son, Robert.

BION M. McCORMICK. A prosperous farmer and representative citizen of Zeandale Township, Riley County, is found in Bion M. McCormick, whose beautiful farm of 160 acres is devoted to general agriculture. He was born September 30, 1867, on this farm, and is a son of Armstead Thompson and Anna (Allen) McCormick.

In recalling the honorable pioneers of this section of Kansas, the name of the late Armstead Thompson McCormick comes quickly to mind. He belonged to that band that may be called the pathfinders in Riley County, coming to this section years before the Civil war, accepting hardships, showing courage and resourcefulness, founding homes and improving conditions and in passing out of life, leaving honorable names and substantial records of having lived.

Armstead Thompson McCormick was born near Huntington, West Virginia, August 18, 1832. His parents were Levi and Phebe (Stuart) McCormick, of Scotch-Irish lineage but natives of Virginia. After their marriage they removed to Wayne County, in what is now West Virginia, and there they passed the rest of their lives. Their family contained eleven children, ten of whom survived to mature years. From this family came a pioneer of 1854 to Kansas, John McCormick making a permanent settlement in Zeandale Township, Riley County, in 1855, and in the fall of the same year he was followed by his brother, Armstead T. McCormick. In the spring of 1856 Armstead T. purchased 160 acres of land in Zeandale Township and on that land lived during the rest of his life with the exception of three years spent as a soldier in the Union army during the Civil war. He enlisted in Company K, Eleventh Kansas Infantry and proved his valor on many a battle-field. On returning from the cares and dangers of army life he resumed civil duties as a farmer. He had come to Kansas a young man seeking future independence and found it here through industry and reasonable prudence. From the raw prairie he developed one of the best farms in the county and prospered in every branch of agriculture. His life was exemplary. He was a devoted husband and father, a good neighbor and popular as such and a citizen above reproach. Although never very active in politics, he possessed force of character and was a strong factor in the republican party for many years.

Armstead T. McCormick was married November 27, 1865, to Anna Allen, who was born in Columbiana County, Ohio, November 11, 1842, and still survives. Her parents were Benjamin and Phebe Allen, who came to Riley County during the period of the Civil war. Four children were born to this marriage, two sons and two daughters: Bion M., Orlen, Phebe, now Mrs. R. V. Allison of Salina, Kansas, and Sadie, now the wife of Frank Short of Topeka, Kansas.

Bion M. McCormick grew to manhood on his father's farm and attended the nearest schools as opportunity offered. In addition to carrying on general farming he has done a large business in raising and dealing in cattle. Under his judicious management the old homestead farm has yearly increased in value, and all told he has 320 acres.

In 1890 Mr. McCormick was married to Miss Ida Hafer, who was born at Wheeling, West Virginia. In 1870 she accompanied her parents to Kansas, in which state they passed their closing years. Her father, William B. Hafer, followed agricultural pursuits. Mr. and Mrs. McCormick have three children: Hazel, Donivan and Kenneth. In politics Mr. McCormick is a republican but not an office seeker. He belongs to the Methodist Episcopal church, and fraternally he is identified with the Masonic bodies at Manhattan, Kansas.

EDWARD BUCKMAN. A few years ago Edward Buckman retired from his farm in Shawnee County, where he had spent the most profitable years of his life, and is now living retired at his home 1516 Guthrie Street in Topeka. The Buckman family has played a very worthy part in developing the lands of Kansas since pioneer times, and Mr. Edward Buckman has also found opportunity at different times to exercise his influence for good in local affairs.

He was born on a farm in Columbiana County, Ohio, June 26, 1853, one of the four children born to Thomas and Susan (Howell) Buckman, both of whom were natives of Pennsylvania. Of these four children the two now living are Edward and his sister Mercy, Mrs. W. H. Coultis of Topeka.

In 1869 Thomas Buckman and his family and also his brother A. Harding Buckman brought their families out to Kansas, locating on adjoining farms in Shawnee County. Thomas Buckman and family for three years lived on seventeen acres on West Sixth Street in Topeka, and in 1872 moved out to the land which in the meantime he had broken up with teams of oxen and horses, and thereafter he gave all his time and energy to the improvement and cultivation of this place. The life and character of the late Thomas Buckman were such that they deserve more than passing mention in any history of Kansas. Politically he was a whig and afterwards an equally active republican. Back in Ohio he held some offices in the city of Alliance, and after coming to Shawnee County he was sent to represent the county in the State Legislature in 1876-77, served as county commissioner during 1886-90, and always gave liberally of his time and means for the support of enterprises that would bring good to the community. He was a charter member of the Grange, and was also affiliated with the Independent Order of Odd Fellows and the Masons. Besides other public service he was a justice of the peace a number of years. Though largely self-educated, he had a remarkable memory, and experience gave him a fund of information and breadth of judgment, so that men naturally reposed their trust in his word and in his judgment. He was reared in the Quaker or Society of Friends,

but later became a Presbyterian and was a deacon in the church in Kansas. Thomas Buckman passed away after a long and useful life in March, 1900.

Edward Buckman was about sixteen years of age when he journeyed to Kansas with other members of the family. He had received his early education in Alliance, Ohio, and he also attended school at Topeka. After school he took his place on his father's farm, and made only one brief excursion outside of agriculture. That was in 1882, when he opened a grocery store on the southwest corner of Tenth and Topeka Avenues. With the burning of this store in 1885, he lost his entire investment, and then resumed farming, where a more abundant success awaited him. He took charge of the old homestead, then consisting of 240 acres, and later added to it until he owned and managed 400 acres, and with this as a foundation, and as a result of hard work and intelligent management, he gained the competency which enabled him in 1913 to retire and move to his city home in Topeka.

Mr. Buckman is an honest, straightforward citizen, stands on his own merits, and his fellow citizens in Shawnee County recognize that he is a man who can be trusted. For ten years he was a member of his local school board, served as township treasurer three years, and is now treasurer of School District No. 22 at College Hill. For twenty years he has been a member of the Ancient Order of United Workmen, is a member of the Grange and the Anti-Horse Thief Association. His wife is a member of the Christian Science Church.

On March 20, 1878, he married Mary L. Howe of Topeka. To their marriage were born six children, one of whom died in childhood. The others are all living in or around Topeka, their names being William Penn, Edward O., Ralph Addy, James Vernon and John Greenleaf.

MRS. HENRIETTA FULFORD (WILSON) KINLEY. In the developing of the beautiful city of Topeka, Kansas, many people who had been born in other states took part and it is surprising how large a number were natives of Illinois. As a rule they were well educated and accustomed to the refinements of life and in their new surroundings their influence was progressive and beneficial. One of these families bore the name of Fulford, a name that became well known at Topeka and which is yet identified with the city's best interests. A well known and highly esteemed member of this sterling old family is found in Mrs. Henrietta Fulford (Wilson) Kinley, residing at No. 1616 Polk Street, Topeka.

Mrs. Kinley was born in Canada and raised at Watseka, Iroquois County, Illinois. Her parents were Abel Fulford and wife, highly respected residents of Iroquois County. They were the parents of eight children and those who reached mature years were: Abel King, Jonathon, Elizabeth, Melissa, Catherine and Henrietta. Abel King Fulford died at Topeka, Kansas, at the age of sixty-seven years, in 1913. He enjoyed a large measure of public confidence and frequently was elected to city offices and was so highly esteemed personally that it was said that everyone was his friend. At one time he filled the office of street commissioner. More than forty years ago he built a house at No. 420 Clay Street and there he died. This house is the home of his brother, Jonathon Fulford. Elizabeth Fulford became the wife of John Gregory. Melissa was married first to Austin B. Lee, who died in 1906 and her second marriage was to Charles Nicely, a well known, substantial citizen of Wabaunsee County, Kansas, for some years but now of Topeka. He is a veteran of the Civil war. Catherine became the wife of Henry Bernard, now a' prosperous farmer in Paulin, Kansas, and for many years an officer of the Topeka Police Department. The parents of the above family lived to the age of eighty-six years and died at Topeka. They were most worthy people and are remembered by their children with the tenderest affection.

Henrietta Fulford attended school in Iroquois County and remained under the paternal roof until her marriage with Robert B. Wilson. He belonged to a very prominent family of Champaign County, Illinois. Mr. Wilson died in 1912. They had a family of eleven children and the following survive: Charles, Ethel, Elmer R., Victor Hugo, Osborne, Glenn, Irvin and Harvey. Gilbert, Leonard and Bell died in childhood. Charles Wilson is a farmer in North Dakota. Ethel is the wife of John R. Wier, of Ashkum, Illinois. Elmer is a railroad man and lives at Rossville, Illinois. Victor Hugo is a member of Company B, Third Regiment Illinois National Guard and is now in camp on the Mexican border. Osborne is a resident of Watseka, Illinois. Irwin was graduated with the class of 1916 from the Watseka High School and will enter the state university at Champaign. He is a young man of great promise. Harvey is attending the home school.

In 1913 Mrs. Wilson was married to Evan Gale Kinley who was born on the Isle of Man. He came to the United States when seventeen years old and has made his own way in the world. He learned the wagon-building trade at Cleveland, Ohio, and from there came to Leavenworth, Kansas, in 1876. In 1885 he located at Topeka and for thirty years has conducted a business here that he has built up honorably. In 1909 the Ford Motor Car Company made him their district agent and, notwithstanding some adverse conditions in the business, he has done exceedingly well. He is a man of quiet manner and unassuming address, honorable in business and sincere in his friendly feeling for others and has a very wide circle of business and personal well wishers.

ELMER BIRDELL GIFT, a native Kansan, spent his active years in educational work. He is now city superintendent of the public schools of Manhattan, and has been a teacher or a student in higher educational institutions continuously for the past twenty years.

He was born on a farm in Smith County, Kansas, April 28, 1874, a son of John and Rachel Ann (Akers) Gift. His parents came to Kansas from Iowa in 1873, settling on a farm. His father was a native of Pennsylvania of German lineage, while his mother was born in Ohio of Scotch and English ancestry. Their respective parents were early settlers in Jefferson County, Iowa, and John and Rachel were married in that state.

The only son in a family of eight children Elmer B. Gift spent the years of childhood and youth on a farm. He was educated in the rural schools, and in 1895 graduated from the high school of Mankato, Kansas. His enviable place in educational circles and his thorough scholarship is the result of many years of alternate teaching and study. What he earned in one season of teaching was extended in a following course of study, and since leaving high school he has paid his own way.

After graduating from high school in 1895 he

spent two years in a country school. Entering the Kansas State Normal at Emporia, he completed the full course in science and graduated in 1900. The fall of that year found him as superintendent of the city schools of Conway Springs. In 1902 he completed the teachers' course at Emporia, and for four years was a teacher at Valley Falls, Kansas.

In the autumn of 1905 Mr. Gift entered the University of Kansas as a student, and in the following year was made instructor in the department of education. In 1907 he graduated A. B. and in 1908 received the degree Master of Arts from the University.

Mr. Gift spent five years as superintendent of the city schools of Alma, and then for one year was Normal Training High School inspector under the state superintendent of public instruction. From the superintendency of the schools of Hiawatha, where he remained two years, he was called to his present post as superintendent of the Manhattan schools in the fall of 1915. Besides the work in the various educational institutions already referred to, Mr. Gift has taken post-graduate work in the University of Chicago, and has also benefited by experience as a traveler. He spent several months abroad in the British Isles and in Continental Europe. He is a member of the Kansas State Teachers Association, of the National Educational Association and the Kansas Schoolmasters Club. Many of his friends know him as a writer, and he has contributed articles both on educational and other subjects to magazines and the current press. He is a Knight Templar Mason and an active worker in the Methodist Episcopal Church. In 1908 Mr. Gift married Miss Mary A. Wentworth. She was born in Kansas, a graduate of Lindsborg College, and has also taught school. They are the parents of two sons, Wentworth and Edgar.

JOHN CHARLES FREY is a dairy farmer in Riley County. He is making a success of that business because he knows how, not only from experience but by close study, and he also brings to his work the indispensable faculty of industry and constant supervision of every detail.

He might well be called the architect of his own destiny. The second oldest of a family of twelve children, and his parents being people of moderate circumstances, he felt the urge of responsibility when only a boy and did almost a man's part in the fields when other children of his age were attending school. Consequently he had limited advantages in the matter of books and schooling.

These early years of toil and industry were in Kansas, to which state he was brought when eight years of age. He was born at Tippecanoe in Miami County, Ohio, April 3, 1870, a son of Michael and Zena (Hauserbrook) Frey. He is of that substantial German stock that in this country and everywhere has shown its capabilities for the hardest problems of life. His parents were both natives of Germany and after their marriage in Ohio lived on a farm for some years and in 1878 came out to Kansas. Their first destination was Junction City, and not long afterward they located on a small farm in Geary County. Four years later they removed to Riley County, settling on a farm in Ogden Township, which was their home until 1894. In that year they returned to Junction City, where the father died in 1904 at the age of fifty-six and where the widowed mother still resides.

Of the twelve children five died in early childhood. The others, all living, are as follows: John C.; William J., of Junction City; Michael, postmaster at Junction City; Mrs. Lida Gerhardt, of Idaho; Mrs. Margaret Grant, of Texas; Hannah, Mrs. Hoyt, of Junction City; and Henry, who also lives in Idaho. The father of these children was a butcher in Germany, but after coming to Kansas indulged in that vocation only to the extent of performing some work for his neighbors. He reared his family on a farm, was a man of excellent character, and was the owner of 240 acres in his home farm.

Having spent most of his early life in Riley County, John C. Frey remained in Ogden Township, and employed all his time and energies in farming, stock raising and feeding up to 1911. In that year he came to Manhattan Township, and has since conducted a modern, sanitary and profitable dairy farm. In politics he is a stanch republican. During his residence in Ogden Township he served as a member of the township board and on the death of the county commissioner from his district he was appointed to fill out the unexpired term. He is a member of the Baptist Church, of the Independent Order of Odd Fellows and of several beneficiary orders.

In 1892 Mr. Frey married Eliza Brewer, daughter of Jesse J. and Ernestine (Green) Brewer. Her father, a native of Ohio, was one of the honored pioneers of Riley County, and after coming to Kansas enlisted for service in Company A of the Ninth Kansas Cavalry. Mr. and Mrs. Frey are the parents of six children: Jesse J., a graduate of the Kansas State Agricultural College; Bertha, Minnie, John, Lester and Wayne.

C. B. GOODRICH. A life of quiet effectiveness, marked by a record of many duties well done and many responsibilities faithfully fulfilled, was that of the late C. B. Goodrich, who died in Lawrence in 1910 at the age of sixty-six. He was one of those quiet unassuming men, rarely known to the world in general, but worthily filling the niche in the affairs of life allotted to them.

Of Canadian nativity, born at Sarnia, he was brought to the United States when very young and was reared in and about Kankakee, Illinois. The first service in his quiet routine came with the outbreak of the Civil war. He enlisted under the stars and stripes as a member of the One-Hundred and Fifty-ninth Illinois Volunteer Infantry, and as a private soldier did his part and share in preserving the Union.

After his marriage to Mary E. Misner, he came to Kansas in 1879, and located near Valley Falls. By good management and industry as a farmer he accumulated a competence, and about 1898 moved to Topeka, where he lived until 1906. He then moved to Lawrence, where he spent his remaining years with his family, honored and respected for his many sterling qualities. He never aspired to public life, but in the round of commonplace accomplishment and in the faithful and intelligent performance of every task that was allotted to him he left a record which may well be envied and admired by the generations that follow him. He read extensively, was an intelligent observer, was loyal to his principles and was especially devoted in his friendships.

Fred E. Goodrich, son of the late C. B. Goodrich was born near Valley Falls, Kansas, in 1881, and spent the first seventeen years of his life there,

receiving his education in the public schools, and later attending the high school at Topeka. While at Salina he learned the milling business, and on returning to Topeka in October, 1911, became identified with the Shawnee Mills, as manager. On July 12, 1916, he accepted the position of manager of The Arkansas City Milling Company, at Arkansas City, Kansas, one of the largest milling plants of the state. Fred E. Goodrich married Miss Josephine Van Amburgh.

ALBERT D. BAUER. One of the veterans of the printing trade and an old time publisher in Kansas, Albert D. Bauer acquired his first experience in "the art preservative of all arts" in a Topeka print shop. That was nearly forty years ago, and for the past twenty-three years he has lived continuously in Topeka.

Mr. Bauer was born in the historic old seat of the Mormons in the Middle West, Nauvoo, Hancock County, Illinois, March 6, 1863. His grandfather John Bauer Sr. was born in Hesse Darmstadt, Germany, coming to America in 1820 and locating as a pioneer in Stark County, Ohio. He was a vineyardist there and engaged extensively in the wine making business. In 1840 he moved with his family to Nauvoo, Hancock County, Illinois, from which locality the Mormons had been only a short time departed. Before leaving the old country John Bauer Sr. married Miss Eber, a native of Hesse Darmstadt. To them were born a large family of fifteen children, twelve of whom grew to manhood and womanhood, and seven of them are still living in the year 1916, thus proving the wonderful vitality of this stock.

John Bauer Jr., father of Albert D., was born in Stark County, Ohio, in 1834. A private school gave him a liberal education, and in early manhood he became a traveling salesman for clothing. He followed that business in various states of the Union, and was a pioneer traveling representative. His death occurred at Butte, Montana, in 1891. In 1857 he married Miss Prudence W. Hussmeyer of St. Louis, Missouri. Her father was a member of the German colony of substantial farmers near St. Louis. John Bauer and wife had four son and two daughters: Alonzo, Frank, Albert, Edward, Anna and Kate. Alonzo, who lives in Topeka, is a traveling engineer for the Santa Fe Railway. Frank died at Wilkesbarre, Pennsylvania, in 1915; Edward is a farmer at Raymondsville, Texas; Anna married Dr. William McVey, one of the prominent specialists in medicine and surgery at Topeka; Kate is Mrs. J. W. Bolt, whose husband is connected with the Burlington Railroad Company at Kansas City, Missouri.

The early life of Albert D. Bauer was spent in his native county of Illinois, but at the age of fifteen in 1878 he came to Kansas and soon afterwards found employment in the printing office of the old Kansas Farmer, whose proprietor was Major J. K. Hodgson. There he served out his apprenticeship and mastered all the intricacies of the printing trade. Practically every printer that learned his trade thirty or forty years ago had at least a period of journeyman experience. Mr. Bauer on leaving Topeka began traveling, following his trade at different places, and in the course of this experience visited nearly every state in the Union.

In 1894 he returned to Topeka and bought out the printing establishment which he has owned ever since. Many periodicals and pamphlets have been published in his shop and in the course of many

years a number of country weeklies have also been printed there. For twenty-two years Mr. Bauer has published a Kansas medical journal. He has a thoroughly equipped office for all kinds of commercial printing, and his success is due to the fact that he has served his patrons adequately.

Mr. Bauer is affiliated with a number of fraternal orders, including the Knights and Ladies of Security, the Woodmen of the World, the Sons and Daughters of Justice and the Fraternal Aid.

I. F. SARVER. It was due to his personal popularity and his high business standing that I. F. Sarver was elected sheriff of Sedgwick County in 1914. It was the first and only office for which he was ever a candidate, and he was elected by a large majority by his wide circle of friends in both parties, and re-elected in 1916 by a large majority.

Sheriff Sarver is almost a native son of Kansas, having been brought to the state when two years of age, and is thoroughly typical of the splendid spirit of this commonwealth. He was born in Champaign County, Ohio, January 24, 1869. In 1871 his parents Mr. and Mrs. Samuel C. Sarver came to Kansas and located near Topeka in Shawnee County. His father is now a resident of Topeka and still owns a section of rich farming land in Shawnee County, besides some valuable business and residence properties in Topeka.

Besides an education in the common schools, I. F. Sarver spent two years in Washburn College at Topeka. He grew up on a farm and while he has a host of loyal friends he has always been strong, vigorous and self reliant in carving out his own destiny. In 1898 he came to Wichita, and for several years was associated with his father-in-law in the hotel business there. As Wichita is one of the chief livestock centers in Kansas, he took up the livestock commission business there, and gave his efforts successfully to that work for six years. During 1911-12 Mr. Sarver was captain of police in Wichita, and it was his creditable record in that office which undoubtedly contributed to the substantial majority which was paid him when he became a candidate for sheriff.

Mr. Sarver is a republican, is a member of Queen City Lodge No. 296, Independent Order of Odd Fellows, and of Wichita Encampment No. 29, for the past seven years has been president of the Sons and Daughters of Justice and is a member of the Sons of Veterans.

On January 2, 1898, he married Miss Mary R. Guyer of Wichita. They have one child, Josephine Bell, born October 3, 1903. Mr. and Mrs. Sarver are active members of the Wichita Presbyterian Church.

JOHNSON S. WILLIAMS is the pioneer of the pioneers. When he arrived he made settlement in what is now Riley County. Besides reclaiming a portion of the land from the wilderness he did other effective work in making Kansas a free state, and afterwards fought for the perpetuation of the Union in the Civil war. Some years ago he retired from active responsibilities, and now resides in comfort at his home at 1203 Colorado Street in Manhattan.

He was born in Henry County, Kentucky, October 25, 1834, and is now at his eighty-third birthday. His parents were Hanson N. and Ann L. (Bell) Williams, both natives of Henry County, Kentucky. The Williams family is of Welsh origin, and first settled in Virginia, though what part of the state they occupied is not now ascertainable. John Williams, the grandfather, came across the mountains

into Kentucky accompanied by his brother Hanson. They were pioneers of the Blue Grass State, John locating in Henry County and his brother at Lexington.

When Johnson S. Williams was still a boy his parents removed to the neighborhood of Covington, Kentucky, where his father engaged in raising truck and small fruits for the Cincinnati market, across the Ohio River. His father was very successful in that line of business, though he rented land instead of owing it. At one time he kept from forty to fifty men employed on his truck garden and in his fruit orchard. It was on that farm that Johnson S. Williams spent his early years. He attended the public schools in the winters, but the rest of the year was spent helping his father and for several years before reaching his majority he was his father's overseer.

It was his early ambition to acquire land for himself and make a home in the West. Led by that desire he came west to Kansas about the time great numbers of people from states both north and south were directing their course into this section of the West for the purpose of solving the problem whether Kansas should be a free or slave state. It was in the second week of March, 1855, that Mr. Williams and others landed in what is now Ashland Township of Riley County. There he drove stakes to a quarter section of land, but subsequently relinquished his right to a land company which proposed to lay out and develop the Townsite of Ashland. When this company failed the land passed to individual ownership, and subsequently Mr. Williams acquired it by purchase. Thus his homestead has considerable historic interest in that section of Riley County. Mr. Williams lived on his farm of 200 acres many years, still owns it, and it represents a large share of his Kansas experience.

In October, 1907, at the age of seventy-five Mr. Williams retired from active farming, and since then has had his home in the City of Manhattan. After getting established in Kansas he wrote a glowing letter of description to his father, and the latter was induced to come also to the new country and arrived with his family in November, 1855. The parents located in Ashland Township, and spent the rest of their days there, being laid to rest in the Ashland cemetery. They were the parents of the following children: Elizabeth, now deceased; Johnson S.; William H.; John W.; Philip M. and Thomas E. All these children were born in Kentucky and four of the sons offered themselves as soldiers in the war for the preservation of the Union.

In 1862 Johnson S. Williams enlisted in Company A of the Ninth Kansas Cavalry, and with that gallant organization he served thirty-five months. The record of his brothers as soldiers is as follows: William H. was in Company G of the Eighth Illinois Infantry; John W. was in Company L of the Eleventh Kansas Cavalry; and Philip M. in Company D of the Third Colorado Cavalry.

For fifty-six years Mr. and Mrs. Johnson S. Williams have traveled life's highway together. They were married on December 9, 1869. Mrs. Williams, whose maiden name was Ruth J. White, was born in McKean County, Pennsylvania, November 29, 1840, a daughter of Dyer and Cynthia M. (Hoag) White. The parents, natives of New York State, arrived in Kansas in 1860, first settling in Miami County and afterwards moving to Riley County where they died. To the marriage of Mr. and Mrs. Williams were born six children: Ernest D., now a successful physician in Kansas City, Kansas; Edith M., deceased; Emmett

A., a farmer of Riley County; Walter F., a ranchman of Colorado; Charles C., a twin brother of Walter, also a Riley County farmer; and Catherine L., the wife of John Graham, a farmer in Riley County.

The patriotism which made Mr. Williams a good soldier in the trying days of the '60s has characterized his entire life in the community of Riley County. He is an active member of the Riley County Historical Society, is a republican, having adopted those principles about the time the party was organized, but has frequently cast his independent vote according to the dictates of his judgment. While he is a member of the Christian Church Mrs. Williams belong to the Baptist denomination.

DAVID L. STAGG. There are many fine farms and prosperous farmers in Riley County and quite a number of them may be found in Ogden Township. One of these is David L. Stagg, who was born in Russell County, Kansas, April 17, 1880, but has spent almost all his life in Riley County. His parents were James and Anna E. (Haynes) Stagg.

James Stagg was born in New Jersey, June 25, 1841, and died in Riley County, Kansas, October 8, 1910. In Illinois he was married to Anna E. Haynes, who was born in Ohio, September 23, 1843, and died in Riley County, September 7, 1905. Four children were born to them in Illinois namely: Harry K., May, Grace and Josephine. In 1877 James Stagg removed with his family from Illinois to Kansas and settled in Russell County and they resided there until 1882 removing then to Riley County. In 1887 Mr. Stagg located on a farm in Eureka Valley, at the foot of what is now known as Stagg Hill, and continued there until within a short time before his death which occurred at Manhattan, where he had established his residence, retiring from a long and active career as a farmer. To his first marriage two children were born after coming to Kansas, David L. and Edith H. His second marriage took place in 1908 to Alice Bergstresser, who survives him.

David L. Stagg was only two years old when his parents came to Riley County and thus almost his entire life has been concerned with the interests and affairs of this section. He attended the public schools and under his father was well trained in agricultural pursuits. He has devoted himself to farming and stockraising and has met with very satisfactory returns.

Mr. Stagg was married March 16, 1910, to Miss Phebe Myers, who is a daughter of Joseph Myers, a prominent citizen of Riley County. They have one son, Joseph Frank. Mr. Stagg supports the candidates of the republican party but is no seeker for political honors for himself. He takes a commendable interest in all that concerns his state and county, and agricultural progress interests him greatly, as he is wide awake and progressive in this line.

ROBERT D. BLAINE, who has had his home in Topeka for a number of years and also maintains a business office there, has been one of the builders of Kansas, his part in .the development of the state being particularly reflected in the magnificent prosperity which during the past quarter of a century has come to the southwestern corner of Kansas. Pratt County in the Arkansas Valley will always have particular reason to remember Mr. Blaine's early activities and influence he directed to the proper development of the resources of that section. For what he has done

and for what he has caused others to do Robert D. Blaine must be accounted one of the foremost men of the Sunflower State.

He was born in Bellefontaine, Logan County, Ohio, a son of William and Agnes (Wallace) Blaine, both natives of Scotland. His father was born in Kirkcudbrichtshire and his wife in the city of Dumfries, both coming when quite young to Logan County, Ohio.

Doubtless it was the inheritance of the Scotch characteristics of patience, determination and energy that have taken Robert D. Blaine with success through all the variations of his experience. He grew up on his father's farm in Logan County, acquiring a common school education, and later took some special courses to better qualify him for commercial affairs.

At the age of twenty, accepting Horace Greeley's advice, he followed the western trail by railway and stage as far as Pawnee City, Nebraska. There he was employed as foreman on an extensive stock ranch. This experience gave him the capital which in 1882 enabled him to start out independently. That year he made his first purchase of land in Kansas, in Nemaha County, and from its subsequent rise in value it proved a profitable investment.

The first tide of immigration into Southwestern Kansas began to flow about the year 1885. Mr. Blaine did not allow this movement to escape his notice. His attention was attracted to Pratt County, which though without railroads, had a vast tract of rich agricultural land. Kingman was then the terminus of the railroad, and it was forty miles to Pratt up the beautiful valley of the Ninnescah. Pratt had few houses and there were no improvements in the entire county beyond a sod house here and there. The manner of transportation was the mountain stage coach operated by the late Colonel or Cannon Ball Green.

Arriving by this old time vehicle, Robert D. Blaine spent a few days looking about the new village, and then buying a claybank pony, saddle and bridle, he started out for the purpose of investigating conditions with a view to establishing an agricultural and machinery business. The months of fall and winter were given over to a personal observation of the entire country within a radius of sixty miles. He then came to the conclusion that it would be a very opportune time and place to engage in the business of furnishing machinery to the settlers of that district.

In the spring of 1886, associating with him his brother the late D. W. Blaine, he established warehouse and yards covering almost a block in the City of Pratt, and had transported by wagon over a distance of forty miles twenty-six carloads of machinery. The quantity of machinery brought in is in itself the best evidence not only of his courage and resolution, but also of his foresight and good judgment based upon the extensive observations he had made. How well justified he was in this investment is found in the fact that the entire lot of machinery was sold the first season. The firm of Blaine Brothers soon established branch stores at different points in the surrounding territory, and the operations of the firm soon placed them among the foremost merchants of Southwestern Kansas.

They operated not only as dealers in machinery but also invested much of their surplus capital in nearby land. Land at that time was considered rather high in price from $1.25 to $10 per acre, but the same land now commands $40 to $75 per acre. Those familiar with the history of Western Kansas during the past thirty years are well aware that the period of ten years from the time Blaine Brothers entered business was one of great uncertainty in crops, of numerous failures in individual cases, and of general financial depression all over the United States. If there were any solid financial rock in that district of Kansas in those years it was the firm of Blaine Brothers. They took their full share of responsibility and hardship in connection with bad crop years, but they stood with their farmers and neighbors through every vicissitude. On two or three occasions they furnished seed to the farmers who had no money with which to buy. In 1889 they distributed a carload of corn for seed to the farmers, and in 1890 brought in sufficient seed wheat to plant about 4,000 acres. Some good crops followed, and the farmers who had received assistance, with few exceptions, paid the cost prices of the seed. It should not be forgotten that the Chicago, Rock Island & Pacific Railway, through the instrumentality of its able adviser Mr. M. A. Low of Topeka, was equally generous in upholding the hands of the farmers in these hard times, and also contributed liberally of seed and in other ways to the deserving settlers. Again and again Blaine Brothers had to extend the time of payment on their notes, and were always ready to assist the settlers beset by circumstances and the misfortunes which were not of their creation.

While the land was very rich, the chief problems with which the early settlers in Pratt County had to contend with was the lack of rain fall and after several years had been spent more or less unprofitably in endeavoring to make the soil produce according to the standard methods long prevailing in the eastern and better watered territories, the people gradually began adapting their methods to soil and climate. A careful study was made of the soil, tests being carried out in different sections, and it was soon learned by experience and observation that the general character of the soil was an intermixture of sandy loam and gypsum. It is well known that gypsum is a natural fertilizer. In later years improved machinery, including tractors and gang plows, have cultivated this soil with great profit, and there has apparently been no depreciation after twenty years of constant croppings in the fertility and productiveness of the land. One fact that was proved during the drought period from 1892 to 1896 was that ordinary clover and timothy could not be depended upon in that locality. Then alfalfa was introduced, and for a number of years Pratt County and that vicinity has been contributing a large share of the Kansas alfalfa crop. Other experiments were carried on for the purpose of discovering some nature of plant which would furnish roughness for the cattle and other livestock. Out of these experiments was introduced kaffir corn, and this led to the trial of other crops of Asiatic origin. Since then kaffir corn has been regularly grown on nearly every farm in Southwestern Kansas.

Mention should also be made in this connection of the various methods of utilizing the grain or seed of the kaffir corn. As Pratt County was one of the chief centers of origin for the kaffir corn crop of Kansas, and as Mr. Blaine himself had a considerable share in introducing this crop, it will not be out of place to notice some things that are perhaps not familiar to the people of the state at large. The grain of the kaffir is now widely used for feeding livestock, but a number of years ago experiments were made for the purpose of testing its qualities as a bread stuff. Several grist mills were adjusted to the experiment, one of these being located on the banks of Elm Creek in Barber County, Kansas. This mill was operated by an aged Frenchman named Koffman. Samples of his flour were sent East and exhibited in public places. The flour was used in various forms and experts gave their testimony that the batter-cakes made from it were equal if not superior to those made of Ohio and Pennsylvania buckwheat flour.

It was thirty years ago when Mr. Blaine identified himself with Southwestern Kansas, and many other developments since then might be noted. Pratt County is now one of the greatest wheat producing counties in the state. The City of Pratt, the county seat, has a population of 4,500 people and some of the finest homes in Western Kansas. The city has a fine sewer and water system, owns its own electric light plant with which it furnishes power to the ordinary industries and lighting to the homes of the city. There are three railway lines in the county seat and five through the county. Some of the best natural roads in Kansas are to be found in Pratt County. In road building an excellent use has been discovered for the gypsum deposit. When used in its pure natural state for surface dressing it becomes very hard on exposure to the weather, and the material is constantly growing in favor among the roadmakers of that county.

Other wonderful discoveries have from time to time been made in the Arkansas Valley. At a depth of about 2,000 feet below the surface is a vast sea of salt. Above that a great strata of gravel and sand, and at a depth of from 40 to 125 feet is a lake of soft water which has been calculated as flowing to the southeast at a rate of about two miles an hour. This volume of water is so far above the salt that is not impregnated and is therefore a great source of water supply. Anyone who has lived in Southwest Kansas knows that a well sunk to this subterranean stream gives not only water in abundance but water of most excellent quality. Throughout Pratt County are now seen on every hand fine modern houses and barns, and some of the largest ranches have private elevators with a capacity of from 5,000 to 20,000 bushels, built for the express purpose of handling the crops of that individual farm. The county is also dotted with silos and herds of fine dairy cattle.

It is only natural that Mr. Blaine should regard with special gratification these various improvements that have taken place since he moved out to Pratt County thirty years ago. Incidentally it should be stated that what is true of Pratt County is true in similar degree of other sections of Central and Western Kansas.

Mr. Blaine was very active in making Pratt County a good place to live. He was elected and served on the city council, and took an active part in ridding that town of objectionable characters, who in the early days flourished in Southwestern Kansas. Such characters, including bootleggers and gamblers, soon found that they were not welcome, and the town was soon cleared of its joints. About twenty years ago the first campaign was undertaken for the building of sidewalks. It is now believed that no city of its size in Western Kansas has more or better first class cement walks. Mr. Blaine was a diligent worker and liberal with his time and money in securing the location of the division point of the Rock Island Railway System at Pratt. Night and day with others he worked in order to secure the bonds for that purpose, and these bonds have proved a splendid investment for the entire community. The relationship between Pratt and the railway have always been mutually agreeable and profitable, and it is a case where advantage to one side has proved equally an advantage to the other. Pratt is now one of the important freight and passenger stations on the Rock Island El Paso line.

Naturally Mr. Blaine was led into politics in Pratt County. For several years early in the present century he served as republican central committeeman. Prior to that time Pratt County had not fared very well in the legislature in the matter of patronage. A fusion representative had been sent from the county for several years, and this representative gave more attention to national affairs than to home talent. It was therefore decided to send a level headed quiet sensible man who would see that the county was properly represented and given its appropriate share of legislative attention. Dr. R. C. Hutchinson, who then resided at Coats, but is now connected with the Kansas Dental College at Kansas City, Missouri, was nominated and elected representative of Pratt County. He was familiar with the network of fresh water streams and lakes which formed the Ninnescah River in Pratt County. That suggested a splendid place for a fish hatchery. A bill was introduced in the Legislature, and after a great deal of mirth on the part of others who did not know the conditions, it was passed with a small appropriation. This was the beginning of one of the largest fish hatcheries in the world. The Ninnescah has never been found wanting. When other streams in Kansas were dry the Ninnescah had a great volume of water between its banks, and more than sufficient to maintain the fish hatchery pond. The hatchery has always been considered one of the leading institutions of Pratt County. Mr. Blaine was an active supporter of Doctor Hutchins in this project, and he lent his active support to the doctor in his candidacy for a second term.

For himself, Mr. Blaine has always been too busy to accept the numerous honors of politics and public affairs which have been offered him and has been content to see that such honors were well bestowed upon others. After nearly twenty years of active connection with Pratt Mr. Blaine determined to make his home in the capital city of Kansas. However, he thought too much of his Pratt County holdings and his old friends there to sell out all his interests. His home on Ninnescah Street, which he occupied for many years and which was one of the fine places of its kind, still remains in his ownership. On coming to Topeka Mr. Blaine bought a fine building site at 1125 Taylor Street, and erected there the modern home in which he and his family reside. He has also made investments in local real estate, and owns a number of properties outright.

The secret of his success is doubtless his ever close relationship with the farming element, and the manner in which he cooperated with the farming settlers around Pratt has been duplicated many times in later years. He has given financial aid to farmers and has assisted many persons around Topeka to engage in the dairy business. His public spirit is above question. He has been an active member of the Commercial Club since coming to Topeka, for almost ten years served as chairman of its immigration committee, and through that committee has exercised an important influence on the welfare of

the city. In municipal politics he has worked for the purpose of getting good men elected to office. Mr. Blaine has also been a liberal contributor to colleges and schools and every movement that affects the vital life and welfare of his home city or state. Several occasions at his own expense he has published important bulletins of information concerning Kansas, Topeka and Shawnee County.

For twenty-five years Mr. Blaine has been a member of the Masonic Order, is a past master of his lodge and is affiliated with the Scottish Rite Consistory No. 1 of Topeka, and takes an active part in its reunion. He attends the Presbyterian Church and is a member of the Brotherhood Bible Club of the Sunday School.

He has an interesting family, consisting of his wife Mrs. Lela L. Blaine, his son William J., who is associated with Frank B. Brown in the publication of the Kansas Trade Unionist, and Robert A. Jr., who is now attending the Polk School. Though fifty-seven years of age Mr. Blaine shows no weight of years, spends practically every working day in his office, and has that spirit which enables a man to grow old gracefully and with little evidence of the passing years. He owns a motor car and another means of keeping himself young is to participate actively in the recreations and sports of the younger generation. In the summer season it is not uncommon to find him with his son Robert, twelve years of age, and several of the latter's young companions, swimming in Gage's Park. An annual vacation has also been one of his rules, and a great lover of travel, he has visited almost all the important points in the United States. Topeka is now considered his permanent home, and there is no more loyal citizen of the capital or of the state than Robert D. Blaine.

A. J. WHITMORE is an old timer in Kansas, having been identified with this state most of the time since 1885. He has been well known both in business and in public affairs, and for a number of years has lived in Topeka.

He was born in Lake County, Illinois, in 1859. His father William D. Whitmore was born in Seneca County, Ohio, in 1836, a son of James Whitmore, who was born in Lockport, New York, in 1794. James Whitmore was an early settler in Ohio, and in 1837 took his family to Illinois and secured a homestead in the extreme northeastern part of the state, not far from Chicago. He died on his old homestead in 1877 at the advanced age of eighty-three. James Whitmore married Martha McNitt. They became the parents of four sons and one daughter. William D. Whitmore at the age of twenty-one married Ann C. Bangs of Lake County, Illinois, a daughter of Herman Bangs. She was a lineal descendant from Edward Bangs who came to Plymouth, Massachusetts, in 1623. A son of Edward was Arthur, who in turn became the father of James, and the latter the father of Herman Bangs, the father of Mrs. William D. Whitmore. William D. Whitmore joined the Union army very early in the Civil war. He enlisted in Company B of the Ninety-sixth Illinois Volunteer Infantry under Col. Thomas E. Champion. His regiment was attached to General Grainger's Reserve Corps. His regiment was also in active service with General Thomas and at the Battle of Kenesaw Mountain near Atlanta, Georgia, on June 20, 1864, William D. Whitmore was killed, and his body now rests in the National Cemetery at Marietta, Georgia. On leaving home he left behind his wife and small son, who was then about five years of age.

This son is Mr. A. J. Whitmore of Topeka. Mr. Whitmore spent the first thirteen years of his life in Lake County, Illinois, and then went to Cedar Rapids, Iowa. From that city in 1879 he went to Chatsworth, Illinois, became a druggist, and after five years returned to Cedar Rapids and from there went to Nebraska. He was first located at Wymore and later was in the lumber business at Odell.

In August, 1885, Mr. Whitmore removed to Kansas, locating at Hanover, where he continued the lumber business. In 1894, while still in business, he was elected register of deeds of Washington County, and filled that office with great credit to himself for four years. On leaving the office he again took up the lumber business, but in 1899 removed to Topeka, where he was appointed chief clerk to the secretary of state, George A. Clark. He filled that office four and a half years during the administrations of George A. Clark and J. R. Burrows. When Mr. Clark became state printer Mr. Whitmore filled the office of assistant state printer for two years.

With the exception of two years spent in Colorado Mr. Whitmore has lived in Topeka since 1899, and for several years has been a traveling salesman. In 1899 he married Elnora F. L. Gilson of Blue Rapids, Kansas. The Gilson family are very well known in that section of the state. Mrs. Whitmore is a graduate of the medical department of the Northwestern University of Chicago and was in general practice five years after her graduation, but has since given up the practice with the exception that for a number of years she has held the very important office of supreme physician in the Order of the Royal Neighbors of America. This organization has more than 375,000 members and is still rapidly growing. Mr. and Mrs. Whitmore for the past eight years have resided in a very attractive home at 835 Lane Street in Topeka. Mr. Whitmore is a member of the Masonic order, being both a York and Scottish Rite Mason, also a Knight Templar and Shriner, and is a past master of Blue Star Lodge, No. 69. He is also a member of the Modern Woodmen and the Ancient Order United Workmen and of the United Commercial Travelers. Mrs. Whitmore is a member of the Congregational Church.

DAWSON W. COOLEY is president of the Oxford Bank in Sumner County. His home has been in Kansas for upwards of half a century, and while his years have been chiefly employed in the banking business, he has also identified himself with various other enterprises for the good and upbuilding of this state.

Mr. Cooley is one of the surviving veterans of the great Union army during the Civil war. He served during the first two years of that struggle in one of the noted regiments of New York State. His enlistment was in Company C of the Ninth New York Volunteer Infantry, known as the Hawkins Zouaves. It was a two-year regiment, and its arduous service was indicated by mention of the more prominent battles in which it was engaged, as follows: Big Bethel, Virginia, the capture of Hatteras on Roanoke Island, Elizabeth City, Newbern, Camden, South Mountain, Antietam, Fredericksburg and Suffolk. Mr. Cooley was with his regiment in all these movements and campaigns, and at the expiration of his enlistment returned home and for a short time was in the employ of the Erie Railway Company. He then went to Nashville, Tennessee, and was in the military railroad service of the Federal Government until the close of the war.

He was born on a farm near Attica in Wyoming County, New York, August 11, 1839, being the oldest of the five children of John B. Weltha A. (Winchester) Cooley. His parents were also natives of New York State. His grandfather, Grove Cooley, came from Connecticut into eastern New York and later removed to the western part of the state, being one of the first settlers on the Holland purchase. Mr. Dawson W. Cooley owns the old land warrant which was written from Amsterdam. John B. Cooley followed farming and in later years the commission business. From New York State he went to northern Wisconsin, and for a time was captain of a steamboat on some of the rivers. He was a very successful business man, and was always ready to give his time and energies to any public good in his community. After the war he removed to Brookfield, Missouri, where he was a merchant, but subsequently retired and died at Rogers, Arkansas, in 1888. His wife survived him and died at Buffalo, New York, in 1905, at the home of her youngest daughter. John B. Cooley was a very active Methodist.

Up to the time he enlisted in the army Dawson W. Cooley lived at home in New York State and gained an education in the local schools. After the war he engaged in business at Brookfield, Missouri. In 1869, after the opening of the Osage Indian reserve in Kansas, he started with Captain L. C. Myers and a Mr. Pettijohn and traveled overland from Brookfield in covered wagons into southeastern Kansas. They were two weeks on the road. Mr. Cooley took a claim adjoining what is now called the City of Wellington. The government surveyor was just engaged at that time in laying out the chief lines marking the county boundaries. Mr. Cooley went through all the vicissitudes of pioneering in Kansas. He and his young wife lived on a claim of 160 acres seven years and in spite of hard times, grasshoppers and droughts he managed to prosper. On leaving the farm he spent three years as a traveling representative for a Quincy shoe factory, and he then located at Oxford in Sumner County.

For more than thirty years Mr. Cooley has been successfully engaged in banking. In 1883 he organized the Oxford Bank, was its cashier for thirteen years and has since been president. This is one of the strongest banks in a town of its size in the state, and its creditable record expresses at every point the personality, the integrity and the thorough business ability of Mr. Cooley. When movements have been launched in Oxford and Sumner County for some community enterprise, they have always had Mr. Cooley's advice and practical assistance.

He could not be called a politician in any sense of the term, though he has consistently supported the democratic party for many years. His chief service in any office has been on the school board. For half a century he has been identified with the Masonic order, is a member of the Knight Templar Commandery at Wellington, served as master of his lodge for eighteen years, and is an honorary member of the Thirty-second degree Consistory No. 2 at Wichita. He and his wife are also active in the Eastern Star. In 1870 Mr. Cooley married for his first wife Estelle Temple, who was born in New York State and died at Oxford in 1885. In 1886 he married Annie Milner, who came from Ohio. Mr. and Mrs. Cooley have no children. Mrs. Cooley is connected with the various activities of the Methodist Church and is well known socially in Oxford. The Sunday School has always found her one of the leading workers. Outside of his bank and some town property Mr. Cooley owns 800 acres of farming land, and this is operated by renters.

ORLEN McCORMICK. One of the substantial citizens and enterprising and successful farmers and stock-raisers of Zeandale Township, Riley County, is Orlen McCormick, who resides on his fine farm of 160 acres situated near the old McCormick home-stead where he was born November 27, 1869. He is the second son of Armstead and Anna (Allen) Mc-Cormick.

In recalling the early pioneers of this section of Kansas, the name of the late Armstead Thompson McCormick comes quickly to mind. He belonged to that band that may be called the pathfinders in Riley County, coming to this section years before the Civil war, accepting hardships, showing courage and resourcefulness, founding homes and improving conditions, and in passing out of life leaving honorable names and substantial records of having lived.

Armstead Thompson McCormick was born near Huntington, West Virginia, August 18, 1832. His parents were Levi and Phebe (Stuart) McCormick, of Scotch-Irish lineage but natives of Virginia. After their marriage they removed to what is now Wayne County, West Virginia, and there passed the rest of their lives. Their family contained eleven children and ten of these reached mature years. From this family came a pioneer of 1854 to Kansas, John McCormick, who made a permanent settlement in Zeandale Township, Riley County, in 1855, and in the fall of the same year he was followed by his brother, Armstead T. McCormick. In the spring of 1856 the latter purchased 160 acres of land in Zeandale Township and on that land lived during the rest of his life, with the exception of three years spent as a soldier in the Union army during the Civil war. He enlisted in Company K, Eleventh Kansas Infantry and proved his valor on many a battlefield. On returning from the cares and dangers of army life he resumed civil duties as a farmer. He had come to Kansas a young man of twenty-three years, in search of future independence, and found it here through industry and reasonable prudence. From the raw prairie he developed one of the best farms in the county and prospered in every branch of agriculture. His life was exemplary. He was a devoted husband and father, a good neighbor and popular as such, and a citizen above reproach. Although never very active in politics he possessed force of character and for many years was a strong factor in the republican party.

Armstead T. McCormick was married November 27, 1865, to Anna Allen, who was born in Columbiana County, Ohio, November 11, 1842, and still survives. Her parents, Benjamin and Phebe Allen, came to Riley County during the period of the Civil war. Four children were born to this marriage, two sons and two daughters, all of whom have domestic circles and homes of their own, worthy representatives of the old stock. They are: Bion M. and Orlen, of Zeandale Township; Phebe, now Mrs. R. V. Allison, of Salina, Kansas; and Sadie, now Mrs. Frank Short, of Topeka, Kansas.

Orlen McCormick was reared on the home farm and attended the township schools in boyhood. He was well trained in all farm industries and he has been able to make them very profitable. His farm, like that of his brother, is well supplied with mod-

ern farm machinery, and the farm improvements are substantial and practical. He has altogether 320 acres.

In 1893 Orlen McCormick was married to Miss Olive Foltz, who is a native of Kansas and a daughter of Cyrus Foltz, an early settler of Riley County, who is now deceased. Mr. and Mrs. McCormick have two children, Lenore and Helen. Mr. McCormick is a Master Mason and also a member of the Benevolent and Protective Order of Elks. In politics he is a republican, and he and family belong to the Methodist Episcopal Church.

HON. JOHN LEVI HUNT. It may be said that Hon. John Levi Hunt, assistant attorney-general of Kansas, and member of the leading law firm of Wheeler, Switzer & Hunt, is one of the fortunate men of Topeka. He was fortunate in having a good parentage, a fair endowment of intellect and feeling, a liberal education, in attaching himself to one of the learned professions, and in casting in his lot with the people of Topeka when her enterprises were probably at their fullest tide of development, and under circumstances which enabled him to co-operate in her material growth. While he has borne a fair share of the labors of professional and public life, he has at the same time preserved his love of letters and his indulgence in the amenities of a refined and gentle life.

Mr. Hunt was born at Chicago, Illinois, February 22, 1869, one of the six children of Homer C. and Anna (Gleed) Hunt, the former a native of New York, and the latter of England, from whence she came to this country in 1857. A number of the Hunts took part in the Revolutionary war, but Homer C. Hunt was suffering from ill health at the time of the Civil war and was thus unfit for service. After his marriage in New York, Homer C. Hunt lived in Wisconsin for a few years, and then went to Illinois, where, at Chicago, he soon became one of the important factors in business affairs. The time of his locating in the western metropolis was when railroads were experiencing the period of their greatest expansion, and with foresight and judgment he identified himself with the firm of Crerar, Adams & Company, which subsequently developed into probably the largest concern in the handling of railroad supplies in the world. In 1871 he took up his residence at Evanston, the exclusive Chicago suburb, and there his death occurred December 29, 1910, Mrs. Hunt surviving until January, 1913. The house is still owned by the heirs. Mr. Hunt was a deeply religious man, and for fifty years prior to his death had served as an elder in the Presbyterian Church. For fifteen years he had shown his friendship for the cause of education as a member of the Evanston Board of Education, and during that time did much to secure better schools for his community. He was one of the substantial men of Chicago and held a high place in the esteem and confidence of a wide circle of friends and business associates.

John Levi Hunt attended the public schools of Evanston, whence he was taken as a child of two years, and was then sent to Northwestern University. Before he had completed his course he went to work for the Jones & Laughlin Steel Company, in the offices of which concern he worked his way upward from office boy to stockman, and then resigned and reentered Northwestern University, this time as a law student. After one year and one-half he received his degree of Bachelor of Laws, graduating with the

U. G. Charles

class of 1895, and in the same year was admitted to the bar. His first professional connection was with the firm of Peck, Miller & Start, probably at that time the most prominent legal combination practicing at the Illinois bar. John B. Miller, of this firm, was later one of the counsel for the Standard Oil Company, in its famous $29,000,000 litigation at Chicago. Mr. Hunt remained with this firm for two years and secured a training that has since been invaluable to him. However, at that time, the Gleeds took over the 'Frisco Line, and, needing assistants, sent for Mr. Hunt, who is related to the family. On coming to Kansas, in 1897, he became assistant attorney to J. W. Gleed, at that time Kansas attorney for the Kansas 'Frisco Lines, and subsequently became associated with the law concern of Gleed, Ware & Gleed, which, in 1910, became Gleed, Hunt, Palmer & Gleed. Mr. Hunt was a member of this leading firm until 1915, when he was appointed by Hon. S. M. Brewster to the position of attorney-general of Kansas, the first public office he has held and one which he still retains. At that time he formed the firm of Switzer, Wheeler & Hunt, with which he remains today. Mr. Hunt, as a legist, is thoroughly grounded in elementary knowledge, is industrious, patient in research and of sound and stable judgment, powerful in forensic contests, both before juries and in the more formal argument before the court. In spite of his many qualifications, he has never been one to thrust himself forward for public office, being domestic in his tastes and rather quiet and unassuming in manner. He is a stand-pat republican in politics, is fraternally affiliated with the Benevolent and Protective Order of Elks, and his religious connection is with the Presbyterian Church. Mrs. Hunt belongs to the Episcopal church.

On March 22, 1906, Mr. Hunt was united in marriage at Hays, Kansas, at the home of the bride, to Miss Minnie Straily. One son has been born to this union: John Homer, who is attending school.

GEORGE BELL and members of his family have been prominently identified with various localities in Kansas for thirty-five years or more. The family now reside in Topeka.

The birthplace of George Bell was Darlington, Yorkshire, England, where he was born in 1845. He grew up at Darlington, and while there he lived on an estate where Queen Victoria's three noted grandsons came to hunt. George Bell came to know these distinguished European characters very well. They are now the Czar Nicholas of Russia, Emperor William of Germany and King George of England.

George Bell in 1877 came to America, was first located at Beecher, Illinois, and in 1880 came to Kansas. In Leavenworth County he became a successful farmer and stock raiser and specialized in fine livestock.

In 1880 Mr. Bell married Miss Jean M. Christy. They were married in the city of Brantford, Ontario, Canada. Mrs. Bell is a member of a very prominent Canadian family. Her grandfather Robert Christy was a man of prominence in Canada and died there in 1876 at the age of ninety-seven. Her father, Hon. David Christy, was one of Canada's distinguished statesmen. Born in the city of Edinburg, Scotland, in 1818, he had been brought to Canada in 1834 when a boy, lived in Brantford, became a school teacher at Hamilton, but afterwards entered politics and rose rapidly in the scale of prominence. At one time he served as speaker of

the Dominion Senate and held many offices under the crown, being at one time secretary of state. Hon. David Christy came to Kansas during Governor St. John's administration, and became well known to the public men of that day. A man of wealth he invested in about 4,000 acres of land in Marion County, and sent his two sons Robert and William to manage the ranch. Not long after making this investment in Kansas real estate David Christy died suddenly at the age of seventy-five. After his death the big Marion County ranch was sold to Lord Sculley. While his sons Robert and William were in Marion County their sister Jean came to visit them, and there she met Mr. George Bell, whom she married in 1880.

Mr. and Mrs. Bell had born to them three children, and the family now reside at 1617 Mulvane Street in Topeka. The children Margaret, Edna and Robert are all talented young people, Margaret and Edna have taken special courses in Washburn College and Robert, though employed in the Santa Fe offices is also continuing his work in Washburn College.

U. G. CHARLES. One of the oldest of the refining and civilizing agencies of man is architecture, the art which constructs for beauty or utility or com-

MENTHOLATUM BUILDING, WICHITA

bines both. While it has necessarily been regulated by natural conditions and configuration of the country in which it is exercised, the development of a modern palace, either for residence or business, step by step from the ancestral cave or tent, is one of the great and interesting romances of civilization. Of the masters of this art who have contributed much to the past of Wichita, and who, because of their superior equipment and talents, may be counted upon to share in the development of the future of the city, more than passing mention is due U. G. Charles, than whom there is to be found no more talented man in the profession in the state.

The Mentholatum Building was the first complete reinforced concrete building to be erected in Wichita, and is now known as The Home of Mentholatum. The style of architecture is the Spanish Mission style. This building contains a steam heating plant and also a cooling device for hot weather, the interior being designed especially for the compounding of Mentholatum, and all business connected therewith. It was constructed in 1908, and has stood as an excellent monument for reinforced concrete work. It is only one of many such structures that Mr. Charles has designed.

U. G. Charles was born March 10, 1865, near Salem, the county seat of Washington County, Indiana. His early education was secured principally in night schools, for his boyhood and youth were largely given over to serving a long and thorough apprenticeship to the trades of cabinet maker and general mechanic in two of the leading passenger coach works of the United States. His duties included the inside finishing of passenger coaches, a work which required workmanship of the greatest exactness and perfection. In this line he eventually became so proficient that in 1894 he was made master mechanic for the Northwestern Car and Machine Works, at Oshkosh, Wisconsin, where he had full charge of the designing department.

Mr. Charles remained with that plant for some time and gave the utmost satisfaction, but finally resigned to become an architect with offices at Oshkosh. Not long thereafter, he was tendered and accepted a position with The Morgan Co., the second largest manufacturers of sash, doors and blinds in the United States, and for five years was engaged with this concern in doing special detail and art design work, in which he gained experience that has been of the greatest assistance to him in his profession. When he left The Morgan Co. he accepted a like position with the Radford Company, who also conducted a large plant of the same kind. In 1901 Mr. Charles decided to begin independent operations, and accordingly came to Wichita, where he opened an office as an architect. During the sixteen years that he has been engaged in the practice of his profession at Wichita, Mr. Charles has achieved a phenomenal success, and his business now extends to practically every state in the Union. In Wichita he has designed about 100 of the beautiful residences for which the city is noted and upwards of forty of the city's business blocks. He specializes in residences and important construction work in iron, steel and cement, and his accomplishments also include the designing and erection of many large school and other public buildings. Recognized and acknowledged as an expert and authority in his profession, Mr. Charles has been called frequently into court to give expert opinions along lines of mechanical engineering and structural work in the settlement of court matters. His contributions to various magazines and periodicals on technical subjects have been of the greatest value to the profession, and for about two years he was the publisher of a monthly architectural magazine at Wichita which attracted great interest among architects everywhere. He is interested in several business enterprises of Wichita. Mr. Charles has identified himself with measures of great public usefulness, having realized that public improvements are the outcome of intelligent and concerted effort on the part of progressive citizens who recognize the debt a community owes as a whole to its people, and thus endeavor to discharge it in a way that will benefit the majority.

In 1890 Mr. Charles was married to Miss Rosa M. Yazel of Wichita. They have one son, Merlin Y., who is interested in his father's professional business and his assistant in the office. Merlin Y. Charles married Clara Alma Fay August 9, 1916. Since the beginning of Mr. Charles' business in Wichita, Mrs. Charles has been his constant and capable co-worker,

and the attainment of his success is to a great extent due to her intelligent co-operation in the handling of the office work.

LLOYD S. FRY. When he came to the City of Manhattan in 1883, Mr. Fry engaged at once in the work which had occupied him for a number of years in Pennsylvania and Kansas and which brought him an enviable place among the state's leading educators. He was employed as a teacher in the College Hill School, and in 1886 was elected superintendent of the city schools of Manhattan, a position he held two years. His record as an educator included two years in charge of the schools of Randolph, one year at Atwood, three years at Hays City. In all this time he was also an important factor in school institute work, and showed unusual ability not only as an instructor but in broadening and uplifting the general standards of school management in his county.

When he gave up teaching in 1894, Mr. Fry went to farming. For eighteen years he conducted a general farm and dairy in Manhattan Township of Riley county, and that was a business congenial as well as profitable, so that in 1912 he was able to retire from his active duties as a farmer and has since lived in a comfortable home in Manhattan.

Lloyd S. Fry was born near Millerstown in Perry County, Pennsylvania, April 25, 1855, a son of Simon H. and Catharine A. (Bretz) Fry. His parents were natives of Pennsylvania and of old Colonial families. The chief lineage of his ancestry is Netherland Dutch, though there is an admixture of Scotch-Irish. Both the Fry and Bretz names were represented by soldiers in the Revolutionary war and also the War of 1812. History mentions John Bretz as an aide-de-camp to General Washington. Simon H. and Catharine A. Fry had five children, one of whom died in infancy. The others are: Clarence, who died in 1881; Lloyd S.; E. Bertha, the wife of A. B. Eells, their home being now in California; and Jennie C., who married Robert J. Fleming and they also live in California. Simon Fry was also a successful teacher, having taught in Pennsylvania for a number of years, and he also managed a farm in that state. His death occurred in 1880, at the age of fifty-seven. In 1884 his widow and some of her children came out to Kansas, locating in Riley County, where she died in 1902, when nearly seventy-seven years of age.

The early education of Lloyd S. Fry was acquired in his native state. In 1882, he was graduated from one of the Pennsylvania state normal schools. He had in the meantime acquired considerable experience in teaching, and on graduating from the normal school was granted a life license as a teacher in Pennsylvania. He also holds a certificate in Kansas, granted him in 1884.

While a man of plain and unassuming disposition, Mr. Fry is, nevertheless, progressive and public spirited to a high degree, and has allied himself with several progressive movements in his home county and state. For many years he was active in the Grange organization, belonged to the Kansas State Grange, and was elected in 1912 lecturer of the Kansas State Grange and held various other offices. He is a republican, but has never sought political honors, but has held township offices. He is a Presbyterian and a member of the Ancient Order of United Workmen and the Anti-Horse Thief Association.

In 1886 he married Miss Mary L. Griffing. Her father was the distinguished Kansas Methodist missionary, Rev. James Sayre Griffing, now deceased. Mr. and Mrs. Fry have two children. Clarence G., who graduated from the Kansas State Agricultural College in 1912, married a classmate, Viva M. McCray; they now reside in Miami, Oklahoma, where he is principal of the city high schools, with his wife as principal of a ward school. Velora A., the younger child, graduated in domestic science in 1915 from the Kansas State Agricultural College and married Merrill L. Gould. They graduated in the same class in the college at Manhattan. They now reside near Jamestown in Cloud County, Kansas, where Mr. Gould is a farmer.

RICHARD HENRY KIMBALL. One of the widely known and highly esteemed residents of Manhattan Township, Riley County, Kansas, is Richard Henry Kimball, who has been a witness of the development of the great West and has borne his part in the work that transformed the unbroken prairie into the richly cultivated fields that make Manhattan Township notable as an agricultural section. Not alone as an early settler is Mr. Kimball worthy of consideration, important as that is in the truthful annals of Kansas, but he is also a veteran of the great Civil war, in which he risked life and health for three years as a soldier in the Union army.

Richard Henry Kimball was born at Goffstown, New Hampshire, May 12, 1838, and his parents were John and Sally Collins (Putnam) Kimball. The father was a native of New Hampshire and the mother of Massachusetts. She came of Revolutionary stock, her maternal grandfather being General Collins, who signalized himself as a gallant soldier in the Revolutionary struggle, and her kindred on the paternal side including the brave Gen. Israel Putnam, of Revolutionary fame, whose character is well depicted by the words inscribed on his tomb, "He dared to lead where any dared to follow."

Richard Henry Kimball and his brothers were reared in New Hampshire and attended the district schools. In the spring of 1856, J. Augustus and John Melville Kimball, older brothers of Richard, ventured as far west as Kansas and located in what is now Manhattan Township, Riley County. Joseph Augustus was accidentally killed in June of that year. Following his brothers, Richard Henry Kimball came also to Riley County, reaching what is now Manhattan Township on December '30, 1856. He soon acquired a land claim in the township and in the spring of 1857 his parents and the rest of their children came also to this section. Before settling down to the hard work that he knew awaited him on his farm, Mr. Kimball explored farther west and made two trips across the plains in the sixties, before enlisting on August 13, 1862, as a private in Company G, Eleventh Kansas Volunteer Infantry for service in the Civil war. This regiment afterward became the Eleventh Kansas cavalry and he followed its fortunes until the close of the struggle, participating in many battles, including the battle of the Blue, West Port and Mine Run. and received his honorable discharge in June, 1865. He is a member of Lew Grove Post, Grand Army of the Republic.

When Mr. Kimball was released from military service, his duty well done, he soon made a journey to New Hampshire, where he knew that a beloved maiden awaited him, and on July 12, 1865, was united in marriage with Miss Elizabeth F. Greer. She was born at Goffstown, New Hampshire, January 17, 1839. Immediately after marriage Mr. and Mrs. Kimball came to Kansas and settled on the farm in Manhattan Township on which they have since lived and where they had the privilege of celebrating together their golden wedding anniversary in 1915. Unto them were born the following children: Fred Greer Kimball, who is a resident of Manhattan, Kansas; Sarah Bertha, who is the wife of Prof. Albert Dickens, of the Kansas State Agricultural College; John Benjamin Kimball, who manages the paternal farm; and Stella Victoria, who is the wife of W. P. Tucker of Florida.

Mr. Kimball has always taken an active interest in public affairs in relation to improvement and development of this section. His vote has always been cast independently and according to his own intelligent judgment. In former years he was prominently identified with the Grange movement and also with the Good Templars but as a rule fraternal organizations have had no appeal to him. He has seen wonderful changes come to Kansas, changes which have justified his foresight in making this state his permanent home, and the part that he has performed has been one that has been creditable to himself, his family and his community. Mr. and Mrs. Kimball spend their winters in Florida.

DAVID CRAWFORD THOROMAN. The first of his name to come to Kansas, the late David Crawford Thoroman was for many years engaged in school teaching and farming in Coffey and Osage counties, and is still remembered by the older residents as a man of upright character, possessed of a high sense of justice. His experiences during the Civil war had placed upon him the handicap of being weak physically, but his energetic spirit and industry helped him to overcome this in large part, and throughout his career he was a useful member of whatever community he made his home.

David C. Thoroman was born in Adams County, Ohio, in 1824, of English descent, and when a young man went to Lewis County, in the northeastern part of Kentucky, where he was married to Katherine Murphy. Thus early he was a schoolteacher and agriculturist and was so engaged when the Civil war broke out. Mr. Thoroman enlisted in Company E, Twenty-second Regiment, Kentucky Volunteer Infantry, and had his baptism of fire in Cumberland Gap, where he took part in a severe engagement. Subsequently he was in the battles around Vicksburg, including Milliken's Bend, Big Black River and the numerous encounters leading up to the surrender of the besieged city, and later took part in the engagement at Arkansas Post. Just prior to the Red River expedition under General Banks, in which his regiment took an active part, Mr. Thoroman was forced to resign, owing to the ill effects of a sunstroke. By that time he had been advanced to the rank of lieutenant, through bravery and faithful service, and had a decidedly commendable war record.

On his return to his home, Mr. Thoroman spent some months in recuperating and then again resumed farming in Kentucky. In 1871 he left that state and came to Kansas, first settling in Osage county and two years later coming to Coffey County. For almost twenty-eight years, Mr. Thoroman was a teacher in the public schools of these counties, practically all of this time in the winter months, while his summers were devoted to farming. The evil effects of his army life, in regards to his physical health, never left him, but he was able to make a place for himself among the men of comfortable circumstances in his community, while as a citizen he held the respect and confidence of all with whom he came into contact. Mr. Thoroman was a man of the highest integrity, and when he died, in 1909, his community lost a man who had ever been a friend of justice. His first wife died after bearing him three children, and he was again married, wedding Rebecca Murphy, a sister of his first wife. She bore him six children, five of whom are now living, including Albert M. Thoroman. She died at Waverly, Kansas, July 31, 1916.

Albert M. Thoroman was born on a farm in Osage County, Kansas, July 9, 1873, a son of David Crawford and Rebecca (Murphy) Thoroman. His early boyhood and youth were passed on farms in Osage and Coffey Counties, and he was given excellent educational advantages in the public schools of Kansas and in the State Normal School, from which he was graduated in 1899, in addition to which he received instruction from his father. His education was completed in the University of Kansas, from which he was graduated in 1909. In the meantime, Mr. Thoroman had taught school, and had served one year as superintendent of the schools of Williamsburg, seven years as superintendent of the schools of Council Grove. He served four years as principal of the Chase County High School at Cottonwood Falls, from 1909 to 1913. In the latter year he was elected secretary of the School Book Commission of the State of Kansas, a position which he still retains and the duties of which he is discharging in an entirely efficient, conscientious and expeditious manner. In this capacity, as co-editor with Prof. H. W. Davis, he has published two volumes now used in the public schools of Kansas: "Classics for the Kansas Schools, Eighth Grade," and the same work for the seventh grade. He has also done editorial work on the Kansas Primer.

Mr. Thoroman is a member of the Congregational Church. He is a republican in politics, and a member of the Kansas Chapter of the Phi Beta Kappa. His fraternal connection is with the Masons, in which he has attained the Scottish Rite degree.

JAMES STEVENSON. One of the substantial and influential men of Shawnee County, is James Stevenson, for the past eight years an esteemed resident of Highland Park but formerly, for many years, a successful farmer in Topeka Township. Unlike many who came to Kansas in the early part of 1882, Mr. Stevenson possessed capital, hardly-won capital that represented years of weary toil and constant self denial.

James Stevenson was born in County Down, Ireland, June 9, 1846, and is a son of Isaac and Nancy (Bradford) Stevenson. His mother died when he was young and his father married again. The latter was a farmer and in very moderate circumstances, and when a second family began to grow about the family hearthstone, James realized that his help on the home acres was not needed and began to plan his independent future. He had been given but limited educational opportunities, had not even thought of learning a trade but he was healthy, cheerful and industrious and that he possessed real courage was shown when he left old Ireland and his people and with no assurance of work ahead, sailed for America and landed at Boston, Massachusetts, with $2.50 in his pocket.

James Stevenson reached the United States in 1869 and it is not likely that he found a more hospitable welcome in the strange city than did hundreds of other foreign born youths who landed in the same year. It is safe to say, however, that none of these sought work more earnestly than he nor performed his tasks with greater faithfulness to his employers. He did not despise any honest job that offered but his first permanent place was as a coachman and ground caretaker on a large estate and in this position he continued for twelve years. During this time he had in view the purchase of land and its improvement, hence was frugal in his expenditures and wholesome and careful in his habits. Therefore when, in 1882 he was ready to come to Kansas he brought with him the sum of $2,400, every cent of which represented honest industry on his part. He used a part of his capital in the purchase of a quarter section of land, paying $10.50 per acre. On his land he built a small house and barn and made other necessary improvements and thus had ready a comfortable home for his bride when, in September of the same year, he brought her to Topeka Township, Shawnee County.

Mr. Stevenson was united in marriage with Susan Dalzell, a most estimable young woman whom he had known for eight years. She was a resident of Boston when Mr. Stevenson formed her acquaintance, having come to the United States from County Down, Ireland, with her brother Samuel, who yet resides in Boston. Mr. and Mrs. Stevenson were married in Topeka. They have had five children: Jane, who is the wife of C. C. Niccum, lives at St. Joseph, Missouri, and has one daughter; Susan H., who is the wife of James Rabe, a farmer in Topeka Township, has three children; James R., who married Josephine Rabe, now deceased, resides in Topeka, and has one child; Isaac Henry, who is a resident of Topeka, married Gertrude Lovell; and Lillian Edna, who is the wife of Melvin McCoskrie, of Topeka, has one son.

By no means does Mr. Stevenson take all the credit for his success in life and the accumulation of his ample fortune. On the other hand he remembers and relates with pride the hearty co-operation of his wife all along the way. She was industrious, prudent and self-denying and her cheerful acceptance of hardships and her encouraging sympathy on all occasions will never be forgotten. On many a humid day of summer she worked over a hot stove to provide the wholesome food which she deemed her hardworking husband and growing children needed, and attended carefully and thoroughly to the other household duties which resulted in bodily comfort for the family. Although the churning of butter was a toilsome operation, its quality made it readily salable and many dollars were thus added to the family income every year. Mrs. Stevenson is a woman who has unselfishly lived deeply in the lives of husband and children, not counting self sacrifice at any time of more importance than their physical and spiritual development. By precept and example she instilled into the youthful minds of her children those principles of right living that have assisted them in making happy domestic hearths of their own.

By hard work and close economy, Mr. and Mrs. Stevenson prospered continuously after establishing their little home in Topeka Township. In time they paid off all the indebtedness incurred on the land and added to it tract after tract until they

now own 640 acres and also own fifteen lots in Highland Park. They continued to reside in the country until 1900, when Mr. Stevenson decided to remove with his wife to Highland Park and since then has devoted his attention mainly to looking after his many interests. His life has not been a selfish one for he has been a liberal supporter of churches, schools, good roads and has always been ready to give encouragement to benevolent and charitable enterprises.

Mr. and Mrs. Stevenson are members of the First Congregational Church of Topeka. He has held minor offices in the county and in politics is a republican.

GEORGE H. HUNTER, a resident of Wellington almost forty years, is one of the leading millers of the state, is president of the oldest bank in Wellington, and has also given much of his time and energies to public affairs, being the present mayor of Wellington.

He was born on a farm near Circleville, Ohio, December 1, 1849, one of the five children of Alexander M. and Sophia (Zepp) Hunter, the former a native of Ohio and the latter of Pennsylvania. Sophia Zepp was of Pennsylvania Dutch extraction, and when a child was brought to Ohio by her uncle and aunt. Alexander M. Hunter enlisted at the outbreak of the Civil war, but on account of physical disability was not accepted for service. He was a republican and a member of the Congregational Church. He came out to Wellington, was associated with his son in the flour mill from 1879 until 1910, and one day while fishing on a railway bridge was killed by a train, being then nearly ninety years of age.

When George H. Hunter was six months of age his parents moved to a farm in Shelby County, Illinois. He had only the advantages of the district schools and his higher education was gained largely through his own efforts and by paying his own expenses through the State Normal University at Normal, Illinois. At the age of twenty he entered that school and was graduated at twenty-three. After one year as a teacher he engaged, in 1872, in the mercantile business and followed it with considerable success for six years in Illinois. Desiring a larger field, and knowing the possibilities of Kansas through some of his friends who had already come to the state, he moved his store to Wellington in 1878. Wellington was then a small village. In 1879 he sold the store and concentrated all his attention upon the flour mill which he had bought in the preceding year.

While at Normal, Illinois, on August 1, 1872, he married Miss Frances M. Beale, who was born in Mason County, Illinois, and was his class mate in Normal School. Mr. and Mrs. Hunter have nine children. Charles W. is now secretary and treasurer of the Hunter Milling Company and has served fifteen years as president of the Board of Education. Lottie M. is Mrs. W. T. Voils of Wellington. George H. Jr. is a rancher at Fargo, Oklahoma. Edna M. is still at home. Frank B. lives at Wellington. Harry is manager of a milling company at Attica, Kansas. Maud M. is Mrs. G. Harris Carr, of Wellington. Fannie S. is Mrs. Foss Farrar of Arkansas City, Kansas. Grace is a student of music and art in a school in Chicago. All the children have had college advantages.

The flour mill which Mr. Hunter bought at Wellington in 1878 was then of the style of equipment known as a buhr mill. It had a limited capacity and was largely employed for the grinding of local grain and feed stuffs. The genius of a capable business man

has raised it from a small local institution until it now ranks as the second largest mill in Kansas outside of Kansas City. The mill has a capacity of 1,500 barrels a day and the product is widely distributed all over the country. When Mr. Hunter bought the mill he had no practical knowledge of milling, but was not ashamed to learn. He brought to the business good judgment, and after mastering the technical details he was soon recognized as an expert miller. He has been active manager of the plant at Wellington since 1879, and has realized his ambition of making the business one of the best of its kind in the state. Besides this mill the Hunter Milling Company has a 300 barrel mill at Attica. The company was incorporated in 1888 with George H. Hunter as president, W. T. Voils as vice president, and Charles W. Hunter as secretary and treasurer.

While a man of unassuming nature, never craving publicity, Mr. Hunter has been very active in public affairs. He is a republican and was a delegate to the National Convention of his party in 1908 and was presidential elector in 1904. For fifteen years he was a member of the Board of Education, a position which has been held for a similar period by his son Charles. He was a member of the city council ten years, served as mayor from 1890 to 1892, also in 1910, and is now on a three year term beginning in 1914. His administration as mayor has been one of marked benefit to the city. During his term a waterworks system has been installed, said to be the finest in the state for the size of the city, and the municipality has also taken over the ownership of the electric lighting plant. These are two conspicuous improvements, but there have been many others. From 1908 to 1912 Mr. Hunter served as a member of the State Senate. During that time he introduced and secured the passage of nine bills, each pertaining to some vital interest of the community or state.

Mr. Hunter is president of the Wellington National Bank, the oldest bank in the city. He also owns considerable property both in the city and in the country. He is enthusiastic in behalf of better highways, and is a member of the executive committee from the Eighth District of the Kansas Good Roads Association. He is a thirty-second degree Scottish Rite Mason, being affiliated with the Wichita Consistory. His happy married life was terminated with the death of Mrs. Hunter on May 6, 1903. She was a devoted mother in the home and was very active in the Congregational Church, with which Mr. Hunter has also been identified for many years and was trustee until his place was taken by his son Charles W.

WILLIAM H. EDELBLUTE. In recalling the worthy pioneers of Kansas, in order to do them due justice and honor, none more deserving of mention in Riley County could be found than the late William H. Edelblute. For many years he was a prominent farmer in Wild Cat Township, a useful and influential citizen, and a veteran of the great Civil war. He was born September 15, 1829, in Huntingdon County, Pennsylvania, and died at his farm residence in Riley County, Kansas, May 28, 1908, in his seventy-ninth year. He was a son of David and Lydia (Conrad) Edelblute.

In tracing genealogy of the Edelblute family, the fact is disclosed that it is of German origin and the name signifies "noble blood." There is a tradition that many, many years ago, a prince of Germany espoused a peasant maid and thereby lost his rank and estates.

Probably before the Revolutionary war the first of this name came to the American colonies and it is found early in the State of Pennsylvania. In that state, David Edelblute, the father of the late William H. Edelblute, was born October 11, 1803, and died in Riley County, Kansas, January 19, 1879. He came to Kansas in 1857 and settled in Riley County in the vicinity of the present Village of Keats. In his native state he had been a charcoal-burner but after coming to this state devoted himself exclusively to agricultural pursuits. In Pennsylvania he was married February 3, 1825, to Lydia Conrad, who was born there November 10, 1809, and died in Riley County, Kansas, September 19, 1866. Their children were as follows: William H.; Nancy Jane, who was born April 29, 1831, is now deceased and was the wife of John Murphy; Eleanora, who was born October 4, 1834, is now the widow of W. W. Walker; Nathan G., who was born June 24, 1837, died in Pennsylvania; Samuel R., who was born February 15, 1840, is deceased; David Henry, whose personal sketch appears in this work; Catherine, who is the widow of William Silver, was born April 10, 1843, and her husband was a Union soldier in the Civil war, a member of Company G, Eleventh Kansas Infantry; Rebecca, who was born October 24, 1847, married George W. Barns and they reside in California; Mary Elizabeth, who was born July 12, 1850, is the wife of W. H. Ashton, of Manhattan, Kansas; and John George, who was born September 11, 1853, is a resident of Idaho.

William H. Edelblute came first to Kansas in 1854 but did not at that time tarry long, going on to Iowa. In 1856 he returned to Kansas and took up a claim in Wild Cat Township, Riley County, where he developed a fine farm from primitive condition, prospered through his industry and at the time of his death owned 400 acres. In 1867 he erected a beautiful residence of stone which stands as a monument to his toil, thrift and enterprise, and it continues to be the home of his widow.

Scarcely had Mr. Edelblute made much in the way of improvement on his Riley County property when war clouds began to gather, times became a little harder and consequently more troubles had to be faced than usually attends pioneering. The Civil war was finally precipitated and Mr. Edelblute soon determined that he would do his full share in preserving the Union, and in August, 1862, he enlisted as a private in Company G, Eleventh Kansas Infantry and served in the struggle until its close when he was honorably discharged. He was a worthy and enthusiastic member of the Grand Army of the Republic, always interested in its affairs and ready at all times to recognize the claims of old army comrades.

On March 4, 1869, Mr. Edelblute was married to Miss Artissima Vashti Ryan, who was born in Clark County, Indiana. She is a daughter of Joseph P. and Elizabeth (Whitson) Ryan, of Irish lineage but born in Indiana. Their respective parents moved to Indiana from Kentucky, originally from Virginia. In 1854 Mr. Ryan removed with his family to Iowa and in 1859 to Kansas and settled first in Riley County but later in Clay County. There he died when aged sixty-one years and there the mother of Mrs. Edelblute died also when aged sixty-nine years. They were the parents of eight children, namely: Thomas G., Athan W., Artemissa Vashti, Elizabeth, Mary, Malcomb, Belle and Edward. Mr. Ryan was a carpenter by trade but also followed farming.

In politics he was a republican. For many years he was a local preacher in the Methodist Episcopal Church.

To Mr. and Mrs. Edelblute were born sons and daughters as follows: William Harvey, who was born September 6, 1870, was graduated from the Kansas State Agricultural College in 1892 and is now following his profession of civil engineer at Rathdrum, Idaho. He has a large ranch in Idaho and he is at this time, November, 1916, colonel of the Second Idaho Infantry on duty on the Mexican border; John Albert, who was born July 16, 1872, is a resident of Manhattan, Kansas; George Clarence, who was born September 4, 1876, resides on the homestead with his mother; Mabel, died in infancy; Merrill Ray, was born September 2, 1885, and Mary Belle, was born June 28, 1888.

William H. Edelblute was a member of the Methodist Episcopal Church and led a consistent Christian life, being kind, considerate and helpful to everyone and honorable and upright in all his business and personal relations. His memory is tenderly cherished by his family and his community can point with pride to a score of his achievements that were for the permanent benefit of the section in which so much of his life had been spent.

CHARLES A. BAKER of Wichita lacked only three or four months of being a native son of Kansas. He has spent practically his entire career in this state, and by close attention to his business as a plumber has built up one of the leading establishments at Wichita, and his business is registered under the state laws.

He was born at Rio, Wisconsin, June 30, 1870, and it was in September of the same year that his parents moved to Arkansas City, Kansas. After a public school education, gained in Wichita, he began an apprenticeship at the plumbing trade, and followed it as a journeyman until 1900. Since then for more than fifteen years he has been in the plumbing business for himself, first at Hutchinson but since 1902 at Wichita.

Mr. Baker is a thirty-second degree Mason and a member of the Mystic Shrine, and is also an Elk. His father was an old soldier, so he has continued the military record of the family and is now serving as a regimental quarter-master with the rank of captain in the Second Kansas Infantry. He has been on the border at Eagle Pass and San Antonio, Texas, since July 1, 1916.

On December 4, 1895, Mr. Baker married Miss Lillie E. Bennett of Wichita. They have a daughter Marcia Helen, who is now a student in the Wichita High School.

Mr. Baker's father, Thomas Baker, was a Kansas pioneer. He was born in Harrisburg, Pennsylvania, grew up in that state and was a farmer, and in January, 1864, enlisted in the Third United States Cavalry for a term of three years. During the last 1½ years of the war his company was stationed along the Mississippi River, and in a skirmish with some guerrillas in Arkansas he was wounded in the hip. When his enlistment expired he set up a barber shop at Rio, Wisconsin, but in 1870 started for Kansas. He went by rail as far as Emporia, and from there by prairie schooner to Arkansas City. He was in the barber business there a few years, then removed to Winfield, and in 1878 came to Wichita, where he worked as a barber until his death in May.

DUDLEY PRATT. Unusual qualities of manhood and character accompanied the successful career of the late Dudley Pratt, who for many years was one of the largest stock buyers in and about Topeka. In many ways Dudley Pratt stood apart and above the average type of stock dealer. He had none of the unscrupulous methods which have so frequently brought that vocation into disfavor. He was fair, he lived the life of the Golden Rule, and in every way he was a fitting representative of the best element of Kansas pioneer citizenship.

Born at St. Mary's, Ohio, January 27, 1832, he was a son of Dr. Seth Pratt. His father was a successful physician in Ohio and of English ancestry.

Spending his early life in his native state, Dudley Pratt received only a practical education in the public schools. He was married in Ohio to Mary Emily Noble. The year following the close of the Civil war he brought his wife and his two oldest sons to Kansas. It was his expectation at the time of making this state his future home. Topeka was then on the western line of civilization, and the terminus of the Union Pacific Railway.

Buying 140 acres of land on the Burlingame road about one mile south of the present site of Washburn College, Dudley Pratt gave $1,100 for that land, which is now worth many times its original purchase price. That was the family home for nineteen years. There the three sons grew to manhood and began the careers which reflect additional honor upon this name. The names of these sons are Henry Fuller, Orange Albion and John Dudley. John Dudley was born on the old homestead near Topeka.

While Mr. Pratt with the aid of his sons operated his farm he was more generally known as a stock man. In time he built up the largest business as a stock dealer in that locality. He transacted business in a period when a dollar meant more to the average man than $5.00 at the present time. In all his dealings he was never known to take advantage of a patron. He never gambled on the rise or fall in the price of livestock. He shared the benefits of an advance with his patrons, and men came to trust implicitly in his word. He acted on the principle that he was entitled to a fair profit and no more. Inherent honesty was his chief characteristic. If a grower asked the price that grower knew that the quotation made by Mr. Pratt was all the market permitted. Long before he died his word was accepted as worth as much as a bond. If for no other reason he deserved to be honored and respected for this splendid quality alone.

Successful in business, he never neglected the welfare of his community. He engaged in every meritorious undertaking, and he was also a man of charity, but acting so that his charity was completely unostentatious and no record was made thereof except in the hearts of the recipients. He was invariably courteous and considerate. For sixty years he was a member of the Independent Order of Odd Fellows.

Dudley Pratt passed away May 23, 1914, when eighty-two years of age. His wife had died in 1902.

Their oldest son Henry Fuller is one of the well known physicians of Shawnee County, living at Rossville. He is father of two children namely Dudley James, professor at Leland Stanford University of California and Esther. The two younger sons are prominent hardware merchants at North Topeka, where they have built up a large trade by exercising the same sterling qualities of character that were so prominent in the life of their father. Orange Albion,

the second son, married Anna Ekel, a daughter of William Ekel. William Ekel at one time operated a lumber yard upon which the Union Pacific Park is now located. Orange A. is an active member of the Christian Church, is a member of the Masonic Order and he and his wife have five children: Leila May, Laura Mayce, Chester Warren, Virgil Thelma and Vivian Mildred.

John Dudley Pratt, the youngest of the three sons of Dudley Pratt, represents the younger generation of Topeka business men who are a credit to that city. He is a Presbyterian, and is a member of the Masonic Order. To his marriage with Miss Anna Allen was born one daughter named Gladys.

To Dudley Pratt in his declining years came the knowledge and satisfaction of having lived a life creditable alike to himself and his state. It was also a matter of gratification to him that his three sons were well settled in honorable careers and living worthy lives.

JOHN WILLIAM DALE has been one of the constructive factors in Sedgwick County. He was one of the founders of the Town of Andale, and has been identified with the little City of Clearwater from almost the beginning of its growth. In business affairs his interests extend to different lines. He was a landowner in the early days, still has interests as a landowner, and is head of the principal banking establishment of Clearwater.

An Illinois man by birth, he was born in DeKalb County of that state December 21, 1847. His father, Frank Dale, was born at Hull, England, in 1812, and was married in Daleville, Pennsylvania, to Marie Webster. She was also born in England.

Frank Dale came to America, and after living a short time in Northeastern Pennsylvania went to Michigan, and after two years there came west to Illinois, locating in DeKalb County in the year following the Black Hawk war, in the early '30s. Frank Dale was a farmer, a merchant, grain dealer, and otherwise a man of more than ordinary importance in that section of Illinois. After a long and honorable career he died at DeKalb in 1886. He and his wife had eight children, four sons and four daughters, a brief record of whom is as follows: Mrs. Clara Metcalf of Isabella, Oklahoma; Mrs. Caroline Bacon of Sandwich, Illinois; Mrs. Mary Watson, a wealthy resident of Mount Hope, Kansas; Mrs. Sue E. Beckwith, who died in Wichita in 1915; Arthur H., a retired farmer at Leland, Illinois; John W.; Frank, a prominent attorney at Guthrie, Oklahoma, and during territorial days in that state was chief justice under the Cleveland administration; and D. M. Dale, who has gained prominence in the law, being a member of the Wichita bar and a former judge of the district court.

During his early years spent in DeKalb County, Illinois, John W. Dale attended the local schools, graduating from the high school at Leland, and for a time was a student in a telegraph college. His first regular employment was as station agent at Leland for the Chicago, Burlington & Quincy Railroad. For one term he was township treasurer of Victor Township in his home county.

Mr. Dale has been a resident of Kansas since the fall of 1876. At that time he settled on a half section of land which he bought from the railroad company in the northwestern part of Sedgwick County. While there he laid the basis of his successful career. He was a farmer and stock raiser for eighteen years, but in the meantime his enterprise had branched out into other fields. In partnership with George Anderson he laid out and founded the Town of Andale, the name being formed by a combination of a portion of Mr. Anderson's name and Mr. Dale's name. Mr. Dale also helped vote bonds for the construction of the Wichita & Colorado Railroad Company. After the establishment of Andale he conducted a brick yard there, and subsequently erected a building which he used for a livery business.

In the spring of 1893, having disposed of his interests in Andale, he moved to a farm three miles north of Clearwater, and resided there six years. In June, 1899, he helped organize the State Bank of Clearwater, and was then elected to his present office, cashier, a post he has faithfully held for more than sixteen years. He is now, and has been for a number of years, principal owner of the bank's stock. Clearwater was only in its infancy when he took a hand in its development, and his influence has been effective in furthering its progress. He erected and sold a number of residences, and in other ways has promoted the growth and general prosperity of the town. For six years he was city treasurer and was mayor eight years.

Mr. Dale is one of the large stockholders in the Uncle Sam Oil Company of Kansas City, Kansas, and for four years was a member of its board of directors. He is also a director in the Farmers and Bankers Life Insurance Company and the Guarantee Trust Company of Wichita.

His first wife was Helen McMurchy, a native of Scotland. She died three years after the marriage, leaving a daughter, Helen M. For his second wife Mr. Dale married Rillie Miller of Mokena, Illinois. They have a son, Frank M., who is now in the drug business in Clearwater.

EMIL B. ROSER is one of those quiet and resourceful business men who accomplishes a great deal and makes very little fuss about it and only comes in for a share of public attention when faithful performance of duty requires it.

Mr. Roser has been in the jewelry business at Wellington since January 10, 1883. He was born in the City of St. Louis January 27, 1867, one of the five children of Henry and Maria Theresa (Seyler) Roser. His father was a native of Germany and his mother of France, both lived for some years in Nancy, France, and in 1852 emigrated on a sailing vessel to New Orleans. Both had relatives in the United States and they finally located in St. Louis, where Henry Roser followed his business as a merchant tailor for several years. Having relatives in Wisconsin, he removed to that state in 1869, and was thus able to give his children the advantages of the fine Normal School at Platteville and later the State University at Madison. Henry Roser was a man of plain and unassuming character, made many friends, and provided liberally for his family. His wife died at Platteville, Wisconsin, in 1893. Henry Roser like many other German Americans did his full part as a soldier of his adopted country during the Civil war. He enlisted in the Thirtieth Missouri Volunteer Infantry, and was in some of the greatest campaigns of the war, including Sherman's march to the sea. He was in the quartermaster's department.

Emil B. Roser had most of his education in the common schools, and since 1878 has been depending upon his own efforts for his advancement in the world. He received considerable experience as clerk in a store and in 1882 he came out to Kansas, where

he had friends. His brother Edward L., had located in Wellington in 1878 and set up in the jewelry business. Edward was in that business at Wellington until his death in 1892. At the death of his brother E. B. Roser continued the business in partnership with his brother's widow, but in a short time bought out the store, and has since made it the leading establishment of its kind in that section of the state. He also owns the building in which his store is located, and at the present time is probably the largest property owner in the City of Wellington.

In 1906 he helped organize the National Bank of Commerce, served as its vice president for two years and has since been president. He is also a stockholder in the Farmers' State Bank at Wellington, is owner of some oil stock and has a large amount of city real estate. He identifies himself with every movement for the improvement and betterment of his community. He is a member and past president of the Commercial Club and is vice president of the Chautauqua Board. Fraternally he is both a York and Scottish Rite Mason, is past master of his lodge, has been officially identified with the Knights of Pythias for the past twenty-five years and for six terms held the presiding office. He is a charter member of the Benevolent and Protective Order of Elks in the Wellington Lodge, which was organized in 1909 and has since been its treasurer. He is also affiliated with the Eastern Star, the Loyal Order of Moose, and other social organizations.

JAMES WOOD. Among her valued citizens Kansas can number yet many of her pioneers, not the floating population of her earliest territorial days, but men who came to the state as homeseekers, even before the outbreak of the Civil war. These courageous and resourceful men are universally held in honorable esteem for the great progress made by Kansas was founded upon their hardihood and energy. One of these is found in James Wood, a representative citizen and a substantial farmer of Ogden Township, Riley County.

James Wood was born in England, September 27, 1844, the eldest son of William and Sarah (Jones) Wood. They came to the United States in 1850, accompanied by their three sons, James, Thomas and William. After living about five years in Greenup County, Kentucky, the family moved to La Salle County, Illinois, thence to Kansas, in the fall of 1857. They settled on the present farm of James Wood, in Ogden Township. Three more sons had been added to the family: Edward and Joseph, both of whom were born in Kentucky, and Charles, who was born in Illinois. The mother of James Wood died in 1862 and the father for his second wife chose Mrs. Elizabeth (Busby) Green, who became the mother of two children: Mary Ann and Ellen Elizabeth. After her death William Wood married a third time but there was no issue of that marriage.

From 1860 to 1866 William Wood was engaged in the freighting business, owning his own outfit and operating between Leavenworth and Fort Dodge. After retiring from this strenuous business he was engaged exclusively until his death in 1883, at the age of sixty-three years, in farming in Riley County. He was a man of true worth, of strong force of character, and his business efforts were attended with satisfying success. He was a consistent Christian, a member of the Methodist Episcopal Church, and was a careful and judicious father and kind and helpful neighbor.

James Wood was but six years of age when his

parents came to America and thirteen when they came to Kansas. Children of pioneers had comparatively few educational advantages and James found his time taken up in attending to clearing up his father's farm while the latter maintained his freighting business. After he was twenty-one years old he embarked in the same business for himself and during the two years in which he was so engaged had some thrilling experiences including two attacks by Indians on him with other freighters. In 1864, at Cow Creek, between Forts Riley and Larned, about 300 Indians opened fire upon the party of freighters which consisted of about 100 men. The fight lasted seven days and resulted in the killing of two of the freighters by the savages. The second attack from the Indians was made at Downer's Station, on the Smoky Hill River, when the Indians numbered about fifty and the freighters twelve. This was a sharp skirmish and the Indians succeeded in killing one of the party and captured two horses. Mr. Wood finally retired from this dangerous business, one that at the time was an absolute necessity because of lack of other methods of transportation, and then went into the peaceful, if laborious business of farming and stockraising. He has been eminently successful and now owns 640 acres of fine Kansas River valley land, on which are modern improvements including a handsome and commodious residence. Mr. Wood owns additionally 200 acres of ridge land, which he uses for grazing purposes.

Mr. Wood was married April 18, 1880, to Miss Amelia Elizabeth Wood, who is a daughter of Job and Eleanor Jane (Honaker) Wood. She was born in Indiana, January 15, 1859. Her father, who was a brother of the late William Wood, was born in England and came to the United States in 1850. He lived first in Kentucky, then in Illinois and later in Missouri, and came to Kansas in 1873 and settled in Ogden Township, Riley County, where he died when aged sixty years.

Mrs. James Wood is one of a family of twelve children born to her parents and was in her fifteenth year when she came to Kansas and was twenty-one when she was married to Mr. Wood, he being then almost thirty-six years old. Mr. and Mrs. Wood are the parents of the following children: William Harry, Elsie Jane, James Clarence, Charles Henry and Job Elbert and Joseph Albert, twins. Job Elbert, Joseph Albert and Charles and William all live with their parents. James Clarence resides at Junction City and Elsie Jane, who is the wife of I. J. Shockley, a farmer, lives in Riley County.

Although nominally a democrat, Mr. Wood has always felt that he had the right to vote independently when his judgment so prompted him. He has never desired public office for himself but has been the kind of citizen that has assisted good and competent men for positions of responsibility. He has long been identified with the Order of Odd Fellows. Mrs. Wood belongs to the Christian Church. Having spent the larger part of his life in Riley County and been a man of influence and importance in all that makes for good citizenship he has a very wide acquaintance and friends of many years standing.

COL. HIRAM W. LEWIS. In many important ways the city of Wichita expresses the life, ideals, and activities of the late Col. Hiram W. Lewis. In his time he was undoubtedly one of the most forceful figures and one of the ablest business men and citizens in the State of Kansas.

When he came to Wichita about 1875 he had already acquitted himself with credit both as a soldier in the Civil war and as a business man. Born near Warren, Ohio, he lived in Ohio during his youth and on May 25, 1863, enlisted in Company E of the One Hundred and Twenty-fourth Ohio Infantry. He went out as a private, becoming corporal, and was in many of the important battles of the great campaigns by which the states of Tennessee and Georgia were wrested from the Confederacy. He was wounded in the arm at Chickamauga. After his honorable discharge on May 15, 1865, he identified himself with the South and bought a plantation near Columbus, Mississippi. He remained on that plantation for ten years, and also took a very active part in public affairs. He served as sheriff of his county, and for several years represented his district in the State Legislature.

Colonel Lewis during his residence in Wichita was primarily a banker. When he came to Wichita he organized the Kansas National Bank, of which he became president. Later with M. W. Levy he organized the State Savings Bank of which he was vice president and cashier. Still later was organized under his direction the Gold Savings State Bank. All these banks are still in operation and have had a long and honorable record. The Gold Savings State Bank, however, is now known as the Union Bank.

In 1893 Colonel Lewis organized the Anchor Trust Company, and was its president until his death on February 12, 1912.

Aside from his work as a financier his life was especially notable for his influence in promoting temperance and education. When he came to Kansas he loyally aided in the temperance movement and it is said that he was probably the strongest factor in his part of the state in securing the adoption of the state-wide prohibition principle. He was also one of the organizers of the old Lewis Academy of Wichita, which was given his name. Some years ago this institution was merged with the College of Emporia, and the Lewis Hall of Science on the college campus now bears his name. During its existence the Lewis Academy served an important end in furnishing a preparatory education to many young men and women of Kansas, and Colonel Lewis was president of its board of trustees. Later he became a director of the College of Emporia and held that office until his death.

Every good cause in the City of Wichita met his hearty approval and gained his support. He was instrumental in organizing a number of mills and factories, in securing the establishment of stock yards, waterworks, and other public utilities, and a complete history of the city could not be written without frequent reference to his name.

Colonel Lewis was twice married. His first wife was Lucy Strong of Massachusetts, who died leaving four children. He married her sister, Kittie Strong, who survives him. Of this union there were five children.

Hiram W. Lewis, Jr., next to the youngest of his father's second children, was born in Wichita February 28, 1891. He graduated from Lewis Academy in 1909, and then took a two-year course in Baker University and finished his schooling at the University of Chicago, where he graduated with the degree Ph. B. Returning to Wichita, he entered the offices of the Anchor Trust Company, and since

1914 has been its secretary and a director. His brother, P. K. Lewis, is president of the Anchor Trust Company. This company handles first mortgages, loans and investments, and is one of the important organizations of the kind in the state. In February, 1915, they opened a branch office at Phoenix, Arizona, which is conducted under the personal supervision of P. K. Lewis.

MAJ. WILLIAM SIMS. The late Maj. William Sims, whose death occurred July 23, 1907, on his farm in Shawnee County, Kansas, had an enviable record both as a soldier of the Civil war and as a citizen in the years that followed that struggle. He was born May 15, 1831, on a farm in Muskingum County, Ohio, and was a son of Mahlon and Myron (Riley) Sims. He grew to manhood in his native community, securing his scholastic training in the common schools, and when still a young man served for a number of years as a clerk in the office of the probate judge. At the breaking out of the Civil war, he enlisted in Company G, Thirty-second Regiment, Ohio Volunteer Infantry, and when the company was organized he was made orderly sergeant. Later a company was taken out of his regiment to man a battery and Mr. Sims was sent back home to recruit a new company to fill the vacancy. While he was absent upon this duty, his regiment was captured at Harper's Ferry. His command then became Company A, Ninth Ohio Cavalry, of which he was made captain, and subsequently he was at the siege of Knoxville, where he was filling the post of major by promotion. Owing to ill health, he was compelled to resign from active service at the front, and from that time until 1866 was employed in the quartermaster's department.

When he received his honorable discharge, Major Sims returned to Ohio, where he engaged in farming, and so continued for two years, then removing to DeWitt County, Illinois, there carrying on agricultural operations until 1872. In that year he came to Kansas and purchased a farm in Mission Township, Shawnee County, of which he was the owner up to his death. Mr. Sims was a thorough, capable and systematic farmer and won success in his ventures as a tiller of the soil, but also was energetic in other directions and filled a prominent place in the affairs of his community. He took an active part in the Grange movement and for many years was treasurer and master of the Kansas State Grange, in this way becoming widely known in state agricultural circles. After serving one term in the capacity of state senator, he became treasurer of the State Board of Agriculture, of which he was subsequently made secretary and acted in the latter capacity some six or eight years. By appointment from Governor Humphrey, he was appointed treasurer of the State of Kansas, to fill the unexpired term of James Hamilton, and for a number of years following the expiration of his tenure of office, was employed as receiver of the Will Knox Bank, administrator of various estates, and in the handling of much similar and important work. Finally, he became president of the First National Bank of Topeka and held that office until the institution went into the hands of a receiver. Prior to this he had been suffering from ill health, and for the last two years of his term as bank president he could give but little thought or attention to bank matters, but it was no act of his which caused the failure of the bank, and throughout his entire career he bore the reputation of an honorable, honest and upright man of the highest integrity and strictest probity.

Major Sims' wife bore the maiden name of Hannah A. Richey and they had two children: John B. and Ella, the latter of whom died in early childhood. Major Sims was a Methodist. Politically he was a republican, and his fraternal connection was with the Independent Order of Odd Fellows. He was always an interested and valued member of the Grand Army of the Republic and a popular comrade of Lincoln Post No. 1.

The only living member of Major Sims' family is John B. Sims, of Topeka, who was born in Muskingum County, Ohio, April 2, 1854. He received a high school education and remained with his parents until coming to Kansas, where for a number of years he was engaged in farming and also bought and sold cattle extensively. He still owns the old home place in Mission Township, a tract of 560 acres, but since 1908 has been devoting the major portion of his time and attention to discharging the duties of his office as secretary and treasurer of the Topeka Pure Milk Company, which in recent years has come to be looked upon as a necessary commercial adjunct. Mr. Sims is a stanch republican and has served two terms in the lower house of the Kansas Legislature, in 1889 and 1891. As business man, citizen and public official, he has won public confidence and esteem, and his name is synonymous with straightforward dealing and loyalty to friendships.

Mr. Sims married Miss Josephine McCracken, who passed over in 1910, leaving three children: John B., Jr., Eleanor, who is the wife of Fred Hill, and Dorothy. Mr. Sims is a Christian Scientist in religious faith.

HENRY FORD HARBAUGH. Even today the great State of Kansas is looked upon as a land of opportunities and a good place for the young man to settle and provide for the future. This is even more true thirty or forty years ago, though it required perhaps a stronger element of individual initiative, courage and ability to endure hardships with patience and fortitude.

It was as a young man looking for a permanent home and a country where his energies and talents would be given the freest exercise that Henry Ford Harbaugh arrived in Kansas in 1878. An uncle was living on a farm near Wellington, and that town was his first choice of destination. He came by railroad as far as Newton, and then by horse and wagon drove over a large part of the western and central portion of the state, and from Wichita arrived in Wellington by stage. He was evidently satisfied, because soon after he reached Wellington he bought 160 acres of land, and started with characteristic vigor to farm it and raise stock. He broke much of that land with horse and ox teams, and his first wheat crop was cut with a cradle. He lived simply and frugally, and adapted himself to the hard conditions which surrounded the early Kansas farmers of thirty or forty years ago. For two years after he came to this state he taught school a part of each year. With that quarter section as a nucleus Mr. Harbaugh has continued to show his faith in Kansas farm land by investing his surplus until he now owns 1,000 acres in Sumner County and also 300 acres in the State of Missouri.

This record of achievement by no means sums up what he has done during the thirty-eight years of his residence in Kansas. In 1888 the Southern

Kansas Mutual Insurance Company was organized, and although he was not present at the meeting Mr. Harbaugh was elected one of its first directors. The following year he was chosen treasurer, and filled that office until 1911, when he was elected president, an office he still holds. The general offices of this company are at Wellington, where Mr. Harbaugh has lived since retiring from the farm in 1914. Mr. Harbaugh stood by the Southern Kansas Mutual through all its ups and downs in the early years, and his associates credit him with much of the success of this company. In 1903 he took the leading part in organizing the Farmers Mutual Telephone Company, and that company now has about three thousand telephones in operation. He has been its president from the time of its organization. He is vice president of the National Bank of Commerce of Wellington, of which he was one of the organizers.

It was only natural that a business man of such standing should be chosen to represent his home people in the State Legislature. He was elected in 1897 on the populist ticket, though his politics is now republican. In 1899 he was father of a bill in the Legislature granting the legal right for hail insurance companies to do business in Kansas. It was as a result of that measure that the Kansas State Mutual Hail Association was organized in 1899. This subsequently has been known as the McPherson Hail Insurance Company. For several years Mr. Harbaugh served as adjuster for the company, then was elected treasurer, and in 1912 was chosen president. He is thus the chief executive in several of Kansas' most substantial insurance organizations.

In 1907 he was again returned to the Legislature, this time on the republican ticket. In that session he was author of several good bills, including one to allow townships to own and operate cemeteries, and also the bill to allow mutual insurance companies to insure schools and churches without paying foreign companies revenue. It should be stated that the McPherson Hail Company is the largest company of its kind in the state and the second largest mutual company. Mr. Harbaugh is vice president of the State Association of Mutual Insurance Companies, and is one of the best informed men in the state on the subject of insurance generally. He was one of the charter members of the Bank of Commerce of Wellington, in which his son is now assistant cashier.

Having considered some of the achievements by which Mr. Harbaugh has become prominent in business and civic affairs in Kansas, something should be said of his personal and family history. He was born at Trenton in Tuscarawas County, Ohio, August 1, 1849, the oldest of the eleven children of Eli and Catherine (Engle) Harbaugh. His mother was a native of Germany, and his father of Ohio. There were four Harbaugh brothers who came out of Germany in the early days and settled in the northern part of the State of Maryland, and subsequently all were soldiers in the War of 1812. From Maryland they went into the State of Ohio and became pioneers there. Eli Harbaugh was a cabinet maker by trade, having learned that occupation from his father. In 1852 Eli Harbaugh went as a pioneer to the State of Iowa, locating in Washington County, where he took up a claim, and his family joined him there in the next year. They made the journey by river as far as Keokuk, and thence overland to Washington County. The family lived in a log house there for a number of years, and that old home and its surroundings are among the first conscious recollections of Mr. Henry F. Harbaugh. The father broke his land

with ox teams, and he was able to serve the early community of farmers by his pronounced ability as a mechanic and inventor. He converted an old boiler into shovels, and manufactured a number of single and double shovel plows that were in great demand by the farmers in his section. Thus the early life of Henry Ford Harbaugh was spent in a pioneer home in Iowa. He attended a school supported by subscriptions paid by the parents of the scholars, and while it is now many years since he left school he has always been a constant student and a man who reads books with a discriminating judgment. When he left Iowa to make a career of his own he went out to California in 1875, but was not satisfied with that state as a permanent residence, and in 1877 returned to Iowa and the following year began his adventures in Kansas.

On March 10, 1880, soon after getting settled on his homestead near Wellington, he married Elizabeth Blattner, of Iowa. They are the parents of four children. Nellie M. is the wife of G. F. Elsass, of Wellington. George E. is now assistant cashier in the Wellington Bank of Commerce. John P. operates the old homestead southeast of Wellington. Edward H. lives at Wichita.

Besides his other public service Mr. Harbaugh served four years as township trustee of Greene Township, Sumner County. He is an active Mason, a member of the Lodge and of Wichita Consistory of the Scottish Rite, is chairman of the board of trustees of the Grand Lodge of the Ancient Order of United Workmen, a position he has held ten years, and was formerly vice president and is still a member of the Kansas division of the Anti-Horse Thief Association. For fully thirty years he held a place on the school board of his home district. Mr. and Mrs. Harbaugh are members of the Presbyterian Church, and have brought up their children in that faith.

JAMES M. MAY. A great and forceful influence was removed from the religious affairs of the State of Kansas in the death of James M. May, which occurred at his home in Manhattan August 17, 1915. The best work of his life was performed as a Sunday School and church organizer and missionary. However, he had a wonderful adaptability and resourcefulness, and might have been successful as a mechanic, a farmer or in almost any line of business, had not his earnest devotion to the cause of religion kept him in that field of effort during all his active years.

He was born in Adams County, Ohio, September 6, 1848, a son of Henry and Margaret (McClung) May. He was of Holland Dutch ancestry in the paternal line and through his mother inherited Scotch-Irish stock. His father was born in Pennsylvania and his mother in Ohio. His father was a carpenter and farmer, and the late Mr. May grew up on a farm in Southern Ohio. The limited education which he was privileged to receive from the common schools he supplemented in after years by private study and wise reading, but his knowledge of men and the motives that move mankind always transcended any of the lore obtained from books. However, he was a great book lover, and to the end of his days enjoyed the communion with the great thinkers of the past.

As a young man he learned the trade of carpenter. That together with farming furnished him an occupation and means of livelihood until he was past forty years of age. When very young he left home to fight the battles of life for himself, but he faithfully contributed of his earnings to the support of his parents until he was thirty years of age or until he established a home of his own.

From early manhood he lived in the West. For a few years he was employed in bridge building for railroads. His proficiency in that work brought him the offer of a good position with large opportunities for the future, but he refused to consider employment which would require his services on Sundays.

While in Hamilton County, Nebraska, he took up a homestead, was married there, and he and his wife settled down to work their claim. Thereafter for a dozen years or so he alternately followed farming and carpentering, and in the meantime his parents came out to Nebraska and located in the same county and spent the rest of their days there. From that time in his youth when he united with the Presbyterian Church the life of James M. May was distinguished for his earnestness and zeal and his devotion to the great cause of Christ. In 1889 he entered the official work of the church as a Sunday School missionary. His first labors were performed in New Mexico, where he spent six months, then for nearly twenty years he was employed in the presbyteries of Western Kansas, where his name became familiar to nearly every Presbyterian home and others as well. Before removing to Manhattan in 1907 he lived at Lincoln and Minneapolis, Kansas, those two towns being his home during his many years of connection with the Presbyterian Board of Sabbath School Work.

In Western Kansas numerous Sunday schools and churches have become permanent organizations and stand as monuments to his labor. The following brief report of his work was found among his papers: 161 new schools organized and 85 revived, with 897 teachers and 7,883 scholars; 549 mission schools and 401 church schools visited and encouraged; 607 Bibles and Testaments, and 10,621 books of the board distributed, and 375,313 pages of religious tracts and papers given away; 9,421 homes visited; 2,452 addresses made; 215 conversions made in Gospel meetings held with mission schools; 117,100 miles traveled in doing the work; Presbyterian churches developed from Sunday schools organized—Kanapolis, Mundon (Bohemian), Elkhorn, Harmony, Aurora, Spring Valley, La Plata (New Mexico); Presbyterian missions developed, Shiloh, Summerville, Pleasant Ridge, Walnut Grove, Stagg Creek, Lindsey; Methodist churches developed, Langley, Appleville, Macyville, Talmage; Evangelical churches developed at Vine Creek and Longford; United Brethren churches at Elm Grove and Melville; and German Baptist at Russell—in all twenty-seven churches.

"They that are wise shall shine as the brightness of the firmament, and they that turn many to righteousness as the stars forever." To "turn many to righteousness" the late Mr. May made the mission of his life. He was a wonderful personal worker, his influence was marvelous and will abide. He exemplified in faith and practice the essentials of the Christian life, and his own career is a splendid testimony to the power of goodness actuated by Christian principles.

"The dear Lord's best interpreters
Are humble human souls;
The Gospel of a life like his
Is more than books and scrolls."

January 15, 1878, Mr. May was united in marriage with Lucy J. Fye. Six children were born to them: Gertrude, a popular teacher in the primary department of the Manhattan City schools; Nellie, postmistress at the Kansas State Agricultural College; Jesse D., in charge of the farm near Manhattan which is now the home of the family; Mary, who completed the high school course in the State School for the Blind and afterwards took a two years' post-graduate course; John M., who graduated from the Kansas State Agricultural College in 1910 and is now at the head of the department of the School of Agriculture at River Falls, Wisconsin; and Henry, who died when ten years old.

Mrs. May, who survived her husband, resides with the family at Manhattan, was born in Pennsylvania April 6, 1856, daughter of John H. and Mary (Reynolds) Fye. Her parents were born in Pennsylvania, and when she was seven years of age they moved to Illinois, and ten years later to Nebraska, settling in Hamilton County, where Mrs. May lived until her marriage. In ancestry she inherits Pennsylvania Dutch stock through her father and English through her mother. Mrs. May and her children are all members of the Presbyterian Church except John M., who in the absence of a Presbyterian church in his community affiliates with the Congregational Society.

GEORGE A. GREENE, M. D. One of the most widely known physicians of Kansas is Dr. George A. Greene, of Wichita, proprietor of Greene's Pathological Laboratory for cancer research. He is a physician of wide experience and learning, and has been in practice in Kansas for the last fifteen years. Few men enter the medical profession with a better equipment than Doctor Greene. In his early career he was a teacher, later studied law, but never practiced it, and laid a very scholarly foundation to his work in the medical field. He was born in Jackson County, West Virginia. After leaving the public schools he entered Anthens College at Athens, West Virginia, where he completed the course, and followed this with another course in Barbersville College. For several years he taught in different parts of his native state, and then began the study of law. He was admitted to the bar in Kentucky. The knowledge of law has proved valuable to him in various ways, though he has never practiced it as a profession. He had realized in the meantime that his real inclination and natural talents were for medicine.

After coming to Kansas in 1902 he was in general practice for a time, but on moving to Wichita he concentrated all his efforts upon his specialty. In fact the purpose guiding him when he chose the medical profession was that he might assist in the solution of the cancer problem. To that end he has been studying and experimenting for many years. After coming to Wichita he established Green's Pathological Laboratory for cancer research, an institution devoted to the non-surgical treatment of cancer. This is located at 1306 North Market Street. Few institutions of the kind have a better record as to results. Cancer patients from nearly every state in the Union have been treated there, and apart from individual cures Doctor Greene has contributed a large amount of knowledge to the problem connected with the cure and treatment of this malignant disease.

During his college career Doctor Greene perfected himself in Greek, Latin, German and French. On

Mr & Mrs W. H. Reed.

September 6, 1905, he married Miss Alma E. Taylor, who was born in Lane County, Kansas. They have one son, J. Orville.

CALVIN M. HILL. One of the long established business houses of Topeka; and one which has established itself firmly in the confidence of the public by reason of the honorable manner in which its affairs have been conducted, is the wholesale wall paper and retail paint business of Calvin M. Hill. Mr. Hill has been a resident of Kansas for thirty-four years, having come here with his parents in 1882, and, with the exception of four years has been identified with the painting and decorating business throughout his career. His present enterprise was started in a small way sixteen years ago, and from its start has prospered and developed.

Mr. Hill was born at Carrollton, Greene County, Illinois, October 27, 1867, and is one of eight children (of whom six are still living) born to Samuel B. and Mary (Hutchins) Hill. His parents came to Kansas in 1882, locating at Marion, where his father was engaged in the painting business until his death. The mother still survives. Calvin M. Hill was primarily educated in the public schools of Illinois and was fifteen years of age when he accompanied his parents to Kansas. He was graduated from the Marion High School in 1889, subsequently spending one year in study at the State Normal School, Emporia, and thus prepared himself for teaching, which he thought to make his regular calling at the outset of his career. For three years he taught in the country schools and was then made principal of the school at Marion, but after one year in the latter capacity turned his attention to the painting, paper hanging and decorating business. Mr. Hill learned the mechanical part of this calling under the preceptorship of his father, and in 1900 embarked in business at Topeka, in a small store on Seventh Street. His unflagging energy and excellent workmanship soon attracted to his concern a good custom and Mr. Hill found it necessary to enlarge his establishment, equipment and stock. This has since occurred on several occasions, and the concern is now one of the leaders in its line in the city. Mr. Hill not only does all kinds of high class painting, paper hanging and decorating, but sells paint, glass, oils, etc., in a retail way, and has built up a large business in handling wall paper wholesale. His name upon a piece of work is an assurance of high quality and an evidence of perfect fulfillment of contract, and in business circles he is well known for his integrity. From 1909 until 1916 Mr. Hill had a second establishment, located at Oklahoma City, Oklahoma but this he disposed of in the latter year. A democrat in his political views, he is primarily a business man and not a politician, although while living at Marion he held several minor offices. Mr. Hill holds membership in the Knights and Ladies of Security, the United Commercial Travelers, the Rotary Club and the Commercial Club, and is a thirty-second degree Scottish Rite and Royal Arch Mason and a Noble of the Mystic Shrine.

In 1891 Mr. Hill was married to Miss Mabel Foote, of Marion, Kansas, and they have three children: J. Jay, Harriet and Margaret. Mr. and Mrs. Hill and their children are members of the Episcopal Church.

WILLIAM H. REED. By reason of the extent and quality of his usefulness, his commercial soundness and acumen, his public spirit, his integrity, and his nearness to the fundamental requirements of citizenship, William H. Reed affords in his career an excellent and encouraging example of success gained through the proper use of every day abilities and opportunities. He laboriously climbed every round of the mercantile ladder, and so ably did he make use of his opportunities, that he was able to retire from activities in the evening of life, and is now quietly residing at his comfortable home at Topeka.

Mr. Reed was born at Bedford, Pennsylvania, January 30, 1830, and has been a resident of Kansas since 1869. He was one of three children born to Dr. William and Elizabeth (Reed) Reed, natives of Pennsylvania, and not related before their marriage. Doctor Reed was a physician and surgeon, and followed his profession throughout his life in the Keystone state. After securing his education in the public schools of Bedford, William H. Reed mastered the carpenter's trade, at which he worked until a severe injury to his hand caused him to seek some other occupation. As a young man he had gone to Warsaw, Illinois, where he was married June 9, 1853, to Miss Elizabeth Davis, who was born at Watertown, New York, daughter of Luther H. and Nancy H. (Bliss) Davis, natives respectively of Pittsfield and Rutland, Vermont, and pioneers of Illinois. Her uncle, a native of Vermont, and an early pioneer in York state, was a soldier in the War of 1812, and he told many interesting stories of early American history still remembered by Mrs. Reed. He settled near Lafargeville on a farm, where he resided until his death, at the age of eighty-four. Another of her uncles, the Rev. E. W. Bliss, was a Baptist minister at Philadelphia and later of Washington, District of Columbia, where he died at the age of ninety-four, after having preached for sixty-three years. Luther Davis took his family from New York state overland by way of wagon as far as Ottawa, Illinois, and there selling the wagons and other paraphernalia, embarked on a boat down the Illinois River and thence up the Mississippi to Warsaw, where for many years Mr. Davis was prominent as a commission merchant, buying goods all over the surrounding country. Mrs. Luther Davis had two sisters: Mrs. Capt. James Comstock, wife of a Civil war veteran; and Mrs. Filley Jenner. Mrs. Reed had three brothers in the Civil war. One, Edwin, was captured during Sherman's march to the sea and was starved and frozen to death in Libby prison, though shortly before he died he was removed to David's Island. Her oldest brother, Emmerson Davis, after Lincoln was assassinated, was taken for J. Wilkes Booth on account of a striking resemblance to that notorious assassin, and he barely escaped with his life. He was arrested and closely guarded until he was identified and the real Wilkes Booth had been discovered.

Mr. and Mrs. William H. Reed had four children: B. F. Reed, a prominent wholesale business man at Ellensburg, Washington, is president of the Cascade Irrigation Canal and an extensive land holder in Ellensburg and Seattle; he is also prominent in the Masonic order, and has two children; Emma, who married W. M. Dignon has four children; Nona, who became Mrs. Quinon has one child, Joseph, of Topeka; Etta Gertrude, who died in infancy.

For a number of years after their marriage Mr. and Mrs. Reed resided at Warsaw, Illinois, and were there during the Civil war. In 1869 they sold their grocery store and came to Topeka on the Union Pacific Railway, crossing the river on the old corduroy bridge. They bought property at 912 Kansas

Avenue, on which they built the home which they still own. Subsequently Mr. Reed entered the furniture business at 510 Kansas Avenue with B. F. Reed, and the business was built up to large proportions, the partnership continuing for nine years. B. F. Reed then sold his interest to Mr. Tomlinson, who continued with William H. Reed for nine years, following which Mr. Reed carried on the business alone for a like period and then retired. In the meantime he had been investing heavily in real estate and farm lands, and these interests became so important as to demand all his attention, although the furniture business had been a most successful one and had made Mr. Reed one of the leading merchants of Topeka.

Mr. Reed is now living in retirement, having reached his eighty-seventh year. Although he has not been in good health for the last year or two he is still remarkably well preserved and takes a keen interest in all matters affecting his community. He is a republican, but has never been a politician, and his only public office has been that of constable, which he held while residing at Warsaw, Illinois. He has no fraternal connections. In business circles he is looked up to and respected as a man of high principles and absolute integrity. During the active years of his life he gave of his money, his ability and his time in the support of movements for civic and general betterment and deserves an established place among the men who made Topeka the great city that it is today.

Mrs. Reed remembers many interesting stories in regard to the struggles which she and Mr. Reed had in getting a foothold in the early days. For a number of years, to aid her husband, she conducted a boarding house, and as the hostess of such entertained many senators and representatives as well as other prominent men of young Kansas. Perhaps in this way she developed her extraordinary business ability, for she now handles all of her husband's property interests in a manner that leaves no doubt as to her acumen and good judgment. They have two farms, each of 160 acres, also considerable city property, including two houses, one on Twelfth and Clay streets and the other at 617 West Tenth Street; their own residence and another dwelling at 934 Quincy Street.

Mrs. Reed has been a Methodist all her life and has been active in religious and charitable work. She is a charter member of the Ladies Auxiliary of the Grand Army of the Republic, and was president and vice president of the ladies branch of the Young Men's Christian Association at Topeka before the Young Women's Christian Association was formed. She also belongs to the Maccabees, and is a charter member of the Toltec Rites of the Masonic Order.

HON. JAMES MCDERMOTT. The career of James McDermott, now a retired resident of the City of Winfield, has been one remarkable in many ways, and his life story contains many interesting chapters. From newsboy on the streets of New York to leading lawyer and member of the Kansas Legislature, his active career led him through many of the most important battles of the Civil war, as well as through the struggles of political life, and through it all he has maintained a reputation for courage, fidelity and absolute fearlessness.

Mr. McDermott was born in New York City, New York, June 6, 1841, and is a son of Hugh McDermott, who was a native of Ireland and who became an extensive contractor in this country. He was taken to Kentucky when about twelve years of age. It was

here that he attended his first term of school, and completed his education largely by private study until he qualified as a teacher and taught in several schools in Kentucky. When the Civil war threatened the destruction of the Union and the families of his neighborhood were rent by dissenting political opinions, he cast his lot with the Union, and in July, 1861, became a member of Company I, Second Regiment, Kentucky Volunteer Infantry, of which he had been one of the organizers. At the time of the organization of the company he was made orderly sergeant, and later he was promoted second, and then first lieutenant, and during the last three years of active service commanded his, and incomplete fragments of other companies. Mr. McDermott participated in the battle of Mill Springs, Kentucky, and Fort Donelson; arrived too late to get into action at Shiloh; was in the Vicksburg campaign, and then took part in the engagement at Chickamauga, where he received a severe gun-shot wound through the groin, from which he has ever since been a sufferer. In November he had recovered sufficiently to rejoin his command, and although he was compelled to be carried to the front by soldiers, fought as commander of his company in the severe engagement of Missionary Ridge. He continued under the command of General Thomas thereafter until the close of the war. After the battle of Chickamauga, his command was mounted, and from that time forward he had under his orders 250 men employed in scout duty. Later Mr. McDermott fought in the battles of Franklin and Nashville, his last, and received his honorable discharge when peace was declared.

Returning to Kentucky, Mr. McDermott began the study of law at Vanceburg in the office of George Thomas, then a judge and later a congressman. After being admitted to the bar he practiced at Vanceburg until the spring of 1870 when he moved to Kansas, took up a claim near Dexter, and engaged in practice at Winfield. He was married in Vanceburg to Miss Mary Bertram and to this marriage there were born three children: James A., county attorney of Cowley County and city attorney of Winfield; Catherine, who is now Mrs. John G. Davidson; and Mary. Soon after his arrival in Kansas, Mr. McDermott became interested in politics, and was recognized to be constructed of official timber. He was sent to the Kansas Legislature and was county attorney for Cowley County and city attorney for Winfield. Mr. McDermott built up a large law practice, but in 1912, owing to declining health and advancing years, retired from the active practice of his profession and was succeeded by his son, James A. Mr. McDermott's first wife died in 1883, and he subsequently married Miss Tirzah Henderson, by whom he became the father of two children: George Thomas and William F.

Mr. McDermott is one of the stalwart republicans of Kansas, and by religion is a Baptist. He is a man of undoubted integrity, of very aggressive views and with courage that has been proven in actual battle and in legal and civic strife. His predominating characteristics are, perhaps, his uncompromising honesty and his antagonism to anything savoring of double dealing or chicanery.

George Thomas McDermott a son of James McDermott by his second marriage, was named after the Union general and the man under whom his father read law. He is himself one of the rising lawyers of Kansas, and is now a member of the well known Topeka law firm of Stone & McDermott.

ENOCH HASSEBROEK. As proprietor of a large general store, at Riley, Kansas, Enoch Hassebroek is a leading factor in the town's commercial life. The business of modern merchandising is a more or less complex one and experience counts for much. Mr. Hassebroek was carefully trained by his merchant father and for the past fifteen years has been at the head of his own establishment. The modern merchant needs large capital behind him because, an account of the awakened demands of twentieth century customers, he must go to the ends of the world to secure his goods, and he must know how to buy closely, and watchful of the markets, in order to sell profitably. Mr. Hassebroek's reputation for reliable merchandise has carried his name all over this section of the country. He was born in Ogle County, Illinois, July 4, 1872, and is a son of Casper W. and Ida (Groenhagen) Hassebroek.

Casper W. Hassebroek was born in Oldersum, Prussia-Germany, August 23, 1836, and died in Riley County, Kansas. He was a son of William and Ann (Freerks) Hassebroek, who emigrated to the United States in 1853 and settled in Ogle County, Illinois, where they spent their last years. Their family contained the following children: Fritje, Frederick, Johanna, Wiemke, Casper W., Albretje, David, Grytie and Wilkea. Casper W. was seventeen years old when he accompanied his parents to the United States and to Ogle County, Illinois. In his own land he had attended the excellent schools and in mental preparation was far beyond youths of his own age among the farmer boys in Ogle County. There he followed agricultural pursuits until 1874, when he came to Riley County, Kansas, subsequently purchasing 160 acres, situated in Madison Township. This land he cultivated until 1877, when he came to the Village of Riley where he was one of the pioneer merchants. He was not only a successful merchant and efficient financier, but a man whose strict integrity won for him the esteem and respect of all who knew him. He was one of the founders of many enterprises and the encourager of many civic movements that advanced the place in which he chose to make his home and his name will long be remembered.

While a resident of Illinois, Casper W. Hassebroek was married to Ida Groenhagen, who survives him. She was born in Sickwerum, Ostfriesland, Hanover, Germany, November 17, 1838, and came to the United States with her parents in 1857. To the above marriage the following children were born: William, who died in infancy; Grytje (Hattie), a widow, who is a resident of Riley; Anna, who is the wife of Frank O. Clark, who is a farmer in Madison Township; Hermina, who is deceased; William (2), who is a resident of Salt Lake City, Utah; Enoch; Mary, who is the wife of Doctor Goodwin, of Riley; Lydia, who is deceased; Johannas, who lives at Riley; and Ida, who lives at Clay Center.

Enoch Hassebroek may almost be claimed as a native by Kansas as he was only two years old when brought to the state and has lived here ever since and all his interests are here. He received a good common school education and then entered his father's store and was trained to be a merchant. In 1901 he embarked in business for himself and now operates a first class general store, conducting it along the same honorable lines that his father established many years ago.

Mr. Hassebroek was married in 1896 to Miss Ellen Griffith, a lady of Welsh ancestry, and they have five children. He is a member of the Presbyterian Church. In politics he is a republican and fraternally he is an Odd Fellow and a Master Mason.

ROBERT C. FOULSTON, while one of the younger members of the Wichita bar, has made a name for himself by the able manner in which he has handled some important cases, and he has also been retained in the interests of the city government in a number of important trials.

A native of Kansas, born at Leoti, Robert C. Foulson started life with a sound physical training and environment, and with a liberal education. In 1908 he graduated from the high school at Moline, Kansas, then entered the liberal arts department of the Kansas State University, and soon transferred his studies to the law department, where he graduated June 7, 1911, with the degree LL. B. Since September, 1911, Mr. Foulston has been in practice at Wichita. In December, 1915, he formed a partnership with William E. Pepperell, a son of W. H. L. Pepperell, the internal revenue collector for this district. The firm is now Foulston & Pepperell. From April 7, 1913, to April 7, 1915, Mr. Foulston served as city prosecutor.

In March, 1915, he married Juanita W. Taylor. Mrs. Foulston is the daughter of Dr. O. J. Taylor, who for many years was in active practice as a physician at Wichita, having located in that city in the early '80s.

SADLIER J. HODGINS. In the practical everyday business world few Topeka citizens have achieved better results and have succeeded in making their careers more effective in the face of obstacles and through constant and hard fighting than Sadlier J. Hodgins. Mr. Hodgins is now head of one of the large commercial establishments in Topeka and has been prominently identified with the business and civic life of that city for a number of years.

He was born in County Tipperary, Ireland, June 1, 1867. After the death of his mother in the old country the family emigrated to the United States in 1877 and came direct to Topeka, where his father William R. Hodgins followed farming and stock raising in Dover Township of Shawnee County. William R. Hodgins, who died in 1881, belonged to a very prominent family in Ireland, and while in the old country was a banker and employer of men. He and his wife had a large family of children, as follows: William H., now deceased; Georgina E., wife of Walter Richards of Topeka; Charles J., deceased; Lillie G., Mrs. George H. Chessman, of Pasadena, California; Hugh A., of Topeka; Richard F. of Topeka; Sadlier J.; Tottenham H. of Doylestown, Pennsylvania; J. Arthur of Topeka; and Fred H. of Kansas City.

Sadlier J. Hodgins has known no other home than Kansas since he was ten years of age. From the time he was eleven he had to depend upon his own efforts and if any man can be called self-made he deserves that title. When he was about sixteen years of age he found employment in the surveying department of the Santa Fe Railway, and is one among many successful Kansas men who had a part of their early experience with that great railway system. He was connected with the railroad work for about seven years. He was next appointed a carrier in the Topeka postoffice and for fifteen years was one of the popular postmen of the city. Following that he made his experience count in a business way and for two years was salesman for the Topeka Paper Company. In 1907 he was elected register of deeds of Shawnee County, and by re-election filled that office with admirable efficiency for four years. During his first term in the office he organized the Central Paper Company, which subsequently bought the Topeka Paper Company and the two were consolidated under the name of the Central Topeka Paper Company. This is now one of the largest establishments of its kind in the State of Kansas, and Mr. Hodgins is president and treasurer.

Besides his participation in local politics and his service as register of deeds, Mr. Hodgins has constantly used his influence in behalf of the commercial and civic welfare of Topeka, and in 1912 was president of the Topeka Commercial Club. He is also a member of the Country Club, and in politics is a republican. He stands high in Masonic circles, being a past master of the Lodge, past high priest of the Chapter, is a Knight Templar York Rite Mason and a thirty-second degree Scottish Rite and also belongs to the Mystic Shrine.

In 1895 he married Jessie L. Burgess. Her father, Colonel James Burgess, was a prominent early pioneer of Kansas, served as a lieutenant colonel in the regiment of Indiana volunteers of which Benjamin Harrison was colonel, and he succeeded Harrison when the latter was made a brigadier general. Mr. and Mrs. Hodgins are members of the First Christian Church at Topeka.

ARCHIE W. LONG. Of the men who have contributed to the business importance and civic development of the various thriving communities of Kansas, one the value of whose services may not be gainsaid is Archie W. Long, of Manhattan. A resident of this city for nearly a quarter of a century, he was for a long period identified with the milling interests here, and now has large oil holdings and directs his energies toward the development of his enterprises connected with that industry. If he has been a contributor to the business development of the community, he has done even a greater service in the line of civic advancement, for it was during his term in the mayoralty chair that Manhattan's present excellent street and sewerage systems were inaugurated.

Mr. Long is a native of West Virginia, born at Ravenswood, Jackson County, March 17, 1872, a son of George W. and America E. (King) Long, who still reside at Ravenswood, where their sons were reared. The family is an old and respected one of the Old Dominion State, and an interesting bit of its history is found in the fact that the paternal grandmother of Archie W. Long, a native of Culpeper County, Virginia, as a young lady of fourteen years of age, in 1822 was a guest at a reception held in honor of LaFayette, the French friend of America and patriot general. George W. Long has long been engaged in blacksmithing and wagonmaking at Ravenswood, and from him his son inherits a decided mechanical turn of mind.

Archie W. Long was given a public school education, and as a young man learned the milling business in all its branches. At the age of nineteen years, he left the parental home to begin the battle of life for himself and went to North Dakota, where he remained for two years, engaged in milling. In August, 1892, he came to Manhattan, Kansas, where he has since resided and where he has risen to a high position in business and political affairs. On locating at Manhattan, he became the founder of the Manhattan Milling Company, with which he continued to be identified until 1903 and then disposed of his interests. Subsequently, for ten years, he was a member of the Long-Barner Milling Company, retiring from the milling business in 1913. For two years thereafter, he was engaged in farming, and March 1, 1915, turned his attention to the oil industry. His business ventures have been attended by gratifying success.

In matters concerning the public welfare, Mr. Long has always manifested a commendable spirit. In politics he is a democrat, and has always been active in the councils of his party in Riley County, taking the lead in political campaigns and bearing much of the burden of losing fights, his party being in the minority in the county. He was twice the candidate of the democrats for the Kansas Legislature, but, although on each occasion he made a credible race, was unsuccessful of election, and, in fact, made the campaigns without any great hope of overcoming the great republican majority. In the city of Manhattan, however, he has been more successful. He was elected a member of the city council for one term, and, later, was sent to the mayoralty chair for one term. As the chief executive of the city administration he rendered acceptable and important service, as after years have witnessed. During his administration many excellent measures were inaugurated and carried through to a successful issue, even against the strongest opposition, chief among which were sanitary and street improvements. The city, at the time he went into office was without sewerage, and Mayor Long installed a sewerage system and improved the water works toward the end of raising the sanitary conditions of the city to the highest standard, now the pride of Manhattan. No less commendable and important was the stand he took in the matter of street improvements, which he undertook and successfully carried out. Street improvements then and subsequently made have made Manhattan one of Kansas' cities of best improved thoroughfares, thus adding not only to the comfort and convenience of its people, but to civic beauty and sanitation. Mr. Long is a thirty-second degree Mason and a Noble of the Mystic Shrine.

In 1903 Mr. Long was married to Miss Laura Engel, a daughter of the late Carl Engel, a pioneer and for years a highly respected citizen of Manhattan, where Mrs. Long was born, reared and educated.

HENRY H. QUANTIC. One of the well known and highly respected citizens of Riley, Kansas, is Henry H. Quantic, a substantial retired farmer. For thirty-two years he has been a resident of Kansas and during this time has witnessed many wonderful changes, and he has done his part in bringing about many that have been beneficial. He was born in the old Town of Kingsbury, in Somersetshire, England, June 10, 1841. His parents, who lived and died in England, were Job and Hannah (Bonning) Quantic, who had a family of thirteen children, five of whom reached mature years. Henry H. was the eldest of the sons, the others being: Thomas G., John, Job and Samuel, and of these, Henry H., Thomas and Job, the last named being deceased all came to America.

Henry H. Quantic was the first of his family to cross the Atlantic Ocean to the United States, making the voyage in 1862, at the instance of Job Bradford, an Englishman, who had previously located on a farm in New York and there prospered. During a visit to his native land he proposed to Henry H. Quantic a plan whereby the young man could borrow from him the sum needed for his traveling expenses and repay it by working on Mr. Bradford's farm for $10 per month. The offer was accepted and duly carried out and it seemed so sensible a plan that subsequently Mr. Quantic brought his brother Thomas to the United States under like conditions, and two years later, in 1868, also aided his brother Job in the same way.

Mr. Quantic continued to follow farming in New York until 1884, when he came to Riley County, Kansas, settling in Wild Cat Township, in the Valley of the Wild Cat. There he secured land which he subsequently developed into a fine farm and through hard work, frugality and good business management added greatly to his original holding and became one of the county's large landowners. For a number of years he engaged profitably in farming and stock raising, but the time came when ease and comfort began to look attractive and therefore he sold his country property and moved into the pleasant Town of Riley, retiring entirely from active business.

In 1868 Mr. Quantic was married to Dorcas Ann Trebley, who was then a resident of New York, but her birth took place in England, April 2, 1842. To this marriage the following children were born: Charles H., Florence A., Effie T., Maude E. and Myrtle Hannah. Both Mr. and Mrs. Quantic are members of the Methodist Episcopal Church and they are counted among the most active and benevolent residents of their Christian body. In politics Mr. Quantic casts his vote with the republican party but has never consented to hold a public office. His life has been one of industry and honesty, with strict regard for the rights of others, and temperate in all things and a strict observer of the moral code, he has reached advanced age in good health and thereby is able to fully enjoy the ease which is his portion and which he has earned.

GEORGE W. ROBINSON of Wichita has been a Kansan forty years. His first work in this state was as an educator at Winfield, continuing from June, 1876, to June, 1879. He soon turned to the more congenial work of a business career. The field in which his energies have found their most successful issues has been in banking, and there are a number of flourishing institutions in the state which were organized or at some time in their career have received the benefit of his excellent judgment and financial ability.

Born February 20, 1855, in Piqua, Ohio, he went to Illinois when a boy and was a student in Hedding College at Abingdon, in that state, until 1873. While in Illinois he taught in the country schools of MacDonough, Fulton and Adams counties, and during the school years of 1874-75-76 was principal of schools at LaPrairie, Illinois.

He next accepted the superintendency of the schools of Winfield, Kansas, and held that position from June, 1876, to June, 1879. In June of the latter year he became associated with his uncle, M. L. Read, and brothers, M. L. and W. C. Robinson, in the M. L. Reads Bank at Winfield. Since then his business record has been almost exclusively in the field of banking. In July, 1884, the M. L. Reads Bank was merged into the First National Bank of Winfield, with M. L. Read, president; M. L. Robinson, vice president; W. C. Robinson, cashier; and George W. Robinson as assistant cashier. Later he was promoted to vice president and cashier.

During the years 1901-02 he was cashier and

Vol. IV—7

president successively of the Pueblo National Bank at Pueblo, Colorado. Selling his interests there in November, 1892, he returned to the First National Bank at Winfield.

One of the greatest achievements of his banking career was his work as receiver of the First National Bank of Arkansas City, Kansas. He was appointed receiver July 3, 1893, by the late James H. Eckles, who was then comptroller of the currency under Cleveland's administration. In less than eight months he had reopened the bank, in February, 1894, and had paid every depositor in full, and with 4 per cent interest. Having accomplished this task in so satisfactory a manner Mr. Robinson returned to the First National Bank of Winfield as cashier, and was associated with that institution until he sold his interests in 1899. In that year he engaged in the wholesale grocery business at Winfield, and conducted it until January, 1902, when he came to Wichita.

At Wichita Mr. Robinson organized the National Bank of Wichita, serving as cashier until September 1, 1905. During the year 1906 he organized the Wichita State Bank, the Merchants State Bank of Wichita, and the National Bank of Commerce of Wellington, and had all three of them in a flourishing condition before he sold his interests in 1910. In that year he organized the Security State Bank of Wichita, of which he is now president, and he was also president of the Reserve State Bank of Wichita, which he organized in 1912. His last achievement in financial affairs was the organization in 1916 of the Kansas Cattle Loan Company of Wichita.

On April 27, 1880, Mr. Robinson married Miss Ella E. Holmes of Winfield. They have one daughter, Edith L.

JAMES CUTHBERT. One of the oldest and best known general contractors in the state is James Cuthbert of Topeka, which city has been his home and the center of his widely extended activities more than thirty-five years. As his name indicates, Mr. Cuthbert is a sturdy Scotchman, and his many associates and friends in Kansas say that he exemplifies all the best traits of the race.

He was born in Nairnshire, Scotland, July 14, 1849, a son of James and Jane (Bowie) Cuthbert, who spent their lives in Scotland. He grew up among his native hills and heather, had a public school education, and after reaching his majority attended evening schools in Glasgow. At Elgin, Scotland, he served a four years' apprenticeship at stone cutting, and subsequently worked as a journeyman in Glasgow.

In order that he might find those abundant opportunities which he had long heard existed in America, he carefully saved his money to enable him to cross the Atlantic and make a home in the New World. Through the influence of Mr. Coats, whose name is familiar throughout the world as the inventor of the Coats thread, he went to Canada in March, 1872, and for a time worked at Peterboro, Ontario. After six months in Canda he came to the United States, and for about a year followed his trade in Cincinnati. It was in Cincinnati that he made the acquaintance of the late John Sargent, who for many years was his associate in the contracting business at Topeka. From Cincinnati Mr. Cuthbert went to Indianapolis, and after working at his trade took up contracting. During the panic of 1873 he experienced some difficulty in obtaining all his savings from the bank which had temporarily closed. His next location was in St. Louis, where he began working on the government postoffice, and was afterwards at Little Rock.

From Little Rock in July, 1879, Mr. Cuthbert arrived in Topeka. His first work here was in setting stone on the west wing of the State Capitol. Afterwards he was a sub-contractor on the Topeka Federal Building and the Kansas City Federal Building. In 1883 he became a member of the contracting firm of Smith, Sargent & Company. Three years later when Mr. Smith moved to California, the firm became Cuthbert & Sargent, and that was the title of the firm of general contractors known all over the State of Kansas until March 1, 1910. Since that date Mr. Cuthbert has been head of the contracting firm of Cuthbert & Sons. Cuthbert & Sons built the Rice County Court House at Lyons, Kansas, the court house at Phillipsburg, Kansas, a school building at Hays for the State of Kansas, a church at Lyons, and numerous other public and private structures including the Loman Hill M. E. Church at Topeka. The firm also has the contract for building the new Lincoln Junior High School at Topeka.

During his long residence in Kansas Mr. Cuthbert has been distinguished by his constant industry and readiness to aid in all laudable undertakings for the benefit of Kansas. In politics he is a republican. While away from his home city on a visit to Scotland he was elected a member of the Topeka School Board. He is a Presbyterian, a Knight Templar Mason and Shriner and a member of the Modern Woodmen of America. For thirty years he has served as a trustee in the Presbyterian Church of Topeka.

On May 29, 1877, he married Samantha C. Fitzpatrick. To their union have been born eleven children: Mary Jane, Mrs. A. C. McKitrick; Jessie May, Mrs. N. G. Edelblut; Katie Bell; William F.; Mabel, Mrs. A. G. Dunham; James B.; John A.; George M.; Charles D.; Elsie W.; and Robert, who died in infancy. Several of the sons are members of Cuthbert & Sons and for years have been actively associated with their father.

CHARLES REYNOLDS LOVE. A former Topeka citizen well remembered for his activity in business and his benevolence and splendid character was the late Charles Reynolds Love. Mr. Love came to Kansas a great many years ago, and spent many years in Topeka, where he died April 15, 1910.

He was of an old and prominent Pennsylvania family and was born at Newcastle in that state August 23, 1848. His parents were John Brown and Maria (Chenoweth) Love, both natives of Pennsylvania. Maria Chenoweth was the daughter of Arthur and Maria (Reynolds) Chenoweth, both of whom were natives of Virginia. This branch of the Chenoweth family is descended in direct line from Oliver Cromwell. The Chenoweths were among the first settlers around Newcastle, Pennsylvania, and the old farm owned by the family included land on which the courthouse now stands. The Chenoweth family has furnished many statesmen and makers of history all down the line. Charles R. Love had two brothers who saw active service in the Civil war. Alfred W., one of these brothers, is now deceased, and George Pearson lives in California. Alfred was in Sherman's army, participated in the great Atlanta campaign and the march to the sea, having enlisted from Illinois. George Pearson ran away from home at the

age of sixteen in order to enlist. There was also one sister who died at the age of eighteen years.

Charles R. Love received his early education in the public schools of Newcastle, Pennsylvania, and Laharpe, Illinois. His father for a time was a hat maker in Illinois, and afterwards engaged in the mercantile business at Newcastle until death. The first business experience of C. R. Love was in a nail factory at Youngstown, Ohio. One of the proprietors of that factory was his uncle. The business was conducted under the name of Brown, Bonnell & Company, and the old organization is now part of the United States Steel Corporation. This firm conducted large plants both in Newcastle, Pennsylvania, and Youngstown, Ohio.

Mr. Love was in that line of business in the East until 1876. He married Alice J. Houk, a daughter of John and Jane (Fulkerson) Houk, natives respectively of New Jersey and Pennsylvania. John Houk was an early settler at Newcastle, and his old farm is still owned by the family. Mrs. Love's maternal grandparents possessed strong anti-slavery ideas, and had left Virginia to avoid association with the institution of slavery. Arthur Chenoweth brought the first colored man to Lawrence County, Pennsylvania. This negro had been given his freedom, but his love for his former master caused him to live on the same farm until his death. Mrs. Love's great-grandfather Houk was a veteran of the Revolution and her grandfather was a veteran of the War of 1812. Clare Houk, an aunt of Mrs. Love, married Captain Leslie, a pioneer Ohio River steamboat captain and later founder and proprietor of the Leslie House, a noted old hostelry at Newcastle, Pennsylvania, which is still standing.

On account of ill health John Houk brought his family, consisting of his wife and two sons and Mr. and Mrs. Love, to Kansas, and secured 320 acres of raw prairie land sixteen miles from Larned, which was their best market place, and seven miles from Kinsley. Here the various members of the family engaged in general farming, and for several years they lived in a sod house and put up with all the discomforts associated with early Kansas pioneering. There were no schools or churches, and neighbors were few and far between. John Houk died on that farm August 14, 1887. His son Horace Greeley Houk had died September 28, 1881, as a result of the hardships incident to the development of a new farm in Kansas. Mrs. Houk, the mother of Mrs. Love, died in Topeka September 16, 1896. All the deceased members of the family now rest in the Garfield cemetery in Pawnee County.

Two years after coming to Kansas Mr. Love left the farm and removed to Topeka. Here he became identified with the construction department of the Santa Fe Railway as a foreman. After the death of Mrs. Love's brother in 1881 he returned and located in the Town of Kinsley near the old homestead. There he followed employment as clerk in a hardware store until the death of Mrs. Love's father, when the old farm was sold and Mr. and Mrs. Love then removed to Topeka. In the capital city Mr. Love engaged in the wall paper and interior decorating business and built up a very large and successful establishment.

In character he was kindly and generous, was greatly loved by children and both young and old, and was continually sacrificing his own interests in order to be helpful to others. He was also a man of splendid business judgment, and soon after coming to Topeka he bought valuable real estate at the corner of Thirteenth and Van Buren streets and built

Charles R Love

there the home which he and his family occupied for a quarter of a century. Later he bought the home at Thirteenth and Harrison streets, where Mrs. Love still resides. Politically he was a republican, was a charter members of the Knights of Pythias and the Ancient Order of United Workmen, was a devout Christian and closely identified with the Methodist Church.

Mr. and Mrs. Love had one daughter, Bertie M. Love, who became the wife of Prof. C. R. Forbes, of the School of Mines of the Missouri State University. Mrs. Forbes was born in Youngstown, Ohio, received her early education in Kinsley and Topeka, Kansas, and became very active in church work and was a social favorite. Her services and the hold she had upon the affections of many people made her death on February 27, 1913, almost a public calamity. She had her father's disposition and qualities of character. The late Mr. Love was a man of great patience and was never known to complain of reverses and hardships. The Rev. Mr. Estey of Topeka, who had been intimately connected with the family ever since they took up their home in that city, paid Mrs. Forbes a beautiful tribute, praising her splendid character, the life of helpfulness and service which she had led and particularly her charity, unostentatious and sincere, bestowed upon poor and needy people.

J. CARROLL MONTGOMERY, M. D. In the office of Doctor Montgomery at Manhattan is a large map of Riley County showing in detail all the features of the county and particularly those which are the work and evidence of man's activities. A number of different colored pegs or pins are usually found dotted about over this map.

It is in this way that Doctor Montgomery as county and city health officer of Manhattan and Riley County keeps track of the district under his jurisdiction, a glance at one of these charts indicate the location of all infectious diseases prevalent in the county at the time, and other pegs show the status of sanitary conditions as to drainage, sanitary equipment, etc. By means of this and other methods Doctor Montgomery has a complete and immediate record or census of health conditions in the county.

He has himself inaugurated many measures for the protection and safeguarding of public health and has introduced other systems which have been tried and approved elsewhere in the state or in other states. His own work may be credited with an important share in the reduction of the death rate of the county. At the same time a campaign of education has been carried on not only among the older but particularly among the younger generations. Many of the facts of hygiene and sanitary standards are now familiar knowledge where a few years ago they were either unknown or ignored. It was Doctor Montgomery who originated the so-called "Junior Health Officer System" in the public schools of Riley County and in the state at large. Under this system every school elects from its pupils one to whom Doctor Montgomery issues a certificate naming him junior health officer. Twice each week Doctor Montgomery sends out a bulletin which is read and posted in each school, and this is of vastly more benefit than all the old time methods of instruction in physiology and hygiene. Under his supervision during the past few years the cess-pools of the towns and cities have been reduced to a minimum. All the privies and water-closets of the public schools have either been regulated in accordance with standard sanitary policies or have been connected with sewer drainage. His office has also extended to the improvement of other conditions, and all of this has contributed to the noticeable decline of the death rate in Riley County. In every school of the county Doctor Montgomery annually delivers one or more lectures on hygiene.

For many years the name Montgomery has been one of influential associations in the medical profession of Manhattan and Riley County. Dr. J. Carroll Montgomery was born at Macon, Missouri, April 25, 1874, the only son and child of Dr. Edward R. and Mary E. (Walker) Montgomery. His father was born in Ohio and his mother in Missouri, and they were married in the latter state. Dr. Edward R. Montgomery took up the medical profession comparatively late in life, and was graduated in 1886 from the American Medical College of St. Louis. He did some preliminary practice in Missouri, but in 1886 came to Kansas. After about six years he moved to Kansas City, Kansas, where he was located three years, then lived for two years in Clay County, after which he was in active practice at Manhattan until his death in 1901 at the age of fifty-two.

In the various localities where his father practiced Dr. J. Carroll Montgomery received the advantages of the public schools. When only a boy he had made up his mind to become a doctor, and he carried on his studies under the direction of his father. In 1896 he entered the College of Physicians and Surgeons at Kansas City, Kansas, and his studies there were supplemented by some valuable practical experience for two years under his father at Manhattan. In 1901 he graduated M. D. from the College of Kansas City, and then located at Tampa, Kansas. In the fall of 1904 he returned to Manhattan, and that city has since been his home and the center of his large work and influence as a physician and surgeon. Doctor Montgomery has been city health officer since 1907 and county health officer since 1909. By virtue of this office he is also secretary of the County Board of Health.

He is widely known as a sanitarian and was formerly president of the Kansas State Association of Public Health Officers and has always taken an active part in that organization. He is a member of the Riley County and the Kansas State Medical societies, and is affiliated with the Benevolent and Protective Order of Elks. He is a member of the Congregational Church and in politics a republican. In 1901 Doctor Montgomery married Miss Delpha M. Hoop.

JOHN WILLIAM CHELANDER is junior member of the furniture and undertaking firm of John Chelander & Son at Randolph, Riley County. He has had a very successful career, and for a young man has shown a wonderful amount of ability and is as public spirited as he is thorough in the performance of his duties as a merchant.

He was born in Sweden, May 6, 1885, and as an orphan child was brought to America at the age of three months. At the age of four he was adopted by John Chelander and wife, and grew up at Randolph, where he gained his education. What he learned in school was supplemented by practical vocational training in the shop and business of his foster father, John Chelander. In 1905 he was made a partner, and has since assumed many of the heavier responsibilities of the firm of John Chelander & Son. In 1907 he married Jessie J. Larson.

His foster father, John Chelander, was born at

Hedemora, Sweden, September 17, 1844, and during his youth in Sweden he learned the cabinet maker's trade. After coming to America he was employed in that line in St. Joseph, Missouri, for seven years. While living there he married Bertha Catharine Johnson.

The name Chelander has been closely identified with the business affairs of Randolph for forty years. In 1876 Mr. John Chelander located there, and he soon afterward opened a cabinetmaker's shop and furniture store. A natural extension of the business was undertaking, and in 1905 he entrusted a share of the business responsibilities to his son, John William, forming the partnership of John Chelander & Son. Besides their business at Randolph they conduct a branch store at Cleburne.

Mr. John Chelander is a genius in mechanics. He is not only a skilled worker in wood, but has shown almost equal proficiency in the manipulation of metal in various forms of useful construction. He is a practical inventor, and is now engaged in perfecting an automobile driven by steam power. He is one of the most highly thought of citizens of Riley County.

FRED BURRIS of Wichita is county poor commissioner of Sedgwick County. He has been a resident of that city ten years, and previously had acquired an extensive acquaintance in Kansas as a traveling salesman.

Something more than passing mention should be made of his administration as county poor commissioner. He has introduced new methods and system and has given distinction to his method of handling the routine cases which come under his jurisdiction. For many years he has taken a deep interest in charity work and in his trips to other cities and other states has observed how the problems incident to the care of the poor were solved and handled. In his present office he is thus putting his previous experience and observation to practical use. For one thing, Mr. Burris has inaugurated a tabulated system showing a complete record of each individual case of the 1,100 families who are helped through his office each year. This system requires the co-operation of the superintendent of schools, the United Charities and the police department and has been the means of accomplishing a maximum of good at the least possible cost to the county. Another special policy of his deserves attention. In the case of school children who are in need of clothing, shoes and other supplies, if their parents were unable to secure these necessities for them, Mr. Burris has furnished such supplies, but has bought new apparel instead of second hand goods. This is a decided departure from an old established custom, and his office is probably the only one in the state that has put this reform into practice and its merits and advantages are too obvious to need explanation.

Fred Burris is a Missourian by birth, born in Livingston County, March 1, 1864. He was liberally educated, attending Avalon College and the State University at Columbia. On leaving school he spent a few years in the cattle business at Avalon, and then entered the services of a Kansas City, Missouri, lumber firm as traveling salesman. For a number of years he traveled over Kansas and other states selling lumber to retail dealers.

In December, 1906, he moved to Wichita and soon afterward established a local collection agency, which he made a profitable business and conducted for a number of years. He was appointed county poor commissioner of Sedgwick County in February, 1913, and is now giving practically all his time to the management of this office.

Mr. Burris is a republican, and in 1912 served as secretary of the Republican County Central Committee. He is a member of nearly all the fraternal societies, including the Masons, Odd Fellows, Knights of Pythias, Benevolent and Protective Order of Elks, and the Improved Order of Red Men.

On May 15, 1889, he married Mary Hayes of Avalon, Missouri. They have one daughter, Lucy.

JASON CLARKE SWAYZE. Judged by the standard which must be applied to the men of his time and circumstances, Jason Clarke Swayze had many of the elements of greatness. He guided his life through a period of tense factional struggle, and always kept his rudder true and in the direction which his conscience told him was right and just. Kansas, and the City of Topeka particularly, has a just pride in recalling the record of this man.

His home was in Kansas at Topeka from 1873 until his tragic death on the streets of Topeka. He was born in 1830 at Hope, New Jersey. He learned the printer's trade under Horace Greeley on the old New York Tribune. For a time he conducted a weekly periodical in New York City. About that time he married Kate Edwards, who was then a well known actress upon the American stage, and after his marriage he engaged in writing plays and was also manager for his wife. During their residence in the East two children were born: Julia Harriet and Oscar Kepler.

Late in 1860 Mr. Swayze went south with his family to tour the Southern States. Their plays were somewhat tinged with Northern sentiment, and consequently did not prove popular in the South. The outbreak of the war in 1861 found Mr. Swayze at New Orleans, where he was conscripted for service in the Confederate army. Watching for his opportunity, after about three weeks he escaped to the Union lines. In the meantime he had been allowed to bring his family as far as Griffin, Georgia, where he was compelled to leave them. At Griffin another child was born, while he was away, and named Annie Laurie. The mother died there in May, 1862.

After his arrival within the Union lines, Jason C. Swayze volunteered in the Union army, being mustered in as a captain and assigned to the staff of General Sherman as a scout. He served until the close of the war in that capacity, and as scout penetrated the enemy's lines many times, and was of material assistance to the Federal cause. A price was set on his head by the rebel authorities, but he was never captured nor wounded.

After peace was declared he made his way south to Griffin, Georgia, where his wife was buried and where his children were living. He then bought the Griffin Citizen and conducted it under the name The Bugle Horn of Liberty. From a quarto he changed it to a sixteen-page magazine. After publishing two issues, the establishment was raided, the office wrecked and the press and fixtures destroyed, and the proprietor was ridden on a rail through the streets, was then mounted on a barrel and given a limited number of minutes to live unless he foreswore allegiance to the United States Government and hurrahed for Jeff Davis. He proudly refused, and succeeded in fighting his way clear of the mob. At that time in addition to his position as editor he was also United States Commissioner of the District of Georgia, and agent of the Freedmen's Bureau. Though constantly persecuted until about the time he left, he never wavered in his determination to hold fast and try to carry out the undertaking which had brought him South. Upon the reorganization of his office he founded and published the American Union, which in 1868 was moved to Macon, where he continued it with no small degree of success until 1873. It is a proof of his remarkable courage, persistence and determination when it is recalled that in publishing this newspaper he was unable to secure the services of a single white man. One white boy came to him and served as an apprentice, but all the rest of his help was colored people, except his own children, who became printers.

He had always been a great admirer of Horace Greeley and in 1873 acted upon that editor and statesman's famous advice to "go West." He removed his newspaper plant to Topeka and began the publication of the Topeka Blade. Its diminutive size, and the fact that it was printed in nonpareil type, led the public to nickname it the "Postage Stamp." That "postage stamp" has an interesting place in the history of the Kansas press. It was enlarged and changed hands from time to time, and now it is the great and influential Topeka State Journal.

Mr. Swayze conducted this paper as long as he lived. Forty years ago Topeka was still almost a frontier town. Conditions of society had not become thoroughly settled after the terrible times of "bleeding Kansas" and its position on the western frontier also served to keep alive some of the border ruffianism. If he had one trait more than another it was that of dauntless courage. He was also incorruptible, was outspoken, called a spade a spade, and his courage of action was not less than courage of speech. He proved an outspoken foe of fraud and graft in every form, and naturally antagonized certain elements and the more so because the expression of his paper could not be controlled or influenced by money. He attacked men regardless of the position they occupied, and as he could not be silenced by bribes, his death was an almost inevitable result.

Jason C. Swayze was murdered on the streets of Topeka March 27, 1877. For his second wife he married Jennie Erwin. She became the mother of two sons, Horace Greeley Swayze and J. Clarke Swayze, Jr.

Oscar Kepler Swayze, a son of this distinguished Kansan, has long been prominent in journalism and in public affairs at Topeka. He was born at Brooklyn, New York, January 19, 1860, and was thirteen years old when the family came to Topeka. Practically all his education has been acquired in the school of experience. He grew up almost in a newspaper office and has been a printer and newspaper man most of his active career. For two years he was city editor of the Topeka Daily Capital and was foreman in that plant for three years.

He has inherited the strong political tendencies of his father and is a stalwart republican. In 1912 he was elected county clerk of Shawnee County and was reelected in 1914. Mr. Swayze is a Knight Templar Mason, a Shriner, a member of the Modern Woodmen of America, the Improved Order of Red Men, the Maccabees and belongs to the Topeka Commercial Club and the Topeka Press Club. On November 30, 1884, he married Hetty McPherson of Brownstown, Indiana.

MICHAEL FLOERSCH. In the year 1854, the late Michael Floersch, then a young man of twenty-one years, came from Missouri to Kansas and homesteaded a claim in the Pottawatomie country. He had been reared in Missouri, where his parents had settled on coming to the United States when he was eight years old. He was born in Germany, in 1833, and was reared in the faith of the Catholic Church, to the teachings of which he consistently adhered through a long, active and exemplary career. When Mr. Floersch came to Kansas he was without capital other than indomitable courage, unlimited energy and worthy ambition, but these served to carry him through the first few years and served as the foundation upon which his fortunes were builded.

At the time of his arrival Mr. Floersch pre-empted land in Pottawatomie County and began to develop a farm. He succeeded, not only in the formation of a large and valuable country estate, but in co-operating with strong and capable men in the business world, and in addition to being a skilled and thrifty farmer and a large live stock dealer, was prominent in business affairs. As a pioneer of Kansas, he took a conspicuous part in the development of the section of the state that was so fortunate to secure the benefit of his judgment and foresight and to be the scene of his business activities. The Town of Flush, in Pottawatomie County, is located on land formerly a part of his farm, and the town was named in his honor, but the Federal postoffice department changed the name from Floersch to Flush because of easier spelling. True to his religious training, Mr. Floersch donated grounds for the Catholic Church parish house and cemetery at Flush and always continued to be a generous and ready responder to appeals for contributions for worthy movements. In politics he was a republican, but he never cared for nor held public office. He and his wife reared a family of five sons and two daughters. In 1896 Mr. Floersch retired from farm life and removed to Omaha, Nebraska, for the purpose of raising his youngest son, now Doctor Floersch, of Topeka, Kansas. The death of Michael Floersch occurred at Omaha, in January, 1906, when he was seventy-two years of age.

Joseph B. Floersch, president of the Union National Bank of Manhattan, Kansas, is a worthy son of an honored father. He was born on the homestead place in Pottawatomie County, Kansas, September 28, 1864, and is a son of the late Michael and Mary (Dekat) Floersch. He was reared on the home farm, attended the public schools during the winter terms, and in 1884 was graduated from the splendid Catholic school at Saint Mary's, in his native county. At that time he engaged in farming not far from his father's place, but April 15, 1889, removed to Manhattan, Kansas, where he has since made his home and where he has been engaged in the banking business for a period of more than twenty-seven years. On coming to Manhattan, Mr. Floersch, in company with his father and other gentlemen, organized the Union National Bank, of which he became bookkeeper. From that position he worked his way steadily to the position of president, which office he assumed in 1906, having been for six years previous to that time the cashier of the institution. Politically he adheres to the principles of the republican party, but is not a politician and has not sought preferment at the hands of his party. In church faith, like his father, he is a communicant of the Catholic Church and has always been a generous supporter thereof, as well as of the cause of education.

* In 1893 Mr. Floersch married Miss Mary C. Donnelly, and they have one of the largest, handsomest and most modern homes of Manhattan, a city of fine residences, among whose prominent and highly esteemed citizens they have long been numbered.

PETER G. JOHNSON. The years 1858 and 1859 were particularly important ones in the history of Kansas. With the adoption of a constitution in the latter year, the peaceful, homeseeking settlers who had come from afar, even from other lands, to establish themselves on these wide prairies, as yet uncrowded as were older sections, found assurance of settled conditions and of the opportunity of preserving the homes they had founded. In the spring of 1858 the parents of Peter G. Johnson, one of Riley County's most respected citizens, settled in Butler County, Kansas. They were natives of Sweden who emigrated to the United States in 1856.

Peter G. Johnson was born in Sweden, March 15, 1834. His parents were Carrie and John Peterson, the son, according to Swedish custom, taking the surname of Johnson, from his father's Christian name. The father was twice married, two sons being born to his first union, Peter G. and August, the latter of whom is deceased. Unto his second marriage four children were born: Victor, Oscar, Christina and Tilda. August and Victor both fell victims of savage Indians, in Indian Territory, in 1862.

During early manhood Peter G. Johnson followed the sea. He was twenty-three years of age when he accompanied his father to the United States, with whom he tarried in Marshall County, Illinois, for two years before coming to Butler County, Kansas, where the father died soon afterward. This domestic calamity served to break up the family and the sons all adventured further in the West, Peter G. locating in Montana. He was variously engaged there until 1865, and in 1866 he came to Riley County and located upon a tract of land in Madison Township. It was there that Mr. Johnson settled down and lived for many years, devoting himself to farming and stock raising. He carried on his operations with vigor and industry and as the years passed prospered with them and at one time owned more than 500 acres of fine land, well improved. Some of this land he has parted with but retains 200 acres. Since retiring from active life Mr. Johnson has been residing near the Town of Riley.

In 1870 Mr. Johnson was married to Anna L. Shillerstrom, a widow and a native also of Sweden. By her first marriage she had two children, namely: Hilman and Melshior. Mrs. Johnson died February 15, 1916, leaving Mr. Johnson one son, Peter A.

Mr. Johnson has been a man of influence ever since coming to Riley County. He has studied public questions far more than has the average citizen and formerly was quite active in politics and was nominated by the greenback party for representative to the Legislature, failing of election by but one vote and many believed he had that vote. He is a student of socialism, with interest watching its effect on public affairs.

SILAS R. DAGUE. As president of the Dague Business College, in the City of Wichita, Mr. Dague has been the potent force in the development and upbuilding of one of the admirable and influential educational institutions of the Sunflower State, and the college of which he is the executive head is maintained at the highest modern standard, with the best of material facilities and with a corps of instructors who are notable for distinct efficiency in the work of the respective departments to which they are assigned.

Mr. Dague was born in Will County, Illinois, on the 17th of February, 1884, but he has maintained his home in Kansas since early childhood, his parents having removed to this state in 1891, when they established their residence at Wilson, Ellsworth County. In the public schools at Wilson Silas R. Dague continued his studies until he had been graduated in the high school, and for two years thereafter, 1903-04, he was a student in Baker University, at Baldwin, this state. For several years thereafter he taught private schools in various cities in the Middle West, and he then, in consonance with his ambitious purpose, entered the Louisville Business College, in the metropolis of the State of Kentucky, where he completed a thorough course in bookkeeping and higher accounting. Thus effectively fortified, Mr. Dague then established his residence at Wichita, in 1914, and that year recorded the founding of his present institution, the Dague Business College, the affairs of which he has directed with marked discrimination and progressiveness, with the result that he has brought its functions up to the most approved standard and gained to it a large and appreciative supporting patronage.

The well appointed headquarters of the Dague Business College are in the Bissantz Building, in the heart of the business section of Wichita, and the well lighted and ventilated rooms are of spacious order—well adapted for the uses to which they are applied. The corps of instructors in the college numbers five efficient teachers, and all departments are equipped for the training of students in a practical and effective way, fitting them fully for the assuming of positions of responsibility in the business world. The courses of study include not only the curriculum usually to be found in institutions of the kind but also one specially designed for preparing students for work under the civic-service system. The enrollment of students for the year 1916 is more than 600, and this fact indicates the splendid growth of the college and the high estimate placed upon it by those desirous of obtaining thorough business education.

Mr. Dague is not only an energetic and progressive young business man but is also a loyal and public-spirited citizen who takes lively interest in all things pertaining to the civic and material welfare of his home city, where he is distinctively popular in both business and social circles.

Mr. Dague married Miss Grace B. Cooper, of Dorrance, Kansas, and they have one child, Virginia Belle.

WILLIAM GREEN. A Topeka merchant whose name has become synonymous in that city with the highest quality of wares and the most reliable methods of merchandising, William Green came to Kansas in 1885 from Green County, Wisconsin. For more than thirty years he has been identified with the material progress of Topeka and his name would undoubtedly be considered among the first mentioned as foremost citizens.

A native of England he was born in Derbyshire on November 17, 1844. When he was about six

GEORGE C. PRITCHARD

years of age, in 1851, his parents Joseph and Ruth (Cooper) Green left their English farm and emigrated to America. The ship Florida, a sailing vessel, brought them over in thirty days. Going to Green County, Wisconsin, Joseph Green was a farmer there a few years, and afterwards operated a water power flouring mill at Dayton, Wisconsin, where both he and his wife died.

Reared on a Wisconsin farm, and in his father's mill, William Green had limited opportunities for an education. When he was about nineteen years of age his loyalty to his adopted country was put to the test and he enlisted March 31, 1864, in Company C of the Thirty-seventh Wisconsin Infantry. He served with that regiment until the close of the war. Going out as a private and mustered in as eighth corporal, he went through the five grades of sergeant, was promoted to second lieutenant, and was finally discharged in September, 1865, as first lieutenant. He went to the front at Cold Harbor, Virginia, in June and on the seventeenth of that month got his baptism of fire. In the engagement which followed his command was repulsed in a charge from the enemy, and on the following day the charge was successfully repeated. His entire service was in the Army of the Potomac. On July 30, 1864, he participated in the blowing up of the fort in front of Petersburg. He was at Hutcher's Run and numerous minor engagements, including the defense of Fort Steadman on March 25, 1865. On April 2, 1865, he was in his last engagement, the capture of Petersburg, the surrender of Appomattox occurring only a few days later.

Returning to Wisconsin after the war on April 1, 1866, Mr. Green opened a general stock of merchandise at Moscow, but a year later became associated with his father in merchandising at Dayton. He finally purchased his father's interests and eventually moved his store to Albany.

Thus it was with a record of nearly twenty years of successive business in Wisconsin that Mr. Green came to Kansas in 1885. At Topeka he resumed business as a retail grocery merchant, and has steadily conducted one of the best stocks and best organized grocery houses of the city for more than thirty years.

He has been a member of the Topeka Commercial Club since it was organized. To many people in Topeka his name suggests valuable public service. For many years he was a member of the city council, and some years ago, without solicitation on his part he was nominated and elected mayor of the city. His administration of three years meant much in the way of public improvement and the progress of Topeka in all departments. Politically he is an independent republican and official honors have come to him without the manifestation of any desire on his part, beyond that of doing his duty as a citizen. While in Wisconsin Mr. Green passed the chairs of the Blue Lodge and in Kansas has attained the thirty-third and supreme degree in Scottish Rite Masonry. He has also served as eminent commander of Topeka Commandery No. 5 of the Knights Templar. He is a member of the First Congregational Church.

In November, 1868, a few years after he returned from the war, Mr. Green married Sarah Dalrymple, Mrs. Green died in 1904. She was the mother of four sons: Arthur, who died at the age of 2½ years; John J., a traveling salesman, who married Bessie Miller and has one daughter; Albert L. S., a partner with his father in the grocery business at Topeka,

who has two daughters by his marriage to Ada Pulley; and William Hartley, who is unmarried and makes his home in Topeka.

GEORGE C. PRITCHARD. Farmers and stockmen throughout Shawnee County and over the state at large recognize in the name of George C. Pritchard a man whose services as a doctor of veterinary surgery were extensively employed in the interests of individuals and the entire state for a great many years. Doctor Pritchard is one of the oldest veterinarians of Kansas, has stood at the top of his profession, but is now retired and is devoting himself to the care and management of a fine stock farm near Topeka.

Born in Lorain County, Ohio, January 12, 1852, he is a son of. Eli B. and Julia Ann (Edwards) Pritchard. When he was thirteen years of age, in 1865, his parents removed to Gratiot County, Michigan. That was then a practically untouched forest of pine timber. It was in the lumber woods of Michigan therefore that Doctor Pritchard grew to manhood. As a boy he had attended the graded schools in Huntington, Ohio, and afterwards the district schools of Michigan. His father was a physician, and the plan most cherished by the parents was that the son should follow the same profession.

However, the son had special tastes and inclinations of his own. For eight years he acted as manager of the John Jeffrey Estate, consisting of extensive land and stock interests, and for another two years he was in the livery business at Sheridan, Michigan. From early boyhood he had been interested in stock, and his early experiences fortified him in the resolution to become a veterinarian. He did his preliminary reading and study with Dr. A. J. Chandler of Detroit. He then entered the Ontario Veterinary College at Toronto, Canada, where he was graduated veterinary surgeon in the spring of 1886.

For the following year he practiced in association with his former preceptor at Detroit. Then in May, 1887, nearly thirty years ago, Doctor Pritchard located in Topeka and his ability and skill gradually became recognized throughout the country districts surrounding that city. For twenty-seven years he actively practiced his profession, and besides his large private clientage he was appointed to many of the delicate and important responsibilities of larger service to the state.

Governor Llewellyn in 1893 appointed him state veterinarian. He filled that position two years until the office was abolished by legislative enactment. Then in 1895 the State Livestock Commission appointed him inspector at Albuquerque, New Mexico, for the purpose of guarding Kansas against the importation of infectious livestock diseases. In these positions and elsewhere Doctor Pritchard had to exercise a great deal of tact, moral courage and firmness and during nearly all the years of his practice he had almost constantly to combat prejudices and open hostility from those whose interests were contrary to the general welfare. His work as veterinarian covered a wide area, and his service involved work of the hardest kind. For a number of terms he was elected and served as president of the Kansas Veterinary Medical Association.

In 1914 Doctor Pritchard bought a tract of 200 acres six miles south of the city on Topeka Avenue. There he owns one of the finest country residences in the entire state. It is equipped with every modern convenience and the surroundings are such as to constitute a model country estate. Having retired from the active practice of his profession he is now free to devote his attention to farming and stock, and is especially interested in the breeding and raising of thoroughbred Holstein cattle. He also has other livestock and has a well developed and thoroughly proportioned farm.

In 1889 Doctor Pritchard married Miss Mary Charles of Hutchinson, Kansas. She died in 1912. In 1913 he married for his present wife Mrs. Lavina (Zimmerman) Sampson. Doctor Pritchard is a republican in politics.

SAMUEL FREMONT GOHEEN. When the City of Manhattan inaugurated the commission form of government in 1912 they chose as the head of the new municipal system a man who had already given efficient service in public office. The people have since kept him in office, and it is to the credit of the city as well as to the man that so capable a public servant as Samuel Fremont Goheen should be entrusted with such responsibility. Mr. Goheen has been a resident of Riley County more than thirty years, has witnessed and has been an important factor in the progress of those years, and filled a responsible post in the county government before his election as mayor of the city.

Mr. Goheen was already grown and a man of considerable business experience when he came to Kansas. He was born in Armstrong County, Pennsylvania, May 2, 1855, a son of George W. and Elizabeth (Holler) Goheen. His parents were also natives of Pennsylvania. In 1883 the family came out to Kansas and settled near Manhattan in Riley County. Mrs. Elizabeth Goheen died there in 1891 at the age of sixty-five. The father died ten years later at the age of eighty-five. In Pennsylvania George Goheen had followed merchandising, but was a farmer in the Sunflower State.

As a boy in Pennsylvania Mayor Goheen acquired an academic education. His first business experience was with his father in a store in Pennsylvania, and the horizon of life was broadened for him by the teaching of four winter terms in the country schools. He married in Pennsylvania and brought his little family to Kansas at the same time with his father. He was then twenty-eight years of age. The first twenty-three years of his residence in Riley County Mr. Goheen spent as a farmer and stock raiser, and a very successful one at that.

His business ability becoming widely known, and his trustworthiness receiving increasing appreciation, he was elected in 1906 as the republican candidate for the office of county treasurer. He filled that post with commendable efficiency for two years. He was then re-elected for a second term. Mr. Goheen left the office of county treasurer in the fall of 1911, and in the spring of 1912 was honored by the citizens of Manhattan by election as mayor. He was elected mayor or head of the commission in 1912 and in 1916 was returned for another term.

On his election as county treasurer Mr. Goheen moved to the City of Manhattan. He has one of the attractive homes of that city and he and his family are well known in social circles. In Pennsylvania in 1876 he married Barbara E. Jack, a native of that state. Their children are: Albert J., George G., John H. and Ethel.

HON. WILLIAM F. PETER. In recalling the representative men of Riley County, who, during life, were earnest and useful, faithful and efficient and so left an impress on the history of their time that is honorable and creditable, the late William F. Peter is called forcibly to mind. Forty-seven years of his life were spent in Kansas and to her interests he was devoted heart and soul, working personally and in public office to further her progress.

William F. Peter, twice elected a member of the State Legislature of Kansas, was born in Jackson County, Indiana, January 28, 1854, and died in Riley County, Kansas, March 2, 1916. He was a son of Jonas and Barbara (Bruenner) Peter, who were natives of Switzerland. They came as young people to the United States and were married in Jackson County, Indiana, where both subsequently died, the father at the age of fifty-three years, and the mother after the birth of four children, the only survivor being Charles Wesley Peter, a sketch of whom appears in this work.

Reared on his father's farm in Indiana and educated in the public schools of Jackson County, William F. Peter remained a resident of his native place until 1869. Ten years earlier, or in 1859, his father had purchased 500 acres of land in Fancy Creek Valley, in Riley County, Kansas, as an investment. In 1869 William F. Peter came westward and being pleased with the property and seeing evidences that careful cultivation would make it one of the most valuable in this section, decided to locate permanently here and in 1872 he was joined by his brother, Charles W. They labored together in developing productive farms and for seven years managed their own domestic affairs, probably not entirely to their satisfaction because both married in the same year, by that time having comfortable homes to which to bring their brides.

On March 30, 1880, William F. Peter was married to Miss Anna Wiesandanger, who is a daughter of Henry and Elizabeth (Pfeil) Wiesendanger. The father of Mrs. Peter was born in Switzerland. He came to the United States and located first in Wisconsin, coming from there in 1861 to Riley County, Kansas. Four sons were born to Mr. and Mrs. Peter: Edwin, Harry, Leslie and Arthur.

Mr. Peter was successful financially in his undertakings, prospering greatly as a farmer and stockraiser. He was intelligent and public spirited and early manifested interest in public affairs as they related to Riley County and the state, and when called upon to serve in public office was ready to accept such responsibilities as his fellow citizens deemed desirable. He served in such township offices as trustee and later was elected, on the republican ticket, a member of the board of county commissioners. In 1904 he was called still higher, being elected to the State Legislature as representative from Riley County, and as indicative of the value placed on his services, he was re-elected in 1906. In all the public positions to which he was called he served with distinction and was generally recognized as a man of more than ordinary ability, foresight and wisdom, and there was no one who ever doubted his honesty or sincerity of purpose. Broad-minded and generous, fair and just, kind and temperate, his family and community lost a most worthy husband, father and citizen when his earthly life closed.

J. EDWARD COOK. Judicious and legitimate has been the advertising policy that has been utilized in the exploitation of the King Ni-Ko system for the cure of the tobacco habit, and the basis of this advertising has been proved efficacy and definite results. The system of treatment accomplishes all that is claimed for it and this fact constitutes the best of the commercial assets on which has been developed the extensive and beneficent business enterprise of which the popular and progressive proprietor is the well known citizen of Wichita whose name initiates this paragraph.

Mr. Cook was born in Keokuk County, Iowa, on the 13th of November, 1864, and after having profited by the advantages of the public schools he continued his higher studies in turn in Pleasant Plain Academy, at Pleasant Plain, Iowa, and Grillett Academy, at Glen Elder, Mitchell County, Kansas. After due preparation he was ordained a clergyman of the Methodist Episcopal Church, and his first pastoral charge was in Jewell County, Kansas. He later filled various pastorates in two circuits of the Northwest Kansas Conference, and finally he went to Carlsbad, New Mexico, where for a few months he had charge of the Methodist English mission. Thereafter he was engaged for some time in characteristically vigorous and effective evangelistic service, and he next assumed the position of superintendent of a magnetic healing institute at Centerdale, Iowa, from which place he was later transferred to a similar office in connection with the magnetic institute at East Dubuque, Illinois. After severing this alliance Mr. Cook gave further evidence of his executive ability and versatile resourcefulness by serving as a traveling salesman until 1901.

In the meanwhile, with an earnest desire to aid tobacco-users in freeing themselves from the dominion of the narcotic, he devoted much time to scientific research and experimentation for the purpose of evolving a tobacco cure worthy of the name. The result was that unequivocal success attended his benignant efforts, and in 1901 he established his residence at Wichita and began the manufacture and sale of the King Ni-Ko System, which embraces a definite system and provides for essentially individualized treatment. Within its history of about fifteen years this company, of which Mr. Cook is the executive head, has given treatment in cases numbering between 40,000 and 50,000, and where the system was conscientiously followed the percentage of cures has been the full maximum—that is 100 per cent. The well equipped establishment of the company is situated in rooms in the building at the corner of Seneca Street and Douglas Avenue, Wichita, and concerning the Ni-Ko System the following pertinent statements are worthy of reproduction in this connection:

"Probably of all tobacco cures, Ni-Ko is one of the best known. The cure has been sold in every civilized part of the world. The company is deluged by testimonials from grateful patients. During the time that Ni-Ko has been manufactured in Wichita hundreds of other so-called cures have been heralded, but they have come and gone. They lack the legitimate fundamentals that have been included in the manufacture of Ni-Ko. Many of them claim to be a cure in every case with the same treatment. Ni-Ko is a system. Every individual case is treated differently. This is but one phase in which Ni-Ko is different from others. Investigation will prove that it is not a mere cure-all, gotten up for the money, but a legitimate product that has undergone the test of time and will do all and more than its makers claim for it."

On the 15th of April, 1913, was solemnized the marriage of Mr. Cook to Miss Lillian Lane, of Cleveland, Ohio. Mrs. Cook is a niece of the distinguished American artist, the venerable A. M. Willard, who acquired fame through the production of the now well known and often re-produced historical and patriotic painting known as "The Spirit of '76."

The late Rev. Edward C. Cook, the venerable father of the subject of this review, was one of the revered citizens of Wichita. He devoted the years of a significantly long and active career to service as a minister of the Society of Friends; he died at the age of seventy-four years, in 1916, and his wife, whose maiden name was Amy Sharpless, likewise was a minister of the Friends' Church, of which she was a birthright member. This gentle and gracious woman was about sixty years of age when she was summoned to the life eternal, and her memory is revered by all who came within the sphere of her influence. She was a daughter of Dr. Septimus Sharpless, of Philadelphia, and a sister of Evi Sharpless, who was the founder of the Jamaica mission established under the auspices of the Society of Friends at Jamaica, West Indies, where he conducted the mission many years.

PAUL E. WALKER, a son of A. D. Walker of Holton, has been a Topeka lawyer for the past fifteen years. He was born at his father's home in Holton, Kansas, August 27, 1876, grew up in his native city, attending the public schools, and took his college course in California, being a graduate of Leland Stanford University. He took his A. B. degree there in 1898, and then entered the Harvard Law School, where he was graduated LL.B. in 1902.

In the fall of 1902 Mr. Walker began practice in Topeka as assistant attorney for the Rock Island Railway Company. He was promoted to general attorney for this road with jurisdiction over Missouri and Kansas and part of other states.

Mr. Walker married Helen Morrow, daughter of O. S. Morrow, who for many years was a prominent factor in affairs in Kansas.

ELIAS EMERSON MORRIS has for eight years been probate judge of Riley County. To that office he has brought a singularly fair impartiality, and ever since he entered upon his duties the people of the county have recognized that the interests of the widows and orphans have been most capably and honestly administered. Judge Morris is one of the old time educators of Kansas, and has long been identified with some form of official service in Riley County.

He was born in Crawford County, Pennsylvania, November 2, 1859, a son of James S. and Mary (Chamberlain) Morris. His parents were married in Pennsylvania and spent the rest of their lives on a farm there. James S. Morris was born in New York State and of New England ancestry, his English forefathers having been pioneers in Connecticut. Judge Morris' mother was a native of Pennsylvania, and was also of early English stock.

Reared on a Pennsylvania farm, Judge Morris had as a boy the lessons of industry and honesty which have so characterized his later years. As a boy he had a strong ambition for a higher education. After leaving the common schools he entered the State Normal School at Edinboro in Erie County, Pennsylvania, and there prepared for his chosen work as a teacher. He was not yet seventeen when he taught his first school and for three years was actively connected with public school work in Pennsylvania.

A resident of Kansas since April, 1880, he has

spent all the subsequent years in Riley County. For ten years he was a teacher, and many men and women now in middle life recall with special gratitude his influence upon their early years. For eleven years he served as trustee of Wildcat Township. While teaching and acting as trustee he lived on a farm, and farming has been an important part of his life's experience.

After his service as township trustee Judge Morris was elected a county commissioner, filled that place with credit for four years, and in 1908 was elected to his present office of probate judge. He has been regularly re-elected at the end of each two years, and as long as he remains in office the people know that the probate functions will be adequately and carefully discharged. Judge Morris is a man of exceptional ability, and is thoroughly honest and conscientious. He is a republican in politics, and is affiliated with the Masonic Order and the Benevolent and Protective Order of Elks. He also belongs to the First Presbyterian Church of Manhattan.

In 1887 he married Mary Elizabeth Zeller. Mrs. Morris died in 1910, being survived by three children: Edna M., Kenneth W. and Sarah G.

CHARLES H. TROTT, who died at his home in Junction City March 2, 1916, attained many of those ideals for which ambitious men will always strive. He proved a gallant and faithful soldier when the country's integrity was in danger, was a merchant and business man of the finest integrity, was a good friend, a good Christian and a good citizen.

For half a century he lived in Kansas, and at the time of his death was one of the oldest if not the oldest business man of Junction City. He arrived in Junction City in the spring of 1866 a veteran soldier and officer of the Union Army. Junction City was then a thriving little town with splendid promise for the future. There were no railroads and Mr. Trott arrived by stage coach. Soon after reaching the town he was appointed postmaster, an office he filled with the systematic regard for his responsibilities which characterized every act of his life. He remained postmaster until 1871. When he went into the office he also bought the book and stationery store which the preceding postmaster had owned. It was as a merchant in books and stationery supplies that Mr. Trott performed his longest business service in Junction City, and only death stayed his hand and interrupted his active participation, the store having since been continued as a service to the community by his only son.

He was also a banker. At one time he was president of the old Central Kansas State Bank of Junction City and when that institution was reorganized as the Central National Bank in 1890 he became cashier and filled that position until 1896. In 1872 he was elected county clerk and after serving one term declined a renomination.

His lifetime severed a period of nearly eighty years. He was born in the City of Boston, Massachusetts, August 8, 1837. His great-grandfather, of English ancestry, was a watchmaker in Boston, where his son, Andrew Cunningham Trott, and also his grandson, Peter Trott, were workers in the same vocation. Peter Trott was the father of Charles H. Trott, and married Almira Tolman.

The early life of Mr. Trott was spent in Boston, and he graduated from high school in 1853, 'and for the following five years was an employe in the wholesale drug house of Samuel N. and W. A. Brewer. From time to time he was advanced in re-

sponsibilities and only left the business to seek better opportunities in the far West. In 1858 he journey by rail and boat to Iowa, where he arrived without either capital or influential friends. He soon afterwards made a trip to Minnesota, which was then the extreme northwest, and part of that journey he accomplished on foot during the middle of winter. After a brief investigation he returned to Iowa and located at Nashua in Chickasaw County, where in the course of the same year he formed a partnership with Caleb Green under the firm name of Trott & Green. They opened a stock of general merchandise, and in the course of a few years had built up a good trade.

In the early months of the Civil war these business partners, feeling a greater obligation to their country than to their private affairs, locked up their store and went into the army. Mr. Trott enlisted in July, 1861, in Company B of the Seventh Iowa Infantry. This regiment was attached to the First Brigade, Fourth Division, Fifteenth Army Corps, under Gen. John A. Logan. From the summer of 1861 until the close of hostilities Captain Trott was in continuous service. He helped overcome the opposition in the Mississippi Valley states of the Confederacy and afterwards was with Sherman on his historic campaign to Atlanta and the march to the sea, and then up through the Carolinas to Washington, where he marched in the Grand Review. For gallant and meritorious services he was promoted first to quartermaster sergeant, then to second lieutenant and acting regimental quartermaster, then to first lieutenant and regimental quartermaster, and finally to captain and assistant adjutant general. He was recommended for promotion to the rank of major, but the war closing about that time he was not commissioned. He was mustered out with the rank of captain and assistant adjutant general in September, 1865, more than four years from the time he had closed his store in Iowa and started for the front. The winter of 1865-66 he spent in his native City of Boston, and then began life anew in Junction City, Kansas.

Captain Trott was an active member of the Grand Army of the Republic, which organization attended his funeral. Some of the other interests and associations which were a vital part of his career were appreciatively described in a local paper at the time of his death in the following words: "The First Universalist Church of this city has been most actively and loyally supported by Captain Trott for more than a third of a century. Through his efforts and the liberal cooperation of friends this church has grown and prospered. As superintendent of the Sunday School for more than twenty-five years he has labored for Christ and the church. The handsome new church home has become a reality through the untiring efforts of a loyal band of co-workers, among whom he was a leader. An an officer of the local church, a trustee of the Universalist State Convention, he has always been a loyal, faithful, constructive worker. As president of the Highland Cemetery Association for years he has actively helped to make this beautifully located cemetery one of the best and most prosperous associations in the state.

Captain Trott in a quiet way was a man of influence in this community. By intelligent service and unwavering loyalty he proved himself to be a good citizen, a faithful friend, a Christian gentleman."

On December 3, 1867, Captain Trott married Miss Josephine McBratney. Her father was Hon. Robert

McBratney of Junction City, who at one time served as United States attorney and land agent. Mrs. Trott, who was also an active member of the Universalist Church, died August 17, 1912.

Hon. Loring Trott, only surviving son and child of the late Captain Trott, was born at Junction City, August 31, 1869. He was educated in the local schools and in 1890 graduated from Lombard University at Galesburg, Illinois. Since then for over a quarter of a century he has been an active merchant. For about ten years he was in business at Denver, Colorado, and then returned to Junction City to join his father as a partner in the Trott book and stationery store. He was its active manager for several years before his father's death and since then has been sole proprietor.

Mr. Trott takes an active part in local affairs and is a leading republican, as was his father. In 1912 he was elected a member of the State Senate, and his term was a service highly creditable to himself and to his senatorial district. Mr. Trott is a Knight Templar Mason, a member of the Mystic Shrine, and has held the various offices in the local lodges of Masonry. He is a member of the Universalist Church.

WALTER S. EZELL. Contributing to the prestige of the City of Wichita as an educational center are a number of well ordered business and technical institutions, and prominent among the number is the Wichita Telegraph College, which was founded in the spring of 1912 by its present owner and manager, Walter S. Ezell, who as a mere boy had manifested a distinct predilection for the art of telegraphy and who contrived to pass much of his time in the telegraph office of the railway station of which his father was agent in the City of Memphis, Tennessee. As an expert operator his interest has never waned and it was through his appreciation of the educational and practical value of his profession that he was led to establish his present excellent school for the training of others for effective service as telegraphists.

Mr. Ezell was born at Memphis, Tennessee, on the 22d of May, 1872, and as a boy he absorbed a working knowledge of telegraphy under the conditions noted in the preceding paragraph. After having profited duly by the advantages of the public schools of his native city he went to the City of Nashville, Tennessee, where he completed a two years' course in Vanderbilt University. After leaving the university he served as telegraph operator and railway station agent in several southern cities, and he was thus engaged until 1900, when he effected the establishing of the Houston Telegraph College in the City of Houston, Texas. He conducted this school six years, within which period he developed the same into the largest and most important institution of its kind in the South. Impaired health virtually compelled him to dispose of the school, and after selling the same he passed two years in California, where he recuperated his physical energies and where he held the position of train dispatcher at Sacramento for the Western Pacific Railroad. At the expiration of the two years he went to Denver, Colorado, and became traveling representative for the Denver Business College. As an executive he proved specially valuable in this field of endeavor, and later he was similarly retained by other business colleges until 1912, when he established his home at Wichita and became the founder of his present splendidly equipped and successful telegraph college. The in-

stitution under his progressive and able management has had a steady and substantial advancement in the number of students enrolled and it now ranks as one of the best colleges of the kind in the West. Both regular and wireless telegraphy is taught in the school, with the most approved and modern of apparatus and accessories, and graduates of the college are most thoroughly fortified for their work, as shown by the fact that they are able to pass the rigid examinations demanded by the Government for service in its wireless and other telegraph stations. The course in the Wichita Telegraph College is also such as to prepare students for efficient railway-telegraph service and all other phases of practical telegraphic work. Wichita is fortunate in having been made the seat of this excellent school and its proprietor is known and valued as a loyal and public-spirited citizen and successful business man. He was recently elected a member of the Institute of Engineers.

JEREMIAH HAMPTON SQUIRES. One of the old and honored residents of Topeka, to which city he came thirty-seven years ago, is Jeremiah Hampton Squires, veteran of the Civil war, who is now living in comfortable retirement after a long and useful career as a business man and public official. Mr. Squires was born at Southampton, on Long Island, New York, September 11, 1842, and is the only survivor of the four children of Jeremiah and Phoebe (Jaegger) Squires, who were farming people.

Mr. Squires resided on the home farm on Long Island until reaching the age of seventeen years, and during this time acquired his education by attending the public schools and Southampton Academy. In the spring of 1860 he went to Columbus, Ohio, and, with the exception of the time he was a soldier in the Civil war, remained in the employ of one man at carpentering, as an apprentice, journeyman, foreman and partner, for nearly twenty years. Mr. Squires enlisted July 22, 1862, as a private in Company A, Ninety-fifth Regiment, Ohio Volunteer Infantry, and within two weeks of the time he was enlisted was engaged in his first battle, at Richmond, Kentucky. In this engagement twenty-seven men of his company were killed or wounded, and here he received his first and only wound during the war which consisted of a bullet in the left hand. He, with 600 others of his regiment, was here captured and paroled for ninety days. He was then declared exchanged and rejoined his regiment, going into active service at Milliken's Bend, in April, 1863, and being subsequently set to work digging a canal north of Vicksburg. Next he went to Grand Gulf, later to Jackson, and then to Vicksburg, where for six weeks he participated in the siege of that city, which finally fell into the hands of the North. His regiment then took part in the chase of Johnston's army, which it met in the battle of Jackson, where it was ordered to uncover a masked battery. In so doing, Mr. Squires, then a sergeant, saw two officers of the enemy beating a retreat, followed them, and, on discovering them in a tent, covered them with his gun and took them as prisoners to the Union lines single-handed. While on the way from Vicksburg to Jackson, he was ordered to select four men and make a reconnoissance in the neighborhood of Black River, where the enemy were supposed to be occupying a fort on the river bank. Here they were surprised by about twenty-five of the enemy who were in the fort and were fired upon. The handful of Union men responded with a charge on the twenty-five Confederates, who retreated and crossed the river in boats, leaving the unguarded fort to be captured by a force of about one-fourth their own strength, one of the plucky Northerns having been dispatched to the Union commander with information regarding conditions. Later in the day, the commander of the Federal troops relieved the four men and they went on to Jackson as previously related. After Jackson the regiment went back to within about six miles of Vicksburg, where the men went into camp. Mr. Squires was then assigned to the duty of going to Columbus, Ohio, to secure drafted men to fill up the depleted ranks of the regiment, but, as there were none there, he was ordered to recruit. He was relieved in the early spring and rejoined his regiment at Memphis, Tennessee, June 1, 1864, and was then in the expedition sent out to check the advance of the Confederate leader, General Forrest. At Brice's Cross Roads, Mississippi, the Union forces, numbering about 6,000 were defeated by the Southerners, who numbered some 10,000, and 136 men of Mr. Squires' regiment were captured by the enemy, he being among the number. He was started to Andersonville Prison and for several days the only food obtained by the prisoners consisted of corn which they picked up from around the places where the animals had been fed. Finally, they reached the line of the railroad and were packed into box cars and sent to Andersonville stockade, where they arrived June 19, 1864. Mr. Squires experienced all the hardships, sufferings and tortures which incarceration in that awful prison meant, and from the weight of 175 pounds when he went in wasted away to eighty pounds, his weight when finally released. On November 24, 1864, with 10,000 other prisoners he was paroled and returned to Camp Chase, Ohio, to endeavor to regain his shattered energies. While at Andersonville, he had in some miraculous manner succeeded in secreting 60 cents from the search of his guards, and with this he bought writing paper and stamps and sent a letter to his sister, who was then living at Columbus, Ohio. Six months after the letter has been written it was handed to him at Columbus. In the spring of 1865 Mr. Squires rejoined his regiment at Mobile, Alabama, but the war being virtually over, he was stationed at Enterprise, Mississippi, doing guard duty for the rest of his service. He was finally ordered North and discharged at Louisville, Kentucky, August 18, 1865, at which time he held the rank of orderly sergeant.

At Columbus, Ohio, July 27, 1867, the brave young soldier was married to Virginia Elizabeth Schimp. He continued to be engaged at carpentering and contracting in Ohio until 1879, when he came to Kansas and purchased 240 acres of raw land in Pottawatomie County, six miles northwest of Waumega. In the fall of that year his family joined him and he continued to be engaged in farming for six years, since which time he has resided at Topeka. For several years he followed real estate ventures and during that time was elected and served three terms as a member of the Topeka Board of Education, and later was elected and served four terms as city clerk. Mr. Squires is a republican. He is a popular comrade of the Grand Army of the Republic and a valued member of the Independent Order of Odd Fellows, the Knights and Ladies of Security, the Ancient Order of United Workmen and the Modern Woodmen of America. He and his family are members of the Methodist Episcopal Church. Mr. and Mrs. Squires are the parents of three chil-

dren: Ralph W.; Frank C., an achitect of Topeka; and Anna L.

RALPH W. SQUIRES, present register of deeds of Shawnee County, was born at Columbus, Ohio, April 29, 1870, and was nine years of age when brought to Kansas by his parents, Jeremiah and Virginia E. (Schimp) Squires, and for a few years the family lived on the farm in Pottawatomie County. The recollection of the booming of the prairie chickens in the spring when frost covered the earth in the morning, the cries of the plover, and other incidents of pioneer life, left an indelible impress on his youthful mind. He received his education in the public schools and later took up the study of pharmacy, and the retail drug business has been his permanent employment. At the November election of 1914 there were 132 names on the ballot for the various offices, from United States Senator on down, and his name as a candidate for the office of register of deeds received a greater number of votes than any other. He has decidedly made good in the office to which he was elected and is vindicating the confidence of the people who felt him capable of discharging its duties efficiently. Mr. Squires is a thirty-second degree Scottish Rite Mason and has the honor of having served as master of Topeka Lodge No. 17, Ancient Free & Accepted Masons. He is also a member of the Shawnee Golf Club.

Mr. Squires married Miss Jennie Griesen, of Topeka, December 14, 1894, and they have one daughter, Virginia.

WILLIAM H. MOFFIT. In the group of surviving territorial pioneers of Kansas, William H. Moffit of Highland Park, a suburb of Topeka, has an important place. Mr. Moffit carries within his individual recollection practically the entire story of Kansas from the beginning of the border warfare until the present, a period of fully fifty years. He has been a witness of great and stirring events, and in those events has not been himself an inconsiderable participant.

His birth occurred in Henry County, Iowa, January 6, 1842. That date indicates that the family history has been identified with the pioneer times of more than one state. Iowa at the time of his birth was still a territory and very sparsely settled. His parents were Orlando and Catherine Bishop (Beam) Moffit. Orlando Moffit spent his entire life as a farmer but had a varied and interesting career along the frontier. He was a native of New York State, moved first to Ohio, and from there to Iowa when it was a territory. He was living in Iowa when the news of the discovery of gold on the Pacific coast reached the Middle West. In 1849 he started overland as part of the great exodus to the gold fields. Joining a large wagon train at Omaha, he journeyed on across the plains by way of Salt Lake City until he reached the coast. He worked in the mines for a time and afterwards was a lumberman. In 1854 he returned to the states by way of the Isthmus of Panama. During his absence in the Far West his family had used up practically all their means, and as his ventures on the coast had been meagerly rewarded Orlando determined upon another move further west where land was cheap, where the climate was mild and where he might hope to live in peace and reasonable prosperity the rest of his days. Loading two wagons with his household goods, with six yoke of oxen to draw them, and with other domestic animals in the train, he set out for Kansas Territory in the

W. H. Moffet

spring of 1855. Orlando Moffit located in what is now Tecumseh Township of Snawnee County. This country was then an unbroken expanse of prairie with only spots of brush to relieve the monotonous vista and with some timber along the water courses. Here and there, but widely scattered, were the dwelling places of the early white settlers. Topeka was a village of slab shanties, and Tecumseh was the more promising of the two towns. In the beautiful valley of the Shunganung Orlando Moffit built his first house, a log cabin, the logs being cut from the growing timber.

The Moffits were known as "black abolitionists" and Charles Moffit, a brother of Orlando, and still another brother, Erastus, were prominently identified with the greatest abolitionist of them all, John Brown. Charles Moffit was an officer during the border warfare period, and his portrait now hangs upon the walls of the State Memorial Building at Topeka.

In the family of Orlando Moffit and wife were three sons and three daughters, and all but one of them are still living. William H. Moffit was thirteen years of age when he came with his parents to Kansas. His recollections cover the entire period of territorial history, the troubles of the border between the Free Soil and Pro-Slavery element, and the wonderful strides of civilization in the great inventions of sixty years.

His education was limited to such opportunities as he had found in the public schools before coming to Kansas. After arriving here he had to do all he could to keep up the pioneer farm.

He was not yet grown when the war broke out. On August 21, 1862, he became a member of Company H of the Eleventh Kansas Cavalry and was in active service until discharged at Leavenworth on September 13, 1865. Most of his campaigning was done in the states of Kansas, Missouri and Arkansas, and among other battles he participated at old Fort Wayne, Cane Hill, Boston Mountain, Van Buren, Sinibar Hill, Lexington, Little Blue, Big Blue and Westport. At the battle of Lexington he was wounded in the left shoulder by a musket ball.

With the return of peace Mr. Moffit came back to Kansas, and at various times was employed in the stonemason's trade. However, his main vocation has been farming and from that he has won the prosperity which enables him to enjoy life now somewhat at leisure. He owns a quarter section of land in one part of Shawnee County, ten acres in another quarter, and twenty-four lots in Highland Park, where he makes his home.

Much of the history of Kansas might be written from the personal recollections of Mr. Moffit. One of the experiences he recalls occurred in 1860, when with his father and other men he engaged in a hunting trip out toward Salina. During that trip the party encountered twenty-seven herds of buffalo, each herd averaging two hundred animals. The party killed twenty-five buffalo and young Moffit himself killed five out of seven attempts. The best of the buffalo meat was "jerked." "Jerked meat" is a term hardly familiar to modern people. The meat was cut in strips, salted, cured over a slow fire and by the sun, and after that process it would keep for a very long time. The party brought back from this expedition about a ton of jerked meat. Mr. Moffit also recalls a custom of the early days when buckwheat was ground through a coffee mill, the chaff being subsequently sifted from the flour.

On February 11, 1868, Mr. Moffit married Maria S. Beam. To their marriage were born four children: Josephine, Mrs. J. N. Edgar; Ella May, Mrs. R. S. Butner; Lucina, Mrs. A. B. Lange; and a son that died in infancy. Mr. and Mrs. Moffit have twenty-four grandchildren. Politically Mr. Moffit is a republican and he and his wife are active members of the Methodist Episcopal Church. He is a member of Lincoln Post, Grand Army of the Republic. While living on the farm he served as road supervisor, school treasurer and school director a number of years.

GEORGE N. HOLMES. For thirty-two years an employe of the legal department of the Atchison, Topeka & Santa Fe Railroad, at the general offices at Topeka, few men are better known or more highly respected than is George N. Holmes. Prior to the time he entered the employ of this line, Mr. Holmes had many interesting and remarkable experiences, and his career is one which exemplifies the value of perseverance, fidelity and integrity in gaining position and fortune.

George N. Holmes was born at Stamford, Lincolnshire, England, January 11, 1853. His father, George Holmes, was a native of Norfolk, in an adjoining shire, and his mother, Sarah Nelsey, was born at Boston, Lincolnshire. They were the parents of thirteen children, of whom George N. was the seventh born. The two eldest daughters are residents of Hemel Hempstead, England; the third daughter is living at Boston, England; a son, James Robert, is in Western Australia, at Kalgoorlie; the youngest son is living in Vancouver, British Columbia; and the two youngest sisters are living in North Topeka, having come to the United States in 1900. Mr. Holmes belongs to a family noted for its longevity, three of his grandparents having lived to nearly the age of ninety years; and George Holmes was eighty-five at his death.

George N. Holmes received his education in private schools in his native land and there received some business experience as a clerk in a dry goods store. He came to the United States in 1873, and, after a year of the most remarkable experiences and vicissitudes arrived in Kansas, where with good luck, hard work, loyal service and the good fortune of securing a good and faithful woman for a wife, he has advanced to a position of honor and trust.

When Mr. Holmes arrived in America it was during the great panic of 1873, when work was exceedingly scarce. With a companion, also from England, he began tramping to find employment, and in their travels they passed through the states of Pennsylvania, Maryland, West Virginia, Ohio, Indiana, Illinois, Missouri and Kentucky, and finally arrived at Kansas City. While in the tunnel of the Wabash Railroad there, Mr. Holmes became separated from his young companion, whom he never saw nor heard from again. Mr. Holmes arrived at the three bridges, Topeka, on the morning of Sunday, on a fine day in the spring of 1874. He had lost his last "shin-plaster" quarter while sleeping in a haystack in Missouri, and was absolutely without funds. Approaching a house to ask for something to eat, he found the family at morning prayers, and the man of the house, who afterwards proved to be Professor Smith of the Quincy School, was very kind to him and asked him to breakfast. His benefactor then introduced him to Ben White, a blacksmith and fellow-countryman, who invited Mr. Holmes to live at his home, where he remained for a month and assisted the blacksmith in his work. Mr. White then introduced him to W. H. Sprinkle, a farmer, who employed him for nearly two years, or until Doctor Ward, of Silver Lake, heard that he was an old dry goods salesman and engaged him for his drug and general store. Mr. Holmes, however, did not care for this business and after a short time resigned and returned to his farming operations, this time with A. S. Thomas, who at that time was clerk of the United States Circuit Court. Going to Topeka to secure his salary, Mr. Thomas noticed that Mr. Holmes was an excellent penman, and, after a consultation with his deputy, hired him as an assistant in the office, where he remained for six years. There he attracted the attention of George R. Peck, the noted attorney, who, recognizing his ability, persuaded him to enter the legal department of the Atchison, Topeka & Santa Fe Railroad. Mr. Holmes has the utmost confidence of the officials of his company, who have found that they can depend absolutely upon his accuracy, ability and loyalty; and has also gained and retained the friendship of all who have worked with him or have come into contact with him in any way. He has been successful in his investments, and at the present time is the owner of a pleasant home and well improved farm in Soldier Township, where he expects to pass the closing years of his life, after his days of usefulness to the railroad have passed, but which, it may be said, will probably be many years in the future. From the first day of May, 1874, to the present time he has never missed a day's employment.

Mr. Holmes married Miss Cynthia Grace Auld, a daughter of Capt. Dan Caldwell Auld, a pioneer of Kansas who settled in Marshall County in 1856. Captain Auld was born in 1809, in Pennsylvania, from which state he went to Harrison County, Ohio, at an early day, and from the Buckeye State to Kansas. He married his cousin, Jane Auld, whom he had courted for a bashful lover, quite after the fashion of John Alden and Miles Standish. Captain and Mrs. Auld became the parents of eight children, born in Ohio, and two in Kansas, Mrs. Auld dying at the time of the birth of the last child. A few years later Captain Auld married Mrs. Hyde, the widow of the noted Doctor Hyde, who owned the property on which is now situated the Knights and Ladies of Security Building. Captain Auld was an ardent Union man during the Civil war, and organized a company for the Thirteenth Regiment, Kansas Volunteer Infantry, which was commanded by Col. John A. Martin. In his later years Captain Auld held many positions of public trust and responsibility, and was twice sent to the Kansas Legislature. He lived to a ripe old age and died when eighty-seven years old while on a visit to his daughter, Mrs. George N. Holmes. Three children were born to Mr. and Mrs. Holmes, namely: Mary Isabel, who is the wife of Louis Fleischer, whom she married October 15, 1895, the Fleischers being an old and honored pioneer family of Kansas; Anna Maud, who died November 21, 1899, as Mrs. Isaac Robinson; and George, who died in August, 1896.

WILLIAM H. LEWARK was one of the prominent factors in the business and social life of Coffeyville for many years. His death in that city July 3, 1914, removed a forceful and energetic worker and a man whose public spirit had always been uppermost in all his relations with that community from the early days.

He was born in the State of Indiana in 1848, a son of John and Elizabeth Lewark. His father was a farmer and died in Idaho, and his mother died in Indiana.

The late Mr. Lewark was one of the boy soldiers of the Union army during the Civil war. When still in his teens he enlisted and for one year nine months was with his regiment and participated in some of the hardest fought campaigns of the war. He was with Sherman on his march to the sea, and followed that great leader on his progress through the Carolinas and had the distinction of marching in Washington at the Grand Review. He spent his early life near Indianapolis, and in 1872 came out to Kansas, locating at Old Parker. He was married there in 1875, and soon afterwards moved to Coffeyville. With the exception of a year and nine months in the restaurant business in Colorado, he was thenceforward identified with Coffeyville's business interests until his death. He established the leading livery enterprise of the city and was still in that work when death overtook him. In 1913 his stables and all their contents were destroyed by fire, and he had made a fresh start only a short time before his death.

His record of public service is as important as his able management of his private affairs. He served as constable a number of years, was elected police judge and filled that office for ten consecutive years, and for four years was a member of the city council. At the time of his death he was commissioner of streets and parks, and had filled that office nearly four years. He was a democrat, attended the Episcopal Church, and was well known in fraternal circles, being affiliated with Keystone Lodge No. 102, Ancient Free and Accepted Masons, Star Lodge No. 117, Independent Order of Odd Fellows, Camp No. 665, Modern Woodmen of America, Lodge No. 775, Benevolent and Protective Order of Elks, and Lodge No. 279, Ancient Order of United Workmen. As a private or as a member of the chamber of commerce he worked constantly for the welfare of his home city, and was a stockholder in the Montgomery County Fair Association. He also had financial interests in a number of local enterprises.

Mrs. William H. Lewark, who survives her husband was before her marriage Nannie McLees. She was born ten miles northeast of Pittsburg, Pennsylvania, and comes of Scotch-Irish ancestry. Her father John McLees was born at Greensburg, Pennsylvania, in 1829, became a hotel proprietor in Pennsylvania, and in 1868 moved to Iowa, locating on a farm six miles from Centerville. He lived there for two seasons, then sold out and moved to Old Parker, Kansas, where in the early days he was engaged in the freighting service for the Indian Reservation. He afterwards moved to Coffeyville and was associated with Mr. Lewark in the livery business until his death, which occurred in 1912. Mr. McLees was a democrat. He was also an honored veteran of the Civil war. From Pennsylvania he enlisted and served three years with a regiment from that state, and took part in the great battles of Gettysburg, Shiloh, Lookout Mountain and many other noted battles. His brother Joseph McLees was killed at Gettysburg. John McLees married Sarah A. Brown, who was born in County Down, Ireland, in 1830, came to this country at the age of nineteen, her family locating near Pittsburg, and she died at Coffeyville in 1890. Her three children are: Mrs. Lewark; Mattie I., who is unmarried and lives with Mrs. Lewark; and Lillie M., who is also unmarried and lives in the Lewark home at Coffeyville.

Mr. and Mrs. Lewark were married at Old Parker in 1875. Mrs. Lewark is a very active member of the Episcopal Church at Coffeyville, and has served four terms as president of the Ladies Guild. She is a prominent member of the Searchlight Club, the first woman's club organized at Coffeyville, the club being a member of the City Federation of Woman's Clubs. Mrs. Lewark is the mother of three children: J. Harry, who conducts the livery business established by his father at Coffeyville; Russell V., who maintains a taxi cab service at Coffeyville; and Katy H., wife of Frank Halden Weaver, a real estate man at Coffeyville.

WILLIAM M. HUNTER, M. D., has not only gained status as one of the representative physicians and surgeons of Kansas but has also become a widely known authority in the diagnosis and treatment of all phases of catarrh, to which department of professional work he now gives virtually his entire attention. He maintains his home and office headquarters in the City of Wichita but in his special field of practice he draws an appreciable and appreciative clientage from states far distant from Kansas. The doctor is a scion of a sterling family whose name has been identified with American annals from the time of the War of the Revolution. He is a direct descendant from Granson Hunter, who left his home in Ireland and came with the British forces to America to take part in the Revolutionary war. Shortly after arriving in America he became assured of the legitimacy of the cause of the struggling colonies and so great was his disinclination to fight against the brave colonial forces that he deserted from the British army and settled in North Carolina. Later he removed to Greenville, Illinois, and became one of the pioneers of that state. His son William wedded Miss Polly Anne Grace, and the young couple forthwith set forth to establish a home in DeKalb County, Missouri. They made the trip with one horse, which the bride rode, and the young husband compassed the major part of the overland trip on foot. They became the first white settlers in DeKalb County, and there Mr. Hunter engaged in farming and stock-growing. It is worthy of historic note that he was a member of the party who escorted the Mormon leader, Brigham Young, and his followers out of Missouri when they were driven from that state. William Hunter was a man of vigor and strong mind, and he went forth to give loyal and gallant service as a soldier in the Mexican war. At the close of the conflict, in recognition of his services, he was allotted a large tract of land in Texas, and on a part of this tract is now situated the fine City of Dallas. John Hunter, son of William and Polly Anne (Grace) Hunter and father of Doctor Hunter of this review, was born and reared in DeKalb County, Missouri. There, as a young man, was solemnized his marriage to Miss Susan Jane Foster and in 1858, accompanied by his family and his venerable father he made his way to Texas. They established their home on the land that had been granted to William Hunter, and there they engaged in the raising of horses and cattle on an extensive scale. At the time of John Hunter's death, in 1865, he owned about 12,000 head of cattle.

Dr. William M. Hunter was born in DeKalb County, Missouri, on the 8th of May, 1852, and thus he was about six years of age at the time of the family removal to Texas, where he gained his preliminary education in the pioneer schools. Later he attended St. Joseph College, at St. Joseph, Missouri, and in 1878 he was graduated in the great University of Michigan, at Ann Arbor, from which he received the degree of Bachelor of Arts. In prepara-

tion for his chosen profession he entered the Eclectic Medical College in the City of Cincinnati, Ohio, and in the same he was graduated as a member of the class of 1880, with the degree of Doctor of Medicine. In the winter of 1883 he entered the great Bellevue Hospital in the City of New York, and during that and the seven succeeding winters he continued to do effective post-graduate work in this institution, where he gave special attention to the study of catarrh in all of its phases and where he had the best of clinical advantages in pursuing his research. During the intervening summers of this period, and up to the year 1900, Doctor Hunter was engaged in the active practice of his profession in the City of Dallas, Texas, and in the year mentioned he came to Kansas and established his residence at Wichita, where he has since specialized in the treatment of all forms of catarrhal disease, his success in his chosen specialty having been such that he has drawn patients from every state in the Union, so that his reputation far transcends local limitations. The doctor is identified with representative professional organizations and continues a close student of the best standard and periodical literature of his profession.

As a young man, prior to entering college, Doctor Hunter gained his full quota of experience in connection with the varied operations of an extensive Texas ranch, and in season it was his custom to drive about 3,000 head of cattle from the home ranch to Dodge City, Kansas, the nearest available shipping point. At that time there was only one store on the river bank where the thriving City of Wichita now stands, and this store was conducted in a primitive shack.

At Dallas, Texas, was solemnized the marriage of Doctor Hunter to Miss Julia Vaughn, and of their five children only one is living—Annie, who is the wife of William Agnew, of Los Angeles, California.

THOMAS MILBURN HOBSON, JR. has made his mark and impress on the world of affairs as an advertiser, and has built up an organization for poster advertising and general advertising, extending through a chain of towns from Tulsa, Oklahoma, to Kansas City, Missouri. He has also been extensively interested in the theatrical business, though he has recently disposed of all his holdings in that field.

He was born at Paola, Kansas, September 23, 1883, and has spent most of his life in the Sunflower State. His ancestors came from Ireland and were early settlers in Ohio and Indiana. His grandfather, John Hobson was born in Kentucky, was a miller and later carpenter and builder, and died at Utica, Indiana, 1862, before his grandson was born.

T. M. Hobson, Sr., who still lives at Paola, was born at Utica, Indiana, in 1845, was reared there, but came out to Kansas in 1867, and has since had his home for forty-nine years at Paola. He is still active in business, as a house mover and bridge builder. He has taken an active part in local affairs at Paola, having served as mayor and several terms on the council. He was married in 1874 at Fort Scott, Kansas, to Miss Minerva Catherine Tresslar, who was born at Franklin, Indiana, in 1852. He is a republican and connected with the Independent Order of Odd Fellows and other fraternal orders. Their children are: Chattie, wife of John Lanier Frye, a merchant at Vandalia, Illinois; and Thomas Milburn, Jr.

Mr. Hobson had an excellent education as a preparation for his life work. After attending the public schools of Paola, leaving the high school in 1901, he spent a year in the Kimball-Union Academy of Meriden, New Hampshire, and then attended Hiram College in Ohio, an institution of which James A. Garfield was once president. He left college in the junior year and in 1905 took up advertising, a line he has followed ever since, especially in poster advertising. He was first located at Paola and worked at his business in that vicinity and still retains interests there, with a manager in charge. In 1909 he went to Douglas, Arizona, and built up a poster advertising plant and also leased the Orpheum Theater until May 1, 1910. At that date he established his headquarters and home at Independence, Kansas, and has developed the extensive advertising business already noted. As a theatrical man he had interests in theaters at Independence, Coffeyville, Ottawa and Caney. His offices are at 112 West Laurel Street and he owns his home at Fifth and Locust streets and considerable other city property. Mr. Hobson is vice president of the Tri-State Poster Advertising Association.

He is affiliated with Fortitude Lodge No. 107, Ancient, Free and Accepted Masons; Keystone Chapter No. 22, Royal Arch Masons; St. Bernard Commandery No. 10, Knights Templar; Mirzah Temple of the Nobles of the Mystic Shrine at Pittsburg, Kansas; with Council No. 45 of the United Commercial Travelers at Independence; with Lodge No. 780, Benevolent and Protective Order of Elks at Independence; with the Loyal Order of Moose, and is a republican, a member of the Commercial Club and the Country Club, and is president of the Rotary Club.

On December 3, 1912, at Independence, Mr. Hobson married Miss Marie Ziegler, a daughter of W. E. and Jessie Ziegler of Coffeyville. Mrs. Hobson is a granddaughter of Mrs. A. C. Stich of Independence.

JOSEPH F. SAVAGE. There are many things of interest connected with the career of Joseph F. Savage, of Coffeyville, particularly in the line of achievements and success and position gained through individual efforts and with honor. Perhaps the most interesting, however, as well as the most important in regard to the history of Kansas, is the fact that this retired banker made what was really the first treaty here with the Osage Indians, this being in 1868, when Mr. Savage was a "sooner." Since that time his fortunes have grown and developed and he has watched what was once the Indian country develop into a center of civilization, and has done his full share in bringing about the progress that has been made.

Mr. Savage was born in Wayne County, Kentucky, February 2, 1839, and is a son of E. S. and Martha (Minges) Savage. He belongs to a family that originated in England and emigrated to the Shenandoah Valley of Virginia during colonial times, and his grandfather was John Savage, who was born in Virginia in 1765 and became a pioneer of Wayne County, Kentucky. He was a farmer by vocation, fought under General Jackson in the War of 1812, and was wounded at the Battle of New Orleans, and finally passed away, honored and respected at his Kentucky home, in 1855. E. S. Savage was born in Wayne County, Kentucky, in 1795, was educated in his native locality and followed the vocation of farming throughout his life there, dying in 1863. He was a man of sterling qualities of character, and through straightforward dealing and good citizenship won the respect and esteem of his fellowmen. He was a democrat in politics. Mr. Savage married Martha Minges, who was born in 1810, in Virginia, and died in Wayne County, Kentucky, in 1855, and

they became the parents of eight children, namely: John, who died young; Peggy, who married R. L. Davis, a mechanic of Louisville, Kentucky, both now being deceased; Rebecca, who died in Wayne County, Kentucky, as the wife of the late John S. Ragon, who was a farmer; Melissa, who also died in Wayne County, Kentucky, unmarried; Sallie, who died in that county as Mrs. Davis; George, who resides at Bartlesville, Oklahoma, and is a retired mechanic; Joseph F., of this review; and Selby, who is a retired educator and lives at Coffeyville.

Joseph F. Savage received his education in the district schools of Wayne County, Kentucky, and was reared on his father's farm, on which he remained until he was seventeen years of age. At that time he came to the West, locating at Springfield, Missouri, in the vicinity of which place he worked on different farms until the outbreak of the Civil war. In 1862 he enlisted in the Eighth Regiment, Missouri Volunteer Cavalry, and with that command saw much hard fighting, being among others, in the battles of Pea Ridge, Little Rock and Shiloh, the Siege of Vicksburg, and the engagements at Tupelo, Mississippi, Prairie Grove, Arkansas, and Nashville, Tennessee. At Jenkins Ferry, on the Saline River, he was wounded through the arm, but soon rejoined his regiment and continued to fight valiantly until receiving his honorable discharge in October, 1865.

With an excellent war record, the young soldier returned to the duties of peace, and in 1867 settled in Cedar County, Southwest Missouri, where he engaged in farming until 1868. In that year Mr. Savage first came to Montgomery County, Kansas. As a sooner, he settled in the Osage country, building a log cabin two miles north of the present site of Coffeyville, his claim being one-half mile west of Talley Springs. After building his cabin, he returned to Missouri for supplies, bacon, plows, etc., and upon his return found that every bit of his improvements had been removed by the Indians. Nothing daunted, Mr. Savage rebuilt his log cabin, and on the morning after his return he was visited by Chief Claymore, of the Osage Nation, who requested him and his companions, James Phillips and William Sain, to leave the Osage country. In spite of this these pioneers continued their building, and while so engaged received a well-written communication from Chief Claymore the gist of which was that unless they removed from the reservation within ten days, he would come with his braves and drive them out. Mr. Savage, acting as spokesman for the whites, asked Henry, the chief's interpreter, what would be the result if the chief's wishes were not complied with and the braves came. Henry replied that he did not know, and went away. Thus matters stood for a few days, when Mr. Savage met the chief on the prairie and invited him and one of his council, Big Elk, together with Henry, to come the next day to his cabin "when the sun was straight up," and eat with him. The invitation was accepted, and after dinner the pipe was passed around, and, seeing that the chief was in a good humor, Mr. Savage decided upon a plan of action. From his pocket he took two silver half-dollars, and, clinking them together, attracted the attention of Claymore. Silver was then very scarce, the Government paying the Indians in greenbacks, a form of currency which they did not like. The Chief eyed the shining silver with greedy eyes, and finally Mr. Savage made the following proposition: "Claymore," he said, "I have given you your dinner, and now I will give you this dollar, that we three be permitted to remain here with the understanding that we steal nothing from you and you steal nothing from us, and we be not disturbed while the Osages live here." The proposition was accepted, the pipe was smoked, and thus was enacted the first kept treaty for the privilege of living in the Diminished Reserve. Later, Chief Claymore gave the three white settlers permission to plow twelve acres of land apiece for raising wheat. This interesting incident was just about a month before Colonel Coffey, the founder of Coffeyville, made his appearance.

For a period of twenty-two years Mr. Savage continued to engage in farming in that locality. His original farm consisted of 160 acres, and he still owns 320 acres about two miles north of Coffeyville, although this is not exactly his original place, as he has bought and sold on several occasions. In 1890 he became one of the organizers and original stockholders of the First National Bank of Coffeyville, and later assisted in the organization of the Caney Valley National Bank, of which he was made president, a position which he retained for twelve years. With others, he founded and put upon a paying basis the State Bank of Coffeyville, and at one time was one of the best known figures in banking circles in this part of the state, but in 1908 disposed of all his banking interests and retired. He is now living in his comfortable modern home at No. 1012 Maple Street, Coffeyville, where he also owns two modern store buildings and other real estate properties. He has various other interests, both agricultural and commercial, and during his active career showed a great interest in civic affairs, particularly when he was serving in the capacity of chairman of the Commercial Club of Coffeyville.

Mr. Savage is a democrat, but has never aspired to public office. His religious connection is with the Baptist Church. In fraternal circles, he is well and favorably known, being a thirty-second degree Mason and a member of Keystone Lodge No. 102, Ancient Free & Accepted Masons, Coffeyville, of which he is past master; Coffeyville Chapter No. 89, Royal Arch Masons; Lochinvar Commandery No. 52, Knights Templar; Wichita Consistory No. 2, Royal and Select Masters and Ararat Temple Ancient Arabic Order Nobles of the Mystic Shrine of Leavenworth.

In 1867, Mr. Savage was married at Osceola, Missouri, to Miss Matilda Fain, who died at Coffeyville in 1870, leaving two sons: Isaac W., who resides on his farm three miles north of Coffeyville; and Abram F., a retired farm owner living at Winfield, Kansas. In 1873, in Cedar County, Missouri, Mr. Savage was again married, being united with Miss Mary Roberson, who died in 1889 at Coffeyville. In 1900 Mr. Savage was married the third time, his bride being Miss Hettie Hobbs, of Winfield, Kansas, daughter of the late Jacob Hobbs.

HERBERT K. LINDSLEY. Recognized as one of the leading commercial centers of the West, the City of Wichita has advanced rapidly in recent years along particular lines. Its geographical location and railroad facilities have made it the largest market in the world for broom corn. In the handling of broom corn, an important figure is Herbert K. Lindsley, president of the American Warehouse Company, whose career is typical of modern progress and advancement. It is not necessary to seek far for the reason for his success, or his indefatigable energy, close application and progressive methods have not only laid the foundation for the enterprise which he has built up, but have led him into other lines of Vol. IV—8

endeavor, in which he has attained equal recognition and reward.

Mr. Lindsley was born at Muncie, Indiana, June 21, 1875. When he was three years of age he was taken by his parents to Sterling, Kansas, where he received his education, and after graduating from the high school of that place, clerked for three years and for a few years thereafter was agent for the Pacific Express Company at Sterling. He then engaged in the broom corn business at Sterling, that town being at the time the largest broom corn market in the West. In 1904 he came to Wichita, where he was the first to engage in the broom corn business, and subsequently became the organizer and was elected president of the American Warehouse Company of Wichita, a $300,000 corporation for the handling of broom corn. This is the largest concern of the kind in the world, and has branch offices in various of the large cities, its warehouses at Galveston being the largest in that city. During the years of its existence, the company has grown and developed under Mr. Lindsley's able direction and its operations have taken on an importance national in its scope.

While Mr. Lindsley has been primarily interested in the broom corn business, he has also entered other fields of business activity, where his abilities and talents have been enlisted in the promotion and development of institutions of more than ordinary importance. In 1900, while a resident of Sterling, he became the organizer of the Lyons National Bank, of Lyons, Kansas, and was made its president, a position which he still retains. In 1902 he organized the Farmers State Bank, of Chase, Kansas, of which he is also the directing head in the capacity of president. During the years 1910 and 1911 he was the prime mover in the organization of the Farmers and Bankers Life Insurance Company, capitalized at $275,000, and in the five years of the company's existence it has had approximately $15,000,000 worth of business in force. This is an old line legal reserve life insurance company, and from the time of its inception, Mr. Lindsley has directed its affairs from the president's chair.

On June 16, 1909, Mr. Lindsley was united in marriage with Miss Jessie Piper, of Clinton, Missouri. They were the parents of two children: Robert Kitchel, born September 27, 1911; and Herbert Piper, born December 16, 1913. Mr. Lindsley is a Scottish Rite Mason, past commander of Sterling Commandery, Knights Templar, and a member of the Blue Lodge, Chapter and Shrine, and also holds membership in the Independent Order of Odd Fellows, the Knights of Pythias and the Benevolent and Protective Order of Elks. He has always taken a deep interest in the welfare of Wichita, never hesitating to advocate or oppose any measure or project which pertains to modern advancement and improvement, which in his judgment merits endorsement or opposition, and is widely known as a man of substantial worth, whose judgment is sound and sagacity keen.

CHARLES W. BARNES. As reporter and newspaper editor, former state superintendent of insurance and now president of the Kansas Life Insurance Company of Topeka, Charles W. Barnes has had an exceedingly busy and successful career covering almost the entire forty-year period since he came to the state.

He was born on a farm in Coshocton County, Ohio, October 28, 1869, a son of William O. and Maria Louisa (McGruder) Barnes. His grandfather

Charles Barnes was a lawyer, one of the pioneer members of the Ohio bar, and in the early days served as a judge. William O. Barnes was a farmer, and left the farm to serve in an Ohio regiment during the Civil war. In 1877 he brought his family out to Western Kansas, locating in Trego County. He acquired a large acreage of land, but soon found that it was not amenable to the kind of agriculture he had practiced back in Ohio, owing to a lack of rainfall. That was many years before the introduction of modern dry farming. He took up ca'tle raising, but not long afterwards met financial disaster during the severe winter of 1882, when most of his stock was frozen in a blizzard. Having had a lion's share of early Kansas vicissitudes, he then removed to Lyon County, and is now spending his declining years at Osage City.

The only child of his parents, Charles W. Barnes was eight years old when he came to Kansas, and on his father's farm and ranch came to know something of the hardships and privations of the Kansas farmer of that time. Most of his education was acquired after his father moved to Lyon County, where he attended the State Normal School in Emporia. At that time it was his plan and ambition to teach, but he became diverted to a more congenial emp'oyment in newspaper work. He worked on the News, the Democrat, the Republican and the Gazette at Emporia, and was employed in almost every capacity from apprentice to editor.

In 1895 Mr. Barnes came to Topeka as political reporter for the Daily Capital, and for three years kept tab on the political situation in the city and throughout the state. He next went to the State Journal at Topeka, as political reporter, and in fact has never wholly lost his interest in journalism.

In 1903 Mr. Barnes entered the field of insurance as assistant to C. H. Luling, then state superintendent of insurance. Then in 1907 he was elected state superintendent of insurance, and reelected in 1908. Those were stirring years in insurance circles everywhere, and he rendered his state a valuable service in the careful and conscientious administration of his public duties.

In 1913 Mr. Barnes was the chief organizer of the Kansas Life Insurance Company, of which he has since been president. Bringing to this institution his wide experience as an official and as a practical business man, he has succeeded in making it one of the large and safe financial institutions of the state.

Mr. Barnes is affiliated with the Benevolent and Protective Order of Elks, the Knights of Pythias, the Independent Order of Odd Fellows, the Modern Woodmen of America, the Knights and Ladies of Security, and the Sons of Veterans. On Christmas Day, 1899, he married Margaret Holmes Bear. They have two children: Charles W., Jr., and Jack B.

DESIRE DEBACKER. The greatest sources of productive wealth along the Kaw River are the market gardens and fruit orchards. This is an industry which has developed to high proportions in Kansas, and as everyone knows is a business where hard work, careful management, and thorough planning are prerequisites of success. Perhaps no family has made a better record in this field and has shown more of these essentials than that of Debacker, one of whose representatives is named above.

The Debackers are Belgian people. Desire Debacker was born near Brussels in Belgium in 1874. His father was the late John B. Debacker, who was born in the same district of Belgium in 1851. He grew up there, married, and was connected with a woolen goods manufacturing concern. When the children were still small his wife died, and leaving the young people with their maternal grandfather John B. Debacker set out for America. Coming to Kansas he homesteaded in Kingman County, seven miles east of the City of Kingman. A little later his family followed him, and after seven years spent in Kingman County he moved to Rosedale in Wyandotte County, and then three years later to Shawnee County, where the Debackers have since had their home and the scene of their activities. John B. Debacker died at the old place in this county in 1904 at the age of fifty-three. His wife's father, Antone Glibert, had charge of the young children for a time and brought them to Kingman County, Kansas. Antone Glibert lived to the advanced age of eighty-seven and died at the home of one of his sons in the State of Washington, much loved and lamented by the Debacker family. John B. Debacker after the death of his wife had to be both father and mother to his children, and not only did his duty by them but provided them well in material substance and was a highly esteemed citizen.

Desire Debacker came to America and joined his father's family when a child. He spent his early youth partly in Kingman County and partly in Wyandotte County, and took up the real work of his life in Shawnee County. He has developed one of the most extensive market gardens and fruit orchards in the county, and has made a specialty of apples. His orchards have produced as high as 10,000 bushels in a single season. The crop above all others for which the Kaw River valley is famous is potatoes, and Mr. Debacker has raised as high as 5,000 bushels of sweet potatoes in a single season. He has shipped produce to every northern state from Minnesota to the lakes, and one of his crops is spinach, of which he shipped 4,000 bushels during one season, that establishing the record of any one grower in the state.

Mr. Debacker married November 18, 1906, Margaret Corcoran, who was born in Louisville, Kentucky, and they have four children: John B., Catherine, Alvin and Sidney. One son named Martin Edmond died in infancy.

ORVIS MILTON BLOOM, one of the well known oil producers living at Independence, Kansas, has been closely identified with the oil districts of the southwest for over twenty years.

He was born in Clearfield County, Pennsylvania, February 9. 1873, a son of A. W. and Rebecca (MacCracken) Bloom. His mother is now living at Independence. Mr. Bloom was one of a large family of children, and his brother, C. L. Bloom, has been one of the most successful oil operators in the southwest.

When O. M. Bloom was five years of age his parents moved to Fulton County, Indiana, and he attended his first schools there. Later they located in Bollinger County in Southeastern Missouri, and he continued his education in the schools there, and after 1885 was a student in the public schools of Linn County, Kansas, where his parents located. He spent the first sixteen years of his life on his father's farms.

In the fall of 1888 Mr. Bloom went west to California, and at Red Bluff became foreman on a ranch that was known as the Walsh Ranch. He remained there 2½ years, then spent one winter in running a traction engine, and continued farming on the coast until March 14, 1894.

At that date he returned to Miami County, Kansas, and has since been active in the oil fields. He has been through all the grades of service, beginning as

tool dresser and rising to contractor. His work has taken him into the Kansas, Oklahoma, Missouri and Texas fields, and he is a producer of both oil and gas.

Mr. Bloom and his family reside at 203 South Fifteenth Street in Independence, and he owns a house and lot at 613 North Tenth Street. Politically he is independent, and he served as deputy sheriff at Bonner Springs, Kansas, during two administrations, one a republican and the other democratic. He is affiliated with Bonner Springs Lodge No. 366, Ancient, Free and Accepted Masons, the Royal Arch Chapter at Kansas City and the Knights Templar Commandery in the same place, and is also a member of Kansas City Consistory of the thirty-second degree Scottish Rite. Mr. Bloom belongs to Independence Lodge No. 780 of the Benevolent and Protective Order of Elks and was formerly identified with Camp No. 649, Modern Woodmen of America.

On April 23, 1900, in Independence, he married Miss Catherine Early, a daughter of B. P. and Catherine Early, who now reside in Coffeyville, where her father is in business. Mr. and Mrs. Bloom have five children: Margaret, who died in infancy; Francis Milton, born August 9, 1909; Mary Elizabeth, born October 9, 1911; Bernard Leroy, born December 23, 1913; and John Edward, born December 26, 1915.

RAY L. BAILEY is one of the widely known men of Shawnee County, and is now successfully farming a fine place four miles north of North Topeka. He makes farming a real business, understands it in all details, and gives it the same energy and close attention which he formerly paid to his work as a traveling salesman. He was on the road for a number of years, and his firm sent him on a number of missions to Old Mexico. On account of his travel and extensive acquaintance in that southern republic he is well informed as to Mexican internal affairs.

Mr. Bailey was born in Mansfield, Tioga County, Pennsylvania, August 24, 1868, but has been a resident of Kansas since his parents brought him to this state in October, 1872.

M. D. Bailey, his father, has long been a prominent man in Kansas. On coming to the state in 1872 he and his family settled in Pawnee County. He was also a native of Tioga County, Pennsylvania, and the Bailey family were among the pioneers in that district. The father of M. D. Bailey was Benjamin F. Bailey, who was born in Pennsylvania and in early territorial days, before the Civil war, came out to Leavenworth, Kansas, and opened a store. Mr. A. Meyers, who is now living in Meyers Valley, in Pottawatomie County, is one of the men who recalls Benjamin Bailey as a Leavenworth merchant in 1855. Benjamin Bailey finally returned to Pennsylvania, having remained in Kansas only a few years.

M. D. Bailey, after coming to Kansas, was employed in the United States Land Department and subsequently for four years was county superintendent of public instruction. Before coming to Kansas he had served as a Union soldier four years. At the outbreak of the war he joined Company A of the Eleventh Pennsylvania Cavalry, and most of his service was in the Army of the Potomac. It was his rare privilege, while stationed in the vicinity of Hampton Roads, to witness the epoch-making naval battle between the Confederate ironclad Merrimac and the marvelous invention of Ericson, the gunboat Monitor. On account of his previous service as a soldier, M. D. Bailey, when

he took up a claim in Edwards County, Kansas, had to live on it only a year to perfect his title. For many years he filled a place in the pension department, and is now in the National Hospital.

Emory Bailey, a son of M. D. Bailey, was a member of the famous Twentieth Kansas Regiment, organized by Col. Fred Funston at the outbreak of the Spanish-American war. General Funston at the time of his death was chief commander of the American forces on the Mexican border. Emory Bailey served with the Twentieth Regiment in all its gallant part in the Philippine war and returned to this country with his regiment.

WILLIAM M. JAMIESON. Few of the business men of Wichita have had more varied careers than has William M. Jamieson, who, since 1910, has been engaged in the handling of large realty transactions in this city. A Scot by birth, he came to America as a lad, and during the next forty years his activities carried him to many out-of-the-way places of this continent, where he was connected with the construction of some of the largest engineering projects of the time. The broad experience and knowledge of men which he gained during this period of his life have been of great value to him in his later business career, and since locating at Wichita he has steadily advanced to a position of prominence among real estate men.

Mr. Jamieson was born at Lanwickshire, near the City of Edinburgh, Scotland, August 5, 1864. In 1869 his father, Alexander Jamieson, emigrated to the United States and located on a farm in Will County, Illinois, subsequently removing to near Ottumwa, Iowa, where he was engaged in farming until 1883. In that year he came to Kansas, and for ten years carried on agricultural pursuits near Clearwater, his final location being at Deer Creek, Oklahoma, where his death occurred in 1902. He was a sturdy, thrifty farmer, of absolute integrity and merited and held the esteem of his fellowmen. His widow, Mrs. Ellen Mason Jamieson, still resides on the farm at Deer Creek. They were the parents of nine children, of whom William M. is next to the eldest.

William M. Jamieson was about five years of age when brought to this country by his parents, and his education was that afforded by the district schools of Will County, Illinois. At an early age this ambitious and energetic youth became self-supporting, and for some years was engaged in farming during the summer months and in working in the mines in the winter seasons. In 1883 he came to Kansas with his parents, and for four years followed farming, but in 1887 went to Carthage, New Mexico, as drill runner for the San Pedro Coal and Coke Company, a position for which he had been prepared by his former experience as a miner. Mr. Jamieson remained in this capacity for three years and then returned to farming for a few years at Clearwater, and in Oklahoma, and for a time was also in the draying business at Clearwater.

In 1901 he formed a connection that was destined to bring him into many exciting experiences and into touch with life in the rough. In that year he engaged with the May & Jekyll Construction Company, of New York, as superintendent of livestock in the building of the railroad from Porte-au-Prince to Santa Clara, Cuba, a capacity in which he remained for one year and was then made superintendent of construction. He continued as the incumbent of the latter post until the successful completion of the road. In 1903 he was made superintendent of tracks and excavation, in the building of the great filtration plant, by May & Jekyll, for the City of Washington, District of Columbia. Returning to Cuba in the employ of the same company, Mr. Jamieson acted as superintendent of railroad construction in the building of the Nipa Bay Railroad to Punta Baca, Cuba, and when that project was completed engaged with Pierson & Son, of London, England, as superintendent of construction of tunnels "A" and "B" in the great tunnel system then under construction under the East River, connecting New York with Long Island. This was completed in May, 1907, and Mr. Jamieson re-engaged with May & Jekyll and went to South America as superintendent of construction in the building of the Madeira & Mamore Railroad, and remained two years in completing the railroad to the headwaters of the Madeira River, and in 1910 returned to the United States, and, locating at Wichita, realized a long-cherished ambition by engaging in the real estate business. Mr. Jamieson has been the medium through which some of the largest deals of recent years have been consummated, and few realty dealers of the city have a more comprehensive knowledge of land values.

Mr. Jamieson married Miss Susan Jamieson, and they are the parents of five children, namely: Arthur C., who is engaged in the undertaking and embalming business at Bucklen, Kansas; and Ora O., Ethel M., Byron and Theodore, who reside with their parents.

HOMER WARD BOMGARDNER is one of Topeka's leading business men, and is also active in civic affairs and a prominent Sunday school worker.

Much of his life has been spent in Kansas. He was born at Canal Dover, Ohio, February 1, 1865, a son of Benjamin F. and Mary (Ward) Bomgardner, his father being of Swiss ancestry. Reared in Ohio where he obtained an education in the high schools and academies, in January, 1884, Mr. Bomgardner came to Kansas, locating in Smith County, and for seven years was a teacher in the public schools of this state. During that time he continued his efforts toward securing a better education, and practically all his savings were invested in school attendance. In Kansas he was a student at Gould College at Harlan, but in 1891 removed to Topeka and for about ten years was employed in the auditing department of the Santa Fe Railway Company.

A permanent direction to his career was given when he started out on the road, traveling over the Central states selling the Bomgardner lowering device, a device used for lowering the casket from the surface to the bottom of the grave. This device was invented by his brother, Joseph Bomgardner. From 1905 to 1907 Mr. Bomgardner worked as a bookkeeper in the Bank of Topeka, but on the 15th of July, 1907, embarked in the undertaking business, at which he has now been engaged nearly ten years. It was while traveling on the road that he met a large number of undertakers and lecturers on embalming, and it was after much study, practical experience, and a widely extended acquaintance that he began the business for himself at Topeka, for which he is unusually well qualified.

Mr. Bomgardner is a republican and is now serving as precinct committeeman. He also belongs to the Topeka Commercial Club and the Rotary Club, is a thirty-second degree Scottish Rite and Knights Templar York Rite Mason, belongs to the Temple of the Mystic Shrine and to the Independent Order of Odd Fellows. He and his wife are both Presbyterians, he has served as superintendent of the Sunday school, and has been closely and helpfully identified with the city training school for Sunday school workers. He was also chairman of the local committee that managed the preparations for the notable jubilee Sunday school convention in May, 1915, and he also collected and managed the impressive Sunday school exhibit at the Topeka State Fair.

On November 25, 1888, Mr. Bomgardner married Cornie H. Rider, of Harlan, Kansas. Their three living children are Ruth, Lucile and Ralph Ward.

CHARLES JOSEPH BOEGER is without doubt one of the foremost men in the profession of photography in the State of Kansas. Some years ago he located in Topeka, and with his studio at 707 Kansas Avenue has done work that entitles him to his place in the profession, and his career is also dignified by the fact that he represents a pioneer family in this state.

His father is the honored Joseph Boeger of Decatur County. Joseph Boeger was born in Prussia, Germany, in 1850, and before he left the fatherland became well known and highly respected in Westphalia. When very young he was elected a member of the Provincial Parliament, and had the distinction of being the youngest member of that body. In 1875 he married Miss Ida Betheny. The Betheny family had an authentic record of its antecedents extending back for centuries, and a number of generations ago they were closely connected with the Astors, of the same branch from which the American Astors are descended. An enormous estate belongs to the Betheny family in Germany, and in time the Boegers will doubtless get their share.

In 1881 Joseph Boeger brought his family to America, lived in St. Louis until 1885, and then moved out to Decatur County, Kansas. He located on a homestead eighteen miles south of Oberlin, and became a farmer and stockman. After twenty-five years of an industrious, temperate life he had accumulated a fortune, and at one time owned upwards of 25,000 acres, located in several counties. His connection with that section of Kansas had a very important bearing upon the farming and community welfare. He and his son Charles Joseph became successful contractors for the building of schoolhouses, and erected upwards of two score in Decatur County alone, and many others in Sheridan County and other counties in Northwest Kansas. As a pioneer in Decatur County Joseph Boeger experienced all the hardships and vicissitudes of the early days. In the absence of mills and other industries it not infrequently happened that settlers were put to hard straits in order to secure the staff of life, and they often ground corn in a coffee mill. Joseph Boeger experienced poor crops, hot winds, grasshoppers, destructive storms, but his fortitude and perseverance won out in the long run.

To the marriage of Joseph and Mrs. Boeger were born eleven children. The sons were Frank, Charles Joseph, Anthony, Herman and George. Frank is now living with his parents in Sheridan County. Herman, at the time of this writing, had enlisted as a citizen member of the United States navy, joining for a month's cruise from Norfolk, Virginia.

Charles Joseph Boeger was born at Dreburg in the District of Westphalia, Prussia, in May, 1879, and was two years of age when he came with his parents to America. He has many reminiscences of the early life of the family in Decatur County. The Rock Island Line has not yet been built across that county, and the only railroad was the B. & M. short line into Oberlin. Mr. Boeger recalls the fact that when he was a boy one of the most interesting sights was the immense herds of antelopes. In a month's time one could see thousands of these animals, and often in flocks of 100 or 200.

Mr., Boeger is now associated with his brothers, Anthony and George, in the conduct of the photographic studio at Topeka. All these sons are young men of unusual intelligence and special talents, and Charles J. Boeger, in the opinion of men competent to judge, is not surpassed by any in his profession in that state. He has made photography a profession, the object of constant study in order to improve himself and take advantage of every new detail, and has attended many photographers' conventions, at one time visiting Buffalo, New York, for that purpose.

Since coming to Topeka about six years ago he has built up a splendid patronage, and he resides in one of the beautiful residences of the city. Mr. Boeger is a self made man, and never attended any photographic school, acquiring his knowledge of the art from experience. Some years ago he started out as an amateur, traveling in a covered wagon over Western Kansas, and in that way he had a most interesting experience and also laid the foundation for his present success.

The name Boeger has a significance meaning Chief Archer. When Joseph Boeger was a young man in Prussia he joined the army, and was in the regular service for three years. He also learned the trade of cabinet maker, and that was his occupation until he located in Kansas. He is a man of fine intellect, a close student, a lover and reader of history and mathematics, and with all his experience in practical affairs as a farmer and land owner found time to work out the plan formed in his ingenious mind. On September 19, 1905, he received a patent for the invention of a new type of machine gun. It is claimed that this gun is more efficient than any other gun now in use, and it seems highly probable that in time its principle will be adopted by many governments.

THOMAS B. WALL. A resident of Kansas for nearly thirty years, the late Judge Thomas Berry Wall was a man whose fine intellectual and professional attainments enabled him to leave a deep and benignant impress upon the history of this commonwealth. He was numbered among the representative members of the Kansas bar, served with distinction on the bench of the District Court and by his character and ability won inviolable place in popular confidence and esteem. He was one of the leaders of the bar of the City of Wichita at the time of his death, which occurred January 14, 1906, and this publication exercises a consistent function when it pays specific tribute to his memory.

Judge Wall was born in Cumberland County, Illinois, on the 1st of January, 1857, and like many another sterling citizen who has gained prestige in professional and public life, his childhood and early youth were compassed by the benignant influences of the farm. He gained his preliminary education in the public schools of his native county and thereafter was graduated in Lee Academy. In the furtherance of his higher academic education he entered McKendree College, at Lebanon, Illinois, and from this excellent institution in 1895 he received the degree of Master of Arts, though he had attended many years before. In this connection it is interesting to recall that one of his classmates was Hon. Charles S. Deneen, who later served as Governor of

Illinois. At intervals while attending college Judge Wall supplemented his financial resources by devoting his attention to teaching school. With characteristic diligence and ability he applied himself to the study of the science of jurisprudence, in which he made rapid progress, and finally he was admitted to the bar of his native state, upon examination before Judge Scofield.

In 1878 Judge Wall established his residence at Wichita, Kansas, and he became closely identified with the civic and material development and upbuilding of this new prosperous city. Here he became associated with William E. Stanley in the general practice of law, and he soon made himself known as a well fortified counselor and versatile trial lawyer. In 1885, when he was but twenty-eight years of age, he was appointed judge of the District Court, by Governor Martin, to fill the vacancy made by the retirement of Judge Henry C. Sluss. The high estimate placed upon the administration of the able young jurist was shown by his election to the office in the following year, to fill the unexpired term of his predecessor. Upon the enactment of the Federal Bankruptcy Law Judge Wall was appointed, by Judge Hook, to the office of referee in bankruptcy for this district, and of this position he continued the incumbent until 1904. He was a stalwart and effective advocate of the principles of the republican party and his special ability as an orator caused his interposition to be frequently sought in campaign work as well as a speaker upon divers other public occasions. In 1900 he represented Kansas as a delegate to the National Republican Convention, and in this connection he formulated the resolution that was passed by the Kansas delegation, in advance of any other state delegation, demanding the drafting of Theodore Roosevelt as candidate for the vice presidency of the United States. In the practice of his profession Judge Wall long maintained a partnership alliance with Judge D. M. Dale, later he was similarly associated with Charles H. Brooks, and during the last four years of his earnest and successful career he was a law partner of Judge Henry C. Sluss. The proclivities of Judge Wall as a close and appreciative student and reader never seemed to abate in the least their vigor, and he was not only a man of broad intellectual grasp but was also specially well known as a brilliant orator.

The judge never lost his deep interest in the basic industries of agriculture and stock-growing, and just west of the City of Wichita he developed and improved a model farm which is considered one of the best improved and most valuable stock farms in the Arkansas Valley.

On August 15, 1880, was solemnized the marriage of Judge Wall to Miss Kate Alexander, who survives him, and of this union were born two sons, Alexander Berry and Paul Jean.

Alexander B. Wall, the elder of the two sons, was born at Wichita on the 12th of December, 1882, and who was afforded the advantages of the public schools and the Lewis Academy of Wichita, as well as those of Wentworth Military Academy, at Lexington, Missouri. He also attended the Kansas State Agricultural College, at Manhattan, and he is now known as one of the representative agriculturists and stock-growers of his native county. He has the active supervision of the fine farm developed by his father, as previously noted, and there conducts a certified-milk dairy in connection with his general agricultural and stock-raising enterprise.

Paul Jean Wall was born at Wichita on the 19th of October, 1885, and after his graduation in the high school at St. Louis, Missouri, he entered, in 1904, the University of Kansas, in the law department of which he was graduated in 1908 and from which he received the degree of Bachelor of Laws. In June of the same year was recorded his admission to the bar of his native state, and in his chosen profession he is well upholding the prestige of the honored name which he bears. For three years after his admission to the bar he was associated in practice with Judge Henry C. Sluss, his father's former law partner, and since that time he has conducted a successful individual practice at Wichita, his law business being largely in the domain of real-estate, probate and corporation practice. In April, 1914, by Judge John C. Pollock, presiding on the bench of the United States District Court, Mr. Wall was appointed United States commissioner for the District of Kansas, for a term of four years, and in this office he is giving most effective service.

On the 16th of November, 1910, was solemnized the marriage of Paul J. Wall to Miss Alice Duncan, of Kansas City, Misouri, and they having one daughter, Jean, who was born November 30, 1911.

J. H. SPINES. The men who establish, organize and develop successful commercial establishments must possess many qualities out of the ordinary. Their insight into business conditions must be keen and far-reaching, their knowledge of values profound, and their ability to grasp opportunities unlimited. Without industrial and commercial interests no locality progresses, for such enterprises are the very life of a community. The investment and attraction of capital, the employment of labor and the consequent opening of new avenues of endeavor to meet newly created demands, all infuse blood into the veins of a section and endow it with new vigor and strength. That part of West Douglas Avenue, between Main Street and the Arkansas River Bridge, in Wichita, is an excellent example of the above statement. With the location in its midst of an enterprise of the kind mentioned, its business life quickened, new interests were awakened, and it has developed into a prosperous center of the city. The man who is probably principally responsible for this desirable state of affairs is J. H. Spines, proprietor of Spines' Store and one of the most progressive of the younger generation of business men of Wichita.

Mr. Spines was born at Milwaukee, Wisconsin, May 2, 1884. After his graduation from the public schools, his family was not able to help him further in the way of an education, but the youth was ambitious to secure a more comprehensive training and accordingly enrolled as a student at Carroll College, Waukesha, Wisconsin, and succeeded in completing the classical courses by working during all his spare time at whatever employment he could find to do. He was graduated from that institution in 1903, and in the following year went to Chicago, where he secured a position with the great house of Siegel, Cooper & Company. He commenced in the humble capacity of stock boy, but his energy, ability and fidelity soon gained him recognition and he was so rapidly advanced that the end of three years found him occupying the position of assistant merchandise manager.

In was Mr. Spines' ambition, however, to become the owner of an establishment of his own, and he was therefore constantly on the lookout for opportunities. In 1909, having heard glowing reports of the opportunities to be found in Kansas, and particularly at Wichita, he came to this city and sought a location. His capital at that time amounted to something less than $500, but he rented a store at No. 111 West Douglas Avenue, and put in a small stock of gentlemen's clothing and furnishings. From the start the enterprise was a successful one, Mr. Spines having shown rare foresight in choosing a locality in which his establishment filled a long-felt want. He was shortly compelled to employ a clerk to assist him in the handling of his custom, and since then the business has grown by leaps and bounds, so that today he employs eighteen people, and carries a stock of goods worth $40,000. Spines' Store is known throughout this section, and while the same store building is occupied in which he began business, it has been rebuilt and remodeled on several occasions to suit the demands of the constantly-increasing trade.

While his own business has been growing and developing, Mr. Spines has been an important factor in the growth and development of the section of the city in which his establishment is situated. Through his influence and the stimulus of his example, many of the buildings have put on new modern fronts and in other ways improvements are going on that are tending to greatly enhance values and thus, in a definite way, to add to Wichita's prestige. He allies himself with all worthy movements for civic betterment, and his judgment and foresight are respected and referred to in circles where leading business men meet. Mr. Spines is a thirty-second degree Mason and member of the Mystic Shrine and also holds membership in the Benevolent and Protective Order of Elks. He is popular no less with his employes than he is with his business and social associates.

Mr. Spines married Miss Lucille Latham, daughter of Chester A. Latham, a well known patent attorney of Wichita, and they have one daughter, Evelyn.

JOHN S. RHODES. Thousands of people who possess only a passing knowledge of Topeka, including the whereabouts of the State House and a few other important institutions, have a very definite acquaintance with a certain store on Kansas Avenue, the proprietor of which is John S. Rhodes.

Mr. Rhodes has been a resident of Topeka for thirty-six years. It is in no wise detrimental to his dignity to say that he has a "junk" shop. One visiting his establishment is reminded of the "old curiosity shop" of Dickens. His shop contains literally thousands of dollars worth of goods consisting of anything from a sewing needle to a gas engine. It is by no means an ordinary second-hand store. His customers are among the wealthiest people of the country, who go to him or write to him for anything rich and rare that may attract their fancy. Beautiful and costly bric-a-brac, books, works of art and works of practical usefulness, can be found in the Rhodes shop when they might not otherwise be found short of the biggest cities of the country.

Mr. Rhodes has lived in the capital city of Kansas since April, 1880. He is what is termed a "down easter," having been reared in New England. However, he is a foreigner by birth, and as his father neglected to enroll himself as an American citizen

R. J. Lee

the duty of naturalization devolved upon John S. Rhodes when he became old enough to exercise the privilege of franchise. He was born near Manchester in Yorkshire, England, January 29, 1848. His father, William S. Rhodes, a dyer by trade, had come alone to the United States in 1847, spending fifty-six days on an old-fashioned sailing vessel in crossing the Atlantic. In 1849 he sent for his family, and John S. was thus about eighteen months of age when he first saw his father. The maiden name of William S. Rhodes' wife was Elizabeth Schofield. On coming to America the father's first employment at his trade was in Branchville, Pennsylvania. About 1852 he moved to Potters Hill, in Rhode Island, and the family resided there until about 1866, when they removed to Yantic, Connecticut, four miles from Norwich. They finally took up their home in Chester County, Pennsylvania, where William S. Rhodes died December 25, 1885, and his widow on November 5, 1907. Of their eight children five are still living.

The eldest of the children, John S. Rhodes, spent most of his early life in Rhode Island and in Yantic, Connecticut. He was christened a member of the Established Church of England, as were also his brothers and sisters, but at the age of eighteen he joined the Baptist Church. Later as there was no church of that denomination in his home community and in order to keep up his church membership, he became a Methodist on probation.

As a boy he had little opportunity to gain an education such as comes from schools and books. He spent much of his time in the dye shop with his father, and those were years of rigid routine when the horizon of opportunity seemed to get further and further away. At the age of twenty-one he "took his time" and having concluded that there was something better than shop work in store for him, he bound himself out to learn the carpenter's trade at Worcester, Massachusetts. His wages were $5 a week for the first year and $6 during the second year. He worked at his trade and also as a ship joiner in the great ship yards of Chester, Pennsylvania. Somewhat later he was given a contract by a shipbuilding concern to go to Panama and superintend the joining part of the construction of a ship. He completed this satisfactorily within a period of seven months.

Returning to the vicinity of Philadelphia Mr. Rhodes continued his work as a joiner in the surrounding towns, and while there he became acquainted with and on May 3, 1879, married Mrs. Anna (Hicks) Brown.

In April, 1880, Mr. Rhodes and his wife started west for Denver, acting upon Horace Greeley's advice. En route he stopped off at Topeka for the purpose of looking around. The place pleased him, and he concluded to make it his future home and that resolution has been carried out strictly since he has lived there for more than thirty-six years. For a time Mr. Rhodes worked at the carpenter's trade and among other jobs he helped build the west wing of the State Capitol. In 1883 he engaged in the grocery business at the corner of Fourth and Lake streets. That was his business headquarters until 1888, when he bought the southeast corner of Tenth Street and Kansas Avenue, No. 1000 Kansas Avenue, and in that location he has continued the activities which have made him so well known not only in Topeka but throughout the state. He continued the grocery business for some years, but in the meantime incidentally began the buying of sec-

ond-hand goods. Gradually that business entirely usurped the grocery trade. At 1000 Kansas Avenue for many years Mr. Rhodes has conducted one of the most remarkable establishments in Kansas. He handles any and everything, and as a successful medium for the buying and selling of merchandise he has deservedly prospered. Mr. Rhodes is affiliated with the Independent Order of Odd Fellows and the Knights and Ladies of Security.

ROBERT IVES LEE. In the death of Robert Ives Lee, which occurred at Chicago, Illinois, December 19, 1911, there passed away one of the most prominent horsemen of the Middle West. He was born May 5, 1846, at Boston, Massachusetts, and was a son of the late Brev.-Brig.-Gen. William Raymond Lee III, U. S. V., A. M., A. A. S., and Helen Maria (Amory) Lee, of Amory Street, Boston, the former of whom was descended from Henry and Mary Lee.

Henry Lee, the founder of the Lee family of Marblehead, Massachusetts, died at Manchester, that state, in 1675, and was perhaps the nephew of Sir Harry Lee, Bart, and grandson of Sir Robert Lee, Knight, of Hulcote, Bucks, and descended from the Lees of Lea Hall, Cheshire. Col. Richard Lee, the founder of the Lee family of Virginia, had a brother, Judge and Dr. Henry Lee, whose wife's name was Marah, but it is unknown whether Henry Lee of Manchester was the Henry Lee of Virginia, although it was so believed by Gen. Robert E. Lee, who was a classmate at West Point and close friend of Gen. William Raymond Lee. His son, Thomas, was a member of the Canadian expedition of 1690. Henry Lee's son, Samuel Lee, Esq., 1667-1754, was a well known merchant of his time, owned the largest vessels of his town, among them the Swallow (1692), a number of slaves, and was a deacon of the Congregational Church, and a justice of the peace. He married Rebecca Masters, the granddaughter of the Worshipful Mr. John Masters. His son, Justice Samuel Lee, Esq., 1694-1753, was a great merchant and celebrated architect of Marblehead, Massachusetts. In 1732 he was the commissioner of the famous "Dogtown" (Gloucester) dispute. He owned many slaves and ships, had a fine library, and journeyed to England a number of times. He left $500 to educate the poor and served his town in various offices for many years. Justice Lee married Mary, the daughter of Gen. John and Abigail (Abbott) Tarring. His son, David, Harvard 1744-47, was at the siege of Louisburg. Justice Lee's son, Col. John Lee, 1716-1789, was a very prominent merchant and owned many ships, six houses, and a number of slaves, as well as much silver, and was "for many years a representative to the legislature and one of the municipal magistrates of the county." He was chairman of the local committee of inspection, 1774, and correspondence, 1775, and one of the delegates to the Essex County Conventions, 1774, 1776. He was a zealous patriot and marched to Salem at the head of his regiment to defend the town against Colonel Leslie, and also to Beverly when the British vessel Falcon fired upon the town in 1775. He married Joanna Raymond, granddaughter of Capt. William Raymond, a noted French and Indian fighter.

The son of Col. John Lee, Col. William Raymond Lee, 1745-1824, was captain and major of Col. John Glover's famous Marblehead regiment, brigade-major, 1776, and colonel of Lee's regiment, 1777. He was personally in charge of the crossing of the Delaware. He was chief in command of Lord Burgoyne, and invented a new kind of cartridge box used during the Revolution, and was later appointed adjutant general of Washington's army, but declined that position. He was collector of the Port of Salem from 1802 to 1824, and head of the firm of Will R. Lee & Company, as well as a representative to the Legislature in his state. Gen. H. A. S. Dearborn wrote his life. He was also an original member of the Society of the Cincinnati, 1789. He married Mary, daughter of Dr. Joseph and Hannah (Swett) Lemmon, Harvard, 1735. His daughter married Gen. H. A. S. Dearborn, member of Congress, and a son of the famous Maj.-Gen. Henry Dearborn.

The son of Col. William Raymond Lee, Lieut. William Raymond Lee II, 1774-1861, was a merchant of Salem and Boston, and a member of the firm of Will R. Lee & Company. During the War of 1812 he was aide-de-camp on the staff of Maj.-Gen. Henry Dearborn, and was in the battle of Lundy's Lane. He married Hannah Tracy, daughter of the noted patriot, Hon. Nathaniel Tracy and Mary Lee. Nathaniel Tracy, A. M., A. A. S., Harvard 1769, was a great merchant, fitted out the first privateer of the Revolution, and was perhaps the richest man of his day, being worth over $6,500,000 in 1780. He was one of the charter members of the American Academy of Arts and Sciences, and was given the honorary degree of A. M. by Princeton. He married "the greatest beauty of her day," Mary Lee, daughter, of "the illustrious patriot, Col. Jeremiah Lee, of Marblehead," who was a brother of Col. John Lee and a son of Judge Samuel Lee. Colonel Lee was chairman of the Essex County Convention, of the Marblehead delegates to the Provincial Congresses, 1774-1776, member of the famous Committee of Public Safety and Supplies with Samuel Adams and John Hancock, and elected to the first Continental Congress. His son, Joseph, Harvard 1769, was a captain in the Revolution.

Lieutenant Lee's son was Gen. William Raymond Lee III, 1807-1891, who was educated at Norwich University and the United States Military Academy at West Point, 1825-29. He was a civil engineer by profession, was sent in 1830 to Texas, then a province of Mexico, to develop many thousand acres of land, was a veteran of the Florida war, was sent by the United States Government to Canada during the Canadian Rebellion, was appointed in 1850 to adjust the difficulties between the City of Wheeling and the Baltimore & Ohio Railroad, and was the first superintendent of the Boston & Providence Railroad, super-intendent and president of the Vermont Central, superintendent of the New York, Ogdensburg & Champlain Railroad and chairman of the board of directors of the Burlington & Vermont Railroad and its president. He was the first railroad man in the United States to burn coal in engines instead of wood.

When the Civil war broke out, General Lee was commissioned colonel of the Twentieth Massachusetts or Harvard Regiment. Among the officers of his regiment were his kinsmen, Mr. Justice Oliver Wendell Holmes, Jr., of the United States Supreme Court, (lieutenant colonel); Lieut. James Jackson Lowell, Lieut. William Lowell Putnam, etc. He was taken prisoner at Ball's Bluff, led his regiment through the Peninsular Campaign. was at Yorktown, Fair Oaks, Glendale, Malvern Hill and Antietam, and commanded a brigade for some weeks. He was brevetted brigadier general for conspicuous bravery at Antietam. He served as chief engineer to the Massachusetts Volunteer Militia with the rank of brigadier general, his cousin, Henry Lee, Jr., of Lee, Higginson & Company, being a colonel on the governor's staff. He prepared the plans for a system of obstructions at the entrance to Boston Harbor. He was the author of

many letters, many reports in regard to railroads and scientific monographs on the comparative cost of wood and coal, etc., as well as of a memoir of Hon. Paul J. Revere. Harvard gave him the honorary degree of A. M. in 1851, and he was a fellow of the American Academy and a member of the Massachusetts Society of the Cincinnati. He married Helen Maria Amory, daughter of Thomas and Elizabeth (Bowen) Amory, who was descended from the Hon. Jonathan Amory, treasurer of the Province of South Carolina, speaker of the assembly, 1693, speaker of the Provincial Parliament, 1695, Advocate of Admiralty, 1697, and Advocate General. Mrs. Lee's grandfather, Dr. William Bowen, was given an honorary degree by Brown University, about 1801. One son, Arthur Tracy, graduated at West Point in 1865 and died as an officer of the United States army, while aide-de-camp to the President. His daughter, Elizabeth Amory, married Gen. Oswald Herbert Ernst, U. S. A., and their daughter, Elizabeth Lee Ernst, married Maj. William Morton Grinnell, U. S. V., nephew of Vice President Levi P. Morton, Assistant Secretary of State, and chevalier of the Legion of Honor of France.

Robert Ives Lee was born at the old Boston family mansion, May 5, 1846. He was educated at Saint Paul's School, Concord, New Hampshire, in the class of 1864, where he was captain of the crew and of the cricket team and a noted athlete. Among his school friends were the late Nathaniel Thayer, financier of Boston, and Stephen Van Rensselaer Thayer. He was prepared there for Harvard, but never attended that institution. In 1869 he came to the West, first to Jefferson County, Kansas, and then to Topeka, with his uncle, Robert H. Ives, the noted financier of Providence and Newport, he having first gone in 1867 to Illinois with letters to the governor from General Lee's friend, Governor Andrew of Massachusetts. Mr. Ives returned after a few months to Providence, but Mr. Lee remained in Topeka and handled for many months heavy investments for Mr. Ives in Kansas lands. Having inherited an interest in trotting horses, he determined to improve the very low grade of horses then found in Kansas, and made a start in 1871 by purchasing "Hiram Woodruff," at Kalamazoo, Michigan. In 1818 the first public trotting race was held in the United States and Mr. Hemenway's "Boston Blue" won it in three minutes. Mr. Lee's grandfather, William Raymond Lee, Jr., then matched his road horse, "Rat," against Mr. Hemenway's "Boston Blue," with a $1,000 bet and $500 forfeit, and "Rat" won the race in the then unprecedented time of 2:50. In 1873, Mr. Lee purchased Prairie Dell Farm (320 acres), 3½ miles west of Topeka, which was the home of his race horses. Prairie Dell Farm was the site of the old Baptist Pottawatomie Indian Mission. In 1847 the Baptists built a large stone school upon that mission and this stone building, ninety-nine feet long, still remains as the oldest building in Shawnee County. On this site Governor Geary issued the first official Kansas Thanksgiving proclamation in 1856.

Mr. Lee saw the very advantageous position of this place and had rented it for several years before he bought it. While at Prairie Dell Farm, "Hiram Woodruff," the first stallion purchased by Mr. Lee, sired "McW," 2:12 1-2, and "Lucy Woodruff," probably the greatest Kansas-bred brood mare, dam of "Silkwood," 2:07, the world's champion pacing stallion. On January 21, 1873, Mr. Lee bought for $780, a rough, ungainly two-year-old colt, who later became the famous "Robert McGregor," known as the "Monarch of the Home Stretch." This handsome chestnut stallion, by "Maj. Edsall," 2:29, dam "Nancy Whitman," by "Seely's American Star," was foaled at Goshen, Orange County, New York, May 9, 1871, and owned by Samuel Whitman, to whom Mr. Lee was introduced by the well known horseman, Gen. Guy Miller, Mr. Lee having carried letters to General Miller from Hon. Thomas Ryan.

"Robert McGregor" was in the stud in Topeka, 1874, also 1879 to 1884. From 1884 to 1890 Mr. Lee stood him in Lexington, Kentucky, and there sold him to John E. Madden, of Lexington, and William E. Spiers, of Glen Falls, New York, for $33,250 cash, the largest amount then ever having been paid for a horse. His stud book of forty mares at $500 each was full at the time of the sale. "Robert McGregor" was later sold to George J. Ketcham for $75,000, and died at Toledo, Ohio, in 1898, where a simple stone marks the burial place of one of the most famous horses ever bred in America. He was without question the greatest race horse that ever made its home in Kansas and did more toward improving the standard of trotting animals in the Middle West than any other horse. He made a record of 2:17 1-2 in the third heat of a hotly-contested race in late November, 1883, over a rough track and after a full season in the stud. This was the last race in which he ever started. It has been said that probably the only two horses of the period which could compare with him were "Maud S." and "Jay Eye See." These three horses were never matched. He earned his title as "Monarch of the Home Stretch" by the game way in which he always finished his races. He trotted fifty-three heats in 2:30 or faster. He was one of the first ten stallions to trot a mile in less than 2:20. "'Robert McGregor' was individually the most magnificent stallion of his day, the most superbly gaited and the fastest. He won many grand races. No horse ever lived that sired as high an average of splendid trotters. He was a wonderful speed getter. Though never really a popular sire, he had 108 standard performers to his credit, sixty-six producing sons and daughters who produced about 250 performers. He will live forever as a progenitor through siring "Cresceus," still considered by many critics the greatest trotting race horse ever seen and the one stallion that has ever held the world's trotting record. Many sons of 'McGregor' have sired notable trotters. Through his daughters, the blood of 'Robert McGregor' has been built into the trotting fabric as one of its enduring elements. One of the most successful trotting stallions of the present day (1916), 'Jay McGregor,' 2:07 1-4, and one of the most wonderful of living matrons, 'Lady Brussels,' are both from 'McGregor' mares."

"Robert McGregor" was the only one of the first ten 2:20 trotting stallions who produced a 2:15 trotter, i. e., "Bonnie MGregor," 2:13 1-2, who took a silver cup as the finest individual trotter of the Grand Circuit. "Bonnie McGregor's" son, "Planet," 2:04 3-4, was the first Chamber of Commerce winner ($5,000), and long the holder of the world's record for a six heat pacing race. His granddaughter, "Baldy McGregor," 2:06 3-4, was the fastest three-year-old trotter of 1912, a colt of phenomenal speed. His most noted son, of course, was "Cresceus," 2:02 1-4, the world's champion, now exported to Russia, where he is achieving marked success as a sire.

Thirty-three sons of "Robert McGregor" have sired eighty-one trotters in the list and seven pacers in the 2:25 list. He was the sire of more 2:15 trotters, exclusive of pacers, than any horse, living or dead, for many years. Among Mr. Lee's other noted horses was "Fergus McGregor," a son of "Robert

McGregor," and of "Miss Monroe," sister to "Monroe," 2:27 1-2. "Fergus McGregor" stood at the head of all Kansas stallions for many years. "Aaron McGregor," 2:14 1-4, his son, made the 1911 record for Kansas bred stallions over a half-mile track. "Fergus McGregor's" most famous get was "Pansy McGregor," who made a world's record of 2:23 3-4 (1), 2:17 1-2 (2), as a yearling performer. Mr. Lee drove "Pansy McGregor" when she made that notable record which stood unequaled for over seventeen years. "Fergus" was also the grandsire of "Ding Pointer," 2:04 1-4.

Among Mr. Lee's other stallions was "Monroe," 2:27 1-2, by "Iron Duke." "Monroe" won in Denver, in one week, $2,300, five weeks after first coming to Kansas, and the following year won every race in which he started in Michigan, Indiana and Illinois circuits. He twice won the free-for-all champion Stallion Gold Medal in the Illinois Circuit. Other well known trotting sires which Mr. Lee maintained in the stud at Prairie Dell were "Aladdin," "Coriander," "Mountain Mist," "McLeod," "Evan Dhu," "McCallummore," "Flying Bird," "Glenwood," "Shamrock," "Stanley," "Grenada," "Jack Daw," "Arena," "Scythian," etc. "Coriander" was the sire of the dam of "Pansy McGregor," world's champion. "McCallummore," who died after one season, was a younger son of "Robert McGregor" and sired "Mary," (1) 2:36 3-4, (3) 2:20 1-4, a yearling record which was equaled by only two others when made. "Aladdin" sired "Mary's" dam. "Arena" was the fastest trotting stallion owned in Kansas. He trotted halves in one minute flat.

Perhaps the best of all Mr. Lee's later horses was "Jack Daw," 14,297, with a four year record of 2:28 1-2, the sire of "Maxine," 2:08 3-4, the fastest four-year-old trotter of 1902. He is the sire of over twenty in the list, and sired a faster trotter for age than any other stallion in Kansas, Illinois, Missouri, Nebraska, Indiana and Pennsylvania. He was the son of "Jay Bird" and his dam was by "Robert McGregor." He was the grandsire of "Allerdaw," 2:04 1-4, and of "Walnut Grove," 2:04 1-4, and was the greatest sire of extreme trotting speed in the Missouri Valley. He was the Kansas champion sire of trotters and was never beaten in the show ring.

For many years Mr. Lee maintained from five to twenty stallions and from fifty to 150 mares at Prairie Dell Farm. It has been said that more of the get of Prairie Dell Farm are in the 2:30 list than those of all other producing stock farms in Kansas put together. At one time Mr. Lee was the owner of the only stallion in Kansas to beat 2:18. He was the owner also of the first stallion foaled in Kansas to beat 2:30, of the first stallion foaled in Kansas to sire a 2:30 performer, and for years of the only stallion at any time foaled in Kansas to sire 2:30 performers. All of his most noted stallions, save "Hiram Woodruff," were bred, foaled or raised at Prairie Dell Farm and made their initial season there. All 2:10 trotters sired by Kansas bred stallions are directly from Prairie Dell stock, and seven of the eleven Kansas bred sires of 2:10 pacers are of this blood or their 2:10 performers are (1908).

The Capital, of March 5, 1908, had the following to say concerning the last of the two disbursal sales of Prairie Dell stock in which Mr. Lee disposed of over eighty per cent of his standard bred horses: "Today will witness the passing of the most famous horse farm in Kansas, Prairie Dell Farm, and one of the most celebrated in the country. It was the home of 'Paula,' mother of 'Gratton Boy,' 2:08, 'Pansy

McGregor,' the world's champion, 'Robert McGregor,' sire of 'Cresceus,' 2:02 1-4, world's champion, 'Jack Daw,' sire of 'Maxine,' the fastest four-year-old trotter of 1902, and many others.''

Perhaps it is not too much to say that Mr. Lee did more to improve the quality of trotting horses in Kansas, and, probably, in the entire Middle West, than any other man of his day. He was the pioneer breeder of trotting stock in Kansas. He organized the first horse fair in Kansas, which later became the present Kansas State Fair, at Topeka, was an active member of the executive committee of the Fair Association for many years, and was superintendent and general manager of the Fair on several occasions. It is worthy of note that during his administration no liquor or unclean shows were allowed upon the grounds.

Mr. Lee also owned large herds of cattle during the early part of his life in Kansas, and at the time of the great Chicago fire in 1871 had a very large herd destroyed there. He also owned a tract of several thousand acres in Texas and parties went to it nearly every year to hunt black bear. He made various foresighted investments in real estate in Louisiana, Oklahoma and Texas, as well as in Kansas City, Missouri, property. He was a member of various national, state and local breeders' associations and was an officer of one of the first local good roads associations.

Mr. Lee was a well read student of American history, particularly in regard to the Revolution and Civil war. He wrote a number of popular papers on scientific methods of breeding horses and also "The Standard Bred Horse," in the Stockbreeders' Annual for 1905, page 35, and "Robert McGregor," in Volume 17, 1899-1900, of the Twelfth Biennial Report of the Kansas State Board of Agriculture, page 271. He traveled in this country and abroad and was elected to the Massachusetts Society of the Cincinnati. Among others, he was a descendant of Governor and Maj.-Gen. Thomas Dudley and Anne Dudley Bradstreet, the latter the first poetess of America, Governor Simon Bradstreet, Maj.-Gen. Daniel Gookin, the famous Anne Hutchinson, Governor Edward Hutchinson, Governor William Green, Rev. John Cotton and Roger Williams, the founder of Rhode Island. A fund has been pledged to the Washburn College Endowment Fund to found the "Robert Ives Lee Memorial Scholarship."

Mr. Lee was married March 31, 1881, to Abbie Katherine Kimber, daughter of Henry and Jean (Henry) Kimber, of Kimberton, Pennsylvania, who came to Topeka, Kansas, in 1871. She was a granddaughter of Emmor Kimber, who founded the well known Kimber School for Young Ladies at Kimberton. The Kimberton Library was one of the first in Pennsylvania, and Emmor Kimber was one of the incorporators of the Reading Railroad. Mrs. Lee is descended from Col. Richard Kimber, an officer of Cromwell's army. Mr. Lee is survived by his widow, his daughter, Helen Amory, who is the widow of William Henry Van Horn, of Chicago, who was educated at the University of Michigan, and has a son, Thomas Lee Van Horn; his daughter, Anna Louise, of Philadelphia, and his son, Thomas Amory Lee.

THOMAS AMORY LEE, a member of the Topeka bar, graduated from Kansas University with the degrees of Bachelor of Arts and Master of Arts, and from Harvard Law School with the degree of Bachelor of Laws. He practiced law at Boston, Massachusetts, for several years, and has traveled in this country and abroad. He is second lieutenant in the Missouri National Guards, instructor on the Law of Real Property in the Law School of Washburn College, a member of the Massachusetts Society of the Cincinnati, sometime chancellor of the Military Order of the Loyal Legion, ex-member of the Society of Colonial Wars (in Massachusetts), a member of the Military Historical Society of Massachusetts, sometime corresponding secretary of the New England Historic Genealogical Society, Essex Institute, Kansas State Historical Society, Kansas Academy of Science, etc., author of "Gen. William Raymond Lee," "Col. Jeremiah Lee, Patriot," "Col. Wm. Raymond Lee of the Revolution," "The Lee Family of Marblehead," "The Lees of Boston," "Robert Ives Lee," "The Tracys of Newburyport," and "Alfred Washburn Benson, LL. D.," "The Ornes of Marblehead," "The Gallisons of Marblehead," etc., "Nathaniel Tracy, A. M., A. A. S.," "The New York Stock Exchange," (Master of Arts thesis), etc.

Mr. Lee was married June 1, 1916, to Miss Mary Helen Shirer, daughter of Hampton L. and Lilian (Whiting) Shirer, and granddaughter of Albe B. and Katherine (Whitney) Whiting. Mrs. Lee is a graduate of Washburn College, Bachelor of Arts. Albe B. Whiting (q. v.), is sometime president of the Kansas State Historical Society, and a pioneer to territorial Kansas, 1856. He has been a trustee of Washburn College for nearly forty years and is one of its largest benefactors.

GEORGE NEIL. A resident of Topeka for a number of years, George Neil is one of the few remaining pioneers of Williamsport Township of Shawnee County. He came to Kansas as a young man before the Civil war, and is one of the survivors of the glorious Second Kansas Regiment and he made a record as a soldier that his descendants may consider with proper pride.

Few Kansans have been more successful in the handling of their business affairs than George Neil. His prosperity has not been for himself alone. He has been public spirited, kindly and considerate of those less fortunate than himself, and is greatly beloved among his old honored comrades and those who with him have shared in the growth and development of Kansas from pioneer times.

George Neil was born November 26, 1842. He was one of eight sons and one daughter. Their parents were Robert and Sarah (Courtney) Neil. His father was a native of the North of Ireland and his mother of an English family. The parents were married at Belfast.

The late Robert Neil's record also belongs in the story of pioneer things in Kansas. By profession he was a gardener and nurseryman. In early life he came to America. That was in the days of sailing vessels, and he was many weeks in making the voyage. Coming alone, he established a home in one of the eastern states, and then returned to the old country, where he married. He brought his bride to America, and thereafter for about a score of years he lived in Kentucky and followed gardening.

It was in the year 1860 that Robert Neil brought his family to Kansas. He secured a tract of land in Osage County that had been owned under what is known as the Mexican War Grant. In the spring of 1861 he came out to Kansas to make this his permanent home. His principal business in Kansas was that of general farmer and the handling of livestock. He brought with him to Osage County a number of grafts, and developed there one of the first orchards. Fruit was a very scarce article in the early years of Kansas, and the products of.the

Neil orchard were eagerly sought by the settlers. It is related that pears sold as high as $6.00 to $10.00 a bushel.

Robert Neil was a man of strong personality, of more than the average stature, was originally a Scotch Presbyterian but later in life a Methodist, and was an ardent republican. His death occurred in 1906 when he was eighty-eight years of age.

After his boyhood spent in Kentucky George Neil came to Kansas with his parents at the age of eighteen. A Kentucky district school furnished him his early learning. His muscles were hardened and his eye trained and he was given a wholesome discipline on the home farm. It was not long after he came to Kansas before the stirring issues between the North and South were brought to the test of arms.

When President Lincoln issued his first call for 300,000 men to put down the rebellion, George Neil was one of those who responded and enlisted in Company I of the Second Kansas Volunteer Cavalry. Members of the same company were Frank M. Stahl, Martin L. Foltz, who later became Mr. Neil's brother-in-law, and Sylvanus Heberling, whose sister married George Neil. From the date of his enlistment until his discharge Mr. Neil participated in every movement of his command. His first bunk mate was killed and the next two were wounded, but Mr. Neil never received a wound nor had a day's sickness during his entire army career. In fact his record of service was so perfect that he might have received an appointment to the regular army. The Second Kansas Cavalry was a splendid organization of soldiers, and its service has redounded to the credit of the entire state. Mr. Neil was with this regiment until his honorable discharge in June 17, 1865. One of the greatest pleasures enjoyed by Mr. Neil has been in recalling the events of half a century or more ago as he marched and campaigned with the Second Kansas through all its movements between 1861 and 1865. Mr. Neil is an enthusiastic American in all that the term implies, believes in its greatness, is a lover of its vast glories and is extremely optimistic as to its future destiny.

Following the war he took up the active business of stock raising and farming which has furnished the chief outlet for his energies ever since. On November 14, 1867, he married Catherine J. Heberling. Five children were born to their union. Lillian died at the age of four years, and the others are: Oscar; Effie, Mrs. George Overmeyer; Daisy Viola; and Laura, Mrs. Edward Lannin.

From the time he cast his first vote to the present Mr. Neil has never wavered in his allegiance to the republican party. His activities in politics have been confined to voting and never to the seeking of office. His best service since the war has been rendered in a business capacity and in carrying forward and keeping up to a high standard the status of Kansas agriculture and stock husbandry. Altogether he has owned upwards of 20,000 acres of Kansas soil and has been interested in about 3,000 acres of Colorado lands. In Williamsport Township alone he owns over 1,200 acres. About twenty years ago Mr. Neil and his family removed to Topeka and they have one of the very comfortable homes of that city. From there he has directed the management of his extensive stock, farming and mining interests.

As a result of many well spent years he has the means and the leisure for travel, and he and his wife have visited nearly every state and territory and have also traveled abroad. As a Kansan Mr.

Neil has constantly contributed to its progress and development. Schools, churches, good roads, anything for the good of his township, county, state or country, finds in him an enthusiastic advocate and supporter. Fraternally he is affiliated with the Grand Army of the Republic and is a thirty-second degree Scottish Rite Mason.

C. J. SLOOP. In January, 1909, Mr. Sloop was admitted to the bar at Topeka, Kansas, and on July 12th of that year moved to Independence. Since then he has been steadily building up a reputation as a sound and safe counselor and as one who can be trusted with the skillful handling of all important interests entrusted to him, whether in civil or criminal law.

A native of Missouri, Charles Jacob Sloop was born at Queen City, December 10, 1878. His father John B. Sloop was born in Schuyler County, Missouri, November 16, 1845, and he spent his active life there as a farmer and also bought and shipped stock on a large scale. In 1861 he enlisted in a Missouri regiment and in a company commanded by A. J. Smith, and was in the Union army throughout the war. He was once wounded. He was in the battle of Shiloh, siege of Corinth, Meriden raid, through the Vicksburg campaign, participated in the bloody battle of Tupelo, Mississippi, and followed General Sherman on the march to the sea. After the war he returned to Missouri, and took up farming, which engaged his energies until his death at Queen City in October 1906. He served many years on the school board, and was a member of the board of deacons and a trustee of the Lutheran Church. Politically he was a republican and was a member of the Masonic fraternity. He married Mary Anna Miller, who was of German ancestry. She was born in Franklin County, Ohio, August 30, 1849, and now resides at Queen City, Missouri. Her children are John W., a farmer at Queen City; Mary Anna Hickins, lives at Queen City; Frances Elizabeth, wife of E. F. Roberts, in the poultry and produce business at Queen City; Charles Jacob; Lewis Ellison, who was a farmer at Queen City and died at the age of twenty-nine; Pearl Alvin, a farmer at Queen City; and Jessie Esther, wife of John Applegate, a carpenter and contractor at Queen City. Another member of this household who grew up with the children was a cousin, Marguerite Miller, who is now the wife of James West, station agent for the Wabash Railroad at Moulton, Iowa.

Reared on a farm, Charles J. Sloop early conceived ambitions designs for a career and worked long and diligently to secure the proper preparation. He graduated from the high school at Queen City in 1896, and thereafter for two years taught a country school near his birthplace. In 1903 he graduated A. B. from the University of Missouri, and following his university course he was principal of the High School at Princeton, Missouri, and was superintendent of schools at Grandin, Missouri, for three years. Returning to the University of Missouri in 1907, he remained in the law department until graduating LL. B. in June, 1909. In the meantime as already stated he had been admitted to the Kansas bar, and soon after graduation he came to Independence. His offices are in the Booth Building.

He has also acquired some property interest in Oklahoma. He owns a residence at 320 Westminster Street in Independence. Politically he is a republican and was reared in the Evangelical Lutheran Church, but in absence of any church of that denomination attends the Baptist Church in Independence. He is affiliated with Fortitude Lodge No. 107 Ancient Free and Accepted Masons, with Lodge No. 780 Benevolent and Protective Order of Elks, in which he was exalted ruler in 1914. He is also a member of the County Bar Association. In June, 1912, at Springfield, Missouri, Mr. Sloop married Miss Alma Myrtle McGhee, a daughter of James M. and Zillah McGhee, who now reside at Grandin, Missouri, where her father is in the real estate business. Mr. and Mrs. Sloop have one child, William Charles, born February 28, 1916.

LOUIS H. CHAPMAN, commissioner of water and light of Kansas City, Kansas, is the man chiefly responsible for bringing these municipally owned plants to a perfection of service where they completely justify the management and control by the city. Mr. Chapman is an expert electrician and general engineer, and has achieved a significant success through his own energies and ambitions. He has been a resident of Kansas the greater part of the time since 1886.

He was born at Hartford, Connecticut, June 17, 1873, the youngest of the nine children of John Oliver and Louisa E. (Smart) Chapman. His parents were both natives of Connecticut. John O. Chapman was master mechanic of the New York, New Haven & Hartford Railway, but gave up that position and brought his family west to Iowa in 1881. Here he became master mechanic of the Iowa Division of the Chicago Northwestern Railway, with headquarters at Clinton. In 1884 he moved his family to Kansas City, Kansas, and accepted a similar position with the Union Pacific Railway. While in service he was injured, and in 1888 was compelled to give up his position. After that he spent much of his time in travel, and in 1892 removed to Chicago, where he died in April, 1893. He enjoyed large responsibilities, was paid a corresponding salary, but spent most of it liberally to provide home and advantages to his large family of children. He had educated himself, since he came of a family in only moderate circumstances. He belonged to the Masonic lodge and the Independent Order of Odd Fellows, but found his greatest delight in his home circle. His widow died in Kansas City, Kansas, in February, 1913.

Louis H. Chapman was thirteen years of age when his father was incapacitated and being the youngest of the family he did not receive the advantages given to the older children in the way of education. He attended common schools in Connecticut, Iowa, and a private school in Kansas City, Kansas. Most of his education he gained by laborious study at night after a day's employment. His first position was as a messenger boy at the stockyards for the Fowler Packing Company. Later he was at work in the lard department of Armour & Company. In 1889 going to Chicago he found work with the Chicago Northwestern Railway, and for a time was a fireman on the elevated railroad. His next position was trimming lamps at $1.75 a day for the electric light department of Armour & Company, and after six months he was given charge of a gang of workmen at $90 a month. During those early years much of his wages went to support his invalid father and his mother.

On December 16, 1892, Mr. Chapman married Miss Carlotta Drought. Her father, E. S. W. Drought, was a prominent man in Kansas. In 1893 Mr. Chapman became connected with the Commonwealth Edison Company of Chicago as a repair man. He showed such ability as a workman and such responsibility that at the end of six months he was placed in charge of the department with ninety men under him. In April, 1895, having resigned this position, he returned to Kansas City, Kansas, and installed the electric plant at the Kansas City stockyards, being appointed master mechanic of that company. He held that position until 1913, when Mayor Green appointed him commissioner of water and light of the municipality. The light and water plant of Kansas City, Kansas, were taken over by the city government some five or six years ago, and both departments have been placed on a paying basis by Mr. Chapman. As commissioner he has supervision of the labor of 230 men employed in the two departments.

In politics he is a republican, but the only public office he has ever held is the one in which he is now engaged. He is a member of the Scottish Rite bodies of Masonry, belongs to Abdallah Temple of the Mystic Shrine at Leavenworth, and is affiliated with the Benevolent and Protective Order of Elks. He takes much delight in outdoor sports, and aside from his work and profession most of his time is spent in his own home. He and Mrs. Chapman are active members of the Episcopal Church. He also belongs to the Mercantile and Union clubs of Kansas City, Kansas.

JAMES ABRAM GARFIELD SHIRK. Now professor of mathematics in the Manual Training Normal School at Pittsburg, Mr. Shirk has filled many important positions in the public schools and colleges of Kansas, and is a recognized authority on his special subject.

A native of Kansas, he was born at McPherson January 12, 1881. His ancestry is Swiss German. The first of the name came from Switzerland to Pennsylvania in colonial days. His grandfather, John Shirk, spent his life in Pennsylvania, was a farmer, and he also contributed fame to the family name by his service in the War of 1812. He was one of the fighting sailors on the flagship of Commodore Perry in the historic battle with the British on Lake Erie. He was one of the six men who, after the flagship Lawrence was disabled, went with Commodore Perry in a small boat to the ship Niagara, while the battle was still raging. For this distinguished service in assisting to drive the British fleet from the waters of the Great Lakes he was afterwards awarded a medal by Congress.

Joseph Shirk, father of Professor Shirk, was born near Meadville in Pennsylvania in 1833. He was reared and married in his native state, was engaged for a number of years in the lumber business, and he drilled the first well in the Oil Creek oil fields of Pennsylvania. He was one of the pioneers in the oil industry. Afterwards he lived for varying lengths of time in the states of Illinois, Nebraska and was an early settler at McPherson. In that town he was at first in the grain business but later farmed in that vicinity for many years. He finally retired and died at McPherson in 1910. Politically he was a republican, was a member of the Methodist Episcopal Church and one of the trustees, and belonged to the Knights of Honor. Joseph Shirk married Alvira Clark. She was born at Clark's Mills in Pennsylvania in 1840 and is still living, being a resident of Dallas, Oregon. Her children are: Pearl, wife of L. G. Miller, who has been engaged in the lumber business until recently, but now gives his attention to his fruit ranch at Dallas, Oregon; Claude Joseph, who is professor of botany in the Wesleyan University at Lincoln, Nebraska; and James A. G.

Professor Shirk spent his early boyhood on his father's farm in McPherson. While there he attended the district schools and in 1898 graduated from the high school at McPherson. His higher education was acquired in McPherson College, from which he graduated A. B. in 1901 and A. M. in 1902, and later in 1904 he entered the University of Kansas, where he received his Master of Science degree in 1905. In the meantime he had taught mathematics and physics at McPherson College during the two school years from 1902 to 1904. After obtaining his master's degree at Lawrence in 1905 he remained there until the winter of 1906 and then finished out a term of teaching at Leavenworth. In the fall of 1906 he was elected professor of mathematics at Ottawa University, and remained the incumbent of that position until 1912. While at Ottawa he taught mathematics and later had the courses in engineering and physics. In 1912 he was elected assistant professor of physics at the Manual Training Normal School at Pittsburg, and in 1914 was made head of the mathematical department in that institution.

Mr. Shirk for ten years has been a member of the Kansas Academy of Science and was honored with the office of president of that body in 1915. He also belongs to the American Mathematical Society and the Kansas Association of Mathematics Teachers. He is a member and deacon of the Baptist Church. His home is in Pittsburg and he owns a residence at 116 East Lindburg Avenue and some lots adjacent to his home.

In 1908 at Ottawa he married Miss Anna Gevene McCoy, daughter of Mark and Elizabeth (Wallace) McCoy. Her mother died in 1915, and her father resides at Ottawa, where he is a city inspector. Mr. and Mrs. Shirk have one daughter, Alice Gevene born February 12, 1912.

ABRAM A. RAUB, M. D. One of the oldest and best known physicians and citizens of Kansas is Dr. Abram A. Raub of Topeka, who came to this state in 1879. Doctor Raub is a veteran of the Civil war. During part of his service he was assistant surgeon in the army, and has been practicing medicine for fully half a century.

Doctor Raub was forty years of age when he came to Kansas, having been born in 1839 at Blairstown, New Jersey. His father was Philip Raub, also a native of Blairstown. The grandfather emigrated from the Rhine provinces of Germany and settled at Blairstown, he and his son Philip both dying on the old place near that city. Together they had occupied the homestead for nearly 100 years. Philip Raub married Miss Sabra Angel of Warren County, New Jersey. To their marriage were born two sons and three daughters, named Emma, Jacob, Catherine, John and Abram, all now deceased except Doctor Raub. The daughter Emma married George W. Stout. Mr. Stout, who was also a native of New Jersey, was a prominent attorney at Easton, Pennsylvania, and a very successful business man. He left an estate valued at $200,000, and at one time he told Doctor Raub that he started life with only 50 cents. Mr. and Mrs. Stout's son George was a youth of more than usual brilliancy, was graduated first in his class and a gold medalist from the University of Pennsylvania, and his death twenty days after his graduation was a calamity to his parents

and a loss to the world. Doctor Raub's older brother Jacob became a prosperous farmer of Warren County, New Jersey. His sister Catherine married Aaron Vaught, of Bradford County, Pennsylvania. John Raub, who is a graduate of Lafayette College at Eastern Pennsylvania and a graduate of the medical department of the University of Pennsylvania, in 1861 went to Fortress Monroe with the Ninth New Jersey Volunteer Infantry with the understanding that he should be appointed assistant regimental surgeon, but was disappointed and then returned home.

Doctor Raub acquired his early education in the public schools of Blairstown, and began his professional studies in the medical department of the University of Pennsylvania. Before graduating he enlisted in the First Pennsylvania Volunteer Infantry at Lincoln's first call for ninety days men. He was stricken with the typhoid fever, and then returned home, finishing his medical education, and in 1863 received appointment as assistant United States surgeon. He passed the examination and was given the appointment by Secretary of War Edwin M. Stanton. Doctor Raub served from April 26, 1863, to April 27, 1864, his resignation being prompted on account of ill health. Doctor Raub is a very competent and interesting witness on some phases of the early period of the Civil war which received perhaps less attention than they deserve in the usual writings on the war. This opportunity as a witness came during the ninety days service. The North had rushed precipitately against the Southern armies without either proper training or without adequate equipment. Whole regiments, says Doctor Raub, were absolutely without arms, without food, the officers were inexperienced, and the men were marching over the hot dry country without canteens, without blankets, and the only clothing they had was what they wore away from their homes.

On May 2, 1864, a few days after he resigned his commission in the army, Doctor Raub married Miss Ernestine McClure. Her father was city engineer of Memphis, Tennessee. Soon after his marriage Doctor Raub moved to Warren County, Ohio, and began the practice of medicine in the Town of Franklin. The situation was not altogether to his liking, and he then returned to Pennsylvania and practiced at Laceyville, in Wyoming County until 1879. In that year he brought his family out to Cawker City, Mitchell County, Kansas. Mitchell County was then practically on the frontier, and his coming brought to that community a physician of unusual experience and ability. For ten years he remained in active practice there. In 1889 he was appointed through United States Senator Plumb, the Government physician to the Pottawatami Indians with office on the reservation, though his family in the meantime resided in Topeka.

Doctor Raub has had his home in Topeka for many years and has become well known as a citizen not only there but over the state. For eight years he served as chairman of the board of pension examiners of Shawnee County, and for one year served by appointment as county physician. For four years Doctor Raub was the chief surgeon of the Kansas State Soldiers Home at Dodge City.

The family of Doctor and Mrs. Raub contained three sons and two daughters. Their names and birth are: Edgar Lee, born in 1867; Ellen Woodward, 1869; Kenneth, 1872; Trail Green, 1874; and Ernestine, 1876. The daughter Ernestine is now deceased. Edgar until recently was an editor at Montgomery City, Texas. Kenneth has recently been elected county clerk of Shawnee County, and enters that office with a promise of great efficiency, since for twelve years he was employed in the offices of the Santa Fe Railway, nearly all the time under Mr. W. W. Strickland. The son Trail is a boilermaker by trade and for twelve years has been in the Missouri Pacific Railway shops at Sedalia, Missouri. Ellen is the wife of Mr. L. G. Tuttle, an old employe of the Rock Island Railroad Company, at present being chief rate clerk, and when the company's headquarters were moved to Chicago he went with them.

CLARK H. KOUNTZ, of Independence, though a young man, is a veteran in the oil industry, and for over ten years has been a factor in the Kansas oil fields, being now vice president of the Prairie Pipe Line Company.

He was born near Bradford, McKean County, Pennsylvania, August 24, 1883, a son of Frank P. and Maggie E. Kountz. His father was born in 1847, and died in 1911, and his mother, still living, was born in 1849. The Kountz family removed from Western Pennsylvania to Findlay, Ohio, which was then in the center of the Ohio oil fields, and in the public schools of that city Clark H. Kountz acquired his early education. At the age of eighteen, in July, 1901, he became a clerk in the office of the Ohio Oil Company at Findlay.

He grew up in the atmosphere of oil fields, and with four years of business experience in Ohio he came to Kansas in June, 1905. Becoming connected with the Prairie Oil & Gas Company at Independence, he was promoted to secretary of that company in 1910, and in 1915 assumed his present post as vice president of the Prairie Pipe Line Company. Mr. Kountz is also a director in the First National Bank of Independence. He is a member of the Masonic Order and the Benevolent and Protective Order of Elks.

On December 21, 1907, at Independence he married Miss Agnes Casebeer, daughter of Dr. Howard M. and Emma F. Casebeer. Mr. and Mrs. Kountz have one daughter, Marjorie Kountz, born May 30, 1913.

CHARLES WILLIAM TRICKETT. That Kansas City, Kansas, can claim distinction of being the largest city in the United States without a saloon or commercialized vice district is due more to the fearless and strenuous efforts of Charles William Trickett than to any other one man. The people of an entire state committed to the cause of prohibition followed with a great deal of interest and admiration his remarkable campaign, made some years ago while assistant attorney general, for rigid law enforcement and the driving out of the saloons and other commercialized forms of vice which had hitherto enjoyed immunity in the Kansas metropolis.

Mr. Trickett, who has lived in Kansas since early childhood was a banker and business man before he took up the law, began practice at Kansas City, Kansas, in 1896.

On June 8, 1906, Attorney General C. C. Coleman appointed him as assistant attorney general with special jurisdiction in Wyandotte County. The appointment in ordinary circumstances might have had no special significance. When Mr. Trickett consented to accept the office it was with the avowed determination and purpose of inaugurating a program of strict law enforcement and overturning the old regime under which Kansas City, Kansas, had been a

wide open town with saloons flourishing in open violation of the state laws. The day he began his official duties opened the fight on the local liquor traffic. It was a war to the finish. Either the saloons had to go or the attorney general had to acknowledge complete defeat and get out of the town himself. The leaders of the liquor traffic had many sinister ways in which to undermine a public official's career and pervert his active influence. It was not a case in which he stood as the open champion for well organized and solid public sentiment. The city was well divided over the liquor question. He had the state law behind him, but he constantly had to run counter to public opinion and overcome an active and vigilant opposition. He actually took his life in his hands. He and his family were threatened by varied forms of persecution. A threat was made to dynamite his house. Some of his property was actually burned. Danger and intimidation had no effect upon his resolute course. As part of his general program he brought about the election of Doctor Gray on an independent ticket as mayor and committed to a law enforcement platform. Mr. Trickett and his lieutenants worked from 8 o'clock in the morning until 1 o'clock the next morning day after day in dislodging the saloon faction, and finally they put padlocks on the doors of all the saloons, and only then did the saloon men retire from the field. He confiscated and burned upwards of $5,000 worth of liquor and various other property connected with the traffic. Along with the saloons he made equal war on gambling and commercialized vice, and for nearly ten years he continued the fight and brought about the wholesome conditions which now prevail in the city.

Mr. Trickett accepted the office of assistant attorney general temporarily, but once in the fight he continued until victory. He had previously refused such an office again and again, and he was under no illusions as to the difficulties and dangers confronting him when he finally consented to serve. As already stated his first appointment came from Attorney General Coleman, and the succeeding Attorney General Jackson made his first official act the reappointment of Mr. Trickett in 1907. He was again reappointed in 1911 by Attorney General Dawson. He continued in the office until 1913.

In the meantime Governor Stubbs had appointed him special counsel and he was commissioned to assist in the general campaign for the overthrow of the liquor forces throughout the state. In this position he also made a special fight against gambling in Kansas City, Kansas, and succeeded in clearing out about 200 notorious gambling places. Another service which he rendered was the prosecution of the various packing plants of Kansas City, Kansas, as a result of which $178,000 were returned to the county in the shape of unpaid taxes and other sums which the packing companies had unjustly held.

Charles William Trickett was born on a farm in Scotland County, Missouri, February 2, 1861, and came to Kansas in 1866 with his parents Charles Marshall and Martha Ann (Walker) Trickett. He was the third in a family of nine children, two of whom died in infancy, and six are still living. His father was a native of Virginia and his mother of Illinois, and the former followed farming all his active career. The Trickett family goes back to colonial days in the history of this country. Originally there were four brothers, Frenchmen, who emigrated to England, and later one of these brothers or his son came to Virginia. He was a ship owner, and after coming to America the name was changed in spelling from Trickette to the present form. This first ancestor in America was connected with Washington's staff in some capacity during the Revolutionary war, and it is known that he was present at the final battle and surrender of the British forces at Yorktown.

Charles M. Trickett came from Virginia overland and located in Scotland County, Missouri, where he married, and at the close of the war he sold his farm there and after a year spent in Nebraska with his brother-in-law came to Kansas, locating at Louisburg in Miami County. He lived in that town and rented his farm. He was in poor health after he came to Kansas and his sons assumed the responsibilities of looking after the farm. He died in 1878. After coming to Kansas he served as justice of the peace, as overseer of roads and streets, and was an active republican. He was a Methodist and his wife a Baptist.

The common schools of Louisburg furnished Charles W. Trickett his early education. At the age of fifteen he was working for the firm of Reed & Wright, grain and general merchants. For a time he had charge of the grading and price making in their elevator. He remained with that firm until 1880, and the company then buying an elevator in Paola placed Mr. Trickett in charge. In 1882 he resigned his position to enter the Miami County National Bank at Paola, and soon afterwards was made teller and later assistant cashier. In 1887 Mr. Sponable, president of the Miami County Bank, organized the Wyandotte County National Bank of Kansas City, Kansas, and Mr. Trickett became cashier of the new institution. During the panic of 1893 this was the only bank in Kansas City, Kansas, that successfully weathered the storm of financial reverses, and Mr. Trickett shouldered many of the heavy responsibilities at that time and remained with the institution until its resources were thoroughly reorganized when the panic had passed.

An ambition to become a lawyer was one of the early desires of Mr. Trickett. While living at Paola he read law for five years under Maj. Benjamin Simpson. Major Simpson subsequently served as United States marshal of Kansas, later as Supreme Court commissioner, and was one of the ablest lawyers the state ever had. In 1896 Mr. Trickett was admitted to the bar, and selling his interests in the bank he opened an office and began general practice. In 1903 he formed a partnership with Mr. Keplinger, and this firm is still in existence, commanding a large and representative clientage and with offices in the Holmes Building. From 1908 to 1913 in addition to his other heavy responsibilities, Mr. Trickett served as attorney for the drainage board district and had active charge of all the litigation of that time. In 1913 he became Kansas attorney for the Kansas City Stockyards Company, and still retains that position. Mr. Trickett has always been identified with the republican party. While living in Paola he served on the board of education, resigning from that position when he removed to Kansas City, Kansas. December 23, 1880, he married Miss Lillie B. Essex of Paola. Her father J. S. Essex was at the time of their marriage foreman of construction on the Missouri, Kansas & Texas Railway. Mr. and Mrs. Trickett have four children: Nellie is the wife of John Stewart, salesman for the Redenour-Baker Grocery Company of Kansas City, Kansas. Pearl is the wife of John Juhlin, of Kansas City, Missouri, traveling solicitor for the Kansas City Stockyards Company. William E., who married Besse Woolsey

of Kansas City, Kansas, is managing his father's real estate interests. Lawrence G. is in the office of the Kansas City Stockyards Company. All these children have been given the comforts of a good home, the inspiration of high ideals and a liberal education. Lawrence and Pearl are both graduates of the University of Kansas. Mr. and Mrs. Trickett are active members of the Congregational Church, and for seventeen years he served as superintendent of the Sunday school, was for a number of years chairman of the board of trustees and was superintendent of the building of the present edifice occupied by the congregation.

WILLIAM S. HYATT is one of the leading corporation attorneys of Southeastern Kansas, and has handled a large and profitable practice at Parsons for the past thirteen years. He is a native of Kansas and his family have been identified with the state since the early days. The Hyatts were of Scotch descent but came from England to North Carolina in colonial times. One or more of them served with the army of the noted "Swamp Fox" of the revolution, Francis Marion. Mr. Hyatt's grandfather, Benjamin A. Hyatt, was born in South Carolina in 1820. He grew up in that state, was married in Knoxville, Tennessee, and before the Civil war moved to Shoal Creek in Jasper County, Missouri. Like many southerners he was an ardent admirer of racing horses and enjoyed that sport. In Missouri he raised horses for racing purposes. At the outbreak of the war, being a Union sympathizer, he was compelled to leave Shoal Creek, and while his family refugeed into Kansas he went north to Minnesota and Michigan, taking his horses, and did not get in touch with his family again until they had located at Lawrence. After the war he settled in Labette County, Kansas, and was a farmer and stock raiser, chiefly horses, until his death in Hackberry Township of Labette County in 1889. Politically he was a republican. Benjamin S. Hyatt married Melinda Tipton, who was born in Tennessee and died in Labette County. Her ancestry were identified with the very beginning of the revolutionary war. William Tipton was a commissioned officer in the Patriot army, and in one battle had a leg shot off. Later he rode all the way from North Carolina to Washington to present his claim for a pension. This was granted, perhaps by a special act of Congress, in the administration of Thomas Jefferson. Besides the pension he was also repaid for a large quantity of provisions he had furnished the Patriot army during the war. Of the children of Benjamin S. Hyatt now living mention is made as follows. Nathaniel Keener, who is owner of a silver mine at Butte, Montana; John, a merchant at Miami, Oklahoma; William S. Hyatt, Sr., the oldest of the children; Laura, wife of George W. Johnson, a farmer in the Province of Alberta, Canada; Clementine, wife of Chandler Chronaster, who is a farmer in Colorado and assisted in forming an irrigation company there; Sherman, a mechanic living at Vinita, Oklahoma.

William S. Hyatt, Sr., father of the Parsons attorney, is still living on his old farm in Hackberry Township in Labette County. He has had a long and interesting career. He was born May 11, 1845, on Shoal Creek in Jasper County, Missouri. He grew up there, but when his father's farm was sacked by the Confederates in 1862 the responsibility devolved upon him as the oldest son of taking his mother and the other children out of the country. He went with them to Lawrence, Kansas, and soon afterward, following the Quantrell raid against Lawrence, he joined Company G of the Sixteenth Kansas Cavalry. He was in active service until mustered out in 1865, and much of the time was engaged in opposing the Indians on the northwest frontier. He took part in the battles of Little Horn and Big Horn in Montana, and while on duty with the scouting branch of the army had many brushes and skirmishes with the Indians. In 1864 he was with the Kansas troops engaged in opposing the advance of General Price into Kansas.

Following the war he located at Lawrence, and in 1866 returned to Shoal Creek in Jasper County, Missouri, where he found his father's farm in a state of complete devastation, the fences all down and the houses and barn burned. Not long after that he and his brother Keener rode on horseback into what is now Labette County. The Indians were still occupants there, and the surveys were just being made preparatory to the opening of the country to settlement. He and his brother staked claims in Hackberry Township, and after camping there a week returned to Lawrence. They then brought all the family to Labette County, and William S. Hyatt, Sr., received a patent from the Government to 160 acres. He has farmed that place ever since, but in the meantime his prosperity has been measured by increased holdings of land until now his estate comprises 720 acres. He has been a diversified farmer and raises a large amount of stock and is still in the harness. Politically he is a democrat, and in the early days in Labette County served as constable.

The wife of William S. Hyatt, Sr., was Susan M. Clark. She was born at Crystal, Indiana, September 19, 1855, and is still living. Their family of children are: William S. Jr.; Emily May, wife of Edward Switzer, owner of a printing plant in Webb City, Missouri; Francis Marion, a farmer in Hackberry Township of Labette County; Isabelle, wife of J. C. Crane, a farmer in Hackberry Township; Martin Luther, a farmer in Hackberry Township; Mary Ellen, wife of J. Cox, a farmer at Bartlett, Kansas.

Thus it is seen that William S. Hyatt comes of some very sturdy stock. He was born on his father's farm in Labette County July 29, 1876. As a boy he attended the district schools there, and was graduated from the Labette County High School in 1895. The first twenty-one years of his life were spent on his father's ranch. His professional training was acquired in the law department of the Kansas State University, where he graduated LL. B. in 1899. Mr. Hyatt distinguished himself while in university as a debater and there are few attorneys in Kansas with a better command of language, with more practical logic, and with more versatile ability whether on the stump or in pleading a cause before a jury. While in university he took part in a number of inter collegiate debates. He was in the Missouri-Kansas contest in 1898, in the Kansas-Nebraska oratorical contest of 1899, and in 1900 represented the State of Kansas in an oratorical contest at Denver. Preparatory to these debates there occurred a series of elimination contests, and thus Mr. Hyatt had to prove his superiority, over a number of debaters in his home state before representing the state in an interstate contest. On two of the interstate contests he came out victor.

Before leaving university he was nominated on the democratic ticket for the office of county attorney of Labette County and was elected in 1900 and gave one term of efficient service. In the fall of 1900 he moved to Oswego, Kansas, but since 1903

has had his home and office at Parsons. In that time he has handled a large general civil and criminal practice. During his first five years at Parsons he was attorney for a number of gas and oil companies around Parsons and in Shreveport, Louisiana, and since then has been the principal attorney for the Albert Emanuel Syndicate, and the Kansas Electrical Utility Company. His offices are in the First National Bank Building. On two occasions he was appointed assistant attorney general under republican administrations for the trial of special cases.

Mr. Hyatt owns his home at 1516 Corning Avenue, also a fine farm of 160 acres in Hackberry Township, and considerable city real estate at Parsons. He is an active member of the Parsons Chamber of Commerce, belongs to the County, State and American Bar associations, and is affiliated with Parsons Lodge No. 117, Ancient Free and Accepted Masons, Parsons Chapter No. 39, Royal Arch Masons, Parsons Lodge No. 527, Benevolent and Protective Order of Elks, and Parsons Lodge No. 1 of the Ancient Order of United Workmen.

In June, 1911, at Parsons he married Miss Reba Jones, daughter of W. W. and Rebecca (Highfield) Jones. Her parents reside at 1415 Corning Avenue in Parsons, and her father is passenger conductor for the Missouri, Kansas & Texas Railway. Mr. and Mrs. Hyatt have two children: William S., Jr., born February 14, 1914; and Maurine Rebecca, born March 20, 1916.

HENRY HOWELL ISHAM was one of the prominent pioneer merchants of Coffeyville, founded and successfully conducted several business enterprises that were material factors in the growth and prosperity of the city, and on account of his business prominence and his personal character was held in the highest esteem.

His death at Coffeyville November 19, 1906, meant the loss of one of the sterling old time citizens of Montgomery County. He was at that time seventy years of age, lacking three days. His birth had occurred at Colchester, Connecticut, November 22, 1836. He was of New England ancestry, four brothers of the name having come from England and settled in Connecticut or New York during colonial times. His grandfather Charles Isham was born in New York state, and spent his life as a farmer, dying near Watertown, New York. The late Henry H. Isham was a son of Charles and Mary (Rogers) Isham. His father was a farmer and died at Avon, New York. His mother was the daughter of one of the most prominent physicians of Colchester, Connecticut.

Reared at Avon, New York, Henry H. Isham was married February 9, 1865, at Lawrence, Michigan, to Miss Annetta Clark. Mrs. Isham, who still resides at Coffeyville, was born in Lawrence, Michigan, daughter of H. B. Clark, who was born near Watertown, New York, in 1812, and died at Lawrence, Michigan, in 1900. He was a pioneer settler in that section of Michigan and spent most of his career there as a farmer. Politically he was a republican. H. B. Clark married Amanda Marshall, who was born in Herkimer County, New York, in 1805 at Little Falls, and died at Lawrence, Michigan, in 1874. Mr. and Mrs. H. B. Clark were the parents of the following children: Oscar, who was a railway conductor and was accidentally killed while on duty at Cherryvale, Kansas; Charles, a retired farmer at Paw Paw, Michigan; Jeannette, who died at the age of eight years in Lawrence, Michigan; George, who died in childhood in Michigan; Mrs. Isham; Orrie, who lives with Mrs. Isham at Coffeyville, is the widow of L. W. Heath,

Henry H Isham

who was a printer in Chicago; and Tabor, who died at Coffeyville in September, 1914.

After their marriage Mr. and Mrs. H. H. Isham returned to New York and lived in Avon until 1868. They then resided at South Haven, Michigan, until 1871, and in June of that year came to Kansas, spending a few months at Ottawa, and in November of the same year moving to Coffeyville. Coffeyville was then a village out on the frontier, and little more than a trading post for the scattered settlements of Southern Kansas and the Indian inhabitants of Indian Territory. While a resident of Avon, New York, Mr. Isham had conducted a tin shop and small hardware store, and was in the same line of business in South Haven, Michigan. On coming to Coffeyville he opened up a pioneer hardware store, and that grew in time, with the settling up and expansion of the surrounding country, into the leading mercantile establishment of its kind in that part of the state. After some years he sold out his hardware interests to his brother J. T. Isham, and the store is now conducted by Harry Isham, a nephew of Mr. H. H. Isham. From merchandising Mr. Isham turned his attention to banking, and conducted a private bank at Coffeyville for six years. He also operated extensively in loans and real estate and at his death left a large estate.

His public service should not pass unmentioned. He served on the council and school board, and devoted much time to every movement for the betterment of his home city. He was a democrat and later a republican, and a member of the Masonic fraternity at Avon, New York. His home was the center of his life, and he gave to his family his best affection. While he was still in the hardware business the famous Dalton gang raided Coffeyville and his store was one of the objects of their pillage. Mr. Isham armed himself with a gun and assisted in repelling the outlaws, and he has always been credited with having killed the leader of the band.

Mrs. Isham was well educated, having attended the public schools at Lawrence, Michigan, where she was born, and also the State Normal School, but was married soon after completing her course. She has been a very active member of the Presbyterian Church at Coffeyville, and was one of those who organized the Earnest Workers Society, and has been instrumental in furthering the benevolent purposes of that society. Mrs. Isham owns the residence at 114 West Tenth Street, the building in which the hardware store is conducted on Union Street, owns a restaurant and drug store building on Union Street, and other residence properties on Fifth Street and Tenth Street.

Mrs. Isham has one daughter, Frances, wife of C. W. Mansur, who lives at St. Louis, where he was manager for the John Deere Plow Company and is still an adviser of that concern. Mr. and Mrs. Mansur have one child, Charles, who is employed by the Miehle Printing Company of Chicago. Mrs. Mansur completed her education in Bethany College at Topeka and in a private school in Kansas City.

EDWARD S. REA. One of the largest milling concerns in Southern Kansas is the Rea-Patterson Milling Company of Coffeyville. The plant was established at Coffeyville in 1894, and at that time the daily capacity of the mill was 400 barrels. Since then, by gradual additions and improvements, the daily capacity is now 1,800 barrels of uour and 600 barrels of meal, while the elevator capacity is 700,000 bushels, this being one of the largest mills in the state. In fact the product from the Rea-

Vol. IV—9

Patterson Milling Company has a very wide distribution, particularly over the South and Southwest, and the company sends flour to Cuba and the Eastern states. The original capital of the company was $50,000, and it is now $300,000. The plant is conveniently situated with respect to the tracks of the Missouri Pacific, Missouri, Kansas and Texas and Santa Fe railroads.

The officers of the Rea-Patterson Milling Company are: H. W. Read, of Coffeyville, president; Edward S. Rea, treasurer and manager; and F. H. Patterson of Fredonia, secretary.

Edward S. Rea was born at Marshall, Missouri, August 16, 1872. His father, P. H. Rea, a veteran business man and miller still living at Marshall, was the founder of the Rea-Patterson Milling Company at Coffeyville, and is still its largest stockholder. P. H. Rea was born in Carroll County, Missouri, May 3, 1840. Reared in Missouri, and of Southern antecedents, he sided with the South in its struggle during the '60s, and was in the Confederate army with Gen. Joe Shelby under Gen. Sterling Price. His home district was closely divided between Northerners and Southerners, and naturally there was much factional local strife, and on account of the unpleasantness Mr. Rea went out to Montana after the war and for a time conducted an express stage line between Helena and Virginia City, and also had a a store as one of the first business enterprises of the present thriving city of Helena. He also became a factor in local politics, and as a democrat served as the first treasurer of Lewis and Clark counties, Montana. Returning to Missouri in 1870, P. H. Rea settled at Marshall in Saline County, and soon built up a large grocery, agricultural implement and grain business and still conducts an implement and automobile store there, incorporated as the P. H. Rea Implement Company. He is very active in the Christian Church and is teacher of a Bible Class. P. H. Rea was married at St. Louis to Mattie Samuel. She was born near Liberty, Clay County, Missouri, in 1849, and died at Marshall in 1894. Her children were: Florence, who died at the age of two years; Edward S.; Virginia, wife of Philip Ott, who is engaged in the implement and garage business with the P. H. Rea Implement Co. at Marshall; William G., manager of the Rea-Page Milling Company at Marshall of which his father is president; Mattie, wife of Frank A. Baker, who is connected with the Ridenour-Baker Company of Kansas City, Missouri; Catherine, wife of Frank Bigger, first vice president of the Robert Keith Furniture Company of Kansas City.

Edward S. Rea, was educated in the public schools of Marshall, in the Manual Training School of St. Louis, where he graduated in 1890, and on the completion of his education at once entered the milling business with the Rea-Page Milling Company of Marshall. For a quarter of a century he has given all his time and energy to this industry, and during the first four years learned milling in all its details at his home city. On July 27, 1894, he came to Coffeyville, and was bookkeeper until May, 1896, and since then has been manager and treasurer of the Rea-Patterson Milling Company. He is also president of the McAlester-Edward Coal Company at Pittsburg, Oklahoma, and president of the Rea-Read Mill and Elevator Company at Tulsa, Oklahoma.

In politics Mr. Rea is independent, and is active in the Presbyterian Church. On April 15, 1896, at Sweet Springs, Missouri, he married Miss Margaret

Owens. Her mother, Mrs. Sarah Owens was born at Sweet Springs and is still living there at the age of seventy-seven. Mr. and Mrs. Rea have one daughter, Nellie Elizabeth, who was born February 5, 1900, is a member of the Coffeyville High School Class of 1917, and her parents plan her continued education.

ALEXANDER JACOB WALDRAVEN. Among the oldest and most highly respected citizens of Riley County, Kansas, is Alexander Jacob Waldraven, who has spent more than half his life in this state. His remote ancestry was Pennsylvania Dutch, and no more solid and substantial people can be found, but for many years the Waldravens had lived in North Carolina. He was born in Stokes County, which was later divided forming Stokes and Forsythe counties in that state, April 15, 1839, and was reared on the farm of his father, John Henry Waldraven.

Alexander Jacob Waldraven has led an agricultural life. After the close of the Civil war he moved to Missouri and resided on a farm near Lee's Summit, in Jackson County, until 1872, when he removed to Kansas and settled on a farm east of Waterville, in Marshall County. It was in 1881 that Mr. Waldraven came to Riley County, locating at that time on section 13, May Day Township, where he purchased 240 acres of land, which he subsequently developed and improved. After many years of prosperity as a farmer and stockraiser, Mr. Waldraven retired, turning over the active management of his large estate to his youngest son, who is a capable farmer and a graduate of the Kansas State Agricultural College.

In 1861 Mr. Waldraven was married to Martha Susanna Long, and they have the following children: Cora Elizabeth, who is the wife of Rev. David Everett Bundy, a minister in the Methodist Episcopal Church, South; Robert Ulysses, who is a minister and traveling evangelist of the church denomination named above; Ada Belle, who is the widow of James T. Smith; and Luther Watts, who was born in Marshall County, Kansas, October 15, 1878, was graduated from the Kansas State Agricultural College in 1900, and in 1914 was married to Miss Laura L. Wendland. He is now operating his father's farm in May Day Township. The parents of the above children reside with Mrs. Smith in May Day Township.

While Mr. Waldraven has never sought political preferment for himself, he has kept well informed concerning matters of public import and has been intelligently interested. At times he has united with organizations that have sought, by the franchise, to bring about better conditions along many lines, and recognized the excellent underlying principles of both the greenback and populist movements. At present he is nominally a democrat but is inclined to be somewhat independent yet in his support of men and measures. Mr. and Mrs. Waldraven were reared in the Methodist Episcopal Church South but as there is no church of that denomination in their neighborhood, they have united with the Evangelical Association and are active Christian workers. The entire family has high standing in Riley County.

RT. REV. JOHN WARD, Bishop of the See of Leavenworth, but with home at 1228 Sandusky Avenue in Kansas City, Kansas, has been one of the ablest priests and administrators of the Catholic Church in Kansas for over thirty years, and a host of friends and admirers both in and out of the church rejoiced in his elevation as a bishop on November 25, 1910.

Bishop Ward was born in the Village of Westview near Cleveland, Ohio, May 23, 1857. He was the second in a family of three children. His parents were Joseph and Ellen (McGrath) Ward, both natives of Ireland. Joseph Ward followed farming in Ohio. Early in his career John Ward was destined for the priesthood. He attended school in Westview, began his classical studies in St. Mary's College at Cincinnati, continued in Assumption College at Sandwich, Ontario, and afterwards graduated from St. Meinrad College in Indiana. He was ordained July 17, 1884, and was appointed assistant at the Cathedral in Leavenworth. After three months there he was appointed to a pastorate in Marshall County, and from 1888 to 1895 was in charge of the church at Parsons, Kansas. He then came to St. Thomas Church in Armourdale, where he was priest until 1898. For ten years he was rector of the Cathedral at Leavenworth, and then returned to Kansas City, Kansas, as irremovable rector of St. Mary's for a period of three years. From this he was appointed Bishop of Leavenworth and was consecrated to that dignity February 22, 1911, by His Excellency Diomede Falconio, apostolic delegate and later cardinal. His see comprises twenty counties in the northeastern portion of the state. Both as priest and bishop has Bishop Ward had the satisfaction of seeing a large number of parishes relieved of burdens of debt and while his work has not been pre-eminent as a financial administrator he is successful.

JASPER WILLIAM HAYWARD, M. D. Since he earned his privilege of practicing medicine in 1909, Doctor Hayward has become increasingly well known as a physician and surgeon in Kansas City, Kansas. Aside from his attainments professionally much interest attaches to his career because of the valiant struggle he made as a youth to secure an education and win a position in a learned profession against heavy odds.

Doctor Hayward was born in Kingman, Kansas, April 3, 1885, a son of Charles and Kate (Weir) Hayward. His father was a native of Boston, Massachusetts, of English descent, was reared in Boston, and his father Nathaniel Hayward afterward came West locating in Glasgow, Missouri, where he became a member of Gen. Joe Shelby's body guard during the Civil war and was also with General Price's army. He fought as a Confederate soldier in the battle of the Blue. Nathaniel Hayward after the war removed in prairie schooners to the Colorado line and later to Indian Territory, and finally located in Kingman County, Kansas, about the time it was organized. Nathaniel and his son Charles took up claims and in the early days lived in dugouts and went through many privations during the lean years of that country. Charles Hayward married his wife at Glasgow, Missouri, where she was born. In 1885 he sold his farm on account of ill health and in 1887 located in Kansas City, Kansas. He operated in real estate, but died in 1891. His widow is still living, but married for her second husband Frank Williams. At the time of the death of Charles Hayward there were three small children, Doctor Hayward being the oldest. Grace is now the wife of George McCarten, a grocer at Nineteenth and Central streets in Kansas City, Kansas; Harry is a photographer connected with the Kennedy studio.

Doctor Hayward was six years old when his father died. He attended the public schools of Kansas City, Kansas, but at the age of nine began earning his own way in the world. He worked as dishwasher in a restaurant and whenever possible he attended school from 1895 to 1898. Those three years were spent in various kinds of restaurant work from dishwasher and cook to cashier. He next was paid wages of $1.50 a week for his services after school hours in a queensware store. While attending high school he carried a paper route for the Kansas City Star. His earnings from this route were not only sufficient to maintain him while in high school but also while a student in the University Medical College of Kansas City, Missouri. While in medical school he was also employed as night doctor of the Emergency Hospital service. In 1909 he graduated M. D. and the same year passed the State Board of Medical Examiners of Kansas.

On December 25, Christmas Day, 1909, Doctor Hayward married Miss Cornelia Andrews, daughter of J. V. Andrews. Her father has long been well known in banking and real estate circles in Kansas City, Kansas. To their marriage have been born two children: Mary Dorothy, now four years of age; and Evelyn Gertrude, aged two.

Doctor Hayward is a republican, has been interested in political affairs and especially in any matters relating to the good of his community. He is a member of Robert E. Sherman Lodge of Masons in Kansas City, Kansas, and also belongs to the thirty-second degree of Scottish Rite. He is affiliated with the Modern Woodmen of America, the Court of Honor and is physician for the local Aerie of the Fraternal Order of Eagles. He also belongs to the Independent Order of Odd Fellows. In the line of his profession he is a member of the Wyandotte County Medical Society and the State Medical Society and is a member of the Union Club. He is also coroner of Wyandotte County, Kansas.

KEITH EVANS COX is a Kansas newspaper man with wide experience and ability, and is now editor and proprietor of the Cheney Sentinel, in Sedgwick County.

Apart from his own work and the influence he has exercised in journalism, much interest attaches to his name because of his honored father and mother, both of whom were prominent in the early days of Kansas.

His father was the late William Edgar Cox. A Kentuckian by birth, he first came out to Kansas from Frankfort in 1859. He remained only a short time, and on returning to Kentucky during the Civil war period gave offense because of his pronounced Union sentiments to his father, who was a wealthy planter and slave holder. William E. Cox again came to Kansas in 1871, and in 1872 located at Wellington. He was a strong and active opponent of the liquor interests, and a devout Methodist. He had studied law during his early career and for many years served as justice of the peace. He was one of the most highly esteemed citizens of Wellington, where he died June 8, 1902, at the age of sixty.

On March 17, 1875, William E. Cox married Mary Evans. They were married at Wellington, where Mrs. Cox still resides with her two daughters. She was the mother of five children, four of whom are still living. Mrs. Mary E. Cox performed a service worth mentioning in any history of Kansas in settling up the Home Valley District near Belle Plaine, Kansas. She personally induced some twenty-five or thirty families to locate there. That was in the spring of 1872. She was also one of the first primary teacher in Sumner County, and conducted the first millinery store at Belle Plaine in Sumner County. Her father, Elijah Evans, came from Iowa and took

up a homestead at Independence in 1871, but later moved to Wellington, where for many years he held the office of probate judge.

Keith Evans Cox was born at Wellington, Kansas, August 28, 1880. After attending the public schools of his native town, he started to learn the printer's trade in the office of the old People's Voice at Wellington. For the past eleven years he has been an active factor in Kansas newspaper life. In September, 1905, he leased the Monitor at Leonardville, Kansas, a paper he published two years. The following year was spent as manager of the Kiowa Journal. For another year he was proprietor of the Wellington Daily Mail, and after selling out his interests there was special railroad and sporting correspondent for the Newton Kansan for two years. From August, 1911, until July, 1913, he edited the Eldorado Republican. At the latter date he bought the Cheney Sentinel from L. A. McCaffree.

The Cheney Sentinel was established February 27, 1884, the year following the organization of the town. It was first known as the Herald with George W. Brown as editor. Later the name was changed to the Blade, then back to Herald, and finally became the Sentinel. Mr. Cox is making it one of the brightest and newsiest country papers in Sedgwick County.

Fraternally he is a Mason and Modern Woodman. On March 12, 1910, he married Olive Lulu Anderson of Wellington. Their daughter, Harriet Ammazette, was born May 13, 1913.

JAMES J. CORKILL, general superintendent of the Beatrice Creamery Company of Topeka, has spent most of his life in Kansas, and besides his present business connections he has a record of honorable service as a soldier, having been a member of the famous Twentieth Kansas Regiment in the Philippines, and afterwards serving two years with the Thirty-sixth Infantry in those islands.

He was born on the Isle of Man, England, in 1877, but came to America in 1889. His parents were William and Matilda (Kneale) Corkill. His maternal grandfather was J. H. Kneale, whose family were English and came out of Lancashire. William and Matilda Corkill spent their last years in Kansas and the former died in 1914 and the latter in 1912 at Topeka. William Corkill was a man of high moral character, and an exemplary citizen. He and his wife were the parents of five daughters and three sons: William H., Catherine Matilda, Charles Frederick, Eleanor E., Alice Rebecca, Edith Arabelle, Emily Anna and James J. William H. is a contractor and builder at Cleveland, Ohio. Catherine is the wife of Howard Griggs, a prosperous farmer at Maple Hill, Kansas. Federick for the past nine years has been connected with the Beatrice Creamery Company and resides at 119 Tyler Street. Alice is Mrs. W. E. Johnston, whose husband for a number of years was a stone contractor at Dover in Shawnee County, but is now a contractor at Stewart, Florida. Eleanor E. is the wife of John T. Barnes, a farmer in Arkansas. Emily is the widow of Mr. James A May and resides with her brother Frederick in Topeka. Edith is the wife of John T. Reed, their home being at Jacksonville, Florida.

James J. Corkill had his early advantages in the public schools of the Isle of Man. He came to this country at the age of twelve years and went to live temporarily with his uncle and aunt, John and Elizabeth Corkill at Dover in Shawnee County, Kansas, his parents later purchasing farm property at Dover. He continued his education at Dover, afterwards entered the Topeka High School, and from there became a student of Baker University. His first experience after completing his education was in the freight department of the Santa Fe Railway.

In the spring of 1898 Mr. Corkill enlisted and became a member of the Twentieth Kansas Regiment, recruited under Col. Fred Funston. In the summer of that year his regiment embarked from San Francisco for the Philippines, and Mr. Corkill was soon promoted to sergeant of Company E. The record of the Twentieth Kansas in the Philippines is thoroughly familiar to Kansas people. Mr. Corkill fought in the first important engagement in which the regiment was employed, at Caloocan in the Island of Luzon, and participated in various skirmishes, later in the battle of Calumpit, following which there was almost continuous skirmishing until they captured the insurgent capital of Malolos, and ended the campaign by taking San Fernando. After fifteen months of almost continuous fighting the Twentieth Kansas returned to the United States. In the meantime James Corkill obtained his honorable discharge from the regiment while in Luzon, and enlisted in the Thirty-sixth Regiment of Infantry commanded by Colonel Bell, now General Bell. Thus Mr. Corkill had two years of further experience against the Philippine insurgents and in guard duty before he was given his honorable discharge and permitted to return to the United States.

In 1903 he entered the service of the Continental Creamery Company of Topeka. Reference to this great organization is made elsewhere. Showing ability and responsibility Mr. Corkill was promoted from time to time until 1908, when he became general superintendent of the greatest creamery plant in the world. The Beatrice Creamery Company has shipped at a single time as much as a train load of butter by express. It has had contracts to supply practically the entire United States Navy with butter. Mr. Corkill says that the Beatrice Creamery Company products are now used daily on every continent in the world, and shipments go from the various plants to fully one half the countries of the earth, either directly or indirectly.

Mr. Corkill was married in 1908 to Miss Jessie B. Klein. The Klein family were pioneers in Coffey County, Kansas, where they settled more than half a century ago. Their original home was in Scranton, Pennsylvania. Mrs. Corkill's father was George A. Klein, who when a young man made a trip to Colorado and on returning while in Western Kansas was stricken with the fever and died. The Kleins are well and favorably known in Coffey County.

DAVID FRIEDLEY CARSON, a prominent member of the Kansas City, Kansas, bar, is a native of Kansas and his people went through all the harrowing experiences of homesteading and making a living out of the land during the years when Kansas was plagued by grasshoppers, droughts and mortgages.

Mr. Carson was born on a farm near Urbana in Neosho County June 7, 1875. He was the third of seven children, four of whom are still living. His parents, William and Anna M. (Friedley) Carson, were both born in Bedford County, Indiana, where their respective parents were early settlers. William Carson's brother, George W., was a colonel in the Union army during the Civil war, while on the maternal side of the family Madison Friedley was a

captain in the Union army. William Carson learned the trade of blacksmith, while his wife became a teacher. Both of them grew up in Bedford, Indiana, where they married, and in 1869 they started west to find a new home in the State of Kansas. All their worldly goods were in a wagon and they traveled in company with two other young couples. They had hope and ambition and energy, but practically no capital when they reached Kansas. They knew no one in the state and they started out as strangers in a strange land. William Carson took up a homestead of 160 acres, and broke the land with oxen and horses. It required six weeks to make the trip from Indiana to Kansas. The first home of the family in Kansas was a two room house built of clapboards stood on end, and the structure was very loosely put together, admitting large quantities of water during a heavy rainstorm. William Carson was a man among men, was interested in everything for the benefit of the community, was an advocate of good schools and roads, served on the school board, and was absolutely trusted for his uprightness and integrity. He had no ambition for wealth, never speculated, and consequently accumulated more of the esteem of his fellow citizens than he did of material possessions. He cared more for the maintenance of a good home for his family and the affording to his children of good opportunities for education and culture. He helped move the first house into Chanute, which was then known as New Chicago, and has seen that village grow to a village of 10,000 people. He and his wife now live retired at Chanute. His wife is a very devout member of the Christian or Disciples Church. William Carson has always been a republican, has served as a member of the Central Committee, but has never sought office. He has filled various chairs in his lodge of Masons.

David F. Carson had a district school education and as a young man taught in his home district. While teaching and working on a farm he paid his way through the State Normal School at Emporia, and after graduating there in 1901 he went to the Philippines and spent a year as a Government teacher on those islands. In the meantime he had definitely determined to become a lawyer, and on returning to this country he entered the University of Michigan law school at Ann Arbor, where he was graduated in 1905. He was admitted to the bar of Michigan in 1905, but being without funds on graduating he was unable to return to Kansas at once, and he put in a short time writing life insurance. He also worked on railway construction on the Junction City Division of the Missouri, Kansas & Texas Railroad. He finally located at Kansas City, Kansas, and in ten years has built up a substantial law clientage. His offices are in the Stubbs Building.

At the outbreak of the Spanish-American war Mr. Carson enlisted in Company H of the Twenty-second Kansas Infantry. This regiment was sent to Camp Alger, but in November he was mustered out without having seen active field service. Mr. Carson was married September 29, 1909, to Daisy Ott of Greenwood County, Kansas. Mrs. Carson is of German ancestry. They have one child, David William.

Mr. Carson is a republican and has served as chairman of the County Central Committee of Wyandotte County. He is a thirty-second degree Scottish Rite Mason, belongs to the Independent Order of Odd Fellows, and has membership in various insurance societies. His wife takes a very active part in the work of the Methodist Episcopal Church.

FRANK WILLIAM DAVIS. One of the best known among the real estate and insurance men of Fort Scott, is Frank William Davis, who, still a young man, has already gained an enviable position in business circles. A peculiar and particular genius is necessary to the man who would acquire success in the real estate and insurance field. The business is identical with no other, and many men who have risen to prominence in other lines have scored naught but failures when they have entered this field. Mr. Davis, however, possesses the qualities of acumen, a pleasing personality and a knowledge of human nature, and these, combined with business sagacity and tireless energy have made his position secure.

Mr. Davis was born at Fort Scott, Kansas, October 17, 1881, and is a son of Samuel Sturges and Elizabeth M. (Hayes) Davis. His father was born at Providence, Rhode Island, in 1842, a son of Samuel Davis, a prominent woolen manufacturer of that city. Samuel S. Davis received a college education, and at the outbreak of the Civil war, when he was nineteen years of age, left college to enlist in a Rhode Island regiment of volunteer infantry, with which he served during the entire period of the struggle. He participated in numerous heavy engagements and came through without a wound, but while on a forced march contracted white swelling of the knee-cap, and for a time was invalided home. When he had received his honorable discharge and was mustered out of the service, he decided to try his fortune in sheepraising in Kansas, and accordingly came to Bourbon County and homesteaded land. He engaged in farming and stockraising on the first claim filed on Rock Creek, entering enthusiastically into his work. Although he put the best of his energy and effort into an endeavor to win success in this field, he was not fitted for the vocation of farming, and after the wolves had destroyed his flocks and he had met with a number of other reverses, he decided to enter a different field. Mr. Davis was a natural scholar and a great reader, and determined to seek a business that would at the same time make use of his talents and prove congenial. Finally he decided upon an enterprise which he felt would succeed, and accordingly came to Fort Scott, where he opened the first bookstore in the history of the city and established the first circulating library. His knowledge of books and authors proved a valuable asset, and he soon found his business upon a paying basis. Through his circulating library, many families of modest means were able to secure the works of the world's best authors, who otherwise would have been unable to do so. At the cost of a few cents they were allowed to rent books, to be returned within a reasonable time, and thus many people became familiar with the work of Dickens, Cooper and the other great writers. For the greater part the people during an early day in Fort Scott were in modest means and books were a luxury that they could not afford to buy. During the many years that Mr. Davis continued in the business he gained an acquaintance that extended all over the city and even into the surrounding countryside, and all who knew him respected and esteemed him as a kindly, gentle man, generous in heart and always ready to overlook the delinquencies of the unfortunate. He never lost his own love for books, and during his lifetime collected a large and attractive library, which covered a comprehensive number of subjects.

When Mr. Davis finally disposed of his book business, it was to accept a position as bookkeeper with a Fort Scott banking house, with which he continued to be connected for some years, until the bank retired from business. He was appointed city clerk, a position which he held for fifteen years, and, although he was a stanch republican, his worth was so appreciated that he was twice appointed by a democratic mayor. When the office became an elective one, he was chosen by the vote of the people at two elections, and was still in harness, at the close of his second term, when his death occurred April 19, 1899, he being then fifty-seven years of age. Mr. Davis was a great friend of education and did all in his power to better school conditions. He was a member of the Knights of Pythias, and his religious connection was with the Episcopal Church. Mrs. Davis was born in 1855, in Polk County, Tennessee, and was brought to Bourbon County, Kansas, when her people refugeed here during the Civil war. She still resides at the old home at Fort Scott. In her early years Mrs. Davis was a member of the Baptist Church, but in recent years has adopted the faith of the Christian Scientists. There were four children in the family, as follows: Percy, traveling representative for the Belknap Hardware Company, of Louisville, Kentucky, with headquarters at Muskogee, Oklahoma, who married Cora A. Browning; Frank W.; Lina M., who is the wife of Harry H. Hill, of Muskogee, Oklahoma; and Alfred W., connected with the Wells Fargo Express Company, at Kansas City, Missouri, who married Miss Elliott, and has one son, Frank.

Frank W. Davis was educated in the public schools of Fort Scott, being graduated with the class of 1899, and at that time became a telegraph operator for the Fort Scott & Memphis Railroad. After serving for four years in the Fort Scott office, he resigned to accept the position of ticket agent for the Frisco Railroad, and held this position for ten years, being then transferred to Joplin, Missouri, and made city passenger agent for the same line. After two years the office was abolished, and, the road going into the hands of a receiver, Mr. Davis returned to Fort Scott, and September 1, 1914, bought the insurance agency of Turley & Watkins, which concern represented twenty-four leading fire insurance companies. Subsequently Mr. Davis was appointed district manager for the Sunflower State Life Insurance Company, in charge of the counties of Bourbon, Linn, Miami and Anderson, with a number of agents under his supervision. He now carries on a large business in insurance, real estate and loans, and through his own efforts has made his agency one of the leading factors in the realty and insurance field of Fort Scott, while his operations extend all over Southeastern Kansas. On April 1, 1914, Mr. Davis was appointed city treasurer of Fort Scott by Mayor Hesser. He is prominent also in fraternal circles, being district deputy grand master of the Masonic lodge and past master of Rising Sun Lodge No. 8, and also belongs to the Benevolent and Protective Order of Elks, the Loyal Order of Moose and the Home Builders.

Mr. Davis was married June 7, 1909, at Fort Scott, to Miss Lulu May Finley, of this city, daughter of Charles H. and Hilda M. (Peterson) Finley. They have two children: Mary Elizabeth, born April 5, 1914; and Frances, born May 1, 1916. Mrs. Davis is active in the work of the Episcopal Church and its societies and charities.

THOMAS COLEMAN TRUMAN. Among those sterling citizens who have been prominent and influential in connection with the civic and business affairs of

Montgomery County and who are today to be designated as representative pioneers of the county a place must consistently be given to Mr. Truman, who has maintained his home at Independence, the county seat, for more than forty years and who is now living in well earned retirement—a man who has been in the most significant sense the architect of his own fortunes, as he became dependent upon his own resources when but twelve years of age.

Thomas Coleman Truman was born at Parkersburg, Wood County, West Virginia, on the 21st of September, 1844, and is a son of Absalom and Serena (Dila) Truman, both likewise natives of West Virginia and both born in the year 1812, at which time that commonwealth was still a part of the Old Dominion State of Virginia. Absalom Truman was born in what is now Calhoun County, West Virginia, and his wife was born in Wood County. He was a son of Thomas Truman, who emigrated to America from England and who became a farmer in what is now Caldwell County, West Virginia, where his death occurred. Absalom Truman devoted his entire active life to agricultural pursuits and was a resident of Wood County, West Virginia, at the time of his death, in 1888, his wife having passed away in the preceding year and both having been members of the Methodist Episcopal Church, South, the while he was found aligned as a staunch supporter of the principles of the democratic party. Of the children the eldest is Elizabeth, who resides at Independence, Kansas, and who is the widow of Henry Woodruff, her husband having been a prosperous farmer and merchant of Montgomery County; Thomas C., subject of this review, was the next child; Henry is a retired sand and coal merchant and resides at Moundsville, West Virginia; Elmira is the wife of Elihu Lanham and they reside at Parkersburg, West Virginia, as does also Francis Marion, who is the youngest of the children and who is there actively identified with the lumber business.

The early educational advantages of Thomas C. Truman were limited. He attended the common schools of his native state in an intermittent way and when but twelve years of age he began to shift for himself. About the close of the Civil war he became concerned with the lumber industry at Parkersburg, and in the spring of 1868, as a young man of twenty-three years, he came to Kansas and numbered himself among the pioneers of Wyandotte County, where he remained four years and where he was identified with farming and lumbering enterprise. He then removed to Montgomery County and took up a homestead claim of 160 acres, on which he lived until 1871, when he sold the property, after having reclaimed a considerable part of the land to cultivation and made various improvements on the property. After selling his farm Mr. Truman removed to Independence where he purchased a small brewery which had here been established. He sold this a short time later and thereafter he here conducted a prosperous wholesale and retail ice business until February, 1916, when he retired from active business. With the growth and civic expansion of Independence the ice business of Mr. Truman kept full pace, and eventually he controlled three ice plants, which turned out an adequate production of artificial ice and also made provision for cold storage. The last of these ice plants to be erected was the modern establishment built and equipped by the Cole Truman Ice & Cold Storage Company, and this plant, eligibly situated near the Missouri Pacific Railroad tracks, has a capacity of fifty tons of ice. With a desire to meet

fully the ever increasing demands placed upon his ice business Mr. Truman effected, in 1904, the organization and incorporation of the Cole Truman Ice & Cold Storage Company, and of this he was the president and general manager until the time of his retirement from active business. He has made judicious investments in local real estate, and in addition to his own home, at 201 North Second Street, he is the owner of three other improved residence properties in the city, as well as a tract of valuable land along the river and just at the edge of the city.

Mr. Truman has not only found in Kansas ample opportunities for the winning of large and worthy material prosperity but has also shown himself a loyal and progressive citizen. He is a republican in politics and while he has had no political ambition his civic loyalty caused him to give most effective service as a member of the City Council of Independence, an office of which he was the incumbent for a period of fourteen years. He is affiliated with the local blue lodge and chapter, as well as St. Bernard Commandery, Knights Templar, of the time-honored Masonic fraternity, and has further extended his affiliation to Abdullah Temple, Ancient Arabic Order of the Nobles of the Mystic Shrine, at Leavenworth. In his home city he holds membership also in the Independent Order of Odd Fellows, the Benevolent and Protective Order of Elks, the Fraternal Order of Eagles, and is a charter member of the Independence Lodge of the Grand Army of the Republic.

Until this juncture has been withheld record concerning the gallant service given by Mr. Truman as a Union soldier in the Civil war. In 1861 he enlisted as a member of Company K, Second West Virginia Volunteer Infantry, and he continued in active service for a number of months after the definite close of the war, being finally mustered out and given an honorable discharge in 1866, his service after the final surrender of Generals Lee and Johnston having been on the plains of the West. He participated in the memorable Valley campaign in Virginia, under General Sheridan, and was in the brigade commanded by General Milroy. At New Creek, West Virginia, he was captured by the enemy, and after he had been confined for a time in historic old Libby Prison his exchange was effected and he rejoined his regiment.

At Parkersburg, West Virginia, in 1867, Mr. Truman wedded Miss Elizabeth A. Dewey, and she died at Independence, Kansas, in 1883, leaving no children. In 1886 was solemnized the marriage of Mr. Truman to Miss Columbia A. Burke, the marriage ceremony having been performed at Neodesha, Wilson County. Mrs. Truman's parents, William and Sarah Burke, long maintained their home at Parkersburg, West Virginia, her father having been a carpenter by trade, but having eventually engaged in the dry-goods business. Mrs. Truman died April 29, 1915. Mr. and Mrs. Truman had no children of their own but their adopted son, H. H. (Crane) Truman, is now successfully engaged in business at Independence, where he has a factory for the bottling of carbonated beverages, commonly designated as "soft drinks."

INDEPENDENCE DAILY REPORTER. One of the oldest successful daily newspapers in Southern Kansas is the Independence Daily Reporter, which has recently completed the thirty-fifth year of its existence.

In 1881 Independence was a small town, the official and market center for a thrifty surrounding country entirely agricultural. Oil and gas had not yet been developed, and had not been dreamed of. Two attempts had already been made to establish daily papers, but had failed. On September 12, 1881, Ralph C. Harper and Samuel Wassam brought out the first issue of the Daily Reporter. It was printed in the office of the Kansan. The two publishers did all the work on this paper, even to delivering the copies after midnight. It is interesting to recall the fact the first important story in its columns was a report of the death of President James A. Garfield.

In a short time the publishers bought the plant of an old publication known as the Living Age, and in January, 1882, the Reporter was published in its own home.

The Reporter had to meet various financial obstacles and vicissitudes. In 1882 one of the founders Mr. Wassam retired and R. E. Harper, assisted by his wife and son, carried on the paper with great difficulty until the summer of 1885. It was then bought by T. N. Sickles, who was its editor and publisher for eighteen years. During those years the Reporter maintained no job department, and while it steadily prospered in good times and bad, it was an interesting exception to the general rule that a small daily paper could not exist without such a supplement to its business. During those years the Reporter was issued some times as a morning paper and sometimes as an afternoon paper, but finally the custom became permanent of publishing it in the afternoon. Mr. Sickles remained proprietor and editor of the Reporter from 1885 until February, 1904, with the exception of the years 1891-93, when he was connected with the United States pension agency at Topeka, though the paper was published by his son, Walter S. Sickles in the meantime.

The next owners of the Reporter were S. P. DeWolf and Allison M. Oliphant, both of whom came from Northwestern Ohio and from the great oil fields of that state. Kansas was then in the midst of an oil boom, and Independence was the mecca of thousands of oil men. No local newspaper attempted to give the news of the oil field, though that by all means was the most important material for journalistic enterprise. H. G. James volunteered to furnish the Reporter news of the oil business, being allowed $10 a week for expenses. After six months he bought the paper from the owners, and took charge as owner and editor September 1, 1904. He continued to specialize in oil news and made the Reporter the standard authority in the Mid-continent oil field. The Reporter originated the name "Mid-continent" for this great oil district.

On April 1, 1913, the Daily Reporter was bought by Clyde H. Knox, who has continued its editor and publisher to the present time. During the thirty-five years the Reporter has kept its mechanical equipment up to the standards of improvement, and now has a large and handsome plant with all the facilities for the publication of a daily paper. It is distinctively a home paper, though it also covers the important news over a large territory in Southern Kansas, and among many hundreds of its readers is the only source of current news, whether local or foreign. It is a high class newspaper, has the prestige of age and influence, and is one of the oldest daily publications in the state.

MRS. KATE M. DILLEY. The able and honored proprietor of the Dilley Sanitarium, in the City of Wichita, has proved herself one of the vigorous and resourceful business women of the Sunflower State and by the establishing and maintaining of her excellent sanitarium she has made a noble contribu-

tion to the list of valuable medical institutions in the City of Wichita.

Mrs. Dilley was born in Manchester, England. When she was a child of two years her parents removed to Cape Town, South Africa, and in that far distant land Mrs. Dilley passed the period of her girlhood and early youth. She profited duly by the advantages afforded in the excellent schools of Cape Town and finally entered Union College at that place, an institution in which she was graduated as a member of the class of 1895. She next entered Claremont Sanitarium, a splendidly equipped institution at Claremont, South Africa, and in the same she was graduated as a trained nurse, in the year 1898. In the following year she was graduated as a midwife, in the Free Dispensary at Cape Town. In the year that marked her graduation in Claremont Sanitarium she opened a Turkish bath establishment at Cape Town, and this she conducted with marked success for the ensuing ten years. In 1901 was solemnized her marriage, at Cape Town, to O. D. Dilley, an American missionary nurse, and the three children of this union, all born at Cape Town, are Almira, Harlan and Aileen.

In 1908, accompanied by her children, Mrs. Dilley left South Africa and came to the United States. Within a short time after her arrival in America she came to Wichita and established the Dilley Sanitarium, which she has since successfully conducted along the general lines that mark the hygienic and definite technical system of treatment that have given international fame to the celebrated Battle Creek Sanitarium, at Battle Creek, Michigan. Mrs. Dilley is a woman of high professional attainments and much executive ability, so that the success of her enterprise at Wichita has been a natural result. Her sanitarium is eligibly situated at 111 South St. Francis Avenue.

EARLY WHITTEN POINDEXTER. On January 8, 1854, there was born on a farm in Martin County, Indiana, near the village with the euphonious name of Loogootee, a boy whose destiny soon took him away from his father's fields and livestock and in 1885 brought him to Kansas, where now for more than thirty years he has been general agent for Kansas of the Northwestern Mutual Life Insurance Company.

He is recognized as one of the ablest life insurance men of the country. He is one of the leaders in the force of men who are regarded as the most aggressive in any line of business and whose work in the aggregate has been a factor in making the Northwestern Mutual one of the strongest companies in the country. Mr. Poindexter took to life insurance with a readiness and with results that indicated that his talents were not misapplied and as a result of hard and intelligent work and upright methods of doing business has found a success in that field beyond what he might have expected in any profession or other commercial line of endeavor.

An eminent American authority has declared that the finest and most virile qualities of American people have been preserved in the mountain districts of Eastern Tennessee and Kentucky. It was in Eastern Tennessee that Mr. Poindexter's parents were both born, and the respective families probably had lived there for several generations. His parents were Christian and Lourinda (Keck) Poindexter. From the mountains of Tennessee they emigrated to Indiana, and the father acquired 320 acres of land which he devoted to general farming, and he was also a raiser of pedigreed sheep and hogs. He was a man of no little influence in his locality. He became a republican with the formation of that party, served several terms as county commissioner, and did all in his power to promote the upbuilding of churches and schools. He and his wife had a family of seventeen children. Five of them died in infancy, and ten are now living.

The second in age among this large family, Early W. Poindexter, grew up in Martin County, Indiana, attended the common schools, spent his vacations on his father's farm, and in 1871, at the age of seventeen, began teaching district school. After that he taught a term or so every year until 1883. Toward the close of this work he had a normal school of 150 pupils at Bloomfield, Indiana. Some of the proceeds from his work as teacher he invested in further education, and he was a student in the University of Indiana at Bloomington until he graduated in 1879.

It was in December, 1879, that Mr. Poindexter married Miss Molly Hatfield, who was born in Greene County, Indiana. Seven children were born to Mr. and Mrs. Poindexter, and these children have well justified the careful training given them by their parents. All have had the advantages of University as well as the city schools. Clarence H., the oldest, attended the public schools of Topeka, graduated from Princeton College and has since been actively associated in the insurance business with his father, and is also a director of the People's National Bank of Kansas City, Kansas. In 1904 he married Miss Olive Gundry. Urban H., the second son, has also had a university training and is in business with his father. Marlin H. has become a competent insurance man and is now state manager at Madison, Wisconsin. Mildred is the wife of C. R. Miller of Hutchinson, Kansas. E. W. Poindexter, Jr., is a student in the University of Wisconsin. Helen and Mary L. are still at home.

Mr. E. W. Poindexter had his first opportunity to sell life insurance in 1883. He took the local agency of the New York Life Company, and was soon made district agent at Vincennes, Indiana. He soon showed his qualifications for the business and in 1885 there came unsolicited to him an offer of a contract with the Northwestern Mutual for the Kansas agency of that company. He first removed to Leavenworth, but in the same year went to Topeka, and had his headquarters in that city until 1907, since which date his home and offices have been in Kansas City, Kansas. Topeka in 1885 was a comparatively small town. Mr. Poindexter not only directed the work of other agents but also was in the field himself and traveled all over the state, every year writing a large volume of insurance personally. Among other interests he is financially identified with the People's National Bank of Kansas City, Kansas.

While Mr. Poindexter has always taken an active interest in local affairs, is a student of national problems and is a loyal republican, he has never sought any public office. He is one of the prominent Masons of Kansas. In 1901 he received the supreme honorary thirty-third degree of the Scottish Rite at Washington, District of Columbia. He belongs to the lodge and the various York Rite bodies of Masonry at Topeka, and also the Topeka Consistory, and is a member of the Shrine at Leavenworth. He is past eminent commander of the Knight Templar. Mr. Poindexter is affiliated with the Independent Order of Odd Fellows, the Knights of Pythias, the Improved Order of Red Men, has held the state

office of Great Sachem in the Red Men, has been Grand Patron of the Grand Chapter of the Eastern Star, and is Past Grand Counselor of the United Commercial Travelers. He and his wife are active members of the Presbyterian Church. Mr. Poindexter is a member of the Kansas City Commercial Club and his son Clarence is active in the Rotary Club.

HON. WILLIAM FREDERICK SAPP. It is said that the present democratic national committeeman from Kansas when he came to the state in 1879 arrived on foot. He was young then, and not above such strenuous exercise when the purpose involved was search of location for the beginning of his professional career. He soon afterward obtained admission to the bar before the District Court at Columbus, and as a lawyer and citizen has been identified with Galena almost as long as that town has been on the map.

The courage and independence that brought him to Kansas and took him through the difficulties of the early lawyer have brought Mr. Sapp far along the road to prominence and success. He is undoubtedly one of the strongest figures in the democratic party of the state. In 1892 he was a delegate at large to the democratic national convention in Chicago, was democratic candidate in his district for Congress in 1894, and is now in his third successive term as national committeeman from Kansas. His first term ended in 1912, his second in 1916, and at the recent national convention he was again chosen to represent the Sunflower State and this term holds over until the next general campaign in 1920. In 1914 Mr. Sapp was democratic candidate for the United States Senate.

He was born at Grand Rapids, Michigan, August 30, 1856, a son of Rezin, a Methodist minister, and Margaret E. (Peyre-Ferry) Sapp. He is a brother of Judge Edward E. Sapp and the ancestry of the family is told in Judge Sapp's sketch on other pages.

Mr. Sapp received his education in the public schools of Grand Rapids, Coldwater and Kalamazoo, Michigan. He graduated from high school about 1875, and studied law in a Grand Rapids Law Office. For the past thirty-five years he has been in practice at Galena and is now member of the firm of Sapp & Wilson, his offices being at the corner of Sixth and Main streets in the Sapp Building, which is owned by him. He has served as city attorney of Galena, was a member of its school board in the early days, and has many important property interests in and around the city. He owns a residence at the corner of Thirteenth and Main streets, another at Twenty-second and Main streets, has business property with a frontage of 250 feet on Main Street, and has 500 acres of farm and mineral lands in Cherokee County. He is a stockholder in a number of banks and is president and owner of the Battlefield Mining Company and president of the Empire Mining Company.

Governor John Leedy appointed him recruiting officer during the Spanish-American war. Mr. Sapp is a member of the Cherokee County and State Bar associations, of the Community Club at Galena, for thirty-six years has been affiliated with the Knights of Pythias, of which he is past chancellor commander, is past exalted ruler of Lodge No. 677 Benevolent and Protective Order of Elks, and belongs to Galena Lodge No. 195 Independent Order of Odd Fellows.

October 29, 1885, at Quincy, Illinois, he married Miss Mary E. Wood, daughter of Daniel and Mary

(Abernethy) Wood. Her mother is now deceased and her father is a retired farmer and land owner living at Quincy. Her grandfather Daniel Wood was at one time governor of Illinois. Mr. and Mrs. Sapp have four children. Peyre-Ferry Sapp is a graduate of the University of Missouri at Columbia, and has the degrees A. B. and LL. B. from Harvard University, and is now a successful attorney at Kansas City, Missouri. Marienne is a graduate of the Kansas State University with the degree A. B. and is at home. Helen Margaret at home, has also attended the University of Kansas. William, who attended the State School of Mines at Golden, California, and the Kansas School of Mines at Weir City, is practicing his profession as a mining engineer.

THE INDEPENDENCE PUBLIC LIBRARY during the past ten years has succeeded in realizing to a very notable degree the best ideals of a library—that it is not merely a place for books to be preserved and collected, but has a work to do in influencing and cultivating the tastes of the community and in making its rich contents accessible to the homes it serves. An outgrowth of the Ladies Library Association, the public library was opened in the new Carnegie Building November 18, 1907. The building was erected at a cost of $22,500, and with grounds the property is now valued at $35,000. The library is at the corner of Maple and Fifth streets.

The present library board is composed of the following: S. M. Nees, president; Mrs. T. H. Stanford, vice president; L. R. Spradling, secretary; Miss Anna M. Gemmell, librarian; Miss Mabelle M. Bays, assistant librarian. The board of directors are: Mayor R. R. Bittman, ex-officio; S. M. Nees, Mrs. G. C. Chaney, Mrs. A. W. Evans; Mrs. G. T. Guernsey, L. R. Spradling, Mrs. A. C. Stich, N. K. Moody, Mrs. T. H. Stanford. The library committees are: Books—Mrs. G. T. Guernsey, Mrs. T. H. Stanford, Mrs. G. C. Chaney; Buildings and Grounds—Mrs. A. C. Stich, Mrs. T. H. Stanford, L. R. Spradling; Finance—L. R. Spradling, Mrs. A. W. Evans.

The librarian, Miss Anna M. Gemmell, assisted in organizing the library and her executive management has been largely responsible for the generous use and patronage that has been made of its collection of 10,000 books. Few libraries in a city of this size have so well balanced a selection of books. Miss Gemmell as librarian has done her utmost to make the library an essential part of the general scheme for public education at Independence, and has constantly co-operated with the teachers in arranging reading courses and providing reference books to accommodate the program of school studies. During 1915 the library issued to its patrons 85,160 volumes. The number of visitors during that year was 44,785, the number of reference books used was 50,578, and the number of visitors to the art room was 3,830. The art room is on the second floor of the library building, and after the Ladies Library Association had turned over all its collection of books to the public library, it remained an organization for the new purpose, to establish and maintain an art room. The association has fitted up and furnished a room on the second floor for this purpose, and for a number of years art exhibits have been held once or twice a year, and the commissions from the proceeds of the sales have been invested in several excellent oil paintings. During the lifetime of the late A. C. Stich, he and his wife donated three fine paintings to the art room.

Miss Gemmell, ably seconded by the board of directors, has studied and worked constantly to make the library an educational center, ont only for that normal proportion of a community's population that always uses such an institution, but also for the many who ordinarily do not resort to a library either for recreation or for enlightenment. Thus the Independence Public Library has now become popular not only with the school children and the clubs and professions, but also with representatives of the many skilled mechanical trades and with the people in general.

PROF. NATHANIEL A. BAKER. In each line of endeavor, in each of the learned professions, the personality of the man of force of character is revealed. With increasing experience and added years the forceful individual attains a broader grasp upon his subject, and with recurrence of problems and perplexities he is able to handle them in a manner which affords greater satisfaction. Such perfection is not attained in a single day nor in a single year, but the man of parts soon finds his place and forces his way to his cherished goal. In the field of education, Prof. Nathaniel A. Baker has attained merited prominence through ability, scholarship, hard and conscientious work and grasping of opportunities, and from the rank of a humble country schoolmaster has elevated himself to the position of city superintendent of schools of the flourishing and prosperous city of Cherryvale.

Professor Baker was born on a farm in Coffey County, Kansas, January 30, 1869, and is a son of Tim and Addie W. (Woodward) Baker, and a member of a family that emigrated from England to the New England colony before the outbreak of the American Revolution. His grandfather, Alpheus Baker, was born in Vermont, in 1794, fought as a soldier in the War of 1812, and subsequently migrated as a pioneer to Noble County, Indiana, and there passed the remainder of his life in farming, his death occurring in 1888. He was first a whig and later a republican in politics, and while not prominent in public life was considered one of the strong and influential men of his community. He was twice married, his second wife being the grandmother of Professor Baker. The only one of the grandfather's children now living is one by his second marriage, Mary, who is married and lives in Michigan.

Tim Baker was born in Ohio, in 1833, and was a boy when his parents removed to Noble County, Indiana. He was reared in a new country, on a wilderness farm, and his boyhood was filled with much hard work, but he grew to manhood a strong and self-reliant product of the frontier. When he was twenty-eight years of age, the Civil war came on and he left his family and enlisted, in 1861, in the Thirtieth Regiment, Indiana Volunteer Infantry, with which he fought in various engagements until the battle of Shiloh, in which he was wounded in the ankle. After his recovery he was given a furlough, and on his return to the front was made a captain of the Twelfth Indiana Cavalry, with which he served gallantly until the close of the war, in 1865. He also sustained another wound, in a brush with bushwhackers, in Kentucky. With his military service completed, Captain Baker returned to Noble County, Indiana, and resumed the study of law, which had been interrupted by war's demands. He was soon admitted to the bar, but did not long engage in practice, as in 1868 he answered the call of the West and came to Coffey County, Kansas, settling on a homestead of 160 acres, which he had pre-empted in 1858. There he passed the remainder of his active life, although his last few years were spent at Burlington, where he died in 1906. Captain Baker was a republican and one of the strong and influential men of his locality, serving as representative in Indiana from Noble County, at the time of Governor Morton's administration. He was a member of the Masonic fraternity, and wherever known was highly respected and esteemed. He married Addie W. Woodward, who was born in 1837, in New York, and now a resident of Kansas City, Missouri, and they became the parents of the following children: Louman E., formerly a farmer and later a machinist, and now a resident of Larned, Kansas; Jessie W., residing with her mother, widow of W. E. King, who was bookkeeper and auditor for the Metropolitan Street Railway Company, of Kansas City, Missouri; Nathaniel A., of this review; Harold, of Toronto, Kansas, formerly a hardware merchant; Stanley, a locomotive engineer of Champaign, Illinois; and Ernest, a veterinary surgeon of Bucklin, Kansas.

When he began to teach in the district schools of Coffey County, Kansas, at the age of seventeen years, Nathaniel A. Baker was himself possessed of only a district school education, but after two years in the schoolroom as master he went to the Northern Indiana Normal School at Valparaiso, where he furthered his training by one year's work. He then returned to Coffey County and taught for two additional terms, spent three years at Welda and seven years at Kincaid, both in Anderson County, Kansas, and finally spent four years as principal of the schools of Cedarvale, Chautauqua County, During all this time he had been adding to his own equipment by constant and faithful study, and in 1908 came to Cherryvale to accept the position of principal of the high school. Two years later his abilities were satisfactorily recognized by his appointment to the office of superintendent of city schools, a capacity in which he has acted for six years. In this time he has materially improved the public school system of Cherryvale, so that it now compares favorably with those of cities of its size any where in the country. He has under his supervision thirty-one teachers and 1,100 scholars, and has succeeded in instituting a feeling of co-operation that makes educational work run like a well oiled machine and is capable of great results. Professor Baker is a valued member of the Montgomery County Teachers Association and the Kansas State Teachers Association. He is a republican and a Presbyterian, and is well known in Oddfellowship, being past noble grand of Cherryvale Camp No. 142, and a member of the Encampment at Cedarvale. His interest in the welfare of his adopted city has caused him to take an active part in civic affairs, and at present he is acting in the capacity of president of the Commercial Club, a position in which he has been able to promulgate and carry through some civic enterprises of considerable importance.

In 1893, Professor Baker was married at Westphalia, Anderson County, Kansas, to Miss Frankie Hooton, daughter of Mr. and Mrs. M. G. Hooton. The mother of Mrs. Baker is now deceased, but the father still survives and is engaged in the draying business at Westphalia. Professor and Mrs. Baker are the parents of three children: Quin, born October

18, 1894, a graduate of Cherryvale High School, class of 1913, and now a junior in Kansas University; Glen, born May 24, 1896, a graduate of Cherryvale High School, class of 1913, and now a freshman in Kansas State University; and Miss Helen, born February 22, 1902, who is attending the Cherryvale High School. The pleasant family home is located at No. 817 East Main Street.

CHARLES M. BALL. While every type of business man must possess certain qualities to ensure success in his enterprises, those indispensable to the banker rest along such high lines that his position in a community is comparable to no other in importance. As a bank represents the most conservative of all institutions, the honest banker is conservative, thereby safeguarding the interests entrusted to his care. Such bankers are invaluable protectors of the public as well as of the private individual. The steadying influence of a conservative banker has often proved a bulwark to a business community in time of real or anticipated panic. The long financial career of Charles M. Ball, president of the Conlen National Bank, at Coffeyville, Kansas, has given him a wide banking experience.

Charles M. Ball was born at Rochester, in Fulton County, Indiana, November 25, 1865, and is a son of Aaron and Celestina Ball, the latter of whom was born at Akron, Indiana, in 1847 and is a resident of Oswego, Kansas. Aaron Ball was born at Akron, Indiana, in 1842, and died in 1895, at Oswego, Kansas. He came to Kansas in 1879, shortly afterward became engaged in farming and stockraising in Labette County, continuing until the close of his life. On numerous occasions he served in town offices at Oswego. He was a member of the Methodist Episcopal Church and a man whose deeds justified such connection. In fraternal life he was identified with the Odd Fellows and the Modern Woodmen of America. His six children are as follows: Flora, who became the wife of David Jennings, a banker at Oswego, Kansas, and later county treasurer; Charles M.; O. W., who is in a real estate and insurance business at Oswego; Edward C., who is a farmer and fruit grower in Arkansas; Ora J., who is a merchant in Webb City, Missouri; and R. M., who is a merchant in Alberquerque, New Mexico.

Charles M. Ball attended the public schools of Oswego, Kansas, being graduated from the high school in 1885, in the same year attending a business college at Poughkeepsie, New York. Mr. Ball's whole business life has been concerned with banking. On completing his education he entered the Conlen State Bank at Oswego as bookkeeper, shortly afterward coming to Coffeyville, and in September, 1886, he became cashier of the Conlen National Bank. In this position he displayed strictness, fairness and integrity and in the course of years became vice president of the institution and in 1915 was made its president. Undoubtedly his careful, conservative course in every position of trust that he has occupied, has had much to do in the building up of the large business this bank enjoys. While paramount this has not been his only interest however, for he is president of the Coffeyville Furniture Company, is vice president of the Coffeyville Gas and Fuel Company and has other investments.

In 1892, at Harrisonville, Maine, Mr. Ball was united in marriage with Miss Cora G. Fall, who is a daughter of Daniel and Sarah Fall, the former of whom is deceased. The mother of Mrs. Ball resides at Colorado Springs, Colorado. Mr. and Mrs. Ball have three children: Helen, who is a graduate of the Coffeyville High School and also of National Park Seminary, Washington, D. C., resides with her parents; William A., who entered Manhattan College after graduating from the city high school; and Charles, who is a student in the high school. Mr. Ball and family are members of the Presbyterian Church at Coffeyville and he is a church trustee.

In politics Mr. Ball has been a worker in the republican party for many years and has been an influential factor in the interests of harmony in many party councils. He has filled several offices of civic responsibility, serving as city treasurer for some time, also as a very useful member of the school board and additionally has served on the Carnegie Library Board.

HON. F. M. BENEFIEL. The State of Kansas can justly lay claim to many advantages, among these being a general citizenship that is enlightened and discriminating. It knows well how to choose its representative men, those to whom it entrusts its public responsibilities. Occasionally a mistake may be made but when public favor is shown to the same individual year after year and under many changing political conditions, it is made plain that merit and not mere popularity is at the root of such action. Among the favorite sons of Montgomery County is F. M. Benefiel, at present city collector in the water and light departments, Coffeyville, whose interests in the business affairs of his community have been extensive, and whose public activities have been of such importance as to materially affect and bring about beneficent legislation.

Among the early settlers in the State of New York were the Benefiels. They were of Scotch extraction, seven brothers of the name coming from Scotland to the American colonies in 1754. In this as in many other families, useful data, early records were not preserved but, as the name is found in the annals of many states, the family presumably was a prolific one and undoubtedly possessed its national characteristics of perseverance and thrift.

F. M. Benefiel was born in Hendricks County, Indiana, February 24, 1862. He is a son of James R. and Sarah (Page) Benefiel, the former of whom was born in Putnam County, in 1825, and died in Hamilton County, Nebraska, in 1900. The latter was born in Hendricks County, Indiana, in 1826, and died there in 1867. Of their family of ten children F. M. was ninth in order of birth, the others being: Martha, who became the wife of James George and shortly afterward they went to Washington Territory and both died on their farm; Mary, who is deceased, was the wife of John Shepard, a farmer; Isaac O., who is a merchant at Coffeyville; John C., who is in business at Coffeyville; Lina N., who is deceased, was the wife of a Mr. Carty; Peter, who was a farmer, died in Oklahoma; Eliza, who died at the age of eighteen years; Asbury, who died in infancy; and Luella, who is the wife of Edward Burquin, a farmer near Bartlett, Kansas. The father of the above family was reared in Putnam County, Indiana, removing prior to marriage to Hendricks County and engaging there in farming until 1884 when he settled in Nebraska. In his political views he was a republican, scrupulously attending to every responsibility of citizenship but never accepting any public office. He was an active member of the Methodist Episcopal Church.

F. M. Benefiel secured his education in Indiana, completing the public school course and then entering the Central Indiana Normal School then at Ladoga but since removed to Danville, and from that institution was graduated in the class of 1883. After teaching one term of school there he went with his people to Nebraska and taught school for four years in Clay County. Although Mr. Benefiel returned then to Indiana he remained but a short time in his native state and in the fall of 1889 came to Coffeyville, Kansas. Here he embarked in a retail and wholesale meat business and for some fifteen years was extensively interested in the buying and shipping of cattle.

Although Mr. Benefiel so directed his business affairs that prosperity attended his efforts, it is not because of this evidence of good judgment that he is numbered with the representative men of this section. He was reared to believe in the principles of the republican party and after coming to Kansas entered more actively and heartily into politics than formerly. In 1892 he was first elected to the State Legislature and continued a member of that august body, through re-election, during the sessions of 1893-1895 and 1899, taking part in the making and passing of some of the wisest and most urgent laws of that period. It was in 1893 that he secured the passage of the educational bill, he being chairman of the committee on education. It is recalled that a stormy controversy arose between the republicans and populists during this session, legislation being carried on for four days behind barricaded doors, the trouble lasting for six weeks when the republicans gained their point through a decision by the Supreme Court. Mr. Benefiel was joint author, with President Taylor of the Emporia Normal School and President Quail, of Baker University, of the bill to regulate colleges by putting them on the same plane as the state university, which bill became a law. In 1899 he was the author of the anti-bucket shop bill, prohibiting gambling in stocks and futures, and in that year he was speaker of the House, pro tem. In 1896 he was on the state ticket, which met defeat as a ticket, for presidential elector. His whole career in the Legislature was marked with earnest public spirit, honesty of purpose and personal efficiency.

Mr. Benefiel was married in 1883, at Crawfordsville, Indiana, to Miss Lula Hillis, who is a daughter of Samuel H. and Alma Hillis, both now deceased. Mr. Hillis was a carpenter contractor. Mr. and Mrs. Benefiel have a family of six children: Elsie, who is the wife of William Wilkins, a painter and decorator at Coffeyville; Samuel R., who is city salesman at Kansas City, Missouri, for the Cudahy Packing Company; James H., who resides with his parents, is an instructor in the high school at Aetna, Kansas; Lelan, who lives at home, is employed with the Carey Commission Company; Alice, who is a graduate of the Coffeyville High School in the class of 1916; and Frances, who attends the public school in this city. Mr. Benefiel owns city real estate of value among which is included the family residence at No. 5 East Third Street.

Since 1899 Mr. Benefiel has been president of the board of education, and during 1915 was president of the Coffeyville Chamber of Commerce. In 1911 he was appointed collector in the city's water and light department and has offices in the city hall. In fraternal life he is particularly interested in the Masons, belonging to Keystone Lodge No. 102, Free and Accepted Masons, and the Knights of Pythias, being a member of Verdegris Lodge No. 89, locally.

He is serving as chancellor commander and for many years has been a member of the grand lodge and has recently been re-appointed chairman of the state committee.

GEORGE L. BANKS. A sterling pioneer and citizen who is now living virtually retired in the City of Independence, Mr. Banks is specially entitled to recognition in this history. He was one of the early settlers of Montgomery County and has contributed his full quota to its civic and industrial development and progress, and he was long one of the prominent and influential exponents of agricultural industry in this section of the state. High honors also are his for the valiant service which he gave as a soldier of the Union in the Civil war.

Mr. Banks was born in Lake County, Indiana, October 13, 1839. His father, Orin Banks, was born in the State of New York, in 1800, and was there reared to manhood, his marriage having been solemnized in Schoharie County, that state. His entire active career was one of close association with the basic industry of agriculture and he was one of the pioneer farmers of LaPorte County, Indiana, where he established his home in 1845. In about 1850 he removed to Lake County, Indiana, where he died in 1856. He was a supporter of the democratic party until the organization of the republican party, when he transferred his allegiance to the latter. He was influential in community affairs and was called upon to serve in various township offices. Both he and his wife were devout members of the Baptist Church, in which he served as a deacon. Mrs. Banks, whose maiden name was Olive Brown, was born in Schoharie County, New York, in 1803, and thus she was eighty-three years old at the time of her death, in 1891, she having been at the time one of the most venerable pioneer women of Lake County, Indiana. Of the children the eldest was Betsey, who became the wife of Major Atkins, and who died in Lake County, Indiana, in 1866, her husband having long survived her and having been a farmer and capitalist of influence. Charles W., a lawyer by profession, died in 1907, in Chambers County, Texas. Morgan, a farmer and merchant, died in McPherson County, Kansas, in 1890. Elisha, who likewise became a representative farmer in McPherson County, died in 1906. Parley A. is a retired farmer and resides at Crown Point, Lake County, Indiana. Mary C. first married Balsar Keith, a farmer, near Union Mills, Indiana, and after his death she became the wife of Simon White, likewise a prosperous farmer of LaPorte County, Indiana. He likewise is deceased and his widow now resides at LaPorte, that county. William A., who died at LaPorte, Indiana, in 1903, had served six years as postmaster of that city and had been a leading importer of live stock in that section of the Hoosier state. George L., of this review, was the next in order of birth. The next two children were sons, both of whom died in infancy. Nathaniel P. is president of a bank at Hobart, Lake County, Indiana. Sarah Lavina is the wife of W. B. Adams, and they reside at Dearing, Montgomery County, Kansas, where Mr. Adams is vice president of a banking institution.

George L. Banks acquired his early education in the common schools of Lake and LaPorte counties, Indiana, and he continued to be associated with his father's farming operations until he had attained to the age of seventeen years. In the autumn of the year in which he reached this age he went to Min-

nesota and found employment in a pioneer sawmill at St. Anthony, the nucleus of the present great City of Minneapolis. The next year, 1857, found him employed in the lumber woods in the wilds of Northern Michigan, and he then returned to the old homestead farm. In Lake County, Indiana, he did a large amount of contract work in the digging of drainage ditches and for one year there he clerked in a grocery store, and afterward was a clerk in a dry-goods store. He finally resumed farming in his native county and was thus engaged at the outbreak of the Civil war. On the 6th of June, 1861, in response to President Lincoln's first call for volunteers, Mr. Banks enlisted as a private in Company C, Fifteenth Indiana Volunteer Infantry, with which gallant command he proceeded to West Virginia and took part in the engagements at Greenbriar and Elkwater. Later he was a participant in the memorable battles of Shiloh, Perryville, Murfreesboro, Chickamauga and Chattanooga. In the battle of Chattanooga he was thrice wounded but his injuries were not serious and he was incapacitated for a few weeks only. Mr. Banks was color sergeant of his regiment in the storming of Missionary Ridge, and most gallantly did he acquit himself on this historic field. The colors were shot down six times, and Mr. Banks himself was wounded on the first and last of these occasions. He was first shot in the ribs, and after regaining consciousness he was again wounded,—this time through the top of the head. His severe injuries incapacitated him from November, 1863, until January 14, 1864, and on the 25th of June of the latter year he was mustered out. Mr. Banks received and greatly prizes the Congressional medal of honor that was presented to him and that bears date of November 25, 1863, and he also has a letter from Hon. Russell A. Alger, at the time the latter was serving as Secretary of War, many years later, congratulating him on his admirable service during the ever memorable battle of Missionary Ridge. Mr. Banks, as color bearer for his regiment, was the first regimental color sergeant to plant the colors on the enemy's works at Missionary Ridge out of a brigade of six regiments, and for this gallant deed he received a medal of honor from Washington, District of Columbia.

After the close of the war Mr. Banks returned to his native county, where he followed farming until the spring of 1871, when he came to Kansas and numbered himself among the pioneers of Montgomery County. He settled in Fawn Creek Township, where he took up a pre-emption claim of 160 acres, and there he continued his farming operations for sixteen years. He developed and improved one of the fine farms of the county and was specially influential in township and community affairs. To his efforts was due the defining of the school district and the erection of the first schoolhouse of District No. 91, and this pioneer school was named in his honor. He had the supervision of the erection of the school building and was a member of the school board until he left his farm, in the autumn of 1886, when he returned to Indiana and became the proprietor of a hotel at Angola. In the following spring he exchanged his hotel property for a farm in Hillsdale County, Michigan, where he remained six years. He then sold his Michigan farm, or exchanged the same for property in Montgomery County, Kansas, where he again was actively engaged in agricultural pursuits for the ensuing two years. He thereafter passed two years at Independence, the county seat, but in 1896 he returned to his farm, upon which he continued to reside until

1903, when he resumed his residence at Independence. Here he has been engaged in the real estate and loan business and in the supervision of his various properties, so that he is not yet fully retired from active business, idleness and apathy being entirely foreign to his nature. He is the owner of valuable residential property in Independence, including his own attractive home, at 417 North Fifth Street, and near Bolton, this county, he owns 240 acres of valuable farm land, besides having another farm, of 160 acres, south of Dearing, this county, and 300 acres in Chambers County, Texas. On the farm near Bolton Mr. Banks effected the drilling of the first large oil well in Montgomery County, in 1903, and the same is still producing extensively.

Mr. Banks has not only achieved large and worthy success in connection with the practical affairs of life but he has also been most loyal and influential in public affairs in Southeastern Kansas. He served two terms as a representative of Montgomery County in the Kansas Legislature, 1905-7, and made a characteristically excellent record in furthering the interests of his constituent district and of wise legislation in general. He is a progressive republican and is well fortified in his convictions concerning governmental policies. While a resident of Fawn Creek Township he served six years as justice of the peace and later held the office of township trustee, his retirement from the office of justice of the peace having occurred in 1882. He has long been a zealous member of the Presbyterian Church, and is affiliated with the Grand Army of the Republic, the Independent Order of Odd Fellows, and the Anti-Horse Thief Society. Mr. Banks is one of the most appreciative and valued members of McPherson Post No. 4, Grand Army of the Republic, at Independence, and has not only served several terms as commander of the same but also as junior vice commander of the Department of the Grand Army for Kansas. It is worthy of special record that on the occasion of the fiftieth anniversary of his being mustered in for service in the Civil war his surviving regimental comrades presented him with a beautiful silk flag of the United States, this being a tribute that he deeply appreciated. Mr. Banks is one of the representative men of Montgomery County, has inviolable place in popular esteem and is one of the substantial citizens of Independence, and he is a director and the secretary of the Jefferson State Bank, at Jefferson, this county.

On the 8th of October, 1864, was solemnized the marriage of Mr. Banks to Miss Olive W. Chandler, and she was summoned to the life eternal nearly forty years later, while their home was on the farm near Bolton, Montgomery County. She was a gracious and gentle woman who was loved by those who came within the compass of her influence, and she died in the year 1902. Of the children of this union the eldest is William N., who is a representative member of the bar of Montgomery County, and is engaged in the practice of his profession at Independence; Charles B. is engaged in the real estate business at Caldwell, Idaho; and Arthur A. is at Denver, Colorado.

In 1904 Mr. Banks contracted a second marriage, when Mrs. Helen J. (Clarkson) Shoemaker, widow of Philo Shoemaker, became his wife. They reside in an attractive home at Independence, in which city she had resided prior to her marriage to Mr. Banks. No children have been born of the second marriage.

R. W. CATES is a director and assistant cashier in the First National Bank of Independence. By profession he is a lawyer and practiced for a number of years with his father, Joseph B. F. Cates, who is one of the oldest members of the legal profession in Kansas.

Joseph B. F. Cates, who is now general attorney for the Prairie Pipe Line Company, with residence at Independence, was born in Grainger County, Tennessee, April 19, 1840. His parents were Charles and Elizabeth (Lloyd) Cates. Charles Cates was a native of North Carolina, where he was reared and educated, and his English ancestors had settled in the Carolinas when they were English colonies. Charles Cates was a farmer, and from his native state emigrated to Tennessee and became a pioneer settler. His wife, Elizabeth Lloyd, was also a native of North Carolina, and of Welsh ancestry.

The only survivor in a family of three sons and three daughters, all of whom reached maturity, and the youngest of the family, Joseph B. F. Cates, gained his high rank in the profession as a result of many years of constant application and the overcoming of difficulties when he was young. His boyhood was spent in Tennessee, where he attended the common schools, his schooling being mingled with the performance of duties on the home farm. In 1860 he graduated from an old institution of higher training in Eastern Tennessee, Newman College, in Jefferson County. His classical diploma was hardly in his possession when he set out for the West. Before the Civil war broke out he helped survey some of the lands of Nebraska territory, and then took up the study of law at Platte City, Missouri. He was admitted to the bar there in 1867 and soon afterwards moved to Humboldt, Kansas, where he did his first work in the profession as a pioneer lawyer, nearly half a century ago. During his ten years' residence at Humboldt he built up a living practice, but left there in 1877 and opened an office in Kansas City, Missouri. With the exception of a few years spent in Florida he lived at Kansas City until 1892. Returning to Kansas, he located at Chanute, and enjoyed a large practice commensurate with his abilities in that city until 1907. Since then his home has been in Independence.

Since 1900 his time and services have been devoted first to the Prairie Oil & Gas Company as general attorney, and since its organization to the Prairie Pipe Line Company. His has been a successful legal career, and he has had an especially wide range of experience in professional work. He is a scholarly lawyer, a man of broad and generous character and for years has associated with many of the prominent men of Kansas and other states. He is a member of the Episcopal Church and fraternally is affiliated with Fortitude Lodge No. 107, Ancient Free and Accepted Masons, Keystone Chapter No. 22, Royal Arch Masons, St. Bernard Commandery No. 10, Knights Templar, all of Independence, and Mirzah Temple of the Nobles of the Mystic Shrine at Pittsburg, Kansas. He has never sought any honors beyond those connected with his profession.

In 1869 Joseph B. F. Cates married Nettie Wilhoite, daughter of J. H. Wilhoite, of Platte County, Missouri. To their marriage were born five children: Charles Henry received his education in the Virginia Military Institute in Lexington and is now a traveling salesman for a New York house. Lloyd R., who died at Independence July 6, 1913, and for several years previously been egaged in farming in Oklahoma. Philip F. is a graduate of the Kansas City Dental College and is now practicing at Cedarvale, Kansas. The fourth among the children is Mr. R.

W. Cates. Ada E. graduated from the University of Kansas in 1906, afterwards specialized by two years of work in the Platte Institute in Brooklyn, New York, and is now a teacher in the public schools of Independence.

R. W. Cates was born at Humboldt, Kansas, in August, 1876, a short time before his father moved to Kansas City to practice. Most of his education was acquired in the public schools of Fredonia and Chanute, Kansas, and he attended the high schools of both places, being graduated from the Chanute High School with the class of 1894. For another year he attended the Kansas State Normal School at Emporia, and later began his preparations for the law, graduating LL. B. in 1900 from the University of Kansas Law Department. In the same year he went East and did post-graduate work in the New York Law School, from which he received the degree LL. M. in 1902. He continued in New York City for a year acquiring additional experience in the profession, and thus well equipped took up active practice at Chanute with his father in 1903. He has been a resident of Independence since 1907, and in 1908 he took his present post as assistant cashier of the First National Bank. While at Chanute he served as city attorney.

Mr. Cates is a democrat, is affiliated with Fortitude Lodge No. 107, Ancient Free and Accepted Masons, Keystone Chapter No. 22, Royal Arch Masons, and is past commander of St. Bernard's Commandery No. 10, Knights Templar. He is also a member of Lodge No. 780, Benevolent and Protective Order of Elks at Independence, belongs to the Country Club, and is a director in the Commercial Club.

In October, 1904, at Independence Mr. Cates married Miss Edith Allen. Her father, the late E. P. Allen, was one of the most prominent citizens of Montgomery County, and his career is sketched on other pages of this publication. Mr. and Mrs. Cates have two children: Catherine, born September 3, 1906, and Allen, born May 23, 1908.

JOHN MILTON CUNNINGHAM. Of the men who have long lent dignity and progressiveness to the business of ranching and farming in Osage County none are held in higher esteem than is John Milton Cunningham, who is now a resident of Caney and one of that city's leading and influential citizens. During a long and successful career he has been identified prominently with financial matters in several parts of the country, but has always returned to agriculture as a vocation, and in this calling has found his greatest measure of prosperity.

Mr. Cunningham was born in the City of Louisville, Kentucky, November 10, 1857, and is a son of Robert Morrison and Annie Elizabeth (Milton) Cunningham. His father was born in Green County, Alabama, March 13, 1829, and as a lad was taken to Louisville, Kentucky, in the schools of which city he was given a good education. His parents were Joseph Parks and Iliza beth F. (Webb) Cunningham, and he was brought up to habits of industry and honesty. Early becoming interested in financial affairs, he was connected with banking all of his life, and at the time of his death, November 25, 1878, was cashier of the First National Bank of Louisville, of which he had been the organizer. Mr. Cunningham was a deacon in the Presbyterian Church and one of his city's substantial and highly respected citizens. He was married at Louisville, November 7, 1854, to Annie Elizabeth Mil-

ton, who was born at Lexington, Kentucky, January 15, 1832, and died at Louisville, February 22, 1896, and they became the parents of the following children: Bettie Scott, born December 27, 1855, who passed her life at Louisville and died September 18, 1890; John Milton, of this notice; Robert Morrison, born September 11, 1859, a wholesale lumber merchant of Louisville, married October 19, 1886, Frances Marmaduke Barnett, who was born in Jefferson County, Kentucky, July 5, 1862, daughter of Judge Andrew Barnett.

On his mother's side of the family, Mr. Cunningham is descended from one of the oldest families in America, and one which originated in England. A Richard Milton is mentioned in land grants recorded in the State Land Office of Virginia, for the years 1636 and 1638, given to him at Westover, in Charles County, on the James River, and it is possible and even probable that this early settler was the grandfather of Richard Milton, the great-great-great-grandfather of Mr. Cunningham. This latter Richard Milton and his wife, Eliza, were living in Richmond County, Virginia, about the year 1720. On August 10, 1725, a tract of 454 acres in "Stafford county on Buck Hall ranch of Occaquan," was granted to "Richard Melton of Richmond County." This part of Stafford County soon afterward became Prince William County, and Richard Milton's death occurred here about the year 1733.

Richard Milton, son of Richard and Eliza Milton, was born about 1715. He inherited from his father a tract of land "adjoining Couper's Cabin Branch" in Prince William County, Virginia, where he lived and reared a family of nine children. His wife, whose name is mentioned in deeds along with his, was Margaret Ross, and it is said that she came of a Scotch family of that name in Pennsylvania. Her grandchildren remembered her as being tall, spare and very neat in dress and appearance. She lived to be about ninety-five years of age, and when a very old lady was still able to ride on horseback to the home of her son, Elijah, making the distance of forty miles in one day. She was born about 1716 and died in 1811. Shortly after the Revolutionary war, Richard Milton removed to Kentucky with his wife, his son, Moses, and his married daughters, and settled on the Chaplin Fork of Salt River, in Nelson County. There he died about the year 1800.

Elijah Milton, son of Richard and Margaret (Ross) Milton, and great-grandfather of Mr. Cunningham, was born in Prince William County, Virginia, December 23, 1755, and died in Fayette County, Kentucky, November 10, 1833. He was married at Green Hill, Frederick County, Virginia, January 28, 1794, to Catherine Taylor, who was born at Green Hill, June 9, 1776. She died in Fayette County, Kentucky, July 29, 1828. Elijah Milton is said to have served as master of army wagons during the Revolutionary war, being closely associated with General Rochambeau during the latter part of the struggle for American independence. When he removed to Kentucky, about 1700, he took up lands on Elk Horn Creek, in Fayette County, about eight miles west of Lexington, and there passed the remainder of his life as a farmer.

John Milton, son of Elijah and Catherine (Taylor) Milton, and maternal grandfather of Mr. Cunningham, was born in Fayette County, Kentucky, March 24, 1802, and died at Baltimore, Maryland, November 18, 1860. He was married in Frederick County, Virginia, September 7, 1826, to Louisa Ann Taylor, his first cousin, who was born in Loudoun County, Virginia, September 5, 1807, and died at Louisville, Kentucky,

April 6, 1869. Mr. Milton was cashier of the Northern Bank of Kentucky, and an elder in the Presbyterian Church.

John Milton Cunningham received his education in the public schools of Louisville and a college at Danville, Kentucky, and in 1875 received his initiation in the banking business as a clerk in the First National Bank of his native city, with which he remained four years. He then accepted a clerkship in the offices of the Louisville & Nashville Railroad and continued with that road until November 1, 1884, when he came to Independence, Kansas, and for two years was bookkeeper for the First National Bank of that city. For the four years that followed Mr. Cunningham lived on his ranch in Osage County, during which time he and Mrs. Cunningham controlled some 12,000 acres of rich farming country. Returning to financial matters, he came to Caney, where he assisted in the organization of the Home National Bank, of which he was made assistant cashier, and, becoming cashier shortly thereafter, remained in that capacity for about two years. At that time Mr. Cunningham went to San Angelo, Texas, where he was at the head of a private banking house for one year, and then came back to Caney, which has since been his home.

Mr. Cunningham is the owner of a handsome modern residence at the corner of Third Avenue and High Street. While he has a number of important business connections, he devotes his time chiefly to the management of his ranch, which consists of 500 acres of farming land and 1,200 acres of pasture in Osage County, just across the Montgomery County line from Caney. He is a republican in his political views, and has served as treasurer of the Caney School Board. Fraternally he is a member of Camp No. 941, Modern Woodmen of America, and both he and Mrs. Cunningham are prominent and popular in social circles of Caney.

While a resident of Independence, Kansas, February 18, 1886, Mr. Cunningham was married to Miss Rose Irene Brown, who was born at Carey, Ohio, August 22, 1865. To this union there have been born four children, as follows: William Brown, born at Independence, December 21, 1886, who died at Caney, June 13, 1887; John Milton, born at Independence, August 19, 1888, who married May 6, 1914, Miss Lillian Miller, of Kansas City, Missouri; Robert Brown, born April 6, 1899, at Caney; and Robert Morris, born at Caney, November 3, 1900, who died January 13, 1901.

PROF. ROBERT ALLYN REED. It is not given to every individual to find a business career that is entirely congenial. The musical genius too frequently finds that circumstances produce for him an environment in the necessary pursuits of every day life that is not satisfying and that bars him from progress and happiness. Happily, however, this has not been the experience of Prof. Robert Allyn Reed, of Coffeyville, who has achieved great success through a broad and comprehensive training and the possession of exceptional inherent talent, and who, as proprietor of the New York School of Music, occupies a very important place in musical circles of Kansas.

Professor Reed was born February 14, 1871, at Troy, Madison County, Illinois, and was named for Dr. Robert Allyn, who was dean at that time of the Illinois State Normal School. On the paternal side he is of Scotch ancestry, and on the maternal of German descent, the Reeds being of an old Maine family. Professor Reed's branch is of colonial origin and dovetails with the ancestry of Speaker Thomas Brackett Reed. Andrew D. Reed, the father

of Professor Reed, was born in 1832, in Maine, and as a young man removed to Illinois, where he was married. He became a teacher of mathematics and law in the State Normal School at Lebanon, Illinois, but too close devotion to the duties of the schoolroom, and the attendant confinement of such a position, caused his health to break down and he was advised to seek a different climate. Accordingly, in 1872, he removed to Appleton City, Missouri, where he established the first dry goods and clothing store, and continued as a successful man of business there until his death, in 1881. A man of intelligence and broad knowledge of important subjects, he rose to be a foremost citizen of his community, and served on the school board and as a member of the city council. His political belief made him a republican and his religious connection was with the Methodist Episcopal Church, in the work of which he was always active. Fraternally he was a Mason. Mr. Reed married Miss Susan E. Hegler, who was born in Kentucky, in 1838, and who still survives and makes her home at Jefferson City, Missouri. To this union there were born five children: Prof. Robert Allyn; Carrie, the wife of W. P. Morris, yardmaster at the State Penitentiary at Jefferson City, Missouri, in line for promotion to warden; W. D., who is a contractor of Kansas City, Missouri; Edward, who is engaged in the jewelry business at San Francisco, California; and Alva W., who for a number of years was a machinist in the employ of the Pullman Car Company, at Pullman, Illinois, prior to his death at Jefferson City, Missouri, in 1914.

Robert Allyn Reed received his early education in the public schools of Appleton City, Missouri, where he was graduated from the high school with the class of 1889. Later he attended the high school at Springfield, Illinois, for a time, but gave up his literary education to begin the study of music. His first preceptor was Prof. George F. Root, of Chicago, under whom he studied vocal music, and subsequently he was with Professor Friemal, also of Chicago, under whose teachings he mastered various instruments. After much further preparation under other noted teachers of Yonkers, New York, and New York City, he entered upon a very interesting period of his career, being for eight years on the road in operatic work.

In 1905 Professor Reed came to Coffeyville to settle permanently, here establishing the New York School of Music, which has grown and developed into one of the largest and most prominent institutions of its kind in the state. Assisted by his wife and a corps of talented and thoroughly competent teachers, Professor Reed teaches music in all its branches, vocal and instrumental, and many of his pupils have gone forth into the world to achieve fame and success. At this time a band of forty-six pieces is under Professor Reed's direction, as well as five different orchestras, and pupils come to the institution from a radius of forty miles, including such points as Nowata, Oklahoma, Claremore, Jefferson, Caney and Cherryvale, Kansas, and from other cities in Kansas. The school, perfect in its every appointment, and offering attractions and inducements to the students, is attractively located at No. 108 West Tenth Street.

Professor Reed owns a residence two miles west of Coffeyville, with six acres of orchards and shade trees, a beautiful country home. In politics he is a republican, but his only office has been that of music supervisor of the public schools, which he held in 1914. He is a member of the Methodist Episcopal

Church. Fraternally, he belongs to Keystone Lodge No. 102, Ancient Free and Accepted Masons, Coffeyville; Coffeyville Chapter, No. 89, Royal Arch Masons; Lochinvar Commandery No. 52, Knight Templars; Loyal Order of the Moose No. 1193, Coffeyville; and Coffeyville Camp of the Woodmen of the World. He is also a member of the Chamber of Commerce and an active worker in matters pertaining to the civic welfare.

Professor Reed was married October 12, 1905, at Appleton City, Missouri, to Miss Bessie G. Grider, daughter of H. C. and Bianca Grider, of Appleton City, where Mr. Grider is a grain merchant and capitalist. Two children have been born to Professor and Mrs. Reed: Robert Grider, born August 13, 1907, a bright and interesting lad who is making rapid progress in his studies, as shown by the fact that he is already in the fifth grade in the public schools; and Susan Bianca, born April 14, 1914.

ALVA C. STARR. For the past twelve years the grocery establishemnt of Alva C. Starr, at No. 710 North Broadway, has been considered in the light of a necessary commercial adjunct by the people of Pittsburg. Many causes contribute to the success of this popular merchant, not the least of which are a thorough knowledge of his business and a determination to keep his particular branch thereof up to the highest known standard. Mr. Starr belongs to that element of business men who have made their own way to success, without the aid of outside influences, and his high standing in trade and business circles evidences the well-directed manner in which his operations have been prosecuted.

Mr. Starr was born on a farm in Vermilion County, Illinois, January 14, 1871, and is a son of S. P. and Maria Jane (Partlow) Starr. The family is of German extraction, the original American emigrant locating in North Carolina during colonial times. Peter Starr, grandfather of Alva C., was born in the Old North State, but as a young man went to Vermilion County, Illinois, where · he was a pioneer farmer, and where his death occurred before the birth of his grandson. S. P. Starr was born in Vermilion County, Illinois, in 1831, and was there reared on his father's farm and educated in the primitive schools of the day and locality. He followed farming there, and also for a time engaged in mercantile pursuits, and in 1877 became a pioneer farmer of Montgomery County, where he owned a property in the vicinity of Cherryvale. This he cultivated with success until 1881, when he made removal to Crawford, locating near Pittsburg, where he continued his agricultural operations until several years before his death, when he retired from agricultural pursuits and took up his residence at Pittsburg. His death occurred in January, 1897. Mr. Starr was a republican, but not a politician, and a member of the Masonic fraternity. He belonged to the Methodist Episcopal Church, was active in the work thereof, held all the lay offices, and was for some years deacon. In Vermilion County, Illinois, Mr. Starr was married to Miss Maria Jane Partlow, who was born in that county in 1834, and died at Pittsburg, Kansas, July 25, 1916, and they became the parents of six children, as follows: John, who was connected with the Pittsburg Headlight and died at the age of forty-four years; Ella B., who is the wife of D. C. Wood, a foreman in the zinc smelters at Bartlesville, Oklahoma; P. H., who was a gas fitter of Pittsburg and died at the age of forty-four years; J. G., who is a banker of Joplin, Missouri; Alva C.; and Gracie M., who married Albert Stamm, a mer-

chant of Pittsburg, and lost her life with her husband by drowning in an accident near Pittsburg, Kansas, in 1904.

Alva C. Starr secured his education in the public schools of Cherryvale and Pittsburg, and at eighteen years of age left school to learn the plumbing trade. This he followed as a journeyman and carefully conserved his earnings until 1904, working at Weir City and Iola. In the year mentioned he returned to Pittsburg, where he accepted an opportunity offered and embarked in the grocery business at his present location. From modest beginnings his trade has grown and developed to large proportions, and he now has a complete and up-to-date stock of staple and fancy groceries, and occupies a two-story building, with floor space 90 by 24 feet. His establishment is made attractive through the strict observance of cleanliness and order, the courtesy of clerks, moderation of prices and good quality of products. Mr. Starr is well known to the trade, being past president of the Retailers Association and at present a member of the executive board of that body. He is also one of the live and active members of the Commercial Club.

Mr. Starr owns his own home, a new modern residence, at No. 501 West Fifth Street. He supports the republican party with his vote, and on its ticket has been elected a member of the school board for the past three years. He is well known fraternally, being a member of Pittsburg Lodge No. 187, Ancient Free and Accepted Masons; Pittsburg Chapter No. 58, Royal Arch Masons; Pittsburg Lodge No. 1554, Knights of Pythias; Pittsburg Lodge No. 56, Ancient Order of United Workmen; the Modern Woodmen of America; and Pittsburg Tent No. 70, Knights of the Maccabees, in all of which he is popular. In May, 1898, he enlisted in Company F, Twenty-second Kansas Regulars, for the Spanish-American war, and held the commission of second lieutenant.

Mr. Starr was married at Pittsburg, in 1898, to Miss Elizabeth Matson, daughter of Robert and Anna (Robinson) Matson, residents of Pittsburg, where Mr. Matson is interested in mercantile affairs. Three children have been born to Mr. and Mrs. Starr: Grace Marjorie, who is a member of the senior class at the Pittsburg High School; and Jessie and Alva C., Jr., who are attending the graded schools.

THE PRAIRIE OIL AND GAS COMPANY. As one of the largest corporations in Kansas, everyone has more or less knowledge of the Prairie Oil and Gas Company, and repeated reference is made to its activities in these pages. However, some items that might not otherwise be. mentioned should be brought together in a paragraph or two.

The company was incorporated and established in December, 1900, with headquarters at Neodesha, Kansas. Since 1905 the home of this corporation has been at Independence, and the people of Independence take great pride in the fact that this corporation has its home in their city. In July, 1916, was completed the Prairie Oil and Gas Building, one of the finest office buildings in the State of Kansas. This is situated on West Myrtle Street between Ninth and Tenth streets.

The present officers of the company are: J. F. O'Neil, president; W. S. Fitzpatrick, vice president; Nelson K. Moody, vice president; J. A. Hollahan, secretary; and A. T. Patterson, treasurer.

All the organization and equipment of the Prairie Oil and Gas Company are for the purpose of producing and marketing crude oil. Its operations cover the fields in Kansas and Oklahoma excepting the Healdton oil fields. The company operates no refineries, and its essential business is to deliver the crude oil to these refineries.

When it was incorporated in 1900 the company had a capital of $3,000,000. Its present capital is $18,000,000.

The company developed a system of pipe lines from the Mid-Continent fields to a point near Chicago in the State of Indiana, capable of transporting its products for a distance of more than a 1,000 miles. The capacity of that pipe line is approximately 65,000 barrels a day, with a branch line to Sugar Creek with capacity of from 18,000 to 20,000 barrels per day, and another branch line to Wood River near Alton, Illinois, of 30,000 barrels a day. These lines were owned and operated by the Prairie Oil and Gas Company for the transportation of its own oil until August, 1914. At that time by law the pipe lines became common carriers, but were continued under the operation of the Prairie Oil and Gas Company until February 1, 1915. At that date there was organized a corporation under the laws of Kansas, with home offices at Independence, and with capital of $27,000,000, The Prairie Pipe Line Company. The Prairie Oil and Gas Company then sold all its pipe lines and transportation facilities and franchises to the new corporation. The officers of the Pipe Line Company are: W. F. Gates, president; C. H. Kountz, vice president; F. M. Wilhelm, secretary; and B. G. Harris, treasurer. This company has leased offices in the west wing of the new Prairie Oil and Gas Building.

FRED C. CHILDS, now superintendent of the Cudahy Refining Company at Coffeyville, is an oil refiner of almost world wide experience. He has been connected with that industry since youth, and has spent a number of years in the Kansas field.

He was born in Philadelphia, Pennsylvania, October 10, 1867, a son of Caleb O. and Sarah A. (Langdon) Childs. His Childs ancestors came from England to Rhode Island in colonial times. His great-grandfather John Cole Childs was a Revolutionary soldier and an extensive land owner in Rhode Island. His grandfather, Thomas Cole Childs, was born in Rhode Island in 1784, served as sheriff of his county and subsequently moved to Warren County, Pennsylvania, where he was a farmer and mill owner. Caleb O. Childs was born in Rhode Island in 1806, was married at Jamestown, New York, and for a time was engaged in the lumber business in Warren County, Pennsylvania. He was one of the pioneers in the production of oil in the Titusville, Pennsylvania, fields, going there in 1861. He was associated with some of the very prominent men in the early oil industry, and in 1867 moved to Philadelphia. A few years before his death he retired and died at Bradford, Pennsylvania, in 1882. His wife was born at Addington, New Jersey, in 1811 and died in Bradford, Pennsylvania, in 1877. Their children were Calphurnia, who died in Warren, Pennsylvania, the wife of H. W. Childs, who is a retired oil producer; Milo H., who died at the age of three years; Robert H., superintendent of the Petroleum Products Company at Independence; and Fred C.

Fred C. Childs received a public school education at Titusville, Pennsylvania, and in 1885 graduated from the high school at Corey in that state. Since then for a period of over thirty years he has been closely identified with the refining industry, being employed in Northwestern Pennsylvania until 1901. In that year on account of his experience and capability, he was selected to go to Japan and construct a refinery for a Japanese company. He remained in the Kingdom of Nippon for two years. Returning to America he spent the next three years at Parkersburg, West Virginia, and since 1906 has been a Kansan. For several years he had charge of the refinery at Niotaze in Chautauqua County, and since 1908 has been a resident of Coffeyville and is superintendent of the Cudahy Refinery, which is located in the northwestern part of the city.

Mr. Childs has his home just northeast of the city limits. He is a republican and a member of the Lutheran Church, and is an active fraternal man, being affiliated with Keystone Lodge No. 102, Ancient Free and Accepted Masons at Coffeyville, and with Fort Scott Consistory of the Scottish Rite. He also belongs to the Knights of the Maccabees at Warren, Pennsylvania, and to Lodge No. 775, Benevolent and Protective Order of Elks at Coffeyville.

In 1890 at Mayville, New York, Mr. Childs married Miss Nellie Lattimore. Her father, Rev. A. Lattimore, now deceased, was a minister of the Lutheran Church.

JAMES F. BLACKLEDGE. Protective laws are passed in every state that seemingly assure the safety of all money that may be deposited either by the laborer or the capitalist in a bank, and still permit enough latitude in the bank's policy to make the business profitable. On the president of the concern rests the responsibility and thus, at the head of financial institutions of solidity are usually placed men of business experience and known integrity, of sterling character and conservative habit. It reflects credit on Coffeyville, Kansas, that just such a man is president of the Caney Valley National Bank, James F. Blackledge.

James F. Blackledge was born October 29, 1869, at Rockville, Parke County, Indiana, and is a son of William and Phebe (Johns) Blackledge. William Blackledge was born in 1829 in Columbiana County, Ohio, and died in 1913 at Caney, Kansas. He grew up in Columbiana County and worked as a builder and contractor, removing to Rockville, Indiana, prior to the opening of the Civil war. In 1861 he enlisted for service in the same, in an infantry regiment, and continued his soldierly duties until the close of the war when he returned to Indiana. He had survived the many dangers to which he had been exposed but he found business conditions disturbed in his old home and in 1876 removed to Peoria, Illinois. In 1878 he came to Kansas and located at Oswego, subsequently, as his business demanded, living at different places, going to Salina then back to Oswego, then to Carthage, Missouri and to Kansas City, in 1896 settling permanently at Caney, Kansas. In politics he was a republican. He belonged to the Masons and was a member of the Rockville Lodge. He and wife were members of the Presbyterian Church and brought their six children up honest and industrious and gave them every advantage their means would allow.

William Blackledge was married to Phebe Johns, who was born in 1832 in Columbiana County, Ohio, and died at Caney, Kansas, in 1909. The following children were born to them: Nettie, who is the wife of G. Torbert, a retired farmer and vice president of a bank at Altamont, Kansas; Seward, who owns a farm near Chetopa, Kansas, for the past five years has been building mills in Old Mexico; Elmer E., who travels over the country as his trade of millwright demands; Mary E., who is the wife of J. F.

Johnson, a schoolteacher at Altamont, Kansas; Sallie F., who is the wife of A. L. Utterback, who terminated two terms as postmaster of Caney in 1916, is an employe as metal weigher for the American Zinc, Lead and Smelting Company; and James F.

James F. Blackledge attended the public schools of Oswego, Kansas, and then took a commercial course in a business college at Salina. From 1888 until 1893 he was a United States railway official between Fort Scott and Webb City. On May 10, 1893, he came to Caney, Kansas, and became bookkeeper for the Caney Valley Bank. Two months later he was made cashier of the institution and in 1914 he was chosen its president.

The Caney Valley National Bank was established as a state bank in 1886, with a capital of $10,000. Its founders were: Thomas G. Ayres, Joseph Savage, George Slosson and P. S. Hollingsworth, all Coffeyville capitalists. The bank became nationalized in 1900 and its present officers are: James F. Blackledge, president; Charles Owen, vice president; H. V. Balcom, cashier, and R. L. De Hon assistant cashier.

The bank is in a very prosperous condition, with a capital and surplus of $70,000, all made out of the original capital. The bank building is situated on the corner of Fourth and State streets and the bank owns the entire business block which includes the postoffice.

At Independence, Kansas, February 19, 1891, Mr. Blackledge was united in marriage with Miss Martha H. Allen, daughter of the late E. P. Allen of that place. Mr. and Mrs. Blackledge have had four children: Ralph P., who died at the age of thirteen years; Pauline B., who is the wife of Dr. B. E. Fellis, of Chicago; Gwynn E., who is agent for the Studebaker Automobile Company, at Caney, Kansas; and Mercedes, who is bookkeeper for the Caney Valley National Bank. The elder daughter of Mr. Blackledge, Mrs. Fellis, is a graduate of the Columbia School, Chicago, and for two years was with the Redpath Circuit.

In politics Mr. Blackledge has always been a stanch republican, never wavering in his allegiance to party. On numerous occasions he has been called on to serve in public office and capacities and his whole course in reference to every duty has been honorable and efficient. He is treasurer of the board of education of Coffeyville, has served on the city council and as treasurer and for five years was a member of the school board. He has long been identified with standard fraternities and belongs to Caney Lodge No. 324 Ancient Free and Accepted Masons; the Benevolent and Protective Order of Elks, No. 1215, and the Fraternal Order of Eagles, No. 1,000, both at Caney.

The Blackledges are of Welsh, Scotch and Irish extraction but they have been Americans for a very long period, having settled in Pennsylvania prior to the Revolutionary war and participating in it. Both Mr. Blackledge and wife are eligible to membership in the exclusive societies of Sons and Daughters of the American Revolution.

JONATHAN G. MILLER. Ever since the arrival in Crawford County of William Lewis Miller, in 1872, the members of the family bearing this name have been leading factors in the upbuilding of Mulberry and the surrounding community. They have developed its soil as agriculturists, have advanced its prestige as coal operators, have added impetus to its growth along commercial lines as merchants, have contributed to its financial strength as bankers, and to its character have given strength by a fine type of citizenship. One of the worthy representatives of the family of Jonathan Garrett Miller, banker, merchant, landowner, coal operator and public-spirited citizen, than whom no man is better known or more highly esteemed in business and banking circles of this part of the state.

Jonathan G. Miller was born at Mulberry, Crawford County, Kansas, March 18, 1875, and is a son of William Lewis and Mary D. (Sadler) Miller. The family is of German origin, but has been in America for a number of generations. The great-grandfather of Jonathan G. Miller was Jonathan Miller, whose career as a farmer and miller was passed in Greene County, Pennsylvania, where his house, built in 1820, and his barn, erected in 1800, still stand. His son, Asa Miller, was born in Pennsylvania, where he followed the same vocations as did his father, and died at Rosedale, in that state. William Lewis Miller was born October 1, 1839, in Greene County, Pennsylvania, and was there reared on a farm and learned the milling business. During the Civil war he was a captain of State Militia, but his company was never called upon for service. He was married in his native state, and in 1872 came to Kansas, settling at Mulberry when there were but seven or eight families in the little hamlet. Here he became the first merchant of a community which his foresight and judgment told him was to become a thriving commercial center. Subsequently he established a flour mill three miles from the town, the first in this section of the state, and still later interested himself in farming and stock raising. As his interests grew he extended his scope of activity, and soon became recognized as one of the real builders of the community, and his operations as a pioneer coal operator did much to develop the industry in this part of the county. In 1895 Mr. Miller founded what has since grown to be one of the leading concerns in the northern section of Crawford County, that of Miller Brothers & Company. This firm consisted of William Lewis Miller, his three sons, William Henry, Clarence Quinter and Jonathan Garrett Miller, and his daughter, Miss Ada L. Miller. This concern has developed more coal fields and found a market for more coal than any other firm in Kansas. Prior to his death, which occurred December 21, 1915, the father sold out his interests, and the personnel of the concern underwent another change when William Henry Miller disposed of his holdings, prior to his death in July, 1916. The family remained together for twenty years, and Miller Brothers & Company now consists of the two remaining brothers and their sister.

In 1907 the Miller brothers entered the banking field by the establishing of the Mulberry State Bank, which they sold in the fall of 1913. Subsequently, in February, 1914, they founded the Pittsburg State Bank, the officers of which are: C. Q. Miller, president; Dr. J. G. Sandidge, vice president, and J. G. Miller, cashier. This concern has a $50,000 capital and a surplus of $5,000. In February, 1916, the same stockholders took over at Mulberry the Miners State Bank, with a capital of $20,000, the officers being: president, Jonathan G. Miller; vice president, C. Q. Miller; and Dr. J. G. Sandidge, a stockholder.

William Lewis Miller, in 1900, established the first steam shovel to lift the overburden off the top, and was the first to introduce the shovel for stripping. He should also be given credit for the invention of the double shaker machine, which he introduced, but

which he failed to patent. The Town of Mulberry is built upon the first forty acres which he owned in Crawford County and on another eighty acres of the family property, but since the advent of the father here the family holdings have extended all over Crawford County and into Bourbon County, Kansas, and Barton and Vernon counties, Missouri. In politics William Lewis Miller was a democrat, and his religious membership was in the Baptist Church.

Mr. Miller married Mary D. Sadler, who was born in 1841, in Fayette County, Pennsylvania, and they became the parents of the following children: Ada L., who is unmarried and resides at Mulberry; Etta B., who died in 1903, as the wife of Charles Perry, a retired merchant and farmer of Mulberry; William Henry, a member of the firm of Miller Brothers & Company, who died in 1915; Clarence Q., one of the firm and a resident of Mulberry; Florence Q., twin of Clarence Q., and wife of Dr. J. G. Sandidge, a physician, surgeon and banker of Mulberry; and Jonathan Garrett, of this review.

Jonathan G. Miller was educated in the public schools of Mulberry and Fort Scott Normal College, which he attended one year. While still in school he evidenced his commercial ability, and as a student handled hogs and cattle very successfully. He continued in livestock and farming, and in his father's store, until the formation of the firm of Miller Brothers & Company, in 1915, when he became a member. In addition to the enterprises noted above, the concern has two department stores at Mulberry, being the leading merchants of the place, and deals extensively in coal lands, leasing a large amount of property. Mr. Miller is also secretary of the Mulberry Telephone Company, owns a number of farms in Crawford County, and is secretary of the Miller-Cherokee Coal Company, owned by the family and controlling about 1,500 acres of coal land.

Mr. Miller is a democrat and has been active in political affairs. In 1910 he was a candidate for the office of state auditor, and in 1916 was a delegate to the Democratic National Convention at St. Louis and was selected as a committee of one to notify the vice president of his nomination. While his business responsibilities are heavy, entailing an immense amount of thought and labor, Mr. Miller is not indifferent to social relations, and holds membership in the leading clubs and fraternities, in all of which he is popular. His reputation in business circles is one that stamps him as a worthy representative of the honored name he bears, and he is constantly finding something to do that will add to his city's prestige and thus perpetuate the family name in the annals of the municipality. Mr. Miller is unmarried and makes his home with his mother on Military Street, Mulberry.

JOSHUA A. STONE. One of the old time citizens of Montgomery County was the late Joshua A. Stone, who identified himself with Independence and that locality soon after the country was open to settlement, and who impressed his ability and energy upon many local business activities. He was especially prominent in the coal mining industry. Mr. Stone died at his home in Independence April 30, 1914. Mrs. Stone, who is executrix of his estate, has proved herself a very competent business manager, and is one of the highly esteemed women of Montgomery County.

Born in Centerville, Michigan, in March, 1846, Joshua A. Stone was sixty-eight years old at the time of his death. His father, George W. Stone, was born in Scotland in 1800. He came to this country a young man, and at Schenectady, New York, married Mary Jane Minders, who was a native of that city. From New York they went to Centerville, Michigan, and in 1849 he joined in the general exodus to the California gold fields. About 1870 he located in Kansas, homesteading a claim of 160 acres one mile north of Independence. He operated that as a farm for some years, but in 1886 retired to Cherryvale, where he died in 1889. He was a republican, and a very active and influential member in the Methodist Episcopal Church, which he served as a deacon. His wife died in California.

Joshua A. Stone was reared in Michigan, and was a vigorous young man when he came to Independence in 1872. In his early years he followed various lines of employment, being a dry goods salesman and a clerk in Camenga & Anderson's drygoods store at Independence. In 1874 he went back to his father's farm, and conducted it and took care of his father for ten years. In 1884 Mr. Stone engaged in the coal business at Independence. For some years he mined the coal off his father's farm, shoveling it out of the hills after stripping the shallow surface from the vein. That farm of 160 acres, the father's old homestead, was situated one mile north of Independence. Mr. Stone was also the first party to ship coal from shaft or deep mines into Independence from the outside. While engaged in mining he operated a mine at Oolagah, Oklahoma. He also had the distinction of being the first man to prospect for gas in Montgomery County, sinking a well on Rock Creek. He was active in the coal trade until 1902, in which year he turned his attention to the ice business, and three years later established a broom factory, and was manufacturing brooms at Independence until his death. He built a factory at the corner of Twelfth and Sycamore streets, and Mrs. Stone still owns that plant. Mr. Stone attended the Episcopal Church, was affiliated with Camp No. 649, Modern Woodmen of America, at Independence, Lodge No. 780, Benevolent and Protective Order of Elks, and was one of the founders of the Commercial Club.

Mrs. Stone before her marriage was Miss Minerva A. Yates. She was born near Bushnell, Illinois, December 24, 1858, a daughter of Robert and Maria (Hey) Yates. The Yates family originated in Germany and on coming to America settled in Ohio. Her grandfather Richard Yates was a pioneer emigrant, a farmer, and died while a soldier in the Union army in the Civil war. Mrs. Stone's maternal grandfather, Morris Hey, was born in London, England, was a school teacher, and was drowned while crossing a creek on his return home from school. Robert Yates, father of Mrs. Stone, was born in Columbus, Ohio, in 1826, was reared there, and was married in Illinois to Miss Hey, who was born in Ohio in 1835. She died at Bushnell, Illinois, in 1874. In the early days Robert Yates dealt extensively in cattle, and drove them over the Allegheny mountains from Ohio and Illinois to Pittsburg and other markets. In 1876 after the death of his wife he moved to Kansas and was an early settler near Independence, establishing his farm a quarter of a mile north of the city, where he owned 160 acres. He sold this land before his death, which occurred in Independence in August, 1902. Politically he was a democrat. Mr. and Mrs. Robert Yates had the following children: Sarah J., wife of S. T. Doggett, of Independence; Mary E., who lives at Tamora, Nebraska, the widow of S. Wallick; Minerva A., Mrs. Stone; Orabell, who lives at Independence, widow of Carl Hattan, who died at Independence in May, 1915; Martha J., who died at the age of eighteen months; McClellan, a master mechanic in the King Con mines at Park City, Utah; Emma, wife of J. W. Pitts, a farmer eighteen miles west of Independence; Josie Adaline, who lives on a farm southwest of Independence, married B. L. Frost; Robert Wilson, who is an engineer on the Denver and Rio Grande Railroad with headquarters at Lumberton, New Mexico; and Willard L., who was game warden at Silverton, Colorado, at the time of his death in 1915.

Mrs. Stone was educated in her native city of Illinois and after coming to Kansas taught in Montgomery County schools for five years prior to her marriage. She has always taken much interest and an active part in the Methodist Episcopal Church and has taught for years a class of the Sunday school. Mr. Stone during his lifetime built the residence in which his widow now resides, and it is surrounded by twenty-seven acres of ground. She also owns another residence in the city and 200 acres of farming land north of Grabham Station in Montgomery County.

Mrs. Stone has three children: Edna May, who died at the age of eighteen years; Nola Beatrice, who married John Stichman, a clerk in Baden's dry goods store at Independence and residing at 715 Washington Street; and Rollo Alphonso, aged twenty-one years and six months who is now a member of Company K, Kansas National Guard. To defend the flag of his country he left an excellent automobile business which he had built up in Independence.

OSCAR LAWRENCE O'BRIEN during the past ten years has been one of the leading lawyers of Montgomery County, and is distinguishing himself in this profession as his father before him did in his capacity as a pioneer farmer of Montgomery County.

He represents some very old American stock. The O'Briens originally came from Ireland to Virginia during colonial times. His great-grandfather, Elijah O'Brien was born in Virginia, was a gunsmith and clock maker and died in Ohio. The grandfather of the Independence lawyer was Enos O'Brien, who was born in Ohio in 1808, became a surveyor and farmer, and was one of the pioneers who moved to this section of Kansas in 1868. His death occurred in Montgomery County in 1872.

About eight years after the death of his grandfather, Oscar Lawrence O'Brien was born on the old farm in Montgomery County November 7, 1880. His father was the late John O'Brien, who was born in Pike County Ohio, in 1841 and died at Independence in 1905. Reared in Ohio, he came out to Kansas in 1868, first locating at Humboldt and in 1869 establishing his home on a farm west of Liberty in Montgomery County. There he homesteaded 160 acres, but by long continued effort not only provided liberally for his family of children, but also acquired a valuable estate. He lived on his homestead until 1903, and this old place, now comprising 210 acres, is owned by his widow. Included in the estate at the time of his death was another farm of eighty acres west of Cherryvale, and this has since been sold. John O'Brien was a democrat. He married Jennie Broughton, who was born in Indiana and now lives in Independence. Their children were: Claudia, who is the wife of A. B. Slater and lives on the old homestead; Oscar L.; Edwin, who has a farm west of Liberty which was also included in the estate of his father.

Oscar L. O'Brien received his early education in the public schools of Montgomery County, and in 1904 graduated from the Montgomery County High School. He then entered the Kansas State University, where he completed the law course in 1907 and was admitted to the bar in the same year. Since then he has devoted all his time and energies to building up a practice at Independence, and is now one of the leading members of the local bar. His offices are at the corner of Main and Penn avenues. In politics he aligns himself with the democratic party. He is a member of the Montgomery County Bar Association.

His home is at 205 South Fourteenth Street. In 1911 at Independence Mr. O'Brien married Miss Naomi Fowler, who was born near Liberty and grew up and received her early education in Montgomery County. She was a classmate of Mr. O'Brien in the Montgomery County High School, graduating in 1904, and afterwards attended Baker University and the Kansas State University. For three years before her marriage she was one of the teachers in the Independence public schools. Her father, I. G. Fowler is a druggist at Independence. Mr. and Mrs. O'Brien have one daughter, Nettie Jane, born March 22, 1912.

SAMUEL A. BYARLAY. So quickly do great events in the world's history succeed each other, that perchance some may be lost sight of, but it is not possible for any American to forget the dangers that attended pioneering, following the close of the Civil war, on the western frontiers, nor the heroism displayed by volunteer soldiers in defending the peaceful settlers by driving off the savage foe. Among the prominent residents of May Day, Riley County, is a veteran of the Indian campaign of 1868-9, in the person of Samuel A. Byarlay, merchant and postmaster at this point.

Samuel A. Byarlay was born in Jackson County, Indiana, September 15, 1848, and is a son of John M. and Millicent (Bundy) Byarlay. His father was born in Tennessee and his mother in Indiana, in which latter state both were reared, the father from the age of nine years. In 1860, John M. Byarlay left Indiana with his family for Riley County, Kansas. It was his hope and intention to thus provide more comfortably for his large family than he could do in Indiana. The family reached Kansas on the 4th of July, 1860, and the father soon afterward bought a small farm in the Fancy Creek Valley. He was a well educated man and taught one of the first rural schools in this county, holding the sessions in his own house. For some time he served as township trustee. His death occurred in 1872 when his age was fifty-four years. The mother survived many years, her death occurring at Clay Center, when seventy-nine years old. Of their ten children three are living.

Samuel A. Byarlay was not quite twelve years old when his parents settled in Riley County and here he attended school and grew to manhood, giving his father assistance on the home farm. In 1868-9 he served as a member of the Nineteenth Kansas Volunteer Infantry under Generals Custer and Sheridan in the memorable campaign against the Indians on the border, and his recollections of those brave and gallant commanders are very interesting. In that campaign, on account of its danger from a treacherous foe, every soldier was a hero and no one gave a better account of himself than did Samuel A. Byarlay.

In 1878 Mr. Byarlay embarked in a mercantile business at May Day, which he has conducted ever since and for many years has been postmaster of the village. In politics he is a republican but this fact has not disturbed him in official position.

In 1872 Mr. Byarlay was married to Miss Carrie Gridley, and they have four children: Guy H., Mabel

Fern, Mina H. and Linn C. Mr. Byarlay is a member of the United Brethren Church.

JOHN C. FIELDS. Among the worthy farmers of Fawn Creek Township, Montgomery County, whose industry, perseverance and good management have brought them into comfortable circumstances, is John C. Fields. Mr. Fields has been a resident of Montgomery County since 1870, in which year he took up a pre-emption claim in what was then the Cherokee Strip. He has steadily added to his holdings since that time, and is now one of the substantial men of his community, having a well-cultivated property of 650 acres, and being a director of the Tyro State Bank.

Mr. Fields was born in Mifflin County, Pennsylvania, October 11, 1848, and is a son of John and Joanna (Wallace) Fields, and a member of a family the American progenitor of which came to this country from Germany in colonial times and settled in Pennsylvania. Robert Fields, the grandfather of John C., was born in the Keystone State, and passed his life in farming in Mifflin County, where he died prior to the birth of his grandson. On the maternal side, Mr. Fields' grandfather was Robert Wallace, who was born at Belfast, Ireland, and as a young man came to America and settled in Pennsylvania, where during the remainder of his active career he was engaged in farming and stock raising. His death occurred about the year 1863. Mr. Wallace married a Miss Wilson, daughter of James Wilson, one of the signers of the Declaration of Independence.

John Fields, father of John C., was born in 1803, in Mifflin County, Pennsylvania, was there reared and educated, and passed his life as a tiller of the soil. He met with a fair measure of success in his farming and stockraising enterprises, but his early death, in 1848, cut short what promised to be a successful career. He was a democrat in politics and an active member of the Presbyterian Church. Mr. Fields married Joanna Wallace, also a native of Mifflin County, who died there in 1864, at the age of fifty-eight years.

The only child of his parents, John C. Fields was educated in the public schools of his native county, and was reared on the home farm, where he remained until 1869, or until he had reached his majority. At that time he came to Kansas and settled in Brown County, as a pioneer, but in 1870 removed to the Cherokee Strip, taking up a pre-emption claim in Fawn Creek Township, Montgomery County. He experienced all the hardships incidental to life in a new country, passed through the grasshopper plague of 1871, and met with a number of other reverses, but through it all worked perseveringly and gradually added to his holdings as his finances would permit, and erected good buildings and installed improvements on his property. Thus he has become the owner of a farm of 650 acres, on which he has two oil wells now producing, although he gives the greater part of his attention to diversified farming and to the raising of graded stock, having a thoroughbred individual for his Shorthorns. He is known in business circles as a man of foresight and acumen, who is honorable and straightforward in his dealings and who, in succeeding himself, has aided others to honorable success. In addition to his residence at Tyro, Mr. Fields owns a valuable business property, and has also been interested as a stockholder in a number of oil companies. Mr. Fields is a director of the Tyro State Bank, one of the strong financial institutions of this part of the county, which was established in 1904 by R. L. Teegarden and other local men of substance. The present modern brick banking house was erected during that year, and stands on Main Street. The present officers of the bank are Joseph Lenhart, president; F. E. Dobson, vice president, and R. L. Teegarden, cashier, all of Tyro. The bank has a capital of $10,000, its surplus being $5,000 and its undivided profits $3,000. It has shown a gratifying growth since its inception and has an excellent reputation in banking circles of this part of the state, as well as possessing the confidence of the general public. Mr. Fields has done his share in placing this institution upon a sound foundation and in directing its policies along lines of safety and conservatism. He is a democrat in politics and stanchly supports the candidates of that party. His public service has been confined to his acting as a member of the school board, a position which he has held for many years, his friendliness to and interest in education making him a valuable member of the school body of his township. Mr. Fields is fraternally connected with the Independent Order of Odd Fellows, being past noble grand of Tyro Camp, No. 517.

Mr. Fields was married in 1874, in Montgomery County, Kansas, to Miss Rachel Ellis, daughter of C. T. and Mary Ellis, who reside on a farm one-half mile north of that operated by Mr. Fields. To this union there have been born the following children: Theodore, who is engaged in farming one and one-half miles west of the home place, one of his father's farms in Caney Township; A. P., who lives three miles east of his father's homestead and follows the oil fields; Elfa, unmarried, who is engaged in teaching in the country schools of Montgomery County and makes her home with her parents; and John and Frank, who are assisting their father in the cultivation of the home place.

CHARLES M. GIBSON, M. D. During the past decade Dr. Charles M. Gibson has been engaged in the practice of medicine at Franklin, Kansas, and by his devotion to the duties of his profession, his close study and his pronounced skill, has won a liberal and representative practice. His talents and executive ability have gained him recognition in his community, and he has maintained throughout his career a high standard of professional ethics and honorable principles.

Dr. Charles M. Gibson was born at Richview, Illinois, July 6, 1879, a son of Samuel B. and Sarah C. (Hussey) Gibson, and a member of a Scotch-Irish family which came from Scotland to America in colonial days and settled in South Carolina. Samuel B. Gibson was born in Randolph County, Illinois, in 1846, and was there reared, educated and married. He followed farming and stock raising in the Prairie State until 1880, when he brought his family to Crawford County, Kansas, buying a farm and engaging in general farming and stock raising. Because of failing health he went to Texas in 1907, and there his death occurred, at Kingsville, in 1909. He was a republican in politics and a faithful member of the United Presbyterian Church, in which he was an elder and active worker. Mrs. Gibson, who survives him and lives at Pittsburg, Kansas, was born in 1852, at Jamestown, Ohio. To Mr. and Mrs. Gibson there were born twelve children, as follows: J. Albert; Minnie Belle, who is now the wife of R. J. Kirkwood and resides at Spearville, Kansas, where Mr. Kirkwood is a prominent farmer and stockman; Robert E., who resides at Pittsburg, Kansas, and is associated with his brother J. Albert in business; Dr. Charles M., of this review; Lyman C., who is a farmer and stockman of Pawnee County, Kansas, and resides at Larned; Samuel E., who is also engaged in farming and stock raising and resides at St. Paul, Neosho County, Kansas; Roy S., who is engaged in the furniture business at Girard, this state; Dr. Elzie H., who is engaged in the practice of dentistry at Altoona, Kansas; Ethel, who is the wife of Dr. W. A. Goolsby, a dental practitioner of Paris, Texas; Bertice, who has made a special study of music, which she teaches, lives with her mother at Pittsburg; Catherine also lives with her mother, and is a freshman at the Manual Training Normal School, Pittsburg; and Lawrence M., a graduate of the Manual Training Normal School, who is now engaged in teaching school and studying for the law.

J. Albert Gibson, of the above family, was born at Richview, Illinois, received a good educational training, and has for some years been prominent in business circles of Pittsburg, and in the political life of Crawford County. He was elected to the State Legislature in 1912 and re-elected in 1914, and in 1916 was a candidate for state senator, but met with defeat. During his two terms in the Legislature, he was one of the most active members of that body, being chairman of the committees on Banks and Banking, Cities of First Class, Employes', Mines and Mining, Immigration and Judiciary Apportionment. Mr. Gibson introduced a bill pertaining to special improvement of cities of the first class, which subsequently became a law. This amended the existing statutes under which citizens had been paying 2½ per cent for the past ten years, an unjust commission or interest, on all special improvements. The amended law did away with this injustice, and of course has been a great saving to the tax-payers. Mr. Gibson, in all, introduced about nineteen bills looking toward the interests of his constituents. He is a republican in his political views and a consistent member of the United Presbyterian Church, in which he is an elder and trustee. Fraternally, he is affiliated with Pittsburg Lodge No. 187, Ancient Free and Accepted Masons; Pittsburg Chapter No. 58, Royal Arch Masons; Pittsburg Commandery No. 29, Knights Templars, Fort Scott Consistory No. 6, of the thirty-second degree, and Mirza Temple, Ancient Arabic Order Nobles of the Mystic Shrine, of Pittsburg; Pittsburg Lodge No. 412, Benevolent and Protective Order of Elks, and United Commercial Travelers, No. 77. He also belongs to the Pittsburg Country Club and the Pittsburg Commercial Club. As a business man Mr. Gibson is interested with his brother. R. S. Gibson, in the Walker Gibson Coal Company, at Pittsburg and the Gibson & Hibbard Furniture Company, at Girard; and is president of the Pittsburg Fuel and Ice Company. He is married and has three children, namely: Helen Claire, who is attending Monmouth (Illinois) College, specializing in music; Eva Louise, a graduate of the State Manual Training Normal School, class of 1916, who is now teaching school while furthering her education; and Grant Burns, who is in the junior class of the Pittsburg High School.

Charles M. Gibson received his early education in the district schools of Crawford County, following which he attended high school at Cherokee, and was duly graduated therefrom in 1900. He next enrolled as a student at Kansas University, Lawrence, where he received the degree of Bachelor of Art in 1905, and two years later was granted his coveted degree of Doctor of Medicine. Immediately after receiving his diploma, Doctor Gibson began practice at Franklin, where he has since built up a large and representative professional business in general medicine and surgery. He has impressed himself upon the people of his part of Crawford County as a skilled practitioner and a man whose genuine sympathy does much to aid his professional talents. Holding to high ideals in his profession, he devotes himself to his conception of duty, and, keeping himself fully abreast of current events, both in his profession and outside matters, is able to enlarge his field of accomplishment and exert a further influence for moral uplift and the betterment of existing conditions. The doctor maintains well-appointed offices on Main Street. He has been successful in a material as well as a professional way, and is the owner of 160 acres of valuable farming land in the western part of the state. Doctor Gibson votes the republican ticket, but is not a politician. With his family, he attends the United Presbyterian Church. Fraternally, he is affiliated with the Ancient Order of United Workmen, while his professional connections include membership in the Crawford County Medical Society, the Kansas State Medical Society, the American Medical Association and the Southeastern Kansas Medical Society.

In 1908, at Lawrence, Kansas, Doctor Gibson was married to Miss Edith L. Irwin, daughter of the Rev. W. H. and Elizabeth (Smith) Irwin. Reverend Irwin, who was a minister of the Baptist faith, is now deceased, but Mrs. Irwin still survives him and resides at Lawrence. Doctor and Mrs. Gibson are the parents of one daughter: Dorothy L., who was born at Franklin, Kansas, January 29, 1911.

CHARLES SUMNER RISDON. Among the men who have lent dignity to the educator's profession in Kansas, Charles Sumner Risdon is deserving of more than passing mention. Throughout his career he has been a resident of the Sunflower State, and from the time of his earliest ambitions for a career as an educator until he realized the attainment of his goal, he attended the educational institutions of the state. His standing in his profession was recognized in 1901, when he was appointed superintendent of schools of Independence, and this office he has filled so capably, that there has been no thought of a change.

Mr. Risdon was born on a farm in Clay County, Kansas, January 3, 1874, and is a son of J. T. W. and Mary Catherine (Rumple) Risdon. The family is an old and honored one in this country, the original ancestor having come to America from Wales and settled in Vermont during colonial days. David Risdon, the grandfather of Charles S. Risdon, was born in the Green Mountain State, from whence he migrated as a young man to the Western Reserve, his death occurring in Ohio when his son, J. T. W. Risdon, was still a child. J. T. W. Risdon was born March 5, 1835, at Tiffin, Ohio, and after the death of his father was taken to Iowa. There he was educated and reared, and after his marriage, in 1873, came to Kansas and settled at Clay Center, Clay County. He was a pioneer farmer and stockraiser of that community, an honorable and industrious man, and through a long career of faithful labor gained a handsome and valuable property. In politics Mr. Risdon was a republican, but he has never cared for public life, preferring to devote himself without interruption to the duties of his farm and his home. He was married in Iowa to Miss Mary Catherine Rumple, who was born in Ohio, December

11, 1842, and was taken by her parents when she was ten years of age to Iowa. Mr. and Mrs. Risdon became the parents of the following children: W. W., who is state mining inspector for New Mexico, with headquarters at Albuquerque; W. M., who had been engaged in farming and stockraising in the vicinity of Jetmore, Hodgeman County, Kansas, until his death at the age of forty-seven years; Dora, who became the wife of M. C. Porter, M. D., and resides in Topeka, where Doctor Porter is a prominent surgeon; Mary, who is the widow of the late R. M. Losey, a farmer of Clay County, and now resides at Clay Center, Kansas; Gertha, who is the wife of Clem Tolbert, engaged in the commercial business at Los Angeles, California; Charles Sumner, of this notice; and Dr. J. W., who is a well known physician and surgeon of Leavenworth, Kansas. The mother of these children still survives and makes her home at Independence, at the residence of her son, Charles Sumner.

Charles S. Risdon received his early education in the district schools of Clay County, Kansas, and remained on his father's farm until he reached the age of eighteen years. In the meantime he secured an education that enabled him to obtain a teacher's certificate, and in 1893 and 1894 he taught in the schools of his neighborhood during the winter months, while assisting his father in the work of the homestead in the summer seasons. Previous to this, in the school year 1892-93, he had taken a course at the Kansas State Normal School, located at Emporia. In 1895, to further himself for his chosen work, Mr. Risdon entered the Salina Normal University, from which he was graduated in August, with the degree of Bachelor of Arts, and in 1901 he was honored by the degree of Master of Arts from this same university. In 1898 and 1899 and again in 1900 and 1901, he acted in the capacity of principal of the high school at Thayer, Kansas, and his efficient work while there attracted such favorable attention that he was appointed superintendent of schools of Independence, a position which he has retained to the present time. In this capacity Mr. Risdon has under his superintendency five schools, fifty-four teachers and 2,000 scholars, and has succeeded in building up the school system here so that it is second to none in any city of the same size in the state.

In the line of his profession, Superintendent Risdon is a member of the National Educational Association, which he joined in 1900; the Montgomery County Teachers Association; and the Kansas State Teachers Association, being a director of the last-named and its president in 1908. He is also a member of the District Teachers Association, and was representative of the Third Congressional District for the Kansas State Teachers Association for a period of four years. His offices are maintained in the Washington School Building. A stanch republican, he has never aspired to any political honors, although always active in matters of public polity, and is an earnest and consistent advocate of temperance and other civic and social virtues. His activity, however, in politics and like affairs, is tactful and considerate, and has never been regarded as "offensive partisanship." Superintendent Risdon's religious affiliation is with the Presbyterian Church. He belongs to Fortitude Lodge No. 107, Ancient Free and Accepted Masons, of which he is past master; the Modern Woodmen of America, Thayer Camp; and Lodge No. 17, Ancient Order of United Workmen, of Independence, while his connection with club life includes membership in the Commercial and Rotary clubs of Independence.

Mr. Risdon was married at Omaha, Nebraska, in 1898, to Miss Myrtle May Starr, daughter of J. C. and Wilhelmina Starr, the latter of whom now resides at Scott City, Kansas. Mr. Starr, a former well known newspaper man and politician, is now deceased. Three children have been born to Professor and Mrs. Risdon, namely: Myrtle Anita, who is a sophomore in the high school at Long Beach, California; and Mary Catherine and Wilhelmina Christine, who are in the second grade of the public school there. The family home at Independence is the scene of many social events.

WILLIAM ROLLIN YENAWINE. Farming has been the business of William Rollin Yenawine. He has given to that vocation the same qualities of enterprise and energy which a successful merchant gives to his store or a manufacturer to his factory. His success has followed as a matter of course. Mr. Yenawine is now the owner of "Brook Side" farm in Ashland Township of Riley County. It is said that the really busy man has more leisure than the one who pursues every undertaking with frantic haste and wastes his efforts on small accomplishment. This is perhaps the reason why Mr. Yenawine, while strictly a farmer and a successful one at that, found time to devote himself to public affairs. He has long been one of the active republicans of Riley county. For four years he held the office of county commissioner, and his creditable administration of that office brought him election as county treasurer. He filled that post four years and met all the most sanguine expectations of his many friends. After leaving the county treasuryship he again devoted his time to farming and stock raising, but in 1916 his friends urged him to become a candidate for the republican nomination in the August primaries for the office of county clerk. He won the election and took office January 8, 1917.

Mr. Yenawine is almost a native son of Kansas. He was born in Hancock County, Illinois, June 27, 1869. When less than two years of age his parents, Seth J. and Anna E. (Moore) Yenawine, moved to Riley County, locating on a farm in Ashland township. That was in 1870. The parents had their home there for many years, but a few years ago removed to the city of Manhattan, where they now reside. Seth Yenawine is actively engaged in the real estate and loan business.

Reared in Riley County on a farm, William R. Yenawine attended the common schools and also spent two years in the Kansas State Agricultural College and a similar period in Baker University. Though liberally educated, he found his most congenial task on the farm, and is one of the men who have helped to raise the general standard of agriculture in this section of the state. As a young man he taught one term in the rural schools. Fraternally he is a Master Mason, and also belongs to the Modern Woodmen of America and the Fraternal Aid. He is a member of the Methodist church.

In 1897 he married Miss Sallie A. Dix. Mrs. Yenawine was born in Riley county, Kansas, a daughter of Mr. and Mrs. O. T. Dix, who came to Kansas from Illinois about 1869, locating in Ashland township, where they have since continued to reside. They represent one of the early farming families of the county. Mr. and Mrs. Yenawine have one son, Chester E. The family reside in Manhattan, and are active social members of that community.

WILLIAM H. SHEPARD. When William H. Shepard left college he chose the work which seemed most congenial and for which he had the greatest apparent adaptability, and entered a bank in Illinois. For thirty consecutive years he has applied himself to the subject of banking, and his business success and prominence is largely due to this concentration of effort along one line.

Mr. Shepard is now vice president of the First National Bank of Coffeyville, and is identified with several other important concerns which might be classed as public utilities in that part of Kansas. His branch of the Shepard family came from England and settled in New York State prior to the Revolution. His grandfather Chauncey J. Shepard was born in 1801, lived for a number of years in Vermont, was a farmer and died at Norfolk, New York, in 1881.

William H. Shepard, Sr., father of the Coffeyville banker, was born at Norfolk, New York, October 19, 1836. Three months after his birth his parents moved to Fairfax, Vermont, where he grew up and where he married. He taught school there, studied law, was admitted to the bar, and almost at the outset of his professional career moved west to Cambridge, Illinois, where he was engaged in the successful practice of his profession the rest of his life. He died at Cambridge, October 5, 1888. As a republican he represented his home district in the Illinois State Senate for two terms. He was a member of the Masonic Order. The senior Mr. Shepard married Mary Jackson, who was born at Westford, Vermont January 30, 1840, and is now living at Kansas City, Kansas. The second of their two children was Frederick J., who died when one year of age, and William H. Shepard, Jr., is the only survivor.

William H. Shepard, Jr., was born at Cambridge, Illinois, May 13, 1865, was educated in the public schools of that city, graduating from high school in 1883, and then entered and pursued the regular academic course in Knox College at Galesburg, Illinois, where he was graduated in 1887.

On returning home from college he was granted an opportunity to learn the banking business, beginning at the bottom, in the First National Bank of Cambridge, was soon made bookkeeper, and held that position until the fall of 1889. For about two years after that he was cashier of the bank at Florence, Alabama, and then in September, 1891 arrived in Coffeyville.

This city has been his home and the stage of his larger business activities for a quarter of a century. Beginning as teller in the First National Bank he was promoted to assistant cashier in 1894, to cashier in 1900, and since 1905 has been vice president.

In the meantime his energies have been extended to other affairs. In March, 1904, with his brother-in-law, George W. Chain, as partner, he took up the manufacture of ice, and the Shepard & Chain Ice Company now supplies the bulk of the artificial ice consumed in Coffeyville and by the railroad companies, and also in several of the surrounding towns. Mr. Shepard is president of the company with George W. Chain as secretary and treasurer. They have one plant of thirty tons daily capacity, located at the corner of Spruce and Fourteenth streets, while the other plant, with a daily capacity of fifty tons, is east of Coffeyville, where the Missouri Pacific crosses the Verdigris River. Each plant has its own storage house.

Mr. Shepard is also manager and treasurer of the Coffeyville Gas and Fuel Company, whose offices are at 110 West Eighth Street. He became manager of the old People's Gas Company in January, 1905, and remained with the reorganization under the present name of Coffeyville Gas & Fuel Company. This company supplies Coffeyville with natural gas obtained from the Kansas Natural Gas Company. The other officers of the company are: W. C. Hall, president; and C. M. Ball, vice president.

In politics Mr. Shepard is a republican. He is past master of the Keystone Lodge, No. 102, Ancient Free and Accepted Masons, and a member of Coffeyville Chapter, No. 89, Royal Arch Masons, Lochinvar Commandery, No. 52 Knights Templar, Abdallah Temple of the Nobles of the Mystic Shrine at Leavenworth, and belongs to Lodge No. 775, Benevolent and Protective Order of Elks. Mr. Shepard and wife reside at 804 Beech Street. On April 12, 1894, at Coffeyville he married Miss Elfrida Hoffman. Her parents Charles and Minnie Hoffman are now living retired at Coffeyville.

WILLIAM NELSON JOHNSON, M. D. A physician whose career has been one of devotion to his profession and the interests of his patients in Cherokee County for over twenty years, and whose ability ranks him among the leaders in medical circles in that section, Doctor Johnson is a man who throughout his career has made the best of his resources and in the best sense of the term is a self-made man.

He was born on a farm in Franklin County, Missouri, August 29, 1853, and his early youth was spent in the troubled conditions during and subsequent to the Civil war. Consequently he had little opportunity to gain an education, and his learning was largely picked up from actual contact with the world and from the study of books which were within his reach. He did not attend public school until after the war. For twenty-five years he lived on his father's farm, and then began the study of medicine and pursued it diligently until he was permitted to practice as an under-graduate. In 1888 he began his under-graduate practice at Crestline, Kansas, and from time to time took courses of medical lectures in the Kentucky School of Medicine at Louisville, from which institution he received his degree of M. D. in 1894.

In 1895 Doctor Johnson left Crestline and moved to Columbus, where years have given him an increasing reputation and he has enjoyed a large general medical and surgical practice. His offices are in the Burke Brothers Building, and he is president of the Burke Brothers Drug Store Company. In professional circles he is a member of the County, State and Southeastern Kansas Medical societies and the American Medical Association.

Doctor Johnson is a republican in politics, has served as a member of the Columbus School Board, is active in the Commercial Club, and a number of years ago took his first degree in Masonry, but went no further in that order. He owns one of the city's comfortable homes at 319 South Indiana Avenue.

Doctor Johnson represents an English family. His great-grandfather, emigrated from England to Virginia in the early days. His grandfather, Thomas Johnson, was born near Richmond, Virginia, was a planter, served at one time in the Virginia State Militia, and died near Richmond when about forty-five years of age. His death occurred before Doctor Johnson was born.

Payton B. Johnson, the father of Doctor Johnson, was born in 1816 near Richmond, Virginia, was

I. T. GOODNOW.

reared there but when a young man went West and settled on a farm in Franklin County, Missouri. Besides farming he followed his trade of a saddle and harness-maker, and he lived an honorable and straightforward life until his death in 1895. In politics he was one of the old-line whigs, but later became affiliated with the democratic organization. During the Civil war he served as a member of the Missouri Home Guards. His church was the Presbyterian. In Franklin County, Missouri, he married Rebecca Patton, who was born in that county in 1825 and died in Columbus, Kansas, in January, 1914. Their children were: Louisa, wife of L. C. Coxie, a carpenter and contractor at Columbus; Doctor Johnson; Mary, wife of William Miller, who is engaged in mining at Galena, Kansas.

In December, 1889, at Crestline, Kansas, Doctor Johnson married Miss Mamie Patterson, daughter of John P. and Eliza (Garrison) Patterson. Both her parents are now deceased, and her father was for many years a United States commissioner in North Carolina.

Four children have been born to Doctor and Mrs. Johnson: Sadie Helen is the wife of George Kerr, who is clerk with Greenfield Brothers, a large clothing house at St. Louis; Nelson is connected with Burke Brothers Drug Store at Columbus; Margaret is in the Freshman class of the Cherokee County High School; and Robert Wayne is a student in the public schools of Columbus.

ISAAC T. GOODNOW. There are certain names that should be preserved in the annals of Kansas with testimonials of pride and admiration, and one of these is Isaac T. Goodnow, who was a member of a notable group of liberty-loving men whose efforts had much to do with making Kansas a free state and opening the way for her to become the great and prosperous commonwealth she is now. He assisted in the founding of educational and religious institutions, he co-operated with others for business expansion and in every way during a long and singularly useful life displayed those qualities which promote comfort, peace and happiness.

Isaac T. Goodnow was born at Whitingham, Windham County, Vermont, January 17, 1814, and died at Manhattan, Riley County, Kansas, March 20, 1894. He was the fourth child of William and Sybil (Arms) Goodnow. His father was born at Petersham, Massachusetts, and was a descendant of one of three brothers who came to the Massachusetts Colony from England at an early day. When a young man he went to Vermont and for many years was a successful merchant at Whitingham. There, in 1806, he was married to Sybil Arms, a schoolteacher and a daughter of Josiah Arms, one of the early settlers of Brattleboro, Vermont.

When fourteen years of age heavy responsibilities fell upon Isaac T. Goodnow because of the death of his father. The support of the family devolved on him in a large measure, necessitating much self denial on his part as his hopes had already been centered on collegiate training and a life in one of the professions. Nevertheless he went to work as a clerk in mercantile establishments, faithful to his duties during the day and applying himself to study at night, hopefully looking forward and in the best way he could preparing himself for the wider environment that his ambition craved.

In 1832 Mr. Goodnow removed to the Town of Coleraine, Vermont, where he was converted and united with the Methodist Episcopal Church, of which he ever after remained a devoted and useful member. The religious emotions that had come to him aroused new hopes and aspirations for every day as well as a future existence and especially created a desire to secure a better education and with this end in view he became a student in the Wesleyan Academy at Wilbraham, Massachusetts, attending during the summer sessions, and taught in the public schools in the winter. Finally he became an instructor in the academy and was identified thus with the institution down to 1848, having been graduated therefrom and for ten years was a professor of natural science and of languages. In 1848 he was elected professor of natural science in Providence Seminary, Rhode Island, and remained there until 1855, when he resigned to go to Kansas with the avowed purpose of helping to make it a free state.

Carrying this project into execution, Professor Goodnow became in 1855, one of the founders of the City of Manhattan, Kansas. He joined the New England Emigrant Aid Company in their long journey to the far West, and with a colony started westward March 13, 1855, reaching Kansas City, Missouri, on March 18 after five days of steady travel. From there a committee of seven was appointed, its members being: Isaac T. Goodnow, Luke P. Lincoln, Charles H. Lovejoy, N. R. Wright, C. N. Wilson, A. Browning and Joseph Wintermute, as the advance guard of the emigrants and they pushed forward into Kansas.

It was a historic event, when, on March 24, 1855, just as the sun was setting, the travelers ascended Bluemont from the north, and from its summit looked down upon what is now the site of the beautiful and prosperous little City of Manhattan. This committee soon learned that there was a prior claimant to the land they sought. In the fall of 1854, George S. Park, of Parkville, Missouri, had located a town site on the Kansas River, on the southwestern part of the present site, and had named it Poliska. Also, on the northeastern part of the town site and upon the Big Blue River, in the same fall, Samuel Dexter Houston, of Illinois, S. W. Johnson, of Ohio, J. M. Russell, of Iowa, H. A. Wilcox, of Rhode Island, and E. M. Thurston, of Maine, had located the Town of Canton. Soon after this the Boston Colony arrived upon the scene and were invited to join the earlier immigrants to help build the town. They accepted the invitation and the name of the town, Manhattan, was agreed upon, this being done to comply with a clause in the constitution of the Cincinnati and Kansas Land Company, which had also arrived.

In 1857 Mr. Goodnow returned to the East and spent the summer in the New England states, raising, in the meantime, the sum of $4,000 for the building of the first Methodist Church edifice west of Lawrence, Kansas. Next, in connection with the plans of Rev. Joseph Denison and Rev. Washington Marlatt, he conceived the idea of establishing a college at Manhattan, to be under the auspices of the Methodist Church. Mr. Goodnow spent the years 1858, 1859 and 1860 in the East, and through his pleas raised the funds for the building of Bluemont College and for its equipment. The college was opened for students in the latter part of 1859, but Baker University, at Baldwin, Kansas, another Methodist institution, had, in the meantime been established, and it was deemed not wise to endeavor to maintain two Methodist colleges in the state, hence plans were made and carried to the end of making Bluemont College the nucleus of what is now the Kansas State Agricultural College. For many years Mr. Goodnow served on the board of trustees of Baker University.

As a lover of liberty, Isaac T. Goodnow ventured his all to help to make Kansas a free state and by men such as he, the end was accomplished. Not to him nor to any of his coadjutors did it appear what historic work they had a hand in achieving.

In the fall of 1862 Mr. Goodnow was elected state superintendent of public instruction and was re-elected in 1864. This office was one for which he was eminently fitted, and he was influential in shaping the educational policy of the state as to the public school system, its colleges, university and normal school. The Kansas State Agricultural College began its existence in July, 1863, while he was state superintendent of public instruction. In 1867 Mr. Goodnow was selected agent for the disposal of the 90,000 acres of the agricultural college lands and this position he held until 1873 with great success. For nearly seven years he was land commissioner for the Missouri, Kansas and Texas Railroad, and during that time, from 1869 to 1876, he sold a great deal of land. While thus occupied he lived at Neosha Falls, Kansas.

Isaac T. Goodnow was married August 28, 1838, to Ellen D. Denison, of Colerain, Massachusetts. She was a daughter of Maj. David and Lucy (Avery) Denison, and was a sister of Rev. Joseph Denison, whose name is closely identified with the early history of Kansas. They were not blessed with children of their own but they reared as a cherished daughter a niece of Mr. Goodnow, Miss Harriet A. Parkerson, who survives them and is a universally esteemed resident of Manhattan, a lady of culture and many accomplishments. Mrs. Goodnow survived her husband for six years, leaving in her passing from life memories of noble qualities and a blameless existence.

In his political views Mr. Goodnow was a pronounced republican and had been an important factor in the party at times, but after 1876 he accepted no office of public responsibility. The evening of his life was passed in the city he had helped to found and was serene and unclouded, surrounded by all the comforts that loving care could bestow, and upheld by the consciousness that he had not lived in vain. Few men of his day were more widely known in Kansas, and also in the eastern states his acquaintance was wide and his friends many. Almost from childhood he unselfishly bore burdens for others and his public efforts were all directed toward helpfulness for those in need and not to advance his own fortunes nor add luster to his name.

HUGH ELLSWORTH WEST has been one of the most prominent citizens of Independence for many years, though his interests as an oil operator have extended far and wide and now include valuable holdings in perhaps half a dozen states. The family were pioneers in Indiana, in which state in Clinton County Hugh E. West was born December 11, 1864. His great-grandfather William West was a native of Kentucky, and went into Indiana when almost the entire state was a wilderness. He died in Clinton County when ninety-six years of age, while his wife lived to be ninety-one. The West family came originally from Scotland and from Virginia moved across the mountains to Kentucky, where they were identified with the first settlement. The grandfather of Mr. West was also named William and he was born in Indiana in 1819, spent his life as a farmer and died in Clinton County in 1874.

Samuel M. West, father of Hugh West, was born

in Clinton County, Indiana, in 1843, was reared and married there, and at the beginning of the Civil war in 1861 enlisted in the Twenty-sixth Indiana Infantry. In the Battle of Prairie Grove, Arkansas, he was badly wounded, was incapacitated for further service, and never completely recovered his strength. In 1870 he moved to Elk City, Kansas, and was engaged in the real estate business for many years. He died at Elk City in August, 1915. He was a member of the United Brethren Church. Samuel M. West married Marie P. Hamilton, who was born in Boone County, Indiana, in 1844, and died at Elk City, Kansas, in 1880. Their children were: Hugh E.; Glendora, wife of Joe Johansen, who is in the milling business at Independence; W. M. West, a blacksmith in South Dakota; and O. M. West, an oil producer living at Wann, Oklahoma. For his second wife Samuel West married Katy Arnold, who came from Indiana and is still living at Elk City. Their one child, Othel H., is now connected with the Cleveland Oil and Gas Company at Cleveland, Oklahoma.

Hugh E. West was about fifteen years of age when his parents came to Kansas, and after the death of his mother, which occurred soon afterwards, he went to work on his own account. Thus he had very little schooling, and has really educated himself by study and observation and practical experience. For a time he was employed in a brickyard, and then became connected with the Deering Harvester Company of Chicago and traveled for several years on the road. In 1892 he had advanced so far as to be able to buy a farm in Chautauqua County, Kansas, and he lived on and conducted that place for five years. In 1897 he moved to Peru, Kansas, and conducted a marble yard and sold tombstones until 1902.

After selling his farm of 200 acres in Chautauqua County and his interests in the marble business, Mr. West went to Chautauqua County, Kansas, and there first became actively identified with the oil industry. Since 1906 he has had his home and headquarters in Independence. His oil holdings now extend throughout the state, and also to Oklahoma and other states. He is a director in several oil companies. In Oklahoma his holdings are in Washington, Nowata, Osage and Tulsa counties, while in Kansas they are located in Chautauqua, Montgomery and Miami counties. All these properties are producing oil, and in addition he has leases to considerable oil lands. He has also acquired extensive holdings of farm lands in Chautauqua County, Kansas, Tulsa County, Oklahoma, Little River and Desha counties, Arkansas, and has other lands in East Carroll and Webster parishes in Louisiana.

Mr. West is a stanch republican. He has been a member of the school board continuously for twenty-two years excepting eight months, and is now on the board at Independence and takes much interest in school affairs. Since 1889 he has been a member of the Modern Woodmen of America at Peru, Kansas. In 1915 he was associated with R. S. Litchfield and A. C. Stich, both of whom have since died, in erecting one of the finest mausoleums in the state at Independence.

Mr. West and family reside at 618 West Maple Street. In 1889 at Elk City he married Miss Mollie A. Piper, daughter of R. H. and Elizabeth Piper, both of whom are now deceased, her father having been a farmer. To their marriage have been born two children: Helen, wife of W. H. Eyssen, a contractor at Independence; and Della, wife of H. P. Decker, who lives at Independence, and is associated with Mr. West in the oil business.

It should perhaps be mentioned that Mr. West together with William E. Connelly of Topeka were at the head of the association which brought about the investigation and legislation against the Standard Oil Company in Kansas during the years 1904-05.

WILLIAM COCHRAN HALL, M. D., has lived at Coffeyville nearly thirty years. As a physician and surgeon he has been successful, as is indicated by the numerous professional relations he has enjoyed as physician and surgeon to a large number of the railway companies and other industrial organizations of that section of the state. But Doctor Hall's usefulness has not been confined entirely within the lines of his profession. He is one of the men who have made Coffeyville a city. He has helped bring many of its industries and organizations, and has aided in numerous worthy enterprises inaugurated for the welfare of the community. He helped bring in manufacturing plants, helped to establish the opera house, and his influence and means have been connected in one way or another with many industrial plants of the city. As a member and president of the Commercial Club he was especially forward in this work, also assisted by taking stock in many business organizations.

Representing in ancestry some of the flower of old Virginia and colonial stock, Doctor Hall was born at Bell in Highland County, Ohio, October 29, 1860. As a boy he attended the public schools of Highland and Adams counties, Ohio, and took summer courses in different normals. Like many successful professional men he did his first work as a teacher. In 1880 he graduated from the normal department of the National Normal University at Lebanon under Professor Holbrook. He did his first school work as a teacher at the age of seventeen. He taught four terms and in the meantime took up the study of medicine at West Union, Ohio, and in 1885 was graduated M. D. from the College of Physicians and Surgeons at Baltimore. With all the heavy demands made upon his professional time, not to speak of his business and civic responsibilities, Doctor Hall has kept pace with the advance made in medical affairs during the thirty years since he graduated. In 1896 he took a course in the Chicago Policlinic and has pursued other courses in the medical schools of Chicago. He located for practice at Latham, Ohio, but after nine months, while still retaining the practice he had built up in that community, he moved his home to Sinking Springs, Ohio, where he remained about a year.

On April 25, 1887, Dr. Hall arrived in Coffeyville, which was then a comparatively young city, and deriving some of its chief importance from its position as the gate city into Indian Territory. Since that date, for thirty years, he has enjoyed a large general medical and surgical practice, but his reputation is particularly based upon his skill as a surgeon. His offices are at 818 Maple street, and he resides at 402 West Ninth street.

Doctor Hall is a member of the County and State Medical societies, the Southeastern Kansas Medical Society, and has served as president in both the County and Southeastern Kansas medical societies and the American Medical Association. He is division surgeon for the Missouri Pacific and St. Louis, Iron Mountain & Southern Railway companies, is local surgeon for the Missouri, Kansas & Texas Railroad, for the Santa Fe Railway Company, and is also surgeon for the Rea-Patterson Milling Company and the Lodowici-Celadon Company, and for several brick plants, smelters and other large corporations.

In a business way he is financially interested in the Mecca Hotel at Coffeyville and has some very extensive real estate holdings in the city besides a farm of 330 acres near Coffeyville. He is a director in the Condon National Bank, is president of the Coffeyville Gas and Fuel Company, and served as president of the Coffeyville Commercial Club, and it was during the time of his membership of this club that the organization succeeded in bringing to Coffeyville so many factories and industries. He also served as president of the board of education and as health officer. Fraternally Doctor Hall is affiliated with Coffeyville Lodge No. 102, Ancient Free and Accepted Masons, and was made junior warden the same night he completed his third degree. He is also a member of Wichita Consistory No. 2 of the Scottish Rite, and was originally a member of the Temple of the Mystic Shrine at Leavenworth, but now belongs to Mirzah Temple at Pittsburg, Kansas. He is a charter member of Coffeyville Lodge No. 279, Ancient Order United Workmen, a charter member of Camp No. 665, Modern Woodmen of America, a charter member of the Royal Neighbors, and a charter member of Coffeyville Lodge of Elks. He was formerly affiliated with the Knights of Pythias.

On June 15, 1887, Doctor Hall was married in Highland County, Ohio, to Miss Sarah H. Hite. Her father was the late Rev. Addison Hite, a Methodist minister. Mrs. Hall died at Coffeyville in April, 1906, leaving two children: Levera May, wife of George F. Lisle, manager of a dry goods store at Chetopa, Kansas; and William Carlton, who was in the Kansas State University during 1914-15, and is now a student in the Manhattan Agricultural College. In August, 1907, at Golden, Illinois, Doctor Hall married Miss Nellie E. MacCord, daughter of Mr. and Mrs. Morris F. MacCord. Her father, who died in 1913, was the oldest school teacher in Oklahoma, and had been active in that profession for fifty years. Mrs. Hall's mother still lives at Golden, Illinois. Dr. and Mrs. Hall have a daughter, Norroena Helen, who was born January 25, 1914. During Cleveland's second administration, Doctor Hall was a member of the board of pension examiners. Politically he is an active democrat.

Some reference should now be made to his parents and ancestors. The Halls came originally from England to New Jersey, then moved to Virginia, and still later to Ohio. His great-grandfather, George Hall, a native of New Jersey, acquired a tract of land in old Virginia along the frontier, was a participant in some of the early Indian wars, and about 1806 was accidentally killed while cleaning his gun. Doctor Hall's grandfather, Jacob M. Hall, was born near the historic battleground of Point Pleasant in old Virginia, now West Virginia, in 1802. When he was a boy the family moved across the Ohio River into Ohio, and he became a farmer and stockman in the latter state. He lived for many years at Bell, Ohio, where Doctor Hall was born, and was still a resident there at the time of his death in 1877, though his death occurred at Dunkinsville. He was a whig and afterwards a republican. Jacob M. Hall married Polly Cochran. She was born in Washington, Kentucky, in 1800, and died at Bell, Ohio, in 1880. Her ancestor, John Cochran, was a sea captain and came from Scotland, and one of the Cochrans served as a soldier in the Revolution, being one of the direct ancestors of Doctor Hall, who is thus eligible to membership in the Sons of the American Revolution. There are two children of Jacob M. Hall and wife still living: Louisa, wife of John Frump, who was a veteran of the Civil War and now a retired farmer near Bell, Ohio; and Matilda, who resides at Bell, and first married a Mr. Frump, who died as a Union soldier in the war, and afterwards married L. G. Douglas, now deceased.

Carey F. Hall, father of Doctor Hall, was born at Bell, Ohio, in October, 1837, and died in Scioto County, Ohio, in December, 1895. He grew up in Highland County and one of his play and school mates as a boy was Hannah Milburn, who was born in Highland County in 1839. When school days were past they married, and Carey Hall then took up merchandising, was also a dealer in real estate, and in 1868 moved to Adams County, Ohio, and in 1893 to Scioto County, where he spent his last days. During the war he was a Home Guard and took part in the pursuit of Morgan during the latter's raid through southern Indiana and southern Ohio. He was a man of fine integrity of character, was highly esteemed by his neighbors. For many years he held the office of justice of the peace and few ever had reason to appeal from his careful decisions to higher courts. He was a democrat, a member of the Methodist Church and a Mason and Odd Fellow. He and his wife, who is now living at Coffeyville, Kansas, had the following children: Dr. William C. Hall; Luella Nora, wife of John Clinton Price, a traveling salesman at Coffeyville; Laura Collier, who died at the age of eighteen; Verdie R., wife of Hardy E. Stanfield, a conductor on the interurban system and living at Coffeyville; Cary Franklin, a music dealer at Coffeyville.

Hannah Milburn, the doctor's mother, is a daughter of Daniel Milburn, who was born in Pennsylvania in 1812, and died at Bell, Ohio, in 1894. He was reared and married in his native state, then went to Highland County, Ohio, and as an early settler cleared up a tract of land adjoining the estate where Doctor Hall's paternal grandfather lived. Daniel Milburn was a whig and republican, and was extremely devoted during all his active years to the Methodist Church. He held all the lay offices and did much to strengthen the influence of the church in his community. Daniel Milburn married Esther A. Rice, who was born in Pennsylvania in 1814, and died near Bell, Ohio, in 1901. Their children now living are: Mrs. Hannah (Milburn) Hall, the doctor's mother; Hester, who resides near Hillsboro, Ohio, widow of Andrew Holt, who was a veteran of the Union army; Valinda, wife of William Ream, a retired carpenter and builder near Hillsboro, Ohio; Aaron W., who occupies the old Milburn homestead in Ohio; Melissa, who is unmarried and lives with her sister Hester at Hillsboro; Angeline, wife of A. W. Lucas, a farmer and stockman near Hillsboro. Two other Milburn children are deceased, a daughter having died at the age of two years, and Martilla, after her marriage to Jacob Butler, who is also deceased. The Milburn ancestors came originally from Germany and settled in Pennsylvania in colonial times. Doctor Hall's great-grandfather in the maternal line was Andrew Milburn, who was born in Pennsylvania in 1786, and was one of those who pioneered into the wilderness of Highland County, Ohio, where he helped clear away the timber and break up the soil. He died in that county in 1876 at the age of ninety.

THADDEUS CONSTANTINE FRAZIER, M. D. A useful life crowded with activity and crowned with achievement both as a physician and as a citizen,

Dr. Thaddeus C. Frazier, of Coffeyville, may still further be considered because he is the pioneer medical man of this city. For forty-two years he has been a physician and surgeon here and additionally has been a leader in all forward movements, accepting public positions as a helpful means of progress for the city, encouraging educational movements and through his stability of character conferring honor upon this whole section.

Doctor Frazier was born in Henry County, Tennessee, December 14, 1841. His parents were William and Judith Ann (Sheb) Frazier. The Fraziers were of Scotch extraction but the founders of the American branch came from the North of Ireland and settled in Virginia and North Carolina in colonial days. The grandfather of Doctor Frazier, Julian Frazier, was born in North Carolina. He removed to Tennessee where he subsequently died leaving a large estate to his children. He had been an influential man in politics and at one time served as a member of the Tennessee Legislature.

William Frazier, father of Doctor Frazier, was born in North Carolina, in 1812, and died at Wichita, Kansas, in 1895. He married Judith Ann Sheb, who was born in Henry County, Tennessee, in 1815, and died there in 1845. They were the parents of four children: Samuel V., who died in 1872, in Green County, Missouri, was in business as a country merchant; Thaddeus C.; William M., who is a resident of Los Angeles, California, is a wholesale dealer in fruit and produce and has business houses in Wichita, Hutchinson and Anthony, Kansas; and a daughter that died in infancy. When young the father of the above family accompanied his parents to Knoxville, Tennessee. In early manhood he removed to Henry County and there was a farmer and stockman. In 1874 he came to Kansas. In politics he was a democrat. Both he and wife were members of the Christian (Disciples) Church.

In boyhood Thaddeus C. Frazier attended the public schools and later had academic advantages at Paris, Tennessee, following which he became a student in the state university at Columbia, Missouri. Shortly after entering this institution the Civil war was precipitated and in June, 1861, the youth went to the front as a member of the Eighth Division, Missouri State Guard, in which he served until the battle of Wilson's Creek, on August 10, 1861, in which he lost his right arm. It is not for the biographer to say what such a loss must have been on the threshold of manhood. It has been said that courage is a tremendous constructive force and seemingly Doctor Frazier has proved in his career the truth of this assertion. The seriousness of his injury kept him an invalid for some time and he went to Texas and remained there until 1868, in the meanwhile preparing for the practice of medicine, completing his medical course in the Louisville Medical University.

After practicing for a few months as an undergraduate, in Greene County, Missouri, in 1869 Doctor Frazier came to Montgomery County, Kansas, locating in the old Town of Parker, situated three miles from the present City of Coffeyville, coming to the latter place in the beginning of its history, in 1874, the first resident physician and surgeon. His practice has been general in character and his territory has covered a considerable field, this being especially the case in earlier years.

Politically Doctor Frazier is a democrat but his conceptions of civic duty and responsibility have not confined him to party lines in the administration of public office. For four years he served as mayor of Coffeyville, during which time many measures of public welfare were adopted and wise laws enforced. For one year he was a member of the city council and for one year served as commissioner when such office was a part of city representation. For eight years he served as city physician. In his long professional career Doctor Frazier has accumulated some valuable real estate, included in which is his residence at 1411 Maple Street, in which he maintains his office. He is unmarried. He assisted in the organization of the Montgomery County Medical Society and later was active in its reorganization.

For many years Doctor Frazier has been prominently identified with the fraternal order of Odd Fellows in both branches, is past noble grand in encampment and canton, present deputy commander patriarch militant of Kansas; has served as grand patriarch of the encampment of the state and served one term as grand warden of the Grand Lodge of Odd Fellows of Kansas. Formerly he was a member of the Knights of Honor. He is one of the representative men of Montgomery County.

HARRY W. BOUCK. The proprietor and editor of the Crawford County Enterprise, at Girard, Kansas, is a worthy representative of the younger journalistic element of Crawford County. To a very considerable extent, it is this element in any community, especially outside of the larger cities, which infuses spirit and zest into the activities of the place. It is this element whose entrance upon the arena of active life dates not farther back than a decade and a half of years which monopolizes most of the vigor, zeal and pushing energy which keeps the nerves of the newspaper world ramifying through all the lesser towns of the country strung to the full tension of strenuous endeavor. A pronounced type of the class of tireless workers thus described, Mr. Bouck has been identified with the newspaper business since his thirteenth year, and, in spite of his youth, his experience has been broad and his training comprehensive.

Harry W. Bouck was born at Greeley, Anderson County, Kansas, May 10, 1892, and is a son of William and Zua (Wilcox) Bouck. The family originated either in Germany or Holland, and it is probable that the great-great-grandfather of Harry W. Bouck was the original emigrant to New York. His great-grandfather was Aaron Bouck, a carpenter and builder of the Empire state, who died at Albany, in 1879. Christopher Bouck, the grandfather of Harry W., was born in 1842, in Broome County, New York, and was there educated, reared and married. In 1861, he was among the first to answer President Lincoln's call for volunteers, and, enlisting in a New York regiment, went to the front in time to take part in the disastrous defeat of the Union army at Bull Run. Later he fought all through the Civil war, participating in many important engagements, and on one occasion being captured by the enemy and confined in the notorious Libby Prison. At the close of the war, with an excellent military record, he returned to Albany, where he operated a grain elevator until 1873, in that year making his way to the West and settling in Iowa. In the following year he moved on to Greeley, Kansas, where he built the only grist mill ever operated at that place, but after two years sold out his interests and engaged in the threshing machine and sawmill business, which he followed until his retirement. His death occurred at Greeley in 1903. Mr. Bouck was a good man of business and a citizen

who had the esteem and respect of those with whom he came into contact. He was a "greenbacker" in politics and was fraternally identified with the Knights of Pythias. In New York he was married to Miss Mary Elizabeth Engle, who was born in 1846, and still survives him at Greeley, and they became the parents of three children: William; Jessie, who became the wife of the late W. A. Savage, from whom William Bouck learned the jewelry business; and Grace, who married J. R. Brady, and resides at Greeley.

William Bouck was born November 16, 1867, at Albany, New York, and was still a lad when the family moved to Iowa. A few months later, in 1874, they came to Kansas, and at Greeley the youth received his educational training. He learned the jeweler's trade there and followed it successfully until 1908, when he came to Girard and established himself in business. He has built up a good patronage here and is known as one of the city's most substantial merchants. In politics he maintains an independent stand. Mr. Bouck is an active member of the Commercial Club, and is very prominent in fraternal circles, having been for eleven years a member of Coronado Lodge No. 163, Knights of Pythias, in which he has held all the important offices, having been a representative to the Grand Lodge of the state four times, and now being past chancellor commander. Mr. Bouck married Miss Zua Wilcox, who was born in 1867, at Ashtabula, Ohio, a daughter of the late John Wilcox, who was for many years a river pilot. Mrs. Bouck died in a hospital at Kansas City, Missouri, in 1903, and was laid to rest in the cemetery at Greeley. Of the four children born to Mr. and Mrs. Bouck, Harry W. is the only survivor, the other three having died young.

Harry W. Bouck was educated in the graded schools of Greeley and the high school at Girard, and from the age of thirteen years has been identified with newspaper work. He served his apprenticeship on the Lawrence World and the Topeka Capitol, and has followed his trade of printer at Platte City, Missouri, Garnett, Kansas, and at other places. In 1912 he secured a one-half interest in the Alma Signal, at Alma, Kansas, and continued with that paper until January 1, 1915, when he returned to Girard and bought a one-half interest in the Crawford County Enterprise, later becoming sole owner of the plant and paper by purchase. This newspaper, which was brought from Hepler, Kansas, in 1913, is a weekly republican organ, the county seat paper, and circulates in Crawford and the surrounding counties. Its well-equipped plant, in which modern machinery has been installed, is located on South Ozark Street, near the Square. The Enterprise, as conducted by Mr. Bouck, is one of the helpful influences in promoting Girard's welfare and progress. Its columns are always open to matters which affect the city and the county and it supports unreservedly those things which make for better citizenship, higher morality and an elevation of educational standards. While a supporter of the republican party, it endeavors to give to its readers an unbiased view of the questions of the day. Its editorials are timely and concise, and its local matter interesting and reliable. Connected with the plant is a job printing establishment capable of turning out first-class work.

Mr. Bouck is widely known in journalistic circles, being a member of the Kansas State Editorial Association and secretary of the Crawford County Editorial Association. He served one term as president of the local typographical union and is a member of the International Typographical Union. Mr. Bouck is also vice president of the Girard Commercial Club and a member of the publicity committee. He is unmarried. Politically, his support is given to the republican party, and his fraternal connection is with Coronado Lodge No. 163, Knights of Pythias.

MARK D. MITCHELL, who was born at Franklin, Pennsylvania, April 15, 1871, is a lawyer by profession, but has used his legal knowledge chiefly to further his interests and those of his associates as an oil producer in Kansas. He has operated in various fields both East and West, and is now one of the prominent business men of Independence.

His father, John L. Mitchell, was born in Center County, Pennsylvania, in 1836, a son of Thomas Mitchell, also a native of Pennsylvania, but who died at Ashtabula, Ohio. John L. Mitchell died in Franklin, Pennsylvania, in 1898, having spent most of his life in that city, where he was a banker, a prominent citizen, and a leader in the republican party. He married Harriet Raymond, who was born at Utica, Pennsylvania, in 1837, and died at Franklin in January, 1915. Their children were: John R., a banker at St. Paul, Minnesota; Lida, who lives at Cleveland, Ohio; Mark D.; Thomas, an oil producer living at Franklin, Pennsylvania; Lynn, a banker at St. Paul, Minnesota.

Mark D. Mitchell graduated from the high school of Franklin, Pennsylvania, in 1890 and then entered Amherst College, where he completed the regular course and graduated Bachelor of Science in 1894. His education was continued in the New York Law School, from which he holds the degree LL. B., granted him in 1896. For about two years after leaving university he engaged in various occupations, but since 1898 has been identified almost altogether with the oil industry. He was an operator in Pennsylvania fields, but since 1907 has had his home at Independence, Kansas. He now has extensive leases in Wayside, Chanute, and Humboldt districts in Kansas, and in the Ramsey Pool and Aluwee, Oklahoma. He is president of the Amherst Oil Company, which operates in the Wayside field and has headquarters at Independence, and is president of the Second Oil Company of Aluwee, Oklahoma.

At Independence, Mr. Mitchell resides at 325 West Main Street. While living at Franklin, Pennsylvania, he served on the school board. He is a republican, and has been a trustee and very active member in the Presbyterian Church. He is affiliated with Myrtle Lodge, Ancient Free and Accepted Masons, at Franklin, Pennsylvania, with Franklin Chapter, Royal Arch Masons, Franklin Commandery, Knights Templar, and with Mirzah Temple of the Nobles of the Mystic Shrine at Pittsburg, Kansas. He also belongs to the Delta Upsilon College fraternity. In 1900 at Franklin, Pennsylvania, he married Miss Margaret C. Brown, daughter of Rev. T. Edwin and Elizabeth Brown, who reside with their daughter, Mrs. Mitchell. Her father is a retired minister of the Baptist Church. Mr. and Mrs. Mitchell have one daughter, Jane, now in the public schools.

JOHN F. FOSHA. Some of the finest lands of Riley County are responding to the intelligent management of John F. Fosha as a farmer and stock raiser. His home is in Madison township, and his record of enterprise in that locality covers a period of nearly twenty years. In that time he has had the usual vicissitudes which beset Kansas farmers, such as dry weather, floods, poor markets, but through good years and bad he has contrived to prosper and is now the owner of a splendid estate comprising 1,040 acres. He is one of the large crop raisers of the county, and in live stock his specialty is Hampshire hogs.

The presence of the Fosha family in Kansas is accounted for by the investment of a prosperous Illinois farmer in the lands of this state. About thirty years ago John F. Fosha, Sr., visited Riley County, and acquired three and a half sections of land in the vicinity of the town of Riley. He never became a permanent settler of Kansas, but after making this investment he returned to his home in Stephenson County, Illinois, where he had become wealthy as an Illinois farmer and where he spent the rest of his days. Because of his extensive investments in Kansas and the presence here of several of his children, it is appropriate to quote some portions of an article which appeared in the Freeport (Illinois) Democrat following the death of Mr. Fosha, Sr., which occurred at his Illinois home near Freeport in December, 1901. "John Fosha was a German by birth, and his birthday was January 12, 1834. When but a small child he was brought by his parents, Mr. and Mrs. Fred Fosha, to America. They settled in Maryland first, and afterwards moved to Virginia, where they remained until 1848, when the family came overland to Ogle County, this state, and began farming near Mount Morris. John Fosha lived at home and helped to develop the farm until after his marriage to Miss Mina Schueneman, which occurred in this city, February 24, 1856, the Rev. William Wagner officiating, after which he became a farmer on his own account, and was one of the most prosperous and successful ones this part of the state ever produced. He lived in Ogle County until his death.

"Few men, and especially farmers, achieve the financial success that Mr. Fosha did. He began life with absolutely nothing and died one of the heaviest land owners and wealthiest men of the county. His homestead of 640 acres is one of the best and most highly improved farms in Northwestern Illinois, with the very best class of farm buildings that add greatly to its value. Besides that he owned a considerable amount of land in Ogle County, and 2,240 acres in Riley County, Kansas, divided into ten large farms, some of which are held by his sons and others rented. And almost from the organization of the institution he has been a heavy stockholder in the German Insurance Company, having served on the directory for twenty-two years continuously, except for one or two years when his brother took his place. He was also a director of the German bank.

"As well as being a most successful business man, Mr. Fosha was a man of the highest character, and had an important place in the county's history. He was held in the highest regard by every one and was a genial, companionable man in social life. He was a democrat in politics, and one of the county leaders, but always declined any office except road overseer and school director."

He reared a family of four sons and four daughters. His widow survives him and is still occupying the old Illinois home. Of their children three reside in Riley County: John F.; Henry, of Grant Township; and Mrs. F. C. Otto.

It was on the old homestead in Stephenson County, Illinois, that John F. Fosha, Jr., was born April 19, 1875, just 100 years of the day after the battle of Lexington which ushered in the war of the Revolution. His early life was spent on an Illinois farm, and his education came from the public schools. In 1897, when about twenty-one years of age, he came to Riley County and has since made a remarkable success as a farmer and stock raiser.

It was about the time that he located in Riley County, in 1897, that Mr. Fosha married Miss Anna Stadel. Mrs. Fosha is a daughter of Mr. and Mrs. Fred Stadel, who also came from Illinois to Kansas, becoming settlers in Riley County, and they now live in Bala township, a few miles north of Riley. Mr. and Mrs. Fosha are the parents of four children: Ervin, Eddie, John and Amelia. The parents and their children are members of the Presbyterian church.

RICHARD YATES KENNEDY. A man of genial presence, of manifest sympathy, of resourceful brain and high educational standards, is found in Richard Yates Kennedy, principal of the Coffeyville High School. He has had many years of experience in the educational field, some thirty-three more or less continuous, and there are few problems of a teacher's life that he has not, at one time or another, successfully solved. Professor Kennedy has been a resident of Kansas since 1887, has valuable property investments in Montgomery County, and social, business and civic interests at Coffeyville.

Richard Yates Kennedy was born in Whiteside County, Illinois, February 16, 1862, and is a son of Robert M. and Martha P. (Roberts) Kennedy, and a grandson of John Kennedy. The grandfather was born in Pennsylvania, of Scotch parentage, and died in that state many years ago. By trade he was a cabinetmaker and he lived in Franklin County.

Robert M. Kennedy was born in Franklin County, Pennsylvania, in January, 1823, and died in Whiteside County, Illinois, in December, 1912. At the age of seventeen years he went to Lawrenceburg, Indiana, and while living there worked as a carpenter and farmer. In 1855 he removed to Whiteside County, Illinois, securing a homestead on which he lived during the rest of his life. In many respects he was a man to be looked up to and his fellow citizens recognized his sterling character and superior judgment by frequently electing him to offices of trust in his township. He served as a justice of the peace and for fourteen consecutive years was township assessor. He was a consistent member of the Presbyterian Church, belonged to the Masonic fraternity and to the Caledonian Club, a social organization.

At Lawrenceburg, Indiana, Robert M. Kennedy was married to Miss Martha P. Roberts, who was born there in 1826 and now resides in Whiteside County, Illinois. To this marriage the following children were born: Joseph, who enlisted in 1861 for service in the Civil war, as a member of the Forty-sixth Illinois Infantry, died of dysentery, at Natchez, Mississippi; William E., who is a contractor doing business in Whiteside County, is a veteran of the Civil war, enlisting in the Seventy-fifth Illinois Infantry and suffered incarceration in Libby prison; Alice, who is the wife of Wesley Sayers, a retired merchant of Dayton, Washington; Henry G., who died in 1863, at the age of seventeen years; Catherine, who is the wife of William E. Brown, who has a large ranch near Waitsburg, Washington; Alfred, who died at the age of two and one-half years; Luther, who died in infancy; H. M., who died in 1905 at the age of forty-two years, was a farmer in Whiteside County; Richard Yates; Clara, who is the wife of James Crom, who is a prominent citizen of Twin Falls, Idaho; and

Grace, who is the wife of Edward Janvrin, a prosperous farmer and stockman of Whiteside County, Illinois.

R. Y. Kennedy in boyhood attended the excellent public schools of Whiteside County. Subsequently he entered the State Normal School at Bloomington, Illinois, and still later became a student in Dixon College, Dixon, Illinois, from which institution he was graduated in 1890, with the degree of Bachelor of Science. Since then he has frequently attended summer sessions at the Chicago University and the Kansas State University, the acquisition of learning being his ideal of enjoying a vacation.

In 1883 Mr. Kennedy began to teach school and continued to teach in Whiteside County for the next four years. In 1887 he came to Kansas and bought a farm, largely as an investment because his field of preferred labor was educational. He resumed teaching and continued in the schools of Montgomery County until 1894. In that year he accepted a teaching position in one of the city schools of Coffeyville and in 1905 became teacher of history in the Coffeyville High School and two years later was made principal of the high school. To this office Principal Kennedy brought solid learning and broad vision as an instructor and combines with teaching efficiency the practical qualities which are equally needed in one who is at the head of such an institution. He has under his supervision 20 teachers and 430 pupils.

In Whiteside County, Illinois, in April, 1886, Mr. Kennedy was united in marriage with Miss Axa B. Wink. Her parents were Sanson and Elizabeth Wink, the former of whom, once a prosperous farmer in Whiteside County is now deceased. The mother of Mrs. Kennedy, now aged eighty-six years, resides at Sterling, in Whiteside County. Mr. and Mrs. Kennedy have seven children, as follows: Ola M., who is a resident of Twin Falls, Idaho, is bookkeeper for Charles Munson, a wholesale dealer; Flossie, who is a graduate of the Coffeyville High School and the Kansas State Normal School at Emporia, is teaching in the schools of Tulsa, Oklahoma; Florence, who is a graduate of several institutions, is the wife of Charles N. Brooks, who is superintendent of construction for the W. S. Dickey Clay Company of Chattanooga, Tennessee; Dewitt, who is employed at Coffeyville in the Cudahy Refining Company's plant; Leah, who is a graduate of the Coffeyville High School, is a sophomore in the State Normal School at Pittsburg, Kansas; Gretchen, who is a student in the Coffeyville High School; and Maxon, who is a pupil in the Eighth Grade in the city public school.

In politics Mr. Kennedy is affiliated with the republican party. Formerly he was an active member of the Modern Woodmen of America and the Knights of Pythias but more recently has confined his attention to organizations connected with his profession and is a member of the Kansas State Teachers' Association, the Kansas Southeastern Teachers' Association, and the National Association of High School Principals, the last named being a newly formed body. With his family Mr. Kennedy belongs to the Presbyterian Church and is a member of the sessions. Interested in everything that promises intellectual advancement and additional culture in his city, he consented to be a member of the directing board of the Carnegie Library. He still retains his farm of 160 acres situated one-half mile north of Bolton, and owns his comfortable residence at 106 West First Street, Coffeyville.

PROF. JAMES ANDERSON YATES. From England to North Carolina, in colonial times, the Yates family may be traced by generations as it extended into Tennessee and Kentucky and 1916 finds it firmly and honorably established in other states. For two decades this name in Kansas has been connected with the educational field, the scholastic attainments of Prof. James Anderson Yates, the head of the departments of chemical and physical sciences, in the State Manual Training Normal School at Pittsburg, having won recognition in this and in other large institutions of learning. Professor Yates enjoys a wide acquaintance with the leading scientists of the country and is valued as a member of numerous scientific bodies.

James Anderson Yates was born October 24, 1865, at Bush, in Laurel County, Kentucky, and is a son of James F. Yates and a grandson and namesake of Anderson Yates. The latter was born in 1810, in North Carolina, and died in 1885, in Grainger County, Tennessee, in which he had been an early settler and farmer. He married a member of the Mitchell family.

James F. Yates was born in 1835, at Rutledge, Grainger County, Tennessee, and died at Bush, Kentucky, in August, 1903. He was reared in Tennessee but during the Civil war went to Kentucky. When the war opened in 1861 he enlisted for service in the Union army, entering the Third Tennessee Volunteer Infantry, and during his three years of military service met with many of the serious hazards of war. He was first wounded in an engagement at London, Kentucky, and subsequently was captured by the enemy but was paroled and later exchanged. He was wounded again at Resaca, Georgia, and was sent to a hospital. As long as he lived he took pride in remembering that he "marched with Sherman to the sea." After he returned to Bush, Kentucky, he engaged in agricultural pursuits and they interested him until the close of his life. In politics he was a republican but never a seeker for office. As a consistent member of the Baptist Church, his fellow men found him true to his faith and a man honest and upright in all his dealings. He married Temperance Smith, who was born in 1835, in Laurel County, Kentucky, and died at Bush, in March, 1901. They had children as follows: James Anderson; Sarah Jane, who is the wife of Israel Howard, a farmer near Goodman, Missouri; George W., who is a farmer, cattle raiser and stockman and lives at Bassano, Alberta, Canada; William F., who lives at Bush, Kentucky, is a merchant and farmer; one child who died in infancy; and one child who lived to the age of five years.

James Anderson Yates attended the common schools at Bush, Kentucky. Following this he taught in district schools in Laurel and Clay counties, Kentucky, for six years and then entered the Kentucky State University, at Lexington. He was graduated from that institution in 1890, with the degree of B. S. and immediately became principal of Laurel Seminary, where he remained for two years. Professor Yates was then called to Cumberland College, where he organized a science department and remained there as its head for five years.

In 1897 Professor Yates became identified with Ottawa University, Ottawa, Kansas, as head of the department of natural sciences and continued in that relation for ten years. It was in 1907 that he came to Pittsburg as head of the chemical and physical sciences departments in the great industrial and normal college here, and since then he has bent every energy in making progress along these lines for the benefit of the state's future men and women. For this

work he is equipped by natural bent and training, by experimental study and association with those whose aims and talents are like his own. He has attended the Chicago University for six summer quarters and has won many quiet honors, and in 1899 received the degree of M. S. from the Kentucky State University.

At Somerset, Kentucky, June 19, 1895, Professor Yates was married to Miss Elizabeth Bryant, of that place, and they have three children: Julia Anna, who belongs to the graduating class of 1917, in the Kansas State Manual Normal Training School; Charles Robert, who is in the sophomore year in the same institution; and Gladys, who is a student in the high school at Pittsburg.

In his political attitude, Professor Yates is a republican. While residing at Ottawa, Kansas, he filled the office of city chemist, as he does at Pittsburg. In 1915 he was made president of the board of welfare, at Pittsburg, organized in large measure for the supervision of public entertainments, and through him the society was largely instrumental in obtaining the passage of the law giving cities rights to maintain such boards of welfare and to license exhibitions and other civic enterprises. In many other ways he has shown the sensible, unselfish public spirit that indicates the good citizen.

For many years Professor Yates has been identified with Masonry and has served in high offices. He belongs to Pittsburg Lodge No. 187, Ancient Free and Accepted Masons; Pittsburg Chapter No. 58, Royal Arch Masons; Pittsburg Commandery No. 29, Knights Templar, and Mirza Temple, Mystic Shrine, Pittsburg. He is a past high priest of the Chapter and a past eminent commander of the Commandery. He is a deacon in the Baptist Church and is chairman of the advisory board and a leader in the benevolent enterprises and wide charities that distinguish this religious body.

Since 1896 Professor Yates has been a member of the American Chemical Society. He is a member of the National Geographical Society, is a life member of the Kansas Academy of Science and past president of the same, is a Fellow in the American Association for the Advancement of Science, in 1899 was a member of the Union Pacific Fossil Field Expedition, and is a member of the National Educational Association. He has never made the accumulation of wealth a leading impulse in his busy life but, nevertheless, has shown the foresight that leads to comfortable independence, just as needful for the scientist as for the ordinary individual, and has secured some valuable property in the way of desirable real estate at Pittsburg, this including his attractive residence at No. 115 East Fourteenth Street. He is also the fortunate owner of an apple orchard of ten acres, situated at North Yakima, Washington.

ALFRED WORREL. One of the prosperous farmers and stockraisers of Zeandale Township, Riley County, Kansas, is Alfred Worrel, one of the best known residents of this section and a highly esteemed citizen. Mr. Worrel was born in Harrison County, Kentucky, September 24, 1859. His parents were William and Susan (Moore) Worrel, both natives of Kentucky.

William Worrel was born in Harrison County, September 12, 1825, and died at his home in Zeandale Township, Riley County, Kansas, July 2, 1901. He was the third eldest in a family of ten children born to his parents, Richard and Jane (Snodgrass) Worrel, both of whom were born and reared in Harrison

ALFRED AND ELLA WORREL AND FAMILY

Taken in 1908

County, Kentucky. They were married there and remained until 1840, when they moved to Hendricks County, Indiana, where the wife of Richard Worrel died in 1870. Richard Worrel subsequently came to Kansas and died at the home of his son William, in 1885.

William Worrel was fifteen years of age when he accompanied his parents to Indiana and remained there until he was twenty-one and then returned to Kentucky and resided there for the next thirty years. In March, 1870, on the death of his mother he returned to Indiana, immediately afterward coming to Kansas and taking up his abode in what is now Zeandale Township, Riley County. In due time, through prudence and industry, he became the owner of 1,700 acres of land. He devoted himself entirely to agricultural pursuits after coming to Kansas but back in Kentucky, for several years and including the Civil war period, he was the operator of a grist, flour and saw mill. Instead of abandoning his mill to enlist in the Union army, where his sympathies were, he continued to operate his mill in order to provide food for the families of soldiers taken by the war. He was drafted however, but provided a substitute and continued his milling business, proving himself a man of judgment and of benevolence. In Harrison County William Worrel and Susan Moore were united in marriage. She was born in Bracken County, Kentucky, November 2, 1835, and died at her home in Riley County, Kansas, July 6, 1886. Unto this marriage five children were born: Richard, Alfred, Sallie, Alice and Charles.

Alfred Worrel was in his eleventh year when his parents came to Zeandale Township, Riley County, and here he has made his home ever since, farming and stockraising being his business. He obtained but limited schooling but a man who has been able to cope successfully with agricultural problems, who has known how to safeguard the fertility of his land, to increase the yields of crops and the production of livestock, may be said to have lost little by not having early book knowledge and that lack in Mr. Worrel's case, has long since been overcome by reading and association with other intelligent men. He owns 480 acres of some of the best cultivated and most valuable land in his township. He served as a member of the township school board for twenty-four years and was township trustee for seven years, honesty and efficiency marking the performance of every public duty. He has resided on his present farm since 1885. Politically he is an independent democrat.

Mr. Worrel was married April 22, 1882, to Miss Ella Lee, who was born at Binghamton, New York, September 30, 1862. Her parents were John and Hannah (Pendergast) Lee. John Lee was born in Ireland in 1836 and died in Pottawatomie County, Kansas, in 1907. His parents were James and Catherine Lee. He came to America in 1848 and while living in New York City served an apprenticeship to the bridge-building trade, at which he was employed during the Civil war by the Union army. He came to Kansas in 1869 and settled in Riley County, removing subsequently to Pottawatomie County. In 1854 he was married to Hannah, daughter of John and Margaret (Conway) Pendergast, of Irish lineage but Mrs. Pendergast was born in New York. Mr. and Mrs. Lee had ten children: James, Catherine, Margaret, Ella, John, Mary A., Rosanna, Charles, William and Thomas.

Mr. and Mrs. Worrel have six children: Charles, who is a resident of Kansas City, Missouri; Phoebe,

who is Mrs. Charles Teel, of Zeandale Township; William J., who is a farmer in this township; Katy, who is the wife of Samuel Moon, of Dayton, Ohio; Lillian, who is the wife of G. E. McCormick, of Riley County; and Albert H., who is a farmer in Zeandale Township.

HERBERT J. CORWINE has long been one of Topeka's most popular citizens, was formerly pastor of the Third Christian Church of that city, and in 1916 he became widely known all over the First Congressional District as democratic candidate for Congress, running in opposition to Congressman Anthony of Leavenworth. To elect a democrat from this district would be to perform a miracle in politics, but Mr. Corwine made a very strong bid for popular support and secured a handsome aggregate of votes, thought impartial observers would have conceded the election of his republican opponent before the ballots were counted. Mr. Corwine was by far the strongest candidate of his party at the primaries in August, 1916, and particularly in those counties where he was personally known he secured a large number of normally republican votes.

Mr. Corwine was born in Pike County, Missouri, at the Town of Frankfort, September 25, 1876. His is a very interesting ancestry. He is a son of John Brooks Corwine, who was born in Mason County, Kentucky, in 1841, and for more than forty years was one of the ablest ministers of the Christian Church. He did his first work as a pastor in Macoupin County, Illinois. He also organized the First Christian Church at Bowling Green, Missouri, and one of its charter members was the distinguished Missouri and national statesman, Champ Clark. Thereafter an intimate friendship existed between Mr. Clark and Mr. Corwine. John B. Corwine was left an orphan and was reared by his relative, Thomas Brooks. Thomas Brooks was a son of John A. Brooks, who at one time was candidate for vice president of the United States on the prohibition ticket and in his prime was considered America's greatest temperance orator. Another relative of John B. Corwine was the illustrious Tom Corwin of Ohio, who stood in the front rank of a group of Ohio men as leaders and molders of public opinion in the crucial period of the Civil war. John B. Corwine himself was a man of more than ordinary ability, talent and intelligence, though extremely modest, a quality which may have prevented the fullest exercise of his abilities so far as his individual promotion was concerned. He had the faculty of attaching young men to him, and he brought thousands of members into the Christian Church. For a number of years he was a member of the faculty of the Christian University of Canton, Missouri, and for ten years was president of the State Sunday School Association.

The wife of John B. Corwine was Martha Goode. Her father, Doctor Goode, was at one time an army surgeon, lived in Macoupin County, Illinois, and later in life became a minister of the Christian Church. To the marriage of John B. Corwine and Martha Goode were born eight sons and one daughter, namely: Willie, who died in infancy; Harry B., who died in Bozeman, Montana, in 1909; Edward L., a resident of Frankfort, Missouri; Bertrand B. and Arthur E., ranchers in Montana; Herbert J. and Homer D., twins, the latter a banker at Frankfort, Missouri; Joel B., in the real estate business at Shelbina, Missouri; and Mary, wife of Mr. Ira Lake of Hannibal, Missouri.

Herbert J. Corwine received his early education in the common and high schools of Frankfort, Missouri, and started life with a definite purpose and resolution to make his personality and talent count for something in the world. For nineteen years he was active in the ministry of the Christian Church, and for several years of that time was pastor of the Third Christian Church at Topeka. He has always been deeply interested in social problems and social amelioration and for 2½ years he served as parole agent for the State Industrial School, having been appointed to that office by the governor of Kansas. For the past year Mr. Corwine has been agency supervisor of the Equitable Life Assurance Company of the United States.

GEORGE S. HINE is state dairy commissioner of Kansas with office in the State Agricultural College at Manhattan. His early life was spent on a Wisconsin dairy farm. Thus he is in a measure a dairyman to the manner born, as well as a man of thorough technical training and wide experience in that field. He had gained considerable distinction as a technical expert in his chosen profession in Wisconsin before he was called to Kansas, and has been identified with the dairy department of the state for the past six years.

He was born on his father's farm near Fairchild in Eau Claire County, Wisconsin, January 25, 1885. He was the oldest of the five sons of Rivilla C. and Kittie E. (Foster) Hine, the former a native of New York, and the latter of Wisconsin. His father was a practical dairyman and horse raiser in Wisconsin.

As a boy George S. Hine alternated between his father's farm and the public schools of Fairchild. On leaving the high school he entered Wisconsin University, where he specialized in the agricultural department and received his degree, Bachelor of Science of Agriculture, in 1907. In determining to secure a university training Mr. Hine carried out his ambition largely through means of his own earnings, and practically paid all his expenses while at Madison. During the last year of his university course he was student instructor in agriculture. After graduating he was appointed assistant instructor in feed and fertilizing inspection and dairy tests. That was his work until September 1, 1909, when he went to Marinette, Wisconsin, as principal of the County School of Agriculture and Domestic Economy.

A year later, on September 1, 1910, Mr. Hine was called to the Kansas State Agricultural College as lecturer on dairying in the department of college extension work. In that capacity he traveled pretty well over all the counties of the state, particularly those where dairying was an important industry, and the dairymen of the state, who had thus become acquainted with him personally and with his work as an instructor, hailed with much satisfaction his appointment in 1912 as state dairy commissioner.

During his administration as commissioner Mr. Hine has brought about many improvements of conditions affecting the dairy interests of Kansas. In particular should be mentioned the adoption of a system for grading cream. Up to that time all cream had looked alike and had been accepted as of a uniform quality. Now cream is sold according to grade, and thus a matter of justice is done those dairymen who seek to produce the best quality of creamery product. All creamery men and station operators are compelled to grade cream, according to standards established by the state dairy laws. ·

Mr. Hine is a member of the National Dairy Instructors' Association, of the Kansas Creamery Improvement Association, of the International Dairy and Milk Inspectors' Association, and has served as secretary of the Kansas Dairymen's Association. He is a member of the Kappa Alpha Beta fraternity. In 1911 he married Miss Edith Dahlberg.

THE COFFEYVILLE PUBLIC LIBRARY. Second to no city of its volume of population in education and culture, Coffeyville maintains a fine public library of 9,000 books affording enjoyment and instruction in almost every field that literature offers.

The Coffeyville Public Library was organized and established by the Women's Federated Clubs and was opened in April, 1912, with about 2,000 volumes. Its organization was made possible by a gift from Andrew Carnegie, the philanthropist. There are about 7,500 patrons, which is the average circulation, about one-half being of juvenile readers, an encouraging proportion and a larger per cent than libraries usually show. The library is situated on the corner of Eighth and Spruce streets, an attractive building of brick construction with Carthage stone trimmings.

Miss Myrtle Becker is the librarian and Mrs. Maud Dana, first assistant.

JOSEPH DAVID PETTET, M. D. With scientific progress shown on every side, medicine has been making wonderful strides forward, discoveries and inventions almost changing methods of practice and broadening the viewpoint of both practitioner and patient. The modern man of medicine no longer confines his efforts to alleviating the temporary ailment, but searches for the seat of the trouble, and prescribes right living, exercise and open air quite as often as medicine. To practice according to the enlightened idea of the present century, requires not only more careful training, but a certain, sure aggressiveness, and no physician of Crawford County has this and other admirable qualities more fully than has Dr. Joseph David Pettet, of Arcadia. Doctor Pettet is practically a newcomer to Arcadia, but has already impressed himself upon the people of the community not only as a thorough, learned and enlightened practitioner, but as a citizen desirous of assisting his adopted locality to better things.

Born in Daviess County, Indiana, April 16, 1875, Doctor Pettet is a son of George W. and Nancy E. (Greer) Pettet. The family originated in France and its early members were pioneers of Indiana, where the grandfather of Doctor Pettet, also a physician and surgeon, passed his life. George W. Pettet was born in 1839, in Boone County, Indiana, where he was reared and educated, and as a young man removed to Morgan County, in the same state, where he was married. Subsequently he went to Daviess County, Indiana, and engaged in farming until 1877, in which year he brought his family to Kansas and located as a pioneer farmer in Montgomery County, seven miles west of Independence, the county seat. For more than twenty years he continued to cultivate the soil of that locality, overcoming many obstacles and stubbornly fighting his way to success, typified by the ownership of a large and valuable farm. In 1898 he retired from active labor, and since then has lived in comfort at his attractive home. Mr. Pettet is a republican. He was reared in the faith of the Quakers, or Society of Friends, a sect which does not believe in war, but when the call came for troops to defend the Union, his patriotism overcame his religious scruples and he enlisted, in · 1861, in Company E, Twenty-sixth Regiment, Indiana Volunteer Infantry. Mr. Pettet served as a soldier for nearly five years and established an excellent record for bravery and faithful performance of duty. Among his battles were such notable ones as Pea Ridge and Vicksburg and he also took part in the Red River campaign. Mr. Pettet married Miss Nancy E. Greer, who was born in 1849, in Morgan County, Indiana, and they became the parents of three children: Jennie, who is the wife of L. L. Garr, a farmer near Havana, Kansas; Lou, who is the wife of John Ross Blair, a real estate man, who has made a fortune out of the promotion of the Town of Columbus, New Mexico, where they have their home; and Dr. Joseph David, of this review.

After securing his primary educational training in the public schools of Montgomery County, Joseph D. Pettet entered the high school at Independence, but remained only one year. He had determined upon a career in medicine, doubtless inheriting his predilection for this profession from his grandfather, and after some preparation entered the College of Physicians and Surgeons, at St. Louis, Missouri, from which he was duly graduated in April, 1900, with the degree of Doctor of Medicine. This was later supplemented, in 1910 and 1911, by post-graduate work at the Kansas City Post-Graduate School. Doctor Pettet began practice as a physician and surgeon at Mound Valley, Kansas, in 1907, and that continued as the scene of his labors for seven years. From that time forward, for about eight years, he was located in various communities, gaining experience and adding to his store of knowledge, so that when he came to Arcadia, in the fall of 1915, he was well prepared to take his place among the leading practitioners. He has built up an excellent practice during the short time he has been located here, and has won the confidence of the people by a strict adherence to high principles in his professional work. A man of broad and comprehensive reading, he is eager to grasp new ideas, but does not put them into general use until he has convinced himself as to their efficiency and merit.

Doctor Pettet has attractive offices on Race Street, where he has a large and valuable medical library and all instruments and appliances for the performance of even the most delicate operation. He realizes the value to the physician of membership in organizations of the calling, and belongs to the Crawford County Medical Society, the Kansas State Medical Society, the Southeastern Kansas Medical Society and the American Medical Association. His fraternal connections include membership in Arcadia Lodge No. 329, Ancient Free and Accepted Masons; the Modern Woodmen of America, at Humboldt, Kansas; and the Knights and Ladies of Security, of Arcadia. How strongly he has taken hold of affairs here is shown in that he is one of the foremost citizens of the place in promoting the city's welfare, in the capacity of secretary of the Arcadia Boosters' Club. Doctor Pettet is a member of the Methodist Episcopal Church. He is a republican in politics, and at various times has held public office, having served as coroner while a resident of Labette County, county health officer there, and a member of the city council at Mound Valley.

Doctor Pettet was married December 9, 1900, at Mound Valley, to Anna M. Williams, daughter of R. H. and Emma Williams, residents of Humboldt, Kansas, where Mr. Williams is a carpenter and builder. Doctor and Mrs. Pettet have one son, Joseph W., born April 1, 1906, who is attending school.

AMOS ALBERT BELSLEY has been a spirited factor in the business and civic life of Wellington, Kansas, for the past fourteen years. He is one of the leading real estate men of that section, and is a former mayor of the city.

His birth occurred on a farm in Woodford County, Illinois, near Roanoke, August 24, 1878. He was the sixth in a family of nine children born to Peter and Cathrine (Schertz) Belsley. His father was born and reared in Woodford County, Illinois, and the grandfather, Peter Belsley, came from Alsace-Lorraine and settled in Illinois in 1830. Peter Belsley, the father, spent his active career as a general farmer and stock raiser, and died in October, 1899, while his wife now lives in Peoria, Illinois. He was very prominent as a democrat, and filled many places of trust in his community. He was president of the Roanoke Coal Mining Company of Roanoke, Illinois, from 1882 until the time of his death in October, 1909.

Amos A. Belsley grew up on a farm, attended district school, and from the age of eleven to eighteen he had the opportunity of attending school for only three months each year. Later, as a preparation for his business career, he took a course in the Brown Business College of Peoria, Illinois.

It was in 1902 that Mr. Belsley came to Kansas and located at Wellington. For a time he was bookkeeper in the Farmers Bank, and in 1906 he and others organized the National Bank of Commerce, and he was assistant cashier and a director of that institution until 1909. When he left the bank in 1909 he entered the real estate business, and in that line has been very successful and has a host of friends and well wishers in this part of the state. In 1911 he formed a partnership under the name of Belsley & Fetters, but since 1916 has been alone.

On February 10, 1909, Mr. Belsley married Kathryn Hazel Herrig, of Wichita, Kansas. He has always remained true to the political faith in which he was reared, the democratic, and has been a rather active party man since coming to Kansas. His service as mayor of Wellington was for three years, from 1911 to 1914. That administration marks an epoch in municipal improvements. The water plant was started, the beginning of a city park system, much paving was done and the Carnegie library movement begun while he was mayor. Whether in office or as a private citizen Mr. Belsley has been more than willing to share his time and service for the benefit of the public welfare. He is a member of the Scottish Rite body of Masonry, and is also a Lodge, Chapter and Commandery Mason, being a past officer of the Chapter and Commandery. He belongs to Wichita Consistory No. 2 and to the Midian Temple, Ancient Arabic Order of Nobles of the Mystic Shrine at Wichita, Kansas. He is a past exalted ruler of the Benevolent and Protective Order of Elks of Wellington Lodge No. 1167, Wellington, Kansas, and is a member of the Knights of Pythias Anchor Lodge No. 9, Wellington, Kansas, and a Modern Woodman of America. He and his wife are loyal church workers in the First Congregational Church at Wellington, Kansas.

CHARLES F. REED, manager of the Ball Manufacturing Company's branch house at Independence, is an alert young business man whose proved abilities and varied experience have well qualified him for some of the larger and more important responsibilities of commercial life.

The family of which he is a member originated in Germany and was transplanted to Pennsylvania prior to the Revolutionary war. Mr. Reed himself was born at East Lynne, Cass County, Missouri, April 7, 1892. His father is W. B. Reed, now a resident of Kansas City, Kansas, and a merchant there. He was born in Pennsylvania in 1851 and at the age of seventeen went west of Illinois and engaged in farming near Decatur. From 1880 to 1905 he was in the hardware business at East Lynne, Missouri, and has since lived in Kansas. He farmed at Grainfield from 1905 to 1908, then spent two years as a merchant at Natoma, and has since been in the shoe business at Kansas City, Kansas. He is a democrat, a Mason and a member of the Methodist Episcopal Church. W. B. Reed married Martha J. Weigle, who was born in Illinois in 1859. J. D. Reed, the first of their children, is a carpenter and builder at Kansas City, Kansas; W. H. Reed is in the real estate and fire insurance business at Kansas City, Kansas; H. J. Reed is general foreman of the store department for the Frisco Railroad, with home and headquarters at Springfield, Missouri.

The youngest of the family, Charles F. Reed, spent his early life at East Lynne, Missouri, and in Kansas, graduated from the grade schools of Natoma and attended high school two years, and in 1910 began teaching. He taught a term at Laton, Kansas, then worked a year in his father's store at Natoma, and from there moved to Kansas City, Missouri, and was employed for two years in the Jones-Post mail order house. Another line of experience came to him as a representative of the Prudential Insurance Company at Kansas City, Kansas. From there, in December, 1915, he came to Independence to act as manager of the Ball Manufacturing Company, whose wholesale and retail general merchandise establishment is located at 200-202 West Main street in Independence.

This is one of the twenty-six branch stores operated by the Ball Manufacturing Company of Kansas City, Missouri. These stores are in Iowa, Missouri, Kansas and Oklahoma, and it is one of the largest general mercantile houses of the Middle West. The executive officers of the company at Kansas City, Missouri, are: Dr. S. E. Ball, president; E. E. Bessire, H. S. Batchelor, Mr. Crone, T. A. Banker, vice presidents.

Mr. Reed takes an active part in the Independence Commercial Club. He is one of the stockholders in the Ball Manufacturing Company. Politically he is independent, is a member of the Methodist Episcopal Church and belongs to Ben Hur Lodge No. 322, Ancient Free and Accepted Masons, at Argentine, Kansas. His home is at 505 South Tenth Street in Independence, and he has a wife and two children. In July, 1912, at Kansas City, Kansas, he married Miss Sadie B. Rhode, daughter of Charles and Ella Rhode; who are residents of Kansas City, Kansas. Their two children are: Marie, born May 20, 1913, and Margaret, born May 21, 1915.

HAROLD McGUGIN. The McGugin family came from Ireland to the United States many years ago, the first of the name in America appearing in Pennsylvania. Removal was subsequently made to Ohio and the family records do not definitely prove whether David McGugin, the grandfather of Harold McGugin, one of the able young attorneys of the

Coffeyville bar, was born before or after the family exodus. He was a farmer and a merchant and died in Montgomery County, Kansas, prior to the birth of his grandson. He may thus be numbered with the pioneers of this section.

William McGugin, son of David and father of Harold McGugin, was born in 1861 in Knox County, Ohio, and there grew to manhood and worked as a farmer. From Ohio he moved to Ringgold County, Iowa, where he was married and engaged in farming there until 1885, when he came to Montgomery County, Kansas, and settled on a farm near Independence. On that farm he remained for three years and moved then to another in the neighborhood of Liberty where he remained for twenty years. He owns two farms in Liberty Township and two farms in Cherokee Township and still resides on one of the latter but is making preparations to remove to Coffeyville. In politics he is a republican and has always taken a good citizen's interest in public matters. He was married to Caroline Bickel, who was born in Iowa in 1863, and they had two children born to them: Eldon D. and Harold, the former of whom is a traveling salesman for the John Deere Plow Company but resides at Coffeyville.

Harold McGugin was born November 22, 1891, in Montgomery County, Kansas, and in boyhood attended the local schools. He early decided on a professional career and after being graduated from the Coffeyville High School in 1912, directed his studies in preparation for the practice of law. For two and one-half years he attended the Washburn Law School at Topeka, Kansas, and in 1914 was admitted to the Oklahoma bar and in February, 1915, to the Kansas bar. He maintains offices at 818½ Walnut Street, Coffeyville, and has built up an excellent practice both civil and criminal. He has made so many friends and his ability is so generally recognized that his candidacy for the office of county attorney, on the republican ticket, meets with general approval. He has been quite active in the republican party and in 1914 was treasurer of the Young Men's Republican Club of Kansas. He represents the younger element in public life, the alert, educated class, able to make his way professionally but with enough public spirit to desire responsibility in politics as a helpful factor in forwarding movements for the public welfare. Such desire surely is commendable and Mr. McGugin is admirably qualified. He is identified fraternally with two organizations, the Loyal Order of Moose and the Modern Woodmen of America.

JAMES G. SANDIDGE. In the colonial history of the United States may be found frequent mention of names that are familiar and even distinguished at present throughout the great Middle West. They ring with achievement as in the old days, and although generations have passed since their first bearers lived and labored and increased on American soil, the stock is the same and the vigor of the younger branches gives testimony to the strength of the parent root. A long line of notable men have borne the name of Sandidge, from the founding of Jamestown, Virginia, and the early settlement of Charleston, South Carolina. A well known representative of this old and prominent family is found in Dr. James G. Sandidge, surgeon, banker and capitalist, who for almost a quarter of a century has been a foremost citizen of Mulberry, Kansas.

James G. Sandidge was born November 12, 1870, in the City of New Orleans, Louisiana. His parents

of beautiful character, kind and devoted as wife, friend and neighbor.

A staunch republican, Mr. Patterson freely admits his political preferences but he has never been willing to accept any public office for himself. He is a valued member of Lew Grove Post No. 100, Grand Army of the Republic.

RICHARD MEYER. When he was twenty years of age Richard Meyer came to Kansas with his parents and since then, for thirty-six years, has been a resident of Riley County. He was born at Freeport, Illinois, March 3, 1860, and was reared and received his education in that locality.

Farming, stock raising and stock feeding have given him abundance of opportunity to work out his destiny, and the work has not only been congenial but on the whole profitable. Mr. Meyer probably ranks as one of the chief stock feeders in Riley County. The spirit of progressiveness has kept him out of the ruts of agricultural industry, and while some of the experiments that he has made have not proved financially profitable, yet they have been not without benefit to himself and others. He has developed some original methods and plans of farm husbandry, and has reached a promising degree of financial success. Along with his inclination to take some of the untried and untested methods of doing business, he has shown a great deal of courage and determination and resourcefulness in the face of difficulties and misfortune. Some years ago an unsuccessful deal in cattle caused him the loss of his entire farm. That was not a permanent setback. He immediately began retrieving his lost possessions, and gradually paid off the indebtedness until he now owns the farm again and unincumbered. This place is a highly improved farm just south of the Town of Riley, comprising 440 acres.

The quality of enterprise which he has shown throughout his career was undoubtedly inherited to a large degree from his father, Richard Meyer, Sr., who also became well known in Riley County. He was born at Emden in the Kingdom of Hanover, Germany, April 28, 1827. While he was an infant his parents both died, within a month or so of each other. Though left an orphan he was taken into the home of relatives and given a careful rearing and the best advantages afforded by the schools of his native town. From 1848 to 1850 he was a soldier in the army under the king of Hanover. At the close of his service, and at the age of about twenty-four, in 1851, he emigrated to the United States. Thousands of his fellow countrymen had come to America in the preceding years, and it was in hope of enjoying the blessings and opportunities of the new world that he crossed the ocean. After landing in New York City he found employment in different lines for four years and then went out to Stephenson County, Illinois. After farming for a time he gave up that in favor of a position as clerk in a store at Freeport. His unbounded spirit of enterprise is illustrated when a little later he went into business for himself on a capital said to have been only $10. Success attended his career as a merchant, and he built up a large business at Freeport and remained in active control until 1879. In the meantime, in 1866, he and three other men had organized the German Insurance Company of Freeport, and he became its first secretary and so served for several years.

In 1880 Richard Meyer, Sr., brought his family out to Riley County, Kansas, and invested largely in

lands in the vicinity of Riley. He afterwards made a number of changes of residence, several times returning to Illinois, and his death occurred in that state at an advanced age.

He was married in February, 1853, in New York City to Miss Hannahrika G. de Graf. She was born at Leer, Germany, in 1827, and she also was left an orphan. It was about two years after their marriage in 1855 that Richard Meyer, Sr., and wife came West and settled in Stephenson County. Five children were born to them: Cornelia, Alida, Richard, Henry and Ida L. The three now living are Richard and Henry, both residents and farmers of Riley County, and Ida L., wife of A. S. Houghton, of Manhattan Kansas.

Richard Meyer, Jr., has been too busy a man to concern himself greatly with politics, though he has always been an ardent democrat, and for four years filled the office of township trustee. He is a Master Mason, a member of the Independent Order of Odd Fellows and the Benevolent and Protective Order of Elks, and of the Farmers Alliance.

In 1883 he married Miss Margaret Beta Raven. They were married in Washington County, Kansas. After they had journeyed life's highway together for nearly thirty years, Mrs. Meyer died in 1910, being survived by five children: Richard, Jr., who was graduated in 1905 from the Kansas State Agricultural College and is now actively associated with his father as a farmer and stock man and in 1916 was nominated by the democratic party as candidate for county clerk; Joseph Arthur, on his father's farm; Ella M., who graduated from the Kansas State Agricultural College in 1907, and is now postmistress at Riley; Amelia, at home; and Margaret Beta, also at home. One child, Willie, died at the age of sixteen.

RALPH L. JAMES. A comparative newcomer to Kansas, Ralph L. James has been identified for the past six or seven years with the city of Independence, where for a time he was connected with the First National Bank and is now assistant to the general manager of the Petroleum Products Company.

He comes of a New York State family. His grandfather, John Hugh James, was born in Wales in 1815, came to this country at the age of ten years with his parents, and grew up in Oneida County, New York, on a farm. He became a farmer and died at Farmersville, New York, in 1888.

In Franklinville, New York, Ralph L. James was born February 8, 1886. His father is R. E. F. James, who was born in New York State in 1860, and now lives at Scio, that state. For many years he conducted a cheese factory at Franklinville, and in 1906 began conducting a creamery and condensed milk factory. From Franklinville he moved to Belfast, New York, and in 1913 to Scio. He is a republican, and has served on school boards in his home state and is an active Methodist, having been trustee of the church at Belfast. He is affiliated with the Knights of the Maccabees. R. E. F. James was married to Marcia Carpenter, who was born at Farmersville, New York, in 1865. Their children are: Ralph L.; Lee T., who is associated with his father in business at Scio and is a graduate of the high school of Portville, New York; and Margaret, now a senior in the high school at Scio.

Educated in the public schools of Franklinville, graduating from the Tenbroek Academy and in 1902 taking a business course in the Westbrook Academy at Olean, Ralph L. James began his business career with 'ample equipment in the way of practical training. In 1903 he was employed in the civil engineering department of the Erie Railroad Company at Cuba, New York, and remained there until 1909. In that year he came to Independence, Kansas, and was made secretary to Mr. R. S. Litchfield, then president of the First National Bank. In 1911 he was promoted to assistant cashier, but on account of poor health and the confining nature of his duties, he resigned in September, 1915, and has since been with the Petroleum Products Company as assistant to the general manager.

Mr. James is a republican, has served as trustee of the First Presbyterian Church of Independence, and is affiliated with Fortitude Lodge No. 107, Ancient Free and Accepted Masons, Keystone Chapter No. 22, Royal Arch Masons, and St. Bernard Commandery No. 10, Knights Templar. He is also active in the Commercial Club and the Country Club of Independence, and was formerly connected with the Wayfarers' Club, a flourishing organization until the need of its existence diminished: It was organized in order that young men who had no homes of their own might have a wholesome environment and meeting place.

At Paola, Kansas, September 6, 1911, Mr. James married Miss Nelle Numbers. She was born at Paola, was educated in the public schools there, graduating from high school in 1903, and in 1907 finished the course of the State Normal School at Emporia, receiving a life teacher's certificate. While pursuing her studies and afterwards she taught in the Paola schools five years, and for three years was connected with the public schools of Kansas City, Kansas. In that time she was an active member of the Kansas Teachers' Association. Since her marriage she has identified herself with local organizations at Independence, is a member of the Country Club there, is treasurer and a member of the year book committee of the Ladies' Library Association, and in the Presbyterian Church is a teacher in the Sunday School. She was one of the organizers and is actively connected with the Philathea, a national organization for young women.

Mrs. James is eligible to membership in the Daughters of the American Revolution through her maternal ancestry. Her maternal grandfather was W. P. Finney, who was born in 1832, and is now living retired at Galion, Ohio. W. P. Finney married Almyra Chambers, who was a daughter of Andrew and Isabel (Marshall) Chambers. Isabel Marshall's father was Captain John Marshall, who was commissioned March 4, 1776, as captain in General Miles' regiment, serving with that organization two months, nineteen days, and later was commissioned captain in Colonel Walter Stewart's Thirteenth Pennsylvania Regulars. He fought in the battle of Brandywine, where he was wounded. He was retired in December, 1778, and was given a pension May 8, 1818. He died upon the Marshall homestead in Richland County, Ohio, and is buried in a private cemetery on that homestead. Mrs. James is also a cousin of Warren G. Harding, who is a member of the Ohio State Senate from Marion, and was recently chosen to "sound the keynote" at the Republican National Convention to be held in Chicago in 1916. Mrs. James is a daughter of Charles T. Numbers, who is a resident of Paola, Kansas. He was born at Galion, Ohio, May 1, 1858, was reared and married there, and in 1885 became an early settler on a farm in Miami County, Kansas. From his farm he moved to Paola where for fifteen years he was in the mercantile business and for the past ten years has been a real estate and insurance

man. He is a stanch republican, and has served as county clerk and as justice of the peace in Miami County, and in Paola has been a member of the city council, and on the school board. He is trustee and treasurer of the Presbyterian Church, with which he has been actively connected for many years, and has also been superintendent of its Sunday school. He is a Master Mason and an Odd Fellow. Charles T. Numbers married Flora A. Finney, who was born in Galion, Ohio, June 1, 1859. Their children are: Dr. D. M. Numbers, who graduated from the Paola High School, the State Normal School of Emporia, and the Western Dental College of Kansas City, Missouri, and is now a practicing dentist at Paola; Mrs. James, the second in age; Lela May, a graduate of the Paola High School and in music from the Ursuline Academy, and is still at home with her parents; Hazel Vera, who is a graduate of the Paola High School, took vocal instruction in the Ursuline Academy, and has also finished a commercial course.

WILLIAM C. KANDT, a native of Kansas, and member of a pioneer family in the state, has been a banker all his active career, and while he maintains offices and has his home at Independence he is active cashier of the Wayside State Bank and president of the Citizens State Bank of Elk City.

His birth occurred in Dickinson County, Kansas, August 24, 1877. His grandparents, John and Mary Kandt were German people who came to this country in the early '50s and in 1857 pioneered into Dickinson County, Kansas, where they were among the first to break the virgin soil and where they lived as farmers the rest of their lives. A. F. Kandt, father of the Independence banker, was born in Germany in 1850 and was brought to this country when three years of age. His parents first lived in Wisconsin, and he was about seven when he came to Kansas. Reared and educated in Dickinson County, he has followed an active career as a farmer and stock raiser, but since 1906 has lived retired at Herington, in Dickinson County. He is a democrat and has filled various township offices, including the office of treasurer. He is a member and deacon of the German Lutheran Church. A. F. Kandt married Fannie Kux, who was born in Austria in 1852. Her father, Ignitz Kux, brought his family to America when she was very young, settling in Chicago and afterwards becoming an early farmer in Marion County, Kansas. A. F. Kandt and wife were married in Dickinson County, and their children were: William C.; Ida, wife of W. F. Ziebel, a retired farmer and cattle man at Herington, Kansas; Fannie, wife of A. F. Holfgren, a banker at Lincolnville, Kansas; Sophie, who is at home with her parents.

William C. Kandt received his early education in the public schools of Dickinson County, and at the age of nineteen finished a general business course at Salina, Kansas. His first employment after leaving business college was in teaching in a commercial school at Fort Smith, Arkansas, for one term. He then became connected with the bank of Herington as bookkeeper, and since then for a period of twenty years has been almost continuously identified with banking. He was bookkeeper at Herington for two years, then helped organize the Tampa State Bank of which he was cashier a year. Selling out his interests, he organized the Woodbine State Bank in 1901, and was its cashier two years. His next activities as a banker were in organizing the First National Bank at Byars, Oklahoma, of which he was cashier seven years. While there he was also connected with the American Trust Company, of which he was president, and was president of the Rosedale State Bank of Rosedale, Oklahoma. Disposing of his interests in these concerns in 1908, he opened an office in Oklahoma City and was in the loan and brokerage business there until 1914.

In that year Mr. Kandt organized the Wayside State Bank at Wayside in Montgomery County, also the Citizens State Bank at Elk City, being cashier of the one and president of the other. The Wayside State Bank, which has a capital of $10,000 and surplus of $2,000, has the following officers: George I. Hess, president; A. D. Berry, vice president; and William C. Kandt, cashier. The officers of the Citizens State Bank of Elk City which has a capital of $15,000 and surplus of $1,500, are William C. Kandt, president; J. A. Brown, vice president; and E. E. Lugenbeal, cashier.

In political matters Mr. Kandt is a republican. While living in Dickinson County he served as treasurer of Lyon Township. He has been a deacon in the German Lutheran Church. Besides his interest as a banker he is district agent for the Franklin Life Insurance Company, and has offices in the Kress Building at Independence. His home is at 212 South Sixth Street in Independence.

In 1901 at Herington, Kansas, Mr. Kandt married Miss Ollie Mencke, a daughter of Rev. O. and Josephine Mencke. Her father is a German Lutheran minister and he and his family reside at Bremen, Kansas. To Mr. and Mrs. Kandt have been born seven children: Raymond, born in 1902, and now in the public schools; Edgar, born in 1904; Persis, born in 1906; Alton, born in 1908; Serena, born in 1911; William, born in 1913; and Josephine, born in 1915. All except the three youngest are attending the public schools of Independence.

LUTHER HENRY WADDLE. One of the greatest influences existing in a community, and particularly in those localities removed from the larger cities, is that exerted by the newspaper. To it the people look for their information regarding questions of importance, and, in a large degree, their own stand is based upon that taken by it. It is therefore desirable that the newspaper of a community be in the hands of capable, reliable and right-thinking men, and in this respect Weir City, in Cherokee County, is particularly fortunate in that the Weir City Journal has as its editor and publisher Luther Henry Waddle, under whose management it is being conducted in a manner that will redound to the credit of the locality and the benefit of its people.

Mr. Waddle was born four miles north of Ash Grove, Greene County, Missouri, September 10, 1881, and is a son of Hon. J. D. L. and Elizabeth E. (Black) Waddle. In the family the blood of several races combine, English, French and Scotch, and the earliest settlement in this country was made in Kentucky, where members of the family were pioneers. Young Dee Waddle, the grandfather of Luther H., was born in 1820, in Carroll County, Northern Missouri, and died near Ash Grove, Missouri, in 1886. He was a school teacher and preacher by vocation, and traveled around to various communities, and became prominent in public life and political affairs, being a member of the Legislature of Arkansas at the time of the outbreak of the Civil war. He was one of those who believed in the preservation of the Union, and did all in his power to prevent Arkansas from seceding, but, failing in this, enlisted in the army of the North, and during his service acted in the capacity of clerk to his captain. He was nominated for Congress at Fayetteville, Arkansas, during the period of the war, but did not return to that state, the remainder of his life being passed in Missouri. He was a stanch republican and a man who was held in the highest esteem and respect in his community. Mr. Waddle married Miss Floyd, and the following children were born: J. D. L.; E. G., who is engaged in farming near Ash Grove, Missouri; Fannie, who is the wife of George Davis, a retired farmer of Wichita, Kansas; Mattie, who is the wife of Robert Leeper, a farmer near Ash Grove, Missouri; Elizabeth, unmarried, who is a writer of considerable note and lives near Ash Grove; and James O., who is a farmer and brilliant newspaper writer of near Ash Grove.

J. D. L. Waddle, father of Luther H., was born October 22, 1850, at Bowers Mills, Lawrence (then Greene) County, Missouri, and as a child was taken to near Fort Smith, Arkansas, where he resided until reaching the age of fifteen years, in the meantime securing a public school education. When he embarked in business it was as a handler of insurance, but subsequently turned his attention to the newspaper business, and, with his son, published the Advance, at Ash Grove, Missouri, for four years. While living in that state, Mr. Waddle became actively interested in republican politics. He is proud of the fact that he has always been a stanch supporter of the principles of the Grand Old Party, and was one of the stand-pat variety until his death, December 9, 1916. While at Ash Grove he was elected justice of the peace, an office which he filled for several years. He was also elected county judge, an office which he held for two terms, or eight years, and was then deputy county clerk of Greene County for eight years. He always was a believer in good roads, and it was he who originated the system of working the county's prisoners on the roads. Greene County now has one of the best systems of highways to be found in Missouri. On September 1, 1906, Judge Waddle came to Weir City, Kansas, and purchased the Weir City Journal, which he assisted in editing until June, 1916. Afterward he lived in retirement until his death. He owned a half interest in the paper. This organ was established in 1888, under the name of the Tribune, and is a republican sheet, circulating in Cherokee and the surrounding counties. The plant, with its modern machinery and equipment, is situated on Washington, corner of Pine Street, and in addition to its newspaper presses has a fine job printing department. Judge Waddle is a member of the Methodist Episcopal Church, and is fraternally affiliated with Ash Grove Lodge, Ancient Free and Accepted Masons, and Camp No. 714, Modern Woodmen of America, of Weir City. Judge Waddle married Miss Elizabeth E. Black, who was born in 1850, in Greene County, Missouri, and died at Weir City, Kansas, in February, 1914, and they had four children: Roxie E., who died at the age of ten years; a boy who died in infancy; Luther Henry, of this notice; and Ella L., who married William Shannon, a railroad man of Nevada, Missouri.

Luther Henry Waddle was educated in the schools of Springfield, Missouri, where he attended the high school, but left in 1900 four months prior to his graduation. At that time he entered the newspaper business at Ash Grove, beginning to publish the Advance, and two years later was joined by his father in this enterprise. In 1904 Mr. Waddle gave up newspaper life for a time, being for two years engaged in farming in Missouri, but in 1906, on coming to

Weir City, began editing the Weir City Journal, with which he has been identified ever since. This has been developed into a strong and influential organ of the republican party, and a newspaper that is known for its reliability and sound worth. Under Mr. Waddle's management its subscription list is showing a pleasing growth each year, and the merchants and professional men are showing their appreciation of Mr. Waddle's efforts by good advertising support. The paper has always been a good booster for its community's interests and those of the people and has been a valuable factor in the securing of civic improvements and general benefits.

Mr. Waddle is a stalwart republican and is prominent in the ranks of his party, having formerly served as precinct committeeman and now serving his second term as treasurer of the Republican Central Committee. He has been a member of the school board of Weir City for six years, and during the last year has occupied the office of president thereof. Fraternally he belongs to Weir City Camp, No. 714, Modern Woodmen of America, of which he is past consul. He is also an ex-member of the International Typographical Union, and belongs to the Weir City Commercial Club.

Mr. Waddle was married at Weir City, Missouri, in June, 1902, to Miss Ella Neergaard, daughter of T. A. and Ella (Lybarger) Neergaard, the former of whom, a farmer, is deceased. Mrs. Waddle's mother married again after her first husband's death, and is now Mrs. B. M. Foust and resides near Elk City, Oklahoma. Two children have been born to Mr. and Mrs. Waddle; Lamar, born December 24, 1903, a freshman in the Weir City High School; and Vivian, born November 3, 1908, who attends the graded schools.

JOHN MILLIGAN JOHNSON. Recently there died at Manhattan a Kansan whose character was even more important than his material achievements. He came within four years of living a century and he was a figure in the activities of the frontier until the frontier had passed away. But more important than all his experiences were the moral forces that emanated from his life, and the things he stood for, believed in, and worked to bring about. It is therefore as a character sketch that the following paragraphs are offered, and they find an appropriate place in the history of Kansas.

John Milligan Johnson was born at Pickneyville, Perry County, Illinois, January 29, 1820. His grandfather was a companion of Daniel Boone in his adventures through the western wilderness. His parents were natives of Kentucky and sometime prior to 1832 they moved to Northern Illinois, settling in the vicinity of Rock Island. When the Black Hawk war came on in 1832 they were still living there. This gave the boy an opportunity to see this small war with the Indians. To the end of his life he remembered many incidents of those stirring times. Having a keen sense of humor, nothing of the ridiculous escaped his attention. He would tell of a certain siege. The people were gathered in a fort. One new recruit was afraid to stand up to the port-hole and take aim at the foe. He would put his gun up to the port and fire at random. He was admonished by an old frontiersman and Indian fighter who said to him: "John, those Indians are not up in the sky flying around turkeys, as you seem to think, if your shooting is any sign. They are down here on the ground where any soldier with courage and sense can see them; take good aim and shoot at them."

His father was a Free Will Baptist minister. The son joined the church of the same faith. While he was of a religious turn he was also a good thinker, and his soul was ever filled with mercy. The doctrine of eternal punishment and endless misery did not appeal to him. He was so constituted that he could never keep from speaking out plainly and denouncing any abuse coming to his knowledge. He spoke his mind on the matter of future punishment. This did not please his church and he was dismissed because he would not change his views and confess that he was in error.

Mr. Johnson was a vigorous and independent American citizen. He thought for himself on all subjects. He had little faith in blind partisanship. It was his judgment that the salvation of the country did not rest with any particular party. He believed in the broad application of the laws of humanity to political conditions. He believed that every man should have opportunity to work and that he should receive liberal compensation for the labor he performed. To him the fact that there was industrial oppression of the great mass of the people was plainly evident. And Mr. Johnson was a man who never evaded any responsibility. He believed it was his duty to help remedy any existing wrong. This caused him to align himself with the liberal movement in politics. He was in the greenback, union labor and populist parties. He voted for James G. Birney and Horace Greeley for President. In the later years of his life he was of the opinion that the emancipation of the laborers of America from social and industrial thraldom would come through socialism, and he became a member of the socialist party. He was no dreamer. He did not deceive himself. He did not expect to live to see the movement he championed succeed in his day. He did his duty to society and to his country as he saw it. He performed his duty as his conscience directed, and trusted the future for the benefit he was sure would result to humanity. Only such men are real leaders. It requires a sublime courage to stand for those things which only bring success in the far future. But it is the salvation of the world that there have always been such men.

In 1859 Mr. Johnson removed from Missouri to Nebraska. There he engaged in freighting across the great plains. In this business he continued for seven years, driving over the old Oregon trail to Denver and Salt Lake City. His integrity was well known. Shippers knew that every pound of freight entrusted to him would be delivered at its destination in good condition if it was in the power of man to do it. He dealt justly with the Indians, but was also firm in requiring them to be just to him. He came to be well known among them and they respected him and protected his trains. He saw the plains black with millions of buffalo. Sometimes he was obliged to stop and permit them to pass on before he could resume his journey. He was disgusted with the wanton slaughter of these great game animals. He saw them slain by thousands, for their hides only. Against this cruel practice he protested, and he refused to kill them. He was proud to say that he never killed a buffalo.

Mr. Johnson moved to Kansas from Nebraska and settled on a farm in Pottawatomie County. There he lived until age began to weigh him down. He was twice married. All his children by his first marriage are dead. One of them, Bird Johnson, was long connected with the Rocky Mountain News. Of the children by his second marriage four are still living:

John W. Johnson, 820 Lincoln Street, Topeka; Jesse R. Johnson of Lincoln, Nebraska; Oscar Johnson; and Mrs. Fred Hulse of Manhattan, Kansas. John W. and Jesse are connected with the Capper publications at Topeka.

This good citizen and pioneer in three states lived to extreme old age. He died from an accident at Manhattan, April 2, 1916, aged ninety-six years. At his funeral the minister said:

"He did not believe that in heaven where God's will is done, that the rum power was allowed to exist, and so he was among the first to try to wipe this evil from the face of the earth.

"He did not believe that in heaven where God's will is done, men have greater privileges than women and so he always favored female suffrage.

"He could not believe that in heaven where God's will is supreme that some live in luxury while others suffered in want and misery and so he reasoned that socialism was right, because it was the only way to have God's will done on earth, as it is in heaven. And to you, his children and grandchildren, I will say weep not, his work is done. Listen to the voice of one that spoke as never man spoke and I believe in spite of doctrines and dogmas that he has received that welcome plaudit 'as you did it unto the least of these you have done it also unto me, enter thou into the joy of the Lord.' He has left to you neither lands nor gold but he has given you an inheritance of greater value. And I ask you to improve those splendid qualities of heart and mind inherited from a noble sire and go forward as he did battling for the right, as God gives you to see the right. Until our Father's will is done on earth as it is in heaven, or until your earthly career is ended and you will find, as did your father, that on the flowery path of duty there is no dark river to cross. 'I care not for your temples and creeds, one thing hold sure and fast, 'tis in the many ample days and deeds that soul of man is cast.'"

CLAYTON A. SWIGGETT is a mechanical engineer both by college diploma and by long and practical experience gained in many localities and in many positions. He is now superintendent of the Western States Portland Cement Company at Independence, and is contributing his ability towards the making of that one of the great industries of Kansas.

The Western States Portland Cement plant began operations at Independence in 1905, and from time to time it has been enlarged and improved until its annual capacity is now a million barrels. About 250 men are employed and the pay roll is one of the chief assets of local property. The plant is situated a mile southeast of Independence, while the offices are in the plant with a branch office in Kansas City. A dozen buildings make up the group of the plant, while the limestone quarry and the clay mines are immediately on the premises. The officers of this company are: A. W. Shulthis, of Independence, president; D. F. Henry of Lamar, Colorado, vice president; C. B. McVay, secretary and treasurer, and C. A. Swiggett, superintendent.

In 1624 Herman Swigert came from Germany and settled in New Amsterdam, now New York City; in 1700 his son, Otto Swigert, settled in Pennsylvania, now Delaware; in 1760, grandson of Otto Swigert, James Swiget, settled in what is now Casey County, Kentucky; in 1829, Nathan Swiget moved from Kentucky to Pike County, Illinois, with one son, George Swiget, then three years old. It was during this time

the additional letters crept into the name which is now spelled Swiggett.

Andrew Swiggett, son of George Swiget, was born May 27, 1854, at New Salem, Pike County, Illinois, and moved to Kansas in 1872, and married Celia A. Mooney, December 31, 1876; from which union there were three children, Floyd P., Clayton A., and Mary E.

Andrew Swiggett first located at Towanda, afterward moving to Eldorado, Kansas, and in 1905, to Wichita, where he still resides; he is a hotel proprietor, a progressive in politics, and a member of the Masonic fraternity.

In the maternal line, the Mooneys originated in the Isle of Man, and were New Jersey settlers also in colonial days. Isaac Mooney, Celia Mooney's father, was a native of Illinois, moved to Kansas in the early days and helped found the town of Towanda, Butler County. He died there; he was a Christian minister and for many years was president of a Christian college in Northern Kansas.

Clayton A. Swiggett received his early education in the public schools of Butler County, Kansas, graduating from the High School of Eldorado in 1901; found his first employment in the Santa Fe shops in New Mexico. He spent three years learning the trade of machinist from a practical standpoint. After that he worked at his trade in old Mexico, California, through the gold fields of Alaska, in the Cour D'Alene mining district of Idaho, and then returned to Kansas. For a year he was a student in the Fairmount College at Wichita, and then entered the Kansas State University, where in 1910 he was graduated and given the degree of mechanical engineer.

Since leaving the university, Mr. Swiggett's work has been identified with the cement industry. As mechanical engineer and assistant superintendent he was connected with the Iola Portland Cement Company at Iola, Kansas, until March, 1916. He then accepted his present post as superintendent of the Western States Portland Cement Company at Independence.

Politically, Mr. Swiggett is an independent democrat. He is a member of the American Society of Mechanical Engineers, and is affiliated with the Iola Lodge No. 569, Benevolent and Protective Order of Elks. At Iola, in 1915, he married Miss Florence Setterstrom, daughter of Judge J. P. and Mrs. Setterstrom, who reside at Elsmore, Kansas. Her father is a prominent citizen of Allen County, being a farmer, a dealer in real estate, and also probate judge.

C. B. McVAY is secretary and treasurer of the Western States Portland Cement Company of Independence. He has been identified with the manufacture and sale of cement for over fifteen years, that having been the chief work of his life.

He was born in Yankton, South Dakota, in 1878. His ancestors, the McVays, were Scotch people who settled in Pennsylvania more than a century ago. The father, William H. McVay, was born at Pittsburg, Pennsylvania, in 1839, was reared and married near Warren County, Ohio, his wife, Rebecca Rutan, being a native of Trumbull County, Ohio. In 1876 he moved out to Yankton, South Dakota, and was a well known banker of that city until his death in 1907. His widow now resides in Portland, Oregon. Politically he was a republican and was a member of the Masonic fraternity. The five children were: Mary, wife of George Wilson, a farmer living at Portland, Oregon; William H., connected with a wholesale hardware house at Portland, Oregon; C. B. McVay;

Samuel D. Houston

H. G. McVay, a mechanical engineer at Portland; and Catherine B., living with her mother.

Mr. McVay attended public school in Yankton and for two years was a student in Yankton College. Leaving school in 1900, he came east to Union City, Michigan, and was assistant chemist of the cement plant there for three years. Returning to Yankton, he spent seven years as chemist and sales manager in the cement plant of that city, and in 1910 identified himself with the Marquette Cement Plant in La Salle, Illinois, remaining with that concern a year as a salesman. He was next sales manager for one year with a cement concern at Dallas, Texas, and from there came to the Western States Portland Cement Company of Independence, and on January 1, 1916, became its secretary and treasurer.

Mr. McVay and family reside at 300 East Locust Street in Independence. Politically he takes an independent stand in local matters, but generally is a republican. He is a member of the Country and Rotary clubs of Independence, belongs to the United Commercial Travelers, and is affiliated with St. John's Lodge No. 1, Ancient Free and Accepted Masons, at Yankton, with Mirzah Temple of the Mystic Shrine at Pittsburg, Kansas, with Oriental Consistory No. 1 of the Thirty-Second Degree Scottish Rite at Yankton, and also with Elks Lodge No. 994 at Yankton. In his native city in South Dakota in 1908 he married Jennie Gamble, daughter of H. S. and Eva Gamble. Her father, now deceased, conducted a loan and insurance business at Yankton. The mother still resides in that city. To their union have been born three children: Chester B., born August 1, 1911; Jennie A., born July 15, 1914; and Hugh G., born January 14, 1916.

BERT L. HORTON, whose full name is Hubert Lee Horton, has spent about thirteen years of his life in Kansas and is one of the large oil producers in Montgomery County. His home and many of his business interests are at Wayside.

He is of Pennsylvania birth and ancestry. There were three Horton brothers back in colonial times who came from England. Mr. Horton's grandfather, Thomas Horton, was reared in New York State, where for a time in the early days he conducted a distillery, but subsequently moved to Tioga County, Pennsylvania, where he engaged in farming until his death.

It was in Tioga County, Pennsylvania, that Hubert Lee Horton was born November 23, 1876. His father Hector Horton was born in New York State in 1823, went to Tioga County as a young man, was married there, and followed farming and stock raising until his death in August, 1898. He was a republican. The maiden name of his wife was Permelia Emmick, who was born at Babb's Creek, now Morris, Pennsylvania, and is still living in Butler County of that state. Their children were: Charles A., an oil producer in Butler County, Pennsylvania; Frank, in the pipe pulling business in the Tulsa oil fields and a resident of Tulsa, Oklahoma; Maria, wife of A. C. English, who has a fruit farm at La Porte, Texas; George E., an oil well driller at Bartlesville, Oklahoma; F. J., who is one of the very successful men of Iola, Kansas, where he is known both as a farmer and as an oil and gas producer; May, who died unmarried in 1899 in Tioga County, Pennsylvania; and Bert L.

In his native Pennsylvania County Bert L. Horton acquired his early education, and spent his youthful years on his father's farm. In 1900 he came to Kansas, first to Allen County, where he worked in the gas fields for two years. Since 1902 his home has been at Wayside in Montgomery County. He laid the foundation of his success as a contractor in the drilling of oil and gas wells, and for the past seven years has been an important producer. He now has forty-three producing wells. His prosperity is also reflected in the ownership of considerable real estate, including the old home farm of 160 acres in Tioga County, Pennsylvania. He has 144 acres in Neosho County, Kansas, and his place at Wayside includes a town home and 80 acres of land.

Politically he is a republican and he takes much interest in Masonry, being affiliated with Iola Lodge, Ancient Free and Accepted Masons, Wichita Consistory No. 2 of the Scottish Rite, and Mirzah Temple of the Nobles of the Mystic Shrine at Pittsburg, Kansas.

In November, 1907, at Wayside Mr. Horton married Miss Lillian Frances Jones. Her parents, Thomas H. and Mary Jones are both now deceased, her father having been a pioneer in Montgomery County, a school teacher in early days, and later a farmer. Three children have been born to their marriage: Lucine Permelia, born in April, 1909; Wilma Mary, born in February, 1911; and Ruth, born September 8, 1914.

SAMUEL DEXTER HOUSTON. One of the very first settlers in Riley County, Kansas, was Samuel Dexter Houston, who located a claim on Wildcat Creek and built a cabin there, in December, 1853. He was one of the county's foremost citizens for more than a half century and his name is linked with some of the most important events in its early history and with those of other representative men of his time. He was conspicuous in the councils that worked on the construction of the Kansas State Constitution.

Samuel Dexter Houston was born at Columbus, Ohio, June 11, 1818, and died at the home of his daughter, Mrs. Luke Parsons, at Salina, Kansas, February 29, 1910. He was a son of Caleb and Elizabeth (Purdy) Houston. His father was born in New Hampshire, from which state he emigrated to Ohio in 1812 and there married Elizabeth Purdy, who was a native of Pennsylvania.

When Samuel Dexter Houston was twelve years old, his parents removed to Illinois and there he grew to manhood. His first visit to Riley County was made in the winter of 1853 and his impressions of the country were so favorable that he located a claim that was situated not far from the mouth of what is still known as Wildcat Creek. On the shore of this secluded little sheet of water he built his primitive log cabin. He returned then to Illinois but in the spring of 1854 brought his family to the pioneer home and for many years they lived in the cabin in the fertile valley of Wildcat Creek.

In 1842 Mr. Houston was married to Miss Mary Jane Rankin, who was a daughter of Rev. William C. Rankin. She died March 8, 1848, in Iowa, where Mr. Houston was engaged in farming. They had the following children: Catherine Amanda, who was born January 10, 1843, is the wife of Luke Parsons and they reside at Salina, Kansas; Annie Elizabeth, who was born November 22, 1845, resides with her sister, Mrs. Parsons; and Sarah Hunter, who died in infancy.

Mr. Houston returned then to Illinois and on May 20, 1850, was married there to Tabitha Kimble, who was born at Cadiz, Ohio, June 10, 1825, and died in Riley County, Kansas, November 18, 1904. To this marriage the following children were born: Loretta, who died in infancy; Samuel Dexter, Jr., who was born July 11, 1852, is now residing in Texas; Mary Luellen, who was born November 1, 1853, is unmarried and lives at Denver, Colorado; Charles Sumner, who was born June 20, 1855, in·Riley County, has always resided in this county and with his sister, Mrs. Charles A. Green, occupies the old family homestead; Angelica, who died in infancy; Lawrence Nile, who was born July 9, 1858, is a resident of Okmulgee, Oklahoma; Ulysses Grant, who was born November 23, 1860, was graduated in 1881 from the Kansas State Agricultural College and is now a lecturer, his home being at Enid, Oklahoma; Hortense L., who was born April 8, 1863, is the wife of A. G. Martin, of Miami, Oklahoma; and Lablanche, who was born January 17, 1869. She is the wife of Charles A. Green, who was born in Sweden, November 29, 1873, and at the age of six years was brought to America by his parents. Mr. and Mrs. Green reside on the old parental homestead in Manhattan Township, Riley County.

Dipping into the authenticated history of Riley County it is proved that Samuel Dexter Houston played an important part in public affairs. In the fall of 1854 he, with Judge S. W. Johnson, of Ohio; Judge J. M. Russell, of Iowa; E. M. Thurston, of Maine, and Dr. A. H. Wilcox, college graduates, met at the mouth of Blue River and located a town site and named it Canton. On March 24, 1855, Isaac T. Goodnow, Luke P. Lincoln, C. H. Lovejoy, N. R. Wright, C. N. Wilson and Joseph Wintermute, committee of a New England company, appeared upon the scene. They were soon followed by the other members of the New England company and the new town they named Boston. In April, 1855, a Cincinnati colony appeared. Mutual agreement was made between the parties and eventually the name Manhattan was accepted. Mr. Houston aided in laying out what is now the prosperous City of Manhattan and one of its principal thoroughfares was named Houston in his honor.

In July, 1861, Mr. Houston was appointed by President Lincoln, receiver of public moneys at the Junction City Federal land office. An ardent anti-slavery man, he bore an active and influential part in the struggle that made Kansas a free state, and, as previously mentioned, assisted in formulating the first state constitution. When the republican party came into existence he felt that he could safely unite with an organization that so entirely expressed his own principles and he continued this affiliation until the close of his long life. He was the first state senator from Riley County and represented Riley and Pottawatomie counties in the state Legislature from 1860 to 1862. At the outbreak of the Civil war Mr. Houston participated in the military movements that succeeded in keeping the Confederate General Price and his legions off of Kansas soil.

Mr. Houston was a man of great force of character and courageous in advocating the principles he believed to be right. He was a fine organizer and so judicious and so enlightened, having been well educated, that his opinions were acceptable to any body of his fellow citizens whose aims were as high as his own. As a husband and father he met every demand and as a neighbor his helpfulness, especially in the early days when assistance was needed on every side, made strong bonds of friendship. His finely improved property including a handsome, commodious stone residence, have long been admirable examples of what the early settlers of the county produced notwithstanding pioneer hardships, and probably his homestead farm ranks with the very best in the county. An exemplary citizen and in every sense a worthy man, he ranked with the builders of the great State of Kansas.

PROF. HARRY W. SHIDELER. For the reason that the journalistic and educational professions are in many ways so closely allied, it is a happy combination of talents that allows an individual to participate in the work of the schoolroom and at the same time to devote a part of his abilities to the editing of a newspaper. Prof. Harry W. Shideler, superintendent of schools of Girard, Kansas, has for many years been well known in educational circles as a thorough and learned instructor, and in more recent years has entered the field of journalism as one of the proprietors of the Girard Press, a newspaper of acknowledged influence and wide circulation. Both as an educator and an editor he is doing much for the progress and advancement of his community, and his record in public life and as a private citizen is one which gives him merited prestige among the helpful men of this part of Crawford County.

Harry W. Shideler was born in Clay County, Indiana, January 14, 1873, and is a son of Henry and Sophia (Harbaugh) Shideler. The family in America traces its lineage back to the year 1730, when Johanne Shideler, a native of Germany emigrated to this country and took up his residence in Pennsylvania, where he followed farming. Later the family branched out to other states, notably Ohio, where, in 1818, the grandfather of Prof. Shideler, Daniel Shideler was born. He was a farmer and blacksmith in Ohio, later moved to Clay County, Indiana, and finally came west to Cherokee County, Kansas, where his death occurred in the fall of 1881. He was married first to Miss Lowrey, a native of Ohio who died in that state, and among their children was Henry Shideler. The grandfather contracted a second marriage with Miss Culler.

Henry Shideler was born in 1845, near Berlin, Ohio, and when he was but a boy was taken by his parents to Clay County, Indiana, where he lived on a farm and was educated in the district schools. When still a young man he learned the wagonmaker's trade, was subsequently engaged in teaching for several years and finally turned his attention to farming. In the fall of 1881 he came to Kansas and located in Cherokee County, where he purchased 120 acres of land, and this he has since increased to nearly 300 acres. He still continues to cultivate his property, and is known as one of the substantial agriculturists of his locality. Mr. Shideler is a republican, on the ticket of which party he was elected township trustee while residing in Clay County, Indiana. In Cherokee County, he has served as a member of the county high school board. In 1863, Mr. Shideler enlisted in the Fifty-ninth Regiment, Indiana Volunteer Infantry, with which he served until the close of the Civil war, participating in numerous engagements and being with General Sherman on his famous march to the sea. Mr. Shideler was first married to Miss Sophia Harbaugh, who was born in 1853, in Clay County, Indiana, and died in 1885, in Cherokee County, Kansas. To this union there were born four children: Harry W.; Dora, who married Frank Painter, a farmer of Crawford County, Kansas; Daniel W., a farmer of this county; and John W., who is superintendent of the schools of Vermillion, South Dakota. Mr. Shideler was again married to Mrs. Susan (Oglesby) Huffer, who still survives, and they became the parents of two children: Floyd I., who lives with his parents on the home farm; and Goldie May, a teacher in the public schools of Cherokee County.

Harry W. Shideler gained his primary education in the public schools of Cherokee County, and when seventeen years of age began teaching in the country districts. In the following year he entered the Kansas Normal-College, at Fort Scott, which he attended for five years, and from which he was graduated in 1896, but in the meantime had not given up his teaching, the greater part of which had been done in Cherokee County, although for one year he was at Swan Lake, Idaho. Thus, combining his work as a teacher with his study as a pupil, he gained an excellent preparation for what he had decided upon as his career. In 1896 Mr. Shideler became professor of economics and history in the Kansas Normal College, and after two years thus spent resigned to enlist, in 1898, in the Twentieth Regiment, Kansas Volunteer Infantry. He went to the Philippine Islands as second lieutenant of his company, and after a year returned to San Francisco and was honorably discharged and mustered out of the service wearing the shoulder-straps of a captain, in October, 1899. At that time he came to Girard, and in the winter of 1900 became principal of the high school here, a position which he retained for two years. Professor Shideler next went to Fort Scott, where he had his first experience in the newspaper business, but after one year was elected superintendent of schools in Girard, an office which he has retained to the present. He has under his supervision 3 schools, 21 teachers and 800 pupils, and has done much to improve the system and to elevate educational standards. In 1904 and 1905, to fill out the unexpired term of Harry E. Hornaday, he acted in in the capacity of county superintendent of schools. He is a member of the state board of education, belongs to the Kansas State Teachers' Association, and in 1907 was president of the Southeastern Kansas Teachers' Association.

In the fall of 1915, Professor Shideler purchased an interest in the Girard Press, a republican sheet which was established in 1866, and which now circulates in Crawford and the surrounding counties, with an exceptionally large foreign list. The paper is published by the firm of Wasser & Shideler, and its modern offices and plant are situated at the corner of Forest and Summit avenues. The Press exerts a strong influence in the territory in which it circulates, and is a well-printed, well-edited organ, giving its readers live and authentic news in regard to questions and happenings both local and national, possessing an editorial page of marked merit, and devoting a good deal of its space to matters calculated to be of benefit to Girard and Crawford County. It has the reputation of being an excellent advertising medium.

Mr. Shideler is a pronounced republican, and has been more than ordinarily active in the affairs of his party. He served as a member of the Girard City Council for four years, and in 1909 was sent to the Kansas Legislature to represent Crawford County. His record in that body was a good one, and his labors were strenuous and fruitful of good results as a member of the ways and means, educational, military affairs and public health committees. Mr. Shideler and the members of his family belong to the Christian Church. He is fraternally affiliated with Girard Lodge, No. 93, Ancient Free and Accepted Masons, of which he is past master, and the Ancient Order of United Workmen, and also holds membership in the Girard Commercial Club. He has been successful in a material way, and in addition to his own residence at 105 Western Avenue, South, and the dwelling next door, owns a valuable farm of eighty acres in Crawford County, located one-half mile south of Girard.

Professor Shideler was married in September, 1897, at Fort Scott, to Miss Iva L. Jessup, daughter of the late Solomon P. Jessup, who for many years was a farmer of Cherokee County. Five children have been born to this union: Harry Kenneth, born June 23, 1898, and now a student at the Kansas Agricultural College, Manhattan; Ralph Jessup, born September 20, 1900, a junior at the Girard High School; Robert Theodore, born October 1, 1902, a sophomore at the high school; Fred Muriel, born September 23, 1904, attending the graded schools; and Frank Jessup, born August 24, 1915.

PROF. EDWARD NORRIS WENTWORTH. Editor, author, and professor of animal breeding at the Kansas State Agricultural College, at Manhattan, Edward Norris Wentworth has accomplished more in the way of adding to the knowledge of mankind, in his twenty-nine years, than have many others in a whole lifetime. His studies have been particularly directed along the line of animal breeding, but, while making this his specialty, he has further broadened his field of knowledge and has won collegiate honors and degrees through high scholarship.

Edward Norris Wentworth was born at Dover, New Hampshire, January 11, 1887, and is a son of Elmer M. and Elizabeth T. (Towne) Wentworth. At the age of six years he was taken by his parents to new homes in the West. They tarried but a short time in Indiana, moved then to Chicago, Illinois, and from there, in 1894, to Marshalltown, Iowa.

It was in Iowa that Edward N. Wentworth grew to manhood. After attending the public schools he matriculated in the Iowa State College, at Ames, and was an apt student, being graduated from that institution in 1907, at the age of twenty years, with the degree of B. S. A. Two years later he received from the same college the degree of M. S. In the fall of 1907 he began his career as an educator, as a teacher in the animal husbandry department of the Iowa State College, where he continued until May, 1913, when he was invited to Chicago and tendered the position of associate editor of the Breeders' Gazette, the leading livestock publication in America. His editorial work on this journal was eminently satisfactory, showing thorough grasp of the subjects that were his specialities, which subjects he made interesting and instructive to its readers. He continued with the Gazette until September, 1914, when he came to the Kansas State Agricultural College to assume the duties of his present position.

As a writer, especially in his own particular line, Professor Wentworth has won an enviable reputation. He is the author of five small volumes, published under the general title, "Cattle Husbandry." In collaboration with Dr. L. J. Cole, of the University of Wisconsin, he is co-author of a text book on heredity in relation to live stock breeding. He leads a busy intellectual as well as practical life, contributing to farm literature, extending the scope of his educational work, and at the same time giving close attention to the every day developments pertaining to his division, one of the most important in the college departments.

In 1911 Professor Wentworth was united in marriage with Miss Alma McCulla, a descendant of Scotch-Irish stock. Through heroic ancestors, Professor Wentworth is a Son of the American Revolution, of which his father was national president in

1916. He belongs to numerous scientific organizations among which are included: the American Society of Zoologists, the American Society of Naturalists, the American Society of Animal Production and others, and is a fellow of the American Association for the Advancement of Science and a member of its council board. He retains full membership in his Greek fraternity of college days, the Sigma Alpha Epsilon, and in the honorary fraternities, the Alpha Zeta (agricultural), the Sigma Delta Chi (journalistic), the Alpha Psi (veterinary) and the Phi Kappa Phi, being a member of the national board of regents of the latter fraternity.

At no time in the world's history has agriculture been of such vital importance as the present and it is encouraging to realize that its development is the chosen work of such able and enthusiastic men as Professor Wentworth. In the solution of the problems to which they give attention lies undoubtedly the future maintenance and preservation of the human race.

FREDERICK WINKLER. The name Winkler has long been prominent in the annals of Riley County and especially in the northern part where, on Franey Creek, the first permanent grist-mill in the county was built by August Winkler, a brother of the late Frederick Winkler. The former came to Riley County in 1857, and the latter in 1860. The Winkler brothers became joint proprietors of Winkler's Mill, which was a landmark, and operated it for many years together. Frederick Winkler continued to operate the mill until within five or six years of his death. Constructed of native stone, the old mill still stands as a monument to the thrift and enterprise of the Winkler brothers, and the near-by village and postoffice of Winkler was named in their honor.

Frederick Winkler was born in Saxony, Germany, January 6, 1836, and died in Riley County, Kansas, November 15, 1900. In the spring of 1860 he came to the United States, following his older brother's example, and immediately joined him in Riley County, Kansas. Perhaps nothing contributed more to the health and contentment of early settlers in any section than the establishing of a grist mill and no doubt the Winkler brothers found many to encourage them in their enterprise. The old mill was patronized well and was a paying property during almost its entire period of use. In addition to his mill interests, Frederick Winkler was a large land owner and became an extensive farmer and stock raiser. His different business undertakings proved successful, but they were never speculative, his ample fortune being amassed along legitimate lines, and he prized his reputation as a man of honest and upright character. He was a faithful member of the German Lutheran Church.

Mr. Winkler was married to Miss Pauline Vogler, who was born in Germany. She survived her husband about thirteen years, passing away at the age of seventy-two, mourned by her children and the community, for she was kind and helpful to every one. She was a member of the German Lutheran Church. Five children survive Mr. and Mrs. Winkler, namely: Flora, Theodore, August, Sophia and Frederick. The present Frederick Winkler resides on the old home place where he was born October 4, 1880, and is considered one of the most dependable citizens and most successful farmers and stockmen in this section of Riley County. In 1913 he was united in marriage with Miss Erna Kunze. Like his late father he is a democrat in his political opinions.

DANIEL LESTER MOWREY of Wayside is a man of extensive experience in the oil districts of the Southwest, and is manager of oil production in this part of Kansas.

His ancestors came originally from Germany and settled in Pennsylvania. The family as a whole has furnished its male members chiefly to the mechanical trades and professions, and the family record is a very worthy one. Mr. Mowrey was born at Emerickville, Pennsylvania, January 20, 1885, and having only recently passed his thirtieth birthday has the promise of many years of usefulness before him. His father, W. H. Mowrey, was born in Pennsylvania in 1844, and died at Emerickville in 1907. His active career was spent as a farmer and stock raiser. As a democrat he was entrusted with a number of township offices, and was also a liberal supporter of the Methodist Episcopal Church. W. H. Mowrey married Catherine Ishman, who was born in Pennsylvania in 1859 and died at Emerickville in 1904. Daniel L. Mowrey of Wayside is their oldest child. The others are: Theodore, a machinist at Sharon, Pennsylvania; Clyde, also a machinist at Sharon; Amor, a steel worker at Sharon; Alvin, who assists his brother Daniel at Wayside; Raymond, still in school at Spartansburg, Pennsylvania. W. H. Mowrey's first wife was a Miss Hunsinger. Her children were: Charles, who is machinist in a paper mill at Johnsonburg, Pennsylvania; Hermann, a farmer at Emerickville; Michael, a farmer at Maysville, Pennsylvania; George, an engineer at Reynoldsville, Pennsylvania; and Mary, wife of Charles McMillan, who is connected with a tannery at Reynoldsville.

Daniel L. Mowrey received his early education in the public schools of his native town in Pennsylvania. He called his education in the common schools completed at the age of sixteen, but in 1903 took a general course in a business college at Reynoldsville. Thereafter for seven years he was in a store at Russell City, Pennsylvania, but in 1910 came to the Southwest and found employment in the Oklahoma oil fields. He was an oil pumper and tool dresser in Oklahoma, but since moving to Wayside, in 1915, has become a successful manager, and now handles the fourteen producing wells of the firm of Lucas & Wiles. Mr. Mowrey is independent in politics and is affiliated with Wayside Lodge, No. 660, of the Independent Order of Odd Fellows. He is unmarried.

J. LOUIS GRISWOLD, M. D. During his long and active practice at Columbus, Doctor Griswold has become a recognized specialist in medical and surgical work, and has well earned a position among the foremost members of his profession in Cherokee County. Doctor Griswold has lived in this section of Kansas for more than thirty years, and was a druggist before taking up his studies and preparations for medicine.

He was born on a farm in Bureau County, Illinois. His Griswold ancestors came originally from Wales and were colonial settlers in Connecticut. His grandfather, Willard Griswold, was born in Connecticut in 1776. He was the son of a soldier of the American Revolution, and other members of the family were also represented in the patriot armies. Willard Griswold became a pioneer farmer in the State of Iowa, where he died in 1874.

Hubbard Griswold, father of Doctor Griswold, has for many years been a well known citizen of Southeastern Kansas. Born in Livingston County, New York, in 1830, he grew up in that state, and spent part of his boyhood as a "bound boy." He worked hard to earn his own living from an early age, and as a young man went west to Michigan. His was a life of varied experience. For a time he was a boatman on the Mississippi River. He became an active farmer prior to the war, and after his marriage in Michigan moved to Illinois in 1855. During the war he tried two different times to enlist, but was rejected on account of disability. In 1868 Hubbard Griswold moved to Northern Missouri, was engaged in farming there for a number of years, and in 1883 moved to Montgomery County, Kansas, where he was one of the early settlers in that now rich and populous district. He is now past eighty-five years of age and is living quietly retired at Caney. He came to his majority in time to participate as one of the first voters of the Republican party, and has always been stanchly aligned with that organization. He is also a Mason. Hubbard Griswold married Susan A. Kinney, who was born in Livingston County, New York, in 1828, and died at Toledo, Ohio, in 1910. There were three children: Alonzo, who is a cattle rancher at Montoya, New Mexico; Dr. J. Louis; and Emma Hopkins, who lives at Toledo, Ohio, where Mr. Hopkins is in the employ of the Standard Oil Company.

Doctor Griswold spent ten years of his early youth in Mercer County, Missouri, and while there received most of his public school training. His father's farm was his home until he was twenty-four, but in the meantime he had been awarded a certificate and taught for four years in the country schools of Northern Missouri.

It was as a school teacher that Doctor Griswold first became known to the people of Southeastern Kansas. He taught one term in Montgomery County, beginning in 1884, and then embarked in the drug business at Crestline in Cherokee County. For twenty years Doctor Griswold owned and operated his drug store at Crestline, and it was from this occupation that he graduated into a professional career. He took up the study of medicine while a druggist at Crestline, and completed his training in the College of Physicians and Surgeons at St. Louis, where he received his Doctor of Medicine degree in 1899. For the next six years Doctor Griswold practiced at Crestline, but since 1905 has had his home in Columbus, and his work in that city has been exclusively as a specialist. He has his offices in the Columbus State Bank Building at the north corner of the Square. Doctor Griswold stands high among his fellow associates in medical circles, is a member of the Cherokee County Medical Society, the State and the Southeastern Kansas Medical societies and the American Medical Association.

While his life has counted much towards the welfare of his fellow citizens, Doctor Griswold has also prospered in business affairs, and besides his home at 626 East Maple Street he owns 320 acres of land in the State of New Mexico. Since coming to Columbus he has served four years in the city council. He is a republican, is affiliated with Prudence Lodge, No. 100, Ancient Free and Accepted Masons, Chapter No. 223, Royal Arch Masons, both of Columbus, and with Columbus Lodge, No. 387, Independent Order of Odd Fellows, and Columbus Lodge, No. 12, Knights of Pythias.

In December, 1895, Doctor Griswold was married in Cherokee County, to Miss Mamie Janney, daughter of William and Mary (Brown) Janney, the latter now deceased. Her father, who is a retired farmer, lives with Doctor and Mrs. Griswold. To their marriage have been born two daughters. Mildred, born July

18, 1897, is now in the first year of the Cherokee County High School at Columbus. Marjorie, born in June, 1903, is in the eighth grade of the public schools.

A. FRANK JOHNSON. During his residence at Independence for thirty-five years A. Frank Johnson has made a most commendable and successful business record, and in many ways has found opportunity to serve the public welfare as a private citizen. For more than twenty years he has been in business as a stock buyer and meat dealer, and is also a bank director and the owner of considerable property.

A Pennsylvanian, he belongs to the branch of the Johnson family which settled in Pennsylvania in colonial days. His grandfather, Roan Johnson, spent his life in that state as a farmer. A. Frank Johnson was born at Strattonville, Clarion County, Pennsylvania, September 10, 1857. His father, Samuel Johnson, was born in the eastern part of the state April, 1818, and became one of the leading farmers and citizens of Clarion County, where he served as county treasurer and sheriff. He died on his farm near Strattonville in September, 1893. Politically he was a democrat, and was a deacon in the Baptist Church. Samuel Johnson married Miriam Owens, who was born in Clarion County, Pennsylvania, in 1816 and died there in 1904. Their children were: Andrew, who served as a soldier of the Union army during the Civil war, afterwards became a pioneer to the State of Minnesota, and died there, being drowned while crossing a river; John also was a Union soldier, was wounded, and died from his injuries shortly after the war in Clarion County; George, who was the third of these brothers to serve their country in the Civil war, is still living at Strattonville, Pennsylvania, a farmer; Martha died young; Curtis was a farmer and died in Clarion County at the age of fifty-eight; Emma is the wife of Edward Loomis, a hotel man at Pipestone, Minnesota; Dr. Samuel was a physician and surgeon in Clarion County, where he died; the eighth child is A. Frank; Rhoda died in childhood in Clarion County; Hayes died in infancy.

A. Frank Johnson spent his early life in his native county, where he attended the public schools. Starting out at the age of twenty-two to make a fortune for himself, he came in 1880 to Kansas and spent the first year clerking in a store at Liberty. Since 1881 his home has been in Independence, and he has been a witness of and a factor in the development of that city from the time it was a village. For nine years he was a clerk in the general store of Henry Baden, and was then connected with a book store for four years. In 1894 Mr. Johnson bought an interest in a meat market situated at 112 North Penn Avenue, and is now head of the firm of Johnson & Goodell. While he leaves the operation of the market itself to others, he employs the most of his time in the buying and selling of livestock. The firm owns the building in which their market is situated, and Mr. Johnson also owns a house at 212 South Eighth Street and his own home at 214 South Eighth. He is a director in the Independence State Bank.

Politically he is a democrat, is a trustee in the Methodist Episcopal Church, is past noble grand of Independence Lodge No. 69, Independent Order of Odd Fellows, a member of the Rebekahs, and of Independence Lodge No. 17, Ancient Order of United Workmen, the Homesteaders and the Commercial clubs.

Soon after coming to Kansas in 1881 at Liberty

he married Miss Carrie Parker, a daughter of C. W. and Marinda Parker. Her father was a farmer and is now deceased, while her mother resides with Mr. and Mrs. Johnson at the age of eighty-six years. Into their household have come five children: Edward L., who died at the age of four years; A. Frank, Jr., a Presbyterian minister now located at Moran, Kansas; Charles T., a graduate of the Western Dental College of Kansas City, Missouri, and now located in Northern Kansas, where he has a successful practice; Edna, who died at the age of eleven months; and Samuel K., still in the family circle.

CHRISTIAN FRANKLIN HERRING. Starting his independent career as a cowboy on the open plains of Texas, later engaging in handling stock in the Indian country, next carrying on farming in Montgomery County, Kansas, and giving this up to be identified with mercantile pursuits and the oil fields of Oklahoma, Christian Franklin Herring finally settled down in his present business, that of proprietor of an automobile garage at Tyro. Mr. Herring's career has been a varied and interesting one and has included the vicissitudes and experiences that make up the lives of the men who have sought and found success in the West and Southwest. The prosperity which has attended his present business indicates that he is firmly established in business life, while that he has placed himself substantially in the confidence of his fellow-citizens was demonstrated in 1915, when he was elected mayor of Tyro for a two-year term.

Christian Franklin Herring was born at Upper Sandusky, Wyandotte County, Ohio, January 20, 1856, and is a son of Christopher and Mary (Ellis) Herring. Henry Herring, the grandfather of Mayor Herring, was born in 1792, in the Canton of Basel, Switzerland, and as a young man served in the regular army of his native land. In 1841 he brought his family to the United States, settling in the vicinity of Upper Sandusky, in Wyandotte County, Ohio, as a pioneer farmer, and there continuing to reside during the remainder of his life. He was well known and highly thought of among the early settlers of that part of Ohio, and through an industrious life won a fair measure of material success. He died in the faith of the Lutheran Church, in 1868, having been active in the work of that denomination throughout his life. In politics he supported the democratic party.

Christopher Herring was born in the Canton of Basel, Switzerland, in 1832, and was nine years of age when he accompanied his parents to the United States. He grew up in Wyandotte County, Ohio, where he received a public school education, and was there reared to farming and married, following which he settled down to the raising of and dealing in stock. In 1871 he sought the broader opportunities offered by the West, locating in Indian Territory (now Oklahoma), but after twelve years returned to Upper Sandusky, where his death occurred in 1904. He was a man of upright principles, honest in his business dealings and true to his obligations, and had the esteem and confidence of those with whom he came into contact. Like his father, he was not a politician, but supported the democratic party's candidates. Also, like him, he was a lifelong member of the Lutheran Church, while his fraternal connection was with the Royal Arch Masons. His operations in farming and stock raising resulted in the accumulation of a property which rendered his old age comfortable. Mr. Herring married Miss Mary Ellis, who was born in Wyandotte County, Ohio, in 1844, and died at Upper Sandusky, in 1902, and they became the par-

ents of four children, namely: William, who died in Ohio at the age of eighteen years; Christian Franklin, of this notice; Mary, who died at the age of fourteen years; and John, who was a moulder in an iron foundry and died in 1908 at Marion, Ohio.

Christian Franklin Herring was educated in the public schools of Upper Sandusky, Ohio, primarily, and later at Caney, where he attended public school for three years while his parents were living in Indian Territory. He was about twenty years of age when he gave up his studies, and at that time left home and went to Texas, where for about nine years he followed the life of a cowboy on the open range. In the meantime, when twenty-five years of age, he had been married, and on his return to Indian Territory settled on a farm, being there engaged in the handling of stock until the territory was combined with Oklahoma and formed into a state. In 1891 Mr. Herring came to Montgomery County, Kansas, and began to devote his attention to farming, a vocation which attracted his activities during a period of seven years. His next venture was in a mercantile direction when, in 1898, he became associated with the Tyro Supply Company, of Tyro, a concern dealing in hardware and agricultural implements. After one year's experience in this line, Mr. Herring disposed of his interests and entered the Oklahoma oil fields, where he labored for four years with some success. He then returned to Tyro and secured a position as clerk in the Deuel Hardware Company's store, and continued with that concern until 1915. In the meantime, Mr. Herring had noted the need of Tyro for a first-class automobile garage, and finally, in 1915, built his present establishment on Main street, where he has an up-to-date establishment, with a floor space 50x80 feet, and all modern equipment for the handling and repair of automobiles. He has built up an excellent business in this direction, owing to his energy and good management. Mr. Herring has his own residence, located opposite the Methodist Episcopal Church, and also owns two other residential properties at Tyro.

Mr. Herring has been well known in public and fraternal life for a number of years. In politics a democrat, he has been active in the ranks of his party, and has been called upon to serve in a number of local offices. While still on the farm he was a member of the board of directors of School District No. 99 for seven years, and since coming to Tyro has acted in a like capacity for several years. In 1915 he became the candidate of his party for the office of mayor and was duly elected by a good majority, and took the oath of office in April, 1915. His term will expire in April, 1917. Mayor Herring has fully lived up to the promises he made prior to his election, and has given Tyro a clean and businesslike administration, bending every effort to the securing of civic improvements. He belongs to Tyro Lodge No. 386, Ancient Free and Accepted Masons; is president of the Anti-Horse Thief Association; has been secretary of the Homesteaders during the past four years, and is one of the leading members of the Independent Order of Odd Fellows, being past noble grand of Tyro Camp No. 517, of which he has been secretary for the past fourteen years, and a delegate to the national convention of Odd Fellows, held at Pittsburg, Kansas, in 1898.

Mayor Herring was married in 1881 at Caney, Kansas, to Miss Jessie B. Wood, daughter of Sylvester and Lydia Wood, the former of whom died on his small farm in 1912, while his widow still survives and makes her home there. To Mr. and Mrs. Herring

the following children have been born: Charles G., who is an oil well driller and follows the oil fields; Howard H., who is an oil worker and resides south of Morris, Oklahoma; Jentia, who married Charles Frost, an oil well operator, living six miles from Nowata, Oklahoma; Keith, who is assisting his father in business and resides at Tyro; Mary Ann, who is unmarried and resides with her parents; and Geneva, who is a senior in the Tyro High School.

SIMEON CECIL CANARY is one of the progressive young business men of Southern Kansas, and is a member of a family that has some of the largest holdings in the ranch and oil districts of Southern Kansas, Northern Oklahoma, and also operates ranches in other states. Simeon Cecil Canary was born at Webber Falls, Oklahoma, May 15, 1892.

His ancestors were among the pioneers of the State of Ohio, where his father, J. D. Canary, was born, in 1869. J. D. Canary was reared in Texas, and in 1898 came to Kansas. He lived for several years on a ranch just across the border in Oklahoma, but has his home in Caney since 1902. J. D. Canary is president of the Canary Oil Company and is general manager of the two large ranches owned by himself and sons. He is an active democrat.

J. D. Canary married Enolia Gibson, who was born at Collin, Texas, in 1872, a daughter of M. W. Gibson. Her father was a native of Texas, was an extensive cotton raiser and owned a number of cotton gins both in Oklahoma and Texas. She died at Waggoner, Oklahoma. The children in the Gibson family were: Mrs. J. D. Canary; James, a farmer at Waggoner, Oklahoma; W. M., Jr., a general merchant and farmer at Webber Falls, Oklahoma; M. W. Gibson, who has extensive farming and mercantile interests at Webber Falls; and Nettie, wife of Omer H. Ellington, a general merchant at Waggoner, Oklahoma. Mr. and Mrs. J. D. Canary have the following children: E. P. Canary, wife of I. D. Williams, who has an orange grove at Lakeland, Florida; Simeon C.; James H., manager of the ranch in Wyoming; Elmira L., who is now a student in the Monticello Seminary at Godfrey, Illinois.

Simeon Cecil Canary received a public school education in Oklahoma, and in 1912 graduated from the Caney High School. In the following year he completed the course at the Culver Military Academy at Culver, Indiana, and then entered the University of Wisconsin, where he specialized in agricultural work preparatory to the large responsibilities he would assume. He remained in the university through the sophomore year. Since July, 1915, he has been engaged in the oil business and in ranching. He is a stockholder in the Canary Oil Company, has interests in the J. D. and S. C. Canary Oil Company, in the J. D. Canary & Sons Oil Company, is a stockholder in the Tyrone Oil and Gas Company. The last named company is operating in the Kansas fields, while the others are principally centered in the fields along the border line between Kansas and Oklahoma. The Canary Oil Company has given a name to an important oil field in Washington County, Oklahoma, as the Canary Oil Field. The officers of this company are: J. D. Canary, president; J. W. Ernest, secretary and treasurer. The J. D. and S. C. Canary Oil Company operates entirely in Oklahoma.

Special mention should be made of the two large ranches controlled by the Canary family. Simeon C. is personally interested in the management and control of the 3,000-acre ranch six miles east and a mile south of Caney. The family has a ranch of

1,500 acres in Wyoming, located in one of the richest farming districts of the state along the North Platte River and at the Town of Saratoga.

Some of the finest cattle in the world have been handled and bought by the Canary interests. A few years ago they paid $8,100 for a bull called Repeater the 63rd. This marks the record highest price ever paid for a yearling bull. Repeater 63rd combines the blood of the greatest sires and dams of the breed, being a grandson of Distributor by Disturber; dam by Lamplighter by Don Carlos; second dam by Don Quixote by Anxiety 4th; third dam by Don Carlos.

Simeon C. Canary owns a fine residence on East Fourth Avenue in Caney, and also three business blocks in the city. He is unmarried. Politically he is a democrat, and is affiliated with Caney Lodge, No. 324, Ancient Free and Accepted Masons, Caney Lodge, No. 1215, Benevolent and Protective Order of Elks, and is a member of the Independence Country Club.

FREDERICK C. OTTO. A prosperous and substantial farmer and a dominating figure in the financial affairs of Riley, Kansas, Frederick C. Otto is also a leading factor in democratic politics in Riley County, at present being the democratic nominee for state senator. The achievements that may be justly credited to Mr. Otto have been fairly won. Deprived early of a father's protection and assistance, he had, in large measure, his own way to make in the world, and it was through a process of struggle that he advanced for many years only step by step. Industry, frugality, efficiency in everything concerning his agricultural operations, made easier the entrance into other lines of business in which he developed still other qualities, and now his position as one of Riley County's best farmers and soundest financiers cannot be questioned. On the same basis his political fortunes have been advanced and he has become his party's choice for a high public office because of his solid qualities and known integrity.

Frederick C. Otto was born August 1, 1862, in Ogle County, Illinois, the youngest of six children born to Christ and Mary (Peperling) Otto. His parents were born in Hanover, Germany, and were married there and remained until after the birth of one child, Dora. In 1858 they emigrated to the United States and settled on a farm in Ogle County, Illinois, and there five additional children were born, namely: Henry, Lewis, August, Mary and Frederick C. The father died in 1863. His widow was a woman of courage and resource. She determined at all hazards, to keep her children together and bravely succeeded, directing the work of the farm and rearing her family wholesomely and to habits of industry. She passed away in 1893.

Frederick C. Otto was an infant when his father died and he grew up under the wise but firm direction of his mother and remained on the home place until he was twenty-seven years of age. Doubtless the lessons he learned through toil during boyhood and youth were admirable as discipline, preparing him in the best way for the wider activities into which his life has merged.

On January 21, 1889, Mr. Otto was married to Miss Johanna D. Fosha, who is a daughter of John and Minnie (Schinneman) Fosha. They were born in Germany and when they came to the United States, settled in Ogle County, Illinois, where Mrs. Otto was born and reared. To Mr. and Mrs. Otto the following children have been born: Dora M., who was graduated from the Kansas State Agricultural College in 1911, and is now first assistant to Dean W. N. Jardine of that college; Edward J., who was graduated from the same college in 1916; and Merton L. and Esther Minnie Gladys.

Mr. and Mrs. Otto came to Kansas in the spring of 1890 and located on a farm just north of Riley on which they have since resided. As time passed Mr. Otto prospered as a farmer and stockman, adding to his landed possessions from time to time and is now the owner of 640 acres of fine land in Riley County, his home farm. He also has 578 acres in Butler County, Kansas, and an interest in 7,000 acres in Finney County, Kansas. In 1911 he completed building a commodious frame residence, handsome in appearance and modern in equipment. In 1892 Mr. Otto bought stock in the Riley State Bank, of which he has been president for a number of years. It is a sound financial institution, and Mr. Otto is a careful, conservative banker.

In politics Mr. Otto has always been identified with the democratic party and his active interest, his loyalty and influence, have made him prominent in its councils and its unanimous choice for the state senate. Fraternally Mr. Otto is a Mason and has taken all the degrees including the Scottish Rite. Mrs. Otto and children are members of the Presbyterian Church. In all that contributes to good citizenship, Mr. Otto takes interest and his fellow citizens never find him lacking in public spirit when occasion for its demonstration occurs. Of genial personality but dignified demeanor, he commands respect and wins esteem from all with whom he has either business or social relations.

JAMES H. PRICE. The large interests which have engrossed the time and energies of James H. Price have brought him to the very forefront among the business men of Crawford County, and particularly of that part lying adjacent to the City of Pittsburg, with which city he has been prominently identified for the past ten or more years. From the very start of his career, he has been interested, in one or another way, with the mining industry, and today he is known throughout Kansas as an extensive coal operator and contractor.

Mr. Price was born in Herefordshire, England, April 9, 1865, and is a son of Thomas and Louise (Lovett) Price, natives of the same place. His father was born in 1838 and was reared on a farm, his education being received in the rural schools of his locality. He was married in his native land and there engaged in farming on his own account, but was not satisfied with the success which attended his efforts and therefore determined to seek his fortunes in America, to which country he came in 1873. He first settled at Brazil, Indiana, where for some time he worked in the coal mines, but later resumed his earlier occupation of farming, and subsequently moved to Montserrat, Johnson County, Missouri, where he purchased a farm. During the remainder of his life he devoted himself to the pursuits of the soil and became one of the substantial farmers and stockmen of his locality. His death occurred on his homestead place, in 1906, when he was sixty-eight years of age. Mr. Price was an industrious, hard-working and God-fearing man, who was representative of the best citizenship of his locality. In politics a republican, he cared naught for political office, but devoted himself whole-heartedly to the development of his farm and the making of a comfortable home for his family. He was an active supporter of the Methodist Church, which he built at

Montserrat, and held all the lay offices therein in addition to being deacon for many years. He was married in his native land to Miss Louise Lovett, who was born in 1847, and died at Montserrat, Missouri, in 1892. They were the parents of the following children: Mary, who married James Oughton, a coal miner, and went to Seattle, Washington, where both passed away; James H., of this review; Francis, who is mine foreman for the Western Coal Mining Company, with headquarters at Pittsburg; William, who is a weighmaster in the coal fields and resides at McCormack, Kansas; George, who is a mine foreman for the Western Coal Mining Company, and lives at Fleming, Kansas; and Elmer, who is engaged in agricultural pursuits in the vicinity of McCormack, Kansas.

James H. Price was eight years of age when brought to the United States by his parents, and his subsequent boyhood and youth were passed at Brazil, Indiana, and Montserrat, Missouri, at which latter place his education was completed in the public schools. His earliest occupation was as his father's assistant on the home farm, on which he remained until he reached the age of twenty-one years, and then entered upon his own career in the field in which he has won such satisfying success. When he left the parental roof, Mr. Price went to Richhill, Missouri, where he entered the mines, and gradually, as the years passed, familiarized himself with every department of the industry. From time to time, as his abilities made themselves felt and his experience warranted, he was advanced, and thus developed into an operator, and as such came to Kansas in 1900. Locating at Pittsburg, Mr. Price began contracting for the sinking of mines, as a contractor, at first in a small way, and later on a large scale. During the time he has been engaged in this business here he has sunk something like 2½ miles of mines in this region, probably as large a work of accomplishment as has been done by any one man in the West. Almost all the mines in the region of Pittsburg have been sunk under contracts handled by Mr. Price, and he has also operated extensively in this way in Oklahoma, Montana and other parts of the United States. Few men know the industry better, and few have a higher reputation for the prompt and efficient fulfillment of contracts. Mr. Price is also the owner of a valuable coal mine of his own, located about two miles north of Pittsburg, and has his own home at No. 605 North Elm Street, and another residence property on East Washington Street.

Mr. Price is a democrat in political matters, but beyond casting his vote takes little part in public matters. He is well known in fraternal circles, being a thirty-second degree Mason and holding membership in Pittsburg Lodge No. 127, Ancient Free and Accepted Masons; Pittsburg Chapter No. 58, Royal Arch Masons; Pittsburg Commandery No. 29, Knights Templars; Fort Scott Consistory No. 6, and Mirza Temple, Ancient Arabic Order Nobles of the Mystic Shrine.

Mr. Price was married in 1888, at Butler, Missouri, to Miss Louisa Frazier, of Belleville, Illinois, and they have had the following children: Anna May, who is the wife of Patrick Drysdale, of Pittsburg, a coal operator; Thomas, who is a mine foreman in the employ of his father and resides at Frontenac, Kansas; Raymond, who is a mining engineer and resides at Pittsburg; William H., who is a member of the senior class at the Pittsburg High School, and resides with his parents; Dewey, who is attending the same school as a sophomore; Irene, who is a freshman at the high school; Eddie, Webster, Edna and Stella, who are all attending the graded schools at Pittsburg, and Maynard, the baby.

WILLIAM P. BROWN, brother of S. Allen Brown, a well known citizen of Independence whose career has already been sketched, has been prominently identified with various business affairs in South-eastern Kansas for nearly forty years, and is now a resident and has his headquarters at Coffeyville.

Born in Pomeroy, Ohio, July 29, 1861, a son of Gen. William R. Brown, he received his early education in the public schools of that state, and came with his parents to Independence, Kansas, in 1874. He was then a student in the Independence High School, but at the early age of seventeen started out in business on his own account and from that time until he was twenty-two was in the lumber business at Independence and then for two years was a grain merchant at Cherryvale. Since 1885 his home has been in Coffeyville, where he conducted one of the extensive lumber yards until he sold out in 1906. Since 1891 William P. Brown has been one of the leading oil and gas operators and producers in the Kansas fields. He owns 325 acres of land with about ten producing oil wells on it.

His home is a fine place at the corner of Eldridge and Walnut streets. This modern residence he built fourteen years ago. He owns several business houses in Coffeyville, and besides the farm already mentioned has a place of 120 acres five miles west of Coffeyville. Mr. Brown's wife is president, while he is secretary and treasurer of the Brown Brokerage Company, a firm that handles real estate both in Montgomery and surrounding counties.

Politically Mr. Brown is a democrat, and fraternally has taken most of the degrees in Masonry, being affiliated with Lodge No. 107, Ancient Free and Accepted Masons at Independence, with the Royal Arch Chapter and with the Knights Templar Commandery No. 10 at Independence, with Wichita Consistory of the Scottish Rite and with Mirzah Temple of the Mystic Shrine at Pittsburg.

In 1883 at Port Washington, Ohio, Mr. Brown married Miss Nannie Kilgore, daughter of John and Elizabeth Kilgore, both of whom are now deceased. Her father was a merchant. Mr. and Mrs. Brown have one living child, a daughter, Violet, who makes her home with them at their country place in Coffeyville.

JOHN W. STANFORD. One of the strongest banks of southern Kansas is the First National Bank of Independence, of which John W. Stanford is cashier. The Stanford family have been prominently identified with Independence for thirty years, since early days in that city, and Mr. Stanford has practically spent his life there and has made himself an important factor in local affairs. The First National Bank was established in 1883 with William E. Otis as president. In 1904 the late R. S. Litchfield became president of the bank. Since Mr. Litchfield's death on March 21, 1916, his successor has not been elected up to the present writing. The active officers of the bank are: E. W. Sinclair of Tulsa, Oklahoma, vice president; John W. Stanford, cashier; and R. W. Oates, assistant cashier. The record of this bank is one of steady and consistent growth and its resources make it one of the financial powers of the state. It has a capital of $100,000, and surplus and profits of $150,000. The bank building, which was

thoroughly remodeled in 1908, is located at the corner of North Penn and West Main streets.

John W. Stanford, who was brought to Independence in infancy, was born at Monticello, Indiana, August 27, 1884, a son of T. H. and Elizabeth (Duffy) Stanford. The paternal grandfather, William Stanford, was born and reared at London, England, came to this country as a young man, and after his marriage located in southern Indiana. Early in the Civil war he enlisted in the Union army and never returned and was never heard from. The maternal grandfather, Patrick Duffy, was born and reared at Dublin, Ireland, was married there, and some years later came to America and followed farming in southern Indiana until his death.

T. H. Stanford has long been one of the prominent business and professional men of Independence. He was born at Independence, Indiana, in 1850, studied law and was admitted to the bar in his native state and in 1885 moved to Independence, Kansas, where for thirty years he has been one of the leading members of the bar. He is a democrat, a member of the Catholic Church, and is affiliated with Council No. 19 of the Knights of Columbus, and Lodge No. 780, Benevolent and Protective Order of Elks at Independence. He is a director in the Commercial National Bank of that city. His wife, Elizabeth Duffy, was born in New Albany, Indiana, in 1854. Their children are: G. T. Stanford, who graduated from Notre Dame University in Indiana and took his law degree from Harvard Law School, and is now associated with his father in the firm of Stanford & Stanford; John W.; L. V. Stanford, in the automobile business at Independence; and F. C. Stanford, who is a graduate of Columbia University and a business man in New York City.

Completing his education in 1900 at graduation from the Independence High School, John W. Stanford took up banking as commercial clerk in the First National Bank. His success is due to the fact that he has applied all his energies since early manhood to one line. In 1911 he was promoted cashier, and has since borne the heavier burdens of the bank's management. He is also a stockholder in the Independence Building and Loan Association, and for the past two years has been treasurer of the Independence School Board. He is independent in politics, is a member of the Catholic Church, belongs to the Commercial and Country clubs, and is affiliated with Council No. 918, Knights of Columbus, Lodge No. 17, Ancient Order United Workmen, and Lodge No. 780, Benevolent and Protective Order of Elks at Independence.

Mr. Standford was married at Bradford, Pennsylvania, to Miss Helen M. Mack, daughter of Patrick H. and Mary Mack, who still reside at Bradford. Her father has been connected with the Bradford Oil Well Supply Company for the past thirty years. Mr. and Mrs. Stanford have two children: Jack, born October 16, 1911; and Mary Jane, born September 1, 1914.

WILLIAM M. ROUNDS. Among the men who have won places of responsibility in the gas and oil business in Kansas, one of the best known is William M. Rounds, district superintendent for this part of Kansas and local manager at Caney of the Prairie Pipe Line Company. From the time of his graduation from high school, twenty-three years ago, Mr. Rounds has been identified with his present line of business, and few men are better informed in its various branches. He has been a resident of Caney since

1915 and has already established himself in the confidence of the people of this thriving city.

William M. Rounds was born in Buchanan County, Iowa, July 25, 1876, and is a son of William M. and Emma (Stalnaker) Rounds. He belongs to a family which, originating in England, was founded in America during Colonial days, the first of the name in this country locating in Vermont. His grandfather, William Seward Rounds, was born in 1809, at Brattleboro, Vermont, subsequently removed to McKean County, Pennsylvania, where he was engaged in farming for a number of years, and in 1862 went to Olean, New York, and enlisted in the Union army for service during the Civil war. He was captured by the Confederates and sent to the awful Andersonville prison, where he died along with hundreds of his comrades, in 1864. William M. Rounds the elder was born in McKean County, Pennsylvania, May 20, 1851, and was there reared to manhood and received a public school education. On attaining his majority, in 1872, he came to Kansas and joined the buffalo hunters on the plains, continuing to be so engaged until the slaughter of these animals was stopped by the Government. Removing then to Buchanan County, Iowa, he was married, and there his two sons were born, and in 1880 returned to McKean County, Pennsylvania, and resumed his activities as an oil operator. In 1912 Mr. Rounds again came west, this time locating at Glen Pool, Oklahoma, where he is now residing and has large oil interests. Mr. Rounds is a democrat in politics, a member of the Methodist Episcopal Church, and is fraternally affiliated with the Knights of the Maccabees. He married Miss Emma Stalnaker, who was born September 20, 1850, in Buchanan County, Iowa, and they are the parents of six children, namely: William M. of this notice; Ernest E., who resides at Jenks, Oklahoma, and is assistant district foreman of the Prairie Pipe Line Company; Grace, who is single and resides with her parents; Bessie, who is also unmarried and at home; Jennie, who is the wife of E. W. Letson, an oil producer and resides at Eldred, Pennsylvania; and Georgia B., assistant principal and a teacher of the Indian Mission School, at Sapulpa, Oklahoma.

William M. Rounds was educated in the public schools of Eldred, Pennsylvania, and after his graduation from the high school of that place, in 1893, entered the employ of Franchot Brothers, oil producers operating in McKean County, Pennsylvania, and Cattaraugus County, New York. He remained with that concern until December 1, 1904, when he came to the West, locating in Oklahoma as connection man for the Prairie Oil and Gas Company, and continued there until July 1, 1915, when he came to Caney, Kansas, to assume the duties of local manager of the Prairie Pipe Line Company. The career of Mr. Rounds has been the career of the average plain, unassuming business man. He has been successful in the things that he has undertaken, is honorable in everything, with scrupulous regard for the sanctity of his given word, and enjoys a large measure of confidence among the men with whom he has been associated. He has been successful because he has given his whole strength to the things which have been entrusted to his care, and because the concerns with which he has been connected have learned to rely upon him absolutely. Politically, Mr. Rounds is a democrat, but he has had little time to engage in public affairs. He is interested in fraternal matters and stands high in Masonry, being a member of Wellsville (New York) Lodge No. 231, Ancient Free and Accepted Masons; Wellsville Chapter, No. 143, Royal Arch Masons; De Molay Commandery, No. 22, Knights Templar, and McAlester (Oklahoma) Consistory No. 2, thirty-second degree.

On October 10, 1907, at Hornell, New York, Mr. Rounds was married to Miss Nora Riley, daughter of John and Elizabeth Riley, of Scio, New York, both of whom are now deceased. Mr. Riley was a miller by vocation. Mr. and Mrs. Rounds have one son: John M., born November 22, 1914.

FRED HARVEY QUINCY. Success in any line of occupation, in any avenue of business, is not a matter of spontaneity, but represents the result of the application of definite subjective forces and the controlling of objective agencies in such a way as to achieve desired ends. Senator Quincy has realized a large and substantial success in the business world, has been given important public office, in which he has served with honor and distinction, and his career has well exemplified the truth of the foregoing statements. He occupies a prominent place in the financial circles of Kansas, is the controlling force in one of its most important banking enterprises, and is one of the distinctively representative men of the state. Progressive and energetic in the management of his various business interests, loyal and public spirited as a citizen, he holds a secure position in the confidence and esteem of the community and has contributed in large measure to the advancement of the City of Salina, in whose still greater commercial and civic prestige he is a firm believer. He is president of the Planters' State Bank of Salina, president of the Salina Chamber of Commerce, and has been twice elected to the state senate from the Thirty-first District, composed of Saline and Ottawa counties.

Fred Harvey Quincy is a native of Wisconsin and was born in Lancaster, Grant County, December 16, 1857, a son of Benjamin E. and Mary E. (Stone) Quincy, natives of Vermont. His ancestors, paternal and maternal, were among the early settlers of America and numbered among them are men who achieved distinction in the frontier life of those early days, the French and Indian war, the war of the Revolution, and the commercial era which followed, and they have filled many positions of usefulness in the town, state and nation. Underhill, Vermont, was founded by members of the Quincy family during the war for independence and here was born Samuel Quincy, the grandfather of Fred H., and who was a soldier in the War of 1812.

Fred Harvey Quincy secured his early educational discipline in the public schools of Grant County, Wisconsin, and Saline County, Kansas, having removed with his parents to the latter state in 1873. Subsequently he completed a course in the State Normal at Platteville, Wisconsin, and was graduated in Bailey's Business College, Dubuque, Iowa, in 1876. The succeeding five years he employed in farming, the winter months, however, finding him clerking in Salina. In 1882 he became a grain buyer and established a profitable business in this line. During 1889-90 he served as sheriff of Saline County, having been elected by a flattering majority in 1889. He was the active factor in the promotion and organization of the Salina Cement Plaster Company in 1893, was elected secretary of the company on its incorporation, and later became president and manager. Mills were built in Dickinson and Clay counties, Kansas, and in Hardeman County, Texas. The output of the mills, "Agatite Cement Plaster," became the standard of quality and the business was a success. In

Fred H. Quincy

1902 the company was merged with the American Cement Plaster Company of Lawrence, Kansas. In 1900 Senator Quincy organized the Planters' State Bank of Salina and was elected president of the institution, and this chief executive office he has since retained. Organized with a capital of $50,000, its business has been of sound and continuous growth. It has at the present writing (1917) a capital of $100,000, and an earned surplus and profits of $50,000, deposits of $1,000,000, and has paid to its stockholders since commencing business dividends exceeding 100 per cent. In the organization, development and administration of the business of the institution Senator Quincy has been the dominant executive and to his progressiveness, energy and resourcefulness is due the strength and high reputation of the organization. He is known in banking circles as an able and discriminating financier and as one who has brought the administrative policy of his bank up to the point of highest efficiency. He is also financially interested in several important commercial enterprises in Salina and has wielded a specially potent influence during the past ten years in the industrial and civic affairs of the city.

To the citizens of the state at large Senator Quincy is best known through his service as a member of the upper house of the Legislature, of which for several years he has been one of the recognized leaders. A lifelong republican, he has been an active force in Saline County since 1889, when he was elected sheriff. In 1904 he was the party's nominee for state senator from the Thirty-first District, comprising Saline and Ottawa counties, and was elected by a handsome majority, being elected for a second term in 1908. As a member of this body he has been industrious, capable, honest and patriotic. It is probable his most important service to the state has been in connection with financial legislation, for which his experience as a banker eminently qualifies him. He drew, without collaboration, and introduced in the session of 1907 a bill to guarantee the depositors of banks against loss. This was the first measure, based upon mutual insurance, permitting voluntary entry of the banks to its benefits, and providing for assessments based upon the past experience of banking loss, ever presented to a legislature in a measure of this nature. The bill, failing to receive attention of this session, was made the object of the special session called by Governor Hoch in 1908, in which it was defeated. The guaranty of bank deposits was made a political issue in the campaign of 1908 and both parties incorporated it in their platforms. In the session of 1909 the bill became a law and has since been declared constitutional by the United States Supreme Court. During the special session of 1908 Senator Quincy drew and was largely instrumental in having passed Senate Bill No. 33, which provides that all state, municipal, county and township bonds and coupons be payable in Topeka, the state treasurer being the authorized fiscal agent of the state. Previously these payments were made in New York City and various banks and officials derived a profit. Under the present arrangement the saving to the state exceeds $15,000 per annum. In 1906 Senator Quincy was one of a committee of five which included W. R. Stubbs, James Troutman, Arthur Capper and R. N. Allen, which planned the organization of the "Square Deal Republican Club." This organization secured from candidates and members of the Legislature an expression of their attitude on the anti-pass, two-cent fare, primary election, and assessment of railway property measures then before the people. These

several measures, were enacted into law during the sessions of 1907-08-09. Senator Quincy was also one of a committee of three appointed by the railway committee of the Senate to draft a bill providing for a public utilities commission, the bill as drawn by them passing in the session of 1911. On becoming a member of the Senate Mr. Quincy was made chairman of the committee on second class cities, which position he has since retained. His committee memberships were: banks and banking, railway, claims and accounts, and taxation. His work in support of the two-cent fare, anti-pass, wheat and corn, maximum freight rates, primary election, and general railway bills was of material assistance in securing their passage. He was also a potential force in securing the enactment of the present tax law. He introduced in the Senate, had charge of, and secured the passage through that body of the so-called "Blue-Sky Law," one of the most important bills ever enacted into law, and which is effecting a saving of millions of dollars to the investors of capital. He is a firm believer in the principle of true representative government and his record of service is one that the district which elected him can contemplate with pride and satisfaction. Senator Quincy has attained the Knights Templar and Scottish Rite degrees in Masonry, is affiliated with Isis Temple Shrine at Salina, and is treasurer of that body as well as of the local Scottish Rite bodies and Salina Commandery. He is a member of the Benevolent and Protective Order of Elks and the United Commercial Travelers, and a director of the Salina Young Men's Christian Association. His religious faith is expressed by membership in the Methodist Church, and he has served as a trustee of the Kansas Wesleyan University. On February 6, 1883, Senator Quincy married Miss Fannie, daughter of John Sprague, a native of West Virginia who was a Union soldier in the Civil war and died in service. Senator and Mrs. Quincy are the parents of two daughters: Lula Sprague, the elder, graduated at Ferry Hall, Lake Forest, Illinois, in 1906, as the honor member of her class. She is the wife of Fred I. Walker, assistant cashier of the Planters' State Bank. Nina, the second child, was also graduated at Ferry Hall, receiving first honors, with the class of 1907. Mrs. Quincy is a woman of broad culture and refinement. Senator Quincy is in all respects a high type of the conservative, unassuming American, diligent in his public duties and commercial affairs and conscientious in all things.

ISAAC S. LIGHTLE. The influence of a sound, conservative banking house is wide and its practical results far reaching. Without such an institution in its midst, no city can hope to take its place among its sister communities, and to it will come no reliable outside concerns. It may be truly said that the growth and development of a community depends largely upon the quality and stability of its banks, and this means the sagacity and integrity of the men who stand at their head. Therefore the thriving community of Arcadia, in Crawford County, is fortunate in the possession of such a stable institution as the Arcadia Home State Bank, at the head of which, in the office of president, is Isaac S. Lightle. Mr. Lightle has had a long and interesting career, which has included participation in the battles of war and peace, and which has invaded various fields of endeavor. He has been successful in the numerous enterprises with which he has been connected, and is representative of the type of men who lend strength to banking institutions because of their personal worth and ability.

Mr. Lightle is of Irish extraction on the paternal side of the family, and of German descent on his mother's side. He was born at Griggsville, Pike County, Illinois, December 9, 1840, a son of James and Maria (Julian) Lightle. The family settled during pioneer days in Ohio, and in Ross County, that state, James Lightle was born, November 3, 1803. He was reared and educated there, engaged in farming as a young man, and was married to Maria Julian, a native of the same county. Shortly after their marriage they removed to Illinois and settled on a farm in the vicinity of Griggsville, Pike County, where the wife and mother died May 2, 1844, aged thirty-three years, two months and ten days. Mr. Lightle continued to carry on agricultural pursuits on the farm which he had broken from the prairie and through hard and faithful work accumulated a modest competence. He died March 6, 1859, aged fifty-five years, four months, three days. A democrat in politics, he was prominent in public affairs of both city and county, and was accounted one of the good citizens and public-spirited men of his locality. Mr. and Mrs. Lightle were the parents of the following children: Margaret, who married first William Burns and second James Miller, both farmers and now deceased, and died at Griggsville, Illinois; William, who spent his life in farming and died at that place; Sarah Jane, who married George Elliott, a farmer and general workman, both dying at Griggsville; Samuel, who followed farming throughout his life and died in Bourbon County, Kansas; Becky, who married John Moulton, a farmer, both dying at Griggsville; Isaac S., of this notice; and James, who also followed the life of a farmer and passed away at Griggsville.

Isaac S. Lightle received his education in the district schools of Pike County, Illinois, and remained on the home farm until he was about twenty years of age, at which time his father died and the young man started out in life on his own account. His first employment was in running a ferry-boat on the Illinois River, this occupation receiving his attention for about two years, when his patriotism led him to enlist in Company H, Seventy-third Regiment, Illinois Volunteer Infantry, for a term of three years or during the war. The Seventy-third saw some hard fighting, including the battles of Perryville, Stone River and Chickamauga, in all of which Mr. Lightle participated, and at the last engagement he received a severe wound in his right arm, which incapacitated him for further service and he received his honorable discharge. When he had recovered, the young soldier occupied himself at whatever honorable employment presented itself, but he felt that he was not making progress and decided to try his fortunes in Kansas. Accordingly, in the spring of 1868, he came to Fort Scott, where he found work in handling cattle, and driving them from Texas, and this he followed for six years, during which time he had many trying and exciting experiences. In 1874 he came to old Arcadia, where he invested his hard-earned capital in a small general store, thus becoming one of the first merchants of the town. He disposed of his interests here in 1877 and went to Barton County, Missouri, where for eight years he was similarly occupied, and in 1885 returned to Arcadia, which community has since continued to be his home and the scene of his success. From 1885 until 1906 he was the proprietor of a successful mercantile business which under his excellent management grew and developed into large proportions and

gave its owner an established prestige as a man of business sagacity and judgment. He retired from the commercial field in 1906, but still retained his grasp upon business and financial affairs as he does today. He is president of the Arcadia Telephone Company, and of the Arcadia Home State Bank, both of which have benefited under his wise, conservative and efficient executive administration. He has large holdings in realty, which include his own residence on Race Street, a building on the same street, near the depot, and a modern restaurant, and in other ways is interested commercially. In politics Mr. Lightle is a republican, and the first town board found him a member. Later he served as a member of the council and of the school board, and his public service was always faithful, efficient and conscientious. He belongs to Arcadia Lodge No. 329, Ancient Free and Accepted Masons.

Mr. Lightle was married in 1874, in Barton County, Missouri, to Miss Eliza Clanton, who died in 1885, at Arcadia, having been the mother of three children, namely: Elsie, who married W. P. Conneff, a meat cutter in a large packing plant at Kansas City, Missouri; Ollie, who died in 1913, as the wife of J. T. Fowler, cashier of the State Bank of Arcadia; and Vernon, who is a traveling salesman with headquarters in Iowa. Mr. Lightle was again married, February 22, 1905, at Kansas City, Missouri, to Mrs. Lydia (Capps) Smith, widow of Stephen Smith, who had been in business at Kansas City for some years prior to his death.

ROBERT E. KENNER. No better lesson relative to the value of honorable effort intelligently directed can be found than that offered by the career of a man who has risen to a responsible position through his own initiative, and in this connection the life of Robert E. Kenner presents an example. Still a young man, he has worked his way to an important post, that of superintendent of the American Zinc, Lead and Smelter Company, at Dearing, Kansas, and in so doing has been dependent only upon his own resource and industry.

Mr. Kenner was born at Eureka, Kansas, August 5, 1883, and is a son of J. W. Kenner and Cora Frances (Cogswell) Kenner, the mother a member of the old Colonial Cogswell family of New England. The Kenners originated in England and at an early day were to be found in Illinois, in which state, in 1815, James Kenner, the grandfather of Robert E. Kenner, was born. He became a pioneer in Kansas of the early '60s, settling on Batchelor Creek, as a homesteader of 160 acres of land. There he passed the remaining years of his active life in agricultural pursuits, and died in 1900, at Eureka. During the Civil war he fought as a soldier of the Union, and assisted in repelling the forces of Price when the Confederates were engaged in their memorable raid. He was first a whig and later a republican, and was an ordained minister of the Christian Church, and active in the ministry the greater part of his life. James Kenner married Judith Willis, who was born in Kentucky, in 1824, and died at Eureka, Kansas, in 1914, and they became the parents of two children: Henry T., who was a farmer all his life and died at Eureka in 1896; and J. W.

J. W. Kenner was born at Albion, Edwards County, Illinois, in 1852, and was still a youth when he accompanied his parents to Kansas. He grew up on the farm located about four miles from Eureka, on Batchelor Creek, and secured his education in the district schools of Eureka and the State Normal

School at Emporia. Later he studied law and was admitted to the bar, served as county clerk of Greenwood County for eight years, and was then employed in the banking business in Eureka and the vicinity for many years. Finally he turned his business talents and legal knowledge to account in the field of real estate and insurance, in which business he is now engaged at Eureka. He is a republican, and his religious connection is with the Congregational Church, of which he is an influential worker and strong supporter. Mr. Kenner stands high in Masonry, belonging to the Blue Lodge, Chapter and Knights Templar of that order. He married Miss Cora Frances Cogswell, who was born at New Orleans, Louisiana, in 1860, and they have four children: Willis Cogswell, who resides at Atlanta, Georgia, and is connected with the Southern Express Company; Robert E., of this notice; Fred, who resides at Atchison, Kansas, and is with the Atchison Champion; and Winifred, residing with her parents, a teacher of piano in the Eureka High School.

Robert E. Kenner attended the public schools of Eureka, where he spent two years in high school, and then entered the Southern Kansas Academy, at Eureka, in which institution he spent two years also. Leaving school in 1905, he secured employment on a farm, on which he worked for about one year, when, becoming interested in the zinc industry, he secured a position in the plant of the American Zinc, Lead and Smelting Company, at Caney, Kansas, as a timekeeper. From that time to the present his career has been marked by constant promotion, won solely through merit and by the display of fidelity, and in 1912 he was made superintendent of the company's plant located one-half mile west of Dearing, with a capacity of 4,480 retorts and employing 400 workmen. Mr. Kenner has thoroughly familiarized himself with every department of the zinc industry and is considered one of the best informed men upon the subject in this part of Kansas. He is thoroughly trusted by his employers, stands high in the confidence of his associates, and has the respect and friendship of the men under him.

Mr. Kenner is a republican, but has been too busy to do more than discharge the duties of good citizenship. His career has been full of hard work, but his labors have been rewarded and he has the supreme satisfaction of knowing that all his work has been well done. Mr. Kenner is unmarried.

EDWIN F. PAUL. Engaged in the retail grocery business at Independence, Montgomery County, Mr. Paul is one of the representative merchants of the younger generation in his native city, his birth having here occurred on the 5th of June, 1886. He is a son of Morgan J. and Della (Kilgore) Paul, the former of whom was born in 1845, in Ohio, where he was reared and educated, and the latter of whom was born in 1862, she being still a resident of Independence, where the death of her honored husband occurred in 1909, the subject of this review being the younger of their two children and being secretary and treasurer of the M. J. Paul Grocery Company, of which his elder brother, John, is president, the extensive business controlled by this firm having been founded by their father, whose name gives title to the company.

Morgan J. Paul came to Independence in the early '70s, and became one of the pioneer merchants of this now important little city, where he engaged in the general grocery trade. For the accommodation of

his growing business he erected a three-story building at the corner of Main Street and Pennsylvania Avenue, and in 1904 the headquarters of the business were transferred to the present eligible location, at 106 West Main Street, where is utilized a floor space of 2,800 square feet, in addition to the basement. Mr. Paul was a progressive business man and loyal and public-spirited citizen, was a democrat in politics, and was affiliated with the Ancient Order of United Workmen. He was highly esteemed in the city where he held prestige as a representative business man for more than thirty years.

Edwin F. Paul continued his studies in the public schools of Independence until he was about nineteen years of age, when he withdrew from the high school to become associated with the large and important grocery business that had been developed under the able direction of his father. He has since given his close attention to the affairs of this enterprise, and he and his brother are well upholding the prestige of the family name, both as progressive citizens and enterprising and reliable business men.

Mr. Paul gives his political allegiance to the democratic party, is a member of the Independence Commercial Club, and is affiliated with the local organizations of the Benevolent and Protective Order of Elks and the Fraternal Order of Eagles. Though he owns an attractive residence property at 200 South Fifth Street, his name is still enrolled on the list of eligible young bachelors in his native city. On the paternal side he is of Welsch ancestry, and his mother is of Scotch lineage. His paternal grandfather was a farmer and the owner of a woolen mill in Tuscarawas County, Ohio, and his maternal grandfather conducted a general merchandise store at Port Washington, that state.

JOSEPH R. BERNAUER. Since assuming the management of the Fredonia Window Glass Company's plant at Caney, Joseph R. Bernauer has been successful in showing excellent financial results, and has evidenced a broad knowledge of mechanical science as well as a wealth of executive ability. Many years of practical experience contribute to his equipment, and during his career he has been connected with some of the leading concerns of this kind in the West.

Mr. Bernauer was born in Baden, Germany, August 13, 1863, and is a son of Raymond and Brigeta (Schlagel) Bernauer. His grandfather, Quirin Bernauer, was born in Baden, Germany, where the family has resided for many generations, in 1800, passed his life as a successful merchant, and died in 1883. Raymond Bernauer was also born in Baden, in 1834, followed the weaver's trade for some years, and likewise engaged in farming to some extent. He was also possessed of much inventive genius, as his invention of the wire screen will testify, but his career in this direction was cut short by his early death, in 1869. Mrs. Bernauer, who was born in 1843, died in 1883, in the faith of the Roman Catholic Church, of which her husband was also a member. They were the parents of three children, namely: Joseph R., of this review; Pauline, who is still a resident of Baden; and Otto, a blacksmith by trade, who died at Fredonia, Kansas, when thirty-five years of age.

Joseph R. Bernauer received his education in the public schools of his native land, after leaving which he served an apprenticeship to and thoroughly mastered the blacksmith's trade. He was only six years of age when his father died, and he did his share early in supporting the family, but on attaining his majority decided to seek better opportunities in the United States, and in 1884 arrived in this country and first located at Wellsboro, Pennsylvania. There he found employment at his trade and in the course of time became the owner of a business of his own, which he built up to substantial proportions. He still has a home in the town in which he first located on coming to America. In 1904 Mr. Bernauer came to the West. He had gradually enlarged the scope of his operations, and was brought to Fredonia, Kansas, to construct the plant of the Fredonia Window Glass Company, subsequently becoming factory manager, a position which he retained for eight years. He next erected a plant for the same company at Coffeyville, Kansas, and in 1913 was employed to build a large machine plant at Okmulgee, Oklahoma. Following this he went to Texas, where for eight months he managed a plant for F. E. Wear, at the end of that time returning to Kansas and locating at Chanute, where he reconstructed a glass plant. Mr. Bernauer remained at Chanute only a short time, however, for he was called to Caney to become manager of the plant of the Fredonia Window Glass Company, in which important position he has since been retained.

The Fredonia Window Glass Company is the owner of the plants both at Fredonia and Caney, and the officers at this time are: C. F. Lutz, president and general manager, Fredonia; B. E. LaDow, Fredonia, vice president; F. E. Wear, Kansas City, treasurer; David Bowie, Topeka, secretary; J. J. Wolever, superintendent of Fredonia factory; J. R. Bernauer, superintendent of Caney factory; C. E. Klock, in charge of the offices at both plants. The company manufactures window glass exclusively, the Fredonia plant having a capacity of forty-eight doors, and the Caney plant of thirty doors. The Fredonia plant, which was established in 1903, is situated in the extreme southwest part of the town, between the Frisco, the Missouri Pacific and the Santa Fe Railways; the Caney plant, established in 1915, is located just northeast of the city limits, on the Missouri Pacific Railway.

Mr. Bernauer is known as a man who is thoroughly familiar with every department of the work in which he is engaged. He has made a close and careful study of all its details, and his natural talents and ingenuity have resulted in a number of improvements and additions to both process and equipment. He is essentially a business man and has not mixed in politics, although he takes an interest in public matters of importance and gives his support to the republican party and its candidates. Fraternally, he is affiliated with the Odd Fellows, at Wellsboro, Pennsylvania; the Red Men, in Texas; and the Brotherhood of American Yeomen, at Fredonia, Kansas. With the members of his family he belongs to the Lutheran Church.

Mr. Bernauer was married in 1885, at Wellsboro, Pennsylvania, to Miss Minnie Loebich, a daughter of Mrs. Anna Loebich, who still resides at Wellsboro. Three children have been born to this union: Elsie, who is the wife of Wallace Ingerick, clerk in the postoffice at Charlestown, West Virginia; Raymond, who attended Kansas University two years, and also attended the University of Wisconsin two years, pursuing the course of mechanical engineer, and now associated with his father; and Minnie, the wife of LeRoy McMullen, of Wellsboro, Pennsylvania, and now attending Olson's Business College, at Parsons, Kansas.

IVY E. HANCOCK, D. O. The ablest representative of the school of osteopathy in practice at Independence, Doctor Hancock, who has been in practice there for the past thirteen years and around her skill and thorough ability has built up a splendid clientele.

Doctor Hancock is a native of Melrose, Iowa. Her great-grandfather came from Ireland and settled in this country in the early part of the last century. Her grandfather, William Vardaman Hancock, was born in Indiana in 1828, and went out to Iowa as a pioneer, following farming and stock raising there until his death at Plano in December, 1906.

J. F. Hancock, father of Doctor Hancock, was born near Gosport, Indiana, in 1856, and soon after his birth his parents removed to Monroe County, Iowa. He grew up and married there, and adopted farming and stock raising as his vocation, in which he is still engaged. From Iowa he moved to Kansas in 1898, locating in Montgomery County, and after farming there for twelve years moved to Chetopa, which was his home for five years, and in 1915 he went to Nowata, Oklahoma, where he still resides. He is a republican. He married Ella Gilbert, who was born in Iowa, and comes of a large family who moved from Indiana to Melrose, Iowa, in 1845. Four of her brothers served in the Civil war. Albert Gilbert served in one of the Iowa cavalries and died in the service from fever, at Little Rock, Arkansas. Henry Clay Gilbert served in Company H, Ira William Gilbert in Company C, and Amasa Gilbert in Company C, Eighteenth Regiment of Iowa. These last three brothers served to the close of the war and lived until a few years ago. Dr. Ivy E. Hancock is the oldest of her parents' eight children. H. H. Hancock is a traveling salesman living at Portland, Oregon; Claude Sumner died at the age of four years; Webster Clay has a ranch at Roy, New Mexico; Rhoda Pearl is the wife of William Stewart, and they live on a ranch at Kremling, Colorado; Albert V. is a merchant tailor and conducts a cleaning and pressing establishment at Sapulpa, Oklahoma; Oliver A. is associated with his brother Albert in business; and William Hobart is a plumber and he and his sister, Doctor Hancock, live together at 329 East Beach Street, where Doctor Hancock owns a residence with four vacant lots adjoining.

From an early age Doctor Hancock's inclinations were for some work which would enable her to be of service to humanity. She attended the public schools in Monroe and Lucas counties, Iowa, finishing her high school in the latter county, and then entered the Still College of Osteopathy at Des Moines, where she was graduated in June, 1903. She began practice at Independence, and her offices are in the Baden Building.

Doctor Hancock is a member of the Christian Church, belongs to the Rebekahs, the Brotherhood of American Yeomen, the Women's Relief Corps, the Ladies' Auxiliary of the Sons of Veterans, and is especially active in the order of the National Americans, having been local examiner for the past eight years and is now national chaplain for the term of four years expiring in 1919. Doctor Hancock is a member of both the state and national associations of osteopathy.

FRED E. DEAL, M. D. Although comparatively recent recruit in the ranks of the Kansas Medical Fraternity, Dr. Fred E. Deal, of Weir City, who possesses the highest qualifications for success in his profession in a natural ability, an inherent energy, a love for his calling and a kind and sympathetic

Dr Ivy C. Hancock.

personality, has already achieved more than ordinary prominence and prosperity. Doctor Deal comes of a family which originated in Germany and settled in Pennsylvania during colonial days, and men of the name have been prominent in business and private life, in public affairs and in the various learned professions.

Fred E. Deal was born at Grenola, Elk County, Kansas, February 15, 1889, a son of J. F. and Laora Alice (Jones) Deal. His grandfather was Peter Deal, who was born in Ohio, in 1830, and removed from that state to Parker, Indiana, where he followed the business of shoemaking during the remainder of his life, and died in 1907. J. F. Deal was born at Parker City, Randolph County, Indiana, in 1859, and there received his early education. In his youth he decided upon a career in the law, and after comprehensive training was graduated from the law department of the Valparaiso (Indiana) University, with the degree of Bachelor of Laws, and in 1883 was admitted to the bar. Like most young legists endeavoring to get a foothold, he was forced to overcome many obstacles and pass through a period of hardships, and in order to tide himself over until he could secure a paying practice, he was forced to teach in the public schools to add to his income. On January 29, 1885, he was married at Parker, and not long thereafter brought his bride to Kansas, feeling that in the West there was greater opportunity for men of ambition and energy. He took up his residence at Grenola, a new community in Elk County, and proceeded to grow with the town. As time passed he built up a practice which developed both in scope and importance, and his reputation as a learned and thorough legist has spread throughout the state, wherever he has appeared in the courts. Mr. Deal was clerk of the District Court of Elk County from 1896 to 1899, being succeeded by Frank Organ, who is now assistant state auditor. He is a republican in politics, and with his family belongs to the Methodist Episcopal Church. Fraternally, he belongs to the Camp and Encampment, and has held the offices also in the Canton and been the representative of his lodge in the Grand Lodge of the state, as well as holding the title of past noble grand. He belongs to the Elk County, Kansas State and American Bar associations. Mr. Deal was married to Miss Laora Alice Jones, who was born at Parker, Indiana, in 1861, and they have three children: Grace Olive, born November 27, 1887, and now the wife of B. O. Scott, a wholesale and retail cigar merchant of Detroit, Michigan; Dr. Fred E.; and Sarah Alene, born January 12, 1905, who is attending the Grenola public schools.

Fred E. Deal was educated in the public schools of Grenola and Howard, Kansas, graduating from the Grenola High School in 1906 and the high school at Howard in the following year. During 1907 and 1908 he attended Baker University, following which he enrolled as a student at the University Medical College, Kansas City, Missouri, from which he was graduated in 1912 with the degree of Doctor of Medicine. Doctor Deal began practice at Arma, Kansas, but after eight months there removed to Radley, Kansas, where he spent a like period. On June 14, 1914, he came to Weir City, and here has since engaged in a general medical and surgical practice, with offices in the Weir Building. Doctor Deal is a man who is living up to high ideals in his profession and is reaping the reward of his careful training. Standing high among his associates he is striving earnestly to prove worthy of the great trust and responsibility which lie in his hands. He is a member of the Cherokee County Medical Society, the Kansas State Medical Society and the American Medical Association. His political support is given to the republican party, and his religious connection is with the Methodist Episcopal Church. He fraternizes with Weir City Camp No. 714, Modern Woodmen of America, the Woodmen of the World, the Ancient Order of United Workmen and the Knights and Ladies of Security, and also holds membership in the Commercial Club. He gives his unqualified support to all movements making for the betterment of his community.

Doctor Deal was married at Slater, Missouri, June 30, 1916, to Miss Winnie Marie George, daughter of Mr. and Mrs. J. C. George, residents of Slater, where Mr. George is engaged in fruit growing.

REV. DANIEL P. MITCHELL was one of the founders of Methodism in Kansas, and for nearly twenty years was the most prominent leader in that church in the state. His was a life of service, not only to his church but to humanity. His name belongs in every history of Kansas, and his good works follow him in the careers of his children. He was the father of Charles Bayard Mitchell, who during his early pastorate was well known in Kansas and was recently elected a bishop of the Methodist Episcopal Church. Doctor Mitchell's daughter Mrs. George T. Guernsey, of Independence, is one of the most prominent women of Kansas and is a national figure in the councils of the Daughters of the American Revolution.

A Virginian by birth, Rev. Daniel P. Mitchell was born near Phillipi in Barbour County in what is now West Virginia, February 2, 1821. His parents were among the solid yeomanry of that mountainous district, and from there he inherited a strong physical organization and endowments of brain and heart which promised for him a prominent position among men. Under the preaching of the pioneer Methodist preachers of that day he was in early life led to Christ, and at the age of twenty-three entered the Pittsburg Conference of the Methodist Episcopal Church. In that conference of strong men he soon became known as a young man of promise, and in a brief period took a foremost place in the church. His appointments were Kingwood, Murraysville, Johnstown, Salem, Coshocton two years, Norman two years, Cadiz two years, Carrollton two years, South Common Church in Allegheny City two years, and presiding elder of Allegheny District two years. The appointment of presiding elder was a mark of distinction in those early days. His last appointment in that conference was Johnstown, Pennsylvania.

Bishop Ames, who knew him best of any of the older bishops, selected him for the Kansas work, and charged him to come to Kansas and help build up the church in this new state. He came to this state with this commission in 1863. He was first appointed to Leavenworth, where he attracted the leading men of the state, preached to large audiences, conducted large revivals and built up the property interests of his church in that city. The next two years were spent as presiding elder in the Leavenworth District, followed by two years as pastor of the Second Methodist Episcopal Church of that city and as chaplain of the state penitentiary. In 1870 he was reappointed to the First Church in Leavenworth. Following this he was pastor of the First Church of Topeka two years, then presiding elder of the Fort Scott District four years, then for four years presiding elder of the Emporia District, for four years presiding elder of the Independence District, and finally took his last charge, Hutchinson, where he completed his thirty-eight years of active service and left a record of work accomplished that few men have equalled. While returning from New Mexico to Kansas in 1881, he died suddenly on the train near Newton, Kansas, August 24, 1881, in his sixty-first year.

He had attained a foremost place in his church in America. He was a member of the General Conference, the law making body of the Methodist Episcopal Church, at four different times, representing each of the three conferences with which he had been connected, and was for several years the representative of his general conference district in the Missionary Society of the church.

Not only was he distinguished as a churchman but as one of the foremost leaders of thought and action in Kansas. He was a prominent candidate for governor of Kansas and for Congress. At one time he received the solid vote of his party for United States senator against his own wishes and best interests. He was universally recognized as the head of the national greenback party of the state, and when the head died the body died also. In all his political career there were no opponents to his views who were disposed to meet him in debate. Some of the strong men who were opposed to his political position, testify that his career was in no wise derogatory to him, either as a man or as a minister of the Gospel. Coming to Kansas during the period of the Civil war, he soon afterward volunteered to assist in repelling Price's raid.

As a preacher he was marked by the unusual mixture of keen logic and glowing imagination. As a reasoner he was clear and concise. As a debater, he had but few equals whether on the conference floor, the platform, the pulpit or in the open field, warding off the sophistries of infidelity. He was a constant worker and literally worked himself to death.

He left a wife and eight children. His wife, whose maiden name was Ann Eliza Baker, born in Pennsylvania, and died in Emporia, was a helpmeet in all his itinerant toils. She was a woman of deep piety and marked intellectuality. She was the daughter of Rev. Henry Baker, a prominent member of the Baltimore Conference of the Methodist Episcopal Church.

A brief record of the children of this worthy couple is as follows: Henry B. was a civil engineer and died in Idaho. Jennie M., now deceased, was the first woman admitted to the practice of law by the Supreme Court of Kansas, became a practicing attorney in Emporia, and afterwards married Judge L. B. Kellogg, who at one time was attorney general of Kansas and is still in practice at Emporia. Joseph T., the third child, is a civil engineer living at Tacoma, Washington. Annie Eliza is the wife of C. H. Aull, who is connected with the Cudahy firm at Omaha, Nebraska. Dr. Charles Bayard, now Bishop Mitchell, having been elected to that office in the General Conference at Saratoga May 19, 1916, was born in 1857, was educated in Allegheny College at Meadville, Pennsylvania, was ordained to the ministry in 1882, and filled numerous pastorates in Kansas and elsewhere. He had been pastor of the St. James Methodist Episcopal Church in Chicago, the largest Methodist church of that

city, prior to his elevation to the bishopric. Bishop Mitchell has long been a distinguished figure in his church, has attended many conferences and conventions in America and abroad, and is a well known lecturer and the author of several books. His home as bishop is at St. Paul, Minnesota. The next younger than Bishop Mitchell is Mrs. George T. Guernsey of Independence. Dove E. is an unmarried daughter and lives at Omaha. Dannetta P. is a teacher of art in the Kansas State Normal School at Emporia and is the wife of Jonas E. Eckdall, proprietor of a bookstore at Emporia.

JAMES A. TEMPLETON. One of the most important industries of the southeastern part of Kansas is the production of oil, a business that has enlisted the best talents of skilled men from every part of this and other states, and of the men who are devoting their energies to this line of endeavor few are better known than is James A. Templeton, of Caney. Mr. Templeton has been engaged in this business from early youth and his success therein has been brought about through a combination which includes a thorough knowledge of conditions, business talent of a high order and constant, unremitting industry.

Mr. Templeton is a native of London, Province of Ontario, Canada, where he was born July 11, 1871, a son of David and Sarah (Sumner) Templeton. The family originated in Scotland, from whence the grandfather of Mr. Templeton emigrated to Canada as a young man. David Templeton was born in 1849, at London, Ontario, and at the age of twenty-five years went to Petrolia, where he still resides. He has been an oil operator all his life, and has followed the opening of new fields in various parts of America, having for several years been largely interested in the Pennsylvania wells. He is still active in business, although now sixty-seven years of age, and through his operations has built up a large business and accumulated a handsome property. Mr. Templeton is a conservative in politics and a member of the Methodist Episcopal Church, and for the past thirty years has been active in church work. David Templeton is a member of the Order of Foresters. He married Sarah Sumner, who was born in 1850, at Armada, Michigan, and they have had nine children, as follows: James A., of this notice; Maude, who married first Alex McAlester, who was killed in South America while drilling oil wells, and she is now the wife of David Clark, a fruit ranch owner and resides at Los Angeles, California; Etta, who married first Arthur Rouse, an oil well driller, now deceased, and she is now the wife of John Battice, an oil producer and oil worker, and resides at Petrolia, Canada; David, an oil producer residing on South Main Street, Caney; Rosa, who is the wife of Arthur Thompson, a tinsmith of Petrolia, Canada; Lula, who is the wife of Earl Sumner, a mechanic in the employ of the Ford automobile factory at Detroit, Michigan; Seth, who is an oil well driller and resides on North Wood Street, Caney; Roy, who is an oil worker of Coffeyville, Kansas; and Ernest, a journeyman barber, who does much traveling in different parts of the country.

James A. Templeton attended the public schools of Petrolia, Canada, until he was fourteen years of age, at which time he began working on a farm, a vocation which he followed for two years. He then entered upon the work in which he was to make his success, his first experience being gained in the Petrolia fields. He next went to the Island of Borneo, where he remained for two years and six months, then returning to Petrolia, where he spent another two years. His next location was Humboldt, Kansas, where he arrived in September, 1903, then to Chanute, Kansas, in 1905, next to Coffeyville, in October, 1909, and finally to Caney, where he arrived in 1910. Since that time he has been located at Caney, devoting himself to the business of oil and gas producing and contracting. He has gradually built up a profitable business, and at this time has fifteen producing oil and gas wells in Chautauqua County, Kansas. In addition to his home, at No. 210 Wood Street, he owns other real estate at Caney and Chanute. Mr. Templeton is a republican. He belongs to the Maccabees of the World, Caney Lodge of Odd Fellows No. 323, Caney Lodge of the Modern Woodmen of America, No. 941, and Caney Lodge of Elks, No. 1215. He also has a twenty-year endowment policy in the Manufacturers Life Insurance Company, whose main offices are at Toronto, Canada. Few men have a larger acquaintance in the oil and gas business than has Mr. Templeton, who is justly accounted an authority in his field.

On September 11, 1900, Mr. Templeton was married at Petrolia, Canada, to Miss Sarah Ann Leach, daughter of the late George Leach, who was an oil producer of the Dominion.

RALPH E. MARTIN. For several successive terms the people of Cherokee County have laid the responsibilities of the office of sheriff upon Ralph E. Martin, who is a native son of that county, and belongs to an old and respected family that has been identified with Kansas since pioneer days. Mr. Martin grew up in Cherokee County, came to know the people and the people have known him since early boyhood, and he has well earned the confidence they have shown him in his repeated elections to this executive office.

Sheriff Martin belongs to old American stock, and the family has exemplified many worthy qualities. It is interesting to note that one occupation has been quite persistently followed by the various generations, and that is the harness-making trade. Sheriff Martin himself learned that occupation and followed it before his election as sheriff.

Ralph E. Martin was born in Cherokee County, Kansas, June 4, 1873. His original ancestors were Irish people who emigrated to Pennsylvania about the time of the Revolution. His great-grandfather John Martin, a native of Kentucky, was a tailor by trade, lived in Ontario, Canada, a number of years and from there pioneered into the State of Michigan. He died in Michigan before Sheriff Martin's father was born. He married Miss Bowles.

Jonathan Martin, the grandfather of the Cherokee County sheriff, was born in Ontario, Canada, in 1808, but was reared in Michigan. He married in Zanesville, Ohio, lived there two years and then went to Carroll County, Indiana, where he followed his trade of a saddler and harness-maker up to the date of his death, in March, 1855. In politics he was a democrat, and that allegiance has characterized nearly all the members of the family in their various generations. Religiously he was a member of the United Presbyterian Church and very active, and was also affiliated with the Independent Order of Odd Fellows. Jonathan Martin married Elizabeth Martin, of the same name but not related. She was born near Zanesville, Ohio, in 1806, of Scotch ancestry. Her father, William Martin, was born in Pennsylvania in 1770, and died in Carroll County, Indiana, in 1856. One of his last acts was to vote for Franklin Pierce for President of the United States.

He was a pioneer farmer in Carroll County, Indiana. The father of this William Martin was a soldier of the American Revolution, and was one of the troops that made the stormy crossing of the Delaware River under Washington on Christmas eve. William Martin married Phoebe Laramore. Mrs. Jonathan Martin, who died in Carroll County, Indiana, in 1870, was the mother of the following children: David, who was a harness-maker and saddler and died at Placerville, California; Pininah, who married Sam Gordon, a farmer, and she died in Kansas City, Missouri; William, who likewise followed the family occupation of harness-maker and saddler and died in Cassville, Missouri; Albert, who died in infancy; B. W. Martin, father of Sheriff Martin, fifth in this family; Henry H., who was a photographer by profession, but for many years was a guard in the United States treasurer's office at Washington, D. C., where he died; Phoebe Ann, who first married George Waggle, a shoemaker, and after his death married Moses Plew, a farmer, also deceased, and she died in Colorado.

Thus it will be seen that a number of this family have been workers in leather, and that was the occupation during his active years of Mr. B. W. Martin, who is an honored resident of Columbus, Kansas. He was born in Carroll County, Indiana, March 26, 1837, was reared there, and was one of the pioneers of Kansas Territory, having come out in 1858, and having homesteaded 160 acres in Miami County. He did not occupy this land long, and returned to Carroll County, Indiana. He settled on a claim in Cherokee County in 1871, and was identified with its management and improvement for a number of years. He finally sold his farm and in 1882 took up his trade of harness-maker in Columbus, and in 1884 engaged in that line of business for himself. After a half century or more of active work he retired in 1915, and is now enjoying the comforts of a well spent career. He is, like other members of the family, a democrat, belongs to the Baptist Church and is affiliated with the Independent Order of Odd Fellows. Mr. B. W. Martin married Sophia Rosenberry, of South Bend, Indiana. She was born in Ohio in 1834, and died in Seneca, Missouri, in 1879. Mr. B. W. Martin and wife became the parents of eight children, briefly mentioned as follows: Roger, who was in the harness business with his father and died in Columbus in 1903; Clara, who married Reuben Evans, a retired property owner living near Los Angeles, California; A. G. Martin, a harness-maker at Miami, Oklahoma; Grace, wife of Samuel Gonzwar, who is an inspector in the city health department of Spokane, Washington; Edward, a bookkeeper at Columbus; Mary, who died at Columbus in 1901, the wife of Kit Beers, who is now engaged in the transfer business at Joplin, Missouri; Ralph E., who is the seventh in order of age; and David, a harness-maker at Columbus.

Mr. Ralph E. Martin has lived in Columbus since he was about nine years of age, and received his education partly in the country schools and partly in the city schools. When eighteen he left his books and studies, spent a couple of years at work on a farm, and then served an apprenticeship at the harness-maker's trade. He was a skillful and able worker in that line at Columbus until he was first elected sheriff in 1909. He was inducted into office January 1, 1910, and served six months. In 1912 he was again the successful candidate for sheriff, and received the largest majority of any man on the democratic ticket in that year. He was re-elected in

1914, and both terms have been characterized by the utmost efficiency and by a conscientious and courageous performance of every duty assigned him.

Mr. Martin is well known in fraternal circles, being affiliated with the Knights of Pythias, the Modern Woodmen of America, the Anti-Horse Thief Association, the Loyal Order of the Moose and the Knights and Ladies of Security at Columbus. He owns one of the comfortable homes of that city.

In 1901, at Columbus, he married Miss Pearl Jameson, a daughter of A. J. and Palina (Strong) Jameson. Her mother is now deceased, and her father, who followed the business of carpenter and contractor, is now living at Columbus. Mr. and Mrs. Martin have four young children: Dale, born in November, 1903; Emery, born in October, 1905; Edith, born September 19, 1908; and Sherry, born August 28, 1911.

MRS. NANCY J. MCNEILL. While the professional career of Mrs. Nancy J. McNeill has covered but a short period of time, she has already demonstrated her right to a place among the learned members of the Cherokee County bar, and, as junior partner of the firm of Skidmore & McNeill, at Columbus, has built up a large and representative practice. Mrs. McNeill was born near the Town of Messer, in Cherokee County, Kansas, and is a daughter of Branche and Mary M. (Fowler) Jones, a descendant of revolutionary ancestors on both sides of the family. The Jones family originated in Wales, and members thereof were found in Virginia during colonial times. Branche Jones was born in Eastern Tennessee, in 1859, and came to Kansas in 1883, settling in Cherokee County, where for a number of years he was engaged in farming and also was employed as a stationary engineer. He is now retired from active pursuits and makes his home with Mrs. McNeill. He is a republican in politics and a member of the Methodist Episcopal Church. Mr. Jones married Mary M. Fowler, who was also born in 1859, in Eastern Tennessee, and to this union there were born two children: Lulu, who died at the age of twenty-seven years as the wife of John Zimmerman, a coal miner of Pittsburg, Kansas; and Nancy Jane.

Nancy Jane Jones received her early education in the public schools of Cherokee County, attending the Cherokee County High School for two years, and then became a teacher in the country schools. Becoming interested in the law, she gave up teaching after two years, and entered the offices of Skidmore & McNeill, where she acted in the capacity of stenographer, having taken a course in the Fredonia (Kansas) Business College. While thus employed she studied law assiduously for four years, and in June, 1916, was admitted to the bar. At the same time she was admitted to partnership in the firm of Skidmore & McNeill, as a member of which she has since practiced. She has demonstrated the possession of qualities which should serve to advance her greatly in her profession, but at the same time stands as a noble refutation of the oft-times expressed belief that the entrance of woman into public life tends to lessen her distinctive character.

By her first marriage to C. H. Warstler, she became the mother of two children: Lee, born March 1, 1903; and Lulu, born February 6, 1905. In 1909, at Columbus, she was married to Edwin V. McNeill, who was born in Ross County, Ohio, January 30, 1857, a son of Corbin A. McNeill. Mr. McNeill belongs to a family which originally came from Scotland to Virginia in early colonial days, and

were later pioneers into Ohio. Corbin A. McNeill was born in 1822, in Ross County, Ohio, and was there reared, educated and married. In 1858 he went to Macoupin County, Illinois, and in April, 1869, to Cherokee County, Kansas, where he became a large landholder and stockman. His home was in Lola Township, and he was the owner of 600 acres of land in Cherokee County. For years he was a recognized leader in republican politics, but never held office. Mr. McNeill married Nancy Ann Kelley, who was born in 1828, in Ross County, Ohio, and died at Columbus, Kansas, in September, 1902. Mr. McNeill's death occurred December 31, 1899, at Columbus. They were the parents of eight children, as follows: John, who engaged in farming in Cherokee County and died at the age of thirty years; William R., who died unmarried, at the age of twenty-two years, in 1874, on the farm of his parents; Edwin V.; Renick, who died in Macoupin County, Illinois; Jacob, a farmer, who died in Linn County, Missouri, aged thirty-nine years; Stronger B., who died at the age of twenty-three years in Cherokee County, where he had been engaged in farming; Mary, who died in infancy; and Corbin A., an attorney of Columbus, Kansas.

Edwin V. McNeill was educated in the public schools of Macoupin County, Illinois, and Cherokee County, Kansas, and remained on his father's farm until he was twenty-two years of age. At that time he went to Colorado, where he ranched, mined and farmed for fifteen or more years, but in 1898 returned to Kansas and settled at Columbus, where he took up the study of law in the office of his brother, C. A. McNeill, and Al F. Williams. Admitted to the bar June 5, 1901, he has since carried on a general practice, with offices in the Logan Security Building. He is known as one of the thorough and capable members of the Cherokee County legal profession and during his fifteen years of practice has been identified with much important litigation. He has served as city attorney of Columbus, an office to which he was elected on the republican ticket. With Mrs. McNeill, he belongs to the Methodist Episcopal Church, and his fraternal connections include membership in Galena Lodge No. 677, Benevolent and Protective Order of Elks, and the Knights of Pythias Lodge of Columbus. The pleasant family home is situated at No. 428 Pennsylvania Avenue.

Corbin Asahel McNeill, brother of Edwin V. McNeill, was born in Macoupin County, Illinois, January 13, 1867, in a log cabin. He received his public school education in Cherokee County, Kansas, following which he attended the State Normal School, at Fort Scott, and became a telegraph operator, a vocation which he followed for a short time. Mr. McNeill read law in the offices of Ritter & Wiswell, attorneys at Columbus, and was admitted to the bar in 1892, and two years later had so favorably impressed himself upon the people that he was elected county attorney, an office in which he served one term. He also served one term as a member of the State Board of Charities, under the administration of Governor W. J. Bailey. Mr. McNeill has had a general civil and criminal practice, and has one of the largest clienteles in this part of the state. He was appointed by Governor Hoch as judge of the District Court, to fill out an unexpired term, and was subsequently elected to that office in 1906 and served four years more. Judge McNeill is a republican. Fraternally, he is affiliated with St. Paul (Kansas) Council, Knights of Columbus; Galena Lodge No. 677, Benevolent and Protective Order of Elks; Galena Aerie of the Fraternal Order of Eagles; and the Loyal Order of Moose, Modern Woodmen of America, Ancient Order of United Workmen and Knights and Ladies of Security, of Columbus. He also holds membership in the Commercial Club. He and the members of his family belong to the Roman Catholic Church, and reside in their modern home at No. 401 South Florida Avenue.

In 1889 Judge McNeill was married to Miss Edna Macy, who died in 1902, leaving one son: Maurice, a graduate of the Cherokee County High School, who read law with his father and is now an attorney of Kansas City, Missouri. In 1904, in Cherokee County, C. A. McNeill was married to Miss Agnes Fleming, daughter of Michael and Fannie Fleming, farming people who are both now deceased. Mrs. McNeill died in 1907, at Columbus, leaving one daughter: Helen, born July 4, 1906. In June, 1910, Mr. McNeill was again married, being united with Miss Clara Schlafy, of Carlyle, Illinois. They have three children: Fred, born February 2, 1911; Zale, born July 7, 1912; and David, born September 27, 1913.

GALUSHA W. ASHBY. Many of the men of Montgomery County who have attained prominence in business life, have had their training in agricultural work and prior to entering commercial, industrial and financial affairs have achieved success as tillers of the soil. In this category is found Galusha W. Ashby, who until 1914 centered his activities in farming in Montgomery County and since that time has given his fine talents to the advancement of the lumber interests of Liberty, as proprietor of the Liberty Lumber Company.

Mr. Ashby was born on a farm in Appanoose County, Iowa, December 23, 1861, and is a son of Thomas and Amanda V. (Fuller) Ashby. On his father's side he is of Scotch descent and on his mother's side of French ancestry, and both families located in Maryland during Colonial times. Thomas Ashby was born in 1834, in Indiana, was reared and educated in that state and Iowa, and in the latter state entered upon his career as a farmer. On May 20, 1871, he came to Montgomery County, Kansas, establishing himself as a pioneer farmer, and here the remainder of his life was passed. He became a substantial agriculturist, accumulated a good property through industry and well-directed effort, and won and held the esteem and respect of his fellow-citizens. His death occurred in 1882. Mr. Ashby was a republican, but took only a good citizen's interest in public affairs. He was an active worker in the Methodist Episcopal Church and a member of its official board. He married Miss Amanda V. Fuller, who was born in Illinois, in 1842, and who still survives him and resides at Liberty. They became the parents of the following children: Galusha W.; D. C., who resides at Kansas City, Missouri, and is a lumberman; J. S., who is engaged in farming in Missouri; Dora, who is the wife of S. T. Woodring, manager of the Kallashu Lumber Company, of Lake Charles, Louisiana; Newton, who is a salesman for the Long Bell Lumber Company, at Kansas City, Missouri; Eliza, who died at the age of six years; and Langton, who died when five years of age.

The public schools of Montgomery County furnished G. W. Ashby with his education, and when nineteen years of age he began farming on his own account. For a period of about thirty years he continued as an agriculturist, winning success by his

own efforts, and while he has disposed of some of his land still holds farming interests. In 1914, desiring to enter business, he came to Liberty, where, in company with John H. Tole, now of Independence, he purchased the yard, stock and equipment of the W. D. Riley Lumber Company, the name of the concern at that time being changed to its present style, the Liberty Lumber Company. Under the new management the enterprise has met with excellent success, and is justly accounted one of Liberty's leading industries. Mr. Ashby has shown himself to be a shrewd, far-sighted business man, alive to every opportunity and with a thorough knowledge of his business. He has also established a reputation for honorable dealing, which has proven a valuable asset in commercial circles. He is a stockholder and director of the Liberty State Bank. In politics he is a republican, but acts rather as a supporter of his party's interests than as a seeker for personal preferment. His religious connection is with the Methodist Episcopal Church.

Mr. Ashby was married in 1888, in Liberty Township, Montgomery County, to Miss Grace Forsyth, daughter of the late Alfred P. Forsyth, a farmer, who was for three terms, or nine years, a member of the Board of Regents of the Kansas State Agriculture College. Mr. and Mrs. Ashby have two children: Edith Beryl, who is the wife of L. P. Guy, a Missouri farmer; and T. A., who resides at El Reno, Oklahoma, and is connected with the Long Bell Lumber Company.

CHARLES H. POCOCK. Postmaster of Tyro, in Montgomery County, a farmer and well known citizen of that locality, Charles H. Pocock for many years was identified with educational work both in Kansas and other states. In character and attainments he is type of man whom the people instinctively respect and repose confidence in, and again and again he has been called to duties of a public nature.

By ancestry he is English, and his grandfather, Elijah Pocock, came from England to Ohio in the very early days. He was a farmer and blacksmith and died in Wayne County.

Mr. Charles H. Pocock was born in Storey County, Iowa, August 12, 1863, a son of E. H. Pocock. His father was born in Ohio in 1834, was reared in that state, and married there Mary Hinkle, who was born in Pennsylvania in 1840 and now resides at Caney, Kansas. E. H. Pocock graduated from the College of Physicians and Surgeons at Columbus, Ohio, with the degree of M. D., and during the Civil war served as an assistant surgeon in that division of the Union army commanded by General Thomas. In 1856 he had moved to Storey County, Iowa, where he practiced his profession for a number of years, and then went back to Ohio, locating at Shreve, and from there to Walnut, Indiana,, where he was engaged in his professional duties for twenty years. Doctor Pocock moved from Indiana to Norman, Oklahoma, where he acquired a farm, and later sold it and retired to Oklahoma City, where he died in 1910. He was an active republican and a Knight Templar Mason. He and his wife had three children: Charles H.; Lee, who was a railroad man and died in Old Mexico at the age of twenty-five; and Frank, who is a farmer at Caney, Kansas.

Though a native of Iowa, Charles H. Pocock spent most of his early years in Ohio and Indiana. He wisely improved his opportunities to obtain an education, and at the extremely early age of fifteen was given his first certificate and taught his first term of country school. He continued teaching for several successive winters, spending his wages during the summer in attending school as a student. In 1882 he completed the teachers' course in the Northern Indiana Normal School at Valparaiso, and from that time forward for nearly twenty years was closely identified with school work. Until 1888 he taught in Indiana, and in that year moved to Kansas and has since been a resident of Montgomery County His first home was four miles north of Tyro, and he continued teaching in Montgomery County until 1901.

In 1898 Mr. Pocock bought a farm of a hundred acres a half a mile west of Tyro, and so far as he has had leisure from other duties has improved and developed it and is still owner, managing it with the aid of his sons. He makes his home on the farm, though for many years his interests have been in the town. From 1901 to 1908 Mr. Pocock was postmaster of Tyro and was again appointed to that official position in September, 1915, taking charge of the office on January 1, 1916. Since 1908 he has carried on a business in real estate, and is one of the reliable dealers and brokers in farm lands in his part of Montgomery County.

Since reaching manhood Mr. Pocock has steadily affiliated with the republican party. For eight years he was clerk of Caney Township, was trustee of the township a term of two years, and has also served on the school board, his interest in school affairs never having been allowed to wane, though he has been out of active school work as a teacher for the past fifteen years.

In 1893, at Independence, Kansas, Mr. Pocock married Miss Minnie E. Brown, a daughter of Andrew J. and Lena Brown. Her father, who was a farmer, died in April, 1916, and her mother still resides on the old farm in Montgomery County. Mr. and Mrs. Pocock have three children: Victor, who was born July 10, 1897, completed the public school course at Tyro and attended the Fredonia Business College, and is now assistant postmaster under his father. John, who was born June 10, 1899, is in the senior class of the Tyro High School. Teddy, born February 27, 1902, graduated at the head of his class from the eighth grade of the grammar schools of Tyro in 1916.

LOUIS R. ROTER. One of the very able business men of Parsons was the late Louis R. Roter, who was president of the Parsons Cold Storage and Crystal Ice Company and had followed merchandising and various lines of business in Kansas and other states for many years.

He died in his fifty-fourth year at Parsons February 3, 1907. He was born in Cincinnati, Ohio, October 2, 1853, a son of Henry Roter, who was born in Germany and died at Dillsboro, Indiana. Henry Roter came to this country a young man, lived in Cincinnati many years, and then moved to a farm at Dillsboro, Indiana.

The first seventeen years of his life the late Louis R. Roter spent on his father's farm and in the meantime acquired an education in the public schools of Dillsboro. He then went to the oil district of Western Pennsylvania, and found employment at Titusville, at first in a grocery store and afterwards in a paint and wall paper store until 1879. From that date until 1881 he was a merchant at Colville near Bradford in the oil district. For many years Mr. Roter carried on a successful business as a general merchant at Abbottsford, Wisconsin. He left there in 1897, and in 1899 located in Parsons, Kansas, where he became actively identified with the ice

business. He did much to develop the Crystal Ice Company and the Parsons Cold Storage Plant, and was president and manager of this corporation at the time of his death. Politically he was a republican and served in the city council of Parsons. He was a member of the Lutheran Church and fraternally was affiliated with Parsons Lodge, No. 117, Ancient Free and Accepted Masons, Parsons Chapter, No. 39, Royal Arch Masons, Coeur de Lion Commandery No. 17, Knights Templar, Parsons Lodge, No. 527, Benevolent and Protective Order of Elks, Parsons Camp, No. 844, of the Modern Woodmen of America, and also belonged to the Sons and Daughters of Justice.

Mr. Roter married for his first wife Alice B. Thompson, who died at Abbottsford, Wisconsin. Her children were: Edith B., wife of Fred P. Hogue, who resides at New Orleans and is general salesman for the Louisiana Red Cypress Company, their children being Fred Louis and Cora Alice; and Alice, the second child of the union, who died in infancy.

In 1855 at Abbottsford, Wisconsin, Mr. Roter married Miss Cora A. Thompson, a sister of his first wife. Mrs. Roter since the death of her husband has continued to live in Parsons and is now president of the Parsons Cold Storage and Crystal Ice Company. She is a very capable business woman, and is also well known socially. She was born at Delaware, Ohio, attended the public schools there and in the State of Pennsylvania, and is a daughter of Joseph B. Thompson. The Thompson family is of Scotch-Irish descent, and its first members in America settled in Pennsylvania during colonial days. Mrs. Roter's grandfather Edward Thompson was born in Pennsylvania, spent many years in educational work in Pennsylvania, and afterwards lived retired in the State of Nebraska until his death. Joseph B. Thompson was born in Reading, Pennsylvania, in 1817, grew up there, and subsequently became a minister of the Reformed Church, preaching in Ohio and Pennsylvania. He died at Canaan, Ohio, in 1879. He was a republican in politics. Joseph B. Thompson married Phoebe Jane Tallman, who was born in Winchester, Ohio, and died in Shannondale, Pennsylvania. Their children were: Alice B., who was the first wife of the late Louis R. Roter; Otho Ferrel, who is superintendent of the Associated Oil Company at Bradford, Pennsylvania; Mrs. Cora A. Roter; Effie Jane, wife of William B. Frost, an oil operator at Muskogee, Oklahoma; Edward U., a painter living at Pittsburgh, Pennsylvania; Nevin H., a bookkeeper at Warren, Ohio; Grace A., who died at the age of twenty-seven, the wife of George Erskine; Birchard D., an oil operator at Simpson, Pennsylvania; Pearl, who died at Pasadena, California, in 1912, the wife of Edwin R. Libert, who was a traveling salesman and is also deceased; and Lulu Maude, who died in infancy.

Mrs. Roter resides in her attractive residence at 1505 Grand Avenue in Parsons. She is an active member of the First Presbyterian Church. Mrs. Roter has two children. Bessie Pearl married Guy B. Bebout, who is an assistant civil engineer in the Federal service, now stationed at Wheeling, West Virginia, and they have an infant daughter named Elizabeth Ann. Charles R., the only son of Mrs. Roter, lives with his mother and is assistant manager of the Parsons Cold Storage and Crystal Ice Company. He and his wife, Bessie R. Roter, have a daughter named Helen Marjorie.

T. C. LONG

T. C. LONG, M. D., now of Independence, has been successfully engaged in the practice of medicine and surgery in Kansas for the past fifteen years. His reputation is especially based on his skill as a surgeon, and he is rated as one of the most proficient in that class of work in Montgomery County.

He was near Portland in Jay County, Indiana, February 5, 1871. His grandfather, who died at the age of forty years, was a native of Ohio and moved from that state to a farm in Jay County. That farm, settled by the family more than eighty years ago, was the birthplace of J. S. Long and also of his son, Dr. T. C. Long. J. S. Long was born in 1838, and has never had any other home than his birthplace. He owns a fine place of 300 acres, and though now nearly eighty years of age still looks after his interests as a diversified farmer. He served in the Union army during the Civil war, has taken an active interest in township and local affairs, and is a democrat and a member of the Reformed Church. J. S. Long married Armenia Frickle, who was born near Portland, Indiana, in 1839 and died on the old homestead farm in 1909. There were seven children in the family: Stephen D., who was a farmer in Jay County, Indiana, died from typhoid at the age of forty; Laura A. never married and is living with her father; Mary F. is the wife of C. P. Strauss, a farmer near Portland, Indiana; H. W. Long is a general merchant at Fort Recovery, Ohio; the fifth in age is Dr. T. C. Long; Jesse is a farmer near Portland; Dr. N. W. Long is a graduate of Barnes Medical College and a physician and surgeon at San Francisco, California.

Educated in the public schools of his native county, Doctor Long also attended the Lookout School of that county, and by working on farms and other occupations finally secured the means to enable him to carry out his long cherished plan of becoming a physician. In 1899 he graduated with the degree M. D. from the Hygeia Medical College of Cincinnati, and in 1901 took his M. D. degree from the Barnes Medical College at St. Louis, Missouri.

After graduating he came to Kansas, and was in practice at Munden until his removal to Independence in December, 1911. In 1909 Doctor Long took a general course in the Chicago Policlinic. As a specialist in surgery, he performs his operations in the Montgomery County Hospital at Independence. He is an active member of the Montgomery County and the Kansas State Medical societies and the American Medical Association.

Doctor Long belongs to the Commercial Club, the Knights and Ladies of Security, the Fraternal Aid, and has membership in Munden Lodge, Ancient Free and Accepted Masons. He is independent in politics. His home is at 311 North Eleventh Street in Independence.

LLOYD LAKIN is one of the prominent young business leaders of Kansas. He is secretary, treasurer and active manager of the Lakin-McKee Manufacturing Company of Fort Scott. This is the largest individual industry in that city, the largest of its kind in Southeastern Kansas, and perhaps the largest in the entire West. The output is overalls. The Lakin-McKee overalls are distributed all over the Middle West. The goods are pre-eminent for quality and service. It is a business built up on character, and to a large degree the constructive and creative ideas of Lloyd Lakin have been fundamental in the success of the business.

The president of the company is Henry P. McKee, while James T. Beatty is vice president. The company was organized in 1908, and they began manufacturing overalls in a small building and on a modest scale, and the great extension of the plant has followed as a natural result of the real demand for the goods. The organizers of the business were the late Charles A. Lakin, father of Lloyd, and Mr. McKee and Lloyd Lakin. Charles A. Lakin was the first president and Mr. McKee was vice president. The plant at the beginning was situated in the outskirts of Fort Scott. In less than two years the business acquired by the company made it necessary to enlarge the plant, and in 1910 was erected a factory building which is a credit to the entire State of Kansas. It is modern in every particular, and special attention has been given to the sanitary and lighting features of the building. The overall factory stands on North Main Street, is three stories high, is of concrete, steel and glass construction, and has a floor space of 21,000 square feet. This industry employs constantly between 150 and 200 people, and their payroll is the largest of any industry in Fort Scott, and nothing in recent years has contributed more to the solid prosperity of the city than the overall factory. They maintain five traveling representatives who are on the road all the year around and cover the states of Kansas, Nebraska, Iowa, Missouri, Oklahoma, Colorado and Arkansas.

Mr. Lloyd Lakin was born in Iola, Kansas, August 24, 1882, and measured in years he is still young and has the promise of most of his life ahead of him, though in point of experience he is a veteran business man. His parents were Charles' A. and Belle (Case) Lakin. His father was born in Indiana and his mother in Kansas. Belle Case's mother was one of the earliest pioneers in Southwestern Kansas, and for some years was postmistress of Osage Indian Mission. Her brother was killed by the Indians in the early days. Charles A. Lakin came to Kansas at the age of twenty, was for a number of years in the drug business at Iola, and later extended his enterprise to general merchandise. He remained at Iola until 1885, and then came to Fort Scott, where he was proprietor of a retail grocery store. Later with J. T. Beatty he established a wholesale grocery house under the name Lakin & Beatty. This firm subsequently merged their interests with the Fort Scott Wholesale Grocery Company, and Mr. Charles Beatty continued a member of that firm until 1907, when he retired. In 1908 he joined his son and Mr. Beatty in organizing the Lakin-McKee Manufacturing Company, but soon after it started his health failed and he died in Fort Scott in 1911 at the age of fifty-eight. He was a splendid type of citizen and business man, and his death was widely lamented, since he was at the time only in the prime of his years. He was an active republican, a member of the Methodist Church, and in Masonry had attained the thirty-second degree and belonged to the Mystic Shrine. His widow still lives at her old home in Fort Scott and is one of the regular members of the Methodist Church. There were only two children, and the daughter Maud Lakin died when twenty years of age.

Lloyd Lakin received his early education in the city schools of Fort Scott, graduating from high school at eighteen, and then took advanced training in the literary department of the University of Kansas at Lawrence. After leaving college he became traveling salesman for the Fort Scott Wholesale Grocery Company. After two years he resigned to take a position in the traffic department of the

Bell Telephone Company at Kansas City, Missouri. He was there until 1908, when he returned to Fort Scott and secured the cooperation of his father and Mr. Beatty in organizing and establishing the Lakin-McKee Manufacturing Company.

Mr. Lakin should be personally credited with the planning and the arrangement of the model factory building which the company erected in 1910. While he left to a skilled architect the actual drawing of the plans, these plans when completed illustrated his ideas and nearly every detail of the building was carefully thought out by him in advance. It was due to him that the features of sanitary arrangement and lighting were especially emphasized.

Mr. Lakin also retains an interest as a stockholder in the Fort Scott Wholesale Grocery Company. He is a republican on national issues, otherwise independent. He is a past exalted ruler of the local lodge of Elks and is a Mason and Shriner, and belongs to the Methodist Church.

On September 20, 1910, at Palmyra, Illinois, where she was born and where her parents still reside, Mr. Lakin married Miss Ethel Smith, daughter of Lafayette and Mary (Duncan) Smith. They have three children, all born in Fort Scott; Lois Isabelle, born May 2, 1912; Meredith Maud, born July 4, 1914; and Barbara Jane, born March 28, 1916. Mrs. Lakin is a working member of the Methodist Church and belongs to the Eastern Star and the C. C. Club.

ASON GITTINGS RICHARDSON. A Kansas pioneer whose name and services were especially identified with Harvey County, Ason Gittings Richardson was one of the strong and noble men of his time. He belonged to the old abolition class of the North, was a man of resolute character and would follow his convictions even in the face of extreme personal danger.

He came to Kansas in 1870 and settled in Harvey County, when that district of Kansas was practically unsettled. His home was in Richland Township. The first religious services held in the county, conducted by Rev. Mr. Roberts, were at his home, and the first Sabbath School was organized in his house on May 1, 1871. When Harvey County was organized Mr. Richardson was appointed by the governor chairman of the original county commissioners for the purpose of organizing the county, dividing it into townships and naming the different subdivisions, and otherwise starting the machinery of local civil government.

He was born at Zanesville, Ohio, May 1, 1830, and died November 11, 1903. His parents were Dr. Rufus Richardson and Jemima Richardson. The family were colonial settlers in America, and his grandfather, Jesse Richardson, fought gallantly as a soldier of the Revolution, and was a pensioner. He served in a Connecticut regiment. After the war he located in Otsego, Ohio, where he died. Dr. Rufus Richardson, while educated for the profession of medicine, seldom practiced except for the poor and needy, and gave his time chiefly to his work as a minister of the Protestant Methodist Church both in Ohio and Illinois. At one time he was president of the North Illinois Conference of his church. He had seen active service in the War of 1812, and in later years he became an active abolitionist and was one of the conductors on the underground railroad in Illinois during the years prior to the Civil war. He was very active in aiding the government against Mormonism when that sect invaded

Nauvoo, Illinois. On account of his ancestry he had membership in the Sons of the American Revolution. Dr. Rufus Richardson was a native of Connecticut, while his wife was born in Virginia.

A. G. Richardson completed his education in Knox College at Galesburg, Illinois, where he was graduated in 1853. In 1855 he engaged in business as a general trader, handling lumber, groceries, real estate and lending money. For a time he lived at Keokuk, Iowa, and while there served as clerk of the city council. In 1863 he removed to Little Rock, Arkansas, where he had his drug store, and in 1866 he removed to Alabama, and bought a plantation engaging in the raising of cotton. He became prominent in that southern state during the years following the war. General Swaine, the military governor of Alabama, appointed him sheriff of Wilcox County. In the political campaign of 1868 he was elected a member of the State Legislature of Alabama, and rendered some effective service. However, the feeling against northern men was so intense throughout the South, and his life was so many times threatened, that he finally left Alabama and came to Kansas in 1870.

His early activities as a pioneer in Harvey County have already been noted. Later he was elected a member of the Kansas Legislature in the session of 1874-75, and at the end of his term was again chosen as county commissioner, an office he filled for many years. Politically he was naturally in thorough sympathy with the republican party, but his political actions were also governed by a strenuous belief in the prohibition principle. In church matters he was a United Presbyterian.

On March 21, 1877, at Zanesville, Ohio, Mr. Richardson married Lida Anderson, who now resides in the City of Wichita. Mrs. Richardson is a daughter of John and Elizabeth Anderson. They were Scotch Irish people and of the old Covenanter stock. Right after their marriage they left the old country, and spent six weeks on a sailing vessel in crossing the ocean. They had already come in sight of America when the vessel was wrecked just off the coast near Halifax, and all their possessions went to the bottom of the sea. It was a time when drafts or checks were not in use, and they brought all their money in coin with them as well as a quantity of household goods. With the shipwreck their own lives were saved, but all these material possessions were lost. In spite of such an inauspicious beginning Mr. and Mrs. Anderson lived to accumulate a competency, and were high minded and honorable people. In their native country they were Orangemen, followers of the Prince of Orange, and in America they became strong abolitionists.

The children of Mr. and Mrs. Richardson were: Rufus Gittings, who married Mary Elizabeth White; Robert Anderson, who married Florence Fay Wolfe; John Levi and Ralph Lovell, both now deceased; and Orpha Edna, who is unmarried and lives with her mother.

JOHN A. BURT. An old and honored resident of Montgomery County was the late John A. Burt, who came to that section of Kansas in the early days and who died at Tyro November 26, 1905. Mrs. Burt and some of her children are still living in the vicinity of Tyro.

Born at Fort Wayne, Indiana, October 24, 1845, John A. Burt was a son of Silas Burt, who was born in Indiana in 1818 and represented a very early family in the settlement of that state. He was a farmer, and died at Fort Wayne in 1850. John A. Burt, after growing up and receiving his early education at Fort Wayne, adopted a career as a farmer and blacksmith, but in March, 1881, moved his family to Southern Kansas and located on a farm three miles east and one mile south of Tyro. There he lived out his active and useful career until September, 1904, when he retired from the farm and during the remaining months of his life was employed by the Tyro Supply Company.

Mr. Burt, though a very young man at the time, was drafted in 1864 from Fort Wayne for service in the Thirty-third Indiana Regiment of Volunteer Infantry, and was in the ranks of the Union army until the close of the war. He afterwards became a member of the Grand Army Post at Coffeyville. Politically he was a democrat, and was affiliated with the Lodge of Odd Fellows at Tyro and the encampment at Coffeyville.

On April 3, 1865, John A. Burt was married at Fort Wayne to Charity E. Cartwright. Mrs. Burt was born at Pickaway, Ohio, where she received her early education, and her parents afterwards moved to Fort Wayne, Indiana, where she was married. Mrs. Burt is an active member of the United Brethren Church, belongs to the Rebekahs, to the Woman's Relief Corps and the Royal Neighbors. She is a woman much beloved not only in her home but in her wide circle of friends and acquaintances.

The children of Mr. and Mrs. Burt have the following brief record: John, who was employed in a mill at Dodge City, Kansas, and was burned to death there April 13, 1914; Mary, who married Hiram Rayl, who now resides in Oregon, and she died in 1894 on their farm three miles west of Tyro; Valancia, who married Wilbur Burt, and resides seven miles north of Coffeyville on a farm; Mattie, who died in 1905 near Tyro. the wife of Ephraim Messersmith, who has a farm four miles east of Tyro; Viola, wife of William Norton, an oil worker, their home being two miles east and one mile south of Tyro; Hettie, wife of Henry Tuggle, they occupying the old home farm three miles east and one mile south of Tyro; Willie, who died in infancy; and Susie, who died September 14, 1910, at Tyro, the wife of John Patchen, who lives at Tyro, and is an oil pumper.

Mrs. Burt's ancestors were Germans who settled in colonial days in old Virginia. Her grandfather, James Cartwright, was born in Virginia in 1793, was a farmer and died in Pickaway, Ohio, about 1853. Her father, James Cartwright, was born in Virginia in 1823, and died at Fort Wayne, Indiana, in 1904. When he was eighteen years of age he moved to Pickaway, Ohio, and followed the occupation of farming and brick manufacture. He was a democrat. James Cartwright married Elizabeth Schivell, who was born in 1838 in Pickaway, Ohio, and died at Fort Wayne in 1910. Of their large family of children Mrs. Burt was the oldest. A brief record of the others is as follows: John, deceased; Armeda, deceased; William, a farmer at Granola, Oklahoma; Minerva, deceased; James, who is employed in a brickyard at Fort Wayne, Indiana; Mattie, who lives at Fort Wayne, widow of Leonard Gaskell, who is employed on city construction work; Emma, wife of Lima Kaler, who is on city construction work at Fort Wayne; Samuel, connected with the brickyard at Fort Wayne; Robert and Thomas, both of whom died in childhood; and Ada, deceased.

Vol. IV—13

STEPHEN ROBERT PING. Kansas is not only famous for its rich lands, its crops of wheat and alfalfa, but also for its untold wealth of resources under ground. and though these resources are comparatively little known even to many of the Sunflower people, Southwestern Kansas is pre-eminently a mineral section. One of the centers of the production of lead and zinc ores is Galena in Cherokee County, Kansas. Galena is one mile from the Missouri state line and ten miles to the Oklahoma state line. In the year of 1916 a strip of country thirty-five miles long and fifteen miles wide, running through a portion of Missouri, Kansas and Oklahoma, produced $34,961,993 worth of zinc and lead ores.

One of the oldest operators there, though by no means an old man, is Stephen Robert Ping. He has been identified with the mining and industrial interests of Southeastern Kansas for nearly thirty years. When he left school he was a poor boy and went to work in the mines for wages. In a short time he had advanced to that degree of skill and business ability where he was operating for himself. For a number of years he was ore buyer for the following smelting concerns: Cherokee Lanyon Smelting Company, American Sheet Steel Company, and the Girard Smelting Company. Perhaps one of his chief contributions to the mining history of Galena has been through the Portia Mining Company, whose scene of operation is right in the Town of Galena. Recently this property was sold to Kentucky people. Mr. Ping put down fifteen drill holes on this land and in six months sold the property and made $50,000 clear. For many years Mr. Ping has done his own mining. He discovered and developed what was known as the Crowe and Ping property on the Southside land at Galena, his associate being the late J. R. Crowe, a well known coal operator of Kansas City. Besides these properties he organized and operated the Mizpah Mining Company and the Ping Investment Company, which were famous mines. Altogether he has built and operated fifteen mining properties in this lead and zinc country.

Mr. Ping is of Colonial American ancestry. His forefather was an Englishman who went to Scotland. married a Scotch woman and later emigrated to America and settled in Kentucky. Stephen Robert Ping was born in Pulaski County, Kentucky, December 25, 1872. His father, Benjamin Franklin Ping, was born in the same county in 1841, was reared and married there, and spent most of his active career as a farmer. In 1878 he moved. from there to Barry County, Missouri, and in 1888 came to Galena, Kansas, where he was identified with mining operations. In 1901 he went back to Barry County, Missouri, but in 1906 again took up his residence at Galena and soon afterwards retired from active business. He died in Galena in 1915. He was a democrat in politics. His first wife, who was born in Kentucky, died in Barry County, Missouri soon after coming out here from Kentucky. Their other children are: Mary, wife of Ed. Hauser, a mine operator who lives in Spring Grove, a portion of Galena; Green Ping, a stationary engineer, lives at Galena; Nannie, wife of G. W. Grant, a merchant, lives at Galena.

Stephen Robert Ping spent his youth in Barry County, Missouri, and Galena, Cherokee County, Kansas. In these localities he received his education from the public schools. While he has been very prosperous in business he has also identified himself with everything that concerns the welfare of his home city of Galena and has done much to build it up, and is an active worker in the Community Club. He was a director in the Galena State Bank until the bank was sold. Besides his fine residence at 607 Washington Avenue he owns $20,000 worth of fine business property in the city and a fine piece of mineral land close to the city.

In matters of politics Mr. Ping is a democrat. He has spent four years in the city council of Galena, is one of the trustees of the Presbyterian Church, is affiliated with Galena Lodge, No. 194, Ancient Free and Accepted Masons, Baxter Chapter, No. 78, Royal Arch Masons, Galena Commandery, No. 46, Knights Templar, Fort Scott Consistory, No. 6, of the Scottish Rite, and was formerly a member of Abdallah Temple of the Mystic Shrine at Leavenworth, having demitted to Mirzah Temple at Pittsburg, Kansas. He is also a life member of Galena Lodge No. 677, Benevolent and Protective Order of Elks. In 1895 Mr. Ping married Miss Lula Vansycle of Galena. They became the parents of three children: Mispah is a graduate with the Degree Bachelor of Arts from Christian College, Columbia, Missouri, and lives at home with her parents; the two younger children, Lucile and Portia, both died in childhood, Portia at the age of four and Lucile at the age of four years and six months.

HOMER CLARE LEMON. Among the prosperous business enterprises of Pittsburg, Kansas, is the Nuttman-Lemon Lumber Company, the organizer and president of which is Homer Clare Lemon, a man of large experience in the lumber industry, and a man of great energy, public spirit and civic zeal. Mr. Lemon was born October 17, 1869, at Cromwell, Iowa. His parents were William Vance and Susan (Carter) Lemon.

The Lemon ancestry is traced to the north of Ireland. Five brothers of the name came to the American colonies and all served in the Revolutionary war from Pennsylvania. One of these patriots was John Lemon, the great-grandfather of Homer C. Lemon, of Pittsburg, Kansas, and the father of John McClannahan Lemon, who was born in Pennsylvania in 1791. He came by way of Kentucky, in pioneer days, to La Porte, Indiana, in which neighborhood he built the old Lemon toll bridge which still spans the stream and preserves his name. He was appointed tollkeeper and while he followed farming as an occupation, he served in important public offices, for four years was receiver in the Indiana Land office and was frequently honored by the democratic party. He had served in the War of 1812. His wife, Jean (McConnell) Lemon, was born in Kentucky in 1789, the first white child born in Woodford County. She died in the old home at the Lemon Toll Bridge, in 1875, having survived her husband for ten years. They had the following children: James, who died on his farm in California; John, who died in 1911, in Sacramento County, California, had been county treasurer for forty years; Mary, who died in Livingston County, Missouri, was the wife of Samuel Gish, also deceased; Sarah, who died at Washington, District of Columbia, was the wife of a Mr. Barkley, who was in the service of the Government; Jane, who died at La Porte, Indiana, was the wife of Charles Cathcart, a farmer, now deceased; Martha, Mrs. Allen, who died at Creston, Iowa; Harriet and Thomas, both of whom died young; and William Vance, who still survives.

William Vance Lemon was born in 1830, in Clark County, Indiana, and in boyhood accompanied his parents in their removal to La Porte, Indiana, and

was reared there. In 1851 he engaged in freighting across the plains to California and followed freighting and mining until 1867, when he went into the lumber business at Cromwell, Iowa, conducting a lumber yard at that point until 1876. For a few years afterward he was in a grain business at Lenox, Iowa, and then moved to Barton County, Missouri, and followed farming there until 1892 when he came to Kansas. For five years he was engaged in a grocery business at Fort Scott and then settled in Arkansas, where he is an apple-grower and general fruit farmer. He casts his vote with the democratic party.

In Union County, Iowa, William V. Lemon was married to Susan Carter, who was born in Ohio in 1843 but was reared in Iowa. She died in 1904 in Washington County, Arkansas. They had four children: Homer Clare; William Carl, a railroad man who lives at Parsons, Kansas; Jessie, who is the wife of William H. Hesser, farmer and merchant at Hermister, Oregon; and John McConnell, who is in the lumber business at Dearing, Kansas.

Homer C. Lemon attended the common schools in Barton County, Missouri, and in 1887 was graduated from the Lamar High School, and during the three succeeding winters taught school. He began work in a lumber yard at Minden, Missouri, where he continued for two years. In 1894 he came to Pittsburg, Kansas, and organized the Sandford Robinson Lumber Company, of which he was vice president and manager and also had an interest in the same for fourteen years. This interest he finally sold and then went to Dearing, Kansas, where he organized the H. C. Lemon Lumber Company and remained president of that concern for four years. In 1913 Mr. Lemon returned to Pittsburg and organized the Nuttman-Lemon Lumber Company. It is well founded financially and does a business in heavy timber over a radius of twenty-five miles and the local trade is very heavy. The plant is well situated for transportation facilities on North Broadway and the San Francisco tracks. Of this company Mr. Lemon is president, S. G. Moore is vice president and A. M. Lent is secretary and treasurer. The company has its trade connections, belonging to the Southwestern Lumbermen's Association, which covers four states: Kansas, Missouri, Oklahoma and Arkansas. For one term Mr. Lemon was on the directing board of this organization.

At Lamar, Missouri, in 1894, Mr. Lemon was married to Miss Anna L. Moore. Her mother was then deceased, and her father, John Moore, a farmer, died afterward at Pittsburg. They have four sons: James M., who was born at Pittsburg, March 7, 1895, after graduating from the Coffeyville High School, spent one year in the State Manual Training School at Pittsburg and is now with the Nuttman-Lemon Lumber Company, and married Miss Grace Crawford, of Pittsburg; John W., who was born at Pittsburg in 1898, was graduated from the high school at Pittsburg in 1916; Robert E., who was born at Pittsburg in 1900, is a senior in the high school; and Walter V., who was born in 1903, is a member of the freshman class in the high school, all representatives of wholesome Americanism.

In politics Mr. Lemon is a staunch democrat. He served one term as a member of the city council and in 1903 was elected mayor of Pittsburg. His administration was marked in its business management and for the bringing about of many civic improvements. His business vigor and acumen make him a valuable member of the Chamber of Commerce. Fraternally he is identified with Pittsburg Lodge No.

187, Ancient Free and Accepted Masons, and with Pittsburg Lodge No. 412, Elks. His handsome private residence is situated on East Fourteenth Street, Pittsburg.

THEODORE WEICHSELBAUM. It is interesting and instructive to chronicle the worthy achievements of so honorable and industrious a life as that of the late Theodore Weichselbaum, for many years active in the business affairs of Riley County, Kansas, for fifty-seven of these being a resident of Ogden. Founded on a sound education, Mr. Weichselbaum's natural sagacity, shrewdness and great business sense were brought into play and he accumulated a vast fortune through entirely legitimate channels.

Theodore Weichselbaum was born June 10, 1834, at Furth, in the Province of Bavaria, Germany, and he died at Ogden, Riley County, Kansas, March 9, 1914. His father, Dr. Moritz Weichselbaum, was born also at Furth, in 1802. He was a graduate of the University of Wurtzburg, Germany, and for sixty-one years was an able practitioner of medicine in his native city. He was fortunate in his choice of wife, marrying Betty Kohn, a native of Wurtzburg. Fourteen children were born to them and she was spared into old age, her descendants still remembering her many virtues.

Of his parents' family Theodore Weichselbaum was the second oldest child. He was given excellent educational advantages according to the efficient methods prevailing in every German province, and to this fact he attributed some of the success that attended his unusual business career. When he left school he engaged as a clerk with a merchant at Furth, Bavaria, serving an apprenticeship of four years, and then engaged in business for himself, accepting a position as traveling salesman for an Amsterdam house, selling mirrors in Holland. He was quite successful in that line of work in which he continued until ambition led him to look into conditions in the United States for enterprising young men and with the result that in June, 1856, he landed in the City of New York. He remained there for ten months and then made his way westward as far as Kansas City, Missouri, where he became a clerk for Philip Rothchild and later purchased his employer's stock and continued the business in his own right. A few months later, however, he moved the goods to Ogden, Kansas, then a promising location, and here Mr. Weichselbaum continued actively in business until the close of his life.

Business foresight was one of Mr. Weichselbaum's essential qualities. In 1869 he began to buy farms offered for sale and eventually in this line alone accumulated more than an ample fortune. He went into extensive farming and became also a breeder of shorthorn and Holstein cattle and horses of Norman and Hambletonian pedigree. In considering his mighty herds the line "cattle on a thousand hills" seemed an appropriate description. He ably managed all his interests but by no means gave all his attention to personal affairs. He became because of his integrity, his stability and earnest good citizenship, a leading man in all that concerned this section especially relating to Riley County and Ogden, and through choice of his fellow citizens frequently assumed the responsibilities of public office. He was treasurer of Ogden Township, was mayor and postmaster of Ogden for many years and at the time of death was a member of the school board. On one occasion he permitted the use of his name as candidate on the democratic ticket for the office of state treasurer, but he was not disappointed when the great republican vote in the state carried all before it. He was reared in the Jewish faith and never departed from its tenets.

Mr. Weichselbaum was married June 10, 1862, to Miss Fannie Blumenstein, who was born in Gunsenhausen, Bavaria. She came to the United States just two days prior to her marriage, her betrothal to Mr. Weichselbaum having previously taken place. She was an admirable woman in every relation of life and her surviving children cherish tender memories of her. To this marriage the following children were born: Josephine; Samuel; Edwin, who died at the age of forty-five years; Bettie, who died at the age of twenty-six years; Albert and Joseph, both of whom died in childhood; and Johanna, who is the wife of J. J. Waxelbaum, of Macon, Georgia. The mother of these children died in 1896 and some years later Mr. Weichselbaum married a second wife who survives him. He was identified with business and benevolent organizations and belonged also to the Odd Fellows and the Knights of Pythias.

Samuel Weichselbaum, eldest son of Theodore and Fannie (Blumenstein) Weichselbaum, was born at Ogden, Kansas, July 24, 1866, and with the exception of brief periods spent in the line of business at Macon, Georgia, and at Chattanooga, Tennessee, he has always lived at his birthplace. Like his late father he is a thorough-going business man and is extensively engaged in farming and stockraising. In 1908 Mr. Weichselbaum was married to Miss Rose Ottenheimer, of Chicago, Illinois. He is a Master Mason and belongs also to the order of Elks.

HON. SOL. A. BARDWELL. Not so often, as in the election and re-election of Hon. Sol. A. Bardwell, has the public choice fallen upon so able and scholarly a man, one so admirably qualified for high public service. For many years Mr. Bardwell was widely known in the educational field, and still later in business circles, his entire training from boyhood leading along lines that develop mental strength and stable character. Accustomed to leadership and responsibility, he entered upon the duties of a legislator with intelligent vision as well as firmness of purpose. Being a careful student, a ready speaker and naturally aggressive, he became a strong number from the first and aided in bringing about much enlightened and constructive legislation.

He was born in Atchison County, Kansas, March 6, 1870, and is one of a family of six children born to Milner and Mary (Washer) Bardwell. Milner Bardwell was born in Massachusetts and came of an old and highly respected family of New England. His father was a Presbyterian minister who was a missionary among the Indians in Mississippi prior to the Civil war, a short time before which he had removed to Indiana. Milner Bardwell was then a young man and in Indiana he was married to Miss Mary Washer, a native of that state. In 1861 Milner Bardwell enlisted in an Indiana regiment for service in the Civil war, in which he was a faithful soldier for three years. Sickness then overcame him and he was sent home but never recovered sufficiently to rejoin his regiment, from which he received an honorable discharge. In 1868 he came to Kansas and resided in Atchison County for five years, in 1873 removing with his family to Riley County, where he pre-empted a homestead and there carried on agricultural pursuits until 1896 when he removed to Clay Center, Kansas, where he resided until his death some years later.

Sol. Bardwell was reared on his father's farm and

can recall the many hardships and disappointments incident to the pioneer days of Riley County. As he grew to school age he attended the district school in the winter time, working during the summer on the farm, and later, continued his studies in the high school at Clifton, Kansas. He was nineteen years old when he first entered the educational field, as a district school teacher and for nearly twenty years followed the profession. In the meanwhile he alternated, for a time attending school and teaching, in this way completing the educational course he had laid out for himself. In 1895 he was graduated from the Kansas State Normal School at Emporia, Kansas. He took a post-graduate course in this institution a few years later. He taught in the district schools of Riley and Clay counties—was principal of the Leonardville schools, later principal of the Randolph schools both of Riley County and then went to Clay County as principal of the New Clay County High School just established. He remained in this position for seven years, which he resigned to enter business.

In 1908 Mr. Bardwell moved to Manhattan, Kansas, and went into the real estate and loan business in partnership with his brother Lou Bardwell, under the firm name of Bardwell & Bardwell. The business was profitable from the first. This association continues and is one of the most prosperous in this city, handling a large amount of outside capital at times that has resulted in fortunate investments and business development at Manhattan.

Mr. Bardwell has always been identified with the republican party. In 1914 he was chosen republican candidate for the legislature in Riley County, to which office he was subsequently easily elected. During his first term he served as chairman of the committee on education and with exceptional ability, and it has been said that at this session of the legislature more extensive and constructive school laws were enacted than ever before in the history of the state. In the second term he was favorably mentioned as an available candidate for speaker, but would not himself become an active candidate.

In 1898 Mr. Bardwell was married to Miss Edith Thomas, a daughter of Dr. F. M. Thomas, of Leonardville, Kansas. Mr. Bardwell is a member of the First Presbyterian Church of Manhattan and is president of its board of trustees. He also served four years as president of the board of education. Fraternally he is a Master Mason and belongs also to the Benevolent and Protective Order of Elks. He is dignified in his manner but frank and affable and his circle of personal friends and well wishers is wide.

SEBA CLARENCE WESTCOTT. With a record of twenty-six years of continuous practice at Galena, Mr. Westcott is secure in those honors and successes that come to the lawyer of ability and character, and is one of the best known men of Cherokee County. He has served in the Legislature and conscientious care and business integrity have marked every relationship of his career.

His people were among the pioneer settlers of Southeastern Kansas. His father, William H. Westcott moved to Baxter Springs, Kansas, in 1869. He died at Baxter Springs in 1872. By occupation he was a farmer, and in politics was a democrat. William H. Westcott was born in Ingham County, Michigan in 1840 and his wife Mary Wright was also a native of that state and died in Ingham County in March, 1867, a few days after the birth of her younger son, Seba Clarence Westcott. The latter was born in Ingham County March 3, 1867. His

older brother is Charles W. Westcott, who was born in 1864 and is an ore buyer and has been connected with the Pitcher firm at Joplin, Missouri, since 1889.

The Westcott family originated in England and came to America in colonial days, settling in New York. Charles Westcott, grandfather of the Galena lawyer, was born in 1810 and was an early settler in Southern Michigan. He was a merchant tailor. He died at Lansing, Michigan, in 1887. William H. Westcott ran away from home twice to enlist in the Union army, and finally succeeded in his plan, going out in 1864 with a Michigan regiment and serving a year and a half.

Mr. S. C. Westcott attended the public schools of Baxter Springs, Kansas, graduating in high school in 1885. Later he entered the law department of the University of Kansas, where he completed the course and was given the degree LL. B. in 1890. After a brief experience in Carthage, Missouri, he moved to Galena in 1890, and has since been connected with some of the important civil cases tried in the local courts. His offices are at the corner of Fourth and Main streets.

He was twice elected to the State Legislature on the republican ticket, serving during the sessions of 1907 and 1909. During his first term he was chairman of the Local Judiciary Committee. Mr. Westcott is a member of the Cherokee County Bar Association, of Lodge No. 677 Benevolent and Protective Order of Elks, Lodge No. 266 Fraternal Order of Eagles, and the Galena Community Club.

In 1893 in Emerson, Iowa, he married Miss Lizzie Sutton, daughter of G. B. and Elizabeth Sutton, both now deceased. Mr. and Mrs. Westcott are the parents of two children: Ralph, born September 22, 1896, is a graduate of the Galena High School and is now a sophomore in the Manhattan Agricultural College; Frances, born October 1, 1899, is a senior in the Galena High School.

DAVID FRANCIS CRAIG. Independence is the home of one of the most widely experienced and prominent contractors and producers in the oil and gas fields of the Southwest. Mr. Craig was born in Pennsylvania, got his first experience in the oil industry there, and has followed the progress of oil and gas development in all the important fields of the United States. A man of great foresight and judgment, and of equally remarkable energy, Mr. Craig has accumulated business interests in various sections of the country, but for a number of years has had his home and business headquarters at Independence.

He was born in Mercer County, Pennsylvania, February 25, 1861. His people were originally Scotch, and his grandfather located in Western Pennsylvania in Mercer County at a very early date and spent his life there as a farmer.

Jacob T. Craig, father of D. F. Craig, was born in Mercer County in 1829, and was one of the prominent farmer citizens of that rugged district of Western Pennsylvania. He acquired two of the old farms of Mercer County, the McElree and the old Irwin homestead, and at his death on March 4, 1911, left an estate of 200 acres. He was a democrat, active in the Methodist Episcopal Church, and a citizen of the highest standing. Jacob P. Craig married Hannah Irwin, who was born in Mercer County in June, 1829. She was a first cousin of the late President McKinley. Her death occurred at Grove City, Pennsylvania, in April, 1916. There were five children in the family: Sadie is the wife of

D. F. Craig

A. J. Wilson, an oil producer, residing at Hanford, California; the second in age is David F. Craig; M. I. Craig is a carpenter and builder in Mercer County, Pennsylvania; Charles B. is still on the old home farm; Homer G. has risen to a place of large responsibilities in the oil industry, and has his home near Vera Cruz, Mexico, where he has charge of the oil interests of the Pearson Company. Homer graduated from the Grove City College of Pennsylvania in the classical course and at the head of his class. During the revolutionary troubles in Mexico in 1914 the company gave him a vacation of five months, when the trouble was at its height, and allowed him a salary of $500 for each month.

David F. Craig spent the first eighteen years of his life on his father's farm in Western Pennsylvania. He attended the public schools of Mercer County, and on starting out for himself went to the oil fields of Bradford, Pennsylvania. Since then the oil fields of many states have attracted his services and presence, and from Pennsylvania he went to Allentown, New York, then to Maxburg, Ohio, following which he returned to the New York fields, afterwards was in Butler County, Pennsylvania, and at Lima, Ohio, and in West Virginia became an independent oil contractor and producer. He operated in the Findlay fields of Ohio and in later years has drilled oil wells all through Colorado, Wyoming and New Mexico. From Boulder, Colorado, he came to Independence in 1903 and from this city as his headquarters has carried on his contracting and producing activities.

As a contractor he put down all the water wells for the Santa Fe Railway Company between Texico and Ricardo, New Mexico. For many years he has been an oil producer on his own account. Only recently he sold most of his producing holdings, though he still owns a considerable acreage in Oklahoma and Kansas. At Sweetwater, Texas, he has some lands and also two business blocks and 220 acres of farm land. He is interested in a 3,500 acre proposition with nine producing gas wells at Mexia, Texas, and owns an interest in the old homestead back in Pennsylvania. Mr. Craig is president of the Southern Oil and Gas Company.

His home is at 204 South Sixth Street, Independence. He is a democrat, and a member of Lodge No. 780, Benevolent and Protective Order of Elks at Independence. His favorite diversion is hunting. He has hunted in California, Old Mexico, New Mexico, Wyoming, Oregon, Southern Texas, and Northern Michigan, and few men in the country know so much about the big game preserves as Mr. Craig.

In 1890 at Mount Morris, Greene County, Pennsylvania, he married Miss Stella Victoria South. Mrs. Craig was born at Mount Morris and was educated there, and prior to her marriage assisted her father in the latter's dry goods store. Her father, Jacob South, who was born in Greene County, Pennsylvania, in July, 1840, and died at Mount Morris in May, 1910, was a school teacher from the age of sixteen to twenty-one, and afterwards was in business as a dry goods merchant. Mr. and Mrs. Craig have one son, Halleck Irwin. He is now making a record for himself as a student and athlete in the University of Kansas. He graduated from the Montgomery County High School at Independence in 1913, with a diploma entitling him to entrance at college without examination. He is now a member of the junior class of the Kansas State University. In 1915 he was the star pitcher on the university baseball nine and made the remarkable record of winning every game pitched. It was through his excellent work that the university

won the Missouri Valley Championship that year. He has also played on the football team and is a member of the Phi Gamma Delta college fraternity. He is pursuing a law course in the university.

MARION J. SIMMONS. To that class of representative citizens who work with the full measure of manly strength for individual success, but also unselfishly endeavor to promote public prosperity, belongs Marion J. Simmons, of Elk City, president of the Citizens State Bank, leading agriculturist, public-spirited citizen and an ordained minister of the United Brethren Church. He has through his abilities and industry accumulated a competency in his individual enterprises, but has always felt it his bounden duty to aid his community and his fellow men, and thus, while holding a position of prestige in the business and financial world, also has a firm place in the esteem and confidence of those among whom he has lived and labored.

Mr. Simmons was born near Bedford, Taylor County, Iowa, February 22, 1860, and is a son of William and Susan (Wininger) Simmons, and a member of a family of French origin which was founded in the colony of Virginia prior to the revolution. His grandfather, John Simmons, was a pioneer to Indiana, where he passed his life in farming, and died in DuBois County before the birth of Marion J. Simmons. None of the grandfather's children survive. William Simmons was born in DuBois County, Indiana, in 1826, and was there reared on a farm and educated in the public schools. Some time after his marriage he went to Iowa and located on a farm in Taylor County, where he resided until 1869, on September 15th of which year he settled on a Government claim of 160 acres on Card Creek, five miles southeast of Elk City. This was before the Government survey was completed and when the Indians were still in the country. Mr. Simmons proved up his claim, developed a good farm, and increased it to 280 acres, which he owned at the time of his death, with the exception of one acre, which he donated to the Simmons schoolhouse, now known as the Card Creek schoolhouse. His death occurred at Elk City, in 1900. Mr. Simmons was an industrious and energetic man and a good citizen. He was an independent democrat in political inclination and never aspired to office, and was an active member of the Methodist Episcopal Church. His doors were always open for public worship in those pioneer days when there were no church houses. The Methodist and the Quakers both held their regular preaching services in his home, and in the winter of '70 both of the above named denominations held their revival meetings there and the results of which were twenty conversions. Mr. Simmons married Miss Susan Wininger, who was born in 1824, in Tennessee, near Cumberland Gap, and died on the farm in Montgomery County, Kansas, in 1889. They were the parents of the following children: Mary, who was married in Iowa to Thomas Freel, a veteran of the Civil war and a farmer, came to Elk City in 1875, where Mr. Freel died, and where Mrs. Freel still resides; J. A., who was engaged in farming for a number of years but later turned his attention to the undertaking business, and is now a retired resident of Yam Hill, Oregon; Marjorie, who died in childhood; Rebecca Ellen, deceased, who married G. W. Carr, a farmer and veteran of the Civil war, who also died in Oregon; George K., who was a farmer and stockman until his death in Oklahoma; Louisa, who was married at Elk City to William Wallace, a veteran of the

Civil war, who died on his farm located near Elk City, in which city his widow still resides; Leonard, who was a farmer and died near Elk City at the age of twenty-six years; William R., who first was engaged in farming near Elk City, but for the past eighteen years has been carrying on agricultural operations in Pottawatomie County, Oklahoma; Marion J., of this notice; Rachel, who married J. C. McCarter and with her husband owns the old homestead formerly belonging to William Simmons; and Dennis P., who died on his farm near Elk City in 1896.

Marion J. Simmons secured his early education under difficulties, being compelled to follow a furrow two miles over the prairie to attend a subscription school, although later he went to the district school in Montgomery County. From boyhood until he was twenty-one years of age he took care of the stock on his father's farm, and upon reaching man's estate embarked in the stock business on his own account, following that until 1915. He has been successful as a farmer and is now the owner of two fine properties of 160 acres each, one located five miles south of Elk City and the other one mile nearer. In addition to these, he owns his handsome residence on Main Street. In 1890 he was ordained a minister of the United Brethren Church, and has preached locally ever since, as well as having ridden the circuit to preach on many occasions. A democrat in politics, he served as township trustee three terms, and without his knowledge was nominated for the offices of probate judge and county treasurer by his friends. Although this is a strong republican district, he made it decidedly interesting for his opponents and in both campaigns cut down the normal republican majority by a large number of votes. Mr. Simmons is a member of William Penn Lodge No. 78, Independent Order of Odd Fellows, of Elk City.

In the early part of 1915, when the Citizens State Bank of Elk City was organized, Mr. Simmons became a stockholder in that institution, and in December of that year was elected its president, a position which he has retained to the present, the other officers being J. W. Brown, vice president; and E. E. Lugenbeal, cashier, both of Elk City. Under Mr. Simmons' direction the bank has prospered and his well known reliability has served not only to gain the confidence of the people in its substantiality, but to give it an excellent reputation in banking circles of Montgomery County. The banking house is situated on Montgomery Street, and the institution has a capital of $15,000 and a surplus of $1,500. Mr. Simmons is a leader in all public-spirited movements launched in Elk City and a promoter of any enterprise that promises to be of benefit to the city or its people.

On August 23, 1881, in Montgomery County, Mr. Simmons was married to Miss Anna B. Davidson, daughter of Asher and Deborah (Curlis) Davidson, farming people of this county who are both now deceased. Mr. and Mrs. Simmons have no children of their own, but have reared two boys: Charles W. Simmons is engaged in farming near Elk City and Marion C. Simmons lives on the old home farm, and is overseer of an oil lease and also engaged in the stock business. These are energetic young men of a high moral standing, and they are sons of Mr. Simmons' brother, the late Dennis P. Simmons.

JOHN C. LARDNER, M. D., is one of the leading physicians and surgeons of Fort Scott, has been a resident of Kansas since 1879, and represents a prominent family of Bourbon County. His parents were highly respected people and reared a family of educated men. Doctor Lardner's brother Hubert is a prominent member of the Fort Scott bar and two other brothers have also become well known in Kansas. Doctor Lardner was born in Muscatine, Iowa, April 1, 1869, of Irish parents. His parents were John and Mary (Butler) Lardner, both natives of County Galway. They came to Kansas in 1879, settled on a farm in Bourbon County, and the father followed farming until his retirement. He died at Bronson, Kansas, in 1903, at the age of seventy-four. The mother passed away at Manhattan December 24, 1915, at the age of eighty-three.

Doctor Lardner from the age of ten years lived on a Kansas farm, acquired his higher literary training in the Kansas Normal College at Fort Scott, where he was graduated Bachelor of Science in June, 1891. From 1888 to 1899 he followed chiefly the vocation of school teacher, and taught in country, village and city schools. He then entered the Kansas Medical College, from which he received his degree Doctor of Medicine in 1902. Since then he has been in active practice at Fort Scott.

Doctor Lardner is a democrat, but has had no aspirations for political service. He is a member of the Catholic Church. On September 6, 1899, at Cherokee, Kansas, he married Miss Marie W. Germain. Mrs. Lardner was born at Girard, Kansas, daughter of Henry and Amanda (Wallace) Germain. Her father was a prominent coal operator owning coal lands in the Pittsburg district and was also connected with the smelters. Doctor and Mrs. Lardner have one child, John Germain Lardner, born at Chanute, Kansas, July 23, 1908.

WILLIAM SHERMAN TIMMONS. One of the highly respected residents and leading business men of Riley, Kansas, is William Sherman Timmons, owner of a lumber yard and dealing also in coal and grain. He belongs to old American stock, his ancestors for generations having resided in one or other of the great states of the Union. There is present in almost every individual, be his station in life what it may, a latent pride of ancestry and a pleasure in being able to trace a clear line far back in the silence of the past. Sometimes men and women offer fortunes to have such a record established. Not so, however, need Mr. Timmons concern himself for he can trace, on both paternal and maternal lines, an honorable genealogical line that connects with the country's early settlement.

William Sherman Timmons was born December 20, 1866, in Saline County, Missouri. His parents were George and Matilda (Baker) Timmons, his paternal grandparents were S. R. and Rachel (Hanshaw) Timmons, and his great-grandparents were Ananias and Ellen (Roten) Timmons. The family doubtless originated in Germany but before the Revolutionary war had settled in Maryland and there Ananias Timmons was born and from there in early manhood went to Ohio and finally settled permanently on a farm in Ross County, married Ellen Roten and they both lived to the age of eighty years. They were among the early settlers there and reared a creditable family, one son S. R., becoming the grandfather of William S. Timmons of Riley.

S. R. Timmons was born in Ross County, Ohio, and passed his life there. In early manhood he married Rachel Hanshaw, who was born in North Carolina but was reared in Ohio, where her parents, Martin and Sarah Hanshaw, were very early settlers and substantial people. S. R. Timmons and wife lived on their farm in Ross County and there he died in 1874 but his widow survived into extreme old age. They had a family of three sons and three daughters, of which George Timmons was the first born.

George Timmons was a native of Ross County, Ohio, born November 30, 1836, came to Kansas in 1878, and died at Clifton, Kansas, in 1911, beloved and respected by all who knew him. He attended the district schools in Ross County and assisted his father on the home farm. He married Matilda Baker, who was born in Jackson County, Ohio, September 23, 1836. Her parents were Josiah and Emma (Schooly) Baker, who were born, reared and married in Jackson County, Ohio. They lived there until 1865, when they removed to Saline County, Missouri. Mrs. Timmons was the first-born of their five children. The paternal grandparents of Mrs. Timmons were Rev. Joseph and Mary (Hankins) Baker, natives of Kentucky, and of German ancestry. Rev. Joseph Baker was a farmer and also was a minister of the Christian Church. He served as a soldier during the Mexican war. Both he and wife lived into old age. Soon after their marriage, George Timmons and wife, about 1865, removed from Ohio to Missouri and settled in Saline County. They resided near Marshall, Missouri, for thirteen years, but in the fall of 1878 removed to Clay County, Kansas, and settled on a farm in Mulberry Township, four miles south of Clifton. In the course of time Mr. Timmons acquired a large body of land, carried on extensive operations as a farmer and stockman and not only became one of the county's capitalists, but a prominent man in public affairs. In 1895 he retired from active farm life and established his home in Clifton, of which city he subsequently became mayor and also served in minor offices. Throughout life, after it formation, he was a member of the republican party. During the Civil war he was a strong supporter of the Union cause, sending a substitute, voluntarily, because a physical disability prevented his serving as a soldier in the ranks himself. Although he accumulated wealth, at death leaving an estate worth not less than $75,000, it had been secured through honorable methods, fairness and justice ever marking his dealings with others. He was widely known and because of his many admirable qualities, was sincerely respected and esteemed. He is survived by his widow and his nine children: Josiah, Emma E., Mary A., Welcome C., William Sherman, Arvina J., Rachel Ota, Daisy H. and Sarah M., all of whom have domestic circles of their own.

William Sherman Timmons was reared on his father's farm and attended the public schools. He continued to follow farming until 1905, when he removed from the old homestead in Clay County and came to Riley, having purchased a lumber yard here, which he has operated ever since. In addition to dealing in lumber, Mr. Timmons operates a coal yard and also a grain elevator, being one of the busy men of Riley. He is an active and loyal republican but has never sought political honors for himself.

In 1890 Mr. Timmons was married to Miss Maggie Gillespie, and they have four living children: Lewis, Birdie, George and Eva.

HARRY E. FLOYD. Prior to coming to Caney, Kansas, in 1907, Harry E. Floyd had been without experience in the journalistic field. He was familiar with the business of farming, had known the cattle ranches for ten years, and for several years had been identified

with mercantile affairs, but the newspaper business was one in which he had not engaged. However, since taking hold of the Caney News, Mr. Floyd has built it up to be one of the strong papers circulating in Montgomery and the surrounding counties, and that he has been able to do so may doubtless be explained by the fact that he knows his country, is well informed along general lines, possesses inherent talent for work of an editorial nature, and has within him an inexhaustible stock of energy and perseverance, these latter being very desirable and necessary qualities in the make-up of the man who would successfully conduct a public print.

Mr. Floyd was born in Chautauqua County, Kansas, February 15, 1877, and is a son of Martin Van Buren and Nancy (Steele) Floyd, and a descendant of Scotch ancestors who emigrated to America during colonial times and were pioneers in the State of Kentucky. Martin Van Buren Floyd was born February 22, 1847, in Bond County, Illinois, and was there reared and married. He was a lad of fifteen years when he succeeded in passing the recruiting officer and enlisting for service in Company C, Twenty-Sixth Regiment, Illinois Volunteer Infantry, during the Civil war, and subsequently fought with that command for four years. He participated in some of the hardest fighting of the war, including the engagements of Lookout Mountain and Missionary Ridge, and those attendant with Sherman's March to the Sea, and at the close of the war participated in the Grand Review, at Washington, D. C. On receiving his honorable discharge, the brave young soldier returned to Bond County, where he took up the duties of farming, remaining there until 1870, in the spring of which year he came to Kansas. After a short stay in Wilson County, he found conditions not to his liking and moved on to Chautauqua County, where he became a pioneer homesteader, settling on 160 acres. This he brought under the plow, and as the years passed he added from time to time to his holdings, until he now is the owner of 720 acres, located 4½ miles southwest of Sedan. He is now retired from active pursuits, and is comfortably enjoying the rest that his labors have brought. Mr. Floyd is one of the substantial and highly respected men of his community, and has served in several local offices, among them those of justice of the peace and census enumerator. He is a republican in his political opinions. A pillar of the Baptist Church, he helped to organize the First Baptist Church at Sedan, and has steadily and generously supported its movements. His only fraternal connection is with the Knights and Ladies of Security. Mr. Floyd married Miss Nancy Steele, who was born in Illinois, in 1851, and they have been the parents of the following children: Olive, who is the wife of Bert Casement, a stockman and leading capitalist of Sedan; Dicie, who is the wife of Thomas Brunger, a prosperous agriculturist of the vicinity of Sedan; Calvin W., who carries on operations in stock at that place; Robert, who is engaged in the harness and leather goods business at Sedan; Harry E., of this review; Albert, a general merchant at Sedan; Lee, also of that place, who is a handler of live stock; Louis, twin to Lee, who is identified with the Provident Association of Topeka, Kansas, in the office of secretary; Clara, who is the wife of Ernest Bennett, a teacher in the Kansas State Normal School, at Pittsburg, Kansas; Alice, twin to Clara, who for a number of years has been a teacher in the public schools of Chautauqua County, now filling the position of deputy county treasurer, and residing with her parents; and Grace, the wife of William Kinnamon, of Sedan, assistant cashier of the State Bank of that place.

Harry E. Floyd received his education in the public schools of Chautauqua County, Kansas, which he left at the age of nineteen years, and from that time until he was twenty-one years of age resided on his father's farm. On attaining his majority, he went into the Indian Territory and the next five years of his life were passed in connection with the cattle business there and in Oklahoma, where he gained much experience and gathered together a little capital. Returning to Kansas, he established himself in business at Sedan, and this he conducted with some measure of success until 1907. In that year Mr. Floyd came to Caney and purchased the Caney News, a paper which had been founded in 1904 by Fred C. Trillingham. This is a weekly paper circulating through Montgomery and the surrounding counties, with a large subscription list, including the most representative people of this part of the state. Under Mr. Floyd's management, it has grown and prospered, has improved in every way, and is on a substantial financial basis. It is considered an excellent advertising medium, and is freely patronized by the merchants and professional men of Caney and the surrounding towns and villages. The News is conducted under a republican policy, but endeavors to give a fair and unbiased presentation of all the news, whether local, state or national. Aside from his business ability in making the paper a success, Mr. Floyd, in his editorial capacity, gives his readers a clean, neatly printed and well edited sheet, with pithy and timely comments upon things of moment and of interest. The offices of the plant are at No. 116 South State Street, while Mr. Floyd's residence is at No. 417 North State Street. He is the owner of a number of city lots in Caney. Mr. Floyd is a member of the Baptist Church and a contributor to its movements. Both personally, and through the columns of his paper, Mr. Floyd supports all movements making for civic betterment and progress. He is well known in fraternal circles, belonging to Sedan Lodge No. 136, Ancient Free and Accepted Masons; Jewell Chapter, Royal Arch Masons, of Sedan; Sedan Lodge No. 141, Independent Order of Odd Fellows; Camp No. 941. Modern Woodmen of America, Caney; Caney Lodge No. 160, Ancient Order of United Workmen, and the Havana Country Club.

Mr. Floyd was married in 1909, at Sedan, Kansas, to Miss Anna Hosford, daughter of I. N. and Olive Hosford, the former of whom was a retired farmer and is now deceased, while the latter still survives and resides at Sedan. Mr. and Mrs. Floyd have one child: Eugene, born August 23, 1910.

THOMAS KENNEDY. The door of opportunity is everywhere opened to the man of enterprise. The most characteristic industry in the State of Kansas was built up by a young machinist who came to Galena nearly thirty years ago and somewhat later established a factory for the manufacture of perforated metals. The Thomas Kennedy Company of Galena is the only concern of its kind west of the Mississippi River as far as the Pacific Coast.

Mr. Kennedy created in his own mind the idea for the machines that are now at work in his plant. He realized the need of perforated metal in various industries, and set his mind to working out the details of a piece of machinery which would accomplish the work economically and efficiently.

In 1892 he set his first factory in operation. His plant now contains a battery of four perforating machines, each weighing twenty-five tons. One of these machines is capable of taking a sheet of metal four feet wide and ten feet long and when it comes from the machinery it is perforated with ⅜-inch holes. It is possible to secure all sizes of perforation and the industry supplies a demand for such commodities all over the United States. The main source of the business is in supplying perforated metal sheets for screens used in the mines. The plant, which is located at 103 North Main Street, between the Frisco, and the Missouri, Kansas & Texas tracks, has floor space of 175x250 feet. About fifteen men are employed in the plant and several of Mr. Kennedy's children are also active helpers in the office and business.

Thomas Kennedy was born in Ontario, Canada, July 22, 1865. Up to the time he was twenty-one years of age he had the advantages of the public schools of Ontario. On leaving school he learned the trade of machinist, and it was experience and observation that finally opened the way for his enterprise and the building up of a successful industry in Kansas. He followed his trade in Ontario, afterwards in Detroit, Michigan, and St. Louis, Missouri, and arrived in Galena in 1887.

Mr. Kennedy is a stockholder in the Galena National Bank and is owner of 1,100 acres of mineral lands in Cherokee County. His home is on Windsor Heights. He has at the same time not neglected those duties which come to the public spirited citizen. He has been a member of the city council, is an active republican, and is affiliated with Lodge No. 677 Benevolent and Protective Order of Elks, the Ancient Order of United Workmen, the Woodmen of the World, the Sons and Daughters of Justice, the Knights of Pythias, the Independent Order of Odd Fellows, being a member of these various organizations at Galena.

In 1892, the same year that he started his factory at Galena, Mr. Kennedy married Miss Nellie Coldwell. Six children constitute the household of Mr. and Mrs. Kennedy. Claude is a graduate of the Galena High School and is a young machinist in the Thomas Kennedy Company. Nellie is also a graduate of the high school and assists in the office of her father. Richard has completed his high school course and is also employed in the business. Catherine is a graduate of the high school, Thomas is still in high school and Mildred, the youngest, is in the grammar school.

CHARLES F. SPENCER. One of the most prominent among the coal operators of Pittsburg, Kansas, is Charles F. Spencer, under whose able and experienced management a number of the leading coal companies are being conducted. Mr. Spencer has been identified with this line of business all his life, and few men have a more thorough or more intimate knowledge of the industry. He was born in Cherokee County, Kansas, January 14, 1873, and is a son of J. W. and Ambrosia (Favor) Spencer.

The branch of the Spencer family to which Mr. Spencer belongs had its origin in England, from which country the first American ancestor emigrated in Colonial times to Vermont, from whence members of the family have journeyed to many other states. His grandfather, Daniel Spencer, was born in 1810, in Vermont, and went as a young man to Illinois as a pioneer, there following farming and stock raising until his death, which occurred at Centralia, Illinois, in 1883. J. W. Spencer was born at East St. Louis, Illinois, in 1840, and in 1862 enlisted in the Thirteenth Illinois Cavalry, with which he served for three years, principally along the border, his numerous engagements including the battle of Pea Ridge. At the close of his military service he returned to Illinois, but in 1866 came to Kansas and settled in Cherokee County, where for many years he dealt in cattle and farmed. He is now living in retirement at Columbus. He is a republican in politics and a member of the Methodist Episcopal Church, in which he has held all the lay offices. Mr. Spencer married Miss Ambrosia Favor, who was born in 1843, in Southern Wisconsin, and died in Cherokee County, Kansas, in 1911. They became the parents of two children: Charles F.; and Lyda, who married Charles Akres, a manufacturer of clay products, and resides at Akron, Ohio.

The graded schools of Cherokee County and the high school at Columbus furnished Charles F. Spencer with his educational training, and after his graduation from the latter, in 1891, he at once embarked in the coal business, in which he has been engaged ever since. He has worked his way to a position of prominence, and as an operator at the present time is president of the Columbus Coal Company, of Columbus; the Spencer-Newlands Coal Company, of Mulberry; and the Pittsburg and Midway Coal Mining Company, of Pittsburg. As president of the last-named concern he maintains offices in the Globe Building, Pittsburg. Mr. Spencer is a republican and a member of the Methodist Episcopal Church. Fraternally, he is affiliated with Columbus Lodge, Ancient Free and Accepted Masons, and he also holds membership in the Chamber of Commerce and the Pittsburg Country Club. Mr. Spencer owns his own residence at No. 1002 South College Street. 1,800 acres of farming land in Crawford County, 240 acres of farming land in Cherokee County, and 200 acres in Oklahoma.

In October, 1896, at Columbus, Kansas, Mr. Spencer was married to Miss Clara Hughes, daughter of Joseph and Margaret (Wharey) Hughes, the former a merchant, now deceased, and the latter now residing with her daughter and son-in-law. Mr. and Mrs. Spencer have been the parents of three children: Harold, a graduate of the Pittsburg High School, class of 1916, and now a freshman at Kansas University, Lawrence, where he will take up the study of mining engineering; Kenneth, a freshman at the Pittsburg High School; and Galen, who is attending the graded schools.

WILLIAM H. RHODES. As proprietor of the Sunrise Stock farm, comprising 230 acres, situated near Manhattan, in Riley County, Kansas, William H. Rhodes occupies a prominent place among agriculturists in this part of the state, the products of his farm because of their standard merits having a wide distribution. Mr. Rhodes was born in Atchison County, Kansas, March 31, 1869, but was reared in Marion County, Kansas. His parents were John M. and Martha (Kuhn) Rhodes.

John M. Rhodes was born in Franklin County, Pennsylvania, and died in Marion County, Kansas, in 1914, when aged seventy-nine years. His father, Christian Rhodes, was born in Germany and after coming to the United States lived always in Pennsylvania. John M. and Martha (Kuhn) Rhodes were married in Franklin County, Pennsylvania, and came to Kansas in 1866. They located first in Atchison County but four years later removed to Marion County, and there Mrs. Rhodes yet lives, being now aged eighty years. Mr. Rhodes for forty-four years successfully carried on farming and stock-raising, a quiet, industrious man, a good neighbor and a valued citizen. In politics he was affiliated with the republican party. Both he and wife were members of the Presbyterian Church. They had four children: Christian E., who is a banker at Elmo, Kansas; William H.; Mary E., who is the wife of H. H. Banker, who is a merchant at Brownsville, Texas; and J. Frank, who is a farmer and stock-raiser on the old homestead in Marion County.

William H. Rhodes was reared to be a farmer and very early, on his father's homestead, began to learn the practical details that are a necessary equipment for success in this vocation. He obtained a common school education but on the farm he has learned more than the books of his boyhood could teach him, for it is a fine training school. Mr. Rhodes has shown its worth by developing into one of the most accurate, careful and enterprising farmers and stockraisers in Riley County. For fifteen years he successfully operated a fine stock farm in Marion County, near Tampa, which he sold in 1908, coming then to Riley County and purchasing his present farm situated near the Kansas State Agricultural College and now known as the Sunrise Stock Farm. He raises exceptionally fine stock consisting of Percheron horses, Hereford cattle and Berkshire hogs.

In 1908 Mr. Rhodes was married to Miss Viola Cromer, who was born in Illinois, and they have two children: Aileen and Harlan. They are members of the Presbyterian Church. Mr. Rhodes is not active in politics but votes the republican ticket and is a dependable citizen in lending his influence, when occasion arises, toward forwarding enterprises promising to advance the general welfare.

HERSCHEL V. BOLINGER. The assistant cashier of the Home National Bank, Herschel V. Bolinger, f Caney, is by inheritance and training well equipped for his responsible position. He comes of a family given to valuable and practical accomplishment, particularly in the line of agricultural effort, which has resided in this country for many generations. Since leaving the schoolroom Mr. Bolinger has been connected with financial institutions, and at Caney has also been identified with railroad affairs and with civic duties.

Herschel V. Bolinger was born at Shelburn, Sullivan County, Indiana, March 19, 1884, and is a son of W. T. and Arpy (Curry) Bolinger. The Bolinger family originated in Germany, from whence the founder came to the United States at an early date in this country's history and took up his residence in Pennsylvania, from which state members of the family made their way south and west. The branch to which Herschel V. Bolinger belongs drifted to Kentucky, where, near Maysville, Mason County, W. T. Bolinger was born in 1851. He was given his early education in his native place until he was fourteen years of age, at which time he accompanied his parents to Shelburn, Indiana, in the vicinity of which town his father had purchased a farm. On starting his independent career, W. T. Bolinger adopted the vocation of farming, which he followed throughout his career, accumulating a good property in Sullivan County, Indiana, before coming west in 1912 to locate at Caney. Mr. Bolinger has been an industrious man who has made his efforts count and whose good management has resulted in his becoming the owner of a satisfying competence. In his political views he is a republican, but has never been a politician. His religious faith makes him a Baptist, and fraternally he is an Odd Fellow, belonging to the Encampment at Shelburn, Indiana, and the Caney Camp No. 323. Mr. Bolinger married Miss Arpy Curry, who was born near Shelburn, Indiana, in 1861, and they are the parents of three children, namely: Herschel V., of this notice; Flossie, who is the wife of A. D. Hunt, connected with the Cudahy Refining Company, at Coffeyville, Kansas; and Gladys, who is a freshman at Caney High School.

After securing his early training in the public schools of Shelburn, Indiana, Herschel V. Bolinger furthered his training by attending the Indiana State Normal School at Terre Haute. Later, he took a special course at the State Normal School, at Danville, Indiana, which institution he left in 1904 to accept the position of bookkeeper with the First National Bank of Shelburn. Later he was advanced to assistant cashier, a position which he held for three years, or until going to Copan, Oklahoma, as cashier of the Bank of Copan, a post which he occupied for over a year. Mr. Bolinger came to Caney, Kansas, in 1908, to become secretary of the Kansas & Oklahoma Railroad, an office which he still retains. In 1915 he entered the employ of the Home National Bank of Caney, in the capacity of assistant cashier, which position he still retains. He also has various other interests, among which may be enumerated the Panama Crude Oil Company, of which he is secretary. Mr. Bolinger may be said to be somewhat of a departure from the long accepted type of banker, having a degree of adaptability and public spirit seldom associated with his prototype of some years ago. He relieves the arid and unchangeable routine of his labor with participation in business, politics and society, in all of which he wields a sane and progressive influence. Politically a stalwart republican, he has taken an active part in civic affairs, and has served as a member of the city council of Caney and in other offices. Fraternally, he is affiliated with Caney Lodge No. 324, Ancient Free and Accepted Masons, and Caney Lodge No. 1215, Benevolent and Protective Order of Elks, in both of which he is very popular. In 1910 he was united in marriage with Miss Lutie Porter, daughter of S. M. Porter, a sketch of whose career will be found elsewhere in this volume. To Mr. and Mrs. Bolinger there has been born one son: Billie Porter, born June 6, 1914.

William H. Bolinger, the grandfather of Herschel V. Bolinger, was born in Pennsylvania, in 1821, and as a young man went to Maysville, Kentucky, where he became a pioneer farmer. There he made his home and followed his vocation until 1865, when he took his family to Shelburn, Indiana, and that vicinity continued to be his home until his death in 1904. In politics he was at first a whig and later a republican, and wielded some influence in his home community. Mr. Bolinger married Miss Victoria Close, who was born in France, and died at Shelburn, Indiana, and they became the parents of six children, as follows: John, who is engaged in farming in Sullivan County, Indiana; J. Sam, who also carries on agricultural pursuits near Shelburn; Charles, who is president of the First National Bank of Shelburn and has large farming and stockraising interests; Nettie, who is the widow of G. All and resides at Terre Haute, Indiana; W. T., the father of Herschel V. Bolinger; and Fred, who resides at Shelburn, Indiana, and is a farmer.

JAMES HENRY BOICE. In 1877 the late F. S. Boice arrived at Galena, and from that time forward was actively engaged in the mining operations that have always formed the basis of the prosperity of that city. For fully forty years the family has been prominently represented at Galena both in the mining industry and in mercantile and other affairs, and the work which was begun by the late F. S. Boice has been continued along even broader lines by his son James Henry.

This is a family whose origin was in Scotland. From that county the father of F. S. Boice came in the early days, became a merchant in Ohio, and died in that state. F. S. Boice was born in Ohio in 1838, was reared and married there and while in that state gained a knowledge of the furniture and undertaking business. A few years after the close of the Civil war he determined to seek a new location in Kansas. His destination was Fort Scott. In the absence of a railroad he reached that town by stage coach. He soon afterward opened a stock of furniture, and extended his business by handling agricultural implements. Then in 1877 he removed to Galena, and was identified with the mining and business affairs of that city until his death in 1909. He was one of the organizers of the Citizens State Bank of Galena, and for many years served as its director. Politically he was a republican and was a member of the Independent Order of Odd Fellows. He married Margaret Mahala Ross, who was born in Ohio and died at Fort Scott in 1874. Of their four children James Henry Boice, the youngest, and who was born at Waverly, Ohio, April 29, 1863, is the only survivor. The oldest child, William, died at the age of three, Annie died when six years old, and Libby died at the age of four.

James H. Boice spent his early years in Fort Scott and also in Galena, and his education was acquired in the Fort Scott public schools. When only thirteen he left school to work in the mines, and from 1877 to 1900 he was one of the active men in the Galena mining district, at first as an employe and afterwards as an independent operator. Mr. Boice had the first sludge mill on Short Creek, at the location that is now the City of Galena. In the management of his business affairs he has been highly prospered. He was one of the originators of the Wyandotte land and still owns that tract. He is director and secretary of the Citizens Bank of Galena, owns 340 acres of mineral lands, in Cherokee County, and has considerable city property, including his home at 500 Joplin Street at the corner of Fifth Street; a dwelling at 907 Wall Street and another at 600 East Fifth Street, and also one at 205 East First Street, and others at the corner of Twelfth Street and Bellevue Avenue and the corner of Third Street and Galena Avenue.

Since 1898 Mr. Boice has been one of the merchants of Galena, and has conducted the leading furniture store of the town. He also owns the building in which his store is situated at the corner of Sixth and Main streets.

In matters of politics he is independent. He served three terms without opposition as treasurer of the school board. He is a member of the Galena Fire Department, and fraternally is affiliated with Lodge No. 677 Benevolent and Protective Order of Elks, and has been chairman of its house committee for the past seven years; with Galena Lodge No. 194, Ancient Free and Accepted Masons; with Galena Lodge No. 195, Independent Order of Odd Fellows; Mineral Lodge No. 3, Knights of Pythias; Aerie No. 266 Fraternal Order of Eagles; Camp No. 804 Modern Woodmen of America; with the Woodmen of the World, with the Sons and Daughters of Jus-

Marie J. Tanguay M.D.

tice, the Kansas Fraternal Citizens, the Degree of Honor, and the Pythian Sisters.

In December, 1887, Mr. Boice was married at Empire a locality now known as Galena Heights, to Miss Emma Garner. She is a daughter of A. J. and Rebecca (Cole) Garner. Her father, now deceased, was a pioneer miner and mine owner, in this section of Kansas, and during the Civil war had served as first lieutenant of the Second Arkansas Volunteer Cavalry. Mrs. Boice's mother is living with her daughter Mrs. Boice. They have one child, F. Garner Boice, who was born September 20, 1892, was graduated from the Galena High School in 1909, spent two years in the University of Kansas at Lawrence and is now assisted with his father in business. This son is a member of Galena Lodge No. 194, Ancient Free and Accepted Masons, and Baxter Springs Chapter No. 78, Royal Arch Masons.

MAMIE J. TANQUARY, M. D., of Independence is one of the leading woman physicians and surgeons of Kansas. She comes of a family that has supplied several able members to the profession, and her work throughout the fifteen years she has practiced at Independence shows her capabilities are on a plane with her own brothers and her professional brethren throughout the state.

. Doctor Tanquary, whose maiden name was Edwards, was born at Water Valley in Hickman County, Kentucky, April 29, 1870. She is of old Southern stock, but her first ancestors in the Edwards line came from England of Scotch-Irish lineage and were pioneer settlers in Tennessee. Through her paternal grandmother she is related to the noted Brigham family. The grandfather Edwards was a native of Tennessee, and had a plantation worked by slaves in that state before the war. He died in Tennessee.

W. H. Edwards, father of Doctor Tanquary, was born in Tennessee November 6, 1828. He spent the first twenty-one years of his life in his native state, and he then went with his parents to Hickman County, Kentucky, where he married. Prior to the war he owned a number of slaves, and conducted his planting operations by slave labor. Soon after the birth of his daughter, Doctor Tanquary, he moved out to Kansas, and became one of the early settlers in Chanute, and the homestead he took up and developed there was sold after his death. He died at Chanute March 10, 1914. He was a democrat and an elder in the Presbyterian Church and was also a member of the Masonic fraternity. W. H. Edwards married Antoinette A. Alexander, who was born in Hickman County, Kentucky, in 1834, and died at Chanute May 7, 1913. Doctor Tanquary was the eighth in a family of nine children, and some reference should be made to her brothers and sisters. The oldest, Maude, died in Hickman County, Kentucky, at the age of three years, and Flavius died there at the age of four years. Luna died unmarried at Chanute at the age of forty-nine. Sallie is the wife of S. J. Paul, who is now retired from business and lives at Hollywood, California. Eudora married J. R. Francis, a merchant at Carthage, Missouri. R. S. graduated from the Bennett Medical College at Chicago with the degree M. D., and while still active in his profession is giving much of his time to his fruit farm at Grand Bay, Alabama. J. B. Edwards, now one of the leading members of the medical profession at Chanute, and owner of the Chanute Hospital, graduated from the Louisville Medical College, afterwards took courses in the Chicago Post-Graduate School and the Chicago Policlinic, studied under the famous

Mayo brothers at Rochester, Minnesota, in 1911, and interrupts his practice every year for some special course in some of the leading medical centers of the country. Walter, the youngest child, died at the age of nine years in Chanute, Kansas.

On February 21, 1871, when W. H. Edwards brought his family to Chanute, his daughter Mamie was not yet a year old. She grew up at Chanute, attended the public schools there, also the State Normal School at Emporia, and her first work outside of home was teaching. She spent one year in Neosho County and four years at Neodasha in Wilson County. From early years she had felt that her mission was to serve her fellow men through the profession of medicine. After leaving the schoolroom she entered the Kansas Medical College at Topeka, where she spent two years, and in March, 1901, graduated M. D. from the College of Physicians and Surgeons at Kansas City, Kansas, a school now affiliated with the Kansas State University. Doctor Tanquary is not the type of physician who rests content with present attainments and in 1905 she spent several months in the Chicago Post-Graduate School, specializing in diseases of women and children, and in 1911 visited the clinics of the Mayo brothers at Rochester. For the past four years she has found much of her practice as a specialist in eye, ear, nose and throat diseases. She is a member of the County and State and American Medical associations. Since beginning practice at Independence on May 15, 1901, Doctor Tanquary has had her time and energies almost completely occupied by the increasing calls made for her services both as a physician and as a surgeon. Her offices are in the Booth Building, and she resides at 317 North Eighth Street. Doctor Tanquary also owns a farm of 160 acres seven miles southeast of Independence, and operates that through renters. She is a member of the Independence Commercial Club, and is affiliated with Eva Chapter No. 18 of the Order of Eastern Star and with the Royal Neighbors. She is a member and liberal supporter of the Methodist Church. On May 5, 1897, at Chanute she married Earl D. Tanquary, who was born in Indiana, received his early education at Neodesha, Kansas, and graduated M. D. from the College of Physicians and Surgeons in Kansas City. Doctor Tanquary has one daughter, Blendena, who is now a sophomore in the Central College at Lexington, Missouri.

HARRY E. COULTER. One of the old and reliable business establishments of Chanute which has enjoyed a steadily increasing patronage ever since the time of its inception is the Coulter Transfer and Storage Company, in which two generations of a family have been interested. Founded by the father, the policy of the business under his direction was based upon strict honesty and honorable principles, and this same course has been followed by the son. The present owner of the business is Harry E. Coulter, a man of broad and diversified experience in business, and a citizen who has contributed through his activities to the material and business welfare of the city of his adoption.

Mr. Coulter was born at Chatsworth, Livingston County, Illinois, May 9, 1867, and is a son of W. J. and Jane (Ririe) Coulter. He belongs to a family which has resided in this country from Colonial days, when the original emigrant from Germany located in Pennsylvania. W. J. Coulter was born in 1834, in Pennsylvania, and was reared in the Keystone state, where he received a public school

He stands very high in Masonry. He has served three years as master and is now past master of Caney Lodge No. 324, Ancient Free and Accepted Masons; is a member of Overbrook Chapter, Royal Arch Masons; Topeka Commandery, No. 5, Knights Templar; Topeka Consistory No. 1 of the Scottish Rite and has also received the honorary degree for services K. C. C. H.; and Caney Chapter of the Eastern Star. His membership is also in Havana Lodge No. 343, Independent Order of Odd Fellows, and the Havana Country Club. His politics is republican.

In his native Missouri County Mr. Rippetoe married Miss Lucinda Harris, a daughter of John Harris, a farmer. Mrs. Rippetoe died in Jackson County, Kansas, in 1883, leaving three children. Rosa B., who died at Hoyt, Kansas, May 12, 1915, was the wife of E. C. Lyon, a carpenter at Havana. Benjamin went to the Philippines with the army and now has a Government position there. Flora E. is the wife of James Randels, a cement worker at Overbrook.

In 1884 at Meriden, Kansas, Mr. Rippetoe married Mary F. McDowell, daughter of Barton and Ava McDowell, both now deceased. Her father was a farmer. By this marriage there were six children: Franklin H., who graduated from the Stricklin Business College of Topeka, where he is now bookkeeper for the Chicago Lumber Company; Everett O., a manager of the Howe Lumber Company at Sedan, Kansas; Ava, who is a graduate of the Colorado Springs Academy, is the wife of Clifford E. Hileman, a mail carrier at Topeka; Robert H., a graduate of the Dougherty Business College of Topeka, is manager of his father's lumber yard at Wayside; Walter Leslie is manager of his father's business at Havana; Charles W. a student at Kansas State Agricultural College.

GEORGE W. LONG is postmaster at Galena. Prior to his appointment to that office during the present administration he had become known as a young and vigorous business man and merchant.

He practically grew up in the grocery trade and knows its every detail not only from the point of view of a salesman but also from the business office. He first became known to the citizens of Galena in 1897 when he entered the service of one of the grocery stores and was employed as a clerk up to 1904. He gave up his work long enough during that year to attend the Joplin Business College, and fortified with this training he returned to Galena and resumed employment in a store for six months. Then in 1905 he set up in business for himself and now owns that excellent market known to all the people of Galena at 923 East Seventh Street. He also owns his residence at 915 East Fifth Street.

Mr. George W. Long was born in Barry County, Missouri, January 18, 1884, and his family were among the early settlers in that section of Southern Missouri. The Longs came originally from England and first settled in the Carolinas and afterwards were pioneers in the State of Tennessee. His grandparents Washburn and Margaret Long were both natives of Tennessee. His grandfather was born in 1831 and died in Barry County, Missouri, in 1909. He went to Missouri in 1853, and spent the rest of his days there as a farmer.

Aaron Long, father of George W., is a well known citizen of Galena. He was born in Barry County, Missouri, in 1850 reared and married there, and took up merchandising which he followed in Missouri until his removal to Galena in 1898. For a time he was a grocer in Galena, later proprietor of a hotel, and

is now back in the grocery business, having a store at Tenth Street and Euclid Avenue. His political support has always been given to the democratic party and during his residence in Missouri he served on the County Central Committee. He is a member of the Christian Church and belongs to the Masonic Lodge at Cassville, Missouri. Aaron Long married Lucy Ethridge, who was born in Marion County, Illinois, in 1852. Their children are: Charles, a farmer in Barry County, Missouri; Ida, wife of W. M. Hemphill, a Barry County farmer; Anna, wife of E. P. Moore, who is employed in the grocery business at Galena; Edna, wife of Dow Moore, a wholesale grocer at Galena; George W.; Lena, who lives with her parents and is employed as a bookkeeper; Stella, who died unmarried at Galena at the age of twenty-six.

The early life of George W. Long was spent in Barry County, where he received his early education in the public schools. His life has been one of varied interests and every worthy movement finds in him a loyal advocate. He is active in the First Christian Church at Galena as a deacon, is a member of the Galena Community Club, and is affiliated with Lodge No. 195 Independent Order of Odd Fellows, Lodge No. 677 Benevolent and Protective Order of Elks, and Lodge No. 266 Fraternal Order of Eagles, all of Galena. For two years he served as chairman of the City Democratic Central Committee. He was city alderman one term and was treasurer of the board of education two terms.

In 1907 in Galena he married Miss Ethel Raines, a daughter of George W. and Naomi (Page) Raines. Her mother died in May, 1916, and her father is a farmer in Cherokee County. Mr. and Mrs. Long have one child, George Aaron, born December 4, 1908.

OSCAR C. BAIRD, M. D. Kansas is justly notable for the skill, learning and high character of the men who compose its medical fraternity and the profession here numbers among its members those whose scientific attainments are far beyond the ordinary. Among those well known during the past sixteen years is Dr. Oscar C. Baird, of Chanute, whose career is typical of modern advancement, his having been a broad field of medical service. Doctor Baird is a native of Van Buren County, Iowa, and was born December 29, 1871, his parents being Nathan and Lorinda (Jones) Baird.

Doctor Baird is of Scotch descent, his original American ancestor having emigrated from Scotland to America during the Colonial era and settled in Pennsylvania. In that state, in 1812, was born the Doctor's grandfather, Josiah Baird, who was a blacksmith by trade, migrated in young manhood to Noble County, Ohio, and later went to Iowa, where he became a pioneer of Van Buren County and there spent the remainder of his life at his trade. His death occurred in 1892, when he had reached the age of eighty years. Nathan Baird, father of Dr. Oscar C., was born in 1839, in Ohio, and was there reared to young manhood. He accompanied his parents on their western migration to Van Buren County, Iowa, and not long thereafter enlisted in the Iowa State Militia, with which he served as a soldier of the Union during the Civil war. When his military duties were completed, he returned to the duties of private life, and for many years was engaged in agricultural pursuits, in which he won success through perseverance and hard labor. His death occurred in Van Buren County, in 1908. Mr.

Baird was a republican in politics. He was a member of the Presbyterian Church, lived his faith every day, served as elder for many years, and was strict in his interpretation of the church's rules. While he was stern and unbending in his belief, he never asked others to do what he himself would not, and his probity and integrity did much to influence others to better lives. Mr. Baird married Miss Lorinda Jones, who was born in 1839, in Ohio, and who still survives in her seventy-first year and lives on the old home place in Van Buren County, Iowa. To this union there were born children as follows: J. F., who is a general mechant and prominent business man of Odell, Illinois; L. C., who is a farmer of Florida and resides at Bairdsville, a town which is named in his honor; Howard, who is carrying on agricultural pursuits in Van Buren County, Iowa; Seth, who is also a well-known farmer of that community; Dr. Oscar C., of this notice; Dr. J., a graduate of the State University of Iowa, degree of Bachelor of Arts, and of the Eclectic Medical College, Cincinnati, Ohio, degree of Doctor of Medicine, and now a well-known medical practitioner of Coffeyville, Kansas; Flo, who is the wife of Harry Gleason, a prosperous jewelry merchant of Boston, Massachusetts; and J. N., a graduate of the State University of Iowa, degree of Bachelor of Arts, and of the law department of the University of Michigan, Ann Arbor, degree of Bachelor of Laws, and now a prominent practicing attorney of Kansas City, Missouri.

Oscar C Baird received his public school education in Van Buren County, Iowa, and there grew up on his father's farm. Later he took his preparatory work at Keosauqau Academy, from which he was graduated in 1890, and attended the Nebraska State University. He next entered the Eclectic Medical Institute, Cincinnati, Ohio, and completed a full course, graduating with his medical degree in 1896, since which time he has taken post-graduate courses at the Chicago Policlinic and the New York Polyclinic. Doctor Baird began his professional career at Medoc, Missouri, where he remained in practice for four years, and in 1900 came to Chanute, which has since been his field of practice. He has built up an excellent clientele as a general practitioner in medicine and surgery and has rapidly risen to a foremost place among Neosho County's men of medicine. His offices are at No. 16 South Lincoln Avenue, where he has an extensive and valuable medical library and all instruments and appliances for the handling of the most difficult cases and the most delicate operations. Doctor Baird belongs to the Neosho County Medical Society, the Kansas State Medical Society, the American Medical Association and the Southeastern Kansas Medical Society. He has been honored on frequent occasions by his fellow-practitioners, having been president of the State Eclectic Medical Society several times, treasurer thereof for a number of terms, and president of the Chanute Lecture Course Association, a post which he occupies now and has for several years past. He is a member of the Kansas State Board of Health and is now city health officer of Chanute. In the early part of 1914, Doctor Baird took a trip with 200 other physicians through France, Germany, Switzerland, England, Belgium and Holland, visiting Austria and all the various provinces of Germany. This was a most interesting trip, and the Doctor was in Europe when the great European war broke out, June 13, 1914. When the Archduke Francis Ferdinand of Austria and his wife, the Duchess of Hohenberg, were shot and instantly killed,

Doctor Baird attended the funeral, as he did also the golden wedding ceremonies of the Emperor Francis Joseph. Doctor Baird is a republican, with progressive tendencies. He is the owner of his own home, at No. 201 Lincoln Avenue, a number of other dwellings at Chanute, and a business building at No. 14 South Lincoln Avenue. He is an active member of the Chanute Commercial Club, and is prominent in fraternal circles, belonging to Cedar Lodge No. 103, Ancient Free and Accepted Masons; Cedar Chapter No. 21, Royal Arch Masons; Chanute Camp No. 63, Woodmen of the World; and Chanute Lodge No. 96, Ancient Order of United Workmen. He is a citizen whose worth is widely recognized not only on account of the good he has done in professional lines, but also because of the active co-operation which he has given to public affairs. He keeps well informed in regard to the new ideas advanced by the medical fraternity, keeps in touch with the progress that characterizes the profession, and is today a most capable and skilled physician, his large patronage being an indication of the confidence reposed in him by his fellow-townsmen.

Doctor Baird was married in 1896 at Omaha, Nebraska, by Dr. Frank Crane, now of Chicago, to Miss May Wilson, daughter of Mr. and Mrs. William Wilson, farming people who are now deceased. They have one child: Anna Opal, a sophomore at Northwestern University, who attended the Young Women's Christian Association conference at Geneva in 1916 as a delegate.

EDGAR L. FARRIS, though one of the younger business men of Independence has utilized his opportunities to the best advantage and is now a partner in one of the leading insurance firms of that city.

He was born in Clarksville, Arkansas, May 16, 1891. His family is of old southern stock, and settled in Alabama about revolutionary times. Grandfather Jasper Farris was born in Alabama in 1824, was a farmer and stockman, and in 1875 moved to Clarksville, Arkansas, where he died in 1900. F. M. Farris, father of Edgar L., was born in Alabama in 1856 and was nineteen years old when he went with his parents to Clarksville, Arkansas, where he still resides. For many years he has been in the commission fruit business in that city. A few years ago he had charge of an extensive advertising campaign conducted by the state government of Arkansas, and took the exhibit "Arkansas on Wheels" to all the neighboring states. He is a democrat and a member of the Baptist Church. He was married at Russellville, Arkansas, to Miss Jennie Eggleston, who was born in Alabama in 1859. Their children are: Eugene, in the bottling business at Pottsville, Arkansas; Edgar L.; Lena, a teacher in the high school at Clarksville, Arkansas; and Marion, a teacher in Spadra, Arkansas.

After graduating from high school at Clarksville in 1908, Edgar L. Farris continued his higher education in Cumberland College in Arkansas, for two years. His first business experience was acquired under his father in the commission business. He remained with his father until 1913, and was then connected for two years with J. W. and Robert Meek, wholesale dealers in cigars, candy and similar goods at Fort Smith, Arkansas. In 1915 he removed to Independence and is now a member of the firm of Kandt & Farris, in the general insurance business with offices in the Kress Building.

Mr. Farris is a democrat, and is a member of the Independence Country Club. He is unmarried.

SAMUEL H. BARR. Some men have such initiative and adaptability for the handling of diversified business that it is difficult to classify them or hold them in one profession. That is true of Samuel H. Barr of Caney. By profession he is a lawyer, practiced law successfully for some years, and has the taste and inclinations for the profession. Before he was a lawyer he was an equally successful school teacher in Montgomery County. From the active practice of the law he was called by his increasing connections with important business affairs and is now at the head or officially connected with some of the big industries in that section of the state. Among other positions he is assistant treasurer and local manager for the Caney Gas Company.

Almost his entire adult career has been spent in Kansas. He was born in the Town of Virginia, Cass County, Illinois, April 16, 1861. His father, Robert Barr, was born in Ireland, was reared in that country, and on reaching maturity became a member of the Irish constabulary. In order to better his own and his family's condition, he determined to emigrate and come to America. In 1858 he located at Virginia in Cass County, Illinois, subsequently moving to Beardstown and then to Rock Island in the same state. In 1878 he sought the opportunities of the great Sunflower State, and established his home near Independence. He died on his farm there in 1890 at the age of fifty-eight years. Besides being a farmer he was a machinist by trade. Robert Barr married Jane Lord, who was born in Ireland and lives on the old home place a mile and a half west of Independence, being now eighty-one years of age. Their children were: Mary E., who died at Independence, Kansas, in 1891, the wife of Rev. Joseph S. Grimes, a Presbyterian minister, also deceased; Samuel H.; Robert L., who is a graduate of Marietta College at Marietta, Ohio, and is now a Presbyterian minister at Bruno, M'nnesota; James, a merchant at Independence; Charles, also in the mercantile business at Independence; Fannie, who died at Independence in 1902, unmarried; Edward B., a machinist at Joplin, Missouri; and the youngest child was a daughter that died in infancy. The father of this family was a democrat in politics, and was very active in the Presbyterian Church, which he served as deacon.

During his youth spent in Illinois Samuel H. Barr received a good public school education and wisely improved his early advantages. He made his education count when at the age of twenty-two he became a teacher, and for several years was one of the most progressive school men in Montgomery County. For four years he taught country schools in the vicinity of Independence, taught one term at Caney, and during the school year of 1887-88 was principal of the Fourth Ward School at Independence.

He gave a whole souled devotion while he was in the profession, but his ambition had already taken the direction of the law, and during part of his school work he was pursuing his studies under the guidance of Hon. S. C. Elliott at Independence. Admitted to the bar in 1889, he opened his office at Caney in the same year. His success was practically assured from the beginning, and many of his earlier clients have always regretted the fact that he did not continue in general practice. During the past quarter of a century Mr. Barr has always been foremost in everything connected with the welfare of the City of Caney. Again and again he has been foremost in movements for its progress and upbuilding and has never stayed his enthusiasm or effort because

of a dark outlook and has enheartened others in carrying forward a work whose results are now in evidence in one of the most thriving towns along the southern state line.

His rapidly developing interests in business and industrial fields obliged him to give up active practice in 1901. Mr. Barr is secretary, treasurer, stockholder and director in the Kansas Oil Company, a company operating in the Oklahoma fields but with headquarters at Caney. He is president of the Barr Gas Company, which has its headquarters at Independence and operates west of that city. From 1902 to 1912 he was president of the Caney Brick Company.

His most important connection, however, is as assistant treasurer and local manager of the Caney Gas Company. This company was organized in 1901, and Mr. Barr became its first secretary. The company was organized for the purpose of prospecting for gas in the vicinity of Caney. Leaders in the organization were E. B. Skinner, former State Senator S. M. Porter, and Mr. Barr, together with W. C. Meeker, G. F. St. John, John Todd, W. F. Gleeck and G. N. Sumner, all of Caney. An enterprise of this kind required great faith and enthusiasm and constant effort to make it a success. Mr. Barr is credited with a large share of the work which laid the foundation for the present industry. He spent weeks and months in the preliminary investigation and organization, until the company had blocked up 18,000 acres of leases around Caney. Then followed the development of the field. The third well drilled produced gas, and later the company brought in some of the biggest gas wells ever known in Kansas. Obtaining a franchise they piped Caney and Tyro, Kansas, and after making the field one of the largest in the Southwest they sold in 1904 a majority of the stock to the Kansas Natural Gas Company. Mr. Barr now holds his position as assistant treasurer and local manager of the original company under the auspices of the Kansas Natural Gas Company. His offices are Fourth Avenue, at the corner of Main Street, and his home is in the Palace Hotel.

With all his strenuous activity in business affairs Mr. Barr has a natural taste for politics and has been exceedingly helpful in past years to his party, the democratic. He was chairman of the County Central Committee in 1898-1900, and his work in unifying the party called for special appreciation. It was his success in his home county that led to his selection as a member of the State Central Committee for the years from 1900 to 1902, and in this larger sphere of politics his influence was hardly less noteworthy. From 1897 to 1911 Mr. Barr was a member of the Caney Board of Education, first being clerk of the board, and was president when he retired. He is a former member and now a supporter of the Presbyterian Church, and fraternally is affiliated with Caney Lodge No. 324, Ancient Free and Accepted Masons; Caney Chapter No. 90, Royal Arch Masons; Caney Chapter No. 105, of the Order of Eastern Star; Caney Lodge No. 160, Ancient Order of United Workmen; Caney Camp No. 041, Modern Woodmen of America, and Lodge No. 780, Benevolent and Protective Order of Elks, at Independence. He is also a member of the Independence Country Club and the Havana Country Club. Mr. Barr has one of the best selected law libraries and general reference libraries in Montgomery County, and it is probable that if his business interests can ever be satisfactorily arranged so that he can spare the time, he will re-enter the practice of law, for which he is eminently fitted.

GRANT WAGGONER is a specialist in mining law with office and practice at Baxter Springs, Kansas. He has claimed his home at Baxter Springs since 1909, but did not open his law office in that city until 1912. While most of his practice is connected with some phase or other of the mining industry, he also handles a general civil and criminal practice.

In 1914 Mr. Waggoner was elected from his district as representative in the State Legislature. He proved an able champion of all progressive legislation enacted during his term, and was particularly at the front in all matters concerning his particular district, which is largely a mining and industrial section. He was chairman of the Mines and Mining Committee and a member of the Judiciary Committee, Railroad Committee, Private Corporation Committee and Roads and Highways Committee. He was very active in securing the passage of the dynamite bill which regulates the sale of dynamite and other high explosives in Kansas.

Mr. Waggoner was born in Montgomery County, Illinois, May 29, 1888. His family had lived in Illinois since pioneer times. The original seat of the Waggoner family was at historic Bingen on the Rhine in Germany. From there three brothers of the name crossed the ocean and in colonial days settled in Delaware. Mr. Waggoner's grandfather George W. Waggoner was born in Hardin County, Kentucky, in 1826, spent his life largely on a farm in Montgomery County of that state and died there in 1867.

George B. Waggoner, who is now a retired resident at Baxter Springs, Kansas, was born in Montgomery County, Illinois, December 2, 1857, and spent all his active career as a farmer. He removed from Illinois to Baxter Springs in 1909. Politically he is a republican. He was married in his native county to Emily F. Long, who was born in Montgomery County, Illinois, December 24, 1859. Their children were: George F., who is a graduate of the University of Chattanooga, Tennessee, and is now practicing law at Waggoner, Oklahoma; Grant; and Grace, wife of R. F. Gresser, who is assistant in the National Bank at Baxter Springs.

Mr. Grant Waggoner gained his early education in the public schools there, also attended Shurtleff College at Alton, Illinois, and in 1908 completed his course and received the degree LL. B. at the University of Chattanooga, Tennessee. For two years he practiced at Tulsa, Oklahoma. Mr. Waggoner is attorney for the Building and Loan Association of Baxter Springs. He owns a 160 acre farm in Oklahoma. His offices are on Military Street. He is a member of the Baxter Springs Commercial Club, of the Cherokee County Bar Association, is affiliated with Baxter Lodge No. 71, Ancient Free and Accepted Masons, is High Priest of Baxter Chapter No. 78, Royal Arch Masons, a member of Galena Commandery No. 46, Knight Templars, and also belongs to Baxter Springs Lodge of the Independent Order of Odd Fellows. He is unmarried.

ARTHUR W. EVANS, M. D., is a native of the Sunflower State, a scion of a pioneer family of this commonwealth and has here achieved definite success in his profession, as one of the representative physicians and surgeons engaged in practice in the City of Independence.

Dr. Arthur Whiting Evans was born at Lawrence, Kansas, on the 26th of October, 1870, and is a son of Arthur and Mary (Leishum) Evans, the former of whom was born in Lancastershire, England, in

Vol. IV—14

1841, and the latter of whom was born in Wales, in the same year, she having been a young girl when her parents immigrated to America and established their home at Baltimore, Maryland, her marriage having been solemnized in the City of Cincinnati, Ohio. Arthur Evans was a resident of Eureka, Kansas, at the time of his death, which occurred in a hospital at Kansas City, Missouri, in January, 1905, he having gone to that city for medical and surgical treatment. His widow still maintains her home at Eureka. Arthur Evans was a boy when he accompanied his parents from England to the United States and after remaining for a time in New York City the parents established their home at Cincinnati, Ohio, where the son was reared to adult age and acquired his early education. There he learned the trade of tinsmith and also became familiar with the varied details of the hardware business. At the time of the Civil war he served as a member of the Ohio Home Guard and assisted in repelling of the invasion of General Price, the Confederate raider. Two of his children were born in Ohio and in 1868 he came with his family to Kansas and numbered himself among the pioneer business men of Lawrence, where he was long and prominently identified with the substantial business conducted by a leading hardware firm. In 1880 he removed to Eureka, where he engaged in the hardware business in an independent way and where he continued to hold secure vantage-ground as an honored and influential citizen until the time of his death. He was a stalwart supporter of the cause of the republican party and while a resident of Lawrence he not only served as a member of the board of aldermen but also one term as mayor of the city. He was a most zealous member of the Congregational Church, as is also his widow, and in the same he served many years as a deacon. He was a Master Mason and was a charter member of a lodge of the Independent Order of Odd Fellows in the City of Cincinnati, Ohio. Of the children the eldest is William Henry, who is engaged in the hardware business at Eureka; Lucy Isabelle, the wife of Dr. A. F. Higgins, a prominent physician and surgeon at Emporia, died in that city; Dr. Arthur W., of this review, was the next in order of birth.

Doctor Evans acquired his early education in the public schools of Eureka, and in 1888 he was graduated in Southern Kansas College. In preparation for his chosen profession he entered the celebrated Hahnemann College of Physicians & Surgeons in the City of Chicago, and in this institution he was graduated in 1892, with the degree of Doctor of Medicine. The following year he completed an effective post-graduate course in Rush Medical College, Chicago, and in 1900 he took another post-graduate course, in the A. & M. Medical College, New York City.

For the first four years after his graduation Doctor Evans was engaged in the practice of his profession in Kansas City, Missouri, and he then, in 1896, established his residence at Independence, where he has since continued in active general practice. He is uniformly accredited with being one of the leading physicians and surgeons of this part of the state and his offices are in the old Opéra House Building. He owns his attractive residence property at 121 South Pennsylvania Avenue, and also a residential property at Caney, in the same county. The doctor is actively identified with the Montgomery County Medical Society, the Kansas State Medical Society, and the American Medical Association. In his home city he is affiliated with the following named Masonic organizations: Fortitude Lodge, No. 107, Ancient Free & Accepted Masons; Keystone Chapter, No. 22, Royal Arch Masons; and St. Bernard Commandery, No. 10, Knights Templars. He holds membership also in the allied organization, Abdullah Temple, Ancient Arabic Order of the Nobles of the Mystic Shrine, at Leavenworth. At Independence the doctor is likewise a member of the Knights of Pythias, the Modern Woodmen of America, the Benevolent and Protective Order of Elks, and the A. H. T. A., besides holding membership in the Commercial Club and the Country Club.

In 1896 was solemnized the marriage of Doctor Evans to Mrs. Carrie L. Wallace, a daughter of Mrs. Benjamin Armstrong, of Wichita.

WILLIAM ERNEST BARKER, M. D. Prominent among the medical men of Southeastern Kansas is Dr. William Ernest Barker, who since 1881 has been engaged in practice at Chanute. During this long period of devotion to his profession he has built up a large and representative professional business, and is justly regarded in medical circles and by the general public as a thoroughly learned, skilled and reliable physician and surgeon. Doctor Barker is a native of Birmingham, England, and a son of William and Martha (Timmins) Barker.

William Barker was born in England, served in the regular army during his youth, and became the owner of an iron works and of several iron and coal mines. Some years prior to the Civil war he came to the United States and located at Cleveland, Ohio, where he was foreman of an iron foundry until his death. His wife died in England, and had been the mother of four children: William Ernest; Mary Ann, of England, the widow of Alfred Bridle, a railroad man; Martha, who is the wife of Professor Crosby, of Paris, France; and Eli, a resident of Birmingham, England.

William Ernest Barker received his early education in the Protestant schools of England, and after graduation from the high school commenced to read medicine, although at that time he was serving an apprenticeship to the general foundry business. Shortly after the close of the Civil war he came to the United States and first located at Mahanoy City, Pennsylvania, from whence he went to Cleveland, Ohio. In 1869 he removed to Kansas City, Missouri, and not long thereafter went to a farm northeast of Burlington, Kansas, where he resumed his medical studies. He subsequently attended the St. Louis Medical College, where he received the degree of Doctor of Medicine and first practiced at St. Louis, from whence he went to Thayer, Kansas. After five years in that city, in 1881 he came to Chanute, and here has continued in a general medical and surgical practice ever since, with the exception of two years (1884-1886) when he was in England, perfecting himself in medicine and surgery at the London Hospital, under Superintendent Treeves. Doctor Barker is local surgeon for the Atchison, Topeka & Santa Fe Railroad, the Pacific Mutual Insurance Company, the Travelers of Hartford, and the State Life Insurance Company of Indianapolis. He belongs to the American Medical Association, the Southeastern Kansas Medical Society, the Kansas State Medical Society and the Neosho County Medical Society, of which last-named he was president for two terms in succession. The doctor is well known in fraternal circles, holding membership in Cedar Lodge No. 103, Ancient Free and Accepted Masons; Chanute Chapter No. 21, Royal Arch Masons; Chanute Commandery No. 44, Knight Templars; Topeka Consistory No. 1, thirty-second degree; and Mirza Temple, Ancient Arabic Order Nobles of the Mystic Shrine, of Pittsburg, Kansas; Chanute Lodge No. 806, Benevolent and Protective Order of Elks; the Fraternal Aid Union, and Blackfoot Tribe, Improved Order of Red Men. He also belongs to the Chanute Commercial Club. Doctor Barker has been successful in a material as well as a professional way. He is a stockholder in the First National Bank of Chanute, and the holder of much valuable property, including an 800-acre farm two miles north of Chanute; a farm of 160 acres south of the city; a sixty-acre tract five miles southeast of here; his own residence at No. 17 South Lincoln Avenue, a dwelling at 418 South Malcolm Avenue; another house at No. 15 North Central Avenue; his business office at No. 15 South Lincoln Avenue, and the business block at Nos. 11-13 South Lincoln Avenue. In political matters he is a republican, but his only office has been that of member of the school board. As a professional man and a citizen he has always been held in the highest esteem, and has been a leader in many movements for the city's betterment.

Doctor Barker's first wife died leaving two sons: Jesse W. and Frank. Jesse W. Barker is a graduate of the Chanute High School, studied for a time at Northwestern University, Chicago, in the medical department, and received his degree of Doctor of Medicine from the Kansas City Medical College in 1900. He began practice as a physician and surgeon at Topeka, went then to Las Cruces, New Mexico, for one year, and in 1902 came to Chanute, where he has since been engaged in practice in association with his father. He is one of the leading members of the profession in Neosho County among the younger generation. He married Jessica Eaton, of Chanute, and they are the parents of six children: LeRoy, a junior in the Chanute High School; William Ernest, who died at age of two years; Wilma, who died aged nine months; Eileen, who is attending the public schools; and Vivian and Ralph Ernest. Frank Barker received his education in Birmingham, England, and is now a baker in the employ of the Bon Ton Bakery at Chanute. He married Mary Costa, and they have five children: Jesse, who attended the Chanute High School and is now a drug clerk in an establishment at Coffeyville, Kansas; George, who is a junior in the Chanute High School; Gordon and Mary, who are attending the graded schools; and Rose.

Doctor Barker was married in 1900 to Miss Lillian Godden, who was born at Janesville, Wisconsin, a daughter of William and Anne (Rumble) Godden. She is a great-granddaughter of James Godden, who was a musician and passed his life in London, England. Mrs. Barker's grandfather was Robert Godden, who was born in 1810, at West Lavington, England, and in that country was the owner of a small farm. About the year 1866 he came to the United States and located in the vicinity of Janesville, Wisconsin, where he was engaged in farming until his death in 1885. On the maternal side, Mrs. Barker is a granddaughter of John Rumble, who was born in 1804 at Beaching Stoke, England, where he died in 1879. He was the village schoolmaster and the owner of a small farm.

William Godden, the father of Mrs. Barker, was born in 1837, in West Lavington, England, and was there educated and reared. Shortly after his marriage, in 1862, he came to the United States and located at Chicago, where he became connected with the Chicago & Northwestern Railroad. He was superintendent of several departments in this system and in that capacity was transferred to Janesville, Wisconsin, where he passed the remaining years of his life, his death occurring in 1899. He was a republican in politics, a member of the Odd Fellows, and an Episcopal in religion, holding the positon of senior warden of his church for a number of years. Mrs. Godden, who was born in 1836, at Beaching Stoke, England, died at Chanute in 1915. They were the parents of five children, as follows: Mary Rebecca, widow of Hans Lyche, who was an editor and Unitarian minister, Mrs. Lyche now being a resident of Christiana, Norway, formerly a minister of the Unitarian Church for eight years, and now a teacher of English in the University of Christiana; William Robert Edgar, who was a traveling salesman and died at Hartley, Iowa, in 1904; Lillian, the wife of Doctor Barker; John Henry, the proprietor of a wholesale and retail marble works at Emmetsburg, Iowa; and Ella Louise, who is the wife of Prof. George S. Parker, a banker and attorney of Anderson, Indiana.

Mrs. Barker is a woman of remarkable attainments and talents. She received her primary education in the public schools of Janesville, Wisconsin, and after her graduation from the high school there went to the Chicago Normal School, the Chicago Kindergarten Association and the Chicago Art Institute, and in 1892 graduated from the Art Academy of Chicago. She taught school at Janesville and Chippewa Falls, Wisconsin, for several years, and holds a life teacher's certificate for Wisconsin and Missouri and also in schools of Chicago. Following her experience as an educator she was retained by D. C. Heath & Company, of Chicago, and during the seventeen years which she traveled for this firm she had charge of its art department and visited every state and territory in the Union. She had charge of the state institute work in Washington, Oregon, California and other points in the country, and in 1899 secured the first state adoption for her company's books in Kansas. In 1911 Mrs. Barker was appointed head of the art department in the Springfield (Missouri) State Normal School, where, as the first art teacher, her work was phenomenal. She succeeded in building up that department to a high state of efficiency, it now being the largest in the State of Missouri, and in 1915 enrolled over 800 students. In that year she was granted a leave of absence, and in 1916 resigned.

ROBERT H. CHILDS, now superintendent of the Petroleum Products Company plant in Independence, is one of the veteran oil men of America. His father was a pioneer in the oil fields of Western Pennsylvania, and Mr. Childs himself grew up in that environment, and took to the work as naturally as a New England youth goes to sea. There is probably not an important oil field in the country with which he has not been identified in some capacity or another.

The Petroleum Products Company established a plant in Independence in 1908. The general officers of the company at Chicago are: H. J. Halle, president; R. J. Dunham, vice president; and Ed C. Ennis, secretary and treasurer. The general manager and superintendent at Independence is Mr. Childs. This plant refines oil products and its output is an important list of standard petroleum products, which are sold throughout the Middle West. The plant at Independence has a crude oil capacity of 5,000 barrels daily, this oil coming from the Oklahoma and Kansas fields. About 200 men are regularly on the pay roll.

Robert H. Childs was born at Enterprise, Warren County, Pennsylvania, January 8, 1851. He comes of old and substantial American stock. His ancestors came from England to Rhode Island in colonial times. His great-grandfather John Cole Childs served with credit in the War of the American Revolution. He owned extensive bodies of land in Rhode Island and died at Warren in that state. Thomas Cole Childs, grandfather of the Independence business man, was born in Warren, Rhode Island, in 1784, and for many years served as sheriff of that county. Later he moved to Warren County, Pennsylvania, where he took up farming and the operation of a mill, and finally retired to Camp Point, Illinois, where he died in 1867.

Caleb O. Childs, father of Robert H., was born at Warren, Warren County, Rhode Island, in 1806, grew up there, was married at Jamestown, New York, and then moved to Warren County, Pennsylvania, where he was engaged for a time in the lumber business. In 1861 going to Titusville, Pennsylvania, he identified himself with oil production when that industry was in its infancy. He became associated with such notable men in the oil industry as Jonathan Watson and Dan Fletcher, and he was in business both at Titusville and Philadelphia, removing to the latter city in 1867. A few years before his death he retired and resided at Bradford, Pennsylvania, where he died in 1882. He was an active member of the Christian Church, was a thirty-second degree Mason, and an Odd Fellow and a republican. In 1830 at Jamestown, New York, he married Sarah A. Langdon, who was born at Addington, New Jersey, in 1811, and died at Bradford, Pennsylvania, in 1877. Their children were: Calphurnia, who died in Warren, Pennsylvania, as the wife of H. W. Childs, who is now a retired oil producer, living in New Jersey; Milo H., who died at the age of three years; and Robert H.

Robert H. Childs gained his early education in the public schools of Titusville, Pennsylvania, graduating from the high school in 1866, and later attending Kentwood College, where he completed the course in 1870. Then began his active career which has led him into various fields and into many responsibilities. For four years he was a manufacturer of lamp burners, sockets, fruit jars, and similar ware at Kensington, near Philadelphia. After that a few years were spent in the cattle business near Denver, Colorado. Returning to Titusville, he had charge of the business of Raydure-Watson Company at Tidioute, and then for five years was an oil producer in McKean County, Pennsylvania, residing at Bradford in the meanwhile. Going to Quarry, Pennsylvania, he helped build the Clark and Warren Works, remaining several years during their construction. His next location was in Warren, where he bought and remodeled the Warren Refining Company's refining plant in North Warren, and conducted it for six years. The next three years were spent with the Bear Creek Refining Company at Pittsburg. Then another three years were passed with the Leader Refining Company at Taylorsville, Pennsylvania.

He was an oil producer in the fields about Marietta, Ohio, for several years, spent two years in the oil fields of California, and then went to Beaumont, Texas, where he built the United Refining Company's plant and conducted it about four years, and for nine months had supervision of the building of the Gulf Refining Company's pipe lines for a distance of sixty-six miles. In 1908 Mr. Childs came to Kansas. At Chanute he remodeled the Chanute Refining Company's plant. Next he built the Kansas Oil Refining Company's plant at Coffeyville, using the material torn down at Chanute. From 1911 he spent a year and a half at Kansas City in charge of the Kansas City Refining Company's plant, and then spent a year building the Purified Petroleum Company's plant at Shreveport, Louisiana. Following that he was with the Phoenix Refining Company's plant at Sand Springs, Oklahoma, and in 1913 came to Independence, where he has since been superintendent of the Petroleum Products Company.

Mr. Childs is a republican, a. member of the Presbyterian Church, and is affiliated with Fortitude Lodge No. 107, Ancient Free and Accepted Masons, Keystone Chapter No. .22, Royal Arch Masons at Independence, St. Bernard Commandery No. 10 Knights Templar, Lodge No. 69, Independent Order of Odd Fellows at Independence, and is a member of the Independence Country Club.

In 1873 at Tidioute, Pennsylvania, he married Miss Sarah M. Meade. Her parents Goodwin and Harriet Meade are both deceased, her father having been an oil producer and hotel proprietor at Tidioute. Mr. and Mrs. Childs have three children: Harriet, who died, at the age of twenty-two; Sarah G., wife of G. N. Moore, reference to whom is made on other pages; and Roberta H., now a freshman in the Independence· High School.

GEORGE N. MOORE, who is general manager for the Petroleum Products Company and of the Standard Asphalt and Rubber Company at Independence, has spent practically all his adult life. in connection with the oil industry and for many years was with the Standard Oil Company in eastern states.

Born at Raymilton, Pennsylvania, November 18, 1878, he is a son of Nelson and Ada (Bell) Moore, who are now living retired at Richmond, Virginia. The Moore family came from Scotland to New York state several generations ago. Nelson Moore, who was born at Rochester, New York, in 1845, was reared and was married in Butler County, Pennsylvania, his wife being a native of the latter county, and in 1883 he moved to Warren, Pennsylvania. He was long connected with the Standard Oil Company in official capacities, but ten years ago retired and has since lived at Richmond, Virginia. During the Civil war he spent three years in a New York regiment of infantry.

George N. Moore received his early education in the public schools of Warren, Pennsylvania, graduating from the high school in 1893, and at once beginning the career which has brought him to his present responsibilities as an oil man. His first work was done for the Buckeye Pipe Line Company, and he spent 19½ years with the Standard Oil in Pennsylvania, West Virginia and Ohio. Moving to Independence, Kansas, January 1, 1913, he has since been general manager for the Petroleum Products Company and the Standard Asphalt and Rubber Company.

The Standard Asphalt and Rubber Company, which has its offices in the same building as the Petroleum Products Company at Independence, was established in 1906. Its plant occupies 200 acres of ground, and approximately 200 men are on the pay roll. This industry is located a mile south of the city. Its special output is asphalt paving, fillers for asphalt streets, and mineral rubber used for compounding with natural rubber. About 10,000,000 tons are produced annually.

Mr. Moore is a republican and a member of the Presbyterian Church, and enjoys many active relations with civic, commercial and fraternal societies. He is a member of the Country, Rotary and Commercial clubs of Independence, is affiliated with Fortitude Lodge No. 107, Ancient Free and Accepted Masons, Keystone Chapter No. 22, Royal Arch Masons, St. Bernard Commandery No. 10, Knights Templar, all at Independence, and Mirzah Temple of the Nobles of the Mystic Shrine at Pittsburg, Kansas, and Eva Chapter No. 18 of the Order of Eastern Star at Independence. He is also a member of Lodge No. 780, Benevolent and Protective Order of Elks at Independence.

At Bemis Point, New York, in 1901, Mr. Moore married Miss Sarah Childs, daughter of Robert H. and Sarah M. Childs, her father being superintendent of the Petroleum Products Company at Independence. Mr. and Mrs. Moore have one child, Robert M., who is now in the public schools of Independence.

HARRY HAYNES CULMER, superintendent of the Standard Asphalt and Rubber Company at Independence, is one of the expert technical men connected with the oil industry and has had a wide range of experience in his profession both in the United States and Canada.

. He came to Independence in 1906, and laid out the works of the Standard Asphalt and Rubber Company, which he has since served as superintendent and chemical engineer.

Mr. Culmer was born in Salt Lake City, Utah, October 30, 1878. He comes of notable ancestry. Records show that the Culmers go back to the year 862 A. D., when the original ancestors came to England with the Danes. They were converted to Christianity under Emperor Augustine who baptized them, and many of the later generations were actively associated with the Church of England. The great-grandfather of Harry H. Culmer was George Frederick Culmer who was a commodore in the navy and connected with the North Irish fleet. He was killed at Sligo, Ireland. The grandfather, Frederick George Culmer, who died at Salt Lake City, Utah, came from England, where he had followed the trade of shipbuilder, and in Salt Lake City was a cabinet maker.

G. F. Culmer, father of the Independence citizen, was born at Kent, England, in 1850. When sixteen years of age he came to America, prior to the advent of his father, and crossed the plains in an ox wagon to Salt Lake City. Later he went to Chicago, to Texas, then back to Chicago, and in 1906 moved to Independence, Kansas, where he is still living. He has been a prominent oil producer and has built a number of refineries in different parts of the country. He enjoys the highest rank in the United States in the Independent Order of Odd Fellows, his local membership being in Salt Lake City Lodge. G. F. Culmer married for his first wife Anna Haynes. She was born in Derby, England, in 1848, and died at Independence, Kansas, in 1913. She also came to this country at the age of sixteen and went west to Utah on the first train that ran into that state. Her children are: Frederick George, who died at the age of three years; G. C. K., who is a retired oil manufacturer and asphalt expert living at Philadelphia; Winifred Haynes, who died young; Florence

Emily, who died in childhood; and Harry Haynes. The father married in 1914 Miss Gilby.

Harry Haynes Culmer graduated from the Salt Lake City High School in 1893 and from the Utah School of Mines in 1896, with the degree mining engineer. Not content with his technical acquirements, he entered the University of Chicago, from which he received the degree chemical engineer in 1897. His technical studies were carried on under his father, and also under such authorities as Doctor Neff, Doctor Stiglietz, Doctor Langfield of the University of Chicago, and under Doctor Franklin, the curator of mineralogy at the Field Museum of Chicago. He specialized in hyro-carbon chemistry and geology, and is undoubtedly one of the leading American experts in the petroleum industry. At one time he was a member of the Society of Chemical Industry of London, England.

He has the distinction of having drilled the second oil well near the state line in McKean County, Pennsylvania. His father furnished the lumber for his derrick. Since 1897 Mr. Culmer has been connected with the petroleum industry in Canada, and in the states of Indiana, Illinois, Texas, Oklahoma and Kansas. He is a member of the Presbyterian Church, and has held all the offices except that of master in Fortitude Lodge No. 107, Ancient Free and Accepted Masons at Independence, and all the offices in Keystone Chapter No. 22, Royal Arch Masons, except high priest. He is also affiliated with St. Bernard Commandery No. 10, Knights Templar, and with Eva Chapter No. 18, Order of Eastern Star at Independence, and served as patron of the Eastern Star Chapter in 1910-11.

In 1900 at Chicago, Illinois, he married Miss Frances May Isaacson, daughter of Holstein and Jane Isaacson, both now deceased. Her father was a cattle raiser and also a hotel proprietor in Minnesota and Wisconsin. Mr. and Mrs. Culmer have three children: Winifred Haynes, who is now in the Montgomery County High School at Independence; Jane Frances, also in school; and George Frederick.

JOHN WESLEY WHEELER. Forty-five years ago when the greater part of Kansas was still an unbroken prairie and open cattle range, John Wesley Wheeler pioneered into the southern part of the state, and his subsequent activities as a homesteader, farmer and stock raiser, have enabled him to amass a competence sufficient for all his future needs. In the meantime he has provided liberally for his family, has borne an upright and commendable part in local affairs. He is now living retired at Havana in Montgomery County.

He is descended from Scotch-Irish ancestors who located in Pennsylvania. Mr. Wheeler himself was born at Findlay, Hancock County, Ohio, April 11, 1839. His father, Jesse Wheeler, was born in Pennsylvania in 1788, about the time that the American colonies were confederated under the United States Constitution. He was reared and married in his native state, and moved from Little York, Pennsylvania, to Seneca County, Ohio, where he was a very early settler. He afterwards moved to Hancock County, Ohio. His early years, from eighteen to twenty-one, were spent according to the fashion of the times, as a "bound boy" in apprenticeship to the carpenter's trade. That trade gave him an occupation for all his subsequent years, and he followed it until too old to work any longer. He began voting as a democrat, but when the republican party was formed sixty

years ago he became aligned with that organization. For many years he was active in the Methodist Episcopal Church. His death occurred in Findlay, Ohio, in 1874. He married Elizabeth Edgar, and three of their children were born in Pennsylvania before they removed to Ohio. She herself was born in Pennsylvania in 1806, and died in Hancock County, Ohio, in 1872. A brief record of the children is as follows: William H., who was a merchant from boyhood up in Findlay, Ohio, but late in life went to Georgia for his health and died in that state; James Jackson, who died in Findlay, Ohio, was a painter by trade, and later became a merchant associated with his brothers, W. H. and O. P. Oliver Perry, who died at Findlay, learned the carpenter trade when young under his father and later became a merchant with his brothers; Adam Clark also learned the carpenter's trade from his father, went out to California in 1850, and died in that state in 1852; Edward Smith, who died in Webster City, Iowa, was a merchant with his brothers back in Ohio and afterwards had a store of his own in Iowa; John Wesley was the sixth in age; Mary Elizabeth married A. M. Pence, an attorney, who died in Paris, France, while her death occurred at Chicago, Illinois; Samuel M. spent his early years clerking in his brothers' store in Ohio, and in 1871 moved to Colorado, where he was engaged in mining until his death at Leadville in 1912; Jesse B. was a consumptive and spent some years as a sheep herder at Leadville, Colorado, where he died.

Gaining his early education in the public schools of Findlay, Ohio, John Wesley Wheeler had his first practical experience as an employe in the store conducted by his brothers. He worked in the store from the age of fourteen to the outbreak of the war. Mr. Wheeler is one of the honored veterans of the great Civil war. He enlisted at the first call for troops on April 27, 1861, and went out with the Twenty-first Ohio Infantry, a three months' regiment. When this term expired he re-enlisted October 9, 1861, and became a member of the Fifty-seventh Ohio Infantry. At the second enlistment he was made a first lieutenant, and afterwards was promoted to captain of Company B of his regiment. He was in service until April 14, 1863, for nearly two years. During those two years he took part in the siege of Corinth, in the battle of Pittsburg Landing, or Shiloh, was through the siege of Vicksburg, and also at the battle of Missionary Ridge.

Having discharged his duties faithfully and well as a soldier of the republic, he returned to Findlay and continued his employment in the store there until the spring of 1870. At that time he moved to Kansas, spending a few months at Fort Scott, and in October, 1870, took a claim of eighty acres in Chautauqua County, Kansas. That claim, now developed as a fine farm, Mr. Wheeler still owns. After nearly forty years of capable management of his farming interests, Mr. Wheeler retired into Havana in 1909, and now lives in a residence which he owns on Main Street. For his military services he also enjoys a pension from the Government. Politically he is a democrat.

In 1885 at Independence, Kansas, Mr. Wheeler married Miss Anna Rogers, who came from Indiana. Her father, James Rogers, now deceased, was also a veteran of the Civil war. Mrs. Wheeler died in 1892 on the old home farm. Her children were: Mary, wife of A. H. Hartman, an oil worker living at Eldorado, Kansas; Bessie and Etta are still at home with their father; James spent three years on a large wheat ranch in the State of Washington, and is now a farmer near Nampa, Idaho.

ROBERT E. ROSENSTEIN of Baxter Springs is a man of varied talents and abilities and has successfully performed the services of a minister of the Gospel and lawyer at the same time. And though his time and attention are now given to the law, he occasionally preaches and is widely known over several states in the ministry of the Christian Church.

While Mr. Rosenstein spent most of his early life in Texas, he was born at Cairo, Illinois, January 4, 1871. His father Rudolph Rosenstein was born at Mecklenberg-Schwerin, Germany, in 1826, and came to America at the age of nineteen, settling in Monroe County, Tennessee. He was a machinist by trade, and it was that occupation that took him from place to place over various states. He lived a time at Cairo, Illinois, and finally located at Tyler, Texas, where he died in 1889. He was a democrat in politics and was reared in the Jewish Church. During the war between the states he served in the Confederate army, enlisting from Tennessee, and for a time was under General Marmaduke of Missouri. He was married in Tennessee to Elizabeth M. Webb, who was born in the eastern part of that state in 1830 and died at Tyler, Texas, in 1906. Their children were Hannah, who is the wife of James K. Boman, a farmer in Barry County, Missouri; Emma, wife of A. D. Beeler, a music teacher at Houston, Texas; William C., who is a contractor and builder and died at Los Angeles, California, in 1912; E. P. Rosenstein, a farmer in East Tennessee; H. N. Rosenstein, who was a tin and coppersmith and died at Tyler, Texas, in January, 1914; Robert E.; Laura, wife of J. W. Powell, a locomotive engineer living at Waco Texas; Rosa, twin sister of Laura, wife of W. H. Hudson, a car repairer living at Tyler, Texas; and J. F. Rosenstein, who is foreman in a tin and copper shop at Tyler, Texas.

The public schools of East Texas gave Robert E. Rosenstein his early education, and he afterwards took a two years course in the old Christian University at Thorp Springs, Texas. He had also begun reading law before he entered the ministry. After leaving Christian University he was pastor of different Christian churches in Texas, Missouri and Kansas. In 1898 he became pastor at Howard, Kansas, where he remained two years, and then successively spent three years at Manhattan, one year at Burlington, and then returned to Texas for one year. Coming back to Kansas he was located at Chanute one year and then removed to Oklahoma, where he engaged in the active practice of law until March, 1916, at which date he located at Baxter Springs. Mr. Rosenstein has a large general practice, and his offices are on Military Avenue.

While he was pastor of the church at Manhattan, Kansas, he read law in the office of Judge A. M. Story, and continued his reading at Burlington with the firm of Ganse and Hannon. He was admitted to the bar September 8, 1902.

Politically he is a democrat, is a member of the Baxter Springs Commercial Club, and is affiliated with Lodge No. 416 Ancient Free and Accepted Masons at Skiatook, Oklahoma, and also belongs to the Royal Arch Chapter. On October 29, 1891, at Tyler, Texas, he married Miss Effie Gould of a West Virginia family. They have two children. Claude H., is a graduate of the Oklahoma University at Norman in the law department and is now practicing law at Tulsa. Aretta who lives at home and assists in her father's office, is a graduate of the high school of Skiatook, Oklahoma.

JAMES BURTON TURNER has covered a wide field, including nearly all the states between the Allegheny and Rocky Mountains, as a worker, operator and producer in the oil fields. He was a pioneer operator in the Mid-Continental fields of Southern Kansas and Oklahoma. Mr. Turner is prominently known among the leading oil men of the country and since January, 1903, has been a resident of Chanute. From that city he has extended his various operations as a producer and contractor, and has drilled hundreds of wells in the fields of Kansas and Oklahoma.

At the present time Mr. Turner has some productive property east of Chanute, including ten active wells, has a lease five miles east of Chanute including eight wells, and a lease at Shaw of two wells. He was born in Crawford County, Pennsylvania, close to the great Pennsylvania oil fields, on November 28, 1863. His ancestors came from England and were colonial settlers in the State of Maine. His grandfather Enoch Turner was born in Maine, in 1791, and afterwards penetrated the wilderness across the Allegheny Mountains and found a pioneer home in Crawford County, Pennsylvania, where he died in 1890, when nearly a hundred years of age.

A. F. Turner, the father of James B., was born at Syracuse, New York, in 1818, and it seems likely that he will live to a greater age than his father. He is still living, in his ninety-eighth year, and a resident of Rouseville, Pennsylvania. When he was two years of age his parents removed to Crawford County, Pennsylvania, he was reared there, and after his marriage located on a farm and was identified with its cultivation and management until he retired to his home at Rouseville. He still owns the farm of 240 acres. Politically he has been a democrat, and has been voting steadily for over seventy years. In the course of his experience as a citizen he has held all the township offices in his home community. He was formerly a member of the Methodist Church and belonged to the Equitable Aid Union until that organization became defunct. A. F. Turner married Jane Lang, who was born in Crawford County, Pennsylvania, in 1823, and died at Rouseville, September 11, 1899. They were the parents of six children: J. E., who was an oil operator and was killed in a boiler explosion at Chanute, Kansas, in 1905; E. O. Turner, a farmer in Crawford County, Pennsylvania; D. E. Turner, a merchant at Rouseville, Pennsylvania; May, who lives at Rouseville, widow of E. F. Grosser, who was an oil operator; James B.; and W. L. Turner, an oil operator at Healdton, Oklahoma.

James Burton Turner spent his early life on the old farm in Crawford County. He had the advantages of the public schools. At the age of eighteen he left home and began working in the Pennsylvania oil fields, and from there his experience has gradually extended to cover nearly all the important oil districts of the country. Mr. Turner owns his home at 1321 South Edith Avenue in Chanute.

He is a democratic voter, is affiliated with Hector Lodge, Independent Order of Odd Fellows, at Chanute, and with the Benevolent and Protective Order of Elks, at Robinson, Illinois.

In 1883 in Warren County, Pennsylvania, Mr. Turner married Miss Kittie Manderville. She died at Rouseville, Pennsylvania, in 1888, the mother of four children: Charles, who is an oil operator living at Chanute; Leo, who died young; Lulu, who died at

C, C, Seerber M. D,

the age of two years; and Marie, who died in infancy. In 1897 at Clymer, New York, Mr. Turner married Miss Ida Gibson, daughter of William and Elizabeth (McNutt) Gibson. Her mother is living at Rouseville, Pennsylvania, and her father, who was an oil operator, is deceased. Mr. and Mrs. Turner have two children: Rowene and Leona, both of whom are in the junior class of the high school at Chanute.

O. F. WALKE who has spent most of his life in Kansas has developed a very substantial business career, and for several years has been proprietor of the Independent Laundry, one of the best equipped establishments of its kind in the southern section of the state.

He is of Scotch-Irish ancestry, and his great-grandfather came from the North of Ireland, and was an early farmer in Ohio. Mr. Walke's grandfather, William Walke, was born in Ohio in 1840, came to Kansas about a quarter of a century ago, and was an active farmer until he retired and died at Columbus, Kansas, in 1912. He made a record as a soldier during the Civil war, enlisting in an Ohio regiment of infantry in 1862 and serving until the close of hostilities. He was a member of the Christian Church, and was a stanch republican of the old school. He was also affiliated with the Modern Woodmen of America. His wife, Caroline Walke, was born in Ohio in 1843 and died in Columbus, Kansas, in 1911.

Mr. O. F. Walke was born at Woodstock, Champaign County, Ohio, April 2, 1888. His father is W. H. Walke, who was born in Ohio in 1856. He was reared in Ohio, where he married Miss Rella McDougal, who was born in that state in 1862. They have two sons: O. F. and D. E., the latter a traveling salesman living at Oklahoma City. In 1890 W. H. Walke came to Kansas and for a time was employed in the Kansas Steam Laundry at Wichita. From there in 1895 he moved to Leavenworth, and operated the first steam laundry in that city. Selling out three years later he returned in 1897 to Wichita, was again in the employ of a laundry, and later became a commission salesman. In 1908 he removed to Independence and in partnership with Will Owens owned the Independent Laundry until the early part of July, 1912, when his son bought him out. Since his removal to Columbus, Kansas, W. H. Walke has owned the greenhouses of that city and does an extensive business as a truck gardener. He is a member of the Christian Church, and has a life membership in Wichita Lodge of the Benevolent and Protective Order of Elks. His certificate is No. 2, but his is really the first life membership since he paid for his certificate, while No. 1 was complimentary. He is also affiliated with the Fraternal Order of Eagles, the Independent Order of Odd Fellows, and the Modern Woodmen of America at Wichita.

O. F. Walke gained his common school education at Wichita and in 1904 completed a course in the Wichita Commercial College. From there he went to Kansas City, Missouri, and his first regular business experience was gained in the offices of the Rock Island Railroad, where he remained three years and eight months. Returning to Wichita he spent one year managing his father's moving picture theater, which was the second institution of the kind established in Wichita. Following that came three years of employment in the sales department of the

Cudahy packing house. On June 3, 1912, he identified himself permanently with the City of Independence, and after four weeks bought his father's interest in the laundry and is now sole proprietor. This is one of the best equipped laundries of Montgomery County and has all the modern appliances and machinery for first-class work. It has a large share of the city business and outside business already averages $75 a week and the trade is constantly growing. The Independence laundry was established about 1900 by Will Owens. It is situated at 212 West Main Street.

Mr. Walke is independent in politics, and with his wife is a member of the Catholic Church. He is a member and carries insurance iff Independence Council of the Knights of Columbus, is a member of the Commercial Club, of the Duck Club, a hunting and shooting organization, and is also affiliated with Independent Lodge No. 780, Benevolent and Protective Order of Elks, and the local organization of the Fraternal Order of Eagles.

At Providence, Rhode Island, October 26, 1911, Mr. Walke married Miss Fannie Gertrude Mahan, daughter of Thomas and Sarah Mahan, and granddaughter of Anna Mahan, who is now living at the extreme age of eighty-nine at Wichita, Kansas. She came to this country from Ireland. Mrs. Walke's father was the founder of the Mahan Mercantile Company at Wichita, and is now deceased. Mrs. Walke's mother is now living at Providence, Rhode Island.

CASSIUS C. SURBER, M. D. An exceptionally long and valuable service in the field of medicine has been rendered by the Surber family in Kansas. The late Dr. David Surber was a distinguished physician in Kansas during the territorial period and afterward. The son, Dr. Cassius C. Surber, has been in practice more than thirty years, the greater part of that time at Independence, and is undoubtedly one of the ablest surgeons in the state.

Originally in Germany, the Surbers were colonial settlers in America, and the family subsequently became pioneers in the Territory of Indiana. Dr. C. C. Surber's grandfather Henry Surber was born in Indiana in 1808. He became a minister of the Campbellite or Christian Church, and carried the gospel into the new State of Iowa and afterwards continued his pioneer labors as a missionary and minister in Kansas. He died in Leavenworth County, Kansas, in 1876.

The late Dr. David Surber was born in Indiana in 1828. He was reared in his native state, but went in young manhood to Iowa, and in 1856 graduated from the Scudder Medical School of Cincinnati. He lived a time in Iowa, where he married, and in 1858 came to the Territory of Kansas and was one of the first to practice medicine in Clinton, Douglas County. From there he removed to Lawrence in 1867, later to Perry in 1868, and after more than half a century of devotion to his profession he retired and passed away at Bonner Springs in 1912. His prominence in the profession over the state is indicated by the fact that in 1888 he served as president of the Kansas State Board of Health. He also had a record as a soldier, having served in the Kansas Cavalry, and was with his command in pursuing the guerilla chieftain Quantrell and was also called into service when General Price made his spectacular raid through Missouri and Eastern Kansas. He was a member of the Douglas County and State Medical his first opportunity for service and work as a school teacher. He taught in Linn County one year, and two years in Franklin County.

Already his ambition was set upon the law as a career. Entering the State University at Lawrence, he pursued the studies of the law department until graduating LL. B. in 1898. In July of that year he began practice at Oswego, and was one of the rising young attorneys of that city for seven years.

Since removing to Cherokee County in 1905 Mr. Morgan has looked after a large general civil and criminal practice, having his home and offices in Galena. He has a suite of offices, rooms 8 to 13, in the Shoman-Moore Building. Besides his private practice Mr. Morgan was elected in 1906 and served one term as county attorney, and has also filled the office of city attorney.

His early life was spent in his native State of Ohio. He was born at Piketon December 17, 1873, attended public schools in Pike and high school in Scioto County, and it was soon after the conclusion of his school work there that he came to Kansas. This branch of the Morgan family is of Irish stock. His ancestors came to Pennsylvania in colonial days. Mr. Morgan's grandfather Thomas Morgan was born in Beaver County, Pennsylvania, in 1803, settled in Jackson County, Ohio, in 1837 and was a farmer in that state until he died in Pike County in 1878. He married Nancy Lutton who was born in Pennsylvania and died in Pike County, Ohio.

Robert Morgan, father of the Galena attorney, was born in Beaver County, Pennsylvania, April 22, 1835, and was two years of age when his parents removed to Jackson County Ohio, where he was reared. He also followed the pursuit of agriculture. After his marriage in Jackson County he moved to Pike County, and farmed there until his death September 28, 1892. He was a republican, very active in the Methodist Episcopal Church, which he served as trustee and steward many years, and for a long time was superintendent of the Sunday school. Fraternally he was affiliated with the Independent Order of Odd Fellows. The maiden name of his wife was Maria A. Daniels, who was born in Jackson County, Ohio, February 1, 1838, and died at Baxter Springs, Kansas, February 19, 1911. There were just three children in the family, Edwin B. being the youngest. His oldest brother M. L. K. is an optometrist at Bartlesville, Oklahoma. The second brother, Thomas, is a painter and decorator living at Columbus, Ohio.

Edwin B. Morgan since reaching his majority has been identified with the republican party. He is a member of the Presbyterian Church. In fraternal matters he is a member of several organizations but takes the greatest interest in Masonry. His affiliations are with Baxter Lodge No. 71, Ancient Free and Accepted Masons; Baxter Chapter No. 78, Royal Arch Masons; Galena Commandery No. 46, Knights Templars, of which he is eminent commander; Mirza Temple of the Mystic Shrine at Pittsburg; Amy Chapter No. 165 Order of Eastern Star; also Galena Lodge No. 677, Benevolent and Protective Order of Elks, of which he is Past Exalted Ruler; Anti-Horse Thief Association and Knights and Ladies of Security. Mr. Morgan joins in the activities of the Commercial Club of Galena, and is a prominent member of the Cherokee County Bar Association.

August 1, 1899, at Oswego, he married Miss Florence Skinner. Her parents both deceased, were Amos and Mary (Bird) Skinner, her father having been a contractor and builder. Mr. and Mrs. Morgan have two children: Robert, born March 16, 1902; and Richard, born December 22, 1906.

WILLIAM WUTTS O'BRYAN. Around the old Catholic mission which has since developed into the City of St. Paul, a number of prominent Catholic families have lived since the Indians gave up their possessions and set out for the Indian Territory. One of the best known of these is the O'Bryans, and as an individual representing the family the name of W. W. O'Bryan has been chosen because of his well-deserved prominence as a citizen of Neosho County and his extended activities as a stock dealer and business man.

The American beginning of this branch of the O'Bryan ancestry originated in William O'Bryan, great-grandfather of William W. of St. Paul. This William O'Bryan was born in Ireland in 1760, and was three years of age when his parents came and made settlement in the Colony of Maryland, where his father died. William O'Bryan, about 1800, moved to Kentucky, and died in Marion County of that state in 1848. He was both a farmer and school teacher.

The next generation was represented by Francis L. O'Bryan, who was born in Nelson County, afterward known as Marion County, Kentucky, in 1805. He spent his life in his native state as a farmer, was an active democrat and a member of the Catholic Church. He died in Kentucky in 1891. His wife was Sarah A. Lancaster, who was born in Kentucky in 1811 and died there in 1881. Her name introduces another interesting lineage. Her father, Ralph Lancaster, who died in Marion County, Kentucky, in 1857, at the age of eighty-seven, was born in Maryland. He was an early farmer settler in Kentucky. A brother of Ralph Lancaster was John Lancaster, who was a surveyor by profession, and while on his way from Maryland to Kentucky was captured by the Indians and remained a prisoner for one year. All his companions taken by the Indians were killed, being burned at the stake. The Indians promised to burn John Lancaster after a year, but in the meantime he made his escape, and making a rude boat out of two logs he drifted down the Kentucky river to Louisville, where he arrived among friends. This John Lancaster was the grandfather of the late John Lancaster Spaulding, Catholic bishop of Peoria, Illinois.

Francis L. O'Bryan and wife had the following children: Sarah Ellen, who died in Marion County, Kentucky, in 1858; John E., who died in infancy; John R., who became a merchant, was born in 1833 in Marion County, Kentucky, and died in 1864; Henry M., mentioned below; W. R., who was a physician and surgeon, and was born in Marion County, Kentucky, in 1836, and died there in 1868; and Catherine A., who was born in 1839 and died in 1884, her husband, J. M. Ballard, having been a merchant, a successful politician, a cattle dealer and for several terms filled the office of sheriff in Marion County, Kentucky.

Henry Wuyts O'Bryan, who was born in Marion County, Kentucky, March 15, 1835, is now living, at the venerable age of eighty-one years, in St. Paul, Kansas. As a boy he attended one of the old subscription schools of Kentucky. He went to school in the winter and the summers were spent in hard work on his father's farm. Later he attended St. Marys College in Marion County. At the age of nineteen he took up the business of handling and dealing in cattle and merchandise, and was prospering until the war came on. On October 8, 1871, Henry W. O'Bryan, with his family, arrived in Kansas, locating at old Osage Mission, now St. Paul. There he built the house on Central Avenue where he still resides. He is a democrat, a member of the Catholic Church and of St. Paul Council No. 760, Knights of Columbus. For many years he has handled stock, and has been more or less actively associated with his sons, but is now retired.

In 1858, in Marion County, Kentucky, Henry W. O'Bryan married Miss Susan E. Hagan, who died at St. Paul, July 28, 1896. Their children were: Sydney F., who was educated at St. Francis Institute in St. Paul, at St. Marys College in Pottawatomie County, finished his theological course in the University at St. Louis, and was ordained to the Catholic priesthood in 1884, devoting many years to the service of his church and dying in Chicago, in 1901. Annie M., the second child, died in infancy. John E., born in 1864, was killed in a runaway accident in 1871. The fourth in the family is William W. Nicholas L., born in 1871, died in infancy. Annie M., born in 1873, is the wife of J. A. Smith, a stock trader at Stark, Kansas. Henry L., born in 1876, is a prominent resident of Chetopa, Kansas, where he is a stockman and is now serving as postmaster. G. I. O'Bryan, born in 1879, is a stock buyer at St. Paul. In 1900 Henry M. O'Bryan married for his second wife Mrs. S. E. (Newton) Worland, daughter of David K. Newton, who was a farmer and is now deceased. Mrs. O'Bryan was born in Indiana.

Of such ancestry and with such a record of family achievements to encourage him during his early years, William Wuyts O'Bryan was born in Marion County, Kentucky, near Loretto, January 27, 1867. He has lived in Kansas since early childhood. His early training was gained in the Jesuit schools, known as St. Francis Institute, at Osage Mission, but at the age of fourteen he left his books and studies to take up the work which has always more or less engaged his active energies. He was at first a cattle herder, and at the age of eighteen began buying and selling cattle for himself, and it is said that during the past thirty years he has handled more cattle than anyone else in this part of the State of Kansas. His operations are on a large scale. Adjoining the Town of St. Paul he has 700 acres of land, where he raises some fine beef cattle every year, and he also has 1,280 acres devoted to pasturage in Bourbon County. Mr. O'Bryan is a director in the St. Paul State Bank. He and his family reside in a very attractive home on Central Avenue. He has served as county commissioner of Neosho County, is an active democrat, a member of the Catholic Church; of St. Paul Council No. 760, Knights of Columbus; of Vulcan Lodge No. 29, Ancient Order of United Workmen, at St. Paul, and has always been generous of his time and energies in behalf of any enterprise promising benefit to the community.

On April 25, 1893, at St. Paul, Mr. O'Bryan married Miss Grace May, daughter of William and Mary Jane (Rodman) May. Her parents are both deceased. Her father was one of the early merchants at Osage Mission, along in the '70s, and subsequently became a banker. Mr. and Mrs. O'Bryan have a most happy and charming household, and eleven children have been born to their marriage. Frank, born February 19, 1894, is a farmer on a place adjoining St. Paul. Edward, born March 8, 1896, is a dealer in live stock. Paul, born July 28, 1898, assists his father. Alice, born November 1, 1900, is attending St. Francis School. Ruth, born January 12, 1902, is also in St. Francis School, and the younger children, several of whom have already begun their education, are as follows: William, born September 9, 1904; Joseph, born March 9, 1907; Charles, born December 27, 1909; Thomas, born March 3, 1911; Grace, born August 28, 1912; and John, born January 20, 1914.

CALVIN L. LONG. When Calvin L. Long came to Montgomery County thirty-seven years ago he found himself associated with the very early pioneers, and is one of the residents of that county who have witnessed practically every phase of development and progress. Mr. Long is one of the oldest men in the real estate business at Coffeyville, and his reputation as a reliable dealer and man of unusual judgment and experience in that line has been in full proportion to his years of activity.

Born in Delaware County, Indiana, July 12, 1852, he grew up on a farm, attended country schools, spent two years in Ridgeville College, a Baptist institution at Ridgeville, Indiana, and in 1871 entered the Northern Indiana Normal School at Valparaiso, where he took both the teachers' training course and a business course, graduating in 1873. Meanwhile he had begun his work as a teacher, which he followed for a number of years. As teacher he faced the scholars of a country school in Delaware County for the first time on December 4, 1869. Altogether he taught eight years in Delaware County. He was then in the stock business and farming from 1879 until 1882.

Coming to Montgomery County he found Coffeyville little more than a frontier village and market town for cattle men, with perhaps 1,000 inhabitants. For the first two years he was in the livery business. Mr. Long opened the first skating rink at Coffeyville in 1884. That was when the roller skating craze first struck the country. He conducted that about two years, and was also in the grain and feed business for a similar time. He early became associated with politics in Montgomery County, and in the early days was candidate for district clerk with three rivals for the same office.

It was on January 1, 1888, that Mr. Long opened his office to handle real estate. His first office was at the corner of Union and Eighth streets, but he now has his headquarters in the Odd Fellows Building. In the meantime he has acquired some very extensive properties of his own, and has handled some of the largest real estate transactions in the city and in Montgomery and surrounding counties. He handles city property, farm lands in Kansas and neighboring states, and has sold a number of business buildings. He owns his present residence at 509 West Ninth Street, also his old home at 511 on the same street, has another residence property at 504 West Twelfth Street, and interests in other houses, and also in a fruit farm in California.

Politically he has always acted with the republican party. He served on the city council several years, was city treasurer four years, justice of the peace five years, and was once nominated for mayor. At that time the people's party was in the ascendency in Kansas, and he was therefore defeated. He was a member of the old board of trade organization, and has served as secretary of the present Commercial Club. On December 25, 1877, in Wheeling, Indiana, Mr. Long joined the Methodist Church, and has always been closely identified with that society. In 1876 he became a member of New Cumberland Lodge of Odd Fellows in Indiana, and is now a member of Star Lodge No. 117, Independent Order of Odd Fellows at Coffeyville, which he has served as noble grand, and is past chief patriarch and member of the board of trustees of Gate City Encampment No. 80. For many years he has been affiliated with Coffeyville Lodge No. 279, Ancient Order of United Workmen of which he is past master workman.

On February 16, 1887, at Coffeyville Mr. Long married Miss Alice C. Irvin, who was born in Hancock County, Illinois, in 1858 and died at Coffeyville May 19, 1915. Her parents were Samuel and Margaret Irvin, both now deceased. Her father was an early settler at Coffeyville and a wagon maker by trade. Mr. Long has one child, Glenna M., who was born at Coffeyville December 7, 1892, is a graduate of the eighth grade of the Coffeyville public schools, now lives with her father, and has been connected with "The Earth" printing office.

Mr. Long has an interesting ancestry. In the paternal line his people were of Scotch origin, and located in Pennsylvania during colonial times. His grandfather, Robert Long, was born in York County, Pennsylvania, July 1, 1779, and died in Delaware County, Indiana, March 6, 1852, at the age of seventy-two years, eight months, five days. He was reared in York County, then moved to Bourbon County, Kentucky, later to Ohio, and was married in Butler County of the latter state January 10, 1805, to Jane Cartmil. She was born in Augusta County, Virginia, April 19, 1780, and died in Delaware County, Indiana, June 13, 1852, aged seventy-two years one month twelve days. She was killed in a runaway accident. Soon after their marriage Robert Long and wife moved to Delaware County, Indiana. That was before the county was organized, and while Indiana was still a territory. In fact the Indians were the chief inhabitants of that district, and the original Long home was one of the few outposts along the frontier and a number of years passed before settlers had become so numerous as to constitute a complete defense and protection against the red men. Robert Long was a sterling pioneer character, and in the early days of Eastern Indiana he made his home a station on the underground railroad and aided many a slave who escaped from the South to Canada. He was a whig, and was a member of the Christian Church. He and his wife were the parents of the following children: Joel, who was a farmer and died in Delaware County, Indiana; Simeon and Austin, both of whom were Delaware County farmers; John C., mentioned below; Lucinda, who died in Delaware County, the wife of Amos Wilson, a minister of the Christian Church, now deceased; Charlotte, who died in Delaware County, the wife of Mr. McLaughlin, a farmer also deceased; Mrs. Brandt, who died in Delaware County, where her husband was a merchant.

John C. Long, father of the Coffeyville citizen, was born in Clinton County, Ohio, May 9, 1820, and was a child when his parents moved to Delaware County, Indiana. He lived in Delaware County the greater part of his life, and died there August 16, 1892. He was a practical farmer, and in the early days went into the green woods along the Mississinewa River and cleared up a homestead of 160 acres. There he spent the rest of his days, and enjoyed a gratifying prosperity. When he began voting it was to favor the whig party, and he later became a republican. He was also a deacon in the Christian Church.

Ruth Caroline Cox who became the wife of John C. Long, represented a colonial family early established in Tennessee. Her father, Isaac Cox, was born in Tennessee in 1796, and died in Delaware County, Indiana, in 1876. He was reared and married in Tennessee, moved from that state to Ohio, and later to Delaware County, Indiana, during the early '50s. He entered a tract of land in Delaware County through the Fort Wayne land office. He was a whig and member of the Presbyterian Church, and had served as a soldier in the War of 1812. Isaac Cox married Mary Helm, a native of Tennessee, who died in Delaware County, Indiana. Their children were: Sarah Ann, who married Mr. Lansing, and both are now deceased, their home having been on a farm in Delaware County and later in Porter County, Indiana; Jane married William Adsit, both now deceased, and they were farmers in Delaware County and later in Iroquois County, Illinois; Eliza married Doctor Helm, a prominent early physician and surgeon at Muncie, Indiana; Joanna married Isaac Sleeth, a Delaware County farmer, and both are now deceased; the fifth in age was Mrs. John C. Long; William was a farmer and stockman and died in Delaware County, Indiana.

Mrs. John C. Long was born in Washington County, Tennessee, January 13, 1827, and died in Delaware County, Indiana, in 1895. She was the mother of the following children: William A., a farmer and stockman at Dewey, Oklahoma; Calvin L.; Robert S., a farmer and stockman in Delaware County, Indiana; Jennie, deceased wife of Leonard Roderick, a farmer in Delaware County.

SAMUEL MORSE PORTER. The career of Samuel Morse Porter is largely identified with the history of Caney, and no record of either man or community would be complete without full mention of both. A resident of this locality since 1881, and of the city itself since 1896, he has seen the little town grow and develop to substantial proportions, and may take a proprietor's pride in this advancement, for it has been a part of his life work. With his own hands he has aided in the building up of what promises to be an important center of commercial and industrial activity; his faith in it has been strong from the first. Mr. Porter is one of the best known business men of Caney, where he has large moneyed interests. At the age of sixty-seven years he is stronger in mind than most men of fifty, and intensely acute and active in all the cares of business life. The success which he has achieved as lawyer, legislator, railroad builder and financier should be a spur to the ambition of every boy in the country.

Mr. Porter was born at Metamora, Lapeer County, Michigan, December 14, 1849, and is a son of Moses Green and Maria M. (Morse) Porter. His paternal grandfather was Moses Porter, a native of near Bristol, England, whence he emigrated to America prior to the Revolutionary war, settling in Ontario County, New York. He participated in the winning of American independence, serving seven years in the patriot army, during six years of which time he was on the staff of Gen. George Washington, and when the struggle was closed returned to his Ontario County farm and lived in peace until his death.

Moses Green Porter was born in 1819 on his father's farm in Ontario County, New York, was there reared and educated, and as a young man removed to Metamora, Michigan, where he was married. Shortly after the birth of his son, Samuel M., he went to Oakland County, Michigan, where he settled as a pioneer on a new farm, and after clearing it from the timber engaged in agricultural pursuits. He met his death in a runaway accident at Walled Lake, in

1884. Mr. Porter was one of the strong men of his day and locality. First a whig and later a republican, he took an active part in political affairs, and at various times held local offices, among them those of supervisor and justice of the peace. He was a devout member of the Baptist Church, of which he was a deacon for many years, and belonged to the Union League and to several clubs which had their inception in the feeling that arose on issues identified with the Civil war. Mr. Porter married Maria M. Morse, who was born in 1818, in Cortland County, New York, and who died at Walled Lake, Michigan, in 1896. Their children were as follows: John Albert, who is engaged in farming at Wixon, Oakland County, Michigan; Samuel Morse, of this review; Edward W., who is a prominent practicing attorney of Bay City, Michigan; and Sarah, who is the wife of Homer Chapman and resides on the old home farm in Oakland County, Michigan.

Samuel Morse Porter attended the district school in the vicinity of his home in Oakland County, Michigan, and, after graduation from the Northville Union High School, enrolled as a student at Hillsdale College, where he pursued an academic course for two years. In the meantime, to add to his income, he had spent three winters in teaching in the country schools. He was graduated from the law school of the University of Michigan, Ann Arbor, in the class of 1874, receiving the degree of Bachelor of Laws, under the late President James B. Angell, who died in 1916. At the time of his graduation, Mr. Porter commenced practicing law at Saginaw, Michigan, and continued to be so engaged there until 1881, when, recognizing the possibilities and opportunities of the West, he made his way to four miles east of Caney, then in Indian Territory, and settled on a new farm. This he developed into a handsome and valuable property, and in the meantime he practiced his profession in his community, handling many cases of importance among the early white settlers here. In 1896 Mr. Porter came to Caney to establish his permanent residence, and here his name has since been identified with many of the most important enterprises which the city has known.

Mr. Porter is associated in business with a number of large corporations, being counsel for a number of gas, oil and glass and brick industries. He maintains well-appointed offices in the Porter Building, which he erected, owns a fine modern brick residence on Fourth Avenue, has three business blocks and a number of city lots on that thoroughfare, and is the owner of a farm of 182 acres 2½ miles east of Caney, another property of 142 acres 1½ miles further east, and eighty acres of good land seven miles northeast of Caney.

As a promoter and builder of railroads Mr. Porter has done much for Caney and the surrounding country. He is president of the Kansas & Oklahoma Southern Railway Company, now in course of construction, which will open up new country in Oklahoma to the south and southwest of Caney; and, assisted by Jacob H. Bartles, for whom Bartlesville, Oklahoma, was named, built the Bartlesville branch of the Santa Fe Railroad, running from Havana to Tulsa. He was also president of the Caney Glass Company, vice president of the Caney Gas Company and of the Caney Gas, Oil and Mining Company, and was formerly president of the Caney Brick Company.

A republican in politics, Mr. Porter's first official position was that of city attorney of Caney. In 1908 he was elected a member of the Kansas State Senate,

and in that body demonstrated the possession of great legislative ability. He was chairman of the oil and gas committee and a member of the judiciary and other important committees, and at all times was very active in behalf of the interests of his constituents. He introduced state refinery legislation and other important bills, but the work which showed to the fullest extent his abilities was that connected with railroad legislation, this including the two-cent fare bill and the general supervision of railroads. This latter, which was the real start of the public utilities control of railroads, has been called the best bill the State of Kansas ever had passed, and as one of the framers of the law Mr. Porter is entitled to the gratitude of the public.

Mr. Porter is a member of the Presbyterian Church and has been generous in his support of its movements. In the line of his profession he belongs to the Montgomery County Bar Association, the Kansas State Bar Association and the American Bar Association. He is a leading Odd Fellow and Pythian Knight, and stands high in Masonry, being a member of Caney Lodge No. 324, Ancient Free and Accepted Masons; Caney Chapter No. 90, Royal Arch Masons, both of Caney, and St. Bernard's Commandery No. 10, Knights Templar, at Independence.

In 1874, at Walled Lake, Michigan, Mr. Porter was united in marriage with Miss Susie Hoyt, a daughter of the late Dr. J. M. Hoyt, a physician of that place, now deceased. Mrs. Porter died at Walled Lake in 1878, leaving two children: May, who married E. C. Johns, of Detroit, Michigan, a farmer who is also connected with the United States postal service; and Grace, who married J. W. Dodge, owner of the Dodge Electrical Company, of Tulsa, Oklahoma. In 1884, at Caney, Kansas, Mr. Porter married Miss Elthea Smith, daughter of the late David H. Smith, who at the time of his death was a retired farmer of Caney. Mrs. Porter is the executrix of her father's estate and is the owner of a business block and several residence properties at Caney. Mr. and Mrs. Porter have had the following children: George F., a graduate of Missouri University Medical College, and now a practicing physician and surgeon of Caney; Margaret, a graduate of Caney High School, and formerly the wife of J. T. Jaynes; Lucinda, who is the wife of H. V. Bolinger, assistant cashier of the Home National Bank of Caney.

JOSEPH HENRY HOOPINGARNER has for twenty-five years been identified with the Methodist Conference in Kansas, though he has not spent all of that time in the active ministry. He is a large property owner and is now pastor of the leading church at Baxter Springs.

He comes of a very interesting family of pioneers in Southeastern Kansas. Rev. Mr. Hoopingarner himself was born in Crawford County, Kansas, April 3, 1871, only a few years after the real settlement of that region began. His ancestry goes back to Wuertemberg, Germany, where his great-grandfather Coonrad Hoopingarner was born. Coonrad and a brother came to America, and while the brother settled in Ohio, Coonrad located in Indiana, near Terre Haute. John Hoopingarner, grandfather of Rev. Mr. Hoopingarner, was born in Indiana, spent his life as a farmer in that state, and died near Terre Haute.

James Patterson Hoopingarner was the pioneer in Southeastern Kansas. He was born near Terre Haute, Indiana, August 31, 1826, was reared and married in Illinois, and for a number of years was a pilot on the Mississippi River being a contemporary in that occupation with Mark Twain. It was in 1856 that he came to Kansas locating on the "Neutral Strip" in what is now Crawford County. He was one of the pioneers who settled there by arrangement with the Indian owners, and his homestead comprised a quarter section of land. He remained there during the troubles which beset the settlers of the Neutral Strip, also through the war, and was an active farmer until 1903, when he retired and was living at Arcadia when he died in June, 1909. During the war he was a member of the Kansas State Guard under Captain Coffman, and took the field when Price made his raids on Missouri and Kansas. He was an active democrat and a loyal supporter of the Christian Church.

While a pilot on the Mississippi River he was married at Piasa, on the Illinois side of that river, to Sarah Ellen Sherman. She was born at Piasa, Illinois, in November, 1837, and is still living in her eightieth year with home at Arcadia. She was the mother of seven children: Sarah Jane, who lives on her farm near Goodnight, Oklahoma, the widow of Michael Stufflebeam, who was a farmer; Mary Paulina, who died near Goodnight, Oklahoma, the wife of Seymour Marshall, a farmer in Oklahoma; James Louis a farmer near Oaks, Oklahoma; Eliza Ellen, wife of A. J. Sheffield, a retired farmer at Arcadia, Kansas; Ida Viola, wife of Thomas B. Basham, a retired farmer at Arcadia; Joseph Henry; and Nellie Irene, wife of Leonard West, a farmer near Tryon, Oklahoma.

Joseph Henry Hoopingarner spent his early life in Crawford County, attended the public schools there, and lived on his father's farm until he was twenty-six years of age. The year 1891-92 he spent in Baker University, and in 1892 did his first work in the Methodist ministry. He preached one year at Stark, Kansas, and following that was again on the home farm for two years. He next took the three year course in the old Kansas Normal College at Fort Scott and followed that with another year on the farm. Mr. Hoopingarner was pastor at Scammon, Kansas, a year and at Gridley, Kansas, two years. Then came another period of three years spent on the farm. In 1903, removing to Kansas City, Missouri, Mr. Hoopingarner engaged in the life insurance business five years and for two years was a piano salesman. In 1910 he returned to Arcadia to settle up his father's estate, and that having been satisfactorily completed he reentered the ministry in 1912. For two years he was stationed at LaCygne, Kansas, and in 1914 took charge of the Methodist Church at Baxter Springs.

Besides his share of the old homestead in Crawford County, Mr. Hoopingarner has 200 acres of land in Ottawa County, Oklahoma. He is a very progressive and loyal citizen and lends his support to every community enterprise. He is a member of the Baxton Springs Commercial Club, of the Fraternal Aid Union, is a democrat, and is affiliated with Arcadia Lodge No. 329, Ancient Free and Accepted Masons, and with Valley of Topeka Consistory No. 1 of the Scottish Rite bodies.

In 1904 at Kansas City, Missouri, Mr. Hoopingarner married Mrs. Effie D. (Werts) Kiser. She died at Kansas City in 1910, leaving one daughter, Jessie Marie, who was born June 22, 1905. In November, 1911, at Arcadia, Kansas, Mr. Hoopingarner married Miss Caroline May Wilkinson daughter of William and Rosa (Haynes) Wilkinson. Her mother is now deceased and her father a miner,

lives at Coalvale, Kansas. Mr. and Mrs. Hoopingarner have one child, Rosemary Ellen, born August 8, 1916.

WILLIAM E. ADAMSON has been a resident of Southeastern Kansas for thirty years, and his career in Neosho County has been marked by splendid service rendered as an educator and also as a civil engineer. For many years he has filled the office of county surveyor, and is still engaged in the official duties of that position with home at Erie.

The Adamson family originated in England, and this branch settled in Virginia in colonial days. Others of the family also located in Pennsylvania. His grandfather, Simon Adamson, was born in Virginia in 1763, and became one of the pioneer settlers of Western Indiana. He was a farmer in that state and he also saw some active service in the Indian border wars. His death occurred at Terre Haute, Indiana, in 1838.

Simon R. Adamson, father of William E., was born at Economy, Indiana, in 1830. In 1834, when the son Simon was four years of age, the family moved to Illinois, near Paris, and Simon Adamson was fourteen when he left there and returned to Economy, Indiana. He was married in his native town, learned the trade of hatter, but gave most of his time to farming. He was among the early settlers of Neosho County, Kansas, where he arrived in 1883, buying a farm of 160 acres five miles east of Erie. That farm is now owned by his son William. Simon R. Adamson died in Neosho County in 1906. He was a veteran of the Civil war, having enlisted in 1862 in the Sixty-ninth Indiana Regiment of Infantry. After fourteen months of service he was mustered out on account of disability. In the meantime he had participated in part of the siege of Vicksburg under Sherman and at Richmond, Kentucky, he had been captured by Gen. Kirby Smith, but was afterwards paroled and exchanged. He was a member of the Grange while living in Indiana, was also affiliated with the Independent Order of Odd Fellows, was a republican and had been brought up in the faith of the Quaker Church by his parents. Simon R. Adamson married Elizabeth J. Starbuck, who was born at Economy, Indiana, in 1828, and died on the old farm in Neosho County in 1904. Lydia Alice was their oldest child and she died in infancy. William E. Adamson was the second of their five children. Sarah E., who now lives at Eugene, Oregon, is the widow of John W. Gwinn, who served as a soldier in the Civil war and afterwards was a carpenter. Lillie A. married Cyrus A. Gwinn, a brother of John W. Gwinn, just mentioned, and they live at Salem, Oregon, Mr. Gwinn being a retired farmer. Charles A. died when four years of age.

William E. Adamson was born at Economy in Wayne County, Indiana, March 5, 1855. He grew up in that district, which was largely composed of thrifty settlers of the Quaker religion. He attended public school at Economy, graduated from high school, and was then appointed to a cadetship in West Point Military Academy, where he remained two years, but left in the spring of 1876 before graduating. After returning from the military academy he took up teaching in Indiana, and in 1886 came to Neosho County, where he continued his work in the schoolroom. Altogether Mr. Adamson taught for twenty-seven years. He had received a thorough training in civil engineering while at West Point, and he has practiced in that line for many years. Since 1906 his home has been at Erie. For upwards of twenty years he has been closely connected with the office of county surveyor. He was first elected county surveyor in 1899, serving

S. W. Shelton, M. D.

two terms or five years. The two following years were spent as deputy surveyor and he was again elected for two successive terms or four years. Then came another interim in which he was a deputy, and in 1914 was elected to the office and is still serving.

He has also prospered in a material way. Besides the old homestead which he owns his home on Neosho Street, another dwelling house in Erie, and a tract of six acres adjoining the town.

Mr. Adamson is a republican, and is a deacon and member of the Christian Church. Fraternally he is affiliated with Erie Camp No. 1101, Modern Woodmen of America, with Kansas Fraternal Citizens, with the Anti-Horse Thief Association, and he belonged to the Grange while living in Indiana.

In 1881, at Richmond, Indiana, he married Miss Lizzie E. Dunham. Her parents, James and Mary (Austin) Dunham, are both now deceased, her father having been a cabinetmaker.

Mr. and Mrs. Adamson have reared six children who do them credit, and most of them are highly educated and have been successful as teachers. The oldest, Louie, died in infancy. Charles R. Adamson, who was graduated from the State Normal School at Emporia in 1911 and is now a member of the senior class in the Agricultural College at Manhattan, lives at Erie and is a teacher. Jennie E., who lives with her parents, and teaches at St. Paul, Kansas, is a graduate of the Erie High School and has attended the State Normal School at Emporia. Virginia M., also a teacher at Erie, is a graduate of the local high school, holds a state teacher's certificate and is a member of the senior class in the State Normal at Emporia. Nellie D., a graduate of the Erie High School and of the Emporia Normal, is a teacher at Muskogee, Oklahoma. Grace M., who graduated from the Erie High School, married H. J. Six, a jeweler at Erie. Ethel A., who taught two years in Walnut, Kansas, is now a senior in the State Normal at Emporia.

FRANK McCLELLAN. After many years employed as an educator in Kansas, Frank McClellan turned his attention to business affairs at Coffeyville, and now has one of the leading offices there for insurance and loans.

His birthplace was Bedford, Pennsylvania, where he was born January 21, 1860. His grandfather, Abraham McClellan, was born in Edinburgh, Scotland, in 1798, came to the United States when a young man, becoming a farmer and stock raiser in Pennsylvania. He died at Rainsburg, Pennsylvania, in 1883. On account of his service in the state militia he was familiarly known as Captain McClellan. Captain McClellan married Elizabeth Morgan, who was born near Everett, Pennsylvania, in 1801, and died near Rainsburg in 1884.

William D. McClellan, father of Frank, was born at Bedford, Pennsylvania, in 1834, was reared and married there, and spent all his active career as a farmer and stock raiser. For a long time he specialized in Shorthorn cattle. In 1875 he moved to Alaska, West Virginia, and died there in 1877. He was a democrat in politics. William D. McClellan married Sarah A. Kerr, who was born at Everett, Pennsylvania, in 1842, and died at Kansas City, Kansas, February 3, 1915. She too was of Revolutionary stock. William D. McClellan and wife had the following children: Frank; William E., who was a music dealer and died in 1887 at Butler, Missouri; James B., whose whereabouts have been unknown to his family for the past fifteen years; Clarence P., a foreman of bridge construction living at Nevada,

Missouri; and Robert K., a farmer near Bonner Springs, Kansas.

Frank McClellan was educated in the schools at Rainsburg, Pennsylvania, graduated in 1875 from Allegheny Seminary, and then took up his career as a teacher for two years in the country schools. In 1884 he graduated from Shenandoah College of Middletown, Virginia, and in the following year reached Kansas.

In this state he has had his home for over thirty years, and fully half of that time was devoted to school work. His first location was Winfield, and for two years he was superintendent of schools at Geuda Springs, then at Pleasanton four years, at Garnett five years, and at Coffeyville two years. Mr. McClellan has lived at Coffeyville since June, 1897, and after leaving school work was in the hardware business three years, was connected with a foundry and machine concern for two years, and for another two years was auditor of the Coffeyville Vitrified Brick and Tile Company. Since then he has given all his time to the insurance and loan business with offices at 820 Walnut Street.

Since coming to Coffeyville Mr. McClellan has identified himself with all those movements and organizations that best represent the civic and social life of the community. He is a member of the Commercial Club, is a republican, Presbyterian, and is affiliated with Coffeyville Lodge No. 102, Ancient Free and Accepted Masons, Coffeyville Chapter No. 89, Royal Arch Masons, Lochinvar Commandery No. 52, Knights Templar, and also belongs to Camp No. 665, Modern Woodmen of America, Lodge No. 279, Ancient Order of United Workmen, Lodge No. 775, Benevolent and Protective Order of Elks, and the Anti-Horse Thief Association.

In 1887 at Warrensburg, Missouri, Mr. McClellan married Miss Margaret Sparks, a daughter of A. B. and Clarissa Sparks. Her father was a farmer, now deceased, and her mother resides at Holden, Missouri. Mr. and Mrs. McClellan have one daughter, Bee, who is a young woman of musical talent and training, being a graduate of Oswego College in 1906, and a graduate in music in 1910 from Bethany College at Lindsborg. She now has charge of the musical department of New Jersey Academy located at Logan, Utah.

FRANK WINFRED SHELTON, M. D. One of the institutions which serve to give metropolitan character to the City of Independence is the Independence Hospital, the founder and builder of which was Dr. Frank Winfred Shelton, one of the most prominent surgeons of Southern Kansas.

Doctor Shelton built this institution in 1906. It is situated on a commanding site at 706 South Fifth Street and in equipment and service, considering its accommodations, it is one of the best hospitals in the state. Besides the hospital building proper, Doctor Shelton erected a special building to serve as nurses' dormitory, storerooms, laundry and other purposes. The Independence Hospital is an incorporated institution, with Doctor Shelton as president, while the late R. S. Litchfield was vice president, George Gilmore is secretary and treasurer, Mrs. Doctor Shelton is a director, and another director was E. P. Allen, who recently died. The hospital has accommodations for twenty patients and there is a staff of eight regular nurses and a training school for nurses is maintained. To this hospital come patients from a radius of 100 miles about Independence and many of them come from points in Oklahoma, particularly Tulsa and Muskogee.

Several generations of the Shelton family have been identified with Kansas. Doctor Shelton's family originated in England, located in Virginia in Colonial times, and many of the family are still found in the State of Missouri. His grandfather, Elias Shelton, was born in Virginia in 1796 and died in Wilson County, Kansas, in 1888. He made his home in Missouri until the death of his wife, and then lived retired at the home of his daughter, Mrs. Lydia Williams, in Wilson County, Kansas. He was successful as a farmer and stock raiser. Although an old man at the time, he possessed such a rugged constitution that he was accepted for service in the Civil war, going out with a Missouri regiment, and in one battle he received a gunshot wound in the leg. After the war he returned to Cass County, Missouri, and lived near Lone Jack. The youngest of his children and the only son still living is Stephen Shelton, father of Doctor Shelton. Stephen Shelton's sister, Lydia Williams, the only other member of the family still living, is the wife of John Williams, and they were substantial farming people of Wilson County, Kansas, just west of Chanute, but now live retired in Chanute.

Doctor Shelton was born in Miami County, Kansas, May 7, 1876, on his father's farm. Stephen Shelton, his father, was born in Cass County, Missouri, in 1846, grew up there, and in 1862 enlisted in a Missouri regiment on the Union side, serving until the close of the war. He was once taken prisoner, but was soon released or escaped, and rejoined his command. Soon after the war he pioneered to Kansas, becoming a farmer and stock raiser in Miami County. In 1882 he removed to Wilson County, but in 1896 returned to Miami County and since 1906 has been retired from active business cares and lives in Paola. He has been quite influential in local affairs, has filled several township offices as a republican, and is an active member and deacon of the Baptist Church. The maiden name of his wife was Marilda Hinds, who was born in Illinois in 1856. Their children are: Archie, who is now register of deeds of Miami County, living at Paola; Dr. Frank W.; Ollie, who died in 1903 in Miami County, was the wife of William Goebel, manager of the plant of the Uncle Sam Oil Company at Kansas City, Kansas, and a son of P. W. Goebel of Kansas City; Ora is the wife of Eugene Hunt, a clerk in a real estate office at Kansas City, Missouri; Nell, who died June, 1913, as the wife of Don Brown, a furniture dealer at Paola, Kansas; Luetta, deputy register of deeds at Paola; and Palmer, a member of the senior class of the Paola High School.

Frank Winfred Shelton gained a liberal education, partly through the advantages furnished him by his father and also by such means as he earned through his work as a teacher. He attended the public schools in Wilson and Miami counties, graduating from the high school at Louisburg in Miami County in 1895, and for two years was a student in the Kansas State Normal at Emporia. While attending the Normal and afterwards he spent four years as a teacher in Miami County. In 1899 Doctor Shelton entered the Kansas City Medical College, now the medical department of Kansas University, and graduated M. D. with the class of 1904. During that year he went East and took special work in bacteriology in Cornell University, and in 1915 he did post-graduate work in the New York Post-Graduate School. While at Kansas City Medical College he

was in St. Joseph's Hospital three years, and during two of those years was house surgeon, an experience which gave him special opportunities at that stage in his career for the practice of general surgery, and did much to develop a skill which has subsequently characterized his active practice. Doctor Shelton has been in practice at Independence since 1905, and in the following year he established the Independence Hospital. He is a member of the County and State Medical societies and the American Medical Association.

Politically Doctor Shelton is a republican, is a member of the Presbyterian Church, belongs to the Independence Country Club, and is affiliated with Fortitude Lodge No. 107, Ancient Free and Accepted Masons, the Benevolent and Protective Order of Elks, No. 780, Lodge No. 69, Independent Order of Odd Fellows, the local camp of the Modern Woodmen of America, and the Fraternal Aid.

At Independence, Missouri, in 1904, he married Miss Violetta Gilman, daughter of John and Sallie Gilman. Her father is now deceased and her mother resides in Independence, Kansas. There are two children: Frank W., Jr., born February 3, 1906, attending public schools; and Gilman, born September 14, 1910.

CHARLES OWEN. The production of oil and gas forms one of the most important industries in the State of Kansas. It is not only a source of great wealth, but at the same time serves as a medium of employment for a great many men and a means of livelihood for a great number of dependent families. In this respect Montgomery County is one of the busiest and most productive portions of the state. The cultivation of its fertile farms and the operation of its almost inexhaustible gas and oil wells go hand in hand to make it one of the prime contributors to the bountiful prosperity of a great region. To supervise all the details of the working of one of the concerns engaged in the production of oil and gas requires a man of more than ordinary energy, sound judgment and thorough knowledge, and such an individual is Charles Owen,' president of the Caney Pipe Line Company, and one of the best known figures in oil and gas circles of Southern Kansas and Oklahoma.

Mr. Owen was born at Lynchburg, Campbell County, Virginia, in February, 1870, and is a son of Dr. William O. Owen. His father was born at Lynchburg, in 1820, was educated for the medical profession, graduated from the College of Physicians and Surgeons, New York City, and for many years was engaged in practice at his native place. During the entire period of the Civil war he acted as senior surgeon of the medical corps of the Confederate hospitals in Virginia. At Lynchburg after the war he continued to follow his profession until his death, in 1891. The impression seems well founded that among the sturdy upbuilders of the State of Kansas such accessories as ancestors or family traditions count for little as a community asset. There is something about the prairies that makes a man want to rely upon himself, to develop his latent talents and to draw upon his innate resources. However, no class of men are more appreciative of honorable forebears, and in this connection Mr. Owen is no exception. The Owen family can not only be traced back to the earliest times in American history, but also in England, where it originated, for some generations. Colonial Virginia was the home of its early members, and a number bearing the name fought as soldiers in the Continental army during the Revolutionary war. On his mother's side of the family Mr. Owen traces the line back to the Cherokees, one of his ancestors being a full-blooded member of that tribe who visited England and received honors at the hands of King George the Second. Mr. Owen, however, has never made a display of his ancestry, for, while proud of his origin, he believes that what a man is and does for himself is the best evidence of manhood, particularly in a comparatively new state like Kansas.

The early education of Mr. Owen came from the public schools of his native place, following which he enrolled as a pupil at Lynchburg College, and was duly graduated therefrom. In 1899 he turned his face toward the West in search of position and fortune, and eventually located on the prairies of Oklahoma, where he embarked in business as the proprietor of a ranch. In this direction he continued with a fair measure of success for something more than four years, when, recognizing the trend of the times and hearing the knock of opportunity, he entered the oil business. In 1904 he came to Caney and this place has since been the center of his activities and here he has developed into one of the leading oil and gas producers in the Kansas and Oklahoma fields. An indication of the extent of Mr. Owen's activities, is found in the fact that he was recently granted a lease on 165,760 acres of gas lands in the Osage Indian Nation, Oklahoma, the lease, granted by the Osage Council, being subsequently approved by the Secretary of the Interior, at Washington, District of Columbia. In 1912 Mr. Owen became the prime mover in the organization of the Caney Pipe Line Company, of which he has since been president, the other officials being G. W. Connelly, vice president, and W. H. Edgrett, secretary and treasurer, both of Caney. The company, which is capitalized at $10,000, supplies gas for industrial and domestic service at Caney and the immediate surrounding territory. Mr. Owen has various other business interests. He is president of the Owen Zinc Company, which established a three-block smelter in the northern part of Caney in 1913, and of which G. W. Connelly is vice president. The company was organized for the manufacture of spelter, the raw material coming from all quarters of the United States, while the finished product is shipped all over the world. Mr. Owen is also secretary of the Connelly Glass Company, of which G. W. Connelly is president and A. Loriaux, vice president, and the factory of which was established at Caney in 1914. This a plant of thirty shops, manufacturing window glass, with its market in all parts of the country to the north and west of Caney. Mr. Owen maintains his business headquarters for the Caney Pipe Line Company, on Fourth Avenue. He is known as a progressive, enterprising man of business, quick and accurate in his judgment and possessing a full measure of tactful discretion, one upon whom his associates may rely in matters of importance. He has been the builder of his own fortune and his business activities have served to materially aid in the development of the natural resources of the community which he has adopted as his home. Politically he is independent, and business cares have thus far demanded his attention to the exclusion of participation in public matters, but he takes a lively interest in everything that promises to affect his community. His religious connection is with the Episcopal Church. In fraternal affairs he affiliates with the lodges of the Masonic order and the Elks.

Vol. IV—15

Mr. Owen was married in 1904, at Nowata, Oklahoma, to Miss Pauline Webb, daughter of the late Hon. George W. Webb, who for some years was a judge of Galena, Kansas.

W. A. BLAIR, editor and proprietor of the Oswego Independent, has had a long and successful experience in Kansas journalism, has owned several papers in the southeastern part of the state, and has always been a live and vigorous citizen and for four years was county clerk of Labette County.

He is a native Kansan, having been born in Washington County January 30, 1879. His paternal ancestors were Irish. His grandfather Andrew Blair was born in County Antrim, Ireland, and spent his life there. For many years he was engaged in the limestone industry and also owned a large amount of land. He was the father of thirteen children altogether. Two of his daughters came to America and both are married, one living in Nebraska and another near Chicago. One son, James, came to this country at the age of forty-five and now resides on a farm near Chicago.

David Blair, the father of W. A. Blair, was born in County Antrim, Ireland, in 1849. He came to America about 1866, landing in New York City and going west to Ohio. He lived on farms in the vicinity of Sandusky until 1869 and in that year came out to Kansas and was one of the homesteaders in Washington County. He proved up on his claim of a quarter section, subsequently sold it and in 1888 moved to Labette County, where he bought 160 acres. He finally sold that tract, and at the present time is living at Edna in Labette County, and owns many broad acres, most of them in this county. Since 1910 he has been in the lumber business at Edna associated with J. C. Justice. Mr. Justice organized the Citizens State Bank of Edna, and David Blair was one of its original stockholders. He is a highly successful business man and has always been influential in civic matters. He has held various township offices, is a republican, was reared a Presbyterian, and has been devoted to the Masonic Order, having served as master of Edna Lodge for at least twenty-member of the Modern Woodmen of America. David Blair married Luella Phillips, who was born at Upper Sandusky, Ohio, in 1856. Their children are: Anna, wife of H. W. Burgess, who is a business man at Edna; W. A.; R. C. Blair, a druggist at Mound Valley, Kansas; D. F. Blair, of Seattle, Washington; Ruby, wife of R. T. McGee, Jr., a general merchant at Edna, Kansas; and Vivian who is unmarried and resides with her parents.

Mr. W. A. Blair received his early education in in the public schools of Labette County, and has lived here chiefly since he was nine years of age. He graduated in 1899 from the Labette County High School at Altamont. He had some experience as a teacher himself, having taught for one term in District No. 97 of Labette County. His chief work, however, has been journalism. He bought and conducted until December, 1904, the Edna Enterprise, and in the meantime established another paper at Coweta, Oklahoma. On January 1, 1905, he leased the plant and moved to Oswego to accept the place of deputy county clerk. He filled that position four years and was then elected county clerk of Labette County. Mr. Blair gave a most creditable administration for four years. In September, 1913, he bought the Oswego Independent, and has given all his time and energy to its management since that date.

The Oswego Independent was established June 22, 1872, by B. F. McGill, and with nearly forty-five years of existence it is one of the very old and influential papers in Southeastern Kansas. It is issued weekly, has circulation in Labette and surrounding counties, and politically is a republican organ. Mr. Blair owns the well equipped office and plant at 309 Commercial Street. He also owns his home at 523 Michigan Street in Oswego.

Mr. Blair is president of the Oswego Fellowship Club, a flourishing organization for the betterment of the town which was founded by a Presbyterian minister in 1909. Politically he is a republican and is a member of the school board. Fraternally he is affiliated with Edna Lodge No. 345, Ancient Free and Accepted Masons, is past high priest of Oswego Chapter No. 15, Royal Arch Masons, and is past eminent commander of Oswego Commandery No. 7, Knights Templar. He also belongs to Camp No. 164, Modern Woodmen of America at Edna.

At St. Louis, Missouri, September 16, 1903, Mr. Blair married Miss Mabel Preston, daughter of W. E. and Rose (Higginson) Preston. Both her parents are now deceased and her father was a music teacher by profession. Mr. and Mrs. Blair have five children: Therese, born February 18, 1905; Robert, born May 29, 1906; Clarice, born October 20, 1908; Fredah, born November 19, 1913; and Billy Bryce, born February 28, 1915.

ALFRED QUINCY WOOSTER. At some time in the life of almost every normal American boy there comes a longing for a "printing outfit." It is a temporary phase of youth. Sometimes it is satisfied by an indulgent parent who buys a toy press and font of type and the production of a few ink smeared cards is about as far as the son usually gets in mastering the printing trade. Other boys satisfy themselves with work around a real printing office, as a devil, and from this class is recruited some of the real editors and printers of the country.

In the case of Alfred Quincy Wooster, now editor and proprietor of the Erie Sentinel, his youthful experience in mastering the printing trade at home turned him to a permanent career. He had spent his early life on an Iowa stock farm. He was well educated, and taught school for a few terms. Then in 1883 he secured the equipment of a job press and some type and other appliances, and at his father's home in the country, he issued his first three-column folio newspaper, the first copy being dated October 18, 1883. January 16, 1884, his paper was enlarged to a six-column quarto and in October, 1887, the size was increased to a seven-column paper. By 1889 there was a circulation of 2,500. Quoting from an old history of Monona County, Iowa, "it was an ably edited, cleanly printed and tastily dressed journal, a credit to the owner and the town."

All his early experience of Mr. Wooster as a newspaper man was in or near the Town of Mapleton, Iowa. From Mapleton he removed to Sioux City, Iowa, in 1890, and there had something approaching a metropolitan exchange in the newspaper field There he published the Liberty Bell, a union labor paper, for two years. The Liberty Bell was then consolidated with the old Tribune at Des Moines, and given the new name, The Farmers' Tribune. Mr. Wooster was its managing editor for two years, during the campaign of 1892. April 1, 1894, he took an interest in The Farmer and Miner at Oskaloosa, Iowa, and one year later bought the paper and changed the name to the Oskaloosa Journal, with a weekly issue. In 1897

he started the Oskaloosa Daily Journal. Mr. Wooster was proprietor of both the Daily and Weekly until December 1, 1904.

In the meantime he had studied law and was admitted to the Iowa bar January 17, 1900. He had carried on his law studies over a period of a number of years. After 1904 he gave his entire time to his practice and to the real estate business. It was failing health that caused him to leave his profession and for two years he lived as much as possible out of doors, engaged in mechanical employment and in the building trades.

In June, 1907, having recovered his health, Mr. Wooster came to Kansas and bought the Erie Sentinel. He is its proprietor and editor today, having as partner his son, Lester A. The Erie Sentinel was established in 1883 as the Neosho County Democrat. Its first home was at Osage Mission, now St. Paul. When Erie was made the county seat of Neosho County the paper was moved to Erie and subsequently changed its name to the present form. It is a paper supporting the democratic policies and is issued both daily and weekly, the daily having been established July 1, 1909. It is one of the leading papers of Southeastern Kansas, and circulates all over Neosho and surrounding counties.

While Mr. Wooster has had a very successful career he undoubtedly owes much to the influences that surrounded him as a boy and especially to the fine character of his father. His father, Quincy A. Wooster, was born September 4, 1839, in West Burke, Caledonia County, Vermont, a son of John and Fanny R. (Stebbins) Wooster. His grandparents were natives of Vermont and Connecticut respectively. John Wooster was a Congregational minister, though in the intervals of that occupation followed farming. He made his home largely in Vermont and New Hampshire until his death. His wife died at West Burke, Vermont, February 26, 1888, at the age of eighty-four.

Third in a family of four children, Quincy A. Wooster had an excellent education, both in the common schools and in an academy. From early boyhood he was a student of books and newspapers, and always kept well posted on the topics of the day and was an original thinker as well. He could form his own conclusions and his career throughout shows an independence and sense of responsibility which make him a type of American citizenship to be admired. At the age of eighteen, after the custom of the time, he was "given his time" by his father, and the following three or four years were spent in the lumber woods of the State of Maine. There he applied himself to the heavy task of the old-time lumbering industry. In the summer of 1860 he started for the Far West. Minnesota at that time was on the frontier of civilization, and locating in Fillmore County he helped make a farm out of the bare prairie. He was living there during the period of the Civil war. In the Indian uprisings that began in 1862 and culminated in one of the greatest massacres that have stained the annals of the West, Quincy A. Wooster volunteered his service and was a member of a volunteer company gathered from Winnebago City, Madelia, South Bend and Mankato and did his part in defending the settlements.

In the spring of 1865 he removed to Iowa, locating in Monona County and taking up a claim on section 6 of Maple Township. He was a rugged pioneer, accustomed to hardships, and in his early years he could perform the heaviest tasks of physical labor. By his own labor he opened up three farms from the wild prairie, and his later years were spent in the cultivation and the care of some fine livestock on his beautiful farm of some 446 acres in Maple Township of Monona County. On his first claim in that county he broke up about thirty acres and built a home, but in 1867 he sold that and bought and improved a farm now in the south half of section 12 in the same township. In 1892 he removed from Iowa and went to the Gulf coast country of Southern Texas. His place of settlement, five miles due north of LaPorte, not far from Houston, Texas, is called Wooster, the postoffice having been named in his honor. In that locality he spent his last years and died in the spring of 1908. Quincy A. Wooster was a remarkable man not only for his material achievements but for his mental vigor and his civic leadership. For many years he was affiliated with the republican party. In 1872, the year that Horace Greeley was a candidate for president and during the liberal republican movement, he followed the fortunes of the great editor, and in 1876 and in 1880 he was a prominent supporter of the greenback party, working earnestly for the election of both Peter Cooper and James B. Weaver. In 1884 he was a delegate to the Chicago Convention that nominated Benjamin F. Butler for president. He became closely identified with the union labor movement in Monona County, Iowa, and was a delegate to various state conventions at different times. In the fall of 1879 he received the nomination of the greenback convention for member of the Legislature, and though defeated, he had the satisfaction of reducing by at least 50 per cent the normal majority against the ticket. In his home county he held the office of county supervisor, and was chairman of the board for two years and filled nearly all the offices in Maple Township. For a time he was connected with the People's Press at Mapleton. Fraternally he was affiliated with Amicable Lodge No. 289, Ancient Free and Accepted Masons at Smithland, Iowa; with Gem City Assembly No. 10,029, Knights of Labor at Mapleton.

On October 5, 1862, Quincy A. Wooster married Miss Catherine M. Monroe, who was born in Bradford County, Pennsylvania, July 1, 1839. She was the daughter of John M. and Roxy (Willis) Monroe, who were both natives of New York State and were married July 28, 1833. From New York the Monroe family removed to Bradford County, Pennsylvania, and in the spring of 1852 settled in Fillmore County, Minnesota, where John M. Monroe and his wife died. The children of Quincy A. Wooster and wife were: Alfred Quincy, the first in age. Fremont M., born May 26, 1866, is still living at Mapleton, Iowa. Nellie M., born October 7, 1867, twice a widow and now resides at Long Beach, California; her first husband was Grant Gallup, a farmer, and her second was Dr. Charles Wheeler, a physician of Blencoe, Iowa. Levi F., born June 5, 1869, is proprietor of a transfer business at Corvallis, Oregon. George C., born May 9, 1871, is a farmer at Molalla, Oregon. Ida J., born August 31, 1872, is the wife of W. J. Shreckengaust, a carpenter at Houston, Texas. Fanny R., born April 2, 1874, is the wife of Steve Steinman, a farmer living at Erie, Kansas. John L., born February 6, 1876, is a farmer at Molalla, Oregon. Dora E., born April 14, 1878, died at Houston, Texas, in 1906, the wife of George E. Richmond, who lives at Houston, and is an all around mechanic, machinist, electrician and inventor. Martin E., born February 11, 1884, died in 1896. Ellen M., born May 1, 1889, died July 24, 1889.

Alfred Quincy Wooster was born while his parents were living in Fillmore County, Minnesota, on June 14, 1863. He was still an infant when they moved to Iowa in the summer of 1865 and his youth was spent on his father's pioneer farm in Maple Township. He learned a great deal about farming as a boy and that knowledge has never entirely left him. He attended the common schools, and before reaching the age of eighteen had taught several terms. In the fall of 1882 he entered the Southern Iowa Normal School and Business College at Bloomfield, and was graduated in the commercial course March 22, 1883. Then followed a brief term of teaching, after which he got into the newspaper business in the manner already described.

Mr. Wooster is an active democrat, was his party nominee for the Legislature in Neosho County in 1914, and in 1916 was nominated for the State Senate to represent Neosho and Wilson counties. He was chairman of the democratic county central committee from 1908 until the fall of 1914 and in 1912 was presidential elector for Wilson. While living at Mapleton, Iowa, he served as town clerk. Mr. Wooster owns the building at the corner of First and Main streets in Erie, where his newspaper plant is located, and also his residence on North Main Street. Fraternally he is a member of Erie Lodge No. 109, Knights of Pythias; and Mapleton Division No. 33 of the Uniform Rank Knights of Pythias. He is past noble grand of Erie Lodge No. 44, Independent Order of Odd Fellows, past consul of Erie Camp No. 1101, Modern Woodmen of America, and belongs to the Kansas Fraternal Citizens, the Anti-Horse Thief Association and to the Printers' Union.

On December 9, 1883, only a few weeks after he had made his pioneer adventure as a journalist, Mr. Wooster was married at the residence of J. W. Hall in Monroe County, Iowa, to Miss Lucy Cox. Mrs. Wooster was born in Putnam County, Missouri, February 19, 1860, a daughter of S. G. and Clarissa (Coffern) Cox. Her parents were both natives of Kentucky, were married in Missouri in the spring of 1857, moved to Monroe County in 1864, and five years later went to Appanoose County, Iowa, living at Moravia. Mrs. Wooster's mother died in Appanoose County and her father at Bentonville, Arkansas.

Mrs. Wooster, who was the youngest in a family of seven children, laid the foundation of her education in the common schools of Appanoose County and finished with two terms in the Southern Iowa Normal School and Business College, where her husband also completed his education. Prior to her marriage she taught several terms of district school. Mr. and Mrs. Wooster have five children. The first child died unnamed a few days after its birth, September 19, 1885. Vera Anna, born January 1, 1888, is the wife of P. A. Rettig, superintendent of an oil company at Chanute, Kansas. Lester A. was born November 26, 1890. He attended the public schools, also the high school at Oskaloosa, Iowa, and was graduated from the Erie High School in Kansas in 1909. Since leaving school he has been in business with his father and assists in bringing out the Erie Sentinel every day and week. He is a member of the Knights of Pythias, the Modern Woodmen of America, the Order of Praetorians, the O. M. B. A., and the Mystic Workers. Lester Wooster married Anna M. Gardner, who comes of a family of Crawford County, Kansas, pioneers, but she was living at Erie prior to her marriage. Her parents were Henry and Sarah E. (Crosby) Gardner, her father having come to Crawford County, Kansas, when the Indians were still there, and he preempted a farm of Government land. Both her parents are now deceased. Mr. and Mrs. Lester Wooster have four children: Alfred Eugene, born September 5, 1909; Homer Lee, born November 27, 1911; Anita

Ellen, born January 8, 1913; and Lester Arnold, born November 29, 1916.

The two youngest children of Mr. and Mrs. Alfred Q. Wooster are: Bernice, who died in infancy in 1896; and Gladys June, who was born June 28, 1898, and is still in school.

EMIL KUDER, M. D., is a man of distinction not only on account of his long practice for over thirty years in Kansas but also for his thorough scholarship and the varied experiences and associations of his career. He is a product of the best technical and university training of Germany, and prepared for the practice of medicine and surgery under some of the greatest masters of those subjects in Europe, before coming to America.

He was born at Stuttgart, Germany, August 31, 1851. His father, Joseph Kuder, was born in 1809 at Eslengen, Germany, and died in 1874 at the manufacturing Village of Gmund in Wuertemberg, not far from Stuttgart. Joseph Kuder was a soldier, and for forty-two years was a member of the regular army of his native kingdom or of the German Empire. At his death he ranked as colonel in the Thirteenth Regiment. He served actively in the War of 1866 against Austria and was in the Franco-Prussian war of 1870-71. Colonel Kuder married Magdalene Nagel, who was born at Gmund in Wuertemberg in 1809, and died there in 1864.

The only child of his parents, Dr. Emil Kuder had the best of advantages both at home and in German schools and institutions. He attended the public schools, the Lenten School, and prepared for college in the Real School, which would correspond to an American manual training school. He then entered Tuebingen University, where he was graduated in 1876 with No. 1 A degree, one of the highest degrees in medicine and surgery. This required a seven years' course. In the meantime during 1870-71 he had fought with the armies of the Empire through the Franco-Prussian war, as a member of the One Hundred and Twentieth Regiment of Infantry. For two years he attended the clinics of the famous Doctor Muller at Stuttgart, and had his first individual experience in practice in that German city.

Doctor Kuder came to America in 1879. For two years he was located in practice at Philadelphia and for another two years at Hazelton, Pennsylvania. Following that came a year at Williamsport, Pennsylvania, and since 1883 he has been a Kansan. He practiced at Wichita until 1893, and since then has been a resident of Coffeyville, where he has enjoyed a special prestige as a physician and surgeon. His offices are in the Carey Building at the corner of Ninth and Walnut streets. He is an active member of the Montgomery County Medical Society.

Doctor Kuder has for the past twenty-three years been a member of Star Lodge No. 117, Independent Order of Odd Fellows, belongs to the Patriarchs Militant, Canton No. 114, and is captain of the Military Rank of Odd Fellows and assistant surgeon from the State of Kansas. His religious affiliation is with the German Lutheran Church, and politically he is independent, formerly having supported the democratic and for the last two elections the republican ticket.

Doctor Kuder's home is at 116 West Seventh Street in Coffeyville. In 1881 at Hazelton, Pennsylvania, he married Miss Elizabeth Wagner. Her father, Fred Wagner, was a shoemaker and died in 1881. Doctor and Mrs. Kuder are the parents of six

children: Fred, who was born in Wichita in 1884 and is now connected with the Missouri Pacific Railway at Wichita; Eugene, born in 1887 at Wichita, a druggist at Parsons, Kansas; Katy, who was born at Wichita in 1889, married Fred Bixler, a merchant, and both are now deceased; Fannie, born at Coffeyville in 1892, is the wife of William Conner, a painter and decorator living at Okanogan in the State of Washington; Julia, born at Coffeyville in 1898 and still at home; and Fern, born in 1902, and with his brother Eugene in Parsons.

GEORGE H. WARK, who has been in the practice of law at Caney for the past thirteen years, and in the fall of 1916 was elected a member of the State Senate, is a native of Montgomery County, where his father established a home about the time the Indians moved out of the country into Indian Territory.

The substantial ancestry of which he is a representative was from Scotland and was transplanted to the American colonies, living in New York State and afterwards in Pennsylvania. Grandfather William Wark was born in Allegheny County, Pennsylvania, in 1808. In his early years he became a settler in Stark County, Ohio, and from there moved to Indiana. He was a farmer and died in Owen County, Indiana, in 1863. His wife, Margaret Sweeney, was born in Ohio. Of their marriage there are three children still living: Samuel, a retired farmer in Washington state; Luther, who was a pioneer homesteader in Thomas County, Kansas, where he is now a stockman and farmer; and Lizzie, wife of Louis Norman, a wagonmaker at Emporia, Kansas. Of those now deceased besides the father of Senator Wark: George, who died at Spencer, Indiana, in 1915, was a lawyer; Aaron and John were farmers; Margaret, who died in Brazil, Indiana, in 1914, married Mr. Travis, a merchant, who is also deceased.

George H. Wark was born on a farm near Liberty, Montgomery County, Kansas, December 19, 1878. His father, Emanuel M. Wark, was born near Canton, Ohio, in 1842 and was twelve years of age when his parents in 1854 moved to Owen County, Indiana. He was reared there and in 1862 enlisted from Owen County in the Sixth Indiana Cavalry. He served over three years until the close of hostilities. In the Army of the Cumberland he fought at Chattanooga, through the Atlanta campaign and the battles around Atlanta, and was then sent with General Thomas' army into Tennessee, completing his army service in the conquest of the Mississippi Valley and in the battles of Nashville and Franklin. He was in nearly every engagement in which his regiment was engaged. With the close of the war he returned to Indiana, where he married, and lived as a farmer in Owen County until 1868. He then removed to the vicinity of Sterling, Whiteside County, Illinois, but in the spring of 1870 arrived in Southeastern Kansas and was among the very first to locate permanently in Montgomery County. Just before he arrived the Osage Treaty had been consummated, but the lands had not yet been officially surveyed by the Government. E. M. Wark came to Kansas in typical pioneer type. He drove a prairie schooner and in establishing his home contended with all the usual hardships that the old-time Kansas farmer had to meet. The old homestead is situated three miles west of Liberty. The late E. M. Wark, who died at Independence June 24, 1915, was a republican, was a member of the Modern Woodmen of America and for a number of years was active in politics. His widow, who is still living at Independence, was Lydia Long before her marriage, and was born in Owen County, Indiana, in 1846. Her children are May, wife of T. W. Hurst, in the milling business at Yates Center, Kansas; George H.; Marien E., wife of E. J. Jones, a farmer and stockman near Independence; and Neleah, who lives with her mother and is a stenographer and bookkeeper.

George H. Wark grew up in Montgomery County on the old farm, attended the district schools, and in 1900 graduated as a member of the first class to complete the course in the Montgomery County High School at Independence. From high school he entered the University of Kansas, and from that institution took his degree LL. B. in 1903. Mr. Wark is a member of the Phi Delta Phi honorary Greek letter fraternity.

In October, 1903, a few months after leaving law school, he established his office at Caney, and since then has been making a name and reputation for himself as an able lawyer, both in the civil and criminal branches of practice. Being so close to the Oklahoma line he has handled much litigation in Oklahoma as well as in Kansas. His offices are in the Porter Building, and he resides at the Palace Hotel.

Mr. Wark owns some land in Oklahoma and some real estate at Caney, but has made his profession less a means for accumulating money than for rendering service to his fellow men. He has served as president of the Montgomery County Bar Association, and was the first member of the Alumni Association of the Montgomery County High School to be elected a member of its board of trustees. For the past eight years he has been city attorney of Caney, and has also held a commission in the Kansas National Guard, being first lieutenant of the company from Caney. Very recently he has been commissioned captain in command of Company D, Third Infantry, Kansas National Guard. He entered the field of state politics in 1916, when he became a candidate for the State Senate to represent the Twelfth Senatorial District. He is an active republican, is a member of the Presbyterian Church, and is a prominent fraternity man, being affiliated with Caney Lodge No. 324, Ancient Free and Accepted Masons; Caney Chapter No. 90, Royal Arch Masons; Coffeyville Commandery, Knights Templar; Mirzah Temple of the Mystic Shrine; the Independent Order of Odd Fellows; Lodge No. 160, Ancient Order of United Workmen; Camp No. 941, Modern Woodmen of America, and is exalted ruler of Lodge No. 1215, Benevolent and Protective Order of Elks, all at Caney. He is a member of the Havana Country Club and belongs to the Kansas Historical Society.

ELMER E. LIGGETT, M. D. Doctor Liggett's place in the medical profession of Labette County is not due only to his more than thirty years of active practice there, but also to many enviable qualities of heart and mind and the possession of splendid skill and a wide range of experience both as a physician and surgeon. As a surgeon he is regarded as one of the most competent in Southeastern Kansas.

Most of his life has been spent in Kansas, though he was born near Marysville, Ohio, March 22, 1861. The Liggett family came from Scotland and settled in Virginia in colonial days. The father William Liggett was born in Virginia in 1808. He married his first wife there, and then moved to Pennsylvania, where he married his second wife, the mother of Doctor Liggett. William Liggett was a cooper by trade. He finally settled near Marysville, Ohio, in 1863 moved to Monmouth, Illinois, where he was engaged in farming, and the winter of 1865-66 he spent at Olathe, Kansas, and from there moved to Paola, where he continued farming. On January 4, 1870, he moved to Chetopa and in 1872 to a farm near that town. He finally retired to a town residence at Chetopa in 1882, and died there the following year in 1883. He was one of the very early settlers in Southeastern Kansas and altogether was quite successful as a farmer and reared and provided for a large family of children. He was a republican and an elder in the United Presbyterian Church. His first wife whom he married in Virginia had three children: John, Alfred and Sarah, all of whom are now deceased. In September, 1843, William Liggett married at Marysville, Ohio, Jane M. Henderson. Doctor Liggett may well take pride in the many sterling qualities of his mother. She was born at Punxsutawney, Pennsylvania, May 13, 1816, and died at Denver, Colorado, February 18, 1916, aged ninety-nine years nine months five days. Her intellect and qualities of heart and mind were equal to her physical vigor. For seventy-five years she was a member of the United Presbyterian Church. She was well educated and even to the last years continued to read a varied literature and kept in close touch with current affairs. She had a remarkable memory, and in the closing years of her life could recount in detail many things that happened ninety years ago. She was nearly ten years of age when the first railroad was constructed in the United States and when the Erie Canal opened the first important highway to the west from the eastern colonies. She was a mature woman when the telegraph was invented, had completed the half century mark about the close of the Civil war, and lived on to witness the remarkable achievements of the last half century in the field of electricity and many other marvels. A few days before her death she told about the phenomenal fall of stars which occurred in 1833, and which she and her sister had witnessed at their home in Pennsylvania. She was descended from a fine old Scotch family, including the first Earls of Caithness and Fife. Some of her forefathers had participated as soldiers in the war for American independence, one of her brothers was a major in the Mexican war, and her son Robert Seldon was a soldier in the Civil war and her step-son Alfred also participated in that struggle. She was the mother of the following children: Anna A., who died in 1872 at the age of twenty-eight, the wife of George Elliott, who is also deceased and who was a farmer; Robert S. who is a market gardener living at Joplin, Missouri; Virginia V., of Denver, Colorado, the widow of J. P. DeJarnette, a harness dealer by trade; Nina, who died in the Park Avenue hotel fire in that city in 1908, unmarried; Wilbur T., who is a physician and surgeon, a graduate of the College of Physicians and Surgeons of Keokuk, Iowa, with the class of 1887, and now engaged in practice at Goldfield, Nevada; Vashti E., who is unmarried and lives in Denver, Colorado; Georgia M., wife of Edwin C. Allen, a traveling salesman with home at Denver; and Dr. Elmer E., who is the eighth and youngest of his mother's children.

Doctor Liggett's earliest memories and associations are identified with the State of Kansas. He began attending public school at Paola, then a district school near Chetopa, and for two years was in the high school at Chetopa. The first eighteen years of his life he spent on his father's farm. For two years he operated a well drill. With his ambition set upon medicine he entered the College of

Physicians and Surgeons at Keokuk, Iowa, where he graduated M. D. in 1884. Doctor Liggett has never allowed himself to grow stale in a professional routine. He has been a constant reader of the best standard literature and has accepted all the opportunities to benefit by broader associations with his fellow practitioners. In 1893 he received a second diploma after a course of work in the Bellevue Hospital Medical College of New York City. He spent parts of the years 1904 and 1905 specializing in surgery in the New York Post-Graduate School.

He began practice at Oswego in 1884, and since then for a period of thirty-two consecutive years has carried on his duties as a professional man and citizen in that locality. His offices are in the Condon State Bank Building. He is an active member of the Labette County and State Medical societies, the Southeast District Medical Society, the American Medical Association and the Medical Association of the Southwest.

Besides his home on Michigan Street and Second Avenue Doctor Liggett owns a fine farm of 200 acres in Cherokee County, Kansas. He is a member of the Good Fellowship Club and the Cooperative Club of Oswego, belongs to the Methodist Episcopal Church and is affiliated with Camp No. 23, Modern Woodmen of America, and with the Ancient Order of United Workmen at Oswego.

In 1887 at Oswego he married Mrs. Mary (Parsons) Maynard, widow of Cyrus Maynard, who was a merchant at Oswego. Mrs. Liggett was born in Indiana, and by her first marriage has a daughter Margaret, now the wife of W. P. Farley, a stockman living at Oswego. Doctor and Mrs. Liggett have one child, Ruth Ellsworth, who is a graduate of the Oswego College for Young Women and lives at home.

WILLIAM C. CECIL, M. D. A really successful merchant, doctor, lawyer or farmer is the man who enjoys a just and adequate compensation for important service rendered in his particular field. It is that kind of success which is enjoyed by Dr. William C. Cecil of Stark, Kansas. He was the pioneer doctor in that community and for thirty years has given his services to rich and poor, and especially in the early days at the cost of much physical hardship to himself.

Doctor Cecil is descended from a notable American family. There is a county back in Maryland named Cecil, and his ancestors furnished that name. The Cecils were originally English people, and a branch of them came over to Maryland at the time of Lord Baltimore, the founder of the colony. Doctor Cecil's grandfather, William Cecil, was born in Cecil County, Maryland, moved from there to North Carolina, and died about 1828 when his son Reuben was six months old. This Grandfather Cecil at one time owned a distillery in North Carolina.

Reuben Cecil, father of Doctor Cecil, was born in North Carolina in 1828. His early years were spent near High Point, North Carolina, and at the age of twenty he came west and found a home in Hancock County, Illinois. He was married there, and for many years followed the trade of blacksmith, and was a citizen of much influence in the community. He held the offices of township clerk and township treasurer and nearly all the other local responsibilities. He was one of the leaders in the United Brethren Church in that county. Though coming from the South he was a pronounced Union man, and in 1864, though nearly past military age, he enlisted for service in the Forty-seventh Illinois Infantry and remained in the army until the close of hostilities. He participated

with Sherman on the glorious march to the sea. After the war he returned to Illinois and died at Plymouth, that state, in 1906. Reuben Cecil married Frances Fortner. She was born in 1830, and died at Colchester, Hancock County, Illinois, in 1911. Reuben Cecil and wife had nine children. Henry A., the oldest, who was a farmer and died in McDonough County, Illinois, enlisted when very young in 1861 in the Seventy-second Illinois Infantry and served throughout the war, participating in thirty odd battles, was once wounded, and was with Sherman in the Atlanta campaign and march to the sea, had served with Grant at Shiloh and Vicksburg, and made an enviable record as a fighting soldier. Margaret, the next in age, died in Hancock County, Illinois, the wife of Wilburn Melton, who is now a farmer at Creeksville, Missouri. The third in age is Doctor Cecil. Thomas L. is a carpenter and contractor at Bazine, Kansas. Sarah married Dr. V. P. Stookey, a physician and surgeon at Colchester, Illinois. Louisa Jane is the wife of William Shanks, a farmer in Wisconsin. A. W. Cecil is a hardware merchant at Elmwood, Kansas. Perry is a truck gardener at Mannette, State of Washington. Ella is the wife of Grant Jeffreys, a farmer and rancher in Nebraska.

Dr. William C. Cecil was born at Plymouth, Hancock County, Illinois, November 15, 1850. Most of his early education was acquired in the public schools of McDonough County, Illinois, and the first twenty years of his life were spent on his father's farm. He has had a great variety of experience, including three years of practical farming in Hancock County. While farming he took up the study of medicine, and afterwards attended lectures in the Eclectic Medical Institute of Cincinnati, where he was awarded his degree Doctor of Medicine in 1875. He at once began private practice, but in 1878 returned to his alma mater for post-graduate work, specializing in diseases of women and children.

His first practice was done at Basco in Hancock County, Illinois. In 1879 he removed to Kansas, and was in practice at Morrill in Brown County, until 1888. Since that year, almost thirty years ago, Doctor Cecil has served the community at Stark, where he was the first permanent physician, and where he has always enjoyed a large medical and surgical practice. He owns his office building on Main Street, also his home in the south part of town, and has ten acres of land just outside the corporate limits where he indulges his fancy as a small farmer.

Doctor Cecil has been too busy with his professional interests to permit the intrusion of politics. However, while in Brown County he served on the school board and is a republican voter. He is a member of the County and State Medical societies, and belongs to Virginia Lodge No. 315, Ancient Free and Accepted Masons at Savonburg, Kansas, and is a member of Fort Scott Consistory No. 4, of the Scottish Rite body.

Doctor Cecil has been twice married. In 1868 in Hancock County, Illinois, he married Miss Sarah E. Robinson. They shared their joys and sorrows together for thirty-six years, until her death at Stark, Kansas, in 1904. On May 15, 1912, at Erie, Kansas, Doctor Cecil married Miss Nell Rumbeck, daughter of Mr. and Mrs. George Rumbeck, who are farming people in Allen County, Kansas. By his first marriage Doctor Cecil had three children. Lena, who died at the age of thirty-five in 1904, married Charles Barnes, who is also deceased and who was a railroad telegraph operator and station agent. The two sons are both railroad men. Ralph is a conductor for the Missouri, Kansas & Texas Railway, living at Parsons, and Hugh, who lives at Stark, is also connected with the Missouri, Kansas & Texas.

JOHN KOSSUTH BEATTY. Before the Indians had been completely removed from Southeastern Kansas across the line into what is now Oklahoma, the Beatty family established its residence in Montgomery County. It is an old and honored name in this section of the state. It is probable that John K. Beatty, a prominent real estate man of Coffeyville, is the oldest native of Montgomery County still living who has spent his entire active career within the limits of that civil division. To speak of him as being the oldest native son is by no means to credit him with age, since Mr. Beatty is barely in the prime of his active career, and only recently passed his forty-fifth birthday. But forty-five is a long time in the history of such a new country as Southeastern Kansas.

His family has an interesting record of participation in the frontier activities of several American states. His grandfather, Walter Beatty, was born of Scotch-Irish ancestry near Nish in Ireland in 1799. When past middle age in 1850 he brought his family to America and settled in Ohio, and from there a few years later moved to Lynn County, Iowa, near Palo. He was both a farmer and a minister of the Methodist Church. His death occurred in Lynn County, Iowa, in 1877. Walter Beatty married Annie Armstrong, who was born in Ireland and died in Lynn County, Iowa. Their children were: Charles, who was a farmer and stock man and died in Benton County, Iowa, having married Mary McAlester, and two of his brothers also married McAlester sisters; Adam, who is the pioneer Kansan of the family, was the father of John K. Beatty; John, who never married and died on the old home farm in Lynn County, Iowa, February 11, 1916, at the age of eighty; James, who died in Benton County, Iowa, where he was a farmer and stock man, and married Ellen McAlester; Annie, who died on the old farm in Lynn County, Iowa, unmarried.

In the next generation comes Adam Beatty, who was born in March, 1833, in Ireland and was about seventeen years of age when his parents came to Iowa and settled in Ohio. In 1855 he moved out to Lynn County, Iowa, was just entering upon his vigorous young majority at the time and able to take an active part in the pioneer work of farming in the new state. In 1864 Adam Beatty came to Kansas, settling first at Ottawa, and in 1868 going to Montgomery County. He was one of the pioneer cattlemen and farmers of this section, and his operations extended across the line into Indian Territory. Later he bought the old homestead farm, 2½ miles southeast of Coffeyville, comprising 120 acres. This was subsequently increased to 410 acres, and he also owned 200 acres four miles southwest of Coffeyville. All this land is still a part of his estate. He died on his farm 2½ miles southeast of Coffeyville February 15, 1911. Some of his land was also platted as the Beatty addition in the north part of Coffeyville, and he acquired some valuable holdings there. Adam Beatty had the character and personality of a true pioneer. His extensive business interests naturally made him a man of prominence, but he exercised hardly less influence as a citizen. He was distinguished by strict and regular habits, by wholesouled and hearty participation in any line of business he undertook, and also by a striking generosity which led him to loan his money freely to less fortunate

men, and he lost many large sums by such liberality. At one time he operated 2,000 acres of ranch land in Oklahoma, and grazed 3,000 head of cattle. It is said that he employed more men in the cattle business than any other individual of Montgomery County. Without having any particular membership in a church, he was a devout Christian with the soul of morality, and his integrity was never questioned. He took a great deal of interest in political affairs. Originally a republican, he aligned himself with the greenback movement, afterwards with the labor party, at another time with the people's party, and then became an independent voter. He was one of the first trustees of the Montgomery County High School. Fraternally he was a member of the Masonic order. During the Civil war he enlisted from Iowa in Company H of an Iowa Regiment of Infantry and served one year until discharged on account of disability. While Adam Beatty had attended school only thirty days, he passed among his fellowmen as a person of thorough education, and this was due to the fact that he was almost constantly a student and read widely in the general field of literature.

Adam Beatty married Margaret McAlester, who was born in Ireland in 1846, and came to the United States with her parents when she was eleven years of age. The family first settled in Coshocton County, Ohio, and afterwards moved to Iowa, where she and two of her sisters became wives of three of the Beatty brothers. She died on the old farm near Coffeyville July 17, 1914. Her children were: James Lincoln, who was born at Ottawa, Kansas, and is now a merchant and live stock dealer at Talala, Oklahoma; Ella, who died at Ottawa, Kansas, at the age of two years; Theresa, who was born at Ottawa and is the wife of Robert Pine, living on a farm four miles south of Coffeyville; John K., who together with all the younger children, all born on the home farm near Coffeyville; Charles W., who is in the cattle business and lives at Coffeyville; Amanda, a teacher by profession with home at Coffeyville; Mary, who is unmarried and resides on the old home place; Annie, who died at the age of four years; Addie, wife of Fred W. Moore, a merchant at Coffeyville; Alsonette, who lives with her brother Charles; and three who died in infancy.

John Kossuth Beatty was born on the Beatty homestead, 2½ miles southeast of Coffeyville, January 1, 1871, being born on New Year's Day, which was Sunday. Reared at home, he spent the first thirty-five years of his life with his parents, and in the meantime attended a public school and the Coffeyville High School. On May 6, 1906, Mr. Beatty moved to Coffeyville and established an office for dealing in real estate. While he has handled extensive tracts on his own account, he has also built up a brokerage business that in volume of sales is one of the largest concerns of its kind in this section of the state. He handles both city property and farm lands in Montgomery County and surrounding counties. His offices are at 114-116 West Ninth Street in Coffeyville. Besides his own residence at 408 Second Street, he owns a number of other residence properties, has a farm of forty acres northwest of Independence, and another of 120 acres in Oklahoma.

Politically Mr. Beatty has always been identified with the democratic party. He is active in the Coffeyville Commercial Club, and is affiliated with Lodge No. 775, Benevolent and Protective Order of

Elks, and Camp No. 665 of the Modern Woodmen of America.

On August 20, 1913, in Coffeyville he married Mrs. Eva (McCormick) Bruce, daughter of Mr. and Mrs. James McCormick, who are now living on their farm near Elk Falls in Elk County, Kansas. By her former marriage Mrs. Beatty had one daughter, Faye, who is now a student in the public schools of Coffeyville.

J. F. DANIEL. He whose name initiates this paragraph is known and valued as one of the progressive business men and public-spirited citizens of Wichita, in which city he is vice president and general manager of the Daniel Shoe Company, which is destined to represent one of the most important industrial enterprises of commercial value to this thriving city.

Mr. Daniel was born at Belton, Arkansas, and in the public schools of that place and Arkadelphia, Arkansas, he acquired his preliminary educational discipline. At the Baptist College in the latter place he pursued a higher academic course of study, also completing there an effective course in the Draughn Business College. For a time he was employed as clerk in a general store at Prescott, Arkansas, going from there to the City of St. Louis, Missouri, where he entered the employ of a wholesale hardware concern. Later he became traveling representative in Kansas for the Wolf Brothers Shoe Company, of Columbus, Ohio, and, after an association with this company for three years he assumed a similar position with the well known Hamilton-Brown Shoe Company, of St. Louis. With the latter corporation he continued his alliance from 1908 until 1915, in the meanwhile becoming a stockholder of the company and a member of its advisory committee. In addition to his duties as traveling salesman, he gave effective service as one of the corps of designers for the company. It was through these various associations that Mr. Daniel gained a broad and accurate knowledge of the various details of shoe manufacturing. Becoming convinced that a profitable enterprise could be developed by establishing a shoe manufactory at some eligible point in the Southwest, he at once made his conviction one of action, finally selecting Wichita as the ideal location for the projected industry. Here he enlisted the co-operation of local capital, and on the 1st of July, 1915, was effected the organization of the Daniel Shoe Company, which was duly incorporated under the laws of the state, with a capital stock of $25,000. Within six months the capital stock had increased to $250,000, and on this basis was instituted the development of the important manufacturing enterprise. As already noted, Mr. Daniel is vice president and general manager of the company, and it should further be stated that the president of the corporation is F. C. Hoyt, who likewise is president of the Union Bank of Wichita. In the manufacturing plant of the Daniel Shoe Company employment is given to a corps of 150 skilled operatives, and the pay roll amounts to fully $100,000 annually. The six traveling representatives of the company cover the states of Kansas, Missouri, Arkansas, Louisiana, Texas, New Mexico, Arizona and Colorado. The products are meeting with a ready and appreciative demand throughout this extended trade territory. The plant has a capacity for the output of seven hundred pairs of men's and boys' welts a day, all of which are in every respect of highest grade. The factory is running to full capacity and is the only shoe manufactory in Kansas. The company has recently found it necessary

to enlarge its thoroughly modern plant by the erection of a two-story brick building, with basement, on the lot adjoining the original factory site. Here authoritative dictum has stated that there is to be found the best equipped and most modern shoe factory of the Middle Western States. The concern gives all assurance of developing into one of the most important as well as one of the most extensive industrial enterprises of the State of Kansas, and at its helm stands a man of marked technical and administrative ability, Mr. Daniel.

WILLIAM F. COON, M. D., whose talents and qualifications have brought him into prominence as a physician and as a citizen of Caney, came to this state from Minnesota, where he was in practice several years, and by birth he is a Wisconsin man.

Born at Eau Claire, Wisconsin, September 20, 1875, he is a son of William F. Coon, and a descendant of ancestors who came from England to the United States in colonial times. His grandfather died in New York State. William F. Coon, Sr., was born in New York in 1825, grew up there, and when a young man went to Eau Claire, Wisconsin, at that time one of the foremost centers of the lumber industry in the state. He was a farmer and also bought and sold horses on a large scale. Politically he was a republican. When nearly fifty years of age he married Emily M. Roberts, who was born in 1853, and is still living at Eau Claire. Doctor Coon was the older of their two sons. His brother, John R., is a resident of Dallas, Texas, and is cashier and adjuster for the Southern Rock Island Plow Company.

It was largely through his own determined efforts that Doctor Coon acquired a liberal education. He attended the public schools of Eau Claire, also Wayland Academy at Beaver Dam, Wisconsin, and his schooling was then interrupted by two years of work for self-support. In 1899 he entered the medical department of the University of Minnesota, and was graduated M. D. in 1903. Additional experience preparatory to practice was given him during a year he spent as interne in the Asbury Methodist Hospital at Minneapolis. Doctor Coon is a member of the medical profession who is never content with present attainments, and does not miss an opportunity to associate with the leading men of the profession. In the fall of 1908 he did post-graduate work in the Chicago Post-Graduate School, and took another course there in 1916.

After entering practice he was located for four years at Elysian, Minnesota. In the fall of 1908 he went to Minneapolis and from there in the spring of 1909 came to Caney, Kansas, where he has since enjoyed a large general medical and surgical practice. He has served as vice president of the County Medical Society and is a member of the State Society and the American Medical Association. His offices are at the corner of Fourth Avenue and Spring Street and he owns his home at the corner of Main and Taylor Avenue.

Doctor Coon is a stockholder in the Kansas Life Insurance Company. He is a member of the Caney Country Club, and though reared a Baptist, in the absence of an organization of that denomination at Caney he attends the Presbyterian Church. He filled the chair of master in the Lodge of Masons at Elysian, Minnesota, and is now affiliated with Caney Lodge, Ancient Free and Accepted Masons, and also with Caney Lodge No. 1215, Benevolent and Protective Order of Elks.

On August 2, 1905, at Downers Grove, Illinois,

Doctor Coon married Miss May Prescott. Her father, the late Rev. B. L. Prescott, was a Baptist minister. Doctor and Mrs. Coon have one daughter, Zula Evelyn, born June 12, 1907.

HARRY L. O'BRYAN is a Chetopa business man who has made himself very active in local affairs there for a number of years. He is a banker, an extensive farm owner, and operator, his name is associated with several of the leading business and commercial enterprises, and at the present writing he is serving as postmaster of the city.

He is of Irish descent. His great-grandfather came out of Ireland as early as 1760, settled in Maryland, and about 1800 moved across the mountains into the new State of Kentucky. Mr. O'Bryan's grandfather Sydney Francis O'Bryan was born in Kentucky in 1804, spent his life in that state as a farmer, and died in 1889.

The head of the next generation is Henry Miles O'Bryan. His career has been identified with the old locality in Southeastern Kansas now known as St. Paul, formerly the seat of the Osage Nation School when the Osage Indians lived there. He was born in Nelson County, Kentucky, in 1835. He grew up and married there, became a farmer, but during the Civil war was proprietor of a hotel at Loretto, Kentucky. In 1871 he came out to Southeastern Kansas and located at Osage Mission or St. Paul as it is now known. For a time he was clerk in a store there, and later bought a farm and engaged in the livestock business, raising and shipping livestock, until he retired about 1906. For the past ten years he has enjoyed the comforts of many years of labor and industry. Politically he is a democrat, has filled various town offices of St. Paul, and was a delegate to a Kansas State convention a number of years ago which declared for Grover Cleveland as president. He is an active member of the Catholic Church and is an honorary member of the Knights of Columbus. H. M. O'Bryan married Susan E. Hagan, who was born in Marion County, Kentucky, in 1837 and died at Osage Mission, Kansas, in 1896. Their children were: Sydney F., who was born in 1860 and died at St. Louis, Missouri, in 1903, having been educated in St. Louis University and having been a zealous and devoted Catholic priest; William W., who was born in 1867, is now the father of eleven children, and is a successful livestock man at St. Paul, Kansas; Annie M., born in 1873 and now the wife of Lon Smith and the mother of eight children, her husband being a farmer and stockman at Stark, Kansas; Harry L., who was the fourth in age among the children; and George I., who was born in 1879 and is a farmer and stockraiser at St. Paul.

Harry L. O'Bryan was born at old Osage Mission now St. Paul in Neosho County, Kansas, April 1, 1876. As a boy he received part of his education, especially along commercial lines in the Jesuit College at Osage Nation. He then took up an active business career with his father and older brother and was successfully identified with livestock raising and dealing until 1901. Since that year his home has been at Chetopa and here also he has become widely known as a live stock man, feeding and shipping livestock on a large scale. In February, 1914, Mr. O'Bryan was selected by President Wilson as postmaster at Chetopa, and since then he has made the postoffice more important than any private considerations or business interests, and is giving a very efficient administration, one generally satisfactory to all patrons.

Besides his city home at the corner of Sixth and Plum streets, Mr. O'Bryan owns a 200 acre farm west of town in Labette County, eighty acres adjoining Chetopa. He furnishes the land and its equipment while a partner operates the farm for dairy purposes. It is one of the best conducted dairy farms in Labette County. The dairy herd comprises eighteen cows, principally Holsteins. Mr. O'Bryan is also vice president of the Farmers and Merchants Bank of Chetopa, and is treasurer of the Cooperative Creamery of Chetopa.

He is a democrat and is widely known in politics over his part of the state. For three terms he served on the city council at Chetopa, was for four years chairman of the County Central Committee of the democratic party, was secretary and treasurer of the Congressional Committee in the Third District in 1912. He is a member of the Catholic Church and belongs to St. Paul Council No. 764 of the Knights of Columbus and to the Anti-Horse Thief Association. In 1901 at St. Paul he married Miss Lizzie Brogan, daughter of Dr. Robert A. and Mary (Farran) Brogan. Her father, who was a well known physician and surgeon, is now deceased. Her mother, who was born in Ireland, is now living with Mr. and Mrs. O'Bryan at Chetopa. Mr. and Mrs. O'Bryan have four children: Robert B., born January 8, 1904; Henry Miles, born August 28, 1906; Elizabeth, born August 23, 1909; and Harry Leo, born December 20, 1915.

HENRY EDWARD REECE, M. D. Five years of effort to maintain the health of a considerable portion of the population of Thayer has drawn the career of Dr. Henry Edward Reece within the fold of a large and emphatic need, giving him an increasing outlet for a wealth of professional and general usefulness. When he came to Thayer, in 1911, he was well equipped to take a position among the foremost physicians and surgeons of this city, and since that time has maintained such a place through his ability, fidelity and devotion to the best principles and ethics of his calling.

Doctor Reece was born at Jefferson, the county seat of Greene County, Iowa, December 27, 1877, and is a son of Michael H. and Sarah (Burden) Reece. He comes of an old American family, which was founded by his great-grandfather, a native of Wales, who, on coming to this country, settled in New York State, and, following his trade of wheelwright, assisted in the building of Perry's fleet for the War of 1812. The paternal grandfather of Doctor Reece was George Reece, who was born in Pennsylvania and was a stone mason by trade. Early in life he developed the wanderlust, and his journeyings took him through Pennsylvania, Ohio, Iowa, Kansas, Missouri and Oregon, in which last-named state he died before the birth of his grandson.

Michael H. Reece was born in 1840, in Dayton, Ohio, and was there reared and educated, and in young manhood went to Holden, Missouri, where he was married. He had learned the carpenter trade in his youth, but at the outbreak of the Civil war was in Colorado, where, in 1861, he enlisted in the Second Cavalry. With this organization he fought for three years and eight months, his service being principally in Missouri and along the border, and including the repelling of Quantrell's raid. At the close of the war he returned to Missouri, but in 1867 moved to Jefferson, Iowa, where he engaged in farming principally, although at times he also followed his trade. In 1882 he came to Chanute, where he worked as a carpenter and assisted in the erection of numerous buildings in the little town, many of which still stand as monuments to his good workmanship. His death occurred at Chanute in 1892, when he was fifty-two years of age. Mr. Reece was a republican in politics, but never sought public office, being content to express his political sympathies by his vote. He belonged to the Campbellite Church, as did also Mrs. Reece, and was fraternally affiliated with the Independent Order of Odd Fellows, which he had joined in his youth. He belonged also to the Grand Army of the Republic. Mr. Reece was married at Holden, Missouri, to Miss Sarah Burden, who was born at that place in 1848, and who still survives him and resides at Chanute. They were the parents of seven children, as follows: William Felix, who is a night foreman in the shops of the Atchison, Topeka & Santa Fe Railroad, at Chicago, Illinois; Thomas Michael, who is a locomotive engineer and resides at San Antonio, Texas; Charles F., who is a locomotive engineer for the Atchison, Topeka & Santa Fe Railroad and resides at Chanute; Dr. Henry Edward, of this notice; Mell C., who is a locomotive engineer for the Galveston, Harrisburg & San Antonio Railroad and resides at Houston, Texas; Buren J., a resident of Chanute and a locomotive fireman on the Santa Fe, who has secured his engineer's papers; and Omer A., who is also a resident of Chanute, a fireman on the Santa Fe and possessed of engineer's papers.

Henry Edward Reece was educated in the public schools of Chanute, primarily, being graduated from the high school there in 1897. He next entered the University Medical College, of Kansas City, Missouri, from which he was graduated in 1900 with the degree of Doctor of Medicine, and since that time has taken post-graduate courses in 1915 and 1916 at Kansas University, Rosedale, Kansas. Doctor Reece began the practice of his profession at Collinsville, Oklahoma, in 1900, and remained at that point for 2½ years. Having passed over what is considered the hardest part of a young physician's career, he then went to Harmony, Oklahoma, where he spent two years, and then changed his field to Bigheart, Oklahoma, where he spent four years. In 1908 he located at Galesburg, Kansas, but after two years again left the state, going at that time to Palacios, Matagorda County, Texas, on Matagorda Bay. That community, however, did not attract him and in 1911 he returned to Kansas and settled permanently at Thayer, where he has since been in the enjoyment of a constantly increasing general medical and surgical practice. His well appointed offices are in the First National Bank Building, where he has every modern instrument and appliance for the handling of even the most delicate and difficult of cases. He has attracted to him the patronage of some of the best families of Thayer, and his professional standing is deservedly high, as he has always lived up to the highest professional ethics. Doctor Reece was the first secretary of the Osage County Medical Society, in 1908, and now belongs to the Neosho County Medical Society, the Kansas State Medical Society and the American Medical Association. He has invested in Thayer real estate, being the owner of a residence on Main Street and other property, as well as farming land in Oklahoma. Fraternally, the doctor belongs to Thayer Lodge No. 149, Ancient Free and Accepted Masons, and Fort Scott Consistory No. 4, being a thirty-second degree Mason, and also holds membership in the Independent Order of Odd Fellows.

Doctor Reece was married in 1901, at Collinsville,

Oklahoma, to Miss Elizabeth Quinton, daughter of Felix and Julia (Sanders) Quinton, the former, a farmer, now deceased, and the latter a resident of Pawhuska, Oklahoma. Doctor and Mrs. Reece are the parents of two children: Halley, born September 12, 1902; and Ethel, born March 8, 1904.

JAY BAIRD, M. D. The medical profession of Kansas has one of its able representatives in Dr. Jay Baird of Coffeyville. Doctor Baird is a man of broad experience, splendidly equipped professionally, and has acquired success and high standing in this state, and is particularly well known among eclectic physicians, and in 1915-16 served as president of the State Eclectic Medical Association.

Some generations back his ancestors were prominent Scotch people, and in that country enjoyed the distinction of a coat of arms marking them one of the ancient clans of Scotland. This coat of arms represents a bull and boar rampant. From Scotland the Bairds came to Pennsylvania in colonial times.

Josiah Baird, grandfather of Doctor Baird, was born in Pennsylvania, in 1802, and when he was quite young his parents moved to Muskingum County, Ohio, where he married and where he took up the trade of blacksmith. A number of years later, along in the '50s, he moved out to Iowa with his son, the father of Doctor Baird, and lived in Van Buren County of that state until his death in 1886. In religion he was a stanch old Covenanter Presbyterian. Politically he was a republican. Josiah Baird married Mary Thompson, who was born in Ohio in 1806 and died in Van Buren County, Iowa, in 1892. Their children were: Nathan; Cephas, who was a minister of the Lutheran Church and died in California; Letitia, who married Uriah Law, and both are now deceased, she having died at Troy in Davis County, Iowa.

Dr. Jay Baird was born near Keosauqua, Van Buren County, Iowa, October 23, 1870. His father, Nathan Baird, was born in Ohio in 1838, grew to manhood in that state, where he married his first wife, and along in the '50s moved out to Van Buren County, Iowa, where he was one of the pioneer settlers and until the close of his life, which occurred on his home farm in Van Buren County in 1900, he followed farming and stock raising. He'was a very active member of the United Presbyterian Church, and in politics was a republican. During the Civil war he was a member of the Home Guards. Nathan Baird married for his first wife Susan Liming, who was born in Ohio and died in Van Buren County, Iowa. Their children were: Jefferson F., a merchant at Odell, Illinois; Luther C., a merchant at Sioux City, Iowa; Howard, a stock man in Van Buren County, Iowa. For his second wife, Nathan Baird married Lurinda Sophia Jones, who was born in Ohio in 1852 and still lives on the old farm in Iowa. Her children were: Seth, who is a farmer near the old place in Iowa; Oscar, who graduated from the Eclectic Medical College at Cincinnati and is now a physician and surgeon at Chanute, Kansas; Dr. Jay Baird is the third of the children; Rufus, the next younger died at the age of five years; Flo is the wife of Harry L. Gleason, a jeweler in Boston, Massachusetts; Clay runs the old home farm in Van Buren County, Iowa, his farm comprising a quarter section of land; Justice graduated from the University of Michigan, where he received his law degree and received the degree of Bachelor of Science from the State University of Iowa and is now in active practice at Kansas City, Kansas.

From a varied early experience as a farmer boy, student and teacher, Dr. Jay Baird pointed his career toward medicine. He attended district schools in his home county in Iowa, graduated from the Keosauqua High School, and for three years taught in Van Buren County. This was followed by a year spent in the State Agricultural College at Ames, Iowa, and another year in the State Normal School at Cedar Falls. Earning his way by teaching, he began his medical education in the State University of Iowa, where he spent two years, and beginning with 1897 practiced medicine as an undergraduate at Vilas, Kansas. He was there for a year and a half. He finished his medical course in 1900 in the Eclectic Medical College at Cincinnati, where he was graduated M. D. After graduating 2½ years were spent in Nebraska, but in 1902 he located at Coffeyville, and has been steadily in practice there both as a physician and surgeon ever since. A large part of his practice in recent years is as a specialist in diseases of children. In 1914 he took a special course in that department of medicine in the Chicago Policlinic. Doctor Baird has his offices at 126 West Ninth Street, and is a member of the County and State Medical societies and belongs to all the medical associations of the Eclectic School, county, state and national.

Besides his residence at 105 West First Street, Doctor Baird owns a fruit farm of forty acres in the Bitter Root Valley of Montana, also a tract of land in Oklahoma, and some 600 acres in Arkansas. Politically he is an independent republican, and is a trustee and active supporter of the Methodist Episcopal Church. He is affiliated with Camp No. 665, Modern Woodmen of America at Coffeyville, belongs to the Commercial Club, and for four years was a member of the City School Board. While on the school board he was instrumental in raising the general standard of the local public schools.

In 1900 in Iowa Doctor Baird married Miss Ida K. Minear, a daughter of George and Emma Minear, both now deceased. Her father was a farmer and stockman in Van Buren County, Iowa. Doctor and Mrs. Baird have three children: Byrle, born November 15, 1902, and a student in the public schools; Bruce M., born August 9, 1906, and also in school; and Lois Catherine, born November 9, 1913.

L. M. ROOME is an oil producer and contractor whose activities have brought him considerable success in Kansas territory and whose business headquarters are at Tyro, in Montgomery County. His first experience in the business was gained in the Illinois oil district, and he came to Kansas about two years ago.

His ancestors came originally from England and settled in old Virginia during colonial days. His grandfather, Edward Roome, was born in Pennsylvania, spent most of his life as a farmer in West Virginia, where he died.

Mr. L. M. Roome was born in Sistersville, West Virginia, July 23, 1886, and for a young man of thirty has made an enviable business record. His father is E. M. Roome, now a resident of Tyro, Kansas, who was born in West Virginia April 7, 1861. He grew up in his native state and a number of years ago became connected with the oil business as a producer, following that work in West Virginia, Illinois and Oklahoma, and since 1915 has continued in the same line with headquarters and home at Tyro, Kansas. He is very strongly grounded in the faith of the democratic party and is a member of the Methodist Episcopal Church. In Tyler County, West Virginia, he married Emma Martin, who was born in that county April 1, 1860. Their children are: Maggie, wife of P. J. Garvey, who is in the automobile business at Pine Grove, West Virginia; Edith, wife of E. M. Mayfield, a wholesale grocer who resides at Middleburn in Tyler County, West Virginia; Mr. L. M. Roome, who is third in order of age; Frank, a resident of Okmulgee, Oklahoma, in force, and field foreman for the Carter Oil Company; and Mary, whose home is with her parents, but is now a member of the senior class in the Tulsa High School.

The first school L. M. Roome attended was at Sistersville, West Virginia, where he was born, and he was also in the public schools of Martinsville in that state, and in 1907 graduated from the West Virginia University at Morgantown. The following year he pursued a business course in the Wheeling Business College at Wheeling. For two years he was connected with a bank at Pine Grove, West Virginia, and in 1910 engaged in the oil business as a contractor for the drilling of wells and as a producer. His first work was in the Illinois field, but in March, 1914, he moved to Tyro, Kansas. He now has a field of seven producing wells two miles east and one mile south of Tyro, and recently disposed of a number of wells which he had brought in. As a contractor he keeps his outfit employed in many parts of the Kansas oil field.

Mr. Roome is a democrat, a member of the Methodist Episcopal Church, and in Masonry is affiliated with Tyro Lodge No. 386, Ancient Free and Accepted Masons; Wichita Consistory No. 2, of the Scottish Rite, and with Mirzah Temple of the Nobles of the Mystic Shrine at Pittsburg, Kansas. He also belongs to the United Commercial Travelers at Lancaster, Ohio.

On October 31, 1909, at Pine Grove, West Virginia, he married Miss Elsie Warner, a daughter of A. E. and Delia Warner, residents of Clarksburg, West Virginia, where her father is a wholesale grocer.

ROBERT ORIN DEMING, president of The Deming Investment Company at Oswego, is at the head of one of the largest financial institutions in the Southwest. The Deming Investment Company, which has been built up on a basis of fair dealing continued through a period of more than thirty years, now has branch offices in nearly a dozen of the larger cities of the Middle West, and at the present time has over $15,000,000 of farm loans in force, out of some $35,000,000 loaned in Missouri, Kansas, Oklahoma, Texas, Arkansas and Mississippi. The company has been a bulwark of security for the investors, and at the same time has protected and aided thousands of farm owners in securing necessary capital for acquirement of title, improvements and carrying on their regular business.

To build up such an organization is of itself no small distinction in the business world. Mr. Deming is in fact one of the foremost financiers of the State of Kansas. Besides the investment company he is owner of the Parsons Natural Gas Company, which supplies the City of Parsons with natural gas. He erected the plant in 1897, and has directed the affairs of the company for nineteen years.

Among the large farms of Southern Kansas perhaps none is more conspicuous by its high standards and model equipment than the Deming ranch of 3,500 acres, adjoining the City of Oswego on the north. A large part of this land lies in the Neosho River bottom and it is protected from overflow by the erection of eleven miles of levee. Mr. Deming has directed the tiling of more than 1,400 acres. Some of the highest grades of livestock have their home on this ranch. Mr. Deming raises a herd of from 500 to 1,000 pure bred Poland China hogs, and usually keeps about 500 head of Hereford cattle. The manager of the ranch is L. S. Edwards, a nephew of the late Senator P. B. Plumb. Mr. Edwards took the full four years agricultural and animal husbandry course in the State Agricultural College at Manhattan.

The Deming family came from England, and was introduced to this country by John Deming, who settled in Wethersfield, Connecticut, in 1642. Mr. Deming is a grandson of Orin S. Deming, who was a Vermont and later a New York State farmer.

Robert Orin Deming was born in Pottsdam, St. Lawrence County, New York, July 24, 1860, a son of Aaron N. Deming, who was born in Pottsdam in 1828. His father was reared and married in Pottsdam, and became an extensive dealer in butter and cheese. In 1872 he came to Kansas, owned and managed a hotel at Arkansas City, and spent the rest of his years as a hotel proprietor, being located at Ogden, Utah, Joplin, Hannibal, and Carthage, Missouri, Wichita and Fort Scott, Kansas, Aspen, Colorado, and at other places. He died at Denver, Colorado, in 1903. He was a republican, a trustee and deacon in the Methodist Episcopal Church, and was affiliated with the Masonic fraternity. Aaron N. Deming married Julia A. Noble, who was born at Franklin, Vermont, in 1830 and died at Wichita, Kansas, in 1893. They were married at St. Albans, Vermont. Their children were: Edgar N., who was killed by Indians in Indian Territory in 1874, while in charge of a surveyors corps under Government contract; Mary, wife of C. W. Bitting, who is in the insurance business at Wichita; Robert O.; Julia, wife of R. C. Israel, a real estate dealer at Wichita.

Robert O. Deming received his early education in the public schools of Arkansas City, Winfield and Wichita, Kansas. He gave evidence of his independent character at a very early age, leaving school when thirteen and thenceforward making his own way in the world. For several years he clerked in a store at Wichita.

Mr. Deming came to Oswego and opened an office to handle farm mortgages and loans in September, 1882. He started in a small way, and by the exercise of absolute integrity in all his relations between the investor and the borrower has made his name a synonym for one of the largest farm loan businesses in the West. On January 1, 1888, the Deming Investment Company was incorporated. This company now has branch offices in Wichita, Kansas, at Little Rock, Arkansas; Dallas, Austin and Abilene, Texas; Memphis, Tennessee; Kansas City, Missouri; and Oklahoma City, Muskogee and Durant, Oklahoma. There are more than seventy salaried employes in the home and branch offices. The general offices are in Oswego. The officers of the company are: R. O. Deming, president; D. S. Waskey, vice president; F. W. Stout, secretary; and R. O. Deming, Jr., treasurer.

The finest residence in Oswego and one of the finest in the entire State of Kansas is owned by Mr. Deming and his home and its comforts are in keeping with his high place in business affairs. In 1897-8 he served as mayor of Oswego. He is a republican, and is affiliated with Oswego Lodge, Ancient Free and Accepted Masons, and Oswego Chapter No. 15, Royal Arch Masons.

In 1887 at Oswego he married Christiana Elliott, daughter of Rev. John and Elizabeth Elliott. Her father, who is now living at Oswego, is eighty-seven years of age and for a number of years was pastor of the Presbyterian Church of Oswego. Mrs. Deming's mother died at Kansas City, Missouri. Mr. and Mrs. Deming have three children and have given them every advantage in the way of educational training. Their daughter Julia was graduated A. B. from the Bryn Mawr College at Bryn Mawr, Pennsylvania, in 1916. The son Robert O., Jr., finished his education with a two year course in the State Agricultural College at Manhattan, and is now treasurer of the Deming Investment Company. The youngest, Elizabeth, is still attending the public schools at Oswego.

JOHN H. SPERRY. Among the men who have contributed to the upbuilding and development of Neosho County, and particularly of the City of Thayer, few are entitled to a greater degree of credit than John H. Sperry, ex-president of the Thayer State Bank, veteran of the Civil war, farmer and stockman, and a citizen who has always been representative of the best type of progressive citizenship. While he is now retired from active labors, Mr. Sperry continues to take a keen interest in the community in which he has resided for forty-eight years, and through his influence and example continues to be a force in promoting the things that make for advancement and progress.

On both the paternal and maternal sides of the family Mr. Sperry comes from sturdy German ancestry. He was born November 18, 1841, at Cambridge City, Wayne County, Indiana, his parents being George and Catherine (Delano) Sperry. His father was born in 1804, near the Rhine, Alsace-Lorraine, Germany, and as a youth learned the trade of cabinet maker, which he followed in his native land. There he was married to Catherine Delano, who was born in the same year and in the same locality, and in 1833, with one son, came to the United States and located at Dayton, Ohio. There he continued to work as a cabinet maker and followed that vocation for a time after he had removed to Cambridge City, Indiana, but eventually turned his attention to farming near Strawtown, Indiana, where his death occurred in 1853. He was a republican in politics, and both he and his wife were faithful members of the Evangelical Church. Mrs. Sperry survived her husband for many years and passed away on the farm of her son, near Thayer, in 1885. They were the parents of the following children: George, who fought through the Civil war as a Union soldier, subsequently took up milling at Noblesville, Indiana, and died there as the result of an accident; Samuel Alexander, who was a farmer and merchant and died at Strawtown, Indiana; Catherine, who married Anton McGassi, one of the great "Seven McGassi Brothers," theatrical performers, now deceased, and died in 1915, at Rigsby, Oklahoma; John H., of this notice; Mary E., who married first Amos Cooper, deceased, a farmer, and married second Mr. Crooks, and died on a farm near Cicero, Indiana, where Mr. Crooks still resides; David, who enlisted in the Thirty-ninth Regiment, Indiana Volunteer Infantry, which was later mounted and became the Eighth Indiana Cavalry, and was killed during the McCook raid in the rear of Atlanta, while fighting with the forces of General Sherman; Jacob, who is farming four miles east of Cicero, Indiana; and Charles, who died on his farm near Dennis, Kansas. Rear Admiral Charles S. Sperry belonged to the same branch of the family.

John H. Sperry received his education in the district schools of Hamilton County, Indiana, and the public schools of Cambridge City, but at the age of sixteen years gave up his studies and learned the carpenter's trade, at which he was working when the Civil war came on. He had not yet reached his majority when, in the fall of 1862, he enlisted as John Sperry in Company I, Seventy-fifth Regiment, Indiana Volunteer Infantry, with which organization he served until the close of the war, rising from private to corporal and later to sergeant. This regiment was organized at Wabash, Indiana, and was mustered into the United States service August 19, 1862, and two days later left the state for Lebanon, Kentucky, but retired to Louisville at the time of Bragg's advance. It then moved to Frankfort, Scottsville, Gallatin and Cave City, in pursuit of Morgan, and was in camp near Gallatin during December, moving in January, 1863, to Murfreesboro, being engaged in scouting and brief expeditions with the Second Brigade, Third Division, Fourteenth Army Corps. On June 24th it started for Tullahoma and participated in the Battle of Hoover's Gap, being the first regiment to enter the enemy's works at Tullahoma. Moving then towards Chattanooga, it was engaged at Chickamauga, and remained near Chattanooga during the fall and winter, taking part in the Battle of Missionary Ridge. It moved to Ringgold, Georgia, in the spring of 1864, joined the campaign to Atlanta, and was engaged at Dalton, Dallas, Kenesaw Mountain, Peach Tree Creek, in front of Atlanta and at Jonesboro. At Atlanta Mr. Sperry was severely wounded, when part of his shoulder-blade was shot off by a shell. He was subsequently detained in a hospital for several months, but rejoined his regiment as soon as he was able for service. On October 4 the Seventy-fifth removed with its corps to Pine Mountain and arrived in time to threaten the rear of French's Division of Hood's army, which was investing the garrison at Allatoona, where he was acting captain. The regiment returned in time to join the march upon Savannah and the march through the Carolinas, participating en route in the battles of Fayetteville and Bentonville, and then moved with the advance of the army to Raleigh, thence to Richmond, and finally on to Washington, D. C., where it was mustered out of the service, June 8, 1865, having participated in thirty-seven engagements.

At the close of his military service, Mr. Sperry returned to his Indiana home, and there, in 1866 was married. For one and one-half years he was engaged in the mercantile business there, but in 1869 came to Kansas and pre-empted 160 acres of land eight miles south of Thayer, a farm on which he resided for twenty-seven years, and to which he greatly added. He also accumulated other farms, which he rented, but at the time of his retirement to Thayer, in 1897, disposed of his holdings to a large extent. Soon after coming to Kansas, Mr. Sperry embarked in the stock business, in which he gained a very edifying success. He frequently fed and shipped as many as sixty carloads of cattle during a year, and in the last year that he was actively engaged in that business shipped sixty-four car-loads in four months. He was also in the lumber business for several years and at one time had the exclusive grain business of the section in his control. During the twelve years that he acted in the capacity of president of the Thayer State Bank that institution grew and prospered and held a position second to no state bank in the county. He was urged to retain the presidency, but with increasing years

resolved to transfer the responsibilities to younger shoulders. As a builder of Thayer, Mr. Sperry erected a large proportion of the business section of the city, as well as the first brick house in the community. He is still the owner of much property here, including several business structures, the postoffice building and his own residence on Neosho Street, in addition to which he has two farms in Labette County, comprising 320 acres, and one farm in Wilson County. Fraternally, he is connected with Thayer Lodge No. 339, Ancient Free and Accepted Masons; Parsons Chapter, Royal Arch Masons, and Parsons Commandery, Knights Templar. During his long and active life, Mr. Sperry has lived close to high ideals, and his citizenship has imparted strength and substantiality to all undertakings with which he has been associated. He splendidly stood the tests which the frontier imposed upon those who invaded its remoteness and the new order of things found him in accord with its aims, purposes and inexhaustible opportunities. His career has been an inspiring one, worthy of emulation by any youth who is entering life with his own way to make.

In 1866, on a farm near Strawtown, Indiana, Mr. Sperry was united in marriage with Miss Mary E. Dietrick, a daughter of Mrs. Susan Dietrick, now deceased. Mrs. Sperry died in 1909, the mother of six children, namely: Minnie A., who is the wife of Joseph Horr, a successful farmer and the owner of several farms; Dora E., who is the wife of Charles F. Petri, and lives on a farm near Dennis, Kansas; Pearl D., who is the wife of William Southwick, who has an insurance business at Parsons, Kansas; John F., who is the owner of the telephone exchange at Ness City, Kansas; Albert O., who is identified with the Pryor Bank, at Pryor, Oklahoma; and R. E., who is the owner of the telephone exchange at Fairfax, Oklahoma.

CHARLES T. BICKETT. Well established in business affairs at Coffeyville, with an office for the handling of insurance, collections and also for the discharge of his duties as justice of the peace, Charles T. Bickett has had an unusually wide range of experience and association with Montgomery County, where he has lived since pioneer times.

His ancestry goes back to an old English family, and in fact may be traced to that noted scholar and thinker, Thomas a' Becket, of the fourteenth century. The Bicketts came from England to Virginia in colonial times. From Virginia they spread across the mountains into Kentucky, and Mr. Bickett's grandfather was born either in Kentucky or Virginia and was a Kentucky farmer.

Charles T. Bickett was born at Maryville, Nodaway County, Missouri, February 7, 1860. His father, Hiram J. Bickett, was born at St. Mary's, Kentucky, in 1813, was reared and married there, was a school teacher for several years, and in 1856 became one of the early settlers in Nodaway County, Northwest Missouri. He taught school in that section of the state until 1876, and in that year moved to Kansas, locating at Wellington, and in 1879 buying a farm three miles west of Liberty in Montgomery County, on which he lived until his death October 14, 1884. He was a Kentucky democrat and a member of the Catholic Church. His wife, Cynthia Bickett, was also born in Kentucky and died in Missouri in February, 1860, at the birth of her youngest child, Charles T. Bickett. The older children were: Jerome, who died in Maryville, Missouri, in 1862; James A., who is a retired physician and surgeon at Maryville; Margaret, who died at Maryville in 1864; Susan, who lives at Cherryvale, Kansas, widow of W. H. Linton, who died in 1916; T. S., roadmaster of the Santa Fe Railway Company, living at Trinidad, Colorado; A. D. Bickett, foreman in the car shops at Horton, Kansas; Rose, now living in the State of Washington, is the widow of James A. Wakefield, who was a miller and lumberman and died in 1908; Joseph A. in the fruit commission business at Chico, California; W. A. Bickett, who was foreman on a fruit and nut ranch in California, and was killed at Burbank in that state by a cave-in of an irrigation plant.

The first fifteen years of his life Charles T. Bickett spent in Northwest Missouri, and up to 1875 was a pupil in the Benedictine Brothers School at Conception, Missouri. In March, 1876, he came to Kansas and lived on the farm of his uncle, Anthony Bickett, at Wellington until the fall of the same year, when his father arrived. On December 23, 1878, he arrived at Independence in Montgomery County and soon afterwards went out to the old farm near Liberty. In 1879, at the age of nineteen, he went on a car load of wheat to Kansas City, Missouri, and began work for Parker Brothers, furniture manufacturers, at 4-5 East Levee. He remained with that firm until the spring of 1882. Until December of the same year he was with the Carlat Undertaking Company, and in January, 1883, returned to the home farm, where he remained until the spring of 1884. Since the latter date his home has been at Coffeyville. In August, 1884, Mr. Bickett entered the employ of Lange & Lape, furniture dealers and undertakers, and was with them several years. In 1895 he went to Claremore, Kansas, and opened a furniture and undertaking business for Col. F. A. Neilson, and was manager of the establishment until July, 1898. On returning to Coffeyville he was bookkeeper and salesman in a wholesale house for six years, and then resumed employment with a Coffeyville furniture company, where he remained until June 1, 1909. After that he was with Ragle & Curry, in the insurance business, until July 1, 1912. At the latter date he opened his office to handle insurance and collections and has built up a large clientage in those lines. In the fall of 1912 he was elected justice of the peace, and still discharges the duties of that office together with his other business. His offices are at Room 7 in the Odd Fellows Building. Mr. Bickett has acquired considerable local real estate, including his home at 110 West North Street.

Politically he is an independent democrat. He was reared in and has always been faithful to the Catholic Church, and fraternally is affiliated with Star Lodge No. 117, Independent Order of Odd Fellows, at Coffeyville; with Gate City Encampment No. 80, and Canton of the same order; with Lodge No. 58, Improved Order of Red Men, at Coffeyville; is a life member of lodge No. 305 of the Fraternal Order of Eagles; is a member of the Fraternal Aid Union at Coffeyville; and belongs to Coffeyville Lodge No. 1193, Loyal Order of Moose; and with Anti-Horse Thief Association. He is a member of the Coffeyville Commercial Club.

On November 18, 1883, Mr. Bickett was married at Coffeyville, Kansas, to Miss Chloe B. Shelley, daughter of Mr. and Mrs. William Shelley. Her mother is now deceased and her father, who lives with Mr. and Mrs. Bickett, was a pioneer settler in Montgomery County of 1869, and followed farming until he retired. Mr. and Mrs. Bickett have had four children: Charles, who died at the age of one and a half years; Grace, wife of Fred Felton, a glass worker living at Terre Haute, Indiana; J. O., who was born June 4, 1888, and died in December, 1911, at the age of twenty-three; and Quixie.

LAROY MCCLELLAN PENWELL was born at Buchanan, Michigan, November 25, 1862. He was one of seven children of Eli W. and Mary L. (Rouse) Penwell.

Eli Penwell was born at Elkhart, Indiana. He went with his parents to Michigan when a small boy, and spent most of his life in that state in the lumber business. He died in Kansas in 1886. His wife, Mary L., died in Kansas in 1889.

The subject of this sketch, L. M. Penwell, as he is known, received his education in the rural schools in Michigan, and came to Kansas with his parents when he was but thirteen years of age. At the age of eighteen years, he entered the employ of the Atchison, Topeka and Santa Fe Railway Company, and continued with that company until April 1894, when he launched his present business, that of funeral director. His present business establishment occupies a space of seventy-five feet frontage, is 150 feet deep, three stories high, and is located at 506-508-510 Quincy Street, Topeka, Kansas.

There is no one in the West who has the reputation for more perfect service, and a better and more broadly extended reputation as funeral director and embalmer than has L. M. Penwell. He was one of the organizers of the Kansas Funeral Directors Association, and was its secretary for eighteen years. He has been a member of the National Funeral Directors Association for 20 years, and served as its president in 1905 and 1906. He was one of the men who drafted and secured the passage by the Kansas Legislature of the present laws governing embalmers and funeral directors. He has put his entire energy in making his business establishment one of the most complete in America.

Colonel Penwell has never sought political honors, but at the solicitation of his friends, in 1909, he made the campaign and was elected to the lower house of the Kansas Legislature. He served one term, and declined re-election. In politics he is a democrat. At the election of Governor Hodges in 1912, he was appointed on the governor's military staff, with the rank of colonel, and was reappointed to the same position by Governor Capper in 1914.

Colonel Penwell takes a keen interest in the business affairs of the city and state. He is a director in the Vermont Granite Company, a director in the Shawnee Building and Loan Association of Topeka, and is president of the Kansas State Fair Association of Topeka. He is a director and life member of the Kansas State Historical Society, and is a member of the Topeka Club, the Topeka Country Club, the Lake View Hunting and Fishing Club.

Among fraternalists they call Colonel Penwell a joiner. He belongs to all the bodies of Masons, including the Blue Lodge, the Chapter, the Commandery, the Consistory, the Red Cross of Constantine, and the Shrine. He is a Past Master in nearly all of these orders, including the Shrine of which he is a past potentate; is an honorary Thirty-third Degree Scottish Rite Mason; a past exalted ruler of the Benevolent and Protective Order of Elks, and a member of their Grand Lodge. He belongs to all

LaRoy McClellan Pennwell

J. A. Stearns, M.D.

branches of the Odd Fellows Order, and at this writing is serving as grand master of the state. He is also a member of many of the other orders, including the Eagles, the Moose, Modern Woodmen of America, Woodmen of the World, Knights and Ladies of Security, Royal Arcanum, the Ancient Order of the United Workmen, and Knights of Pythias, and he is a member of all their grand bodies.

Colonel Penwell was married in August, 1888, to Miss Mary H. E. Maston, of Mount Hope, in Sedgwick County, Kansas. She died April 4, 1912, at Topeka, Kansas. He has one daughter, Portia W. who is Mrs. John C. Stapel of Rock Port, Missouri. Mr. Stapel is editor and proprietor of the Atchison County Mail.

Colonel Penwell's home is in Topeka, where he enjoys the distinction of being one of its leading citizens. He has gone through all the hardships and privations that a great many of the early settlers of Kansas experienced.

Colonel Penwell takes an active interest in everything that will benefit his city. He has made no attempt to be other than a common citizen, doing his level best to take his place among men, and to build up the city and state in which he lives. He expects to make Topeka his home until he dies, and is always ready to spend his time and money and ability for anything that will help Topeka or its citizens, and he would rather have his friends than all the money in the world.

THOMAS A. STEVENS, M. D. In the great majority of cases, heredity has no rights which the biographers of successful Americans, especially those of the West, feel called upon to respect. However, in shaping the course of some men it wields a distinct influence, and must be noted when the tendency born in a man is nurtured by an ever-present force in the same lines, crowding other avenues of thought and compelling devotion to a certain vocation or profession. Heredity, supplementing environment and training, has had much to do in shaping the career of Dr. Thomas A. Stevens, a leading physician and surgeon of Caney. Not only his father, but his maternal grandfather, were physicians before him, and the predilection for his calling that has contributed so greatly to his success is but his natural inheritance from men of professional skill and zeal.

Doctor Stevens was born at Corydon, the county seat of Harrison County, Indiana, March 14, 1856, a son of J. D. and Margaret A. (Johnson) Stevens. J. D. Stevens was born in 1835, at Corydon, of Scotch-Irish and French parents, was prepared for his profession at Jefferson Medical College, Philadelphia, and Miami Medical College, Cincinnati, Ohio, graduating from the latter with the class of 1867, and commenced practice at Vincennes, Indiana, whence he had removed in 1860. He successfully followed his profession for many years in Indiana, but in the evening of life came to Kansas, where his death occurred, at Peru, in 1913. He was married in 1855 to Margaret A. Johnson, who was born at Vincennes, Indiana, of Scotch and French descent, daughter of Dr. William Johnson, who was a medical practitioner at Vincennes for forty years and died there when seventy years of age. He was the son of a Revolutionary soldier, Gen. Richard Johnson, who became famous in what was then known as the Northwest. The children of Doctor and Mrs. Stevens were as follows: Thomas A., of this review; Nancy A., who is the wife of John H. Sams, connected with a gold smelter at Victor, Colorado: Dora K., the wife

of R. I. Hillman, a republican ex-postmaster of Peru, Kansas; Dr. J. C., a graduate of Rush Medical College, Chicago, and now a successful practicing physician and surgeon of Tulsa, Oklahoma; Jemima, who is the wife of William Haberly, a farmer of Peru, Kansas; Maude, the wife of O. D. Hicks, a merchant of Las Vegas, Nevada; and Edgar M., a smelter worker residing at Caney, Kansas.

Thomas A. Stevens received his primary education in the schools of Vincennes, Indiana, being graduated from the high school when sixteen years old. At that early age he displayed industry and ability as a teacher in the schools of Indiana and continued as an educator for two years. In March, 1876, he came to Kansas, accepting the position of teacher in the school at Sedan, where he remained for two years more. His next employment was as clerk in a drug store, and it was here that his inherent talent made itself felt and he began the study of medicine. In 1880 he matriculated in the Missouri Medical College, and in 1881-2 attended a course of lectures at the Kansas City Medical College. However, he did not complete the course in the latter year, but began the practice of his calling at Cedarvale, Kansas, where he remained until January 1, 1885. At that time Doctor Stevens came to Caney, where he remained for a period of seven years, although he has been engaged in practice in Southeastern Kansas continuously since.

Being an undergraduate, the reputation and business of Doctor Stevens depended wholly upon his work when he entered upon his career, but so earnestly did he apply himself to the thorough study of every case brought to him for treatment that he soon was well on the way to success. In 1891 he returned to the Kansas City Medical College, now the medical department of the University of Kansas, and was graduated March 15, 1892, with the degree of Doctor of Medicine. In 1899 he took his first post-graduate work in the New York City Polyclinic, and in 1902 returned to New York City, where he did a few weeks' work in the clinics of the various hospitals of the metropolis. In 1902 and 1905 he attended the Policlinic at Chicago. Doctor Stevens was appointed United States pension examining surgeon by President Cleveland in 1893, and retained that position for four years, during which time over 1,200 veterans of the Civil war appeared before him for examination. He was also appointed medical examiner for all the old line insurance companies doing business in the State of Kansas, and in the work of that office his attention was called to the urgent need of an organization of medical examiners in the United States. Accordingly, he addressed 100 letters to as many prominent physicians all over the country, calling their attention to the propriety of such an organization, with the result that June 2, 1900, at Vincennes, Indiana, there was completed the organization of the American Association of Life Insurance Examining Surgeons, which now bears the name of the American Medical Examiners' Association, and which, in point of numbers, ranks second only to the American Medical Association. Doctor Stevens was secretary of the organization for three years. He is also a member of the Caney City Medical Society, the Montgomery County Medical Society, the Southeastern Kansas Medical Society, the Kansas State Medical Society, the American Medical Association and the Santa Fe Railroad Medical and Surgical Society, and is an ex-member of the International Association of Railway Surgeons. He has been local surgeon for the Missouri Pacific and Santa Fe railways, and throughout his work has been successful both professionally and financially. A great deal of his practice has extended to Oklahoma and the Indian Territory, where he has had among his clientele members of the Osage, Cherokee, Delaware, Choctaw, Munsee and Cheyenne Indian tribes. In 1900 Doctor Stevens built and equipped the Caney Sanitarium and Hospital, which, measured by the good it has accomplished, has been one of the most successful of the city's institutions.

Doctor Stevens maintains well-appointed offices on State Street, opposite the postoffice, while his residence, which he owns, is a modern and handsome structure at the corner of Spring Street and Third Avenue. Formerly he' was the owner of a large farm in Montgomery County and fifteen residence properties at Caney, but these he has traded comparatively recently for Kansas City property, which he still owns.

During his residence at Caney, Doctor Stevens has taken a prominent part in public affairs and an active interest in the growth and development of the town, a rapidly developing manufacturing city the growth of which is due to its being the center of one of the most extensive oil and gas fields in the world. For sixteen years he served as a member of the Caney Board of Education, being for nine years of this time its president. In both of President Cleveland's administrations he acted as United States pension examining surgeon. A democrat in politics, he was elected on the ticket of that party to the office of mayor in 1900, and during that and the ensuing year gave Caney a most excellent and efficient administration, conserving its interests and getting the greatest value of good from the city's finances. He was the candidate for county clerk in Chautauqua County on one occasion, and while there is a normal republican majority there of 2,000 votes, met defeat by only sixty-five votes. In February, 1916, Doctor Stevens was appointed postmaster of Caney, an office in which he is giving the satisfaction that only a man of his ability and executive force can grant. Fraternally, Doctor Stevens is prominent, being identified with Caney Lodge No. 324, Ancient Free and Accepted Masons; Caney Chapter No. 90, Royal Arch Masons; Caney Camp No. 941, Modern Woodmen of America; Caney Lodge No. 1215, Benevolent and Protective Order of Elks; and an ex-member of the Ancient Order of United Workmen and the Anti-Horse Thief Association.

Doctor Stevens was married May 16, 1880, at Peru, Kansas, to Miss Luella Sams, daughter of W. C. and Lucy Sams. Mr. Sams was an early stockman of Kansas, and both he and his wife are now deceased. To Doctor and Mrs. Stevens the following children were born: O. V., member of the lumber firm which has several yards in Oklahoma, and manager of the branch at Nowata, that state, an ex-member of the Kansas Legislature, who was elected as representative by more than 1,000 majority on the democratic ticket in a district normally strong for the republican party, and the youngest member in the house during his session; Norene K., who is the wife of W. G. Longtoft, a glass worker of Caney; Mabel C., who is the wife of G. W. Connelly, president of the Connelly Glass Company and vice president of the Caney Pipe Line Company and the Owen Zinc Company, and with other large interests at and about Caney; Maude E., who resides with her parents; Frances, who is the wife of J. H. Wilson of Caney, proprietor of the Bon Ami Lumber Company; Leta B., who is the wife of C. I. Gause, a banker of Mound City, Kansas;

and Thomas A., Jr., of Caney, who is connected with the chemical department of the American Zinc, Lead and Smelter Company.

HON. W. W. THOMPSON. The interests of the widow and orphan are protected and safeguarded so far as is humanely possible in Labette County where W. W. Thompson is probate judge. That is the finest proof of his administration of that office during the last six years. Judge Thompson, while not a lawyer by profession, is a man of judicial temperament, of wide experience in business and public affairs, and has both the personal integrity and impartiality which qualify him so well for his present duties.

He is one of the older settlers of Labette County. He was born in Montgomery County, Illinois, April 3, 1864, and is of Scotch descent. His grandfather Archibald Thompson was born in Scotland, came to America in time to participate in the War of 1812, afterwards settled in Kentucky, where he married, and then moved to Illinois where he followed farming in Clinton County until his death in 1866. Judge Thompson was about two years of age when his grandfather died.

The father, G. W. Thompson, was born in Kentucky January 19, 1839. He grew to manhood in his native state, but was married in Jefferson County, Illinois, where he spent many years as a farmer and stock raiser. He died in Montgomery County in January, 1906. He was a deacon in the Baptist Church and in politics a democrat. G. W. Thompson married Mary J. Rainey, who was born in Tennessee in 1840 and died in Montgomery County, Illinois, in 1876. Their children were: Cynthia A., wife of W. A. Davis, a coal miner at Hornsby, Illinois; Louisa I., who lives in Decatur, Illinois, the widow of J. T. Owens, who was a railroad man, and died November 3, 1914; W. F. Thompson, a Baptist minister now located at Petersburg, Illinois; Judge W. W.; G. W., Jr., a breeder of fine stock at Girard, Kansas; and M. G. Thompson, who recently came from Valparaiso, Nebraska, to Parsons, and has bought a farm in Labette County.

As a boy Judge Thompson spent his time on a farm in Montgomery County, Illinois, attended the public schools there, and in 1884 attended the course of the high school at Litchfield. On leaving high school at the age of eighteen he came out to Kansas and for a time farmed at McCune in Crawford County. For more than twenty years he was successfully identified with farming and the raising of breeding stock in Labette County. Judge Thompson enjoys a high repute among the farmers in this section of Kansas, and is still identified with the industry as the owner of farming land. His principal farm consists of 160 acres and is situated in Liberty Township two miles south of Parsons. He also has a farm in Oswego Township, twenty acres of which are inside the city limits. His own home at Oswego, where he has resided since his election to the office of probate judge, is at 5 Illinois Street.

Since he was twenty-one years of age Judge Thompson has been actively interested in republican politics, and has filled a number of positions both of a political nature and involving public trusts. In 1910 he was proposed as a candidate for the office of county judge, was elected, and has since been regularly reelected at the end of each two years. In 1916 he was reelected for a fourth term with practically no important opposition. While living in Liberty Township he served a number of years on the school board and for four years was justice of the peace. He now has his offices in the courthouse at Oswego.

Judge Thompson is a deacon in the Baptist Church, and particularly in the early days took a very prominent part in the American Horse Thief Association. He was president of Lodge No. 193, A. H. T. A. in Liberty Township for seven years, was elected seven consecutive years as a state delegate and was a national delegate in 1909 at Fort Smith, Arkansas, and in 1910 at Jacksonville, Illinois. Judge Thompson is one of the five members of the Board of Public Welfare Club at Oswego, and for the past three years has served as a member of the city school board. He belongs to the Oswego Commercial Club. In 1886 in McCune, Kansas, he married Miss Alice M. Ross, daughter of R. M. and Jane (Marshall) Ross. Her father, now deceased, was a farmer in Crawford County, and her mother resides in McCune. Judge and Mrs. Thompson have six children: F. R. Thompson, who operates his father's old farm and stock ranch two miles south of Parsons; Grace L., wife of O. L. Gray, a farmer five miles south of Parsons; E. R. Thompson, who lives on his father's farm in Oswego; A. R. Thompson, who is a student in the Kansas State University at Lawrence, graduated from the Oswego High School in 1915, and is his father's deputy during vacations; Myrtle M., is a senior in the Oswego High School; and Mabel, the youngest, is in the eighth grade of the public schools.

KARL E. BAUERSFELD. One of the most prominent among the younger generation who are contributing to the advancement and prosperity of the smaller communities of Southeastern Kansas is Karl E. Bauersfeld, mayor of the thriving and progressive Town of Earleton, Neosho County, and cashier of the Earleton State Bank. Mayor Bauersfeld has been a resident of Earleton for but a little more than five years, but during this time has thoroughly established himself as a capable and energetic man of business, and in his official capacity has done much to aid civic advancement.

Karl E. Bauersfeld was born August 12, 1890, in Woodson County, Kansas, and is a son of G. and Martha (Shriber) Bauersfeld. His father was born near the City of Berlin, Germany, in 1858, and was twenty years of age when he came to the United States, settling in Wilson County, Kansas, as one of the early residents of that community. There he purchased 320 acres of land, which he developed into one of the fine properties of the section, and which he increased to 400 acres. He continued to be engaged in agricultural pursuits until his retirement, and is now living at Yates Center, Kansas. Mr. Bauersfeld is a republican and has served in the capacity of township treasurer. He is a member of the Evangelical Church and very active in its work. Mrs. Bauersfeld was also born in Germany, in 1861, and has been the mother of three children: A daughter who died in infancy; Karl E.; and Fred, who resides at Kansas City, Missouri, and is connected with the Kansas City Star.

Karl E. Bauersfeld grew up on his father's farm, and attended the public schools of Woodson County until he was eighteen years of age, at which time he enrolled as a student at the Central Business College, Kansas City, Missouri. On completing his course at that institution he became bookkeeper at the Gridley (Kansas) State Bank, but after one year the bank was sold and Mr. Bauersfeld entered a store at that place in the capacity of clerk. In 1911 he came to Earleton in the capacity of bookkeeper of the Earleton

Vol. IV—16

State Bank, and his faithful service and fine ability won him promotion to the cashiership in 1914, a position which he occupies at the present time. The Earleton State Bank was founded March 29, 1907, at which time the officers were: J. R. Chambers, president; J. Y. Converse, vice president; and A. W. Cook, cashier. The present officers are: J. R. Chambers (represented by estate as Mr. Chambers is deceased), president; O. M. Balch, vice president; and K. E. Bauersfeld, cashier. The bank has a capital of $10,000 and a surplus of $2,000, and is housed in a new brick bank building on Neodesha Street, which was erected in 1911. Mr. Bauersfeld is a careful and conservative banker, and is careful of the interests of the depositors, among whom he is very popular because of his unfailing courtesy and obliging manner.

Mr. Bauersfeld has always voted the republican ticket and wields a strong influence in politics in his community. In the office of mayor, to which he was elected in 1915, he has endeavored to give his adopted community a clean and serviceable administration, and his efforts have been productive of good results in the way of civic improvements. He belongs to the Evangelical Church, and is fraternally affiliated with the Ancient Order of United Workmen of Earleton and to Chanute Camp No. 64, Independent Order of Odd Fellows.

Mr. Bauersfeld was married in June, 1916, at Portland, Oregon, to Miss Pearl Brocaw, of that city, who was born at Burlington, Kansas.

M. S. McNABNEY, secretary-treasurer and manager of the Kansas Wholesale Grocery Company of Coffeyville, has had a very progressive career as a Kansas business man. He has lived in this state for thirty years or more. When a young man his ambition was to become a lawyer. There were others to think of besides himself, and in providing for them he had to give up such career and he thus found himself on a homestead claim in Western Kansas. From one step to another he made his way in the business world, and about ten years ago founded the wholesale grocery house which is now known to retail merchants all over Southeastern Kansas and is one of the important institutions of Coffeyville.

He was born at Coulterville, Perry County, Illinois, January 10, 1862, a son of James and Elizabeth A. (McNabney) McNabney. His parents bore the same surnames but were not related, and both were of Scotch descent, the name being originally spelled McNab. Both parents were born in the northern part of Ireland near Belfast. James McNabney was born in 1809, came to America in 1857, and died in Perry County, Illinois, in 1881. In Ireland he pursued the trade of cabinet maker, but was a farmer and stock raiser in Perry County, Illinois. After becoming an American citizen he voted the republican ticket, and was a very active member and supporter of the United Presbyterian Church. His wife survived him a number of years and died in Western Kansas in 1893. Their children were: Robert, who became a farmer and died in Lyon County, Kansas, at Americus in 1912, aged about sixty-eight; Elizabeth A., who is now living at Greeley, Colorado, the widow of John M. McMillan, who was a farmer; William, a retired land owner at Liberal, Kansas; Rebecca, wife of Rev. Mr. Blodgett, a minister of the Seventh Day Adventist Church, and they reside at College View, Nebraska; Anna is the wife of James Irvin, a retired farmer at Americus, Kansas;

Maggie married W. J. Craig, a farmer at Evans, Colorado; the seventh in age is M. S. McNabney.

At the time of his father's death M. S. McNabney was nineteen years of age. In the meantime he had attended the public schools of Perry County, Illinois, and for three years was a student in an academy. After leaving school he farmed from the age of eighteen until 1884, and then moved out to Kansas, and spent six years in Lyon County as a farmer. For one year of that time he read law, but having the responsibility of caring for his mother and sister he gave it up. From Lyon County he moved to Western Kansas and took up a claim of 160 acres. For three years he improved and cultivated that land, and was also engaged in the hardware and implement business.

Preparatory to the next step in his progress he went to Topeka and finished a course in shorthand, typewriting and bookkeeping in the Topeka Business College. During the next ten years Mr. McNabney was connected with the Davis Mercantile Company of Topeka. His experience in mercantile lines was also continued for several years with the Coffeyville Mercantile Company. In April, 1907, Mr. McNabney organized the Kansas Wholesale Grocery Company, and this firm started out on a modest scale with headquarters near the Missouri Pacific depot. In December, 1910, the company completed its new offices and warehouses, a two-story and basement building 70x160 feet, at the corner of Thirteenth and Willow streets near the Missouri Pacific station. The officers of this company are: H. W. Read, president; A. J. Robertson, vice president; and M. S. McNabney, secretary, treasurer, manager and buyer. Mr. McNabney is in fact the mainspring of the company's activities and success. He has built up the business until it supplies a large share of the local grocery trade in and around Coffeyville and is rapidly extending its territory. Mr. McNabney is also secretary of the Mission Oil Company and is a director of the Basement Sample Store.

He owns an attractive residence at 605 West Fifth Street, and some other residence property on West Ninth Street. Mr. McNabney is a republican, is a member of the Coffeyville Library Board, and has given much of his time for years to the interests of the Presbyterian Church. He has served as elder, was a trustee of the church nine years, and for eleven years was superintendent of its Sunday School. His fraternal affiliations are with Camp No. 665, Modern Woodmen of America, with the Triple Ties, with Lodge No. 1193, Loyal Order of Moose, with the Woodmen of the World, with the United Commercial Travelers, with the Sons and Daughters of Justice, all these organizations being represented at Coffeyville.

In 1893 at Topeka Mr. McNabney married Miss Maggie Wilson. Her father S. T. Wilson is a grocery merchant at Emporia, Kansas. To their marriage have been born five children: Grace, a senior in the Emporia College at Emporia; Roy, who graduated from the Coffeyville High School in 1916; Warren, a freshman in high school; Raymond and Margaret.

E. L. GRAHAM. The large industries of Coffeyville have brought to that community many men of ability from all parts of the world. One of those to be named in this class of energetic citizenship is E. L. Graham, treasurer and manager of the Acme

Foundry and Machine Company. Mr. Graham was the real founder of this business, and is an experienced foundry man, having served his apprenticeship many years ago in Kansas.

A native son of Kansas he was born at Neodesha June 25, 1877. This branch of the Graham family came originally from Scotland and lived for many years in the State of Ohio. His father L. H. Graham was born at Mount Sterling, Ohio, in 1847. He grew up in that state, and in 1871 became a Kansas pioneer, locating at Neodesha, where he followed the cattle and butcher business for a number of years. He left Neodesha in 1884, lived for a time at the old Village of Litchfield, which is no longer in existence, and in 1893 moved to Pittsburg, where he died in 1903. He was an active republican, a member of the Ancient Order of United Workmen and the Modern Woodmen of America, and industry and integrity characterized his career throughout. L. H. Graham married Marian A. Knapp, who was born in Ohio in 1855 and is still living at Pittsburg, Kansas. They reared a large family of children: Harry C., who is in the butcher and cattle business at Pittsburg; E. L. Graham; Frank, who died in infancy; Marian, who died unmarried at Pittsburg in 1913; Corresta, wife of Arthur Fletcher, an electrical engineer employed by the Jackson-Walker Coal and Mining Company at Frontenac, Kansas; Taylor and Lemuel, both of whom died in early boyhood; and Ray, who is bookkeeper and cashier for the Acme Foundry and Machine Company at Coffeyville; Ruth and Irma, both of whom live at Pittsburg with their mother, and the latter is a teacher in the public schools in Pittsburg.

The public schools of the old town of Litchfield, Kansas, supplied E. L. Graham with his early education, but left school and books at the age of thirteen and entered upon a practical career, spending three years with his father in the butcher business. After that he was engaged in mining coal up to 1896. Seeking a new trade and a larger field for his abilities, he learned the pattern maker's trade, and having become proficient was advanced in 1903 to the position of superintendent of the United Iron Works at Cherryvale, Kansas. Mr. Graham remained in that responsible position until 1913, and in 1914 came to Coffeyville and organized the Acme Foundry and Machine Company.

This is an industry of more than local importance. It does a general foundry and machine business, manufactures iron, brass and aluminum castings, and all kinds of machinery pattern works. The shops are located at the corner of Thirteenth and Beech streets. The executive officers of the company are: C. M. Hodshire, president; E. L. Graham, treasurer and manager; and Ray Graham, brother of E. L., secretary and cashier. Mr. E. L. Graham is also manager of the Coffeyville Salvage Company.

He shows a decided interest in local affairs, is a working member of the Chamber of Commerce, is a republican and is affiliated with Council No. 141 of the United Commercial Travelers at Independence, with Lodge No. 780 Benevolent and Protective Order of Elks at Independence, and Keystone Lodge No. 102 Ancient Free and Accepted Masons at Coffeyville.

On June 5, 1901, at Pittsburg he married Miss Maude Huff. Her father, now deceased, was a gardener and her mother is still living at Pittsburg. To their marriage have been born four children: Ethan C., born August 3, 1902; Glen, born July 26, 1906; Marie, born August 28, 1909; and Kenneth, born April 25, 1915.

FRED PERKINS. To acquire a name that is a synonym of business integrity and honor and that is entitled to the respect of an entire community is of itself one of the highest goals to which the ambition of a man can aspire. It is not something that can be attained in a few short years. It is the result of long continued energy, fair dealing and strict probity.

The people of Labette County know Fred Perkins not only as an old settler of that section but as a man who has carried a fine force and wholesomeness of character into all his relations with the community. For many years he has been and still is an active farmer in the county and in later years has built up an extensive business in farm loans and is president of the State Bank of Oswego.

He is one of the comparatively few Kansas men who can trace their ancestry in an unbroken line to the time when the Massachusetts Bay colony was established. His original American ancestor was John Perkins, who was born at Newent, Gloucestershire, England, in 1590. He sailed from Bristol, England, on December 1, 1630, with his family, and landed at Nantucket, Massachusetts, in May, 1631. He died in 1654. His son, Jacob Perkins, was born in England in 1624 and was six years of age when the family left England. He died in Massachusetts in 1699. The next generation was headed by Matthew Perkins, who was born in Connecticut and died in Chaplain of that state in 1773. Matthew Perkins, who was a farmer, married his wife when she was fifteen years of age, and their first child was born when she was sixteen. She became the mother of twelve children and lived to be eighty-seven years of age.

In the next generation was Ephraim Perkins, who was born at Chaplain, Connecticut, in 1745, spent his life as a farmer and died at Becket, Massachusetts, in 1813. Becket was the home of a number of generations of this family. Ephraim Perkins was the great-grandfather of Fred Perkins. The grandfather was Origen Augustus Perkins, who was born at Becket in 1785 and died at Becket in 1854. He spent all his life as a farmer.

Fred Perkins was born at Becket, Massachusetts, September 16, 1845, and is a son of C. O. Perkins. His father was born at Becket, September 22, 1820, and died at Thomasville, Georgia, in May, 1887. He was reared and married at Becket and was not only a farmer but a prominent business man of his town. His home throughout his life was at Becket, though his interests led him to various other states. He paid his first visit to Kansas in 1871, and spent much of his time in this state thereafter. In his home state and town he served as chairman of the school board many years, and was a republican and a member of the Congregational Church. C. O. Perkins married Serepta C. Snow, who was born in Becket in 1824 and died there in 1845. Of their marriage Fred Perkins was the only child. The father then married a sister of his first wife, Olive C. Snow. She was born in 1818 at Becket and died there in 1884. She became the mother of two children: Belle died in girlhood at Becket; Blanche lives at Dorchester, Massachusetts, the widow of R. F. Alger, who was a minister of the Baptist Church.

His early life Fred Perkins spent in his native Town of Becket. He attended the public schools there and in 1865 graduated from the Wilbraham Academy. For two years he was also a student in the University of Michigan at Ann Arbor. Mr. Perkins has been continuously identified with Southeastern Kansas since 1870 and was thus one of the early pioneers of Labette

County, locating there soon after the Indians left, and the land was open for settlement. He began farming at Oswego, and farming is the vocation that furnished him at least the foundation for his generous prosperity. He still owns about 900 acres, divided into several high class farms, situated north, south and west of Oswego. He devotes this land to diversified farming and is one of the leading raisers of Hereford cattle in the county. His comfortable home is situated on North Street in Oswego. He also owns the office building on Commercial Street where his own offices are. He is president of the State Bank of Oswego, and is senior member of the firm of Fred and C. S. Perkins, dealers in farm loans. They are one of the old and reliable firms in this line, and their business covers Southeastern Kansas, Southern Missouri, Northern Arkansas and Eastern Oklahoma.

While getting his creditable success Mr. Perkins has not neglected the public welfare. For fifteen years he served as a member of the city council of Oswego, and is president of the Labette County Good Roads Association. He is an independent republican, a member of the Oswego Commercial Club, and in Masonry is affiliated with Oswego Lodge No. 63, Ancient Free and Accepted Masons; Oswego Chapter No. 13, Royal Arch Masons, and Oswego Commandery No. 7, Knights Templar.

In September, 1869, at Becket, Massachusetts, Mr. Perkins married Miss Mary E. May of Woodstock, Connecticut. Her father, Thomas May, was a farmer. Of the seven children born to Mr. and Mrs. Perkins three now survive. A brief record of the children is as follows: Thomas, who died at the age of fourteen months; Charles Snow, who is a graduate of the State Normal School at Emporia and is now junior member of the firm of Fred and C. S. Perkins, farm loans, at Oswego; Clitus, who died at the age of eleven months; Olive May, who died at the age of one year; the fifth child died in infancy unnamed; Kate S., a graduate of the Oswego Woman's College, is the wife of W. E. McGregor of Oswego; Elizabeth M., also a graduate of Oswego College, is the wife of Ray Taylor, a jeweler at Oswego.

MARTIN J. KELLY. The removal of the Kelly family to Kansas nearly fifty years ago brought a remarkably virile and substantial stock of people into the state. Martin J. Kelly, who was a child at the time of the family removal, and for thirty years or more has kept himself very busily employed at farming, contracting, and banking, and is now cashier of the St. Paul State Bank at St. Paul. There were fourteen children, and as a family these children have made a mark in the world.

Their father was William E. Kelly, who was born in Tuam, Ireland, in 1839. He had all the natural wit and wisdom of the true Irishman, and was never at a loss for means to make himself independent in the world. When he was a small child his parents came to America and settled in Butler County, Ohio, where he was reared and married. He farmed there for a time, but soon after his marriage removed to Peoria County, Illinois. It was on the farm in that county that Martin J. Kelly was born August 17, 1865.

Four years later, in 1869, the family came to Kansas and located near Gardner in Johnson County. There William E. Kelly bought 160 acres of practically unimproved land, and made it the nucleus of a farm which had few peers in that populous and highly improved agricultural section. He was a very successful farmer, and in 1904 he retired and moved to Olathe, where he died in March, 1911. At the time of his death he owned 453 acres, and that body of land is still administered as an estate. William E. Kelly was a republican, a member of the Catholic Church and of the Knights of Columbus, and he had a great host of loyal friends and few enemies. He married Catherine Dowd, who was born in Connaught, Ireland, in 1838 and died at Olathe, Kansas, in November, 1910.

The pride which these parents took in their children was entirely justified. As already stated there were fourteen of them. Brief reference to their names and respective positions in the world is as follows: William H., a grain dealer at Edgerton, Kansas; Mary I., wife of W. D. Hendricks, who is in the insurance business at Olathe; J. D. Kelly, a general contractor at Kansas City, Missouri; Thomas T., whose name is known all over Kansas by his former service as state treasurer and is a contractor at Paola; Edward E., who died on the old farm at Gardner, Kansas, at the age of twenty-five; Margaret, who died at Wichita in 1912, the widow of William Sherr, who was a farmer; Martin J.; Rev. Bernard S., who is pastor of the Catholic Cathedral at Leavenworth, Kansas; Ella C., wife of Martin Geer, a rancher in Montana; Marian, a Sister of Charity at Topeka; Joseph A., in the real estate and loan business at Kansas City, Missouri; Anna, wife of J. A. Marshall, a farmer and livestock auctioneer at Gardner; Frank X. and Charles M., both on the old farm in Johnson County.

Martin J. Kelly spent the first twenty-one years of his life on his father's farm. In the meantime he attended the public schools of Johnson County. On starting out for himself he and his brother Thomas began farming a place in partnership in Miami County, and they remained there eight years. After that for fifteen years Martin Kelly was associated with his brother, William H., in the milling and grain business at Edgerton. He and his brother, Thomas, again resumed relations as partners, and joined the Lantry Contracting Company of Strong City, Kansas, and for eighteen months they were engaged in building one of the most monumental pieces of railway construction in America, Raton Tunnel, near the City of Raton, New Mexico.

Since then Mr. Kelly has given his principal attention to banking. From 1900 until September 1, 1915, he was president and cashier of the Edgerton State Bank, and on October 1, 1915, became cashier of the St. Paul State Bank.

The St. Paul State Bank was established in 1892, its first officers being Paul Kimball, president; Walter Petty, vice president; and H. C. Carpenter, cashier. In October, 1915, a consolidation was effected between this bank and the Mission Bank. The present officers are: Patrick Diskin, president; B. B. Fitzsimmons, vice president; and Martin J. Kelly, cashier. The bank has its paid up capital stock of $20,000 and surplus and undivided profits of $6,500. The bank is well situated on Central Avenue at St. Paul.

Mr. Kelly is also a stockholder in the Midwest National Bank of Kansas City, Missouri. Politically he has always been a republican. For eight years he served as mayor of Edgerton. He is a member of the Catholic Church, and of St. Paul Council No. 760 of the Knights of Columbus. He and his family reside in a comfortable residence which they own on Main Street. In February, 1895, at Edgerton, Mr. Kelly married Miss Grace Scott. Her father, G. W. Scott, is a retired lumber dealer living at Kansas City, Missouri. Mrs. Kelly died at Edgerton in 1900, leaving two children, Paul, who assists his father in

the bank, and Harold, who is a student in the St. Francis School at St. Paul. In 1912, at Kansas City, Missouri, Mr. Kelly married for his present wife Miss Minnie Harrington, daughter of D. A. Harrington, a retired contractor living at Kansas City, Missouri. Mr. and Mrs. Kelly have three children, Martin J., William H. and Mary Catherine.

THOMAS C. HARBOURT. A resident for thirty-eight years is not the only distinction of Thomas C. Harbourt at Coffeyville. He is a man of wide interests and activities, has been a contractor and builder, has filled many local offices with credit and efficiency, and is one of the best known men in fraternal circles in Southeastern Kansas. He is still active in business, handles real estate, and is also a justice of the peace.

His earlier years were spent in Ohio. His people were of German stock, lived in old Virginia some years, and afterwards identified themselves with the abolition movement in Ohio. Thomas C. Harbourt was born in Jefferson County, Ohio, September 25, 1849. His grandfather Peter Harbourt was born in Germany in 1783, came to this country when a young man, lived in old Virginia for some years and about 1840 established his home in Jefferson County, Ohio. He served all through the war with Mexico, but his chief pursuit was as a farmer. Of his children the only one now living is Cromwell O., who is a retired oil producer and operator in Harrison County, Ohio. Mr. Harbourt's grandfather in the maternal line was Samuel McClain, who was born and married in Scotland, and soon after his marriage emigrated to America, becoming a farmer, and afterwards moving to Jefferson County, Ohio, where he died before Thomas C. Harbourt was born.

John B. Harbourt, father of Thomas C., was born near Hot Springs, Virginia, in 1814. He grew up in that locality, but in 1839 moved out of Virginia across the Ohio River into the rugged country west of Wheeling in Jefferson County. He remained there and conducted his farm until his death in 1892. Like many of the people living in the hills west of the Ohio River in Jefferson County he was an ardent abolitionist, and his house was one of the stations on the underground railway whereby many a fugitive slave from the South found refuge until his progress toward freedom in Canada could be advanced. John B. Harbourt was an intimate friend of Alexander Clark, editor of the Pittsburg Christian Advocate. He voted for Harrison, the whig candidate, in 1840 and afterwards became a republican. He filled a number of local offices, was a member of the state militia, and was a very devout Methodist and class leader in the church. John B. Harbourt married Rachel McClain, who was born in Washington County, Pennsylvania, in 1817 and died in Jefferson County, Ohio, in 1898. Their children were: Catherine, who died in Jefferson County, Ohio, at the age of thirty-nine; Thomas C.; George H., a farmer in Columbiana County, Ohio; Mary E., wife of Samuel Watt, a farmer in Jefferson County, Ohio; John W., a railroad man connected with the Wellsville and Cleveland Railroad, with home at Wellsville; Thursa E., wife of John Swickard, a farmer of Jefferson County; W. W. Harbourt, who has been a farmer and now lives in Columbiana County, Ohio; Ida M., wife of John Miler, of Hammondsville, Ohio; and the ninth and youngest, a daughter died in infancy.

During his early youth spent in Jefferson County,

B. F. Dawson

Thomas C. Harbourt attended the district schools, and after reaching his majority went to Richmond, Ohio, and was a student in the United Presbyterian College, paying his way all through the course and graduating in 1871 with a teacher's certificate. Though qualified for teaching, he never followed that profession, and instead, in January, 1872, removed to Defiance County, Ohio, where he entered the lumber and milling business.

In March, 1878, from Ohio Mr. Harbourt came to Coffeyville, Kansas, and was thus identified with that community in the very early days, when the town was in fact as well as in name the Gate City to Indian Territory. For a number of years he carried on an extensive business as a contractor and builder, and many of the homes and other structures in and around Coffeyville testify to his workmanship.

The honors of office fell upon him early during his residence at Coffeyville, and he served as chief of police in 1880, again in 1883, 1897, 1901 and 1902. He was marshal of the court of Coffeyville from 1903 to 1908. For ten years at different times Mr. Harbourt has served as justice of the peace and is now discharging the duties of that office. In connection he handles real estate, and has his offices in the Odd Fellows Building. His residence and home is at 116 West Second Street. As an officer of the law he had some interesting and exciting experiences particularly in the early days, and from 1888 to 1892 rode as deputy United States marshal for the Fort Smith court when Judge Parker was judge of that tribunal.

A believer in the principles of fraternalism, he has been identified with different orders and has done much effective work in maintaining them. For thirty-six years he has been affiliated with Star Lodge No. 117, Independent Order of Odd Fellows at Coffeyville, has filled all the chairs of the local lodge, has been representative in the Grand Lodge five times; is a member of Gate City Encampment No. 80, with which he has been identified for twenty-five years, and belongs to Canton No. 14, Patriarchs Militant at Coffeyville, and is now serving as secretary of the Department Council of Kansas with the rank of lieutenant colonel. He is also a charter member of the Ancient Order of United Workmen at Coffeyville, which was founded there twenty-seven years ago on May 29, 1889, and he has filled every office in Lodge No. 279, and is now recorder, and for several terms was master workman and has also represented the local order in the grand lodge. For the past thirty years Mr. Harbourt has been affiliated with Coffeyville Lodge No. 89, Knights of Pythias, of which he is past chancellor commander. He was one of the charter members of the A. H. T. A. at Coffeyville, has been one of its most active workers, and is the oldest man in consecutive membership of the local order. He was formerly a member of the Coffeyville Commercial Club, and belongs to the Montgomery County Fair Association at Coffeyville.

In 1871 in Richmond, Ohio, Mr. Harbourt married Miss Jennie S. Shelly, daughter of Benjamin Shelly, now deceased, who was a farmer. Mrs. Harbourt died January 12, 1914, leaving two sons: Charles R., who is a graduate in pharmacy from the University of Kansas, and is now owner of the Kane drug store at Coffeyville; W. W. Harbourt, who is a contractor and builder at West Coffeyville. On October 12, 1915, Mr. Harbourt married Mrs. Josephine (LeCroix) Podvant, widow of L. A. Podvant.

BENJAMIN FRANKLIN DAWSON. Among the early settlers in Kansas was Benjamin Franklin Dawson, who came to the state in 1855 and selected a home in what is now Shawnee County and maintained it here throughout life. He was one of the sturdy, solid men of his time and was justly admired and respected for his honorable and upright life, for his many acts of benevolence and charity, and for the example he set of worthily filling the place allotted to him by Divine decree.

Benjamin Franklin Dawson was born in Terre Haute, Vigo County, Indiana, December 2, 1828. His father, Thomas W. Dawson, was a native of Virginia but moved with his people to Indiana in the formative period of that commonwealth, and in the early history of Illinois, located in Edgar County and subsequently took part in the Black Hawk war. In their declining years he and wife moved to Topeka, Kansas, and there passed the remainder of their days.

On the home farm in Illinois, Benjamin F. Dawson passed his youthful days, assisting his father and attending the district schools in the neighborhood. From a scholastic standpoint, he would 'not, at the present time, have been considered a well educated man, but as he was gifted with more than the average of intelligence, read much and had a retentive memory, he was generally considered far better informed than the average among his neighbors. He inherited, perhaps, a pioneer instinct, and in 1855 his acquired interest in the West, especially Kansas, led to his determination to come to the state and secure a home on her beautiful prairies near one of her life-giving rivers.

Mr. Dawson's journey to Kansas from Illinois was made in one of the pioneer "prairie schooners" made familiar to every present day schoolboy through poem, romance and moving picture, and six weeks elapsed from the time of departure until his arrival. The present stately City of Topeka was not then on the map and the site was merely a frontier village. Mr. Dawson lost no time in preempting the southwest quarter of section 27, town 11, range 16, and here he passed the subsequent years of his life, toiling early and late to make a home worthy of his loved ones. On this place he spent sixty busy years and it was a source of satisfaction to him, as age crept on, that they had not been lived in vain. In the matter of worldy acquisition, Mr. Dawson was successful. As a citizen, he bore more than his share of the burden of aiding in the erection of churches and schoolhouses, of road building and general improvement. He was a member of the school board for forty years and helped build three school houses.

In the dark days prior to the breaking out of the Civil war, Benjamin F. Dawson was known as a stanch Unionist. When General Price invaded Kansas, Mr. Dawson enlisted in the state militia and was a member of Captain Huntoon's company in the regiment commanded by Colonel Veale. In the movement to check the advance of the enemy, Mr. Dawson was made a prisoner, at the Battle of the Blue, but was shortly afterward paroled.

The domestic life of Mr. Dawson was one of happiness and content. He was united in marriage to Susan M. Wade, whose father, William B. Wade, was a member of the first Kansas Territorial Legislature and a prominent factor in early days in this state. Six children were born to Mr. and Mrs. Dawson: Carrie, Mary, Mrs. Emma Lanham, Mrs. Julia Gill, William T., and Frank N. Mr. and Mrs. Dawson and their family were all members of the Presbyterian Church.

Mr. Dawson's life covered a remarkable period in the history not only in Kansas but in the whole world. In his way and in his own environment and limited only by circumstances, he did his part. In his own avocation he saw the sickle succeeded by the cradle in the gathering of the harvests, the first crude harvesters come into use and the modern triumphs of farm machinery succeeding. He witnessed the great strides in human achievement in the development and use of steam and electricity, and, with a profound faith in the illimitable power of the One who had so wonderfully directed his own life, he set no limit to the progress future ages may disclose.

William T. Dawson was born on the home farm March 3, 1871. He and his brother and all his sisters were born on that homestead. He received his early education in Topeka schools and business college, and for a number of years has had active charge of that old homestead. For the last eleven years he has been identified with the real estate business in Topeka, and for the past three years has been assessor of real estate in that city.

Mr. Dawson is an active member of the Second United Presbyterian Church, is a member of the Independent Order of Odd Fellows and a republican. On September 25, 1902, he married Miss Edna Ione Reed, daughter of Joseph Reed. Their two children are Louise and Eleanor.

WILLIAM B. WADE. When the pioneers of 1854, who were men of solid worth, as was William B. Wade, later a member of the First Territorial Legislature of Kansas, came to Shawnee County, it was for the peaceful conquest of the soil and for the establishing of permanent homes in which they could rear their families to succeed them with credit to state and parentage. These pioneers were home-seekers, not restless, irresponsible wanderers, and, while many brought a measure of capital, all came with sturdy, industrious habits insuring the earning of it. The historian of today looks back over the intervening period and may, with admiring wonder, contemplate some of the hardships which faced our pioneers of sixty years ago that they overcame through their courage and resourcefulness. History on many a printed page, has told the story of danger and conflict that ensued with the coming of the white man into Kansas, and in 1854 there was still serious menace. While pioneer life was necessarily simple, the most primitive demands of existence made striving necessary, and in Shawnee County self denial was obligatory and the merest comfort a luxury. With no adequate means of heating the rude log cabins, into which came frequently the deepest mysteries of life (birth and death), with no machinery and often with no tools with which to clear or cultivate the wild land secured from the government, with no modern methods of transportation and often with no reachable markets for sale of products or purchase of supplies, the mere preservation of life presented serious problems. Added to the strain of hard labor, social recreations as such, were often unknown and the tension on strained nerves was as harmful as on overworked muscles.

Nevertheless, with knowledge of such conditions and unawed by them, William B. Wade left the comforts and civilizating influences of his eastern home and in 1854 came to Kansas. In his native state he had been a man of some importance and the time came when, from situations as above pictured, in his new home he developed public order and secured financial independence. His superiority in education, judgment and faithful devotion to public interests were soon acknowledged by the other settlers and he was chosen their representative in that remarkable body of statesmen, the First Territorial Legislature of Kansas. There were no railroads through Shawnee County at that time and Mr. Wade rode on horseback, as did our distinguished legislators in colonial days, to attend the session and take part in its deliberations.

William B. Wade was born near Richmond, Wayne County, Indiana, and was a son of Thomas and Mary Wade. Undoubtedly they were of New England ancestry and probably of old Quaker stock. Indiana still claims many of the name. An agricultural life was chosen by William B. Wade but the spirit of enterprise also possessed him and hence removal was made first to La Salle County, Illinois, and from there, in 1854, to Kansas. He located first on a claim on Rock Creek, near Meriden, in Jefferson County. The trip was a long and tiresome one at that time, the travelers finding railroad accommodations only to St. Louis, Missouri. They journeyed up the river to Leavenworth and there hired teams to take them to their destination. During the three years that they lived on Rock Creek a one-room cabin was the family home. It was often visited by the Indians and the wild beasts of the prairies had not yet been exterminated. It was while he yet lived on Rock Creek that Mr. Wade was elected to the territorial legislature and helped to build the constitution of the state. In 1857 he removed with his family to the northwest corner of what is now Tecumseh Township, Shawnee County. During his declining years he sold the place and removed to Topeka, living a retired life in that city until his death in 1895, when aged eighty-two years.

William B. Wade was united in marriage with Caroline Burbank, who was born in Vermont. Seven children were born to this union, six of whom grew to maturity, and of the three survivors one is Mrs. Susan Dawson, who is the widow of Benjamin Franklin Dawson, formerly of Shawnee County.

William B. Wade was a stanch Free Soil man and many political battles were fought in those early days between the Free Soil and the Pro-slavery factions. Mr. Wade never relinquished his principles and in this regard had the hearty cooperation of two of his sons, Samuel B. and Spencer P., both of whom are now deceased. He was influential in the Masonic fraternity. Generosity and kindness marked his personal attitude to every one. No history of Shawnee County would be complete without honorable mention of this early settler and legislator.

CHARLES O. TALLMAN, one of the leading business men of Fort Scott, is a son of the late Thomas W. Tallman, whose career reflects much of the history of Fort Scott and Bourbon County from pioneer times until the present century.

Bourbon County never had a more forceful character nor a man of greater popularity, than the late Thomas W. Tallman. He was born in Burlington County, New Jersey, October 25, 1826, and was eighty-nine years of age when he passed away December 27, 1915. His parents were Woodmanse and Elizabeth (Read) Tallman, also natives of New Jersey. Woodmanse Tallman's father was Thomas Tallman, an Englishman, who came to America and was a man of large means. He had a large family of sons and when Woodmanse Tallman received his inheritance he moved out to Logan County, Ohio, settling on a farm, where he continued prosperous and successful and reared eleven children. The late Thomas W. Tallman was the fifth of these eleven sons, and was five years of age when his parents moved to Logan County. His early life was spent in that pioneer district, and he attended one of the subscription schools held there. He grew up on a farm but at the age of eighteen became a trader, buying and selling horses and also conducting a livery stable, and he spent much of his time at West Liberty and Bellefontaine. At Bellefontaine he met and in October, 1855, married Catherine Austin.

In the spring of 1856 Thomas W. Tallman made his first trip out to Kansas. There were no railroads at that time and from Kansas City he and five other men drove a team and wagon to Fort Scott. Fort Scott was then important mainly as the seat of the land office and as a military post. His first view of Fort Scott was obtained April 20, 1857, and soon afterward he bought 160-acre claim on the east side of the old town. He filed on this claim and proved it up. He bought other land, and on his claim he erected one of the best log houses then seen in that entire country. The following year he brought his family from Ohio. They journeyed by railroad to the terminus at Jefferson City, Missouri, and from there they came with wagon and team to Fort Scott. Thomas W. Tallman was one of the pioneer farmers of Bourbon County, and his enterprise enabled him to develop one of the best farms in the county in early years. He had hardly become well established when the border troubles broke out, and for eight or nine years his home was more or less constantly in danger. He often did guard duty at Fort Scott, and he kept his family in the city much of the time. When he first arrived at Fort Scott there were not more than 200 people in the town, and most of them lived within the boundaries of the old fort.

In the course of time his farm land became more valuable for other purposes than raising crops, and the eastern portion of the present city is built upon the land once owned by Thomas W. Tallman. When the Kansas City, Fort Scott & Gulf Railroad came through the company bought 100 acres of the Tallman Estate for the purposes of yards and roundhouse, and subsequently other portions of the land were laid out in city lots.

Soon after he became a resident of Fort Scott the territorial governor appointed him one of the county commissioners to lay off Bourbon County into townships, and he filled that office three years. He was elected in 1878 to the State Legislature and served two terms. He was always an ardent democrat and though living in a strongly republican district, his personal popularity and the confidence reposed in him by his fellow citizens, gave him official honors without regard to partisan questions. While in the Legislature he was one of the few democrats who voted for submitting the questions of state wide prohibition to the people and then and always he labored consistently and energetically on behalf of the prohibition cause. Thomas W. Tallman was the first democrat who was ever elected to the office of sheriff in Bourbon County, and he filled that office with characteristic efficiency for four years. There were any number of stanch republicans in Bourbon County who would never fail to give their vote for Tom Tallman.

In 1890 Mr. Tallman bought the Chicago Lumber Company, which had been established in 1887 during the boom days in Fort Scott. He acquired this business largely to give his sons a business start, and was only to a slight extent identified with its management personally. Thomas W. Tallman was a charter member of the Independent Order of Odd Fellows, in the lodge organized at Fort Scott in 1858, and at the time of his death was the last of the original charter members. His wife died May 26, 1900, at the age of seventy-four. Five children were born to their marriage, and the following paragraphs contain some individual reference to these different children.

Emma, the oldest, who died at Fort Scott, married William M. Davis, and her only surviving daughter Catherine is now the wife of Rev. J. H. Gross, a Presbyterian minister, and they reside in Marietta, Ohio.

Frank A. Tallman, who was born in Bourbon County, January 1, 1859, was educated in the country schools and in the schools of Fort Scott, and his first business experience was in association with his brother Charles in the commission business at Salt Lake City, Utah, where they remained two years. After selling out his interests in Salt Lake he spent several years in the commission business at Helena and Butte, Montana, and then returned to Fort Scott to take charge of the lumber business previously acquired by his father. Since Thomas W. Tallman's death his sons Frank and Charles have continued the lumber business, and it is now the largest concern of its kind in the city. Frank Tallman married Mrs. Sarah (Stevenson) Baker. Politically he is a democrat.

Charles O. Tallman, who was born in Bourbon County November 20, 1860, was educated in the local schools and in the old Kansas Normal School, and began his career as a fireman on the Kansas City, Fort Scott and Gulf Railroad. He was promoted to freight and then to passenger engineer, and he had for several years a run on the old Memphis and Missouri Pacific System between Fort Scott and Topeka. For seven years he continued railroading, and then resigned to enter the commission business at Salt Lake City with his brother Frank. Later he was manager of the Capital Hotel at Boise, Idaho, for two years, and also spent some time in Seattle, Washington, and Portland, Oregon. Since his return to Fort Scott he has had an active share as a partner with his brother Frank in the lumber business. Mr. Charles O. Tallman is also a director of the Citizens National Bank, a position which his father held for many years. He is an active democrat, served two years as city treasurer, two years in the city council, and in 1915 was elected a city commissioner.

On November 17, 1899, at Fort Scott Charles O. Tallman married Miss Leota Noel of Bourbon County. Her father Eli Noel, who was born in Indiana, settled near Uniontown in Bourbon County and was a farmer there until some years ago and is now manufacturer of the Noel automobile at Kansas City, Missouri. Mr. and Mrs. Charles Tallman have two sons: Thomas Noel Tallman and Harry Tallman.

Elizabeth L. Tallman, the fourth child of Thomas L. Tallman, died after her marriage to George E. Ware of Fort Scott, and left three children, Ida, Thomas and Mary Ware.

Fannie Tallman, the fifth child, who died in 1900, was the wife of John H. Crain, a well known attorney of Fort Scott. They had three children: Helen

E. Crain born April 26, 1891; John Tallman Crain born March 4, 1892; and Margaret E. Crain, born May 3, 1890, and now the wife of Roy S. Johnson of Newkirk, Oklahoma.

CHARLES SAMUEL BENDURE, M. D. One of the best known families in Southeastern Kansas is the Bendures. Many of the name have gained honorable distinction in their several vocations, and among them is Charles Samuel Bendure, one of the widely known physicians of Labette County, who has practiced for a quarter of a century at Bartlett.

He traces his descent along the Bendure line to France originally, but the family has been represented in America since colonial times and were among the pioneers of the Green Mountain state. His grandfather, Stephen Weeks Bendure, was born in Vermont in 1803. He was reared in that state, was an early settler in Ohio, thence moved to Indiana and later to Illinois, and he died while on a visit in Cowley County, Kansas, in 1877. By occupation he was a farmer.

W. H. Bendure, father of Doctor Bendure, was born in Xenia, Greene County, Ohio, March 16, 1838. In 1852, when he was fourteen years of age, his parents moved to Marshall County, Indiana, and he was reared and married there. He was both a farmer and carpenter, and was one of those faithful and skillful masters of the latter trade who had a mechanical efficiency such as few carpenters of the present day could measure up to. It is said that he would go into the timber, hew the logs and then convert them into frames for a house, performing practically every step in the building of a home from the time the timber was standing in the forest until the house was ready for occupancy. W. H. Bendure moved to Kansas and arrived in Neosho County on May 29, 1870. He homesteaded a claim of 160 acres there, and while developing it also followed his trade for ten years. In 1880 he moved to Longton, Kansas, where he was in the mercantile business for a year, and then traded for a farm in Elk County, on which he lived three years. In 1885 he went south into the old Indian Territory, taking a lease upon some land thirty-five miles south of Vinita. He remained there until 1889, the year when the original Oklahoma was first opened to settlement. Returning to Labette County, Kansas, he bought an eighty-acre farm which he occupied two years, and on selling that engaged in the hardware and implement business in Bartlett. He was one of the pioneer merchants there, but after three years sold his stock and on September 16, 1893, participated in the opening of the Cherokee Strip in Oklahoma. He made the run and was successful in obtaining 160 acres. After proving up his claim and occupying it as a farm until 1899 he sold out and bought another farm north of Howard in Greenwood County, Kansas. At the end of three years he sold that and went to Dutch Mills in Arkansas, buying a farm nearby and a residence in the town. That was his home until his death on December 18, 1913. W. H. Bendure was an active republican, but after the war became a democrat and actively supported that party until 1892. He then became aligned with the union labor ticket and with other parties advocating social and economic reforms. He was an active member of the Cumberland Presbyterian Church. W. H. Bendure also made an army record. During the Civil war he was for three years a gallant soldier in the Eighty-fifth Indiana Volunteer Infantry.

W. H. Bendure married Rebecca J. Stallard, who was born in Rush County, Indiana, in 1841, and is still living at Coffeyville, Kansas. Her children were:

Ollie, who died at the age of eighteen months; Dr. Charles S.; C. B., who is a blacksmith by trade and is now street commissioner and city marshal at Mound Valley, Kansas; Ida Rosetta, wife of C. L. Lane, an auctioneer living at Coffeyville; N. F., who is a teamster in the factory of the National Sash and Door Company at Coffeyville; A. E., a blacksmith at Independence, Kansas; W. V., who is employed by the Cudahy Refining Company at Coffeyville.

One of these children, Dr. Charles Samuel Bendure, was born near Plymouth in Marshall County, Indiana, August 3, 1860. He received his early education in the schools of Kansas, and for the first twenty-two years of his life lived on his father's farm. In 1882 he entered the University Medical School at Kansas City, remained there for a time, and by private instruction was qualified for practice. He practiced one year at Sedan, Kansas, then at Harts Mills three years, looked after the welfare of the residents around Vinita, Oklahoma, for four years, and in 1889 returned to Kansas and identified himself permanently with Bartlett in Labette County. Since then he has conducted a general medical and surgical practice. Doctor Bendure graduated from the University of Kansas Medical Department with the degree of M. D. in 1897.

His offices are on Main Street, and he owns his home at the corner of Sixth and Hackberry streets. For many years Doctor Bendure has served as city health officer of Bartlett. He was clerk of the school board in 1890 when the district was formed out of five other districts, and has always taken a great interest in schools and every other institution reflecting the welfare of the community. He is a member in good standing of the Labette County Medical Society, the Southeastern Medical Society, and politically is a socialist.

In 1883 in Elk County, Kansas, Doctor Bendure married Miss Ellen M. Ashmore. Her father, Judge R. N. Ashmore, was for many years probate judge of Elk County, but is now living retired at the age of eighty-six in the State of Washington. Doctor and Mrs. Bendure have four children: Harl W., who is connected with the Topeka Iron Bridge Works and spends much of his time on different contracts for that company in various localities; Harvey Leonard, who is a brakeman with the Missouri, Kansas & Texas Railway living at Parsons; William N.; Gertrude May, who lives at home and is attending the public schools of Bartlett. The son, William N., is now postmaster at Bartlett, and is one of the brilliant young men of Southeastern Kansas. He has recently been admitted to the Kansas bar, and has for a number of years been active in democratic politics. He was born at Bartlett in 1890, and has depended upon his own exertions to push him ahead in the world. For a time he read medicine under his father, but gave up the idea of becoming a physician and studied law. He worked hard at other occupations while getting his legal education, and was graduated from the Hamilton College of Law at Chicago in 1916. He has been postmaster of Bartlett since November 23, 1914, and in 1915 was journal clerk in the State Legislature. Will N. Bendure was married July 2, 1913, to Miss Estella M. Long, who was a well known teacher in Labette County before her marriage. Mr. and Mrs. Will Bendure have one child, Mary Ellen, born June 22, 1915.

WILLIAM N. BENDURE is now serving as postmaster at Bartlett, and is one of the young but very influential figures in democratic politics in that section of the state. He was admitted to the bar in January, 1917.

Mr. Bendure was born at Bartlett, February 6, 1890, a son of Dr. Charles Samuel Bendure, a prominent physician of Bartlett for many years. Doctor Bendure was born in Marshall County, Indiana, August 3, 1860, a son of W. H. and Rebecca J. (Stallard) Bendure. W. H. Bendure had a very notable career and was one of the very earliest settlers of Labette County. He first came to Kansas in 1870, lived on a homestead in Neosho County for ten years, then went to Longton, and after varied experiences in Kansas he entered the Indian Territory in 1885 and was engaged in farming there for four years. He was one of the pioneer business men of Bartlett in Labette County, but afterwards sold out and made the run into the Cherokee Strip in 1893. He finally bought a farm in Arkansas, where he died.

Dr. Charles S. Bendure, who was the second in a family of seven children, spent his early life on his father's farm, chiefly in Kansas, and began the practice of medicine nearly thirty-five years ago. He practiced in Kansas and also in Oklahoma, but since 1889 has been caring for a large general practice at Bartlett. He was given the M. D. degree in the College of Physicians and Surgeons at Kansas City, Kansas, in 1897. Besides practicing medicine he has also been a prominent worker in the civic ranks of Labette County and his home town. Doctor Bendure was married in 1883 to Miss Ellen M. Ashmore, whose father, R. N. Ashmore, was for many years probate judge of Elk County, Kansas. Doctor Bendure and wife had a family of four children: Harl W., Harvey Leonard, William N. and Gertrude May.

William N. Bendure was born at Bartlett, Kansas, February 6, 1890. He received his early education in the public schools of his native village, and graduating at the age of fourteen he had the equivalent of a high school education. He has been self supporting since he was eleven years of age, and is a man of good natural gifts and abilities and of a great degree of energy to make the best use of all his opportunities. In 1905 he attended the Fredonia Business College.

For a year and a half Mr. Bendure studied medicine with his father. From Bartlett he then moved to Oswego, where he took up the study of law with the Hon. Francis M. Brady, first assistant to the United States district attorney of Kansas City, Kansas. After his return to Bartlett Mr. Bendure took extension work, and in 1916 was awarded the degree LL. B. by Hamilton College of Law at Chicago.

He is a very active democrat and on November 29, 1914, Thanksgiving Day, was appointed postmaster at Bartlett, an office he still fills with credit to himself and in a most satisfactory manner to the patrons of the office. During the session of 1915 Mr. Bendure was journal clerk of the State Legislature.

He was formerly a stockholder in the Conklin Mortgage Company of Wichita. He is affiliated with Lodge No. 458 of the Independent Order of Odd Fellows at Bartlett, in which he has held several of the chairs. He organized the Citizens Concert Band at Bartlett for the purpose of boosting the town and he has always played one of the instruments in that band of thirty-four pieces, which has a more than local reputation as a musical organization. Mr. Bendure belongs to the Sons and Daughters of Justice and to the Rebekahs.

On July 2, 1913, at Carthage. Missouri, he married Miss Estella M. Long, a daughter of Addison and Mary (Detchon) Long, both of whom are now deceased. Her father was at one time a retired farm owner at Chetopa, Kansas. Mr. and Mrs. Bendure have one daughter, Mary Ellen, born June 22, 1915. Mrs. Bendure is a graduate of the Chetopa High School and the Kansas State Manual Training Normal at Pittsburg, and has a life teacher's certificate. She taught one year in Bartlett and three years in Chetopa before her marriage. Mrs. Bendure was born in East Palestine, Ohio, and her parents moved to Kansas in 1890, locating in Chetopa. It was in Chetopa that she grew to womanhood and received most of her education. She is an active member of the Rebekahs and of the Bartlett Band Boosters Club.

CHARLES SAMUEL STRAHAN, M. D. While Doctor Strahan has the distinction of having been the mayor of Galesburg, Kansas, his high standing in that community is chiefly due to his long and active practice as a physician and surgeon. Doctor Strahan fought many battles with circumstances before he was able to gain his ambition and enter upon the practice of medicine, and throughout life has been a hard worker, conscientious in all his dealings, and has thoroughly deserved every item of his success.

The Strahan family is of Scotch-Irish origin, and Doctor Strahan's grandfather, Robert, was a native of Scotland, came to America and settled in Virginia and afterwards went across the mountains into Kentucky, and followed farming until his death in Fleming County, Kentucky. He died before Doctor Strahan was born.

The next generation of the family is represented by Samuel Strahan, who was born in Virginia in 1812. He grew to manhood in Fleming County, Kentucky, where he married. In early years he was a stock buyer, but in 1844 he removed to Randolph County along the east line of the State of Indiana and was a farmer there until his death in 1896. He was a republican voter and a member of the Methodist Episcopal Church. Samuel Strahan married Martha Hunt, who was born in Fleming County, Kentucky, in 1821 and died in Randolph County, Indiana, in 1894. She became the mother of seven children: Clement R., who died in Randolph County, Indiana, in 1913, was a tile manufacturer and also postmaster at Huntsville, Indiana, and saw active service, though a boy at the time, in the Union army during the Civil war; Russell P., is a resident of Muncie, Indiana; Basil H. is in the livery business at Parker, Indiana; the fourth in age is Dr. Charles S.; Nathan U. lives on a farm near Winchester, Indiana, and at one time held the office of sheriff of Randolph, County; Mrs. Hattie French lives in Indianapolis; James F. is a farmer near Winchester, Indiana.

Charles Samuel Strahan was born on his father's farm in Randolph County, Indiana, October 19, 1861, and up to the age of seventeen he lived with his parents on that farm. During that time he improved the advantages afforded by the public schools. Without means to pursue his higher education, he began doing for himself, farming, working out by the month, and attending school at brief intervals every winter. That was his general experience up to the age of twenty-one. For two years he pursued the reading of medicine under Dr. H. C. Hunt at Huntsville, Indiana. After that he was able to take a term of lectures in the Indiana Eclectic Medical College at Indianapolis, and for two years he gained some knowledge useful in his subsequent work by employment in a drug store at Farmland, Indiana. In 1890 Doctor Strahan came out to Kansas, lived in the western part of the state for a time, then at Mound Valley, and in 1892 he identified himself with the community of Galesburg, where he has since practiced medicine and surgery along general lines.

Doctor Strahan owns his office building on Main Street, his home on Center Street, and also has another house in the west part of town.

As already stated he was the first mayor elected by the City of Galesburg and filled the office to the satisfaction of all concerned for four years. He was a member of the school board for fifteen years and part of the time was treasurer. He is a democrat, and is affiliated with Galesburg Lodge of the Independent Order of Odd Fellows.

On June 26, 1886, at Winchester, Indiana, he married Miss Rebecca Boyer, who is a native of West Virginia. They have a family of five children: Edna O., wife of Arthur Trammell, who is connected with the Missouri, Kansas & Texas Railway and lives at Parsons; Effie May, wife of Earl Locke, and they live on their farm 2½ miles west of Galesburg; Clay C., a rural mail carrier out of Galesburg; Lela, who was born in 1901 and now attends the high school at Thayer; and Bernice, born in 1904, and a student in the public schools of Galesburg.

J. CLARK HICKS. When 600 live and progressive business men of such a city as Fort Scott, all members of the Fort Scott Chamber of Commerce, choose one of their number as president, the choice is in the nature of one of the highest compliments and honors that could be paid, and is a responsibility which any man would appreciate. Recently the Chamber elected as president Mr. J. Clark Hicks, who is by no means one of the oldest business men of the city, but who by hard work and progressive methods has built up what is appropriately considered one of the largest and most complete exclusive furniture houses in Southeastern Kansas.

Mr. Hicks spent his early life on a farm in Bourbon County. His opportunities he largely made for himself. He began his commercial career in the humble role of a clerk. No hours were too long for him to work, and no problem that arose was too difficult for him to solve. He has made a success by conscientious performance of those duties which lie nearest and which are the important things in the life of any man.

Mr. Hicks was born at Lena in Stephenson County, Illinois, October 13, 1876. His parents Edward L. and Clementine (Weary) Hicks, were also born in the same county and were married there. They lived on a farm until they removed to Bourbon County, Kansas, and here the senior Mr. Hicks has since successfully followed farming. Some years ago he became associated with his son Clark in the furniture business at Fort Scott. He is a stanch republican and he and his wife are members of the Methodist Church. Their children are: Minnie, wife of Louis Gwinn of Kansas City, Missouri; J. Clark; and Edward Bailey Hicks, who is employed in the furniture business of his brother.

J. Clark Hicks gained his early education in the Bourbon County schools and in the old Kansas State Normal. At nineteen he left the farm and found place as a clerk in the furniture store of Requa & Sons at Fort Scott. He remained with that one house, steadily employed and advancing to larger responsibilities, for a period of ten years. During that time he had not only thoroughly learned the furniture business in every detail, but he had also carefully saved something from his earnings, and what was even more important had gained a confidence which

established his credit. Then in 1908 he started out in a modest way as a furniture dealer on his own account, and every year since then has seen some increase or enlargement to his business. He has made it practically an exclusive furniture house, and it is now one which would do credit to any larger city. He has a fine location on Main Street, and his store has 15,000 square feet of space devoted to the show and storage of his complete stock. A staff of eight or ten people find employment in this store.

It was this ability to build up a successful business of his own and the spirit of enterprise which has always characterized him that caused his fellow associates in business affairs to elect him president of the Chamber of Commerce. The Chamber has its headquarters in the newest and most modern office building in Fort Scott, and a paid secretary and stenographer are employed to handle the business of the organization. This Chamber is doing a great deal for the city, and the membership is loyally devoted to the best interests of the community. Mr. Hicks is a member of the republican party, belongs to the Order of Elks and is a member of the Episcopal Church.

On March 3, 1908, at Fort Scott he married Miss Nellie Mitchell, daughter of Charles W. and Mary (Graff) Mitchell. The Mitchell family came to Fort Scott in the early '60s and were among the pioneers. Charles W. Mitchell for over twenty years has been clerk of the school board of Fort Scott, and has been a leader in all local educational affairs. Mrs. Hicks takes an active part in the Episcopal Church. They are the parents of one child, Marion, born at Fort Scott December 4, 1908.

THOMAS JAMES HANLON has achieved a place as a prominent attorney in Southern Kansas, and is now senior member of the firm of Hanlon & Hanlon at Coffeyville, being associated in practice with his younger brother.

Kansas is his native state. He was born at Howard in Elk County July 27, 1882. His ancestry is Irish. His grandfather Thomas Hanlon was a stone mason by trade, emigrated from Ireland to the United States in 1847, lived for a time in Massachusetts, and afterwards near Peoria and Quincy, Illinois, in which state he died. He was a democrat in politics. His children now living are two in number: Jerry, a farmer and stockman at Woodhull, Illinois; and R. C., a banker and stockman at Galva, Illinois.

Thomas J. Hanlon, Sr., father of the Coffeyville lawyer, was born in Ireland in 1842 and was five years old when he was brought to America. He spent most of his early youth in Illinois, and was married at Quincy in that state. In 1880 he moved out to Elk County, Kansas, and was one of the early farmers in that section, and afterwards was in the drug business at Howard. For a time he was in business in Kansas City, and in 1892 he moved to Coffeyville and had an office as a dealer in real estate there until his death in September, 1896. He was a democrat and a member of the Catholic Church. The senior Mr. Hanlon married Maggie O'Brien, who was born in St. Louis, Missouri, in 1856, and is still living at Coffeyville. Of their children two died in infancy, and the only survivors are Thomas J. and his brother F. B. Hanlon, members of the firm of Hanlon & Hanlon, attorneys at Coffeyville.

Thomas James Hanlon was educated in the Kansas public schools, graduating from the Coffeyville

High School in 1901, and then entering the law department of the Kansas State University. He also attended Notre Dame University in Indiana. Winning his LL. B. degree at Kansas University in 1904, he at once set up in practice at Coffeyville, and has found generous opportunities to win success as a member of the Montgomery County Bar. He has a large practice both in civil and criminal law. The offices of the firm are in the Conlon National Bank Building.

Besides his home at 401 East Ninth Street, Mr. Hanlon owns some other real estate in Coffeyville, and also a farm of over 100 acres near that city. During his practice he served for a time as deputy county attorney. He is an independent democrat and a member of the Catholic Church, belongs to the Chamber of Commerce, the County and State Bar associations, and is affiliated with Coffeyville Lodge No. 775, Benevolent and Protective Order of Elks. Mr. Hanlon is also president of the Park and Amusement Company which conducts the natatorium, dancing and skating rink and other amusement facilities at Coffeyville.

COL. J. B. COOK. In all Southeastern Kansas there is no better known figure than Col. J. B. Cook of Chetopa. For more than forty years he has been recognized as one of the old and reliable and standard real estate dealers. He was one of the pioneers in Labette County, and lived on and improved a claim there before taking up his present business.

He is not only an interesting character because of his long and honorable record in business, but for a life of varied service and experience. Many who know him well in real estate circles have only such knowledge of his early career as is reflected in his title of colonel. That is by no means a complimentary title. It was won by the hardest kind of fighting service in the Civil war. He has spent most of his life on the western frontier, and is one of the few men who knew the exciting life of California in the days following the discovery of gold there. His friends and business acquaintances by the hundred will appreciate even the necessary brevity of a review of his life as given in the following paragraphs.

Jeremiah B. Cook was born in Lancaster County, Pennsylvania, at Pleasant Grove, June 22, 1834, and has already passed his eighty-second birthday. His ancestors were English people who emigrated to Pennsylvania in colonial times, and were of the old Quaker stock of that province and state. His grandfather, William Cook, was born at Warrington in York County, Pennsylvania, was a Quaker farmer, and died at Pleasant Grove. Colonel Cook's father, Allen Cook, was born at Warrington, York County, in 1808, and died in Lancaster County in 1847, while the Mexican war was still in progress. He was a farmer, an old line whig, a Quaker, and among other activities was a director of the schools in his locality. He married Rachel K. Brown, who was born at Goshen in Lancaster County, Pennsylvania, in 1810. Her father, Jeremiah Brown, who died in Lancaster County, Pennsylvania, served as a member of Congress during Harrison's administration. He was a whig, and owned a large farm in Lancaster County. Mrs. Allen Cook died in Labette County, Kansas, in 1885. There were a number of children. Edwin, the oldest, died in California at the age of twenty-three, having been one of the early seekers after gold in that state. The second in the family is Colonel Cook. Anna Mary, who died in 1914, and is buried at Chetopa, married Capt. J. J. Slaughter, who served as first lieutenant

in the One Hundred and Thirteenth Illinois Infantry during the Civil war, afterwards became a farmer in Labette County, Kansas, and is also deceased. William, the fourth child, is now a retired resident of Oswego, Kansas, was for three years a soldier in the Second Colorado Cavalry during the Civil war and served two terms as sheriff of Labette County. Charles is a retired farmer at Strawn, Kansas. Henry C. lived for a number of years at Vinita, Oklahoma, where he was cashier in a bank, and died in North Missouri. Julia, the seventh and youngest child, died at the age of eleven years.

Colonel Cook received his early education in the public schools of Lancaster County, Pennsylvania, and spent the first fifteen years of his life on his father's farm. With a disposition that craved excitement, and with the wonderfully stimulating events then going on in the western part of the United States, he could not quietly bide at home but ran away to seek such adventure as came in his path. It was in April, 1849, he left his home in Lancaster County. He was then fifteen years of age. His first experience was on the canals of Pennsylvania, and he boated on several of these thoroughfares during 1849-50. He then crossed the mountains to Pittsburg, became a flatboatman, traveled down the river to Louisville and Cincinnati, and at the age of seventeen, in the fall of 1851, went as a flatboat hand as far as New Orleans. In the fall of 1852, after an absence of several years, he returned to his father's home and spent the next year in managing the farm.

In November, 1853, Colonel Cook went out to California by way of the Nicaragua route. He was then nineteen years of age. He spent three years in the Far West mining and herding cattle, and he is one of the few survivors of that time who can relate from personal recollection the episodes of California experience as have been painted by Bert Harte and others writers of the time. When he returned to the states in 1856 it was by way of the Isthmus of Panama, and he paid $48 in gold to secure transportation across the isthmus.

A brief residence in Pennsylvania, and he was again in the West. In April, 1857, he arrived in Kansas City, or what is now Kansas City, since the metropolis of that name could hardly have been said to have existed in that year. He went by boat up the river to Jefferson City, which was then the western limit of the Missouri Pacific Railway. Colonel Cook lived in Kansas City until March, 1860. He bought a property on what is now Grand Avenue and owned it until the spring of 1860. He had a prominent part in the border war between Missouri and Kansas. He was a free state man but attended one of the meetings which the Missourians held for the organization of a company to go into Kansas and drive out the Yankees. Colonel Cook says that he passed a very critical examination. By his extensive experience in the West and South he was a master of the Missouri dialect, and could answer all questions regarding county officers in Jackson County, where he claimed that he was "bohn and raised." He was able to recall the sheriff's name because he had seen that official sell some niggers. The meeting which he attended was held at Nevada, Missouri, and he would surely have been hanged had his motive for attending it or joining the company been known.

In 1860 Colonel Cook went to Illinois, where his mother had bought a farm in Tazewell County. While there he bought 160 acres of prairie land, and began the converting of it into a farm. He was thus engaged when the war broke out in 1861. Then followed the intensely interesting chapter of his military experience.

In September, 1861, he went as a private into the Fourth Illinois Cavalry, Company H. He was afterwards promoted to corporal and later to sergeant in that company. He was with his regiment under General Grant at Fort Henry, Tennessee, and there had command of twenty men comprising the extreme advance guard of the army. He was at the head of this little company and was the first Union man to ride into Fort Henry, where he pulled down the Garrison flag within 400 yards of the rebel infantry who were moving out of the fort. Colonel Cook has among his prized trophies of a long life this flag. With his little squad of followers he pursued the rebels, passing a twelve pounder Napoleon gun which was mired down, and he soon afterwards picked up the silken banner of the Tenth Tennessee Infantry. He was also in the four days fighting around Fort Donelson, was actively engaged both days at Shiloh or Pittsburg Landing, and within a year after his enlistment was promoted to second lieutenant of Company F in the Fourth Illinois Cavalry. On account of the illness of his captain and the absence of the first lieutenant he commanded this company in every engagement for about a year after September, 1862. During that time he and his company captured more Confederates than any other company in the command. On one occasion he and his men charged Company B of the Third Texas Cavalry, captured eight of them after a three-mile chase, Colonel Cook having only fifteen men on this brilliant excursion. During the siege of Vicksburg he was engaged in raiding the country around, and before going into Vicksburg captured 200 cars and sixty engines at Grenada, Mississippi.

When the Third United States Colored Cavalry regiment was organized at Vicksburg, Mississippi, Colonel Cook was promoted to major of that command, and as the colonel soon afterwards became a brigade commander and as there was no lieutenant colonel he had active command of the regiment in every engagement except one. This negro regiment was officered by men every one of whom had a fighting record in the Fourth Illinois Cavalry, being non-commissioned officers who proved worthy of every promotion conferred upon them.

While commanding this regiment of colored cavalry, Colonel Cook continued his notable record. On March 5, 1864, at Yazoo City, Mississippi, he fought and defeated Gen. L. S. Ross' Brigade of Texas Rangers, comprising the Third, Sixth, Ninth and Twenty-eighth Texas Cavalry. He and his men charged with drawn sabres the Holmes Louisiana Battery at Woodville, Mississippi, October 5, 1864, and captured the guns, officers and men. On November 27, 1864, came another notable exploit. He captured the Big Black River bridge on the Illinois Central Railroad about fifty miles north of Jackson, Mississippi. He made this charge with his men dismounted and they had to face the fire from a stockade fort on the opposite bank of the river and on both sides of the railroad track. For this gallant exploit he was made lieutenant colonel by a general order of the War Department No. 303. That was the only order of that kind issued by the war department during the year 1864. There are almost countless incidents in Colonel Cook's experience as a soldier which might be related. Three different times he led charges against the famous Texas Rangers, and twice he captured some prisoners, and once he narrowly escaped capture himself.

In May, 1865, Colonel Cook was made brigade commander at Memphis, Tennessee, of the Third Brigade Cavalry Division District of West Tennessee. This brigade comprised the Fourth Illinois Cavalry, the Third United States Colored Cavalry and the Second Wisconsin Cavalry, altogether 2,300 men. That promotion came to him when he was not yet thirty-one years of age. Colonel Cook served with these different regiments for nearly a year, and was finally mustered out on January 26, 1866.

After the war he spent a year managing a cotton plantation of 800 acres eighteen miles north of Memphis, Tennessee. He then went back to Illinois and undertook the improvement of his 160 acre farm at Delavan. He was successfully identified with its management for several years, until there came a strong and insistent call for him to go to Kansas.

In the fall of 1870 Colonel Cook arrived in Labette County, and in the following spring located at Chetopa. Here he bought 320 acres ten miles west of Chetopa, improved that as a farm, but since the fall of 1873 has lived in Chetopa and since 1874 has been engaged in the land and loan business. Colonel Cook is the type of man whom everyone implicitly trusts. He has therefore not only gained a worthy success, but has rendered a splendid service in the real estate field. He has been the friend both of the investor and the borrower, and though more than a million dollars have been loaned through his agency there has never been recorded a loss of any importance. In the past ten years it has never been necessary for him even to make a foreclosure. It is not strange therefore that hundreds of the best pieces of property in Southeastern Kansas have been listed with Colonel Cook.

Colonel Cook owns an attractive residence on Maple Street and Seventh Street in Chetopa, and also the Cook Building at the corner of Fourth and Maple streets, where he has had his offices for more than thirty years. He traded a part of his old homestead in Labette County for this business property.

His career has been prominently identified with the civic growth and material development of Southeastern Kansas. For seven years he served as an efficient mayor of Chetopa. He was in two sessions of the Kansas Legislature, in 1885-86. Colonel Cook was one of the projectors of the Missouri Pacific Railroad through Chetopa, and was first vice-president of the company which built that branch of the road. He is a class leader in the Methodist Episcopal Church, is a prohibitionist in politics, and was the first commander of Post No. 27, of the Grand Army of the Republic. At one time he was also president of the Neosho Valley Investment Company. Fraternally he is affiliated with Chetopa Lodge No. 27, Ancient Order of United Workmen, and with Chetopa Lodge of the Knights of Pythias.

In November, 1871, in Decatur, Illinois, Colonel Cook married Mrs. Hannah (Pitts) Prosser. She died in a hospital at Omaha, Nebraska, in December, 1892, and is buried in Chetopa. Colonel Cook has no children by his first marriage. In September, 1894, at Chicago, Illinois, he married Miss Rose Dorland, a daughter of Nathan Dorland, now deceased, who was a farmer at Bartlett in Labette County. Colonel and Mrs. Cook have two children: Harry D., who is a stenographer for the secretary of the Prairie Pipe Line Company at Independence, Kansas; and J. B.,

Jr., who is a stenographer for the Western States Cement Plant at Independence.

WILLIAM W. GRAVES. It is as a publisher, author and editor that William W. Graves has made his mark in Kansas. Until he was about twenty-two years of age he had concerned himself with the business of getting an education, working in his father's store at St. Paul, Kansas, and with teaching.

Then came his decision to learn the printer's trade. The publishers of the Pittsburg World expressed a willingness to "take him on" as an apprentice, allowing him to work as hard as he pleased, but he was to receive no wages at the first and was to board himself. He stuck to his resolutions, completed the contract, and then his name was entered upon the payroll.

The Pittsburg World was a daily paper, but in 1893 it was moved from Pittsburg to Girard, Kansas, and Mr. Graves went along with it as local editor. The World suspended publication in 1895, and that was the first jolt Mr. Graves had sustained in his ambitions as a newspaper man. The first day of January, 1896, found him connected with the Neosho County Journal, a weekly published at St. Paul and owned by the Fitzsimmons Brothers. He had acquired a one-fourth interest, but in August of the same year he purchased the rest of the stock and has since been the paper's editor and owner. On becoming chief of the office he changed its name to the St. Paul Journal. The St. Paul Journal was established in 1868 by John H. Scott. It is democratic in politics, and furnishes the news and sings the praises of St. Paul and Neosho County.

Had he done nothing more, still Mr. Graves would be considered one of Kansas' successful journalists. However, on January 6, 1902, he was elected editor of the official paper of the Anti-Horse Thief Association, Kansas Division, and was given the contract for publishing this paper by a special committee appointed at the state meeting of the order held at Independence, Kansas, October 16-17, 1901. Many predicted that the paper would fail. Doubtless Mr. Graves is the chief reason it has not failed, and the prosperous condition of the Anti-Horse Thief Association Weekly News today flatly contradicts all doubts and ill omens of fifteen years ago. This paper started with a circulation from Mr. Graves' office of 700 copies, all paid for. There was a rapid expansion, until the circulation reached 7,000, and for the past ten years the average has been 5,000. The News has since been recognized by the officers of the Missouri, Oklahoma, Arkansas, New Mexico and Illinois divisions of the order as the official paper of their respective divisions.

At the beginning of this article Mr. Graves was referred to as an author. Many know him only in that capacity. He has written a great deal besides in the columns of his home paper, and has published his own and books of other writers from his plant at St. Paul. He has written "The Tricks of Rascals," published in 1905, and now in its second edition; "The Law for Criminal Catchers," published in 1907; "On the Trail," published in 1908; "Graves' Manual," a compilation of parliamentary rules for the Anti-Horse Thief Association, now in its second edition; "Origin and Principles of the Anti-Horse Thief Association," published in 1915; "Early Jesuits at Osage Mission," published in 1916. He is also publisher of "The Degree of Honor Messenger," a monthly paper, of "A Prince of His Race," by Oscar Graham, and "The Call of the Master," by Rev. Raymond O'Keefe, C. P.

William W. Graves was born near Blencoe, Washington County, Kentucky, October 26, 1871. His ancestors came from England to Maryland about the time of Lord Baltimore, and a later generation moved over the mountains to Kentucky. His father, James P. Graves, was also born in Kentucky, in the year 1852, and married Minerva Ballard, who was born in Kentucky in 1853. In 1881, these parents left Kentucky and moved to Neosho County, Kansas. James Graves was engaged in business as a merchant at St. Paul, but somewhat later removed to Montgomery, Indiana, and is now living at Bicknell in that state. His wife died at Linton, Indiana, in May, 1910. Their children were: William W.; Addie, wife of George Haag, a coal miner at Linton, Indiana; Alice, wife of George Fitzpatrick, a coal miner at Linton; Charles, in a lumber yard at Linton; Edward, a chemist who lives in Columbus, Ohio; Ida, who is unmarried and lives in Chicago; Joseph, who is studying medicine in Valparaiso, Indiana; and Lillian, who lives with her brother Edward at Columbus, where she is attending school.

The early education of William W. Graves was acquired in the district schools of Kentucky, and in 1891 he graduated from the St. Francis Institute of St. Paul, Kansas. As already mentioned his first business experience was as clerk in his father's store in St. Paul, and for one year he had the entire management of the store. Then for a year he taught school, and from that turned his attention to mastering the printing trade, as already described.

On April 30, 1895, Mr. Graves married Miss Emma Hopkins, who was a native of New York and came to Kansas with her parents in 1874. Her parents were Joshua B. and Charille Hopkins.

In politics Mr. Graves is a democrat, and individually and through his paper has found many opportunities to serve his home community. He has been township clerk of Mission Township, and in 1896 and 1897 was elected a member of the St. Paul civil council. He owns fifty shares of stock in the Kansas Casualty and Surety Company of Wichita, has his own residence on Lafayette Street in St. Paul, another dwelling on the same street, and the building in which his offices and plant are located on Fifth Street. He is also owner of the opera house on that street, and has a good farm of 110 acres 1½ miles south of St. Paul. Another business connection is with the firm of Sork & Company, harness dealers of St. Paul. Besides printing and publishing a first class newspaper, Mr. Graves has been in the fire insurance business for the past fifteen years, and represents the following standard companies: Hanover Fire, American Central, Springfield, Cleveland, Queen, Phenix of Hartford, Fidelity-Phenix, National and the Hartford.

His active relations with the Anti-Horse Thief Association have already been mentioned, and he is a member of local branch No. 29 of St. Paul. He is a charter member of Council No. 760, Knights of Columbus, is a charter member of the Royal Neighbors, No. 753, of St. Paul, has for twenty years been affiliated with the Modern Woodmen of America and has served as clerk of Camp No. 296 of St. Paul, and is past master workman of St. Paul Lodge No. 26, Ancient Order of United Workmen, and four times has been sent as a state delegate to that order.

JOHN P. DAVIS, TOPEKA. A resident of Kansas for forty-four years. Mr. Davis has in his career set an example of all that is best in American citizenship, not only to his immediate family but to the public in general. He has been prominent in public and business affairs, and has discharged the responsibilities which have fallen to his lot in a conscientious and able manner. His most potent influence for good has been exercised in business as well as in every day life. By his extensive business connections and his extended personal acquaintance he is one of the well known men of Kansas.

Mr. Davis was born in Ashland County, Ohio, January 20, 1839, a son of Amos and Nancy (Crawford) Davis, both of whom were born and reared in Columbiana County, Ohio. His father was a farmer, a man who had the confidence and respect of all who knew him, and a citizen of more than ordinary importance in his community.

The record of the life of John P. Davis is not without difficulties met and overcome. He spent his early life on the home farm, attended public schools, and when a young man moved with his parents to McDonough County, Illinois, where he engaged in farming and teaching.

Mr. Davis was married to Miss Sarah Horrabin at Blandensville, Illinois, February 11, 1858. Mrs. Davis was born at Egbeth, England, February 3, 1838, and came to the United States with her parents at the age of twelve years. Her father, Hon. Humphrey Horrabin, was a prominent citizen of Central Illinois and served as a useful member of the State Legislature.

In the fall of 1873 Mr. Davis and family came to Kansas from Illinois. He bought and located on a half section of land in Brown County near Hiawatha, and for nine years engaged in farming and the livestock business. Mr. Davis was twice elected a member of the Kansas Legislature, being chosen on the republican ticket. His service in that body was a notable one. He was an active member and the author of several important bills which became laws. One of these is known as the Transfer Record Law. This law has saved to the State many thousands of dollars, which prior to that time had been lost through imperfect land descriptions. It required all the work and influence which Mr. Davis could bring to bear in order to get this measure passed through both houses and finally signed by Governor Anthony. He was author of a game law protecting native birds; and several other important measures introduced by him became laws and were written in the statute books.

In 1882 Mr. Davis moved to Hiawatha and was instrumental in laying out the Knapp, Moon and Davis Addition to Hiawatha, in which he lived. This addition is one of the choice resident districts of that city. During the same year through the influence of Mr. Davis the Kansas Mutual Life Insurance Company was organized. The late Governor Morrill and many other prominent Kansans were members of the Board of Directors. Mr. Davis was made president, Mr. W. M. Welleome, vice president, and Mr. John E. Moon, secretary. The company made rapid growth and in the spring of 1892 moved to Topeka on account of that city being a better location. About forty people came with the moving of the company from Hiawatha to Topeka. In 1905 the Kansas Mutual was transferred to the Illinois Life Insurance Company of Chicago. At that time the company had over twelve million dollars of insurance in force, one hundred thirty-four thousand dollars in surplus above all liabilities, and total assets amounting to about eight hundred thousand dollars.

In 1904 Mr. Davis, his son Byron H. Davis, and Mr. W. M. Wellcome formed a partnership under the firm name of Davis, Wellcome & Company for the handling of real estate and farm loans. In 1906 the real estate part was discontinued and the business of the company devoted to the handling of farm loans exclusively. The company was incorporated under the name of The Davis-Wellcome Mortgage Company, and through the efforts of Mr. Davis became state correspondent for the Prudential Insurance Company of Newark, New Jersey, for the loaning of that company's money in Kansas. Later on Missouri was also placed under their control. Loaning in these two states, the Davis-Wellcome Mortgage Company of Topeka has made a steady and substantial growth, and is one of the large financial institutions of the State of Kansas.

While living in Hiawatha Mr. Davis was president of an organization known as The Business Men's Club, and after coming to Topeka assisted in organizing the Topeka Commercial Club, of which he is one of the five charter members. The Commercial Club has recently become the Chamber of Commerce.

For the past twenty-two years Mr. Davis has been a member of the Board of Trustees of Baker University, and for many years vice president of the Board. He has been a liberal contributor to the material support of that college.

A rare and wonderful personality was that of the late Mrs. John P. Davis. Mr. and Mrs. Davis celebrated their golden wedding anniversary amid a host of friends and relatives. They traveled life's highway together for fifty-three years. Thirty years of that time Mrs. Davis had spent as an invalid, being afflicted with rheumatism. She lived during all those years in a wheel chair, but always bore her lot with such fortitude, cheerful and uncomplaining patience, and radiated so much of the real significance of the Christian virtues, that it can be safely said that the period of her physical misfortune was the period of greatest growth and development in mind and heart and the source of untold blessing to her family and all who came within the sphere of her presence. She was the mother of eight children, seven of whom survived her, one child having died in infancy. Those who survived their mother were: Byron H.; Alonzo L.; Cora F., (Mrs. Charles G. Colburn); Viola M., (Mrs. Robert T. Herrick); Frank S.; Myrtle M., (Mrs. William Stephens, deceased); and Ivah B., (Mrs. Thomas B. Frost).

During the many years they spent in Kansas Mr. and Mrs. Davis acquired a large circle of friends among the prominent citizens of the state, including many of the notable figures in Methodism throughout the country, who paid tender tribute of respect to the memory of Mrs. Davis at the time of her death January 7, 1911.

A distinguishing feature of Mr. Davis career has been his religious life. While he has lived this every day without ostentation, his has been the worthy part of vitalizing and making effectual the practice of Christianity and its harmony with the best things of life. He has been a member of the Methodist Episcopal Church for sixty years and of its official board for over fifty years. During all that time he has been active in Sunday School work, and has taught the same Bible class for the last twenty years. He has taken a very active interest in the affairs of the Young Men's Christian Association, and has done much to contribute to its welfare, having been a member of the board of directors over twenty years. Mr. Davis has been permitted to live beyond man's average earthly tenure, and the world continues to be better because of his having lived in it.

WILL R. BLACK is a native Kansan, grew up and received his education in this state, and is now one of the capable oil inspectors under the state government, with headquarters and home at Coffeyville.

He traces his ancestry back to a family of Scotch origin, and one that was planted in Virginia during colonial days. His grandfather Andy Black, was born in Pulaski County, Virginia, in 1814, was reared and married in that state, and in 1838 went to Western Indiana, where he followed farming and stock raising until his death. He died at Greencastle, Indiana, in 1872. He was a democrat and a member of the Baptist Church. Andy Black married Clara McCammack, who was born in Virginia in 1816 and died in Indiana in 1878. Their children were: James, mentioned below; Jackson, who served with a Kansas regiment in the Civil war and has since followed farming in this state; Seleta, who died at Welda, Kansas, the wife of H. T. Hill, also deceased, who was a farmer and stock raiser; Robert, who lives at Welda, Kansas, was with an Indiana regiment in the Civil war and is a farmer; Thursa, who died at Welda, Kansas, unmarried; and Nellie, who died at Welda also unmarried.

James Black, father of the deputy state oil inspector, was born October 12, 1835, in Pulaski County, Virginia, and was about three years of age when his parents moved to Indiana. He grew up in that state, and in 1855 came as a pioneer to Kansas Territory, locating first at historic Ossawatomie, and in 1857 locating at Garnett. Settlers were just beginning to come into that section of Kansas, and James Black secured a homestead of 160 acres. A few years later he took his place in the ranks of the state militia and was in service in repelling Price's raid through Kansas and Missouri. From pioneer times until advancing years compelled him to lay aside active responsibilities he was a farmer and stock raiser. In April, 1913, being an invalid, he went to the home of his son Will and died in Coffeyville January 3, 1916, when in his eighty-first year. While living in Anderson County he served two terms as county commissioner. He was a democrat and a member of the Independent Order of Odd Fellows. James Black was married in 1858, the year after he located on his homestead at Garnett, to Ellen Norris, who was born in Ohio January 18, 1838, and is still living, making her home with her son Will. The children were: Albert L., who was born in 1861, was a cigar manufacturer at Garnett for several years and later farmed near Texarkana, Texas, where he died in 1906; F. J. Black is a newspaper man, connected with the Kansas City Star and living at Coffeyville; Nellie N. is the wife of John W. Hedley, a jeweler at Altus, Oklahoma; Ella M. married Charles H. Paxton, a jeweler at Paola, Kansas; Osroe died in Garnett, Kansas, in 1889, and was born in 1872; the sixth and youngest of the family is Will R. Black.

Born at Garnett April 17, 1878, Will R. Black received his early education in the public schools of his native town, and left high school in his junior year to begin life on his own responsibilities. He found plenty to do and a means of making a satisfactory livelihood as a farmer and stock raiser near Garnett. In 1913 he was called from his farm by appointment from former Governor G. H. Hodges as a deputy state oil inspector. Mr. Black is now filling the office of oil inspector under civil service rules. He is a democrat.

On May 28, 1899, at Garnett he married Miss Rhoda I. Ellis, daughter of H. M. and Cynthia Ellis, her mother now deceased. Her father served as a soldier in the Civil war in the Ninth Kansas Volunteer Cavalry, and is now living retired at Garnett.

EDWARD E. DIX. The vocation of railroading continues to attract many ambitious young men when they enter upon life's activities, and this field of activity has often proven rich in opportunity to those who have possessed the inclination to work industriously and faithfully, to scorn hardships, to face heavy responsibilities, and to give absolute devotion to the interests of the great systems which employ them. There is no place for those who do not thus prove themselves. Among the officials of almost every other line of business there are found men of sterling worth who would have succeeded well in almost any field of activity, but for railroading there must be natural inclination, and this must be supplemented by hard, practical experience. In this connection may be cited the career of Edward E. Dix, general agent of the Frisco Railroad at Fort Scott, Kansas, who has won promotion from the very bottom of the ladder through the possession of the qualities noted above as being necessary for success in the life of a railroad man.

Mr. Dix was born at Lawrence, Douglas County, Kansas, March 21, 1860, and is a son of Ralph C. and Jette (Graham) Dix, the former born at Wethersfield, Hartford County, Connecticut, and the latter at Freeport, Stephenson County, Illinois. Ralph C. Dix had learned the trade of mechanic in the East but felt that his field was too restricted and therefore decided to try his fortunes in the great West. From his native state he went to Illinois, and, in 1855, in company with the father of Frank Faxon of Kansas City, Missouri, drove overland from Chicago to Kansas City, subsequently coming to Lawrence, Kansas, where he at once began the manufacture of plows. This was the first industry of the kind started in Kansas, and at first his principal trade was with the Indians, and the early white settlers were already beginning settlement and there is no doubt but that Mr. Dix would have built up a large and prosperous business had his life been spared. However, this was not to be, for when the notorious Quantrell and his band came to Lawrence, the family home, adjoining the Johnson house, was at the point of the fiercest fighting and was burned to the ground and Mr. Dix and one of his brothers were killed. Mrs. Dix was left with three small children: Edward E., and twin daughters, Belle and Lucy. Belle later married the Hon. George H. Edwards of Kansas City, and Lucy is the wife of W. S. Kinnear of Columbus, Ohio. Subsequently, Mrs. Dix married W. J. Flinton, editor of the Lawrence Gazette, and still lives in that city, in advanced years.

The public schools of Lawrence furnished Edward E. Dix with his educational training, but he was fatherless and it was necessary that he do something to support himself, and he therefore had no chance for an academic or college training. At the age of sixteen years he put aside his school books and began his connection with railroad work in the capacity of messenger boy in the employ of what was known as the Saint Louis, Lawrence & Western Railroad. This was but a modest start, but the youth possessed ambition and energy, and his employers soon recognized these traits, together with his inherent ability, so that he was advanced from time to time until he reached the position of telegraph operator. In this capacity he was stationed at different points along the line, each one

of more responsibility than the one which had preceded it, and thus he secured practical and diversified
experience which stood him in good stead in later
years. When he was stationed at Carbondale, the
railroad went into the hands of a receiver and the
line between Carbondale and Lawrence was given
up. Mr. Dix, disappointed, but not discouraged, returned to Lawrence, where he worked as an operator
until 1878, and in that year transferred his services
to the Frisco Railroad, with which he has been connected ever since. With this line he resumed his
activities as an operator, taking various posts along
the line of the road, and in 1882 came his reward
for fidelity in the shape of an appointment to the
office of agent at Fort Scott. During the next
eighteen years he discharged the duties of this position faithfully and efficiently, and in 1900 he was
advanced to the post of general agent, a position
which he has continued to occupy to the present time.
Mr. Dix has made railroading his life work. That
he has continued in the same vocation that he adopted
in his boyhood shows him to be possessed of the
true spirit of the trainman. Being a close student
of railroading, he is justly accounted one of the
best informed men upon the subject in the state,
as well as one of the most competent and reliable.
He has been constantly interested in the growth and
development of Fort Scott, and as a helpful participant in local affairs has served as president of the
Fort Scott Business Men's Association, a position
in which his progressive ideas as to the problems
of the day did much to advance civic and commercial
interests. He is prominent in Masonry, having reached
the thirty-second degree and being a member of the
Shrine, and also holds membership in the Benevolent
and Protective Order of Elks. Always a republican,
he has been stanch in his support of that party, and
in 1900 was appointed by Governor Stubbs as a
delegate to the National Conservation Congress, which
met that year at Minneapolis.

On October 21, 1900, Mr. Dix was united in marriage with Miss Sarah Miller, who, prior to her
marriage, was superintendent of music in the public
schools of Fort Scott. She was born and reared in
Indiana, and is a lady of culture and refinement.
One son has come to Mr. and Mrs. Dix: John Perry,
who was born June 2, 1902.

MRS. J. H. STEPHENS. As president of the City
Federation of Women's Clubs, an active factor in the
Current Club and a member of the Carnegie Library
Board, at Coffeyville, Mrs. J. H. Stephens occupies a
prominent position in the social, civic and intellectual
life that has made this city one of the centers of
cultural interests in the state.

Mrs. Stephens (Esther Logan) comes of an old
colonial family of English origin. The Logans were
pioneers in Kentucky, in which state Mrs. Stephens'
grandfather was born and died. Her father, G. H.
Logan, was born in Somerset County, Kentucky,
January 6, 1840. In early manhood he accompanied
his widowed mother when she removed to Nodaway
County, Missouri, where he later engaged in merchandising. In 1889 he went to Oklahoma and was the
pioneer merchant at Kingfisher and continued there
until 1906 when he came to Kansas and is the senior
member of the Logan-Stephens Mercantile Company
at Coffeyville. He married Julia Bradford, who was
born August 25, 1849, in Missouri, and died at
Coffeyville in March, 1914. They had one child,
Esther, who became the wife of J. H. Stephens.

J. H. Stephens was born in Linn County, Missouri,

December 18, 1871, and was educated in the public
schools. He entered business at Linneus, in his
native county. For several years he was a cashier in
the employ of the New York Life Insurance Company and for three years was a merchant at Kingfisher, Oklahoma. In 1904 he came to Coffeyville
and entered the mercantile business being now the
junior member of the firm of the Logan-Stephens
Mercantile Company located on Ninth Street, one of
the largest establishments of its kind in this city.
In his political sentiments he is a democrat.

In 1900 Mr. Stephens was united in marriage with
Miss Esther Logan, who was born at Burlington
Junction, Nodaway County, Missouri. Mrs. Stephens
attended the public schools of Lexington, Missouri,
and later had the superior educational advantages
offered by the Lexington Female Seminary. Mr.
and Mrs. Stephens have two children, a son and
daughter: John Logan, who is a student in the city
high school, and Julia Virginia, who is yet in the
grade school. Mrs. Stephens is an active member of
the Presbyterian Church in which she was reared.

Perhaps it is because Mrs. Stephens exemplifies
the womanly attributes which have ever adorned her
sex, as well as that she possesses the wide vision and
high ideals of the intellectual modern progressive
woman, that she has been selected for the presidency
of such a representative body as the City Federation
of Women's Clubs. She has the personality that
creates admiration and wins esteem.

ORLIN M. BALCH. The mercantile interests of the
thriving and prosperous Town of Earleton, in Neosho
County, are well represented by Orlin M. Balch, who
has resided in this community all his life and is
known to its citizens as a business man of ability
and a citizen who has played his part in the town's
development. Mr. Balch has other interests here, being president of the Earleton State Bank, and his
record is one that is creditable both to himself and to
his community.

Orlin M. Balch belongs to a family of Scotch-
Irish origin, which was founded in America in colonial
days, the original emigrant locating in Virginia. From
the Old Dominion state the family migrated with the
western tide of civilization to Illinois, and in that
state, in Coles County, George Balch, the father of
Orlin M., was born in 1832. He was reared and
educated in his native community, but about the time
of the outbreak of the Civil war went to Wisconsin,
where he enlisted in the Third Regiment, Wisconsin
Volunteer Infantry, and served nearly four years
as a Union soldier. These four years were ones
crowded with hard fighting, for the Third Wisconsin
took part in some of the most important campaigns
and battles of the great struggle, being, among others,
at Shiloh, Vicksburg, Lookout Mountain and Chickamauga, and with Sherman on his great march to the
sea. On one occasion Mr. Balch was wounded and
taken prisoner by the enemy, but later his exchange
was effected. At the close of his military service, or
shortly thereafter, Mr. Balch came to Kansas, and in
1865 homesteaded 160 acres near the Town of Earleton, in Neosho County. The splendid record which
he had made as a soldier was duplicated as a civilian,
and his agricultural labors, prosecuted industriously
and managed ably, brought him into possession of a
fine tract of land. He continued as a farmer up to
the time of his death, in 1909, when he was the owner
of 440 acres of land. Mr. Balch was always a republican, and while he did not seek office, took an active
interest in the success of his party. He belonged to

MR. AND MRS. ABRAHAM D. BERRY

the United Brethren Church. Mr. Balch married Miss Sarah Stevens, who was born in 1845, near Paris, Indiana, and she still survives her husband and resides on the old home farm near Earleton. They became the parents of four children, as follows: G. T., who is connected with the Cudahy Refining Company and resides at Chanute; E. F., who resides with his mother and superintends the operations on the home farm; Orlin M., born at Earleton, November 4, 1877; and Mattie, who is the wife of A. L. Skinner, a merchant of San Diego, California.

During his boyhood Orlin M. Balch resided on the home farm, on which he worked during the summer months, while in the winter he attended the district schools near Earleton. Subsequently he enrolled as a student at the Chanute High School, from which he was graduated in 1893, and then went to the State Normal School at Emporia, where he completed the course of the junior year. He commenced his career as an educator, and for four years taught in the country schools of Neosho County, but his first business experience was with the Long Bell Lumber Company of Chanute, with which he remained four years. In 1910 Mr. Balch became a proprietor on his own account, when he purchased a store building on Neodesha Street, near the depot, at Earleton, and installed a stock of up-to-date merchandise. From small beginnings this has grown to good proportions, and four clerks are now necessary to handle the business, which comes from a radius of eight miles. The store building is 40x70 feet, has all modern accommodations and conveniences, and reflects the progressive spirit of its owner. The goods are well selected, attractively arranged and fairly priced, and have been purchased with an idea of meeting the demands of his trade. Mr. Balch is a business man with an excellent reputation for integrity and fair dealing, and his name connected with the Earleton State Bank, in the capacity of president, does much to inspire confidence in the solidity of that institution. He is the owner of a residence one-half block east of his store building on Neodesha Street and of a well-cultivated 80-acre farm, situated 2½ miles east of Earleton. In politics he is a republican. He has always been ready to serve his city in public office, and has been a member of the township board of trustees and the board of school directors. Fraternally Mr. Balch is well known and has many friends among his fellow-members in Chanute Camp, Independent Order of Odd Fellows; Chanute Lodge No. 806, Benevolent and Protective Order of Elks; Earleton Camp No. 5070, Modern Woodmen of America; and Cedar Lodge No. 103, Ancient, Free and Accepted Masons.

In 1907, at Earleton, Mr. Balch was united in marriage with Miss Lizzie Foetisch, daughter of Charles and Mary (Potts) Foetisch, both of whom are deceased. Mr. Foetisch was a pioneer of 1869, when he homesteaded a tract of 160 acres in Neosho County. Mr. and Mrs. Balch have one child, Joe, born February 26, 1913.

ABRAHAM D. BERRY, who now enjoys prosperity as a farmer and oil producer at Wayside, is one of the men who became acquainted with this part of Kansas when the Indians were reluctantly giving it up as a hunting ground. He has been a resident of Kansas almost continuously for forty-five years. As a pioneer he helped lay the foundation for the present magnificent prosperity of Kansas.

Born in LaGrange County, Indiana, May 10, 1847, he went as a small boy with his parents to Livingston
Vol. IV—17

County, Illinois, received his education there, and spent the first twenty-one years of his life on his father's farm.

It was in 1870 that Mr. Berry first came to Kansas. His first location was at the old trading post in Linn County. He found employment in different lines for several years, but in 1872 returned to Illinois for a couple of years. He made his permanent settlement in 1874 and after his marriage at Trading Post in Linn County he moved in the same year to what is now Wayside. At that date, forty-two years ago, he located on his present farm. Mr. Berry owns 320 acres in Rutland Township in the suburbs of Wayside, besides a farm in Caney Township, and a Texas farm in the Rio Grande Valley. On his farms in Rutland and Caney townships there are now fifty-eight producing oil wells, and these would give him a fortune apart from his substantial interests as a farmer and stock man.

His farms are thoroughly developed, and he has a complete equipment of buildings, modern machinery, and for years has carried on diversified farming and the raising of blooded horses and cattle. Mr. Berry is also vice president and a stockholder and director in the Wayside Bank. Politically he is a republican. He is one of the leading men to support the Baptist Church in his community and fraternally is affiliated with Havana Lodge, No. 640, Independent Order of Odd Fellows, with Anti-Horse Thief Association, and was formerly a member of the Good Templars.

Several generations ago the Berrys came from Germany. His great-grandfather was the founder of the family in this country and probably settled in Virginia. Mr. Berry's grandfather, Alexander Berry, was a Revolutionary soldier, afterwards followed farming, and died in Indiana.

Samuel Berry, father of A. D. Berry, was born in Ohio in 1815, and was also a pioneer in Kansas. Reared and married in his native state, he soon afterwards moved to LaGrange County, Indiana, from there to Livingston County, Illinois, locating near Streator, and in 1874 came to Montgomery County, Kansas. Here he followed farming and stock raising on his farm two miles southwest of Havana on Bee Creek. This place of 240 acres was originally known as the George Ripley farm, and is now owned by a grandson of Samuel Berry, Walter Deffenbaugh. Samuel Berry died on that farm May 26, 1892, aged seventy-seven years, one month and twenty-nine days. As a republican he took much interest in civic affairs, and held various township offices. He is an active member of the Methodist Church. He first married a Miss Hinton, and both their children, Isabella and Alexander, are now deceased. For his second wife Samuel Berry married Elizabeth Deffenbaugh, who was born in Ohio and died in Illinois in 1854. Her children were: George, who died at the age of ten years; Catherine, wife of T. S. Clark, living at Coffeyville, Mr. Clark having been a railroad engineer for the past thirty years; Samuel, who died in childhood; Susan, who resides at Independence, widow of James Deffenbaugh, formerly of Wayside, who was a farmer and stock raiser; Margaret Delilah, who died in Illinois in January, 1915, the wife of D. S. Robins, who is also deceased and who is a farmer and stockman; A. D. Berry, who is the sixth in age; Emma, who died in 1892, married John D. Hiner, deceased, who owned a farm in Oklahoma and gave much of his time to a machine for manufacturing cement; Charles, who was a farmer in Chautauqua County, Kansas, and died in 1899.

A. D. Berry was married April 8, 1874, at Trading

Post on Magazine River to Miss Mary A. Hall, a daughter of Joseph and Sarah Hall. Joseph Hall, who was a blacksmith and farmer, had a notable military record, having served through the Mexican war and afterwards fighting with the Twentieth Kansas Infantry in the Civil war. He was a lieutenant in the Civil war. To the marriage of Mr. and Mrs. Berry were born three children: Annie, wife of Bert Gibson, a farmer and stock raiser living near Nowata, Oklahoma; Martha May, who died in childhood; and Mary Etta, wife of Arthur Banks, formerly a nurseryman and they now reside at Houston, Texas.

LOREN E. HARVEY for nearly ten years has been chief of the fire department of Coffeyville. No municipal service has been more highly developed in efficiency and equipment than that for fighting fires, and none is of greater usefulness to the property and welfare of citizens. Mr. Harvey is one of the veterans of the fire department of Coffeyville, and by his leadership among his men and also his influence in equipping and keeping up the best standards of service, is performing a most valuable part in the life of that city.

Though he was born at Sheldon, Missouri, November 21, 1880, he has spent most of his life in Coffeyville, and attended the public schools there until he was fifteen years old. In the meantime he had acquired some experience helping his father, and at the age of fifteen took upon himself the responsibilities of earning his own way, and for the next four years worked in a grocery store. In earlier years Mr. Harvey was well known among professional baseball circles. He played baseball with the Western Association, and for several seasons was catcher for the Pittsburgh and Iowa teams.

It was in August, 1901, a little before his twenty-first birthday, that Mr. Harvey joined the Coffeyville fire department. After six years in the ranks and with a record of capable performance at every call to duty, he was elected chief in 1907, and it is a tribute to his leadership and also to the general efficiency of the department that in the past ten years Coffeyville has had only one serious fire. That was in 1912 when the Lewark livery barns were destroyed at a loss of $25,000, and but for the prompt and hard work of the department the fire would have spread to adjoining buildings and entailed a much greater loss. Coffeyville has now two fire stations. The Central Station, built in 1904, at Seventh and Union streets, is the headquarters for Chief Harvey and he has eight paid firemen under his supervision. The equipment consists of one automobile hose wagon, equipped with chemicals and other implements, and carrying 1,000 feet of 2½ inch hose; an automobile ladder service truck, with 210 feet of ladder, with life net, chemicals, electric wire cutters, tin roof cutters and other implements; and a chief's auto, carrying two thirty-five gallons of chemicals and 150 feet of chemical hose. Station No. 2, at 507 West Twelfth Street, has a team and hose wagon, with chemicals, small ladders and 1,000 feet of hose. In the years since he entered the fire department of Coffeyville Mr. Harvey has allowed no other interests to interfere with strict and regular performance of his duties.

His Harvey ancestors were pioneer settlers of Kentucky. His grandfather was a native of Kentucky, but went as an early settler into Missouri, lived for a couple of years with his son in Kansas, but then returned to Missouri and died on his farm

near Sheldon. One of his sons, Thomas Harvey, served as a soldier throughout the Civil war and died in Sedalia, Missouri.

Samuel Harvey, father of Loren E., was born in Kentucky in 1845, but grew up near Sheldon, Missouri, where he married. As a boy he had some extensive experience as a cowboy in Kansas, Texas and Indian Territory. He was about sixteen years of age when the war came on and though eager to enlist was prevented until toward the close, when he went out and was with the army for the last three months of the war. While living at Sheldon in Missouri he was a deputy sheriff, and in performance of his duty was shot by a horse thief, being severely wounded through the arm and hip, and the bullet he carried to his grave. He was only twenty years of age when this occurred. In 1883 Samuel Harvey moved from Sheldon, Missouri, to Anthony, Kansas, where he followed farming and also conducted a hotel. In 1887 he came to Coffeyville, and during the early days following the development of the first gas wells, was in the plumbing business. In 1912 he retired and moved to Nowata, Oklahoma, where he died January 3, 1913. He was a republican in politics and a member of the Baptist Church. Samuel Harvey married Nannie Dungan, who was born in 1863 and is now living at Nowata, Oklahoma. Their children were Loren E.; Emmett, who was a traveling salesman for the Carey Commission Company and died at Bartlesville, Oklahoma, in July, 1912. Fred, who served for three years ten months under his brother Chief Harvey at Coffeyville, and for the past four years has been chief of the fire department at Nowata, Oklahoma. Floyd, in the laundry business at Nowata.

In politics Mr. Harvey is an independent republican, and his fraternal affiliations are with Lodge No. 775 Benevolent and Protective Order of Elks, No. 305, Fraternal Order of Eagles, No. 1193 Loyal Order of Moose, and Lodge No. 104 of the Homesteaders, all of Coffeyville. His home is at 514 South Walnut Street.

In 1904 at Cherryvale, Kansas, he married Miss Carlie Casort, daughter of Charles and Sarah Casort. Her mother is now deceased and her father, who is a molder in the Coffeyville foundry, lives with Mr. and Mrs. Harvey. They have one child, Lawrence, born November 24, 1907, and now a pupil in the public schools.

EDWARD BELL PAYNE, M. D. With an understanding of what is awaiting the man of science, the many doors yet unopened which will lead to the further amelioration of the ills of mankind, and the constant yearning to add to his store of knowledge, it is practically impossible for the conscientious physician and surgeon to arrive at a state of mind where he is satisfied with what he has accomplished and, of necessity, he keeps on striving for perfection as long as life lasts. A long list of accomplishments in his profession have marked the career of Dr. Edward Bell Payne, one of Fort Scott's leading medical men, who, still in the prime of life, may be looked to for further and greater achievements.

Doctor Payne was born in Miami County, Kansas, on a farm near Paola, October 9, 1866, and is a son of Rev. James M. and Mary A. (Cantwell) Payne. The latter, who was born in 1843, was a daughter of Andrew Cantwell, a native of the South of Ireland, who emigrated to the United States at an early date and settled in Illinois, where he farmed until moving to Linn County, Kansas. There he followed agricultural pursuits during the remainder of his life. Rev. James M. Payne was born in 1843, on a farm in Indiana, and as a young man moved to Illinois and engaged in farming. When the Civil war came on he enlisted in Company G, Second Regiment, Illinois Volunteer Cavalry, with which organization he served four years, five months and fourteen days as a private. In 1866 he came to Kansas and settled on a homestead near Paola, Miami County, where he engaged in farming. Being of a deeply religious nature, he studied for the ministry and was ordained in the Methodist Church in 1878. His ministerial labors began in Miami County and for many years he preached in Eastern and Southeastern Kansas. From 1893 until 1898 he was pastor of Grace Methodist Church, at Fort Scott, and in the latter year was appointed chaplain of the National Military Home, at Leavenworth, Kansas, a position which he has retained to the present time. Reverend Payne is beloved by all, and counts hundreds of friends in all walks of life and of all religions and creeds. Mrs. Payne, a woman of culture and refinement, is a devout Christian and has been of great assistance to her husband in his religious and charitable labors. They had three children, of whom two died in infancy.

Edward Bell Payne began his education in the country schools of Miami County, following which he attended Baker University, at Baldwin, Kansas. He next began his medical studies in the University Medical College of Kansas City, Missouri, from which he was graduated in 1889, and then took his degree in Bellevue (New York) Hospital in 1890. Doctor Payne started practice at Galena, Kansas, in the fall of 1890, and remained there until 1905, during which time he was the recipient of numerous honors, being at various times president, vice president and secretary of the Cherokee County Medical Society, and for five years a member of the school board of Galena, during which time he was instrumental in having built two splendid school buildings. For thirteen years he served as superintendent in the Methodist Sunday schools and in various other ways held a prominent place in the life of the community. In 1905 Doctor Payne came to Fort Scott, where he has since advanced to a leading place in the ranks of his profession. Holding to high ideals in his professional service, his work has always been characterized by a devotion to duty and with an appreciation of the responsibilities resting upon him. He is interested in all that pertains to modern progress, both in and outside of his calling, particularly along intellectual, moral and material lines, and his charities assist many worthy enterprises. He belongs to the American Medical Association, the Kansas State Medical Society and the Bourbon County Medical Society, and has served Bourbon County as coroner for six years. Politically, the Doctor is an adherent of republican principles. He stands high in Masonry, belonging to the Knights Templar and the Shrine at Leavenworth. He has continued his religious labors at Fort Scott, where he is trustee of the Methodist Church and has been superintendent of the Sunday school for ten years. As a relaxation from the exacting duties of his calling, Doctor Payne engages in agricultural work, having a natural love for farming and being the owner of a handsome property at Redfield, Bourbon County, where he raises the standard crops and also breeds good livestock.

Doctor Payne was married July 6, 1898, at Baxter Springs, Kansas, to Miss Rose Luckey, a native of Illinois, and a daughter of John and Susan Luckey, who came to Cherokee County, Kansas, direct from Illinois. Doctor and Mrs. Payne have one daughter, Mary Esther, who was born at Galena, November 11, 1903, and is now attending school. Mrs. Payne is well known in social circles of Fort Scott, and, like her husband, takes an active part in religious and charitable work, being district president of the Methodist Episcopal Missionary Society.

CLARK NICHOLAS STARRY, M. D. Representing the first class ability and skill of his profession and enjoying a large general practice, Clark Starry has devoted all his active lifetime to medicine as a profession, and began his career with an excellent equipment, the test of real practice finding him well qualified for important service. For the past fifteen years he has practiced at Coffeyville.

He represents a family that came originally from England and settled in Virginia during colonial days. Clark Nicholas Starry, M. D., was born in Marshfield, Indiana, February 28, 1871, and his parents soon afterward came to Kansas and were early settlers in Miami County of this state. His grandfather Nicholas Harvey Starry was born in Virginia in 1800, was reared in that state, but early in life went to Indiana, where he followed farming, and then when quite well advanced in years, about 1870, came out to Kansas and bought 160 acres of land in Miami County, where he lived until his death in 1879. He was independent in politics, a very active member of the Christian Church, which he served as elder, and lived his many years usefully and well. He married Margaret Cashman, who was born in Pennsylvania in 1800 and died on the old farm in Miami County, Kansas, in 1876. None of their children are now living.

Nicholas Harvey Starry, Jr., father of Doctor Starry, was born in Warren County, Indiana, in 1842. He grew up and married in his native state and became a Warren County farmer. In November, 1871, a few months after the birth of Doctor Starry, he came to Miami County, Kansas, settling on a farm of 160 acres, and afterwards increasing his holdings by the purchase of another quarter section. He was one of the leading farmers and stock raisers of that county for many years. He had a family of four daughters and two sons, and to the girls he deeded all his real estate, while his personal property was divided between the two boys. Not all his life was devoted to farming and money getting, and he should be remembered as one of the sterling and upright citizens who impressed their influence for good upon one of the early communities of this state. He was especially active as a member and elder in the Christian Church, and he and his wife were among the thirteen charter members who organized a church of that denomination in Miami County in 1873, and he was the last of the thirteen to die. Politically he was independent. Nicholas H. Starry enlisted in 1862 in the Eighty-sixth Indiana Infantry, and after nine months with his regiment was transferred to the signal service, and continued in that corps until the close of the war. He had a long and honorable participation in the campaigns for the preservation of the Union. He fought in the battles of Chattanooga, Missionary Ridge, in the many battles leading up to Atlanta, and then was on Sherman's march to the sea. He married Sarah G. Bonebrake, a relative of the noted old time citizen of that name of Topeka. She was born in Ohio, August 2, 1845, and died on the home farm in Miami County, Kansas, September 6, 1909. Their children were: Maude, who married Isaac Wise, and she died on their farm in Miami County, where Mr. Wise still lives; Leona is unmarried and lives at Louisburg, Kansas; the third in age is Doctor Starry; Beverly C. is in the grocery business at Louisburg; Alta is the wife of Jacob Ring, and they live on a farm adjoining the old homestead in Miami County; Effie is unmarried and lives at Louisburg with her sister Leona.

Doctor Starry grew up in Miami County, had the familiar environment of a Kansas country boy, and beginning in the districts schools graduated from the Louisburg High School in 1888. Among his early experiences was teaching a term of school in Miami County for three months. In 1893 he graduated with a life teacher's certificate from the Emporia State Normal School, and thereafter for one year was principal of the schools at Bucyrus, Kansas.

All this work was preliminary to his preparation for the career of his choice. Entering the Kansas City Homeopathic Medical College, Doctor Starry was graduated Doctor of Medicine in 1897. For the first two years he practiced at his old home town, Louisburg, then spent a year in Ossawatomie, and on June 2, 1900, located in Coffeyville. He is one of the leading representatives of the Homeopathic School of Medicine in Southern Kansas, and has always enjoyed a fine practice both in medicine and surgery. His offices are in the Columbia Building. Doctor Starry is a member of the County and State Medical societies, the Southeastern Medical Society and the American Medical Association. He has never aspired to political honors, and is merely a voter of the democratic ticket. He is affiliated with Coffeyville Lodge, No. 775, Benevolent and Protective Order of Elks, and other lodge societies.

Doctor Starry and family reside at 617 West Eighth Street. On May 8, 1906, he was married at Astoria, Oregon, to Miss Alice May Morgan, daughter of David and Mary (Walsh) Morgan. Her father was a very prosperous business man, now deceased, and her mother still lives in Astoria, Oregon. Doctor and Mrs. Starry have three children: Sara, who was born July 17, 1909, and is now a student in the Coffeyville public schools; Nicholas, born November 14, 1912, and Alice Clark, born November 4, 1916.

JOSEPH A. WELLS was one of the earliest settlers in Neosho County. He moved into that section in March, 1866, less than a year after he was discharged with an honorable record as a soldier of the Union. On April 4, 1866, he took up his claim of a quarter section of land three miles northwest of the townsite of Erie. For over half a century he has been identified with that community.

After farming for a year and a half, Mr. Wells sold his claim, and moved to Erie. In the meantime he had been elected to the office of probate judge, and filled that position with credit for two years. Since then he has been engaged in the real estate, insurance and law business. In 1873, at the time of the panic of that year, he left Kansas and went into Texas, where he followed contracting for a couple of years.

Mr. Wells is of very old American stock. His immigrant ancestor John W. Wells came from England to Virginia in colonial days and during the Revolution was a member of Washington's body guard. In the next generation Philip Wells, great-great-grandfather of Joseph A. Philip, lived in Georgia and was a shoemaker by trade. The great-grandfather was Carter Wells, who died in Tennessee, where he was a very early settler. Grandfather Philip

Wells became a Baptist minister, and died at Walkerville, Illinois.

Samuel Wells, father of Joseph A., was born at Brush Creek, thirty miles west of Nashville, Tennessee, in 1800. He lived a long and useful life and died at Walkerville, Illinois, in 1892. He spent his early years farming on Brush Creek in Tennessee and married his first wife there. In 1832 he removed to Walkerville, Greene County, Illinois, and was one of the first to clear up a tract of land and engage in farming in that locality. For fifty years he was one of the leading citizens of that community. A democrat by inheritance and individual belief, late in life, when James Blaine was a candidate for President, he supported that statesman and ever afterwards voted the republican ticket. He was one of the leaders in the Baptist Church and built and paid for the church across the road from his old home in Illinois. His first wife, Mary Smith, had four children, all now deceased. For his second wife he married Mary Powers, who was born in Tennessee in 1812 and died at Walkerville, Illinois, in 1849. Their children were: Joseph A., John C., deceased, Elizabeth, Sarah and George W., deceased, so that Joseph A. Wells is the only surviving member of his mother's family. Samuel Wells, in 1852, married Sarah Sullivan, who is now deceased. There were twelve children by that union, and all are now deceased except David W., who resides on the old home farm in Walkerville. At the time of his death Samuel Wells left a fine estate of 500 acres.

On his father's farm at Walkerville in Greene County, Illinois, Joseph A. Wells was born March 24, 1838. As a boy he had the advantages of such education as was imparted in a log cabin schoolhouse at Walkerville. Until he was twenty-two he lived on and worked on his father's farm. Then for one year he was engaged in farming for himself.

Mr. Wells had been married a little over two years and was becoming comfortably settled when the tocsin of the war sounded and called him into active service to preserve the Union. August 8, 1862, he enlisted in Company H of the 91st Illinois Infantry. Much of his service was spent in guarding the border of the Southwest, and he was in New Mexico a part of the time. He also, with his regiment, took an active part in the operations around Mobile Bay, in the siege and capture of that city, and he was a participant in the battle that followed the succeeding day when Whistler, Alabama, was captured and large quantities of munitions fell into the hands of the Union forces. His muster out from the army came July 12, 1865.

A few weeks after his return home he went to Northern Missouri and bought a farm, but remained on it only until the following spring, when he came and joined the settlers of Neosho County. Mr. Wells has given his time and resources to a number of business affairs, and was one of the men responsible for the opening of the oil and gas fields around Erie. He has some fine property, including forty acres of alfalfa bottom land a mile west of Erie, a residence at the corner of Seventh and Main streets, another dwelling house at the corner of Seventh and Grant streets, and an office building on Main street.

Mr. Wells recalls the exact date of his conversion from the democratic party to allegiance with the republican organization. It was after he enlisted in the army and came as a definite decision on December 22, 1862. Since then for fifty-four years he has actively supported and worked with the republican organization. He is a member of the Presbyterian

Church, has served as master seven times of Erie Lodge No. 76, Ancient Free and Accepted Masons; is a member of Fort Scott Consistory No. 4 of the thirty-second degree Scottish Rite; of Valley Chapter No. 11, Royal Arch Masons at Humboldt; of Erie Camp No. 1101, Modern Woodmen of America; Lodge No. 275, Ancient Order of United Workmen; and Lodge No. 77 of the Sons and Daughters of Justice at Erie.

On March 25, 1860, at the age of twenty-two, Mr. Wells married Miss Matilda Wood, daughter of Pleasant and Cynthia (Caid) Wood. Her father was a farmer and both parents are now deceased. Mr. and Mrs. Wells have lived together more than fifty-five years and in that time have reared some children who have gained distinction. Loyal T., who was a farmer, died at Erie in 1899. Seth G., a resident of Erie and a printer by trade, served one term as state auditor of Kansas. Byron C., who died at Erie in 1898, was deputy postmaster. Logan H. is an attorney and in the insurance business at Muskogee, Oklahoma. Jay C. is a horseman at Reno, Nevada. Jennie E., the only daughter, is the wife of James E. Rogers, who is bookkeeper in the office of the state treasurer at Topeka.

JOSEPH EDWARD EXNER, now president of the Coffeyville Shale Products Company and especially identified with a number of other manufacturing and business concerns of Montgomery County, is a veteran railroad man, having retired from the hazardous and responsible position of locomotive engineer some thirteen years ago to take up a career as a manufacturer at Coffeyville.

He is an Eastern man, though most of his experience in railroading and business has been gained in the West. His Exner ancestors had their original seat of residence in Germany. During colonial times two brothers of the name came to New York State, while another brother went to Australia. At Savannah, New York, Joseph Edward Exner was born November 10, 1861, a son of Edward Exner. His father was born at Clyde, New York, in 1829 and was a successful farmer and stock raiser at Savannah and Port Byron, New York. His death occurred at the latter place in 1902. He was a democrat and a member of the Methodist Church. Edward Exner married Mary Jane DeVoe, who was born at Montezuma, New York, in 1841 and died at Savannah in that state in 1869. Their children were: Maitie, wife of Willis M. Frost, a retired farmer at South Butler, New York; and Joseph E.

Reared on a New York State farm, until he was eighteen years of age Joseph E. Exner attended the public schools of Savannah. His first experiences were one summer spent in work on a farm, then a year in a wagon factory at South Butler, and in 1882, at the age of twenty, he entered railroading as a brakeman for the New York Central Railway. He spent two years as a brakeman, one year nine months as a fireman, and in that brief time earned promotion to the rank of locomotive engineer. He was made an engineer December 5, 1886; and the following year was given promotion to the responsibility of piloting the engines of the White Mountain Express, a passenger train running between Oswego and Norwood, New York, there connecting with the Ogdensburg and Lake Champlain Railroad. He handled the throttle on that run for an entire summer, living at Watertown, New York. In the summer of 1887 he was engineer on the Buffalo, Rochester and Pittsburg Railway. On December 25,

Christmas Day of 1887, Mr. Exner arrived at Little Rock, Arkansas. This was his first introduction to the West. After making one trip over the Iron Mountain Road in order to familiarize himself with it, he took the post of engineer and for two years ran an engine out of Little Rock. He was then transferred to the Kansas and Arkansas Valley Railroad between Fort Smith and Coffeyville, Kansas. Mr. Exner has many interesting incidents to relate of his career as a railroad man, particularly while an engineer on Southwestern railroads, which at the time and place were much exposed to the danger of attacks from bandits and outlaws.

After twenty-two years of faithful railroad service Mr. Exner resigned his position in January, 1903, and at the same date established his family residence at Coffeyville. Entering business, he established a brick yard at Coffeyville, first known as the Coffeyville Shale Brick Company. In 1914 it was reorganized as the Coffeyville Shale Products Company, and its output is now hollow building tiles. The plant is situated a mile and a half northwest of Coffeyville. The officers of the company are: Joseph E. Exner, president and general manager; A. N. Kellogg, vice president; and L. A. Florea, secretary and treasurer. This is one of the industries which helped to give Coffeyville its pre-eminence as a brick manufacturing center. The plant has a capacity of 100 tons for each ten-hour day, and the products are shipped over a radius of 300 miles around Coffeyville, some of it going as far as Omaha, Nebraska.

Mr. Exner is also vice president of the Denison Clay Company of Coffeyville, a company manufacturing hollow building tile with their plant two miles northwest of Coffeyville. He is president of the Exner-Dodge Packer Company, manufacturing all oil and gas well swage nipples and supplies. This is a large and important industry, the fine new factory being located at Fourth and Santa Fe streets. Another concern of which he is the chief executive officer is the Will-Pur Mining and Milling Company at Harrison, Arkansas, which owns 160 acres and has eighty acres under lease, and is rapidly developing promising prospects for mineral development. Mr. Exner also has an interest in 2,200 acres of gas leases near Van Buren, Arkansas. In Coffeyville he and his family occupy an attractive residence at 602 Lincoln Street. His own plant manufactured the brick for the construction of this modern home in 1905. He owns another dwelling house on Spring Street.

Politically Mr. Exner is a republican, is a member of the Presbyterian Church, and fraternally is affiliated with Keystone Lodge No. 102, Ancient Free and Accepted Masons at Coffeyville, Coffeyville Chapter No. 89, Royal Arch Masons, Lochinvar Commandery No. 52, Knights Templar, and Little Rock Consistory No. 1 of the Scottish Rite. He is a member of the Chamber of Commerce, and belongs to the Good Fellowship Club at Coffeyville.

On January 29, 1884, Mr. Exner was married at Fairhaven, New York, to Miss Nannie R. Worden, of Spring Lake, New York. To their marriage were born three children. Blanche Estelle, born August 7, 1888, is the wife of Ben H. Morgan, a salesman for the Rea-Patterson Milling Company, with Coffeyville and Independence as his territory, and they reside at 610 West Fifth Street in Coffeyville. Maitie Evangeline was born April 20, 1899, and is now a senior in the Coffeyville High School. Louise Evelyn was born November 24, 1902, and is in the freshman class of the Coffeyville High School.

JOHN H. CRIDER. A continuous practice as a member of the Fort Scott bar since 1882 gives John H. Crider a distinction not only as one of the oldest members of the local bar, but also as one of the most successful. From the first Mr. Crider has looked upon the law not so much as a vocation as a profession requiring all the loyalty and service of his nature and throughout has kept his work in full accord with the high standards and dignity of his vocation. It may be a matter of interest to recall that Mr. Crider earned his first fee of $100 from Hon. Eugene Ware, "Ironquill," this amount being paid him for his services as referee in proceedings in aid of an execution.

Mr. Crider was born in Lancaster, Ohio, March 2, 1859, son of Dr. Henry L. and Sarah Ann (Weisz) Crider. The founder of the Crider family in the United States was Jacob Crider, who was born in Germany in 1768, and was an early settler in Fairfield County, Ohio, where he followed farming until his death in 1824. He was the great-grandfather of the Fort Scott attorney. His wife, Barbara Weaver, was also born in Germany and died in Fairfield County, Ohio, in 1844.

Jacob Crider, grandfather of John H., was born in Fairfield County, Ohio, February 12, 1807, and died there in 1868. His wife, Elizabeth, died in Fairfield County in 1862.

Dr. Henry L. Crider, who was born near Lancaster, Ohio, in 1827 and was reared on a farm near that town, died there in 1896. He was a physician but spent most of his career in the practice of dentistry. He married Sarah Ann Weisz, who was born June 30, 1826, and died October 7, 1897. She died in the same house in which she was born. She was a daughter of Rev. George and Catherine (Shuman) Weisz. Rev. George Weisz was born June 21, 1793, and died in Lancaster, Ohio, March 10, 1859. His wife, Catherine, was born May 16, 1799, and died in Lancaster March 30, 1868. The Weisz family was a large and prominent one in that section of Ohio, and Rev. George Weisz was a minister of the German Reformed Church. Catherine Shuman was a daughter of John Shuman, who was a son of George Shuman, who, with his first wife and first born son, Michael, came from Germany about 1760 and settled on a farm on Turkey Hill in Manor Township in Lancaster County, Pennsylvania. They reared a family of five sons: Michael Shuman, who was born in Wuertemberg, Germany; John, Henry, Adam and Andrew, born in Lancaster County, Pennsylvania, were the names of these sons. George Shuman, their father, married a Manning. Her brother, John Manning, was also a settler on Turkey Hill, and John Manning's wife was a sister of George Shuman. John Manning and George Shuman were thus brothers-in-law in a double sense and their wives were sisters-in-law in the same degree. The Shumans and Mannings reared large families and they were numerously represented in Manor Township of Lancaster County, Pennsylvania. George Shuman's second wife was Catherine Pfeiffer, and to this union was born six children, namely: Christian, Elizabeth, Jacob, Mary, Frederick and George, Jr.

Dr. Henry L. Crider did not enlist in the regular army during the Civil war on account of his wife being an invalid and requiring all his faithful care. He was an ardent supporter of the Union cause and organized a company for the express purpose of capturing General Morgan. He brought this company into camp and on account of his enthusiasm was promoted to colonel by Governor Tod of Ohio. However, the company never got into active service. Doctor Crider was a splendid specimen of physical manhood, was over six feet tall and proportioned accordingly. He was an ardent republican. He and his wife had six children. One of them, William, died in infancy; Catherine Elizabeth died at the age of thirteen, and Dr. George S. Crider died in Lancaster, Ohio. The three now living are: John H.; Jacob W., a banker of Charlestown, West Virginia; and Lida A., widow of Henry Ellsworth Varney.

Mr. John H. Crider received his early education in the public schools of Lancaster, Ohio. In 1880 he graduated in the scientific course from Heidelberg College at Tiffin, Ohio. His law studies were pursued at Lancaster under Col. John M. Connell, who had served as colonel in the Seventeenth Ohio Regiment in the Civil war, and was a brother-in-law of Gen. Thomas Ewing, who subsequently became chief justice of the Supreme Court of the State of Kansas.

Admitted to the bar in 1882, Mr. Crider at once came to Fort Scott and began the practice which has kept his time and energies engaged now for almost thirty-five years. For two years he was a partner with H. A. Pritchard under the name Crider & Pritchard, but aside from that he has always conducted an individual practice.

For six years he held the office of city attorney, his first term being in 1889-90, and he was again in the office from 1895 to 1899. In 1904 he was chosen elector at large on the republican ticket for Kansas, and in 1914 was an unsuccessful candidate for Congress from his district. He is a polished orator and his services have been in demand in many campaigns. For ten years he has served as grand master workman for Kansas of the Ancient Order of United Workmen, his first term being from 1897 to 1901, and his second from 1905 to 1911. He is a Lodge, Chapter and York Rite Mason, a Knight of Pythias and a Modern Woodmen of America. He is also one of the charter members of the Fort Scott Chamber of Commerce and belongs to the Knights and Ladies of Security.

On December 19, 1888, near Fort Seneca, Ohio, he married Miss Ida A. Abbott. Mrs. Crider was born in Seneca County, Ohio, daughter of Francis E. and Melissa (Ingraham) Abbott. She is a descendant of the old and prominent Massachusetts family of Abbotts, and through that lineage has membership in the Daughters of the American Revolution. She is a member of the Presbyterian Church. Mr. and Mrs. Crider have six children, three of whom are deceased. One died in infancy; Robert W. died at the age of three years, and Ida Louise at the age of sixteen. All the children were born at Fort Scott. Frances Eugenia is the wife of Thomas W. Moreland of Fort Scott. John M. Crider and Marian Abbott Crider are both graduates of the Fort Scott High School.

WILLIAM HENRY FRANCIS. Among the men foremost in Montgomery County identified with industrial enterprises, those who have become widely known by reason of the magnitude of their operations and the extent of their trade connections, few are better known than is William Henry Francis, superintendent and manager of the Coffeyville Vitrified Brick and Tile Company's plants at Coffeyville, Collinsville, Cherryvale and Fort Smith. Mr. Francis has spent his entire career in the business in which he is now engaged, and is maintaining the prestige in business circles attained by his honored father, the late George Francis.

William H. Francis was born at Danville, Pennsylvania, February 10, 1867, and belongs to a family which originated in Ireland and was founded at an early day in Ohio, where the grandfather of Mr. Francis was born. The grandfather was a brick manufacturer of Pennsylvania and fought as a soldier during the Civil war. George Francis was born at Danville, Pennsylvania, November 30, 1844, and received his education in the public schools. As a young man he became interested in the brick business, and continued to engage therein in Pennsylvania until the latter '80s, when he came to Coffeyville, Kansas. He first started a small dry press brick plant in the northeast part of the city, where the National Refinery now stands, and later on built a small hand press plant on the site now occupied by the big modern plant of the Coffeyville Vitrified Brick and Tile Company. It was while operating the small hand press plant that Mr. Francis discovered the shale that has since helped to make this section famous as a brick manufacturing center. Up to that time the shale had been thought to be a formation of soapstone, but Mr. Francis conceived the idea of burning some of it as an experiment and it proved to be one of the finest of brick making shales. The hand plant at that time was not adequate for the manufacture of this high quality of brick, and he therefore interested C. M. Ball, W. H. McMahan and George Picker in the enterprise, the result being the organization of the Coffeyville Vitrified Brick and Tile Company. This company installed a modern plant and the manufacture of paving and building brick was carried on extensively, the business growing to such an extent that four years later the capital stock was increased to $40,000 and the plant of Stich & Shulthis, at Independence, was taken in by a stock absorption. The company next built a plant at Cherryvale and then one at Chanute, but the latter was closed down a few years ago and a new one opened at Collinsville, while just before closing down the Independence plant the company acquired the plant at Fort Smith, Arkansas, and all four were operated at the same time.

George Francis not only enjoyed the reputation of being the discoverer of brick-making shale west of the Mississippi River, but also of being the first to burn it with natural gas in this part of the country. For years he was general foreman of manufacture for the company at all its plants and at the time of his death held the position of vice president of the company. Necessarily his duties were arduous and heavy, but he found time for many charities and was an ardent church worker. He was kind and sympathetic with the army of men that worked under him and enjoyed their warmest affection at all times. He was a loyal supporter of the First Methodist Church of Coffeyville and was largely responsible for the building of the present handsome edifice of that denomination. Quiet and unassuming, he was a man not of words but of actions, and his true worth was known only to those who knew him best. Mr. Francis was a republican in politics, but his inclinations did not run toward a political life. For a period of fourteen years he was president of the Young Men's Christian Association at Coffeyville. At the time of his death, which occurred May 18, 1915, he was the owner of his own fine brick residence at No. 312 West Tenth Street, as well as another residence on South Willow Street, and had large oil interests in Kansas.

Mr. Francis was married in 1866, in Danville, Pennsylvania, to Miss Ella Ethlyn, who died in 1900, at Coffeyville, and they had three sons: William Henry, of this notice; Charles, who is general manager of the Francis Brick Company of Muskogee and Boynton, Oklahoma; and Harry, also connected with the Francis interests at Boynton, and a brick manufacturer. Mr. Francis was again married in October, 1904, to Miss Nettie (Irwin) Stamper, who survives him.

William Henry Francis received his education in the public schools of Everett, Pennsylvania, where he was graduated from the high school in 1886. He then became interested in the brick business at Everett, where he remained with his father until 1887, at that time coming to Coffeyville, where he assisted his father in the organization of the Coffeyville Vitrified Brick and Tile Company. Since his father's death he has succeeded him as superintendent and manager of the Coffeyville, Collinsville and Cherryvale plants, with headquarters at the latter place, where is also his residence, at No. 510 East Fifth Street. Mr. Francis has inherited many of his father's sterling qualities and is rapidly making his name as well known in brick manufacturing circles as was the elder man's. His associates place the greatest faith in his knowledge, ability and judgment and his efforts are doing much to advance the business of the company. Mr. Francis has other business interests and holdings and his real estate properties include a residence at No. 513 Fifth Street.

Politically, Mr. Francis is a republican, although, like his father, he has never sought public honors. He is well known and popular in fraternal circles, and holds membership in Cherryvale Lodge, No. 137, Ancient Free and Accepted Masons; Cherryvale Chapter, No. 86, Royal Arch Masons; and Saint Bernard Commandery, No. 10, Knights Templar, of Independence; Cherryvale Camp, No. 142, Independent Order of Odd Fellows; and Jayhawker Camp, No. 913, Modern Woodmen of America, Cherryvale. He is likewise an active worker in the Commercial Club and gives his stanch support to all measures calculated to benefit Cherryvale or its citizens.

Mr. Francis was married in 1891 at Coffeyville, to Miss Julia A. Skinner, daughter of James Skinner, who is engaged in the draying business at Coffeyville, and to this union there have been born children as follows: Chester, who resides at Cherryvale and is the proprietor of an automobile garage; Mildred, who lives with her parents, a graduate of the Cherryvale High School; Connett, who assists in the Cherryvale plant of the company of which his father is superintendent; Helen, a graduate of the Cherryvale High School, class of 1916, and now residing with her parents; Georgia, who attends the high school as a member of the junior class; and Wilma and Robert, who are students of the graded schools.

J. Walter Clark. In no state in the Union, perhaps, have the public schools in recent years been given more careful consideration than in Kansas, and this is evidenced by the fact that school boards all over are insisting on higher qualifications and efficiency than ever before. They demand teachers not only of scholarship, but of high moral character, of equable temperament and conventional deportment, rightly contending that these instructors have lasting influence on the youth that is entrusted to them at the most impressionable age. Well qualified in every way is Prof. J. Walter Clark, who, for the past two years, has been superintendent of the schools of Buffalo, Kansas. Entering the teacher's profession when but sixteen years of age, he has continued in the educational field because he loves the work. No effort has been too great when it has enabled him to add to his store of knowledge, and, although yet a young man, he has many university honors to his credit, and prior to coming to Buffalo, had already admirably filled educational positions of responsibility.

J. Walter Clark was born November 6, 1888, at Piedmont, Wayne County, Missouri. His parents are D. M. and Charity L. (Chilton) Clark. The early ancestors came to Virginia, in colonial times, from England, moving later into Kentucky and still later to eastern Missouri. This name is honorably borne in many sections of the country at the present time in business, professional and public life.

D. M. Clark, father of Professor Clark, was born at Brunot, Wayne County, Missouri, in 1862, and was reared and educated there and later became a farmer and stockman in Wayne County. In 1912 he located at Benedict, in Wilson County, Kansas, subsequently removing to Scott City, where he yet resides and continues to be interested in farming and stock. He was quite prominent in politics in Wayne County, serving for a time as county clerk and also was a member of the state legislature representing Wayne County, elected on the democratic ticket. He married Charity L. Chilton, who was born at Brunot, Missouri, in 1868, and six children were born to them, as follows: Cleveland, who is his father's partner in business; H. L., who is a farmer and also a real estate agent at Chaonia, Missouri; J. Walter, of Buffalo, Kansas; Samantha R., who is the wife of T. R. Wilkinson, a farmer near Piedmont, Missouri; D. W., who is a farmer residing at Anahuac, Texas; and Myra, who resides with her parents and at present is interested in her studies, taking postgraduate work in the high school at Scott City.

J. Walter Clark attended the public schools at Piedmont, Missouri, until he was graduated from the high school in 1905, and in 1908 he was graduated from the Normal school at Cape Girardeau. Later he attended summer courses in the following educational institutions: two summers in the University of Colorado; one summer in the University of California, and one summer in the University of Michigan at Ann Arbor.

In the meanwhile Professor Clark had been devoting himself to the cause of education as a teacher, almost without cessation from his sixteenth year. Before coming to Kansas in 1911, he had taught school for five years in Missouri, for one year in Oklahoma, and one year in Arkansas, and afterward, for three years he was superintendent of schools at Benedict, Kansas. He built up a fine school system there and made hosts of professional and personal friends. The only political office he has served in was that of deputy county clerk under his father in Wayne County, Missouri.

Professor Clark was married in 1915, at Lindsborg, in McPherson County, Kansas, to Miss Julia G. Fordice, who is a daughter of W. S. and Julia (Stover) Fordice. The father of Mrs. Clark is a retired farmer and he and wife live at Lindsborg. Since he was twelve years old, Professor Clark has been a member of the Baptist church and as teacher of the men's class in the Sunday school, at Buffalo, he proves that he is versatile enough to instruct and interest those of mature years as successfully as he has directed youth for so long a time. Earnest, alert and enthusiastic in his professional work, he is also pleasant and companionable with all with whom he is associated in other ways.

CAPT. DAVID STEWART ELLIOTT. For more than half a century the name Elliott has been one of important associations with Kansas history. The quality of public service has distinguished the family in all generations. The first of the name in Kansas was a Pennsylvania soldier, also named David Stewart Elliott, who was killed by Quantrell's band of raiders during the Civil war. The late Capt. David Stewart Elliott of Coffeyville, long known as a lawyer, editor, fraternal organizer, and soldier, also gave up his life as a sacrifice to the country during the Philippine war. Several of the children of the late Captain Elliott are filling worthy places in their respective spheres, including his daughter, Miss Leila C. Elliott, who is now city treasurer of Coffeyville.

David Stewart Elliott, father of the late Captain Elliott, was born at Lewistown, Pennsylvania, was reared and educated and married in that state, and was an editor by profession. He served as a soldier in the Mexican war; and though quite an old man at the time he enlisted in 1861 in a Pennsylvania regiment of infantry. He was in the service in Kansas, and his company was on its way to Fort Smith to assist in repelling the Price invasion of Missouri and Kansas when he was killed by Quantrell's men at Baxter Springs. This was in 1864. He and others of the command were captured by the Quantrell raiders, were lined up against the wall and all shot. This Pennsylvania soldier whose record deserves special mention in any history of Kansas had only one child, the late Capt. David Stewart Elliott. The mother of Captain Elliott was born at Everett, Pennsylvania, in 1822 and died at Coffeyville in 1892.

At Everett, Pennsylvania, Capt. David Stewart Elliott was born December 23, 1843. When about fifteen years of age he entered a newspaper office to learn the printing trade and in April, 1861, enlisted in Company G of the Thirteenth Pennsylvania Volunteer Infantry. That was a three months' regiment, and at the end of his term he re-enlisted in Company E of the Seventy-sixth Pennsylvania Volunteers, and was with that command for more than three years. In 1868 he became editor of the Bedford County Press at Everett, Pennsylvania, and continued in that capacity until 1873. On February 9, 1869, he was admitted to the bar of Bedford County, but after practicing a few years resumed his work as editor and was editor of the Everett Press from 1881 to 1885.

In May, 1885, Captain Elliott became a member of the Montgomery County Bar, locating at Coffeyville, but soon answered the call to his old profession as a newspaper man and from June 5, 1885, to September 1, 1897, edited the Coffeyville Weekly Journal. Early in 1892 he established the Daily Journal, and was also its editor until 1897.

In May, 1898, the Twentieth Kansas Regiment was enlisted for the Spanish-American war, and Company G was recruited at Independence, consisting for the most part of Montgomery County boys. The officers of the company were: D. Stewart Elliott, captain; H. A. Scott of Sycamore, first lieutenant; and William A. McTaggart, son of Senator McTaggart, second lieutenant.

As every Kansan knows, the Twentieth Kansas made its record of achievement in the Philippines. Captain Elliott, whose qualifications as a military leader were enhanced by his previous service in the Civil war, went with the regiment to the Philippines early in 1899, and while in line of duty at Calocan, just north of Manila, on February 28, 1899, was shot by a Filipino sharpshooter and died a few hours later. His remains were brought home and on April 14, 1899, were laid to rest at Coffeyville with military

D S Stewart Elliott.

honors. He had entered the Civil war at the age of seventeen, and he was in his fifty-sixth year when death came to him in the Far East.

Something of Captain Elliott's talents and characteristics can be learned by a brief quotation from an old history of Montgomery County: "After locating in the county Captain Elliott devoted only a portion of his time to the practice of law. His tastes led to the formation of his fellow men into associations, political parties and other organizations, and the promulgation and advocacy of their principles, rather than to the irksome and methodical work demanded in the practice of law. For this work of his choice he was by nature admirably equipped. He was a fluent and pleasant speaker and at once took a leading part in meetings to effect such organizations, or to advocate their tenets. As a writer he was terse, graceful and effective, and as a soldier enthusiastic and courageous. During his residence in Coffeyville Captain Elliott was its attorney for one or more terms and a member one term of the lower house of the Kansas Legislature, where he was at once a conspicuous member. At his death he was a member of sixteen lodges."

Captain Elliott was a republican, and was filling the office of city clerk at Coffeyville at the time he resigned to enlist for service in the Spanish-American war. As an active member of the Methodist Episcopal Church he served as president of the Epworth League and superintendent of the Sunday school, and held all the lay offices in the church. Among the fraternities of which he was an influential member were the following: Keystone Lodge No. 102, Ancient Free and Accepted Masons; Coffeyville Chapter No. 89, Royal Arch Masons; St. Bernard's Commandery No. 10, Knight Templars, at Independence; with the Scottish Rite bodies of Masonry; Coffeyville Lodge of the Independent Order of Odd Fellows; Camp No. 665, Modern Woodmen of America; Woodmen of the World; Select Friends; Knights and Ladies of Security; Knights of Pythias; Lodge No. 279, Ancient Order of United Workmen; Post No. 90, Grand Army of the Republic; also the organization of Sons of Veterans.

Captain Elliott married Miss Clara Barndollar, who is still living at Coffeyville with her children. She was born at Everett, Bedford County, Pennsylvania, September 24, 1846, and represents an old American family. One of her ancestors was John Williams, who served as a private under Capt. David Hendershot in the First Battalion of Bedford County during the Revolutionary war. Another of her revolutionary ancestors was Capt. Richard Dunlap, who was captain of the Bedford Company in the First Battalion of Militia commanded by Col. William Parker, Captain Dunlap was killed while fighting at Frankstown, Pennsylvania, on June 3, 1781. Another ancestral connection of interest was Capt. James Martin. He married Sarah Thomas, the great-grandmother of Mrs. Captain Elliott, and they were married at the home of Benjamin Franklin on October 19, 1759. Captain Martin was a first lieutenant and afterwards promoted to captain of a company from Pennsylvania in the Revolution.

A brief record of the children of the late Capt. David S. Elliott and wife is as follows: John B., who was a member of his father's company and who is now superintendent of the Pullman Company at Kansas City, Missouri; Miss Leila C.; Irene, who lives at Coffeyville with her mother; James Russell, who enlisted in his father's company at the age of fifteen, and was the youngest soldier in the American army

during the Spanish-American war; Grace, at home with her mother; and David S., Jr., who was educated at Baker University and is the republican nominee for county clerk of Montgomery County.

Miss Leila C. Elliott, now city treasurer of Coffeyville, was born at Everett, Pennsylvania, but was reared and educated at Coffeyville. She possesses unusual business ability and efficiency in the routine and detail management of public offices, and for a time was deputy city clerk and afterwards was elected and served as city clerk for three years. In 1913 she became city treasurer, and is giving a most excellent administration of that important office. Miss Elliott is a member of the Daughters of the American Revolution, and is active in the Methodist Episcopal Church.

CHARLES W. KENT of Coffeyville is a veteran newspaper man of Kansas. His has been an interesting past. He served as a boy soldier in the Union army, and several of his brothers also bore arms for the Stars and Stripes. In a half century of active experience he has largely been identified with the newspaper business, and has been in Southern Kansas about a quarter of a century.

On July 7, 1893, he established and brought out the Gate City Independent, the forerunner of the present weekly Independent. For a number of years Coffeyville was familiarly known as the Gate City, since it was in fact the gateway leading from Kansas into old Indian Territory. Since its establishment Mr. Kent has been sole owner and editor of this old and influential newspaper. He now has a modern plant and equipment at 208 East Ninth Street. He also owns the building from which the paper is published. Starting out with a weekly issue, six months later Mr. Kent changed it to a semi-weekly paper, and six months later still he made it a daily and semi-weekly. Since the Spanish-American war the daily has been discontinued and in 1908 he abandoned the semi-weekly edition. It is now a weekly, and this change was made largely to adapt the paper to the needs and demands of the farming community surrounding Coffeyville. The Independent has a splendid country circulation, and goes to patrons on the farms and in the nearby towns all over Southeastern Kansas and Northern Oklahoma. It is essentially a home newspaper and specializes in news of the farms and in country correspondence. Another feature is the fashion department maintained by the McCall Company, and this appeals to the farmers' wives and to women generally. Politically it is an independent republican paper.

Charles W. Kent was born May 1, 1848, in Richland County, Illinois. His ancestors came originally from England. In fact there were two brothers of the name who came to this country at the beginning of English settlement. Mr. Kent's direct ancestor came over in the Mayflower, landing at Plymouth Rock, while the other brother went to Jamestown, Virginia. John G. Kent, father of the Coffeyville editor, was born in Ohio in 1808, was reared in that state, and was a cabinet maker by trade. In 1844 he moved to Southern Illinois in Richland County, where he followed his trade, and in 1854 located at Cuba, Illinois, where he died in 1862. He was an old line whig and later a republican, and very active in the Methodist Episcopal Church. At one time he also served in the state militia. John G. Kent married Margaret Hannah Gardner, who was born in Ohio in 1812. She died in St. Louis, Missouri, in 1900. Of their children Eliza A., who died in Canton, Illinois, married Hiram Myers, a farmer, who is also deceased. The son John F., who died at Canton, Illinois, saw three years of active service in an Illinois regiment during the Civil war, was taken prisoner on April 6, 1862, at the battle of Shiloh, was sent to the Confederate prisons in Belle Isle and at Cahaba, Alabama, being paroled after a year, and finally rejoining his regiment; by trade he was a carpenter. David was also a soldier and was killed the morning of the first day of the great battle of Shiloh on April 6, 1862, and his brothers John F. and Elmer were taken prisoners while carrying him off the field. Next in age after David were Elmer G. and Charles W. Sarah first married James Barricklow, who was a merchant in Coffeyville, Kansas, at the time of his death, and she is now the wife of William Bowers, an electrician living at Davenport, Iowa.

Charles W. Kent received most of his early training in the public schools of Cuba, Illinois. When about sixteen years of age on May 4, 1864, he enlisted in Company D of the One Hundred and Thirty-seventh Illinois Volunteer Infantry. He re-enlisted February 11, 1865, in Company B of the One Hundred and Fifty-first Illinois Infantry, and was finally mustered out January 24, 1866. In a fight at Memphis, Tennessee, August 21, 1864, he was wounded, was taken prisoner, but was recaptured the same night by his own company. His wound kept him in the hospital until the term of his regiment expired and on his second enlistment he was detailed as Right General Guide of the First Brigade, Second Separate Division, Army of Georgia. The rest of the time he carried a United States flag. From Nashville, Tennessee, to Atlanta, he was in the great campaign leading up to the fall of the latter city, was then on Sherman's march to the sea, and was then assigned to duty with his regiment at Columbus, Georgia, to relieve another regiment which had been sent to the frontier on account of Indian troubles. During the last months of his service he was chiefly engaged in keeping down the guerrillas. He was finally mustered out at Columbus, Georgia.

After the war returning to Canton, Illinois, he was soon working at the printing trade in an office there, and that experience proved valuable not only in giving him a substantial trade but also in enabling him to complete an education which had been necessarily neglected during the war. From Illinois he went south and conducted a republican newspaper at Columbia, Tennessee, during the years of 1876-77. On his return to Canton he was in the newspaper business a year, and then was traveling representative for the Illinois Transcript of Peoria.

Coming to Kansas in 1887, Mr. Kent was first located at Coffeyville for a year, and the following three years were spent in Eureka Springs, Kansas, on account of his ill health. For a time he was engaged in the insurance business at Coffeyville until he established his present paper in 1893.

Politically Mr. Kent is a republican, and is an active supporter of the Methodist Episcopal Church. He has held all the offices and is past commander of Post No. 90, Grand Army of the Republic at Coffeyville, and also belongs to Gate City Homestead No. 104, the second largest lodge in the Order of Homesteaders.

In 1869 at Laclede, Missouri, Mr. Kent married Mrs. Mary (Eastwood) Brickel, whose first husband was killed by the bushwackers during the Civil war. Mr. Kent has three children by this union: Leon Ulysses, who is a cigar manufacturer at Elmwood, Illinois; Henry Elmer, a professional musician whose home is in Indiana but who also travels as his profession demands; Lilly May, wife of G. Epley, proprietor of a restaurant at Elmwood, Illinois. At Independence, Kansas, in 1889 Mr. Kent married Mrs. Jennie Thomas, who died the following year. In September, 1893, at Coffeyville he married his present wife, Miss Mary Rout, a daughter of William Rout, who is a retired resident of Coffeyville. Mr. and Mrs. Kent have two children: Harry, who graduated from the Coffeyville High School with the class of 1916; and Ruth, who completed the eighth grade of the public schools, took a business course at Muskogee, Oklahoma, and is now living in California.

DAVID PRAGER. It was the influence of his personality and character as much as his successful business activities that made David Prager so useful and valuable a citizen of Fort Scott, where he resided for over forty years. His career illustrates the fact that the successful man is not necessarily the selfish man. He did not keep the resources of his heart nor of his material means to himself, but dispensed them with free hand among his family, his friends and the entire community. He was one of Fort Scott's most beloved and best known citizens.

David Prager was born in a village in Bavaria, Germany, June 7, 1834. He lived in Kansas from territorial days until his death at his home, 224 South Crawford Street, in Fort Scott, November 26, 1911. His death, due to heart failure, came suddenly, and though in his seventy-eighth year at the time, it was a heavy blow to the community.

His early education was acquired in his native land. At the age of fifteen he came to the United States and joined an older brother at St. Louis. He also lived for a few years in Peoria and Alton, Illinois. On coming to this country he began an apprenticeship as a jeweler and goldsmith. He finished the apprenticeship at Alton, and in 1858 arrived at Lawrence, Kansas, then the chief center of the free state community of Kansas. He was a prosperous jeweler of Lawrence when Quantrell made his famous raid. The Prager store was one of those looted by the bandit and guerilla, and the entire stock, valued at $4,000, was carried away. That his life was not taken always remained a circumstance considered miraculous by Mr. Prager. The raiders at first proceeded to his home, and from there marched to the store. Mrs. Prager, then a young wife, never expected to see him again. He himself had a premonition that his life would be spared, and told her he would soon return. He was made to unlock his store, and was then told to get home quickly. He lost no time in obeying this order, and thus his only loss was his stock of jewelry. Some years later the state reimbursed him to the extent of $1,800.

After the Lawrence raid he soon removed to Leavenworth, and for a few years was in the hardware business in that city. David Prager came to Fort Scott in 1869. He opened in that year the jewelry store which he conducted until the time of his death, though for several years he had been practically retired, two of his sons having assumed the main responsibilities of the business.

All the kind words and tributes spoken of him at the time of his death were more than justified. He had hundreds of friends, and all knew him to be a man of worth and integrity. Those closely associated with him, either socially or in business affairs, during the forty-two years he lived in Fort Scott, held for him the highest respect and esteem, and it is probable that he had not a single personal enemy. Devoted to family and friends, he had that cheerful disposition and jovial good will which made him not only a practical friend but a spiritual tonic to all who came within the boundaries of his influence. He lived a long life, and this was due to the fact that he was even tempered, had clean standards, and possessed an almost perfect poise of mind and body. He was always young in spirit, even after years accumulated a heavy load upon his shoulders. His youthfulness was not a pose, but a direct outflowing of an eternal spring deep in his nature. He spent much of his time with younger people. All the boys on the street esteemed it an honor to be his friend. He had a kindly word, a jest or a token of sympathy for all. His generosity was not confined to words alone. Some years ago, it is recalled, he learned that a young friend, in whom he took a special interest and whom he had assisted previously, was in a tangle of financial difficulties. He came to his aid, and it was assistance well bestowed, and by his act the young man was permanently set on his feet, and he afterward repaid every cent Mr. Pregar had advanced him. He was not the type of man to make money-getting an end in itself. He enjoyed the prosperity that came to him, and lived comfortably, and beyond that he asked nothing more. In many ways he exemplified that spirit of service to his family and fellowmen which must always be placed in the scale above mere riches.

David Prager was long affiliated with the Masonic order, and at the time of his death was one of the four surviving charter members of the Eastern Star Lodge of Fort Scott, which had been organized thirty-five years previously.

In a business way Mr. Prager built up the finest jewelry store in his section of the state. He was also one of the men who helped to make Fort Scott a city. During the great era of prosperity in the early '80s, he and J. E. Westervelt and N. Greenfield built in 1883 the Union Block, and since its completion the Prager jewelry store has been a constant tenant of the building. About the same time Mr. Prager put up the fine residence on South Crawford Street, where he lived until his death. For over fifteen years he was a member of the public library board.

At Lawrence, Kansas, September 30, 1859, he married Miss Hattie Briggs, of that city. Mrs. Prager died in 1906. She became the mother of eight children, and all these are still living.

Minnie Prager, the oldest of the family, is now the wife of L. A. Rucker of Coffeyville, Kansas.

William Prager, the second child, was born at Lawrence, December 31, 1862; was educated in the Fort Scott public schools, and at the age of seventeen entered his father's store and learned the trade and business of jeweler. He remained with his father until the latter's death, and in the meantime he and his brother, Louis, became active partners in the business and since their father's death have succeeded to the old established house. William Prager is a democrat, but believes that there is good in both parties, and has often exercised freedom of choice in the matter of candidates. He is a thirty-third degree Mason and also a member of the Scottish Rite, belongs to the Chapter and Mystic Shrine, and is also a member of the Benevolent and Protective Order of Elks. On February 24, 1897, at Fort Scott, he married Miss Lillie Stadden, daughter of Col. Isaac Stadden, of Fort Scott.

Fannie, the third child, is the widow of W. J. Smith of Fort Scott. Stella is the wife of Mr. Oscar Rice, the well-known insurance man of Fort Scott. Nettie married Mr. E. E. Reid of Fort Scott. Louis Prager has already been referred to as the associate of his brother, William, in the jewelry business established by their father.

Walter Prager, also a merchant at Fort Scott, married Miss Helen Kishler, who was born in Kansas City, Missouri, daughter of Samuel P. and Jane (Templeton) Kishler, now residents of Chicago. One son was born to their union, Samuel Kishler Prager, on March 31, 1916. Walter Prager is a member of the Masonic order and the Elks.

Catherine Prager is the wife of E. Clifford Gordon of Fort Scott, and they have two sons, David Prager Gordon and E. Clifford Gordon, Jr.

FRANK MARION HARR is city engineer of Parsons. He is a competent and thoroughly versed man in his profession, and he trained himself for that career.

His Harr ancestors came from Germany and settled in New York State in colonial times. His paternal grandfather, John M. Harr, was born in Ohio in 1820, spent his life as a farmer and died in Van Wert County of the Buckeye State in 1897. He was an active republican in politics. Of his children four are now deceased, and those still living, the uncles and aunts of Frank M. Harr, are: Corwin, a farmer in Van Wert County, Ohio; Demie, wife of Ben Britson, a retired farmer of Van Wert County; Abe, who lives retired in Woodward County, Oklahoma; Ad, a carpenter in Van Wert, Ohio; John M., engaged in the furniture business at Springfield, Missouri; Mary, wife of E. H. Snyder, a clothing merchant at Convoy, Ohio; Emma, wife of Burt Stewart, a retired farmer in Van Wert County; and P. A., a hardware merchant at Aurora, Missouri.

U. S. Harr, father of the Parsons city engineer, was born in Van Wert County, Ohio, November 13, 1856, and died at Parsons, December 11, 1913. His early life was spent in Van Wert County, and in 1880 he moved to Parsons and was married there. He was for thirty-three years in the employ of the Missouri, Kansas & Texas Railway as bridge and building foreman. An active republican, he was also a prominent fraternal man and was affiliated with Parsons Lodge, No. 117, Ancient Free and Accepted Masons, Parsons Chapter, No. 39, Royal Arch Masons, Coeur de Leon Commandery, Knights Templar, Fort Scott Consistory, No. 4, of the Scottish Rite, and also belonged to Parsons Lodge, No. 1, of the Ancient Order of United Workmen. U. S. Harr married Belle M. Waters. She was born in Champaign County, Illinois, March 11, 1861, and is still living at Parsons, where she married Mr. Harr. Her children are: C. A., a rodman at Parsons; Frank M.; Ethel Maude, wife of Fred Jarrell, a machinist at Osage Junction, Oklahoma; and Reba Kathleen, wife of W. H. Franklin, a railway brakeman living at Parsons.

Frank Marion Harr was born at Parsons, November 9, 1887, and has spent practically his entire life within the limits of that city. He attended the public schools, including the high school, but left his books and studies at the age of eighteen to take up the practical duties of the world. Mr. Harr began as driver of a delivery wagon, and followed various occupations for several years. In 1907 at the age of twenty he secured his first experience in engineering as a rodman, and by the competency displayed and the faithfulness to the discharge of every duty was advanced from one grade of the service to another until he became assistant engineer for Parsons in 1909, and on April 17, 1916, was appointed to his present post as city engineer. Mr. Harr in this capacity has charge of all the important details of municipal improvement. His offices are in the courthouse.

He is a democrat, is affiliated with Parsons Lodge, No. 117, Ancient Free and Accepted Masons, Parsons Lodge, No. 1, Ancient Order United Workmen, and his home is at 1327 Chess Street. On April 9, 1911, at Parsons he married Miss Kathryn Dempsey, daughter of E. H. and Mary Dempsey of Fairfield, Iowa. Her father is associated with The Cable Lumber Company. Mr. and Mrs. Harr have two children: Reba La Vaun, born March 25, 1912; and Frank Emert, born February 7, 1914.

CALVIN ARTHUR DAVIS. The superintendent of the Cudahy Refining Company at Chanute, Kansas, Calvin Arthur Davis, is one of the sons of the Sunflower state who has worked his own way to position and independence. A product of the farm, when he started upon his career his equipment consisted of ambition, determination and good common sense, and these qualities he directed so well that he soon became recognized as a man from whom large things could be expected. Promotion naturally followed, and his career has since been one of constant advancement.

Mr. Davis was born on a farm south of Fort Scott, in Bourbon County, Kansas, August 24, 1880, and is a son of Calvin and Hattie H. (Peterson) Davis. The family came originally from Wales and settled in Virginia, during the Colonial era, later branching out to Kentucky and other southern states. Luther Davis the grandfather of Calvin A., was born in 1815, in Kentucky, and prior to the Civil war was a planter and slaveholder near the city of Lexington. From Kentucky he went to Cumberland County, Illinois, where he farmed until the spring of 1877, at that time coming to Kansas and homesteading a tract of 160 acres of land in Butler County. There he passed the remaining years of his life in agricultural operations, becoming one of the substantial and highly respected citizens of his community. His death occurred on his farm, in 1885.

Calvin Davis, father of Calvin A., was born on his father's farm near Lexington, Kentucky, and was educated in the public schools of Cumberland County, Illinois, to which locality he was taken by his parents when a lad of seven years. He was reared as an agriculturist and followed that vocation in Illinois until the spring of 1878, when he came to Butler County, Kansas, as a pioneer, and homesteaded 160 acres of land near Eldorado. He remained there for only two years, however, and in the spring of 1880 took up his residence in Bourbon County, near Fort Scott, where he bought a partly-improved property. This he farmed until 1883, when he made another move, this time locating in Woodson, near Toronto, where he has a well-cultivated tract of eighty acres. Mr. Davis is still actively engaged in farming and stockraising and is known as a practical and progressive farmer and as a citizen who takes an interest in the community welfare and assists in beneficial movements. He is a democrat, but has not held office, and his fraternal affiliation is with the Modern Woodmen of America. He has held a number of lay offices in the Christian church, of which he has been a member since youth. Mr. Davis was married in Cumberland County, Illinois, to Miss Hattie H. Peterson, who was born in that county in 1852, and they have had the following children: Luther,

who resides in Woodson County and is a farmer; Calvin Arthur; Audrey, who is the wife of John Harris, an oil tank builder of Oilton, Oklahoma; Omar, who is engaged in farming in Woodson County, Kansas; Orian, also an agriculturist there; Louis, who likewise follows the vocation of farming in Woodson County; and Mabel and Caroline, who reside near Toronto with their parents.

Calvin Arthur Davis received only ordinary educational advantages in the public schools of Woodson County, where he completed the eighth grade course. However, he has made the most of his opportunities, and through observation and reading has made himself a well educated man. He was reared amid agricultural surroundings, remaining on the home farm until he was twenty-two years of age, but did not care for the life of a farmer and, accordingly, in 1902, came to Chanute, where he accepted a minor position with the Atchison, Topeka & Santa Fe Railroad. During the three years that he was identified with this line he was promoted several times, and in 1905 left the employ of the railroad to enter the service of the Kansas Oil Refining Company, with which he remained two years, gaining a good working knowledge of the refining business. In 1907 he entered the employ of the Chanute Refining Company, and steadily worked his way upward to the position of superintendent, which office he has held since May, 1914. The plant was purchased by the Sinclair Oil Refining Company, in June, 1916, and the name changed to the Cudahy Refining Company, Mr. Davis being retained in the capacity of superintendent, a position for which he is singularly fitted by training and experience. The plant of this concern is situated one and one-half miles south of Chanute, and has a daily capacity of 2,700 barrels, oil coming from the Oklahoma fields. Mr. Davis is the owner of his own residence, at No. 1302 South Forest Avenue, Chanute, and a valuable farm of eighty acres four miles south of Chanute. In politics he is a democrat, but has found his time occupied with his business to an extent that keeps him from taking more than a good citizen's interest in public matters. He is fraternally affiliated with Cedar Lodge No. 103, Ancient Free and Accepted Masons, and Chanute Camp No. 852, Modern Woodmen of America.

In 1904 Mr. Davis was married at Yates Center, Kansas, to Miss May Austin, daughter of Steve and Rachel (Rhoades) Austin. Mr. Austin, who was a farmer, is now deceased, but the mother still survives and makes her home at Toronto. Mr. and Mrs. Davis have two children: Fay, born April 21, 1907, and Clair, born August 11, 1910.

JAMES L. McCoy has for many years been identified with the lumber industry both in Kansas and Arkansas, and manages his extensive interests from his home and headquarters at Coffeyville.

Nearly all his active career has been spent in the West and in the early days of Oklahoma he went there as a pioneer and opened a farm. James L. McCoy was born in Atchison County, Missouri, May 21, 1869. Four generations of the McCoys have lived in this country, having come originally from Scotland, and the family were early settlers in the State of Ohio. Mr. McCoy's grandfather, Andrew Cartwright, who was born in Maryland and followed farming in Ohio, was a cousin of Peter Cartwright, the famous Methodist evangelist of the early days in Southern Ohio and other states.

William McCoy, father of James L., was born in Pike County, Ohio, in 1836, and died at Coffeyville· in 1905. He came out to Kansas and located at Coffeyville in 1886, and for many years was in the general merchandise business with store at the corner of Eighth and Walnut streets. He built the fine business block known as the McCoy or Junction Building at the corner of Eighth and Walnut streets. That building is still included in his estate, as are also two dwelling houses, one at 601 Willow Street and another at Third and Union streets.

Reared and receiving his early education in Pike County, Ohio, James L. McCoy came west in 1885, and in 1887 went to Arkansas, where he engaged in the lumber business a few miles out of Fayetteville on the Frisco Railroad, about the time that railroad was constructed. Some five years later he went to the southern part of the state and established his mills in Horatio. He still owns extensive interests in the pine lumber districts of that section. Since 1906 Mr. McCoy has had his home in Coffeyville, and has operated extensively as a retail lumber dealer. His yards are on Eighth Street near the Santa Fe Railroad tracks. Mr. McCoy also has sawmills at Horatio, Arkansas, and another lumber yard at Angola, Kansas.

He is executor of his father's estate and individually he owns a row of flats on Maple Street, forty acres of farm land east of Coffeyville, and one of the most attractive modern brick residences in Coffeyville at 410 Elm Street. Mr. McCoy for the past two years has been a trustee in the Methodist Episcopal Church. He is a democrat, a member of the Masonic order and belongs to the Lumberman's Fraternity, the Hoo Hoos.

Mrs. James L. McCoy has for a number of years been one of the recognized leaders in women's affairs at Coffeyville, and has accomplished a great deal in making woman's influence effective in behalf of a cleaner and better city and more wholesome conditions throughout the community. Mrs. McCoy, who married Mr. McCoy in 1891, at St. Paul, Arkansas, was before her marriage Miss Katie Bretz. She is in the fifth generation from her ancestor Bretz who came from Holland and.settled in Pennsylvania in colonial times. This ancestor was Philip Bretz, who located in Lancaster County, Pennsylvania, in 1765. Mr. McCoy has a complete and authentic record of all the generations subsequent to the Bretz family on American shores.

Mrs. McCoy was born at Moccasin, Effingham County, Illinois, was educated in the public schools there, was a teacher in the schools for three years, and then for two years before her marriage was connected with the schools at St. Paul, Arkansas, where she met Mr. McCoy.

Mrs. McCoy is one of the active workers of the Methodist Episcopal Church at Coffeyville, teaches a class in the Sunday School and is conference treasurer of the Home Missionary Society. She is a member of Coffeyville Chapter No. 112 of the Order of the Eastern Star. Her name is especially familiar in connection with woman's club affairs. She belongs to the Culture Club, which is affiliated with the State Federation of Woman's Clubs, and is a member of the City Federation of Woman's Clubs. Again and again her work and ·influence have been helpful in promoting many movements for the advantage and improvement of her home city.

All this she has accomplished together with the rearing and training of a large family of promising children, many of whom are already on their own responsibilities and making good in the business world. Mr. and Mrs. McCoy have one grandchild.

The oldest of their ten children is Clarence, who was born December 20, 1892, is manager of his father's sawmill at Horatio, Arkansas, and at Horatio married Ethel Millwee, by whom he has one child, J. L. McCoy, Jr., born March 9, 1915. Lawrence, the second son, was born December 24, 1893, and conducts his father's lumber yard at Angola, Kansas, he being a graduate of the Coffeyville High School. Katie Ray was born August 18, 1897, and died December 10, 1902. William was born November 20, 1899, and is a junior in the Coffeyville High School. Elizabeth was born June 8, 1901, and died in early infancy. Ruth, born August 26, 1903, is making rapid progress as a scholar and is now in the eighth grade of the public schools. Esther, born November 18, 1904, is also a remarkably bright child and is in the eighth grade. Frank was born October 9, 1906, and George on January 9, 1909, both being in the grammar schools. Ralph, the youngest, born November 19, 1912, and died October 3, 1914.

Mrs. McCoy's father is John Bretz, who was born at Akron, Ohio, June 12, 1836, and is now living at the venerable age of eighty years at Abbott, Arkansas. He grew up and married his first wife in Ohio, was a farmer for a number of years, moved to Illinois in 1862, where he followed farming and the drug business, and in 1887 entered the sawmilling industry in Arkansas, where he is still living, being now retired. Mr. John Bretz is a democrat, and has held the various lay offices in the Methodist Episcopal Church. He is a Royal Arch Mason. His first wife was Julia Hoffman, and her two children were: Jennie, the widow of Thomas Kramer, who was an Illinois farmer and died in 1915; and George, a farmer at Shields, Kansas. For his second wife John Bretz married Angeline Mahin, who was born in Illinois in 1845 and died at Moccasin in that state in 1879. Her children were: Sarah and Lizzie, both deceased; Mrs. James L. McCoy; Edward, deceased; Bertha, who lives in Louisiana, the widow of William Shanklin, who was in the mining business in Missouri associated with his uncle Nathaniel Shanklin, who still lives there; Frank, a sawmill man at Horatio, Arkansas; and Effie, now deceased. John Bretz married for his third wife Mary Culler, and the only child of that union is Fannie, who is unmarried and lives at Massillon, Ohio. For his present wife John Bretz married Lizzie Lucas.

WILLIAM A. CORMANY. During a period covering more than a half century William A. Cormany has been a resident of Fort Scott, and in this time has been closely identified with the agencies that have made for progress along material, educational and moral lines. Coming here a veteran of the Civil war, in 1866, he entered newspaper life as owner of the Fort Scott Monitor, and since then his activities have branched out in various avenues of business. He is one of the few remaining of the early settlers of the city, and looks upon its present prosperity with the eye of a proprietor.

Mr. Cormany is a son of William and Margaret (Coldsmith) Cormany, the former of whom was born in Edinburg, Scotland, in 1810, and the latter in Pennsylvania, of Dutch descent, in 1813. William Cormany was brought to the United States in 1813, by his parents, the family settling in Pennsylvania, where he met and married Margaret Coldsmith, and in 1840 they started for Ohio in a covered wagon. When they were twelve miles from the little Town of Lithopolis, Fairfield County, Ohio, the wagon broke down, and before the journey could be resumed, the son, William A., was born, January 27, 1841. Several weeks later the little party again got under way and finally reached their destination, at Lancaster, Ohio, where the father worked at his trade of harnessmaker and also engaged in the manufacture of black-snake whips, contracted for by the United States Government. In 1862 the family went to Illinois, and there the mother died in the following year. She really grieved herself to death over the fact that she could learn nothing as to the fate of her three sons, George, Jacob and William A., who served through the Civil war as Union soldiers. Jacob Cormany was given a medal of honor for carrying his wounded captain from the field of battle under fire. The father survived the mother for some time, dying in 1880. He had been a soldier during the Mexican war, while William A. Corman's maternal grandfather was an American soldier during the War of 1812.

William A. Cormany attended the public schools of Lancaster, Ohio, but never graduated therefrom, the greater part of his education having come from the school of experience. As a youth he was bound over to a printer at Lancaster, where he served three years, during which time he received $30 per year for his services. After ten years of service he received a diploma, as was the custom of that day, signifying that he was a full-fledged journeyman printer. Armed with this, he went to Cincinnati, Ohio, but soon found out he had much to learn in regard to the printing business. His first salary at Cincinnati was $5 per week, and as his board and room cost him $4.75 it left the young man little for himself, but he was persevering and ambitious and decided to ''stick it out.'' His persistence was rewarded, for after several months he was placed in the showbill department of the Cincinnati Commercial, and there made splendid headway, soon becoming considered as an expert in the art of show-bill printing. At this time Mr. Cormany's career was interrupted by the Civil war. He came of good fighting stock on both sides of the family, and when the call came for volunteers to defend the Union, he responded, and April 12, 1861, enlisted in Company D, Sixth Regiment, Ohio Volunteer Infantry. This regiment was one of the first to go into action at the front and participated in the engagements at Laurel Hill, Carrick's Ford, Elkwater, Muzo Flats, Shiloh, Corinth, Perryville and Stone River, at which last-named battle Mr. Cormany was captured by the enemy, and held prisoner for nine months, the last three months of which time he was incarcerated in the notorious Libby Prison. That he suffered all the hardships and privations that were the portion of captured Union soldiers is shown in the fact that when captured he weighed 140 pounds, and when released weighed 89¾ pounds. After his recovery he fought at Chickamauga, Brown's Ferry, Orchard Knob and Missionary Ridge, and two days before his regiment was mustered out of the service, in June, 1864, was promoted second lieutenant for conspicuous bravery in leading a charge on Fort Resaca. When the Sixth Ohio was mustered into the service it totalled 1,031 men, and when mustered out but 327 of the original muster remained, and this regiment was the first in point of general health in the entire Northern army.

At the close of his military service, Mr. Cormany returned to Cincinnati, but soon became dissatisfied with his condition and believing that he could better himself in the West, in 1866 he came to Fort Scott,

where, on March 1, he purchased the Monitor. With this publication he contined to be identified for many years, building it up to be one of the strong and influential newspapers of the state. Later various other business ventures secured the benefit of his ability and energy, and at the present time he is one of the best known men in Fort Scott in the fire insurance field. It was but natural that a man of Mr. Cormany's ability should be called upon for public service, and as city councilman, and finance commissioner under the commission form of government, he accomplished much for the advancement and general good of his adopted city. Mr. Cormany is a republican, and is affiliated with the Baptist Church. He belongs to the Grand Army of the Republic, the Benevolent and Protective Order of Elks and the United Commercial Travelers, and is prominent in Odd Fellowship, being past grand master of the Grand Lodge of Kansas.

On August 27, 1864, Mr. Cormany was married at Mount Carroll, Illinois, to Miss Susan Emmert. Mrs. Cormany's brother was Hon. D. B. Emmert, who was elected in the fall of 1869 as state senator of Kansas. He was a noted man in public life, a brilliant writer, and a close friend and associate of Hon. Eugene Ware, eminent Kansas lawyer and poet. Five children were born to Mr. and Mrs. Cormany: Ora, who is the wife of Grant Frankenburger, of Cimarron, New Mexico; Grace, who is the wife of W. B. Shirk, of Kansas City, Missouri; Charles E., of Milwaukee, who fought as a soldier during the Spanish-American war; Ada, who is the wife of C. E. Warner, who was adjutant of the Twentieth Kansas Regiment under General Funston, in Cuba, during our late war with Spain; and W. N. Cormany, of Fort Scott, who is commercial freight agent of the Missouri Pacific. Mr. and Mrs. Cormany have fourteen grandchildren and three great-grandchildren. They celebrated their Golden Wedding Anniversary in the mountains of New Mexico, August 27, 1914.

JOHN McEWEN AMES. One of the leading business institutions of Caney, Kansas, is that operating under the name of Kan-o-Tex Refining Company, an industry which has contributed materially to the importance of this city as a center of business activity. The credit for the success of this enterprise is largely due to its president, John McEwen Ames, a man of broad experience and marked business talents, who, until coming to Caney in 1915, had been identified with large business corporations in the East.

Mr. Ames was born in New York City, New York, February 12, 1867, and is a son of John Hubbard and Sarah Lucy (Hyde) Ames. He belongs to a family which originally came from England to Weathersfield, Connecticut, during colonial times, and on his father's side has Revolutionary ancestors, one being Ithiel Battle, the grandfather of his maternal grandmother, who enlisted in the patriot army from Tyringham, Massachusetts; while another was Josiah Harvey, a surgeon's mate who enlisted from Connecticut, and who was the father of Mr. Ames' grandfather's mother. Mr. Ames is also directly descended from Mayflower ancestors, as is shown in the following genealogy: John Tilly and wife were on the Mayflower, and both died a little after coming ashore. Their daughter, Elizabeth Tilly, was married in 1620, when fourteen years of age, to John Howland, aged twenty-eight years, also of the Mayflower. Their daughter, Hope Howland, of Plymouth, was married in 1646 to Elder John Chipman, Boston, 1631; Barnstable, 1649; Sandwich, 1684-1708. Desire Chipman, daughter of Elder John and Hope (Howland) Chipman, born February 26, 1673-4, died 1705, married February 23, 1692, Col. Melatiah Bourn, of Sandwich, born 1673, died 1742. Bathsheba Bourn, daughter of Col. Melatiah and Desire (Chipman) Bourn, born in 1703, married William Newcomb, born in 1702, died 1736. Their daughter, Sarah Newcomb, born in 1729, married October 19, 1760, Benjamin Fessenden, born 1729, died 1783. Lucy Fessenden, daughter of Benjamin and Sarah (Newcomb) Fessenden, born in 1770, died in 1852, married April 25, 1793; Alvan Hyde, D. D., born in 1768, died in 1833. Joseph Hyde, son of Alvan and Lucy (Fessenden) Hyde, married Catherine McEwen. Sarah L. Hyde, daughter of Joseph and Catherine (McEwen) Hyde, married John H. Ames, and they became the parents of John McEwen Ames.

John Hubbard Ames, the father of John McEwen Ames, was born at Housatonic, Massachusetts, December 27, 1838, his parents being William Henry Ames of Housatonic and Lucy Bartlett of Lee, Massachusetts. Entering Williams College in 1856, he discontinued his course in 1858 to go abroad in company with George Fuller, the artist of Deerfield, Massachusetts. At the outbreak of the Civil war, in 1861, he applied for examination and was commissioned in the United States Navy as engineer of the third grade and assigned to the Connecticut for blockade duty. His service continued throughout the war in this duty, except for the time during which he, with others, was detailed by the Government to experiment with superheated steam on boats plying between Baltimore and Fortress Monroe. At the close of the war he started on the Minnesota to circle the globe, but the ship broke down and had to return to New York, and Mr. Ames resigned his commission as past assistant engineer to become superintendent of the Yale Lock Company, then located at Shelbourne Falls, Massachusetts. In 1871 he was superintendent of the Herring Safe Company, New York, and in 1872 was made superintendent of the Grant Locomotive Works, at Paterson, New Jersey. As representative of this concern he was sent to Odessa to erect a consignment of locomotives purchased by the Russian Government, the first ever exported by an American concern. The Grant Company failed while he was abroad and in 1875 he again became superintendent of the Yale Lock Company, at that time located at Stamford, Connecticut, which position he held until 1879, when he was employed by the Northern Pacific Railroad Company in the purchase of rails and locomotives. In 1881 he was made purchasing agent of this company and was transferred to Saint Paul, Minnesota. Mr. Ames retired from the position in 1890, as his health was failing, and shortly thereafter moved back to the East, dying April 14, 1908, at his home at Ware, Massachusetts. Mr. Ames was a member of the Loyal Legion. He made the designs for the first government postoffice boxes for the Yale Lock Company and secured a number of patents, among others a steam separator for boilers, a Yale padlock, a refrigerator, an automatic brake for railroad cars, a railway signal apparatus and a pneumatic transmitter for store service.

At Clifton, Staten Island, December 26, 1861, Mr. Ames was married to Sarah Lucy Hyde, and they became the parents of the following children: William Henry, who is connected with the M. B. Farrin Lumber Company, of Cincinnati, Ohio; Joseph Hyde, with the American Car and Foundry Company, of Chicago, Illinois; John McEwen, of this review; George Fuller, with the freight department of the New York Central Railroad, at Rochester, New York; Henry Olmsted, connected with the St. Paul Fire and Marine Insurance Company, St. Paul, Minnesota; Lucy Bartlett, who is the wife of Remsen McGinnis, treasurer of the Holly Sugar Company, of Denver, Colorado; and Catherine McEwen and Sarah Hyde, unmarried, who reside with their mother at Ware, Massachusetts.

After some preparatory education, John McEwen Ames entered the Shattuck School, at Faribault, Minnesota, from which he was graduated in 1887, following which he pursued a course at Johns Hopkins University, where he secured the degree of Bachelor of Arts and graduated in the class of 1890. While at college he was a member of the Alpha Delta Phi Greek letter fraternity. In the spring of 1891 he started his business experience with the Peninsular Car Company, as a draughtsman, at Detroit, Michigan, and with the organizing of the Michigan Peninsular Car Company, was made chief draughtsman, a position which he retained from 1894 until 1899. In the latter year he accepted a position as mechanical engineer of the American Car and Foundry Company, and went to New York City, acting in that capacity until coming to Caney, in October, 1915.

In the meantime, in 1909, he had become president of the Kan-o-Tex Refining Company, a concern which had been organized that year for the purpose of refining crude oil from the Kansas and Oklahoma fields. Jacob Bartles had built the original plant at Caney, while Bennett & Miller had erected a plant at Longton, Kansas, and the new organization purchased the two plants, dismantled the one at Longton, and brought both together at Caney, where the main offices and plant are now located beside the Santa Fe Railroad tracks. The company now has machinery of the latest invention and manufacture, and the capacity of the plant is 1,000 barrels per day, with the force working up to capacity output practically all the time. The present list of officers includes: president, John McEwen Ames; vice president, Wilbur Munn, of Orange, New Jersey; secretary, Frank Heilig, of Caney, Kansas; treasurer, Robert R. Cox, of Caney; superintendent of refineries, E. S. Dorrance, of Caney; superintendent of leases, Clyde M. Boggs, of Bartlesville, Oklahoma; directors, John McEwen Ames, Wilbur Munn, H. M. De Lanoie of New York City, Frank Heilig and Robert R. Cox. In addition to being the directing head of this large and important enterprise, Mr. Ames has various other interests, being a director of the American Car and Foundry Export Company of New York City, and president of the Columbia Bolt and Nut Company of Bridgeport, Connecticut. He has a broad and firmly established reputation as a mechanical engineer, and has been the patentee of a number of ingenious inventions. He belongs to the American Society of Mechanical Engineers, the New York Railroad Club and the Engineers' Club of New York City, and to the Alpha Delta Phi Club of New York City, and the Havana Country Club. Politically, he is a republican, and his religious support is given to the Protestant Episcopal Church, of which he has long been a member.

On January 5, 1907, Mr. Ames was married at Williamsport, Pennsylvania, to Miss Josephine Bowman Coleman, daughter of Fletcher and Millicent Coleman, both of whom died at Williamsport, where Mr. Coleman was engaged in business as a lumber merchant.

WILLIAM M. JARDINE, Dean of the Division of Agriculture and Director of the Agricultural Experiment

Station, Kansas State Agricultural College, was born January 16, 1879, on a ranch in Oneida County, Idaho, where his parents, William and Rebecca (Dudley) Jardine had settled as pioneers in 1871 at the time of their marriage. William Jardine was born at Paisley, Scotland, in 1849, and came to this country when fifteen years of age. Rebecca Dudley was born at Willard City, Utah, in 1855, of Welsh parentage. William M. Jardine, their fourth child and eldest son, found it necessary at an early age to assume unusual responsibilities which were destined to give him invaluable experience and an unexcelled practical training. At that time Southern Idaho was an almost unbroken range covered with timber or sage brush. From twelve years of age until he finished his college course, his range of activities included breaking colts, driving horses long distances to market, cutting timber, stacking hay, milking cows, breaking sod covered with sage brush, using horses for power, and performing any and all of the varied services required by ranch life in a new country. The greater part of the three years preceding his first attendance at college was spent on a ranch in Big Hole Basin, Montana, where the sole enterprise consisted in cattle raising with its attendant features of broncho breaking and round-ups, and where, as a supplement, great quantities of prairie hay were yearly cut and stacked for feed.

In mid-winter, the year he was nineteen years of age, he entered the Utah Agricultural College as a sub-freshman. His previous schooling had consisted of a term each winter of from two to three months in the country schools of Idaho. The close of college in the spring found him with funds exhausted. He felt it hopeless to try to continue college work, but during his brief residence, various members of the college faculty had become impressed with his native genius and potential possibilities, and brought forces to bear which subsequently enabled him to return to college. Following friendly advice, he went home, secured a country school with a six months' term, and at its close, leased his father's ranch, giving his parents opportunity for an extended vacation, and during the remainder of the year so applied modern and progressive ideas in its management as to astonish his family and friends with its pecuniary returns. The next fall he re-entered college and continued in attendance without further interruption until graduation in 1904 with the degree of Bachelor of Science in Agriculture. The summer of 1906 he attended the Graduate School of Agriculture of the University of Illinois. September 6, 1905, at Salt Lake City, Utah, he was married to Effie Nebeker of Logan, Utah.

Following the completion of his college course, William M. Jardine, became interested in the possibilities of successfully farming western lands on a large scale through the use of big machinery, such as the traction engine and the combined harvester. He became a charter member of the Utah Arid Farming Company, a Utah corporation, the first organization in that state to test the practicability of so employing machinery. He was manager of the Utah Arid Farming Company during 1905. A few years later he became a charter member of the Northern Pure Seed Company, a Montana corporation operating a tract of several thousand acres of land near Forsyth, Montana, on the Yellowstone River, and was director of the Company from 1908 to 1915. The Northern Pure Seed Company also made a specialty of using large machinery in its operations. In the course of his agricultural work in the West, W. M. Jardine became

one of the leaders in introducing and growing profitably on a large scale, hard winter wheat in Montana.

Notwithstanding his great and continued interest in practical farming, the chief activities of W. M. Jardine have been educational. In 1904, while a senior student in the Utah Agricultural College, he became an assistant in the Department of Agronomy; the following year he was made instructor and then professor of agronomy, in which position he continued until the close of 1906. He served as Assistant United States Cerealist in charge of dry-land grain investigations from 1907 to 1910. During this period his residence was in Washington, D. C., but the greater part of his time was spent in the field superintending the work of substations and studying dry-land agriculture in the different western states and in Canada. In 1910 he became agronomist at the Kansas State Agricultural College, and in 1913 was made Dean of the Division of Agriculture and Director of the Agricultural Experiment Station. He was lecturer in field crops at the Graduate School of Agriculture, Michigan Agricultural College, 1912.

The reclamation of the dry lands of the West attracted the interest and attention of W. M. Jardine from the beginning. While connected with the Utah Agricultural College he helped to establish a series of substations for the State of Utah, at which stations the first comprehensive investigations in dry-farming were conducted. Two years later, as expert in dry-land agriculture and Assistant in Cereal Crops in the United States Department of Agriculture, he assisted in the establishment of similar stations in other western states. These stations are now operated by the Department of Agriculture in co-operation with the several states in which they are located.

The work of reclaiming the arid lands of the West was made possible through the development of the system of farming known as dry-farming, whereby crops are produced without irrigation in areas of limited rainfall. The fundamental principles of this system were developed through studies made at the dry-land experiment stations first established by individual states and later by the federal government. W. M. Jardine has been closely identified with the dry-farming movement from its inception and has become a recognized authority on the subject. He was one of the founders of the International Dry-Farming Congress, has served on its Board of Governors almost continuously, and was president of the organization during the year 1915-1916.

W. M. Jardine has been author of numerous papers on dry-farming and other subjects related to agriculture and of numerous bulletins published by the Utah Agricultural College, the United States Department of Agriculture, and the Kansas State Agricultural College. He was elected president of the American Society of Agronomy at its ninth annual meeting, November 13-14, 1916. He is a member of the honorary fraternities, Alpha Zeta and Phi Kappa Phi, and the social fraternity, Beta Theta Pi. He is a fellow of the American Association for the Advancement of Science, and a member of the National Institute of Social Sciences, the Masonic order, and the Grange. He is a member of the Cosmos Club, Washington, D. C., and the Commercial Club of Manhattan, Kansas.

W. M. Jardine is a comparatively young man whose untiring energy, indomitable courage and initiative, combined with a winning personality, a student attitude, and a unique ability to apply science effectively to the most practical farm problems, have amply

the sights of the town, discounted the wind, the bullets and the bad men, and pointed out that the most favorable place in the whole world for a young man to make his fortune was right at Hugoton. But the young reporter couldn't see it that way and was up before daylight to catch the stage for Lakin, and he never returned to that country until he became a candidate for governor.

From the publication of the weekly Mail and Breeze it was but natural for an active newspaper man to drift into the daily publishing business, and when the Bank of Topeka found itself the owner of the Topeka Capital it picked the likeliest newspaper man in the state. Whatever the purchase price, only $2,000 in real money changed hands the day the deal was made. That was all Arthur Capper had. He was given all the time he wanted to pay the balance.

It was a long and hard pull to get the Capital out of the fire. But Arthur Capper kept at it until he had made that paper one of the most profitable newspaper enterprises in the state. Along with the Capital he built up the Mail and Breeze until it became the biggest farm paper in Kansas. From time to time there has been added the Missouri Valley Farmer, Capper's Weekly, Nebraska Farm Journal, Missouri Ruralist, the Household and the Oklahoma Farmer.

The management of the business and editorial affairs of all these papers could be successfully handled by one man only if he were trained in practically every department of the publication business. That is where Arthur Capper showed himself to be a smart man when he quit work at $25 a week in the composing room to take a reporter's job at $10 a week. Besides the newspapers there is the big job printing establishment and also the big engraving plant, all operated under the direct supervision of Mr. Capper.

After getting his business well organized the young man decided to see for himself just how he had the business in hand. So he went into politics, leaving the men he had trained to actually manage his papers, printing plant and engraving company. The big properties continued to run just as smoothly and just as profitably as when Mr. Capper was in active charge all the time, which indicates a wonderful genius for organization and the picking of men who can be depended upon.

Five years ago he built the big new building for all his properties. It is a five story building and was thought to be large enough to handle the business for years. It is already overcrowded.

In politics Arthur Capper has always been a republican. But he has been on the side of progress at every turn, and all but bolted the party several times to make it swing from standpatism to progressivism and the cause of advancement. He stood by the progressive wing of the party even in defeat and when it cost him hundreds of votes of the stand-pat element of the party. He has always supported business in the administration of state, county and city affairs and when he became governor it was upon the express promise to do for the state as he had done for his own business, as far as he was able. Two years in office showed him the folly of a real business administration in state affairs with the system of government that permitted changes of officers every two or four years and divided responsibility where derelict officials could blame others for their failure to perform their sworn duties. At the opening of his second term Governor Capper announced a program of progressive measures intended to make government simpler, more effective and less expensive to the taxpayers. The budget system of state appropriations, the consolidation of boards and commissions with more direct responsibility, the city-manager plan and a change of county governments to remove numerous useless and expensive offices, were included in his program.

Governor Capper has been interested in almost everything that makes Kansas a better place to live in. He fought for the pensions for mothers and the child hygiene department and when he found there was a joker in the mother's pension law set about to remove this and make the law a real benefit to the women and children of the state. He has been an active member or an officer in the various peace movements and was a vice president for Kansas for the National Welfare League. He has always been a booster for good roads and for prohibition in the state and nation. He helped put through the workingmen's compensation law amendments, and fought for a minimum wage and shorter hours for the women workers of the state. In fact, there has been nothing that makes for better government, better homes, better society that he has not taken an active interest in. He is also an ardent lodge man, belonging to several secret orders and is one of the governors of Mooseheart, the Moose home in Illinois.

In 1892 Mr. Capper married Miss Florence Crawford, daughter of the late Samuel J. Crawford, the third governor of Kansas. For many years they lived in an old frame home at the corner of Topeka Avenue and Eleventh Street. This was recently torn down, and an elegant and comfortable home was built on the grounds.

ANDY CURRY has been a resident of Montgomery County for thirty-four years. To an older generation of the people of this county he is well remembered as a successful teacher. For nearly a quarter of a century he has been in the insurance business at Coffeyville and has built up one of the largest local agencies in the state for general insurance.

His ancestors were Irish people who came to America and settled in Kentucky in the very early days. From Kentucky the family moved to Southern Indiana, locating in the Wabash valley, and it was in Sullivan County, Indiana, that Andy Curry was born December 2, 1855. His grandfather, Samuel Curry, was born in Mercer County, Kentucky, in 1789, the year that George Washington was inaugurated as the first president of the United States, and a date which attests the very early settlement of the Curry family in the blue grass region. Samuel Curry crossed the Ohio River and settled in Sullivan County, Indiana, along with the first movement of population into that region, was a farmer there, and died in 1869. He was a strong democrat, and a consistent member and elder of the Presbyterian Church. Grandfather Curry married Sallie Thompson, who was born in Virginia and died in Sullivan County, Indiana, at the age of ninety years. None of their children are now living.

John S. Curry, father of Andy, was born in Kentucky in 1817, and was a small child when his parents moved to Sullivan County, Indiana. He grew up there, married in that county, and became a carpenter and builder. In that trade he assisted in constructing a great many houses and other buildings throughout the district south of Terre Haute. He died in Sullivan County in 1871. He was a democrat and a member of the Presbyterian Church. John S. Curry married Nancy C. Wilson, who represented another pioneer family of Sullivan County, where she was born in 1826. She died at Terre

Haute, Indiana, in 1891. Their children were: Samuel, who became a farmer, later retiring to Terre Haute, where he died in 1908; Sarah, who died at Shelburn, Indiana, married John Siner, a farmer, also deceased; Margaret, who died in Sullivan county, married Anderson Mitchell, a retired farmer in Vigo County, Indiana; Martha, who lives with her brother Andy at Coffeyville, has lost three husbands, John Adams, a farmer, Jeptha Baldridge, a merchant, and James McKee, a farmer; H. W. Curry is a teacher living at Terre Haute; John F. died at Shelburn, Indiana, in 1874, at the age of twenty-two; the seventh in age is Andy; Robert B. died at the age of fourteen; Arpa is the wife of William T. Bolinger, a retired farmer at Caney, Kansas; Nancy, who died at Terre Haute, was the wife of Spencer McGrew, a hardware merchant, now deceased.

Reared in the country districts of Sullivan County, Andy Curry acquired a common school education, and availed himself of such opportunities as were presented to him not only to secure an education, but also to qualify as a teacher of others. For several terms he attended the Indiana State Normal School at Terre Haute. In the meantime he had begun teaching in the country districts and followed that vocation in Indiana for six years. In March, 1882, Mr. Curry arrived in Coffeyville, Kansas, and during the next eight years was a teacher in the country schools of Montgomery County, and during part of that time also followed farming.

Since the spring of 1890 he has lived in Coffeyville. In that city for seven years he was clerk in a clothing store, was in the wholesale cigar business for two years, and has since been an insurance man and has built up a large business in the city and also operates as a broker. His offices are in the Terminal Building. His home is at 708 Willow Street.

While living in Parker Township, as a teacher and farmer, he served two terms as township trustee. At Coffeyville he has been honored again and again with a place on the school board and also as a member of the city council. The citizens of Coffeyville remember to his special credit his work as mayor, an office to which he was elected in 1913 for two years. One feature of his administration was the construction of a large dam at the waterworks and the introduction of such improvements as to make the city water plant one of greatly increased efficiency. While mayor he insisted upon a strict enforcement of the laws and ordinances and the city was so well governed that there was no occasion for state officials to intervene in local affairs.

Mr. Curry is a democrat, is a member of the Coffeyville Commercial Club, and is affiliated with Lodge No. 117, Independent Order of Odd Fellows, Camp No. 665, Modern Woodmen of America, and Lodge No. 775, Benevolent and Protective Order of Elks, all of Coffeyville.

In October, 1879, in Vigo County, Indiana, Mr. Curry married Miss Ella E. Seldomridge, daughter of John M. and Alice Seldomridge, both now deceased. Her father was a miller and afterwards a farmer. Mr. and Mrs. Curry have one daughter, Bonnie, who is a graduate of the Coffeyville High School, and is now the wife of R. K. Long, an oil producer and operator living at Coffeyville.

HARRY S. BROWN. A lawyer of twenty years' experience, Harry S. Brown has been identified with the Coffeyville bar the greater part of his professional career and he has shown a remarkable capacity for handling litigation entrusted to him and is a leading citizen as well as a lawyer.

He represents an old Indiana family of English origin. His first American ancestors came to South Carolina in colonial times. Through his grandmother Mr. Brown is of Scotch descent. One of his Brown ancestors was a captain in the English navy and lost his life at sea. His grandfather, John Brown, died near Frankfort, Indiana, and was a native of South Carolina, having established his home on a farm in the Hoosier state during the '30s.

Mr. Harry S. Brown was born at Wanamaker, Indiana, September 16, 1870. His father, Samuel M. Brown, was born in South Carolina in 1822, and was about eight years of age when his parents moved to the vicinity of Frankfort, Indiana. He became a physician and surgeon, graduating M. D. from the Cincinnati Medical College and practiced continuously and usefully at Wanamaker for a period of fifty-six years. He was a democrat, very active in the Baptist Church, a member of the Masonic fraternity and at one time was a candidate for the State Legislature. Dr. Brown's first wife was a Miss Brady, who died at Wanamaker, leaving the following children: Henry J., a merchant, who died at Wanamaker in 1915; Edorus O., a money broker at Indianapolis; Corydon S., a physician and surgeon at Wanamaker; Arthur V., an attorney and a member of the Indianapolis bar; Charles A., a civil engineer living at Indianapolis. For his second wife Doctor Brown married Marilda McGaughey, who was born near Hamilton, Ohio, in August, 1841, and now resides at Indianapolis. Her children were: Harry S.; Edward A., a physician and surgeon at Indianapolis; Frank T., a member of the Indianapolis bar; and Ruth, wife of Daniel S. Adams, a physician and surgeon at Indianapolis.

Harry S. Brown as a boy attended the public schools of Wanamaker, and took a six years' course in Butler University at Irvington, a suburb of Indianapolis. He was graduated Bachelor of Science in 1893 and in 1896 completed his course and received the degree LL. B. from the Indiana School of Law at Indianapolis. After his admission to the Indiana bar in 1896 Mr. Brown practiced at Indianapolis for five years, and in 1901 moved to Coffeyville. He soon acquired a living practice in that city and remained there in the profession until 1910. From that year until 1915 his home was in Lebanon, Missouri, and from 1912 to 1914 he served as prosecuting attorney of LaClede County, Missouri. He then returned to Coffeyville and now has a substantial general civil and criminal practice in Montgomery County. For one term he served as city attorney of Coffeyville. Mr. Brown's offices are in the McCoy Building, and he resides at 806 West Third Street. He owns considerable property in Coffeyville and is one of the public spirited members of the community. For one year he served as clerk of the Coffeyville City Court. He is a democrat, and was his party's nominee for city judge on two separate occasions and was also candidate for police judge. He actively supports the Methodist Episcopal Church and fraternally is a member of Acton Lodge, Ancient Free and Accepted Masons, in Indiana, the same lodge of which his father was a member. He also belongs to the Life and Annuity Association, and was formerly affiliated with the Benevolent and Protective Order of Elks and the Knights of Pythias.

In 1902, at Coffeyville, Mr. Brown married Juanita N. Matthews, a daughter of John W. and Mary

Matthews. Her father, now deceased, was a miller and her mother resides at Neodesha, Kansas. Mr. and Mrs. Brown are the parents of five children: Juanita N., born October 24, 1903; Samuel E., born August 11, 1905; Mary R., born December 6, 1908; Harriet O., born March 6, 1911; and Ella Louise, born March 6, 1914.

SHERIDAN M. DICK. By choosing a line of activity and sticking to it closely for many years Sheridan M. Dick has attained an enviable position in business affairs. He is now foreman of the Baldwin Shirt Factory at Parsons. This industry is probably the largest of its kind in the State of Kansas.

Mr. Dick was born in Indiana County, Pennsylvania, May 10, 1866. He is of Irish descent, his Grandfather William Dick having been born in Ireland and having come to the United States when a young man. He spent his life as a farmer in Indiana County, Pennsylvania, where he died in 1870. The father of S. M. Dick was John W. Dick, who was born in 1819, also in Indiana County, Pennsylvania. He lived there the life of a farmer, and though quite an old man at the time and past military age he gave three years of faithful service to the Union army during the Civil war. In 1884 he moved out to Kansas, farmed in Douglas County near Lawrence, and was still a resident there when his death occurred. He died in Indiana County, Pennsylvania, in 1907 while on a visit to the scenes of his birthplace. He was an old school republican and a member of the Presbyterian Church. John W. Dick married Isabelle Sleppy, who was born March 4, 1833, in Indiana County, Pennsylvania, and died at Lawrence, Kansas, in 1905. Their children are: Isaac, a rancher at Tulare, California; James N., who was for many years with the Pennsylvania Railroad Company and died at Johnstown, Pennsylvania, in 1912; Abram, a granite cutter living at Grand Rapids, Michigan; Mrs. Lizzie Bryan, who lives in Indiana County, Pennsylvania, a widow; William Lincoln, a railroad man at Grand Rapids, Michigan; John, a farmer in Indiana County, Pennsylvania; Grant, who died at Grand Rapids, Michigan, in 1915, and was also a marble and granite cutter; Sheridan M., who is the eighth in order of birth; Harry, who is connected with the Cambria Iron Company at Johnstown, Pennsylvania; Chalmers, who was an employe of the Pennsylvania Railroad Company and died at the time of the great Johnstown flood from the effects of exposure while performing rescue work; Mrs. Maggie Grumbling, of Johnstown, Pennsylvania, the wife of a contractor and builder; Kate Rosa, wife of an employe of the Pennsylvania Railroad, their home being near Pittsburg, Pennsylvania; Mattie, wife of Rolla Ferris, a farmer in Chautauqua County, Kansas. As will be seen all the members of the family have filled substantial places in the world and have given a worthy account of themselves.

S. M. Dick received his early education and training in the public schools of Indiana County, Pennsylvania. The first twenty years of his life he spent on his father's farm, and then came west and for two years was employed in a grocery store at Lawrence, Kansas. After that business experience he took up his real work in the world. Entering the shirt manufacturing business with the firm of Wilder Brothers at Lawrence, he learned the trade of shirt cutter, and spent seventeen and a half years with that concern. During the last two years he was foreman, and in July, 1907, was called from Lawrence to Parsons to take a similar position in the manufacturing department of the Bald-

win Shirt Factory. This is a well known company, and its president is E. B. Stevens and the manager is George B. Karr. The Parsons plant, located at 2400 Broadway, makes only high grade shirts, night shirts and pajamas, and the market for the output is found in twelve states. Fifteen traveling representatives are kept on the road, and there are forty-five employes at Parsons. The factory over which Mr. Dick has active supervision has a capacity of 1,200 shirts per week.

Mr. Dick is a member of the Parsons Chamber of Commerce, is a republican of the progressive type, and is affiliated with Lodge No. 94 of the Independent Order of Odd Fellows at Parsons, Lodge No. 7 of the Ancient Order of United Workmen at Lawrence, and Camp No. 14 of the Woodmen of the World at Parsons. He owns a comfortable home at 2609 Belmont Avenue in Parsons.

In 1887 at Lawrence Mr. Dick married Miss Sophia Nelson, daughter of John and Sophia Nelson, both of whom are now deceased. Her father was a cabinetmaker. To their marriage have been born six children: Ralph, a shirt cutter in the Baldwin shirt factory at Parsons; Phillip, who is a moulder by trade and lives at Kansas City, Missouri; Frank, a shirt cutter in the Baldwin shirt factory; Fay, who graduated from the Parsons High School in 1916; Ella, a junior in the high school; and Teddy, the youngest of the family.

WILLIAM HENRY TESTER was born in Burgess Hill, a town nine miles north of Brighton, County of Sussex, England, on July 4, 1869. He received the common school education as given by the parochial schools under the care of the Church of England. Six years of his life were spent in Weston Super Mare, situated on the Bristol Channel in Somersetshire. As a boy of ten or twelve, reading of the wonderful things of America—her immense mountain ranges, her Great Lakes and wonderful Niagara Falls, and last but not least of that Great American Desert as shown on the maps of the late '60s—a strong desire to become a partaker of the things offered by that promised land possessed him, and he often found himself gazing westward from the seashore watching the sun as it sank into the western sea, and saying to himself, "Some day I shall follow to that wonderful land of promise." The father of the family also became interested, not for himself so much, as he often said, but that his children might come into that inheritance of better things that great English-speaking continent offered those who sought her shores with a desire for the really good things of life and were willing to do their part.

William Tester, the father of William H., was born at Burgess Hill (St. John's Common) August 4, 1840, is still living, and for the last thirty-four years has lived in St. Louis, Missouri. Sarah Cornford Tester, the mother of William H., was born at Hurstmonceux, near Hastings, County of Sussex, England, on May 18, 1839. In 1865, on May 27th, at the Old Church of Brighton, England, she was married to William Tester. She died at St. Louis, Missouri, June 1, 1890, at the age of 51.

Six children were born to this union: William H., the subject of this sketch; Frances Alice, who died in infancy; Charles Walter, now living in St. Louis; Alfred Lewis, now living at Fort Scott; Annie Alice, now Mrs. William T. Bishop, living in St. Louis; Emma Jane, who died in infancy.

On May 17, 1883, the morn of the family destiny dawned and the old ties were severed, and William

Tester, with his wife Sarah and the four surviving children, set out for the United States from Weston Super Mare, with the town of Jackson in the State of Tennessee as their destination. No one who has never undergone such an experience can form an idea of the momentous seriousness of such an undertaking for a man with his wife and four children, William H., the eldest, not yet fourteen, and the youngest, Annie Alice, but five, entering a new country, unknown and with limited capital, yet with a stout heart, and a mind and disposition for work in his calling, which had prior to his leaving England been that of foreman of a large pottery in Weston Super Mare, where he had enjoyed the confidence of his employer and had on numerous occasions been placed in charge of the plant's exhibits at the various agricultural shows held throughout England and Wales.

On June 1st the family landed in New York. Many deep and lasting favorable impressions were made on the mind of William H. at the entrance into the land. These have since been an inspiration to him, so that his love for the land of his adoption is of such strength, that as he has these many years lived under OLD GLORY he would willingly offer himself for its defense.

The father of the family shortly after arrival in St. Louis in September, 1883, having moved up there from Jackson, Tennessee, on account of a better means of livelihood offering there, took out his first papers or declaration of his intention to become a citizen of the United States. Enjoying thereby the citizen's rights, he overlooked taking out his final papers until seven years had passed. In the meantime William H. attained his majority and it became necessary for him to also take out naturalization papers, which was done at Scott City, Scott County, Kansas, where he was then residing, in 1892.

For several years after reaching St. Louis the subject of this sketch was engaged in industrial pursuits, later going with his father to a farm where three years were spent in active health-giving labor. About this time the matter of a life work began to force itself upon him, and the decision was reached to enter the railway service. A preparatory course was taken in the school then maintained in 1888 by the Missouri Pacific Railway, and in August, 1889, he entered the service as night telegraph operator for that line at New Haven, Missouri. He has been continuously in their service until the present time, having been appointed agent at Coffeyville, Kansas, August 13, 1906.

On January 10, 1894, in Wheeling, West Virginia, he was united in marriage to Miss Virginia Lillian Crawford, the daughter of Mr. and Mrs. M. C. Crawford, who were prominent in the social and business life of that city, as well as being one of the older families there. Two children, Katherine Virginia and Allen Crawford, were born to this union, both of whom survive and are growing into promising young lives. Both have attended the state university.

In private life Mr. and Mrs. Tester have identified themselves with the social and religious life of the community in which they have resided for the last ten years, having been closely identified with the Presbyterian Church of Coffeyville, he serving it as elder and clerk of its session for several years, and serving Neosho Presbytery as one of its lay commissioners to the Grand Assembly at Chicago in 1914.

He has also been actively identified in Masonic life, having been made a Mason at Scott City in 1891, served the Coffeyville Lodge as Master in 1911, and the Coffeyville Commandery as Commander in 1916,

as District Deputy Grand Master of the Eighteenth Masonic District under Grand Masters Elrick C. Cole, Charles H. Chandler, William L. Burdick, and Giles H. Lamb from 1914 to 1917, inclusive, and as Grand Representative of the Grand Lodge of Indiana to the Grand Lodge of Kansas, also as Grand Representative of the Grand Commandery of Vermont to the Grand Commandery of Kansas.

GEORGE F. BOSWELL, who represents a pioneer family of Montgomery County, has spent most of his active career at Coffeyville, was a merchant there for a number of years, and now devotes his time to the management of his extensive property interests and also his holdings in the oil and gas district.

He was born in Atchison County, Missouri, October 29, 1859. The record of his family in America goes back to his grandfather George Finley Boswell, who was born in England of Scotch descent in 1804. After his marriage to Hannah Colter, who was a native of Ireland and of Irish descent, he came to America, settling in Tennessee, where he was a planter and on his plantation he also conducted a hattery. He died in Decatur County, Tennessee, in 1866 and his wife also passed away there. Of their children the only one now living is Mary, who resides at Stoutsville, in Fairfield County, Ohio, the widow of James Chenoweth, who was a farmer by occupation.

The founder of the Boswell family in Southern Kansas, was A. P. Boswell, father of George F. He was born in Decatur County, Tennessee, in 1837, grew up and married there, and from early life was well versed in the business of planting and farming. In 1857 he went to Northwest Missouri and was an early settler in Atchison County. After living there a few years and with the outbreak of the war between the North and the South he returned to his native state and in 1862 enlisted in a Tennessee regiment of the Confederate army. He was in active service until the close of the war. At one time he was taken a prisoner but was soon exchanged. Following the war he farmed in Tennessee, but in 1871 pioneered to Kansas, and was one of the early settlers near Coffeyville. After six years as a farmer, he moved to Coffeyville and was active in business affairs and as a money lender and in 1883 engaged in the hardware and implement business. He was a man of distinctive ability and enjoyed many honors from his fellow citizens. Politically he was a democrat. While living on his farm in Montgomery county he served as township trustee one term, and afterwards was elected and served for nine years or three terms as county commissioner. He also filled the office of mayor of Coffeyville two terms. Among other interests he was vice president of the First National Bank. While a resident of Tennessee he was an active member of the Methodist Church, and was affiliated with Keystone Lodge No. 102, Ancient Free and Accepted Masons at Coffeyville.

In 1855 in Decatur County, Tennessee, A. P. Boswell married Miss Melissa Dudley Kelley, who was born in that section of Tennessee June 22, 1833. She died at Coffeyville February 9, 1914. A. P. Boswell in 1896 made a business trip through Oklahoma and while at Nowata was stricken and died. He and his wife had the following children: George F., Sarah S., wife of A. L. Wagstaff, who has for many years been engaged in the brokerage and real estate business and is now living in Kansas City, Missouri; Andrew A., a resident of Coffeyville; Tina C., wife of E. E. Wilson, who was in the lumber business at Coffeyville and is now a business man of Pueblo, Colorado; Robert, who died in infancy; William A., who was in the hardware business for a number of years and also a trader and died at Coffeyville in 1908.

When George F. Boswell was an infant his parents returned to Tennessee and he spent much of his boyhood in Decatur County. He was about twelve years of age when his father became a pioneer in Montgomery County and he grew to manhood on the farm. In 1876 he finished his early education by graduating from the Coffeyville High School. During the forty years that have followed many interests have engaged his enterprise and active attention. He spent three years as a young man in learning the trade of carpenter, and also gained some valuable experience as a grain buyer. From 1882 to 1895 he was in the mercantile business at Coffeyville. For the past twenty years he has devoted all his business energies to looking after his property as a real estate holder and also the affairs of several large oil and gas corporations. Among local real estate which he owns are his residence at 510 Elm street, other dwelling houses on Walnut, Elm and Willow streets, and some scattered property throughout the city. He is a stockholder in the Coffeyville Gas and Fuel Company; a stockholder and director in the Coffeyville Shale Products Company; a stockholder and director and president of the Georgia Oil and Gas Company; president and stockholder of the Delokee Gas and Oil Company; stockholder and director of the McAlester-Edward Coal Company in Oklahoma; stockholder and president of the Boswell Realty Company; and has interests in the Robinson Packer and Machine Company of Coffeyville.

In political affiliation Mr. Boswell is a democrat. For three terms he served in the Coffeyville City Council, was city treasurer six years, and is now serving as a member of the school board. As a young man he joined the Christian Church, but he now attends the Methodist. For a number of years he was one of the active workers in the Chamber of Commerce. Fraternally his affiliations are with Camp No. 665, Modern Woodmen of America at Coffeyville, with the Kansas Fraternal Citizen, and with the Anti-Horse Thief Association.

In February, 1887, at Coffeyville Mr. Boswell married Miss Alvira Burke, daughter of John Burke. Her father who lived on a farm west of Coffeyville, died November 29, 1916, in his ninety-second year. Mrs. Boswell died at Coffeyville in 1902, being survived by one daughter, Georgia. Georgia Boswell was born in Coffeyville in 1890 and is now the wife of Harry W. McEwen, cashier of the Cuthbert State Bank at Cuthbert, South Dakota.

On May 11, 1904 at Coffeyville Mr. Boswell married for his present wife Miss Leona R. Stephenson, a woman of brilliant mind and social leadership, and with a record of important public service to her credit in her home city of Coffeyville. Mrs. Boswell, who was born at Marietta, Ohio, December 5, 1871, was educated in the public schools of Johnson and Miami County, Kansas, her parents having come to Kansas in the early days. She was a student for two years in the high school at Paola, and then entered the Kansas State Normal at Emporia, from which she graduated in the spring of 1893 with a life teacher's certificate entitling her to teach in practically any state in the Union without further examination. Mrs. Boswell's first experience as a teacher was one year in the grade schools of Coffeyville, another year in the high school, and the third year she was in the Independence High School. Returning to Coffeyville she taught for seven years as assistant principal and principal of the high school. Since her marriage she has ably directed the affairs of her household and the care and rearing of her children, and has also borne many of the responsibilities laid upon the women of the city. She is a member of the Carnegie Library Board, and has filled a place on that board since the library was built, and has ably assisted in its support and maintenance. She is a member of the Coffeyville Culture Club and was president of the City Federation of Women's Clubs when the Carnegie library was opened. The library in fact stands as a monument to the combined efforts of these women's clubs. It fell to Mrs. Boswell to make the presentation speech when the city federation turned over its library and 2,700 volumes and other equipment to the new Carnegie institution. Mrs. Boswell is a member of the Methodist Church and the Royal Neighbors.

Mrs. Boswell is a granddaughter of John Stephenson, who was born 1793, and was one of the pioneer settlers in Southeastern Ohio, where he followed farming. He died at Marietta in that state in 1874. The maiden name of his wife was Gray, and she was born in Ohio and died at Marietta. Of their children the two now living are: Belle, wife of Benjamin Cogswell, of Marietta, Ohio; Jewett, a retired farmer at Gardner, Kansas.

Mrs. Boswell's father was Henry Stephenson, who was born in Marietta, Ohio, in 1837, and died at Arroyo Grande, California, in August, 1908. He was reared and married in Ohio, where he took up farming, and in the summer of 1876 brought his family to Spring Hill in Johnson County, Kansas. The buffaloes were still numerous on the plains when he arrived in Kansas, and he was one of the sterling pioneers who developed this country. Later he moved to Emporia for a year, and in 1890 began his operations as a rancher twenty-five miles southeast of Coffeyville in the Cherokee Nation, where he leased an extensive tract of land and devoted it to wheat raising and the cattle industry. He conducted that ranch until 1898, then removed to Coffeyville, where he had his home for three years, and after that spent three years in Seattle, Washington, in business with his son Russell. Returning to the Osage Nation, he was associated with his son Henry on a ranch there, and afterwards went with his son to a ranch in California, where he died. Henry Stephenson was a democrat and a member of the Baptist Church. He married Rebecca M. Sheets, who was born in Marietta, Ohio, in 1844, and died at Coffeyville in January, 1898. Mrs. Boswell was the third in a family of seven children. Her brother Rodney, now living at Arroyo Grande, California, is a miner and has some mines in Old Mexico, in the state of Sonora, 125 miles from Hermosillo. Her next younger brother, Henry, a resident of Los Angeles, is a manager of five large cattle ranches and is part owner and manager of the ranch at Palomas, which in recent months has attracted so much notice as being the scene of Villa's raid against Columbus, New Mexico. Catherine A., the next younger than Mrs. Boswell, lives in Santa Maria, California; Russell, who died at Santa Maria, California, in January, 1913, was a wholesale and retail meat merchant there. Odell died at Spring Hill, Kansas, in 1882. Sylvester S., the youngest child, spends his time traveling and lives in California.

Mr. and Mrs. Boswell have two children. Catherine Parr was born November 7, 1906, and is now in the public schools at Coffeyville. Berenice Kelley was born October 2, 1908.

MARSHALL MARION McCASLIN is a native of Kansas and has crowded a great many activities and experiences into the thirty years since his birth. He was formerly a farmer, but is now proprietor of the Acetylene Welding Company, one of the important industries of Coffeyville.

The McCaslin family came out of Ireland, were early settlers in America, and for many years lived in the State of Indiana.

Mr. McCaslin was born in Crawford County, Kansas, July 23, 1886. His father, W. M. McCaslin, was born in Illinois in 1860, was reared there. In 1880 he came with his family to Kansas, locating in Chautauqua County, where he married, then going to Crawford County, and coming from there to Montgomery County in 1902. He is a practical farmer and now lives on his place six miles northwest of Coffeyville. He attends the Methodist Episcopal Church and is a republican. W. M. McCaslin married Mrs. Maggie Ellsworth, who was born in Illinois in 1855. Ada, the oldest of their three children, is the wife of Dr. S. Huff, who has a world-wide reputation as a specialist in the treatment of cancer, and is one of the oldest specialists in that field of medicine, his home being at Mound Valley, Kansas. Bertha, the second of the children, is the wife of C. N. Fye, a farmer and railroad machinist living at Pindell, Arkansas.

The only son of the family, Marshall M. McCaslin, attended the public schools while living on his father's farm in Crawford County. In 1907 he took a course in the Coffeyville Business College, specializing in bookkeeping. After one year of experience in the real estate business he took up farming in Montgomery County, and was so engaged until February, 1916, when he sold his farm and became manager and owner of the Acetylene Welding Company. This is a plant which is a growing and prosperous concern, fitted up with mechanical appliances for every sort of welding and also for the repair of automobile machinery. Mr. McCaslin owns the plant and its machinery, the location being at 819 Spring Street.

Politically he is a republican; he is a member of the United Brethren Church and is affiliated with Coffeyville Lodge No. 1193, Loyal Order of Moose.

His home is at 304 East Ninth Street. January 25, 1913, at Coffeyville, he married Miss Bessie Augustine, daughter of John and Julia Augustine. Her parents are farmers, their home being near six miles north and a little west of Coffeyville. Mr. and Mrs. McCaslin have one daughter, Nema, born August 29, 1914.

JOHN PEDROJA. One of the most reliable and progressive of the younger members of the Crawford County bar, who stands high in professional ability as a man of broad business and financial judgment, is John Pedroja, who since 1911 has been engaged in practice at Mulberry. He has also served the public well and conscientiously in the offices of city clerk and city attorney during the past four years, and is a citizen who has done much to advance the interests of his community.

Mr. Pedroja was born at Gnosca, Switzerland, November 27, 1880, and is a son of Charles and Angelina (Rochi) Pedroja, natives of the same place. Charles Pedroja was born in 1855, and was reared and educated in his native place, where he learned the trade of painter and served two years in the regular army of Switzerland. In 1888 he brought his family to the United States and located at once in Greenwood County, Kansas, where for a number of years he was engaged in farming and raising stock. In 1914, in order that his children might receive better school advantages, he located at Lawrence, where he now lives in retirement. Mr. Pedroja has been an industrious and thrifty workman all his life, and is now in comfortable circumstances. He is a democrat in politics and belongs to the Independent Order of Odd Fellows. Mrs. Pedroja, who also survives, was born in 1857. Their children are as follows: John; Charles, Jr., who resides at Hill City, Kansas, proprietor of a drug store; Severence, also a druggist, with a pharmacy at Hamilton, Kansas; Clinton, who is engaged in agricultural pursuits in the vicinity of Hamilton; Frank, who is a druggist at Wakeeney, Kansas; James, of Mulberry, assistant of his brother John; Edward, who is a junior at Kansas University, Lawrence; and Mary, who is in the sophomore class at that institution.

John Pedroja received his primary education in the public schools of Greenwood County, Kansas, and pursued his preparatory course at the Southern Kansas Academy, at Eureka, from which he was graduated in 1898, when he was but eighteen years of age. He next entered Kansas University, where he completed the sophomore year, and next went to Chicago, where he became a law student at De Paul University and graduated in 1907 with the degree of Bachelor of Laws. He began practice at Plainville, Kansas, in 1909, and in 1911 went to Pittsburg, where he formed a partnership with Mr. Smith, under the firm style of Smith & Pedroja, which combination has since continued with offices both at Pittsburg and Mulberry, Mr. Pedroja being the representative of the firm at Mulberry. He has personally represented a number of large interests in important litigation during the last few years and is now an active and successful practitioner. One year after his arrival at Mulberry, he was elected city clerk and city attorney, and these offices he has continued to fill to the present time, giving excellent satisfaction to the citizens of this thriving Crawford County community. Mr. Pedroja's practice has covered a wide range. He has an excellent record in general departments of the law, but his constructive ability, as shown by the various organizations with which he has been connected, has won for him a still higher place in the esteem and confidence of his clients. He is secretary and treasurer of the Mulberry Coal Company, the McGowan Manufacturing Company, the Scammon Coal Company and the Mulberry Building and Loan Association, and a director in all these enterprises. In addition to his own modern home, located on Perry Street, he owns several other residences at Mulberry. Fraternally, he is connected with Pittsburg Lodge, No. 187, Ancient Free and Accepted Masons; Fort Scott Consistory, No. 6, thirty-second degree; and Mirzah Temple, A. A. O. N. M. S., at Pittsburg, and with Mulberry Lodge, No. 417, Independent Order of Odd Fellows. In connection with his profession, he belongs to the Crawford County Bar Association and the Illinois State Bar Association, and, as one of the live, energetic men who are doing things for their community, holds membership in the Mulberry Boosters' Club. He votes the republican ticket.

Mr. Pedroja was married in January, 1915, to Miss

Allie Kurtz, of Mulberry, Kansas, daughter of Philip and Theresa (Schillings) Kurtz, who are now residents of Mulberry, Mr. Kurtz being a retired farmer who carried on successful operations for many years in Cherokee County.

ROLLA EDWIN LONG, superintendent of the city schools of Galena, is an educator of wide and diversified experience in the schools of this state, and has spent altogether upwards of twenty years in a profession which is one of the most important to the welfare of mankind.

In 1916 he entered upon his fourth consecutive year as superintendent of the schools of Galena. The people of that city take special pride in their schools, and Mr. Long has done much to raise the local school standards and improve the different departments of instruction. Under his supervision are six schools, a staff of thirty-seven teachers, and about seventeen hundred scholars enrolled.

The first school he taught was in 1888. It was a country district seven miles southeast of Osage Mission in Neosho County. After the year spent there, he has consecutively taught for two years in the country at Blancheville in Marshall County; two years as principal of the high school at Oswego; three years as principal of the city schools of Irving; two years superintendent of schools at Waterville; six years superintendent of schools at Axtel; six years superintendent at Lincoln; and from Lincoln he came to Galena.

Mr. Long represents a pioneer family both in Indiana and Kansas. His paternal ancestors came from England to Massachusetts in colonial times, and subsequently members of the family went south into North Carolina. His grandfather, Tobias Long, was born in 1790 and about 1827 came west with his family and settled in Greene County, Indiana. He spent his career as a farmer there and died in 1871.

David Long, father of Professor Long, was born near Pilot Knob, North Carolina, October 2, 1824, and was a small child when brought to Indiana. He was reared in Greene County of that state, was married in Lawrence County, Indiana, and after living there until 1872 on a farm came in that year to Kansas. His first settlement was at a point nine miles north of old Osage Mission, now St. Paul, but in the following year he bought a farm of 160 acres two miles north of St. Paul, where he lived quietly engaged in his business as a farmer until his death in March, 1896. He was a republican and a recognized leader in the Methodist Episcopal Church in Neosho County. He served as a steward and trustee of his home church, and in every way gave liberally of his time and means to the support of the church movement. He married Jeannette Lowder, who was born in Lawrence County, Indiana, July 2, 1832, and died at Erie, Kansas, in November, 1910. They were the parents of a large family of children: Mathew Thomas, a minister of the Methodist Church at Shattuck, Oklahoma, and an inventor of more than local note; Lindia Ann is the wife of J. J. Fields, editor and owner of the principal paper at Sentinel, Oklahoma; Cornelius was a teacher and died at Walnut, Kansas, in 1886; Finley was a teacher in the Government Indian schools and died in New Mexico in 1908; H. C. Long is in the real estate and insurance business at Ottawa, Kansas; John R. is a farmer three miles south of Stark in Neosho County, Kansas; Rolla E. Long is the seventh in age among the children; Maggie May is a teacher of domestic science in California; Dr. L. L. is a physician and surgeon at Beaver, Oklahoma.

Rolla Edwin Long was born in Lawrence County, Indiana, April 27, 1869, and was about three years of age when his parents came to Kansas. Largely as a result of his ambition and earnest efforts he has acquired a liberal education. He began attending school in Neosho County, at first the country schools and the town schools of Osage Mission, and finished the high school course in the State Normal School at Emporia. He has received two life teacher's certificates from the State Normal at Emporia, and in 1915 he was awarded the degree Bachelor of Science by the State Manual Training Normal School at Pittsburg, Kansas. He also has a diploma in architecture from the International Correspondence School at Scranton, Pennsylvania. He is a constant student and gained his higher education largely in the intervals of his work as a teacher. He is a man of broad human sympathies and keeps in close touch with every advance made in school affairs.

For many years he has been identified with the Kansas State Teachers' Association and also with the Southeast Kansas Teachers' Association. He is an elder in the Presbyterion Church, a republican in politics, and is affiliated with Axtel Lodge of Masons. His home is at 1005 Short Street in Galena.

On June 3, 1896, at Mound Valley, Kansas, Mr. Long married Miss Edith Brown, daughter of Finley and Rachel (Bonner) Brown, both now deceased. Her father, who was a farmer, died in March, 1916.

WILLIAM WALLACE BROWN, general attorney at Parsons for the Missouri, Kansas & Texas Railway and a director in that railway company, is one of Kansas' prominent lawyers with many well earned distinctions in the profession. The secret of his success has been hard work. He began practice only after a thorough preliminary training of self reliance and after getting his professional education through his own earnings and efforts.

A native of Kansas, he represents a pioneer family. Mr. Brown was born in Coffey County July 29, 1868. He is of English ancestry. His grandfather Robert Brown was born in England, brought his family to America in 1845, and became a contractor and builder in the State of Iowa. While still at work in his business he was struck by a beam and that caused his death about 1857. He died in Iowa.

Charles Brown, father of W. W. Brown, was born at Beverly, Yorkshire, England, November 14, 1832. He was thirteen years of age when he came to America and he grew up at Maquoketa, Iowa. After finishing his education he became a farmer. In 1857 at the age of twenty-five he moved from Maquoketa, Iowa, to Kansas, and was one of the early settlers in the territory. His permanent home was on a farm along the line between Anderson and Coffey counties. A few years after coming to Kansas he enlisted in the Tenth Kansas Regiment of Infantry, and was in active service during the war, principally in Missouri, Arkansas and Indian Territory. He was in the battle of Prairie Grove, Arkansas, and served with the Kansas troops in repelling Price's raid. After the war he homesteaded eighty acres and was married in 1865. He then settled down to farming and proved a man of unusual energy and success in that business. He was both a farmer and stock raiser and eventually he had fully 400 acres of land in his possession. In the early days he was actively identified with the Grange or Patrons of Husbandry, but in later years became somewhat dissatisfied with

W. W. Brown

its management and methods. In his home community he was always active and influential. He served seven years as county commissioner and held all the township offices. He was a prominent republican, and a member of the Methodist Episcopal Church. After a life filled with usefulness he died at his home in Coffey County February 10, 1915, in his eighty-third year. Charles Brown married Miss Mary Isabelle Hinde. She was born in Cattaraugus County, New York, in 1842 and her death occurred on the homestead farm in Coffey County, Kansas, in 1892. Mr. W. W. Brown was the oldest of their four children. The next younger, Louie Grace died in Coffey County in 1895 as the wife of William Sharp, who is now living in Los Angeles, California. Maggie Amanda married H. A. Striegel, and they now live on their farm forty miles west of Wichita near Murdock, Kansas. Fred E., the youngest of the family, now occupies the old homestead in Coffey County.

Though reared on a farm the ambitions of William Wallace Brown early pointed to a professional career. He attended the district schools of Coffey County, the high school at Burlington, and then entered the University of Kansas where he completed the classical course and received the degree A. B. in 1892. The following two years were spent in a schoolroom as teacher, and he was principal of the high school at Abilene, Kansas. Mr. Brown devoted several attentive years to the study of law in a law office at Burlington, Kansas, and in 1896, gained the coveted goal of admission to the bar.

The twenty years since his admission have been years of growing experience and increasing ability in his profession. He practiced at Burlington until 1902, then at Emporia until April, 1905, and came to Parsons as assistant general attorney of the Missouri, Kansas & Texas Railroad Company. In July, 1913, he was advanced to the position of general attorney, and now fills one of the most prized positions in the legal profession in the state. He is widely known as a railroad lawyer throughout the west. His offices are in the General Office Building of the Missouri, Kansas & Texas Railroad at Parsons. Besides his position as legal adviser to the company he is also one of the directors.

Mr. Brown is a successful business man. He owns considerable real estate in Parsons, has a fine farm of 160 acres on the Neosho River near Burlington, and is president of the Burlington Lumber Company. He is a member of the Presbyterian Church, is past master of Emporia Lodge No. 12, Ancient Free and Accepted Masons, and a member of Emporia Chapter No. 12, Royal Arch Masons, Parsons Council, Royal and Select Masters. He is also identified with the Parsons Chamber of Commerce and belongs to the Labette County, the State and the American Bar associations.

In 1906 at Emporia he married Miss Frances Evans. She is a daughter of Judge E. N. Evans, a prominent attorney of Emporia, who has filled the positions of both probate and district judge there.

ASA KNOWLES TALBOT. It is no small distinction in the business world to create and build up a business which is generally recognized as the leader of its kind in a city or county. That is the place occupied by the A. K. Talbot Harness and Manufacturing Company at Coffeyville. It is the leading concern in the handling of harness and other goods in Montgomery County, and Mr. Talbot has also developed a factory for the manufacture of leather

novelties and is at the head of a very successful concern.

While he has spent nearly all his life in Kansas, Mr. Talbot was born near Owensville, Indiana, February 2, 1871. The Talbots are of Scotch-Irish descent. His father, William H. Talbot, who was born in Ohio in 1839, was one of five sons, three of whom identified themselves with southern states and two went to Indiana. William H. Talbot was married at Evansville, Indiana, and in following his trade as plasterer and brick mason resided there, at Owensville, Princeton and other places in the state. He made a most creditable military record, having served throughout the war from 1861 to 1865 with the First Indiana Cavalry. He participated in the early campaigns by which Southwestern Missouri was cleared of Confederate forces, and fought at the battle of Pea Ridge, Arkansas. He was three times wounded. In 1877 he came to Kansas, first locating at Virgil, and in 1890 retiring to Toronto, where he died August 4, 1900. The maiden name of his wife was Elizabeth Knowles. She was born in Georgia in 1844 and is still living at Toronto, Kansas. Her children were: Luella, wife of H. G. Marshall, a merchant at Mead, Kansas; Asa K.; Myrtle, wife of U. S. G. Collins, a telegraph operator at Oklahoma City; Jennie, who lives at Toronto, the widow of Earl Russell, who was a merchant; and Gilbert, an engineer for the Portland Cement Company at Iola, Kansas.

In the public schools of Toronto and Eureka, Kansas, Asa K. Talbot received his early education. At the age of twenty he took up his independent career, learning the harness trade at Toronto, and completing an apprenticeship in 1894. For a number of years he worked as a journeyman, spending six years with Mr. Neill at Sedan, Kansas, and coming to Coffeyville in 1900. At Coffeyville he entered the employ of C. G. Geissler, and was with him a year and a half. In April, 1902, after the death of Mr. Geissler, Mr. Talbot bought the business from his widow, and has since conducted the leading harness house of the city. The business is now conducted under the name of Talbot Saddlery Company, and manufactures all classes of harness and leather novelties which find an extensive distribution over a wide territory. The home of the business is at Tenth and Walnut streets.

Mr. Talbot resides at 404 Elm Street, and also owns a residence at 1117 West Eleventh Street and some other city real estate. Since coming to Coffeyville he has made himself a public spirited and energetic citizen. For five years he served as a director and is still a member of the Montgomery County Fair Association. He also belongs to the Chamber of Commerce, is affiliated with Coffeyville Camp No. 665, Modern Woodmen of America, and Coffeyville Lodge No. 775, Benevolent and Protective Order of Elks. Politically he is a democrat.

In 1898, at Sedan, Kansas, Mr. Talbot married Miss Anna Lee, daughter of John and Nellie Lee. Her father, who was a stockman, is deceased, and her mother is living at Sedan. Mr. and Mrs. Talbot have two children: Nellie, who died young; and Leah, who is a student in the public schools at Coffeyville.

MILLARD FILLMORE WOOD. A little more than forty years ago Millard F. Wood came to Montgomery County, a young school teacher. While he taught school for a time, he also interested himself in improving a homestead claim, and afterwards advanced rapidly in business and also in politics. He is now secretary and treasurer of the Ideal Supply Company.

An Illinois man by birth, he was born at Aviston, Clinton County, November 12, 1850. His grandfather, Wiley Wood, was born in Virginia in 1791, and was a farmer and one of the early circuit riders of the Methodist Episcopal Church. In 1872 he came to Kansas, and died in Mound Valley Township of Labette County in 1876.

William Devers Wood, father of Mr. M. F. Wood, was born in Tennessee in 1822. His early boyhood days were spent in Indiana, and from there he moved to Aviston, Illinois, where he was a merchant and also postmaster. In 1880 he moved from Illinois to Cherryvale, Kansas, and continued the mercantile business there until his death in 1896. He was a republican, a deacon and local preacher in the Methodist Episcopal Church, and when a very young man enlisted and offered his services in the Mexican war, being rejected on account of physical disability. William D. Wood married Naomi Carr Lear, who was born in Lancaster, Pennsylvania, in 1828. She was descended from Charles McMicken, who was a prominent philanthropist and founded and dedicated the McMicken University at Cincinnati, Ohio. He also gave large sums of money to the Methodist bishops who were promoting the colonization of American negroes in Liberia, Africa.

Millard F. Wood spent his early life in Aviston, Illinois, where he attended the public schools, and he finished his junior year in McKendree College at Lebanon, Illinois. The county superintendent of schools then appointed him to a scholarship in the State Normal at Bloomington, and he attended that school in 1871 for one term. On leaving school he taught in Clinton County, Illinois, and in 1873 he moved to Labette County in Southeastern Kansas and from there came to Montgomery County in 1874. Here he took up a claim of 160 acres, and after the first year resumed teaching. From his homestead he moved to Cherryvale, where he was in the drug business for two years, and subsequently added departments of dry goods and groceries, and continued in that business and also as a dealer in livestock until 1880. The firm was known as Anderson & Wood, and it was one of the prominent early firms in the county. After selling his interest Mr. Wood was appointed, in 1880, as census enumerator for the City of Cherryvale and the Township of Cherry, Those duties completed, he was associated with his father in the mercantile business until 1885, in which year he accepted the nomination for the office of county treasurer. Elected, he served two terms of four years, and during that time he lived in Independence. In 1890, on retiring from the office of county treasurer, he became a plumbing contractor and an ice dealer and remained in business along those lines at Independence until 1892. In 1893 he became associated with the First National Bank of Cherryvale. Mr. Wood was the first city clerk of Cherryvale after it became a city of the third class, and filled that office for seven years. He also spent a long time with the board of education and assisted in securing the building of several new schoolhouses at Cherryvale.

In 1894 Mr. Wood again returned to Independence and has since been in the sanitary contracting business. He installed all the steam heating and plumbing of the fine Carl-Leon Hotel at Independence, and has had a number of contracts for the city, including the plumbing in the Independence City Hospital, and has installed much of the work in the modern residences. On November 7, 1916, he was elected county commissioner of the Second District of Montgomery County.

Mr. Wood is a member of the Methodist Episcopal Church, belongs to the Commercial Club and the Elks, and has active fraternal relations with Fortitude Lodge No. 107, Ancient Free and Accepted Masons; Keystone Chapter No. 22, Royal Arch Masons; St. Bernard Commandery No. 10, Knights Templar; Abdallah Temple of the Nobles of the Mystic Shrine at Leavenworth; Lodge No. 17, Ancient Order of United Workmen, and Camp No. 1 of the Woodmen of the World. He is past high priest of the Royal Arch Chapter and is now secretary.

On March 1, 1874, at Cherryvale, Mr. Wood married Ida E. Paxon, a daughter of the late Seth and Mercy (Webster) Paxon. Her mother belonged to the noted Webster family of the same stock which produced Daniel Webster. Mrs. Wood's father was a blacksmith and originally lived near Buffalo, New York. Mr. and Mrs. Wood have two children: Bertha E., wife of Howard G. Jones, a pharmacist; Clarence William is a railway postoffice clerk on the runs between Kansas City and Coffeyville, Kansas, on the Missouri Pacific Railroad, and lives at Kansas City, Kansas.

PROF. HERBERT M. HOWISON. As one of the flourishing cities of Kansas, Parsons has representatives in nearly all the industries and professions. As a developer of its musical interest the city has recently received an important addition in the person of Herbert M. Howison, a prominent professional musician and a man of wide experience as a teacher and devotee of the art.

Professor Howison is a young man of much talent and has been thoroughly trained in many of the best schools and under some of the best instructors of the country. The family have lived in this country for about four generations. The original Howisons were residents of the Scandinavian Peninsula, removed from there to Scotland, and there the stock was fused with the Scotch and English races. On emigrating to America Mr. Howison's ancestors located in New York State. His grandfather was Robert Howison, and was a pioneer cattle drover from New York State to Chicago. On one of his trips through the West he lost his life and is supposed to have been killed by Indians.

Herbert Milford Howison was born at Chippewa Lake, Michigan, November 21, 1888. His father, James Robert Howison, who was born in New York State in 1851, spent the first thirteen years of his life there, and then went with his mother to Michigan. He has been identified with the lumber business all his active career, and chiefly as superintendent of lumber yards. In 1904 he moved his family to Albuquerque, New Mexico, and in 1909 returned to Michigan and located in Saginaw, where he had previously resided for twelve years. After one year he again went to the Southwest and was in business in Chihuahua, Old Mexico, until compelled to leave that country on account of the revolutionary troubles. From there he went to Oregon, but in 1915 located in Lake Charles, Louisiana, where he still resides. He is a member of the Masonic fraternity and the Modern Woodmen of America and politically he is a republican. James R. Howison married Hannah Tubbs, who was born in St. Johns, Michigan, in 1853. They had only two children. Professor Howison's older brother is Charles C., who is a foreman in the DuPont powder factory at Wilmington, Delaware.

Most of his early life Professor Howison spent in Saginaw, Michigan, where he attended the public schools. He was also a student in the preparatory department of the University of New Mexico and from 1904 to 1906 attended the University of New Mexico School of Music. In 1906-07 he was a student in Martin College in Tennessee, and from 1907 to 1912 continued his training for the musical profession in the Oberlin Conservatory of Music at Oberlin, Ohio.

From 1912 to 1915 Mr. Howison was director of the Lake Charles Conservatory of Music in Louisiana, and made a splendid record while there. At Lake Charles he was choir director of the First Baptist Church from 1912 to 1914, and of the First Presbyterian church during the following year. He is well known in musical organizations and in 1914 was chairman of the Standardization Committee, and a member of the Executive Committee and the State Piano Committee of the Louisiana Music Teachers' Association, and in 1915 served as president of the association. During the school year 1915-16 Mr. Howison was director of music in Oswego College for Women in the State of Kansas, and in July, 1915, located at Parsons, where he now has his home and studio and is rapidly building up a large clientage as a teacher.

He is a member of the Association of Presidents and Past Presidents of State and National Teachers' Associations, is a member of the executive committee of the Kansas State Music Teachers' Association and chairman of the program committee for 1917, and holds an accredited teachers' certificate. Politically he is independent, and his church membership is with the Presbyterian denomination.

In September, 1915, at Lake Charles, Louisiana, Mr. Howison married Miss Florence Kinnear. Her parents are Dr. H. N. and Hannah (Tilton) Kinnear, who now reside at Foo Chow, China.

CHARLES V. FITCH. Valeda is one of the flourishing small villages in Labette County and to a large degree the business activities of the place are concentrated in the enterprise of one citizen, Charles V. Fitch, who owns and manages the leading store of that community and is also the present postmaster.

Mr. Fitch was born in Fleming County, Kentucky, May 2, 1875. His Fitch ancestors came from England to Virginia in colonial days. His grandfather, Nathan Fitch, was born in Kentucky, spent his life there as a farmer, and died in Fleming County.

S. E. Fitch, father of the Valeda merchant, was also prominently known in that part of Kansas. He was born in Fleming County, Kentucky, in 1848, was reared and married there, and his early years were spent as a farmer. In 1886 he moved to Valeda, where he continued farming, but for the last twelve years of his life was engaged in general merchandising at Valeda. He died there in 1913. When he first began to cast his vote it was as a republican, but later he identified himself with the populist movement and still later became a democrat. For two terms he served as township trustee of Howard township. He was an active member of the United Brethren Church. S. E. Fitch married Fannie Wallingford, who was born in Fleming County, Kentucky, in 1850, and is still living at Valeda. Her children were: Charles V.; Walter, who died at the age of twenty years, having been drowned near Lenapah, Oklahoma, while engaged in a cattle drive through that territory; Lulu, wife of F. P. McCarty, who is a farmer at Blue Mountain, Arkansas; Mary, wife of F. G. Mulenix, a steam shovel operator living at Denver, Colorado.

Charles V. Fitch received his early education in

Fleming County, Kentucky. He was about eleven years of age when brought to Kansas, and he attended the public schools of Valeda. The first twenty-one years of his life he spent on his father's farm. Then for five years he was an independent farmer at Valeda, and after that became associated with his father in the general merchandise business. After the death of his father the store was turned over to him and he has since managed it and his genial popularity and his ability as a merchant have caused a large volume of trade to center at Valeda in recent years. His store is well situated on Main Street.

In October, 1914, Mr. Fitch was appointed postmaster of Valeda by President Wilson, and is now giving a capable administration of the affairs of that office. He is a democrat, is affiliated with the Independent Order of Odd Fellows at Coffeyville, with Camp No. 7511, Modern Woodmen of America, at Valeda and is also a member of the Homesteaders' Order.

In July, 1896, at Valeda, Mr. Fitch married Anna McCarty, daughter of Isaac and Margaret (Sharp) McCarty, both of whom are now deceased. Her father was a farmer and also a preacher, representing what is known as the Hardshell Baptist denomination. Mr. and Mrs. Fitch are the parents of a fine family of seven children: Claude, born January 26, 1897; Albert, born February 16, 1899; Esther, born June 24, 1902; John, born July 31, 1904; Clifford, born August 28, 1906; Wayne, born June 29, 1908; and Hazel, born May 22, 1910.

A. H. McCARTY. When the Valeda State Bank was organized at Valeda, June 1, 1915, under a state charter, the institution was given a good start not only by reason of its capital of $10,000, and by the subsequent accumulation of a surplus of $2,500, but also because of the excellent men who were its stockholders and original officers and directors. The president of the bank is A. E. Townsend, the vice president W. H. Bollman, and the cashier A. H. McCarty, all well known residents of Valeda and vicinity. The bank erected its home on Main Street in 1915.

The cashier, A. H. McCarty, was born in Des Moines County, Iowa, March 21, 1863. His ancestors were originally from Ireland, but have been in this country since colonial times, first having settled in Virginia. Isaac McCarty, his father, was born in Claiborne County, Tennessee, in 1824. Two years later in 1826 his parents took him to Indiana, in which state he grew to manhood. He then moved to Henry County, Iowa, followed farming for many years in Iowa, and in 1885 came to Oswego, Kansas, and soon afterwards to Valeda, where he continued farming until his death in 1908. He was a democrat and a member of the Baptist Church. Isaac McCarty married Margaret Ann Sharp. She was born in Indiana in 1828 and died at Valeda in 1896.

A. H. McCarty received his early education in the public schools of Des Moines County and Henry County, Iowa. Some years later in 1889 he attended a business college at Burlington, Iowa. He has been a resident of Kansas since 1885 and for thirty years has been one of the leading citizens of Labette County. For five years he served as deputy county clerk, county clerk two years, has been a member of the school board and township trustee, and through all his relations, whether as a farmer, public official or banker has given an excellent account of himself. Besides his position as stockholder and officer in the Valeda State Bank, Mr. McCarty still owns a fine farm of 240 acres a mile south of Valeda, and also has a comfortable residence on Howard Street.

He is a democrat, an active member of the Baptist Church and belongs to the Kansas Bankers' Association. In 1891 at Oswego he married Miss Ida M. Ames, daughter of Asa Ames, now deceased, who was a Kansas farmer. Mr. and Mrs. McCarty have two children: Ira D., who was born February 21, 1897, and was graduated from the high school at Altamont in 1916; and Isaac, born February 25, 1898.

ALBERT ERSKINE WILSON, who is a son of that splendid Montgomery County pioneer, the late Ebenezer Erskine Wilson, has had an active business career at Coffeyville covering a period of twenty years, during which time he has progressed from the position of stenographer and clerk to head of one of the leading elevator companies of Southern Kansas, and has also acquired other business interests.

His birth occurred in Independence, Kansas, February 24, 1876. Mr. Wilson is descended from a family that originally lived in Scotland, and among his direct ancestors were the noted Erskines of Scotland. The Wilsons came from Scotland to Pennsylvania.

His father, Ebenezer Erskine Wilson, was born at Elizabethtown, Pennsylvania, November 21, 1838. Soon after reaching manhood, in 1861, he enlisted as a private in the Second West Virginia Cavalry of the Union army, and was promoted to captain of a company. He was in service throughout the war, in many of the great battles and campaigns, and was with Grant at Appomattox. Soon after the war he went west to Illinois, and while at Galesburg married Miss Betty Braden. She died six months after their marriage.

On August 28, 1869, Ebenezer E. Wilson arrived in Kansas, and as president of the Independence Townsite Company laid out a large portion of that town. The negotiations had hardly been completed for the removal of the Indians from this section of Kansas, and Montgomery County was then on the extreme frontier. During the remainder of his life E. E. Wilson played a dominant part in the activities and affairs of his home city of Independence. He was the second mayor of that city. He and F. D. Irwin built the first store on the townsite and as the firm of Wilson & Irwin conducted a general merchandise stock for a number of years. Later he became assistant county treasurer under Cary Oakes and also under treasurer Joseph Barricklow for four years, and was then himself elected county treasurer and held the office four years. He was associated with the Commercial Bank, and as president of the Independence School Board, laid the foundation of the public school system. He took a great interest in higher education and was himself a man of thorough scholarship, a deep thinker, and by his interest as a historian and writer preserved much of the interesting chronicles of early Montgomery County. He contributed numerous articles to the South Kansas Tribune and his work as a historian can be best appreciated from the Edwards Historical Atlas of Montgomery County which was published in 1881, the historical part of which was written by him.

When the Montgomery County Agricultural Society was organized in 1871 he became its first secretary. He was an active republican, was a member of McPherson Post No. 4, Grand Army of the Republic, and as regular attendant of the Congrega-

tional Church took a great interest in its affairs and helped support it both by his personal influence and in other substantial ways. One of the prominent men of his time, he naturally associated with the makers of history in that section of Kansas, and was a personal friend of L. U. Humphrey, one time governor of Kansas.

Ebenezer E. Wilson died at Independence, Kansas, August 28, 1894. For his second wife he married Morna Moore. Her father, Alexander Hamilton Moore, was the second postmaster of Independence. Mrs. E. E. Wilson was born at Galesburg, Illinois, November 28, 1846, and died at Independence, Kansas, January 29, 1890. Her children were six in number, Albert E. being the second in age. Zell, the oldest, is the wife of A. T. Stewart, who is general freight agent for the Missouri Pacific Railway at Kansas City, Missouri. Floyd M., a resident of Hartman, Colorado, is manager of the Denver Alfalfa Milling and Products Company, which has five plants located at Hartman, Bristol, Wiley, Cornman and McClave, Colorado. Sallie, twin sister of Floyd, is the wife of W. R. Forker, who is general sales agent and a stockholder of the Moreland Motor Company at Los Angeles, California. Jane M. is the wife of Thomas E. Wagstaff, a prominent lawyer of Independence, Kansas. George T., a resident of Los Angeles, is state agent in California for the Alfalfa Milling and Mixing Machinery Company.

Albert Erskine Wilson, who was fourteen years of age when his mother died and eighteen when his father passed away, received his early education in the Independence public schools but left school when a senior in high school on account of the death of his father. Going to St. Louis he finished a six months' course in shorthand in 1896, then in the same year returned to Kansas and became stenographer for the firm of Hall & Robinson at Coffeyville. This firm operated the Missouri Pacific elevator at Coffeyville. He was promoted to bookkeeper, then to superintendent of the elevator, and held that position until July 1, 1913. Mr. Wilson then resigned and organized the Wilson Elevator Company, of which he is president and general manager. He leased from the Missouri Pacific Railroad its terminal elevator at Coffeyville and this is now one of the substantial businesses of the kind in Southern Kansas. The vice president of the company is Thomas E. Wagstaff of Independence and the secretary and treasurer is Mrs. Vera D. Wilson, wife of Mr. Wilson. The offices are at 908 Maple Street.

Politically Mr. Wilson is a standpat republican. He is a member of the Commercial Club, has served as president of the Coffeyville Country Club, belongs to the Presbyterian Church and is affiliated with Keystone Lodge No. 102, Ancient Free and Accepted Masons at Coffeyville, Coffeyville Chapter No. 89, Royal Arch Masons, Lochinvar Commandery No. 52, Knights Templars, and Coffeyville Lodge No. 775 of the Benevolent and Protective Order of Elks.

Mr. Wilson and family reside at 612 Lincoln Street. On June 2, 1909, at Independence he married Miss Vera Doyle. Her parents, both now deceased, formerly resided at Hastings, Michigan. Mrs. Wilson graduated from the Hastings High School and from the Hackley Manual Training School of Muskegon, Michigan, and before her marriage was domestic science teacher in the Coffeyville High School. They are the parents of two children: Albert E., Jr., born December 24, 1910; and Harriet Elizabeth, born August 24, 1915.

HENRY SEYMOUR SEWELL. For a man of forty years Henry S. Sewell has had more than an ordinary record of success in business affairs. He is one of the well known merchants of Independence, owns extensive properties in that city and in other sections of Southern Kansas, and all his prosperity is a result of continued concentrated effort through the years since he left home and started out to carve his own career.

Born in Montgomery County, Kansas, October 4, 1876, Henry Seymour Sewell is a son of J. B. and Mary M. (James) Sewell, and a grandson of J. G. and Catherine (Maybury) Sewell. His grandparents were among the early pioneers of Montgomery County, having arrived here in 1871 and taking up a homestead about twelve miles from Independence. They were Tennessee people, steady, industrious, people of high principles, and in the past forty-five years the family has left its mark on affairs in Montgomery County in many ways. Mr. J. B. Sewell, father of the Independence merchant, is now in the mercantile business and is postmaster at Bolton, and his career is sketched on other pages of this publication.

While a boy Henry S. Sewell attended the public schools of Montgomery County. As he was one of a family of nine children, he saw the necessity of self-support at an early age, and therefore contributed all his labors that he could to helping out his father, who was then in the mercantile business. He learned the trade of butcher and at the age of twenty-one started out for himself. In the meantime he had given all his wages as a contribution to the support of the household.

Beginning at Independence as a meat cutter and clerk, he worked there steadily until 1902, and then for a year was a meat cutter at Tyro, Kansas. The following eighteen months were spent in the oil fields of Montgomery County, and he then resumed his trade in the meat business at Independence for two years.

Hard and persistent work and thrift and saving eventually gave him a little capital which, in 1907, he employed by opening a stock of groceries and meats on his own account. His first store was on West Sycamore Street in Independence, and later he built up a large store on East Main Street, but he has since traded it for a farm of 160 acres in Chautauqua County. His principal store now is at 1001 West Myrtle Street. Besides his farm in Chautauqua County, he has an excellent place of eighty acres ten miles southeast of Burlington in Coffey County, owns a house and four lots in Bolton, and his residence is at 1001 West Myrtle Street.

Mr. Sewell is independent in politics, and is affiliated with Camp No. 649, Modern Woodmen of America, at Independence. On September 22, 1907, at Troy, Ohio, he married Miss Stella Bowers, daughter of W. M. and Mary Bowers, who still live at Troy, Ohio, where her father is a finisher in painting automobiles. Mr. and Mrs. Sewell have two children, William Seymour, born September 2, 1908, and now in the public schools at Independence; and Irene, born April 26, 1913.

RAYMOND WILLIAM MOORE, M. D. Medicine embraces a vast field of knowledge and the successful physician must be a man of varied learning. Never at any time has the healing art demanded more in its practioners than at the present day and never has the profession given so fair an account of itself. Find the leading physician in a community and this acquaintance will indicate, with few exceptions, the man of most intellectual attainments, the keenest mind, the most progressive spirit. In this category stands Raymond William Moore, president of the Crawford County Medical Society, who since 1899 has been engaged in practice at Arcadia.

Doctor Moore was born at Marshall, Saline County, Missouri, September 22, 1872, and is a son of Levi J. and Nancy Priscilla (Horsman) Moore. The family originated in Ireland and settled at an early date in Ohio, probably during colonial times, and the doctor's grandfather, a farmer of the Buckeye State, died there in 1858. Levi J. Moore was born May 1, 1842, in Hocking County, Ohio, where he was reared and educated and where he resided until young manhood, when he removed to Iowa. While living in the latter state the Civil war came on and in 1861 he enlisted in the Third Iowa Cavalry, with which he fought in a number of severe engagements, including the battle of Pea Ridge. Shortly after that engagement he received a severe injury which incapacitated him for further duty at the front, and he was accordingly transferred to the One Hundred and Sixty-ninth Battalion, Veteran Reserve Corps, and did hospital duty during the rest of the war. Following the declaration of peace, he removed to Johnson County, Missouri, where he was employed as a stonemason for several years, and was there married, October 24, 1868, to Nancy Priscilla Horsman, who was born October 2, 1848, in Hardin County, Ohio. Not long thereafter, they went to St. Genevieve County, Missouri, where Mr. Moore also followed his trade, and later to Randolph County, Illinois, where for a time he engaged in farming. In 1885 Mr. Moore returned to Missouri and located in Vernon County, and there continued to be engaged in agricultural pursuits during the remainder of his life. His death occurred on his farm, in 1896. Mr. Moore was a republican, and an active member of the Methodist Episcopal Church, to which Mrs. Moore, who survives him and resides at Nevada, Missouri, also belongs. They were the parents of seven children, as follows: Leon Louis, born November 26, 1870, a mail carrier of Nevada, Missouri; Raymond William; Annetta, born October 26, 1877, who follows photography as a vocation and resides with her mother; Carl H., born October 6, 1880, who is a master mechanic and resides at Pueblo, Colorado; Caswell A., born February 5, 1883, who is identified with the International Harvester Company, at Kansas City, Missouri; Donna V., born October 15, 1886, who is a hospital attendant; and Lynn J., born October 31, 1889, who occupies an excellent position with the Oregon Short Line Railroad, at Portland, Oregon.

Raymond William Moore received his early education in the public schools of Missouri and Illinois, following which he attended the State Normal School at Warrensburg, Missouri. He left that institution in 1893 and for four years taught in the public schools of Vernon County, Missouri, in the meantime prosecuting his medical studies. He matriculated in the University Medical College in September, 1896, and was graduated from that institution in March, 1899. At this time the Spanish-American war came on and Doctor Moore entered the hospital department as hospital steward, and was stationed at Camp Alger, Virginia, and Camp Meade, Pennsylvania, for six months. When this service was completed he returned to Missouri, and in 1897 and 1898 was interne in the University Hospital at Kansas City, and then entered that institution as a student and was graduated in 1899 with the degree of Doctor of Medicine.

On April 3, 1899, Doctor Moore established himself in an office at Arcadia, and since then has built up a large and representative practice in general medicine and surgery. He has continued to be a close and careful student, and in 1910 took a special course at the New York Post Graduate Medical School and Hospital, specializing in diseases of the rectum and physical diagnosis of the heart and lungs. He now maintains well-appointed offices over the Home State Bank, where he has every instrument and appliance known to the profession, and a large and valuable medical library. Recognizing the value of medical societies to the physician, he has long been affiliated with the leading associations, including the Crawford County Medical Society, the Kansas Medical Society, the Southeastern Kansas Medical Society and the American Medical Association, and the high esteem in which he is held by his fellow practitioners is shown in the fact that he is president of the county society. Fraternally, the doctor is affiliated with Arcadia Lodge, No. 329, Ancient Free and Accepted Masons; Fort Scott Consistory No. 6, thirty-second degree; Arcadia Lodge, No. 401, Independent Order of Odd Fellows; the Fraternal Aid Union, and Arcadia Lodge, No. 159, Ancient Order of United Workmen. He has always been a friend of the schools, and at this time is secretary of the board of education. As a republican Doctor Moore was elected twice to the mayoralty chair of Arcadia, and gave the people sound, practical and businesslike administrations, which were characterized by numerous greatly needed civic reforms. He is a director of the Arcadia Building and Loan Association, and in addition to his own pleasant and modern home on Race Street, is the owner of several other dwelling properties. He has always lent his aid to progressive movements and can be counted upon to support all worthy enterprises.

Doctor Moore was married October 22, 1901, at Kansas City, Missouri, to Miss Anna May Downing, daughter of Mrs. Violetta Downing, who divides her time between the homes of Mrs. Moore, at Arcadia, and another daughter, who lives at St. Louis, Missouri. Doctor and Mrs. Moore are the parents of three children: Maude, born September 2, 1902, who is a freshman at the Arcadia High School; Ralph D., born October 27, 1903, who is an eighth-grade student in the public school; and Abby Jane, born September 10, 1907, who is in the fifth grade of the public school.

WILLIAM PAXTON HAZEN, who died at Chetopa, Kansas, April 16, 1909, was for many years a successful Kansas banker. His widow, Mrs. Addie (Glass) Hazen, who survives him, is widely known in women's circles in Kansas, and is especially active in charitable and philanthropic enterprises in her home city.

Mr. Hazen died when at the high tide of his usefulness. He was born in Pittsburgh, Pennsylvania, July 10, 1858. His father, David Hazen, was a lawyer by profession, practiced for many years in Pittsburgh, Pennsylvania, but died in Erie, Kansas. Mr. Hazen's maternal grandmother, Mary Ewing, had her pew in the First Presbyterian Church in Pittsburgh for more than forty years. She was the wife of Judge Ewing, a very prominent attorney of Western Pennsylvania. Mr. Hazen on his mother's side is also a descendant of Roger Williams of colonial history.

William P. Hazen was educated in the public schools of Pittsburgh, and after reaching manhood his parents came west to Otley, Iowa, and while in that state he attended the Agricultural College at Ames. On leaving school he came to Cherryvale, Kansas, in 1880, and from there to Thayer. He was cashier

of a bank in Thayer until 1887, and then helped to build and organize the Farmers and Merchants Bank at Erie, Kansas, in which he held the post of cashier until 1893. After that for three years he was connected with the National Bank of Pittsburg, Kansas, and then for a year was in the brokerage business at Baltimore, Maryland. Returning to Kansas and locating at Arkansas City he was appointed assistant bank commissioner for the State of Kansas, and was still serving in that position when he died. He had 108 banks under his supervision and was regarded as one of the most competent examiners in the state.

The late Mr. Hazen was a man of single purity in his personal and public life. He stood for wholesome ideals in public affairs, and was one of the instigators of the reform party in politics. For six years he edited the Advance at Chetopa. Politically he was a republican of progressive type. He loved Kansas. He loved the Kansas prairies, the flowers, the institutions and the men of Kansas. He was connected with the Chamber of Commerce of Pittsburg, with the Modern Woodmen of America, the Ancient Order of United Workmen, the Bankers Life of Des Moines, Iowa, and with the Knights Templar Masons, Pittsburg Commandery. He held a number of offices in the Methodist Episcopal Church.

Mr. Hazen married Miss Addie Glass. Mrs. Hazen was born in Rockport, Indiana, January 13, 1864, and was educated in the Rockport College. He is an active member of the Methodist Episcopal Church and is one of the organizers of the Wednesday Club of Chetopa. This club is affiliated with both the state and national Federation of Women's Clubs. In July, 1916, Mrs. Hazen returned to Chetopa after seven years spent in Baldwin, Kansas, where she lived while her children were attending Baker College. She owned a residence in Baldwin. In both these cities she is well known for her social prominence and is a member of the school board of the public schools of Chetopa.

Mrs. Hazen is a daughter of T. Milton Glass, a well-known citizen of Chetopa. He was born at Bardstown, Kentucky, April 10, 1835, and when he was quite young his parents removed to Terre Haute, Indiana, where he was reared and educated. He has always been a farmer and farm owner, but has usually lived in some town. He came to Kansas in 1885, locating in Oswego, and bought extensively farm lands between Oswego and Chetopa. Since 1898 his home has been in Chetopa and he now owns 210 acres in Cherokee and Labette counties, having sold the rest of his farm interests. His home is on Plum Street in Chetopa, and he also has a half block of lots in that city. Mr. Glass is a republican and has held a place in the city council of Chetopa for three terms. He is a member of the Methodist Episcopal Church. During the Civil war he enlisted in the Union army at the last call for troops and was with the Twelfth Kentucky Cavalry as a first lieutenant.

Mr. Glass married Melissa Miller, who was born at Patriot, Indiana, March 8, 1841. Their children were: Nellie, who died at the age of fourteen; Mrs. Hazen; Willard, who was murdered by a robber at Welsh, Oklahoma, in 1898; and a daughter that died in infancy. The Glass ancestry came originally from Ireland.

Mrs. Hazen is the mother of three children, all of whom are exceedingly competent young people, and have entered upon very promising careers of usefulness. The son, Willard Glass, was graduated from

Baker University at Baldwin, with the degree A. B., in 1910; spent five years as cashier of the People's State Bank of Baldwin, and in order to familiarize himself with metropolitan banking he resigned to take a position in the Southwest National Bank at Kansas City, Missouri. He is learning banking in its every detail, and plans to make his life work in that field. He is also a director in the Morgan Gardner Mercantile Company at Baldwin, and while a resident of Baldwin served as city treasurer. He is affiliated with the Independent Order of Odd Fellows and the Zeta Chi college fraternity.

Gertrude, the older daughter of Mrs. Hazen, was graduated from Baker University A. B. in 1912, then attended the Margaret Morrison School of the Carnegie Institute of Technology at Pittsburgh, Pennsylvania, where she specialized in domestic science, was awarded the degree Master of Arts by the Kansas University in 1915, and is now in the Howard Payne College at Fayette, Missouri.

Ruth Hazen, the youngest child of Mrs. Hazen, is now a member of the senior class in the Oswego Seminary, has taken 4½ years of instruction in the violin department at the Baker University Conservatory, and is a very proficient musician. Her studies along that line are now being continued on the piano, and she is planning a special course in playground work at Battle Creek, Michigan. Her talent as a musician and her versatile ability in other ways qualify her unusually well for playground work, and she has been a factor through her musical interests in various festivals and religious meetings.

ARTHUR M. THURMAN. As the prosperous and rapidly-growing city of Caney is located almost on the state line between Oklahoma and Kansas, many men who make their homes in the city are the owners of property in the former state, particularly land that is used for agricultural purposes. A large number of these make daily trips between their country estates and their city residences, either by way of train or automobile, and in this class is found Arthur M. Thurman, a prosperous farmer and rancher, who lives at Caney, but whose magnificent property, consisting of 1,280 acres of fertile and productive land, is located nine miles southeast of the city, in Osage County, Oklahoma. When Mr. Thurman came to Caney, then but a farming center, in 1901, he was possessed of no means other than those represented by his ambition and determination, and his first work was as a clerk in a drug store. From that time to the present he has steadily advanced, until now he is justly accounted one of the substantial men of his community.

Arthur M. Thurman was born at Osceola, the county seat of Saint Clair County, Missouri, January 28, 1879, and is a son of Richard Scott and Eliza (Cobb) Thurman. The family originated in Ireland, from whence the first American progenitor emigrated during colonial days, members of the family locating in the Western Reserve of Ohio as pioneers. Joseph Thurman, the grandfather of Arthur M. Thurman, was born in 1776, in Ohio, from which state he enlisted as a soldier in the American army for service during the War of 1812. In 1816 he traveled westward, locating in Missouri, and in his later years became a pioneer farmer of Kansas, and died at Fort Scott, in August, 1862. He had fought under Gen. William Henry Harrison, but was a democrat in his political belief. Mr. Thurman married a Miss Price, who bore him four children, namely: John, who crossed the plains to California during the gold

rush of "the days of '49," and after a short experience as a miner died in that state; Marion, who died in Missouri after a successful career spent in the milling business; Joseph, who was engaged in farming until his death at Nevada, Missouri; and Job, who was also an agriculturist and died at Neosho, Missouri. After the death of his first wife, Mr. Thurman was married to Mrs. Mary (Roberts) Joslin, a native of Kentucky, who died near Joplin, Missouri, and they had three children, namely: Isaac Riley, who followed farming as a vocation and died at Neosho, Missouri; Zacharias, who was a miner and died in the far West; and Richard Scott.

Richard Scott Thurman was born at Saint Charles, Saint Charles County, Missouri, January 21, 1847, and was a small child when taken to Newton County, in the same state, by his parents. There he received a public school education and was reared on the home farm, on which he worked until his activities were interrupted by the coming on of the Civil war. When he was but fifteen years old, in August, 1862, Mr. Thurman enlisted in the Union army for service in the war between the states, becoming a member of Company E, Fourteenth Kansas Cavalry. With this command he saw some hard fighting, including all the engagements incidental to Price's raid, and when he received his honorable discharge and was mustered out of the service, it was with an excellent record for gallantry and fidelity. On his return from the war, the young soldier went to Saint Clair County, Missouri, where for nearly thirty years he operated the ferry on the Osage River. Subsequently, he went to Nowata, Oklahoma, where he engaged for a time in teaming, and July 12, 1905, came to Kansas and located at Coffeyville, where he has been engaged in private teaming and in working for the city with his teams to the present time. He is the owner of his own residence, at No. 303 East Twelfth street, Coffeyville, as well as the lot adjoining. Mr. Thurman has been a man of industry, and while he has not become wealthy, has accumulated a competence for his declining years. He has always been known for his honesty and straightforward dealing, and among those who know him is held in the highest esteem. Politically a democrat, he has never been a politician. His only social connection is with Sheridan Post No. 90, Grand Army of the Republic. Mr. Thurman was married in 1871, at Fort Scott, Kansas, to Miss Eliza Cobb, daughter of David and Martha Cobb, both of whom are now deceased. Mr. Cobb was a veteran of the Civil war, having fought from 1861 to 1865 as a member of the Sixth Kansas Cavalry. The children born to Mr. and Mrs. Thurman are as follows: Walter, who resides near Coffeyville, Kansas, and is engaged in farming; Clara Belle, who died at the age of three years; Arthur M.; Oscar Frank, who was an engineer for a steamshoveling company, and in May, 1914, was so injured in a boiler explosion at San Diego, California, that he only lived forty-eight hours; and H. R., who is a teamster and makes his home with his parents at Coffeyville.

Arthur M. Thurman was educated in the public schools of Osceola, Missouri, where he attended the high school, but at the age of seventeen years left school to go to Nowata, Oklahoma, where he worked on farms for about two years. In 1898 he went to Coffeyville, Kansas, and for three years had experience as a clerk in a store, and in 1901 came to Caney. This community was then only a farming center, but Mr. Thurman had the foresight to see that some day it was destined to be a live commercial and manufacturing community, and he accordingly laid his plans to remain here. His first employment was as a clerk in the drug store conducted by Doctor Booker, but two years thereafter turned his attention to farming and ranching in Osage County, Oklahoma, a line in which he has continued to the present with almost phenomenal success. On his broad acres Mr. Thurman raises blooded stock in horses and cattle, and fancy chickens and turkeys, in addition to which he carries on diversified farming. He maintains his residence on Third Avenue, Caney, and makes daily trips to and from his ranch in his automobile. With his years of experience, his excellent business foresight, and his managerial ability, it is needless to say that Mr. Thurman accomplishes the greatest possible results from the operation of his land. He is a republican in politics, and while he has not cared for public honors, has discharged his duties of citizenship by acting as a member of the school board in the vicinity of his ranch in Osage County for two years. Fraternally, he is connected with Lodge No. 160, Ancient Order of United Workmen, Caney, and Lodge No. 1215, Benevolent and Protective Order of Elks, and also holds membership in the Country Club, situated on Big Caney Creek. He is a man of strong characteristics, public spirited, popular, honorable in all his dealings, and through his upbuilding of his handsome and valuable property is an agricultural factor of widespread influence.

Mr. Thurman was married March 29, 1903, at Caney, Kansas, to Miss Lola Labadie, daughter of Frank and Samantha (Miller) Labadie, and a one-eighth Osage Indian on her father's side. To Mr. and Mrs. Thurman there has come one child, Geneva E., who was born at Caney, March 27, 1906, and is now attending the public schools.

GEORGE A. FANCHER, proprietor of the Fancher Printing Company of Coffeyville is a veteran of the printing art and has followed his trade in many states and towns all over the Far West. For the past thirty years his home and center of activities have been in different cities of Kansas and he is now proprietor of one of the leading job offices in the southern part of the state.

He comes of old and substantial American stock, his ancestors were French a number of generations back, and the family was established in this country by three brothers who settled in New York when it was still a colony. Mr. Fancher's great-grandfather was a soldier in the Revolution.

J. W. Fancher, grandfather of the Coffeyville business man, was born in New York State in 1792. He spent most of his life in his native state as a farmer, and when he retired he moved to Michigan, living with his son J. W., Jr., and died at the latter's home in Buchanan, Michigan, in 1876. He married Eliazbeth Hicks, who was born in New York State and died at Syracuse. She was a Quakeress and a regularly ordained preacher in that faith. The children of these worthy people were: Alva, who enlisted in a New York regiment in the Civil war and died while in service; George H., who became a banker and died at San Francisco, California; Bradley C., who was a lumberman and was killed in an accident in a sawmill at Berrien Springs, Michigan; J. W. Fancher, Jr., father of George A.; Lee R., who is a banker at Merced, California, and was a soldier for four years in a New York regiment of infantry during the Civil war, and the sixth of the family was also a volunteer from New York in the war and was killed in one of the battles in which his regiment engaged.

Mr. George A. Fancher was born at Buchanan, Michigan, February 20, 1868. His father, J. W. Fancher, is now living retired at Merced, California. He was born at Syracuse, New York, in 1838, was reared there, educated in the public schools and afterwards in the schools of Ypsilanti, Michigan. As a young man he went to Buchanan, Michigan, where he married. By trade he was a cooper, and at one time he served as principal of the public schools of Buchanan. He has been a successful business man and now has extensive land holdings in Michigan, Indiana and California. While a resident of Berrien County, Michigan, he served as sheriff and also as chief of police at Buchanan. Politically he is a democrat. J. W. Fancher married Miss Margaret Roe, who was born in 1842 in LaPorte County, Indiana, and died at Davis in that state in May, 1906. Their children were: Alva C., who is a rancher at Athlone, California; Melvin H., who lives on one of his father's farms in Starke County, Indiana; George H., who is the third in age; Willis, a fruit farmer at Los Angeles, California; Clarence, who lives on one of his father's farms at Merced, California; Lona, wife of Doctor Winan, a physician in Chicago; Chloe, wife of Doctor Denaught, a physician at Hamlet, Indiana.

While attending the public schools at Buchanan, Michigan, George A. Fancher learned printing in one of the newspaper offices there, and in 1884, following his graduation from the Buchanan High School, he went to Chicago and had his first journeyman's experience in that city. He had his share of traveling about over the country as nearly all printers do, and from Chicago went to Leadville, Colorado, and in 1886 reached Kansas and secured employment at his trade in Hutchinson. In 1889 he went to Saline, and from there to Winfield in 1891. He followed the trade at Winfield for ten years. In 1901 he moved to Iola, and from there four years later came to Coffeyville, where he has had his home and his business since 1905. At Coffeyville he was employed for four years as a printer in the offices of the Journal.

In 1909 Mr. Fancher established the Fancher Printing Company, which has complete mechanical facilities and an organization of expert printers for all classes of jobs of printing. His plant is at 108 West Tenth Street. Mr. Fancher resides in a country home with ten acres of ground three miles northeast of Coffeyville, and built his attractive residence there in 1910. He also owns a dwelling house at 302 East Eleventh Street and another at 612 East Fifth Street.

Politically he is a republican. He is a member of the Chamber of Commerce and affiliates with Coffeyville Camp No. 665, Modern Woodmen of America.

In 1895 at Winfield, Kansas, he married Miss Anna Brown, daughter of Mr. and Mrs. H. C. Brown. Her father was a farmer now deceased and her mother still lives in Winfield. Mr. and Mrs. Fancher have two children. Alva Keath was born April 20, 1905, and is now in the public schools at Coffeyville. Carl Prentice was born May 14, 1909, and is attending school in the country district near his father's home.

WILLIAM C. HAVERSTICK. One of the oldest families in Montgomery County is the Haversticks, of which William C. Haverstick, for the past quarter of a century connected with the oil business, is a member. Before the Osage Indians had moved from this section of the country the late Samuel Haverstick had brought his family to the northern part of Montgomery County, and a portion of his original homestead claim is still in the Haverstick ownership.

Casper Haverstick, grandfather of William C., was born at Eusfelden, Canton of Argyle, Switzerland, and when a young man came to America and was a pioneer farmer and business man in Ohio. He died at Washingtonville, Ohio, in 1873.

The late Samuel Haverstick, a son of this Swiss immigrant, was born in June, 1836, at Washingtonville, Ohio. He grew up in that state, went as an early settler to Waverly, Iowa, where he was married, and his business was that of farming and mining. In 1862 he moved to Kansas, soon after the admission of the territory to the Union, and first located in Miami County. On April 14, 1869, he arrived in what is now Montgomery County, and secured his homestead of 160 acres in Sycamore Township in the northern part of the county. Of that 160 acres, eighty acres are held in trust in the name of A. E. Haverstick, the youngest son of Samuel. The town of Sycamore is built on the other eighty acres. Samuel Haverstick after a long and active career died on his farm in this county November 4, 1894. He was a democrat and a man of more than ordinary prominence and influence in his home township, serving as township treasurer and in other offices. He belonged to Neodesha Lodge of the Masonic Order. Samuel Haverstick married Sarah Powell, who was born in December, 1837, at Lewiston, Illinois, and died on the old farm February 15, 1910. There were three children: William C.; Addie H., wife of Charles Dugan of the State of Oregon; and A. E. Haverstick, who lives at Sycamore and is a field man for the Hale Pipe Line Company.

William C. Haverstick was born at Waverly, Bremer County, Iowa, June 27, 1858, and was only four years of age when brought to Kansas. Most of his education was acquired in the public schools of Independence, and he graduated from the high school there in 1876. His early ambition was to become a railroad man, and his desire was fulfilled when he was given the position of locomotive engineer with the Union Pacific Railroad, and he was with that company a trusted and efficient engineer from 1880 until 1889. He was then connected with railroads further east until 1891. On November 15, 1891, at Clinton, Indiana, he was severely injured on the head and shoulder in a head-on collision while he was piloting a locomotive over the Chicago & Eastern Illinois Railroad. The collision was due to the mistake of a dispatcher in giving a lap order. To save his life he jumped from the engine and the injuries of the fall incapacitated him for further active railroading.

Returning to Kansas and after recovering he engaged in the oil and gas business. At Neodesha he acquired some extensive interests, but has now sold out his holdings and is engaged in the oil brokerage business with office and headquarters in the Carl-Leon Hotel in Independence. Mr. Haverstick is a democrat, has never aspired to hold an office, is a member of the Brotherhood of Locomotive Engineers, and is affiliated with Kansas City Lodge No. 271, Ancient Free and Accepted Masons, at Kansas City, Kansas.

WILLIAM AARON BRANDENBURG as president of the Pittsburg Manual Training Normal School, has one of the most important positions in the Kansas educational field. While he has been identified with educational affairs in this state only a few years, that time has sufficed to indicate his broad qualifications and his unusual ability as a teacher and administrator. Mr. Brandenburg was formerly superintendent of

Vol. IV—19

schools of Oklahoma City and was also well known as a leader in school work in his native state of Iowa.

He was born in Clayton County, Iowa, October 10, 1869. His ancestry originally had its seat in Berlin, Germany. His great-great-grandfather emigrated in colonial days from Germany and settled in Maryland. Mr. Brandenburg's father Francis Marion Brandenburg was born in the State of Ohio, October 6, 1846. He was reared in McLean County, Illinois, followed farming all his life, and in 1906 retired from the farm and lived at Des Moines, Iowa. He was never a resident of Kansas, but died while on a visit to his son in Pittsburg on April 2, 1916. Politically he was a democrat. He belonged to the Grangers' organization and for many years was an elder in the Christian Church. He was married in Clayton County, Iowa, to Enfield Maxwell, who was born in Clayton County, Iowa, in June, 1844, and is now living at Des Moines. Their children were: William A.; Walter E., who is pastor of the First Christian Church at Parsons, Kansas; A. W., a farmer in Clayton County, Iowa; Dr. George C., who is a member of the faculty of Purdue University, at Lafayette, Indiana; Amy, wife of Henry Carmichael, a farmer in Clayton County; Mrs. Laura Christensen, whose husband is foreman in the Newbury Nursery at Mitchell, South Dakota.

William A. Brandenburg grew up on a farm in Clayton County, Iowa, attended the public schools there and the high school at Volga, and for a year and a half taught in the rural schools of his native county and for two and a half years was assistant superintendent at Volga. His ambition from the start was to get a higher education, and in 1895 he entered Drake University at Des Moines, where he completed the course leading to the degree of Bachelor of Philosophy. On graduating in 1900 he accepted the position of superintendent of the Park Avenue School of Des Moines, where he remained two years. He was then superintendent for three years of the Capital Park School in Des Moines, and from 1905 to 1910 was superintendent of the public school system of Mason City, Iowa.

Since then his active work in the educational field has been in the Southwest. In January, 1910, he was unanimously elected superintendent of the public schools of Oklahoma City, which position he held until August, 1913, when without formal application he was called to the presidency of the State Manual Training Normal at Pittsburg, Kansas, and has since been its able executive.

From 1911 to 1913 Mr. Brandenburg was a member of the State Board of Education in Oklahoma. During the summers of 1903-04-05 he taught in the department of education in the Drake University at Des Moines. He is a member of the National Educational Association, the National Society for the Promotion of Industrial and Vocational Education, and a member of the National Educational Council. Politically Mr. Brandenburg is an independent. When only twenty-two years of age he was elected justice of the peace in Sperry Township in his native county in Iowa on the democratic ticket. He is an elder in the Christian Church and fraternally is a member of Pittsburg Lodge, No. 187 Ancient Free and Accepted Masons, Pittsburg Chapter, No. 58, Royal Arch Masons, Pittsburg Commandery, No. 29, Knights Templar, Mirza Temple of the Mystic Shrine at Pittsburg, belongs to the Knights of Pythias and the Modern Woodmen of America at Mason City, Iowa, and the Brotherhood of American Yeomen at Des Moines.

On June 22, 1893, at Volga, Iowa, he married Miss

Alta Penfield, a daughter of William A. and Lucy A. (Chapman) Penfield. Both her parents are now deceased. Her father was a merchant. Lola, the oldest child of Mr. and Mrs. Brandenburg, is a graduate of the Pittsburg Manual Training Normal School with the degree Bachelor of Science and is now a teacher in the Pittsburg High School. Amy is a sophomore in the Manual Training Normal School. Merrill is in the senior class of the Normal High School, while Harold is a high school freshman, Helen is in the third grade of the grammar school, and William A. Jr., in the first grade.

A. J. LUGEANBEAL has for many years been a successful merchant at Angola, and at the same time has participated actively in Labette County politics and in civic affairs.

Born at Gridley, Illinois, January 12, 1872, Mr. Lugeanbeal has spent most of his life in Kansas. His grandfather, Alexander Lugeanbeal, was born in Germany, came to America and followed farming in Ohio and died at Black Run in that state. A. J. Lugeanbeal, Sr., was born at Marion, Ohio, in 1841, and died at Fredonia, Kansas, in 1902. He was reared and married in Ohio followed farming there, and then moved to Gridley, Illinois, soon after his marriage. While in Illinois he saw active service in an Illinois regiment during the Civil war. He enlisted in 1861 and went through the entire struggle. From Illinois he moved to Fredonia, Kansas, in 1882, and was actively identified with farming there until his death. He was a democrat in politics, a member and deacon in the Christian Church, and was an active Mason, having taken his first degrees in that order while at Camp Butler, Illinois, during the Civil war. A. J. Lugeanbeal, Sr., married Elizabeth A. Kearfoot, who was born at Delaware, Ohio, in 1845, and is now living at Fredonia, Kansas. They had a large family of children, noted briefly as follows: Mary, wife of D. O. Ponsor, a blacksmith of Guilford, Kansas; Rosa, who died at the age of twenty-six years as the wife of George Hutchinson, who is a farmer at Shaw, Kansas; D. C. Lugeanbeal, a merchant at Fredonia; Ella, wife of John W. Smith, a farmer at Fredonia; A. J. Lugeanbeal, Jr.; W. F., a merchant at Bartlett, Kansas; Lizzie A., wife of R. W. Kibler, a farmer at Benedict, Kansas; E. E, who is cashier of the bank at Elk City, Kansas; Pearl, who died at the age of twenty-five, the wife of W. T. Morse, a farmer at Guilford, Kansas; Eva, wife of Henry Woollard, a merchant at Guilford; and Lela, wife of Andrew Ward, a farmer at Parsons, Kansas.

Mr. Lugeanbeal, who was brought to Kansas by his parents when he was ten years of age, completed his education in the district schools of Wilson County in this state. The first twenty-five years of his life he spent on his father's farm and then varied the monotony of farming by engaging in railroad work and also beginning the operation of a farm on his own account. His home has been in Angola since 1902. In that year he bought the building at the corner of Main Street and Watson Avenue which he has ever since occupied, and there established a general stock of merchandise. He has the principal one of the two stores in the town, and has built up a very large patronage over a wide surrounding territory.

Mr. Lugeanbeal has long been a prominent figure in local democratic politics. For ten years he served as township clerk. At the last election he was a candidate for the office of county treasurer, but owing to the fact that he had for an opponent a lady and that she was a candidate for the second term (it being customary to give an incumbent of a county office the second term), he was defeated by a small majority. Mr. Lugeanbeal is affiliated with Lodge No. 237 of the Knights of Pythias at Fredonia, which he served as master at arms for two terms; also belongs to the Dramatic Order of the Knights of Khorassan, the higher branch of Pythianism, is affiliated with Edna Lodge No. 345, Ancient Free and Accepted Masons, with Angola Lodge No. 523 of the Ancient Order of United Workmen, of which he is past master, and for twelve years has served as financier. He is also vice president of the Labette County Good Roads Association.

In the way of property Mr. Lugeanbeal owns both his home and store at Angola. In 1905 at Edna, Kansas, he married Miss Mamie Cave, daughter of H. C. and Julia Cave, who live on their farm near Angola. Mr. and Mrs. Lugeanbeal have two children: Wintress, born August 3, 1906; and Jack Cave, born March 17, 1908.

HENRY A. JOHNSMEYER. One of the worthiest families to receive attention in the annals of Riley County is that of Johnsmeyer, which has been identified with the early settlement, the development, and the civic and community life there for more than half a century. Henry A. Johnsmeyer was born soon after the family came to Kansas, and he has himself prospered to a degree where his extensive landed estate and his large business affairs constitute him one of Riley County's notable men.

His father was the late C. A. Johnsmeyer, who died on his farm in Jackson Township of Riley County in 1911. He was born near Wehrendorf in the Kingdom of Hanover, Germany, September 13, 1840. Reared and educated in his native country, at the close of four years of service in the Sixth Hanoverian Infantry he emigrated in 1865 to America. Of all the various nationalities of the great German Empire that have come to America none has surpassed in virile power and sturdy industry the Hanoverians.

On arriving in New York City C. A. Johnsmeyer was employed for two months in a grocery store as a clerk. His aim was to identify himself with the western country, and on leaving New York City he journeyed by way of one of the early railroads through the Middle West as far as Kansas City. From there a boat took him up the river to Leavenworth and a wagon was his mode of conveyance to Randolph in Riley County. Afterward he invested his modest capital in 160 acres of land in Jackson Township. That was the nucleus of the splendid homestead on which he lived the rest of his life. Only a few improvements had been made on the land and he practically transformed it by industry and thrift into the splendid farm which it now is. It is considered one of the best of the many fine farms in the Blue River Valley. His material accumulations grew out of his broadening enterprise as a farmer and stock raiser, and he was also an influential and highly respected citizen. To his original 160 acres he added until he was the owner of farm lands not only in Riley but in Washington County, though much the greater part was in the former county.

In December, 1865, soon after coming to Kansas, C. A. Johnsmeyer married Miss Anna Bohne. They were married in Jackson Township. Mrs. Johnsmeyer is still living, occupying the old homestead in that township. She too was a native of Hanover, Germany. A brief record of her ten children is as follows: Henry A.; Louisa, widow of Albert Harrisberger, living at Randolph, Kansas; Louis W., a lumberman at Randolph; John F., of Leonardville; Herman H., of Tampa, Kansas; Edward C. of Riley; Amanda, wife of Fred Richter, a Riley County farmer; Carl, of Randolph, on old homestead; Nellie, wife of August Richter of Randolph; and Alma, wife of Reuben Axelton of Randolph. Both parents were reared and were always faithful to the German Evangelical Church. C. A. Johnsmeyer was a republican in politics, and though he never aspired to political office and held only a few minor township positions, he was a man of decided prominence in local affairs. Throughout his long career he was known as a reliable, liberal minded and public spirited citizen.

It was on a farm near Randolph, Kansas, that Henry A. Johnsmeyer was born. He was the oldest of the ten children, and he naturally assumed responsibilities in advance of his years, and bore a sturdy share of the farm work at home until he was twenty-two. He attended the country schools and having acquired the art of farming in all its details, when he started for himself it was on a place in Washington County, Kansas. He was a farmer in that locality until 1903, when returning to Riley County he acquired a farm in the Mill Creek Valley of Grant Township. Ten years later he came to his present home west of the Town of Riley. Mr. Johnsmeyer has for three decades helped to grow the staple crops of Kansas, and has also done an extensive business as a stock raiser and breeder. He is now one of the largest land owners of Riley County. Though a man of ample means he and his family still choose to reside in the country, and they have one of the most beautiful homes in the county, a frame building constructed largely by Mr. Johnsmeyer's own skill and work. This home is less than a mile west of the Town of Riley.

Among other interests he is president of the Farmers State Bank of Riley. He is a stanch republican and he and his family are members of the German Evangelical Church. In 1890 he married Miss Mary Harrisberger, who was born in Center Township in Riley County. Her father, F. Harrisberger, was one of Riley County's early settlers. Two daughters have been born to their marriage: Vera L. and Nora E. Vera is now teaching school and Nora will soon graduate in music.

E. C. GLASS, D. D. S., has been a resident of Independence since 1903, and is one of the leading members of the dental profession in Southern Kansas.

Born January 28, 1876, the year of the hundredth anniversary of our national independence, he was given the name Earl Centennial Glass. His birth occurred near Bois d'Arc, Greene County, in Southern Missouri. His parents are Albert M. and Susan (Van Voorhis) Glass, both of whom are still living, with their home at Bois d'Arc, Missouri. The Glass family came originally from Scotland and settled in Virginia in colonial days, while the Van Voorhis family were Hollanders and originally settled in New York. Albert M. Glass was born in Stark County, Ohio, June 18, 1843, and is a veteran of the Civil war. He enlisted in 1862 at the age of nineteen in Company D of the 115th Ohio Infantry, and served until the close of the war. While in the Tennessee campaign he was taken prisoner, but was later exchanged and rejoined his command. In 1871 he moved his family to Missouri and has spent his active career

there as a general farmer and stock raiser, and is now retired though occupying his farm. He is a republican, and is an elder in the Christian Church. His wife was born near Canton in Stark County, Ohio, November 14, 1844. Their children are: James I., a farmer at Bois d'Arc, Missouri; Dr. E. C. Glass; and Iva, who died February 11, 1914, her husband, Marvin J. Ross, being in the hardware business at Eureka, Kansas.

Doctor Glass while a boy attended the country schools of Bois d'Arc and also the Drury College at Springfield, Missouri. April 30; 1901, he completed his course and graduated D. D. S. from the Western Dental College of Kansas City, Missouri. After some experience in the profession elsewhere, he established his office at Independence in August, 1903, and has since enjoyed a large practice and is recognized as one of the most skillful men in his profession in this part of the state. His offices are in the Booth Building on West Myrtle Street. He is a member of the State and National District Dental societies.

Fraternally he is affiliated with Fortitude Lodge No. 107, Ancient Free and Accepted Masons, at Independence, and belongs to the Methodist Episcopal Church and is a republican. On March 18, 1908, at Sycamore, Kansas, he married Miss Edwina Chandler. Her parents were Edwin and Agnes Chandler. Her mother died in November, 1915, and her father is living retired at Sycamore, Kansas.

WILLIAM S. GOOCH, M. D., has practiced surgery and medicine at Mapleton, Kansas, for the past fifteen years, and in point of experience and general ability ranks as the first and leading member of the profession in that community.

Doctor Gooch is a Missourian and was born at Meadville, in that state February 6, 1875. His family settled in pioneer times in Northwestern Missouri and the original stock came out of England and established themselves in Kentucky along about the close of the Revolutionary war. Doctor Gooch's Grandfather Gideon Gooch was born in Kentucky, moved from that state to Northern Missouri, and when the first news came of the discovery of gold in California he crossed the plains as a seeker of wealth on the Pacific, and died in California in 1848. His wife's maiden name was Foster. She was also a native of Kentucky and died at Meadville, Missouri. Joseph Gooch, father of Doctor Gooch, was born at Meadville, Missouri, in 1844, was reared and married there, and has always followed farming. Since 1902 he has lived in the vicinity of Mapleton, Kansas, where he has a farm. He is a democrat and a member of the Christian Church. He married Nancy J. Evans, who was born in Kentucky in 1850. They have three children: Elizabeth, at home; William S.; and Alma, wife of E. J. Edmundson, Mr. Edmundson being associated with Doctor Gooch in the drug store business at Mapleton.

Doctor Gooch had his first educational advantages in the public schools of Meadville, Missouri. Two years were spent in the Chillicothe Normal School at Chillicothe, Missouri, and he was a teacher for three years in Linn County, Missouri. His ambition from early boyhood had been to become a physician. In 1896 he entered Beaumont Medical College, now called the St. Louis University, where he was graduated Doctor of Medicine in 1900. His first practice was done at Elmer, Missouri, where he remained six months, and in September, 1901, he came to Mapleton, Kansas, and has been looking after a growing medical and surgical practice ever since. His offices are in the Waterman Building. Doctor Gooch is a member of the Bourbon County and the State Medical Societies, the Southeastern Kansas Medical Society and the American Medical Association. He keeps in close touch with all the advances made in his profession.

Doctor Gooch owns a half interest in the only drug store in Mapleton, located on Main Street. He also has a good farm of 100 acres situated a mile and a half east of Mapleton. For a number of years he has served on the local school board, and belongs to Mapleton Lodge of the Masonic Order, the local camp of the Modern Woodmen of America and the local lodge of the Ancient Order of United Workmen. In politics he is a democrat.

Doctor Gooch was married at Wheeling, Missouri, in September, 1901, to Miss Grace Buckner, daughter of James and Elva (Lewis) Buckner. Her parents now reside in Kansas City, Missouri, her father being a retired merchant. Doctor and Mrs. Gooch have two children: Forestine, born January 21, 1906; and Maxine, born May 1, 1911.

SAMUEL S. GLASSCOCK, M. D. That "an institution is but the lengthened shadow of a man" has an unusual and more than nominal application in the case of the Grand View Sanitarium of Kansas City, Kansas. For thirteen years this institution has realized the highest standards and ideals of a real sanitarium because it has been permeated by the personality and the ability of Dr. S. S. Glasscock, whose reputation as an authority on mental and nervous diseases is accepted and credited among the leaders of the profession all over the Middle West.

In 1898, at 26th and Ridge Avenue, F. M. Bidwell began what is now the Grand View Sanitarium. Originally it was designed merely to take care of county cases. At first its capacity was for about eighteen or twenty cases. In 1903 Dr. George M. Gray, S. S. Glasscock and F. M. Tracy, all prominent members of the medical profession of Kansas City, Kansas, leased the property for two years, and converted it into a sanitarium. In 1905 Doctors Glasscock and Tracy bought the property and made a number of changes in the physical structure and equipment. In 1910 Doctor Glasscock became proprietor of the institution and has since held the majority of the stock, the principal minor stockholder being Dr. A. L. Ludwig. In 1911 an addition of twenty rooms with private baths was added, and the institution now has a capacity for fifty patients. The sanitarium is devoted primarily to the care of persons suffering from mental and nervous diseases and drug addicts. The Grand View Sanitarium is a corporation with a capital of $25,000. It occupies a magnificent site, on an elevation near the city, surrounded with grounds of twenty acres, and it is one of the noblest institutions of its kind in the entire Missouri Valley.

From the days when he was a farm boy in Missouri Doctor Glasscock has been constantly under the urge of a great ambition to be of service to humanity through the profession of medicine. His birth occurred on a farm near Excelsior Springs, in Clay County, Missouri, April 13, 1862. He was one of the five children of Archibald and Rachel (Yancey) Glasscock, his father a native of Tennessee and his mother of North Carolina. Both were born in 1822 and both died in the year 1898. Archibald Glasscock was brought to Northwestern Missouri in 1832 and spent the rest of his life as a farmer.

Though all his mature years have been devoted to a profession, Doctor Glasscock knows the practical details of farming, since he became well acquainted

with them as a boy. He also attended district schools, spent two years in the University of Missouri, and after obtaining a teacher's license taught a district school. His mind had already been made up as to the profession he would follow. While teaching he read medicine under Dr. S. R. Keith of Excelsior Springs, and later he secured means to enter the Rush Medical College of Chicago, where he was graduated M. D. in 1887. He returned to begin his practice at Excelsior Springs. After two years, in 1889, he went abroad and took post-graduate work in one of the greatest medical centers of the world, the University of Vienna in Austria. While there he specialized in mental and nervous disorders.

On returning to America in 1890 Doctor Glasscock located in Kansas City, Kansas, and has now been an honored member of the profession in that city for over a quarter of a century. For some years his practice was of a general nature, but since 1903, at which time he acquired his active interest in the Grand View Sanitarium, he has been specializing in mental and nervous diseases, and now confines his entire attention to that branch of the profession.

For five years Doctor Glasscock was a member of the staff of St. Margaret's Hospital, and for fourteen years has been on the staff of Bethany Hospital and is now consulting neurologist. He is professor of mental and nervous diseases in the medical department of the Kansas State University. His name is also well known in medical literature, especially along the lines in which he specializes.

Doctor Glasscock at one time was president of the Kansas City, Missouri, Academy of Medicine and in 1915 was president of the Medical Association of the Southwest. He is also a member of the Wyandotte County and the Kansas State Medical societies and the American Medical Association. He belongs to the Medical College fraternity Phi Beta Pi, and is a thirty-second degree Scottish Rite Mason and a member of the Mystic Shrine. In politics a republican, it has always been his steadfast desire to serve the public through his professional activities, though in 1904 he was elected and served one term in the state legislature from Wyandotte County, and has also been connected with some of the important civic and municipal movements in Kansas City, Kansas. Since 1880 he has been a member of the Methodist Episcopal Church, and in 1915 was president of the Laymen's Association of the Kansas Conference, and in 1916 was a delegate to the general conference at Saratoga Springs.

November 29, 1888, he married Miss Ollie Hunter, who was born in Illinois, daughter of Milton B. and Sallie (Reed) Hunter. Her father was a carriage manufacturer and spent his last years in Kansas City, Missouri. Doctor and Mrs. Glasscock have three daughters: Edith, Rachel and Catherine.

JOHN NORVAL SHERMAN, M. D. Although one of the younger physicians of Neosho County, Dr. John Norval Sherman, of Thayer, has gained the confidence and support of the public by reason of his thorough training for his profession and his fidelity to the ethics of the medical fraternity. He came to his present field of activity in 1916, with five years of experience behind him, and has already built up what promises to be a lucrative and representative practice.

Doctor Sherman was born July 11, 1884, at Lafayette, Madison County, Ohio, and belongs to a family which originally came to America from England and settled in New York before the War of the Revolution. His grandfather was William Sherman, who

Samuel S. Glasscock

was born in 1825, in the Empire State, from whence he went to Kentucky, then to Scioto County, Ohio, and later to Madison County, Ohio, his death occurring in 1885, at Irvin Station, Ohio. He was a pioneer cattle man of the Buckeye State and a good and loyal citizen who served the Union as a soldier during the Civil war. A. W. Sherman, the father of Dr. J. N. Sherman, was born January 10, 1850, at Columbus, Ohio, and was reared in Scioto County, that state. As a young man he went to Madison County, where he was married and engaged in farming until 1888, when he removed to Bardstown, Nelson County, Kentucky, his present home. He has for some years past been engaged in the lumber business, and is one of the substantial men of his community. He is a republican, a strong member of the Baptist Church, and well known in fraternal circles, belonging to the Masons, Odd Fellows and Modern Woodmen of America. Mr. Sherman married Miss Susan Holler, who was born at West Jefferson, Ohio, and they have three children: A. W., Jr., who is engaged in the laundry business at Samuels, Kentucky; Dr. John Norval; and Grover E., who is engaged in merchandising at Samuels, Kentucky.

John N. Sherman received his early education in the public schools of Bardstown, Kentucky, to which community he was taken as a lad of four years. After graduating from the high school there in 1898, he entered the University of Valparaiso, Indiana, where he completed the junior year course, and then took up his medical studies in the College of Physicians and Surgeons. After one year in that institution he went to the University of Louisville, Kentucky, where he spent three years and graduated in 1907, with the degree of Doctor of Medicine, and further advanced his training by doing post-graduate work in the New York Polyclinic Hospital, where he spent eight months in 1908. For two years, 1910 and 1911, he was an interne in the Louisville City Hospital, and in the latter year began practice at Knoxville, Tennessee, where he remained until 1914. Doctor Sherman then did another year of interne work at the Louisville City Hospital, and in 1915 went to St. Louis, Missouri, and later to Kansas City, in both of which cities he practiced for a short time. In July, 1916, he settled permanently at Thayer, Kansas, his offices being located the second door west of the postoffice, on Neosho Avenue. Doctor Sherman has created a decidedly favorable impression upon the people of Thayer, and with his comprehensive training and broad experience it is highly probable that he will build up a large practice. He possesses in large degree the desirable qualifications for his profession, prominent among them being a natural sympathy and kindness of manner, while his devotion to his honored calling makes him a respecter of its best and highest ethics. He holds membership in the Neosho County Medical Society, the Kansas State Medical Society and the American Medical Association, and keeps abreast of all the advancements made in medicine and surgery. Fraternally, he is affiliated with Duvall Lodge No. 6, Ancient Free and Accepted Masons, of Bardstown, Kentucky. He is a faithful member of the Baptist Church, and in politics maintains an independent stand.

Doctor Sherman was married at Bardstown, Kentucky, May 27, 1908, to Miss Palmer Hibbs, the daughter of Arthur and Sally (Bean) Hibbs, residents of Cox's Creek, Kentucky, where Mr. Hibbs is engaged in agricultural pursuits. Doctor and Mrs. Sherman are the parents of one daughter, Eunice, who was born October 19, 1909.

OLLIE EZEKIEL REED. By his work as well as by his position Ollie E. Reed is one of America's foremost authorities on dairy husbandry. He holds that chair in the Kansas State Agricultural College at Manhattan. While Professor Reed has contributed extensively to standard works on agriculture and stock raising, all his writings bear the earmarks of practical experience, and the value of his teaching has been largely as practical demonstrator of the most effective methods to be employed particularly in dairy husbandry.

He has always lived in close touch with the soil and its products. He was born on his father's farm near Fayette in Howard County, Missouri, August 19, 1885. His parents, William L. and Annie E. (Manion) Reed were both born in Kentucky. Reared on a farm, Mr. Reed attended country schools, graduating in 1903 from the high school at Moberly, Missouri, and then continued his education in the scientific and agricultural departments of the University of Missouri, from which he was graduated in 1908 bachelor of science in agriculture. In 1908-09 he taught dairy husbandry at the Missouri State University and in 1909-10 was instructor in the same subject at Purdue University, Lafayette, Indiana. In 1910 the University of Missouri conferred upon him the degree Master of Science.

Since the fall of 1910 Professor Reed has been connected with the Kansas State Agricultural College at Manhattan, at first as assistant professor of dairy husbandry and since 1911 as full professor of that subject. In 1910 he married Miss Lucy Ann Lee.

Among his practical contributions to the science and business of the livestock industry should be mentioned his aid in solving the problem of making silage from alfalfa and also his effective work in building up a dairy herd which is undoubtedly equal to that maintained by any institution in the United States. Many valuable bulletins have been issued under his authorship or editorship. One of these that has proved of greatest value to cattle men is a treatise on sorghum crops for silage. He was also an associate editor in the one volume work on "Dairy Cattle and Milk Production." He contributed the dairy chapters of an agricultural text book now used in Kansas and elsewhere, and is also author of the dairy chapters in Doctor Waters' work on Essential Agriculture.

He is a member of the honorary agricultural fraternity, Alpha Zeta and of the honorary college fraternity Phi Kappa Phi. He is a Master Mason and a member of the Christian Church.

WESTERN TERRA COTTA COMPANY of Kansas City, Kansas, is the only successful industry for the making of this building material, which has had such a remarkable growth of popularity in use during recent years, between Chicago and the extreme Pacific coast, It is an industry which reflects credit upon the growing importance of Kansas City, Kansas, and is the only concern of its kind in the state.

Terra cotta, which is the Italian for "burnt clay," is perhaps the oldest manufactured building material known in history. It has been manufactured in America only during the last forty or forty-five years to any extent. Many improvements have been made in the manufacture, and the modern terra cotta is noted for the beauty of its glazed surface, the variety of color that may be introduced and even more for its practically fireproof qualities. The manufacturers of terra cotta in America are mostly all members of the

National Terra Cotta Society, and that organization has done much not only to standardize much of the manufacture but also to advertise the advantages of terra cotta as a modern building material.

William Timmerman and Paul C. Baltz organized and first established the Western Terra Cotta Company. The business was organized in Kansas City, Missouri, October 12, 1906, but the company found its available location in Kansas City, Kansas, and began operations in December the same year. They started with one kiln and with only five employes. At the present time the company has eighty-five men on its pay roll and the plant, now covering over a block of ground, represents an investment of more than $50,000. Its products are distributed all over the Central West and the output and value of the products have grown steadily since the first year of operation. Mr. Wm. Timmerman is president and general manager of the company, Mr. P. C. Baltz is secretary and treasurer, and since 1916, Walter Timmerman has been vice president. Both Mr. Timmerman and Mr. Baltz are residents of Kansas City, Kansas, and have been effective and loyal citizens and ever ready to engage in any movement for the general welfare.

Mr. William Timmerman was born in Chicago, Illinois, November 6, 1867, one of the six children of Henry and Christina (Lau) Timmerman. His parents were born near Hamburg, Germany, came to America when still single, the mother having been brought by her parents in 1852 in a sailing vessel that was four weeks in crossing the Atlantic. Henry Timmerman for many years was identified with educational work in this country.

William Timmerman had a private school education at Chicago, and early developed his talents for artistic lines. He took courses of instruction in designing and other art work in the Art Institute at Chicago, and for a year was a student of art in Boston. He learned the trade of architectural designer and modeler with the Northwestern Terra Cotta Company, and for several years was head modeler and designer for the Winkle Terra Cotta Company at St. Louis. He also spent twenty years in journeyman work at his trade and is everywhere recognized as one of the American experts in the manufacture of terra cotta.

On November 19, 1910, Mr. Timmerman married Miss Emilie M. Baltz, who was born in St. Louis, a daughter of George and Barbara (Herthel) Baltz. Mr. and Mrs. Timmerman were married in Topeka, Kansas. They have one child, William, Jr., aged four years. Mr. Timmerman is affiliated with Clifton Heights Lodge No. 520, Free and Accepted Masons, is independent in politics, and in religious matters inclines to the Presbyterian Church.

THOMAS JEFFERSON BARKER. The history of Kansas is a generalization of the histories of thousands of individuals whose character and activities made the state what it is. Hardly one of those individuals came into closer touch with the adventures and exciting realities of pioneer times than the late Thomas Jefferson Barker, who was a pioneer of old Wyandotte and for many years one of the leading business men of Kansas City, Kansas. Mr. Barker died at his home in Kansas City, Kansas, August 4, 1913, and was then nearly eighty-five years of age.

He was born in Bedford County, Virginia, December 11, 1828. The Barkers were early settlers in the old Commonwealth of Virginia. His great-grandfather James Barker was one of the Virginia colonials who followed Washington as a somewhat despised contingent of the British regimentals under General Braddock into the western wilds of Pennsylvania, and was present at Braddock's defeat at the hands of the French and Indians. It is believed that this same James Barker afterwards fought with the colonial troops in the War of the Revolution. Mr. Barker's grandfather was Jacob Barker, a native of Richmond, Virginia, and the father was William A. Barker, who was born in Albermarle County, Virginia, March 14, 1796. William A. Barker was a soldier during the War of 1812. William A. Barker married Sarah Hobbs, who was born in Bedford County, Virginia, in 1800, a daughter of James Hobbs who came from England to Virginia about 1794. James Hobbs had fought with the English troops in the East Indies, but after becoming an American citizen enlisted to serve in the American army during the War of 1812. William A. Barker and wife had seven sons and one daughter, among whom Thomas J. was the sixth.

These children were reared in conditions closely approximating poverty. The parents were poor, and it not infrequently occurred that the children went without shoes when snow was on the ground. William A. Barker from 1818 to 1823 was employed as a slave driver for Captain Ed Pate. In 1823 he suffered paralysis from his hips down, and he lived an invalid until his death in 1837. Thus he left his widow and children to make their own way in the world.

Thomas J. Barker when his father died was only nine years of age. All the schooling he ever had could have been covered in six months' time. Nevertheless he made wise use of books, his opportunities to mingle with men and affairs, and in his later life was accounted well read and well posted.

After the death of the father the family removed to Mercer County in what is now West Virginia. That first year was one of poor crops, and Thomas J. Barker at the age of eleven left home to make his own way and also contribute something to the expenses of the household. He was employed at wages of $4 a month by Anderson Peck, and during the second and third years worked at $8.33 a month. Leaving his old locality he went down the Kanawha River to Kanawha, Virginia, and there found employment with Augustus Peck at wages of $25 a month and board. He worked in Mr. Peck's store. Mr. Peck had various stores in that vicinity and young Barker was employed in the one located at Big Coal in Boone County, and also had charge of the postoffice. Later he was made manager of the store in Brownstown.

While thus engaged he reached his twenty-first birthday. About that time he was advised by a friend to go to the gold fields of California, where wages as high as $10 a day were paid. With this in view he set out, going by the Panama route. At Chagris, Panama, he was taken ill with fever and returned to the States. He spent some time in recuperating in his old home at Brownstown.

In April, 1855, he again started West, and again his destination was California. His companion was John Stanley of Mercer County, Virginia. They engaged passage on the steamboat Salem at Brownstown, proceeded down the river to Cincinnati, thence took a boat to St. Louis, stopping at the Virginia Hotel. There Mr. Barker found on the register the name Henry Clay Pate. He proved to be the son of the man for whom his father had previously worked. Introducing himself and his friend to Mr. Pate, it was soon found that Mr. Pate and party were on their way to Kansas for the purpose of swelling the emigration from the South and making Kansas a slave state.

Barker and Stanley were requested to go along, and consequently the trip to California was abandoned and the entire party embarked on the Golden State, a large side wheeler which carried them up the Missouri River to what is now Kansas City. There Mr. Pate and party left the boat, but Stanley and Mr. Barker continued on to Weston, Missouri. There he applied for employment with a Mr. Byrnes, but he having nothing to offer, they continued on to Fort Leavenworth. From there they went to Leavenworth, which was then a town of about 1,000 population, and the main distributing point for Kansas. Here Mr. Barker secured work as cook with a party of United States surveyors under Col. Charles Manners, who had the contract to survey part of the Kansas-Nebraska line. Mr. Barker remained with that surveying party from April to December, 1855. Others in the party were John Stout, William Manners, brother of Colonel Manners, R. L. Ream, Jr., Norman Deifendorf, Mr. Wiley, Mr. Garland, Mr. Hoyt, Mr. Cunningham, Mr. Keller. The party left Leavenworth about May 4th with two teams and wagons. Part of the equipment carried was a cast iron monument which was to be placed at the point previously selected by Gen. Robert E. Lee for the United States Government. Crossing the river at Weston they proceeded up the Missouri side through St. Joseph and Oregon, then recrossed the river on the ferry run by an old Indian where White Cloud is now located. Two miles below that point they set up the monument, which is still standing. That was placed on May 10, 1855. Colonel Manners, who had been an old sea captain, took great pains to be accurate in all his measurements and observations. He spent two days in getting the east and west lines both by sun observations and by comparisons with the north star. From there the party proceeded at the rate of three miles a day, and arrived at a point sixty miles west on June 2. From there they returned to Leavenworth for supplies, and on the return some of the party quit, and their places were filled by others. On the 7th of June they reached the meridian and there began work running a line twenty-four miles north, thence to the Missouri River, then again returning to the guide meridian and proceeding north another twenty-four miles and again east to the river. That took them to a point about a mile and a half north of where Nebraska City now stands. In the meantime Mr. Barker became afflicted with malaria fever, and after recuperating took the stage for the mouth of Platte River. While there he heard that a party of Pawnee Indians had surrounded and killed about half of the surveying party while the remainder had returned to Nebraska City. He joined his old comrades at Nebraska City, and on organizing and returning to the spot where the other half of the party were reported to have been killed by the Indians, they found the report only partially true. The Indians had surrounded them, but the surveyors were as yet unharmed. About the 10th of September Colonel Manners finished surveying the third parallel to the mouth of Platte River, then again returned to the guide meridian, and crossed the Platte a few hundred feet below where the fourth parallel started. About that time twenty-seven Pawnee Indian chiefs demanded that the colonel stop surveying, since he was on Indian land, which the chiefs could not allow him to steal. Colonel Manners persisted in carrying out his instructions, when 500 Indians suddenly sprang up as if by magic and again demanded through interpreters that the work must cease at once, otherwise the chiefs could not be responsible for the actions of their younger men. The Indians were so thoroughly

aroused and hostile, that the surveying party took discretion as the better part of valor and desisted from their task and returned to Omaha. Here Colonel Manners called upon the Indian agent of the Pawnees, and then with two wagons loaded with provisions, lead and powder, and the Indian missionary, they all hurried back to the Pawnee village. An Indian council was held and the agent informed the chief that the Great Father considered buying their lands and had sent this party merely to look it over, measure and value it, and promised that otherwise no disturbance of Indian rights would be made. The chiefs were mollified, and the surveyors finished the work of the fourth parallel, which reached the Missouri River eight miles above Omaha.

Again Mr. Barker was taken ill, and he then had to give up work with the surveying outfit altogether. His next position was digging potatoes for a Mr. Byers, who was also a surveyor. Mr. Byers treated Mr. Barker very kindly and promised him some work in subdividing land. He finally, however, determined to rejoin the surveying party, and started on foot, reaching Colonel Manners and his party at Decatur. On the 30th of November, 1855, the last cornerstone was set, and on top of it was planted a United States flag. Then on the first of December they all started south again, and reached Council Bluffs. From there Mr. Barker, Mr. Wright and Edward Kelly continued to Leavenworth and after many delays and difficulties caused by snow and ice arrived opposite Fort Leavenworth on December 18th. On the 27th of December, 1855, Mr. Barker reached the old Town of Wyandotte, with the ground covered by two feet of snow. Here he was paid off and given his discharge from the surveying work. For a time he remained with the old hotel keeper, Brown, and in January engaged to cook in the Brown Hotel, having two Wyandotte Indians for assistants. This hotel was a log house on Fourth and State streets, and bore the name Catfish Hotel, owing to the preponderance of that fish on the menu. Later Mr. Barker assisted Mr. Jenks as chainman in the work of subdividing three fractional townships in what is now Wyandotte County. He then returned to his hotel work, and afterwards joined Mr. Stuck, who had a contract to subdivide several townships in Johnson County. He was leaving to take up that work when a letter arrived through the postoffice informing him of the death of his brother-in-law. Mr. Stuck then released him and he spent several weeks in looking after the needs of his sister.

Again he was at work as a cook at $1 a day, and it was a long day, from six in the morning until ten at night. On one occasion six Indians under the influence of liquor were at the table, and in a melee which ensued Mr. Barker was struck on the head with a barrel stave and left for dead. In spite of extreme suffering he lived, and had the best of care from his many friends. Before he fully recovered he was engaged as a cutter of wood, patterns for Isaac Zane, the noted blind inventor of Kansas City, Kansas, who was experimenting on perpetual motion machines. Leaving that employment he became a wood chopper and cleared up the ground where the high school now stands in Kansas City. Not long after that he visited his old home in Virginia, and on returning was again engaged by Mr. Brown in the hotel and also drove an ox team. His next employer was Izaha Walker, who had been instrumental in saving his life when the Indians attacked him in the hotel. Mr. Walker owned the store and ferry at Wyandotte, and Mr. Barker became clerk in the store. In 1856 he bought a half interest in the business, and the postoffice was kept in the same building and he had to handle the mail. That old landmark is still standing, 328 Nebraska Avenue.

On April 7, 1857, Mr. Barker was appointed postmaster under President Buchanan. The postoffice was then known as Wyandotte, Leavenworth County, Kansas Territory. The mail was carried on regular routes only as far as Kansas City, Missouri, and from that point it was brought to Wyandotte by trustworthy citizens coming and going between the two towns. In 1858 a stage coach was put in operation between Kansas City, Missouri, and Leavenworth, and that brought the mail regularly every day to Wyandotte. For the first six months the contents of the mail bag was about twelve letters received and sent and about the same number of newspapers. In the fall of 1858 Mr. Barker built a structure at the southeast corner of Third and Nebraska streets and moved the postoffice to that point. In 1861 he was recommissioned postmaster by Montgomery Blair, the postmaster-general in Mr. Lincoln's cabinet. He filled that office until April, 1863, when R. B. Taylor was appointed and took the office. In those early years the receipts of the local postoffice ran between $200 and $480 a year. In fact so meager was the amount of mail that Mr. Barker frequently carried it about in his hat and delivered letters as he found the addressees on the streets.

The Quindaro Townsite Company had built a steamboat named the Otis Webb for the purpose of navigating the Kaw River, from Quindaro as a base. This plan failed, and the boat was subsequently wrecked on the Platte River. In 1863 Mr. Barker bought the wreck and started to remove the machinery, but soon found the machinery had been sold to another man, and Mr. Barker was therefore reimbursed for his original outlay.

He was one of the defenders of Kansas against the Price raid during the war. A short time before that raid was made he went to Leavenworth and drew out what money he had on deposit in the bank, and on his way home was followed by two men who evidently had intentions of highway robbery, but he managed to elude them. During 1864 he found employment in clearing up wood and getting out ties for the Missouri River Railway, now Missouri Pacific Railway. During the war he was a member of the Twenty-third Kansas Militia, serving as quartermaster sergeant in Company A under Izaha Walker and also under Captain Chenault.

In 1865 Mr. Barker married Mary Ellen Hall, daughter of Capt. John L. and Frances (French) Hall. Mrs. Barker was born in New Hampshire and had come to Kansas with her parents in 1857. Her father was a steamboat captain and he and Mr. Barker were associated in a number of business enterprises. To Mr. and Mrs. Barker were born three children, one of whom died at the age of eight years. The two still living are Thomas J. Barker, Jr., and James Edward Barker.

Not only through the pioneer activities already outlined but in many other ways Thomas Jefferson Barker was one of the most influential upbuilders of Kansas City, Kansas. After Wyandotte County was set off from Leavenworth County he served as one of the first county clerks. He was a democrat politically and was elected a member of the State Legislature on that ticket to represent Wyandotte County, at first in 1866 and again in 1880. He was in the Legislature when the prohibition law was passed and he was a strong advocate of that measure. For a time he

was also deputy county treasurer and a member of the school board. Every school and every church established during his time in Kansas City, Kansas, was an institution in which he took a keen interest, and many times he was directly an aid to such improvements. Personally he was a man of modest demeanor, quiet and resourceful, and never sought any of the conspicuous honors of politics or public life.

The foundation of his business prosperity was laid as a lumberman. He conducted a sawmill at Indian Springs, and from its operation he made the money which enabled him to invest in steamboat lines and in extensive tracts of land. At one time he owned a thousand acres of land and a great amount of city property in and around Wyandotte. He was a man of wonderful generosity, an excellent judge of human nature and benefited many men by the employment which he furnished and also by assisting many in getting a start in the world. At one time he was president of the Argentine State Bank, and was also president of the Wyandotte National Bank and was otherwise prominent in financial affairs. In 1875 he engaged in the real estate business and subsequently took in his sons as partners, making the firm T. J. Barker & Sons, one of the oldest and most reliable firms of that kind in Kansas City. One of the last improvements he made was the construction of a building on Minnesota Avenue next to the postoffice, erected in 1906.

At the time of his death he was the oldest member of the Masonic Order in Kansas, having been elevated to the Master's degrees in 1857. Mrs. Barker is still living.

Both the sons were liberally educated, having finished their education in Vanderbilt University at Nashville, Tennessee. Edward Barker studied law in Kansas. Thomas J. Barker, Jr., after completing his education took up a business career, was bookkeeper and assistant cashier in the Wyandotte State Bank, and in 1908 joined his father in business. Thomas J. Barker, Jr., married Catherine C. Rogers. They are the parents of four children: Thomas J., Roger Lee, Clara Beatrice, now Mrs. Alvin Evans of Kansas City, Kansas; and Edward Delbert.

Edward Barker, who married Caroline Mott, is one of the prominent lawyers of Kansas City, Kansas. He was appointed commissioner on the water board by Major Guyer in 1909 and rendered a valuable service in rehabilitating that plant after it came under municipal ownership. Both sons are active Masons, and Thomas J., Jr., has attained the thirty-second degree of the Scottish Rite, and belongs to the Mystic Shrine at Leavenworth. Thomas J. Barker and wife and his mother are active members of the South Methodist Church, and he is a steward and since 1899 has been treasurer.

CHARLES E. SPOONER. When he started upon his wage-earning career, at the age of fifteen years, Charles E. Spooner began at the bottom of the ladder in the capacity of bundle-boy in a department store. No favors were shown him, for he had no important friends or other favoring influences, but his fidelity, energy and ability won him recognition and promotion and he soon grew beyond the opportunities of his immediate environment, and from that time his advancement has been sure and steady. In 1888 he became connected with the Missouri, Kansas & Texas Railroad, in a minor position and in the service of this line he has continued to the present, his position at this time being that of general auditor of the line, with headquarters at Parsons.

Charles E. Spooner was born at Toronto, Ontario, Canada, March 11, 1858, and is a son of J. J. B. and Mary (Brewer) Spooner and a member of a family which originated in England and emigrated to New York during colonial days. His great-great-grandfather, William Spooner, fought as a soldier of the Continental line during the Revolutionary war, and his grandfather was "Col." Alden Spooner, who passed his life at Brooklyn, New York, where he was publisher of the Long Island Star, a pioneer newspaper. J. J. B. Spooner, father of Charles E., was born in 1820, in Brooklyn, and as a lad was adopted by his maternal uncle, George W. Jermain, and was reared at Detroit, Michigan. He was married in the latter state, and there, having inherited his father's journalistic abilities and inclinations, was for some time the publisher of a newspaper. Returning to New York, he located at Lockport and became cashier of the Lockport Bank and Trust Company, a position which he held for a half a century, with the exception of the years 1855 to 1858, when he lived at Toronto, Canada, and was clerk in a hotel. Mr. Spooner's death occurred at Lockport, in 1907, and his loss was universally mourned in his community where he had been a good, strong and reliable citizen. A republican in his political views, he served as deputy county clerk of Niagara County, New York, as city clerk of Lockport, as clerk of the board of supervisors and as deputy county treasurer. His fraternal connection was with the Independent Order of Odd Fellows. Mr. Spooner married Miss Mary Brewer, who was born at Hartford, Connecticut, in 1819, and died at Lockport, New York, in 1900, and they became the parents of six children: Cornelia Jermain, who died unmarried at Lockport, New York, at the age of twenty-nine years; Sarah J., who is a resident of Evanston, Illinois; George A., who is a retired resident of Leavenworth, Kansas, having been formerly a paymaster in the service of the United States army, as well as being a veteran of the Civil war; Mary E., who is the wife of F. F. Dodge, employed in a railroad office at Galveston, Texas; Laura C., of Evanston, Illinois, wife of Prof. Edouard Baillot, who holds the chair of Romance Languages at the Northwestern University, Evanston; and Charles E., of this review.

Charles E. Spooner received his education in the public schools of Lockport and was fifteen years of age when he took his place among the world's workers as a bundle-boy in a department store of his native place. He soon won promotion to the position of clerk, which he held for two years, and in 1876 first came to Kansas and located at Leavenworth, where for six months he was clerk in Clark & Company's private banking house. Returning to Lockport, he was for one year a salesman in a clothing store, and then returned to the dry goods with which he had started his career, although this time in the post of bookkeeper. Mr. Spooner gained one year's experience in this capacity and then went to Indianapolis, Indiana, where he was bookkeeper for the Owen Pixley Company for one and one-half years, and his next position was in Chicago, where for something over a year he was connected with the credit department of Butler Brothers. In 1880 he returned to Leavenworth and secured the position of secretary of the Union Stone Works, but after one year became a member of the firm of George A. Spooner & Brother, books and stationery, for one and one-half years. Disposing of his interests in this concern, Mr. Spooner returned to the East, as office manager at

New York City for the firm of Butler Brothers, and remained in that position for more than three years, when he returned to Kansas, in 1888, and entered the employ of the Missouri, Kansas & Texas Railroad, at Sedalia, as revising clerk. He was next appointed to the joint accounts and then promoted to the office of chief clerk of the ledger desk, next to the auditor's department at Parsons, in 1895, and in 1915 to the office of general auditor of the road, with his offices in the general offices of the line. His promotion has been won by merit alone and in railroad circles he is accounted the right man for the place. Mr. Spooner's home is at No. 1615 Morgan Avenue. He is a republican in politics, and a member of the International and Rotary clubs, of Parsons, and of the Parsons Chamber of Commerce. As a citizen he lends his support to good measures and no worthy movement appeals to him in vain.

Mr. Spooner was married first in 1883 at Leavenworth, Kansas, to Miss Eliza Lucinda Watkins, daughter of the late S. E. Watkins, who was retired at the time of his death. Mrs. Spooner died at Saint Louis, Missouri, in 1894, having been the mother of three children, namely: Mary Elizabeth, who is the wife of F. Glen Taylor, of Little Rock, Arkansas, traveling livestock claim agent for the Rock Island Railroad; Jermain Alden, of Parsons, chief clerk of fuel accounts of the Missouri, Kansas & Texas Railroad; and Charles E., Jr., also of Parsons, ticket clerk for the same road. Mr. Spooner was again married in 1903, at Kansas City, Missouri, to Miss Nellie Inez Buzan, daughter of the late Squire Buzan, who up to the time of his death was a successful agriculturist of Forest City, Missouri. Mr. and Mrs. Spooner have had no children.

ALBERT W. KNOWLES. Topeka recently had cause to mourn the death of two pioneer citizens and able and successful business men, Albert W. Knowles and his brother Charles O. Knowles, both of whom passed away within a few days of each other. At the time of his death on October, 1916, Albert W. Knowles was vice president of the Bank of Topeka, with which he had been identified twenty-eight years, and he had been a resident of Topeka since the age of twenty.

His father was Joshua Knowles, whose name also deserves the distinction of mention in any history of Topeka or Kansas. As a farmer, financier, promoter of good movements and public spirited citizen, Joshua Knowles came and went among the people of his adopted city from the time of his arrival in November, 1859, until the close of his life August 8, 1869. There remained in his wake an impression of usefulness, of genuine dependable citizenship, traceable to his untiring zeal and ready recognition of opportunity.

Member of a family that was founded in America in 1640 by emigrants from England, Joshua Knowles was born in Massachusetts June 23, 1816. He received an ordinary education in his native state, and for many years was engaged in farming there. He first came to Kansas in 1857, taking up a homestead. It was his determination to make the state his future home, but after a year he returned to Massachusetts, and remained there until November, 1859, selling his homestead in Eastham, Massachusetts, to Gustavus Swift, who later became the noted Chicago packer. He came back to Kansas and located in Topeka. Here he engaged in the business of buying sheep, which he rented out to the neighboring farmers on shares. Joshua Knowles was one of the prime movers in the building of the old pontoon bridge across the river at Topeka. He became one of the incorporators of the old Topeka Bank and Savings Institution, and was actively connected with that until his death. Out of this bank grew the present Bank of Topeka.

Joshua Knowles married Lucinda Doane. Her ancestor, John Doane, settled at Eastham, Massachusetts, in 1640. The two sons of Joshua Knowles to reach maturity were Albert W. and Charles O. Joshua Knowles and wife were active members of the Methodist Church.

The late Albert W. Knowles was born in Massachusetts, January 16, 1839. Few men had in their lifetime experience more of adventure, danger and hardship than Mr. Knowles. Like many boys who live along the sea coast, the mariner's occupation was a constant fascination to him, and as early as thirteen he was gaining experience before the mast. As a boy of eighteen he left his home at Eastham and shipped on a sailing vessel bound on a long voyage around the globe. Before attaining his majority he had visited every continent and helped to steer the course of the ship through the waters of every ocean. On returning home he exchanged the adventures of the sea for those of the Far West. At the age of nineteen, in 1858, he arrived in the Territory of Kansas. Here he took up the trade of stone mason and in a practical sense he helped to lay the foundation of the capital city of Kansas. It was his regular occupation until 1872. During that time he assisted in the stone work of the old east wing of the State House.

In the meantime, with the outbreak of the war in 1861, he enlisted for the three months' service in Company A of the Second Regiment Kansas Volunteer Infantry. His time up with this organization, he utilized his previous experience as a sailor, and in 1862 enlisted from Charlestown Navy Yard in the United States navy. He was on the sloops of war Ossipee and Pensacola, and during the greater part of the remaining months of the war was engaged in blockade duty. He received an honorable discharge in 1864.

In 1872 with his brother Charles, Albert W. Knowles engaged in the retail hardware business in Topeka. They conducted one of the old and successful establishments of that kind for sixteen years. Selling his interests as a merchant, Mr. Knowles entered the banking business as vice president of the Bank of Topeka, and he held that position continuously for twenty-eight years until his death. Mr. Knowles was a prominent republican, for a number of years was a member of the Topeka City Council, for eleven years served as city treasurer, and was always ungrudging of his time and energies in behalf of the community where he spent all the mature years of his life. He had long been identified with Topeka Lodge of the Masons, and was also a member of the Grand Army of the Republic.

In August, 1865, he married Miss Mary Sheldon. She died in February, 1905, leaving one son, Reuben Knowles, who is an official in the Bank of Topeka. In 1906 Mr. Knowles married Mrs. Mary A. O'Brien, a native of New York City.

AMOUR LORIAUX. Among the alert and enterprising men who during the last several years have utilized the opportunities offered at Caney for business preferment and who have attained thereby success, is Amour Loriaux, whose career is typical of modern progress and advancement, and who as a man of affairs ranks among the leaders of the younger generation in this live community. Mr. Loriaux is vice president and manager of the Connelly Window Glass Company, a concern which from modest beginnings has grown to large proportions, and has been a resident of Caney since 1908.

Amour Loriaux was born at Charleroi, Hainaut, Belgium, December 24, 1885, and is a son of Joseph and Julia (Haubruge) Loriaux, natives also of that place. His grandfather, Emile Loriaux, was born in 1843, at Charleroi, came to the United States in 1891, and after spending one year at Streator, Illinois, moved to Hartford City, Indiana. He then came to Caney, Kansas, where he is now living in comfortable retirement, still strong and vigorous in both mind and body in spite of his seventy-three years. During his active years he followed the trade of a glass-blower, a vocation which has been engaged in by the members of the family for a number of generations.

Joseph Loriaux was born in November, 1865, at Charleroi, Belgium, where he was reared and educated, and in his youth learned the glass-blowing trade, which he followed during his entire residence in his native land. When he came to the United States, in 1891, he went to Streator, Illinois, where there was a glass factory, in which he worked for one year, at the end of that time moving to Hartford City, Indiana, where he likewise followed his trade. In April, 1908, he came with his family to Caney, and in 1913 went to Bartlesville, Oklahoma, where he now makes his home. Mr. Loriaux at this time is a merchant in the line of meat and groceries, and also has holdings in the oil fields of Kansas and Oklahoma and is a producer. He is a republican in politics, and fraternally a charter member of Caney Lodge No. 1215, of the Benevolent and Protective Order of Elks, and of Caney Lodge of the Fraternal Order of Eagles. Mr. Loriaux married Julia Haubruge, who was born in 1868, at Charleroi, and they have five children, namely: Amour, of this notice; Joseph, who is a window glass worker of Caney; Radolph, who is engaged in merchandising at Bartlesville, Oklahoma; Francine, who resides at that place with her parents; and Eva, who is a student in the Bartlesville public schools.

Amour Loriaux was educated in the public schools of Hartford City, Indiana, and as he proved a bright and attentive scholar, was able to graduate from the eighth grade when he was thirteen years of age. Being anxious to enter upon his independent career, he secured employment in a window glass factory at Hartford City, Indiana, and subsequently held a like position at Danville, Illinois, from whence he came to Caney in 1908. Here Mr. Loriaux secured a place in the plant of the Connelly Glass Window Company, and through the display of ability, industry and fidelity, won steady promotion until, in 1915, he was made manager of the concern, as well as vice president and a member of the board of directors. Still a young man, Mr. Loriaux has established a reputation for sound judgment and keen sagacity. While he never sacrifices a safe conservatism to personal ambitions, yet he has always sought honorable advancement. Few men can speak with more authority upon the glass business, and he has proven his ability to handle the problems that always arise in the conduct of growing enterprises. He holds membership in the National Window Glass Workers' Association. Mr. Loriaux is interested in civic affairs, and has not hesitated to advocate those measures and principles that he believes are best for his city. Accepting modern ideas, he gives his support to movements along material and moral progress.

S N Simpson.

His political views make him a republican, and fraternally he holds membership in the Benevolent and Protective Order of Elks, having been a charter member of Caney Lodge No. 1215.

Mr. Loriaux was married in 1904, at Hartford City, Indiana, to Miss Eva Goossens, a daughter of Victor and Henrietta Goossens, farming people of Hartford City. Mr. and Mrs. Loriaux have two children: Amour, Jr., born December 19, 1906; and Maurice, born August 27, 1909.

JAMES W. REID, assistant general attorney of the Missouri, Kansas & Texas Railway Company at Parsons, is one of Parsons' young lawyers and a man of many brilliant qualifications and of rising reputation.

He was born in Johnson County, Missouri, July 22, 1883. His ancestors came out of England and were early settlers in the State of Ohio. His father J. N. Reid was born in Ohio, and died at Xenia in that state in 1896. Most of his active career was spent in Missouri as a farmer, and he was also a traveling salesman for a number of years. Politically he was a republican and was a member of the Methodist Episcopal Church. J. N. Reid married Elmira Elliott, a native of Ohio. She died in Warrensburg, Missouri.

James W. Reid received his early education in the public schools of Warrensburg, Johnson County, Missouri, graduated in 1900 from the high school at Warrensburg, and then came to Kansas and in 1903 received his degree A. B. from Baker University. Newspaper work formed part of his early experience, and he paid some of the expenses of his law course in that profession. In 1907 he graduated LL. B. from the Kansas City School of Law and was admitted to the bar the same year. He practiced for a time in Kansas City, Kansas, but from 1908 to 1913 was associated with John J. Jones at Chanute, Kansas. Since October, 1913, he has been assistant general attorney with the Missouri, Kansas & Texas with headquarters at Parsons. He is a member of the Labette County and State Bar associations and belongs to the First Methodist Episcopal Church of Parsons. In 1909, at Topeka Mr. Reid married Miss Anna Hoch, daughter of that distinguished Kansan former Governor E. W. Hoch. Mr. and Mrs. Reid have two children: Edward Hoch, born December 27, 1909, and James Richard, born May 1, 1914.

SAMUEL N. SIMPSON. A notable life came to a close with the death of Samuel N. Simpson on November 27, 1915. Important though his achievements were in the field of business and in the development of many useful enterprises and undertakings in the cities of Lawrence and Kansas City, Kansas, it is because his activities and influence were so vitally identified with the primitive period of the territorial Kansas that his individual history bulks so large in the annals of the state and furnishes a chapter that may be read with instruction and profit by every student of Kansas annals.

The story of his early experiences was well told in his own words. He wrote them at the request of his children, and it was due to a modesty which was one of his characteristics that he never used the pronoun I in the entire recital. It is a narrative simply told and with a personal detachment and candor that makes it one of the most illuminating chapters in Kansas history. There is every propriety in permitting the readers of this publication to see

through the eyes of Mr. Simpson the conditions as he saw them in the early territorial period.

He begins his narrative with a brief description of the conditions which prevailed as a result of the struggle between the free state and pro-slavery elements for the possession of Kansas. He tells how by the wholesale importation of voters from Missouri a slavery territorial legislature was elected in 1855, a code of slave laws enacted to govern the territory, and how the machinery of the Federal Government and its army were used to bank up these iniquitous measures. As a result, he says, by the summer of 1856 one-third of the free state settlers had left the Kansas territory because of the enormities of the slave power. From that point his story can be quoted in his own words:

"At this time when there seemed to be total darkness, a man commenced shaping events without knowing it himself or attracting any attention from even his neighbors. A kind Providence now seemed to take matters in hand, using forces that were not appreciated. In September, 1854, he arrived in what is now called Lawrence, having walked through Missouri. He had been reared in New Hampshire. On the first Sabbath after he arrived he organized a Bible class. On the first Sabbath in 1855 he gathered the few children in town together in his office and commenced a Sunday school, which became the Sunday school of the Plymouth Congregational church of Lawrence. During 1855 he organized a Sabbath school at the home of Mr. Lyons, four miles up the California Road. Mrs. Sarah T. D. Robertson and Mrs. Kellogg were teachers.

"In the winter of 1855 and 1856 the Plymouth Congregational church asked this man to go East to raise money for a church building. He accepted, and in raising this money came in contact with Dr. Post of St. Louis; Dr. Thompson, of Buffalo; Henry Ward Beecher and Dr. Bellows in New York and Brooklyn; Dr. Todd, in Pittsburg; Eli Thayer, J. M. S. Williams, Amos A. Lawrence, Leonard Bacon, Dr. Cabbott, Dr. Webb, Edward Everett, Robert Winthrop, Dr. Wallace and many others in New England. In May, 1856, he organized a Sunday school at Franklin, a small town three miles west of Lawrence, settled mostly by families from slave states. Charles Edwards, of Lawrence, was a teacher. During the dark period in 1856 there were some thirty young men from different southern states scattered throughout Douglass county, boarding with families from Southern states. These young men received thirty dollars per month from the states from which they came. Their occupation was to create such a state of society by burning houses, barns, hay and grain stacks, killing stock and occasionally killing a man, as in the case of Barber, Hoyt and Dow, that free state settlers would cease to come to the territory and many of those already there would leave rather than live under such conditions.

"Dr. Charles Robinson and several other free state men were held as prisoners by United States troops in a camp about eight miles west of Lawrence. Dr. Robinson was the leader of the free state cause and party in Kansas Territory during the struggle. This unnamed man visited the camp and talked over the conditions. They agreed that a vigilance committee should be formed with two by-laws, viz: To obey orders and to keep secrets and to make it their first business to force out of the country the men who were committing the depredations and murders.

"This man returned to Lawrence and invited to his office Turner Sampson, a democrat from the

State of Maine, and Milton Guest, of Indiana, both men being over forty-five years of age. The conditions in the county were discussed and it was agreed to organize a vigilance committee with the above by-laws. The three agreed to meet that evening after dark at a vacant house near the Blood Mill. They met and decided upon three persons who should be invited to meet at the same place the next night. At the next meeting there were six persons present and at the next twelve. In a short time the committee had grown to have two hundred members and they wished to elect this man dictator. He refused and a Mr. Green, who operated a saw mill, was elected dictator. Mr. Green was true and brave and very quiet. His orders were law. It is only when society is in desperate straits that it consents to a dictatorship. The organization did its work well and after a few of the marauders had been visited at night the rest left for Missouri.

"One day soon thereafter, when this man was superintending his Sunday school at Franklin, a Southern man, whose children attended the school, asked him to step to one side and said: 'I think that I ought to tell you that an army from Missouri will be up here in a short time to destroy Lawrence. They are using a certain log cabin in town as a fort, and already have a cannon there to use against the town when they come up. Please do not give me away.'

"This unnamed man went up to the camp the next day and informed Dr. Robinson. It was agreed that the fort at Franklin and any others which might be learned of should be taken before the army arrived from Missouri and the cannon secured. The free state party had been on the defensive long enough, and besides, it was known that a company of men under General Lane from the free states was on its way through Iowa and Nebraska to help the free state settlers of Kansas. It was thought well to strike a blow before assistance came. This man returned to Lawrence and the order came to eighty men of the vigilance committee to meet at two points near Franklin after dark the next night. Upon arriving at the points designated one party was to attack the fort at Franklin from the south side and the other party from the north side, and to take it. The men drew near upon their hands and knees so as not to be seen and to expose themselves as little as possible.

"They all had Sharp rifles and they used them but to no good purpose. A space had been left open between the logs of the fort about five feet from the ground and those inside could fire through this opening. One free state man was killed and others wounded. The free state men were obliged to withdraw. And now what should be done? Some said the fort could not be taken without a cannon. The men were wet with the dew upon the grass. It was nearly midnight. The pale moonlight and the dying companions afforded a sad picture. This man declared that the fort must be taken if they had to pry the logs apart. The cannon within must come into their hands. It was finally decided to load upon a wagon some hay and dry fencing and what tar and rosin could be found in town to set the log fort on fire. When the load was ready a call was made for volunteers to draw the fuel against the fort. Captain Bickerton, Caleb Pratt, S. C. Smith, Reuben Randall, Edward Russell, this man and two or three others took hold and drew the wagon close to the fort, then lighting the hay. The light illumined the town. It was agreed that a stream of bullets should be fired steadily into

the door of the fort to prevent those inside from pushing the wagon away from the building. Soon a white flag was run up over the fort, and the cannon captured and taken out with gun carriage and wheels. In the moment of success and victory the cost of victory is forgotten. The men embraced the cannon even in that dark hour.

"After further deliberation it was planned to take by storm before daylight the fort on Washington Creek, six miles south of Lawrence; and that the cannon should be moved west upon the California road to Fort Titus twelve miles west of Lawrence. Kimball brothers and this man returned to Lawrence and fished out of the Kansas river the type which the border ruffians had taken from the office of the *Herald of Freedom*, the *Kansas Tribune* and the *Kansas Free State*, a few weeks before and thrown into the Kansas river at the time they destroyed the Free State Hotel and burned Dr. Charles Robinson's house. The lead was run into three bullets for the cannon to be used at the taking of Fort Titus. All the forces with the cannon must be brought against the last fort and it must be taken before night.

"The company which had come through Nebraska arrived during the night that Franklin and Washington Creek forts were taken and assisted the free state army in taking the last of the three forts. The news of the two victories in the night spread with the morning light and the free state army numbered several hundred armed men before it reached Fort Titus. Colonel Shombry, of General Lane's party, in behalf of himself and his men, offered to take the fort by storm. They were not successful and the colonel lost his life in the attempt. The free state army, out of range of the rifles in the fort now waited for the cannon with the three bullets.

"A man was found who had served in the English army—Captain Bickerton. The cannon was placed in his hands and after loading it he announced that he would give the enemy a copy of *Kansas Herald of Freedom*. The bullet went through the log fort. The cannon was loaded again and with a voice that all could hear the Captain announced that they should have a copy of the *Kansas Tribune*. After this bullet went through the fort up came a white flag. Titus and eighteen prisoners were taken. The return to Lawrence in the latter part of the afternoon with the prisoners and the triumph of the three victories cannot be described.

"Colonel Titus, who was wounded, and the other prisoners were placed in the hands of this man, and he secured Dr. S. B. Prentice to attend to the wounded. The battle of Franklin was the Bunker Hill in the Kansas warfare, except that the victory was more telling and the results came sooner. The prisoners were soon exchanged for free state prisoners who were being held under the bogus territorial government under sham charges that they might be prevented from working for the free state cause. The people of Missouri went on preparing for the taking of Lawrence, for they realized it would be impossible to hold slaves in a state with such a town as Lawrence in it. Three armies were recruited in Missouri and were on their way to Lawrence. This was in September, 1856, and an election for president of the United States would be held in November. The democratic leaders in the East decided that the war in Kansas must be stopped or the party would be defeated. If Lawrence should be destroyed by Missourians, the election would go against them. Governor Shannon, the territorial governor, was withdrawn and Mr. Gerry was appointed to fill his place.

He arrived in the territory while the army from Missouri were on their way to Lawrence. Governor Gerry ordered some United States troops, a battery of flying artillery, from Fort Leavenworth into Douglass county, stationing them near Lawrence.

"The Missouri army was then encamped a few miles east of Lawrence on the Wakurusa Creek and the advance guard was so near Lawrence that it was exchanging shots with the Cabbott Guard Company, which company had been raised by this man. The rifles had been furnished him by Dr. Cabbott, of Boston, in case he could raise a company. Every free state man was in his place and the women of Lawrence were doing their part. On Sunday night or Monday morning the attack would be made, despite the fact that the Missourians had twenty-eight hundred, men to the free state's six hundred. At this stage, Governor Gerry located this battery of flying artillery upon the hill south of Lawrence and asked the Cabbott Guard to support their artillery in case of a battle. The governor then went to the headquarters of the Missouri army and told them they must return to Missouri. If Lawrence were destroyed, then the election would go against the democrats and all would be lost. The officers, supported by the men, informed the governor that they had come to wipe Lawrence from the earth and that they intended to do it. The governor replied that he had the United States troops ready and that he should use them to protect Lawrence; that he had orders from the President of the United States to do so. The Missourians deliberated all night but finally saw that they could not hope to succeed with the United States troops united with the free state men, and so returned to Missouri. Thus ended the contest in Kansas Territory to make it a slave state by force of arms.

"There was fighting in Southern Kansas later which grew out of local difficulties. The successful capture of the fort at Franklin and the other two forts was the death knell of the introduction of slavery into Kansas. The loss of Kansas to the South brought secession. Secession brought the war, and the war brought emancipation. Thus Providence often seemingly employs the most insignificant means to bring about very important results. In this case there has been built a mighty nation which may yet control the governments of the world."

In the veins of Samuel N. Simpson flowed the blood of freemen, and it is not strange that he became an actor of importance in the critical days of Bleeding Kansas. The Simpson family was founded in New England in 1631, the first of the name coming from Scotland. There were Simpsons in the French and Indian war, and John Simpson, grandfather of Samuel N., enlisted from his native town of Deerfield, New Hampshire, at the beginning of the revolution. He arrived in time to take part in the Battle of Bunker Hill, and the family tradition is that he fired the first gun in the battle and was promptly arrested on charge of disobeying orders. Later, on the same battlefield, he was commissioned major. His flintlock musket and his commission descended as heirlooms and were greatly cherished and prized by the late Mr. Simpson of Kansas City.

Samuel N. Simpson was born at Deerfield, New Hampshire, October 3, 1826, a son of Samuel and Hannah (Pearson) Simpson. His father came out to Kansas in 1857, was an early settler at Lawrence, and died there at the age of eighty-two, his wife having passed away at seventy-nine.

Supplementing his own recital of early times at Lawrence, it should be stated that Samuel N. Simpson was one of the party of six persons who were the first settlers of that town. It was at his suggestion that the town was named Lawrence in honor of Amos A. Lawrence, of Boston. Mr. Lawrence, on being informed of this compliment, sent a draft for $10,000, directing that the money be used for educational purposes. The fund later increased to $14,000, and when Kansas established its State University the City of Lawrence offered this fund as an aid to the institution provided it should be located at Lawrence, which was done.

After the war Mr. Simpson engaged in business at Lawrence and he always considered that city his home, though he was a resident for many years of Kansas City, Kansas. He was laid to rest at Lawrence. He organized the Simpson Bank at Lawrence, became prominent in real estate affairs, and in 1877 he extended his business to Wyandotte County. He was the first to propose changing the name of Wyandotte to Kansas City. He also built the first bridge where the new Central Avenue bridge and viaduct is now being constructed. Mr. Simpson was one of the first white men to buy land from Split Log, the Wyandotte Chief, and received from him the right of way for the bridge. The late Mr. Simpson, together with his sons, improved and developed many of the most valuable parts of Kansas City, Kansas, and in the real estate field he was long pre-eminent. Mr. Simpson was devoted to the prohibition cause, was a republican in politics without aspirations for office, and was a sincere and devout Christian, being a member with his wife of the Congregational Church.

In 1864 Samuel N. Simpson returned to Columbus, Ohio, and married Miss Kate Lyon Burnett. Her father, Judge Calvin Burnett, a native of Vermont, was for many years a well-known citizen of Lawrence, Kansas. Mrs. Simpson was a highly educated and cultured woman, and for many years gave the distinction of her presence to one of the most hospitable homes in the State of Kansas. She was born in Vermont in 1833 and died in 1900. There were three children: Charles Lyon, Burnett Newell and Nellie Josephine, an adopted daughter, the latter being the wife of William A. Ackenhausen.

Charles Lyon Simpson was born in the City of Lawrence November 23, 1865, and his brother, Burnett N., was born there in July, 1869. Charles Lyon was a student in the Boston Institute of Technology three years, and then became associated with his father in the real estate business. He is now one of the oldest established men in real estate circles in Kansas City, Kansas, and has promoted some of the largest deals and has brought about some of the most notable improvements on both sides of the state line. He is at the present time actively concerned with something like thirty-five additions in various parts of Kansas City, Missouri. In 1913 he served as president of the National Association of Real Estate Boards, was president of the Kansas City Real Estate Board two years, 1911-12, and is a member of the Country Club, the Blue Hills Club and the University Club. On January 5, 1893, he married Mary Miner Gamble of Kansas City, Missouri. They have two children: Dorothea and Hamilton Simpson, both of whom are attending school at Washington, D. C.

Burnett Newell Simpson is a graduate of Harvard University. After studying law at Harvard University, he began its practice in Kansas City, Missouri, and later formed a partnership with Charles A. Boaley. He is vice president of the Banking Trust Company and represents several large eastern estates in their western investments. He was an incorporator, and for several years, the secretary, of the University Club of Kansas City and also member of the Kansas City Country Club and the Blue Hills Club. In 1903, he married Caroline C. Gamble, granddaughter of Governor Gamble of Missouri.

ALBERT SMITH, M. D. It is practically beyond the possible for the conscientious physician and surgeon to arrive at a condition of mind where he is satisfied with his accomplishments, no matter what their degree, for, with an understanding of what great things are coming to the man of science, the numerous avenues yet unopened which will lead to new realms in the cure of the ills of humanity, and a constant yearning to add to his store of personal knowledge, he, of necessity, keeps on striving for perfection as long as life remains. One of the men of the Kansas profession who has already accomplished much out of the ordinary, but who remains a close student and careful investigator, is Dr. Albert Smith, of Parsons, who has been engaged in a general practice here for more than twenty years.

Doctor Smith was born at Erie, Kansas, July 24, 1870, and is a son of Irvin and Callie (Kennedy) Smith, and a member of a family which assisted in the pioneer settlement of the State of Ohio. His father was born in 1846, in Columbus, Ohio, and was there reared and educated, but as a young man went to Wabash, Indiana, where he was married and established himself in the drug business. In 1868 he came to Kansas and settled at Erie, where for many years he was proprietor of a leading pharmacy, and retired in 1910 and moved to Parsons, where he now resides. He is a republican and a man of intelligence and real worth. Mr. Smith married Callie Kennedy, who was born in 1850, in Ohio, and died at Eldorado Springs, Missouri, in 1886, and they became the parents of three children: Albert, of this notice; Nell, who died at Parsons, in 1905, as the wife of Peter Duffy, now a merchant of this city; and May, who died at the age of two years.

After attending the public schools of Parsons, Albert Smith placed himself under the preceptorship of Professor Hixon, a graduate of Johns Hopkins University, who tutored him in his preparatory work, and thus he was fitted to enter the Kansas University, where he spent one year in studying pharmacy. Next, he entered the Philadelphia College of Pharmacy, from which he was duly graduated with the class of 1890, and then began his medical studies in the Chicago College of Physicians and Surgeons, an institution in which he spent two years. His education was still more further advanced by a course at the famous Hahnemann Medical College, from which he was graduated in 1895, with his cherished degree of Doctor of Medicine. Unlike many physicians, Doctor Smith did not cease to be a student when he had received his degree. On the contrary, he was incited to greater effort in the line of acquiring knowledge, and since his graduation has taken post-graduate courses at the Chicago Policlinic, the New York Polyclinic and the New York Post-Graduate School, and in 1914 went to Europe, visiting the famous institutions of Vienna, Paris, London and Berlin and spending five months in specializing in surgical work.

Doctor Smith began practice at Parsons in 1895, and here has continued without interruption, save during the time he has been engaged in special study. He has a large clientele and carries on a general practice in both medicine and surgery, and is also local surgeon for the Missouri, Kansas & Texas Railroad.

Holding to high ideals in his professional service, his work has always been characterized by a devotion to duty and with an appreciation of the responsibilities resting upon him. He keeps in touch with all recent work in his profession, and his sound judgment and wide experience, combined with the benefits he secured from membership in the various organizations, county, state and national, of his profession, enable him to decide upon what is valuable and that which is unessential in his practice. His well-appointed offices are located at Nos. 1812½ and 1814½ Main Street, and his residence is at No. 1610, on the same thoroughfare. Doctor Smith is a republican, but has not sought public office. He is fraternally connected with the Modern Woodmen of America and the Benevolent and Protective Order of Elks, and also holds membership in the Commercial and Rotary clubs and the Parsons Chamber of Commerce.

Doctor Smith was married at Parsons, in 1896, to Miss Nannie E. Cowden, of this city, and to this union there has been born one son: Albert N., born December 11, 1903, who is a member of the freshman class at the Parsons High School.

JACKSON B. CRANE. Although the founder of the Crane family in Kansas, Jackson B. Crane was neither born nor died in this state, he spent forty-five years here, the best part of his life, and his name deserves preservation in the country's enduring annals. His was one of the first pioneer cabins built in 1854 within a radius of eleven miles west of Leavenworth, then the frontier. He was one of that hardy band that not only dared the privations of the wilderness but had the resolute will that accepted a life that, at that time, positively demanded eternal vigilance because of savage strife. Through his almost fifty years here he worked effectively for the best interests of this section in every way, and courageously advocated reforms when only truly brave men did so.

Jackson B. Crane was born in Ohio, owing his baptismal name, perhaps, to the fact that his birthday occurred on or very near the day that General Jackson captured New Orleans, January 8, 1815. In manhood he left his native state for Iowa, accompanied by his aged father, who died at Muscatine and was buried there. Mr. Jackson Crane remained at Oskaloosa, Iowa, until 1854, in the meanwhile becoming a trusted and valued citizen of Mahaska County, which he served two terms as sheriff. He had always been a democrat, a Jacksonian democrat, but the time came when his opinions changed to some degree on the subject of slavery. This attitude gave him some trouble with his neighbors after he had moved to Kansas, in 1854, but he was unyielding in his views in regard to the further spread of slavery. Hence, when the infant republican party came into existence, in 1856, with its main platform of prohibition of slavery in the territories, it found in Mr. Crane a conscientious supporter, to such an extent that he sent his eldest son back to his old neighbors in Iowa to give them his views, as having had more experience of slavery than they in its practical workings, and to urge them to approve the principles of the new party and vote for its first presidential candidate, John C. Fremont, as was his own intention. It is on record that many of them did so.

Jackson B. Crane and his wife had thirteen children: Columbus, Alexander Pope, James, Miner, Leonard, John, Robert, Stephen, Jackson, William, Ann, Emeline and Mary. After a residence of forty-five years in Leavenworth County, Jackson B. Crane and wife left Kansas and moved to Perry, Oklahoma, where both died in advanced age. 'Of their surviving eleven children, the ages run from fifty-two to eighty-one years.

Columbus Crane, the eldest son of the founder of the family in Kansas, married Miss Permelia Jones, a member of a family that came to Kansas in 1855 from Ohio. To them were born five children, three sons and two daughters: Lafayette Fremont, who was born in 1858; Emma, who is now Mrs. Tork, lives at Holton, Kansas; Josephine, who is Mrs. Blossom, lives at Rutland, Vermont; Alfred E., who was born in 1863, at Leavenworth, is an attorney at Topeka; and Calvin C., who is a temporary resident of Eureka Springs, Arkansas.

Alfred E. Crane married Miss Lillian M. Woodburn, a member of a family that came to Kansas in 1860. Rev. J. A. Woodburn still survives, having been active in the ministry for sixty years. The family and its connections are all prominent in the state. One son, F. T. Woodburn, is a district judge at Holton, Kansas. An uncle of Mrs. Crane, John Quincy Adams Roberts, who was one of the early pioneers, still survives at the age of eighty-seven years, a resident of Newcastle, Indiana. He was a soldier in the Union army during the Civil war. Mr. and Mrs. Crane have one son, Harry Alfred, who was born in 1902.

JOHN HENRY KEITH. From his native state of Kentucky, where his ancestors had lived for generations, and where he was admitted to the bar, John Henry Keith came west about twenty-five years ago, and the greater part of the time has been in active practice as a lawyer at Coffeyville. Along with a large clientage he has developed many interests that connect him with the oil and gas industry of the Mid-Continent field, and he long since reached that position where he can be properly spoken of as a successful and prosperous man.

His birth occurred in Warren County, Kentucky, December 3, 1867. The Keith family originated in Scotland, and in colonial days was transplanted to Pennsylvania. One of the early governors of the Province of Pennsylvania was Sir William Keith. The old home built by Governor Keith in Bucks County twenty miles northeast of Philadelphia is still standing. Mr. Keith had one ancestor, Alexander Keith, who served with a Virginia regiment in the Continental line during the Revolution. Mr. Keith's grandfather, Rev. John Keith, was born in Kentucky in 1816, was for many years an active Baptist minister, and died in Warren County of that state in 1891. He married Mary Edwards, who was born in Virginia, and the Edwards family also furnished soldiers to the Revolution from Virginia.

Ivey Keith, father of John H. Keith of Coffeyville, was born in Kentucky in 1846, and spent his life in that state as a farmer and stockman. During the war he served in the Union army, enlisting in 1863 in Company I of the Fifty-second Regiment of Kentucky Volunteer Infantry, and remained in the service until the close of the war. He was several times wounded, and took part in a number of battles and skirmishes. He was a republican in politics, and an active member of the Baptist Church. His death occurred in Butler County, Kentucky, in 1913. Ivey Keith married Jennie Finney, who was born in Warren County, Kentucky, in 1846, and died on the old farm homestead in that state in April, 1915.

Her father was Jack Finney, who was born in Kentucky in 1814, was a farmer, and died at Allen Springs, Kentucky, in 1854. Jack Finney married Lucinda Thomas, a cousin of Gen. George H. Thomas of Chickamauga fame. She represented a Virginia family and some of her ancestors were soldiers in the Revolution. Jack Finney was a son of Morgan Finney, who was also a Virginia volunteer in the Revolutionary army.

Mr. and Mrs. Ivey Keith had a large family of children, briefly noted as follows: John Henry; Addie, wife of R. B. Lawrence, a farmer and stockman in Butler County, Kentucky; Clay, who was in the oil and cattle business and also a banker and merchant at Lenape, Oklahoma, and was killed in an automobile accident south of Coffeyville in 1914; Euclid, who is a farmer in Butler and Warren counties, Kentucky, and resides in the former county; Emmett, a farmer and cattle man at Lenape, Oklahoma; S. E. Keith, in the oil business at Lenape; William, who resides at Lenape, Oklahoma, and has been engaged in the oil business and also has served as clerk of court.

Reared in Kentucky, John H. Keith attended school at Bowling Green and also Ogden College. He took up the study of law privately in an office at Bowling Green, and in November, 1889, was admitted to the Kentucky bar. After three years of practice at Bowling Green, he moved to Oklahoma, spent some time at Muskogee and Nowata, but on October 1, 1893, established his home and office at Coffeyville, where he has since enjoyed a large civil and criminal practice. His offices are in the McCoy Building at the corner of Eighth and Walnut streets. He is an active member of the County and State Bar associations, and has participated to some extent, chiefly in the line of his profession, in politics, being a democrat. He served as city attorney for Coffeyville for a number of years, and in 1903 represented Montgomery County in the Kansas Legislature. He served on the judiciary, corporations and several other committees. Fraternally Mr. Keith is affiliated with Coffeyville Camp No. 665, Modern Woodmen of America.

Like many successful lawyers he has acquired some very influential and important connections in the business field. Mr. Keith is now president of the Southern Oil and Gas Company, president of the Shufeldt Oil and Gas Company, president of the Emma Oil Company, president of the Cherokee Water Company; secretary of the Dewey Portland Cement Company in Oklahoma; president of the Calumet Mining Company; and a director of the Coffeyville Brick and Tile Company. Besides his home at 814 West Ninth Street, he owns considerable other real estate in Coffeyville, and has about 3,000 acres of farm land situated in Kansas, Oklahoma, Missouri and Kentucky.

Mr. Keith married Miss Elizabeth M. McCoy, a daughter of the late William McCoy, who was one of the pioneer business men of Southeastern Kansas, and whose extensive lumber operations extended into the states of Louisiana and Arkansas.

Mr. Keith has two sons. Walter S., who graduated from the University of Cincinnati with his degree of Bachelor of Laws, is now in active practice at Coffeyville, associated with his father. Paul G., who finished his technical education in the Ohio Mechanical Institute at Cincinnati, is now an oil and gas operator living at Coffeyville.

RICHARD M. KLEINHANS is a veteran railroad man, having been in the active service more than twenty years. He started in his native State of Michigan, worked through various grades of promotion with the Lake Shore Branch of the New York Central lines, and finally came to the Southwest in the employ of the Missouri, Kansas and Texas. He is now car accountant for that road with headquarters at Parsons.

Born in Detroit, Michigan, September 8, 1877, he is a son of George and Cecelia (Hunt) Kleinhans. His father, was born in Pennsylvania in 1813, moved from that state to Ohio, and from there to Michigan. He was a wholesale butcher, a business to which he devoted the best years of his life, and he died at Detroit in 1901. Politically he was a democrat, and was an upright Christian man. His wife was born in Ohio and died in Detroit.

Reared and educated in Detroit, Richard M. Kleinhans after graduating from the Detroit High School in 1893 entered the employ of the Lake Shore Railroad. He was with that company one year and then spent two years with the Michigan Central, following which he returned to the Lake Shore and was continuously in its service for seventeen years. Mr. Kleinhans has always been noted as a faithful worker and early gained the confidence of his superior officials by his diligence and keen and active method of transacting every work entrusted to him. He began with the Lake Shore as car checker was promoted to car distributor, then to traveling car agent, then to chief car agent, and finally to inspector of transportation. In 1912 Mr. Kleinhans removed to Denison, Texas, as inspector of transportation for the Missouri, Kansas & Texas, and in November of the same year was appointed car accountant. In the discharge of those duties he moved his headquarters on May 26, 1915, to Parsons. His offices are in the General Office Building at Parsons. Mr. Kleinhans is very popular among railway men generally and all admired the pluck and efficiency which have brought him various promotions from time to time.

Politically he is independent, and retains his affiliation with Detroit Lodge No. 34 of the Benevolent and Protective Order of Elks. Mr. Kleinhans comes of a family of German origin, but his forbears have been in America for a number of generations. Their first place of settlement was in Pennsylvania. On August 29, 1906, Mr. Kleinhans married Miss Edith Whiteman, a daughter of Charles Whiteman. To their marriage have been born four children: Dorothy, born June 20, 1907; Harry, born February 8, 1909; Alma, born January 10, 1911; and Edith, born November 5, 1913.

EDGAR W. BOARDMAN, M. D. Medicine is constantly making tremendous strides forward, with scientific progress shown on every side, and discoveries and inventions are practically changing methods of practice and broadening the viewpoint of both physician and patient. To practice according to the enlightened ideas of the present century requires not only a most careful training but a certain, sure aggressiveness, and no physician of Parsons has this and other admirable qualities in greater degree than has Dr. Edgar W. Boardman, a practicing physician and surgeon of this city since 1888.

Doctor Boardman was born at Fort Dodge, Iowa, January 10, 1864, and is a son of Dr. H. E. and Susan C. (Locke) Boardman. The Boardmans originated in England, from which country two brothers came to America at an early day in the history of the American Colonies, one locating in Connecticut and the other in Vermont. The old Boardman Hill, at Rutland, Vermont, was a family possession for upwards of 200 years, and it is from this branch that Doctor Boardman is descended. His grandfather was Elijah Boardman, born in 1792, at West Rutland, a farmer by occupation who spent his entire life there and died in 1875.

Dr. H. E. Boardman was born in 1835, at West Rutland, Vermont, and was given the advantages of an excellent educational training. He graduated from Middlebury (Vermont) College with the degrees of Bachelor of Arts and Master of Arts, then took a course at Andover Theological Seminary, from which he was graduated with the degree of Doctor of Divinity, and finally pursued his medical studies at Hahnemann Medical College, Chicago, where he received the degree of Doctor of Medicine. As a young man he went to Sun Prairie, Wisconsin, subsequently to Monroe, in the same state, and in 1865 to Fort Dodge, Iowa, from whence he later removed to Larned, Kansas, and there continued in the practice of his profession until his death, in 1888. He was one of the most scholarly men of his day and community, an honor to his calling and a citizen who won the confidence and respect of his fellow-men. He was a republican in politics, and a member of the Congregational Church. Doctor Boardman married Susan C. Locke, who was born in 1836, at Bellows Falls, Vermont, and who still survives and makes her home with her son, Edgar W. To this union there were born two sons: Dr. Edgar W., of this review; and Horace P., born in 1869, who resides at Reno, Nevada, and holds the chair of civil engineering in the State University of Nevada.

Edgar W. Boardman attended the public schools of Monroe, Wisconsin, where he was graduated from the high school in 1881, and, having inherited his father's inclination for the medical profession, took up his studies at Hahnemann Medical College, Chicago. He was duly graduated therefrom with the degree of Doctor of Medicine, in the class of 1885, and since that time has taken post-graduate courses in the same institution, at the New York Polyclinic, and, in 1915, at Johns Hopkins University, Baltimore, Maryland. On receiving his degree, in 1885, Doctor Boardman engaged in practice at Larned, but three years later, at the time of his father's death, came to Parsons, where he has since carried on a general medical and surgical practice and has built up a large and representative clientele. He holds to high ideals in his professional work, and is in every way worthy of the respect which he has so clearly won. A man of broad and comprehensive reading, he is eager to grasp new ideas, but does not put them into general use until he has convinced himself as to their efficiency and merit. Doctor Boardman maintains offices in the Exchange State Bank Building, and owns his own residence at No. 1711 Belmont Street, in addition to which he has other real estate. He is a republican of the stand-pat variety. In the line of his profession, he holds membership in the Labette County Medical Society, the Kansas State Medical Society, the American Medical Association and the Southeastern Medical Society, and shows his interest in civic affairs by his active participation in the movements of the Parsons Commercial Club. He is prominent fraternally, and belongs to Lodge No. 527, Benevolent and Protective Order of Elks; Parsons Lodge No. 117, Ancient Free and Accepted Masons; Fort Scott Consistory No. 42, thirty-second degree of Masonry; Mirzah Temple, Ancient Arabic Order Nobles of the Mystic Shrine; Parsons Camp, Modern Woodmen of America; the Ancient Order of United Workmen, the Royal

Arcanum, the Knights and Ladies of Security and the Royal Neighbors.

Doctor Boardman was married in 1890, at Parsons, to Mrs. Lillie V. (Holbrook) Long, daughter of the late Dwight L. Holbrook, a manufacturer of school furniture, and widow of the late William Long, a dentist of Parsons. Doctor and Mrs. Boardman have no children.

PROF. PIUS B. HUMPHREY. The claim of Prof. Pius B. Humphrey upon the esteem and confidence of the people of Caney, Kansas, is based upon five years of faithful and efficient service in the office of superintendent of city schools. When he came to this city, in 1911, he was admirably fitted to take charge of the institutions in which the mind of youth is molded and developed, and since that time he has through steady and constant endeavor built up a school system which may be said to be second to none of a city this size in the state. His entire career has been devoted to work of an educational character, and in whatever community he has centered his activities he has always gained the good will and respect of his fellow-citizens.

Professor Humphrey was born in Scotland County, Northeastern Missouri, April 7, 1872, and is a son of Thomas P. and Sarah Jane (Stough) Humphrey. The family originated in England and the original American progenitors came to this country long before the Revolutionary war, being early settlers of Kentucky. From that state the family branched out to other parts of the country, one going to West Virginia, in which state was born in 1803, William Humphrey, the grandfather of Pius B. In 1838 William Humphrey came to the West, locating in Lewis County, Missouri, and twenty years later went to Scotland County. After a long and successful career passed as a farmer and stockraiser, he retired from active pursuits and moved to Knox County, Missouri, where his death occurred in 1885. He was a man of industry and progressiveness, honorable and trustworthy with his business associates, and a man who wielded a distinct influence in his community because of his general information and good judgment. He married Eliza Pettit, who was born in 1801, in West Virginia, and died in Scotland County, Missouri, in 1887, and among their children were the following: Ann, who married David Stice, a retired farmer, and resides at Downing, Missouri; Marten, who is a retired farmer of Hurdland, Missouri; and Thomas P.

Thomas P. Humphrey was born in March, 1832, in Kentucky, and was six years of age when taken by his parents to Lewis County, Missouri, where he was reared and educated. He was brought up to farming pursuits, and on attaining his majority followed in the footsteps of his father and adopted agriculture and stockraising as his life vocations, pursuits in which he was engaged throughout his career, with the exception of several years passed in merchandising. Through good management and industry and operations carried on along well-directed lines, he accumulated a good property and was in fairly comfortable circumstances at the time of his death, which occurred in Scotland County, September 4, 1911. He had been a resident of that county from 1858. Mr. Humphrey was a citizen who always supported measures for the benefit of his community, but did not engage in politics, save to cast his vote in favor of the candidates nearest his ideal. His religious connection was with the Baptist Church.

Mr. Humphrey married Miss Sarah Jane Stough, who was born July 30, 1842, in Ohio, and who died on the home farm in Scotland County, Missouri, May 18, 1916, and they became the parents of the following children: Melissa, who became the wife of Jesse E. Epperson, a farmer and stockraiser of Adair County, Missouri; Bettie Elizabeth, who is the wife of L. H. Ashby, a farmer and stockraiser of Knox County, Missouri, and the rural mail carrier of his community; Marten, who taught school for twenty years before becoming the owner of a large and valuable ranch in Garfield County, Washington, on which he died in 1895; William, the owner of a ranch and a stockraiser in Knox County, Missouri, who has also taught school for many years in his community; Thomas, who is engaged in operations on the old home farm in Scotland County; J. H., who is a resident of Denver, Colorado; Alice, who is the widow of Thomas Cashman, and resides at Keokuk, Iowa; Nora, who is the wife of J. E. Burns, a dairyman of Hannibal, Missouri; Pius B., of this review; Pearl, who is the wife of F. M. Long, engaged in merchandising at La Platte, Missouri; May, who is the wife of Virgil Donoehew, a farmer of Scotland County, Missouri; A. A., who is a farmer and stockman of Adair County, Missouri; Zoe, who died in 1903, in Scotland County, Missouri, as the wife of Ed Donoehew, a brother of Virgil, who now resides in Kansas and is a farmer and stockraiser; Mina, who died young; and P. C., who is unmarried and resides on the home farm in Scotland County.

Pius B. Humphrey received his early education in the public schools of Scotland County, Missouri, following which he took a course at a preparatory college at Hurdland. He began his career as an educator in 1893, in the State of Washington, and remained there during that and the following year, when he returned to Missouri and for seven years taught in the public schools. During that time, in 1902, he entered the Missouri State Normal School, at Kirksville, from which he received a life teacher's certificate in 1906. In 1908 he was given the degree of M. P. from that institution, and three years later the same school conferred upon him the degree of B. S. Mr. Humphrey resumed teaching in 1906 and for two years was principal of the schools at Bolckow, Missouri, then going to Centralia, Missouri, as superintendent of schools, an office which he held for three years. After one year in a like capacity at Lebanon, Missouri, he was brought to Caney, Kansas, in 1911, and here has since held the position of superintendent of city schools. Under Mr. Humphrey's supervision are four schools, thirty-five teachers, and approximately 1,300 scholars. He has done much to improve the system and to elevate the educational standard here, and during his administration several new schools have been erected and a great many improvements installed. Professor Humphrey is a member of the Kansas State, Montgomery County and Southeastern Teachers' associations. He is a democrat in politics, a member of the Presbyterian Church, and fraternally is connected with the Independent Order of Odd Fellows, at Centralia, Missouri.

Professor Humphrey was married in Adair County, Missouri, in 1893, to Miss Lula Rankin, daughter of David and Mollie Rankin, the former of whom died in 1892, while the latter still survives and makes her home at Kirksville, Missouri. Mr. Rankin was a successful farmer and stockraiser. Two children have been born to Professor and Mrs. Humphrey, namely: Cleo, who died in infancy; and Jewell, born Novem-

Vol. IV—20

ber 27, 1898, who is now a member of the junior class at the Caney High School.

WILLIAM STEPHEN McDONALD. The distinctive fact in Doctor McDonald's record as a physician and surgeon at Fort Scott is not the twenty-five years he has practiced there, nor even the exceptional attainments and the skill he has gained in the profession, but more than all these the spirit of service which has animated him in all his work. Such a man never measures his success by fees, but by the satisfaction of doing all he can to alleviate human suffering and by the conscientious performance of his duties to the world and humanity.

Doctor McDonald is of old New England stock. He was born at Prince Edward's Island March 21, 1853, son of Archibald and Mary A. (Bowyer) McDonald. His father, who was of Scotch parentage, was a farmer and also a contractor and builder, and died in Eastern Maine at the age of sixty-eight. The mother, who was of French Huguenot ancestors, died at Portland, Maine.

Fifth in a family of eight children, Doctor McDonald gained a liberal education. He first attended the Wesleyan Boarding School at Redfield, Maine, and then entered the Wesleyan University at Middletown, where he was graduated A. B. in 1882. He received the degree Master of Arts from his alma mater in 1885. After his graduation he took the chair of Natural Science in the East Maine Conference Seminary at Bucksport, and taught there for three years. Having definitely decided upon a medical career, he then entered the Jefferson Medical College of Philadelphia, where he remained until graduating M. D. in 1889. For two years he was an interne in the Jefferson Hospital and thus when he came to Kansas in 1891 he was fortified and prepared for practice by an unusual range of experience and opportunities. Locating at Fort Scott, he has now followed his profession in that city for a quarter of a century.

While in college Doctor McDonald was noted as an expert oarsman and all around athlete. His strong physique was an important aid to him in his early practice. It was especially valuable when it came to attending his patients in the country districts. Doctor McDonald in those early years was never known to refuse to respond to a call regardless of the weather, regardless of whether it was day or night, and regardless of the distance or other difficulties involved in attending his patients. It should be remembered that twenty or twenty-five years ago Bourbon County had few modern highways, few telephones, and the automobile had not yet been introduced to lighten some of the burdens of country practice. In the many years he has spent here, Doctor McDonald has traveled over every country highway and by-path in the county, and there is probably not a farmhouse in the entire county with which he is not familiar. Along with his successful practice he has maintained the character of a warm-hearted and generous gentleman, and has accomplished a great deal of good.

He is a member of all the medical associations, including the American Medical Association, and for several years served as treasurer of the Bourbon County Medical Society. He is local surgeon for the Frisco Railroad, and in 1914-15 was president of the Order of Frisco Railroad Surgeons. His hobby aside from his profession is farming, and in a modest way he looks after a farm near Fort Scott. He is a Scottish Rite Mason and belongs to the Mystic Shrine, and for the past ten years has been chairman of the board of trustees of the Methodist Episcopal Church.

On September 25, 1892, at Fort Scott, Doctor McDonald married Miss Flora Rice, daughter of John Holt and Nancy (Russell) Rice, a prominent Fort Scott family elsewhere referred to. Mrs. McDonald is a member of the Methodist Church and of the Ladies' Aid Society.

PETER J. RINGLER, who is manager and part owner of the Parsons Bottling Works, one of the largest concerns of its kind in the state, has had a very active and successful business career.

He was born in Livingston County, Illinois, December 14, 1868. His grandfather Peter Ringler was born in Kurhessen, Germany, came to the United States about 1876 after his wife had died in Germany, and lived on a farm in Livingston County, Illinois, until his death. In Germany he was a contractor for the building of railroads, and he also served his regular term in the German army.

Peter Ringler, Jr., father of the Parsons business man, was born in Kurhessen, Germany, in 1825. He came to this country about 1843, locating first in Baltimore, Maryland, where he was engaged in the bakery business, and afterwards for several years was connected with the Armour Packing Company in Chicago. He was married while living in Chicago and from there moved to a farm in Livingston County, Illinois. That farm was where he reared his children. In 1882 he moved to Sibley, Iowa, continued farming in that state for a number of years, and in 1906 went to the Northwest, spending a short time in Dakota, and from there went to Minnesota. He died in March, 1915, in a hospital at Staples, Minnesota. He was a democrat, had been honored with various township offices, and was an active member of the Lutheran Church. Peter Ringler married Louisa Strauss, who was born in Hanover, Germany, in 1834, and died at Lake Park, Iowa, in 1904. Her children were: William, who in 1915 moved from Lake Park, Iowa, to Pipestone, Minnesota, and has been a farmer all his active career; Peter J.; John, a farmer at Staples, Minnesota; Rosa, wife of John Card, a carpenter and builder at Staples, Minnesota; Katy, wife of Enos Thorne, a farmer at Staples, Minnesota; and George, also engaged in farming at Staples.

Peter J. Ringler received his early education in Livingston County, Illinois. At the age of fourteen he left school to learn the machinist's trade. He worked out his apprenticeship at Sandburn and Milford, Iowa, and followed the trade of machinist for many years. His home was in Iowa until 1903, and in that year he moved to Wellington, Kansas, in 1910 went to Wichita, to Iola in October, 1914, and since May 20, 1916, has had his home and business headquarters in Parsons. Mr. Ringler has been in the bottling business for the past eighteen years. He conducted a bottling plant at Spirit Lake, Iowa, at Wellington, Kansas, and during his residence at Iola and Wichita was in the real estate business. In May, 1916, he bought an interest in the Parsons Bottling Works from C. O. Humphrey, and is now active manager of this business. The plant has a capacity of 300 cases a day, and that makes it one of the leading concerns of its kind in the state. The plant is fitted with all the up to date appliances and machinery, the motive power is supplied by electricity and other features are a fine sterilizing machine. The plant is located at Twenty-first Street and Corn-

ing Avenue. Mr. Ringler is also a stockholder in the Uncle Sam Oil Company.

His home, which he owns, is at 1407 East Crawford Avenue. Mr. Ringler is a member of the Lutheran Church, served on the school board for two terms while living in Iowa, is a republican, and joined the Woodmen of the World in Camp No. 11 at Wellington, Kansas, and now has membership in the Camp at Iola.

In October, 1897, at Eldora, Iowa, he married Miss Caroline Christoffer, daughter of Mr. and Mrs. Ole Christoffer. Her father now resides at Ellsworth, Iowa, and is a retired farmer. Mr. and Mrs. Ringler have four children: Laurel was born July 21, 1901; Clarence was born August 22, 1903; Celia was born September 16, 1905; and Doris was born April 1, 1910. All the children are now receiving their education in the Parsons public schools.

ROBERT ALEXANDER LONG. It is perhaps not generally known that the humble beginnings of the great Long-Bell Lumber Company was made in Kansas. The home of the corporation for a number of years has been in Kansas City, Missouri, where the splendid R. A. Long office building, one of the finest and most modern structures of its kind in the Middle West, furnishes the headquarters for the business whose operations are widespread all over the Southwest. But for forty years the retail business of the concern has been largely in Kansas and Kansas may properly claim Robert A. Long as one of its greatest business executives.

On April 30, 1875, a carload of lumber was unloaded at the little town of Columbus, in Cherokee County, Kansas. It was consigned to the firm of R. A. Long & Company. This firm consisted of Robert A. Long, Victor B. Bell and Robert White. The senior member of the firm was twenty-four years of age and his partners had not yet reached their majority. The members of the firm had neither surplus capital nor bank accounts. However, Mr. Bell's father was president of the Kansas City Savings Bank and Mr. White's father its cashier. The bank thus gave them the best of recommendations and when cash was required loaned it to them on open account.

In the original yard at Columbus, R. A. Long served as yard manager, bookkeeper and general utility man. He had only the most casual acquaintance with the lumber business. The story is told that when the first invoice was checked, the items "dimensions" and "S. S. & E." were not understood. This was evidently a case in which the man emphasized the broad general and fundamental principles rather than a knowledge of the smaller technical details. In time Mr. Long knew what the details meant and he became a practical retail lumberman. The first year the firm at Columbus earned only $800. In the second year its profits were $2,000. By that time the business was so flourishing as to justify the establishment of a branch yard. In the next six or eight years a number of different yards had been established over Southern Kansas. In 1877 Mr. White, the junior member of the firm, died, his interests being purchased by the surviving partners. In 1884 the company was incorporated with a capital of $300,000. This capital was fully taken up by the earnings of the business. Every year saw a notable increase in the establishment of new yards and the general enlargement of the scope of operations. Whereas, Mr. Long at Columbus forty years ago was content to sell lumber a few hundred feet at a time, the business of the present corporation in its retail

department alone sells millions of feet of rough and finished lumber and mill work, and vast quantities of lime, cement, coal and other products.

In 1889 a wholesale department was added. In 1891 the capital stock was increased to $500,000. Up to that time Mr. Long had acted as superintendent and manager of the company's interests, but with the establishment of the wholesale department Samuel H. Wilson, brother-in-law of Mr. Long, who had come into the old firm in 1887, took charge of the retail department and continued its supervision until his death on October 20, 1903.

It would require a book to describe the detailed development of the business or even to give a full account of its present ramifications. The Long-Bell Lumber Company is now the parent organization of a vast business system. Besides the Long-Bell Lumber Company there are nine allied corporations engaged in the manufacture of lumber, and several other corporations for conducting various activities of the business. The organization now owns immense land holdings in Louisiana, Texas and Arkansas. Its timber interests are chiefly Southern yellow pine and hardwood. The ten sawmill plants have an annual capacity of 500,000,000 feet. The vast extent of cut-over timber lands are handled and marketed by the Long-Bell Farm Land Corporation and the Long-Bell Demonstration Farm Company has for its principal purpose to demonstrate the agricultural value of lands from which the timber has been removed.

While the favors of fortune have been so liberally bestowed upon Mr. Long, perhaps no man has worked harder to deserve them and to constitute his life and influence a more important agency for benefit to mankind. There was a time when he was poor, though never desperately so, and he had as close a fellowship with manual toil and with the adversities of life as thousands of men who have never been able to aspire to financial independence. He was born December 17, 1850, on a farm in Shelby County, Kentucky, near the Town of Simpsonville. His parents were Samuel M. and Margaret K. (White) Long. His mother was a cousin of Senator Blackburn and of Governor Luke P. Blackburn of Kentucky. Mr. Long's father spent his life as a farmer. His father has been described as an intensely practical, methodical and ambitious man, and one who believed in doing, not dreaming. Robert A. Long inherited some of those qualities. He had the imaginative faculty. Imagination has been too frequently confused with idle dreams. As a matter of fact it is the most valuable asset of mental character. Mr. Long to a peculiar degree has been able to translate ideas and plans originating in his brain into practical achievements, has also had the courage of his convictions, and those characteristics perhaps more than anything else have been responsible for his career.

He acquired an education in the common schools of Shelby County and spent fifteen months in a school for boys at Shelbyville. In the usual sense of the term he did not have a liberal education. Some men have been credited with such an education merely because they went through a college and ever afterward ceased to interest themselves in the larger affairs of life. The reverse has been true of Mr. Long. His education really began after he left school and he has been an intense student of life ever since. As a boy he looked beyond the horizon of a simple farm existence, but beyond an unsatisfactory clerkship in a local store found no opportunity to broaden his interests until the age of twenty-two. Part of his boyhood had been spent during the period of the Civil war. Three of his older brothers, Thomas, E. S. and Belvard, had spent a few months in the Union army, but Mr. Long himself was too young for that service.

It was during a visit to Kansas City at the home of his uncle, C. J. White, then cashier of the Kansas City Savings Bank, that Mr. Long had his first big opportunity. How he and the son of Mr. White and the son of Dr. J. B. Bell, president of the bank, made their pioneer venture as lumber dealers has already been described.

Mr. Long is a man of ideas and ideals. He is a constructive thinker, and as a speaker his words are listened to with respect. He is not a one-subject man. He knows lumber but he knows other things as well. A remark of his has often been quoted and deserves quotation: ''Every big business man should write a paper or make a speech at least twice a year on some live subject, not necessarily. connected with his business, that would require investigation. Investigation means more knowledge and knowledge is an asset.'' He has personally applied this truth in many ways. He is identified with many organizations, and his addresses have been listened to by the great bankers of the Nation, by lumbermen's associations, and by many of the civic organizations of his home city. He has always realized the responsibility of wealth and position and has given his time and means unreservedly to the benefit of others. Another remark of his that has been quoted and expresses an important fact of his own character is the following: ''No man will get much out of life who lives wholly for himself. The man who shuts himself away from the world and thinks that he and his family circle are all that matters will find he's in a mighty narrow circle.''

The extent and variety of his interests were aptly indicated by an article that appeared in the Daily Banker and Stockholder: ''To many who know something of the extent of the Long-Bell interests it is a matter of wonderment that Mr. Long and his associates should find time and capacity for direct and close personal supervision of all their manifold business affairs, and still be able to take an active interest in other things. Yet the heads of this big institution are associated with numerous other interests almost as prominently as they are with the lumber business and its allied activities. While consistently avoiding any hint of ostentation, Mr. Long has ever been profoundly interested in religious matters, and in the material advancement of the Christian church in the Middle West his efforts and money have had a larger influence than even his best friends suspect. True to his Kentucky nativity, he is a lover of fine horses, and maintains a lively interest in the famous stables that are under the direct supervision of his daughter, Miss Loula Long. Mr. Long is a breeder of blooded dairy cattle, and one of Kansas City's principal sources of supply for certified milk is 'Longview,' Mr. Long's wonderful country estate near Kansas City. As if these things were not enough to fully employ him outside of business hours, Mr. Long has given much attention to welfare work among the many thousands of Long-Bell employes in the sawmill districts, working with the International Young Men's Christian Association in improving living conditions in the lumber camps and establishing club houses, schools and places of entertainment for workmen and their families.''

Mr. Long is a member of the Blue Hills Country Club, the Mid-Day Club, the Hill Crest Club, the Kansas City Club and the Chamber of Commerce.

He is one of the most liberal benefactors of the Independence Boulevard Christian Church. On December 16, 1875, at Columbus, Kansas, he married Miss Ella Wilson, daughter of George and Eliza (Hughes) Wilson. They are the parents of two daughters: Loula Long, still at home and mentioned above as especially interested in looking after her father's splendid stables, and Sally America, now wife of Lieut. Comm. Hayne Ellis of the United States Navy.

Mr. and Mrs. Long's first home in Columbus was a small three-room cottage with his lumber yard only a short distance away on the same piece of ground. In that home his children were born and he and his wife lived there happily for several years. Later they built a larger and more commanding house also in Columbus, and they remained residents of that little Kansas town upwards of sixteen years. In 1891 Mr. Long came to Kansas City, and his city home here is one of the show places, while his country estate, Longview, comprises about 1,500 acres and is operated as a model dairy farm, with a prize herd of Jersey cattle.

HON. WASHINGTON E. GREGG. The chief executive office of any community is a responsible one and the individual occupying it has resting upon his shoulders not only the numerous burdens connected with the management of a city, but also the accountability for its commercial and moral integrity. As he is, so is his community, for it soon reflects his character and manner of dealing with large problems, and unless he keeps a firm grip upon the reins of office and forces his associates to handle civic affairs in an expeditious and straightforward manner, his administration soon shows the effect of lax principles and the community suffers accordingly. For this reason, of late years the people of the more advanced and progressive cities are choosing their mayors from among their sound business men, for they recognize the effect of example and action, and realize that a man who has accomplished much in a commercial, industrial or financial way, is very liable to be able to carry on the affairs of complicated civic government. The present incumbent of the mayoralty office of McCune, Kansas, is Hon. Washington E. Gregg, who has been engaged in business here for thirty-two years, is proprietor of the largest business establishment in the city, and is president of the McCune State Bank.

Washington E. Gregg was born October 2, 1858, in Madison County, Ohio, and is a son of John Gregg. His father, who is one of the old and highly respected residents of McCune, was born in 1833, in Madison County, Ohio, and was there reared and married. He possessed only an ordinary education, and had neither the advantages of capital or influential friends, so that he was principally employed as a general workman, accepting such honorable employment as presented itself. Through industry and thrift he accumulated enough means to go with his wife and children to Indiana, in 1860, and for eleven years was engaged in farming in that state, but in 1871 became a pioneer resident of Kansas, locating on a farm of 160 acres in Crawford County, which is now owned by his son, Washington E. John Gregg continued to be engaged in agricultural pursuits during the remainder of his active career, at the end of which he gave up his labors and removed to his comfortable home at McCune, where he now resides. He is a republican in politics, and for several terms was a trustee of Osage Township. He belongs to the Methodist Episcopal Church and to Lodge No. 70, Ancient Order of United

Workmen, at McCune. Mr. Gregg was married to Miss Whittaker, who was born in Madison County, Ohio, in 1836, and died August 6, 1865, being buried eight miles north of Williamsport, Indiana. They were the parents of four children: Washington E.; Agnes, who died at McCune in 1898, as the wife of Orin Doty, who resides on a farm west of McCune; A. B., who owns a farm of 160 acres adjoining the old homestead, 4½ miles northwest of McCune; and a boy who died in infancy. Mr. Gregg was married second to Miss Mary Sohn, who was born in 1840, in Germany, and died in 1906, at McCune, Kansas, and they became the parents of five children, as follows: Grant, who is a retired merchant of McCune; A. S., who is an agriculturist and makes his home at McCune; C. C., who is engaged in the coal business at Girard, Kansas; Dora, who is the wife of Doctor Strain, an optician of Parsons; and Edith, who is the wife of William Struhover, a traveling salesman of Marion, Indiana.

Washington E. Gregg received his education in the public schools of Warren, Indiana, and Crawford County, Kansas, and remained on his father's farm until he was twenty years of age, at which time he commenced farming on his own account. In 1884 he came to Fredonia and entered upon the career which has since made him one of the leading business men of the city. His start was a modest one, consisting of a one-half interest in the furniture business conducted by George McCaslin, but after one year he bought his partner's interest, and for two years thereafter conducted the business alone. He then sold a one-half interest to M. S. Austin, but after two years again came into full possession of the establishment, which he has conducted by himself to the present. In 1893 he added a hardware stock to the business, and this hardware and furniture store is the largest in McCune, occupying floor space 45 x 140 feet, and situated on Hamilton Street. The trade extends over a radius of twelve miles, and the business has been built up through honest and straightforward methods, Mr. Gregg's business reputation being an excellent one. As a member of the Commercial Club, he has been active in numerous movements which have added to the commercial and industrial prestige of McCune, and through precept and example has encouraged others to operate along progressive lines. Mr. Gregg is president of the McCune State Bank and vice president of the Mineral (Kansas) State Bank, and his connection with these enterprises has done much to insure their solidity. With supreme faith in the future of McCune and the surrounding country, he has invested his holdings in realty, and is now the owner of a resident on Main Street, the store building in which his business is located, a livery barn on Hamilton Street, 160 acres of farming land 3½ miles northwest of McCune, 160 acres two miles north, and 160 acres one mile north of the city, and also has large coal interests in Oklahoma.

Mr. Gregg has long been one of the leading republicans of Crawford County, and has been called upon frequently to serve in public positions of trust and responsibility. After several terms as a councilman, he was elected mayor of the city, and, with an interval, was again elected to this office and is now serving his third consecutive term therein. During his administrations the electric light plant and electric water works have been installed and numerous other improvements have been made which have made this one of the up-to-date and progressive cities of this part of the state. In his official capacity his ablest abilities and energies have been given to the city's

welfare. He has always been a friend of education, and during the past fourteen years has been a member of the Crawford County High School board. In fraternal circles, Mayor Gregg is equally prominent. He belongs to McCune Lodge No. 237, Ancient Free and Accepted Masons, of which he has been past master three consecutive terms and senior deacon many terms; Cherokee Chapter No. 87, Royal Arch Masons; Cordelia Commandery No. 17, Knight Templars, of Parsons, Kansas; Fort Scott Consistory, No. 6, thirty-second degree; and Mirzah Temple, Ancient Arabic Order Nobles of the Mystic Shrine, of Pittsburg, Kansas; McCune Lodge No. 193, Independent Order of Odd Fellows, of which he is past noble grand; McCune Lodge No. 70, Ancient Order of United Workmen, of which he is past master workman; McCune Camp No. 2870, Modern Woodmen of America; and the Anti-Horse Thief Association. He is also president of the McCune Country Club and a general favorite in club and social circles.

Mr. Gregg was married in 1885, in McCune, to Miss Hannah Harley, daughter of Mr. and Mrs. George Harley, both now deceased. Mr. Harley was a retired farmer and stockman. To Mr. and Mrs. Gregg there have been born three children, namely: Cecil D., a graduate of the McCune High School, who spent one year in the Crawford County High School and two years at Baker University and is now assisting his father in his business enterprises; Minnie, who is a graduate of the McCune High School, spent two years at the Manual Training Normal School at Pittsburg, and is now a teacher of domestic science in the McCune School; and Helen, a graduate of the McCune High School, class of 1916, who is attending the State Normal School.

GEORGE HOWE BECHTEL. Of the men who are maintaining Montgomery County's reputation and prestige in financial circles, few are more highly esteemed as banking officials and citizens than George Howe Bechtel, cashier of the Liberty State Bank, of Liberty. Like many other Kansas bankers, Mr. Bechtel is a product of the farm and of the schoolroom. It would seem that the practicality developed in agricultural life and the mental sharpening acquired in the educator's vocation form a combination happily adaptative to the great and important business of banking. At least, Mr. Bechtel's career and his success support such a view.

Mr. Bechtel was born September 13, 1867, in Atchison County, Kansas, and is a son of William and Emma F. (Thompson) Bechtel and a member of a family that originated in Holland and emigrated to America in Colonial times, settling in Pennsylvania. Joshua Bechtel, the grandfather of George H. Bechtel, was born in the Keystone State, and there passed his entire life, dying in Montgomery County. He followed farming as a vocation and was accounted a substantial man and a good citizen, respected and esteemed by those who knew him. William Bechtel, father of George H., was born in 1825, in Montgomery County, Pennsylvania, and was there reared and educated. In young manhood he went to Cincinnati, Ohio, where he was married, and there followed carpentering and building until coming to Kansas in 1860. He first located at Leavenworth, where he worked at his trade, made sashes for Colonel Anthony to be used in the Times Building, and during the early days of that city assisted in its upbuilding and development. In 1865 he removed with his family to Atchison County, Kansas, and with his earnings purchased a farm of 160 acres, .

on the prairies. This he succeeded in putting under a good state of cultivation, and there he made his home during the remainder of his active life, although at the time of his retirement he went to Valley Falls, Kansas, where his death occurred in December, 1904. During the Civil war Mr. Bechtel served in the Kansas State Militia, with which organization he assisted in repelling Price in his raid through Kansas. He was a republican in his political views, and belonged to the Methodist Episcopal Church, in the work of which he was always active, being a member of the official board for a long period of years. As a citizen he did his full duty by his community, and his sterling traits of character gave him a high standing in the confidence of his fellowmen. Mr. Bechtel married Emma F. Thompson, who was born in Rhode Island, in 1833, and died in Atchison County, Kansas, in 1907. She was a Christian woman of many charities and was beloved by a wide circle of friends. To Mr. and Mrs. Bechtel there were born the following children: Willis, a resident of San Francisco, California; Jennie, the wife of Luman Rutty, who is retired and lives on his orange grove at Pomona, California; Nellie, who is the wife of Lewis Chandlee, a carpenter and builder of California; Emma, who is the wife of William S. Irvin, of Muskogee,, Oklahoma; J. R., a graduate of the Topeka Medical College and now a practicing physician and surgeon of Lawrence, Kansas; George Howe, of this notice; and Edward, who is a carpenter and builder of Kingfisher, Oklahoma.

George Howe Bechtel attended the public schools of Atchison County, the Salina Normal University and the State Normal School, at Emporia, and in the meantime resided on the home farm, where he devoted his summers to the cultivation of the soil. Thus, at the age of twenty-one years, he was equipped physically and mentally for the vocation of teaching, which he followed for four years in Dickinson County and for seven years in Atchison County, and in the latter was for two years principal of the schools of Huron. In 1902 Mr. Bechtel gave up teaching for the business of banking in that year becoming bookkeeper for the Huron State Bank, with which concern he was connected three years. He then became cashier of the Citizens State Bank, of Peru, Kansas, with which he was identified for two and one-half years, and in 1907 came to Liberty to become cashier of the Liberty State Bank, a position which he has since retained. The Liberty State Bank was established in 1904 as a state institution. by C. W. Wingate, Lewis Billings and others, and immediately began to fill a long felt need. In that year the brick banking house was built on Main Street, and the business of the institution has steadily grown under the management of the following officials: president, Lewis Billings, of Cherryvale; vice president, John H. Tole, Liberty; cashier, George H. Bechtel, Liberty; and assistant cashier, G. W. Wingate, Liberty. The capital of the Liberty State Bank is $10,000 and the surplus and undivided profits, $3,600. It bears an excellent reputation in banking circles and is regarded as a safe and conservative institution which will protect its depositors' interests in every way, such an opinion being the result of its past operations and the well known integrity of its officials. Mr. Bechtel is a republican. While a resident of Huron he served as a member of the city counsel, has been a member of the school board at Liberty, and at present is city treasurer. He belongs to the Methodist Episcopal Church and

to its board of trustees. Mr. Bechtel is also a member of the Kansas State Bankers Association.

In 1896, at Nortonville, Kansas, Mr., Bechtel was married to Miss Mabel Mitchell, daughter of Charles and Isabelle (Helm) Mitchell, residents of Baldwin, Kansas, where Mr. Mitchell is a retired farmer. To Mr. and Mrs. Bechtel there have been born the following children: Isabelle, a graduate of Montgomery County High School, class of 1915, and now bookkeeper in the Bank of Liberty; Viola, a senior at the Montgomery County High School; Ruby, a freshman in that school; William and George, who are attending the graded schools of Liberty; and Dorothy, still at home.

JAMES BASSETT was a pioneer figure in Kansas. He arrived in the territory in 1857 and from that time forward until his death which occurred at Dover in Shawnee County, December 26, 1915, he was an upright, conscientious, hard working and successful citizen.

He came to Kansas from Onondaga County, New York. A native of England, he was born in Glastonbury, January 25, 1836, and was one of the nine children of Joseph and Elizabeth (Hale) Bassett. Some years later, in 1849, Joseph Bassett set out for America, determined to establish a home for himself and family in the New World. He found a favorable location in Skaneateles, New York. A year later he went back to England and returned with his family to America. The rigors of a long voyage on board a sailing vessel, which was meagerly provisioned and watered, proved too much for Mrs. Bassett, who died a few days after landing in this country. Joseph Bassett married again, and he and his wife spent the remainder of their days in Skaneateles.

The late James Bassett was thirteen years of age when brought to this country, and altogether he received only eleven months of schooling, but by his wide reading he came eventually to be highly educated, and he kept this up to the end of his long and useful life. He grew up on a farm in and about Skaneateles until about twenty years of age.

In 1857 he started west on a prospecting expedition. By February he had arrived at Leavenworth. From there he walked across the country to Dover, and that community remained his principal home for nearly sixty years. In Dover two of his married sisters had already located, Mrs. Alfred Sage, and Mrs. John Sage. His early employment in Kansas was as a farm hand. He also pre-empted a tract of land, and by developing that as a farm contributed something · to the progress of the state. Though he was a witness of many of the atrocities committed during the border warfare period, he possessed none of the radical views of either side, and so far as was consistent with an honorable course he remained neutral.

His real patriotism was manifested when, on December 1, 1861, he enlisted in Company F of the Second Kansas Regiment of Cavalry. He remained with that regiment throughout its campaigns and service, and was not discharged until January 18, 1865. He left the army at Leavenworth as a corporal. As a volunteer he was many times called upon to do dangerous scout duty and was often under the direct fire of the enemy. He was in the Battle of Poison Springs, from which so few of his comrades escaped alive, and in that hurried retreat through the timber received an injury to his right eye which destroyed the sight later and made it necessary to remove the eyeball.

At the close of the war he returned home, and thereafter made three trips across the plains to Colorado, Pike's Peak being his destination once. Eventually he settled down to the quiet life of a farmer at Dover. In that community he experienced all the hardships incident to pioneer life. He combated drought, the grasshopper plague, the starvation prices of farm produce and engaged in the relentless warfare of the early Kansas settler against the rigid and forbidding conditions of an environment, which as a result of men's continued efforts gradually changed for the better. Through it all by rigid economy and with the help of a good wife, James Bassett contrived to prosper.

He was also an effective unit in his community. He was one of the organizers of the Dover State Bank, of which he was a director until a short time before his death. He was also among those who established the Dover Cemetery. A member of no religious denomination or secret fraternity he believed in and practiced the Golden Rule and hated cant and hypocrisy. He was charitable in thoughts and in deed and for his upright life was universally respected and loved. He was "Uncle Jim" to the community where he had lived for over fifty years, and young and old came to him for advice and counsel, knowing they would get from him the truth without fear or favor.

On November 17, 1866, Mr. Bassett married Ann Sage, daughter of Arthur and Keziah Sage, of a prominent pioneer family of Kansas, who survives him. To their marriage were born four children, two girls and two boys: Miss Mary Bassett, a teacher of ability; Hattie B. Aldrich, M. D., a physician of Caney, Kansas, and wife of Harry L. Aldrich, M. D., a member of Kansas State Board of Health; Albert J. Bassett, a teacher for many years in Kansas, and is now a prominent hardware merchant of Dover; and Harris T. Bassett, the eldest, a director of the Dover State Bank, and a successful farmer of Dover.

ASA MESSINGER. It is not likely that men within the City of Pittsburg, Kansas, have contributed in greater measure to the making of their surroundings than has Asa Messinger. Look where one will, large buildings and small, modest homes and elegant residences, banking houses and industrial plants, churches and educational institutions, structures for the housing of public utilities—these, and more which contribute to the architectural ensemble of a flourishing town, are the product of his brain and hand. And this is not all. In the capacity of commissioner of streets and public improvements, he has added to the city's beauty and safeguarded its people's health in the way of sanitation, and has introduced innovations that would be valuable assets to a city many times the size of Pittsburg.

Mr. Messinger was born at Taylorville, Illinois, November 29, 1876, and is a son of W. S. and Harriet (Flemming) Messinger. His grandfather, Asa Messinger, was a pioneer of Illinois, where he followed farming for many years, and died at Taylorville. W. S. Messinger, father of Asa Messinger, was born in 1851, at Alton, Illinois, where he was reared and educated, and as a young man went to Taylorville, at which place he was married. He engaged in farming in Christian County until 1888, in which year he went to Missouri, and for ten years farmed in the southern part of the state. In 1898, on coming to Kansas, Mr. Messinger located at Cherokee,

where he followed the trade of carpenter, and in 1904 located at Pittsburg, where he is still actively engaged at his trade. He is a democrat, belongs to the Methodist Episcopal Church, and is fraternally affiliated with the Knights of Pythias. Mr. Messinger married Miss Harriet Flemming, who was born in 1846, at Taylorville, and whose death occurred in Southern Missouri in 1890. They became the parents of five children, as follows: Harmon, who died in infancy; Asa; Homer, who died in infancy; L. Dwight, a carpenter and builder of Pittsburg; and Marion, who is also engaged in the same business here.

Asa Messinger received his education in Illinois and Missouri, where he attended the public schools, but this has been greatly supplemented through reading and by contact with his fellow men, so that he may really be said to be self educated. He was only fourteen years of age when he took his position among the world's workers, finding employment in a sawmill in Southern Missouri. He was so engaged for eight years, after which he turned his attention to the trade of carpenter, having inherited mechanical ability from his father and developing it through his work among skilled mechanics. In 1898 he accompanied the family to Cherokee, Kansas, where he continued to work at his trade for two years, and since 1900 has been a resident of Pittsburg, and for the greater part of this time has been engaged in a general contracting business. During the sixteen years of his residence and business activity at Pittsburg, he has been connected with the construction of some of the largest of the city's buildings. Among the many contracts handled by him may be mentioned the following: remodeling of the National Bank; erection of the Masonic Temple; superintending the construction of the Methodist Episcopal Church; rebuilding of the State Normal School and the Presbyterian Church; drawing of plans for the Christian Science Church and the Forest Park Building, the latter a $22,000 structure; remodeling of the Lakeside and Washington school buildings, and the Ramsey, Famous and Degen's dry goods stores; and the building of Ridgeway's, Charles Melette's and Doctor Graves' residences, in addition to many others too numerous to mention. Mr. Messinger is an intelligent, well-informed and broad-minded man, lending to his business a progressive spirit, and to the community an extent of practical usefulness which it is difficult to correctly estimate. In politics, he is a democrat. In April, 1913, he was elected commissioner of streets and public improvements, and during his two terms of office there have been more streets paved than there had been previously since the founding of Pittsburg. One of his greatest works was the installing of the first storm sewer put in at Pittsburg, a $50,000 contract. He has been instrumental in securing the Whiteway, also in the establishing of municipal music and entertainments and was instrumental in securing the first motor driven fire fighting apparatus ever purchased in Pittsburg. In every possible direction he has given himself whole-heartedly to looking after the improvements of the city. That he has aimed to discharge the duties of his office in an economical way and at the same time to get the greatest amount of beneficial results for the municipality, is shown in the fact that he has never employed a foreman or superintendent in his department, but has supervised all work himself. Commissioner Messinger is a member of the Methodist Episcopal Church. He belongs to various fraternal, commercial and social bodies, including Pittsburg

Lodge No. 187, Ancient Free and Accepted Masons; Rescue Lodge No. 393, Independent Order of Odd Fellows; Pittsburg Lodge No. 1554, Knights of Pythias, and Smelter Camp No. 691, Modern Woodmen of America; the Pittsburg Chamber of Commerce; the Pittsburg Automobile Club, and the Pittsburg Good Roads Club. He has a number of business connections and is vice president of the Pittsburg Poster Advertising Company.

In 1896, while a resident of Southern Missouri, Mr. Messinger was united in marriage with Miss Jennie Burriss, daughter of William and Dollie (Snead) Burris, both of whom are deceased. Mr. Burriss was a teamster by vocation. To Mr. and Mrs. Messinger there have been born seven children: William, who resides with his parents and is identified with his father's contracting business; Pearl, who is attending the State Manual Training Normal School, Pittsburg; Paul, who died at the age of ten years; Lee and Helen, who are attending the graded schools of Pittsburg; and Marguerite and John, at home.

PROF. GEORGE W. TROUT, professor of history at the State Manual Training Normal School at Pittsburg, Kansas, was born in Allen County, Kentucky, September 16, 1863, and is a son of Rev. Paton and Amanda (Black) Trout. He belongs to an old and honored family which originated in Ireland, and came to America during the days of the American Colonies, the first forefather in this country settling in Virginia, from whence the family drifted to various parts of the Union.

George Trout, the grandfather of Professor Trout, was born in Sumner County, Tennessee, in 1789, and there spent his entire life on the same farm, dying in 1898. He was a democrat in politics and at one time served as judge of the district which now bears his name. He and his son, George, resided on that farm during the administration of every president of the United States, and the latter still makes his home there. Rev. Paton Trout was born in 1834, in Sumner County, Tennessee, and was reared on a farm, but chose instead the ministry as his vocation and educated himself for this calling. He became a circuit rider in the Methodist Episcopal Church, South, and at one time filled as many as thirty pulpits in a single year, in Allen County, Kentucky, and Sumner County, Tennessee. During the Civil war he enlisted under John Morgan in the Confederate army, but while he consented to fight for the South, would not cross the Mason and Dixon line, and as a result was forced to desert and remain in hiding for several years. In 1882 he came to Kansas and was pastor of churches at Bronson and Fort Scott, but finally retired from active service, and died in 1912, at La Harpe, Kansas. He was a democrat. Reverend Trout married in Allen County, Kentucky, Miss Amanda Black, who was born in 1840, in Sumner County, Tennessee, and died in Allen County, Kansas, in August, 1883, and they became the parents of nine children, namely: Alfred who was a merchant at Odin, Illinois, and died in 1906; Margaret, who married A. J. Myers, a resident of Kansas since 1881 and now a merchant at La Harpe; Josephine, who is the wife of James McGrew, a smelterer at La Harpe; Mary Elizabeth, who died at the age of three years; George W.; Edgar, who is engaged in the butchering business at Odin, Illinois; Mary, who is the wife of William Harry, a dry goods and clothing merchant at Ralston, Oklahoma; Mattie, who is the wife of Thomas Stout, a merchant of Cherryvale, Kansas;

and Ina, who is the wife of O. W. Vandergrif, of Oklahoma City, Oklahoma.

In his youth George W. Trout received only an indifferent public school education, as the family was large and he was expected to contribute to its support. He was only fourteen years of age when he began to do a man's work on the farm, in Marion County, Illinois, thus earning $6 per month. He continued as a farm hand in the fields of Illinois, with gradually increasing wages, until 1882, when he came with the family to Allen County, Kansas, and during the next six years continued to work as a farmer during the summer months. In the winter terms, however, he taught in the country schools, having managed to pick up some education through studying in the hours that were not demanded for farm work, and in 1885 was given a county teacher's certificate. With his appetite for knowledge only sharpened by what he had secured, Mr. Trout determined to gain a thorough education, and in 1893 entered Ottawa University, from which institution he was graduated in 1899, with the degree of Bachelor of Arts. Subsequently, he went to Rochester, New York, where for three years he attended a theological seminary, specializing in history and sociology, and in 1902, on his return to Kansas, located at Pittsburg as pastor of the First Baptist Church, a pastorate which he filled for five and one-half years. In 1908 he was offered and accepted the chair of history in the State Manual Normal Training School at Pittsburg, where he has since remained and where he now has two assistant professors.

Professor Trout is now one of the best known educators in the state, was one of the organizers of the Kansas Sociological Association, of which he is a member, and belongs also to the Kansas State Teachers' Association and the Kansas Historical Association. His political beliefs make him a republican. Fraternally, he belongs to Pittsburg Camp of the Modern Woodmen of America, and to Pittsburg Lodge No. 187, Ancient Free and Accepted Masons, of which he is past master; Pittsburg Chapter No. 58, Royal Arch Masons, of which he is high priest; Pittsburg Commandery No. 29, Knights Templar, of which he is prelate; Mirzah Temple, Ancient Arabic Order Nobles of the Mystic Shrine; Zabud Council, of Topeka; and Fort Scott Consistory No. 6, of the thirty-second degree. He also holds membership in the Pittsburg Commercial Club and allied himself with other progressive and public-spirited citizens in advancing movements for the welfare of the city and its people.

Professor Trout was married in 1887, in Allen County, Kansas, to Miss Mary L. Gilbert, daughter of Edward and Mary (Tucker) Gilbert, farming people, the former of whom is now deceased, while the latter is a resident of Kincaid, Kansas. To this union there have been born nine children, as follows: Deva, who died at the age of three years; Ola, who died when three months old; Alden Camby, born May 5, 1893, a graduate of the academic department of the State Manual Training Normal School, and now a member of the Pittsburg Fire Department; Ruth, born December 28, 1895, who is the wife of James Stillwagh, the proprietor of an ice manufacturing business at Pittsburg, and has one child, Edith Lavon, born January 15, 1915; Anna, born April 4, 1898, who is a freshman at the State Manual Training Normal School; Gilbert, born February 28, 1901, a freshman in the high school department of the State Manual Training Normal School; Ralph, born September 10, 1903, who is in the ninth grade in this school;

Harold, born February 7, 1906, also a student; and Mary E., born July 7, 1910. The family home is at No. 305 West Quincy Avenue.

CHARLES HIRAM COOK. Prominent among the men who have long been identified with the oil industry in Kansas as producers and drillers is found Charles Hiram Cook, of Coffeyville. From the time he left school he has followed the oil and gas fields in various parts of the country, and with the great development of the Kansas fields became interested here and has since played a part in the growth and advancement of the industry. Mr. Cook was born at Springboro, Crawford County, Pennsylvania, January 31, 1863, and is a son of Francis Henry and Emily (Fisher) Cook.

The Cook family originating in England, was transferred to America during Colonial days, when the progenitor settled in Pennsylvania. In that state was born the great-grandfather of Charles Hiram Cook, who followed farming all his life and there passed away. He was the head of a large family, and among his children was George R. Cook, the grandfather of Charles H., born in 1809, at Springboro. He was reared as farmer and followed that vocation for a number of years, but also followed other lines of industry, his abilities and energies carrying him into railroad grading contracting and sawmilling. He was originally a whig and later a republican, and was a very active member of the Methodist Episcopal Church. As agriculturist, business man and citizen he won and held the respect of those with whom he was associated, and in his death, which occurred in 1885, Springboro lost one of its best men. Mr Cook married Miss Maria Soper, who was born in 1813, in Pennsylvania and died at Springboro, July 4, 1876, and they were the parents of the following children: Francis Henry; Naomi, deceased, married J. B. Bradley, also deceased, came to Kansas in the spring of 1870 and located near Topeka, but after perhaps two years returned to Pennsylvania, having been discouraged by the grasshopper plague in 1871, Mr. Bradley then resuming his operations as a real estate dealer and oil producer; William R., deceased, who also came to Kansas in time to be here during the grasshopper year, then returning to the East and locating at Bolivar, New York, where he was cashier in a gas company's office and also an operator in oil, and where his death occurred; Aris, living at Springboro, Pennsylvania, the widow of the late William Sweeney, who was a carpenter and builder; Porter S., who came to Topeka, Kansas, in 1870, engaged in the livery and real estate business and served as sheriff of Shawnee County, and now a resident of Sulphur Springs, Arkansas; Hiram, whose death occurred in 1862, when overcome by gas from an oil well where he was working in Canada; Mary, deceased, who married Arthur Fisher, who came to Kansas in 1870 and were routed by the grasshoppers, then returning to the East. Mr. Fisher now being manager of a gas company at Cuba, New York; and George W., a Kansas pioneer of 1872, who is a farmer and has an undertaking establishment at Dover, Kansas.

Francis Henry Cook was born November 14, 1832, in Crawford County, Pennsylvania, and was there reared and educated. He was brought up on the farm, but in his father's other enterprise conceived a liking for business, and finally entered merchandising as the proprietor of his own establishment. Mr. Cook was married in his native county, and in 1870 removed to Venango, Pennsylvania, there also

engaging in mercantile pursuits. Subsequently, for four years, he followed farming in Venango County, from whence he went, in 1881, to Bradford, Pennsylvania, and Bolivar, New York, at which points he had charge of oil property. In 1886 Mr. Cook took his family to Michigan, buying a farm in Victory Township, Mason County, just outside of the City of Ludington. This farm he cultivated until 1905, and in that year retired and moved to Puyallup, not far from Seattle, Washington, where he now lives in quiet and comfort, enjoying the pleasures which are his by right of his long years of faithful labor. As a man of honor and sterling traits of character, Mr. Cook is highly esteemed by those who have come into contact with him, and he has always been a good citizen. A republican in his political affiliation, while living in Pennsylvania and later in Michigan, he served as a justice of the peace. He is a member of the Methodist Episcopal Church and in his younger days took an active part in church work and for some years served as superintendent of the Sunday School. During the Civil war, at the time General Lee was threatening Philadelphia, Mr. Cook volunteered for the Union army and went to Harrisburg, but was not called upon for service. He married Miss Emily Fisher, who was born in 1843, at Silver Creek, New York, and they became the parents of the following children: Clara, who is deceased; Charles Hiram, of this notice; Hattie, who is deceased; Alice and Aris, who both died of diphtheria; and Mary, who married Mr. Tripp and now makes her home with her parents.

Charles H. Cook attended the public schools of Springboro and Shamburg, Pennsylvania, and Chamberlain Institute, at Rudolph, New York. When he graduated from that institution he at once became identified with the oil and gas business, and followed the fields in New York, Pennsylvania, Ohio and Indiana, until 1912, on July 1 of which year he came to Coffeyville, Kansas. Here he has since carried on operations of an extensive character, both in the line of drilling and operating, and has become one of the well known figures in this field. He likewise has an interest in a lease at Wann, Oklahoma. In politics Mr. Cook is a republican. He resides at No. 101 West First Street, and has numerous friends in that locality, as he has also in business circles.

In 1887, at Lima, Ohio, Mr. Cook was married to Miss Maude I. Best daughter of Mr. and Mrs. P. W. Best, the latter of whom is deceased, while the former is a resident of Ridgeway, Pennsylvania. To them have been born the following children: Myrtle, a graduate of Lima High School, and a graduate nurse of the Beaver County General Hospital, Rochester, Pennsylvania, and residing at home with her parents; Raymond L., an oil well driller, who also lives with his parents; Jessie, who died at Coffeyville, at the age of twenty years; and Marie, a graduate of the Coffeyville High School, who attended the Kansas State Normal School at Emporia for two years and is now a teacher in the high school.

WILLIAM PETERSON, during the last years of his life, lived retired with his wife in a comfortable home at Randolph in Riley County. He had a remarkable range of experience. A native of Sweden, he came to the United States a poor man. He had hardly become accustomed to American ways before he entered the army to fight for his adopted land. Three years of gallant and faithful service as a Union soldier are to his credit. Nearly fifty years ago he came out to the new State of Kansas. He was a homesteader and for years a successful farmer in Pottawatomie County. The fruits of his labors enabled him to retire and enjoy in comfort his declining years.

He was born February 17, 1834. Childhood and youth, the advantages of schools and much of hard work were his portion during the twenty-six years he lived in Sweden before immigrating to the United States.

On August 17, 1860, he landed at the City of Boston. A day or two later he was working at Jamestown, New York. From the tasks which furnished him a livelihood he was called to the higher service of his adopted country. August 27, 1861, a year and ten days after he came to this country, he enlisted as a private in Company A of the 112th New York Volunteer Infantry. That regiment saw some of the hardest fighting during the first three years of the war. Without recalling all the engagements in which he participated, it should be noted that in the battle of Cold Harbor on June 3, 1864, William Peterson was struck by a minie ball in the right shoulder. That was the only important wound received during his service. Mr. Peterson secured possession of the ball after it was extracted from his shoulder, and he afterward kept it as a memento of his military experience. On August 30, 1864, three days after the expiration of his term of enlistment, he was given an honorable discharge with the rank of corporal.

Another soldier in the 112th New York Infantry was Christopher Oakland. Mr. Oakland was in Company E. He had come to America some years before from Sweden, bringing with him his family, including his daughter Emma, who had been born in Sweden September 29, 1843. In the fall of 1864, after his honorable discharge from the army and after he had voted for the re-election of Lincoln for president, William Peterson was married to Miss Emma Oakland at Jamestown, New York.

After his marriage he followed farming on a small piece of land near Chautauqua Lake in Western New York. The great opportunities of the Middle West called him to share in their abundance, and in 1867 Mr. Peterson homesteaded a claim in Pottawatomie County, Kansas. In the development of that claim, in the making of a home, the rearing and training of his children, he was busily occupied until 1901. Having then reached a period in his life when he was amply able to retire, he did so and afterward lived in a comfortable home at Randolph.

For his part in developing a farm and his worthy relationship with the community, Mr. Peterson deserves mention as one of the makers of the great Commonwealth of Kansas. He was long a member of the Grand Army of the Republic, and for more than fifty years actively supported the republican party. For nine years his fellow citizens called upon him to serve as justice of the peace in his home township of Pottawatomie County, and he was once census enumerator in his township. He and his wife were long active members of the Methodist Church. In 1914 they were permitted to celebrate that impressive and beautiful ceremony of a golden wedding anniversary. Twelve children were born to their union, and six of them are still living, all grown to useful and honorable manhood and womanhood.

ALONZO O. BLAIR, M. D. By nearly forty years of practice in Southeastern Kansas Doctor Blair has become widely known as a successful physician and surgeon, and for more than a quarter of a century has been identified professionally and also in a business way with the City of Pittsburg.

By ancestry he is of Scotch-Irish stock. His great-great-grandfather came in colonial times from England and settled in South Carolina. Doctor Blair's grandfather was a native of South Carolina, but was opposed to the institution of slavery and moved from that state to Tennessee and thence to Illinois. He was one of the conductors on the famous underground railroad in the years before the war, a route by which many fugitive slaves escaped to freedom in Canada. He was an early farmer at Sparta, Illinois, where he died.

Illinois is the native state of Doctor Blair. He was born in Perry County September 19, 1852. His father William R. Blair was born in Tennessee in 1824, grew up in that state, and at the age of thirty-four removed to Perry County, Illinois. He followed farming all his life, and died at Perry in March, 1916. He was a man of considerable influence in his home locality, was an active republican, filled the office of justice of the peace, and was a member and elder in the Reformed Presbyterian Church. He married Martha McQuiston, who was born in North Carolina in 1842 and died at Perry, Illinois, in 1856. William R. Blair was a very successful farmer in Illinois and left a large estate, part of which is still owned by his children. These children were: Dr. A. O. Blair, the oldest; Lyman, who occupies part of the old homestead in Perry County, Illinois; James Edwin, who lives on a farm near the old homestead; William Lincoln, farming on a part of the old homestead; Lillian, who is married and lives on a farm south of Wichita, Kansas; and Mabel, unmarried, living in New York City.

The early youth of Doctor Blair was spent on an Illinois farm. He attended public school at Perryville, and in 1873 was graduated from the Colterville Academy. He then entered the St. Louis Medical School, now the medical department of the University of Missouri. He completed a thorough course in that institution and was granted his degree M. D. in 1877. In 1890 Doctor Blair interrupted his private practice and took post-graduate work in the New York Polyclinic. That was shortly before he located in Pittsburg. For the first year of his practice he was located at Colterville, Illinois, but in 1878 came to Kansas, and this state has been the stage of his professional activities and his business success. He practiced at Bavaria from 1878 to 1882 and at Beulah until 1890. In the latter year he removed to Pittsburg, which was then just coming into prominence as an industrial city, and for years he has enjoyed a large share of the general medical and surgical practice in this locality. His offices are at 412½ North Broadway and he owns an interest in the building.

Doctor Blair has used his means to invest largely in local real estate. He owns his home at 513 West Second Street, also a business building on South Broadway, a large brick structure near the Frisco depot, and he and Tom Caffey own the two-story brick building on Locust and Fourth streets adjoining the Santa Fe Railway. He owns other real estate in Pittsburg and has some investments in Port Arthur, Texas.

Doctor Blair is a member of the Crawford County and Kansas State Medical societies, the Southeastern Medical Society and the Medical Society of the Southwest and the American Medical Association. He is a republican and has served as a member of the city council of Pittsburg. He is now a trustee in the United Presbyterian Church. Fraternally his

W. S. Morton

relations are with Pittsburg Lodge No. 187, Ancient Free and Accepted Masons, Pittsburg Chapter No. 58, Royal Arch Masons, Pittsburg Commandery No. 29, Knights Templar, and Mirzah Temple of the Mystic Shrine at Pittsburg. He also belongs to Pittsburg Lodge No. 56, Ancient Order United Workmen, and to Pittsburg Camp of the Modern Woodmen of America.

In Colterville, Illinois, in 1877, the year he was graduated in medicine, Doctor Blair married Miss Elizabeth Hughes, a daughter of John and Elizabeth (Miller) Hughes, both of whom are now deceased. Her father was a farmer. Doctor and Mrs. Blair have two daughters. Florence is the wife of Robert Nesh, who is assistant manager in a brick company at Pittsburg. The daughter Olive is a graduate of the College of Music at Cincinnati, Ohio, is a music teacher and makes her home with her parents.

WILLIAM S. NORTON. Whatever their environment, men of true ability have the power to raise themselves above circumstances, and apparently handicaps and difficulties act only as a spur to increase effort and accomplishment. There are few Kansans whose careers better illustrate the truth of this assertion than that of William S. Norton, who is known so well in Cherokee County as a financier and business man.

Mr. Norton could review by personal recollections practically every phase of life in Southwestern Missouri and Southeastern Kansas during the last half century. He was a Union soldier during the war and the keynote to his success can probably be found in the fact that he has been ever ready to meet danger and difficulty and has always been unusually resourceful in every exigency of a long life.

As to his ancestry it can be stated that the Nortons were English people and were pioneers to the State of Ohio, where they settled before the War of 1812. Their first point of settlement on coming to America was North Carolina.

Mr. William S. Norton was born in Edgar County, Illinois, July 26, 1844. His father was Amos Norton, a native of Mount Vernon, Ohio, where he was born in 1826. After spending the first nineteen years of his life in the vicinity of Mount Vernon, he moved to Edgar County, Illinois, where he married and subsequently identified himself with farming a raw tract of land in that section of the Prairie state. Amos Norton was a Kansas pioneer. The territory was barely opened for settlement when he arrived in 1854 at Fort Scott. He homesteaded a claim there. After working his land for two years, he removed to Buffalo, Dallas County, in Southwestern Missouri. In that rough and rugged district of Missouri he spent his summers in farming and followed the carpenter trade in the winter months. When the war broke out Amos Norton quickly showed his stand for the Union cause. He lived in a part of Missouri where Union sentiment could not be spoken without the hazard of personal danger, but in spite of that he enlisted in February, 1862, in Company B of the Fourteenth Missouri Cavalry. He was elected lieutenant of his company and was soon afterward appointed quartermaster. He was mustered out of this organization in February, 1863, and was soon afterward appointed colonel of the Eleventh Missouri Cavalry. On April 2, 1863, he was captured by a band of guerillas headed by John Turner, and as nothing further of his fate was ever learned it is probable that he was put to death by his captors in Southwest Missouri. Though a Unionist, he was in poli-

tics a Douglas democrat. He was a thorough Christian, an active member of the Baptist Church, and belonged to the Masonic fraternity. In 1843, in Edgar County, Illinois, Amos Norton married Elizabeth Frazier. She was born at Greencastle, Indiana, September 23, 1825, and died at Columbus, Kansas, September 24, 1900. She became the mother of six children: William S., the oldest; Mary Jane, who died at Portland, Oregon, in 1910, the wife of Mr. Cusack, who was a farmer and is also deceased; Serilda Ann, who lives at San Diego, California, the widow of John Crawford, who was a farmer during his active career; John D., who was a miner and died at Galena, Kansas, in 1905; Beverly B., who was pursuing his studies at Dubuque, Iowa, in 1876, when he was killed, being thrown from a horse; and Douglas, who was town marshal at Carle Junction, Missouri, and on November 4, 1884, while on the discharge of his official duties, was killed, being shot by a member of a band of toughs.

From the peaceful scenes of an Illinois community William S. Norton was projected into the rough and oftentimes turbulent life of Southwestern Missouri when he was about ten years of age. Most of his education came from the public schools of Buffalo, Missouri, and a select school at Springfield, that state. At the age of seventeen, about the time the war broke out in 1861, he left school to enlist in Company A of the Independent Mounted Rangers, and his first service with this organization was to act as a bodyguard to the governor of the State of Missouri. Later his company was organized in the Fourteenth Missouri Cavalry, and later he veteranized and became a part of the Eighth Missouri Cavalry. With these different organizations Mr. Norton spent more than four years following the flag of the Union and was mustered out at Little Rock, Arkansas, in September, 1865, under order No. 171. While the great theatre of the war was east of the Mississippi, it is certain that no service was attended with greater hardships and more constant danger than came to those who followed the Union flag in the southwestern country of Missouri, Arkansas and the Indian Territory. Mr. Norton was at the Battle of Carthage, July 5, 1861; at the decisive engagement of Wilson Creek, at Pea Ridge, Prairie Grove, Helena and Poison Springs, Arkansas, and in a number of other minor battles of the campaign in those two states. For ninety-three days and nights he and his comrades were under fire at Four Corners, Arkansas, a point where the states and territories of Arkansas, Missouri, Indian Territory and Kansas adjoin. This engagement followed the Battle of Pea Ridge. During a charge of cavalry at Springfield, Missouri, he was slightly wounded by a sabre cut.

Since the war Mr. Norton has always enjoyed the friendship and communion of his old army comrades, and in 1867 he joined the first Grand Army Post organized at Carthage, Missouri. He has since been an active member of Frank P. Blair Post, Grand Army of the Republic, at Galena; Columbus Post and John A. Dix Post at Baxter Springs, Kansas.

After the war Mr. Norton resumed life in the desolated districts of Southwestern Missouri. Locating south of Carthage, in Jasper County, he followed farming during the open months of the year, and for two years taught winter terms of school. He then moved across the Missouri line and accepted the privilege of becoming one of the first white homesteaders on the lands vacated by the Indians in Cherokee County. He filed on a claim of a quarter section near Baxter Springs, on a part of the head-

right of Chief John Ross, former chief of the Cherokee tribe. After three years spent in improving
and developing his claim he returned to Carthage,
Missouri, and for several years was in the freighting
business. He conducted a freighting outfit between
Carthage and Sedalia, Missouri, and also operated it
through different points in old Indian Territory.
This was in the years before railroads opened up
the southwestern country, and that form of transportation reached Southeastern Kansas in 1871, and he
turned his attention to other lines.

From 1871 to 1877 Mr. Norton was a merchant at
Joplin, Missouri, and also became identified with
the mining districts in that vicinity. From 1877
until 1882 he was engaged in merchandising and mining at Galena, Kansas, and from there removed to
Scammon, Kansas, where he was known as a merchant and coal miner up to 1892. Then, on account
of ill health, he retired temporarily from business
affairs, and for eight years lived at Baxter Springs.
Mr. Norton is a man of wide experience not only in
practical business affairs and in dealing with men,
but also in the law, and during his residence at Baxter
Springs he was a practicing lawyer for a part of
the time. Out of the eight years he spent there he
served as mayor of the town for six years.

On January 17, 1900, Mr. Norton removed to
Columbus, and once more resumed business as a coal
operator and merchant. In 1903 he retired from
the mercantile business and has since sold most of
his mining properties, though still interested in a
small scale in this industry.

Though nominally retired from business, his interests are so widespread as to make him a man of
commanding importance in financial circles. He is
president of the Columbus State Bank, is a stockholder in the First National Bank at Columbus, is
the largest stockholder in the International Life Insurance Company of St. Louis, of which he was a director
for a number of years, is a stockholder in the Prudential Casualty Company of Indianapolis, in the
Casualty Company of Kansas City, and the Great
Western of Phoenix, Arizona, and the Southwestern
Casualty Company of St. Louis. He owns an interest
in the building occupied by the First National Bank
of Columbus and the building occupied by the Columbus State Bank, is owner of the building which is
the home of the Daily Advocate on Kansas Avenue,
and is regarded as one of the largest farm land
owners in Cherokee County. His farming interests
include six different farms and aggregate over 1,200
acres. He also is owner of 100 acres of mineral land
in Ottawa County, Oklahoma. His own home is at
221 North Kansas Avenue, and he has another residence in the western part of Columbus.

His career as a public spirited citizen also calls
for some mention. He has always been a live republican, and in 1888 was elected a member of the Kansas
State Senate. He served four years, and during that
time figured in procuring the passage of a number
of bills for the benefit of his constituents. Coming
from a district of the state where the mining industry
was of great importance, he was author of the "shot
firing bill," a measure which relieved the coal miners
of a large part of the hazard they had hitherto endured. This bill prohibited the firing of shots while
any men were still in the mine. For two years coming, 1907-08, Mr. Norton served as mayor of Columbus. He is active in the Presbyterian Church, belongs
to the Columbus Commercial Club, and fraternally is
affiliated with Prudence Lodge No. 100, Ancient Free
and Accepted Masons; Columbus Chapter No. 223,

Royal Arch Masons; Fort Scott Consistory No. 6 of
the second degree Scottish Rite, and is a charter
member of Mirza Temple of the Nobles of the Mystic
Shrine at Pittsburg, Kansas. He is also affiliated
with Pittsburg Lodge No. 412, Benevolent and Protective Order of Elks.

In 1863, while still serving as a Union soldier,
Mr. Norton was married at Bolivar, Missouri, to
Miss Martha J. McKinney. She died in 1864, and
her only child, Martha J., died soon afterward. On
April 3, 1883, at St. Joseph, Missouri, Mr. Norton
married Miss Mary J. Stahl. Her father was captain
of a company in the Second United States Dragoons
during the war, was wounded and taken prisoner in
one battle, and died while confined in Andersonville
Prison. Mrs. Norton died at her home in Columbus
May 20, 1910, after a happy married life of twenty-
seven years. Mr. Norton has a daughter and son.
Maude, who had completed her education in the Hardin
College at Mexico, Missouri, and was at the entrance
of a promising young womanhood, when drowned near
Baxter Springs, Kansas, June 10, 1905, at the age
of twenty. Claude W., the only child now living, was
graduated from the Military Academy at Mexico, Missouri, in 1905, and is now connected with the International Life Insurance Company of St. Louis.

EDWIN V. LANYON. The president of the National
Bank of Pittsburg, Edwin V. Lanyon, is a dominant
factor in the financial and industrial world and belongs to a family the members of which have figured
conspicuously in the industrial development of Southeastern Kansas for the last quarter of a century. He
is a native of Wisconsin, born at Mineral Point,
December 14, 1863, and a son of Josiah and Jane
(Trevorrow) Lanyon, the former a native of Mineral
Point and of English descent, and the latter a native
of England.

Josiah Lanyon came to Pittsburg, Kansas, in 1882,
and was interested in the smelter development of this
section, but later returned to Mineral Point, Wisconsin. In the public schools of that city Edwin V.
Lanyon received his education, and in 1882 came to
Pittsburg with his father, here assisting him to build
a smelter which they operated together under the
firm style of W. & J. Lanyon until 1897. They also
built a large smelter at Iola, and a number of members of the Lanyon family were interested in these
gigantic projects, in which thousands of dollars were
involved. The Iola plant was operated under the
name of Robert Lanyon & Sons Smelting Company,
as was also the La Harpe plant, and these enterprises
were later absorbed by the Lanyon Zinc Company. In
the spring of 1899, Edwin V. Lanyon of this review
became superintendent of the Lanyon Zinc Company's
smelters at Iola and La Harpe and remained in that
capacity until the year 1902, when he went to Neodesha and, in partnership with his brother, Delos, and
William Lanyon, Jr., built a zinc smelter which they
operated about a year when it was sold to the Grady
M. & I. Company, of St. Louis. He then returned
to Pittsburg, Kansas, and became president of the
National Bank of Pittsburg, with which he had been
associated as a director for a number of years previously. This is one of the substantial banking institutions of Southeastern Kansas and many of the best
known business men of this section have been interested in it for years. While Mr. Lanyon gives the
banking interests the greater part of his attention,
he is still interested in a number of important industrial projects. In 1906, he, with his brother, Delos,
and associates, organized the Lanyon Star Smelting

Company, at Bartlesville, Oklahoma, and constructed a large plant at that place which they still operate. Mr. Lanyon was one of the organizers of the Pittsburg Zinc Company, which purchased a plant at Pittsburg in 1907, which they still operate, and of which company he is president. In 1905, with other interests, he organized the Home Light, Heat and Power Company, of which he was president, but later that concern was absorbed by an eastern company. Beside his banking interests at Pittsburg, he is interested in the Mulberry State Bank, of which he is vice president.

Although his private interests are extensive and important, Mr. Lanyon has found time to devote to the public welfare, and his public spirit has led him to be every ready to support any enterprise tending to make a greater Pittsburg. He has served as mayor of the city one term and is an active member of the Chamber of Commerce, has been vice president of the Commercial Club, and is now vice president of the Carnegie Library board. Fraternally, he is a Knight Templar Mason and a Shriner, and belongs to the Ancient Order of United Workmen, the Benevolent and Protective Order of Elks, the Modern Woodmen of America and the Fraternal Aid Union.

Mr. Lanyon was united in marriage November 27, 1889, with Miss Lydia, daughter of T. L. and Caroline (Neff) Scott, of Pittsburg, Kansas, where her father is a contractor and builder. Mrs. Lanyon was born in Missouri, and came to Kansas with her parents when a child. Mr. and Mrs. Lanyon have three children: Marjorie, who is the wife of T. C. Hill and resides at Pittsburg; and Edwina and Dorothy.

PROF. WILBER A. COCHEL. There is no doubt but that educational education means more to the United States today than any other kind of education and great institutions like the Kansas State Agricultural College are standard bearers in disseminating agricultural knowledge. This college management, with remarkable judgment, has gathered together a group of thoroughly trained instructors covering every phase of agriculture, the agriculture of modern progress. At the head of the animal husbandry division is found Prof. Wilber A. Cochel, a scholar and scientist whose name carries weight in many states of the Union on account of his discoveries and solid achievements.

Wilber A. Cochel was born at Tipton, Missouri, August 7, 1877, and is a son of William H. and Charlotte (Calvin) Cochel. He was reared at Tipton where his father was a hardware merchant and also a farmer. On his father's farm he gained his first practical lessons in agriculture, not unwillingly, for he has always loved the soil and been interested in its development and possibilities. He was afforded educational advantages and after being graduated from the Tipton High School, he entered the academic department of the University of Missouri, from which he was graduated in 1897.

During the succeeding five years Mr. Cochel was mainly engaged in general farming, stockraising and feeding and dealing in cattle. Desiring further scientific knowledge he entered the agricultural department of the University of Missouri and was graduated in 1905. During the St. Louis Exposition in 1904 he was superintendent of the Holstein-Fresian exhibit.

From 1905 to 1909 Professor Cochel was connected with the experiment station at Purdue University, LaFayette, Indiana, in the organization of experiment work. He was the introducer of the silo, which

has revolutionized the system of feeding cattle. He developed a system for the management of feeding beef cattle at a profit, and many other of his ideas have been embodied in modern work along this line. On leaving Purdue University, Professor Cochel went to the Pennsylvania State College, where he continued in charge of the animal husbandry department until July, 1912, when he accepted an invitation to the Kansas State College of Agriculture and has continued a resident of Manhattan ever since.

The outstanding feature of Professor Cochel's work as head of the animal husbandry division and animal husbandry experiment station, includes the determining of a method whereby by-products may be best utilized toward beef production; the use of grain sorghums for feeding livestock, and also of solving the problem of wintering beef cattle. At a glance even the layman can recognize the vast importance attaching to such duties and can recognize that only one thoroughly familiar with the subject, trained along this line, with definite knowledge gained by experience, could ever hope to bring about practical solutions. He has acted as an expert judge of cattle at many expositions and fairs. He has served as president of the American Society of Animal Production; is a member of the American Breeders' Association; of the National Geographical Society; of the National Society for the Promotion of Science, and of the American Genetic Society. He still maintains membership in his old Greek letter college fraternities, the Alpha Zeta and the Phi Kappa Phi.

In 1907 Professor Cochel was united in marriage with Miss Caroline Fahnestock. They are members of the Presbyterian Church. For a number of years he has been identified with the Masonic fraternity but politically has never been active.

JAMES FREDERICK O'CONNOR. The stern competition and exacting conditions of twentieth century business progression have resulted in specialization in every line of industrial and constructive activity. Men of marked ability have proved beyond question of doubt, through consecutive action and comprehensive investigation, that the best and most productive results are secured by a consistent devotion to some particular line of effort. The reason for this is that, with so many competitors it is practically impossible for a single individual to become an expert in all lines. When he entered upon his career, James Frederick O'Connor recognized the fact that the man who dissipates his energies in all directions attains no definite goal, and during his life he has, therefore, practically confined himself to one line of business. His start was given him when he secured the privilege of using an old icehouse, deserted by its former owner, his father. That was a quarter of a century ago. Today, the O'Connor-Hamlin Ice and Cold Storage Company is one of Fort Scott's foremost industries, alike a credit to the city in which it is located and a monument to the consistent fidelity of one who realized the benefit of specialization, through which he has worked out a splendid success.

James Frederick O'Connor was born at Fort Scott, Kansas, November 3, 1868, a son of John and Adelia (Karleskind) O'Connor. His mother was born at Constableville, a little town near Rome, New York, the daughter of Frederick Karleskind, who brought his family from New York to Kansas in 1860, and settled on a farm in Bourbon County, where for many years he was a successful farmer and upright citizen. In his later years he retired to Fort Scott, and there his death occurred. John O'Connor was born in Ireland in June, 1838, and was a lad of sixteen years when he emigrated to the United States. After a short stay at New Orleans, he made his way to St. Louis, Missouri, and there learned the baker's trade, and when he had completed his apprenticeship went to Keokuk, Iowa. In that city he followed the trade of journeyman baker and confectioner, and in 1861 came to Fort Scott, Kansas, where, with a small capital saved from his meager wages, he engaged in business as the proprietor of a small grocery and confectionery. Mr. O'Connor soon recognized the opportunity for the extension of his business and in the winter of 1863 built an icehouse, which he filled with ice during the winter months and distributed this natural article during the summer in connection with his grocery business. In the winter of 1873 there was not enough cold weather to produce an ice crop, and as he was not in good health, and was suffering from an old wound caused by a fractured leg, he sold out his store and moved to a farm that he had purchased some years before, located some three miles from the city. This was in a neglected and run-down condition and needed building up, and during the sixteen years that he operated this property Mr. O'Connor proved a good and practical agriculturist, accumulating a satisfying competence and developing an excellent farm. In his later years he retired from active affairs, and lived comfortably retired in his attractive home at Fort Scott, on North Crawford Street, where he passed away December 26, 1916. Mr. O'Connor has always been a reliable and public-spirited citizen, who has done his share in the upbuilding of the city and county and whose integrity, industry and general worth have brought him many friends and attracted to him the esteem and respect of the people of his community. During the Civil war he enlisted in the Home Guards, his injury preventing him from going to the front. He is a consistent member of the Roman Catholic Church, as is also Mrs. O'Connor, who, like her husband, is greatly respected and esteemed. They have been the parents of eight children, as follows: Francis, who died at the age of four years; James Frederick, of this notice; Elizabeth, who is the wife of Charles P. Hamlin, secretary and manager of the O'Connor & Hamlin Ice and Cold Storage Company; George, who learned the trade of machinist at Fort Scott, in the Fort Scott Foundry and Machine Works, and now a successful manufacturer of machinery at Vancouver, British Columbia; Charles, who is engineer at the ice and cold storage plant; Joseph, who is a clerk with the Fort Scott Wholesale Grocery Company; Anna, who is the wife of J. J. Cummings, assistant superintendent of the Frisco Railroad at Fort Scott; and William, who is engaged in mercantile pursuits at Wichita, Kansas.

James Frederick O'Connor was educated in the parochial school at Fort Scott and the Central Public School, and then entered the old Kansas Normal School, although he did not complete his course there. At the age of eighteen years he gave up his studies to assist his father on the home farm, but after one year went to Pittsburg, Kansas, where he found employment in a dairy. It was at this time that Mr. O'Connor decided to reopen the old icehouse, and, gaining his father's consent, he began the ice business alone in 1892. During the winter months of that year Mr. O'Connor worked with every ounce of energy that he possessed. He had faith in the business and determined to make it succeed, and this faith and determination often kept him at work for thirty-six hours at a stretch. He had only a limited capital and was

unable to hire assistants, but his first year's work brought results, and in 1894 he interested his brother-in-law in the venture, Charles P. Hamlin. Together they continued to labor during the winter months to store up natural ice, and in the summer months to build up a trade, and under their combined efforts the business grew and developed rapidly. By the year 1901 the little venture had grown to astounding proportions, and in that year the present company was incorporated, with the following officers: James F. O'Connor, president; C. B. McDonald, now of Kansas City, Missouri, where he is president of the Peoples State Bank, vice president; and Charles Hamlin, secretary and manager. In that year, 1901, the company planned to manufacture ice, and a 20-ton refrigerating machine was installed in a new modern factory built of brick and insulated with cork board and fitted with concrete floors. In 1904 the business had grown to such an extent that it was necessary to add a 12-ton refrigerating machine, and in 1912 the old machines were replaced by the latest type refrigerating machine of 50-tons daily capacity. In 1916 the company decided that Fort Scott was badly in need of a cold storage plant, and with characteristic energy went about building a modern plant for this purpose, with a capacity of 28,000 cubic feet, the lower floors being used for ice storage and the upper floors being divided into three large storage rooms, leased to the wholesale commission merchants of the city for the storage of fruit, produce, butter, eggs, etc. This innovation was really a boon to the merchants of the city, who hailed its advent with enthusiasm and who have supported it commensurately. The ice business has grown far beyond the limits of Fort Scott and the concern is now supplying towns far distant with ice. Everything about the company's plant and office is modern in every respect. Its deliveries are made with motor trucks and six double-horse wagons, and it has been the pride of the house to make its deliveries expeditiously and to give full value for a fair price. From twenty to twenty-five men are given steady employment, and the business is one that has come to be recognized and appreciated as one of Fort Scott's necessary commercial adjuncts. Thus, from a humble and inauspicious start, within a quarter of a century, has grown a business that has its established place in a city not lacking for important enterprises. Much of its success is due to the fact that Mr. O'Connor is one of those who have supreme faith in themselves, and who does not know what it is to fail in anything that he undertakes. He has centered his energies and ambitions in this enterprise, and has made it his constant aim that all business transactions connected with it be carried on in a manner beyond criticism. Personally, his standing in the business world is of the best, and while such a self-made success often turns the head of its maker, Mr. O'Connor still remains modest and unassuming, retaining his old friendships and making many new ones.

As a citizen, Mr. O'Connor is engaged in a venture that will prove of inestimable value to Fort Scott. In 1915 he conceived the idea of purchasing a tract of eleven acres of land adjoining the company's property, a stretch of ground known as Bridal Veil Park, which has a famous well of excellent mineral water that for twenty-five years has gushed six feet over the surface through a pipe line 960 feet deep. The park and well were in a run-down condition, but after the company had purchased the land, improvements were at once started and a fine swimming pool, built of solid cement foundation, was installed. During the first summer of its existence the pool could not begin to supply the demand made upon it, and was patronized by the best class of citizens of Fort Scott. When improvements now under way are completed the park will be one of the beauty spots of the city. Mr. O'Connor is a democrat in his political views, but has never sought office, having been content to devote himself to his business interests. He is a member of the Fraternal Order of Eagles, and in religious faith is a Roman Catholic.

On November 16, 1892, Mr. O'Connor was married at Fort Scott, to Miss Caroline Hamlin, a sister of Charles Hamlin, who married Mr. O'Connor's sister. Mrs. O'Connor is a daughter of Casper and Adeline (Radell) Hamlin, and a member of a family of pioneer farmers who came to Kansas during the early '80s. Three children have been born to Mr. and Mrs. O'Connor: one child who died in infancy; Irene, born in 1898, at Fort Scott, a graduate of the Fort Scott High School and of Loretta Academy, of Kansas City, Missouri, and now attending the Kansas State Normal School, where she is taking a special art course; and Elmer, born in 1899, who is attending the Fort Scott High School.

ELLSWORTH L. BURTON. One of the very able members of the Kansas Legislature in the session of 1915-16 was Representative E. L. Burton from Parsons. Mr. Burton is an attorney by profession, has spent most of his life in Kansas, and has some very influential and important connections in his part of the state.

He was born at Mattoon, Illinois, April 30, 1868. The Burtons came from England and settled in the Carolinas during colonial days. Mr. Burton is a direct descendant of Cavalier Burton. His grandfather Alfred Burton was born near Guilford Court House in North Carolina, and died in Jasper County, Illinois.

George Burton, father of E. L. Burton, was born in Jasper County, Illinois, in 1841, and spent most of his early youth and manhood there. He enlisted from Illinois in the Seventy-ninth Illinois Infantry, and later was a member of the Ninety-seventh Regiment from that state. Altogether he served three years in the Union army, and among the various campaigns in which he participated was the siege of Mobile. After the war he returned to Illinois, continued farming for several years, but in 1870 moved out to Kansas and was one of the early homesteaders along the line of the Missouri, Kansas & Texas Railroad in Neosho County. He acquired 160 acres there, but subsequently sold that farm and moved to Montgomery County. He finally retired and has since lived at Hallowell in Cherokee County. He is a republican who has served as township trustee a number of terms and also as justice of the peace. He was a member of the board of managers of the Soldiers Home at Dodge City during Governor Stanley's administration and a part of Governor Bailey's term. He has been an active minister of the Christian Church for the past thirty years, having performed those duties in addition to his work as a farmer and his duties as a citizen. He also belongs to the Masonic fraternity. George Burton married Elizabeth Harris, who was born in Jasper County, Illinois, in 1842, and died in Cherokee County, Kansas, in 1901. Of their five children four died in childhood.

Ellsworth L. Burton, the only living child of his parents, was educated in the district schools of Neosho, Montgomery and Cherokee counties. He also attended for a year and a half the old Kansas Normal College at Fort Scott when Professor Sanders was its president and owner. On leaving normal school in 1887 Mr. Burton engaged in the abstract business, and for three years carried on the study of law at Columbus, Kansas. Admitted to the bar in 1890 he has now been in active practice for more than a quarter of a century. For two years he practiced at Columbus, one year at Scammon, and from 1894 to 1907 had his home and offices in Oswego. Since 1907 he has practiced at Parsons and from that city conducts a large civil and criminal practice. His offices are in the White Building.

Besides his law practice Mr. Burton is a stockholder and one of the directors of the Fidelity Coal and Mining Company and of the Fidelity Fuel Company. He served as city attorney while living at Columbus, Scammon, and Oswego, and for four years held the office of county attorney of Labette County. He is an active republican and was elected on the republican ticket to the House of Representatives in 1914. While in the Legislature he has served as a member of the judiciary committee, committee on labor, committee on mines and mining, and chairman of the committee on accounts and fiscal management. He is also a member of the Efficiency and Economy Committee of Kansas. Mr. Burton is an active member of the Kansas State Bar Association, and belongs to Parsons Lodge No. 606, Loyal Order of Moose.

In 1889 at Pittsburg, Kansas, he married Miss Abbie R. Thomas, daughter of F. M. and Elizabeth Thomas. Her mother is now deceased and her father is a farmer in Missouri. To the marriage of Mr. and Mrs. Burton were born five children. George F., the oldest, finished his education by a year and a half in the Kansas State University; read law with the firm of Glasse & Burton, and since his admission to the bar in January, 1913, has been in practice with his father. Elizabeth, still at home with her parents, is a graduate of the Parsons High School, and spent one year in the Kansas State University. Marion T. is a junior in the Parsons High School. Ruth has graduated from the high school and is still at home. Ellsworth L. is still pursuing his studies in the public schools.

FLOYD E. DOUBLEDAY. It has been the fortune of Floyd E. Doubleday to realize many of his worthy ambitions, and through the exercise of good judgment and business ability to wrest from his opportunities financial and general success. For many years he has been interested in the coal industry, and at the present time is accounted one of the leading operators of Pittsburg. Mr. Doubleday was born at Italy, New York, June 23, 1859, and is a son of Guy L. and Caroline (Hobart) Doubleday.

The Doubleday family is of English origin and traces its ancestry back in America to Colonial days, when the earliest ancestor came to Massachusetts. Elisha Doubleday, M. D., the grandfather of Floyd E. Doubleday, was born in 1800, near Binghampton, New York, practiced medicine and surgery all his life in the Empire State, and died at Italy, New York, in 1865. Guy L. Doubleday was born at Italy, in 1827, and as a young man selected the profession of his father for his life work. He secured his degree from the Geneva College of Physicians and Surgeons, and continued in practice throughout his life, dying in 1870, at Italy. He was one of the most prominent men of his community, was a leading democratic politician, and at the time of his death was serving as associate judge of Yates County, New York. He was a member of the Methodist Episcopal Church. Doctor Doubleday married Caroline Hobart, who was born in 1831 at Potter, New York, and died at Penn Yan, New York, in 1908, and they were the parents of four children: Elisha, who died at the age of six months; Leander L., who came to Kansas in 1874 and lived at Columbus until 1898, where he was a banker, then went to Racine and Milwaukee and engaged in the real estate and investment business for twelve years, and finally located at Kansas City, Missouri, where he died in February, 1914; Floyd E.; and Charles E., a graduate of the Syracuse University medical department, and now a practicing physician and surgeon at Penn Yan, New York.

Floyd E. Doubleday was educated in the public schools of Yates County, New York, and the high school at Penn Yan, from the latter of which he was graduated in 1874. Two years later he came as a pioneer to Columbus, Kansas, where he secured a position in a bank and remained thus employed for four years, at that time going to Neodesha, where he was identified with a milling company for two years. Mr. Doubleday received his introduction to the coal business at Litchfield, Crawford County, Kansas, in 1882, and remained there seven years, in 1889 coming to Pittsburg, where he continued in business until 1901 as superintendent and general manager of a number of coal companies. In 1901 he removed to Lawrence, in order to give his children better educational advantages, and in 1908 went to Kansas City, Missouri, where he made his home until 1912. He then returned to Pittsburg, where he has since continued as an operator, being the owner of a mine near Arcadia, in Crawford County. Mr. Doubleday's home is at No. 708 West Euclid Avenue. He is a republican, and in fraternal affairs is affiliated with Pittsburg Lodge No. 187, Ancient Free and Accepted Masons; Pittsburg Chapter No. 58, Royal Arch Masons; Pittsburg Commandery No. 29, Knights Templar; the Ancient Order of United Workmen and the Modern Woodmen of America.

In 1880 Mr. Doubleday was married at Columbus, Kansas, to Miss Elizabeth Phelps, daughter of the late George H. and Celina (Carse) Phelps. Mr. Phelps was a well known attorney of Columbus, and Mrs. Phelps, who survives him, makes her home with her daughter and son-in-law. Mr. and Mrs. Doubleday have three children: Darlene, who resides with her parents and has one child, Elizabeth, born October 3, 1909; Carolina, who is the wife of Robert D. Yates, connected with the Underwood Typewriter Company, of Kansas City, Missouri; and Floyd E., Jr., a graduate of the Lawrence High School, who finished the junior year in engineering at Kansas University and is now engaged in business with his father. Floyd E. Doubleday, Jr., married Miss Alice Wilhelmi, and they have four children: Alice, born December 31, 1910; Floyd E. III, born May 8, 1912; Charles, born September 23, 1913; and Max, born May 18, 1915.

ARTHUR A. HUGHART. The life work of Arthur A. Hughart has been in the educational field. In his native state of Indiana he gained more than a local reputation as an able schoolman, not only as an individual teacher but as a school executive, and it was from that field he was called to the superintendency of the city school of Coffeyville in 1912. Here his influence has been of the greatest value. He has thoroughly reorganized and systematized the work of the city school system, has introduced some new departments and methods, and has made the local schools an object of pride to all citizens.

Born on a farm in Center Township, Porter County, Indiana, August 12, 1864, Arthur Abram Hughart is a son of William A. and Mary (Fulton) Hughart and a grandson of David Hughart. David Hughart, who was of German lineage, and of an old colonial family in Virginia, was born in that state and in 1835 came west and located as a pioneer in Porter County, Indiana. He secured government land in Liberty Township, and in the course of many years of toil and industry made it a fine farm. In 1860 he moved from the farm to Valparaiso, where he was engaged in the buying and shipping of grain. He was a successful business man and a public spirited citizen. He died in Porter County, Indiana, at the venerable age of eighty-nine years.

William A. Hughart, father of Professor Hughart, was born in Westmoreland County, Virginia, June 28, 1830, and was five years of age when brought to Porter County, Indiana. He grew up in that section of Northwest Indiana, attended some of the pioneer schools, and gave his active career to agriculture. He died September 4, 1912. His wife, Miss Fulton, was born in Pennsylvania, a daughter of Abram and Jane (Turner) Fulton. The Fulton family moved to Indiana about 1840, establishing a home in La-Porte County, where Mary Fulton grew to womanhood. She was a woman of fine character, and had a great influence over her children during their youth. She died in 1907 at the age of eighty-three. Of her four children only two reached maturity, the daughter being Ruth, wife of Samuel E. Collins, a building contractor at Valparaiso, Indiana.

The early life of Arthur A. Hughart was spent on a farm. With growing stature and increasing strength he found ample employment in farm duties, and in the meantime attended the district schools. In 1889 he graduated from the Valparaiso High School, and at the age of twenty did his first work as a teacher in one of the district schools of his native county. At an early age he learned to depend upon himself, and he gained his higher education largely through his earnings as a teacher and farm worker. After a thorough four years' course he was graduated in 1893 A. B. from Wabash College at Crawfordsville, Indiana.

On leaving college Mr. Hughart became principal of the public school at Hebron in Porter County, Indiana, and remained there two years. It was his reputation as a successful principal and able schoolman that brought about in 1895 his election as county superintendent of Porter County. For seven years Mr. Hughart filled that position, and in that connection showed the ability for systematic and efficient organization as the management of schools to the best interests of all concerned that have since been his chief characteristics in educational work.

On leaving the office of county superintendent in 1902 he was elected superintendent of the public school system of Valparaiso, Indiana. There he had a large force of teachers and many schools under his direction, and the ten years of his superintendency are still bearing fruit in that progressive Northern Indiana city.

In August, 1912, Professor Hughart came to Coffeyville to accept the superintendency of the city schools, and he now has under his supervision nine schoolhouses, a faculty of ninety-six teachers and an enrollment of 3,500 scholars. Professor Hughart has the faculty of imparting his enthusiasm to all his subordinates, and during the past four years has worked constantly to the ideal of making the city school system an efficient factor in the training of an army of children for their life service.

Under his administration have been established departments for kindergarten and applied arts work in the grades, and at the same time he has gradually broadened and raised the general standards of the city schools. He has secured effective cooperation among his staff of teachers, and has done much to inspire them with the necessity of continued application to the best ideals of the teaching profession. As a result an increasing number of local teachers have been attending the State Normal Schools of Kansas during the summer vacations and working for life certificates in the profession.

Politically Professor Hughart is a republican. He is affiliated with Keystone Lodge No. 102, Ancient Free and Accepted Masons, Coffeyville Chapter No. 89, Royal Arch Masons; Lochinvar Commandery No. 52, Knights Templar, with the council degrees of Masonry at Valparaiso, and with Valparaiso Order of the Eastern Star. During his residence in Valparaiso, Indiana, he served as a trustee of the public library, and has been a member of the Carnegie Library Board at Coffeyville. He is active in the Southeastern Kansas Teachers' Association, which he served in 1914 as president, and in 1915 as chairman of the executive committee. He is a member of the Schoolmasters' Club of the State of Kansas. A working member and elder of the Presbyterian Church, he has charge of the Business Men's Sunday School Class, and his wife is also closely associated with him in his church interests.

August 16, 1893, Mr. Hughart married Miss Ruth Talbortt. Mrs. Hughart died in 1897, leaving one daughter, Lyal, who is now living in the home of her grandparents at Valparaiso. September 26, 1901, Mr. Hughart married Miss Grace Louderback, daughter of John S. Louderback, of Porter County, Indiana. Mr. and Mrs. Hughart have two children: Esther, a freshman in the Coffeyville High School; and Jane.

LEWIS C. NELSON. The large industries in and about Coffeyville have naturally drawn to that city many of the expert technical men as well as business executives, and one of these is Lewis C. Nelson, superintendent of the Ludowici-Celadon Company, manufacturers of hollow roofing tile. Mr. Nelson as a young man became an expert wood worker, later developed a proficiency and familiarity with the pottery industry and for a number of years has been one of the trusted officials of the present company.

His birth occurred in Glasgow, Scotland, July 15, 1871. His father Charles W. Nelson, who was born in the vicinity of Glasgow in 1842 was a weaver in the woolen mills, and died at Glasgow in 1884. He was a conservative in politics and an active member of the Episcopal Church. He received military training as a soldier in the English army. Charles W. Nelson married Ida Froley, who was born near Glasgow in 1847 and died there in 1877.

L. C. Nelson, the only child of his parents, was six years old when his mother died, and thereafter he received a rudimentary training in the public schools of Glasgow. At the age of twelve he was brought to the United States by his uncle John Nelson, who established his home at Boston. Since that time Mr. Nelson has been largely dependent upon his own resources for advancement. For two years he found such work as was fitted for his strength and ability in Boston, and he then began an apprenticeship in ornamental wood carving and modeling. He served a five year's apprenticeship at Boston, and continued with the same firm until he was twenty-one. In the

meantime he had supplemented his early education by courses in the night schools, particularly in drawing and other technical subjects.

As a journeyman worker Mr. Nelson went to St. Louis in 1892. During that and the following year he also followed his trade at Chicago when the World's Fair was in progress, and alternated back and forth between those two cities for six years. In 1898 he moved to Chicago, and spent a year in the Pullman car shops.

In 1899 his services were called to Zanesville, Ohio, as a modeller and designer in the potteries around that city. He spent two years there, and in 1902 became identified with the roofing tile business as a pattern maker. His first employment in that line was at New Lexington, Ohio, and he was soon promoted to foreman of the shops and continued there until 1909. In that year he was transferred to Ludowici, Georgia, as superintendent of the company's plant for two years. In January, 1911, the company sent him to Coffeyville as superintendent of the Ludowici-Celadon Company. The Coffeyville plant of this well known concern is located in the southwest corner of the city. Its output is exclusively roofing tile. At the present time the company operates two plants, one at Coffeyville and one at New Lexington, Ohio, having abandoned the plant at Ludowici, Georgia. The company officials, all Chicago men, are: A. W. Brown, president; J. M. Williams, vice president; C. C. Weiland, secretary; and R. C. Sturdevant, treasurer.

Mr. Nelson since coming to Coffeyville has become one of the genial and popular citizens of that town. He is a member of the Business Men's Accident Association, and is a republican and a member of the Episcopal Church, and fraternally is affiliated with Coffeyville Lodge, No. 775, Benevolent and Protective Order of Elks, with Lodge No. 250, Free and Accepted Masons at New Lexington, Ohio, Charter No. 149, Royal Arch Masons, and Lochinvar Commandery, No. 52, Knights Templar, at Coffeyville.

In 1898 at St. Louis he married Miss Lillian Stanton, daughter of Charles and Catherine (Burgoon) Stanton. Both her parents are now deceased and her father was a carpenter and builder. Mr. and Mrs. Nelson have four children: William S., born in Chicago, April 16, 1900, and now a sophomore in the Coffeyville High School; Virginia, born in March, 1903, at New Lexington, Ohio, and a pupil in the public schools; Mildred, born in November, 1906, at New Lexington, Ohio, and also in school; Louise, born June 19, 1909, at New Lexington and now in the primary grades of the Coffeyville schools.

THE PITTSBURG SASH & DOOR COMPANY. One of the very considerable industries of the City of Pittsburg is The Pittsburg Sash & Door Company, which like many successful concerns had a very modest beginning but is now contributing a great deal of wealth to the city and is furnishing support to many families whose members find employment there. This business was originally started as a hay press by L. N. Mosteller, now a retired business man of Pittsburg.

In October, 1902, Henry R. Ransom arrived in Pittsburg and bought what was then known as the Pittsburg Planing Mill, situated at Fourth and Grand Avenue. Since then the business has been under the direction of the Ransom family, and during the past year its business has been so voluminous that its payroll amounts to $15,000. It has prospered and expanded continuously during the fifteen years since Henry R. Ransom took charge of the industry.

The Ransoms were a colonial English family that

settled first in Virginia. Later they lived in New York State. S. S. Ransom was born at Perrysburg, New York, and is still living now retired at Pittsburh, Pennsylvania. He was reared and married in Perrysburg, New York, and was for many years a traveling salesman. S. S. Ransom married Jennie Strickland, who was born in Ellinsville, Warren County, Pennsylvania.

Henry R. Ransom, head of The Pittsburg Sash & Door Company, is the only child of the above parents. He was born at Perrysburg in Cattaraugus County, New York, March 27, 1870. He received his early education in the public schools of Warren County, Pennsylvania, but at the age of sixteen left school to take up the carpenter's trade. He became a contractor and builder, and began contracting at the age of nineteen. For five years he was in that line of business at St. Louis, a similar time at Carthage, Missouri, and while there was connected with the Carthage Sash and Door Factory. From Southwestern Missouri he moved to Kansas in October, 1902, and bought the industry at Pittsburg which he has since conducted with such notable success. Henry R. Ransom is an active republican and a member of the Methodist Episcopal Church.

On June 17, 1891, at Jamestown, New York, Henry R. Ransom married Miss Gertie N. Kilbourn. The Kilbourn family is of very old American stock. The first of the name came from Wood Ditton, England, to Weathersfield, Connecticut, as early as 1635. The original American ancestor had several children. The great-grandfather of Gertie N. Kilbourn was Robins Kilbourn, who was a minister in Connecticut, and in 1835 moved to Cherry Creek, New York, where he died. He was the father of Mrs. Remmington, who had her home in Ilion, New York; William R.; and several other children not now recalled.

William Robert Kilbourn, grandfather of Mrs. Henry R. Ransom, was born in Connecticut in 1800, and in young manhood moved to Cherry Creek, New York, where he married and where in 1824 he built the first sawmill. He followed that business for many years. He was quite influential in that locality and besides his business connections was an active church member, served as supervisor in 1841-43 and was a leading whig. He died at Cherry Creek in 1875. William R. Kilbourn married Lydia King. who was born in Rhode Island in 1801 and died at Cherry Creek, New York, in 1884. Her parents came to Cherry Creek when she was young, and her father was one of the original purchasers of town lots there. William R. Kilbourn and wife had the following children: William Robert, who was born in Cherry Creek in 1826 and died there in 1883, having followed his father's occupation and never married; Hiram, mentioned below; Mary, who was born at Cherry Creek and died at Watrous, New Mexico, in 1902, the wife of O. A. Hadley, who was at one time governor of the State of Arkansas, owned extensive ranch interests in New Mexico and died at Pasadena, California, in 1915; Mrs. Carr, wife of a farmer at Cherry Creek, where she died; Norman, who was born at Cherry Creek and spent his last years as a farmer in Minnesota; Elisha, who died at his native Town of Cherry Creek in 1892, having been identified with farming and the milling industry; Leonard, who was born at Cherry Creek and died on his farm in Minnesota; Benjamin, who spent his brief life in Cherry Creek.

Hiram Kilbourn, father of Mrs. Henry R. Ransom, was born in Cherry Creek, New York, in 1827, and died in Pittsburg, Kansas, in 1909. He was reared in his native town and his early experiences in business affairs were in conducting a planing mill and in managing a farm. He finally moved west to Waterloo, Iowa, where he was in the millwright business, and in 1869 came as a very early pioneer into Crawford County, Kansas. He took up and farmed a homestead of a quarter section, but in 1875 returned to his native village in New York and resumed business as a sawmiller and chair manufacturer. In 1886 he retired to Jamestown, New York, but in 1902 returned to Pittsburg, Kansas, where he lived until his death. Hiram Kilbourn was an active republican, a member of the Methodist Episcopal Church and the Masonic fraternity. He made a creditable record in the Civil war. In 1862 he enlisted in Company G of the Ninth Iowa Infantry, and was in service practically three years. In the North Georgia campaign he was wounded at Ringgold, and was incapacitated and the war closed before he was fit for service. Hiram Kilbourn married for his first wife Miss Carr, and her children were: Robert, who is a wagon maker at Carthage, Missouri; Mary, who died in Washington Township of Crawford County, Kansas, in 1870. For his second wife Hiram Kilbourn married Hulda Shirley, who was born near Rockford, Illinois, November 15, 1848, grew up there on a farm, and is now living at Pittsburg, Kansas. She is an active member of the Methodist Church and belongs to the Woman's Relief Corps. Her children are: Minnie L., who died at Jamestown, New York, in 1893, the wife of Angus McKenzie, who is still living at Jamestown; Mrs. Henry R. Ransom.

Gertie N. Kilbourn, wife of Henry R. Ransom, was born in Washington Township of Crawford County, Kansas, a mile north of Frontenac, on March 8, 1872. Thus she has the distinction of having been one of the early white children born in this new country of Southeastern Kansas. While she was still an infant her parents returned to Jamestown, New York, where she was reared, attending the grammar and high schools there. She is a regular attendant and a generous supporter of the Methodist Church.

Henry R. Ransom and wife are the parents of three children. Raymond R. was born June 29, 1892, in Jamestown, New York, but has lived in Pittsburg, Kansas, since he was ten years of age; he graduated from the high school in 1909 and then continued his higher education in Baker University, from which he received the degree A. B. in 1913; he is now actively associated with his father in The Pittsburg Sash & Door Company. On December 28, 1913, Raymond R. Ransom married Miss Beatrice Fast, a daughter of Mr. and Mrs. J. C. Fast of Hutchinson, Kansas.

Paul, the second child of Henry R. Ransom and wife, was born in St. Louis, Missouri, December 27, 1896. was graduated from the Pittsburg High School in 1913, and is now a sophomore in the electrical engineering department of the Carnegie Institute of Technology at Pittsburgh, Pennsylvania. Donald, the youngest child, was born in Carthage, Missouri, December 24, 1900, and is now a student in the State Manual Training Normal School at Pittsburg, Kansas.

CLAUDE EMMETT HAMILL, M. D. The first thirty-two years of his life Doctor Hamill spent in gaining a liberal education and in successfully following the industry of farming. His ambition was always fixed on medicine, but various business interests contrived to keep the goal distant until some six or seven years ago. Since 1910 he has been in active practice at Parsons and enjoys a splendid reputation as physician and surgeon.

C. E. Hamill M. D.

His name represents an old and honored family in Kansas. His paternal ancestry goes back to Ireland, where his grandfather, Samuel Wallace Hamill, was born at Dublin in 1776. He came to this country before his marriage, lived a year in New York City, and then went to Cadiz, Ohio, where he spent the rest of his life as a farmer and died in 1872. He married a Miss Graham, who was also a native of Ireland. She died at Cadiz, Ohio, in 1878, at the age of eighty-four. Doctor Hamill's maternal grandfather was John Gallagher, also a native of Ireland. He was a painter and decorator by trade, and came to Kansas after a youth spent in Pittsburg, Pennsylvania. He died at Willow Springs, Kansas, and is buried in Baldwin City, of this state. John Gallagher married Miss Elizabeth Ross, who was born in Scotland and died at Overbrook, Kansas.

Dr. Claude Emmett Hamill was born in Fredonia, Kansas, January 10, 1877. His father, Robert Emmett Hamill, was born at Cadiz, Ohio, in 1838, grew up in Ohio and was one of five brothers, all of whom served in the Civil war in the Union army and one was killed while in service. As a young man Robert Emmett Hamill enlisted in the fall of 1862 for service in the 126th Ohio Infantry. He was in the Union army three years four months. At first he was in the Army of the Tennessee and took part in the great battle of Shiloh. Afterwards he was with the Army of the Potomac and among the more important battles in which he participated were those of Fredericksburg, Cold Harbor, the Battle of the Wilderness, where he was wounded in the abdomen, and was almost constantly on duty until he received his honorable discharge. He as well as his wife were highly educated people considering the time and circumstances in which they were reared. After the war Robert E. Hamill returned to Ohio and completed his education in an academy. For a time he taught school in Illinois at $50 a month, and in 1870 arrived in Kansas. His first settlement was fourteen miles south of Lawrence, where he was engaged to teach a school. He then took up a homestead of 160 acres seven miles from Eldorado at Quito in Butler County. He conducted a general store while proving up his claim. His next removal came in 1876 to Fredonia, Kansas, where he paid $700 for a claim of 160 acres under the pre-emption law, and lived on it six months to prove his title. It was during the six months residence on that claim that Dr. Claude Emmett Hamill was born on January 10, 1877. His birth occurred in a log cabin, his parents residing in a humble home while proving up his claim. All the other children were born in more comfortable houses. Robert E. Hamill next returned to Butler County, where he built a store and was in the mercantile business until the fall of 1880. He then bought 124 acres of land in Douglas County, lived there until the spring of 1884 and moved to his last home, a farm seven miles southeast of Lawrence, where he died September 9, 1884. He is buried at Baldwin City, Kansas. He was a very successful man as the above outline of his enterprises suggest and left a large estate. His widow still owns 620 acres of land in Kansas, including 280 acres in Douglas County, 160 acres in Cherokee County, and 180 acres in McClain, Oklahoma. Robert E. Hamill was a republican and a member of the Methodist Episcopal Church. His wife, Susan Matilda (Gallagher) Hamill, was born at Pittsburg, Pennsylvania, April 14, 1844, completed her education in a college at Pittsburg, and for five years was a teacher prior to her marriage. She is now living on her farm eight and a half miles southwest of Lawrence. Her children

were: Lillian B., who died unmarried at Lawrence August 7, 1892; Bertrand D., who looks after his mother's farm and resides with her, though he is well equipped for the profession of law, being a graduate of the Kansas University Law School; Dr. Claude Emmett, who was the third in age; Estella, who died at the age of one year; and Robert Sylvester, who died in the spring of 1885 at the age of nine months.

Doctor Hamill received his early education in the public schools southwest of Lawrence, and graduated from the high school of that city May 15, 1893. He was with the first class in the high school that took the subject of plane and solid geometry. The year 1893-94 was spent in the Kansas State University. After being out of school a year he resumed his studies and was graduated in the classical course with the degree Bachelor of Arts June 7, 1898.

On leaving college Doctor Hamill spent a year on the farm in Wilson County, made a number of improvements during that time, and then sold. The next spring he went to live on his father's old place in Douglas County and was a farmer there two years. Chartering two cars, he moved his live stock and other goods to the 160 acre farm which he had bought east of Columbus, Kansas. His family still owns that place. About that time he was first able to lay out his plans for a medical training. He spent one term in the preparatory department of the medical school of the Kansas State Medical College, but then gave up his studies and bought a farm he still owns near Kansas, and was engaged in its active management for three years. He then entered the medical department of the Kansas State University but took his last two years in the Northwestern University Medical School at Chicago, where he graduated Doctor of Medicine in 1909. After a year of hospital training in the Wesleyan Memorial Hospital of Chicago he returned to Kansas and in the spring of 1910 opened his office at Parsons. His offices are at 1805½ Main Street and he has a very satisfactory general practice in medicine and surgery. He is a member of the Labette County, Kansas State and Southeastern Medical societies and the American Medical Association.

Doctor Hamill is an independent republican in politics, belongs to the Presbyterian Church and fraternally is affiliated with Camp No. 14, Woodmen of the World at Parsons, New Ideal Council No. 1881 of the Knights and Ladies of Security, the Mystic Workers of the World, the Sons and Daughters of Justice, the National Americans, and is a member of the Parsons Chamber of Commerce. Doctor Hamill is unmarried.

CHARLES S. DENISON. The ordinary, every-day man, engrossed in the business avocation which brings his daily bread, is representative of the nation's citizenship. This is the normal type, and his life begins and ends, perhaps, with nothing more distinctive than is the ripple on the face of the stream when the pebble is thrown into the water. It is the unusual type that commands attention and it is his influence exerted on his community, and the record of his life, that is valuable and interesting as a matter of biography. In the professions, and especially in the law, the opportunities for usefulness and personal advancement depend almost entirely upon this unusually gifted individual, and here natural endowment is as essential as is thorough preparation. The bar of Crawford County is a representative body of Kansas and as such has its full quota of brilliant men,

included among whom may be mentioned Charles S.
Denison, why by inheritance, education, predilection
and thorough training, is fitted to take his place among
the leading members of his calling.

Charles S. Denison, who has been practicing at the
bar of Pittsburg since 1909, was born at the Osage
Mission, Saint Paul, Kansas, August 28, 1878, and
is of Scotch and German descent, the Denisons having
come from Scotland to Pennsylvania prior to the
Revolutionary war. His grandfather, David Denison,
was born in the Keystone State, where he was a millwright, and later in life also followed that vocation in
Illinois, where his death occurred at Sterling, in 1887.
The father of Charles S. Denison, J. L. Denison, was
born in 1837, in Westmoreland County, Pennsylvania,
and was there reared and received his early education, being graduated from the academy at Chambers-
burg. Subsequently he studied for the law at Princeton, Illinois, and in 1859 came to Kansas and settled
at Iola as a pioneer attorney. While residing there
he enlisted in the Ninth Kansas Cavalry, and served
throughout the Civil war, along the Arkansas and
White Rivers, and was once slightly wounded. He
then returned to Iola, but in 1866 went to old Erie,
now two and one-half miles east of Erie, where he
established a trading post and conducted it from that
year until 1876, then going to the Osage Mission,
where he resumed the practice of his profession. He
rose to a high place among the lawyers of his county,
and from 1889 until 1908 was attorney for the Santa
Fe Railroad. He died at Kansas City, Missouri,
August 14, 1908, but was laid to rest at Erie, Kansas. A republican in his political views, Mr. Denison was county attorney of Neosho County for eight
years. He was a member of the Presbyterian Church.
In fraternal circles he was particularly well known,
having been the organizer of the first Blue Lodge of
Masons at Humboldt, Kansas; organized and installed
the first Commandery, Knights Templar, at Oswego,
which has since been removed to Parsons; organized
the Commandery at Osage Mission, which has since
been transferred to Chanute; and organized the first
Chapter in Southeastern Kansas, which was removed
to Chanute. He was a life member in each of these,
and was also a member of the Benevolent and Protective Order of Elks. Mr. Denison married Miss
Martha Hoagland, who was born in 1845, in Wyandotte County, Ohio, and now resides at Erie, Kansas,
and they had three children: Anna, who is unmarried
and resides at Erie; Charles S.; and Todd, who is
employed by the Burroughs Adding Machine Company at Oklahoma City, Oklahoma.

Charles S. Denison received his education in the
public schools of Erie, where he was graduated from
the high school in 1896, and then entered the law
office of his father. He was admitted to the bar in
1902 and engaged in practice at Erie, where he
remained until 1909, in that year coming to Pittsburg. He has been successful in building up a large
general practice and has been connected with some
important litigation in the state courts. His offices
are located at 301 to 305 Commerce Building. While
at Erie, Mr. Denison was district attorney for the
Santa Fe Railroad and local attorney for the Missouri, Kansas and Texas Railway from 1905 to 1909.
He is a republican, but has never sought public office.
His professional connections are with the Crawford
County, Kansas State and American Bar associations.
His home is at No. 603 West Third Street.

On January 21, 1915, at Girard, Kansas, Mr. Denison was united in marriage with Miss Thora Kiehl,
daughter of Chris and Rosa (Baker) Kiehl, residents

of Franklin, Kansas, where Mr. Kiehl is master
mechanic for the Western Coal and Mining Company.

GEORGE WASHINGTON WINGATE. The career of
George Washington Wingate, of Liberty, Kansas,
is an expression of practical and diversified activity,
and in its range has invaded the fields of agriculture,
business, finance, education, politics and society, all
of which have profited by the breadth and conscientiousness which are characteristic of the man
and his work. As a business man he developed
several enterprises into paying ventures, as a banker
he has made an honorable place for himself, in public
life his services have been of exceeding value to his
community, and as a member of society he has constantly endeavored to promote movements for the
advancement of education, morality and good citizenship.

Mr. Wingate was born in Sussex County, Delaware, August 30, 1861, and is a son of Stansbury
Jacob and Annie (Berry) Wingate, and a member of
a family which, originating in England, settled in
Delaware in colonial days. Stansbury Jacob Wingate was born in 1825, in Delaware, was reared and
educated in that state, and was married in Sussex
County, Delaware. In young manhood, he learned
the trade of wagonmaking, and in following that
vocation traveled extensively, gradually following
the tide of civilization to the West as each new
community became more thickly settled. In February, 1862, not long after the birth of George W.
Wingate, he went with his family to Moultrie
County, Illinois, subsequently removing to Macon
County, in the same state, and locating at Decatur.
There he remained until the spring of 1870, when he
went to Illiopolis, Illinois, that community being his
home for three years or until his removal to Berry
Station, Christian County, Illinois, a community in
which he resided and worked at his trade for two
years. His next stop was at Edinburg, Illinois,
and in the spring of 1875 he gave up his trade as a
regular vocation and located on a farm in Christian
County, which he cultivated during the years 1875
and 1876. On January 19, 1877, he arrived at Independence, Kansas, and in the following February
moved on to Liberty Township, Montgomery
County, where he located on a farm. Thus located
on a good farm, in a fertile section of the state, he
gave up his roving and settled down to hard work
in cultivating his fields. He became, through industry and perseverance and the well-directed use of
his natural talents, one of the substantial men of his
community, and well deserved the respect in which
he was held by his fellow citizens. His death
occurred on his farm April 10, 1895, when his community lost one of its good citizens. He was a
democrat in political belief, a member of the Independent Order of Odd Fellows, and an active worker
in the Methodist Episcopal Church, in which he
served as deacon. By his first marriage, to a Miss
Adams, he had one son: Charles H., who adopted
the trade of miller and followed that vocation until
his death at Chicago, Illinois, in 1893. Mr Wingate
was married second to Annie Berry, who was born in
Delaware in 1838, and died in Liberty Township, in
April, 1894. They had five children, as follows:
W. B., who was for many years engaged in the hotel
business and died at Coffeyville, Kansas, in February, 1908; George Washington, of this review; Isaac,
who died in infancy, at Decatur, Illinois; Alice, who
is the wife of W. R. Phillips, a farmer of Alberta,

Canada; and C. H., who is engaged in farming in the same locality.

George W. Wingate began his education in the schools of Illinois, attending the district schools in the various communities in which the family lived. He completed his training in Montgomery County, Kansas, and here came to man's estate on his father's farm. Shortly after attaining his majority, in 1883, he engaged in farming on his own account, continuing to be engaged therein until the spring of 1889, his operations being centered in Montgomery County. At the time mentioned he turned his attention to buying and shipping stock, a business which he followed successfully at Liberty for one year and at Cherryvale for two years, and at the end of that time went to Coffeyville, where he engaged in the hotel and restaurant business. This enterprise he conducted for two years and then returned to the homestead to care for his aged parents in their declining years, remaining with them and looking after their every want as long as they lived. In 1901 Mr. Wingate had his first experience in mercantile affairs when he assumed by purchase the ownership of the hardware and implement business formerly owned by William Heckman, at Liberty. Here, as elsewhere, he made a success, conducting the business for a period of eleven years and then selling out. In the spring of 1912 he rounded and closed up his business connections.

In February, 1913, Postmaster W. P. Livingston died and in the following May Mr. Wingate was appointed under the civil service laws to fill the vacancy and since that time has been faithfully and capably discharging the duties of that office, giving the people of Liberty and the surrounding community an excellent mail service. In addition he is serving as city clerk of Liberty, another office in which he is displaying executive ability of a high order. In fact, a large part of Mr. Wingate's time in recent years has been devoted to the public service, for he was a member of the school board for fifteen years, a justice of the peace for six years and mayor for one term. Politically, he is a democrat. Mr. Wingate was one of the chief promoters and organizers of the State Bank of Liberty, which was organized in 1904, and of which he is assistant cashier and a director, having missed but one directors' meeting from the time of the bank's inception. His foresight and judgment as a business man have been very valuable in the development of this organization and in putting it in a substantial place in public confidence and financial reputation. In addition to his residence on Fourth Street, Liberty, Mr. Wingate is the owner of a three-story brick business building on Union Street, Coffeyville. Public enterprises promising to be of benefit to the city or county may always be sure of his support, for he has been a constant encourager of beneficial movements, and at present is a stockholder in the Montgomery County Fair Association. Fraternally, Mr. Wingate belongs to Lodge No. 279, Ancient Order of United Workmen, and to the North American Union.

On December 15, 1883, Mr. Wingate was married at Radical City, Montgomery County, Kansas, to Miss Ida M. Thornton, daughter of Mr. and Mrs. F. M. Thornton, the latter of whom died in 1877, while the former still survives and resides with his son-in-law, Mr. Wingate. Francis Marion Thornton was born in Smith County, Tennessee, December 10, 1827, and was three years of age when taken by his parents to Schuyler County, Illinois, where he was reared and lived until he had a family of three children. He then removed to Rome, Iowa, where he read medicine and began practice in Jefferson County, that state, continuing to be thus engaged until 1865. Prior to this time, for twelve years, he had been in the ministry. In 1865 he was drafted into the United States service as a soldier during the Civil war, and took up arms as a member of Company H, Fifteenth Regiment, Iowa Volunteer Infantry. With this organization he completed a service of nine months, and when he received his honorable discharge returned to Iowa, but in the spring of 1866 came to Kansas and located in Leavenworth County. Here he practiced until 1872 when he changed his field to Liberty Township, and built up a large practice for which he cared until his retirement in 1890. Doctor Thornton is independent in his political views, and has served as township trustee two terms and was a justice of the peace while in Leavenworth County. As doctor, citizen and public official, he has always commanded the highest respect of his fellow-citizens. He and his family are members of the Baptist Church. In 1851 Doctor Thornton was married to Miss Nancy Scott, of Schuyler County, Illinois, who died at Liberty, Kansas. They were the parents of eight children, as follows: Simeon, who is engaged in blacksmithing at Liberty; Martha, who died at Independence, Kansas, as the wife of R. Grant, who has been engaged in the lumber business at Kansas City and Chicago; Mary, who married first James Van Cleve, deceased, and second L. H. Clevenger, and resides at Hunter, Missouri, where Mr. Clevenger is a farmer; Louisa, who married Charles Kirwin, a retired farmer of Neodesha, Kansas; Ida M., who is now Mrs. Wingate; Abel H., who died aged eleven days; Curtis, who died aged four years; and Sherman Scott, who is a policeman at Coffeyville.

Mr. and Mrs. Wingate have been the parents of five children: Ralph, who is a traveling salesman for the Delaval Separator Company, and is superintendent of nine counties of Kansas, with his headquarters and residence at Parsons; Clarence, who is private secretary to the superintendent of the Prairie Oil and Gas Company of Tulsa, Oklahoma, and has his home there; Frankie, who died at the age of eighteen months; May, who died at the age of seven years; and Nell, who is a junior at the Parsons High School and resides with her parents.

HAMMOND R. HEAL is enrolled among the progressive young business men of Coffeyville, where he is secretary and treasurer of the Kansas Oil Refining Company. An Indiana man by birth, he grew up and received his education in that state, and has been a resident of Kansas the past twelve years. In that time he has acquitted himself creditably in every business and civic relation.

He comes of an old Pennsylvania family, the Heals having come from England and settled in that state during the colonial days. Mr. Heal was born at Marion, Grant County, Indiana, January 18, 1884. His father William E. Heal, who was born in Indiana in 1856, served as county treasurer of Grant County, and in 1902 moved to Kansas, being connected with the Sunflower Glass Company of Coffeyville for a number of years. Since 1910 his home has been in Washington, D. C., where he is in the government service. He is a standpat republican and a member of the Methodist Episcopal Church. William E. Heal married Nancy E. Parrill, who was born in Grant County, Indiana, in 1850 and died at Marion in that county in 1905. Her children were: Orion B., who is district manager for the S. H. Kress Company at Chattanooga, Tennessee; Hammond R.; Elva, wife of C. C. Blue, district agent of the Gypsie Oil Company at Cleveland, Oklahoma; and Jessie, wife of C. A. King, who is connected with the Alluwee Oil Company at Coffeyville.

Educated in the public schools of Grant County, Indiana, and graduating from the Marion High School in 1903, H. R. Heal after another vear spent in the Marion Normal College came to Coffeyville in 1904. For a year and a half he was connected with the Sunflower Glass Company, and then spent two years with the Western Window Glass Company at Independence. Following that he was with the Coffeyville Window Glass Company until the winter of 1912, when he severed his connection and identified himself with the Kansas Oil Refining Company, of which he is now secretary and treasurer. This plant, located in the south part of Coffeyville, has a maximum capacity of 2,000 barrels a day, and refines crude oil brought from the Oklahoma fields.

Politically Mr. Heal is an independent republican. He has no aspirations in the way of political honors. He is a member of the Methodist Episcopal Church, and is affiliated with Keystone Lodge, No. 102, Ancient Free and Accepted Masons, and Coffeyville Chapter, No. 89, Royal Arch Masons. He is one of the working members of the Coffeyville Commercial Club.

In 1907 at Tecumseh, Illinois, he married Miss Carrie Boles. Her father, A. S. Boles, now deceased, was a river pilot and boat man on the Mississippi River. Her mother now resides at Meredosia, Illinois. Mr. and Mrs. Heal have one daughter, Mildred, born July 26, 1906, and now a student in the Coffeyville public schools.

JOSEPH E. STONE. A resident of Montgomery County since 1870, Joseph E. Stone has long been one of the leading farmers and stockraisers of this part of the state, and since 1907 has been president of the Home National Bank of Caney, one of the most reliable and substantial financial institutions of the county. It is difficult to conceive of a more solid combination for the attainment of financial security than a bank founded upon the prosperity and landed values of such a rich agricultural country as Montgomery County. Mr. Stone is one of the largest stockholders in the bank and his status as a farmer and a citizen is typical of the material upon which it rests and which has made the institution of which he is the head illustrative of the best type of bank in a farming community—something founded upon a rock, which the speculations and the panics of the metropolis cannot affect.

Joseph E. Stone was born in Waldo County, Maine, July 26, 1842, and inherits the sterling New England qualities of character, as well as sturdy traits which come from Scotch-Irish progenitors. His paternal grandfather was Jonathan Stone, who was born in Massachusetts in 1771, and died in Waldo County, Maine, in 1856. He followed the sea for many years in his early life, but in later years settled down to farming in Maine and was so engaged at the time of his death. Jonathan Stone, father of Joseph E., was born in Maine and was reared to the life of an agriculturist, a vocation which he followed throughout his long and useful career. He married Sarah Stevens, also a native of the Pine Tree State, and they became the parents of the following children: Joseph E., of this review; Mary Elletta, the wife

of J. H. Freeman, who was connected with the schools of Aurora, Illinois, for many years as superintendent, and also was state superintendent of schools for some time, and now living in retirement at Aurora; Addie E., widow of the late Isaac Struble, who died in 1914, after a long and successful career in the law and in public life, having been for a number of years congressman from the Eleventh Congressional District of Iowa, while his widow now makes her home at Lamar, that state; and Jonathan, who died in 1914, at Vassalboro, Maine, after a career in farming.

Joseph E. Stone was reared in Maine, and when a boy attended the public schools of that state, being at one time a pupil of the late Hon. Nelson Dingley, the author of the famous Dingley Tariff Bill. When sixteen years of age he became a school teacher and for four years followed that vocation, his career as an educator being interrupted by the outbreak of the Civil war. In the latter part of the year 1862, Mr. Stone enlisted in Company B, Twenty-sixth Regiment, Maine Volunteer Infantry, but soon after his enlistment, with others, he was permitted to attend a military academy at Philadelphia, Pennsylvania, for three months, in order to prepare for and become an officer of colored troops in the Union service. After having successfully passed a test examination, he was commissioned second lieutenant, and as such went forward to the field of actual war service with the Forty-first Regiment, United States Colored Infantry. A few months later, he was promoted to the rank of first lieutenant of the same company, which had seen its first battle in the breastworks before Richmond, Virginia. Mr. Stone continued to serve in the Army of Virginia, Twenty-fifth Corps, and won a splendid war record, having been several times in command of his company. He won also an enviable reputation as a driller of recruits and soldiers, and equal distinction for courage, coolness and fidelity on the field of battle. He was present at Appomattox Courthouse when General Lee surrendered to General Grant, April 9, 1865, and in the following May, with his corps, was ordered to Texas, to protect the Rio Grande, or the border from trouble that might arise because of certain complications with Mexico. Later the command was ordered to Louisville, Kentucky, where its members were honorably discharged in December, 1865. Mr. Stone then returned to his Maine home, but in January, 1866, was commissioned first lieutenant of the One Hundred and Twenty-fifth Regiment, United States Colored Infantry, which was sent westward to contend with the hostile Indians of the great plains. The regiment proceeded to Fort McRey, New Mexico, and after a service of twenty months returned to Fort Leavenworth, Kansas, where it was mustered out of the United States service in November, 1867. Mr. Stone is familiarly known as "Captain" Stone, which title comes not from his Civil war service, but from being captain of a company of "Wide-Awakes" at Independence, Kansas.

After receiving his honorable discharge at Fort Leavenworth, Captain Stone again visited his parental home, but after a short stay returned to the West, early in 1868, and located at Lees Summit, Jackson County, Missouri, where he engaged in the commission business with a measure of success until 1870. In that year he removed to Caney, Kansas, and there embarked in farming, breaking the wild prairie land with an ox team and thus beginning what subsequently became a very successful business career. He has continued his farming activities up to the present time and for years has been extensively dealing in cattle, also raising large herds. He owns over 1,000 acres of valuable land and is a holder of interests in numerous enterprises of a business and financial character.

Since 1907 Mr. Stone has been president of the Home National Bank, which was incorporated as a national bank in 1900 and owns its own banking house at the corner of Fourth Avenue and State Street. The present officers of this institution are: Joseph E. Stone, president; G. T. Braden, vice president; Elmer Brown, cashier; and H. V. Bolinger, assistant cashier. The bank has a capital of $40,000 and a surplus of $5,000, and under the direction of Mr. Stone is increasing its deposits each year, and strengthening its reputation as a solid and trusted repository. Captain Stone's successful business career, due wholly to his own individual efforts, and the commendable interest he has taken in all movements for the general welfare and public interests of his community, have united to win for him the deserved respect and universal esteem of his fellow-citizens. He has materially contributed to the upbuilding of the flourishing City of Caney, where he has so long resided and where he has held various positions of honor and trust. He was one of the very first to take an active part in the securing of the glass factories for Caney and to support his interest by taking stock therein.

In politics, Mr. Stone is a "stand pat" republican and has taken a more than ordinarily active part in party affairs. In 1871 he was elected the first sheriff of Montgomery County, an office to which he was re-elected in 1873, and during the entire four years of his incumbency gave excellent service to the county. During the '70s and '80s he acted as a member of the local board of school directors, later was justice of the peace, and for seven years during President Roosevelt's administration held the office of postmaster. Fraternally, he belongs to the Ancient Order of United Workmen, No. 160, of Caney, and is known as the "father" of the Masonic order at Caney, belonging to Caney Lodge No. 324, Ancient Free and Accepted Masons, and to Keystone Chapter, Royal Arch Masons, of Independence, Kansas. The bank of which he is the directing head holds membership in the Kansas State Bankers Association and the American Bankers Association.

At Independence, Kansas, in 1874, Mr. Stone was united in marriage with Miss Anna Van Sandt, also a native of Missouri, who died in 1897. They became the parents of the following children: Arthur F., who is connected with the Ford Antomobile Company, and resides at Kansas City, Missouri; H. G., an employe of the Prairie Pipe Line Company, residing at Caney; Myrtle, of Fort Worth, Texas, wife of Sol Summerfield, a traveling man for a wholesale jewelry and notions house of St. Louis, Missouri; Roy M., of Fort Worth, Texas, connected with the wholesale and retail dry goods establishment of Stripling & Company; and Earl E., of East St. Louis, Illinois, chief auditor of the Western Weighing Association, a concern in which Armour, Swift and other large packers are interested.

HON. JAMES N. DUNBAR. As lawyer, judge, farmer and stockraiser, Judge Dunbar has long been one of the prominent citizens of Cherokee County, and has taken an active and valuable part in local affairs. It was the confidence felt by the people in his judgment and integrity as well as his sterling reputation as a lawyer that brought about his election to the district

bench, and his administration of that position has more than justified the expectations of those who supported him for the office.

Though most of his life has been spent in this section of Kansas, Judge Dunbar was born in McDonough County, Illinois, December 23, 1865. As one might expect from the name, the Dunbars are of Scotch ancestry. Members of this branch of the family immigrated from Scotland to Virginia in Colonial times. Judge Dunbar's grandfather Daniel Dunbar, who was born in Virginia, went as a young man over the mountains into Kentucky, was a farmer in that state for many years, and died there in 1866. For a time he served as a member of the Kentucky State Militia.

The father of Judge Dunbar was W. Dunbar, who was born in Kentucky in 1816, and died in Cherokee County, Kansas, in 1877. During his early life in Kentucky he married his first wife, took up farming there, afterward lived for ten years in Brown County, Illinois, and from there moved to McDonough County. In 1869 he came to Cherokee County, Kansas, and was here about the time the Indians left and the work of progress began under the dominion of the white race. He developed a good farm, and was a highly respected citizen of the county during the rest of his life. Politically he was a republican, and was a member of the Christian Church. By his first marriage he had four children: Cynthia, now deceased; Elizabeth; Elihu, deceased; and William D., also deceased. For his second wife W. Dunbar married Maria Louise Nardin, who was born in Columbus, Ohio, in 1826, and died in Cherokee County, Kansas, in 1886. She became the mother of five children, of whom Judge Dunbar is the youngest. Judge Dunbar's oldest brother, Walter C., was born in McDonough County, Illinois, November 2, 1857, has followed the trade of carpenter, and is now living in Tulsa County, Oklahoma. He is an active republican. For his first wife Walter Dunbar married Hattie Taylor, and their children were: Lulie A., who married W. N. Jordan, a farmer in Tulsa County, Oklahoma; Clifford A., an oil worker in Tulsa County; Mary C., wife of J. Miller, a farmer in the same county; Clyde, a farmer in Tulsa County; Zoa, wife of Frank McCabe, engaged in the oil business in Tulsa County; Blanche, wife of Claude Thorpe, an oil worker in that county; and J. N., also an oil worker in the same county. For his second wife Walter Dunbar married Linda Parker, who is also deceased, and she was the mother of Ernest, Pearl and Ruby, all of whom are living at home with their father. Walter Dunbar married for his present wife Mary K. McNeill. Judge Dunbar's oldest sister, Susie C., is the wife of W. A. LaMaster, a retired farmer in Cherokee County. The next sister, Lula J., is living at Brush, Morgan County, Colorado, the widow of Ed Brehrton, who was a farmer. David Dunbar, the other brother of Judge Dunbar, is a farmer in Cherokee County.

While growing up on a Cherokee County farm Judge Dunbar attended the local schools and furthered his literary training in the Columbus High School. The first twenty years of his life were spent on his father's farm, and then for a time he was engaged in teaching. He also had a course in the Sedalia Business College in Missouri, and was employed in various lines of work for several years. His ambition was finally concentrated upon the law, and his early studies were carried on in the office of Fred BaSom at Columbus. Since his admission to the bar in 1892, Judge Dunbar has carried on a large and profitable practice at Columbus. In 1901-2 he served as county attorney, and he was called to fill large responsibilities when, during 1909-10, he acted as assistant attorney general of Kansas. In 1914 came his election as judge of the District Court, and he has been intrusted with the responsibilities of this office since January, 1915. Judge Dunbar is a member of the Cherokee County and State Bar Association, and is recognized as one of the ablest lawyers of Southeastern Kansas.

He has never lost the keen interest in farming which he acquired when a youth, and his home is now on a stock farm of 160 acres located at the corporate limits of Columbus, on the west side of the city. He employs this farm for the raising of general crops and first-class live stock. In politics Judge Dunbar is a democrat.

In 1893, near Muskogee, then Indian Territory, now the State of Oklahoma, he married Miss Dradie McPhail, daughter of J. B. and Ellen Roger (Ball) McPhail. Her father is a farmer, and both parents now reside in Whatcom County, Washington.

Judge and Mrs. Dunbar take great pride in their fine family of five children. Noel, who was born October 2, 1895, is now completing his last year in the Cherokee County High School. Clare, born September 1, 1901, is in the Freshman class of the high school. Owen was born September 4, 1903, and Quinton was born July 18, 1905, and Dradie, on January 28, 1908, and all these younger children are also attending school.

FRED B. SKINNER has been in the lumber business for thirty years, a period constituting practically his entire adult life. Most of that time has been spent at Coffeyville and he is now sales manager of the National Sash and Door Company.

As to his ancestral record, he represents a colonial branch of the Skinner family that came from England to New York. His grandfather Joseph Skinner was born in New York State June 28, 1814, was reared there, afterwards went to Michigan as a pioneer, and was married in that state January 19, 1837, to Juliatte Bugbee, who was born July 5, 1811, in New York State. Joseph Skinner, who was a farmer, moved from Michigan into the western wilds of Nebraska, and finally retired from his farm and spent his last years in Kansas with his son James in Johnson County, where he died in 1875. His wife died in Nebraska April 4, 1864. A brief record of their children should be given. F. B., born January 15, 1838, served as a soldier in the Civil war, and is now a retired merchant at North Bend, Nebraska. Ellen J., born August 29, 1840, was married September 9, 1857, to William B. Gilson, a farmer at Salem, Oregon. Joseph A., born September 25, 1842, enlisted in the Union army from Nebraska, followed farming as his vocation and died in Southern California; January 18, 1868, he married Maggie McAlester, who is now living at Omaha, Nebraska. The fourth of the children was James L. Skinner, mentioned below. Charlotte A., born March 19, 1846, was married April 30, 1865, to George Lawrence, a farmer in Missouri, and she died in Nebraska.

James L. Skinner, father of the Coffeyville business man, was born in Cattaraugus County, New York, April 3, 1844. When he was fourteen years of age his parents went out to Nebraska in 1858. Nebraska was then a territory and almost unoccupied by white men west of the Missouri River. He grew up in the vicinity of Omaha, became a farmer, and homesteaded a claim of 160 acres. In 1871 he came from Nebraska to Kansas, and was one of the early settlers and farmers of Johnson County. From there in 1874 he moved to Coffeyville, and was likewise identified with the pioneer activities of that then frontier town. Fully forty years ago he engaged in the transfer business at Coffeyville and has conducted it ever since, having the old and reliable establishment of that kind in the city. Although a very young man at the time he enlisted from Nebraska for service in the Union army, and spent nine months in the closing scenes of the war, his service being on the Northwestern frontier against the Indians. He is a republican in politics. James L. Skinner owns his residence at 416 East Ninth Street and also has a small farm east of the city limits. On August 30, 1867, he married Elizabeth Newell, who was born at Amherst, Massachusetts, in 1847. Their children are: Fred B.; Julia, wife of W. H. Francis, superintendent of the Coffeyville Vitrified Brick Company, their home being at Cherryvale; Frank N., who is connected with the Coffeyville Furniture Company; Lela, who resides at Coffeyville, widow of Byron Ritter, who was for a number of years in the employ of the Union Pacific Railway at Omaha, Nebraska; Mrs. Addie Campbell, of Delaware, Oklahoma, her husband being an operator in the oil fields.

Mr. Fred B. Skinner was born at the home of his parents in Blair, Nebraska, October 8, 1868. He was too young to remember when the family came to Kansas and some of his first recollections are of the home at Coffeyville, where his father located when the son was about six years of age. He received his education in the public schools of Coffeyville, leaving school at the age of eighteen and soon after beginning his career as a lumberman. He has been connected with the lumber trade ever since, and since 1909 has been sales manager for local shipments with the National Sash and Door Company.

Many citizens of Coffeyville know Mr. Skinner best through his forceful administration of city affairs a few years ago in the office of mayor. He served as mayor in in 1908-09, and in that office left a very comprehensive program of civic improvement and betterment. He was a member of the city council several times, and for two terms was president of the Chamber of Commerce. During his administration $100,000 fund was raised by the Chamber of Commerce to provide for the location of substantial factories and other industries in the city. Mr. Skinner is a republican, is affiliated with Star Lodge No. 17 Independent Order of Odd Fellows, Lodge No. 775 Benevolent and Protective Order of Elks, both at Coffeyville.

In 1901 Mr. Skinner built his attractive home at 410 East Ninth Street. In 1893 he was married at Coffeyville to Miss Effie Peterson, who died in February, 1902. She was a daughter of A. F. and Jennie (St. John) Peterson and her parents live on a farm northeast of Coffeyville. Mr. and Mrs. Skinner had one son, Jesse Leroy, who was born November 17, 1894, was graduated from the Coffeyville High School in 1913, and is now demonstrator for the Studebaker cars, his home being at 412 East Ninth Street in Coffeyville. Mr. Skinner married in 1904 M. Josephine Keister of Hoopeston, Illinois.

FRANK NEWELL SKINNER, vice president and assistant manager of the Coffeyville Furniture Company, owes his successful position to the fact that he has steadily pursued one line of endeavor since leaving school as a boy.

Geo. M. Gray, M. D.

He was born at Olathe, Kansas, June 2, 1872, a son of James L. and Elizabeth (Newell) Skinner, who moved to Coffeyville about two years after his birth and are numbered among the old settlers of that city. In the public schools of Coffeyville Frank N. Skinner obtained his early education, and after leaving school at the age of eighteen began clerking in a grocery store. In December, 1894, he became identified with the undertaking business and he now has his office at 17 West Tenth Street, Coffeyville.

Mr. Skinner and family reside at 607 Willow Street, having built his home there in 1898. He is a public spirited citizen, served four years on the school board, is a republican and a member of the Presbyterian Church. He also belongs to the Chamber of Commerce, and is widely known in fraternal circles. His affiliations are with Keystone Lodge No. 102 Ancient Free and Accepted Masons, Coffeyville Chapter No. 89, Royal Arch Masons, Lochinvar Commandery No. 52 Knights Templar, and Chapter No. 112 of the Order of Eastern Star. He also belongs to Coffeyville Camp No. 665, Modern Woodmen of America; Star Lodge No. 279, Independent Order of Odd Fellows; Lodge No. 775 Benevolent and Protective Order of Elks; Lodge No. 305, Fraternal Order of Eagles; Tent No. 1193 Loyal Order of Moose; Anti-Horse Thief Association; the Order of Owls; Improved Order of Red Men No. 58; Brotherhood of American Yeomen.

December 2, 1896, at Coffeyville Mr. Skinner married Miss Mabel Cass, daughter of Hardin and Hattie Cass. Her father, now deceased, was a grain merchant at Coffeyville, and her mother lives at 605 Willow Street in that city. Mr. and Mrs. Skinner have four children: Vera A., born September 18, 1898, and now in the Coffeyville High School; Kathleen, born October 31, 1902; Keith who died at the age of three days; and Frank N. Jr., born July 22, 1914.

Louis E. Dodds. Among the well-known native sons of Labette County who have passed their entire careers in this section and who have worked their way to positions of standing in various walks of life, Louis E. Dodds is a representative of the railway element. For more than a quarter of a century, Mr. Dodds has been identified with the Santa Fe Railroad system, and since 1903 has held the position of freight and passenger agent for this line at Cherryvale, where he has become very popular with the patrons of the road.

Mr. Dodds was born in Labette County, Kansas, June 9, 1872, the only child of Abe Z. and Sarah (Barnes) Dodds. His grandfather was Zebra Dodds who, born in Scotland, emigrated to the United States as the first of the family to come to this country, and settled in the vicinity of Pittsburgh, Pennsylvania, where he passed the remaining years of his life in various occupations. Abe Z. Dodds was born in 1838, in Pennsylvania, where he was reared and educated, and in his youth learned the trade of millwright. At the age of twenty years he left the parental roof and went to Spencer, Indiana, where he followed his trade until the outbreak of the Civil war, when he enlisted in a regiment of Indiana volunteer infantry and served gallantly as a soldier of the Union until peace was declared between the North and the South. With an excellent military record, the young soldier returned to his Indiana home and resumed his activities in his trade, but in 1871 answered the call of the West

and came to Labette County as a pioneer. He found a ready need for his services in the erection of mills, and built all the first flour mills that were erected in this section, including structures at Coffeyville, Parsons, Cherryvale and Independence. Mr. Dodds did not live long, however, to enjoy his prosperity, as he passed away in 1874, at Nevada, Missouri, when his career had just begun, the hardships of army life having probably undermined his health and hastened his demise. He was a republican, but beyond exercising his right of franchise took little interest in political affairs. His religious membership was in the Methodist Episcopal Church. Mr. Dodds married Miss Sarah Barnes, who was born in 1845, in Indiana, and who survived her husband for many years, dying at Cherryvale, in 1903. Louis E. was their only child.

Louis E. Dodds received his early education in the public schools of Montgomery County and pursued his high school studies at Cherryvale, where he took nearly a four-year course. Leaving school in 1889, he accepted a position as clerk in a Cherryvale hotel, but in 1890 went to work for the Santa Fe Railroad, with which he has been connected ever since. His first position was that of yard clerk, and he was steadily promoted, as his ability and fidelity became recognized until 1903, when he was made station agent at Cherryvale, an office which he retains. Each year his duties have become more and more important and arduous, but Mr. Dodds has developed with his position and continues to handle its affairs in a manner eminently satisfying alike both to the road and to the traveling public. Both the passenger and freight departments are under his supervision and he has mastered thoroughly all the details pertaining to each, and his uniform courtesy and geniality have served to make him many friends. Mr. Dodds is the owner of his residence at No. 503 East Main Street, in addition to which he has a well cultivated and valuable farm of 160 acres located in Labette County, which he rents. He is a republican, but has never sought public preferment. Fraternally, he is connected with Cherryvale Lodge No. 137, Ancient Free and Accepted Masons; Cherryvale Chapter No. 86, Royal Arch Masons; St. Bernard's Commandery No. 10, Knights Templar, of Independence; and Jayhawker Camp No. 913, Modern Woodmen of America, Cherryvale. He belongs also to the Commercial Club.

Mr. Dodds was married in 1894 at Neodesha, Kansas, to Miss Avarilla Eaton, daughter of the late B. Eaton, who for some years was engaged in the undertaking business at Neodesha, and to this union there has been born one son: Frank, a graduate of the Montgomery County High School, who is connected with the Midland Life Insurance Company, of Kansas City.

George M. Gray, M. D. There is hardly a more eminent physician and surgeon in the State of Kansas than Dr. George M. Gray, of Kansas City, Kansas. He is ex-president of the Kansas State Medical Society, a member of the American Medical Association, and has been accorded the honor of a fellowship in the American College of Surgeons. In 1915 Governor Capper appointed him a member of the State Board of Medical Registration and Examination for Kansas and he is now president of the board. Doctor Gray has been in active practice at Kansas City, Kansas, for more than thirty-five years, and for the greater part of that time has been head of the staff of St. Margaret's Hospital.

His attainments and the service he has rendered in his profession are not the only distinctions to be associated with his name. Doctor Gray is properly considered as the father of the park and boulevard system of Kansas City, Kansas. For years he has worked and planned for an adequate system of driveways and parks, and many of the ideas of the project now being put into execution originated in his mind.

In March, 1907, the Kansas Legislature passed the law giving Kansas City, Kansas, authority to organize a park board, and permitting the board to levy special taxes for a park and boulevard system. A test was made of the law, and it was declared constitutional by the supreme court. When the law went into effect Mr. Gray was serving as mayor of Kansas City, Kansas, and that position gave him the authority to appoint the first park board. His appointees were Dr. S. S. Glasscock, James Sullivan and J. P. Angle. A little later Doctor Glasscock resigned and was succeeded by Doctor Gray as a member of the board. Through all the various steps connected with the original legislation, the organization of the board, and the inauguration of its constructive plans, Doctor Gray's influence was everywhere apparent. He and his fellow members of the board secured the services of one of the most eminent landscape engineers in the country, George E. Kessler, and according to plans drawn up by him the work was started in 1909. It is still in progress, and it is estimated that ten or more years will be required for the completion of the ambitious plans formulated at the beginning. The original park board continued their jurisdiction over the work until this board was supplanted by the commission form of government.

Doctor Gray is a son of the late Rasselas M. Gray and a nephew of Alfred Gray, both of whom were prominent pioneers in Kansas City, Kansas. Alfred Gray, who was born in Erie County, New York, December 5, 1830, a son of Isaiah and May (Morgan) Gray, was well educated in academies of the east, was graduated in law at Albany in 1854, practiced for a time at Buffalo, and in March, 1857, arrived in Kansas, settling at old Quindaro, which was one of the original starting points in the development of the present City of Kansas City, Kansas. He was a farmer there from 1858 until 1873, and in 1872 was elected the first secretary of the Kansas State Board of Agriculture, and formulated the plans and laid the foundation for the magnificent work since carried on by that organization. He had previously served from 1866 to 1870 as a director of the State Agricultural Society. Alfred Gray was secretary of agriculture until his death on January 23, 1880. During the war both he and his brother had served in the Union army. Alfred became regimental quartermaster of the Fourth Kansas Regiment in April, 1862, and later was transferred to the Tenth and subsequently to the Fifth Regiment. He had served as a member of the first state legislature of Kansas, having been elected December 6, 1859. Some years ago the state erected a monument to his memory in the Topeka Cemetery.

Rasselas M. Gray was also a native of Erie County, New York, was one of the early free state men in the territory of Kansas, and settled at Quindaro in 1858. He was one of the last to desert that town, which had so many interesting associations with early territorial days. He lived there until the death of his wife in 1899, being both a farmer and a merchant. After that he lived at the home of a daughter in Kansas City, Kansas, and died March 11, 1911, at the age of eighty-eight years. He was survived by two sons and one daughter, and also by fourteen grandchildren and nine great-grandchildren.

Dr. George M. Gray was born at Waukegan, Illinois, March 4, 1856, a son of Rasselas M. and Susan (Doust) Gray. He was educated in the public schools of Wyandotte County, and at the age of nineteen was working as a clerk in a drug store in Kansas City, Missouri. He aspired to a professional career, studied medicine under Dr. E. W. Shauffler in Kansas City, Missouri, and then took a course in the old College of Physicians and Surgeons of Kansas City. He was graduated in 1879, and then entered Bellevue Hospital Medical College of New York City, where he received a diploma in 1880.

From the time of his graduation Doctor Gray has been continuously in practice both in medicine and surgery, and besides his connection with the local hospitals and his large private practice he has always exerted a strong influence in behalf of adequate health and sanitary laws in his city and state and has been prominent in the making of a great medical school in connection with the University of Kansas.

He is vice president of the Peoples National Bank of Kansas City, is a charter member and the president of the River View State Bank and president of the Security State Bank. He is a member of all the Masonic bodies, and is a republican in politics. In 1907-8 he served as president of the Mercantile Club. While president of this club he had the satisfaction of seeing his ideas concerning a park and boulevard system incorporated into state law and made a part of the charter of the city.

Doctor Gray recalls the fact that when the old Town of Quindaro was laid out forty acres of ground within the city limits were laid out and designated for public parks. He believes, probably on good authority, that this was the first city in Kansas to be provided with grounds for public parks, and as a result of the activities of Rasselas Gray, his father, the land was kept in the original condition as laid out in 1856, and this will eventually become a part of the park and boulevard system of Kansas City, Kansas.

In 1881 he married Miss Caroline Harlan, of Kansas City, Missouri, a daughter of Minerva Harlan, widow of Howard Harlan. Mr. and Mrs. Gray are the parents of three children: Mary, who married Willard J. Breidenthal, a cashier of the Riverview State Bank, son of John W. Breidenthal, who was bank commissioner for two terms and at one time a candidate for governor on the populist ticket; Ruth M., the second daughter, married Thomas M. Van Chave a lawyer of the firm of McAnany & Alden and at the present time assistant city counselor; George, the only son is at present attending the Kansas University with the intention of taking up the study of medicine.

AL F. WILLIAMS. Whether as a lawyer, as a business man or in the circles of the republican party, Al F. Williams is a recognized leader in civic affairs in Cherokee County. His interests have been so many that while some may know him best as a lawyer, others would think of him as one of the most virile personalities in republican politics in the state, and still others would recognize his prominent relations with the business growth and development of his home city.

Born in Appleton City, St. Clair County, Missouri, July 10, 1876, Mr. Williams is of Welsh descent, though his ancestors immigrated to Pennsylvania in colonial days, and afterward became pioneers into Illinois. His father, L. A. Williams, was born in

Southern Illinois in 1850, grew up there, when a young man went to Missouri, lived in Parsons, Kansas, for three years, from 1874, then at Appleton City, Missouri, until 1888, at Lamar, Missouri, until 1899, and then came to Columbus, Kansas, where he was engaged in the grocery business until his death in May, 1901. A republican in politics, he filled a position in the city council of Lamar for several terms, and in every community where he lived took an active part in civic affairs. Fraternally he was identified with the Independent Order of Odd Fellows and the Woodmen of the World. Jennie J. Wylie, who married L. A. Williams, was born in Kansas in 1849, and is still living with her son, Al F. Williams, at Columbus. Her children were two in number. The daughter Edith, is the wife of O. W. Van Zandt, cashier of the Columbus State Bank, and they have one daughter, Ailene, born in 1911.

Al F. Williams spent most of his early life in the State of Missouri, attending the public schools of Appleton City and Lamar and graduating from the high school of Lamar in 1894. For one year he taught school in Barton County, Missouri, and then traveled by way of an old-fashioned prairie schooner to Mountain Grove, Wright County, Missouri, where he established the Mountain Advertiser and conducted that publication until the fall of the same year. Returning then to Lamar, he entered the law office of Thurman & Wray, and diligently pursued his studies up to October, 1896.

Reared as a republican, he became a factor in politics before he had reached his majority. During the McKinley campaign of 1896 he made many speeches in Barton and Jasper counties, Missouri, and in Cherokee County, Kansas.

It was no doubt the acquaintance he formed in Cherokee County during that time that led to his taking up his residence at Columbus, where he finished his law studies in the office of C. D. Ashley, and was admitted to the bar in the spring of 1897.

Since his admission to the bar Mr. Williams has conducted a large civil and criminal practice. His standing as a lawyer is well indicated by the fact that he is local attorney for the Missouri, Kansas & Texas Railroad Company, for the Kansas City Southern Railway Company, the Missouri Pacific Railroad Company, for the Mayer Coal Company, the Central Coal and Coke Company, the Long Bell Lumber Company and the Clemens Coal Company.

His part as a citizen has been not less important than his activities as a lawyer. For the past twenty years he has identified himself actively with every movement for the upbuilding of Columbus. He assisted in getting all the railroads, and has been one of the prominent men in the Commercial Club.

Soon after the outbreak of the Spanish-American war Mr. Williams enlisted, May 2, 1898, in Company F of the Twenty-second Kansas Regiment. He was first lieutenant of his company, and ninety days after his enlistment was made acting quartermaster of the regiment upon death of Quartermaster Lieutenant Lamb. The regiment was commanded by Col. H. C. Lindsey. From Topeka it went to Camp Alger in Virginia, marched through Thoroughfare Gap and camped on the old battlefield of Bull Run or Manasas, and spent the last sixty days in Camp Meade, Pennsylvania. The regiment was mustered out in November, 1898, at Fort Leavenworth, Kansas. With that exception Mr. Williams has been in active practice at Columbus since his admission to the bar.

For two terms he served as city attorney, and administered the office of county attorney of Cherokee County with great efficiency for two terms, from

1902 to 1906. He had already gained a splendid reputation as a criminal lawyer, and was able to render a great service to the county during the term he was official prosecutor.

Mr. Williams is treasurer of the Republican State Committee, is treasurer of the Congressional Committee, is chairman of the Republican County Central Committee, and was recently a candidate for the nomination for attorney general of the state against Mr. Fred S. Jackson. He entered that contest without hope of success, and it was a gratifying tribute to his reputation and personalities that he polled 40,000 votes. He was also candidate for nomination for judge of the Eleventh Judicial District, and though he made no campaign, he lost the nomination by the narrow margin of forty-five votes. In March, 1915, Mr. Williams was elected at the Kansas State Republican Convention one of the Big Four delegates from Kansas, and in that capacity he attended the National Convention in Chicago, where he was assigned to membership on the committee of rules and order of business.

A strong believer in fraternalism, Mr. Williams has been again and again honored in the various orders in which he is a member. He is a past Grand Chancellor of the Knights of Pythias of the state, is past chancellor commander of Columbus Lodge No. 12 of that order, belongs to the Pythian Sisters, to the D. O. K. K., to the Uniform Rank and the Insurance Department of the Knights of Pythias. He is a member of the Kansas Grand Lodge of the Benevolent and Protective Order of Elks, and is past exalted ruler of Lodge No. 677, Benevolent and Protective Order of Elks, at Galena. Other fraternities of which he is a member are Lodge No. 387, Independent Order of Odd Fellows, Camp No. 72, Woodmen of the World, the Rebekahs and the Anti-Horse Thief Association. He is on the executive committee of the Columbus Commercial Club, and is the only citizen of Columbus who has membership in the Pittsburg Country Club. As president of the Old Settlers Reunion Association he brought about the most successful meeting of that organization ever held in the reunion of August, 1916.

Mr. Williams is president of the Columbus Building & Loan Association, is president of the Western Cigar and Tobacco Company, a wholesale organization, is president of the local Chautauqua Association, and has a large amount of property in and about Columbus. His offices are in the Bliss Building at the southeast corner of the square, and he is president of the company that owns the Cigar Building. His own home is at 516 West Walnut Street. Recently Mr. Williams platted an addition at the north side of Columbus situated on the street car line, and these lots are being sold for residence purposes. Besides other real estate in Columbus he owns a farm of seventy-five acres seven miles southeast of the town.

In 1905, at Columbus, Mr. Williams married Miss Kate Weisenbarker, of Pittsburg, Kansas. They have one daughter, June, born June 9, 1913.

ARTHUR FULTON CRANSTON. From time immemorial, the legal profession has attracted to its ranks a large percentage of notably brilliant men. When rightly followed it is one of the noblest callings, affording at once full play to Christian sympathy, and opportunities for helpful public service, and holding a mighty prerogative, that of instigating exoneration of and restitution to the wrongly oppressed, or the administration of just retribution to the guilty. It has no room or opportunity for the weakling, but the strong it strengthens with a keener insight to human thought and feeling, with a more accurate realization of the obligations and responsibilities that are civilization's bequest to modern manhood.

Of the brilliant men in the legal profession of Southeastern Kansas, one of the best known is Arthur Fulton Cranston, of Parsons, legist, legislator, public-spirited citizen and influential republican politician. He was born at Urbana, Champaign County, Illinois, December 14, 1867, and is a son of Capt. W. W. and Jennie (Fulton) Cranston. The Cranston family originally came from Scotland, locating in Rhode Island during Colonial days, and in that state was born in 1804 the grandfather of Arthur F. Cranston, Christopher Cranston. Christopher Cranston became a pioneer of the Western Reserve of Ohio, where he settled on school lands and engaged in farming and the raising of livestock, being particularly interested in the raising of sheep. His death occurred on his farm in the vicinity of Woodstock, Ohio, 1859, when he fell from the loft of his barn. He was one of the substantial men of his day and locality, whose efforts assisted materially in the building up and development of his community and whose example was an influence for good among his fellow-citizens, by whom he was honored and respected. He married first a Miss Parks, and they became the parents of three children: Charles, a farmer and dealer in and breeder of fine horses, who died at Galesburg, Illinois; and Mary and Josephine, the last named dying unmarried. Christopher Cranston was married the second time to Irene Knott, who also died at Woodstock, Ohio, a granddaughter of Ethan Allen, and they had eight children, namely: Christopher, who met a soldier's death on the battlefield of Shiloh, during the Civil war, while wearing a blue uniform; Lew, who followed farming in the vicinity of Woodstock, Ohio, and there passed away; W. W.; Nettie, of near Trenton, Missouri, widow of Mr. Harris, who prior to his death was engaged in farming there; Helen, who married Mr. Sykes, once mayor of Trenton, Missouri, where both died; Ann, who died at Trenton, Missouri, in 1880, as the wife of Mr. Perry Froman, who lives in Oklahoma; and Dr. Otto G., who is engaged in the practice of medicine and surgery at Wewoka, Oklahoma.

W. W. Cranston was born in 1838, at Woodstock, Ohio, where he received his education. As a young man he was interested in mercantile enterprises, beginning at the close of the Civil war. In 1861 he enlisted in the Sixty-sixth Regiment, Ohio Volunteer Infantry, with which he fought until the close of the war. He took part in some notable engagements, including the battles of Chickamauga, Antietam and Chancellorsville, and was with Sherman on his famous march to the sea and participated in the Grand Review at Washington. His service was characterized by bravery and faithful devotion to duty, and during the period of the war he rose from the ranks to be captain of his company. Captain Cranston was the recipient of a medal from Congress for distinguished bravery under fire. With three others, he crept out to a bullet-swept position and brought in a wounded Confederate soldier, who was carried to Chancellorsville church. Unfortunately the risk was useless, as shortly thereafter the church was set ablaze by shell-fire and the wounded Johnnie Reb perished with many others, wearers both of the blue and the grey.

At the close of his military service, Captain Cranston returned to Ohio. In 1867 he went to Urbana, Illinois, and in the vicinity of that place, in Champaign County, purchased a farm. This he conducted until 1877, in which year he disposed of his interests

and went to Gainesville, Texas, where he turned his attention to the cattle business on the open range. He bought and sold several ranches and remained in the Lone Star State until 1882, when he came to Parsons, Kansas, and located on a farm. In 1890 he retired from active pursuits, moved to the City of Parsons, and here passed his declining years in comfort and ease, dying at his home here December 7, 1907. Mr. Cranston was one of the most highly esteemed citizens of his community. He was a republican in his political views, served in the Kansas Legislature in the session of 1889-1891, and was for years a member of the board of school directors. He was a faithful member of the Universalist Church. Mr. Cranston married Miss Jennie Fulton, who was born at Urbana, Ohio, in 1846, and now resides with her son at Parsons. Three children were born to this union: Arthur Fulton, of this notice; Dr. Oscar; and Florence. Dr. Oscar Cranston is a graduate of the Kansas City Medical College, class of 1894, degree of Doctor of Medicine, and is now engaged successfully in the practice of medicine and surgery at Madison, Kansas. He is married and has two daughters, Dorothy and Mildred, both of whom are attending the public schools of Madison. Florence Cranston married Alvah Carter, who was engaged in the sale of school and church furniture up to the time of his death in 1903. Since that time Mrs. Carter has lived in Parsons, Kansas, as do the three children, Jean, who attends the Los Angeles High School, and Ruth and Aleene, who attend the public schools. Mrs. Florence Carter belongs to Hannah Jameson Chapter, Daughters of the American Revolution.

Arthur Fulton Cranston attended school in Illinois for two years, then was a pupil in the subscription schools of Texas, and in 1882 entered the public schools of Parsons, Kansas. In 1887 he enrolled as a student at the Kansas Agricultural College, where he displayed unusual ability by completing the four-year course in three years and was graduated in 1890. For the three years that followed he was a teacher in the public schools of Labette County, and in the fall of 1892 entered the law department of the University of Kansas, where, in the graduating class of 1894 he received the degree of Bachelor of Laws, in the same class being Fred Jackson, Judge E. L. Fischer of Kansas City, Judge Ruppenthal, Judge Raines, and Judge Hogan, of Jewell County, Kansas. Mr. Cranston began a general practice at Parsons in 1894 and since that time has steadily risen to a commanding position at the bar of Southeastern Kansas. He maintains offices in the Karr Building. He resides at the old home, No. 1531 Stevens Street, and owns three other dwelling houses in Parsons.

Mr. Cranston has always been a republican, and is accounted one of the strong men of his party in Labette County. In 1898 he was a candidate for the legislature, but was beaten by a 200 majority by Doctor Gabriel. In 1908 he again ran for the legislature and was elected over Doctor Allison, his subsequent career in the house being an active and distinguished one in which he served on eight committees, including that to inspect state institutions, the Judiciary, the Labor Committee, of which he was chairman, First Class Cities, Mines and Mining, Penal Institutions, and Judicial Apportionment, and two special committees, one of which was to report on methods of economy for the state. He was interested in the State Bank Guaranty measure and railroad legislation, introduced a bill to raise from $10,000 to $25,000 indemnity for railroad employes meeting death in the line of service, and in every way looked after the interests of his constituents. He also introduced a referendum bill, and a bill to call a convention to draft a new state constitution, and both of these passed the House but were killed in committee by the Senate. In 1910 he ran versus P. P. Campbell for a seat in Congress in the primaries, but this was an insurgent year and he met with defeat, although he made fifty speeches in nine counties and prosecuted a most vigorous campaign. He has also served as clerk of the school board of Parsons for six years and was county attorney from January, 1913, to January, 1915. In 1907 he was a candidate for appointment as district judge of the Sixteenth Judicial District.

Mr. Cranston belongs to Parsons Lodge No. 117, Ancient Free and Accepted Masons; Parsons Camp No. 844, Modern Woodmen of America, of which he was clerk six years; Knights of the Maccabees, Parsons Tent, of which he was also clerk six years; Ancient Order United Workmen, Parsons; and the Anti-Horse Thief Association. Mr. Cranston is unmarried. He possesses one of the finest libraries, legal and otherwise, to be found in the city.

GEORGE H. LONG is a business man of Kansas City, Kansas, where he has been located for the past eight years. As an undertaker he has built up a large clientage on the basis of thorough and competent service, and has given to that profession the best of his energies and his conscientious study for a number of years.

Mr. Long is a native of Ohio, born September 30, 1875, at Ripley in Brown County. He was the oldest of the five children of James A. and Jemima (Fluharty) Long. Both parents were natives of Ohio. James A. Long had a brother, John, two years older. They were left motherless when children, and their father, George Long, soon afterward determined to seek a home in Kansas. He came out to the state by ox team and wagon and married here and soon after getting his home established he went back to Ohio to get his children. On returning to Kansas he found that his second wife had died during his absence, and he himself fell a victim to cholera about 1854. His children, James and John, went back to Ohio and were reared there by separate families. John was in the regular army, was injured during service in the West against the Indians, and his subsequent record became lost to the family. James A. Long was a lumberman in Ohio, and for fifteen years served as deputy marshal of Ripley, Ohio. He was a democrat and a man held in the highest esteem throughout his community. He was a Methodist and an active supporter of church and school.

Mr. George H. Long grew up in Brown County, Ohio, attended the common schools at Ripley, also had high school training, and began his career as clerk in a hardware store while still a student in high school. He remained with that store for ten years, and laid the foundation of his substantial business education while there. This early training has proved invaluable to him in his later years.

On September 18, 1899, Mr. Long married Miss Bessie Grim. Her father was a successful undertaker at Ripley, Ohio. Mr. Long soon afterward became associated in business with his father-in-law, and in 1906 they removed their establishment to Hamilton, Ohio, where they continued in business for two years. In 1908 Mr. Long came to Kansas City, Kansas, for the purpose of starting a business of his own. While looking for a suitable location he worked in various places and subsequently bought an interest in the W. B. Raymond Company. He was with that firm

one year, and in 1910 he set up in business for himself on Tenth Street, near his present location.

Mr. Long has succeeded in the undertaking business because he gives every courtesy to his patrons, regardless of their station in life or of their means and circumstances. His business has had a steady growth, and he is now considered one of the leading men in his line in the city.

Mr. and Mrs. Long are the parents of two children, Louis and Martha. Politically Mr. Long is largely independent, though inclined to support the democratic party. He has never filled any official position. He gives his support to those movements which are most closely identified with the public welfare of his community, is exceedingly progressive, and in 1911 he advanced the idea of a city manager plan for the government of Kansas City, Kansas, a method which has been tested successfully in other large cities and eliminates much of the politics and inefficiency from local government. Mr. and Mrs. Long are active in the work of the Central Avenue Methodist Episcopal Church.

WILLIAM MARTIN LADD. Prominent among the younger Government officials of Montgomery County, Kansas, is William Martin Ladd, who is capably discharging the duties of postmaster of the thriving little City of Dearing. Mr. Ladd had as training for his official services an experience in banking, and having attained his position by virtue of successful participation in a civil service examination, is handling the affairs of the mail service in an entirely acceptable manner. He is a native son of Kansas and was born at Vernon, Woodson County, October 4, 1891, his parents being Ira W. and Mina L. (Martin) Ladd.

Mr. Ladd belongs to a family of Scotch-Irish descent, which, it is believed, was founded in this country during colonial times. His grandfather was Ira W. Ladd, who was born in Ohio, and who through a long and useful career practiced medicine and surgery in the Buckeye State. He died at Edgerton, Ohio, in 1866. Doctor Ladd married Alice Thornburg, who was born in 1841, in Ohio, and died at Dearing, Kansas, in November, 1914, and their only child was Ira W. Ira W. Ladd was born in 1868, in Butler County, Indiana, and was there reared and educated, remaining in that community until 1886, when he removed to Vernon, Kansas, where he was married. He was a pioneer farmer of Woodson County and continued to be engaged in agricultural pursuits there for ten years, in 1896 removing to Fort Scott. In that community he continued as a tiller of the soil until 1905, then becoming a resident of Dearing, Montgomery County, where he continued as a farmer until 1913. Since that time he has been a resident of California, being the owner of farming land and orchards in the Golden State. Mr. Ladd is a republican in politics and an active member and supporter of the United Brethren Church. He married Mina L. Martin, who was born near Hyattsville, Bourbon County, Kansas, and William Martin is their only child.

William Martin Ladd attended the district schools of Montgomery County, Kansas, subsequently went to the public schools of Dearing, and completed his education at the Coffeyville Business College, from which he was duly graduated. In 1910, at the age of eighteen years, he entered the Dearing State Bank as bookkeeper, and continued with that institution for two years, following which he continued in the same capacity with other business and financial concerns. In 1915 he took the civil service examination, and October 5th of that year was appointed postmaster of Dearing under President Wilson's administration. He has already improved the mail service greatly here and has won the confidence of his fellow-citizens by his fidelity to duty and their friendship by his uniform courtesy and obliging nature. Mr. Ladd maintains an independent stand in regard to politics, is a member of the United Brethren Church, and is fraternally affiliated with Camp No. 618, of the Independent Order of Odd Fellows, and Camp No. 8141, of the Modern Woodmen of America, both of Dearing.

Mr. Ladd was married in 1911, at Coffeyville, Kansas, to Miss Ethel M. Johnson, daughter of W. C. and Cora J. Johnson, of Coffeyville, where Mr. Johnson is the proprietor of a wagonmaking establishment. Mr. and Mrs. Ladd have one son: Ira William, born July 27, 1912.

HON. BYRON JUDD was a pioneer of Wyandotte County. He established his home in the village of Wyandotte in November, 1857, when Kansas was still a territory. He lived in the village, his capacities expanding with the growth of the community, and his personal position and influence rising as Wyandotte County grew and prospered, and at his death on July 27, 1909, it was generally recognized and appreciated that he was one of the men who had left a permanent impress for good upon Kansas City, Kansas, a great city of which his old home village of Wyandotte had in the meantime become an integral part.

He was nearly eighty-five years of age at the time of his death. He was born at Otis in Berkshire County, Massachusetts, August 13, 1824, a son of Ardon and Sarah (Hubbard) Judd. Both parents lived out their lives in Massachusetts, and both were members of pioneer New England families. Byron Judd spent his youth in the Berkshire Hills. He tried his muscle in cultivating the rough and stony ground of that section. He attended the common schools, also the academy at Southwick, and completed his education in the Massachusetts State Normal School at Westfield. For a time he was a teacher in Massachusetts.

He was about thirty-one years of age when he set out for the West. His first home was at Des Moines, Iowa, where he served a year as deputy county recorder. Then toward the close of 1857 he arrived in that part of Kansas which was ever afterwards his home. He was one of the early land agents and bankers, became active in public affairs, and in 1871, upon the organization of the First National Bank of Wyandotte, was elected president. He continued at the head of that institution, one of the strongest in Kansas, until the weight of years and increasing infirmities obliged him to resign.

In the early history of Wyandotte he served as president of the city council and later as mayor, for five years was justice of the peace, then became trustee of Wyandotte Township, and for four years was county treasurer. He was one of the early incumbents of the office of United States Land Commissioner for the District of Kansas, and in 1872 he was elected a member of the State Senate and re-elected in 1874. Throughout his career he was a democrat in political convictions.

He is recalled not only as a prominent citizen and banker, but as a man of unusual character. He came to exercise large power, but always exercised

it with justice and mercy. He did much for the poor and unfortunate, and until almost the close of his life stood with that group of men who were the real builders and makers of the foremost commercial center of Kansas. He was not identified with any religious denomination, but attended the Congregational Church, of which his wife was a devout member.

In 1865 he married Mrs. Mary Louise (Cooper) Bartlett. At the time of her marriage she lived in Kansas City, Kansas, but was born at Irasburg, Orleans County, Vermont. She died February 8, 1908. There were two children, Sara and Emily. The latter died in 1890. Sara, who is now librarian of the Kansas City Public Library, married Corwin Matthew Greenman, who was a traveling salesman and died in 1900. Mrs. Greenman has three children: Judd, Donald C., and Louise.

HON. WILLIAM Y. MORGAN is one of the men who have attained sufficiency of public distinction so that he might merely give his address as Kansas and every one would know the who's who and who's what about him.

He was born in Cincinnati, Ohio, April 6, 1866, a son of W. A. and Minnie (Yoast) Morgan. His father served as an officer in the Twenty-third Kentucky Regiment in the Union army, and in 1871 brought his family to Kansas. For forty years he was editor of the Cottonwood Falls Leader and at the same time was prominent in public affairs, was a member of the Legislature, the State Senate, and was department commander of the Grand Army of the Republic. Mr. Morgan's mother was department president of the Woman's Relief Corps and was an active newspaper woman and prominent in the public life of women in Kansas.

William Y. Morgan was educated in the University of Kansas, graduating with the degree A. B. in the class of 1885. He has always been deeply interested in the state university, served four years as regent, and is a loyal member of the college fraternity Phi Gamma Delta.

Practical experience in journalism, which has been his chief business interest all his active career, he first gained as a reporter for the Lawrence Journal during 1886-88. In 1888 Mr. Morgan bought the Strong City Republican, but sold it in 1892 and then became proprietor of the Emporia Gazette, which he in 1895 sold to William Allen White. On selling the Gazette Mr. Morgan bought the Hutchinson News, and has been its owner and editor ever since. Thus his real residence, so far as the exact city is concerned, is and has been for years Hutchinson. In 1914 Mr. Morgan was elected a director of the Associated Press. He is one of the principal stockholders and a director of the State Exchange Bank, and has been identified with various Hutchinson enterprises. He has been president of the Hutchinson Y. M. C. A. since its organization in 1909, and has done all he could to forward the work of that organization over the State.

The republican party in Kansas has long felt a special pride in being able to name William Y. Morgan as one of its most influential leaders. He has often served as chairman of county organizations, and in 1916 was a delegate to the Republican National Convention and during the following campaign was director of publicity in the western department for the Republican National Committee. Mr. Morgan is a thoroughly progressive republican.

HON. WILLIAM Y. MORGAN

In 1899 he was elected state printer of Kansas, an office he held four years, until 1903. He served as a member of the legislature from 1904 to 1910, and in 1914 was elected to his present office as lieutenant governor of Kansas. In 1916 he was re-elected, and his present term expires in 1918.

Governor Morgan has served as division commander of the Sons of Veterans, is a Thirty-second degree Scottish Rite and Knight Templar Mason, a member of the Knights of Pythias, Benevolent and Protective Order of Elks and the Loyal Legion. He is a Presbyterian, a member of the University Club of Kansas City, the Press Club of Chicago and the National Press Club of Washington, D. C.

While his interests since early childhood have been so closely identified with Kansas, Governor Morgan has exercised the opportunity for extensive travel. He is the author of three travel books: ''A Journey of a Jayhawker,'' ''A Jayhawker in Europe,'' and ''The Near East.''

Governor Morgan was married at Strong City, Kansas, in November, 1890, to Miss Colie Adair, daughter of Witt Adair. They have one daughter, Claudia.

MORILLO ABIAL SPALDING. In Morillo Abial Spalding the thriving community of Dearing, Montgomery County, has a citizen who has contributed to its upbuilding a conservative and reliable general mercantile business, who formerly, for eight years, carried on the drug business, and whose long experience in a commercial way has been a decided factor in helping his city to better things.

Mr. Spalding was born at Morrisville, Vermont, February 13, 1856, a son of A. W. and Mary (Tenney) Spalding, a grandson of Warren Spalding, a Vermont farmer who spent his life there, and a member of a family, which originating in England, was established in the Green Mountain State in Colonial times. A. W. Spalding was born in Vermont in 1836, and was there educated and reared. He grew up as a farmer and that vocation he adopted upon reaching manhood, subsequently continuing as a tiller of the soil throughout his life. In later years he moved to New Hampshire, and in that state his death occurred in 1896. He was a republican in his political views, a man who took a great interest in the welfare of his community, and one who had the respect and esteem of his associates. He was a faithful member of the Universalist Church. Mr. Spalding married Miss Mary Tenney, born in 1836, in Vermont, who died at Morrisville, that state, in 1896. There were three children in the family: Morillo Abial, of this review; Fred, who is a retired merchant and resides at Minneapolis, Minnesota; and Charles A., who still lives in New England.

After attending the graded and high schools of Morrisville, Vermont, from which latter he was graduated in 1872, Morillo Abial Spalding began work as a clerk in a shoe store, where he received his introduction to business methods and remained four years. At this time he answered to the call of the West and journeyed to Iowa and located at Hamburg, where for many years he was engaged in business and served as postmaster for three years. His next location was Kearney, Nebraska, where for three years he was engaged in teaching band music, and then went to Cook, Nebraska, where he embarked in the drug business, and continued therein until 1906. The next two years were spent at Tyro, Kansas, in a like enterprise, and in 1908 he located at Dearing, where he became the proprietor of a pharmacy and conducted it successfully for eight years, when, in 1916, he disposed of his drug interests in order to open his general mercantile business, which is now the leading establishment on the main street of the town. Mr. Spalding is possessed of the ability to make a success of whatever venture he undertakes, and has already built up a prosperous trade. He stands high in the public esteem and belief in his integrity and good judgment have been variously manifest. Politically he is a republican, but while a supporter of his party's candidates and principles, has not cared to endeavor to push himself forward as a candidate for public preferment. He belongs to the Odd Fellows Lodge at Dearing, of which he is past noble grand, and to the Ancient Order of United Workmen in Nebraska.

In 1884, at Riverton, Nebraska, Mr. Spalding was married to Miss Mary Gooding, and they had one daughter: Lola, who married Mr. Peebles, cashier of a hardware and implement company at Spokane, Washington. In 1901 Mr. Spalding was married, at Riverton, to Miss Irene Harrop, daughter of the late James Harrop, a farmer. They have one daughter, Erbine, born September 8, 1904, who is attending the Dearing graded school.

WILLIAM B. SUTTON. Since he came to Kansas in 1887, as a rancher-lawyer, William B. Sutton has found all the opportunities that an ambitious man could crave for an active, earnest, useful and prosperous career. For many years he has lived in Kansas City, Kansas, and is one of the leading lawyers of that city.

He was born in Indiana County, Pennsylvania, February 12, 1849, the seventh in a family of ten children born to James and Sarah (Stanborough) Sutton. His father was born in the same county of Pennsylvania in 1812, and died in 1870, while the mother was born in Pittsburg and died in 1899 at the age of eighty-four. James Sutton was a merchant, a paper manufacturer, a private banker, and at the time of his death was president of the First National Bank of Indiana, Pennsylvania.

William B. Sutton was educated at Tuscarora Academy in Juniata County, the Elders Ridge Academy in Indiana County, and in 1868 graduated from Washington and Jefferson College at Canonsburg, Pennsylvania. The time of his graduation was distinguished by another important event of his life. June 8, 1868, he married Miss Agnes Black, who was born in Canonsburg, Pennsylvania, daughter of John E. and Alice (Hanson) Black. Her father was a banker at Canonsburg and also treasurer of Washington and Jefferson College.

For the next two years Mr. Sutton studied law with Judge Blair in his native town of Indiana, and on April 20, 1870, was admitted to the bar in the Fifth Judicial District in the State of New York. He then engaged in active practice at Utica, New York, and had gone so far in his profession that in 1880 he was elected judge of Oneida County, and served a term of six years on the bench.

It was partly to get away from the confining work of his profession and also to possess himself of the opportunities of the great West that caused Mr. Sutton to come out to Kansas in 1887. Kansas has been his home now for thirty years. He first located in Russell County, and for two years busied himself with the management of a ranch. He then opened a law office in the town of Russell, and continued the practice of law together with farming until 1897. In 1894 he was elected a member of the State Legislature, serving one term. In the spring of 1895 Mr. Sutton was appointed by Governor E. N. Morrell a member of the State Board of Irrigation, and served in that capacity two years. While a member of the Legislature he was chairman of the committee on agriculture, and had as much to do with the passing of the seed grain law as any other member. From 1891 to 1898 he was a member of the State Board of Agriculture. He was elected and served two years as president of the Kansas Improved Stock Breeders' Association. Thus he has had more than a nominal interest and part in the raising of the standards of agriculture and stock raising in this state.

In 1897 Mr. Sutton removed to Kansas City, Kansas, and since then has devoted his attention largely to the practice of law. He is now senior member of the firm of Sutton & Sutton, his associate being his son, William B. Sutton, Jr. Mr. Sutton is a republican, a Protestant in religion, and a member of the Masonic fraternity.

Seven sons were born to Mr. and Mrs. Sutton, of whom four are now living. Charles E., of Lawrence, is a practical stockman and farmer, and has been president of the State Board of Agriculture; James is a business man at Harper, Kansas; William B., Jr., graduated in 1899 from the university and for a number of years has been associated with his father in practice; Dr. Walter S. Sutton, late of Kansas City, Kansas, whose death occurred on November 10, 1916, was a graduate of the State University and also of the College of Physicians and Surgeons at New York, and was Associate Professor of Surgery in the Medical School of the State University, and Associate Attending Surgeon at Bell Memorial Hospital at Rosedale, and the Christian Church Hospitals in Kansas City, Missouri; Everett B. lives at Independence, Kansas.

ARTHUR RICHARD NASH, M. D. A surgeon whose ability has brought him a rapidly growing reputation in southeastern Kansas, Dr. Arthur Richard Nash has practiced at Parsons for the past four years. He received his degree in medicine nearly twenty years ago, and has had a wide range of experience and opportunity in his profession since then.

He is of Irish stock. The Nashs were English originally and moved from there to Ireland. Doctor Nash is a grandson of a physician, Richard Nash, who spent his life in Ireland as a physician and surgeon. He died in County Tipperary at the age of fifty-two.

Richard Nash, Jr., father of Doctor Nash, was born in County Tipperary in 1840. His mother brought him to the United States in 1843 and he grew up at Chateaugay, New York, and at Pewaukee, Wisconsin. He learned the trade of shoemaker, followed it a number of years and was also a shoe merchant. He was in active business at Oconomowoc, Wisconsin, until 1884, and then engaged in farming near St. Croix Falls in that state and in 1900 moved to Ellsworth, Wisconsin, where he now conducts a drug business. He is a republican, and for a number of years served as justice of the peace. He is also a Royal Arch Mason. Richard Nash married Phoebe Ann Laine, who was born in Vermont in 1849, and died at Ellsworth, Wisconsin, in 1914. Doctor Nash is the oldest of their children. Caroline died at Oconomowoc, Wisconsin, at the age of three years; Francis Ralph is superintendent of the schools at St.

Croix Falls, Wisconsin; Cora Isabelle is the wife of Olaf Sundby, who has the leading general merchandise store at Ellsworth, Wisconsin.

Arthur Richard Nash was born while his parents resided at Oconomowoc, Wisconsin, on April 8, 1871. His parents took much interest in his early training, and from that source and also by making opportunities for himself he gained a very liberal education as a foundation for his professional work. Until he was seven years of age his instruction was looked after by Miss Noble in a select school at Oconomowoc. He then attended the public schools there and in that vicinity, afterwards was in the district schools near St. Croix Falls, and whether in school or on the outside his instruction was always under competent teachers. In 1889, at the age of eighteen he began teaching, and for three years followed that occupation and partly paid his own expenses while in college. Doctor Nash is a graduate of the Northern Indiana Normal School, now Valparaiso University, where he took his Bachelor of Science degree in 1894. He then entered the Rush Medical College at Chicago, the oldest medical college in the Middle West, and though completing the four years work in three be remained another year to get credit for the entire four years course. He graduated Doctor of Medicine in 1897. Beginning as a general practitioner he has gradually specialized and his time is now practically taken up with the work of surgery. He has attended clinics in the famous Mayo Brothers Hospital at Rochester, Minnesota, and has also taken post-graduate work at St. Paul and Chicago.

From 1897 to 1909 Doctor Nash practiced at Ellsworth, Wisconsin. He then spent three years at Del Norte, Colorado, where he was surgeon in the St. Joseph's Sanitarium. Since coming to Parsons in 1912 he has specialized in surgery. His office is at 107½ South Central Avenue. He is an active member of the County and State Medical societies and the American Medical Association, and has served as city and township health officer back in his home town of Ellsworth, Wisconsin, also at Parsons and elsewhere.

Doctor Nash and his family reside at 1725 Chess Avenue in Parsons. He also owns a home in Ellsworth, Wisconsin. Politically he is an independent republican and is a member of the Catholic Church, belongs to the Parsons Chamber of Commerce and to Anamosa Council of the Knights of Columbus in Colorado.

In 1899 at Clayfield, five miles from Ellsworth, Wisconsin, he married Miss Ellen Louise Mallon, daughter of Mr. and Mrs. James Mallon. Her father, now deceased, was a farmer and stock raiser, making a specialty of Shorthorn cattle. Her mother is still living at Ellsworth, Wisconsin. Doctor and Mrs. Nash are the parents of five children: Marguerite Anna, born in 1900; Eleanor, born in 1902; Frances, born in 1904; Richard Arthur, born in 1907; and James Byron, born in 1910. All except the youngest were born in Ellsworth, Wisconsin, while James B. was born at Del Norte, Colorado.

MIDDLETON L. PERRY, M. D. Among the men of Kansas who are carrying on the highly important work of caring for the afflicted and irresponsible members of society, one of the best known is Dr. Middleton L. Perry, superintendent of the State Hospital for Epileptics, at Parsons.

Doctor Perry was born at Lancaster, Dallas County, Texas, August 15, 1868, and is a son of Middleton and Ellen (Ellis) Perry. The family is of English extraction and settled during colonial times in Virginia, where the grandfather of Doctor Perry, Frank-

Arthur R. Nash, M.D.

lin Perry, was born. He was a farmer by vocation and in young manhood moved to Illinois, where he became a pioneer of Greene County and there continued his agricultural pursuits until his death which occurred before the birth of his grandson. Middleton Perry was born in 1814, in Indiana, but as a boy was taken to Illinois, where, in Greene County, he was educated, reared and married. In that state he followed farming, but in 1844, when thirty years of age, went to Texas as a homesteader, and that state continued to be his home until his death, which occurred at Lancaster, in 1892. Mr. Perry took part in the stirring happenings that occurred in the formative era of the Lone Star State and endured the privations and hardships incident to pioneer settlement, and was considered one of the sturdy and self-reliant men of his day who assisted in the development of his adopted commonwealth. He was an industrious man, and through hard and constant work became the owner of a valuable property. Politically Mr. Perry was a democrat and one of the stanch supporters of his party's candidates and principles. He was an active member of the Baptist Church, the movements of which he supported liberally, while his fraternal connection was with the Masonic order. At the outbreak of the Civil war, he enlisted in the Confederate service, and rose to the rank of a captain of a Texas cavalry regiment. Mr. Perry married Miss Ellen Ellis, who was born in 1824, in Illinois, and died at Lancaster, Texas, in 1891, and they became the parents of the following children: Frank, now deceased; Mollie, who is the wife of W. D. Breazeale, engaged in city work at Dallas, Texas; Maggie, who is the wife of W. P. White, a real estate agent of that city; A. L., a farmer, stock raiser and general business man of Duke, Oklahoma; Nona, who married I. E. Stout, a stockman of San Angelo, Texas; W. Y., who is engaged in banking at Lancaster, Texas; Loura, who resides with her brother, M. L.; and Middleton L., of this notice.

The early education of Middleton L. Perry was obtained in the public schools of Lancaster, Texas, where he was graduated from Lancaster Academy in the class of 1885. He next enrolled as a student at the University of Texas, at Austin, where he spent one year, and then entered the medical school of the University of Tennessee, at Nashville, from which he was duly graduated in the class of 1892, at that time receiving his cherished degree of Doctor of Medicine. In 1892 and 1893 he served as interne in the City Hospital, Nashville, Tennessee, and in the latter year also did post-graduate work at the University of Virginia. He then returned to his native state for a short time, but soon went to New York, where he did post-graduate work under private instructors for six months, and also in hospitals there. He next became assistant physician of the State Hospital, Morris Plains, New Jersey, in 1894, and held that position steadily until 1898. In 1898 Doctor Perry went to Europe, where he specialized in neurology at the University of Berlin and the University of Vienna. In 1899 he was appointed pathologist in the State Hospital of Georgia, and remained in that capacity until 1903, when he was sent for to come to Parsons and become superintendent of the State Hospital for Epileptics, of Kansas. The first act of the Kansas Legislature of 1899 was the setting aside of an appropriation and the appointment of a committee for the building of this hospital, one of the most humane and highly important state institutions in the Southwest. The buildings are located in the northwest part of Parsons, and the grounds consist of 640

Vol. IV—22

acres. During his incumbency, Doctor Perry has labored faithfully in behalf of his charges, and at present a new hospital building is being erected, although this is but one of the many benefits and improvements secured through his earnest and indefatigable work. He is nationally accounted an authority on the care and treatment of epilepsy and is frequently called upon to appear before important bodies to read papers and deliver lectures upon the subject. He makes his home in the state residence on the grounds and is therefore constantly in touch with the wards of the state. Doctor Perry is an independent democrat. In line with his profession he belongs to the Labette County Medical Society, the Kansas State Medical Society, the American Medical Association, the Southeastern Medical Society and the Medical Society of the Southwest. He belongs also to the Parsons Chamber of Commerce and is a director of the Exchange State Bank of Parsons.

Doctor Perry was married in 1902 at Milledgeville, Georgia, to Miss Jamie Wimberly, daughter of the late James and Ellen (Guiton) Wimberly, both of whom are now deceased. Mr. Wimberly was for many years one of the successful attorneys of Georgia. To Doctor and Mrs. Perry there have been born two children, namely: Middleton Lee, born December 23, 1903; and Wimberly, born July 29, 1905, both at Parsons.

WINFIELD FREEMAN. Lawyer, author, traveler, leader in republican politics and a business man, Winfield Freeman has been a Kansan for more than thirty-five years. He has long enjoyed a reputation as one of the foremost members of the bar in Kansas City, Kansas.

He was born at London, Ohio, January 3, 1848, a son of James F. and Eleanor (Dawson) Freeman. His early life was spent in Winchester, Ohio, where he attended the public schools and where he read law in the office of Hon. A. Stiver. Admitted to the bar in 1869, at the age of twenty-one, he practiced law for a number of years in Ohio, and in 1878-79 served as prosecuting attorney of Preble County. Since 1879 he has been a resident of Kansas. From 1880 to 1884 he was assistant attorney for the Solomon Valley Railroad Company. In 1881 he was elected mayor of Minneapolis, Kansas. As one of the promoters of the Kansas City Elevated Railroad Company Mr. Freeman removed to Kansas City, Kansas, in 1884, and was actively identified with that transportation service as attorney until 1888. It is forty-eight years since he commenced the practice of law in Ohio in 1869, and his experience is a remarkably long one. He was associated with Silas Wright Porter, now associate justice of the Supreme Court of Kansas, from 1891 to 1899, and was also a partner with Hon. William J. Buchan, who for many years was representative and state senator. Another one of his professional associates was W. A. Johnston, now chief justice of the Supreme Court of Kansas.

Judge Freeman has for many years been one of the leading campaign speakers of the republican party. He was elected to the city council in 1887-89, and from 1890 to 1892 served as city counselor of Kansas City, Kansas. In 1893 he was appointed county attorney of Wyandotte County, and from 1903 to 1907 served as probate judge.

Judge Freeman is a member of the Kansas State Bar Association. He was a delegate to the Universal Congress of Lawyers and Jurists at St. Louis in 1904. For several years he was lecturer on medical jurisprudence before the College of Physicians and Surgeons of Kansas City, Kansas. An active Methodist, he has been a teacher in its Sunday schools for forty-six years.

Judge Freeman made a trip around the world in 1907-08, and has not only traveled extensively but has studied foreign people, and during his world trip he delivered numerous addresses at missionary centers. He is a favorite lecturer on the Orient, and has contributed many articles to the press on Eastern countries and their people. He is also well known for his historical writings. His ''Battle of Arickaree'' is found in Volume 6 of the reports of the Kansas State Historical Society, and is a splendid contribution to the Indian history of Kansas. It is a graphic description of one of the most romantic incidents of the Great Plains.

Judge Freeman was married July 6, 1876, to Miss Reba Silver of Richmond, Indiana. They reside at 749 Washington Boulevard, Kansas City, Kansas.

DAVID HECKMAN. Of the men whose ability, industry and forethought have added to the character, wealth and good government of Liberty, none are better known than David Heckman. Mr. Heckman is a business man, not only by training and long experience, but by preference and natural talent, and all these qualities have been combined to form a force through which he has worked his way to success. He first came to this community in 1870, but it was not until 1877 that he located permanently in Liberty, and since that time his fortunes have been linked indissolubly with those of the growing community which he has watched grow and develop with the eye of a proprietor.

Mr. Heckman was born on his father's farm near Leechburg, Armstrong County, Pennsylvania, January 17, 1847, being a son of Abraham and Esther (Klingensmith) Heckman, a grandson of Philip Heckman, a pioneer Pennsylvania farmer who died in Armstrong County before his birth, and a member of a family which originated in Germany and transferred its abiding place to America many years ago. Abraham Heckman was born in 1812, in Armstrong County, and there his entire life was passed in the vocations of farming and stockraising. He was a man of sound intelligence and force of character, and his abilities were recognized by his fellow-citizens on a number of occasions when they elected him to public positions of trust and responsibility, such as overseer of the poor, township treasurer and numerous other posts. He took a great interest in civic affairs and was prominent in his community as a democratic politician. He died in 1906, in the faith of the Lutheran Church, in which he had been an active worker. Mr. Heckman married Miss Esther Klingensmith, who was born in Armstrong County in 1816 and died there in 1901, and they became the parents of the following children: Gideon, who died in Armstrong County after a long career passed as a tiller of the soil; Henry, who, in following the vocation of schoolteacher, traveled from the Atlantic to the Pacific, and died at Salem, Oregon; Mary Ann, who is the widow of Louis Deiffendeifer, a farmer of Indiana County, Pennsylvania; Peter, who died near the old homestead farm in Armstrong County, Pennsylvania; A. J., who fought as a soldier during the Civil war, subsequently came to Kansas where he was in business with his brother, David, and died at Ossawotamie, Kansas, being buried at Liberty; William, who was in the real estate business and insurance at Coffeyville and died in February, 1916; David, of this review; John C., who was identified with steel mills in Pennsylvania for twenty years before his death in Armstrong County, Pennsylvania, in 1910; Catherine, who is the wife of Albert Klingensmith, a hardware merchant near New Kensington, Pennsylvania; and Margaret, who is the wife of Abraham Shutt, now living retired at Leechburg, Pennsylvania, after many years spent in agricultural pursuits.

David Heckman attended the district schools of Armstrong County, Pennsylvania, and was reared on his father's farm, on which he resided until reaching the age of twenty-three years. In 1870 he left the parental roof to seek his fortune in the West, and arrived in Montgomery County, Kansas, February 14th of that year when he pre-empted from the United States Government a property which was later to become the townsite of Liberty. This he subsequently sold, after a short period, to Captains McTaggart and Herod, and the town was founded in 1871. When he disposed of this land, Mr. Heckman went to Crawford County, Kansas, where for six years he lived on a farm. Conditions there, however, were not entirely satisfactory, and on disposing of his property advantageously, he returned to Liberty, then a full-fledged, growing and prosperous town. In company with his father-in-law, he embarked in the mercantile business, with a stock of goods worth $2,000. From the start the business was successful, the ability, good judgment and foresight of the partners attracting a large volume of patronage and their straightforward dealing and absolute integrity in all matters holding customers that were once made. At one time, during the earlier days, so great had the business grown that trade was attracted from a radius of fifteen miles, and there are still a number of customers who come in from six miles and even farther to deal with this old and reliable concern. A three-story building is occupied, Mr. Heckman owning two floors and leasing the third, and everything is sold from a pin to a thrashing machine or an automobile. The floors have a front of 75 feet and a depth of 80 feet, and the great stock is being constantly rearranged and renewed so that only up-to-date goods of the best quality are kept. Throughout his career Mr. Heckman's name has been synonymous with fair and upright dealing, and this gives him decided prestige in business circles. While the greater part of his attention has been centered in his store, he has other interests, and at the same time has not been neglectful of his duties as a citizen, for he has lent his support to various public-spirited enterprises which have helped Liberty in its growth. He resides in his own home, located in block 9. Mr. Heckman is a democrat in political affairs, and fraternally is well known, belonging to Independent Order of Odd Fellows Lodge No. 105, Liberty, Modern Woodmen of America Camp No. 96, Liberty; Lodge No. 279, Ancient Order of United Workmen, of Coffeyville; the Rebekahs of Liberty and the Anti-Horse Thief Association, of this city.

In 1874, at Liberty, Mr. Heckman was united in marriage with Miss Emma Barnett, daughter of the late Edward Barnett, a merchant of this place. Mrs. Heckman died February 29, 1916, having been the mother of one child, Myrtle, who died aged eighteen months and one adopted daughter, True, who married Frank Love, and resides at Winona, Missouri, where Mr. Love is filling the position of railroad agent.

HENRY E. DEAN came to Kansas in 1885 at the age of eighteen. Then and for a number of years afterwards he was a humble worker in the ranks of the industrial army. Success did not come to him like a lightning flash, but as a result of long, steady and painstaking effort. For the first two years he was employed on farms in Leavenworth and Franklin counties. On removing to Kansas City, Kansas, in 1887, he found a job as teamster for one of the packing plants. Making himself known as one who could be trusted, and diligent in the execution of his duties, he was given positions in the rising scale of importance and financial income, and eventually he became foreman in the curing department of Sulzberger & Sons' packing house.

A boyhood desire to become a lawyer had in the meantime crystalized into a set and fixed determination, and for several years, in addition to the duties of the day, he attended night school in the Kansas City School of Law. From that institution he was graduated June 10, 1900, and was admitted to the Missouri bar and soon afterwards to the Kansas bar.

Even after his admission he felt that it was the wisest course to continue earning money in the old routine rather than endure the starvation period which confronts the average young lawyer while waiting for clients. But in September, 1900, he opened an office in Kansas City, Kansas, and from that time with the exception of three years has been continuously engaged in practice. He was first a member of the firm of Bradbent & Dean, then Getty, Hutchings & Dean, then Hale & Dean, and finally Hale, Dean & Higgins. At present Mr. Dean is engaged in individual practice with offices in the People's National Bank Building. Mr. Dean is well grounded in the fundamental principles of law, has a splendid practice, and both his reputation and position in the profession are thoroughly assured.

With his growing success as a lawyer Mr. Dean has become more and more widely known in public affairs and as a public leader of demonstrated ability. In 1909 he was elected president of the Wyandotte County Bar Association. In 1904 he was appointed auditor of Wyandotte County by Judge Moore, and filled that office for four years. When Kansas City, Kansas, adopted its commission charter, Mr. Dean was elected in 1910 a member of the first city commission, and was re-elected in 1911, serving altogether three years and part of the time as president of the commission. In August, 1913, Governor Hodges appointed him a member of the Panama-Pacific International Exposition at San Francisco and San Diego. He was made secretary of this commission and had the general management of the Kansas interests in that great world's fair.

At the dedication of the site for the Kansas Building in October, 1913, at San Francisco, on the identical spot where the Twentieth Kansas Regiment encamped prior to its departure for the Philippines, Mr. Dean was chosen as the orator to deliver the dedicatory address. It was a notable speech, and was not only appreciated by the many citizens of the Sunflower State who were present at the occasion, but was widely read when republished by the press of the country. Without attempting to quote the address as a whole, some sentences should be extracted that reveal the intrinsic power of literary expression by Mr. Dean, and which also have some permanent interest to Kansans.

"Expositions of the past have been reminiscent in their character, and step by step have recounted the achievements of the long ago. The occasion which engages our attention today is unique in that it departs radically from the celebration of the past and finds its theme in the vital present. Not that we would detract one jot from these great world gatherings of the past, marking, as they have, world epochs, but our present ceremony is one of the preliminary steps to celebrate a material accomplishment from which are to flow blessings to all people of the great round world.

"And so Kansas comes with no halting step or blurred vision to participate in this great celebration which we believe presages these great things for humanity. But realizing with our backs to the past and our faces gazing hopefully into the future we descry shapes and figures which justify the prediction that following fast upon the heels of this marvel of engineering skill are to come yet social, industrial and moral changes that will go far toward the relief of conditions that to the thoughtful are fast becoming intolerable. And so Kansas comes to you today in no spirit of exultation, without bombast, egotism or boastfulness, but with a serene confidence in the future, and believing that we can see through the Golden Gate the crimson streaks which betoken the dawn of a new and better day, in the fullness of which the barriers erected and so long maintained by selfishness and the wrongful use of power are to be broken down, and in their stead shall be installed a reign of progress, justice and equity. And it is in this spirit that we today in the name of the great State of Kansas dedicate this spot, rich in its history of the past and golden with promise for the future."

Mr. Dean has been a sturdy republican, and in 1916 was nominated by his party for the lower house of the State Legislature.

He is a member of the Union and Elks clubs of Kansas City, Kansas, and in Masonry has attained the supreme thirty-third honorary degree in the Scottish Rite. He is master of the Lodge of Perfection, and is also affiliated with the Independent Order of Odd Fellows. Mr. Dean is a lover of outdoor sports, especially of hunting.

Henry Ezra Dean was born at Cold Springs, Kentucky, August 23, 1867, the fifth in a family of eleven children. His parents were Hiram E. and Matilda (McCollum) Dean, both natives of Kentucky. His father was a prosperous farmer in Kentucky and lived there until his death in 1909 at the age of seventy-nine. The mother is past seventy-five and is still living at the old home in Cold Springs. Hiram E. Dean served with credit as a Union soldier during the Civil war, became a republican upon the organization of that party, and both he and his wife were loyal Baptists. It was on the old home farm in Kentucky that Henry E. Dean spent his early years and gained his education in the district schools. Being without means to carry on his ambitious plans for a professional career, he came out to Kansas and put in the many years of hard work on farm and in packing plants until he was able to realize his early dreams.

On October 11, 1893, he married Miss Jennie B. Bown, daughter of William T. and Nancy J. (Johnson) Bown, who came from New Albany, Indiana, to Kansas City, Kansas. Mr. and Mrs. Dean have three children: Helen, who died when six and a half years of age; and Harry E., and John Russell.

DUNHAM O. MUNSON, M. D., is one of the leading specialists of Southeastern Kansas. He has practiced at Pittsburg upwards of twenty years, and while the earlier part of his practice was devoted to general medicine and surgery, for the past five years he has given his time exclusively to the diseases of the eye, ear, nose and throat.

He is a man of splendid attainments in his profession and undoubtedly inherits much from his fine old American ancestry. He was born at Brockport, New York, June 27, 1859, but a part of his early life was spent in Ontario, Canada. He attended the public school and high school at Bowmanville in Ontario, was graduated from high school in 1879 and then removed to Detroit, Michigan, where he spent a number of years as bookkeeper with a music house. He had a long and varied business career before entering his profession. For four years Doctor Munson was in the real estate business at Denver, Colorado. He had long cherished an ambition to enter the field of medicine, and finally removed to St. Louis and became a student in the Marion-Sims College of Medicine, now the medical department of St. Louis University. He was graduated there M. D. in 1896. In the past twenty years Doctor Munson has been continuously a student and a close follower of every advance made in his special line of practice. After beginning private practice at St. Louis in 1896, he has taken post-graduate work in the Chicago Policlinic, the Illinois Eye, Ear, Nose and Throat Infirmary, the Chicago Eye, Ear, Nose and Throat College, and also in the St. Louis University and the various hospitals and clinics there.

Doctor Munson practiced in St. Louis until 1898, in which year he removed to Pittsburg, Kansas. During 1900-02 he also practiced at Cherokee. For about twelve years he looked after a general medical and surgical practice, but has been an exclusive specialist for the past five years. His offices are in the Globe Building at Pittsburg.

For two years Doctor Munson served as county health officer, was city physician of Pittsburg three years, and during his residence at Cherokee was railroad surgeon for the Frisco, served as mayor of that town and as president of the school board. He is affiliated with Girard Lodge of the Masons, Cherokee Chapter Royal Arch Masons, and Palestine Commandery No. 28 Knights Templars at Girard. His church membership is in the Episcopal denomination. He is an active member of the Crawford County and the State Medical Society and belongs to the Pittsburg Country Club.

In 1889 at Greeley, Colorado, Doctor Munson married Miss Magdalene Begert. Her father Jacob Begert, who died at Medicine Lodge, Kansas, in 1914, was a farmer, and his wife now resides in New Sharon, Iowa. The Begert family came to America about 1856 from the vicinity of Lake Luzerne and Berne, Switzerland. They settled in Brockport, New York, where Mrs. Munson was born April 7, 1867. Mrs. Munson is an active member of the State Federation of Women's Clubs. Doctor and Mrs. Munson have one son, Herbert Edwin, who was born in Chillicothe, Illinois, November 6, 1896, is a graduate of the Pittsburg High School, and is now a sophomore in the School of Journalism at the Missouri State University.

By reason of his descent from a line of very prominent and patriotic American ancestors Doctor Munson has membership in the Sons of the American Revolution, the Order of Washington, the Society of Colonial Wars and the Founders and Patriots of America. Eligibility to membership in the order of Founders and Patriots of America is based upon the following qualifications: Twenty-one years of age, of good moral character and reputation, a citizen of the United States, and one who is lineally descended in the male line of either parents from an ancestor who settled in any of the colonies now included in the United States of America prior to May 13, 1657, and one or all of whose intermediate ancestors in the same line, living during the period of the Revolution from 1775 to 1783 adhered as patriots to the cause of the colonies. Doctor Munson is also deputy vice commander for Kansas of the Order of Washington. A candidate for membership in this order must have descended in the male or female line from a male ancestor who assisted the colonies in obtaining independence, and the revolutionary ancestor must have descended in the direct male line from an ancestor who was in the colonies prior to 1750 and who or whose son held at some time an official position during the colonial period or was the founder of a town or was in the military or naval service, or was a minister of the gospel. Probably few persons understand what the qualifications for membership in these various orders are, and it will therefore be of special interest to trace Doctor Munson's ancestry.

I. Capt. Thomas Munson, the ancestor of all the Munsons in the United States, was born in 1612 and died in 1685. He came from England, and in 1637 was one of the forty-two men of Hartford, Connecticut, who served under Captain Mason in the Pequot Indian war. He was of New Haven, where he signed the Fundamental Agreement in 1639. He was lieutenant in 1664-76, served under Captain Treat in the King Phillip war; was captain in 1676 of the New Haven Militia. Captain Thomas was elected to the Plantation Court in 1662. He was foreman of the first grand jury empaneled in New Haven; also a member of the Supreme Court of Appeals. In 1666 he was elected deputy to the General Assembly, serving in this capacity for twenty-four sessions.

II. Samuel Munson, born August 7, 1643, according to the New Haven First Church record, was married according to the town record October 26, 1665, to Martha, daughter of William and Alice (Pritchard) Bradley. Samuel died in 1693 in Wallingford, Connecticut. He was deputy from New Haven to the General Court of Connecticut, 1665, 1678, 1680, 1683. Samuel Munson with thirty-eight others of New Haven founded Wallingford, Connecticut. The General Court of Hartford on May 12, 1669, "doe grant liberty to make a village on the East River." Among the names signed to the agreement appear those of Samuel Munson, Thomas Yale, Thomas Curtis, Samuel Peck and John Peck, Joseph Benham, John Brockett and Nathaniel How. A record of the General Court October 19, 1675, reads: "This court confirms Samuel Munson ensigne Wallingford Traine Band."

III. Samuel Munson, born February 28, 1669, at Wallingford, Connecticut, married Martha ——. She died January 7, 1707. He married the widow of Caleb Merriman, daughter of Eliasaph Preston. She died November 28, 1755. Samuel died November 23, 1741, aged seventy-three, at Wallingford. He was town clerk at Wallingford twenty-nine years. In October, 1712, the General Court divided the Traine Band of Wallingford, "Samuel Munson to be ensigne of the west company of Traine Band."

IV. William Munson, born October 13, 1695, at Wallingford, Connecticut, married Rebecca, daughter of Thomas Curtis of Wallingford. William died July 21, 1773, at Waterbury, Connecticut. Thomas Curtis, whose daughter Rebecca married William

Munson, was born in 1648, died in 1736; was ensigne Wallingford Traine Band 1704, and original proprietor and signer of the Covenant 1669; deputy colonial legislature 1689, 1714, 1717; constable 1681; town treasurer, 1686. Thomas Curtis married Mary Merriman of Wallingford June 9, 1674-5. She was born in New Haven in 1657 and died in Wallingford. John Curtis, father of Thomas, was born in Nazing, Essex County, England, in 1611, died in Stratford, Connecticut, 1707, aged ninety-six. He married Elizabeth Welles, who died in Stratford, Connecticut, March 9, 1681-2. John Curtis was a soldier in King Phillip's war and attained the rank of ensign. He was one of the original patentees of Stratford, Connecticut, and in the patent was called "Sergeant John Curtis."

V. William Munson, born July 5, 1731, at Wallingford, Connecticut, married Sarah, daughter of Isaac Griggs, Wallingford, February 28, 1753. He died May 26, 1815. His wife died October 7, 1806, at Waterbury, Connecticut. William served in the Revolutionary war as a private. He enlisted May 26, 1777, in Capt. David Smith's Company, Connecticut Battalion, served three years, discharged May 26, 1780, as a private from Maj. David Smith's Company, Eighth Connecticut Regiment, Col. Isaac Sherman.

VI. Elisha Munson, born October 10, 1756, at Waterbury, Connecticut, married September 3, 1783, Mabel Homeston, daughter of Joy Homeston (Humestone). Elisha died in 1835 at Prospect, Connecticut. Elisha enlisted with his father William on the same day and in the same company and was discharged on the same day and in the same company. The battles engaged in were Harlem, Germantown and Monmouth. Elisha was pensioned. Both these patriots were with Washington at Valley Forge.

VII. Limus Joy Munson, grandfather of Doctor Munson of Pittsburg, who therefore represents the ninth generation of the family in America, was born at Prospect, Connecticut, in 1800. In 1821 in Canton, New York, he married Lorene Weller. She was born in Canton in 1800, and died in Cobourg, Ontario, Canada, in 1876. Limus J. Munson, who was a carriage manufacturer, died at Cobourg, Canada, in 1835.

VIII. David Ezra Munson, father of Doctor Munson, was born at Prospect, Connecticut, in 1832. He spent his early life in Prospect, and in Cobourg, Ontario, and in Rochester, New York. He also became a carriage manufacturer, and followed that business largely in Canada and died at Gault, Ontario, in 1888. He was a member of the Methodist Church and a thirty-second degree Scottish Rite Mason. In 1856 he married Amy Oekerman; who was born in Belleville, Ontario, in 1834, and is now living at the age of eighty-two in California. Her children were two in number, the older being Doctor Munson. The daughter Frances A. lives in Los Angeles, California, and is the widow of the late Charles Lypps, who was an oil operator and was killed in an automobile accident in Los Angeles May 19, 1913.

STEPHEN E. BEACH. In searching for the facts of history concerning any community, the mind of the chronicler turns naturally to the first things or the initial work accomplished in the formation of that community into a social and political body. An interest always attaches to these first things which is not to be found in anything else historic, and when there has been found the first settler, or the first house, or the first institution, it is looked upon with more than

ordinary respect, and an endeavor is instinctively made to retrace the history of the subject of our interest to its or his beginning. The first things of fifty or sixty years ago are frequently difficult to ascertain, because of the death or removal of the actors and the absence of authentic records concerning them. But occasionally the chronicler has the rare privilege of coming into personal contact with one who has lived through the period of the beginning of things, and who still remains as an active factor in the life of the community. In this connection interest centers in Stephen E. Beach, of Chanute, a resident of Neosho County since 1859, and a witness of the wonderful development of the county since that time.

Mr. Beach is a native of New England, having been born at Wallingford, Connecticut, November 25, 1837, his parents being Nathan and Lucy (Pierpont) Beach. He is a member of a family which traces its ancestry directly to one of the Pilgrims, John Beach, who was born in 1618, was at New Haven in 1643, was married in 1650, was at Stratford in 1650, signed the Wallingford Loan Contract in 1670, and is spoken of as deceased in 1680. While at New Haven he was fined five pounds for carelessly felling a tree whereby the cow of one George Smith was killed. John Beach's son, Thomas, was born in 1650; Thomas' son, Nathan, was born August 8, 1692; and the latter's son, William, was born November 18, 1716. Steven Beach, the son of William, was born October 25, 1760, and died November 17, 1821. He married Miriam Parker who was born July 26, 1753, and died June 25, 1823. Jason Beach, son of Steven and Miriam, and grandfather of Stephen E. Beach, was born December 27, 1775, and died at Wallingford, Connecticut, May 28, 1830. He married Susannah Hotchkiss, April 17, 1800, she born November 12, 1777, and died October 25, 1847. Mr. Beach followed farming throughout his life. The children of Jason and Sarah Beach were: Lucy, born January 29, 1801, died June 29, 1801; William, born May 26, 1802, died October 2, 1853; Roger N. born February 12, 1804, died August 1, 1831; Norman, born March 17, 1806, deceased; Susan, born November 19, 1808, deceased; Lucy, born November 19, 1808, died September 11, 1868; Nathan, born May 17, 1811, died October 3, 1882; and Eliza A. born February 10, 1816, died in 1908.

Nathan Beach, father of Stephen E. Beach, was born at Wallingford, Connecticut, May 17, 1811, followed farming all his life there, and died October 3, 1882. He married Lucy Pierpont, who, like her husband, was a member of an old and honored New England family, and they became the parents of four children, as follows: Joel, who during a long career was engaged in farming, merchandising and the manufacture of spoons, and is now a retired resident of New Haven, Connecticut; Stephen E.; Zerah, who resides on the old home farm at Wallingford, Connecticut, where he has an extensive peach orchard; and Esther, who is the wife of Rienzi Stone, of Wallingford, Connecticut, a retired farmer with a large income derived from his rentals and investments.

Stephen E. Beach passed his boyhood on the home farm, and was afforded excellent educational advantages in one of the best literary institutions of Connecticut. Shortly after reaching his majority, he responded to the call of the West by joining some neighborhood youths in a trip to the Rockies, which venture resulted in his final settlement and residence in Kansas. In 1859 he came to what is now Neosho County, where, after more than half a century has passed, he is still an active spirit in the life of the community. His first experience with the frontier began at Kansas City, upon his arrival there from St. Louis by boat, in company with Elmer Johnson, an eastern friend. Their objective point had originally been Leavenworth, Kansas, but abandoned their original intention upon reaching Kansas City, and, instead, purchased a horse and light wagon and started across the plains for Denver, Colorado, in company with a caravan. Also making the journey with Messrs. Beach and Johnson was Sam Purdy, a youth who joined them at Kansas City. When well out on the plains, near the Arkansas River, they left the caravan and drove on alone, intending to make a camping ground in advance of their erstwhile comrades. While young Beach and a companion were exploring the bluffs for game, keeping their wagon in sight, however, they came to a high point overlooking the river, and were dismayed and disconcerted to see their wagon surrounded by Indians, the whole party retreating from the direction of the two young men and the horse on a trot, a gait that was a usual sign of danger on the plains. The two footmen broke directly for their wagon and decided to give battle when discovered, if it came to the worst. As was expected, a few of the Indians approached, but every time young Beach raised his rifle to shoot, they would yell and make signs and motions for him not to do so. The young men were undecided whether these gesticulations were for a friendly purpose or designed to entrap them alive, but as they did not harm the Indians the adventure ended with no more serious consequences to the young men than a marked reduction in their supply of sugar and other articles comprising their commissary. They joined the ox train from there on to Pikes Peak.

Eventually the little party reached Pikes Peak, but found the country overrun with gold-seekers and settlers, and, as nothing encouraging presented itself, the "one horse tourists" struck the trail for Leavenworth. On their arrival there Mr. Beach and his partner opened a grocery store, which they conducted for two months. Then, loading their stock of goods into two wagons, they moved into what is now Neosho County, where together they established a grocery business at Osage City, later called Rogers' Mills. This was the initial step in a career that from that time to the present writing has been identified with the formation, development and growth of that community as a social and political organization. Thereafter the supplies for the store were obtained at Kansas City, which point Mr. Beach visited as frequently as he needed goods or as was necessary as a freighter for others. The store not proving very profitable, however, he gave it up for other pursuits and purchased his first claim on Beach Creek, which was named in his honor as the first settler upon its banks. This quarter-section he abandoned in 1865, and settled on another tract, bordering on the Neosho River, which tract he deeded, proved and still owns. At this time he possesses 240 acres of farming land, his own residence at No. 801 West Main Street, Chanute, 5½ acres directly opposite his residence in the heart of the city, another dwelling at No. 512 West Third Street, Chanute, and a dwelling and two vacant lots at Colony, Kansas.

Mr. Beach early engaged in the cattle business, and in partnership with Benjamin M. Smith, another pioneer, grazed cattle all over the site of what is now Chanute, the partners having for the salting grounds for their herd that portion which now forms the center of the city. Mr. Beach removed his family to Chanute in 1885 in order to secure better educational advantages for his children. In later years he was identified with the Bank of Commerce of Chanute, was its president for two years, and is still a stockholder therein.

During the Civil war Mr. Beach was a member of the Kansas State Militia and was commissioned ensign by Governor Robinson and third lieutenant by Governor Carney. He was commissioned by Governor Carney a member of Neosho County's first board of commissioners and at the first election called by this board and the county clerk, Mr. Beach was elected superintendent of public instruction for Neosho County, in which capacity he served two years. The first man elected to the office of county treasurer declined to serve, whereupon Mr. Beach was appointed to that office, and by appointment and election continued to fill it for five years. He served as trustee of Tioga Township for four years and has also served as a justice of the peace in that township. He was one of the townsite company which established the Town of Chanute, and it was largely through his efforts that the Atchison, Topeka & Santa Fe Railroad located a station at the junction of that road with the Missouri, Kansas and Texas line.

Mr. Beach has always cast his ballot in accord with his convictions. The Pierponts, his mother's people, were whigs, and the Beach family, although not partisan, have inclined to support the principles of the democratic party. Mr. Beach cast his first presidential vote for a republican and remained with that party until 1872, when he voted for Horace Greeley. Since then he has been identified with no party in particular, voting as an independent. As an independent candidate he was elected mayor of Chanute in April, 1911, by a majority of 676 votes in a republican city. This may be taken as an expression of the high esteem in which he is held in that city, where throughout a long, busy and useful career he has ever been known as a man loyal to truth, honor and right, one whose self respect, probity and integrity have controlled his every act. Mr. Beach is a thirty-second degree, Scottish Rite Mason, and belongs to Cedar Lodge No. 103, Ancient Free and Accepted Masons; Chanute Chapter No. 21, Royal Arch Masons; and Chanute Commandery No. 44, Knight Templars, and has been master of his lodge and high priest of his chapter. He also holds membership in Chanute Lodge No. 96, Ancient Order of United Workmen. He has long been a member of the Methodist Episcopal Church, in which he is now serving as a trustee.

Mr. Beach's first wife was a Miss Sarah Sinclair, whom he wedded February 17, 1862, and who died August 31, 1865, without issue. On March 11, 1866, Mr. Beach was united in marriage with Miss Tressa Burch, who died February 21, 1871. Three sons were born to this union: Elmer, who died May 22, 1888; Charles, an engineer at the cement plant at Iola, Kansas, who married Nellie McKeever; and Harvey E., who has inherited the wanderlust, probably from his father, served a number of years on a revenue cutter in Puget Sound, has taken a whaling voyage up toward the North Pole, and is now a resident of California. On August 3, 1873, Mr. Beach married his third wife, Mary A. Brooks, who died without issue, March 2, 1874. On December 24, 1874, Mr. Beach married Miss Sarah Stanfield, and to this union there were born three daughters and one son: Leona, a graduate of Chanute High School, and valedictorian of her class of twelve students, married Dr. Johannes Rudbeck, a practicing physician and surgeon of

Seneca, Kansas; Sylvia E., a graduate of the Chanute High School, where she was valedictorian of her class of eighteen graduates, attended the State Normal School at Emporia, Kansas, and taught for several years in the Chanute public schools prior to her marriage to W. E. Wilson, a clothing merchant of Chanute; Eunice D., who died young; and Don C., a graduate of the Chanute High School, who later attended Baldwin University, and now a resident and prominent young business man of Chanute, where he is district manager for the Missouri, Kansas and Texas Telephone Company.

FLOYD B. McBRIDE, M. D. Among the young and enthusiastic professional element of Montgomery County is found Ford B. McBride, who, within the short space of seven years, has built up at Liberty a medical and surgical practice as gratifying personally as it is successful financially. The fearless, questioning attitude of the twentieth century nowhere is more strikingly apparent than among the exponents of medical science. The tendency of the latter-day physician is to avoid, above all things, hasty jumping at conclusions or too ready dependence upon formulae, a tendency that is rapidly destroying ancient delusions and thereby placing the health of the nation in the hands of reasoners and independent thinkers. In this class Doctor McBride undoubtedly belongs.

Ford B. McBride was born July 22, 1882, at Sullivan, Indiana, and is a son of T. P. and Lena (Godwin) McBride. The family is of Scotch-Irish origin and, probably in colonial days, first settled in New Jersey upon coming to America. The grandfather of Doctor McBride, William McBride, was born in 1832, in New Jersey, where he was reared to manhood, moved then to Ohio, where he was married, and was a pioneer into Sullivan County, Indiana. A cabinet maker by vocation, he followed his trade in all these states, and during the Civil war served the Union as an engineer, being a member of the Missouri branch of that service. In his declining years he moved to Illinois, and there his death occurred at Danville, in 1908. Mr. McBride was a sturdy pioneer, who combined in his character the sterling qualities of his Scotch and Irish forebears, and whose courage and industry were matched by his rugged honesty and fair dealing which caused him to be a good citizen and won for him the respect of his fellows. He was married twice, and by his first wife had a number of children, of whom three are still living: Agnes, who is the wife of Mr. Schneller, of Paris, Illinois, a veteran of the Civil war; T. P.; and Charles, who is a tonsorialist of Paris, Illinois. He also had several children by his second marriage, and of these three are living: James, who is a barber shop proprietor of St. Louis, Missouri; Florence, who is married and resides at St. Louis, Missouri; and Maude, who is married and resides at Sullivan, Indiana.

T. P. McBride was born in 1858, at Coshocton, Ohio, and was reared in Ohio, where he resided until young manhood then going with his parents to Sullivan, Indiana. For many years he has been engaged in the furniture and undertaking business at Sullivan, and has won his own way from small beginnings until he is considered one of the substantial men of this city. He is a republican politically, but not an office seeker, is a faithful member of the Methodist Episcopal Church, as is also his wife, and belongs to the Independent Order of Odd Fellows and the Knights of Pythias. Mr. McBride

has been a prominent factor in assisting in the development of his city, and is accounted an honorable and straightforward man of business. He was married at Sullivan, to Miss Lena Godwin, who was born in 1860, in Sullivan County, and they became the parents of only one child: Ford B.

Ford B. McBride received his early education in the public schools of Sullivan and graduated from the high school there in 1901. In that year he went to Indianapolis, where for one year he worked for the Laycock Manufacturing Company, but he had not given up his early desire for a career in the medical profession, and in 1902 entered the medical department of the Indiana University, Indianapolis. There he pursued a full course, helping to pay his own tuition, and in 1906 was graduated with the degree of Doctor of Medicine. To further prepare himself for the practice of his chosen calling, he served 2½ years in the National Military Home, at Marion, Indiana, being an interne for one year and assistant surgeon for 1½ years, and at the end of that time returned to Sullivan and entered practice. His experience there, however, was of short duration, for in the spring of 1909, feeling that the West offered better opportunities for the young and struggling medical man, he came to Liberty, Kansas, and this city has since been his field of operation. He now has an excellent general practice in both medicine and surgery, built up by a display of superior skill, broad learning and a natural sympathy for suffering humanity. He owns a residence on Second Street, as well as an office building on Main Street, and is rapidly approaching that material success which his abilities deserve, his professional position being already established. He has continued to be a close and careful student, and keeps fully abreast of the various advancements being made in medicine and surgery by holding membership in the Montgomery County Medical Society, the Kansas State Medical Society, the Southeastern Medical Society and the American Medical Association. Politically a republican, he has not been a seeker for public honors, his interest in matters political being confined to an endeavor to elect good men to hold public office and enact good laws for the government of the community. His fraternal connections include membership in Liberty Lodge No. 123, Ancient Free and Accepted Masons and Cherryvale Lodge No. 989, of the Benevolent and Protective Order of Elks.

In 1911, at Cherryvale, Kansas, Doctor McBride was married to Miss Iva Witham, of that city, daughter of Mr. and Mrs. J. C. Witham, the latter of whom is deceased. Mr. Witham, who for many years was engaged in extensive agricultural pursuits, is now making his home at No. 825 East Fifth Street, Cherryvale, being retired from active affairs. Doctor and Mrs. McBride have no children.

GEN. DUDLEY EMERSON CORNELL. The career of the late Gen. Dudley Emerson Cornell was one characterized by participation in various lines of endeavor and experiences of an interesting and extraordinary character; by faithful devotion to the duties and responsibilities of both peace and war; by success in business; and by a high type of citizenship that won to him the friendship and esteem of men in all walks of life. From 1866 until his death, in 1911, he was a resident of Kansas, and during this time was not only widely known in business circles as a man of sound ability and broad knowledge, but as a public official whose labors were always directed in behalf of the welfare of his community and its people.

General Cornell was born on a farm near Wilton, Saratoga County, New York, January 15, 1837, being one of the four children of Merritt I. and Mercy W. (Howard) Cornell, natives respectively of New York and Vermont. He belonged to one of America's oldest and most highly honored families, having been a descendant from Thomas Cornell, a native of England who, in 1638, to escape religious persecution, left that country and emigrated to the new land across the waters, here joining the colony of Roger Williams, which had been established two years before at Providence. He continued to worship as a Quaker during the rest of his life. Thomas Cornell became one of the large landholders in his day and locality, and in 1640 founded the homestead on Narragansett Bay, which is still held in the family possession. In 1642 he migrated to New Amsterdam, and in 1646 was granted a tract of land by Governor Kieft which is now known as Cornell's Neck. Thomas Cornell was the father of five sons and five daughters, one of the descendants of whom, a distant relative of General Cornell, was the late Ezra Cornell, whose great donations made possible the founding of Cornell College, one of the greatest in the country today.

Merritt I. Cornell, the father of General Cornell, was born in Washington County, New York, and married Mercy W. Howard, a native of Shaftsbury, Vermont, and a sister of United States Senator Howard, who served in that body for a number of years as a representative from Michigan. Mr. Cornell died in 1883, and his widow in 1881, and all their four children are also deceased. In the Empire State, Merritt I. Cornell was a farmer and school teacher and a man of some importance in public affairs, serving as county superintendent of schools and county commissioner for several terms. During the closing years of his life he made his home with his son, Dudley E., and was residing with him at the time of his death. He was originally a whig and later a republican in politics.

Dudley Emerson Cornell, of the eighth generation of the family in America, received his early educational training in the public schools of his native place, subsequently matriculating at Rensselaer Polytechnic Institute, Troy, New York, from which institution he was graduated as a civil engineer. In 1856 and 1857 he followed his profession in Wisconsin, where he was identified with the Milwaukee & Mississippi Railroad, between Madison and the Mississippi River, this line now being a part of the Chicago, Milwaukee & St. Paul system. The year 1858 saw Mr. Cornell one of a party of gold-seekers journeying to California by way of the Isthmus of Panama, and after his arrival in the Golden State he continued to be engaged as a civil and mining engineer until 1860. Returning in that year to New York, at the outbreak of the Civil war he enlisted for a short time in the Seventh New York Cavalry, better known as the "Northern Black Horse Cavalry," but at the expiration of his term, at Hoosic, New York, raised Company A, of the One Hundred Twenty-fifth Regiment, New York Volunteer Infantry, of which he was commissioned captain. He was presented a handsome sword by the citizens of Hoosic, in August, 1862. He had a brilliant military record, and at the close of the war was serving on the staff of Gen. Rufus Saxton and later held the rank of major-general in the Kansas State Militia

to which he had been appointed by Governor John P. St. John.

In 1866 General Cornell again decided to try his fortunes in the West, and in that year came to Kansas and located in Wyandotte County. His former railroad experience and his knowledge of civil engineering gained him a position with the Eastern Division of the Union Pacific Railway, his first title being that of clerk in the general passenger and ticket office. He was promoted to chief clerk in that office, and in 1876, after the road had become an independent line, known as the Kansas Pacific, he was made general passenger agent, a position which he maintained until the consolidation of the Kansas Pacific and the Union Pacific. In 1889 he retired from active business affairs and in 1894 went to live at his country home, "Highland Farm," near Bonner Springs, Wyandotte. One of the leading republicans of his day, he served as mayor of Wyandotte, now Kansas City, in 1883, and was again elected mayor of Kansas City in 1907 and 1908. In 1902 he accepted the nomination of his party for the office of county treasurer and was elected by a large majority and re-elected in 1904, serving until 1906. His public service was an excellent one. General Cornell was a man of business who took advantage of every fair opportunity, but his dealings were always above board, and he was always ready to help the less fortunate and to contribute to every laudable enterprise.

On October 13, 1868, General Cornell was united in marriage with Miss Annie M. Speck, a native of Pennsylvania, and a daughter of Dr. Frederick and Adelaide (Dennis) Speck. To this union there were born six children, namely: Frederick Dudley, who is a well known real estate man of Lincoln, Nebraska; Dr. Howard Merritt, a practicing physician of Las Cruces, New Mexico; Adelaide Marion, who is the wife of Prof. Ernest Blaker, of Cornell University; Dudley Emerson, Jr., who died at the age of two years; Grace, who is the wife of Capt. Fred Bugbee, U. S. A., at present stationed in the Canal Zone; and George Stewart, who is engaged in the insurance business.

Dr. Frederick Speck, the father of Mrs. Cornell, was an old and honored physician of Kansas City. He was born at Carlisle, Cumberland County, Pennsylvania, November 24, 1818, his parents being Dr. Joseph and Mary (Motter) Speck, also natives of that place. His paternal grandparents were Frederick and Barbara (Musselman) Speck, who were born in Lancaster County, Pennsylvania, and the first paternal ancestor to settle in America was a Hollander, the mother's ancestor being a German. The parents of Doctor Speck had three children, of whom he was the eldest child and only son. The mother died in 1838 and his father subsequently married Elizabeth Hollenback, by whom he reared a family of six children, all of whom are now deceased. The father's death occurred April 3, 1875, at Kansas City, Kansas, in which city he had located in 1857. He was a graduate of Dickinson College, Carlisle, Pennsylvania, and of the Baltimore Medical College, and practiced his profession for over forty years, during two years of which time he was a surgeon in the Union army during the Civil war.

Dr. Frederick Speck spent his early life in his native place and received his literary education at Dickinson College, from which his father had graduated many years before. His first knowledge of medicine was acquired under the preceptorship of the elder man, and when still in early manhood, he

completed a course at Franklin Medical College, Philadelphia, being graduated therefrom with the class of 1847. Doctor Speck began the practice of his beloved calling at Fremont, Schuylkill County, Pennsylvania, but after five years there and a similar length of time spent at Selin's Grove, Snyder County, that state, he came to the West and took up his home at Kansas City, Kansas, where he continued in active practice right up to the time of his death, September 16, 1893. For forty-six years he has been a devotee of the healing art and during thirty-six years of this time has resided at Kansas City, where he was widely known socially and professionally and was greatly beloved by those who had been attracted to him by his many excellencies of mind and heart. Doctor Speck and his wife had come to the West in June, 1857, on the boat Edinburgh from St. Louis to Wyandotte.

Doctor Speck was married June 8, 1848, to Miss Adelaide M. Dennis, who accompanied him to the West and died here March 8, 1882, leaving four children: Annie M., Mary C., Joseph B. and Richard D. On December 31, 1885, the doctor married Mrs. Frances L. Battles, a daughter of Hon. Marsh Giddings, former governor of New Mexico, and widow of Augustus S. Battles, of Philadelphia, Pennsylvania. Doctor and Mrs. Speck were members of the Episcopal Church, and he was the first vestryman of the First Episcopal Church of Kansas City. A prominent Odd Fellow, he was honored with the rank of grand master and grand chief patriarch of the state, and grand representative to the grand lodge of the United States at Baltimore, Maryland, in 1873, and at Atlanta, Georgia, in 1874. He was also a member of the Masonic and Knights of Pythias fraternities. Politically a stanch republican, he served four terms as mayor of Kansas City and several terms as a member of the council, and his public services included numerous other helpful activities. For ten years he was pension examiner, and was a member of the board that built the Blind Asylum, served as one of its trustees for several years, and was its physician from the time of its inception until his death. Professionally, as in every other way, his standing was excellent, and he was one of the most honored among the members of the Kansas State Medical Society and the American Medical Association. His friendships included some of the most prominent men of his day. His home life was beautiful. In his death Kansas City lost its most useful and most greatly beloved man.

Mrs. Cornell is a leading figure in social and club circles of Kanusas City. For two years she was regent of James Ross Chapter, Daughters of the American Revolution, and organized and was president for four years of the United States Daughters of 1812 for the State of Kansas. She is a charter member of the Social Science Club, which was organized in 1881, and a life member of the Kansas State Historical Society. She takes an active part in the various activities of the Episcopal Church, of which she has been a member for fifty years.

ROBERT BURNS GIBB, M. D. As a surgeon one of the foremost in Kansas in point of ability and prestige is Dr. R. R. Gibb of Pittsburg. Doctor Gibb is still a young man, not yet forty, yet has had the experience and training which have matured his unusual natural gifts and ·his reputation and position are now well assured.

Coming to Kansas after he had completed his medical course, Doctor Gibb was born at Fairbury. Illinois, December 15, 1878. He is of Scotch ancestry.

His grandfather John Gibb was born in Chapel Hall, Scotland, in 1812. He was in the coal business in Scotland for many years and coming to this country in 1846 located at Lonaconing, Maryland, and afterwards moved to Fairbury, Illinois. He was a well known coal operator, and his relations with that business finally brought him to Pittsburg, Kansas, where he died in 1898. He married Jeannette Stevenson, who was born at Chapel Hall, Scotland, in 1812 and died in Woodson County, Kansas, in 1890.

John Gibb, Jr., father of Doctor Gibb, was born in Scotland in 1840, and was brought to America at the age of six years. He spent his early life at Lonaconing, Allegany County, Maryland, and also at Fairbury, Illinois. At Fairbury he became identified with the coal business, and in 1882 removed to Miles City, Montana, where he still resides. He has been very prominent in civic and political affairs in Miles City, being a republican. For four years he served as sheriff of Custer County, Montana, represented his district one term in the legislature and has attended many county, state and national conventions of his party. He is a Mason and a member of the order of Elks. John Gibb married Anna R. Ireland, who was born in La Salle, Illinois, in 1842. Their children are John F., who is associated with a leading newspaper at Miles City, Montana; William, who is a graduate of the Louisville, Kentucky, College of Dentistry, and is now practicing his profession at Miles City; Daisy married James Campbell, assistant superintendent in the smelter at Great Falls, Montana; and Doctor R. B. Gibb.

Taken to Montana when about five years of age, Doctor Gibb attended the public schools of Miles City and spent two years in a high school there. He then entered the medical department of the Central University of Kentucky, from which he was graduated Doctor of Medicine June 28, 1900. He received the highest honors in his class and also individual honors in surgery and diseases of women. Even while in the university his promising career in the field of surgery was definitely anticipated. By competitive examination he won an internship in the City Hospital of Louisville, and had that special advantage for one year before beginning practice.

For the past fifteen years Doctor Gibb has accepted every opportunity to observe and study the best methods of surgery and to associate with the leaders in that field. In 1909 he spent a year abroad, visiting hospitals and clinics in many of the leading medical centers, especially Vienna, Berlin, Paris, Budapest, Glasgow and London. He has taken post-graduate work with the Mayos at Rochester, Minnesota, in the New York Post-Graduate School and has attended clinics in Philadelphia, Boston and Cleveland.

Towards the close of 1900 Doctor Gibb located at Pittsburg and began a general practice. For the last ten years, however, he has specialized in surgery and diagnosis and in those departments he has few peers in southeastern Kansas. His offices are in the Kirkwood Building at Seventh Street and Broadway.

Doctor Gibb is a member of the Pittsburg, the Crawford County, the Kansas State and the Southeastern Medical societies, the American Medical Association, the International Surgeons Society of Rochester, Minnesota, and belongs to ·the Clinical Surgical Society of America. Membership in this last named organization is one especially prized by American surgeons. To qualify for election as a member formerly it was necessary to contribute some original device, discovery or paper to the science of surgery. Membership in that society also makes Doctor Gibb eligible to the American College of Surgeons. He is a republican in politics and fraternally is identified with Pittsburg Lodge No. 187, Ancient Free and Accepted Masons, Pittsburg Chapter No. 58 Royal Arch Masons, Pittsburg Commandery No. 29 Knights Templar, and Mirzah Temple of the Nobles of the Mystic Shrine at Pittsburg.

In 1903 in Kansas City, Missouri, Doctor Gibb married Miss Ray N. Kirkwood, a daughter of the late Archibald B. Kirkwood, one of the distinguished citizens of Pittsburg whose career is sketched on other pages. Doctor and Mrs. Gibb have one daughter, Eleanor G., born March 7, 1911.

ARCHIBALD B. KIRKWOOD. In the death of Archibald B. Kirkwood on May 16, 1916, the City of Pittsburg and southeastern Kansas lost a very prominent business man and citizen. He was one of the pioneers in the development of the coal resources of this section of the state. At one time he was general manager of the Wear Coal Company and president of the Standard Mercantile Company of Pittsburg. Of later years his interests were rather widely diffused and long before his death he had acquired a generous competence which would have enabled him to take life easily and leisurely.

In many ways he had a remarkable career. He entered the coal industry at the age of thirteen. He worked in the mines and about them in practically every capacity. He was a master of the business before he reached his majority, and not only had a thorough grasp of every detail of coal mining but was also a master in the handling of men and large material resources.

He was born at Lonaconing, Allegany County, Maryland, August 20, 1859. and was still comparatively young when death overtook him. His parents were John and Rachel (Gibb) Kirkwood. His father was born in Glasgow, Scotland, and the mother was also a native of that country. As a young man John Kirkwood came to the United States, locating in Maryland. He had learned coal mining in Scotland, and had come to America to find a larger field. About 1862 he brought his family to Fairbury, Livingston County, Illinois, and there he opened and operated the second coal mine in that district. He conducted it under the name of the Central Coal Company. After many years as one of the leading operators in that part of Illinois he came toward the close of the '80s to the coal fields of Kansas, and served as superintendent of the Osage Coal Company at Scranton for some time, and in 1893 moved to Pittsburg, where his son Archibald had previously located. He died in Pittsburg.

The early life of Archibald B. Kirkwood was spent chiefly in Fairbury, Illinois, where he gained a limited education in the local schools. At the age of thirteen he was given his first occupation in a coal mine, keeping a trap door. Later he drove mules to the coal cars, and from that graduated into a practical coal miner. He went through the various positions from pit boss, mine foreman, superintendent, up to general manager. There was nothing about a mine in its construction or operation which he did not understand, and he was not only a mining engineer but also had a practical knowledge of general engineering. This was evidenced by the fact that in 1880 ne became a subcontractor in the construction of the Big Horn tunnel of the Northern Pacific Railroad in Custer County, Montana. That work kept him engaged for about nine months.

Following this bit of experience in the northwest, Mr. Kirkwood came to Kansas, and located at Carbondale in Osage County. The coal mining industry was just beginning to attract attention in that section. He became mine foreman for the Kansas Carbon Coal Company, which was the coal department of the old Kansas Pacific Railroad. He next moved to Scranton in the same county and was made foreman for the Osage Mining Company, the coal department of the Santa Fe Railroad. It was during his early years in Kansas that Mr. Kirkwood met Mr. Frank E. Wear, and their acquaintance was subsequently developed into a business partnership. Mr. Kirkwood remained at Scranton until 1888, and then associated with Mr. Wear went to Liberal, Missouri, where they leased and operated a mine. Three years later they opened up the No. 1 mine, known as the Sunshine, at Minden, Missouri.

In the meantime in 1890 the Wear Coal Company had been organized, and in 1891 Mr. Kirkwood became superintendent of its mines at Pittsburg. In 1900 he was elected general manager of all the mines controlled by the Wear Coal Company including nine mines in the Pittsburg district, besides others at Collinsville, Oolagah and Poteau in Indian Territory and also mines in Arkansas and Missouri. 1,100 men were employed by the Wear Company in the Pittsburg district alone. Mr. Kirkwood was one of the large stockholders as well as general manager of the Wear Coal Company for many years.

He was also president of the Standard Mercantile Company of Pittsburg, which operated what was then said to be the largest department store in Kansas. After retiring from the coal business Mr. Kirkwood gave up serious work of all kinds for nine months and spent the time traveling through Europe. After his return he devoted himself chiefly to real estate and merchandising. He erected the Kirkwood Building at Seventh and Broadway in Pittsburg. This structure was destroyed by fire in 1911, but he at once rebuilt it and made it one of the largest and handsomest business structures in Pittsburg. He was also president of the Kirkwood-Hammett Hardwood Company, whose store was in the old Kirkwood Building and its stock was destroyed by the same fire that burned the building. Mr. Kirkwood was a promoter of the Syndicate Building at Seventh and Broadway.

He was always prominent in local affairs, and served as mayor of Pittsburg in 1907. He was a man who in later years seldom betrayed the hard experiences of his early youth when he was a humble laborer in one of the most hazardous occupations that engage men. He was a man of very affable manner, was genial and a good companion, and was extremely generous and sympathetic especially with those who saw only the unfortunate side of life. He was affiliated with the lodge, chapter, council and commandery of the Masonic order at Pittsburg and with Ararat Temple of the Mystic Shrine at Kansas City. He also belonged to the Elks, the United Commercial Travelers, the Improved Order of Red Men and the Fraternal Order of Eagles.

At Windsor, Illinois, March 30, 1880. Mr. Kirkwood married Miss Ida M. Bowman. Mrs. Kirkwood survives her honored husband and makes her home in the Kirkwood Building. To their marriage were born three children. Ray N. is now the wife of Dr. Robert B. Gibb, a prominent surgeon of Pittsburg. Edna married D. M. Hammett and they live in Shreveport, Louisiana. Roy was at the time of his father's death a sailor in the British marine.

GEORGE W. GABRIEL, M. D., of Parsons had his first medical experience as a hospital steward and soldier during the Civil war. He is now the oldest active medical man in the state, having practiced continuously for over forty-five years. Doctor Gabriel is one of the pioneer physicians of Parsons, and has identified himself with that community not only in a professional capacity but also as a public spirited man of affairs. He is a former state senator.

He was born in that old center of education and culture of the Ohio Valley, Athens, Ohio, on November 17, 1841. The Gabriels were French Alsatians, but settled in Pennsylvania during the colonial days. His great-grandfather Abraham Gabriel was a Pennsylvania soldier in the Revolution, and thus Doctor Gabriel is eligible to membership in the Sons of the American Revolution. His grandfather Elias Gabriel was born in Pennsylvania in 1786, and as a young man went to Southeastern Ohio and settled at Athens. He saw active service in the War of 1812 and thus the Gabriel family has been represented in every important war of this country beginning with the establishment of the independence of the United States. Elias Gabriel was a stone mason and farmer and died at Athens, Ohio, in 1864. He married Susan Bane, who was born in Pennsylvania and died at Athens.

Moses Gabriel, father of Doctor Gabriel, was born at Athens, Ohio, in 1814, and spent his life as a farmer and stock raiser in that section. He died there in 1879. He was a consistent member of the Methodist Episcopal Church, and politically was a democrat. His wife, whose maiden name was Mary Johnson, was born in 1813 in Ireland, was brought to this country when a child by her father, and lived at first in Muskingum County, Ohio, but afterwards in Athens. She died at Athens in 1900. Doctor Gabriel was the second in a family of six children. His older brother Elias came to Kansas in 1868 and is now a retired farmer at Erie in this state. His younger sister Susan resides at Nevada, Missouri, the widow of James Wells, who was a farmer. Christiana married James Dixon, a retired farmer of Athens, Ohio. Elmer was a farmer and died at Athens in 1896. Emmet died while still pursuing his studies at Athens.

Educated in the public schools of Athens, Doctor Gabriel graduated from the high school at the age of fifteen, and his first twenty-one years were spent on his father's farm. In 1862 he enlisted in the Army Hospital Corps and in that capacity was able to render efficient service at many battles. He was at the battles of Gettysburg and Antietam, to mention only two of the more important engagements, and after his honorable discharge came to Topeka in March, 1864, and enlisted in the Seventeenth Kansas Volunteer Infantry. He was with that command 100 days, and in that time fought at the battle of Westport, Missouri, against Prices Confederate troops.

After the war Doctor Gabriel lived in Topeka, and then spent two years in the Starling Medical College at Columbus, Ohio. From 1868 to 1870 he practiced at Ladore in Neosho County. Continuing his medical studies he was graduated M. D. from the Kansas Medical College in 1871. He has always been a keen student, and his studies together with his wide range of experience have qualified him in an unusual degree for successful work. He has attended clinics and lectures since his graduation at Cincinnati, at Columbus, Ohio, and in the Kansas City Medical College. Doctor Gabriel located at Parsons in 1870, when that was a small village and just at the beginning of its career as a railroad center. He has his offices and

home in the Haynes Building on Main Street. Doctor Gabriel is a member of the Labette County and State Medical societies and the American Medical Association.

He has prospered in a business way, being a stockholder in the Parsons Commercial Bank, is the owner of two small farms in Labette County, and has real estate in Parsons.

In many ways he has been a civic leader. For seven terms he filled the office of mayor, and those terms marked a period of great progressiveness in municipal affairs. He was also a member of the State Legislature three times, and represented his home district in the Senate during 1901-03. Doctor Gabriel is a democrat in politics. He also served one term as county commissioner and in 1871 was appointed to a place on the school board, and thus helped to influence the early establishment of schools in the city. He is especially well known in the Masonic order, being affiliated with Parsons Lodge No. 117, Ancient Free and Accepted Masons, Parsons Chapter No. 39, Royal Arch Masons, Coeur de Lion Commandery No. 17, Knights Templar, at Parsons. Progress Chapter No. 49, Order Eastern Star, at Parsons, and Mirzah Temple of the Mystic Shrine at Pittsburg, Kansas. He is also a member of Camp No. 844, Modern Woodmen of America, at Parsons, and Parsons Camp No. 14, Woodmen of the World.

In 1869 at Ladore, Kansas, Doctor Gabriel married Mrs. Elizabeth (Hager) Hallowell. Mrs. Gabriel died at Parsons in 1891, leaving two children. The son, Harry E., is division superintendent of the Frisco Railway Company, with home at Willow Springs, Missouri, and is a graduate of the Parsons High School. The daughter, Mary, is the wife of Alfred Noyes, who is engaged in the insurance, real estate and musical instrument business, and resides on a farm near Parsons. Mrs. Noyes is a graduate of the Clinton Academy in Missouri. In 1894 at Parsons Doctor Gabriel married Mrs. Mary (Cassady) Brown, who died at Parsons in 1906.

JOHN J. JONES. Actively connected with a profession that has an important bearing upon the progress and stable prosperity of any section or community, and one which has ever been considered as conserving the public welfare by furthering the ends of justice and maintaining individual rights, the reputation of John J. Jones, of Chanute, as a lawyer has been won through honest, earnest labor, and his standing at the bar is a merited tribute to his ability. For a quarter of a century he has been engaged in practice at Chanute, and during this time has been connected with much of the important litigation that has been brought before the courts of city, county and state. Mr. Jones was born at Pinckneyville, Perry County, Illinois, August 22, 1869, and is a son of Dr. John R. and Frances Gertrude (Gillis) Jones.

The Jones family is of Welsh origin and the branch to which John J. Jones belongs was founded in America preceding the Revolutionary war. It early settled in Kentucky, from which state Mr. Jones' grandfather migrated to Illinois as a pioneer in 1818 and located on a farm in Perry County, where he passed the remainder of his life in agricultural activities. Dr. John R. Jones was born October 6, 1836, at Pinckneyville, Illinois, and was given good educational advantages. In his youth he decided upon the medical profession as his life work, and after some preliminary training entered the Missouri Medical College, from which institution he was duly graduated with his degree. He was married in Illinois, and in 1876 came to Chanute, Kansas, as one of the first physicians and surgeons of this part of Neosho County, and here continued in practice for thirty years, his death occurring October 12, 1906, when he was six days past seventy years of age. Doctor Jones became widely and favorably known throughout this section, not alone as a skilled practitioner and a steady-handed surgeon, but as a kindly, generous friend, always ready to assist the unfortunate and to give of his services in the alleviation of human ills. He belonged to the Neosho County Medical Society, the Kansas State Medical Society and the American Medical Association, was a close student all his life, and observed strictly the highest ethics of his honored and humane calling. As a fraternalist, he stood high in Masonry, belonging to Chanute Lodge No. 103, Ancient Free and Accepted Masons; Chanute Chapter No. 21, Royal Arch Masons; and Chanute Commandery No. 44, Knights Templars. His religious faith was that of the Methodist Episcopal Church, which he supported generously, and as a voter he was a republican. Doctor Jones married Miss Frances Gertrude Gillis, who was born July 7, 1846, and she still survives and has her home at Chanute. To their union the following children were born: an infant daughter who is deceased; Humphrey B., who died at Chanute at the age of sixteen years; Lydia, who is the wife of William Irwin, chief of police of Chanute; John J.; Dr. F. W., a successful practicing physician and surgeon of Girard, Kansas; Gertrude, who died at Saint Margaret's Hospital, Kansas City, Missouri, being the wife of Grant Blair, a farmer living west of Chanute; D. R., who is a successful oil operator in the Oklahoma fields; Itie L., who is unmarried and makes her home with her widowed mother; Frances V., who is also unmarried and lives with her mother, and is chief saleslady and buyer of the Racket Store, Chanute; and B. F., who married Ruth Hough and lives on a farm located west of Chanute.

John J. Jones was less than seven years of age when he was brought to Kansas, and here his early education was secured in the graded and high schools of Chanute, from the latter of which he was graduated with the class of 1889. Following this, he began the study of law, for which calling he had always had a predilection, and in 1892 was graduated from the law department of the Kansas University with the degree of Bachelor of Laws. In that same year he was admitted to the bar, and from that time to the present has been engaged in a general civil practice that has grown as great in size as it has in importance. He maintains offices in the First National Bank Building, and in addition to his large private practice acts as local attorney for the Atchison, Topeka & Santa Fe Railroad, the Missouri, Kansas & Texas Railroad, and George F. Sherrett, receiver for the Kansas Natural Gas Company, of which concern Mr. Jones was formerly general attorney. He is likewise general counsel for the Union Traction Company, the line of which runs from Parsons to Coffeyville, and of the Kansas-Oklahoma Traction Company, which extends between Coffeyville, Kansas, and Nowata, Oklahoma, in both of which lines he holds a directorship. He belongs to the Kansas State Bar Association and the American Bar Association, and enjoys an excellent reputation in the ranks of his fellow-practitioners. Politically, Mr. Jones is a republican, but has never aspired to office, nor has he allowed his name to be used as a candidate for public honors. He has supreme faith in the future of Chanute, as is evidenced by the fact that much of his capital is invested in real estate in this

city. In addition to his own home, at No. 907 South Highland Avenue, he owns the residence at No. 203 East Tenth Street, Nos. 934 and 936 South Lincoln Avenue, and Nos. 401, 406 and 501 Evergreen Avenue. Likewise he is the owner of the old homestead of 240 acres, situated three miles west and one-half mile north of Chanute, a thoroughly modern farm, which has been so highly improved and includes such fine buildings and handsome equipment that it is one of the show-places of the section, people coming for many miles to view its beauties. Fraternally, Mr. Jones is a life member of Lodge No. 806, of the Benevolent and Protective Order of Elks.

On June 3, 1896, at Chanute, Mr. Jones married Miss Belle Wilson, daughter of W. L. and Louise (Benjamin) Wilson, the latter deceased, and the former making his home with Mr. and Mrs. Jones. Mr. Wilson was for many years engaged in agricultural pursuits in Neosho County, but has now retired from active labors. Mr. and Mrs. Jones have no children.

WILL R. BURGE. Trained faculties and an enlightened understanding are necessary requisites of a newspaper man in these modern days. The responsibility resting upon the man in charge of the policy and editorial branch of a newspaper is heavy and should not be lightly assumed. From the time of the discovery of the art of printing, the power of the Fourth Estate has been great, and fortunate indeed is the community whose newspapers are directed and controlled by men of real worth, integrity and knowledge. In Will R. Burge, the City of Cherryvale has a newspaper man of this enlightened class. As proprietor and editor of the Cherryvale Republican he is doing much to forward the interests of his community, and under his management the sheet is becoming a power in Southeastern Kansas affairs.

Mr. Burge was born in a log house in the Chickasaw Nation, Indian Territory, October 18, 1880, and is a son of S. B. and Josephine (Grubb) Burge. The Burge family originated in Germany, where the name was originally spelled "Buradge," and during the days preceding the American Revolution was founded in this country, one of the early members settling in Ohio. John Burge, the grandfather of Will R. Burge, was born in Ohio, and for many years followed farming in Paulding County, Ohio. Although past middle age when the Civil war came on, he enlisted in a regiment of Ohio volunteer infantry, and met a soldier's death on the field of battle while wearing his country's uniform. John Burge married Mary Meeks, who was born in 1817, in Ohio, and they became the parents of five children, namely: Reuben, who taught an Indian reservation school and died in Oklahoma; S. B.; Mary Ellen, who is deceased; John, who died on the home ranch in Oklahoma, where he was living with his mother; and W. W., who lives on a ranch near Pontotoc, Oklahoma.

S. B. Burge was born in 1840, in Paulding County, Ohio, received his education in the public schools and was reared on the home farm. He was married in his native locality and for some years engaged in farming there, but in 1879 went to the Chickasaw Nation, where he homesteaded a claim and resided until 1887. In that year he came to Kansas, and for about fourteen years was engaged in cultivating the soil near Burlington, but in 1901 retired from active pursuits and moved into the city, where he now resides. He took part in much of the early development of this locality and Oklahoma and experienced many of the hardships incident to pioneer life, but by hard work and good management succeeded in the accumulation of a property that insures his comfort in his declining years. Mr. Burge is a member of the Methodist Episcopal Church. He is a man universally respected for his honorable and straightforward dealing, as well as for his good citizenship and his fidelity to friendships. He was married in Paulding County, Ohio, to Miss Josephine Grubb, who was born in that county, in 1847, and they became the parents of six children, as follows: Franklin S., who died in infancy; Geddes M., who died at the age of twenty-six years, at Siloam Springs, Arkansas, having for several years been a farmer in Coffey County, Kansas; Mary, who married Charles Knoblock, a farmer and ranchman of Coffey County, Kansas; S. A., who is a contractor at Burlington, Kansas; Will R.; and Minnie, who died at Burlington, at the age of nine years.

Will R. Burge was educated in the public schools of Burlington, where he was graduated from the high school with the class of 1899, and in the following year gained his first newspaper experience in the printing office of the Burlington Courier. During the four years that he remained with that paper, he became thoroughly familiar with the mechanical department of newspaper publication, and in 1904 started on a trip that took him through California and to various towns along the Pacific Coast, working at the printer's trade. Mr. Burge returned to Kansas in 1906 and secured the position of foreman with the Cherryvale Republican, and in the years that followed became more and more interested in it, until July 1, 1914, he purchased the paper and plant and became its owner and editor, it having been formerly owned and edited by H. J. Powell. The Republican was founded in 1871 and conducted merely as a weekly until 1898, when it became a daily, although the weekly has not been abolished. As its name indicates it supports the grand old party and is one of the chief adherents of republicanism in this part of the state. The plant, at No. 104 East Main Street, is equipped with the most modern presses and machinery, making possible the issuing of a clean, attractive and well-printed paper. This circulates freely in Montgomery and all the surrounding counties, and is sent in every direction in the country. Mr. Burge gives his readers clean and up-to-date news matter and editorials that are timely and virile. Local movements for advancement always find support in the Republican's columns. Mr. Burge is a stanch republican, and a member of the Baptist Church. Fraternally, he is affiliated with Cherryvale Lodge No. 137, Ancient Free and Accepted Masons, and also holds membership in the Commercial Club, in the work of which he has been active.

On October 20, 1906, at Cherryvale, Mr. Burge was married to Miss Katheryn Patterson, daughter of A. W. and Elizabeth Patterson, the latter now deceased and the former a resident of Kansas City, Kansas. To this union there have been born two children: Madeline, born August 29, 1907, and now attending the Cherryvale public schools; and Josephine, born June 10, 1916.

ALBERT MEBUS. It demands a large measure of business discernment to enter an old field, already well occupied, and to be able within a few years to harvest success and not only that but to stand second foremost with all competitors. It was in 1909 that Albert Mebus, who is now the second largest insurance handler in Kansas City, Kansas, went into business for himself and his rapid progress in the insurance line, proves great business capacity and keen foresight. Not only, however, in his private affairs has Mr. Mebus manfully responded to business opportunities, but publicly as a progressive citizen, he has demonstrated his system and efficiency and is one of the most prominent advocates of the good roads movement, so important in the further development of Kansas as well as the nation.

Albert Mebus was born in the Village of Aubrey, in Johnson County, Kansas, July 27, 1876, and is a son of John F. and Christina (Anderson) Mebus. The father was born in the City of Copenhagen, Denmark, and came to the United States in 1866 and the mother was born in Sweden and came to America in 1871. John F. Mebus went first to the lumber camps in Michigan and worked at logging until 1871, when, remembering an old acquaintance who had located in Johnson County, Kansas, he decided to seek him out and perhaps in the new state he might find better working opportunities than he could in Michigan. He found his countryman, who was a shoemaker, and was welcomed and given work in his shop and later was admitted to partnership. Mr. Mebus was industrious and frugal and the time came when he had enough capital to buy his partner's interest and he continued his own shoe store at Aubrey until 1883, when he moved to Kansas City. There he expanded into a large shoe dealer and as he was a man of excellent business judgment, he amassed an ample fortune before retiring in 1894. As opportunity had offered he had invested in farm lands which he then sold and bought real estate in Kansas City. He educated his two sons so that they were prepared for a business life and in every way was a good father and an admirable citizen. He married Christina Anderson and they had two children: Albert and Alfred G., the latter of whom lost his life in 1910, while serving as fire captain in a disastrous fire at Kansas City.

Albert Mebus attended school regularly until he was sixteen years of age and then went into business and for two years was proprietor of a grocery store. Although he was successful in this enterprise, he found the responsibilities too heavy for his years and finally sold his stock. About this time he became a member of the Kansas City fire department and continued so connected for eight years, during the closing three being captain of Engine House No. 5. In 1902 he went with the firm of Merrian, Ellis & Benton, real estate and insurance men, as all-around man and rent collector, and won the confidence of the firm through his energy and business integrity and remained in that office for seven years, during this time gaining an insight into this line of business that prepared him for an enterprise of a similar character on his own account. This he entered into in 1909 as junior partner in the firm of Morrison and Mebus, owning a half interest, which continued for two years as a general insurance business. Since then Mr. Mebus has been alone and has so widened his field that he is rated as the second largest insurance dealer in this city.

Not only has Mr. Mebus developed his private business solidly and carefully, but he has identified himself with measures of great public usefulness, notably the good roads movement. All public improvements are the outcome of intelligent and concerted effort on the part of progressive citizens. These movements must have leaders. In 1910 Mr.

Mebus was one of the organizers of the Kansas State Automobile Association, of which he was vice president for a number of years. As a good roads enthusiast, he is vice president of the Kaw Valley Improved Road Association, and vice president of the King of Trails Association. He also was one of the organizers of the Kansas State Good Roads Association and was one of the prime movers in its activities. Mr. Mebus was one of the reorganizers and a director of the Minn Avenue State Bank, and is a stockholder in many other local concerns.

On October 14, 1896, Mr. Mebus was married to Miss Carrie Maulding, who was born at Kansas City and is a daughter of M. M. Maulding, who is a farmer and gardener, and they have three children, aged respectively fourteen, twelve and seven years: Dorothy, Thelma and Albert, Jr. Mr. Mebus plans to give his children every possible educational advantage. The family belongs to the Lutheran Church.

Mr. Mebus is a thirty-second degree Scottish Rite Mason, belonging to Abdallah Shrine. At the present time he is exalted ruler of Kansas City Lodge No. 440, Benevolent and Protective Order of Elks.

ERNEST EVERETT STONECIPHER. A Kansas educator of fifteen years' experience, Mr. Stonecipher has taught in country schools, has been principal of village and city schools, and with increasing capabilities and growing reputation has been preferred to some of the larger responsibilities connected with school work in Cherokee County. He is now county superintendent of public instruction in Cherokee County, and his place in the profession is well indicated by the fact that he is also serving as president of the Southeastern Kansas Teachers Association, the largest organization of school workers in the state.

Mr. Stonecipher was born in Cherokee County, in Ross Township, September 5, 1880, and had a rural environment during his youth. He is of old American stock, although the Stoneciphers originally came from Germany and settled in the Carolinas in colonial days. His grandfather, Samuel Stonecipher, was born in Tennessee, in 1815, was a farmer and blacksmith in Marion County, Illinois, for many years and died there in 1898.

J. C. Stonecipher, father of Professor Stonecipher, is one of the old and honored residents of Cherokee County, now living on a farm in Pleasant View Township. He was born in Marion County, Illinois, March 26, 1856, grew up there, but in 1875, at the age of nineteen, came to Sheridan Township of Cherokee County and for a time was employed on the farm of his brother, Doctor Ezra Stonecipher, and also attended school at Oswego. He was married in Ross Township, Cherokee County, in 1879, and then settled down to farming in Ross Township. For a number of years he conducted a threshing outfit. While living in Ross Township he served as township trustee four years, and held a similar office in Pleasant View Township, where he has been engaged in farming since 1896. He served as township trustee for four terms, and was an active figure in democratic circles, having been several times a member of the County Central Committee. He belongs to the Baptist Church, and is affiliated with the Independent Order of Odd Fellows and the Anti-Horse Thief Association. J. C. Stonecipher married for his first wife Lucy E. Hamblin, who was born in Illinois June 17, 1860, and died in Ross Township of Cherokee County in 1891. Her two children were Ernest E. and Norah L. The latter is the wife of Luther H. Stukey, a farmer and stockman

in Elk County, Kansas. In 1895 Mr. Stonecipher married for his second wife Mrs. Belle (Moon) Devena, widow of the late James Devena, a railroad man. To this marriage have been born four children: Joseph Edgar, a teacher in Cherokee County; Lucy E., now a senior in the high school in the Cherokee County High School; Bessie E., a sophomore in the high school; and Marion E., who is still in the grammar school.

The most of his early school training Ernest E. Stonecipher acquired in Cherokee County, but has been a constant student whether a pupil or teacher. In 1916 he received the teacher's state certificate from the State Manual Training Normal School of Pittsburg, Kansas.

His work as a teacher began in 1902, when he taught a year in Wirtonia, in District No. 32 of Cherokee County. Another year was spent in Rising Sun, District No. 65, two years at Lawton, Kansas, for two years he was principal at Lowell, and for three years principal at Galena. Thus by experience he was well qualified for his duties when he was elected in the fall of 1910 as county superintendent of public instruction. He took office in May, 1911, and by re-election in 1912 and 1914 has continued to administer his duties to the general satisfaction of all the people of Cherokee County interested in the schools. From his office in the Court House in Columbus he has under his supervision 100 school districts with 143 teachers and 5,000 scholars enrolled.

Mr. Stonecipher is an educator in the largest sense of the word, being equally and sincerely interested in everything that makes for human progress and welfare. He has been elected for the year 1917 president of the Southeastern Kansas Teachers Association, which has a membership of 2,800 active educators. He served as a member of its executive committee in 1914, and the association placed him in charge of the basket ball tournament in 1914 and 1915. He is a member and clerk of the Baptist Church at Columbus, is especially active in Sunday school affairs, being superintendent of the school in his home church, and a member of the executive committee of the County Sunday School Association. Fraternally he is a past grand of Columbus Lodge No. 387, Independent Order of Odd Fellows, belongs to the Anti-Horse Thief Association and to the Knights and Ladies of Security. He is also interested in business affairs, being a stockholder in the Cherokee County Lumber Company, and he owns a good residence at 618 West Elm Street in Columbus.

In 1909, in Moniteau County, Missouri, he married Miss Mattie M. Dale, whose father, George F. Dale, was a pioneer farmer in that section of Missouri. Mr. and Mrs. Stonecipher have two children, one daughter, Nadine, born February 3, 1911, and one son, Joseph Dale, born September 29, 1916.

HON. JAMES McGREW was one of the historic characters of Kansas, has a place in the history of the state at large because of his early activities and influence as a free state man, and his service in the office of lieutenant governor, while locally he is to be credited with much of the enterprise which entered into the foundation of the present metropolis Kansas City, Kansas.

He was born in Adams County near the great battlefield of Gettysburg, Pennsylvania, January 26, 1822, and died at his beautiful old home, erected in the early days, and known as McGrew's Grove, on Quindaro Boulevard in Kansas City, Kansas, January

Henry McGrew

19, 1911, aged eighty-eight years, eleven months, twenty-three days.

He was reared and educated in Pennsylvania, and in 1844, at the age of twenty-two accompanied his parents to the Sac and Fox Indian Reservation in the Territory of Iowa. His parents both died in that state. James McGrew early identified himself with mercantile activities, and was practically a life-long merchant. He conducted a general store at Lancaster in Keokuk County, Iowa, and in September, 1857, came to Wyandotte County, Kansas. He was associated with the party headed by Thomas H. Swope in organizing the old City of Wyandotte. He was one of the first merchants there, and from 1860 to 1870 had both a wholesale and retail grocery business. A special distinction is due to him in the fact that he was one of those who originated the packing industry in Kansas City, Kansas. He built and operated the first packing house at the mouth of the Kaw River. Until recently the building in which his operations as a packer were conducted still stood on Fourth Street near Freeman Avenue.

As a free state man he took an active interest in shaping the affairs of the Territory of Kansas. He served in the territorial legislature in 1859 and 1860, was mayor of the City of Wyandotte two terms, was elected to the State Senate in 1862 and in 1864 was chosen lieutenant governor of Kansas. It may be of interest to recall the fact that in 1864 there were two republican state tickets in Kansas. Mr. McGrew was the nominee on the regular republican ticket, and he defeated Hon. John J. Ingalls, who was candidate on the union republican ticket. It was one of the few political defeats registered against the classic Kansas orator, and in this case Mr. McGrew triumphed by about 4,000 votes. As lieutenant governor he was in office during the administration of Samuel J. Crawford, the war governor of Kansas. From the beginning of the party organization Governor McGrew was a stanch republican.

After retiring from office in 1867 he thereafter devoted himself steadfastly to his various business interests. He had first become interested in politics while living in Keokuk County, Iowa, and served as one of the early sheriffs of that county.

In 1848 at Lancaster, Iowa, Governor McGrew married Miss Mary Doggett, who died in 1863. In April, 1870, at Alliance, Ohio, he married Miss Lida Slaven, who survived him. Governor McGrew was the father of five children: Josephine E., who married H. H. Smalley; Henry McGrew, who married Julia M. Townsend; Louise, who married Thomas S. Moffett; Grace, who married Capt. William F. Clark of the United States Army; and Mary McGrew, who is unmarried and still resides in Kansas City, Kansas.

HENRY McGREW, a son of the late Governor James McGrew and his wife Mary (Doggett) McGrew, has spent practically all his life in Kansas City, Kansas, was formerly prominent as a member of the bar of that city, and is still one of the leading business men.

He was born at Lancaster, Keokuk County, Iowa, April 18, 1857, the same year that his father came as a pioneer to Wyandotte, Kansas. He grew up at Wyandotte, attended the public schools, and had all the advantages that a young man of ambition would crave as a preparation for a career. Determining upon the vocation of lawyer, he entered the University of Michigan at Ann Arbor, where he was graduated LL. B. with the class of 1879. He engaged in practice at Kansas City, Kansas, and while

in active practice he served five years as city attorney of Wyandotte and for two years 1891-92 was county attorney of Wyandotte County. In the meantime he became actively interested in the management of extensive real estate and other properties and business affairs, and since 1904 he has been practically retired from his legal practice. Mr. McGrew has done much to develop some of the best sections of Kansas City, Kansas, for residence and business uses, and is one of the men first in influence and power in the general commercial life of the city. He is connected as a stockholder or director with several of the leading banks, and is also general manager of the Bonner Portland Cement Company, with offices in the Victor Building.

Mr. McGrew has been classified politically as a standpat republican. He is a thirty-second degree Scottish Rite, a member of the Mystic Shrine at Leavenworth and belongs to the Congregational Church.

On January 6, 1881, at Kansas City, Kansas, he married Miss Julia M. Townsend, who was born at Racine, Wisconsin, daughter of Joseph and Annie (Batten) Townsend. Both her parents were natives of England. Mr. and Mrs. McGrew have three sons: George W. McGrew, who married Mayme Maher; Joseph T. McGrew, who married Jessica Jones; and Homer A. McGrew, who married Virginia Young.

C. O. ROSS. In a conspicuous place on the roll of men who have become successful through their connection with the oil and gas industry is found the name of C. O. Ross, a native of the Buckeye state and a splendid type of the alert, progressive and public-spirited men whose records are indications that success is ambition's answer. His long and prominent connection with the oil business began at the time of his majority, when he started in at the bottom to make his way to a position of prominence, and no oil producer in Kansas has a better record for high and straightforward business conduct, or for success won with honor. With the exception of six months spent in Colorado he has made Coffeyville his home and the center of his activities since 1907.

Mr. Ross was born on a farm in Wesley Township, Bartlett P. O., Washington County, Ohio, January 16, 1875, and is a son of James and Martha (Heald) Ross. Thomas Ross, his grandfather, was born in 1796, in Scotland, and as a young unmarried man came to America, making his way from New York to Virginia, where for some years he was engaged in farming. In later life he removed to Illinois, where he continued in agricultural pursuits until his death in 1876, when he was eighty years of age. With native thrift and industry, Mr. Ross accumulated a satisfying property and was known as one of his community's solid and substantial men. He was married in Virginia, and became the father of two children: Sarah, the widow of Elwood Lambert, who died in 1914, resides in California, eight miles from Los Angeles, on an English walnut farm; and James.

James Ross was born in 1834, in the Shenandoah Valley of Virginia, where in later years he was to visit wearing the uniform of his country. He was a small lad when his parents removed to Belmont County, Ohio, and not long thereafter his mother died. Subsequently he went to Washington County, Ohio, and there was married. Mr. Ross, in his younger years, taught school during the winter terms and farmed in the summer months, and continued to be so engaged until the outbreak of the Civil war, when he shouldered a musket and marched to the front with other patriotic young men from his neighborhood. During four years he fought under the flag of the Union and in this time his command saw some of the most important and decisive fighting that marked the entire struggle, its engagements including, among others, the fighting at Gettysburg, Missionary Ridge and Vicksburg and on Sherman's famous March to the Sea. Mr. Ross was twice wounded, once at Gettysburg, but on each occasion rejoined his company as soon as possible and resumed his post of duty. He established an excellent record for courage and soldierly qualities and won alike the respect of his officers and the admiration of his comrades.

When he returned from the war, a seasoned, hardened veteran, Mr. Ross found it difficult to resume his old habits of life. The duties of the schoolroom and the farm seemed prosaic and lifeless after the stirring experiences through which he had passed, and he therefore sought an employment in which more action was promised. Accordingly he joined a bridge construction gang, with which he was working when the accident occurred that nearly cost him his life. A hand-car on which he was riding was struck by a freight train and in the subsequent wreck Mr. Ross lost one of his arms and nearly lost a leg. Nothing daunted by a misfortune which would have discouraged the great majority of men, Mr. Ross began the study of law, and so closely did he apply himself that within a reasonably short period he was admitted to the bar and began practice. He still follows his profession, in which he has gained a decided success, and is now one of the leading members of the Bartlett (Ohio) bar. Mr. Ross exercises his right of franchise in behalf of the candidates of the republican party. His religious belief makes him a member of the Methodist Episcopal Church. Mr. Ross married Miss Martha Heald, daughter of "Billy" Heald, a Quaker farmer of Washington County, Ohio. Mrs. Ross was born in that county in 1844, and died in 1901, the mother of the following children: Glenn, and William T., who are engaged in farming in Washington County, Ohio; Edgar A., who is engaged in the practice of medicine and surgery at Bartlett, Ohio; L. A., who is a farmer of Comanche County, Oklahoma; C. O.; Hattie, who is the wife of Ezra Walker, a foreman in the mines of Pittsburgh, Pennsylvania; and Grace, who is the wife of Charles Meadows, a farmer of Montgomery County, Kansas.

C. O. Ross attended the public schools of Washington County, Ohio, until he was eighteen years of age, at which time he entered upon his independent career as a worker. For several years he was variously employed, accepting such honorable positions as granted emolument with a promise of betterment. It was not, however, until he was twenty-one years of age that he became identified with what was to prove his life work. At that time he accepted a position dressing tools in the oil fields of Ohio, subsequently working through the fields in the Buckeye state and in Kentucky as well. In 1903 he came to Kansas, first locating at Peru. In the meantime he had become a producer, in which capacity he shortly went to Nowata County, Oklahoma, where he spent four years. Returning then to Kansas, he established his headquarters at Coffeyville, and, with the exception of six months spent in Colorado, this city has been the scene of his success to the present time.

The advancement of Mr. Ross in business circles has been almost phenomenal. He has rapidly added to his holdings as a producer, and at the present time has 350 wells producing oil in Chautauqua County, Kansas, and near Bartlesville, Oklahoma, as well as an equal amount of wells as anyone else has in the Peru Sand fields. Likewise, he owns a 900-acre ranch; a river-bottoms farm in Montgomery County, which is used for alfalfa growing and consists of 377 acres, other tracts of land in Kansas; a forty-acre fruit farm in Colorado, of which twenty acres are devoted to apples; and his own residence, at No. 1904 South Walnut Street, Coffeyville. He is secretary, treasurer and general manager of the Interstate Oil and Gas Company and has other important business connections. In industrial and commercial circles his name is synonymous with fair dealing and adherence to high business standards, and he has the added prestige that accrues through a man's having made his own way. Mr. Ross is a republican but not an office seeker. With his family, he belongs to the Methodist Episcopal Church. His fraternal connections are with Sedan Lodge, Ancient Free and Accepted Masons; Wichita Consistory No. 2, thirty-second degree; Oklahoma City Temple, Ancient Arabic Order Nobles of the Mystic Shrine, and Modern Woodmen Camp of Peru. He is an active participant in movements making for civic betterment and a hard worker in the Chamber of Commerce of Coffeyville.

Mr. Ross was married at Bartlett, Ohio, in 1896, to Miss Ida Miller, daughter of Oliver and Laura (Arnold) Miller. Mr. Miller, who was a farmer and a veteran of the Civil war, is now deceased, but Mrs. Miller still survives and makes her home near Bartlett. To Mr. and Mrs. Ross there have been born the following children: Edith, born June 28, 1896, married Glen Walton, manager of his father-in-law's fruit farm near Montrose, Colorado, and has one child, Evelyn; Ralph, born July 23, 1898, residing with his parents, a junior at the Coffeyville High School; Hazel, born September 20, 1900, a freshman at Coffeyville High School; Clifford, born October 3, 1905, attending the graded school; Kenneth, born April 17, 1908, also attending public school; and Charles, born September 16, 1910.

OLIVER DENIOUS, a resident of Erie, Kansas, since 1894, has lived a life full of activity. His experiences have been in the role of a farm laborer, soldier, farmer, business man, public official, and wherever and in whatever place destiny has put him he has given a good account of his ability and character.

He was only twelve years of age when he became self supporting. That was back in Stark County, Ohio. His first work was to hire out to neighboring farmers, and though extremely young, he often did a man's work. Naturally enough he had limited advantages to obtain an education, and the public schools he attended were in Stark County. After four years working for others he returned to his father's place and put in one year after the age of sixteen on the old homestead.

His birth occurred at Greensburg, Summit County, Ohio, July 8, 1844. Although the Denious family came from Germany to Pennsylvania in early days, their ancestry was principally Scotch. Judge Denious' grandfather was Michael Denious, who was born in Pennsylvania in 1790 and became a pioneer settler in Summit County, Ohio. He was both a farmer and blacksmith. He saw some active service as a soldier

OLIVER DENIOUS FAMILY GROUP

during the War of 1812, and his death occurred at Greentown, Ohio, in 1863.

Levi Denious, father of Oliver, was born in Summit County, Ohio, July 9, 1818, and in 1846 he removed to Stark County and died at New Berlin in that county July 17, 1903. During most of his years he followed the trade of carpenter and joiner, and during the winter months he worked at cabinet making. He was a democrat, a member of the Methodist Episcopal Church, and in every sense a good citizen. His wife Nancy Raber, was born in Stark County, Ohio, in 1818, and died at Greentown in that state in 1899. Of their six children, the first, a son, died in infancy. Lovina, who died at Akron, Ohio, was the wife of Martin Stover, who is a retired blacksmith at Akron. The third in age is Mr. Oliver Denious. Catherine, who lives at Greentown, Ohio, is the widow of George Krieghbaum, who was a lumberman and farmer. Leonard is a real estate man at New Berlin, Ohio. Sadie died at Greentown, Ohio, unmarried.

Oliver Denious at the age of eighteen left the farm to become a soldier of the Union. He enlisted in 1862 in the One Hundred and Fourth Regiment of Ohio Volunteer Infantry, being mustered in August 8, 1862, and serving nearly three years, until his honorable discharge on June 12, 1865. He was both an efficient and brave soldier. He fought in some of the greatest campaigns of the war, including the advance upon Atlanta with Sherman, and he was afterwards sent back into Tennessee and participated in the bloody battles of Franklin and Nashville. From there he and his command were sent into North Carolina and were in the Carolinas when the war closed.

The first year out of the army he spent farming in Stark County. He bought a saw mill at Mogadore, Ohio, and after operating it for sawing lumber two years he converted the machinery into a clay mill, and for eight years was a manufacturer of pottery goods. His next experience was in the City of Cleveland, where he followed the carpenter's trade, and also worked as an employe of the Street Railway Company.

Mr. Denious has lived in Neosho County, Kansas, since 1883. The first five years he spent as a practical farmer and helped to develop some of the fertile soil of this region. In 1888 he was appointed postmaster of Galesburg, Kansas, and held that office through the Harrison administration and until Cleveland was elected for the second term. The people of Neosho County then elected him to one of the most important offices in the county government, that of probate judge, and he remained the incumbent two years until the populistic landslide of 1896 defeated him for re-election.

At the beginning of his term as probate judge he came to Erie in 1894, and on leaving office he bought a furniture and undertaking business. He now confines his attention entirely to undertaking, and has a first-class equipment and is one of the leading men in that business in the county.

Among other interests Judge Denious is president of the Building and Loan Association of Erie. His offices are on Third Street and he owns his residence on Fourth Street. In politics he is a republican, and while living in Ladore Township of Neosho County served as a member of the school board. Fraternally his affiliations are with Erie Lodge No. 676, Ancient Free and Accepted Masons; Akron Chapter, Royal Arch Masons, Erie Lodge No. 175, Ancient Order United Workmen, and with the Fraternal Aid Union. He is a member of Erie Post No. 311, Grand Army of the Republic, and is a past commander.

Vol. IV—23

In 1866 at Greentown, Ohio, he married Miss Martha Moore, daughter of Joseph and Elizabeth (White) Moore. Both her parents are now deceased and her father spent his life as a farmer in Stark County, Ohio. Judge Denious and his wife have been married half a century, and their children are all grown and established in homes of their own. Ada is the wife of Robert E. Miller, who has charge of the Rock Island Implement Company's branch offices at Omaha, Nebraska, where he resides. Lillie lives in Oklahoma and married Robert Hamilton. Wilbur is a successful attorney at Denver, Colorado. Jesse is editor of a paper at Dodge City, Kansas.

JUSTUS NATHAN BAIRD. Since his admission to the Kansas bar in February, 1909, Justus Nathan Baird has concentrated every energy upon the worthy task of building up a clientage and reputation at Kansas City, Kansas, and the esteem paid him by his fellow lawyers and the large practice he enjoys is ample evidence of his success. He practices in all the courts of the state and has offices in the Husted Building.

Mr. Baird is a graduate in law from the University of Michigan, and was influenced to locate in Kansas by the presence in this state of two brothers, both of them prominent and well known physicians. One of them is Dr. O. C. Baird, of Chanute, and a member of the State Medical Board and the other is Dr. J. Baird of Coffeyville.

One of nine children Justus Nathan Baird was born on a farm near Keosauqua in Van Buren County, Iowa, March 17, 1882. He is grateful for the fact that his life was spent in the invigorating and wholesome atmosphere of the country. His parents were Nathan and Lucinda S. (Jones) Baird, both natives of Ohio, and of New England and Pennsylvania Dutch ancestry. The respective families were established in this country in colonial days. Nathan Baird was an Iowa pioneer. He went from Ohio overland with ox teams to that state in 1854 and took up a homestead of 150 acres of Government land. He used his oxen to break that land and later was joined by his parents in Iowa. He was married in Iowa to Miss Jones, and he lived on his farm until his death in 1900. The old homestead is still owned by his children. Nathan Baird was not only a successful farmer and stock raiser, but a man of much influence in his home community. He worked for the success of republican principles and candidates, though for himself he never sought office. His name became a byword for practical wisdom and for honest and upright character, and of course there were not wanting those who were willing to take advantage of his fairness and honesty. He brought up his children to frugal and honorable standards of life, and his name is a benediction to them all. He and his wife were members respectively of the Presbyterian and Methodist denomination. His widow still lives on the old Iowa farm.

All the children were trained to make the best of their opportunities, and several of them aspired to professional careers. Justus N. Baird after leaving the common schools entered the Iowa Wesleyan University at Mount Pleasant, where he remained three years, and in 1906 he graduated A. B. from the University of Iowa at Iowa City. He then entered the law department of the University of Michigan, where he was graduated LL. B. with the class of 1908, and at the same time was admitted to the Michigan bar. A few weeks later he arrived at Kansas City,

Kansas, and has been in active practice since February, 1909. Mr. Baird has practiced alone.

Unlike many young lawyers he has shown no inclination to enter political life, though he is a stanch republican. He has held various chairs in the lodges of the Independent Order of Odd Fellows, is a member of the Knights of Pythias, and is always ready to help forward any public spirited enterprise. He and his wife are active in the Methodist Episcopal Church.

On October 19, 1911, Mr. Baird married Miss Amelia Ware. Mrs. Baird, who was born in Kansas, is a daughter of one of the greatest of Kansans, the late Eugene Ware, whose place as a great lawyer, a great poet, and a public leader will always entitle him to a conspicuous position in Kansas history. Mr. and Mrs. Baird have one child, Justus N. Baird, Jr.

EDWIN E. SAPP. There has been a Sapp connected with the bar of Cherokee County almost since the City of Galena was founded. Coming to that town in January, 1884, after having worked and studied earnestly to prepare himself for the bar, earning his own living in the meantime, Edwin E. Sapp in a comparatively brief time had won the approbation and favor of a considerable clientage.

In the years that have followed hardly a member of the Cherokee County Bar has been shown greater honors and has been accorded a larger and more profitable share in the civil practice of the courts. As long as his private interests would permit, his fellow citizens kept him employed in some phase of public life. He served as city attorney of Galena twelve years, was probate judge of Cherokee County two terms, judge of the Court of Common Pleas one term, and for another term sat on the district bench as judge.

In later years his business interests have become paramount to his professional. Judge Sapp is president of the Giant Mining and Royalties Company, a director in the George L. McCullagh Lead and Zinc Company, a director in the Lockport Lead & Zinc Company, director in the Scarlet Kid Mining Company, and the Pioneer Lead & Zinc Company. He has acquired some large property interests. His law offices are in the Sapp Building at Galena and he owns his home at 705 Galena Avenue, four other dwelling houses in Galena, two farms aggregating 200 acres in Cherokee County, and owns some mineral lands in the same county.

Judge Sapp is descended from some very fine families. His paternal ancestry came originally from Holland and located in Virginia in colonial times. He was born after both his grandfathers died. His paternal grandfather George Sapp was born in Ohio and died in Knox County of that state. The maternal line is one of special interest. His maternal grandfather was Peter Pierferry, who was born at the old artillery training ground and fortress of Le Fere. At one time the town and its environs were part of the feudal possessions of the Ferry family. Thus it was that Peter Pierferry became the hereditary colonel of the Le Fere Regiment. He was a graduate of the St. Croix Military College and the Berna Military College, and a fellow student in these colleges with him was the young Corsican, Napoleon Bonaparte. It is a matter of particular interest that Napoleon after his graduation became a sub-lieutenant under Col. Peter Pierferry in the Le Fere Regiment. In fact these two men were in a number of campaigns together. After Napoleon reached the pinnacle of his career and became emperor, Colonel Pierferry, be-

ing a Royalist in sympathy, abandoned his cause and securing a passport from Napoleon came to America and settled on Belle Isle in Lake Erie. That was in 1811. In 1812 he removed to Sandusky, Ohio, on account of Indian troubles. He was a member of the Ohio State Militia during the War of 1812. From Ohio he removed to Fort Raisin, near Monroe, Michigan, and was variously honored there, serving several terms as county treasurer.

Judge Sapp's father was Reason Sapp, who was born near the site of Kenyon College in Knox County, Ohio, in 1816. He was reared there, and subsequently became a minister of the Methodist Episcopal Church. He was a member of the old Ohio Conference when its jurisdiction extended over Michigan. After his marriage in Monroe, Michigan, he spent most of his time in the service of the Michigan Conference, and died at Grand Rapids in 1873. He was a republican and a Mason. The maiden name of his wife was Margaret Pierferry, who was born at Sandusky, Ohio, in 1821, and died at Galena, Kansas, in 1897. Their children were: Perry, who became a farmer and died at Ionia, Michigan, in 1881; Dexter T., who served for three years in the Seventh Michigan Cavalry during the Civil war and is now an attorney practicing at Gunnison, Colorado; William F., a veteran attorney of Galena, Kansas, mentioned elsewhere; Judge Edwin C.; Charles, a manufacturer of automobiles at Jackson, Michigan; John, an attorney at Gunnison, Colorado.

Judge Edwin E. Sapp was born in the home of his parents at Jackson, Michigan, July 12, 1858. He attended public school at Grand Rapids, but at the age of thirteen became dependent upon his own resources. His father died about that time and he had to hew out his own career. Many lines of work contributed to his support, and he worked as a gardener, at the printing trade, and finally secured by his own efforts the opportunity and means to study law. He carried on his law studies in the offices of one of the oldest and best known law firms in Chicago at the time, Dexter, Herrick & Allen. The two younger members of that firm died recently, and were among the foremost lawyers of Chicago.

Judge Sapp was admitted to the bar in 1883, and in January of the following year came to Galena. In politics he is a democrat, is a member of the Cherokee County and American Bar associations, belongs to the Community Club of Galena and to Lodge No. 677 of the Elks.

In 1885 at Galena he married Miss Mary E. Aldrich, daughter of Mr. and Mrs. H. B. Aldrich of Catskill, New York. Both her parents are now deceased. Her father was for many years in the livery business. Judge and Mrs. Sapp have three children: Dexter is a graduate of the law department of the Missouri State University and is now practicing at Galena. Vira graduated from the State Manual Training Normal School at Pittsburg, Kansas, and Christian College at Columbia, Missouri, and is still at home. Thomas is a graduate of the Kansas School of Mines and is a mine operator, with home at Galena.

SAMUEL BAUGHMAN. In the career of Samuel Baughman, now one of the leading real estate and insurance men of Chanute, there are found those qualities which make for success in business life. Industry, perseverance, a wise direction of talents and a quick grasp of opportunities have always characterized his actions, and throughout his life he has governed his operations by principles of fair dealing, so that his reputation in business matters is one which places him in an enviable position. He has been interested in a number of lines of endeavor, and in each has made a success, and the same statement applies to his management of the affairs of several public offices in which he has served.

Samuel Baughman was born in Westmoreland County, Pennsylvania, January 6, 1842, and is a son of Peter C. and Barbara (Heck) Baughman. He belongs to a family which came from Hessen-Castle, Germany, in 1746 and located near the City of Philadelphia, from whence it removed to the western part of Pennsylvania in 1764. Peter C. Baughman was born in 1807, in Westmoreland County, Pennsylvania, and was there reared and educated and for many years was engaged in agricultural pursuits. In 1850 he removed to Illinois, and engaged in farming in the vicinity of Rock Island, and in 1874 made his way to Altoona, Wilson County, Kansas, where he continued his agricultural operations. Later he moved on to Neosho County, and in the evening of life retired from active pursuits and took up his residence at Chanute, where his death occurred in 1895. Mr. Baughman was an industrious and energetic man, a skilled agriculturist who readily became conversant with conditions in the various communities in which he carried on his operations and a citizen who assisted his home vicinity's interests to grow and develop. He was a republican, although not active as a politician or seeker for personal preferment, and was a strong member of the United Brethren Church, the faith of which he brought into his every-day life. Mr. Baughman married Miss Barbara Heck, who was born in 1807, in Westmoreland County, Pennsylvania, and there reared and educated, and died at Shaw, Neosho County, Kansas in 1889. Mr. and Mrs. Baughman were the parents of the following children: Elizabeth who died at Moline, Illinois, in 1910, as the wife of the late Henry Truxell, who was a mechanic; Daniel, who came to Kansas in 1874, became a farmer and died in Wilson County in 1881; J. W., who came as a pioneer farmer to Kansas in 1869, and now a retired resident of Chanute; Margaret, who is the widow of Adam Fries, a carpenter and mechanic of Moline, Illinois; Catherine, who died in Wilson County, Kansas, in 1906, as the wife of the late Aaron Gamble, a farmer; Samuel; and Lydia, who married first George Pearce, a farmer, now deceased, and is now the wife of W. A. Golden, a retired mechanic of Moline, Illinois.

Samuel Baughman was educated in the graded schools of Rock Island and the high school at Moline, Illinois, and was nineteen years of age when he answered the call of his country and enlisted in Company C, Fourteenth Regiment, Missouri Volunteer Infantry. Later he veteranized in the Sixty-sixth Regiment, Illinois Volunteer Infantry, his service extending from his first enlistment, in September, 1861, until his final muster out, in June, 1865. During this time he participated in numerous battles, including Fort Donelson, Shiloh and both Corinths. He was with General Sherman at Missionary Ridge and Resaca, all the battles that took place in the great march to the sea, and Atlanta, and in North Carolina, during Sherman's campaign in that state, was at one time taken prisoner by the enemy, but managed to make his escape. His record was an excellent one, both for bravery and faithful performance of duty, and he returned to his home a seasoned soldier and better man, steadied by the stern discipline of the army and with a better understanding of life's responsibilities.

After a short stay at his home at Moline, Mr. Baughman went to Davenport, Iowa, where he attended Bryant & Stratton's Commercial College, and shortly after completing his course in that school engaged in the butchering business at Milan, Illinois. This he conducted until 1874, when he came to Wilson County, Kansas, and began farming in the vicinity of Altoona, a vocation to which he devoted six years. In 1880 he was elected sheriff of Wilson County and served in that capacity for two terms. When he retired from that office Mr. Baughman built the Gold Dust Hotel, at Fredonia, Kansas, and continued as the proprietor of that popular caravansery until 1893, when he traded the establishment for a large tract of land in Dent County, Missouri, and again took up farming as his vocation. After two years, however, he disposed of this land and came to Chanute, where he again took up his first business, that of butchering, and continued to be engaged therein for six months. Following this, he embarked in a wholesale bakery and ice cream business, with his son, Walter S., and continued therein for seven years, and was then elected police judge of Chanute and acted in that capacity four years. Since that time he has devoted his attention and talents to the real estate and insurance business, in which he has met with unqualified success, his offices being at No. 113½ West Main Street. Mr. Baughman handles much Chanute and Neosho County land, residential, business and farming, and owns his own residence at No. 711 South Highland Avenue, and dwellings at No. 110 South Steuben Avenue and 101 South Lafayette Avenue. He has an excellent knowledge of realty values, and in the insurance line is the representative of all the large and reliable companies.

Mr. Baughman is a republican. In the offices to which he has been elected he has shown a conscientious desire to discharge his duties faithfully, and his public record is as clean and creditable as those which he established as a soldier, a business man and a citizen. With his family he belongs to the Presbyterian Church. Mr. Baughman is widely known in fraternal circles, having joined the Masonic fraternity more than a half century ago, at Corinth, Missouri, while in the Union army, at which time he was given a traveling charter. He now belongs to Cedar Lodge No. 103, Ancient Free and Accepted Masons, Chanute; Chanute Chapter No. 21, Royal Arch Masons; Chanute Commandery No. 44, Knight Templars; Mirza Temple, Ancient Arabic Order Noble Mystic Shrine, at Pittsburg, Kansas; and the Council at Iola, Kansas. He is a member of Chanute Post No. 129, Grand Army of the Republic, of which he is past commander, and is now one of the state officers in the council of administration of the State Department of the Grand Army of the Republic.

Judge Baughman was married in 1868, at Moline, Illinois, to Miss Lenora F. Kidder, daughter of Nelson and Marinda (Curtis) Kidder, both deceased, Mr. Kidder having been a mechanic. Mrs. Baughman, who was a member of the Daughters of the American Revolution, and a lady of many graces and accomplishments, died at Chanute in 1912. Judge and Mrs. Baughman were the parents of the following children: Nellie Z., who married Charles S. Reed, for twelve years a judge of the Court of Common Pleas, at Sandusky, Ohio, who resigned from the bench to form the leading law firm of Reed & Eichelberger, at Cleveland, Ohio; Walter S., who was formerly engaged in business with his father at Chanute, but now engaged in farming four miles north of Chanute; Ernest, who died at the age of three years; Mabel, who died when 4½ years of age; and Elsie B., who is the wife of B. B. Blackburn, of 711 South Highland Avenue, Chanute, a locomotive engineer in the employ of the Atchison, Topeka & Santa Fe Railroad. Both Mrs. Reed and Mrs. Blackburn are members of the Daughters of the American Revolution and were delegates to the national convention of that organization held at Washington, District of Columbia, in 1915. Mrs. Reed is prominent as a club woman and speaker and has gained national prominence. She was Grand Ruth of the state lodge of the Order of the Eastern Star, and was a member of the party which accompanied Charles Evans Hughes in his trip through Ohio, during his political campaign.

JOSEPH L. STRICKLER. In reviewing the lives of the business men of Cherryvale, especially in regard to the establishment and growth of the oil industry, it who have taken part in this work have been those who have brought with them from other parts of the state and country reputations for honorable dealing, and capability for accomplishment of purpose. Associated with the oil industry of this part of the state is the name of Joseph L. Strickler, who came to Cherryvale in 1902 and is now probably the largest independent producer in this locality. Mr. Strickler has been identified with the oil business practically since he started upon his career and has had experience in various fields. He was born in Fairfield County, Ohio, December 19, 1872, and is a son of William Baker and Mary (Foutz) Strickler.

The Strickler family is of German origin and was founded in America previous to the Revolution, the American progenitor settling in the colony of Virginia. John Strickler, the grandfather of Joseph L., was born in 1808, in the Shenandoah Valley of Virginia and was a marble cutter by trade, but on going as a pioneer to Fairfield County, Ohio, took up farming as his vocation and homesteaded 160 acres. He also built the old half-way house between Lancaster and Pleasantville, which he conducted for many years, and there continued to reside during the remainder of his life. He was equally successful at his trade, as the proprietor of his tavern and as a farmer, and was a man of some influence in his community, and rounded out a full and useful life, dying in 1887, at the age of eighty-eight years. Mr. Strickler was a stanch democrat. His children were as follows: Lew, who followed the trade of marble cutter and died at the old family place in Fairfield County, and who fought as a soldier for three years during the Civil war; John, also a marble cutter, who saw three years of service in the Civil war as a Union soldier and died at Columbus, Franklin County, Ohio; Ad, a marble cutter by trade, who retired in his latter years and died at Bremen, Fairfield County, Ohio; Dan, who is a retired contractor and builder of Franklin County, Ohio; Job, who is a retired carpenter of Nelsonville, Hocking County, Ohio; Joe, who was a blacksmith and died at Rushville, Fairfield County; and Katie, who died at Basil, Fairfield County, in 1908, as the wife of Henry Swarner, a retired farmer.

William Baker Strickler, who now resides on his farm one mile north of Cherryvale, was born May 29, 1842, in Fairfield County, Ohio, on his father's farm. He was reared thereon, and like several of his brothers early adopted the trade of their father, that of marble cutting, which he followed for a number of years. This brought him into contact with men engaged in large construction jobs, and he gradually developed into a contractor and for many years was well known in handling heavy stone work for county bridges, etc., in Ohio. In 1911, feeling the effect of advancing years, he decided upon a partial retirement and at that time came to Kansas and purchased the small farm upon which he now has his home. He is still hale and hearty and is a familiar figure on the streets of Cherryvale, where he has made numerous friends. Mr. Strickler is a republican of the "stand pat" variety, and a member of the Christian Church, in the work of which he was active during his younger days, having served as deacon. He took some prominent part in public affairs while in Ohio, having been postmaster at Rinville for a number of years and also running the first mail route out of Corning, Ohio. For the past fifty years he has been a valued member of the Independent Order of Odd Fellows. In 1862 Mr. Strickler answered his country's call for volunteers, joining Company I, One hundred and Twenty-Sixth Regiment, Ohio Volunteer Infantry, with which he served until the close of the war. Attached to the Army of the Potomac, the One Hundred and Twenty-Sixth took part in some of the hardest-fought engagements of the entire struggle, including the battles of the Wilderness, Shiloh, Lookout Mountain and Gettysburg. Although he received a wound at the Wilderness, Mr. Strickler never lost a trick of duty by being compelled to go to the hospital, and his entire service was characterized by a brave and faithful discharge of duty. He married Miss Mary Foutz, who was born in April, 1847, in Licking County, Ohio, and they became the parents of the following children: Bertha, a graduate of the Corning High School, who married Dan E. Ten Eyeick, a florist of Crawford County, Ohio, and the owner of five large greenhouses; Sedda, a graduate of the Corning High School, who taught school until her marriage to C. D. Hemery, a sheep raiser of Woolton, Wyoming; Joseph L., of this notice; Walter, master mechanic and foreman in the railroad shops at Crestline, Ohio; and Cora, a graduate of the Corning High School, who taught school for several years, and died at Osawatomie, Kansas, in 1916, as the wife of J. A. Rogers, an oil well driller now residing at Cherryvale.

Joseph L. Strickler received his education in the public schools of Corning, Ohio, but at the age of fifteen years gave up his studies to enter upon his career. His first position was that of collector for J. G. Stallsmith, of Corning, in whose employ he remained three years, and at the end of that time secured an introduction to the business which he was destined to make his life work. His start was a tool dresser and later he began drilling wells, both oil and gas, following the various fields through Ohio, West Virginia and New York. In 1899 he became a contractor in drilling wells and after running tools in Ohio, came to Parsons in the same year. Subsequently, he ran tools, drilling wells for gas at Humboldt, Burlington, Iola, and many other towns, and in 1902 came to Cherryvale, which has since been the center of his operations. He has been drilling ever since, all over Montgomery, Labette, Wilson and Neosho counties, in Kansas, as well as in the Oklahoma fields, as a contractor, and personally has sixteen oil producing wells in Montgomery and Labette counties, making 400 barrels per day, the largest production in this section. On one lease he pumps a 250 barrel tank every day. This is all Mr. Strickler's own production, and he has no companies with whom he has to divide his profits. In addition to his oil interests, Mr. Strickler has devoted his fine business talents to the development of several important enterprises in other lines of endeavor, and at the present time is president of the Cherryvale Iron Works and of the San Antonio Packing Box Company, of San Antonio, Texas.

Politically, Mr. Strickler is a republican, and he supports his party stanchly, but has not found time from his business cares to enter actively into politics or public life. He is prominent in Masonry, having attained to the thirty-second degree, and belongs to Cherryvale Lodge No. 137, Ancient Free and Accepted Masons; Cherryvale Chapter No. 86, Royal Arch Masons; Saint Bernard Commandery No. 10, Knights Templar, of Independence; Fort Scott Consistory No. 4, Royal and Select Masters; and Abdullah Temple, Ancient Arabic Order of Nobles of the Mystic Shrine of Leavenworth, of which he is a life member. He is also a life member of Cherryvale Lodge No. 989, Benevolent and Protective Order of Elks, and belongs to the Cherryvale Commercial Club.

In 1900, at Burlington, Kansas, Mr. Strickler was married to Miss Anna Marcella ("Tot") Huddleson, daughter of Robert J. and Anna Huddleson, the latter of whom resides with her daughter and son-in-law. Mr. Huddleson, who was a stationary engineer by vocation and a pioneer of Burlington, died at Cherryvale in 1908. Mr. and Mrs. Strickler have two children: Russell, born January 26, 1906; and Nellie, born July 14, 1909, both attending public school. The family home is situated at No. 331 West Third Street.

COL. LEWIS C. TRUE. Some interesting distinctions belong to this veteran soldier and lawyer who now lives retired at Kansas City, Kansas. He came to Kansas soon after leaving the army, and spent several years combating the hardships and plagues which afflicted the farmers in that period in Franklin County. Unable to make progress as a farmer, he took up the study of law, and in 1871 was admitted to practice in Cherokee County. He spent five years in general practice at Chetopa, and was then elected county attorney of Labette County.

Kansas had just enacted its state wide prohibition law. Colonel True went into office committed to the duty of upholding the laws of the state and as a gallant soldier he could see no other course before him but to perform his duty. Personally he has always been a stanch advocate of prohibition, and he at once proceeded to employ the instrument of public office to carry out and enforce the state law. Though the law imposed equal obligations upon every county attorney in the state, Colonel True was the only incumbent of such an office during the first two years who rigidly applied the provisions of the new laws. It was a most ungrateful task, but he was not deterred by any of the difficulties or the dangers attending prohibition enforcement. His enemies burned his house and set in his path every other possible obstacle, and at at the end of his first term they succeeded in defeating him for re-election. That defeat is really one of the greatest tributes ever given to Colonel True. It should be recalled that he shared defeat along with Governor St. John, who had been re-nominated on the prohibition ticket.

Since 1882 Colonel True has been a prominent member of the bar of Kansas City, Kansas, and practiced actively there until a few years ago. He was the first city attorney of Kansas City after the consolidation of several towns under a city charter.

Lewis Corbin True was born on a farm in Coles County, Illinois, April 4, 1842. He was one of the six children of Frederick G. and Cynthiana (Wigginton) True. His brothers and sisters who are still living are: J. F. True of Topeka; J. W. True of Eureka Springs, Arkansas; Mrs. Ollie Gould, wife of George Gould of Mattoon, Illinois. His parents were both natives of Frankfort, Kentucky. His grandfather John W. True was born in Virginia. Colonel True's mother died when he was a child. His father was an active leader among the abolitionists of Illinois and was one of the sympathizers with the underground railway. He was a successful and prosperous farmer, having acquired his land by direct purchase from the Government in Coles County, and he subsequently secured a section of railway land, giving him altogether 800 acres, which he devoted to general farming and cattle raising.

The old farm in Coles County was the environment in which Colonel True spent his early years. He attended the common schools, worked in vacations on the farm, and at the age of eighteen entered Illinois College at Jacksonville, where he remained about a year. At the outbreak of the war in 1861 he enlisted as a private in Company E of the Thirty-eighth Illinois Volunteer Infantry. In the fall of 1862 he was transferred to the Sixty-second Illinois Infantry. It was with that regiment that he made his splendid record as a soldier. On the basis of merit he was promoted successively to the positions of adjutant, captain of Company D, major, lieutenant colonel, and when the regiment after three years of service veteranized and re-enlisted he became colonel. While lieutenant colonel he was placed in command of the Third Brigade in the Department of Arkansas, and the record of this command is a part of the official records of the War of the Rebellion, found in Volume 48, page 266, Series 1, part 2. Colonel True participated in several of the important campaigns by which the country on both sides of the Mississippi River was conquered from the Confederacy, and he was in a number of notable engagements. At the close of active hostilities he remained in the service with his veteran regiment performing duty largely in Indian Territory, and was granted his honorable discharge in August, 1866. He was the youngest officer of his rank among the entire armies of the Union.

After the war he determined to make Kansas his home, and locating in Franklin County he became associated with his brother James F. True and also with that famous Kansan, Hon. E. D. Coburn, in conducting a livestock ranch. The operation of a Kansas farm is a simple matter now compared to what it was fifty years ago, and Colonel True soon left the farm and going to Chetopa engaged in the study of law under William P. Lamb. He is now one of the oldest attorneys in the state. After removing to Kansas City, Kansas, his private practice was uninterrupted except for the time he served on the bench as judge of the Common Pleas Court, and one term as judge of the second division of the District Court of the Twenty-ninth Judicial Circuit. Seven years ago he gave up his office and practice, and now spends practically all his time at his comfortable home at 563 Freeman Avenue.

In November, 1865, before leaving the army, Colonel True married Miss Annie Keeler of Pine Bluff, Arkansas. Her father George Keeler was a well known planter in Arkansas where Mrs. True was born. They have two living children: Frederick G., of Peoria, Illinois, and George L., of Amarillo, Texas.

Colonel True has always been an active republican, has taken part in a number of campaigns, and has always been a fighter for prohibition and temperance. He and his wife are members of the Presbyterian Church and Mrs. True is a member of the Ladies Aid Circle No. 86 of Kansas City, Kansas. Twice Colonel True has served as commander of Burnside Post No. 28, Department of the Grand Army of the Republic; and the Sons of Veterans organization at Kansas City, Kansas, bears his name.

HON. EDWARD ALEXANDER ENRIGHT. Distinguished as a statesman as well as for his achievements at the bar, Edward Alexander Enright is an honored, valued and admired citizen of Kansas City. For almost a quarter of a century he has been a prominent factor in the law and in public affairs, and his name stands foremost among the leaders who have organized, fathered and vitalized many of the progressive movements which have made Kansas the great commonwealth it now is.

Edward Alexander Enright was born September 17, 1858, at West Burke, Vermont, the seventh in a family of nine children · born to Rev. Joseph and Katherine (Weir) Enright.

Rev. Joseph Enright was born at Kilrush, in County Clare, Ireland. He attended school there and being of studious habits and serious mind, very early dedicated himself to the ministry, accepting the faith of the Methodist Episcopal Church. It is probable that at that time but small encouragement was given in County Clare to the missionary efforts of the young preacher and naturally his thoughts turned to another country, in which he had learned there was a wider field of opportunity. Hence, in 1840, with little capital except faith, hope and innate goodness, he embarked for Canada on a sailing vessel, and after a weary voyage was safely landed in the Province of Quebec and settled in the hamlet of Waton, near Danville. There he not only preached the gospel but lived it, doing all in his power to bring comfort and happiness into the lives of people who had seldom experienced either. It was there that he met the admirable woman who became his wife, Katherine Weir. Her father was Rev. Alexander Weir, who was also a Methodist minister. In many ways the Weir family has been prominent in English history, not only in religious bodies but in public affairs and some of its members have sat in the Parliament.

About 1850 Mr. Enright removed with his family to Vermont and became a member of the Methodist Conference in the district in which the Town of West Burke was situated. He accepted the hard, laborious life of the itinerant Methodist preacher and as the conference decided he moved his home from place to place and thus served many churches in Vermont before his useful life came to a close, at Windsor, Vermont, in 1895. He was a self made man but during his long life attracted men of high scholarship; he never sought a public office of any kind, but so won the confidence of public men that they sought his advice and followed his counsel, this notably being the case on many occasions when an honored senator of the United States laid legislative plans before him before giving them support. Following the Golden Rule and ever allying himself with movements for the betterment of humanity, Mr. Enright never accumulated a large amount of worldly goods, but, through prudence and industry in conducting a farm, was able to give his family a comfortable home and to lay aside enough to assure the education of his children, this being one of the ambitions of his life. During the progress of the Civil war he gave a great deal of time to administering to the sick and wounded and although not connected officially with any military body, he held himself ready for any emergency and through his agency sorrowing families far from the battle field many times derived comfort from the knowledge that he had tenderly performed the last rites over the hero soldier's grave. He was a man of simple, unaffected dignity and his memory still lingers in the section where his life of devotion was mainly spent.

Edward Alexander Enright attended first the public schools of Windsor, Vermont, and in 1878 was graduated from the high school and entered the University of Vermont, from which institution he was graduated with the highest honors of his class, in 1882. This made him an honorary member of the Phi Beta Kappa Greek letter fraternity. After graduation he taught school until 1883, at Cavendish, in Windsor County, Vermont, and then came as far west as Iowa and for one year was principal of the Smithland schools, in Woodbury County, going from there to Albion, Nebraska, where he was principal of the high school and one year later was elected county superintendent of Boone County and continued to fill that office for four years. During his teaching years he had devoted his leisure time to the study of law and had been admitted to the bar.

Although it would be a matter of pride to claim that Mr. Enright chose Kansas City as his home after considering the advantages of many others, the truth is that he located here in an accidental way, as it were. A beloved sister was a resident and she fell ill and Mr. Enright left excellent prospects in Nebraska in order to remain at her bedside. This was in 1890 and he soon determined to open a law office and enter into practice here and from that day to the present his name and fame have belonged to Kansas City.

Politically a republican, in 1897 he was elected chairman of the republican central committee. In 1898 he was elected county attorney for four years and it was during this time that he had arrested one William Atkins for violating the eight-hour law of the state and personally conducted this as a test case, advising therein with the attorney general of the state. By appeal this case was taken to the Supreme Court, which affirmed the constitutionality of the act, thus causing Mr. Enright to win his case. Another widely heralded case was that in which he gave his name as plaintiff in prosecuting a suit of injunction to prevent the Metropolitan Railway Company from securing a franchise which failed to secure to the citizens of Kansas City their just rights. He also gave his name in suit of mandamus compelling the board of county commissioners of Wyandotte County, Kansas, to raise the personal taxes of large corporations in the county.

Mr. Enright was first elected to the State Legislature in 1903, serving in the special session of 1904, and in 1907 was again elected a member of the Legislature and served through the special session. During his legislative period he was the father of numerous most important bills and through his earnest support and hard work many admirable laws were placed upon the statute book. He introduced bills concerning prison reform; for protecting cities against dishonest paving contractors and to guarantee factory protection for laborers. He was entrusted by labor commissioners of the state with special labor legislation and through his efforts many advantageous and labor reform laws were formulated. He supported the primary law; the anti-pass law, and introduced and had charge of bills authorizing Kansas City, Kansas, to purchase the franchise of the Metropolitan Water Company, thus establishing municipal ownership in the city. He was especially interested in the passage of bills protecting policy holders in insurance contracts, and in all measures that brought about right and justice especially to the oppressed.

Mr. Enright had been put forward as his party's candidate for governor in 1902. He held other public offices than those mentioned and during the administration of President Theodore Roosevelt served four months as Indian commissioner at Checota, Indian Territory. He resigned this office in order to return to his law practice, which had grown to large proportions. Having given much attention to insurance law he has done a large amount of court business for fraternal organizations in which insurance is a feature. He is known all over the country as an able representative of leading fraternal orders in the courts of the land, not only because of his powers as a public speaker, but because of his absolute understanding of every technicality of the law. Aside from his other interests, Mr. Enright is interested in various prospering industries of the state and is a director of the Home State Bank and the Minn Avenue State Bank, both of Kansas City.

Mr. Enright is a thirty-second degree Mason. He belongs to the Knights of Maccabees of the World; to the Brotherhood of American Yeomen; to the Knights of Pythias; to the Royal Neighbors, in which he was chairman of the beneficiary committee for five years; and has been a member of the law committee of the Modern Woodmen of America for a longer time than any other individual; and has held committee appointments and been a delegate to the Supreme conventions of the order of Ben Hur and other bodies.

Mr. Enright was married July 26, 1888, to Miss Myra Belle Brewer, who is a daughter of H. W. and Martha Brewer, of Red Cloud, Nebraska, and they have one daughter, Myra Alice, a most attractive young lady and a social favorite. Mrs. Enright is a member of the Methodist Protestant Church.

Mrs. Enright's parents were pioneers in Wisconsin. From there they removed to Stark County, Illinois, and afterward to Red Cloud, Nebraska, where Mr. Brewer was a grain buyer for forty years and was also in business at Kansas City, Missouri. His death occurred March 27, 1900, after which Mrs. Brewer made her home with Mr. and Mrs. Enright until her death, on May 22, 1912.

Perhaps no woman in the United States is better known in the great fraternal order of the Royal Neighbors than is Mrs. Enright. She has been officially identified with the Eastern Star, the Yeomen and the Young Women's Christian Association, but her special work has been with the Royal Neighbors of America. She is a charter member of Laurel Camp No. 84, of Kansas City, Kansas, which now has a membership of 700 and increasing each year. She has been officially connected with this organization since 1897, having served two years as supreme chancellor; two years as a member of the law committee; two years as supreme receiver; eight years as a member of the board of supreme managers, being its chairman for three years and continuing officially after the terms were changed from biennial to triennial. She has been supreme oracle or president of the national organization since 1911, receiving at the time of her first election, three-fourths of the vote cast and at her second election

the vote was unanimous. During her administration membership has increased from 200,000 to 375,000.

It is a law of the Royal Neighbors that only women shall fill the offices. Mrs. Enright takes an interest in everything looking toward betterment and uplift and is active in civic clubs and associated charities.

WILLIAM CLYDE TOMLINSON. As one of the representative and old established undertakers of Southeastern Kansas, William Clyde Tomlinson, of Chanute, belongs to that class of men in his line who have elevated the calling to a profession and conduct their work scientifically and expertly. Mr. Tomlinson established his business in Chanute seventeen years ago and with the exception of an interval of three years, has been here continuously since. During this time has witnessed remarkable advancements made in his field of endeavor. The modern undertaker and embalmer must be the possessor of qualities which fit him for his calling, for he must not only thoroughly understand it, but must be possessed of infinite tact and sympathy of manner. He is called into a family at a time of greater grief, when ordinary duties are suspended and there is a necessity for kindly action and expert advice. As the possessor of these qualities Mr. Tomlinson is gratefully remembered in many homes which have been visited by death.

William C. Tomlinson was born in Mercer County, Illinois, April 19, 1865, and is a son of Joseph F. and Adelaide (Randall) Tomlinson, and belongs on both sides to families which have long been residents of this country and who have been distinguished in a number of fields of endeavor. On the paternal side the family is traced to three brothers who emigrated to America during colonial days, one locating in Vermont, one in Kentucky and one in North Carolina, William C. being descended from the last-named ancestor. Henry Bishop Tomlinson, his grandfather, was born in North Carolina, in 1796, and as a young man went to Boone County, Indiana, where he was engaged in practice as a physician for many years. He retired after a long and honorable service to his calling, and located at Chanute, Kansas, where he soon died, in 1881. His first wife, who was the grandmother of William C. Tomlinson, died when her son Joseph F. was but five years old, and the grandfather took for his second wife Polly Hacker, who died at Girard, Kansas.

Joseph F. Tomlinson was born November 8, 1843, in Boone County, Indiana, and was there reared and educated. He was still a young man when he left the parental roof and went to Mercer County, Illinois, in which community he was married, while home on a furlough during the war. He was living in that state when President Lincoln issued his first call for volunteers to defend the Union, and showed his patriotism by enlisting in Company I, Seventeenth Regiment, Illinois Volunteer Infantry, although then only seventeen years of age. His service as a wearer of the blue uniform of his country covered a period of three years and two months, and during this time saw much active fighting, including the engagements of Fort Donelson, Shiloh, Pittsburg Landing, Corinth, Holly Springs and the Siege of Vicksburg. When his service was completed, the brave young soldier returned to Mercer County, Illinois, where he engaged in farming, and in 1872 went to Iowa, there continuing his agricultural operations in Guthrie County until 1878, in that year going to Keokuk County, Iowa, as a farmer. Mr. Tomlinson came to Chanute in 1886 and on a farm in Neosho County he continued to carry on operations until 1899. At that time he left the farm and removed to the city, where he established the undertaking business now conducted by his son. He did not live long enough to carry the business through to the proportions which he had planned, as his death occurred June 20, 1900. Mr. Tomlinson was a man who was respected and esteemed for his many admirable qualities of mind and heart, and for the honorable manner in which he always conducted his business operations and his private activities. He was a republican in his political views, although not an active politician, and was a devout and faithful member of the Methodist Episcopal Church. He always maintained his interest in the fortunes of his former comrades in the Union army, and was a popular member of Neosho Post No. 129, Grand Army of the Republic, at Chanute.

Mr. Tomlinson was married in Mercer County, Illinois, to Miss Adelaide Randall, who was born February 12, 1845, at Rochester, New York, a member of a family which settled at Providence, Rhode Island, when that place was founded by Roger Williams, in 1636. Stephen Randall, Jr., the maternal grandfather of William C. Tomlinson, was born in 1811, in Rhode Island, and shortly before the birth of his daughter, Adelaide, removed to New York and located at Rochester. In 1847 he went with his family to Mercer County, Illinois, and engaged in farming, but in the evening of life removed to near Sigourney, Iowa, where he passed away in 1896, at the age of eighty-five years. He married Rachel Trumbull, who was born in either Connecticut or Rhode Island, and died at the homestead in Mercer County, Illinois. Mr. Tomlinson belonged to a military training company, as had his father before him, and several members of the Randall family saw military service. Stephen Randall, Sr., the great-grandfather of William C. Tomlinson, was born in 1787, at Providence, Rhode Island. He removed with his son Stephen to New York, and his great-grandson still possesses a memento of his visit in the Empire State, in a tomahawk which was picked up by him at Sackett's Harbor, and which had been used in the War of 1812. In 1847 he went as a pioneer farmer to Mercer County, Illinois, and there his death occurred in 1870.

Mrs. Adelaide Tomlinson died in Keokuk County, Iowa, in 1884, having been the mother of the following children: William C., of this review; Ira W., who was engaged in farming in Keokuk County, Iowa, until his death at the age of twenty-five years; Charley E., who was also a farmer in that county and died when thirty-four years of age; Leona A., who died at Trinidad, Colorado, in 1898, as the wife of the late R. S. Lawrence, who until his death was a machinist in the employ of the Atchison, Topeka and Santa Fe Railroad; and Lucy, who died in 1884, at Sigourney, Keokuk County, Iowa, aged seven years. Joseph F. Tomlinson was again married, to Miss Jane Jessup, now a resident of Sigourney, Keokuk County, Iowa, and they had one son: W. Elmer, who is credit man for the International Harvester Company, with headquarters at Columbia, South Carolina.

As a boy and youth William C. Tomlinson divided his time between assisting his father on the home place during half of the year and spending the rest in the public schools, both in Illinois and Iowa. In the winter of 1886 he attended the United Presbyterian Academy, at Washington, Iowa, and on leaving that institution entered upon his own career. His first experience was as a country school teacher in

Iowa, where he remained one term, and in 1887 he came to Chanute and for six years taught in the Neosho County schools. He continued as an educator in the Neosho and Wilson County schools for nine years and the Wyandotte County schools for three years, and in 1899 located permanently at Chanute, where he began business as a dealer in second-hand furniture and stoves. The sudden death of his father, in 1900, caused him to give up his business in order to take charge of the undertaking establishment, of which he has since been the owner, the offices being located at No. 201 West Main Street. One of the most modern of undertakers, Mr. Tomlinson is always on the alert to secure every improvement or advantage of new discoveries, and keeps his equipment abreast of the times in all particulars. His residence is at No. 221 Southwestern Avenue.

Mr. Tomlinson is a republican, and at various times has been called upon by his fellow-citizens to serve in public positions, having been township clerk of Canville Township for one term of two years, and a member of the Chanute Board of Education for seven years. His religious faith is that of the Baptist denomination, and he has for several years been a trustee of his church. Mr. Tomlinson is particularly well known in fraternal circles, belonging to Cedar Lodge No. 103, Ancient Free and Accepted Masons; Chanute Lodge No. 852, Modern Woodmen of America; Hector Lodge No. 64, Independent Order of Odd Fellows; Chanute Lodge No. 63, Woodmen of the World; the Fraternal Aid Union; Council No. 44, Sons and Daughters of Justice; Chanute Lodge No. 688, Loyal Order of Moose; and the Anti-Horse Thief Association; and also holds membership in the Chanute Business Men's Club and Abe Lincoln Camp No. 83, Sons of Veterans, of which latter he is past commander.

Mr. Tomlinson was married in 1889 at Earleton, Kansas, to Miss Louvisa Williams, daughter of John and Lydia (Shelton) Williams, retired farming people who reside at Chanute. Three children have been born to Mr. and Mrs. Tomlinson: Vernie A., who received a high school education and is now the wife of George C. Young, who is connected with Wade & Stanley's furniture store at Chanute; Bertha C., a graduate of the Chanute High School, who taught school for one year in Neosho County and two years at Chanute, before her marriage to Roy E. Cowen, who is manager of the National Supply Company, of Colorado, Kansas; and Bernice, who is attending the Chanute High School as a member of the junior class.

GRANVILLE S. HOSS, JR. Since his appointment to the office of postmaster of Cherryvale, in 1915, Granville S. Hoss, Jr., has been discharging the duties of his responsible position in a capable and conscientious manner that has given the people of the city no reason to complain of their mail service. Prior to assuming the duties of this office, Mr. Hoss had been connected with several business houses and had displayed ability that brought him favorably forward as made of official timber.

Mr. Hoss was born at Nevada, Missouri, December 28, 1885, and is a son of Granville S. and Julia (McBride) Hoss. The Hoss family has been in America since 1756, in which year Johannes Hoss emigrated from Germany and settled in Pennsylvania, from whence the family drifted to the West and South. Samuel B. Hoss, grandfather of Granville S., was born in 1819, in Greenville, Tennessee, and was there reared, educated and married. When still a young man he migrated to Missouri, where he taught school

for some years, but finally turned his attention to· farming and developed a good farm, on which he carried on operations until his retirement from active affairs. He died at Southwest City, Missouri, in 1904. Samuel B. Hoss married Almeda Snell, of the well-known family of that name in Tennessee, in which state she was born, and they became the parents of the following children: A. B., who is a banker of Southwest City, Missouri; Granville S.; Emma, who is the wife of L. O. Ellis, D. D. S., a retired dental practitioner of Kansas City, Missouri; O. H., an attorney of Nevada, Missouri; and Fannie A., the wife of Willam Arnold, a teacher of the State of Washington.

Granville S. Hoss, Sr., was born October 29, 1850, in Pettis County, Missouri, and was there reared and educated and admitted to the bar. Prior to his marriage he removed to Vernon County, in the same state, and for a number of years carried on a successful practice at Nevada, from whence, in 1897, he went to Saint Louis, and formed a law partnership with Senator Stone. This combination became one of the strong ones of the city and continued until 1905, when Mr. Hoss gave up his legal work and came to Cherryvale, where he bought the Cherryvale Telephone Company, of which he has since been owner and manager. He is a democrat in politics, and while in Vernon County, Missouri, served in the capacity of prosecuting attorney for several years. He belongs to the Masonic fraternity and to the Presbyterian Church. His home is at 426 East Main Street. Mr. Hoss married Julia McBride, who was born August 6, 1856, at Paris, Missouri, and they are the parents of four children: Granville S., Jr.; LeRoy K., who is wire chief for the Cherryvale Telephone Company; and Margaret and Julia, who reside with their parents.

Granville S. Hoss, Jr., enjoyed good educational advantages in his youth, attending the public schools of Nevada and Saint Louis, Missouri, and Smith Academy, now a part of Washington University. This latter institution he left in 1904 to become a clerk in the office of the Colonial Security Company, of Saint Louis, but in 1905 accompanied his father to Cherryvale and was made secretary of the Cherryvale Telephone Company. This office he retained until 1915, when he was appointed by President Wilson as postmaster of Cherryvale, and took charge of the duties of the office March 1st of that year. Mr. Hoss is a democrat in politics and stanchly supports the candidates of his party.

In January, 1916, Mr. Hoss was married at Columbus, Kansas, to Miss Pearl E. Bornhouser, daughter of William and Hattie Bornhouser, the latter of whom is deceased, while the former resides in Oklahoma and is a contractor and builder. Mr. and Mrs. Hoss reside in their modern home at No. 206 South Neosho Street.

WILLIAM ELLIOTT BARNHART, who has lived in Kansas City, Kansas, since 1887, has held many large responsibilities in connection with transportation lines, both urban and general railway companies, and has also regulated his private affairs so as to give time for much public service to his home city.

His personal career has been one of many interesting experiences and achievements and his ancestry is also an appropriate matter of record. Mr. Barnhart was born at Cedar Valley in Wayne County, Ohio, December 8, 1857, a son of Frederick William and Clarissa (Gooding) Barnhart.

The paternal ancestry goes back to his great-grandfather Johann Wilhelm Bernhardt. From the German Palatinate, now including chiefly Baden and Rhenish Bavaria, this ancestor emigrated on May 12, 1764, and settled in Westmoreland County, Pennsylvania. A son of Johann Wilhelm was Philippe Bernhardt, who served as a soldier in the War of 1812. Philippe's wife was Elizabeth Rice, whose father, Frederick Rice, was a gallant soldier of the War of the Revolution and when he died at Wooster, Ohio, in February, 1848, he was accorded burial with the honors of war. The old family bible of Johann Wilhelm and of Philippe Bernhardt is now in the possession of Mr. Barnhart of Kansas City. About a hundred years ago the family name was changed from Bernhardt to Barnhart so that the spelling and pronunciation might conform.

On the maternal side Mr. Barnhart is descended from George Gooding, who was born in England in 1632, and emigrated about 1650 to Plymouth Colony, settling at Dighton, Massachusetts. Five generations of the Goodings are buried at Dighton. Mr. Barnhart's maternal grandfather, William Gooding, was one of the early settlers of Ohio. The descendants of George Gooding and of Miles Standish of Mayflower fame frequently intermarried. The Goodings served in all the Colonial wars and the War of the Revolution. It is a fact not generally known that the popular "Yankee Doodle" was composed during the French and Indian war by an English army officer as a satire on a company of Massachusetts militia commanded by Captain Gooding of Dighton.

The home of Mr. W. E. Barnhart during his childhood and youth was at Cedar Valley and Wooster in Wayne County, at Seville and a farm near Chippewa Lake in Medina County, Ohio. He also spent a part of his youth in Brooklyn, New York. He was an office boy employed in New York City during the great panic of 1873, and was standing on the steps of the banking house of Jay Cook & Company in 1873 when that institution closed and precipitated a panic which for widespread consequences was one of the greatest this country has ever endured. For his higher education Mr. Barnhart returned to Ohio and entered Oberlin College, where he was graduated in 1878 at the age of twenty. He was the youngest member of his class. While in college he paid nearly all his expenses by teaching country school and by tutoring in Greek and Latin at Oberlin and Elyria.

His career since leaving college covers a period of nearly forty years. His first ambition was to become a lawyer. He studied law at Elyria and while a student supported himself by teaching. Going to St. Louis, in 1879, he entered the office of the United States district attorney as a clerk. Somewhat later he realized that the law was not entirely to his liking as a permanent occupation, and in October, 1879, he entered the railway mail service. For about a year he was a postal clerk on the Missouri Pacific Railway. He was then detailed to the office of superintendent of the Seventh Division, Rural Mail Service. One promotion followed another rapidly, and in 1883 he was made chief clerk, later assistant superintendent of the division, and given assistant supervision over the postal service of seven states. In 1884 Mr. Barnhart was sent by the United States Government to the City of Mexico to arrange a better interchange of mails between the two countries. A few months later he received an offer from the Diaz administration to take charge of the railway mail service of the entire Republic of Mexico. This offer on account of family reasons he declined.

It is well known that the Government service in America, even the postal service, does not offer the opportunities for a career such as are found in the English civil service for instance. Mr. Barnhart early realized the limitations, and not desiring to pass his entire life as a Government employe, he resigned and moved to Kansas City, Kansas. He has had his home in that city from October 1, 1887.

At Kansas City, Kansas, Mr. Barnhart became identified with the street railway system during its constructive period. At different times he served in the following capacities: Land agent, secretary, auditor and as superintendent. In 1897 he entered the service of the Kansas City, Pittsburg & Gulf Railway, now the Kansas City Southern, and filled consecutively the offices of special agent in charge of mail service and insurance, chief clerk to general manager, and tax commissioner. In 1901 Mr. Barnhart became identified with the Kansas City, Mexico & Orient Railway as right of way, townsite and tax commissioner. He is still connected with that company, though most of his time is now devoted to his private interests in the oil fields of Louisiana. While making some land purchases for the Kansas City Southern Company in 1900, Mr. Barnhart had the distinction of discovering the Caddo oil fields in Louisiana.

While his business interests have lain largely outside of Kansas City, Mr. Barnhart has become widely known for his active participation in local affairs. In 1894-95 he was chairman of the Wyandotte County Republican Central Committee. In 1895 he was elected a member of the Kansas City, Kansas, Board of Education, was on the board nine years, and seven years of that time was president. While he was in office the city high school building, the Carnegie Library, and many ward school buildings were erected.

Mr. Barnhart was president of the Mercantile Club of Kansas City, Kansas, during the year 1914-15, and in 1915 was elected president of the Associated Charities of the city, an office he still retains. For many years he has served as a trustee of the Congregational Church.

At Elyria, Ohio, April 27, 1881, Mr. Barnhart married Mattie Lake Johnston. Mrs. Barnhart was born at Elyria, Ohio, September 13, 1861, daughter of Charles W. and Mary (Fisher) Johnston. In the maternal line she is a distant relative of Grover Cleveland. Mrs. Barnhart is descended from Peter Johnston, who was born in Lockerby, Annandale, Scotland, in 1735. He emigrated to America and located in Saratoga County, New York, in 1773. Soon afterward he proved his devotion to the Colonial cause by serving as a soldier in the Revolution in Captain Ephraim Woodworth's company of the Thirteenth Regiment of Albany County Militia. Mrs. Barnhart for many years has been prominent in the Woman's Club and the general social, civic and church life of Kansas City, Kansas.

Four children were born to their marriage: Marian Florence, born August 1, 1885, was married March 19, 1908, to Samuel Stewart, Jr. Oliver Frederick Johnston, born June 23, 1894, is now a student in the State Agricultural College at Manhattan. Alice Clarisse, born June 16, 1896, is now finishing her education in Oberlin College, Ohio. Charles Eugene, born January 6, 1899, died January 28, 1913.

AUSTIN H. JENNINGS. For many years the name of Jennings has been honorably associated with busi-ness enterprises of importance in Kansas City, through the efforts of Austin H. Jennings, who is president of the Crystal Springs Ice, Fuel & Grain Company and is interested in other concerns that occupy a prominent place in the commercial field. Although not quite so active as in earlier years, Mr. Jennings continues one of the most stable and dependable of the city's business men and one of the most reputable and highly esteemed citizens. Mr. Jennings was born May 25, 1850, on a farm near Delaware, Ohio. His parents were Austin H. and Jane H. (Pratt) Jennings.

Austin H. Jennings was born in Ohio, a descendant of an old north of Ireland family that had emigrated to the United States in colonial days. The parents of Mr. Jennings were pioneers in Delaware County, industrious but of limited means, and he had no educational opportunities in his youth, in fact was educated by his wife after their marriage. All his life he had the highest respect for every educational measure and was one of the willing organizers of what became the Ohio Wesleyan University, in which institution a number of his children were educated, assisted by their father as he was able, but of enough enterprise and independence to earn the means for themselves. Mr. Jennings was a farmer and through his industry and prudence acquired enough land to assure him a competency and was considered a man of means for that time when he died. He was married to Jane H. Pratt, who was born in Devonshire, England, and accompanied her parents to Ohio. Her father was a cooper and followed that trade all his life. After marriage, Mr. and Mrs. Jennings settled on land that was yet in the wilderness, paying $1 an acre for the same. They endured every pioneer hardship, from having to travel on pack horses all the way from Virginia to Zanesville, Ohio, to building a primitive log cabin and subsisting as best they could until Mr. Jennings had succeeded in clearing land and getting in a crop. In this primitive home, later replaced by a comfortable one, thirteen children were born and of the eight survivors Austin H. Jennings is the oldest.

It was from homes like this that brave and hardy young men responded when President Lincoln called for soldiers to preserve the Union. Although Austin H. was too young to be a soldier, he can recall when his oldest brothers, Robert P. and Harvey S., enlisted as privates in Company C, Fourth Ohio Volunteer Infantry. Robert P. had already completed his medical education and was prepared to enter into practice, but his patriotism, in spite of somewhat impaired health, led him to set aside a career to which he had looked forward long, and enter the army. After four months he was discharged for disability but later was appointed an assistant surgeon in the Fifty-first Regiment and served in this capacity until the Civil war was over. Harvey S., the second of the soldier brothers of Mr. Jennings, served with such conspicuous bravery throughout the entire war, that after the battle of Chancellorsville, when he captured two of the enemy, he received a commission as second lieutenant by a vote of Congress. He never accepted this commission because of his unwillingness to be separated from his comrades in General Hancock's corps, in the Army of the Potomac, with whom he had fought on the battlefields of Winchester, Gettysburg and at other points. He was thrice wounded and did not recover sufficiently to return home until three months after the war ended.

Austin H. Jennings attended the public schools in Delaware County and after completing the high school course, decided on a year at college. Not to be out-done by his older brothers, who had worked their way through college, he determined to be equally independent and in order to secure this college train-ing accepted honest labor of any kind, such as shov-eling gravel and shearing sheep. After his collegiate year was completed he made his way to Illinois with Gibson City as his objective point as he had secured a school to teach there. He walked the distance of thirty miles from Bloomington to Gibson City and during the year he remained there, teaching the first school, the town was laid out.

Mr. Jennings returned then to Ohio and for one year was a student in the Ohio Wesleyan University. He then spent four years as a clerk in a clothing store and during this time was able to accumulate enough capital to warrant his embarking in business for himself, but just then a partnership was offered and probably if his health had not failed, Kansas would never have been able to claim one of its worthiest citizens.

In 1878 Mr. Jennings came to Kansas to look over the country with an idea of locating here and became well satisfied and returned to Ohio in order to settle up his affairs and for his family, but his father's sudden death interfered with his plans. It was nec-essary for him to assist in closing his father's estate and it was not until 1883 that he returned to Kansas, accompanied by his family, and located at Winfield, in Cowley County, which was then the home of a brother, who was engaged there in the practice of law. The country in that vicinity was new and Mr. Jennings acquired the ownership of six farms. He became interested in several ways and rebuilt his health while living in the open for a year. An in-vestment in wheat proved a fortunate venture and later he went into the business of buying claims and renting them out and subsequently drifted into the real estate and bond business, in which he continued to be interested for eighteen years. He was ap-pointed during this time, receiver for the McCollum-Cochran Company of Winfield and cleared up the case, paid all debts and returned the store to the owners. He resided on his farm land for six years and during this time introduced the first alfalfa in Cowley County, Mr. Jennings' foresight continually leading him along progressive ways and seldom directing him wrong.

Mr. Jennings was married February 9, 1876, to Miss Laura Sidle, who was born in Pleasant Valley, Ohio. Her parents were natives of Pennsylvania and Ohio. Mr. and Mrs. Jennings have two sons, Austin H., Jr., and Frank H. It was in order to give his sons better educational advantages that Mr. Jennings moved to Kansas City, Missouri, and resided there two years. He then became interested in the Crystal Springs Ice, Fuel & Grain Company, building up the plant in 1902. He went into this business with no previous experience but his general knowledge of business made the undertaking successful. He is president of the company, while Frank H. is vice president and Austin H. is general manager. The ice is wholesaled to retailers and the business is now conducted by the two young men. Mr. Jennings was the organizer of the Northwestern Garage & Storage Company, of which Frank H. is general manager. The elder son, Austin H., is also in the employ of the Government and has charge of the handling of mail and parcel post packages at Kansas City, Kansas.

Mr. Jennings has additional interests to those al-ready mentioned, being the owner of much city prop-erty both business and residential. He was one of the organizers of the Peoples National Bank, Kansas City, Kansas, and for several years was one of its directors. In his own material prosperity he has not been unmindful of the wants and needs of others, ever being generously disposed and has been a liberal supporter of education and religion. In 1886 he was instrumental in having a meeting called to secure the location of a Methodist school at Winfield, and donated the first $500 for the purpose. It is now a flourishing institution and bears the name of the Southwestern University of Winfield and he has been a constant supporter of the same from its beginning.

Politically a republican, Mr. Jennings supports this party from principle, never having been willing to accept any public office. He belongs to the Blue Lodge in Masonry, while both sons have advanced to the thirty-second degree. Both he and wife belong to the Methodist Episcopal Church and in earlier years were very active in its various departments of work. They naturally have a wide circle of friends.

THOMAS. E. DONNELLAN of Parsons has the active supervision of all Southeastern Kansas, Eastern Okla-homa and Southwest Missouri for the International Harvester Company. He has been general agent for that great corporation for the past fifteen years. Mr. Donnellan is a Kansas man, is a birthright farmer and knows the practical side of farming, an experi-ence which has proved valuable to him as representing a great agricultural house.

His family on both sides came to Kansas in ter-ritorial days. His father, John Donnellan, who was born in County Clare, Ireland, in 1824, came to this country at the age of twenty years, and for several years was employed in the lumber camps of New York State. It was in March, 1856, that he came to Kan-sas. Kansas was then a territory and the scene of the great struggle which earned for the territory the name "Bleeding Kansas." His first location was in Miami County, where he secured 160 acres of an old Indian reservation and for two years was en-gaged in cultivating it. The activities of the Bush-whackers drove him away from that land, and he then moved to Atchison County. Subsequently he sold the quarter section in Miami County and in Atchison County he bought a farm of 160 acres a half mile west of Lancaster. Thereafter he was one of the leading farmers and citizens of Atchison County until his death in 1894. John Donnellan was a republican, and was one of the first justices of the peace in Atchison County and for many years served on the school board. For twelve years he was township treasurer of Lancaster Township. John Donnellan and all his family were members of the Catholic Church. During the war he was a member of the Home Guards, in the Union army, and helped repel the invasion of General Price. The wife of John Donnellan was Mary Davidson, who was born in Uniontown, Pennsylvania, in 1828 and died in Atchi-son County, Kansas, in 1895. Her father Robert M. Davidson was born in Pennsylvania in 1807 and was of Scotch ancestry, the Davidsons having come to Pennsylvania in colonial times. Robert Davidson spent his early life in Pennsylvania, was a carpen-ter and builder by trade, and in 1857 migrated to Atchison County, Kansas. For a number of years he was a general merchant there and died at Lancas-ter in 1889. The children of John Donnellan and wife were Anna, wife of Albert Ostertag, a travel-ing salesman living at Atchison, Kansas; Thomas E.; William R., who has a hardware and implement store at Lancaster; Emma, who is cashier in a store at

Atchison; Margaret, wife of August Mangelsdorf, who is in the wholesale seed business at Atchison; and Juniata, wife of John Cleary, a farmer in Atchison County.

Born in Atchison County, Kansas, April 16, 1864, Thomas E. Donnellan spent the first twenty-one years of his life on his father's farm. He attended the public schools, and himself became a school teacher, following that work in his native county for five years. He was one of the young and progressive farmers of Atchison County four years, and also filled the position of under-sheriff there four years.

After two years in the coal and lumber business at Atchison Mr. Donnellan in 1901 entered the service of the International Harvester Company, becoming general agent for Kansas. He has since represented this corporation and in December, 1914, moved to Parsons, from which city he supervises a force of fifty-four men in Kansas, Eastern Oklahoma and Southwestern Missouri. There are five other branch offices in the State of Kansas under his jurisdiction. Mr. Donnellan's offices are on Twentieth Street and Broadway.

His home is at 1631 Corning Street. Mr. Donnellan is a republican, and besides the official service already mentioned was township trustee and township treasurer of Lancaster Township in Atchison County. He is a member of the Catholic Church, and belongs to Council No. 723, Knights of Columbus at Atchison, to Lodge No. 647 of the Benevolent and Protective Order of Elks at Atchison, to the Modern Woodmen of America and the Knights of the Maccabees at Atchison, and the Woodmen of the World at Topeka. He is also an active member of the Parsons Commercial Club and the Rotary Club.

In Atchison County on April 4, 1888, Mr. Donnellan married Miss Emma Schletzbaum, daughter of Francis and Elizabeth Schletzbaum. Mr. and Mrs. Donnellan are the parents of three children: John F., who is a graduate of St. Benedict's College at Atchison, is now advertising manager for the Coast Banker and lives at San Francisco; Rosalia is a student in the Parsons High School; Robert E., a graduate of St. Benedict's College at Atchison, is now a traveling representative of the International Harvester Company.

JAMES H. DE COURSEY. Many of the great commercial houses of the world have been built up from a small foundation, and a young law student's enterprise in nourishing and developing a business idea of his own, is responsible for the most extensive ice cream and butter manufacturing plant in the State of Kansas. It is located at Kansas City and is the property of the De Coursey family, and its able manager, James H. De Coursey, was also its founder.

The De Coursey name has been one held in high regard in Kansas for three generations. The first of the family, James De Coursey, was born in Louisiana, undoubtedly of French stock, and in the gold rush of 1849 traveled by wagon to California from Illinois. He returned by water and after marrying in Illinois, came again to Kansas, the appearance of the state having pleased him when he had crossed overland on his way westward. He located on a farm in Johnson County, near Edgerton, broke up his land with oxen and bore many hardships there before moving to Leavenworth, in 1859, after selling his farm. There he engaged in the grocery trade and also became interested in dairying and he is credited with founding the first creamery in the state, in 1879. During the Civil war he was a member of the Home Guards. He was

the father of four sons and three daughters, and three sons and one daughter survive.

Edwin E. De Coursey, son of James and father of James H. De Coursey, accompanied his father to Kansas but in 1879 went to Colorado and for some years was a mine operator at Leadville and became interested also in ranching. He came back to Kansas and located at Leavenworth in 1898 and at present is a resident of Kansas City, Kansas, but he still retains his interests in Colorado. He is a democrat politically and was quite active in public affairs in Colorado, serving there as chairman of the county central committee, also as assessor and as water commissioner.

Edwin E. De Coursey was married in Colorado to Miss Mary E. McCormick, and they have five children: James H., Frank C. and William B., all interested in the De Coursey Ice Cream Manufacturing Company; Edward J., proprietor of a hotel at Mexia, Texas; and Mary, residing at home.

James H. De Coursey attended the public schools and St. Mary's College and then entered upon the study of law in the offices of E. S. McAnany and M. L. Alden, at Kansas City, and subsequently worked his way through the Kansas City School of Law. It was during his student days that he began experimenting in a small way at No. 330 Seventh Street, in the manufacture of ice cream, his quarters being too small for much expansion. He gradually was able to interest his father in his enterprise and then his brothers, and in 1908 the business partnership was formed that has been the means of adding one more important manufacturing plant to Kansas City. The normal demand for this dainty is large in every section and when it is marketed under the De Coursey brand, its handling is found profitable everywhere.

James H. De Coursey is one of the younger business men of Kansas City, his birth having taken place at Alma, Colorado, July 29, 1883, but practically his life has been spent here. Outside of his creamery interests he is otherwise concerned, being a director of the Riverview State Bank and of the Peoples National Bank, and is president of the Kansas Ice Cream Improvement Association. Politically he is a democrat and is president of the Wyandotte County Democratic Club.

In 1910 Mr. De Coursey was married to Miss Julia McManus, who was born in Kansas City and is a daughter of Michael McManus, one of the pioneer residents. They have two children: Edwin and Mary. Mr. and Mrs. De Coursey are devout members of the Catholic Church. He belongs to the Knights of Columbus, to the Elks and to the Merchants Club, and is ever ready to testify to his public spirit by assisting in laudable public movements.

WILLIAM HENRY HITE. In some individuals the business sense is remarkably developed and this proves the medium through which they may attain an eminence not to be gained by those who try to control affairs for which they have no aptitude. It is now generally recognized that no one reaches unusual success who works against his natural inclinations, and when competition is so keen men need every assistance that developed talent can give in order to take profitable advantage of offered opportunities and to be able to develop legitimate business chances. Especially is this true in communities where strong and able men gather, such as Cherryvale, where although the field of operation is broad, the rivalry is intense. Among the men of Cherryvale who have won success through the possession of marked business talent is William Henry Hite, proprietor of the Globe Clothing Store. When he entered upon his career at the early age of twelve years, he followed his inclination for business, and as his talents have developed he has fitted into his opportunities, so that now, in the prime of life, he finds himself at the head of the largest establishment of its kind in this part of the state.

Mr. Hite was born in Wheatland, Missouri, March 20, 1869, a member of an early Missouri pioneer family, probably from Virginia, and a son of William Henry and Martha (Van Noy) Hite. His father was born in Missouri, in 1849, and was reared on a farm, and naturally when he entered upon his own career chose farming as his vocation. Mr. Hite was an indirect victim of the Civil war, for while he never enlisted or fought as a soldier he was killed in a skirmish with ''bushwhackers'' in the disturbed time that followed the close of the great struggle, and died from the effect of a gun-shot wound in May, 1869. He was a democrat. Mr. Hite married Martha Van Noy, who was born in 1850, in Tennessee, and she still survives him and resides at Cherryvale with her son by a second marriage, Harry Kimey.

William Henry Hite was an infant of two months when his father died, and he was reared in the home of his maternal grandmother, Mrs. Mary Van Noy, at Wheatland, Hickory County, Missouri, where he received his education in the local school. The fact that his wages were needed and that he was anxious to enter upon his career caused him to leave school when but twelve years of age, and the greater part of his education has come in the school of experience and through coming into contact with men of real practical knowledge, with whom he has been forced to match wits in the business world. His first position was as a clerk in a general store at Wheatland, and during the six years that he held this position he became more or less familiar with almost every type of article which may be sold, the stock comprising a wide variety of goods. In 1888 he advanced himself when he went to Clinton, Missouri, and after one year spent as a clerk there went to Deepwater, Missouri, where he remained as clerk in a clothing store for nine years. He had been connected with what was known as the Globe Clothing Store, and in 1898 the firm sent him to take charge of their branch at Pittsburg, Kansas, with which he was identified four years. During all this time Mr. Hite had been carefully saving his earnings with one end in view—that of becoming the proprietor of an establishment of his own. His opportunity occurred in 1902, when he came to Cherryvale and formed a partnership with G. K. Withers, opening an establishment under the firm name of the Globe Clothing Store. The start was modest, but the people soon appreciated that the house was one where they could receive good value for their expenditures, and trade grew rapidly. The partnership continued until 1909, when Mr. Hite bought out his partner's interest and since that time he has been the sole proprietor. The store, situated at the corner of West Main and Neosho streets, has appointments of a modern character, with a well selected and carefully arranged stock of clothing, shoes, hats and furnishings, and the original policy of the store, to give full value for money received, has never been changed. The business has grown steadily until now it not only commands a large trade in Cherryvale, but attracts patronage from Thayer, Parsons and Mound Valley, and the Globe splits the trade of this section with the large establishments of Coffeyville and Inde-

pendence. In business circles Mr. Hite is accounted an astute business man, alive to every opportunity, but honorable in every way.

A republican in politics, Mr. Hite has been active in the ranks of his party, and has served as ward committeeman, and as delegate to county and state conventions, and was a delegate to the State Convention at Topeka, Kansas, in 1916. He is a member of the Presbyterian Church. Fraternally, he is also prominent, being a thirty-second degree Mason, and a member of Cherryvale Lodge No. 137, Ancient Free and Accepted Masons; Cherryvale Chapter No. 86, Royal Arch Masons, of which he is past high priest; Saint Bernard Commandery No. 10, Knights Templar, of Independence; Fort Scott Consistory No. 4; and Mirza Temple, Ancient Arabic Order Nobles of the Mystic Shrine, of Pittsburg, Kansas. He belongs also to Cherryvale Lodge No. 989, Benevolent and Protective Order of Elks; Cherryvale Camp No. 142, Independent Order of Odd Fellows; Cherryvale Camp No. 154, Woodmen of the World; and Jayhawker Camp No. 913, Modern Woodmen of America. He has been an active member of the Commercial Club for a long period, and his standing in business circles is indicated by the fact that he was president of this organization for about six years, and that he is now secretary and treasurer of the Kansas Retail Clothiers Association. He owns his own modern home, at No. 419 East Main Street.

At Austin, Missouri, in 1894, Mr. Hite was married to Miss Dell Woodard, daughter of Mr. and Mrs. Ichabod Woodard, who still live at Austin. Mr. Woodward, who is now a farmer, was a merchant at Austin and near Kansas City during the Civil war period. Mr. and Mrs. Hite are the parents of the following children: William Blaine, born September 21, 1895, a graduate of the Cherryvale High School, and now a sophomore at the University of Kansas; Woodward Van Noy, born September 6, 1897, a graduate of Cherryvale High School, who is a freshman at Lawrence University; Chester Henry, born August 17, 1910, attending the graded school; and Mary Elizabeth, born November 22, 1913.

ANTHONY C. FASENMYER, now retired, has been a constructive factor in the commercial affairs of Kansas City, Kansas, and many of the results of his thirty-one years of activity still stand and have entered permanently into the life and well being of the community.

Mr. Fasenmyer was born at Fryburg in Clarion County, Pennsylvania, January 10, 1857. He was the third of five children whose parents were Jacob and Frances (Fletcher) Fasenmyer. His grandfather Balthaser Fasenmyer lived near Strassburg in Alsace, France. He spent seven years as a soldier under the great Napoleon. From there he emigrated to America and located at Fryburg, Pennsylvania, having come from a town of a similar name in Baden, Germany. He was a farmer. Jacob Fasenmyer was for fifty years a merchant in Pennsylvania. His children attended the little red schoolhouse in the country and that was the only advantages they had outside of a good home training.

After leaving school Anthony C. Fasenmyer clerked in his father's store and thus acquired a fundamental knowledge of merchandising. At the age of seventeen his father started him in a store in a small country town near Fryburg, and he was identified with that business until he removed to Kansas.

It was due to the persuasion of Father Kuhls, of St. Mary's Hospital in Kansas City, Kansas, and an old friend of the Fasenmyer family, that Anthony Fasenmyer came out to the West and with his wife and one child settled at Wyandotte, now Kansas City, Kansas. His first business was handling real estate in partnership with Dan Rooney, and Dan Furlong. The firm was known as Rooney, Furlong & Fasenmyer. With the collapse of the boom in Kansas this firm was one of many that was caught in financial straits, and Mr. Fasenmyer lost practically all he had gained by his previous years of effort and the year following he spent as manager of the Kansas Catholic, a local publication, and then with money borrowed from the A. M. Northrup Banking Company he once more engaged in business for himself at 530 Minnesota Avenue. That was his business home for twenty years, and in 1911 he sold out and retired. His two brothers Frank P. and Joseph G. Fasenmyer, also conducted a clothing store in the same block and on the same side of the street. All these three brothers made comfortable fortunes as business men of the city.

Mr. Anthony Fasenmyer was one of the organizers of the Commercial Bank and of the Kansas Trust Company and Citizens Savings Bank, and was vice president and a director in each organization for fifteen years. He has acquired a large amount of real estate, and owns the two story building at the corner of Seventh and Minnesota avenues which he built and which bears his name.

On January 13, 1885, Mr. Fasenmyer married Mrs. Mary (Sterner) Groner. She was born at Fryburg, Pennsylvania. Nine children were born to them, two of whom died in infancy. Cornelius is a business man in Kansas City, Kansas, and Eugene G. is also a young business man, both the sons having risen to commendable prominence in local affairs. Louisa is the wife of Harry Mauk of Orlando, Florida, where he followed contracting, and they have two children. Christinia lives at home. Mary is a Sister of Charity at Butte, Montana. Julia and Frances are trained nurses at St. Joseph's Hospital in Kansas City, Missouri. Anthony is a student in the electrical engineering and mechanical department of Notre Dame University, in Indiana. Collette is still at home. Mr. Fasenmyer has given his children liberal advantages in the way of education and all the comforts of a good home.

Mr. Fasenmyer has always exercised his independent judgment in politics, has stood for everything that would make a better and greater community, but has never sought any office. He and his family are active members of St. Mary's Catholic Church and Mrs. Fasenmyer is one of the foremost church workers and has done much to alleviate the conditions of the poor and needy in her home city.

GEORGE W. KIDDER, who, excepting for the earliest years of infancy, has spent his entire life in Crawford County, has had a long and varied and extremely useful relationship with business affairs in various towns of that county and particularly in Pittsburg. Mr. Kidder is now secretary of the Chamber of Commerce and is also secretary of the Retail Merchants Association.

The Pittsburg Chamber of Commerce, which was established in 1881 at the beginning of the town when Pittsburg was nothing more than a coal camp, has been in continuous operation ever since. They performed a great work and the city itself in many ways stands as a monument to the cooperative endeavors of this organization. It now has about 300 members representing every business, professional and mechanical pursuit, and these men are associated in such a way that their united efforts constitute a tremendous power for the upbuilding and advantage of Pittsburg. Many notable results have been accomplished by the organization.

In recent years the Chamber has brought about the construction of thirty-five miles of paved streets, the construction of a big storm sewer drainage system caring for a large portion of the city, the building of curbing, guttering and concrete bridges, and the improvement of several beautiful parks for the recreation of the citizens. The purchasing of the waterworks of the city, the extension of its mains to remote parts of the towns, extension and improvements of roads leading in every direction beyond city limits, the adjustment of railroad rates, the additional improvements placed in the city schools and in the State Manual Training Normal. The advocating and attending to of civic improvements with a view to continuous beautification—all these are a few of the notable results accomplished through the combined efforts and influence of the Chamber of Commerce. Analytical and practical tests have recently been made through this organization of the various clays abounding in great quantities in this part of Kansas. These tests have demonstrated to practical pottery manufacturers the great possibilities of a clay product business at Pittsburg. Pittsburg is an ideal situation for such industries. It has unusual natural advantages in the way of raw material and cheap fuel, has unexcelled shipping facilities and an enormous territory demanding such product and within easy reach by rail from factory to consumer. One of the objects now being pursued with great energy by the Chamber is the building up of this particular industry at Pittsburg. The Chamber of Commerce is a very live organization and its secretary Mr. Kidder has taken special pains to render it a medium of reliable and prompt information to all interested parties.

The Retail Merchants Association of Pittsburg, of which Mr. Kidder is also secretary, has for its object the closer relations and betterment of the merchants of Crawford County. This association furnishes to its members all legal and proper information which the individual merchants might require for their protection or for other business purposes. Thus this association has on file for the use of its members ratings on patrons, collection accounts statistics, information on bogus check writers and forgers, maintains a strict censorship on all special advertising plans presented, on all special sales systems by trading stamps, coupons, etc., and the association also makes weekly reports on chattel mortgages. The present officers of the association are: J. M. Leipman, president; F. D. Barker, vice president; G. W. Kidder, secretary; and H. Degan, Sr., treasurer.

George W. Kidder was born in Adams County, Illinois, June 8, 1868, and was brought to Southeastern Kansas about three years later. His father L. H. Kidder, who was born in Adams County, Illinois, January 11, 1843, was descended from an English family that came from England to Maine in colonial times. L. H. Kidder spent his early life as a farmer and school teacher in Adams County, and in 1871 he arrived on the full tide of early settlement in Southeastern Kansas. He located on a farm four miles south of Pittsburg in Baker Township of Crawford County, and being one of the early arrivals he was able to select a good tract of 160 acres at a cost of only $1.25 per acre. Some years later he sold his farm and was engaged in the grocery business at Girard and later at Pittsburg. He was also well known in public affairs, and for four years was clerk of the District Court of Crawford County and held various township offices. Politically he was a republican, was a member of the Methodist Episcopal Church, and belonged to Pittsburg Lodge No. 56 Ancient Order of United Workmen. He now resides at 106 East Park Street in Pittsburg and is engaged in the grocery business at 108 West Third Street. L. H. Kidder married Miss Matilda H. Moore, who was born in Muskingum County, Ohio, January 6, 1843, and is still living. Their children were: George W.; Alice, who died at the age of 4½ years; Charles Watson, who lives at Pittsburg but is a traveling salesman for the Ridenour-Baker Grocery Company of Kansas City, Missouri.

The early education of George W. Kidder came from the public schools of Crawford County. He finished the junior year in the Girard High School, but left school in 1888 to begin his practical commercial and mercantile experience. He spent one year with the firm of Kidder & Merriweather, and another year with the successor of that firm T. F. Gregg. For a year he clerked in a grocery and shoe store at Girard, and then had charge of the grocery department of the A. W. Barker department store at Girard until April, 1892. At that date Mr. Kidder came to Pittsburg, and was engaged in the mercantile business with his father from 1894 to 1896. He then sold his interest to the older Kidder and spent a year in the mechanical department of the Kansas City Southern Railroad Company and for four years was head bookkeeper in the coal department of that road. He was next employed as head bookkeeper a year and a half by the Pittsburg Daily Headlight. Ill health compelled him to give up that work. He was then in the real estate business under the firm name of Kidder and Coulter until 1908. The panic of that year brought on hard times which compelled him to sell out to his partner, and for the next two years he had charge of the general office of W. W. Cook & Sons, contractors for light, water and sewer plant. In 1910 Mr. Kidder returned to the Headlight as solicitor, but in a short time took charge of the new business department for the Home Light Heat and Power Company. He spent two years with that concern. In February, 1912, he was elected secretary of the Pittsburg Chamber of Commerce and since 1913 has been secretary of the Crawford County Retail Merchants Association. He is also secretary of the Crawford County Good Roads Association. His offices are in the Globe Building.

Mr. Kidder is a republican, and from 1900 to 1908 had a place on the city council. He is a steward in the Methodist Episcopal Church, and is superintendent of the Intermediate Department of the Sunday School. Among other business interests he is a stockholder in the new Cornelia Copper Company at Calumet, Michigan, and in the Elgin Motor Car Company of Chicago. Fraternally he is affiliated with Pittsburg Lodge No. 187 Ancient Free and Accepted Masons, and Pittsburg Chapter No. 58 Royal Arch Masons.

On July 8, 1896, at Girard, Kansas, Mr. Kidder married Miss Emma Purdun. Mr. and Mrs. Kidder have three children: Clarence H., who graduated from the Pittsburg High School in 1914 and is now a student of the State Manual Training Normal School at Pittsburg. Maurice A. is in the freshman class of the high school, while Elizabeth A. is in the sixth grade of the grammar schools.

JOHN L. ROBINSON. The absolute honesty, the feeling of community interest, the intelligent public spirit that belong and illuminate the best type of citizen, are all qualities demanded of men who enter the banking field. The close relation between banks and a community's prosperity makes the banking business one of paramount importance. One of the well known financiers of Neosho County, Kansas, is John L. Robinson, president of the Fidelity State Bank, at Chanute, a business man of long and honorable experience. Mr. Robinson was born June 25, 1865, in Delaware County, Iowa, and is a son of A. M. and Josephine (Sprague) Robinson.

Without doubt the Robinson family came to the American colonies from Scotland. They settled in the State of New York and in the main have been agriculturists. A. M. Robinson, father of John L. Robinson, was born in New York State in 1820, and died at Buffalo, in Wilson County, Kansas, in 1898. In 1834 he accompanied his parents when they removed from New York to Michigan, and still later to Lee County, Illinois, where he grew to manhood and acquired farming land, which, in 1871 he traded for a quarter section of wild land situated 2½ miles east of Buffalo, in Wilson County, Kansas, on which he resided until 1885 and then retired and came to Chanute. For many years he was active in the affairs of the Methodist Episcopal Church, in which he was a class leader.

A. M. Robinson was married in Illinois to Josephine Sprague, who was born in the City of Quebec, Canada, in 1827, and died at Chanute, Kansas, in 1890. They had three children: Solomon E., who is a farmer in the Saskatchewan country; Josephine, who died at the age of six years; and John L., of Chanute, Kansas.

In the public schools of Wilson County, John L. Robinson made such rapid progress that when but sixteen years old he secured a certificate that enabled him to teach school and he alternated teaching and farming until 1885, when he came to Chanute. Here he became a clerk for the grocery firm of Lindsay & Anderson and continued there for nine years, making many personal and business friends and gaining solid knowledge along business lines. Later he purchased the grocery stock of Samuel Foster and subsequently entered into partnership in the grocery line with J. R. Copple, under the firm name of Copple & Robinson. They continued in business for two years, their store being located on the corner of Main Street and Highland Avenue, in the heart of the city. After the dissolution of this partnership, Mr. Robinson conducted a general store at Vilas, Kansas, for eight months, removing his business then to Buffalo, where he continued for five years and one month, under the firm style of Shirley & Robinson.

Mr. Robinson returned then to Chanute as a better business field, buying at that time an interest in the Bank of Commerce, becoming assistant cashier of the same and continuing until 1902, when he sold his interest. He did not leave the financial field, however, but in February, 1903, organized the Home State Bank, becoming cashier of this institution and remaining such until January, 1907, when he accepted the same office in the Peoples Home State Bank. In October, 1914, Mr. Robinson sold his interests here and remained out of business until November 9, 1915, when he opened the Fidelity State Bank. The bank has had a very prosperous career. Its officers are men in whom the public has complete confidence, John L. Robinson being president, Adam Lock, vice president, and C. C. De Bolt, cashier. The capital is $25,000, and the surplus $2,500.

In 1916 Mr. Robinson erected the handsome modern building, of brick and stone construction, which is the home of the Fidelity State Bank. It is a two-story building, situated on the corner of East Main Street and Lincoln Avenue, and is fitted and equipped especially for bank, office and store purposes. Other valuable property owned by Mr. Robinson includes his residence at No. 127 North Forest Avenue, a dwelling on the corner of Second Street and Forest Avenue, and a third dwelling at No. 514 North Steuben Street.

Mr. Robinson was married in 1892, at Le Loup, in Franklin County, Kansas, to Miss Paulina Bodley, who is a daughter of the late O. J. Bodley formerly a farmer in that county. Mr. and Mrs. Robinson have three children, namely: Gladys J., who is a student in the junior year in Lawrence University; Gerald F., who is a student in the Chanute High School; and Mildred, who is completing the eighth grade studies in the public school. Mr. Robinson and family belong to the Methodist Episcopal Church at Chanute and he is a member of the board of stewards.

In politics Mr. Robinson, like his late father, is a republican. He has always been a wide awake, interested citizen wherever he has resided but has never desired public office, consenting, however, to serve on the board of education at Chanute. Fraternally he belongs to Cedar Lodge No. 103, Ancient Free and Accepted Masons and Chanute Chapter No. 21, Royal Arch Masons, and is identified also with Chanute Lodge No. 96 Ancient Order of United Workmen, and with the Fraternal Aid Union. He has always been a liberal benefactor of worthy projects in the community and has been mindful ever of the claims of charity.

WILLIAM E. H. ANDERSON. The importance of the practical real estate man to any community is very well demonstrated in the recognition which he receives in his locality, a recognition which is based upon his activities in developing his city and county and of interesting outside capital in its realty. While, unfortunately, there are some who take an unfair advantage of their position, the men who really succeed are those, whose advice and recommendations can be depended upon by investors. Cherryvale is one of the communities which has been largely built up by this class of men, among whom, in a prominent position, stands William E. H. Anderson, who has occupied a leading place in real estate and insurance circles here since his advent in 1895.

Mr. Anderson was born at Danville, the county seat of Vermilion County, Illinois, June 1, 1861, and is a son of John F. and Ordella (Fairchilds) Anderson. The branch of the Anderson family to which he belongs originated in Ireland, and the first emigrant to America was his great-grandfather. His grandfather was William Anderson, who was born in 1795 and who became a pioneer into Vermilion County, Illinois, where he located during Indian days and experienced all the dangers and hardships incident to the life of the intrepid settlers opening up a new country and paving the way for civilization. Mr. Anderson was possessed of courage, industry and perseverance, and reclaimed a property from the wilderness, developed a good farm and accumulated a satisfying competence. He passed his life in that community and there his death occurred about the time of the close of the Civil war. He was first a whig in politics and later a republican, and while not an office seeker or politician, wielded some influ-

ence in his community. He was the father of the following children: Lizzie, of Danville, Illinois, the widow of Mr. Martin who was engaged in farming for many years in Vermilion County; Kate, also of Danville, who is the wife of Mr. Hoover; Jennie, who is the wife of Simon Lanham, a farmer near Oklahoma City, Oklahoma; Lou, who is married and resides at Wichita, Kansas; Frank, who was a farmer in South Dakota when last heard from; and John F.

John F. Anderson was born in 1830, in Indiana, and was a lad when he accompanied his parents to Vermilion County, Illinois. His education was secured in the primitive subscription schools of the then sparsely settled community and his boyhood and youth were replete with exciting experiences. In the rugged life of the frontier he learned the value of hard work and honesty and, being a natural mechanic, learned the trade of cabinet maker, which he followed for some years in his younger life. Later, however, he turned his attention to farming, and this remained to be his vocation until his early death, which occurred in Vermilion County, June 3, 1865. He had inherited his father's traits of industry and perseverance and would, no doubt, have made a success of life had he been spared. Like his father, also, he was a republican, but public life held out no attractions to him. Mr. Anderson married Miss Ordella Fairchilds, who was born in 1832, in Vermilion County, Illinois, and she still survives, in good health and spirits, at the advanced age of eighty-four years, her home being at Cherryvale. To Mr. and Mrs. Anderson there were born the following children: two sons who died in infancy; Charles M., who passed his life in agricultural pursuits and died in Indiana; William E. H., of this review; Wesley E., who resides at Danville, where he is engaged in mechanical work as an electrician; John F., who is a general workman and lives at Ambia, Indiana; and Russell H. Lindsey, who resides at Louisville, Kentucky, where he holds a professorship in the Spencerian Business College.

William E. H. Anderson attended the district schools of his native county and his earliest work was found in the fields of the neighboring farmers, on which he was employed during the summer months. He was eighteen years of age when he left school to devote his entire attention to farming, and this he followed in Illinois, both as employe and owner of farms until 1899, in January of which year he came to Cherryvale and established himself in the real estate and insurance business. His enterprise was started in a modest way, but his ability and energy, combined with an inherent initiative carried him safely through the first lean years, and he soon found himself at the head of a paying business. As the years have passed it has extended its scope and what was first strictly a venture confining its activities to Cherryvale is now one which covers the whole surrounding territory and extends to other counties and into other states. Mr. Anderson maintains offices in the McCormick Building, at the corner of West Main and Neosho streets, sometimes known as the Globe Building. In addition to handling real estate of all kinds, both as owner and agent, he represents several old line fire and life insurance companies and has built up a large and lucrative business in this direction. He has been the medium through which some large and important transactions have been consummated, and has been a factor in influencing outside capital to invest in Cherryvale realty and institutions. He is a republican in politics, like his forebears, and for eight years served in the capacity of justice of the peace. He belongs to the Methodist Episcopal Church, of which he has been steward and treasurer of the board of trustees for seven years.

Mr. Anderson was married in May, 1912, at Kansas City, Kansas, to Miss Effie Lukindill, daughter of T. H. and Mary Lukindill, the latter of whom is a resident of Cherryvale. Mr. Lukindill, who was the proprietor of a painting and paperhanging business at Cherryvale for some years, is now deceased. Mr. and Mrs. Anderson are the parents of one daughter: Jewell Lucile, who was born at Cherryvale, August 29, 1915.

JAMES H. LUSCOMBE is present county attorney of Wyandotte County. He was elected in 1916 by a majority of 1,070 on the democratic ticket. He has been practicing law at Kansas City, Kansas, for the past eighteen years and entered the law after a long service as a plaster contractor. The chief factor in his success either as a mechanic or as a lawyer has been hard work. He is noted for the zeal and efficiency with which he handles every interest entrusted to his charge, and his uprightness of character and other qualifications made him one of the strongest men on the county ticket in the last general election in Wyandotte County.

Mr. Luscombe has lived in Kansas since 1883. He was born in the City of St. Louis, Missouri, February 24, 1863. He was the oldest of nine children born to James and Sophia (Cordier) Luscombe. His father was born in England in St. David's parish of Exeter. He was a plasterer by trade and in early youth came to America. He lived in Canada for a time and was always a lover of travel and change of scene and seldom remained long in any one place. As a journeyman he followed his trade in the States, located at St. Louis, where he married, and remained in that city from 1859 to 1863. In the latter year he came to Leavenworth, Kansas, and joined a regiment of cavalry, taking part in the battle of Westport under the command of General Pleasanton during Price's raid. James Luscombe though he fought for the Union cause and was in every way an exemplary citizen carried out to the end his resolve to remain a subject of Great Britain. He refused to sign the muster roll while in the army for fear that action would make him automatically an American citizen. He was also a noted swimmer and he many times accepted wagers to swim the Missouri River. From Leavenworth in 1872, he went back to St. Louis, and from 1875 to 1878 lived at Springfield, Illinois, where he was employed as a plasterer on the State Capitol Building. After that he was in Salina, Kansas, for eight months, following which the family had their home in Kansas City, Missouri, for four years and in 1883 moved to Kansas City, Kansas. James Luscombe after his children had grown up indulged his fancy for travel and wandering about the country and his death occurred in Los Angeles in 1889. He and his wife were devout members of the Episcopal Church.

James H. Luscombe received his early education in the common schools of Leavenworth, St. Louis and Springfield. He did his first work in the plasterer's trade at the age of thirteen. At that time he carried a hod during the construction of the Illinois State Capitol at Springfield. Altogether he followed his trade for twenty-three years, and at many points over the United States. When his father left home

he became the head of the family, and contributed a large share of his income to their support. When he was twenty-one years of age he did contracting, and among other contracts he did the plastering work on the old Orpheum Building at Ninth and Delaware streets.

When he was a boy of thirteen and living at Springfield, Illinois, Mr. Beveridge, secretary of the Capitol Commission, and brother of Governor John Beveridge, showed much interest in the boy and desired to secure his appointment to a cadetship in the Naval Academy at Annapolis. The boy had a natural fondness for water and ships but the plan to make him a naval cadet was interfered with by his father and was never carried out. As a diversion Mr. Luscombe has made many models of battleships.

He was thirty-three years of age when he determined to take up the study of law. As a student he carried on his studies with the firm of McGrew, Watson & Watson at Kansas City, Kansas, and was admitted to the bar in April, 1897. He did not begin active practice until December, 1898, and he continued his work as a plasterer and contractor until he was firmly established as a lawyer. He has had a good general practice, and in 1908 he served as assistant county attorney under Joseph Taggart, continuing in that office until 1913. He was then appointed divorce proctor by James M. Meek.

As a democrat he has taken much interest in party politics, especially in his home county. He has held various chairs in the Knights of Pythias and is chairman of the judiciary committee of the grand lodge. He is also affiliated with the Modern Woodmen of America. He and his wife are members of the Episcopal Church. Mr. Luscombe's mother is also living in Kansas City, Kansas.

On October 9, 1888, he married Miss Anna Laverie who was born at Geneva, New York. Her parents came to Kansas City, Kansas, in 1881. Her father was a farmer. Mr. and Mrs. Luscombe have four children: Louise, now Mrs. A. E. Joy of Kansas City; J. H., Jr., who is a machinist with the Union Pacific Railway Company; Robert L. and Charles T., both in high school. It has been Mr. Luscombe's worthy ambition to give his children much better educational advantages than he himself enjoyed as a boy, and he has succeeded in doing that and also in providing them with a happy home surrounding.

JAMES D. PETERS is a successful member of the Parsons bar. Business and clients came to him generously when he established himself in private practice. Anyone familiar with the facts of his life will say that Mr. Peters' prosperity has been well earned. From early boyhood he gained his education and made his own way in the world, and in climbing upward to success has helped others along the way.

He was born in Westmoreland County, Pennsylvania, June 5, 1867. His father John Peters, who was born in County Antrim, Ireland, in 1811 and died in Westmoreland County, Pennsylvania, in 1882, was of a very long lived family. He himself attained the age of seventy-one, and yet was an exception to the normal lifetime of his brothers and sisters. He had four brothers and three sisters and every one of them lived to be more than a century. Mollie was 112 years old in 1909. She spent her life in Ireland. In 1835 John Peters came to America, and followed the trade of butcher which he had learned in the old country. He first located in Indiana County, Pennsylvania, and in 1864 moved to Westmoreland County. For a number of years he handled overland mail contracts. He was a republican and a member of the Covenanters Church. John Peters married Rachel Steele, who was born in County Londonderry, Ireland, in 1839. A short time before she was born her family moved from Scotland to Ireland. She died in Parsons, Kansas, in 1903. She had been brought to America by her mother in 1849 and lived in Philadelphia until her marriage.

James D. Peters is the only child of his parents. His only education as a boy from schools was obtained during three winters when he attended school in Westmoreland County. Aside from that he has educated himself by laborious study and hard thinking. When eleven years of age he went out to work on farms in Pennsylvania and followed that occupation in his native state until 1890. In that year his mother moved to Philadelphia, and there he was employed at the carpenter's trade. Mr. Peters and his mother came to Parsons, Kansas, in 1893, and for the next three years he was in the special agency department of the Missouri, Kansas & Texas Railway Company.

In 1896, when nearly thirty years of age, Mr. Peters found opportunity to begin the preparation for the career on which he had long set his heart. In that year he entered the law offices of M. Byrne, and was engaged in the study of the various authorities until 1899. In that year he qualified and was admitted to the bar, and since then has conducted a general civil and criminal practice with offices in the Karr Block at Parsons.

Mr. Peters is a republican, a member of the Presbyterian Church and belongs to Parsons Lodge No. 561, Loyal Order of Moose, and to the Fraternal Mystic Circle. His home is at 1600 Gabriel Avenue. In July, 1898, at Parsons he married Miss Minnie Davis, daughter of J. B. and Willie A. (Burdett) Davis. Her parents live at Parsons, where her father is in the stock department of the Missouri, Kansas & Texas Railway. Mr. and Mrs. Peters have four children. John W. is still at home and learning the tinner's trade. William is in the sophomore class of the high school. Florine attends the First Ward School in Parsons as does also the youngest daughter, Gertrude.

TILLMAN E. DALE. Distinguished as the oldest oil contractor and driller in the mid-continent fields, Tillman E. Dale, one of the substantial men of Chanute, Kansas, is one of the best known oil men in Kansas, Oklahoma and Wyoming, having operated in every field in earlier days in the business and is the pioneer in Neosho County. Mr. Dale was born March 1, 1862, in Buchanan County, Iowa. His parents were George and Mary Robinson (Davey) Dale, both natives of England.

George Dale, the paternal grandfather, was born in England in 1807 and remained in his own country until he found a young family growing up about him for whose welfare he was concerned and it was to the great land across the Atlantic Ocean that he looked to provide comfortable conditions for his children. Possibly about 1835 he brought his family to the United States and settled among the pioneers in Wisconsin, not far from Monroe. In 1856 he came to Allen County, Kansas, and worked on what is now known as the old Doctor Wakefield farm, near Humboldt. He died in Wisconsin in 1864.

George Dale, second, father of Tillman E. Dale, was born in England in 1828 and was only a boy when his parents came to America and settled in Wisconsin. He became a carpenter and builder and owned a sawmill in Wisconsin. In 1856, accompanied by his own family and probably by his father, he came to Humboldt, Kansas, and acquired a sawmill. This mill was burned during Price's raid, in the early days of the Civil war. Deprived of his means of livelihood, and considering the neighborhood dangerous for his family, Mr. Dale started with them for Lawrence, driving the whole distance with an ox-team, and from Lawrence went to Buchanan County, Iowa. He enlisted for service in the Civil war in Wisconsin in 1863, joining a Wisconsin regiment, and was wounded in battle and died in the hospital from the effects of his wounds. In 1869 his widow and children returned to Humbolt, Kansas, where she died in August, 1904. Her maiden name was Mary Robinson, and she was born in 1829, in London, England.

John Robinson, the maternal grandfather of Tillman E. Dale, was born in London, in 1799, and died in California, in 1887. He came to the United States accompanied by his family and was an early settler in Wisconsin, near Monroe. He resided there as a farmer until 1868, when he removed to Humboldt County, California. His daughter, Mary, was twice married, first to a Mr. Davey, who succumbed to cholera which was epidemic in New York City when they landed, and the two first-born children, a daughter and a son, also died of this dread disease. There were two other sons, William and John Davey, the former of whom died at Humbolt, Kansas, and the latter in Iowa shortly after completing his service in the Civil war. The second marriage was to George Dale and three children were born to this union, namely: J. E., who resides on a farm situated nine miles northeast of Chanute; Lucy, who is the wife of J. B. Burns, of Humboldt, Kansas, who is a rural mail carrier; and Tillman E.

At the age of thirteen years Tillman E. Dale closed his school books and began to work as a man when many youths consider themselves entitled to a much longer season of irresponsibility and play. For seven years he was engaged in the fatiguing tasks entailed by running and herding cattle on the range and following this became a stationary engineer for a flourmill operating at Humboldt. Mr. Dale continued there for ten years, when he became interested in his present line of business, drilling for gas and oil, and, as mentioned above, has operated in almost every field in the Mid-continent space that has seemed promising, and has drilled hundreds of wells. In 1898 Mr. Dale came to Chanute and has maintained his home here ever since, owning a handsome residence at No. 723 Evergreen Street. Although his time is very fully occupied both as contractor and producer, Mr. Dale finds opportunity to look after his farm of forty acres, which is situated nine miles southeast of Chanute. When Mr. Dale came to Chanute the city had voted the sum of $5,000 to pay for expert drilling for gas and he did the work, and of the four wells drilled, three were satisfactory and paying propositions.

Mr. Dale was married April 29, 1891, at Texarcana, Arkansas, to Miss Laura Hellinghausen, who is a daughter of the late William Hellinghausen, a stonemason by trade. Mr. and Mrs. Dale have one son, Edwin, who assists his father.

In politics Mr. Dale is a republican and as an earnest citizen gives attention to public affairs, particularly when laws are formulated that affect the industries of Kansas. He is a valued member of a number of organizations, including the Ancient Order of United Workmen, the Anti-Horse Thief

Association, and formerly belonged to the Odd Fellows and at present is identified with Lodge No. 806, Benevolent and Protective Order of Elks, at Chanute. He has traveled all through the western country, visiting California at least five times, and probably no more thoroughly or correctly informed oil or gas operator and producer could be discovered in this great belt. Many have a superficial knowledge of conditions, but it is to men like Mr. Dale that capitalists turn when they desire facts.

ALLEN DALE HILEMAN. Belonging to that class of business men whose practical education, quick perceptions and great capacity for painstaking industry have advanced them to positions of business prominence formerly occupied only by men many years their seniors, Allen Dale Hileman, while representing the vigorous and resourceful present of Kansas, gives promise of participating in its more enlightened future, more especially at Cherryvale and in Montgomery County, where he is engaged in a well-established real estate, loan and insurance business and also connected with the Montgomery County National Bank.

Allen Dale Hileman, or Dale Hileman, as he is universally known, was born in Andrew County, Missouri, June 3, 1875, a son of John S. and Mary J. (Briggs) (Shelby) Hileman. The Hilemans came originally from Germany and settled in the colony of Pennsylvania prior to the Revolutionary war. In that struggle fought the great-great-grandfather of Dale Hileman, while his great-grandfather was a soldier in the Mexican war. Daniel Hileman, the grandfather of Dale Hileman, was born in Pennsylvania, in 1808, and was there educated, reared and married. He was a man of diversified talents and at different times during his life followed the vocations of farming and carpentering and the profession of medicine. Mr. Hileman was a pioneer into Ohio as a young man and subsequently moved on westward to the State of Missouri and took up his residence in Andrew County on a farm, which he cultivated while also following the vocation of physician. He became widely known throughout the countryside, and no weather was too inclement for him to fare forth on horseback to ride perhaps miles across the prairies to minister to some sick person. During the Civil war he became a member of the Home Guards in Missouri, and in his later years drew a pension from the Government for the services thus rendered. In 1881 he left Missouri and came to Kansas, settling in Labette County, on a farm of 320 acres, which is now occupied by his son, D. O. Hileman, and on which the grandfather died in 1899. He became a man of substance and importance in his community and was highly esteemed by all who knew him. In politics a stanch republican, he always warmly supported the candidates and principles of his party, and prior to the Civil war on one occasion served as presidential elector. He was a lifelong member of the Methodist Episcopal Church. Mr. and Mrs. Hileman were the parents of the following children: Erskine, who enlisted in the Union service during the Civil war and died while in a Confederate prison; John S., the father of Dale Hileman; Dallas, who is a veteran of the Civil war and a retired farmer and now lives near Baxter Springs, Kansas; D. O., who is engaged in agricultural pursuits on the old homestead of his father near Oswego, Kansas; Anna, deceased, who married Wallace Crockett, also deceased, a veteran of the

Civil war and a farmer of Labette County; and one daughter who died in infancy.

John S. Hileman was born in Ohio, in 1845, and received his education in the public schools of his day. He was a young man when he accompanied the family to Andrew County, Missouri, and was little more than a lad when, in 1861, he enlisted for service in the Union army during the Civil war, as a member of the Thirty-fifth Regiment, Missouri Volunteer Infantry, an organization with which he remained for over three years. He saw some hard fighting, including the engagement at Helena, Arkansas, and established an excellent record for courage, fidelity and the display of soldierly qualities. When he received his honorable discharge he returned to Andrew County, Missouri, and there continued to be engaged in farming until 1882, when he removed to Labette County, Kansas. There he was a successful farmer and stockraiser until 1896, at that time leaving the farm and going to Edna, where he has since been engaged in the real estate and insurance business. He has been successful in his business enterprises, being possessed of acumen and foresight and his name is an honored one in business circles. He has also been prominent in republican politics, and for one term represented Labette County in the Kansas Legislature. His religious connection is with the Methodist Episcopal Church, in which he is serving as a deacon. Mr. Hileman is a member of the Independent Order of Odd Fellows and of the Grand Army of the Republic. He married Mrs. Mary J. (Briggs) Shelby, who was born in Ohio, in 1841, daughter of Hanover Briggs, of Northwest Missouri. To this union there have been born three children, as follows: Gertrude, who is the wife of Rev. H. W. Todd, a minister of the Methodist Episcopal Church, stationed at Altamont, Kansas; Lora H., who is the wife of J. H. Lower, president of Montgomery County National Bank, of Cherryvale, Kansas; and Allen Dale, of this review.

Dale Hileman attended the public schools of Labette County, Kansas, the State Normal School at Emporia for one year and the Southwestern College of Winfield, Kansas, for two years, then entering, in 1897, the Gem City Business College, at Quincy, Illinois. While he was attending this latter institution, the Spanish-American war came on, and Mr. Hileman joined the First North Carolina Regimental Band, with which he served six months in Georgia and Florida. On his return he again located in Labette County, but in 1900 went to Columbus, Kansas, where he received an introduction to abstract and insurance work and remained in an office of that nature for four years. He had a natural liking for this business, assimilated its principles readily, and soon perfected himself in his chosen vocation. In 1904 he came to Cherryvale and established his present business, in real estate and insurance, which has since grown to large proportions and is justly accounted one of the leading enterprises of its kind in the county, the business being mostly confined to Cherryvale and the vicinity. Mr. Hileman maintains well-appointed offices in the Ringle Building, while his home is situated at No. 624 East Main Street. Mr. Hileman has engineered some of the most important real estate transactions in this section. He is shrewd and far-sighted, has a thorough knowledge of city and town land values and is well posted as to the resources and advantages at the disposal of people contemplating settlement or change of location at Cherryvale.

Mr. Hileman has always been a republican and at

various times has been honored by his fellow-citizens who have sent him to serve in positions of public trust. He has for nine years been a member of the school board, for the past five years has been a justice of the peace, was city clerk of Cherryvale for one year, and in 1914 was strongly urged to run for the mayoralty, but declined because of pressure of business. In the discharge of his official duties he has displayed excellent executive capacity and a conscientious endeavor to serve his community to the best of his powers. He is an active member of the Presbyterian Church. Fraternally, Mr. Hileman belongs to Cherryvale Camp No. 142, Independent Order of Odd Fellows, of which he is past grand; Verdigris Encampment, Independence, Kansas; and Edna Camp, Modern Woodmen of America; and also belongs to the Commercial Club. He is the leader of the Cherryvale Band, an organization of twenty-four pieces, and known as one of the best musical associations in this part of Kansas. Mr. Hileman is also local agent for the Aetna Building & Loan Association of Topeka.

On December 31, 1901, Mr. Hileman was married at Cherryvale to Miss Eve Fair, daughter of E. W. and Rachel (Shunk) Fair. Mr. Fair, who died November 19, 1914, was a Union veteran of the Civil war, and Mrs. Fair still survives him and resides at Cherryvale. Mr. and Mrs. Hileman are the parents of two children: H. Dwayne, born August 8, 1903, who is in high school; and Keil E., born March 10, 1906, who also attends the public schools and is in the sixth grade.

WILLIAM BEGGS, now county clerk of Wyandotte County, and with a long and honorable record of public service, has been a resident of Kansas City, Kansas, since early boyhood and found his work for many years in connection with some of the packing industries of the city. There is hardly a better known citizen of the city or county, and his ability to do things and get things done and his personal integrity have long made him a man of mark.

He was born in the northern part of Ireland May 27, 1867, the oldest of seven children of Richard and Mary Ann (Leamon) Beggs. The parents, seeking to better the conditions for themselves and their children, set out in 1872 and came to the United States. At Chicago Richard Beggs secured employment with the Fowler Packing Company, but soon afterward was transferred to Kansas City, Kansas, where he became head of the dry salt pork cellars, responsibilities which he continued to hold until he retired from active work in 1906. He is at the present time making his home with a son in Kansas City, Missouri. His beloved wife died in 1906 at the age of sixty-eight. The seven children are still living: William; James L., now city commissioner of streets and public highways of Kansas City, Kansas; Charles, chief clerk of the H. P. Wright Investment Company of Kansas City, Missouri; Richard, Jr., connected with the Armour Packing Company of Kansas City; Mrs. Ernest E. Haight, wife of a real estate man of Kansas City, Missouri; Robert, superintendent of the Colorado Packing and Provision Company at Denver; and John, a salesman for Swift & Company at New York.

It was the ambition, which he worthily realized, of Richard Beggs to provide a good home and give his children good educational advantages, and the value of his citizenship is to be appreciated not only for what he has done himself but for what he has assisted his family to do. He is a republican, and

twice served as a member of the city council of Kansas City. He is active in the Ancient Order of United Workmen, in the Masonic Lodge, the Eastern Star and Scottish Rite degrees, and also in the Fraternal Aid Union. He is an active Methodist as was his wife.

William Beggs was five years of age when brought to America, and acquired his early education in the schools of Chicago and Kansas City, Kansas. When fourteen years of age he left school to become an apprentice in the tinning department of Armour's Packing Plant. After learning his trade he continued work as a tinner for twenty years. In 1904 he was appointed to a position in the State Grain Inspection Department, and was in the state service in that capacity for two years. In 1906 and again in 1908 Mr. Beggs was elected trustee of Wyandotte Township, and was the only republican elected in the township during those years. Then in 1910 came further evidence of his personal popularity and the confidence reposed in his ability as a public official when he was chosen register of deeds of Wyandotte County. He was re-elected three successive terms and had the distinction of being the first person ever to fill the office for that length of time. In the fall of 1916 he was elected county clerk. He has always been a loyal republican in his voting affiliations.

Mr. Beggs was married April 20, 1890, to Miss Emily Ahlstedt, who was born in Moline, Illinois, daughter of Gustave and Matilda Ahlstedt. Her parents were both natives of Sweden and Mrs. Beggs was the second in their family of eight children. Her father was a cabinet maker by trade. Mr. and Mrs. Beggs have five children: Ruby, wife of Clarence Falstrom, an employe of the Commercial Bank of Kansas City, Kansas; Pearl, wife of Lester Franklin, of Kansas City, Kansas; Charles Richard, at home; Robert Emmett; and Dorothy Helen. All the children have had the advantages of the high school and have enjoyed the inspiration and culture of a good home.

Mr. and Mrs. Beggs are active members of the Methodist Church. He is a Scottish Rite Mason, a member of Sherman Lodge, Ancient Free and Accepted Masons, has been financial secretary for nine years of Chelsea Lodge of Odd Fellows, and also belongs to the Modern Woodmen of America and other insurance orders.

JOHN PELLEGRINO. Among the men of high merit that the State of Kansas has called to responsible position, is John Pellegrino, of Pittsburg, Kansas, state mine inspector. From the age of fifteen years to the present, Mr. Pellegrino has been identified with mines and mining, with the exception of two years, during which interval he served faithfully as a United States soldier in the Philippine Islands. He has had a wide field of experience, and by hard, practical work in the mines and by persistent study in different institutions of learning, he has thoroughly qualified himself for the important post he fills.

John Pellegrino was born June 3, 1878, at Coblentz, on the Rhine, in Germany, to which country his grandfather, Giovanni Pellegrino, had brought the family from Italy. He was born near Turin, Italy, in 1814. He was a farmer and died in 1891 in Luxemburg, Germany.

Michael Pellegrino, father of John Pellegrino, was born in Germany in 1847, and died May 2, 1894, at Esch sur L'Alzette, in Luxemburg, Germany. He married Josephine Paulus, who was born in 1851, near Bingen, Germany, and died in 1890 in the same province as did her husband. Michael Pellegrino was a merchant and inn-keeper. He had two sons, John and Peter, the latter being an electrician at Esch sur L'Alzette, Germany.

John Pellegrino attended the excellent public schools of his native land and had high school advantages for two years. He was fifteen years old when he became a coal miner and all through the succeeding years the coal mining business has occupied his main attention, having for him the attraction that other vocations and professions have for other men. He came to the United States and on July 4, 1892, reached Yates Center, in Woodson County, Kansas, later in the same month coming to Crawford County. In 1898 he enlisted in Company F, Twentieth Kansas Volunteer Infantry, in General Funston's command. This regiment was sent to the Philippine Islands and while there Mr. Pellegrino saw hard service. He returned to the United States and was mustered out by reason of the muster out of the regiment.

In the same year of his return, Mr. Pellegrino resumed his coal mining interests. Not satisfied with the mass of practical knowledge gained through personal labor and investigation, Mr. Pellegrino determined to become completely informed in relation to mining science in every branch, beginning his technical studies by taking a course in mining under the direction of the International Correspondence School, at Scranton, Pennsylvania. This he is supplementing through an extension course in mining in Kansas University, at Lawrence.

On February 16, 1900, at Litchfield, Kansas, Mr. Pellegrino was married to Miss Mary Kuplen, who is a daughter of August and Jennie (Oberton) Kuplen, who reside on their farm at Breezy Hill. To the above marriage five children have been born: John, in 1901; Peter, in 1903; Josephine, in 1905; George, in 1908; and Harold, in 1911, all of whom are pupils in the public schools at Pittsburg.

In politics Mr. Pellegrino is a republican. During his residence in Lincoln Township, Crawford County, he served in the office of township trustee. On May 1, 1915, he was appointed state mine inspector but otherwise has accepted no political office. He is a Mason and belongs to the different higher branches of the order at Fort Scott. He is identified also at Pittsburg with the order of Eagles and is a member of Camp No. 23, United States War Veterans.

OLIVER MORTON WILLIAMS, one of the younger citizens of Kansas, has played his part efficiently as a teacher and business man, and is now manager and part owner of the Coffeyville Business College. This college is an institution noted for its thorough work in training young men and women for responsible positions in commercial affairs.

A native of Kansas, Mr. Williams was born at Oak Valley, October 24, 1887. Several generations back his ancestors were living in Wales, and after coming to the United States settled perhaps first in New York, and afterwards went to Maryland. The great-great-grandfather's name was Timothy Williams, and he was of Welsh descent. He was a Revolutionary soldier and also had three sons in the Continental army. The three sons were captured by the British and taken to Montreal, Canada, to the British prison. One of them was a physician, and he was soon taken out of the prison. The reason for this removal was not known by the other brothers but they supposed for service in the British hospitals, and they never heard of him afterward. The other two were kept in the prison for three years and three months, then were released and came back home.

Great-grandfather Benjamin Williams was born in Pennsylvania about 1770. He was too small to serve as a soldier in the time of the Revolution, but he could mold bullets and watch port-holes while the soldiers rested. He was also captured by the British and Indians. An Indian took him and a little girl about his size to keep with the tribe, but a British officer, not wanting to be burdened with the children on the march, bought them of the Indian for a red bandanna handkerchief each, and sent them back with the women to their homes. This great-grandfather afterward moved to Ohio and died there at the age of eighty-six. His oldest son was a soldier in the War of 1812, afterwards moving to Illinois, and dying there about 1840.

Mr. Williams' grandfather, Benjamin Williams, was born in Maryland in 1800, and died in Lake County, Indiana, at the age of seventy-two. He was reared and married in his native state, then went to Ohio, in 1837 moved to Missouri, and nine years afterward took up a permanent home in Lake County, in the extreme northwest corner of Indiana, where he followed farming and stock raising. He died there at the age of seventy-two. He was a Presbyterian. Benjamin Williams married Miss Miller, who was born in Maryland and died in Lake County, Indiana, about the same time as her husband. Only two children of this venerable old couple are still living, Benjamin, Jr., a retired farmer in Lake County, Indiana, eighty-five years of age; and C. S. Williams. One of his sons Wm. A. Williams, served under General Taylor in the Mexican war. After his discharge, in 1849, he returned home, stayed but a short time, then went to Iowa. Later he moved to Kansas, and in the border warfare he helped to drive the southerners from the state. When the Rebellion broke out, he enlisted in the Union army, was discharged at the end of his term of enlistment, and re-enlisted for the second term, and was finally mustered out late in the fall of 1865. Several years afterward he moved to Dewey, then in the Indian Territory, and died there at the age of seventy-three. Another son, T. C. Williams, enlisted in the fall of 1864, as a recruit in the Seventeenth Indiana Infantry and served about a year. After his discharge, he came home and lived in Indiana until about 1880, moving then to Chicago, where he died in 1904, at the age of sixty-five.

C. S. Williams, father of Oliver M., was born in Morrow County, Ohio, October 20, 1836. His present home is at Longton, Kansas. He was about ten years of age when his parents removed to Lake County, Indiana, and he grew up and married there. He has an honorable record as a soldier of the Union during the Civil war. In 1861 he enlisted in the Fifth Indiana Cavalry, and was in service until near the close of hostilities nearly four years later. His regiment participated in some of the early campaigns in Eastern Tennessee and Kentucky, being at the siege of Nashville, and he was under General Stoneman in the celebrated raid through Georgia, and was captured at Macon, Georgia, by the Confederates under Gen. Joe Wheeler. For seven months after his capture he was kept in the Confederate prisons at Savannah and Andersonville, and was finally turned over to General Terry's army at Wilmington, North Carolina, and was exchanged just before the close of the war.

Returning to Lake County, Indiana, from the South, he married and settled down to farming. In 1870 he and his wife and two daughters came to Longton, Kansas, where they were among the early pioneers. He followed farming in that locality for many years, but in 1915 retired to the comforts of a town home. He is a standpat republican, and at three different times served as township trustee in Elk County. He is a member of the Grand Army of the Republic. In 1866 C. S. Williams married Margaret Andrews, who was born near Joliet, Illinois, May 2, 1850. Their children are: Alma, wife of L. W. Young, a farmer at Buxton, Kansas; Ida, wife of E. E. Estey, who is employed in a smelter at Bartlesville, Oklahoma; Kate, wife of C. C. Clawson, a carpenter and contractor at Wichita, Kansas; and Oliver M.

Professor Williams secured his early training in the public schools of Oak Valley, Kansas, and spent three years in the Kansas State Normal at Emporia. He began teaching early, spending three years in the public schools of Elk County, and in 1909 completed a course in the Independent Commercial College under L. H. Schmidt. With this preparation for a business career, he found work with the Jacob Dold Packing Company at Wichita, and was sent to the branch houses of this company at Little Rock, Arkansas, and Atlanta, Georgia, and was in the service until 1913. During the winter of 1913-14 Mr. Williams and R. F. Riley bought the Coffeyville Business College, of which Mr. Riley is president and Mr. Williams active manager. Together they have brought up the equipment and general standard of this school so that it ranks among the first schools of commercial education in the state. The college is situated at 711½ Walnut Street. Besides its principals two assistant teachers are employed, and there are accommodations for about a hundred students. Business men and firms generally have come to appreciate that graduates of this school are thoroughly trained in all the branches of commercial work.

Mr. Williams has his home out on West Eighth Street at Stop No. 2 on the Union Traction Line. He is a republican, a member of the Methodist Episcopal Church and is affiliated with Camp No. 665, Modern Woodmen of America at Coffeyville. In 1910, at Elk City, he married Miss Myrtle E. Wheeler, daughter of G. H. and Hannah J. Wheeler, who still lives at Oak Valley, Kansas, her father being a blacksmith. Mr. and Mrs. Williams have three children: Claire, born April 17, 1911; Marguerite, born February 22, 1913; and Clifford, born February 10, 1915.

BYRON WILLIAMS. The mention of the name of Byron Williams calls up associations as one of the foremost livestock men of the State of Kansas. Mr. Williams is comparatively young, only forty years of age, but in the years since he started out on his own responsibility has shown a remarkable ability in all branches of the live stock industry. He has operated extensively as a rancher and raiser of horses and cattle, his dealings have made him a familiar figure in all the leading markets of the Middle West, and he is undoubtedly one of the best known men in the business in Southern Kansas. His headquarters are at Coffeyville.

He represents a family that has pioneered in several different states. He was born in Litchfield, Illinois, June 9, 1876, a son of Joseph and Mary E. (Ash) Williams. His great-grandfather Walker Williams came from Wales in the early days and spent his last years near Litchfield, Illinois. The grandfather, Thomas Williams, was born in Kentucky in 1812, was reared in that state until his parents moved as pioneers into Illinois, and his active career was spent as a farmer. He died at Altamont, Kansas, in 1901. He had two children, Joseph and Henry. Joseph is the father of Byron Williams. Henry came out to Kansas in 1879, locating in the central part of Labette County, and remained a resident of that community until 1900. He then went back to the vicinity of his birthplace north of Litchfield, Illinois, bought a farm there, and still occupies it. Byron Williams' grandfather on his mother's side was William Ash, who was born in 1825, lived in the State of Illinois from the time he was thirty until he was fifty-five years of age, and thereafter on a farm at Lee Summit, Missouri, where he died in 1906. The Ash family came to the United States in colonial times, and many of its members have enjoyed a conspicuous success in business and general industrial affairs. Byron Ash, maternal uncle of Byron Williams, is a resident of Carthage, Missouri, and has been one of the men most prominent in the development of the mineral resources of Southwest Missouri. He was one of the first to develop the Joplin and Carthage mining districts, and is still an important factor in that business. Joseph Williams, father of Byron, was born in Macoupin County, Illinois, in 1845. He grew up and married in his native state, but had previously at the age of seventeen in 1862, enlisted for service in the Union army with the Twenty-second Illinois Volunteer Infantry. He was with the army until the close of the war and came home with a splendid record of service. He participated in the battles of Shiloh, Gettysburg, Lookout Mountain and a number of others. He was married at Jacksonville, Illinois, to Miss Mary E. Ash, who was born at Collinsville, Illinois, in 1847. After his marriage he farmed in Macoupin County, Illinois, and then identified himself with the newly developing Kansas City, Missouri, where he did teaming for construction work. Returning to Jacksonville, Illinois, in a short time he finally located six miles north of Litchfield, where he lived until four of his children were born. In 1880 Joseph Williams brought his family to Kansas, making the journey in prairie schooners and locating in the center of Labette County. For $1,100 he bought 160 acres of some of the best land of that county. That farm he kept for twenty-five years, developed it to a high state of cultivation and improvement, and when he sold it he received what amounted to a fair competency as a reward for his early foresight and judgment and for his many years of industry. On selling his farm he bought a residence in Cherryvale and is now living there retired. He is a republican, and for many years has been a devout member of the Methodist Church, of which he is a deacon. He and his wife have the following children: Charles H., who is assistant cashier of a bank at Lakeland, Florida; Clarence J. died at the age of twenty years, six months, while attending Rohrbaugh's Business College at Omaha, Nebraska; Byron Williams is the third in age; May is the wife of Fay Green, and they live on their ranch in the Big Horn Basin near Sheridan, Wyoming; Frank is in the livestock business at Vinita, Oklahoma; Hattie married Charles Fagleman, who for the past eleven years has held the position of head freight clerk in the Santa Fe freight office at Coffeyville; Ora, with the Cudahy refinery; and Delbert, the youngest son, is connected with his brother Byron selling stock at Prescott, Arkansas.

F, M, Watkins

With an education supplied by the district schools of Labette County, Byron Williams, who has lived in Kansas since he was four years of age, turned his early attention to farming and stock raising, and gained much valuable experience during the eighteen years spent on his father's farm. For a time he lived and operated in Labette County, and was then associated with J. A. Jones in the buying and selling of horses and mules at Altamont, Kansas, until 1903. Since that year his home and business headquarters have been in Montgomery County, and two very successful years were spent as a member of the firm of Coverdale & Williams, at the end of which time he bought out Mr. Coverdale's interest and continued the business alone at Coffeyville until 1913. He then formed a partnership with John M. Grant of Kansas City, Missouri, making the firm of Grant & Williams. This firm has some very extensive interests including the operation of the old Grant farm and ranch near Oswego, Kansas, and also the large livestock ranch which Mr. Williams had in the meantime acquired five miles west and a mile north of Independence on the Elk River. Mr. Williams enjoyed three very successful years with Mr. Grant until the latter retired from business on account of ill health.

In January, 1914, Mr. Williams moved to Independence, and continued his business from his headquarters there until November, 1916, when he moved to Coffeyville. Besides his extensive business as a buyer and shipper of livestock, he produces much stock on his own farm. He has a half interest in 320 acres twelve miles southeast of Coffeyville in Oklahoma; owns 155 acres three miles east of Sedan, Kansas; has a half interest in 160 acres five miles north of Cedarvale, Kansas; a half interest in the Elk River farm of 265 acres; and is also identified with oil development, owning a quarter interest in a producing lease at Alluwee, Oklahoma, and some extensive undeveloped leases in both Kansas and Oklahoma. Mr. Williams has bought the grounds on South Walnut Street, Coffeyville, where he has shipping connections with all the railroads. He is building large barns and yards for his horses, mules and cattle.

Mr. Williams has a very attractive home at Coffeyville, located at 508 Willow Street. Politically he is a republican, has been a deacon in the Christian Church, and his wife is also an active worker in the same church. Fraternally he is affiliated with Coffeyville Lodge No. 104, Ancient Free and Accepted Masons; Fort Scott Consistory of the Scottish Rite; Mirzah Temple of the Mystic Shrine at Pittsburg; with the Camp of the Modern Woodmen of America at Altamont and with the Anti-Horse Thief Association. He is also a member of the Independence Commercial Club.

In September, 1898, at Altamont, Mr. Williams married Miss Lina D. Duckworth, daughter of Robert and Martha Duckworth. Her mother is still living at Altamont. Her father, who spent his active career as a farmer and stock raiser, was a gallant soldier throughout the period of the Civil war, and on April 15, 1864, was commissioned captain of Company D of the Thirty-eighth Regiment. Mr. and Mrs. Williams have three children: Robert Lloyd, born August 28, 1899, and now a freshman in the Montgomery County High School; Byron, born December 10, 1903, and attending the grade schools; and Enola Irene, born May 3, 1909, and also in school.

FRED M. WATKINS, M. D. It is not every individual who possesses in his make-up the characteristics that make for success in widely diversified callings, but in the person of Dr. Fred M. Watkins there is found a combination of qualities that have brought him equal success in the profession, in business undertakings and in the vocation of farming, and he has likewise made an important place for himself in the field of politics.

Dr. Fred M. Watkins, president of the Cherryvale Ice and Cold Storage Company, of Cherryvale, Kansas, was born November 22, 1868, at Lawton, Van Buren County, Michigan, a son of H. J. and Mary R. (Hall) Watkins. His forefather was Capt. Nathan Watkins who came to America as an officer in the British army, but after his arrival in this country became a convert to the cause of the Colonists and finally deserted the English army and became a captain in the continental army under General Gates. He served until the close of the Revolution and then settled in New Jersey, where he made his home until his death. He had three sons, one of whom went to Ohio, one to Michigan and one to the State of New York. James Watkins, a grandson of Capt. Nathan Watkins, and grandfather of Doctor Watkins, was born in 1794 in Michigan and passed his entire life in that state as a farmer, dying at South Haven, in 1878.

H. J. Watkins was born at Lawton, Michigan, in 1848, and was reared, educated and married in that community, where he was engaged in agricultural pursuits until 1871, then coming to Kansas as a pioneer of Nemaha County. There he homesteaded a property of eighty acres and developed it into an excellent farm, installing many improvements and raising fine crops. He was a man of industry and energy and was held in high esteem as a citizen. In 1906 he disposed of his farm land holdings, which had increased to considerable size, and retired from active labors, taking up his home at Cherryvale. There his death occurred in 1909. He was a stanch republican in his political views, but was never an aspirant for public office, preferring to devote himself to his agricultural labors. While not a member of any particular religious organization, he was a Christian, God-fearing man, and attended church regularly. His fraternal affiliation was with the Independent Order of Odd Fellows, the meetings of which he attended at Goff, Kansas. Mr. Watkins married Miss Mary R. Hall, who was born in 1848, in Michigan, and she still survives and resides at Cherryvale. They became the parents of the following children: Dr. Fred M., of this review; Frank, who is a real estate agent and farmer and resides at Goff; Floyd, who died at the age of seventeen years; Ena, who is the wife of R. J. Flemming, a farmer of Alta Vista, Kansas; G. A., who resides in Florida, where he has land holdings; G. E., who is associated with his brother in the Cherryvale Ice and Cold Storage Company; and J. J., of Cherryvale, who is also identified with the same concern.

Fred M. Watkins attended the district schools of Nemaha County, Kansas, to which community he was brought as a child of three years, but returned to Lawton, Michigan, and was graduated from the high school of that place in 1889. At that time he began a career as a schoolteacher and for a number of years taught at Lacota, Michigan, and Goff, Kansas, and then for a short period entered business life, building the first elevator at Goff and founding the Goff Grain Company, of which he was president for one year. During this time he had not given up the idea of engaging in the medical profession, and when he left the grain and elevator business it was to enter the Central Medical College, St. Joseph, Missouri, from which he was graduated in 1897, with the degree of Doctor of Medicine, subsequently taking post-graduate work at the Chicago Policlinic. In 1898 Doctor Watkins embarked in medical work at Wetmore, Kansas, where he built up a fine practice and established his reputation as a thorough, reliable and skilled physician and surgeon. During the five years he was thus engaged, however, he had become interested in business affairs, and in 1904, seizing an opportunity, came to Cherryvale, where he became connected with the manufacturing business. The Cherryvale Ice and Cold Storage Company had been established by his brothers, G. A., G. E. and J. J. Watkins, in the previous year, and Doctor Watkins accepted an invitation to become connected with the concern. Since that time there have been a number of changes in the personnel of the officials, and the present officers consist of Dr. F. M. Watkins, president; and G. E. Watkins, secretary and treasurer. The plant, which is both wholesale and retail, is situated just south of the town, being a large, modern structure, with the largest ice-making machinery and abattoir with a capacity of ten head of cattle and twenty-five head of hogs per day. They also have a large feed yards for both cattle and hogs. The plant is now manufacturing twenty-three tons of ice daily and supplies Cherryvale and the country in the vicinity with both meat and ice. Under Doctor Watkins' management it is prospering and growing steadily and has become recognized as a necessary commercial adjunct. In politics a republican, Doctor Watkins wields considerable influence in Montgomery County, and at present is a member of the legislature, representative of the Twenty-sixth District. He has been a member of the school board for several years, and has given his support to all movements for the advance of education, as well as to other worthy and beneficial enterprises. His religious connection is with the Presbyterian Church, of which he is one of the trustees. Fraternally he is affiliated with Cherryvale Lodge No. 137, Ancient Free and Accepted Masons; Topeka Consistory No. 1, thirty-second degree Masonry; Abdullah Temple, Ancient Arabic Order Nobles of the Mystic Shrine; Modern Woodmen of America, Jayhawker Camp No. 913; Camp No. 154 Woodmen of the World; and the Mayflower Camp No. 312, Royal Neighbors of America. He is also a member of the Commercial Club. Doctor Watkins has offices at No. 101 East Main Street, and owns his residence at No. 503 on the same thoroughfare, in addition to a farm of 200 acres in Labette County and another farm of 300 acres in Montgomery County.

In 1893 at Wetmore, Kansas, Doctor Watkins was married to Miss Ola Frazey, daughter of W. D. and Susan (Zook) Frazey, the latter a resident of Hiawatha, Kansas. Mr. Frazey who was a carpenter and farmer by vocation, is now deceased. To Doctor and Mrs. Watkins there have been born three children: Ray, a senior at the Cherryvale High School; Dale, who is in seventh grade in the public schools; and Chester, in the primary grade.

TIMOTHY MCSHANE, who came to America from his native Ireland when a young man of twenty years, has found or made his opportunities in life, and by a strict course of self reliance and integrity has become one of the leading business men of Kansas City, Kansas, where he is vice president and manager of the Bargain Lumber Company at Tenth and State streets. He has been a resident of Kansas City since 1884, and resides at 240 North Eighth Street.

He was born on a farm in County Donegal, Province of Ulster, September 15, 1860. He was one of a large family of ten children. Only four are now living, three of them in America and one in Ireland. The parents Cornelius and Mary (Meehan) McShane, spent their lives quietly on an Irish farm.

Timothy McShane received his education in Ireland, and at the age of twenty in 1880 he and his brother Patrick came to this country to join an older brother John, then living in Missouri. Patrick afterwards became a priest of the Catholic Church and is now located at Lincoln, Nebraska.

On coming to America Timothy McShane found work with the Byrne Lumber Company for a short time, and has followed the lumber business almost continuously for thirty-five years. After locating in Kansas City in 1884 he was identified with various firms but in 1912 he and his son Leo P. McShane organized the Bargain Lumber Company. Leo is secretary and treasurer of the company, while Timothy is vice president and active manager. It is one of the leading concerns of the kind in the city, and is a business which in earlier years was owned by Doctor King of Kansas City, Missouri. Both Mr. McShane and his son have an accurate and thorough knowledge of the lumber business in all its details.

On June 27, 1888, Timothy McShane married Miss Margaret Vaughn. She was born in Virginia, but was reared at Marysville, Missouri, daughter of John and Catherine (Duggan) Vaughn. Her parents were farmers in Northwest Missouri, and both were natives of Ireland. The father is deceased and her mother still lives in Marysville, Missouri.

Mr. and Mrs. McShane have seven children: Mary, Leo P., John, Kathleen, Thaddeus, Bernard, Edward. All the children still live at home with their parents. All have had good educations and have been well prepared for the serious responsibilities of life. Leo P. is a very ambitious young business man, and by night study worked his way through the Kansas City School of Law, being graduated in 1914. He has not taken up active practice, but has engaged in the lumber business with his father and is also secretary and treasurer of the Rule Investment Company.

Mr. Timothy McShane is a democrat in national politics, but strictly independent in local affairs and follows his individual convictions as to the best man and the best local policy. He has supported movements of a laudable nature for improvements, and is a wholesome as well as successful citizen. He and his wife are active members of the Catholic Church. He is affiliated with the Woodmen of the World and served as its council commander for seven years.

WILLIAM LANYON. More than any other the name Lanyon is distinctive of the zinc industry in Southeastern Kansas, particularly at Pittsburg. The Lanyon family had been prominent in this particular industry for several generations. To a large degree the importance of Pittsburg as a zinc manufacturing center is due to the enterprise of the Lanyons who came to this part of Kansas more than thirty years ago from their original home in Southern Wisconsin, where they had operated extensive mining and manufacturing industries.

Though he was one of the earliest of the family to

take an active part in the zinc industry in Southeastern Kansas, Mr. William Lanyon gave up many of his interests in that field some years ago, and is now best known as a banker and leading citizen. He is vice president of the National Bank of Pittsburg and is now serving as mayor of the city. He was born at Mineral Point, Wisconsin, December 26, 1862. His father William Lanyon was a native of England, where he was born in 1830. Six years after his birth his parents came to the United States and finally settled in Mineral Point, Wisconsin. He grew up there, married, and was first engaged in the grain business. Coming to Pittsburg, Kansas, in 1882, he was a pioneer in the development of the coal fields and the operation of the zinc industry, and was closely associated with those phases of the city's growth and development. However, he always kept his home at Mineral Point, Wisconsin, where he died in June, 1908. He was a republican, a member of the Methodist Episcopal Church, and belonged to the Masons and the Ancient Order of United Workmen. William Lanyon, Sr., married Miss Maria Thomas, who was born in Mineral Point, Wisconsin, in 1837 and died there in 1914. Their children were: William; Ella, wife of Henry Vaughn, a broker in New York City; Myrtle, wife of J. A. Meserole, a retired druggist of Mineral Point; Colonel, who resides at Iola, Kansas, and was formerly closely identified with the Iola State Bank; Daisy is the wife of Thornton Posey, who is a buyer for the American Tobacco Company and lives in New York State.

William Lanyon received his early education in the public schools of Mineral Point, Wisconsin, graduating from the high school in 1882. In the fall of the same year he arrived in Pittsburg, and thenceforward was closely identified with the great Lanyon zinc smelters until 1908. The Lanyon Company also had zinc works at Iola. Several years ago these industries were sold to the United Zinc Company. Mr. Lanyon then built a zinc plant at Neodesha, Kansas, but finally sold that. He is still treasurer of the Pittsburg Zinc Company. After retiring from the zinc business largely he returned to Pittsburg and bought an interest in the National Bank of Pittsburg, of which he is now vice president.

Politically he is a republican. He served eight years altogether as member of the city council and as city commissioner. In April, 1915, he was elected mayor and is handling the affairs of the city in a very progressive and enlightened manner. He belongs to the Methodist Episcopal Church, to Pittsburg Lodge No. 187, Ancient Free and Accepted Masons, Pittsburg Chapter No. 58, Royal Arch Masons, Pittsburg Commandery No. 29, Knights Templar, Mirza Temple of the Nobles of the Mystic Shrine at Pittsburg, and to Valley of Wichita Consistory No. 1 of the Scottish Rite. Everything connected with Pittsburg's welfare finds a ready and generous supporter in Mr. Lanyon. He has been a working member of the Chamber of Commerce and the Retailers Association, and also belongs to the Country Club and the Kansas Bankers Association.

In 1883 at Mineral Point, his native town, he married Miss Amelia Spratley, a daughter of Mr. and Mrs. A. J. Spratley. Her father, who was a merchant, is now deceased and her mother still lives in Mineral Point. Mr. and Mrs. Lanyon have four children: Roy, who is employed in the zinc business at Bartlesville, Oklahoma; Lynnett is the wife of A. C. Ellsworth, who operates a steam shovel in the mines about Pittsburg; Wilma is a graduate of the Pittsburg High School and is now attending the Belmont Seminary for Young Women at Nashville, Tennessee; Helen is a senior in the Pittsburg High School.

JOHN WILBUR LAPHAM. The life record of John W. Lapham, postmaster, attorney and ex-mayor of Chanute, Kansas, stands in contradistinction to the old adage that a prophet is never without honor save in his own country, for Mr. Lapham is a native son of the county and city in which he has directed the efforts of his successful career. The son of a leading member of the Neosho County bar, he has followed in his father's footsteps in the legal profession, as well as making a success in business life and as a public official.

John W. Lapham was born at Chanute, Kansas, May 29, 1887, and is a son of Hon. Amos S. and Josephine (Bonham) Lapham. The family traces its ancestry back to the sixteenth century in England, and the first American ancestor was John Lapham, who emigrated to this country from Worcestershire, in 1607, and settled in Rhode Island. For many years the family was well and prominently known in the New England States, but with the western tide of civilization went to Ohio, where it took root and flourished. At Woodstock in that state, on April 7, 1845, was born Amos S. Lapham, the father of John W. Lapham.

On February 14, 1874, Judge Lapham was married at Chanute, Kansas, to Miss Josephine Bonham, who was born at Springfield, Illinois, February 14, 1854, and to this union there have been born four children: W. A. who is an automobile salesman of Chanute; Miss Agnes; John Wilbur; and Mary, who resides with her parents. Miss Agnes Lapham, who is now giving concerts and instruction at Chicago, Illinois, is a national figure in musical circles. A graduate of the University of Kansas in piano instruction, she spent three years in study in Germany, where her talents were developed under the teachings of the famous Madame Ziesler. She is a young woman of remarkable accomplishments and a wonderful performer, and has been heard in many of the leading cities of the country.

John W. Lapham attended the public schools of Chanute as a boy, and after his graduation from the Chanute High School, in 1903, entered the University of Kansas, from which he received the degree of Bachelor of Arts in 1907. He had inherited his father's predilection for the law, and his legal studies were prosecuted in the law schools of the University of Chicago, and of the University of Michigan, at Ann Arbor, from which he was graduated in 1910 with the degree of Bachelor of Laws, and in July of the same year was admitted to the Kansas bar. In January, 1911, he was appointed city attorney of Chanute, an office in which he served for four months, during which time he revised and compiled the city ordinances of Chanute. He then became a candidate for mayor of Chanute, to which position he was elected April 1, 1912. As he inaugurated the commission form of government, he had but one year to serve, and then returned to private life and the practice of his profession. However, he was not allowed to remain long out of the public eye, for on January 8, 1915, he received the appointment from President Wilson to the office of postmaster of Chanute, his term to run to January 12, 1919. In the postmastership, as in his other public offices, Mr. Lapham has displayed energy and conscientious desire to render real service to the community.

Mr. Lapham resides in his own home at No. 714 South Highland Avenue. He is well known in fraternal life, belonging to Cedar Lodge No. 103, Ancient Free & Accepted Masons; Wichita Consistory No. 2, thirty-second degree; Mirza Temple, Ancient Arabic Order Nobles of the Mystic Shrine, of Pittsburg, Kansas, Lodge No. 806, Benevolent and Protective Order of Elks, Chanute; the Fraternal Union; Chanute Camp No. 852, Modern Woodmen of America; and is a past president of the local lodge of the Anti-Horse Thief Association, the largest in the state, and is a member of the Kansas executive committee of the Anti-Horse Thief Association. Mr. Lapham is manager of the Lapham interests in the oil and gas fields east of Chanute.

On December 23, 1911, at Chanute, Mr. Lapham was married to Miss Jennie Purdy, daughter of J. N. and Alice (Wiley) Purdy, residents of Chanute, where Mr. Purdy is engaged in the livery and automobile storage business. Mr. and Mrs. Lapham have one child: Alice Virginia, who was born September 13, 1914.

C. H. FORTNER, M. D., has long enjoyed a well-earned reputation and position in the medical profession at Coffeyville. He entered practice with a thorough and comprehensive training and his fine talent soon attracted to him a patronage that has grown steadily in volume and importance, while his participation in progressive movements has made him one of the community's most valuable and valued citizens.

Doctor Fortner represents an old Indiana family. His ancestry goes back through several generations to some Fortners who came from Germany, and the family has lived in this country since colonial times. His grandfather, Aaron Fortner, was born in Indiana in 1831. His people located in Howard County of that state at an early date and he grew up there, followed the trade of wagon maker, and was also a farmer. Politically he was first a whig and later a republican. Aaron Fortner died in Howard County, Indiana, in 1911. His children were: E. L. Fortner, faher of Doctor Fortner; Emma, who lives in Howard County, Indiana, widow of James Roby, who was a farmer; Mattie, who died in Howard County, and her husband, William Myers, a farmer, is also deceased; Dora, lives in Los Angeles, California, the wife of Albert McReynolds; William R. is a mechanic living at Indianapolis; Lillie Washington lives at Alto, Indiana; Grant is also a resident of Indiana.

It was at Kokomo in Howard County, Indiana, that Doctor Fortner was born July 16, 1872. His father, E. L. Fortner, who now resides in Victoria, Texas, was born in Howard County, Indiana, in 1850, and was reared and married there. He grew up as a farmer, and subsequently became an active minister of the Seventh Day Adventist Church. In that capacity he came to Kansas in 1886, locating at Sterling in Rice County. As a minister his services took him from place to place over the state, and in 1898 the Foreign Missionary Board sent him to South America, where he spent two years in evangelical labors. Returning to Kansas he continued active in the ministry in that state and in Missouri, but finally resumed farming in Montgomery County for about two years, and in 1911, largely on account of his wife's health, went to Texas and is now farming and stock raising near Victoria. Rev. Mr. Fortner is a republican. He married Nannie B. Edwards, who was born in Howard County, Indiana, in 1851. Their children are: Doctor Fortner; Otho, who is now living at Cape Town, South Africa,

representing American manufacturers in their efforts to establish a market for their goods in South Africa; Rose is the wife of W. E. Dixon, a furniture dealer at Wichita, Kansas; Roy L. is a farmer and stock raiser at Victoria, Texas.

Doctor Fortner spent the first fourteen years of his life in Indiana, attending the public schools in the meanwhile, and after his parents moved to Kansas he was in the high school at Sterling. He gained a sturdy constitution during the twenty years he spent on his father's farm and when the family moved to Kansas City he entered the Medico-Chirurgical School, an institution subsequently merged with the Kansas University. He attended medical college three years, graduating M. D. March 31, 1899. For the first two years Doctor Fortner practiced out in Western Kansas in Norton County, following which he was in practice at Kansas City, Missouri, two years. He then took post-graduate studies for a year in the University Medical College, during 1904, and at the end of his term moved to Coffeyville, where his ability soon won him rank as a skillful physician and surgeon. He now carries on a general practice with offices at 127½ West Ninth Street and home at 605 Elm Street. He is an active member of the County and State Medical Societies and the American Medical Association.

Doctor Fortner has been very successful as a business man and now owns and controls a large amount of property, principally farm lands. He owns a farm of 240 acres three miles northeast of Coffeyville, another place of 150 acres in Seward County, a farm of 100 acres in Nowata County, Oklahoma, and a farm of 260 acres in Victoria County, Texas. His holdings also include residence property at 215 West Seventh Street in Coffeyville, and two houses at the corner of First and Maple streets.

Though reared a republican, Doctor Fortner has always voted the democratic ticket. For a time he served as city physician at Coffeyville. In Masonry he is a member of Amsterdam Lodge, Ancient Free and Accepted Masons, Fort Scott Consistory No. 4 of the thirty-second degree Scottish Rite, and Abdallah Temple of the Mystic Shrine at Leavenworth. He also belongs to Coffeyville Lodge No. 775, Benevolent and Protective Order of Elks, and to the Commercial Club of that city.

In 1902 at Amsterdam, Missouri, Doctor Fortner married Miss Jessie Wintermute, daughter of Mr. and Mrs. A. C. Wintermute, who live at Grand View, Missouri. Her father is a general merchant.

JOHN THOMAS SIMS, who many years ago secured prestige as one of the most forcible lawyers of the Kansas City, Kansas, bar and is now serving as judge of the Probate Court of Wyandotte County has had his share of the slings and arrows of outrageous fortune. His early life was one of hard and continuous work, often ill repaid, and again and again overtaken with calamity or disaster. He tried farming in the early days of Kansas, and various other occupations, and again and again when prosperity seemed to smile upon him he was put back at the beginning by drought or some other of the numerous calamities which are so familiar in Kansas history.

Judge Sims was born at Robinson, Crawford County, Illinois, December 31, 1804. He was one of eleven children, four of whom are still living, and is the only one in Kansas. His parents were Thomas Jefferson and Arminta McComas (Elledge) Sims. His father was born in Virginia, was a blacksmith and wagon-maker by trade, and for a number of years followed merchant milling, having a mill on the banks of the Wabash River on the Illinois side. He lived in Illinois until his death about 1877. Judge Sims' mother was born in Kentucky in 1828 and died at Robinson, Illinois, in 1884. The father was a democrat until the war, and then joined his allegiance with the republican party. The only public office he ever held was that of tax collector. He was an active member of the Christian or Disciples Church. Several members of the family have attained distinction. Judge Sims' sister Mrs. Ellen May Firebaugh, wife of a physician, was herself graduated from Rush Medical College at Chicago but did not practice after her marriage. She attained most note as a literary woman, was author of ''The Physician's Wife'' and has contributed to various magazines. Stella Sims, a younger sister of Judge Sims, is a graduate dentist and has practiced that profession very successfully.

Judge Sims received his early education in Robinson, Illinois. At the age of seventeen he left school and first aspired to be a farmer. While farming some land he paid another farmer $1.50 a week board, and during all that time lived on flap-jacks and sorghum, corn-dodgers and maple syrup. It was a bad season, but he worked hard while others loafed. Altogether it was an unsuccessful venture, and he then began teaching school. He taught twenty-two days a month and was paid wages of $25 a month. At the end of the year he took Horace Greeley's advice and came west to Kansas. This was in 1884. Locating at Parsons, he worked on a farm for a time, and also taught in Labette and Pratt counties. At Pratt he became interested in land dealing, associated with J. W. Ellis. Continued dry weather brought his efforts in that direction to a failure and he then returned to Parsons and subsequently to Joplin, Missouri. There he was reduced to financial extremities, and as a last resource he came to Kansas City, Kansas, and sought employment with Swift & Company, packers.

Judge Sims has been a resident of Kansas City, Kansas, since 1895. He has studied law while teaching, and in 1895 was admitted to the bar. He has handled some of the most important litigation tried in the local courts. He was the principal attorney in the noted Casper Compensation case and was also legal representative for the Grand Lodge of the Ancient Order of United Workmen in the case against the State Lodge which was compromised.

Besides his private law practice Judge Sims has spent much of his time in public office. He was three times elected to the office of justice of the peace, and served until the office was abolished. In 1905 he was elected judge of the Police Court and was re-elected in 1907 and again in 1909. He resigned in December, 1910, during his third term, consequent upon his election in November, 1910, as probate judge of Wyandotte County. He has been kept in that office, which requires so much care and delicacy of administration, to the present time, and in 1916 was made the recipient of the largest majority ever given to any candidate for office in the county. His majority in that election was 8,000. For some time Judge Sims practiced in partnership with Col. L. C. True. Even after he came to Kansas City and became well established as a lawyer, his experience with disaster was not over. In 1903 he lost practically all his property in the flood of that year.

Judge Sims has long been an active worker in the republican party, has been delegate to various conventions, and for two years was secretary of the Republican Central Committee of the Second Con-gressional District. He is a member of the Wyandotte County and the Kansas State Bar associations. He belongs to numerous fraternal societies, including the Masons, in which he has attained the Knight Templar degree, the Elks, the Knights of Pythias, the Modern Woodmen of America, and the Ancient Order of United Workmen, in which he has served as chairman of the law committee. He and his wife are active members of the Presbyterian Church.

On October 24, 1893, Judge Sims married Miss Cora Anna Petri of Parsons, Kansas. Mrs. Sims was born in Ohio and her people came originally from Alsace-Lorraine. She is of both French and German ancestry. Her parents were prosperous farmers and finally came to Kansas, locating at Parsons. Judge Sims met his wife at Parsons, and their first meeting was during a severe storm. To their marriage were born three children. The only one now living is Elizabeth Arminta, who was born August 1, 1894, and is now a student in the Emporia College.

PAUL PHILLIP MACCASKILL. One of the younger members of the Kansas bar, in active practice at Parsons, Paul MacCaskill has already had a wide range of experience in his profession and in public affairs. While studying law and since he spent a good deal of time in the service of public men, at Topeka and elsewhere, and in 1915 was secretary to Hon. Bailie P. Waggener, the Atchison County representative in the State Senate.

He is of a fine strain of Scotch ancestry. The name MacCaskill, or MacAskill, is of Norse origin, meaning Anses Kettle, or sacrificial vessel to the gods. The MacCaskills were a sept of the powerful MacLeod clan who prior to 1715 owned the Isle of Skye and other holdings in the Hebrides as well as on the mainland. The MacCaskills lived on the Isle of Skye, and Mr. MacCaskill's great-great-grandfather Malcolm MacCaskill came to this country in 1811 and located in a Scotch settlement at Fayetteville, North Carolina. He followed planting through his career. The grandfather, Allen A. MacCaskill, was born at Fayetteville, North Carolina, in 1828 and died there in 1904. His active career was spent chiefly as a planter and prior to the war he owned a number of slaves. He was also a man of deep scholarship, was a Presbyterian minister, and was well versed in the Gaelic languages and was an instructor of them. During the war between the states he was a chaplain in the Confederate army and was present with General Lee at Appomatox. This scholarly old southerner married a Miss Jackson, a relative of Gen. Stonewall Jackson.

It was in Fayetteville, North Carolina, that Paul MacCaskill was born July 7, 1890. His father is Walter Scott MacCaskill, who now resides at Parsons, Kansas. His father was born at Fayetteville in 1866, grew up and married there, and followed farming until 1891, when he became a fireman with the Chicago, Milwaukee & St. Paul Railroad, running out of Savannah, Illinois. In 1897 he was promoted to engineer with the same road, and in 1904 came to Parsons, and has since been one of the efficient and trusted engineers of the Missouri, Kansas & Texas Railroad. He owns his residence at 318 North Twenty-third Street in Parsons. He is a democrat of the old school and attends the Methodist Episcopal Church. Walter S. MacCaskill married for his first wife Mary Virginia Gurly, who was born at Goldsboro, North Carolina, and died in 1897. Her only child is Paul MacCaskill. For his second wife W. S. MacCaskill married Ida Overholtser of Perry, Iowa.

Her children were: Caryl, who was born October 1, 1899, and is a member of the junior class in the Parsons High School; Frank O., who was born in 1904, and is in the public schools; and Alice, born in August, 1907.

Paul MacCaskill received his education in several different localities. His mother died at Perry, Iowa, and he attended school there for a time. For two years he lived in the home of his uncle J. B. Moll, who was general roadmaster of the Chicago, Milwaukee & St. Paul with headquarters at Chicago. From Chicago he returned to Perry, Iowa, then went to Marion, Iowa, and attended school in all these places. In 1904 his father brought him to Parsons and he left the high school of that city in 1907. During the two years from 1907 to 1909 he was engaged in farming in Whiteside County, Illinois, and then spent a year on a plantation at his birthplace in Fayetteville, North Carolina. Returning to Parsons he spent part of the year 1910 in the Parsons Business College, and then entered the law office of W. S. Hyatt. The school year 1911-12 was spent in the law school of the Kansas University. In the fall of 1912 Mr. MacCaskill took an active part in assisting the campaign of Hon. George W. Hodges. During the legislative session of 1911 he was committee clerk for James Orr. In 1913 he was clerk to Senator I. M. Hinds in the Senate. At the close of that session he was appointed private secretary to A. E. Helm, commerce counsel of the Public Utilities Commission.

Taking the bar examination in January, 1913, and being admitted to the bar, he resigned his place as private secretary in July of that year, and has since been in active practice at Parsons. As a democratic candidate he made the race for county attorney, and though Labette County is nominally republican his defeat was accomplished by a very narrow margin. Mr. MacCaskill has his offices in the First National Bank Building and resides at 1416 Appleton Avenue. He is a member of the Methodist Episcopal Church, belongs to the Phi Alpha Delta law fraternity, and to Parsons Lodge No. 1 of the Ancient Order of United Workmen.

On September 3, 1913, at Lawrence Mr. MacCaskill married Miss Gladys Rearick, daughter of Mr. and Mrs. John Rearick. Her father is still living and is station agent for the Missouri Pacific Railway at Altoona, Kansas. Mr. and Mrs. MacCaskill have one son, Paul Hyatt, born August 2, 1914.

JOHN B. FAVOR, present sheriff of Sumner County, has been a resident of Western Kansas for over forty-five years, and though he was a small boy when the family moved here he knows both by recollection and personal experience all the vicissitudes and trials that beset the early pioneers.

This story of a pioneer Kansas family begins with the removal of Gaines and Susan (Lavender) Favor from their native state of Tennessee to a farm near Cairo, Illinois, in 1855. On that farm in the southern part of Illinois was born on January 22, 1860, John B. Favor, first mentioned above. A little more than a year later Gaines Favor, who had got well started as a farmer in Southern Illinois and was recognized as a man of some prominence, was killed by the explosion of one of the old-fashioned threshing outfits known as "Groundhog" machines. This was, of course, a calamity in the family history. Besides his widow he was survived by an older son and two daughters in addition to John B. Favor. The work of the farm then fell upon the widowed mother and

her children. To make their situation the harder the war broke out, and they were hard pressed to make a living during that period. Selling the Illinois farm and acting on the advice of some uncles and brothers-in-law who were living in Kansas, Mrs. Favor took her children to a claim of 160 acres on the raw prairie twenty miles southwest of Abilene, on the old Chisholm cattle trail from the south. It is important to remember some of the conditions of that year, 1870. Not a single railroad had penetrated Indian Territory to the Red River, Abilene was still in the high tide of its eminence as one of the main cattle shipping points and the terminus of the great Chisholm Trail over which thousands and thousands of cattle were driven every year from the plains and ranches of Texas. Thus the situation along the old cattle trail, while in some respects an advantage, was also exposed to some of the dangers incident to the wild and reckless life that characterized the old days of the range and trail.

Nothing daunted, however, Mrs. Favor established her home there, broke some land, and hers was the fourth family to locate in that section along Holland Creek. She and her children lived in a simple dugout home of that date. Three years later they moved to a more elaborate dwelling, but it was still a dugout. The early people along the frontier had too many things to think of to consider schools. Mrs. Favor, however, was very ambitious for her children, and in order to get them educated she deeded an acre from her land and by subscription a schoolhouse was erected, being used both for church and school purposes. In that old schoolhouse Mr. John B. Favor received many of the early lessons of his youth. After two years on the first farm Mrs. Favor moved to eighty acres at another location on Holland Creek, and there she remained for a number of years. While there the family engaged in the stock business and general farming, and in spite of the widespread sufferings caused by grasshopper years and the drouth, they managed to keep their cattle from starvation by grazing them on the foothills and in the draws. As there was no father or husband to look after the family it was characteristic of the generous and bighearted Texas cowboys and rangers that they offered their services in every way for the protection and safeguarding of this lonely woman and her children, and furnished some of the feed necessary to bring their cattle through the winter.

In 1880 the family removed to Abilene. Her older son subsequently married and removed to McDonald County, Missouri, where he is now a prominent fruit farmer and has seven children. The mother, desiring to be with this son, moved to Missouri, leaving John B. Favor in Abilene.

John B. Favor for several years conducted a transfer and teaming business in Abilene. On January 6, 1884, he married Miss Alice Looker in Abilene.

He has long been active in public affairs. In 1890 he was appointed city marshal of Abilene, and two years later was elected by the populist party and held that office continuously for fourteen years. He proved an efficient officer in the preservation of law and order, and had many interesting experiences, though of course Abilene had become a greatly changed town from the wild and riotious period when it was exclusively a cattle town. In 1904 Mr. Favor was elected on the republican ticket to the office of sheriff of Dickinson County, and in 1906 was elected for another term of two years.

On leaving the office of sheriff in Dickinson County, in 1908, he removed to Wellington, and there, associated with J. W. Julian, opened the Bungalow restaurant. He continued in this business for two years until after he began his duties as under sheriff with J. M. Lingenfelder. He was under sheriff four year, and in 1914 was elected to the office of sheriff of Sumner County, and was re-elected in 1916 for a term of two years on the same ticket.

Sheriff Favor has long been prominent in fraternal work. He has filled all the chairs in the Independent Order of Odd Fellows, in the Ancient Order of United Workmen and the Modern Woodmen of America, and is past master of the Blue Lodge of Masons at Abilene, and has held all the offices in the Royal Arch Chapter at Abilene and all the chairs except that of eminent commander in the Knights Templar Commandery. At three different times he has served as assistant state lecturer, and has been patron two times of the Eastern Star. Mrs. Favor is also prominent in the various auxiliaries connected with these orders, and is worthy matron of the Eastern Star and also belongs to the Women's Christian Temperance Union. Mr. and Mrs. Favor are members of the Presbyterian Church, and in many ways have proved themselves valuable factors in the communities where they have lived.

CHARLES T. CARPENTER is one of the pioneer bankers of Coffeyville, and for thirty years has been closely identified with what is now known as the Condon National Bank, being vice president of that institution. Mrs. Temple W. Carpenter, his wife, is one of the prominent women of Southern Kansas, has been a leader in religious, social and public affairs, and is president of the Carnegie Library of Coffeyville, and is the only woman who has ever been honored with a place on the school board of that city.

The Carpenter family is a very old one in America, having been transplanted from England to Rehoboth, Massachusetts, as early as 1632. From there its descendants moved to Pennsylvania, and into North Carolina and Kentucky. Mr. Carpenter has ancestors who fought in the Revolution.

Charles T. Carpenter was born at Palmetto, Tennessee, December 9, 1858, and belongs to a substantial stock of people who were extensive planters in early Tennessee, but were stanchly aligned with the Union cause and in the difficulties that grew out of the Civil war moved north of the Ohio River. Peter Carpenter, grandfather of the Coffeyville banker, was born in North Carolina in 1790. He was reared and married in his native state, became a planter, and moved his family to Tennessee, establishing a homestead on an eminence long known as Carpenter Hill. He was a stanch whig, and on account of his pronounced advocacy of the Union cause he had to refugee from Tennessee during the war, and lived at Bloomfield, Iowa, where he died in 1865. Peter Carpenter married Margaret Ramsey, who was born in 1805, and died at the old estate at Carpenter Hill in Tennessee in 1845. She was of Scotch-Irish descent and her ancestors had come to America at the beginning of the nineteenth century.

Samuel Carpenter, father of Charles T., was born at Knob Creek, North Carolina, in 1826, and was reared and educated near Palmetto, Tennessee. He became a merchant, and in 1874 moved out to Kansas and locating at Oswego established one of the early general mercantile stores there. He retired from business in 1887 and died at Oswego in 1901. He was a republican, and was practically a lifelong

member of the Presbyterian Church, serving as a member for forty years. Samuel Carpenter married Sarah Montgomery, who was born in Tennessee in 1831 and died in Oswego, Kansas, in 1907. Their children were: Laura C., wife of Dr. W. H. Belt, a physician and surgeon at Oswego, Kansas. Robert P., in the real estate and insurance business at Oklahoma City; Charles T.; Mary, wife of L. J. Van Alstyne, who is connected with the Carpenter & Van Alstyne mercantile establishment at Oswego, Kansas; Samuel, Jr., also a member of the firm of Carpenter & Van Alstyne at Oswego; Margaret, a teacher in the Central High School of Kansas City, Missouri.

Charles T. Carpenter had his first schooling in a private institution at Palmetto, Tennessee. After his parents moved to Kansas he continued his education in the State University at Bloomington, Indiana, where he was graduated A. B. in 1876. He then came out to Kansas to join his parents at Oswego, and spent five years in the employ of his father. While at Oswego he became connected with his real work in life, and served two years as cashier of the Condon Bank there. In 1886 he came to Coffeyville as one of the partners in the Condon Bank, which was then a private institution and had been established at Coffeyville that year. The bank took out a state charter in 1898, and since 1903 has been the Condon National Bank. Its present officers are: C. M. Ball, president; Charles T. Carpenter, vice president; C. A. Walker, cashier; and F. S. Mitchell, assistant cashier. This is one of the old and reliable banks of Southern Kansas, and has a capital of $100,000 and surplus and profits of $50,000. In September, 1916, the bank completed its handsome new home, a two-story terra cotta building at 814 Walnut Street in Coffeyville.

Mr. Carpenter is also senior partner in the Charles T. Carpenter Insurance Agency, the largest agency of the kind in Montgomery County, and handling life, fire, hail, cyclone, accident, plate glass, and practically every line of insurance. For twelve years Mr. Carpenter served as president of the Coffeyville Board of Education and is still a member of the board. He is trustee of the Montgomery County High School at Independence. Politically he is independent, is a member of the Presbyterian Church, which he has served as trustee and elder, and has made himself an influential factor in everything that concerns the better life and progress of his home city.

In 1892 at Rockport, Indiana, Charles T. Carpenter and Miss Temple West were united in marriage. Mrs. Carpenter was born in Pike County, Indiana. Her ancestors, the Wests, came from England to Virginia in colonial times. Her grandfather, Hugh West, a native of Virginia, saw active service in the Mexican war, and spent his life as a farmer in Kentucky and Ohio. He died in Clermont County, Ohio. He was a whig in politics. Hugh West married Rosanna Boyd, who was born in South Carolina and died in Indiana about 1867.

J. D. West, father of Mrs. Carpenter, was born in Clermont County, Ohio, in 1828, grew up there, but when quite young went to Pike County, Indiana, where he was a successful farmer and stockman, and where he died in 1900. He was a republican. In 1861 he enlisted with an Indiana regiment and served all through the war, first under the command of Grant and later under Sherman. In one battle he was taken prisoner, and was confined at Andersonville until exchanged. J. D. West married Sophronia Brock, who was born in Virginia in 1834 and died in Pike County, Indiana, in 1870. Their children were: Joshua, who was a farmer and died in Pike County, Indiana; Mrs. Carpenter; Leander, who is employed in an elevator at Mount Carmel, Illinois; Eva, who died at Rockport, Indiana, in 1875, unmarried.

Mrs. Carpenter received her early education in Rockport, Indiana, graduating from the high school there in 1882, and in the same year entering the State University at Bloomington, where she completed the course and received the degree Ph. B. in 1886. She is a member of the college sorority, Kappa Alpha Theta. For several years before her marriage Mrs. Carpenter taught at Rockport and also at Minneapolis, Minnesota. In addition to the conscientious care of her home and family, Mrs. Carpenter has accomplished a great deal in the sphere of woman's activities. Since early girlhood she has been a worker in the Presbyterian Church. For a number of years she has served as treasurer of Chapter No. 112 of the Eastern Star at Coffeyville. Mrs. Carpenter is one of the charter members of the Searchlight Club, the original woman's club of Coffeyville, and was its president for a long time. She has been closely associated with local affairs, particularly those affecting the educational progress of the city, and is president of the Carnegie Library Board. Reference has already been made to the fact that she is the only woman who ever served on the board of education, and she filled that important post in local affairs four years.

To the marriage of Mr. and Mrs. Carpenter were born seven children: Walter Thomas is a director and bookkeeper in the Condon National Bank, being a graduate of the Coffeyville High School, as are all the other older children; Samuel is in his father's insurance office; Charles T. is also learning the insurance business under his father's direction; Hugh is now in the junior class of the Kansas University at Lawrence; Margery, after finishing the high school course in 1916, entered Oswego College for Women; William is a freshman in the Coffeyville High School; Sarah is in the seventh grade of the public schools.

JOEL H. RICKEL. Among the citizens of Chanute, one who has had a most interesting career is Joel H. Rickel, a resident of this city since 1896, and now the owner of a carriage and repair shop and the owner of a valuable farm. Mr. Rickel is a veteran of the Civil war, and has been a prominent figure in Grand Army circles, being a past commander of several posts in Kansas and a past department commander of the State of Kansas. He was born in Ashland County, Ohio, December 8, 1844, and is a son of John S. and Jane (Fulks) Rickel.

The Rickel family, which originated on the Rhone, Germany, was founded in this country during Colonial times, and three bearing the name fought with the Patriot army during the war of the Revolution, one meeting his death at the battle of Brandywine. Michael B. Rickel, the grandfather of Joel H. Rickel, was born in 1776, in Tuscaraugus County, Pennsylvania, and became a pioneer into Ohio, where, in Ashland County, he entered a farm from the Government. There he passed the remainder of a long and industrious life, and died in 1868. John S. Rickel was born in Ashland County, Ohio, in 1813, in the same house in which was born his son, and was reared and educated in the community. He was a mill-

wright by trade and a civil engineer by profession, and in 1841 went to Kosciusko County, Indiana, where he cleared a farm from the heavy timber. There he spent the remainder of his life, and died in 1853. He was a whig in politics and a member of the Masonic fraternity. Mr. Rickel married Miss Jane Fulks, who was born in 1813, in Wayne County, Ohio, and died in Kosciusko County, Indiana, in 1858, and they became the parents of three children: Joel H.; Rebecca Jane, who is the widow of Dick Peek, who was a farmer, and resides in Shelby County, Illinois; and J. M., president of the Chanute Tank Company, of Chanute, Kansas.

Joel H. Rickel was reared on his father's farm in Kosciusko County, Indiana, until he was ten years of age, at which time he returned to Ashland County, Ohio, and was there given a common school education. After the death of his father he resided on the farm of his grandfather until he was fifteen years old, at which time he struck out for himself, but his career was interrupted by the outbreak of the Civil war. In 1861 he enlisted in the Twenty-fourth Regiment, Ohio Volunteer Infantry, with which he served until June 19, 1864. During this period he saw some of the severest fighting of the entire war, taking part in no less than twenty-two engagements, including such notable battles as Shiloh, Corinth, Murfreesboro and Chickamauga. At Stone River, Mr. Rickel was shot through the right foot, and September 19, 1863; he was again wounded, this time seriously, three ribs being broken. He was unconscious when found, and his comrades thinking him dead, prepared for his burial. He laid on the funeral pile for fourteen hours, when they discovered that life was not extinct. He was five months recovering from this injury, but rejoined his regiment as soon as he was able. Mr. Rickel's war record was one of which any man might well be proud. He was courageous in battle, earning the admiration of his comrades, and his faithful performance of whatever duty was imposed upon him gained him the respect of his officers.

At the close of the war the brave young soldier returned to Ashland, Ohio, but he had seen enough of the outside world to desire to see more, and also felt that the West held out opportunities that his home community could never give him. Accordingly, in 1866, he went to Blackhawk County, Iowa, where he engaged in farming for three years, and in 1869 located on a farm in the vicinity of Flora, Illinois. After one year of agricultural work, he moved into the town, where he followed carpentry for three years, and in 1873 first came to Kansas, settling in the vicinity of Emporia, where he farmed with some degree of success for two years. At the end of that time he went to Wabaunsee County, Kansas, and during the next ten years was engaged in the real estate and loan business, an enterprise in which he met with success. Mr. Rickel's love of adventure, however, remained unsatisfied, and at that time he went to sea, fishing for turtles, under a contract with the Fulton Turtle Cannery, of Rockport, Texas, which called for all the turtles weighing over 200 pounds that he could catch. In this capacity he fished all along the coast of Mexico and Central and South America and his catches were phenomenal during the three years of his contract. While thus engaged he brought many strange fish and curios to the surface of the waters, and eventually decided to make a collection of curios, which he brought back to the United States. These included a dolphin whale, a hammer-head shark, a man-eating shark, a black shark, and a mammoth sawfish twenty-one

Yours Very Truly
Joel Henry Rickel

feet long and weighing 2,500 pounds. All of these he had mounted by a taxidermist, and a large collection of radiates, zuphites and molusca, which were subsequently placed on exhibition in Texas, Arkansas and Kansas, and finally were established at Chanute. Many of these curios have since been sold to exhibitions, museums and dealers, but Mr. Rickel still possesses 800 of the smaller specimens, including rare and valuable species of the finny tribe, which form a most interesting collection and have been viewed by thousands of people, many of whom came from long distances solely to see them. Mr. Rickel has added other features to the collection, including a piece of rosewood veneering which was taken from the first piano (or spinnet) ever shipped to America.

Mr. Rickel came to Chanute in 1896, and here has since been the proprietor of a carriage and repair shop. He is also superintending the operations on his farm, which lies one mile west of the limits of Chanute, a handsome property which has been brought to a high state of cultivation and yields a good income. He likewise owns other real estate, including a brick flat building at No. 318 East Main Street. Mr. Rickel is a stand-pat republican, and cast his first vote for Abraham Lincoln, since which time he has given his ballot to every presidential candidate of his party. He is a member of the Odd Fellows and the Triple Tie, and stands high in the councils of the Grand Army of the Republic, being a past department commander of the Grand Army of the State of Kansas. He is now a member of Chanute Post No. 129, of which he is past commander, as he is also of two other posts in the state.

Mr. Rickel was married in December, 1890, at Guthrie, Oklahoma, to Miss Mary A. Hardy, daughter of William and Ann (Garrity) Hardy, farming people, both of whom are now deceased. By a former marriage Mr. Rickel had three children: Henry E., who is the editor of a newspaper at Eskridge, Kansas; B. G., who is a contracting painter at Portland, Oregon; and Willard H., who is engaged in the real estate and loan business at Eskridge, Kansas.

THOMAS J. WHITE, a lawyer of high standing in both Kansas City, Kansas, and Kansas City, Missouri, has been a resident of Kansas forty-eight years. He had his experience as an early homesteader, was in railway service for a number of years, and gained a very thorough knowledge of public men and national politics in his relationship as confidential clerk to Senator Ingalls. He has been a lawyer for nearly thirty-five years.

Mr. White was born at Whitstable, a town on the seacoast in County Kent, England, January 27, 1842. He was the second in a family of seven children born to Joseph and Jane (Collar) White. He was the only member of the family to come to America. His father Joseph was a sea captain. Mr. White was reared in England and in the English schools and largely through his own persistence and studious habits acquired a good education. While in England he learned shorthand. He acquired proficiency in this by arduous work often by candle light, and also commenced the reading of law. He married in England, and two years later, in 1867, determined to seek his fortune in the New World.

After landing in New York he proceeded West, settling for a time in Illinois and taught a term or so of school at Neponset in Illinois. In 1869, with his wife and in company with two other families he left Illinois, journeyed by railroad to St. Joseph, Missouri, and from there by horse and wagon, over-

land to Washington County, Kansas. He homesteaded a claim of 160 acres. He and his family lived in a small house on the claim for about 2½ years, endured the privations and hardships characteristic of those years, and finally proved up by commuting the claim.

The art of shorthand which he had acquired in England proved the key by which he entered into a broader life. In 1871 he was requested to become secretary to W. F. Downs, superintendent of the Central Branch of the Union Pacific Railway, now a part of the Missouri Pacific system. He accordingly removed to Atchison, and held various positions, including secretary to the superintendent, claim agent, purchasing agent, chief clerk and finally general auditor. He remained in railway work until Jay Gould bought the road and made it part of the Missouri Pacific System in 1880. His Railway Auditorship gave him a thorough and practical knowledge of accounting.

In 1880-81 Mr. White was in charge of the office of a large hardware house at Atchison. In 1881, at the invitation of U. S. Senator John J. Ingalls, Mr. White became his private secretary; and he was also made clerk of the Senate Committee of the District of Columbia in Washington. He continued as Mr. Ingalls' private secretary and clerk of said Senate Committee for nearly seven years. While in Washington he enrolled as a student in Georgetown University School of Law. Previously, in Atchison, Mr. White had taught a night school in shorthand. He also served as a member of the school board there two years and was city clerk there two years.

Mr. White was graduated from the Georgetown University Law Department with the degree LL. B. in 1882 and in 1883 received the degree of LL. M. He was admitted to the bar of the District of Columbia in 1882, and a year or two later, to the bar of the Supreme Court of the United States. Mr. White was in practice at Atchison from January 1, 1888, until the summer of 1889, when he removed to Kansas City, Kansas, and for twenty-seven years has successfully practiced there with particular attention to real estate and tax law. He has always been a great student with a high reputation for industry, method and exactness in all of his business and professional matters; strictly temperate and regular in his habits; all of which have resulted in giving him a very high standing among the successful lawyers of the State. From 1889 to 1891 he was a partner of F. D. Mills, but with that exception has practiced alone.

Among other fruits of his relationship with Senator Ingalls Mr. White acquired much knowledge of the bankruptcy law, and in 1898 was appointed referee in bankruptcy by Judge Foster, and filled that position until 1904. Mr. White was a member of the Kansas City, Kansas, school board from 1905 to 1908 and served as president in 1905.

Outside of his professional and business interests the inspiration of his life has been his home and family. Mr. and Mrs. White have been married fifty-one years. They were married in England at Speldhurst, Tunbridge Wells, Kent, April 17, 1865. Her maiden name was Mary Elizabeth Willett. They have four children: Frank W., president of the Lyman Drug Company of Manistee, Michigan; Nellie E., at home; William F., a real estate man at Seattle, Washington; and Mary L., at home.

Mr. White has been a loyal republican and has done much to support his party organization in Kansas. He and his wife are active in the affairs of St. Paul's Episcopal Church and he has served as superintendent of its Sunday school for over twelve years. Prior to coming to Kansas City he was superintendent of the Congregational Church Sunday School at Atchison for twelve years. In Masonry he has become affiliated with the various bodies of the Scottish Rite, has served as master of the Consistory and is a member of the Kansas City, Kansas, Mercantile Club.

Mr. White has made nine long trips back to his native England, sometimes accompanied by his wife, sometimes alone, and at other times by one of his sons or daughters. They have spent much time in travel both in this country and abroad. Mr. White has always taken a great interest in the history of Kansas, and he cherished for many years one relic of pioneer times in the form of the original key to the jail in which John Brown was confined before he was hanged, but which he has recently donated to the Kansas State Historical Society at Topeka, Kansas.

CHARLES MANVILLE SAWYER, chairman of the board of directors of the Federal Reserve Bank at Kansas City, Missouri, began his banking career in Kansas and is perhaps as widely known over the state as any one banker. The Federal Reserve Bank at Kansas City, Missouri, serves the district comprising the states of Kansas, Nebraska, Colorado, Wyoming and the greater part of Oklahoma, and portions of Missouri and New Mexico.

Mr. Sawyer was born on a farm near Streator, Illinois. His is an old American family and some of his ancestors fought as officers in the revolutionary war. His parents were Lewis M. and Salanda (Moon) Sawyer, the former a native of New York and the latter of Illinois. They were the parents of eight children. Lewis M. Sawyer had come to Illinois in 1842 and for many years was a successful farmer, stock raiser and also interested in several banks. He retired from active business in 1898 and moved to Evanston, Illinois, in which handsome city he still resides at the age of eighty. His wife died January 19, 1915. Lewis M. Sawyer while living at Streator took an interest in republican politics and served as a member of both the House of Representatives and the Senate of Illinois.

His father being a man of considerable wealth for the time and of substantial social position, Charles Manville Sawyer had excellent opportunities during his boyhood. However, he was the only one of his parents' children who did not go to college. He contented himself with the district schools and the high school of Streator. He lived on a farm in 1885-86 and in the spring of 1887, through the influence of his brother-in-law, Mr. E. E. Ames, afterwards prominent in Kansas, came out to this state and located at Norton. Norton, then a frontier town along the line of the Rock Island Railroad in the northwest part of the state, was just rising to importance as the center of a rapidly settling district. Charles M. Sawyer was just twenty-one years of age, but soon justified the confidence of the directors who made him cashier of the First National Bank of Norton. He filled that post until July, 1893, and during that period he gained a wide acquaintance with the people of Northwestern Kansas and came in touch with the early settlers during the series of hard years which beset them. In July, 1893, Mr. Sawyer was appointed a national bank examiner. That position gave him exceptional opportunities for acquaintance and association with bankers all over the state, and he continued the work

until 1897, when he resigned to return to Norton and become president of the First National Bank. He was called from that position by Governor Hodges in 1913, and appointed bank commissioner of the state. In 1914 he was elected a governor of the Federal Reserve Bank at Kansas City, Missouri, and in 1916 became chairman of the board.

As an associate of Mr. E. E. Ames Mr. Sawyer has been identified with the management and control of a number of banks in Northwest Kansas. He was a member of the executive council of the American Bankers' Association from 1903 to 1906 and again in a similar position from 1908 to 1911. In 1898 Mr. Sawyer was honored by election to the office of president of the Kansas Bankers' Association.

In politics he is a democrat, and was a delegate at large to the Democratic National Convention at Denver in 1908, and was also a member of the convention of 1912 at Baltimore.

On May 22, 1889, Mr. Sawyer married May Holmes. She was born at Streator, Illinois, daughter of Frank Holmes, the first merchant of that city. Mr. and Mrs. Sawyer have four children. Lewis M., Jr., is a graduate of the University of Kansas and the Yale University Law School, and since March, 1915, has been a state bank examiner of Kansas. Margaret, Frances and Catherine are Mr. Sawyer's daughters. Frances is now a student in the Kansas University, while Catherine is attending Miss Barstow's School.

Fraternally Mr. Sawyer is a thirty-second degree Scottish Rite Mason, a member of the Mystic Shrine at Salina, and also belongs to the Modern Woodmen of America, the Blue Hills Country Club, Knife and Fork Club, Mid-Day Club, Bankers' and Automobile clubs of Kansas City, Missouri. Mrs. Sawyer is a member of the Episcopal Church.

GUY E. TRUITT. To the real lover of nature there is no vocation known to mankind which furnishes more interesting possibilities than the nursery business. Developments in recent years along this line have been as wonderful as they were formerly unexpected and unbelievable. Yet even to the man who labors faithfully to maintain high standards already established there is that satisfaction in accomplishment possible only when an individual works in collaboration with nature and the elements of creation. Kansas has had its full quota of earnest, painstaking men in this vocation who have delighted in their labor and have contributed liberally to the well-being of the community, but few concerns have enjoyed a longer or more prosperous career than the Chanute Nurseries, which have enlisted the activities of two generations, and which are now being conducted at Chanute under the able management of Guy E. Truitt, a man who is perfectly and sincerely in sympathy with his work.

Mr. Truitt was born in Greenup County, Kentucky, July 2, 1876, and is a son of James and Ella E. (Griece) Truitt, and is of English descent. His father was also a native of Kentucky, born in 1838, and was reared on a farm, where he learned to love and understand the works of nature. During his youth he engaged in farming, but gradually turned his attention more and more to the nursery business. When the Civil war came on he enlisted in the Home Guards, but saw little service, and when peace was declared went happily and contentedly back to the cultivation of his plants, his shrubs and his trees. In 1878 he came to Chanute as a pioneer, having become impressed with the possibilities of this region, and not long thereafter founded the Chanute Nurseries. His start was a small one, if compared with business enterprises of the present day, but through persistent labor and with the help of his growing sons he built it up to large proportions, and the business became recognized as one of the city's regular institutions and one which contributed to Chanute's prestige. Mr. Truitt passed away at Chanute in February, 1914, universally respected and esteemed, a man whose life among the growing things had put his heart into attune with nature's best moods and had developed his natural qualities of sympathy and kindliness. Mr. Truitt was a stanch republican, and a member of the Masonic fraternity. He was married in Kentucky to Miss Ella E. Griece, who was born in 1842, in Ohio, and who survives her husband and resides at Chanute. They became the parents of five children, as follows: a son who died in infancy; William, who was associated with his father and brothers in the nursery business and died at Chanute in March, 1914; May, who conducts the greenhouse at No. 219 North Steuben Avenue, the only one in Chanute, where there are 35,000 square feet of glass; Walter, a resident of Chanute, who was formerly connected with the nursery business with his father and brothers; and Guy E.

Guy E. Truitt was educated in the public schools of Chanute, and was graduated from the high school here with the class of 1894. At that time he accepted a position with the Atchison, Topeka and Santa Fe Railroad, in the service of which line he continued for a period of twelve years, then entering the nursery business with his father and his brothers, William and Walter. Mr. Truitt is now the sole owner of the business, which he has developed into large proportions. The storage plant is situated at No. 28 East Chestnut Street, and its dimensions are 57x112½ feet and 97x112½ feet, the offices being located in the same building. The stock, which includes all manner of trees, fruits, bushes, shrubs, vegetables, flowers and plants, is grown all around Chanute, and is shipped all over the United States, the Chanute Nurseries having a lively market in practically every state in the Union. Many of these products are grown on Mr. Truitt's own farm, a handsome, well-cultivated tract of 120 acres, lying two miles south of Chanute, where he has all the latest improvements and most modern machinery. He has experimented in the growing of various products and has been successful in producing some new varieties.

Mr. Truitt is a republican, but not an office seeker, although he has always been ready to contribute of his services in the advancement of public-spirited movements. He is affiliated fraternally with Cedar Lodge No. 103, Ancient Free and Accepted Masons; Chanute Chapter No. 21, Royal Arch Masons; Chanute Commandery No. 44, Knights Templar; and Chanute Lodge No. 806, Benevolent and Protective Order of Elks.

Mr. Truitt was married at Emporia, Kansas, in 1906, to Miss Nellie C. Smith, daughter of W. B. and Josephine (Truitt) Smith, of Emporia, the latter being a distant relative of the Truitt family of this notice. Mr. Smith is a foreman in the employ of L. W. Lewis, a bridge contractor. Mr. and Mrs. Truitt reside in their pleasant home at No. 503 N. Highland Avenue.

HARRY C. WEIBLE. When it is stated that Harry C. Weible moved out from Pennsylvania to Independence about thirteen years ago, it will be readily

surmised that he is connected in some way with the oil or gas industry, and he is in fact one of the large oil producers in the Mid-Continent field and from his headquarters at Coffeyville directs extensive operations not only in Southern Kansas but in Oklahoma and Texas.

Practically reared in the oil fields of Western Pennsylvania, he is the son of a veteran of the industry. Mr. Weible was born in Allegheny City, Pennsylvania, January 16, 1858. He was still a child when his grandfather Weible died. His grandfather was born in Allegheny County in the very early days, and died there after a career as a farmer. He married a Miss Ferguson, who died in Allegheny County, and of their children the only one now living is William Weible, an uncle of Harry C., and a retired oil producer at Allegheny City. The Weibles came originally from Germany and settled in Pennsylvania in colonial times.

Isaac Weible, father of Harry C., was born in Allegheny County, Pennsylvania, in 1821. He was reared and married in his native locality, took up farming as his first vocation, and with the discoveries of oil in the western counties of his native state he entered the fields as a producer and operator in Venango and Butler Counties. For many years his home was at Karns City in Butler County, where he died in 1894. He held a number of town offices there, and was an active republican, and was one of the leading members and supporters of the Methodist Church. Isaac Weible married Catherine Myers, who was born in Allegheny County, Pennsylvania, in 1819 and died at Karns City in 1903. George, the oldest of their children, now a resident of Mannington, West Virginia, for many years was a gauger along the pipe lines for the Standard Oil Company. Charles, the second in age, is an oil producer in Butler County, Pennsylvania. Thomas lives at Greenville, Pennsylvania, has also been in the oil business, has several large farms, and is one of the noted horsemen in his section of the state. Mary first married Dr. Beard, a meat dealer and a traveling representative for a wholesale meat house, who died when quite young; for her second husband she married Mr. Adams, who was a railroad contractor and is also deceased, and she now makes her home at Allegheny City, Pennsylvania. The fifth in age is Harry C. Weible of Coffeyville. William H. lives near Toledo, Ohio, and is foreman for the Ohio Oil Company. Margaret is the wife of D. C. Macon, an oil producer in California. Jennie married A. D. Sutton, a resident of Lima, Ohio, and a buyer for the Standard Oil Company.

With nearly all the members of his family in some way connected with the oil industry, Harry C. Weible grew up in the atmosphere of the oil fields of Western Pennsylvania, and at the age of fifteen left the public schools of Venango County and began as a pumper. With experience he developed into a contractor and later was a producer in Butler and McKean Counties of Pennsylvania and also in the fields around Lima, Ohio. In 1903 he came to Independence, Kansas, but after a short time moved in July of that year to Coffeyville, where he has since had his home and business headquarters. At the present time Mr. Weible has productions in the Ohio fields, in the Kansas and Oklahoma fields, and some gas interests in Texas. He owns a farm in Oklahoma and has some oil wells upon it.

Mr. Weible is president of the Texas Central Gas

Company, of the Robert Packing Machine Company of Coffeyville, is vice president of the People's State Bank of Coffeyville, and is manager of the Sequoyah Oil Company, of the Condry Oil Company, the Weible and Coovan Oil Company and the Weible and Hoffman Oil Company.

His home is at 603 Elm Street in Coffeyville. Mr. Weible is a republican, a member of the Methodist Church, and his fraternal affiliations are with Keystone Lodge No. 102, Ancient Free and Accepted Masons at Coffeyville, Coffeyville Chapter No. 89, Royal Arch Masons, Lochinvar Commandery No. 52, Knights Templar, and Mirzah Temple of the Mystic Shrine at Pittsburg, Kansas.

In December, 1884, at Franklinville, New York, Mr. Weible married Miss Paula Hazzard, daughter of John and Ellen (Latham) Hazzard. Both her parents are deceased and her father was in the lumber business. Mr. and Mrs. Weible have two children. Fern finished her education in the Hardin College for Young Women at Mexico, Missouri, and is now the wife of Leonard Hoffman, a resident of Little Rock, Arkansas, where he is chief clerk to the superintendent of the Iron Mountain Railroad. Merl, a resident of Coffeyville, graduated from Baker University, attended the law department of the Kansas State University at Lawrence, where he took his LL. B. degree in 1915, and while building up a practice at Coffeyville is also assisting his father in the oil business.

RUFUS E. CABLE was born in Pittsburgh, Pennsylvania. He came to Kansas City, Missouri, in 1856, and was employed as a clerk in the establishment of W. E. Proctor, who was the proprietor of a general store. The store of Mr. Proctor and all other business houses in Kansas City, Missouri, were at that time on the levee along the south bank of the Missouri River. The residences were scattered about on the hills back of the business houses. At that time M. J. Payne was mayor of Kansas City, Missouri. Mr. Cable in 1865 moved to Wyandotte, now Kansas City, Kansas, where he has continued to reside to the present time. Wyandotte was then a small village and Mr. Cable has lived to see it become the metropolis of Kansas, with a population of more than 100,000. He has been a factor in this growth and has done his full share of the work required to build up the city.

Mr. Cable has been active in politics, and was a member of the board of education and the city council. For many years he was justice of the peace and he served as mayor of Wyandotte. For several years he was probate judge of Wyandotte County. He was a good officer in every position he held. Since he retired from the office of probate judge he has not been engaged in any regular business, but has been employed in looking after his property in Kansas City, Kansas, and Wyandotte County.

He has always been outspoken on any question affecting the destiny of Kansas City, Kansas, and the public interests generally. He is one of the most respected citizens of the city and enjoys the confidence of the community.

EDWARD R. CALLENDER, proprietor of the Callender Printing Company of Kansas City, Kansas, has lived in this state for over thirty-five years and for a quarter of a century has been a resident of Kansas City, Kansas. He learned printing when a boy, and his name is widely known through his connection with the printing trade and also at different times as a publisher of newspapers.

Mr. Callender was born at Berlin, Wisconsin, August 31, 1867, the third in a family of six children whose parents were John H. and Marian (Russell) Callender. His father was a native of Canada and his mother of New York State. The grandparents came from Scotland, lived in Canada, and afterwards moved to Wisconsin. John H. Callender grew up in Ripon, a city where the first political organization took the name republican and thus gave substantial claim to the distinction of being the birthplace of the party. John H. Callender became a dentist. He practiced at Ripon for a number of years and then seeking a change of climate and a more active life he came to Kansas when the Osage District was opened. In 1878 he located near Anthony when only a few houses stood on the townsite. He brought his household furniture and lumber from Wisconsin, carrying the goods on a wagon sixty-five miles to Harper County. He took up a claim of 160 acres, proved up on it, but as a result of several years of successive drought he had to abandon farming and resume his practice as a dentist. Later he sold his farm and gave his entire attention to his practice at Anthony. He finally retired to Wichita and died there in 1903. His widow died in 1909. Doctor Callender was a republican, was a member of the Masonic order and was always interested in the welfare of schools and churches. He was a Methodist, was trustee of his church many years and also superintendent of the Sunday school.

Edward R. Callender attended school in Wisconsin and had later the advantages of the dugout schools at Anthony. He was also a student in the Wellington High School. It was a mere accident that he formed a connection which became permanent with the printing trade. Without any specific intentions as to the future he worked for a time as a printer's devil on the Belle Plaine News, and having learned the trade put in three years there and since then has never been long separated from printing and newspaper work. At Anthony he worked on the Anthony Republican, and in 1887 established with a partner named Markwell the Anthony Free Press. This paper was published daily. Anthony was then enjoying a boom, and the paper was highly successful. After two years he sold his interest and having realized that Kansas City, Kansas, had exceptional advantages of location he moved to that city and in 1890 opened a printing shop on Minnesota Avenue. He began there with modest equipment and on a small scale, but from year to year increased the business and enlarged his service until the was competing on terms of equality with the larger printing shops of the city. Associated with the Greer boys he established the Kansas City Tribune. He operated the daily for about a year and then sold to Judge Charles E. Lobdell. From the Tribune he once more devoted his attention to the printing business opening a new shop on Sixth Street in the basement of the Husted Building. His plant and facilities were enlarged from time to time and he finally removed to his present location at 708-710 North Sixth Street.

In October, 1891, Mr. Callender married Louise Cable of Wyandotte County, daughter of Judge R. E. Cable, elsewhere referred to. They are the parents of four children: Harold, who is assistant city editor of the Kansas City Times; Leonard, teller in the People's National Bank of Kansas City, Kansas; Louise, now in high school; and Edward, a pupil in the graded schools.

Mr. Callender in Masonry has attained the thirty-second degree of Scottish Rite, belongs to the Mystic Shrine at Leavenworth, to the Knights of Pythias, the Ancient Order of United Workmen, the Modern Woodmen of America, and the Maccabees. He has held all the chairs in the Knights of Pythias. He is well known in business and social circles of the city, is a member of the Mercantile Club, a former director of the Rotary Club, and belongs to the Union Club. The only public office he ever consented to accept was clerk of Circuit Court, the result of an appointment by Governor Hoch. He remained in the office one year. He is a republican and is an active member of the Christian Science Church.

WALTER GORDON CADMUS is one of the prominent business men of Parsons. He has had a long and active career in varied lines of enterprise, but now for many years has been a factor in the Parsons Cold Storage and Crystal Ice Company, of which he is secretary, treasurer and general manager.

His Cadmus ancestry had its original seat in Holland. His great-grandfather emigrated from Holland and settled at Plainfield, New Jersey, soon after the close of the Revolutionary war. His Grandfather Andrew L. Cadmus was born at Plainfield, New Jersey, in 1809, became a physician and surgeon, practiced for many years in New York City, and while still a resident there he died at Saratoga Springs, New York, in 1881.

Daniel F. Cadmus, a son of this physician and father of the ' Parsons business man, was born in Hoboken, New Jersey, in 1834. He spent his early life in Hoboken, New York City, Jersey City, and that vicinity. In 1854 he moved to Henry, Illinois, located on a farm there, and was married. He subsequently moved to Boone County, Iowa, where he conducted a sheep ranch. His business interests took him to the states of Illinois, Missouri, Alabama, Virginia, and in 1869 he paid his first visit to Kansas. He remained in the state from 1873 until 1881, when he went to Alabama, and his death occurred in 1888 at Sunnyside, Arkansas. He was independent in politics and a member of the Presbyterian Church. He married Phoebe A. Hoagland, who was born in 1830 in Plainfield, New Jersey. She died at Selma, Alabama, in 1882. Of her children Charles, the oldest, died at the age of twenty-six in Pratt County, Kansas, where he was a rancher. Mary J. married J. E. Mays and they live on their ranch at Garden Plain, Kansas. The third in age is Walter G. Harriet C. is the wife of James H. Weigley, a merchant at Richland Center, Wisconsin.

Walter Gordon Cadmus was born October 27, 1862, while his parents lived in Boone County, Iowa. He grew up and gained his early education in different localities. From 1873 to 1877 his parents lived at Sedgewick in Harvey County, Kansas, and while there he attended the public schools. He received a high school education, finishing his schooling in Iola and Oswego, Kansas.

On leaving school in 1881 he became clerk for the Oswego Coal Company and was located at Weir for two and a half years. The next five and a half years he spent on a ranch in Pratt County. For one year the Corbin Banking Company of New York employed him as a special inspector of the company's loans in Arkansas and South Carolina. Mr. Cadmus then resumed the coal business, and for four and a half years was connected with the Kansas & Texas Coal Company at Leavenworth.

His home and business headquarters have been in Parsons since August 1, 1895. For a number of years he was connected with the coal and grain firm of Busby & Smith Company. On January 1, 1904, he engaged in the ice business as part owner of the Parsons Cold Storage and Crystal Ice Company. He is one of the principal stockholders in this corporation, and is its secretary, treasurer and manager. The company was organized in 1892, and had a capital of $50,000 until 1905, when it was increased to $75,000, with corresponding enlargement of the capacity of the plant. From 1892 to 1903 the company supplied ice all over Southeastern Kansas and Northeastern Oklahoma. Since 1903 the local business has taken practically the entire output. The company now manufactures 70 tons of ice a day, and has storage capacity for 1,200 tons. The plant is at North Boulevard and Lincoln Avenue and the offices are at 200 North Central Avenue. The officers of the Parsons Cold Storage and Crystal Ice Company are: C. A. Roter, president; J. F. Steele, vice president; and Mr. Cadmus secretary, treasurer and manager.

Besides his own home at 321 South Twenty-fifth Street Mr. Cadmus owns a dwelling house at 1824 Felix Avenue. Mr. Cadmus is a progressive in politics. While living in Pratt County he served a year as township trustee of Richland Township and in Parsons has been a member of the board of education for 3½ years. He was on the board when the white and colored children were separated in the public schools. He belongs to the Parsons Commercial Club, and fraternally is affiliated with Parsons Lodge, No. 117, Ancient Free and Accepted Masons, Parsons Lodge, No. 12, Ancient Order United Workmen, and Parsons Lodge, No. 62, Anti-Horse Thief Association.

In 1885 at Independence, Missouri, he married Miss Sarah E. Crawley, daughter of D. S. and Sarah Crawley. Her father, now deceased, was a minister of the Latter Day Saints Church. Mr. and Mrs. Cadmus have four children. . Clara, a graduate of the Parsons High School, is still at home with her parents. Daniel H., who graduated in mining and engineering at the University of Kansas, is now superintendent of mines for the Central Coal and Coke Company at Huntington, Arkansas. Charles E., who resides at 2316 Belmont Avenue in Parsons is assistant cashier at the local offices of the International Harvester Company. Walter G., Jr., is a student in the University of Kansas, taking a course in architectural engineering.

W. W. KANEY. In the career of W. W. Kaney, of Chanute, there is found an excellent illustration of the rewards that may be attained through industry and perseverance, for his has been a life in which achievements have been self gained and in which outside assistance has played no part. With but an indifferent education he started out in the world to make his own way when he was but a lad, and has steadfastly worked his way to a position of prominence as one of the leading oil producers of this part of Kansas.

Mr. Kaney was born June 4, 1867, near Cuba, Cattaraugus County, New York, on an Indian reservation of 160 acres, and is a son of William and Mary (Dunkin) Kaney. His grandfather was Seraphim Kaney, who was born in Germany and came to the United States in young manhood, locating in Pennsylvania, where he passed the remainder of his life in agricultural pursuits, and died on his farm 2½ miles from Saltsburg, that state, in 1870. William Kaney was born in 1836, at Tarentum, Pennsylvania, and was there reared and received a public school education, and when still a young man went to Cattaraugus County, New York, where he was married. He was one of the pioneers of the oil industry in the United States, having drilled the third well ever sunk for oil in this country, and followed the drilling of wells in New York, Pennsylvania, Georgia and Alabama, Governor's Island, New York, and in Bohemia and Hungary, Europe. The entire active period of his career was devoted to the same line of business, but he is now retired and lives at Saltsburg, Pennsylvania, where he has a comfortable home. Mr. Kaney is a member of the Masonic fraternity. During the Civil war he enlisted in a Pennsylvania volunteer infantry regiment, with which he served for eleven months, taking part in several engagements and in the siege of Vicksburg. He married Mary Dunkin, who was born near Cuba, Cattaraugus County, New York, in 1846, and died at Titusville, Pennsylvania, in 1894, and they became the parents of three children, namely: W. W., of this review; Harry, who is a constructing engineer of electrical and power plants for the Westinghouse Electric Company, at Staten Island, New York; and Susie, who is the wife of Bert White, a traveling salesman with headquarters on a farm in Michigan.

W. W. Kaney received his education in the public schools of Titusville, Pennsylvania, which he left at the age of thirteen years. While this completed his school training, through observation and reading he has accumulated a vast store of worth-while knowledge, so that he is today a well-educated man. In his youth he was ambitious and industrious, anxious to get out among the world's workers, and when only thirteen years of age left home and since that time has made his own way. His first employment was in a barrel factory, where, for long hours, he was paid a wage of 70 cents a day. He held this position until the barrel factory was destroyed by fire, when he entered upon a career in which he has since won prominence and success. His first connection with the oil business was a pumper of wells, for which hard labor he received $15 per month, but as he was only fifteen years old at the time, he considered his earnings good. From that position he rapidly rose to others, and remained in the Pennsylvania fields until 1892, when he went to Europe, and for twenty-two months was in Bohemia and Hungary, where he worked by the month. Returning to America in the fall of 1893, he drilled in Indiana and Ohio, and in January, 1896, took up his residence in Kansas, where his fortune awaited him. His first location here was with the Kansas Division of the Forest Oil Company, at Neodesha, and he continued with this concern until he began contracting on his own account in 1898, in which year he came to Chanute. Mr. Kaney continued contract drilling until 1912, and since that time has been a producer. He has twenty-seven oil wells producing and eleven gas wells between the Kansas, Missouri & Texas Railroad and the Neosho River, east of Chanute. This lease of over 1,200 acres, all proven, is the nearest field to Chanute of any of the gas and oil producing properties. He has also leases west of Chanute and to the north, in Allen County, and is known as one of the most thoroughly informed oil men in this part of the country. As a business man Mr. Kaney has always been held in high esteem by his associates, by reason of the straightforward manner in which he has conducted his affairs.

Mr. Kaney's present residence at No. 602 West Main Street, is a modern home, and is made interesting and attractive by a fine yard, exceptionally well kept, in which he has a long series of cement tanks, in which he grows lilies and breeds goldfish. Here he has sixteen varieties of pond lilies, both the tender and hardy, the night and day bloomers, a rare and interesting collection that has been viewed with much interest by botanists from all over the country. He also breeds a new species of goldfish, a cross between the Ribbontail and the Japanese Fringe-tail. Here he raises also the Egyptian lotus and the water hyacinth, the latter known as "the million dollar weed" because the United States Government spent in the neighborhood of $1,000,000 in trying to rid the St. John's River of this flower. Mr. Kaney has from 100 to 200 pond lily blossoms per day from May until the frost kills them.

Mr. Kaney is independent in politics and has never cared for public life. He is a life member of Chanute Lodge No. 806, Benevolent and Protective Order of Elks. Mr. Kaney always gives his support to measures calculated to aid the community, and is a friend of education and religious movements.

In 1887, at Perry, New York, Mr. Kaney was married to Miss Jennie L. Hack, daughter of Mr. and Mrs. Adam Hack, the former of whom is a retired tinsmith of Perry, New York, while the latter is deceased. To Mr. and Mrs. Kaney there has been born one daughter: Laura May, a graduate of the Chanute High School and an expert bookkeeper, who resides with her parents.

PRATT BARNDOLLAR, a cattle dealer at Coffeyville, has some very interesting connections with the country and the people of Southern Kansas and of Old Indian Territory.

His father was the late J. J. Barndollar, who built up by energetic business methods a large estate consisting of mercantile, manufacturing, mining, banking and other business properties, and was one of the leading men of his time in Southern Kansas and Northern Oklahoma. J. J. Barndollar was born at Everett, Bedford County, Pennsylvania, in 1842, and came west when a young man. He arrived at Humboldt, Kansas, in 1869, and in 1871 went into Osage country of Indian Territory around Pawhuska. He afterwards lived at Parker, Kansas, and at Coffeyville from the establishment of that town. He was a merchant and Indian trader, and for a number of years was connected with some of the principal trading stores in the northern part of old Indian Territory. He was a member of the firm of Barndollar, Bartles & Gibson at Pawhuska; of Barndollar, Bartles & Neilson at Claremore; and of J. J. Barndollar & Company at Nowata, Oklahoma. He was also president of the Coffeyville Furniture Company, president of the A. P. Boswell Hardware Company, and director in the Condon National Bank. He died October 23, 1904, in New Mexico, while traveling for his health in that state and in Texas.

The late J. J. Barndollar was a republican in politics, and was affiliated with Keystone Lodge No. 102, Ancient Free and Accepted Masons at Coffeyville, with Topeka Consistory of the thirty-second degree Scottish Rite and with Abdallah Temple of the Nobles of the Mystic Shrine at Leavenworth. He was a soldier throughout the Civil war, serving as a lieutenant in a company of Pennsylvania Infantry.

J. J. Barndollar married Nonie Pratt, who is now living at Coffeyville and is executrix of the large estate left by her late husband. She was born in

Leavenworth, Kansas, and is a quarter-blood Delaware Indian. She has a close relationship with some of the most prominent members of that tribe. Her grandfather Maj. J. G. Pratt was Indian agent at Piper, Wyandotte County, Kansas, for the Delaware Indians and of the Wyandotte tribes. She is also, a granddaughter of Rev. Charles Journeycake, the famous chief of the Delawares. She received her education in Leavenworth and Shepardson College of Granville, Ohio. Mrs. J. J. Barndollar's mother is now Mrs. N. M. Bartles of Dewey, Oklahoma. Bartlesville, Oklahoma, was named for Mr. Bartles, and all these families, the Journeycakes, Bartles and Pratts were very prominent in both early and late history of Kansas and Northern Oklahoma. Mrs. Barndollar is now Mrs. A. H. Gibson, and lives at the old homestead at Coffeyville, and has a large estate to look after, including city property, oil lands, and farms. She is a daughter of the American Revolution.

Pratt Barndollar, only son and child of the late J. J. Barndollar, was born at Coffeyville April 23, 1891, and resides at 301 West Eighth Street, just east of the old homestead where he was born and reared.

He received his early education in the Coffeyville public schools, attending the high school, the Culver Military Academy in Indiana and the William Jewell College at Liberty, Missouri, leaving school in 1909 to take up an active business life. Since then he has handled cattle and also oil interests, and has assisted his mother in the management of the estate.

He is an independent republican, is a member of the Baptist Church, and stands high in Masonry, being affiliated with Keystone Lodge No. 102, Ancient Free and Accepted Masons at Coffeyville, Coffeyville Chapter No. 89, Royal Arch Masons, Lochinvar Commandery No. 152, Knights Templar, Fort Scott Consistory of the Scottish Rite No. 4 at Fort Scott, and Mirzah Temple of the Mystic Shrine at Pittsburg, Kansas. He is also a member of the Coffeyville Commercial Club, and has a life membership in the Kansas Society of the Sons of the American Revolution and is the lineal descendant of six revolutionary ancestors.

SAMUEL BOWMAN, now of Coffeyville, where he is engaged in the real estate, insurance and loan business with his sons, is a Kansas resident of nearly thirty-five years and was long prominent in Labette County, where he served two terms as probate judge.

His Bowman ancestors were German people who came to Pennsylvania in Colonial times. His grandfather, Benjamin Bowman, a native of Pennsylvania, was a farmer and cabinet maker, also a minister of the Dunkard Church, and spent many years in the Shenandoah Valley of Virginia, where he died some years before Judge Bowman was born.

It was in the valley of the Shenandoah, a mile from Harrisonburg, Virginia, that Samuel Bowman was born May 18, 1846. His father, John Bowman, was born in the same locality in 1790, and spent his life in that famous valley, engaged in farming and stock raising. He died at Harrisonburg in 1873. Though a resident of Virginia he was not in sympathy with the South on the issue of slavery, was a stanch Union man, and a whig and republican in politics. He was an active member of the Dunkard Church. John Bowman married Rebecca Wine, who was born in the Shenandoah Valley in 1802, and

died on the old farm near Harrisonburg in 1872. A brief record of the children is as follows: Daniel, who was a Virginia farmer and died in that state; Catherine, who died in the Shenandoah Valley as the wife of Joseph Miller, also deceased. Elizabeth, who died in Virginia in 1915, and her husband Daniel Thomas, who was a farmer, is also deceased; John W. and Benjamin were both Virginia farmers and died there: Isaac is living on a farm near Harrisonburg; Joseph, died in Virginia; Susanna resides in Eastern Virginia, the widow of Abram Hinegardner, who was a farmer; and the ninth and youngest of the family is Judge Samuel Bowman.

As a boy he attended the public schools near Harrisonburg, and also lived for a time at Hagerstown, Maryland, where he worked on a farm and attended school in winter. In 1864 he moved to the vicinity of Dayton, Ohio, and spent four years on a farm there. While there he married, and afterwards took his wife to Illinois and settled on a tract of raw prairie in 1869 and developed that as a good farm before leaving it. After twelve years as an Illinois farmer, Judge Bowman came to Kansas in 1882, spent the first year in farming in Crawford County, and then moved to Labette County.

Judge Bowman had a farm in Labette County and occupied it until 1904, but has since sold it. In 1904 the citizens of Labette County elected him probate judge and during the next four years he gave a careful and conscientious administration of the many delicate responsibilities imposed by this office. In the spring of 1909 after leaving office, he went East and for nearly a year visited the scenes of his early youth and relatives in Virginia and elsewhere.

Since 1910 Judge Bowman has lived in Coffeyville and has been associated with his sons, W. G. and A. C. Bowman in the real estate and insurance business. Their offices are located in the Traction Building on Eighth Street. Besides city property they handle farm lands over a large district from Coffeyville to Colorado and into Oklahoma. They represent a number of insurance companies, and also handle an extensive volume of loans.

Judge Bowman during his residence in Labette County served twenty years as a member of the school board, and also filled the various township offices there, including justice of the peace. He is a republican, is affiliated with Lodge No. 279, Ancient Order United Workmen at Coffeyville and is an active member of the Commercial Club.

In 1868 near Dayton, Ohio, he married Miss E. J. Roadarmer, daughter of William and Barbara Roadarmer, both of whom are now deceased. Her father was a farmer. The oldest child of Mr. and Mrs. Bowman is Lula, who resides at Coffeyville, the widow of S. C. Neale, who was connected with the Kansas Land Company of Coffeyville. Ray, the oldest son died at the age of twenty-three years in Labette County, after he had begun a very promising career. The two younger sons W. G. and A. C. are both associated in business with their father as already stated.

DAVID S. GILMORE has been connected with the publishing and editing of newspapers in Southern Kansas for a quarter of a century or more. For upwards of twenty years he has been proprietor and editor of the Northern Lyon County Journal at Allen, and is one of the leading citizens of that town.

He is a son of one of the very prominent pioneers

and early builders of Emporia, the late D. S. Gilmore. D. S. Gilmore was born in County Dundee, Scotland, in 1841, a son of William Gilmore, who was a cabinet maker and who brought his family to America, living for a time in Rochester, New York, and in 1858 settling among the pioneers of Southern Kansas. D. S. Gilmore was also connected with the printing trade, and as a pressman helped move the first power printing press up the river to Leavenworth and thence to Topeka, this being the first press of the kind brought into Kansas. There were no railroads in the state at the time. For some time D. S. Gilmore was joint owner with Mr. Statler of the Emporia News. At the first call for troops he enlisted in a Kansas regiment of infantry and was a Union soldier until the close of the war, and his widow now receives a pension for his services. Following the war he was in the newspaper business at Emporia and later for twenty years was in the furniture and undertaking business. He was also associated with W. T. Soden in the manufacture of furniture, their factory being located on the river at Emporia.

D. S. Gilmore also took a prominent part in public affairs. He served as county clerk of Lyon County and as commissioner, also filled the office of mayor of Emporia, and was one of the leading republicans in this section of the state. He was a member of the Christian Church and of the Masonic order and the Independent Order of Odd Fellows. He married Margaret L. Brown, who was born in Indiana in 1846 and still lives in Emporia. Their children were: Jean, wife of William White, a hardware salesman living at Seattle, Washington; Stella, wife of W. H. Brooks, who for the past thirty years has been a grocery merchant at Emporia; Anna, wife of R. H. Lewis, a merchant at Kansas City, Kansas; Helen, wife of Eugene W. McGain, an attorney at Pawhuska, Oklahoma; David S.; John, a salesman for W. H. Brooks Grocery Company at Emporia; and Margaret, wife of E. C. Ryan, secretary and treasurer of the Mutual Building and Loan Association of Emporia.

David S. Gilmore was born at Emporia, August 16, 1868, and gained his early education in the public schools, being graduated from the Emporia High School in 1888. He took up the printing trade, and for a time was on the Emporia Republican for C. V. Eskridge, and was then with the Emporia Gazette, when it was owned by J. R. Graham, and afterwards when W. Y. Morgan, now lieutenant governor of Kansas, was its proprietor.

In 1896 Mr. Gilmore entered journalism as an independent profession, establishing a paper called the Admire Journal at Admire, but two years later he removed the plant to Allen and changed the name to the Northern Lyon County Journal. This is one of the influential newspapers of Lyon County and has a circulation over a tier of six townships in the northern part of the county and also goes into many homes and other adjacent counties. The offices of the plant are on West Fifth Street. It is a weekly paper and is independent in politics.

Mr. Gilmore himself is a member of the socialist party. He attends the Methodist Church and belongs to the International Typographical Union. In 1892, at Emporia, he married Miss Minnie L. Thomas, daughter of Samuel and Margaret Thomas, both of whom are now deceased and who were of Welsh descent. Her father was a stone mason by trade. Mr. and Mrs. Gilmore have six children: Phyllis, wife of C. M. Certain, who is connected with the street railway company at Emporia; D. Sam, Jr., a printer for the Sanders-Cook Printing Company at Pittsburg, Kansas; Dorothy, a freshman in the State Normal School at Emporia; Helen, a freshman in the Allen High School; and Clarissa and William.

WILLIAM HENRY CRADDOCK. As the greatest calamity ever suffered by Kansas City, Kansas, was probably the flood of 1903, that year will always be memorable in the city's history. Another event associated with that year was the death of William Henry Craddock, who had just completed a service of two years in the office of mayor. Mr. Craddock was stricken on March 2, 1903, and his death occurred on the 4th of the same month at the Savoy Hotel in Kansas City, Missouri. He was mourned by the entire city, and never any similar occasion in the city has brought out such a tremendous concourse of citizens of all classes to pay respect to one who was taken away from the midst of a valuable service and position of influence. He was a man of rare ability, was a splendid type of business man, and had a bigness of heart and soul commensurate with his material activities.

His birth occurred on a farm near Louisville, Kentucky, December 25, 1851. His parents were William W. and Edna (Smith) McGaryhill Craddock. Edna Smith McGaryhill was the granddaughter of one of the signers of the Declaration of Independence and a leading figure in the revolutionary period of American history. Mr. Craddock's father and grandfather bore the name William W., both were successful lawyers, and they also rendered distinguished service on the bench. Mayor Craddock's father was for some years a law partner with the famous Joe Cannon of Illinois.

When William H. Craddock was ten years of age his parents removed to the Craddock settlement at Mattoon, Illinois. They made the journey on a river boat, the steamship Starlight, which sank in the middle of the Mississippi River, and the family had a very narrow escape from death.

Mr. Craddock was educated in the public schools of Mattoon and also attended a college in Illinois. In 1870, when nineteen years of age, he accompanied his four brothers out to Wichita, Kansas. He soon secured a clerkship in the courthouse of Sedgwick County, and was the youngest employe of the county government. Mayor Craddock's father had seen active service in the Mexican war as adjutant general.

William Henry Craddock came to Kansas City, Kansas, in 1880, six years before the city of that name was incorporated. At 200 North James Street he established the Craddock Mercantile Company, and thus founded a business which until 1903 was one of the largest of its kind in either of the two adjoining cities. He subsequently brought his brothers into the business and he himself removed to Aurora, Illinois, where he bought a large ranch of 2,700 acres. There he found profit and pleasure in the management of his farm and in the raising of fine livestock.

Returning to Kansas City, Kansas, in 1896, Mr. Craddock became president of the Western Realty Company, an office he retained until his death. In all his work he was characterized by large ideas, a practical efficiency in carrying out his plans, and he brought about some of the largest real estate deals in both the Kansas cities. At one time he owned all the property from Twelfth to Eighteenth streets on the right side of Grand Avenue in Kansas City, Missouri, but this was lost through litigation.

On December 20, 1881, he married Mary Elizabeth Cuthbert. They were married in Wisconsin, but Mrs. Craddock was born in Ohio and her parents were farmers in that state and later in Illinois. Mr. and Mrs. Craddock had three children: Harry Hubert, William Henry, Jr., and Laura Cuthbert. Politically Mr. Craddock was a democrat. When he was elected mayor of Kansas City, Kansas, in 1901, he was given the compliment of the largest majority ever given a candidate for that office. The choice was well justified, for he distinguished himself by the rare executive ability in which he handled the administration of the municipality, during the next two years. In 1902 Mr. Craddock was an unsuccessful candidate on the democratic ticket for the office of governor of Kansas. His name was again discussed at a later time for the same office, but he refused to allow it to be considered. He had attained Supreme Honorary Thirty-third degree in Scottish Rite Masonry and was a member of many orders and organizations. He was also a member and officer in St. Paul's Episcopal Church, and one of the liberal contributors to its support.

JOHN MAHLAN MOORE has long been prominently identified with financial affairs in Kansas, was one of the leading bankers of Wichita and assisted in the organization of many banks in that section of the state and remained a resident of Wichita until a few years ago when he was translated to a higher sphere of banking in the metropolis of the Missouri Valley at Kansas City. Mr. Moore is now vice president of the Southwest National Bank of Commerce of Kansas City, Missouri.

His successful career in banking affairs in the Middle West is not due to a wealthy or influential environment as a boy. Like many of the eminent business men of America he was born on a farm. His birth occurred in Shelby County, Kentucky, October 31, 1859. He was the second in a family of eight children. His parents were Thomas H. and Mary Elizabeth (Weekley) Moore, both of whom were natives of Kentucky, their ancestors having come into that state from Virginia. John M. Moore had a country training and only the advantages of the common schools and for two years an academic course. At the age of seventeen he left the farm to become clerk in a store. He remained with one firm at Shelbyville for ten years, part of the time as bookkeeper. There he laid the foundation of his business experience.

Finally a farm loan company felt such confidence in his ability as to employ him to go to Kansas and represent them. As their representative he located in Wichita and for five years had the supervision of his company's loans on farm property. He was at Wichita during a period of years marked by many rapid and dramatic if not tragic reversals of prosperity, and he knew that section of Kansas at its low tide and its high tide.

In 1892 he was elected cashier of the Fourth National Bank of Wichita. When he took that position the Fourth National had deposits of about $28,000. It was a successful bank in a way, and reflected at the time the low average of material prosperity in that part of Kansas. Mr. Moore remained its cashier until 1908. He had the pleasure of witnessing the remarkable growth and expansion of the surrounding country, the development of Wichita as a great industrial center, and he assisted in the corresponding growth and development of the Fourth National Bank. When he left the institution its deposits aggregated $3,000,000. It is now one of the most substantial financial institutions in Kansas.

In 1908 Mr. Moore was elected cashier and vice

president of the Southwest National Bank of Kansas City, Missouri. He was one of the Charter members and organizers of this bank. In 1912 its resources were merged with those of the Southwest National Bank of Commerce, and since then Mr. Moore has been first vice president of the larger institution.

Among the other banks in which Mr. Moore has had a part in organization or management are the following: Benton State Bank, State Bank of Goddard, Valley Center State Bank, Garden Plains State Bank, Pechi State Bank, Furley State Bank, Murdock State Bank, Bank of Peck, Florence State Bank, and he still retains interests in some of these institutions. Mr. Moore also owns a Texas ranch of several thousands of acres.

He has long been identified with Masonry, is a life member of the Scottish Rite Consistory and the Mystic Shrine and a life member of the Benevolent and Protective Order of Elks. He has held the office of treasurer in the various Masonic bodies and was one of the organizers and was treasurer and director of the Wichita Perpetual Building and Loan Association. While living in Wichita he belonged to the First Baptist Church, was one of its active members, and gave his liberal support and encouragement to every social, religious and public movement in that city. Politically he is a democrat, but has never held any office.

Mr. Moore was married July 3, 1893, to Mrs. Eva (Chenault) Stinson. Her first husband was J. L. Stinson, a prominent business man at Wichita. By that marriage Mrs. Moore has two children, Harry and Douglas.

RUFUS J. HILL. There are many points of historical interest pertinent to the personal career and ancestral record of this venerable pioneer citizen who is now living practically retired in his pleasant home at Independence, Montgomery County. On both the paternal and maternal sides he is a scion of fine old American colonial stock and individually he has precedence as being one of the pioneer members of the Kansas bar, as well as a broad-minded and public-spirited citizen who has played well his part in connection with the civic and material development and progress of the Sunflower State, within whose borders he has maintained his home for virtually half a century.

Rufus Joel Hill was born in St. Lawrence County, New York, on the 16th of February, 1838, and is a son of William and Anna (Meader) Hill, the former of whom was born in Vermont, in the year 1784, and the latter of whom was born in Rhode Island, in 1792, both having been representatives of families that were founded in New England in the early colonial period of our national history. William Hill was reared and educated in the old Green Mountain State and during the course of a long and active career he was known not only as a business man of marked ability but also as a loyal and liberal citizen of exceptional intellectuality. As a young man he went to the Province of Quebec, Canada, and about the year 1832 he established his residence in St. Lawrence County, New York, where he became a citizen of prominence and influence and where he passed the residue of his long and useful life, his death having there occurred in 1878.

William Hill took a deep interest in public affairs and was aligned with the old whig party until the campaign of 1848, when he espoused the cause of the free soil party, which nominated Martin Van Buren for the presidency of the United States. In the next national campaign, that of 1852, the free soil party virtually changed its title to the free democracy, and as a representative of the latter Mr. Hill was a delegate to the convention that nominated John P. Hale, of New Hampshire, for the presidency. He united with the republican party at the time of its organization and was a delegate to its first national convention, that of 1856, when Gen. John C. Fremont was made its standard-bearer as nominee for the presidency. He attended also, though not as a delegate, the republican national convention of 1860, in Chicago, where Abraham Lincoln was made the presidential nominee. It is worthy of note in this connection that his son, Rufus J., immediate subject of this review, accompanied him to this historic convention. William Hill had the further distinction of having served as a soldier in the war of 1812. As a young man he enlisted as a member of a Vermont volunteer regiment, and with the same he participated in the Battle of Plattsburg, one of the memorable engagements incidental to the second conflict with England. The wife of William Hill long survived and continued to maintain her home in St. Lawrence County, New York, until she too was summoned to the life eternal, in 1892, at the remarkable age of 100 years. Of the children of this union each lived to be over twenty-one years of age. The names of the children are here indicated in the respective order of birth: Betsey, Elmina, William O., Chester, Sarah, Sophronia and Jane are all deceased; Lafayette is a retired farmer and resides at Pine River, Minnesota; Rufus J., of this review, was the next in order of birth and his twin sister, Rua R., is the wife of Angus McMillan, who is still actively engaged in the harness and saddlery business in St. Lawrence County, New York; Patience is deceased; Anna is the wife of George W. Burt, of St. Lawrence County, her husband being a merchant; Andrew is a representative farmer in St. Lawrence County; and Mary is deceased.

Rufus J. Hill acquired his early education in the schools of his native county and in 1856, when eighteen years of age, he went to Minnesota, where he gained a due quota of pioneer experience as a farm employe, in the meanwhile continuing to attend school during the winters. In consonance with his ambitious purpose he finally entered the law department of the celebrated University of Michigan, at Ann Arbor, in which he was graduated as a member of the class of 1865 and from which he received the degree of Bachelor of Laws. For eighteen months thereafter he was engaged in the practice of his profession at Ripon, Wisconsin, and he then, in 1867, came to Kansas and numbered himself among the pioneers of Linn County. In the following year he removed to Fort Scott and became one of the early members of the bar of Bourbon County, where he was associated with W. C. Webb and Gen. Charles W. Blair in the general practice of law until 1871. In the winter of the year last mentioned Mr. Hill initiated the erection of the house that was to constitute his place of residence in Independence, and in the spring of 1872 he here took up his abode. He thus became one of the pioneers of Independence and one of the prominent and influential representatives of his profession in Montgomery County. He built up and long controlled a substantial and important general law practice and he is now one of the most venerable members of the bar of this section of the state. Though he continues to give more

or less attention to the incidental activities of his profession he has been virtually retired from active practice since 1911. He has long been known as a strong trial lawyer and as one specially well fortified as a counselor, his being a broad and accurate knowledge of jurisprudence, as he continued a close student of the law during the many years of his active practice. In 1874 Mr. Hill was retained to look after the legal interests of the Osage Indians of this section, and in this capacity he continued his effective services for the government until the election of President Cleveland in 1884. In 1868 he had been present at the time when the Dunn Creek treaty was effected between the government and the Osage Indians, and this led to his being later engaged in looking after the tribal affairs of the Osage Indians, with a number of the leaders of which tribe he had become acquainted at the treaty mentioned. He continued to be associated with the legal affairs of the Indians until 1911, with secure place in the confidence and respect of the tribe, and since that time he has been practically retired from active professional work. He is well known throughout this section of Kansas and is familiarly designated as Judge Hill.

Mr. Hill has been a resourceful force in connection with political affairs in Kansas, is a stalwart advocate of the principles for which the republican party ever has stood sponsor in a basic way and his first presidential vote was cast for Abraham Lincoln. He formerly maintained active affiliation with Fortitude Lodge, No. 107, Ancient Free and Accepted Masons, at Independence, and also with the local lodge of the Independent Order of Odd Fellows. He is still in active affiliation with the local organizations of the Modern Woodmen of America and the Woodmen of the World, both he and his wife being zealous members of the Presbyterian Church and being numbered among the best known and most honored pioneer citizens of the vigorous and prosperous little city that has represented their home for more than forty years and in which their circle of friends is coincident with that of their acquaintances.

At Ripon, Wisconsin, on the 27th of June, 1867, was solemnized the marriage of Mr. Hill to Miss Annie Hargrave, daughter of William and Emma (Redfern) Hargrave, who were sterling pioneers of that state. Mr. Hargrave was born in Scotland and was a lad of fourteen years at the time of the family removal to the Province of Quebec, Canada, where he was reared to maturity and where his marriage was solemnized. He was identified with mercantile business in the City of Quebec for a number of years and finally removed with his family to the City of Toronto, where his daughter, Annie, wife of the subject of this review, was born. In reference to the ancestry of Mr. Hill it may further be stated that his paternal grandfather, a native of the southern part of England, was sent to the West Indies in the employ of the British government, and at the time of the American Revolution he had started for his old home in England, but the vessel on which he had embarked was captured by the Americans and he was taken to Providence, Rhode Island. He remained loyal to his king but after the close of the Revolution he established his home in Vermont, his death having occurred at Rutland, that state. He was a man of superior education and became a successful teacher in the schools of the old Green Mountain commonwealth.

In conclusion is given a brief record concerning the children of Mr. and Mrs. Hill: Annie is the widow of William Whiteman, who was employed as a telegraph operator in the service of the Atchison, Topeka & Santa Fe Railroad, and she now remains with her venerable parents in their pleasant home in Independence; William died at the age of ten months; Emma is the wife of Harry Brown and their attractive home at Independence was presented to them by Mr. Hill; and Ellen died at the age of seven years.

JOHN C. KIRBY, M. D. For the past fifteen years the name of Dr. John C. Kirby has been increasingly identified with the best tenets of medical and surgical science in the city and vicinity of Cedar Vale. By many of the longest established and most conservative families his skill, resource and obliging temperament have come to be regarded as indispensable, and there exist many who are indebted to him for their restoration to health, happiness and usefulness. Doctor Kirby has the zeal which recognizes no limitations in his profession, and the great unrest which projects him into ever-widening channels of research. His most prized attributes in part are inherited from colonial sires, who braved the perils of early Carolina and whose successors, when duty called, followed the martial fortunes of Washington in the winning of American independence.

John C. Kirby was born in Benton County, Missouri, January 7, 1864, and is a son of Robert and Nancy J. (Davis) Kirby. The earliest American ancestor of the family came to North Carolina from England, prior to the War of the Revolution, in which the great-grandfather of Doctor Kirby fought as a soldier of the Continental line. Robert Kirby, the grandfather of the Doctor, was born in North Carolina, fought as an American soldier during the War of 1812, became a pioneer into Tennessee, and in 1843 moved to Benton County, Missouri, where he passed the remainder of his life as an agriculturist and died before the birth of his grandson.

Robert Kirby was born in 1832, in Tennessee, and was eleven years of age when taken by his parents to Benton County, Missouri. There he was married and engaged in farming, and had just gotten himself nicely started upon an agricultural career when the Civil war came on to interrupt his forward march to prosperity and to end his life. As a son and grandson of soldiers he enlisted in the Home Guards, in Missouri, and in 1865, while endeavoring to assist his comrades in the capture of a band of roving guerrillas, was treacherously shot and killed by these free-booters, who were wearing Federal uniforms. Mr. Kirby was a stanch republican and a faithful member of the Christian Church. He married Nancy J. Davis, who was born in 1833, in Kentucky, and died in 1907, at Sedan, Kansas, and they became the parents of five children: Jacob, who was an employe of the Missouri Pacific Railroad and died in 1899, at Arkansas City, Kansas; Emory D., who was a college professor at Battle Creek, Michigan, for a quarter of a century and died in 1915, in New Mexico, whence he had gone to restore his health; James J., who is manager of the Fitch Manufacturing Company, at Boone, Iowa; Lucinda, of Berrien Springs, Michigan, widow of William Curtis, who was an Adventist minister; and Dr. John C., of this review. The mother of these children was again married, being united with O. H. Sheppard, a farmer of Sedan, Kansas, who died at that place in June, 1912. They became the parents of four children, as follows: O. H., who is engaged

in farming in the vicinity of Geary, Oklahoma; Cornelia, who is the wife of R. Heinebaugh, a retired merchant of Sedan; Alice, who is the wife of Herbert Comer, in the United States mail service at Sheridan, Wyoming; and Annette, who is also married and a resident of Wyoming.

John C. Kirby received his early education in the country schools of Butler County, Kansas, to which locality he had been brought as a child of eight years by his mother and step-father. Subsequently he went to the Kansas State Normal School, at Emporia, where he took the academic course, and following this spent a part of one year at the Kansas University. He then commenced his medical studies at Iowa State University Medical College, from which he was graduated with the class of 1892, and receiving the degree of Doctor of Medicine, and since that time has taken two post-graduate courses in the Chicago Post-Graduate Medical College, one in 1901 and one in 1907.

Doctor Kirby commenced the practice of his profession at Barnston, Nebraska, where he remained two years, and where he passed through a part of his career that is always the most difficult for the young physician. He next changed his field of activity to the community of Verona, Illinois, and remained there for eight years, and in 1901 came to Cedar Vale, where he has since remained. He has been engaged in a general medical and surgical practice at Cedar Vale, and the community has generously and readily responded to his bid for co-operation with commendable promptness and mutual benefit. His offices are located in the Dosbaugh National Bank Building, and his home, which he owns, is on Maple Street. Doctor Kirby belongs to the American Medical Association, the Kansas Medical Society and the Chautauqua County Medical Society, and his high standing among his fellow practitioners is evidenced by the fact that he is president of the last named association. He has been successful financially, as well as professionally, and is the owner of valuable farming interests and oil lands. Formerly he was vice president of the Alene Oil Company, of Oklahoma. A prominent and popular fraternalist, he belongs to Barnston Lodge No. 165, Ancient Free and Accepted Masons, of Barnston, Nebraska; Cedar Lodge, Independent Order of Odd Fellows, of Cedar Vale; Cedar Vale Lodge, Ancient Order of United Workmen; and Cedar Vale Camp, Modern Woodmen of America.

In 1898, at Verona, Illinois, Doctor Kirby was married to Miss Lois Dondanville, who died at Cedar Vale in 1907. They had three children: 'Louise, born November 24, 1899, now a junior at the Cedar Vale High School; Jeane, born November 24, 1899, twin of Louise, and a member of the same high school class; and Evelyn, born in April, 1903, who is attending the graded schools. In 1909, at Winfield, Kansas, Doctor Kirby was married to Miss Bertha McNeely, a daughter of William and Sarah (Houston) McNeely, residents and retired farming people of Cedar Vale. Dr. and Mrs. Kirby are the parents of one son, John Paul, born April 19, 1910. Energy, adaptability, gentleness and sympathy have blazed the way for a gratifying realization of professional ambitions, and by the same token it may be said of Doctor Kirby that much is promised to a man who has, in addition, the maturity, practical experience and broad outlook upon life of fifty-three years.

FREDERICK H. IRELAND. For many years Fort Scott has been recognized as one of the leading commercial centers of Kansas, being splendidly fitted for such preeminence by its location in regard to transportation facilities. This supremacy, which is recognized even in the old eastern cities, has been brought about and maintained by the aggressive business men who have chosen this city as the field of their operations, many of which are far-reaching in their results. Among the men belonging to this class of citizens is Frederick H. Ireland, of the Ireland & Rollins Planing Mills Company, whose career is one typical of the city's progressive spirit and advanced commercialism.

Frederick H. Ireland was born in Clermont County, Ohio, not far from the City of Cincinnati, September 21, 1861, a son of Robert and Sophia (Morgan) Ireland. His father was born in Dublin, Ireland, where he learned the trade of coppersmith, and as a young man emigrated to the United States, where, at Philadelphia, Pennsylvania, he met and married Sophia Morgan. He was of a roving disposition and traveled all over the West on horseback, following his trade and practicing medicine, and finally died at Cincinnati, in 1864, of copper poisoning. Sophia Morgan was born in London, England, and was brought to the United States as a girl, the family coming to this country on a sailing vessel which took two months in crossing the Atlantic. Her father was Thomas Morgan, a young man of family, who had studied medicine in his youth, and who passed away at Philadelphia. After the death of her husband, Mrs. Ireland moved with her children to a farm in Clermont, Ohio, where the elder sons supported the family by farming for several years, and then sold out and went to Illinois, locating on a farm in Macon County. There they remained eight years and then again disposed of their land and went to DeKalb County, Missouri, traveling overland in a covered wagon and arriving at their destination in 1869. Mrs. Ireland made her home with her son, William, in that county from 1869 until 1891, in which year she went to Allen County, Kansas, and there her death occurred. Mrs. Ireland was a devout Baptist, a good Christian woman, who bore her trials bravely and patiently, and who reared her children to lives of honesty and industry. Of the seven children, three are deceased, the survivors being: William, a retired farmer of Bronson, Bourbon County, Kansas, who has been afflicted with total blindness for a number of years; David, a resident of Sacramento, California; Ellen A., who is the widow of William Clark, of Buffalo, Kansas, who fought as a Union soldier during the Civil war; and Frederick H.

Frederick H. Ireland was the youngest of his parents' children, and was three years old when his father died. He secured as good an education as the means of the family would permit, attending the public schools of DeKalb County, Missouri, and Stewartsville (Missouri) College, and at the age of twenty-one years began to learn the trade of carpenter. In 1882 he came to Kansas and in his first season assisted his mother on the home farm in Allen County, following which he was occupied at his trade in that county until 1887. He next went to Bronson, Bourbon County, and worked as a journeyman carpenter, and in 1897 came to Fort Scott, where, in April of that year, he formed a partnership with Elisha J. Rollins. This formed the nucleus for the great business now known as the Ireland & Rollins Planing Mills Company, which has become the largest enterprise of its kind at Fort Scott. The business began in a small way, but gradually developed under the careful handling and energetic labor of the partners, and its plant now occupies a floor space of 20,000 square feet, and employs from twenty-five

to thirty mechanics in the manufacture of special designs of store fixtures. During the past ten years the company has been under special contract to manufacture fixtures for the S. H. Kress Company, of New York City, but this is only one angle of the business, for its products are sent throughout the South to Florida and as far west as Arizona, with an immense business in the Middle West. Mr. Ireland is well deserving of the title of self-made man. He owes his success to his hard work, to the following out of a well-defined idea, to his business acumen and judgment and to a strict integrity that has given him high standing among leading business men all over Kansas. Independent in his political views, he has served Fort Scott as a member of the city council. He is connected with several fraternal organizations, and his religious relationship is with the Christian Science Church.

Mr. Ireland was married May 20, 1887, at Bronson, Kansas, to Miss Emma E. Ellis, a native of Anderson County, Kansas, and a daughter of Charles Ellis, of Garnett, Kansas. They have one daughter, Paulina, who was born at Fort Scott, September 29, 1895, a post-graduate of the Fort Scott High School, and now a student at Horner's Institute, Kansas City, Missouri.

Elisha H. Rollins, partner of Mr. Ireland in the proprietorship of the Ireland & Rollins Planing Mills Company, and one of the progressive and energetic business men of Fort Scott, was born March 15, 1859, on Prince Edward Island, a son of John and Mary (Harker) Rollins, natives of that place, who passed their entire lives there in agricultural pursuits. The father died in 1909, at the age of seventy-five years, while the mother passed away many years before, being forty-seven years old at the time of her demise.

The fourth in a family of nine children, Elisha H. Rollins received a public school education, and in his youth learned the trade of carpenter, which he followed at his native place until 1876. In that year he came to Kansas City, Missouri, where he followed his trade for three years, and then came to Fort Scott and continued at his trade as a journeyman until he joined Mr. Ireland in the planing mill business. Like his partner, Mr. Rollins is a man of foresight and good judgment, a thorough business man, and a citizen of high character and standing. He is a republican in politics, a Presbyterian in his religious faith, and a member of the Independent Order of Odd Fellows and the Fraternal Union.

On August 30, 1886, at Fort Scott, Mr. Rollins was married to Miss Jennie Margrave, daughter of Hon. William and Sarah (Hefton) Margrave. They have one son: William M., born October 22, 1888, a graduate of the Fort Scott High School and the Kansas State Normal School, of Pittsburg, who has taught three years in the public schools of Fort Scott and two years in the Wichita High School.

Hon. William Margrave, father of Mrs. Rollins, was born in Barton County, Missouri, January 17, 1818, studied law, was admitted to the bar in Missouri in 1851, and in 1854 came to Fort Scott. In November of that year he was appointed justice of the peace by Governor Andrew Reeder, and his subsequent service in that office has never been equalled in continuity, for had he lived but a few months longer he would have rounded out a half century in that position of honor and responsibility. His death occurred September 29, 1904, when the people of city, county and state mourned. Coming to the town of

W. J. Grove, M. D.

Fort Scott when it was still in its infancy, he watched its growth and development through the passing years, and did much to assist in its transformation into one of the leading cities of the West. He was the first justice of the peace in the State of Kansas, and, unlike many who came after him, had a thorough knowledge of civil and criminal law, so that he was able to dispense justice in a fair manner, as evidenced by the fact that his decisions were seldom reversed. He was a remarkably fine judge of character and human nature, and while he was stern and courageous in his handling of law-breakers, was at heart kindly disposed and a stanch and tried friend of the unfortunate. In his death Fort Scott lost one of its first and foremost citizens, a man universally respected and beloved.

WILLIAM WESLEY ROBB, who is superintendent of the electric light plant at Chanute, began his career as a locomotive fireman and has filled many positions of responsibility, chiefly as a manager of machinery and plants, and much of his service has been rendered in the State of Kansas.

He is of Scotch ancestry. His great-grandfather came from Scotland and was an early settler in Ohio. His grandfather, James Warren Robb, was born in the State of Illinois, in 1824, and died in Mercer County in that state in 1902. By profession he was an attorney, but many years ago he came out to Kansas with his son and and took up a homestead in Dickinson County, where he lived about eighteen years. He then removed to Wisconsin and afterwards to Illinois.

Rev. J. W. Robb, father of William Wesley, has spent a large part of his life in Kansas, and was a participant in the pioneer activities in the western part of the state. He was born in 1851 in Mercer County, Illinois, grew up there, and when a young man went to Minnesota. He became a minister of the Presbyterian Church, and was married in Minnesota where he preached the gospel for several years. He was also pastor of a church in Illinois. It was in 1873 that he brought his family to Kansas and located in Dickinson County. He conducted a Presbyterian mission there, and he preached at many points in the western part of the state. He was a real pioneer and ministered not only to the spiritual but to the material needs of his early neighbors. He helped them build their sod house homes, took off his coat and worked alongside the harvest hands in the wheatfield, and every Sunday would preach a sermon and conduct the religious services of the community. From Kansas he removed to Nebraska, spent about eight years there, then went to Wisconsin, and in 1902 returned to Kansas and for several years was a minister of the gospel at Iola. He is now living in comfortable retirement at Fort Scott. He is a republican and a member of the Masonic and Independent Order of Odd Fellows fraternities. Rev. Mr. Robb married Miss Alwilda Andrews, who was born in Minnesota in 1853 and died in Wisconsin in 1911. A brief record of their children is as follows: W. H. Robb, who is chief engineer of a cement plant at Syracuse, Indiana; William W.; Mary, wife of Henry Wertz, a locomotive engineer living at Colorado; Eva, wife of Lon Brown, a practicing physician at Western, Kansas; Lucy, wife of Merton De Forest, who is a locomotive engineer with the Chicago Northwestern Railway, living at Green Bay, Wisconsin; Clarence K., engineer of the city water plant at Chanute; and Addie, wife of

Arthur Powell, a railroad telegraph operator living in Illinois.

William Wesley Robb was born at Janesville, Wisconsin, November 27, 1872. The first school he ever attended was in Dickinson County, Kansas, and the school was held in a private home. Afterwards he continued his education in Nebraska, graduating from the high school at Hastings in that state. He also spent three years at the Poynette Academy at Poynette, Wisconsin.

On leaving the academy, in 1894, Mr. Robb took employment with the Chicago and Northwestern Railway, and for four years was a locomotive fireman. Coming to Kansas, he became a stationary engineer at Fort Scott, where he remained four years, and after that was at Iola four years, at Independence one year, and Neodesha three years. Mr. Robb is a very expert mechanic and has shown a great deal of capability in every task assigned him. On coming to Chanute in 1910 he accepted the superintendency of the electric light plant. Mr. Robb and family reside at 223 South Santa Fe Street, and he also owns a dwelling house at 1601 South Ransom Street in Fort Scott. In politics he is a republican voter and is affiliated with Cedar Lodge No. 103, Ancient Free and Accepted Masons at Chanute and with the Scottish Rite bodies at Fort Scott.

In 1902, at Fort Scott, Kansas, he married Miss Ollie Hedges. She was born in Ontario, Canada. To their marriage was born one child, James William, on December 4, 1911.

WILLIAM THOMAS GROVE, M. D. Doctor Grove has been one of the foremost physicians and surgeons of Eureka for twenty-two years. He is a man of high attainments in the profession. While most of his work has been in general lines he is a recognized expert in diseases of the eye, nose and throat and has largely specialized in that department of practice. His standing as a citizen is not less than that he enjoys in his profession.

Doctor Grove found the road to a professional career somewhat uneven and punctuated with difficulties. He began working for his own living when a boy, and had experiences as a farm hand, teacher, clerk and in various other lines before he reached the goal of his ambition.

He was born in Everett, Pennsylvania, April 7, 1867. His ancestors came originally from Holland in colonial days. There were three Grove brothers, one of whom settled at York, Pennsylvania, another in Maryland and another in Virginia. Doctor Grove is descended from the Pennsylvania branch. His grandfather was born in Pennsylvania, and died at York in that state, where for many years he kept a tavern.

Robert C. Grove, father of Doctor Grove, was born in Pennsylvania in 1842, was reared and married in that state, and at the outbreak of the Civil war he enlisted in a Pennsylvania regiment of infantry. After his career as a soldier he became a school teacher, and has followed that profession for fully half a century. Soon after the war he moved to Gallatin, Missouri, where he taught school, and is now a resident of Springfield, Missouri. In politics he is a republican. Robert C. Grove married Harriet Hannah Jane Woodcock. She was born in Pennsylvania in 1839. Doctor Grove was the second in a family of three children. His older sister Sadie E. is the wife of James A. Deavor, who is a stationary engineer by trade and is in the employ of the Dupont Powder Company with home at Princess Ann, Maryland. Jesse Amos, the only brother of Doctor Grove, was formerly at Amaranth, Pennsylvania, but is now living at Eureka, Kansas.

Doctor Grove spent part of his youth at Princess Ann, Maryland, where he attended the public schools five years. On leaving school he worked for three years on a farm at Salisbury, Maryland, and during that time he had the privilege of attending school during the brief winter months. His next instruction came from the public schools of McConnellsburg, Pennsylvania, where he remained two years. He also spent a year in the County Normal School there. With this preparation he became a teacher, working in that occupation for a year in Fulton County, Pennsylvania. He then was one year on the home farm and then for one year was clerk in a store at Clear Ridge, Pennsylvania.

When Doctor Grove came to Kansas his first location was at Virgil, where he arrived November 4, 1887. He spent three months on a farm, then taught a spring term of school and for two years was in the country district schools near Virgil. In the meantime he attended Baker University for one year.

All these experiences were merely preparatory to his real career. Doctor Grove was a student in medicine at Rush Medical College in Chicago for one year, and the following year entered St. Louis University, where he graduated M. D. March 26, 1893. Since then he has taken a considerable amount of post graduate work. He spent some time in the Manhattan Eye and Ear Infirmary of New York City, in the Chicago Eye and Ear College, and had considerable experience in the West Side Hospital of Chicago. He has also taken general courses in the St. Louis University, but wherever possible has enlarged his knowledge and ability of his specialties.

From 1893 Doctor Grove practiced at Virgil, Kansas, for 2½ years, and since then his home and office have been in Eureka. His offices are at the corner of Third and Elm streets, a block east of the Hotel Greenwood.

Doctor Grove has been prospered in a business way, and besides his home at First and Mulberry streets he owns two farms aggregating 380 acres in the State of Oklahoma. He served a number of years as health officer at Eureka, and is now in his second term as county coroner. He was first elected in 1912 and re-elected in 1914, his present term expiring January 1, 1917. He is a member of the Lyon County, the State and Southwest Medical societies and the American Medical Association.

Doctor Grove is a republican in politics. He takes much interest in fraternal affairs. He has served as senior deacon of Fidelity Lodge No. 106, Ancient Free and Accepted Masons, is a member of Eureka Chapter No. 45 Royal Arch Masons, has held offices in Eureka Commandery No. 54, Knights Templar, belongs to Wichita Consistory No. 2 of the Scottish Rite, and he and his wife are members of Queen Bess Chapter No. 56 of the Eastern Star. From 1902 to 1907 Doctor Grove was head physician for the State of Kansas of the Modern Woodmen of America. His local membership is in Beetle Camp No. 858. He also belongs to the auxiliary of that order. In 1893 at Virgil, Kansas, he was initiated in the Independent Order of Odd Fellows and has been left support of the Vice Grand and right support of the Noble Grand at that organization. Doctor Grove is a member and trustee of the Methodist Episcopal Church at Eureka.

On August 31, 1893, at Virgil, Kansas, he married Miss Minnie I. Dalton, daughter of Thomas and Sarah (Osborn) Dalton, both of whom are now deceased. Her father was an early farmer settler near Virgil. Doctor and Mrs. Grove have five children: Gladys is now a senior in the State Agricultural College at Manhattan. Harold Thomas is in the junior class of Baker University. William Paul is a bill clerk in the freight office of the Santa Fe at Wichita. Harriet Elizabeth is in the second grade of the public schools at Eureka. The baby of the family is Wendell Dalton.

GEORGE J. PFISTER. The tireless business activities of some men constitute a greater service to a community than a long service in public office, and that is true of George J. Pfister of Coffeyville, one of the old time citizens of Montgomery County, formerly prominent as a cattleman and rancher, and one of the largest property owners in and around Coffeyville. In building up his prosperity it is a well known fact that Mr. Pfister has been guided by a constant desire to benefit the public as well as himself, and at every point his public spirit and devotion to the welfare of his community have equalled his material success.

A resident of Kansas since he was a child, George J. Pfister was born near New Harmony in the southwest corner of Indiana, May 17, 1866. His father was Frank L. Pfister, who was born in Luxembourg, Germany, in 1842. When fifteen years of age in 1857 he came to the United States with his parents, who settled near New Harmony, Indiana, on a farm. Frank was the oldest of eight children, the others being: Alees, who is a retired farmer living in Southwest Indiana and served as a soldier in the Civil war with the Union army; Michael, who is still living a retired farmer in Southwest Indiana, was also a soldier of the Civil war; Captain Martin served with the rank of captain of a company in the Union army, later became a farmer in Southwestern Indiana, and his death occurred as a result of an injury when he fell from a tree; John is a retired farmer at Carmi, Illinois; Joseph lives on his farm in Southwestern Indiana; Mary lives at Mount Vernon, Indiana, widow of John Coon, a farmer, deceased; Lizzie lives in Indiana and is a widow.

While Frank L. Pfister was coming across the ocean in 1857 he became acquainted with Miss Kate Woolhater, who with her parents was a passenger on the same vessel. She was born near Luxembourg, Germany, in 1844. The Woolhater family also settled near New Harmony, Indiana, and Frank L. and Kate were married there. From Indiana they moved to Iowa, and in the fall of 1869 arrived in Kansas, settling as pioneers in Labette County eight miles east of the present site of Coffeyville. This part of Kansas was then out on the frontier, and was still in a sense Indian land. Frank L. Pfister took up farming and stock raising, and became very prominent in the livestock industry, especially as a raiser of cattle and hogs. He retired to Coffeyville in 1885, and died there in 1906. He was a democrat, but never aspired to hold any political office, and was a member of the Catholic Church. His wife died on the old farm in Labette County in 1882. Their children were: Louis, a retired farmer at Mount Vernon, Indiana; Joseph, who was a farmer and died near Mount Vernon in 1880; George J. Henry, who graduated in dentistry from a college in Kansas City, practiced for a time with Dr. Wassam in Topeka, and then for the sake of his health went to the Island of Cuba, where he died in 1892;

Lizzie died in Coffeyville at the age of twenty-five, having graduated from St. Mary's Seminary at Leavenworth, Kansas; Frank had nearly completed his studies at St. Mary's Kansas, when he died at the age of twenty-two, and John, who died in in-infancy.

George J. Pfister began his education in the country schools of Labette County, Kansas. He was reared on his father's farm until eighteen, and then spent two years in the Osage Mission School at what is now St. Paul, Kansas. On leaving school he entered the cattle business in Indian Territory, in the old Cherokee Nation. He was extensively identified with ranching and stock raising in what is now Oklahoma for ten years. Since 1896 Mr. Pfister's home has been in Coffeyville. From this city as a center his operations have been widely extended both as a practical farmer and in the handling and management of large real estate interests. He has acquired over 1,200 acres of land in the vicinity of Coffeyville, and now owns 800 acres a mile and a half north of the city on Verdigris River; his residence is at 1002 Spruce Street in Coffeyville, his home being a fine eleven-room dwelling built in 1905; he owns six business brick buildings along Eighth Street in the business district; a 30-foot frontage on Eighth Street; a 100-foot frontage on the corner of Ninth and Maple streets; a fifty-foot front in Block 49 on Ninth Street; a seventy-five-foot front on Eighth Street in Block 49; a lot 50x110 feet in Block 53 on East Eighth Street, and a number of other scattering properties. The tax valuation placed on his properties is over $80,000. Mr. Pfister has been an active operator in the real estate field since 1896. He formerly owned the Coffeyville paint and wall paper store on Eighth Street, but that is now owned by his son, Stafford.

At different times a number of local enterprises have benefited from Mr. Pfister's assistance and support. Anything that will improve and make a better town has his hearty cooperation. He is president of the Montgomery County Fair Association. Politically he is independent, and has been content to serve the public by his private activities and not through an office. For the good of his home city he once consented to serve as a member of the city council. He is a member of the Catholic Church and belongs to the Fourth Degree of the Knights of Columbus, Council No. 991 at Coffeyville. He is also a member of Coffeyville Lodge No. 775 Benevolent and Protective Order of Elks.

In 1888 at Emporia, Kansas, Mr. Pfister married Miss Rhoda E. Jones, daughter of Edward and Bridget Jones, both now deceased. Her father was a farmer. Mr. and Mrs. Pfister have four children, Hazel, Stella, Stafford and Raymond. Hazel, who is still at home with her parents, is a graduate of the Coffeyville High School; Stella graduated from the high school and from Loretto Academy of Kansas City, and is now living at Ponca City, Oklahoma, wife of James Ryan, who is in the oil refinery there with his father; Mr. and Mrs. Ryan have one child, James, born in 1914. Stafford attended the high school, St. Mary's College at St. Mary's, Kansas, and is now proprietor of the Coffeyville paint and wall paper store. Raymond after leaving high school entered St. Benedict's College at Atchison, Kansas, and is now operating one of his father's farms. He married Velma Furnish.

THOMAS E. TRIGG. "A map of busy life" mused the poet Cowper more than a hundred years ago, over his newspaper. The description yet holds good, a century of existence only having widened its field and strengthened its power. With its modern perfected machinery for the garnering of news, and with its vivid portrayal of the world's happenings, it is, indeed, a map of swiftly passing events, one that has become a necessary vitalizing element and an indispensable factor of every day living. How surely the development of a newspaper in a community marks the latter's progress. A name well known in journalism in Kansas, is that of Trigg, and a worthy bearer of this honored name is found in the owner and proprietor of the Elgin Journal, Thomas E. Trigg, who has been identified with newspaper work for more than a quarter of a century.

Thomas E. Trigg was born at Albia, Iowa, September 15, 1862. His parents were William Allen and Mary Elizabeth (Ware) Trigg, the latter of whom died at Garnett, Kansas, in 1901. The paternal grandfather, Thomas E. Trigg, was born in Virginia, of remote Irish ancestry, in 1809, and died in Linn County, Kansas, in 1891. His people had been early and substantial settlers in Kentucky, and Trigg County, in that state, commemorates their importance. Prior to the Civil war, Thomas E. Trigg was a large planter and a slaveholder in Kentucky. From there, in 1871, he moved to Linn County, Kansas. His wife was a member of the Gohegan family, of Virginia, and she died before his removal to Kansas.

William Allen Trigg, father of Thomas E. Trigg, of Elgin, Kansas, was born in Kentucky, in 1838, and grew to manhood and was educated in his native state. From Kentucky he went to Albia, Monroe County, Iowa, and there engaged in teaching school for several years and then removed to Centerville, in the same state and took charge as superintendent of a woolen mill, remaining there for six years and then resumed school teaching in which he continued until 1878, when he located at La Cygne, in Linn County, Kansas. He spent one year there as a school teacher, and one year as a farmer and then was elected probate judge. This caused him to remove to Mound City to reside, and he remained on the bench for two terms of four years.

Judge Trigg then entered the newspaper field by purchasing the Linn County Clarion, which he ably edited for ten years and for some time after removing to Garnett still retained the ownership of the Clarion. After locating at Garnett he bought the Eagle, published there, and during his long connection with that journal built up an influential newspaper for that section of the state. He subsequently served one term in the State Legislature. In 1904 he retired from the newspaper business. In politics he has always been a republican. In religious faith he is a Methodist and both at Garnett and at his present home, Westphalia, Kansas, he has served in the lay offices of the church. Fraternally he is identified with the Ancient Order of United Workmen and the Odd Fellows. At Bonaparte, Iowa, he was married to Mary Elizabeth Ware, who was born in Ohio in 1843, and they became the parents of four children: Thomas E., Clarence J., who resides at Kansas City, Missouri, where he is clerk of the city courts; Fred C., who is a member of the editorial staff of the Kansas City (Missouri) Star and Times; and Anna Stewart, who is the wife of Lee P. Cayot, who is a general merchant at Westphalia, Kansas.

Thomas E. Trigg attended the public schools at Mound City, Kansas, and subsequently completed his sophomore year at Lane University, Lecompton, Kansas. In 1882 he became a railroad telegraph operator, for the Missouri Pacific system, and continued until 1888. At that time his father was interested in the Garnett Eagle and he went into the printing office and learned the business and contiued with the Eagle until the property was sold in 1904, in which year he went to Cedar Vale and for the four succeeding years was foreman on the Cedar Vale Commercial. Mr. Trigg then decided to become the owner of his own journal and when the Chautauqua Globe came into the market in 1907, he purchased the paper and conducted it very creditably until 1909, when he sold that in order to move to Cedar Vale, where he purchased the Cedar Vale Commercial. This enterprise not proving entirely satisfactory, he disposed of the Commercial in 1910, and bought the Mirror, at Latham, in Butler County, Kansas, which, during his ownership of six years he developed into a paying property. In April, 1916, Mr. Trigg came to Elgin and founded his present admirable newspaper, the Elgin Journal. He has found here an appreciative public and is giving Chautauqua County a fine journal, well edited with all its departments up-to-date and practical. While its policy is republican in politics, its editor is not bigoted and is able to discuss questions of public concern from more than one standpoint.

Mr. Trigg was married at Kansas City, Kansas, in 1892, to Miss Ella B. Vincent, who was born in Macon County, Missouri, and was educated in the public schools of Bates County in that state. Her parents were Capt. A. B. and Nancy (White) Vincent. Captain Vincent was born near Cincinnati, Ohio, in 1836, and died at Ottawa, Kansas, in May, 1912. He married Nancy C. White, who was born in June, 1838, in Macon County, Missouri, and died at Ottawa, Kansas, in December, 1911. As a young man Captain Vincent taught school in Ohio and in Missouri and after coming to Kansas was a farmer and dealer in livestock. At one time he was mayor of Foster, Missouri, and there served in numerous offices to which he was elected on the democratic ticket. He honorably secured his title, having enlisted for service in the Civil War in 1861 and remained in the army for four years, during which he was made captain of Company C, Fifty-third Ohio Volunteer Infantry.

To Mr. and Mrs. Trigg one son was born, Thomas Clyde, on May 26, 1893. He was educated in the public schools of Latham, Kansas, and had completed a part of his high school course when he accepted an opportunity to visit Honolulu and make a trip up the Pacific coast, completing his far-journeying by going as far east overland as New York and back. At present he occupies the important office of assistant superintendent of a division of the Metropolitan Street Railway Company, at Kansas City, Missouri. In March, 1916, he was married to Miss Pearl Whitmeyer.

Mr. Trigg is connected with numerous political and journalistic organizations, and fraternally is identified with Latham Lodge No. 401, Ancient Free and Accepted Masons, and Elgin Chapter, and the Kansas Fraternal Citizens Association.

PROF. HENRY CLAY DALE No person in a community wields a greater influence in the molding and shaping of character than does the school teacher. The capable, conscientious instructor stands nearer to the hearts of his charges than does any other persons. On entering the schoolroom the child's mind is as plastic clay and is as readily made to take shape in the hands of the skilled educator. Therefore his great responsibility, and; therefore the honored position which he holds in the community when his duties are faithfully discharged. Of the educators of Columbus, Kansas, Prof. Henry Clay Dale is one of the leaders. He has devoted his entire career to his profession, in the ranks of which he has steadily advanced until at this time he is principal of the Cherokee County High School.

Professor Dale was born on a farm in Jasper County, Missouri, August 30, 1882, and is a son of Henry Clay and Emma J. (Barker) Dale. The founder of the Dale family in America was Sir Thomas Dale, first governor of Virginia, and a prominent citizen during colonial days. The great-grandfather of Professor Dale was Elijah P. Dale, a son of George Dale. He was the father of Robert J. Dale, who was for many years engaged in farming but who lived retired for several years before his death, which occurred at Carthage, Missouri. At that place was born his son, Henry Clay Dale, April 6, 1848. He was reared and educated in Missouri, where he was married, and as a young man adopted farming as his life work, having been reared amid agricultural surroundings. For a number of years he cultivated the soil of a fine farm in Jasper County, Missouri, but in 1890 met with a serious injury which caused him to retire from farm work, and in the following year he came to Galena. This, however, was not his first visit to this locality, for as early as 1871 he had come to the same section and cultivated a farm on the present site of Galena, in addition to which he taught school before the cities of Empire and Galena were founded. On his arrival at Galena in 1891, Mr. Dale engaged in the real estate business, and for some years served in the capacity of justice of the peace, but at this time is manager of the business of his son, Oliver C. He is a democrat, and a member of the Baptist Church, in the work of which he has taken an exceedingly active part, and formerly having been church treasurer at Galena. Mr. Dale married Miss Emma J. Barker, who was born in Central Missouri, in November, 1851, and to this union there have been born eight children: Oliver C., born December 23, 1871, who has made a large fortune, owning with his children 1,000 acres of land in Payne County, Oklahoma, with large oil interests, and also the owner of the home estate south of Carthage, a tract of 300 acres on which he is mining for lead and zinc; Charles R., born October 20, 1873, who is a plumber of Galena, Kansas; Arthur L., born January 30, 1875, who died in August, 1898; Magdaline, born November 3, 1877, who died in 1909, as the wife of Jesse Lewman, connected with a grocery store at Galena; Canzada, born October 18, 1880, who died March 24, 1915, as the wife of J. W. Jarrett, a miner of Galena; Prof. Henry Clay; Gordon Alfred, born December 30, 1884, who is manager at Yale, Oklahoma, for the general merchandise house of his brother, Oliver C.; and Willie Anna, born November 3, 1886, who is the wife of Morris Peteet, engaged in the general merchandise business at Yale, Oklahoma.

Henry Clay Dale, the younger, received his early education in the public schools of Galena, Kansas, and in 1905 was graduated from the academy at Ottawa, this state. He next entered Ottawa University, from which he was duly graduated in 1909, with the degree of Bachelor of Arts, and in that year began his teaching career in the public schools of Galena. In 1915 he left the position of principal, which he had held at Galena for one year, to become principal of the Cherokee County High School, a most important and responsible office, in which he has under his charge seventeen teachers and 420 pupils. Professor Dale is a member of the Southeastern Kansas Teachers' Association and the Kansas State Teachers' Association, and has gained more than a local reputation as an educator. He has sought to better conditions in every way and to elevate the educational standard. A thorough student of the science of education and possessed of a natural instinct for child psychology, he has made his school a living, growing organism responsive to the best in the teacher and pupil. He possesses in marked degree the supreme gift of the teacher, combining a natural aptitude for teaching with the executive force necessary to energize a body of teachers. In politics Professor Dale is a democrat. He is active in the work of the Baptist Church, in which he is a chorister in both church and Sunday school. His fraternal connections include membership in Galena Lodge No. 194, Ancient Free and Accepted Masons, and the Knights and Ladies of Security.

In 1912, at Galena, Kansas, Professor Dale was married to Miss Edith Ina Mitchell, daughter of William and Martha (Hinchcliffe) Mitchell. Mr. Mitchell, who was a miner, is now deceased, but Mrs. Mitchell still survives and resides at Strafford, Missouri. Professor and Mrs. Dale have one child: Ina Maxine, who was born June 6, 1915.

FRANK A. BARDWELL. A large majority of the men who are engaged in working the oil fields of Kansas have been devoting their energies to this line of work all of their lives, whether as employes, employers, contractors, drillers or producers. They have had the experience from early youth and it is but natural that they should meet with success in their undertakings granted that opportunities are the same. But there is another class among the men who are making this one of the great industries, this being formed of the men who had their training in other fields of business endeavor, and who have had their own problems to work out and their commercial battles to fight with men who by reason of their experience were better equipped. In the cases where these men have won, their success is more than creditable. In the latter class of Kansas producers is found Frank A. Bardwell, of Chanute, whose uniformly successful career has invaded various avenues of business life.

Mr. Bardwell was born at Ottawa, the county seat of LaSalle County, Illinois, August 11, 1870, and is a son of A. G. and Mary (Drake) Bardwell, and is of English descent, the family having come to America from England previous to the American Revolution and settled in New York. His grandfather was a native of Pennsylvania, who carried on the lumber business throughout his life and died in the Keystone State prior to the birth of his grandson. A. G. Bardwell was born at Tunkhannock, the county seat of Wyoming County, Pennsylvania, in 1833, and was reared in his native state. As a young man he sought his fortune in the West, locating at Ottawa, LaSalle County, Illinois, where he interested himself in farming. While there the Civil war came on and he enlisted in the One Hundred and Fourth Regiment, Illinois Volunteer Infantry, with which he served for three years, and established a fine record for courage and faithful discharge of duty. He took part in numerous skirmishes, was with his regiment in all its long and wearisome marches, and participated

in the great battles of Shiloh, Lookout Mountain, Bull Run, Chickamauga and Cold Harbor, many smaller engagements, and the siege of Vicksburg. At the close of the war he received his honorable discharge and returned to Illinois, where he resumed his activities as a farmer and also engaged in buying and selling livestock. In 1881, on coming to Kansas, he located at Humboldt, in the same line of business, and later went to Erie, where he was also a stock dealer. After several years at the latter point, he retired from active business affairs and removed to Chanute, where he now lives in retirement. Mr. Bardwell is now eighty-three years of age, but is still in good health and spirits and alive to all the important public questions of the day. He is a "standpat" republican, belongs to the Masons and the Grand Army of the Republic, and is a faithful member of the Presbyterian Church, in which he has served as an elder. During the active years of his career he was industrious and energetic, so that now, in the evening of life, he is able to enjoy the comforts that belong only to those whose careers have been characterized by hard, well-directed work. Mr. Bardwell married Miss Mary Drake, who was born in 1834, in Bradford County, Pennsylvania, and died at Thayer, Kansas, in 1911. To this union there have been born five children, namely: Mary, who is the wife of R. B. McCutchan, an attorney of Longton, Kansas; Charles H., an oil operator of Chanute; Cora, who died at Chanute, in April, 1914, as the wife of O. L. Holley, a traveling salesman with headquarters at Parsons, Kansas; Dora, twin of Cora, who is the wife of A. G. Liddle, an oil operator of Independence, Kansas; and Frank A.

Frank A. Bardwell was given good opportunities for a thorough educational training in his youth, being sent to the graded public school of Ottawa, Illinois, and Humbolt, Kansas, and the country schools of Neosho County. He then went to Baker University, where he completed the junior year's course, but left the college in 1892 to enter upon his business career. This was commenced at Savonsburg, Kansas, where for six years he was cashier of a bank, and in 1898 he embarked in the stock business at Longton, Elk County, where he remained until 1906. After two years he realized the opportunities extended by the oil business, and made his initial venture in the Independence community, where he remained for three years, although in the meantime he also gained some experience in the Oklahoma fields. He next spent two years at Paola, and in 1914 came to Chanute, not long after which he disposed of his Paola holdings. He is now a producer in the Augusta, Butler County, fields, and is opening up a new territory. During the time Mr. Bardwell has been connected with the business, he has learned all of its branches thoroughly, and may be accounted a thoroughly qualified man in any angle of the industry. He has made many friendships in the fields, and has established an enviable reputation for integrity and square dealing. In addition to his own residence at No. 221 West Elm Street, he owns a dwelling at No. 108 North Garfield Avenue, and 320 acres of land in Colorado. Politically he is a republican, his religious faith being that of the Presbyterian Church, of which he is a generous supporter, while his fraternal affiliations are with the Masons and the Odd Fellows, the latter being with Hector Lodge No. 64.

Mr. Bardwell was married in 1896, at Erie, Kansas, to Miss Ida Farrell, daughter of J. W. and Jennie (Chase) Farrell, the former of whom is a retired farmer of Manhattan, Kansas, and the latter is deceased. Mr. and Mrs. Bardwell are the parents of one son: Charles A., who was born September 30, 1906.

T. W. TRUSKETT. The real estate brokerage business established by Thomas W. Truskett, in 1908, has gone hand in hand with the development of Caney since its inception and undoubtedly has contributed largely toward the advantageous disposal of property and the honorable and satisfactory placing of loans, as any concern of the kind in Montgomery County. Mr. Truskett is one of Caney's substantial citizens; his success is self-made and in its scope and usefulness directs attention to qualities of perseverance, business integrity and ability and high regard for the welfare of the community.

Mr. Truskett was born in Monroe County, Ohio, March 28, 1852, a son of Thomas W. and Elizabeth (Williams) Truskett. His paternal grandfather was a native of England who on coming to the United States located in the State of Maryland and there passed the remainder of his life, while on his mother's side his grandfather Betts was a German emigrant to Pennsylvánia. Thomas W. Truskett the elder, was born in Maryland in 1823, and was reared and educated in his native state, from whence, as a young man, he went to Monroe County, Ohio. There he became a pioneer farmer, married, and established a home, and continued to be engaged in agricultural pursuits until 1859, when he removed to Cooper County, Missouri, again becoming a pioneer. In 1862 he enlisted in the First Regiment, Nebraska Volunteer Infantry, for service during the Civil war, and joined the command of Gen. John Seaton, with which he participated in a number of the most important engagements of the war, including the battles of Shiloh, Helena and Fort Donelson, and the siege of Vicksburg. He was taken prisoner by Shelby's men near Springfield, Missouri, but was shortly thereafter exchanged and rejoined his regiment, with which he fought until the close of the struggle. He established an excellent record for bravery and fidelity, and when honorably discharged and mustered out of the service, at Omaha, Nebraska, returned to his Missouri home. Mr. Truskett continued to be engaged in farming in Cooper, Morgan and Moniteau Counties, Missouri, until 1870, and in that year went to Vernon County, where he made his home and carried on his agricultural activities until 1890. In that year he located in Washington County, Oklahoma, settling on a farm ten miles south of Caney, Kansas, consisting of 100 acres, where he was living at the time of his death, in 1896. He was laid to rest in the cemetery at Caney. Mr. Truskett was a republican and a faithful member of the Christian Church. He was married in 1841, in Ohio, to Miss Elizabeth Williams, who was born September 1, 1820, at Crabapple Orchard, Pennsylvania, and was a schoolmate of the great statesman and politician, James G. Blaine, at one time a candidate for the presidency of the United States. Mrs. Truskett died at Caney, Kansas, in September, 1894, having been the mother of eight children, as follows: John O., born in 1843, enlisted in 1862 in the First Nebraska Infantry, was discharged for disability, recuperated and re-enlisted in the Second Kansas Cavalry, took part in many engagements, was again discharged because of disability toward the close of the Civil war, returned to Missouri and engaged in farming, and died in Nevada, that state, in 1885; James H., born in 1845, who is engaged in farming on Hog Shooter Creek, Washington County, Oklahoma; Joseph I., born in 1847, who is engaged in farming at Mulberry, Kansas; A. A., born in 1851, is now retired and resides at Montverde, Lake County, Florida; Mary E., who died at the age of seventeen years; Thomas W., of this notice; H. A., born in 1855, was a farmer and grain and lumber merchant, founder of the Home National Bank of Caney and one of this city's most prominent citizens, and died in 1906; and Harriet M., who married first Jacob Russell, a barber, now deceased, and now the wife of John Wyatt, a retired farmer of Independence, Kansas.

Thomas W. Truskett received his education in the public schools of Missouri, and was reared as a farmer, remaining on the homestead until he was twenty years of age. When he started upon his career, however, it was as a school teacher, and for five years was engaged in teaching in Missouri and Kansas. He first came to this state in 1873, when he took charge of a school at Godfrey, in which vicinity he remained two years. In 1875 he engaged in farming along the Drywood Creek, twelve miles south of Fort Scott, where he remained for five years, then removing to near Elgin, Kansas, where he farmed for three years. About this time Mr. Truskett's wife died, and for a period thereafter he did not have a settled home, although he was engaged for a time in the shoe business at both Independence, Kansas, and Joplin, Missouri. From the latter point Mr. Truskett went to Washington County, Indian Territory, and engaged in farming and the cattle business for twelve years, and in 1891 came to Caney, which city has since been his home and the scene of his successful operations.

On first coming to this city, Mr. Truskett engaged in business as the proprietor of a livery barn, but after two years thus spent turned his attention to mercantile lines, and founded what has since become the leading store in its line in the city, located at the corner of Fourth Avenue and Spring Street. There he successfully handled general dry goods and groceries and through good management and honorable dealing built up a prosperous establishment. In 1908 Mr. Truskett disposed of the business to his nephew, W. O. Truskett, although he still owns the building. He has since devoted his attention to the real estate brokerage business, handling properties in Colorado, Old Mexico, Florida and Montgomery County, Kansas. He is the owner of five residences at Caney, these being among the finest in the city, two smaller residences, and his own handsome home at the corner of Sixth and Main streets, four of Caney's business buildings, and 966 acres of valuable land in Old Mexico. He also has various other interests, prominent among which may be mentioned his flourishing feed business, which has also been built up under his personal direction.

Mr. Truskett was formerly a republican in his political views, but is now an independent democrat. He served one term as mayor of Caney, during which time he displayed abilities that won him the respect and esteem of his fellow-citizens. On another occasion he was a candidate for a place in the Kansas State Assembly, but was in a district which had a republican majority of 800 and met defeat with the rest of the democratic ticket. Mr. Truskett is an active member of the Christian Church and generously supports its movements. He is well known in fraternal circles, and was the first past president of the state organization of the Fraternal Order of Eagles, and at the time of his retirement from his official position was presented with a handsome watch charm as a memento and appreciation of the services he rendered that organization.

Mr. Truskett was first married June 5, 1876, to Mrs. M. J. Gepford, the widow of Silas Gepford. She died November 20, 1880, leaving three children: Metta May, born November 20, 1877, died in Texas, married L. L. Peterson, who now resides at Caney and manages the feed store in partnership with Mr. Truskett, and had four children: Orin, a graduate of the Caney High School, class of 1915, and now attending the Manhattan State Normal School, Jennie and Dora who are attending the Caney High School, and Charles, a student in the graded schools; Harvey A., born March 26, 1879, who died in infancy; and Harriet E., born October 10, 1880, and now the wife of Dr. C. E. Wyatt, a practicing dentist of Independence, Kansas. Mr. Truskett was again married February 13, 1887, to Miss Theodosia V. Ross, of Missouri, who died April 22, 1904, leaving two children: Benjamin O., born October 31, 1888, who has graduated from a school of embalming and is now associated in business with his father; and Beatrice, born January 16, 1901, who is attending the public schools. Mr. Truskett was married the third time March 15, 1908, to Miss Bertha Berger, a native of Belgium, and they have one daughter: Cleo Lenora, born September 13, 1910.

GEORGE K. REID, who has been a resident of Kansas nearly thirty-five years, has built up and maintained what is unquestionably the largest business at Howard in abstracts, loans and insurance. When it is stated that Mr. Reid is the son of a minister, there is no need to explain that he was not reared in a home of luxury or wealth, and as a matter of fact from an early age he has been dependent upon his own resources and has made good.

His Reid ancestors at one time lived in England, moved from there to Scotland, thence to northern Ireland, and from County Tyrone, Ireland, they came to America just after the revolution. They first settled in Kentucky and from there moved to Ohio. Mr. Reid's paternal grandfather, John Reid, was born in Pennsylvania in 1798. He went in the early days to Ohio and followed farming there. He did in Cedarville, Ohio, in 1879.

George K. Reid was born at West Barnet, Vermont, August 7, 1863. His father, Rev. William H. Reid, who was born at Cedarville, Ohio, in 1828, was reared and married there, and entered the ministry of the Presbyterian Church. He was a graduate of Miami University at Oxford, Ohio. Nearly all his service during a long and active life was as a missionary. He endured almost endless hardships and struggles as a pioneer religious teacher and preacher. He preached in Vermont, in Pennsylvania, Iowa, Minnesota, in Ontario, Canada, and also in Indian Territory. His death occurred at Fort White in the State of Florida in 1899. In politics he was a republican. Rev. Mr. Reid married Julia A. Harbison, who was born at Cedarville, Ohio, in 1840, and died at the old Dwight Mission in Indian Territory in 1887. The children were: Hugh M., who became a farmer and died at Fort White, Florida, in 1898; George K.; Mary, who died at the age of six years; William P., who was an employe of the Chicago, Milwaukee & St. Paul Railway Company and died at Milwaukee, Wisconsin, in 1900.

George K. Reid spent his early years in various localities, wherever his father happened to be sojourning. He received the bulk of his early education in the public schools of Bloomington, Indiana, and also attended high school there. In the meantime he had worked for a time for the Adams Express Company at Cincinnati. In 1880 he went to Ontario, Canada, finished his course in a high school in that province in 1881, and the following two years were spent as a salesman of subscription books.

On coming to Howard, Kansas, in 1883, Mr. Reid began his real career. For the first five years he was deputy county clerk of Elk County, then became bookkeeper in the First National Bank and for six years was connected with the Howard National Bank. Since 1894 he has been in the real estate, abstract, insurance and loan business, and his long experience and his thorough integrity as a business man enabled him to render an expert service to his large clientage. His offices are in the First National Bank Building. He has prospered in a business way, and besides his home at the corner of Elk and Perry streets, he owns a farm of 320 acres seven miles north of Howard, and has an interest in 360 acres at another location in Elk County.

Mr. Reid is a member of the Howard School Board and is its clerk, is city treasurer, and lends his co-operation and support to every movement for the public welfare. He is a republican, is active in the Presbyterian Church, being a member of the Session, and the Board of Trustees. His fraternal relations are with Hope Lodge No. 155, Ancient Free and Accepted Masons at Howard, and with Lodge No. 124, Ancient Order of United Workmen at Howard.

In 1881 at Wroxter, Ontario, Canada, Mr. Reid married Mary Lees. Her parents, Andrew and Mary (Hislop) Lees, came to Kansas many years ago and her father still lives on his farm a half mile south of Howard. He is ninety years of age, and his wife died at the age of eighty-one. Mr. and Mrs. Reid have reared some children who do them credit. Mary is the wife of Dr. R. E. Cheney, who is now engaged in the practice of dentistry at Eureka, Kansas. Julia, the second child, died at the age of six months. Robert J. is a graduate of the University of Kansas in the law department and is now practicing at Kansas City, Missouri. Frank R., who attended the University of Kansas two years and is a graduate of the Kansas City Dental College, is now building up a fine practice as a dentist at Howard. George R., the youngest, died at the age of seven years.

CLIFFORD C. NESSELRODE, M. D. In 1906 there came to Kansas City, a young graduate in medicine who entered St. Margaret's Hospital as an interne. Very modest was this young man as to his acquirements but not much time elapsed before his medical knowledge and his surgical skill were noted and approved, and at the present time no practitioner enjoys more public confidence or personal esteem than does Dr. Clifford C. Nesselrode. In addition to attending to a large and constantly increasing private practice, he is on the staffs of St. Margaret and Bethany hospitals and on the surgical staff of the University of Kansas School of Medicine at Rosedale. Doctor Nesselrode was born February 25, 1880, near Conway Springs, in Sumner County, Kansas. His parents were James Harvey and Anna (Moulton) Nesselrode.

The progenitor of the Nesselrode family, the great-grandfather of Doctor Nesselrode, came to America from Germany and settled in Pennsylvania.

There Samuel Nesselrode was born and there married a member of the old German family of Fisher, who proved an admirable wife. They, in course of time, moved to Ohio and in that state their son, James Harvey was born and in 1866 accompanied his parents to Kansas. Samuel Nesselrode purchased 160 acres of land in Johnson County, near Spring Hill, and that property has never since been out of the family.

To Johnson County about this time came an attractive young lady, Miss Anna Moulton, a native of Wisconsin, to visit her brother. Instead of returning to her native state she was married to James Harvey Nesselrode. In 1878, with their first child, Gertrude, who is now the wife of J. M. Holcomb, a farmer in Johnson County near her parents, together with Mrs. Nesselrode's brother and wife, they journeyed in a covered wagon to Sumner County. They took up adjoining claims near Conway Springs, broke up the land, proved up and built frame houses. In 1883 however, Mr. Nesselrode sold his land and returned to Johnson County and there bought his father's old farm and continues there still engaged in farming and dairying. He is recognized as a man of sterling character. In politics he is a republican from principle, never accepting any public office except on the school board.

Clifford C. Nesselrode attended the district schools in Johnson County until prepared to be a teacher himself. Early deciding upon a professional life, he felt it no hardship to provide his own college expenses. But Nature soon asserted her preference for medicine and surgery and in 1902 he entered the Kansas City Medical College and continued a student in the Kansas University, alternating study and teaching. In 1905 the above school was made the medical department of the University of Kansas and Doctor Nesselrode was engaged as a student-teacher in laboratory work and continued until he was graduated in 1906. In this year he became an interne in St. Margaret's Hospital and in the following year entered Dr. George McGray's office, since when he has maintained his own office and has been connected with the institutions above mentioned. His practice absorbs all his time, being connected with many professional bodies and called on for many services such as fall to the humanity of the physician even if not classed directly with charities. He is a Fellow of the American College of Surgeons and belongs to the Kansas State Medical Society, of which he was vice president one year and for three years was chairman of the committee on health and public education; of the American Medical Association; was the representative from Kansas to the Clinical Congress of the Surgeons of North America; and is a member of the Southwest Medical Association, of which he was vice president for one year. Doctor Nesselrode is a specialist in surgery and in 1910 took a special course in surgery in the Harvard Post Graduate School.

On January 1, 1908, Doctor Nesselrode was married to Miss Ella Allen, of Lenexa, Johnson County, Kansas. Her father, George Allen, is a prominent farmer in that county. Doctor and Mrs. Nesselrode have a three-year-old daughter, Mary Jane. Doctor Nesselrode is a stockholder in several banks. He is president of the Mercantile Club and one of its directors, is an active member of the Rotary Club, is a Mason, and retains membership in his old college fraternity, the Phi Beta Pi.

GEN. JOSEPH KENNEDY HUDSON. One of the ablest soldiers of Kansas and most determined fighter for the free-state movement, the late General Hudson will have a lasting fame not only for what he did in the trying years of Kansas' youth, but also as founder and for many years editor of the Topeka Capital. It was his resourcefulness as a practical newspaper man and his wonderful ability as an editor and molder of public opinion that gave the Capital its wide influence and standing as a journal, and the history of the Kansas Press has no more notable figure than Joseph Kennedy Hudson.

It is not the purpose of this article to describe in detail the history of the Topeka Capital. That belongs to other pages. But something should be said of General Hudson's personal relations with that journal and also of his ability and personality as an editor. It was in 1873 that he purchased the Kansas Farmer and moved it from Leavenworth to Topeka. He continued to edit and publish this paper until 1879. In March of the latter year he began the publication of the Topeka Daily Capital, now owned by Governor Capper. To the task of making a metropolitan daily paper with at least a state wide influence, General Hudson brought keen foresight, rare judgment, magnificent courage and a fund of energy and endurance that was a marvel to his associates. In a few years he had made the support of the Capital almost indispensable to any general movement in state politics or affairs, and he also elevated it to the position of one of the foremost journals in the West. The Capital under General Hudson had its part in much that now distinguishes Kansas as a state. The adoption of prohibition was probably due more to the ardent advocacy of General Hudson through the Capital than any other one factor. General Hudson himself was a radical in politics, and possessed the courage of his convictions. As a fighter he neither asked nor gave quarter. He used his pen with a vigor and freedom that made it felt in every cause he championed. And yet he did not have the narrowness which often distinguishes radicalism. He would contend for the cause or principles he believed to be right, and yet when experience justified a change in course, he would readily yield or modify his personal convictions. He stated what he regarded to be the truth at the time regardless of what had been his course or belief in the past. It was inevitable that he should be bitterly hated by political opponents and was often the object of savage attack. His honesty was never doubted, and he came to number among his warm personal friends some of his bitterest political foes. Many Kansas newspaper men grew up under the prospering care of General Hudson, and no one ever worked with the Topeka Capital who did not have the greatest of admiration and even of love for him.

Joseph Kennedy Hudson was born at Carrollton in Carroll County, Ohio, May 4, 1840, and died May 5, 1907, at the age of sixty-seven. His early life was spent at Salem, Ohio. It was a Quaker community, and was a stronghold of abolitionism. His father John Hudson published the Anti-Slavery Bugle, at Salem, the organ of the Western Anti-Slavery Society. As a boy there Joseph K. Hudson joined the John Brown League, a secret organization which had for its purpose the destruction of slavery throughout the Union. It was this early connection which subsequently brought him out to Kansas for the purpose of joining the army under Gen. James H. Lane.

At the age of twenty-one he enlisted as a private in the army and finally attained the rank of major. He enlisted at Fort Leavenworth, July 30, 1861, in Company E of the Third Kansas Regiment of Infantry. In 1862 the Third and Fourth Regiments were

B. Rockwell

LADIES' READING CLUB HOUSE, JUNCTION CITY, KANSAS,
BUILT AND GIVEN THEM BY BERTRAND ROCKWELL
Dedicated September 1, 1896

consolidated, becoming the Tenth Kansas Infantry. In that regiment Mr. Hudson was commissioned first lieutenant of Company C, and the regiment became part of General Lane's Brigade in the Army of the Frontier.

From the organization of the regiment at Fort Scott, Kansas, in 1861 until July, 1863, General Hudson participated in the various skirmishes and battles of the Division through the campaigns in Missouri, Indian Territory and Arkansas. He was at the engagement at Dry Wood, Newtonia, Old Fort Wayne, Cane Hill, Van Buren and Prairie Grove, all of which mark important stages in the progress of the campaigns through the Southwest. He was at different times under the command of General Fremont, General Hunter, General Blount, General Herron and General Schofield.

Col. William Weer, commanding the Second Brigade, First Division, Army of the Frontier, in the course of a report dated December 12, 1862, made the following recommendations: "To my Acting Adjutant General, Lieutenant J. K. Hudson of the 10th Kansas, I cannot award too high praise. He was my only aide, and was everywhere at duty's call, carrying orders, cheering and rallying the men. His worthy qualities in camp as well as upon the field entitle him to promotion."

In the meantime, in 1862, he had been appointed acting assistant adjutant general of the Second Brigade of the Army of the Frontier. In 1863 he was appointed to the same office in the First Brigade. He was aide on the staff of Brig. Gen. Thomas A. Davis and was later on the staff of Major General Schofield, commanding the Department of Missouri. December 21, 1863, he was commissioned major of the Sixty-second United States Colored Infantry. At the time of his promotion to major his regiment was ordered down the Mississippi River to join Banks in the Red River campaign. He saw active service at Morganza Bend, Baton Rouge, and Port Hudson on the Mississippi River, and at Roca Chica Pass, Brownsville, and on Brazos Santiago Island in the southern end of Texas along the Rio Grande. On detached service he commanded six companies of Infantry at Roca Chica Pass and Ringgold Barracks. General Hudson participated in the battle of Palmetto Ranche on the Rio Grande River May 11, 1865. That was the last engagement of the war, and curiously enough was fought close to the point where the initial engagement of the Mexican war was contested. In July, 1865, General Hudson was given his honorable discharge.

After the war he engaged in farming and stock raising on a large scale in Wyandotte County for about eight years. During a portion of that time he served as a regent of the State Agricultural College. General Hudson had much to do with reconstituting the management and plan of the college at Manhattan. He believed that the theoretical and sectarian interests which were emphasized in the original management of the institution would in time have destroyed its usefulness, and he worked consistently to get the college on a basis of administration which would best serve the original object for which the appropriation had been designed.

In 1871 he was elected to the Kansas House of Representatives, and in 1874 received twenty-four votes on a joint ballot for United States senator. As proprietor and editor of the Topeka Capital he gave nearly thirty years of his active life to journalism. In 1895 he left the newspaper business and afterward spent most of his time looking after his mining and land interests in Missouri.

In 1895 General Hudson was elected state printer of Kansas and held that office two years. On May 29, 1898, President McKinley commissioned him a brigadier general of volunteers to serve in the war with Spain. For this honor he received the almost unanimous endorsement of the people of Kansas and his appointment was urged by the governor, by both United States senators and by the entire congressional delegation without regard to politics. Considering the many excellent qualifications of General Hudson as a military man, it is to be regretted, and it was a keen disappointment to him and his friends, that the path of duty did not take him to the actual battle front during the war. Soon after his appointment he was assigned to the Fourth Army Corps, under command of Major General Coppinger at Tampa, Florida. While in command of the Second Brigade of the Second Division Fourth Army Corps his most important duty was to prevent demoralization and disaster due to the illness which afflicted the unseasoned troops in the summer camps in a tropical climate. Both at Tampa and later at Huntsville, Alabama, General Hudson performed the duties assigned him in such manner, as to receive the highest commendation from the commanding general. He was mustered out in November, 1898, and at once returned to his home in Topeka.

General Hudson was long identified with the Grand Army of the Republic. He was a republican in politics.

At Wyandotte, Kansas, April 5, 1863, General Hudson married Mary W. Smith, also of Salem, Ohio. General Hudson had an ideal home life. Mrs. Hudson was a talented woman, has written for magazines and other publications, and with all her outside interests she was a devoted wife and gave the best of her character and talents to her home and family. General and Mrs. Hudson had four children. The three now living are: Mrs. Dell Keizer of Kansas City, Kansas; Paul Hudson; and Mrs. William C. Smith. Mrs. Hudson, the widow of General Hudson, is now living at Fresno, California. The only son, Paul Hudson, is editor of the Mexican Herald, in the City of Mexico.

BERTRAND ROCKWELL, who has had his home at Kansas City, Missouri, since 1906 was one of the constructive figures in Kansas from the close of the Civil war until he retired from business. Apart from the individual interest of his career, his activities have had the greatest value in connection with Junction City and that section of the state.

Before he had reached his majority he had left school and entered the army, and came out with the rank of captain. Two weeks after being mustered out, in September, 1865, Captain Rockwell reached Leavenworth, Kansas. From there he was carried by one of the Kansas stage line stages to various towns and cities, visiting Lawrence, Topeka, Manhattan, Junction City, and Council Grove. His object was to find a suitable location for business. He finally cast his lot in with beautiful Junction City, then a town of 300 or 400 people. His first task was to erect a frame building 20 by 50 feet. Ten feet at the rear was partitioned off for a sleeping room. He was then unmarried and for several years he lived and worked in one building. The rest of the space he filled up with a stock of groceries and men's furnishing goods. This frame building gave way to a larger and better structure, and B. Rockwell & Company attained its position among the foremost merchandise firms over all that section of Kansas. For twenty-five years Captain Rockwell put in sixteen hours a day at his business and his success grew in proportion to his energy and enterprise. His father was also associated in business with him for a time, and subsequently George A. Rockwell, a brother of Captain Rockwell, became a partner. In 1892 the business was incorporated as the B. Rockwell Merchandise & Grain Company, with Capt. Bertrand Rockwell as president, George Rockwell, his father, as first vice president, and George A. Rockwell was second vice president. Captain Rockwell retired from the active business in February, 1905, and was succeeded by George A. Rockwell as president. This is one of the oldest commercial enterprises of the state, with a record of more than half a century of existence. Measured by the annual volume of its trade transactions, the business was hardly second to any similar establishment in the larger cities of Kansas.

A number of years ago Captain Rockwell gave to Junction City a handsome token of his loyalty to that community. He built for the Ladies Reading Club a neat stone club house. It is the only recorded instance in which such a structure was built and donated by a man for a ladies organization. The building was dedicated September 1, 1896. The president of the club at the time was Mrs. Newell F. Green. The principal address of the evening was given by Noble L. Prentis, and it was an occasion long to be remembered by those who attended, since there were a number of people of prominence in Kansas who participated in the program, much of which was made up of reminiscences of bygone years in Kansas life.

Capt. Bertrand Rockwell was born at Warsaw, Hancock County, Illinois, April 25, 1844. He is a son of George and Catherine Cole (Westlake) Rockwell. His father was born at Ridgefield, Connecticut, October 12, 1815, and his mother was born at Newburgh, New York, November 16, 1820. This branch of the Rockwell family goes back to John Rockwell who came from England to the Massachusetts colony about 1640 and subsequently resided at Stamford, Connecticut. He died at Rye, New York, in 1676. In the earlier generations the lineage is traced to Sir Ralph De Rocheville, a Norman knight who went to England in the train of Queen Maud. John Rockwell the first American of the name, was the father of John Jr., who died at Stamford, Connecticut, in 1673; Thomas, son of John Jr., was born in Stamford, Connecticut, in 1667, and died there June 17, 1712; Thomas Jr., in the next generation, was born in Norwalk, Connecticut, December 13, 1708, settled at Ridgefield, Connecticut, and died there November 4, 1779; Lieutenant James, son of Thomas, Jr., and great-grandfather of Bertrand Rockwell, was born at Ridgefield in 1750, attained his rank as a soldier in the War of the Revolution, and died at Ridgefield November 25, 1808; Thomas H. Rockwell, son of Lieutenant James, was born at Ridgefield May 2, 1776, was a cabinet maker and farmer, and died at Ridgefield in 1865. George Rockwell, father of Captain Rockwell, was a teacher in Connecticut and Illinois, in 1840 established a drug store at Warsaw, Illinois, and a few years later became a participant in the Mormon war in Illinois. He was with the troops which killed Joseph and Hyrum Smith at Carthage, Illinois, June 27, 1844. He also served three years in the Civil war, being with the Seventh Missouri Cavalry in Missouri, Arkansas, and Louisiana. He participated in numerous battles and skirmishes and was mustered out as a captain of the Seventh Missouri Cavalry. Soon after the war he disposed of his business interests at Warsaw and joined his son Captain Rockwell at Junction City, Kansas. He died there January 13, 1896.

Catherine C. Westlake, mother of Captain Rockwell, was a daughter of Rev. George Westlake, formerly of Newburgh, New York. George Rockwell and wife had several children who attained prominence. Their daughter Anna Frances became the wife of Lieut.-Gen. Adna R. Chaffee of the United States Army, who commanded the American forces in China when Pekin was captured. Dr. Thomas H. Rockwell rose to distinction as medical director of Equitable Life Assurance Society of New York City.

Capt. Bertrand Rockwell received his early education in the Warsaw public schools of Illinois. He left school in order to enlist in the army. In August, 1861, he went with the Iowa Home Guard from Chariton, Iowa, to Northern Missouri to repel the rebel invasion. On July 23, 1862, he enlisted as a private in the Thirty-fourth Iowa Infantry, and was in service until mustered out as captain September 5, 1865. He was in Missouri, Tennessee, Alabama, Florida, Arkansas, Louisiana, Texas, and Virginia, and took part in battles and skirmishes in all these states except Virginia. He had the unusual experience of witnessing five surrenders of Confederates. These surrenders were: Arkansas Post, Arkansas, January 11, 1863, where 4,760 Confederates surrendered; Vicksburg, July 4, 1863, 31,600; Fort Gaines, Alabama, August 8, 1864, 900; Fort Morgan, Alabama, August 23, 1864, 1,000; and Blakely, Alabama, April 9, 1865, 4,000. The Thirty-fourth Iowa Infantry had the honor of receiving the surrender of Morgan, and Captain Rockwell's Company was the first to take possession of the fort after its surrender. He also participated in the last charge of the War of the Rebellion at Blakely, Alabama. Lee had surrendered three hours before the charge was made. On the right of the Union lines was a brigade of colored troops under General Pile. The Confederates seeing these colored soldiers advancing at double quick with fixed bayonets, ran from that portion of the line in order to surrender to white soldiers.

Since the Civil war Captain Rockwell has been a merchant, banker, lumber dealer, and contractor for state and army supplies. In all those years there was only one in which expenses were more than income. That was in 1874, the year grasshoppers devoured every green thing in Geary and adjacent counties of Kansas and laid waste the entire state. For several years Captain Rockwell was president of the First National Bank of Junction City, Kansas, and has been a director in other national banks.

He is a man of broad interests and has cultivated these interests by a varied participation in business and civic life and by much travel. Captain Rockwell has made four trips to Europe and made one tour to China, Japan and the Philippines. Though always interested in local affairs he never held office. A stanch republican, he was a delegate to the National Republican Convention at Chicago in 1904, when Theodore Roosevelt was first nominated for president. He is a member of Union Lodge No. 7 Ancient Free and Accepted Masons at Junction City, is a Knight Templar Mason, belongs to the Military Order of the Loyal Legion of the United States, Commandery of Kansas, and was its commander in 1900, and is affiliated with Grand Army Post No.

132 at Junction City. At Kansas City, Missouri, he has membership in the Kansas City Country Club, the City Club, the Knife and Fork Club. Captain Rockwell attends the Episcopal Church.

At Junction City, Kansas, September 29, 1870, he married Julia Marshall Snyder. She is a daughter of George Snyder of Philadelphia, Pennsylvania, and Mary Love Scott of Bush Hill, Fairfax County, Virginia. Her mother's grandfather, Gustavus Scott, was a very prominent man in the early life of our nation. In 1795 he was one of the three commissioners to erect public buildings, including the capitol in Washington. In 1797 at the request of President Washington he gave his private name as collateral security to Holland bankers who were not satisfied with the state securities of Virginia and Maryland which were being furnished to complete a capitol building of the United States in Washington, District of Columbia.

Captain and Mrs. Rockwell have five daughters, all of whom are living: Mrs. James R. Edwards of Santa Rosa, California; Signora Carlo Gino Venanzi of Assisi, Italy; Miss Mary Rockwell of Kansas City, Missouri; Mrs. Francis H. Crosby of San Francisco, California; and Mrs. John Beyers Love of Kansas City, Missouri.

MARTIN VAN BUREN CAGNEY, whose home has been in Emporia for the past thirty years, is an old time printer, having first taken up the art of typography when a boy before the Civil war, and has followed his trade under many changing conditions and in many localities. For many years he has been proprietor of a commercial printing establishment at Emporia, and has also been frequently honored with positions of trust and responsibility in that city.

His own career has the interest of much variety and he belongs to an interesting family. His father Maurice Cagney was born in Ireland in 1818, and became a sailor, and as a captain navigated different vessels owned in Boston. His home for many years was on the Massachusetts coast, chiefly at Salem, in which historic city his son Martin Van Buren was born June 8, 1843.

In 1848 the family left Salem and removed to Chicago, where Maurice Cagney owned and operated a line of hacks and transfer wagons in that then young and vigorously growing city. He later moved to a farm twenty-two miles west of St. Louis. There he found himself in somewhat unpleasant surroundings. He owned no slaves, was opposed to the institution, but all his neighbors were slave owners and they made it so unpleasant for him that in 1855 he left the farm and went to Keokuk, Iowa, where he resumed the transfer business. During the war he removed to Kansas City, Missouri, where for the last thirty years of his life he was retired from business. His death occurred in Kansas City in 1909, when at the age of ninety-one years three months. Politically he acted as a Douglas democrat before the war and afterwards was a republican. He was a member of the Presbyterian Church. Maurice Cagney married Mary Quinlivan, who was born in Scotland in 1814 and outlived her husband, reaching the remarkable age of ninety-eight years three months. She died at Kansas City in 1912. Her five children were: Mary, who died while the family were living near St. Louis, her death occurring in a St Louis hospital; Martin Van Buren; Thomas L., who enlisted and served during the last two years of the war in a Missouri regiment of infantry, is now a member of Warren Post Grand Army of the Republic at Kansas City, Mis-

souri, where he resides and for many years was a first engineer on steamboats plying both the lower and upper courses of the Mississippi and Missouri rivers, retiring from that vocation many years ago and now owning real estate in Kansas City which enables him to live in ease and comfort; T. M. Cagney, who is a car builder at Kansas City; and Rose, wife of John Crotty, of Kansas City, who is an expert blacksmith and in earlier years was employed in making fine steel chases.

Mr. Cagney spent his childhood and youth partly on the Massachusetts coast, at Chicago, near St. Louis and at Keokuk, Iowa. At the age of thirteen he left the public schools and entered a printing office in Keokuk, where he learned the printer's trade. He went with the family to Missouri early in the war, and served in the Missouri State Militia, being discharged with the rank of lieutenant in Company E Sixty-fifth Regiment, Missouri State Militia.

After the war he followed his trade as a journeyman in Indiana, Ohio, Illinois and Missouri, and in 1886 came to Emporia, where for two years he was foreman of the Emporia Republican, edited by ex-Governor Charles V. Eskridge. He then bought a printing establishment which he has conducted ever since, and his shop has been headquarters for high class job printing for fully a quarter of a century. His place of business is on Commercial Street between Sixth and Seventh avenues.

Mr. Cagney was for some years a member of the Emporia City Council and while a councilman was elected mayor, filling that office two years. He is a republican, a member of the Lutheran Church, and is affiliated with Emporia Lodge No. 12, Ancient Free and Accepted Masons, Emporia Chapter No. 12, Royal Arch Masons, Emporia Commandery No. 8, Knights Templar, Emporia Lodge No. 84, Ancient Order United Workmen, and his interests have matured in the Triple Tie Insurance Organization.

In 1888 at Emporia Mr. Cagney married Miss Amanda Weesner, daughter of Cyrenus and Rebecca (Allen) Weeser. Her parents reside at 728 Exchange Street in Emporia. Mr. Weeser is employed by the Santa Fe Railroad Company. Mr. and Mrs. Cagney have one daughter, Edna, wife of Luther Myser, a resident of Des Moines, Iowa. Mr. Myser travels for a wholesale china house and also owns a half interest in the Myser Brothers China Store at Emporia.

WILLIAM FRANK FLACK, M. D. While the medical profession for centuries has enlisted some of the most profound minds of all times, modern discoveries and developments have opened up new fields for the brilliant physician and surgeon, and many of this profession have turned their attention to particular branches, specializing along certain lines. This development has been necessary, for the problems presented in the calling today are so serious and difficult of solution that the average physician has not the expert knowledge to handle all satisfactorily. For some years past William Frank Flack, the pioneer physician of Elk County, has been specializing in diseases of the eye, and while he also carries on a general medical and surgical practice at Longton, where he has been located since 1885, it is perhaps in his particular field that he has achieved his greatest distinction.

Doctor Flack was born at Wooster, Wayne County, Ohio, April 18, 1857, and is a son of John and Nancy (Russell) Flack. The Flack family came from Germany to America during Colonial days and located in Pennsylvania, while the Russells had representatives in the patriot army during the War of the Revolution. James Flack, the paternal grandfather of Doctor Flack, was born in Pennsylvania, and was a pioneer into Ohio, where he built the first mill in Wayne County. This was owned by Mr. Flack and was operated by water power, and in connection therewith he also carried on large farming operations, being the owner of much property. He died at Wooster, Ohio, before the birth of his grandson.

John Flack, father of Doctor Flack, was born in Pennsylvania, and was still a youth when he accompanied his parents to Wayne County, Ohio. There he was engaged in farming until 1862, in which year he removed to Greene County, Indiana, and in 1881 located in Kansas, where he began farming near Independence. His death occurred in that locality in 1883. He was a republican in politics, and his religious faith was that of the United Presbyterian Church. Mr. Flack married Miss Nancy Russell, who was born in Ohio, and died at Independence the same year as her husband, and they were the parents of the following children: William Frank; Mary, who died at Independence, Kansas, as the wife of the late Tom Clifford, who was a farmer; James, who was a farmer and mail carrier and died at Longton; Gordon, who is superintendent of the water works at Caney, Kansas; Mattie, who is the wife of Frank Brewster, a leading contractor and builder of Independence, with numerous large contracts to his credit; John, who is proprietor of a plumbing establishment at Bartlesville, Oklahoma; and Ella, who lives in California.

The early education of William F. Flack was obtained in the public schools of Greene County, Indiana, and at Bloomington (Indiana) High School. In 1881 he came to Kansas and for a short time worked at the carpenter's trade at Independence, but soon resumed his studies, this time for the medical profession, and in 1885 was graduated from the Electric Medical College, Cincinnati, Ohio, from which he was graduated with his degree. He first began practice at Longton, and here has continued to carry on his profession, with ever increasing success. When he began practice here he started as a stranger in a new field, and has grown in reputation and patronage until he now commands the entire confidence of the people all over this locality. He has kept well abreast of modern developments in medicine and surgery, and having a complete library and all the current professional publications, has continued his medical researches with constancy and assiduity. In the search for clearer vision and larger capacity for usefulness, he has taken post-graduate courses at the Chicago Policlinic, in 1892 and 1893, specializing in diseases of the eye, and in this field is widely known. In manner he is genial and optimistic, traits which contribute materially to his business as well as social success. Doctor Flack holds membership in the Elk County Medical Society, the Kansas State Medical Society, the American Medical Association and the Eclectic Medical Society of Kansas. He has frequently been the incumbent of official positions of trust and importance in connection with his profession, having been a member of the Board of Medical Examination and Registration of Kansas, under Governor Bailey, and serving as health officer of Longton for fourteen years. He also was a member of the school board for seven years, during which time much was done to improve the local school system. In political matters he supports the principles and candidates of the republican party. As a fraternalist, Doctor Flack is a prominent Mason, belonging to Longton Lodge, Ancient Free and Accepted Masons; Howard Chapter, Royal Arch Ma-

sons; Saint Bernard Commandery No. 10, Knights Templar, of Independence; and Abdullah Temple, Ancient Arabic Order Nobles of the Mystic Shrine, of Leavenworth. In addition to his residence on Fifth Street, he is the owner of a farm of 120 acres located 1½ miles northeast of Longton.

Doctor Flack was married at Kansas City, Missouri, in 1886, to Mrs. Sarah (Brown) Switzer, daughter of the late W. A. Brown, of Michigan, who was an agriculturist. To this union there have been born two sons: Dr. Frank, a successful practicing physician and surgeon of Coffeyville, Kansas; and Russell, who resides at Elk City, Kansas, and is engaged in business as an insurance agent.

WILLIAM LESTER KELLOGG. The superintendent of motive power of the Missouri, Kansas & Texas Railroad, William L. Kellogg, has worked his way to his present position through his own initiative. At the outset of his career he had no favorable influences to assist him, and he has depended upon no happy circumstances to aid him in his promotion. The chances he has had have been the chances that have come to every man who has been placed in a position similar to his own; the reason that he has gone further than some of his fellow workmen is due to the fact that when these chances arose he had the foresight to recognize them and the ability to fill the positions which they offered.

William Lester Kellogg is an Ohioan, born at Alliance, February 3, 1869, a son of Franklin J. and Catherine M. (Mather) Kellogg. He is of Scotch descent and is a representative of a family which was founded in America prior to the Revolutionary war. His grandfather, William Kellogg, was born in 1787, in Pennsylvania, from which state he removed to Ohio, where he was a superintendent of mines. He retired in 1877 and moved to his home at Alliance, Ohio, where he died in 1881. Franklin J. Kellogg was born in 1832, in Pennsylvania, and was reared and educated in the Keystone State. He went to Alliance, Ohio, as a young man and was there married, beginning his career upon a farm in the vicinity of that city, where his enterprise led him into the operation of a dairy and a general store. His inclinations led him to Kansas in 1883, and, settling at Eldorado, he became one of the most substantial men of the community, both from the standpoint of holding property and from the viewpoint of good citizenship. He accumulated large properties in city realty and farm properties in different parts of Kansas, in order to take care of which he removed to Topeka in 1890 and resided in that city until 1894. In 1896 he retired and took up his residence at Los Angeles, California, where his death occurred in 1914. Mr. Kellogg was a republican who voted the straight ticket but did not look for favors at the hands of his party. Throughout his life he was an active member of the Methodist Episcopal Church. He married Miss Catherine M. Mather, who was born at Alliance, Ohio, in 1839, and died at Topeka, Kansas, at the age of fifty-four years, and they were the parents of two children: Daniel P. and William L. Daniel P. Kellogg, like his brother, has been a railroad man all of his life. He started at the bottom of the ladder in learning the railroad business with the Missouri Pacific Railroad, in Kansas, and at the present time is master mechanic for the Southern Pacific Railroad at Los Angeles, California.

William L. Kellogg received his education in the public schools of Eldorado, Kansas, and he and his brother had as a classmate the noted William Allen

White, now of Emporia, Kansas. A warm friendship sprang up between the three boys and time has not served to chill its glow. After his graduation from the Eldorado High School, in 1887, Mr. Kellogg devoted himself to learning the machinist's trade, in the shops of the Missouri Pacific Railroad, at Fort Scott and Eldorado. He gained some valuable experience as a locomotive fireman, but left this position in 1891 to go to St. Paul, Minnesota, where, after a short period of firing he was given an engineer's run, and subsequently was promoted to foreman of the roundhouse. His all-round ability, fidelity and extensive knowledge combined to gain him still further promotion, and he was made road foreman of engines at St. Paul, holding that post until 1900, when he went to the Iron Mountain Railroad as master mechanic. After 1½ years, Mr. Kellogg was recalled to the Missouri Pacific, where he remained as master mechanic, with headquarters at Fort Scott, Kansas, until 1905. That year saw his appointment as superintendent of motive power for the Pere Marquette and Cincinnati, Hamilton & Dayton Railroad, at Detroit, Michigan. His excellent services there were recognized and appreciated by the Missouri, Kansas & Texas Railroad, which sent for him to take a like position with them in November, 1912. He now has his headquarters at Parsons and has charge of the locomotive and car departments of the entire system. Mr. Kellogg holds a responsible position, and it is one for which his training and experience well fits him. Having worked his way up from the bottom he is able to appreciate the difficulties surrounding the various departments and is capable of rectifying any discrepancies.

Mr. Kellogg is a railroad man through and through. He is a member of the Master Mechanics Association, the Master Car Builders Association, the Traveling Engineers Association and the American Railway Fuel Association. The spirit of fraternalism has led him into Masonry, in which he has attained to the thirty-second degree, being a member of Cincinnati Lodge No. 542, Ancient Free and Accepted Masons; Cincinnati Chapter No. 97, Royal Arch Masons; Cincinnati Commandery No. 3, Knights Templar; Valley of Cincinnati Consistory; and Syria Temple, Ancient Arabic Order Nobles of the Mystic Shrine, of Cincinnati. He also holds membership in the Commercial Club, and is a republican in his political allegiance. He is interested as a stockholder in several oil companies.

Mr. Kellogg was married in Old Trinity Church, New York City, in 1911, to Miss Sylvia Woodruff, daughter of Mr. and Mrs. Frank Woodruff, both of whom died in 1912. Prior to his death Mr. Woodruff had charge of the water service department of the Pere Marquette Railroad at Saginaw, Michigan. Mr. and Mrs. Kellogg are the parents of three children: William Howard, born January 19, 1912; Clara Louise, born October 21, 1914; and Russell Harding, born October 21, 1914, the latter two twins.

FRANK E. BODLEY. The men upon whose shoulders rest the responsibility for prosperity and advancement along every line of commercial and industrial activity are the captains of industry and finance who are in command of the armies which are fighting to preserve the nation's standing among the countries of the earth, as well as against those foes to established currency and methods of transacting business. Without them and their sound, conservative policies, the country would be at the mercy of every irresponsible, unscrupulous speculator or visionary idealist. As is but natural, the financiers of the country's great cities

are the ones called upon principally to bear the greatest amount of this responsibility, but the smaller communities contribute their share according to their size and progressive spirit, and throughout the State of Kansas there are found communities whose citizens are serving faithfully and well in the financial ranks. Among these at Chanute in Neosho County is found F. E. Bodley, president of the Peoples-Home State Bank of Chanute and a well and favorably known banker whose operations have been extensive and important and whose reputation rests upon many years of upright and honorable dealing.

Mr. Bodley was born April 24, 1859, at Princeton, Illinois, son of O. J. and Amelia (Uhler) Bodley. In 1889 he became interested in banking, at Quenemo, Osage County, where he remained for years as president of the Farmers State Bank. In 1905 he came to Chanute to become vice president of the Bank of Commerce and resigned that position and was made president of the Peoples-Home State Bank, an office which holds at the present time. Mr. Bodley is widely known in banking circles as a man of high ability, careful, conservative, farseeing and possessing excellent judgment. The Peoples-Home State Bank, the policies of which he is so ably directing, was established in 1906 as the Peoples State Bank and was merged with the Home State Bank in 1907, the latter having been established in 1903. Today the capital and surplus is $60,000 and deposits are over one-half million dollars. The officers are: F. E. Bodley, president; J. L. Barnes, vice president; H. C. Bodley, cashier; and J. E. Wood, assistant cashier. The banking house was erected in 1906 by Mr. Bodley for the bank, and he still owns it, this structure being situated at the corner of Main Street and Santa Fe Avenue. It is a modern bank building, of brick and Carthage stone, the bank being located on the first floor of the building.

In 1886, near Ottawa, Kansas, Mr. Bodley was married to Miss Laura Copple, daughter of the late John and Emma (Rasdell) Copple, and to this union there has been born one son: Harold C., a graduate of St. John's Military Academy, Salina, Kansas, who is cashier of the Peoples-Home State Bank of Chanute and one of the prominent and rising young business men of the city.

HON. BEN S. PAULEN. Each individual, under a democratic form of government, possesses an equal chance for public advancement. There is no reason why any man, providing that he possess real ability and sound judgment, cannot aspire to the highest position in the land, but while this is true theoretically, in actuality it is the one who has always been a little in advance of his associates and has developed his faculties beyond the ordinary who forges ahead and is placed by the people in positions of honor and responsibility. In this connection the foregoing is true of Hon. Ben S. Paulen, one of the leading merchants of Fredonia and vice president of the Wilson County Bank. Long prominent in commercial and financial circles, he demonstrated that he was possessed of abilities far beyond the ordinary, and reached an honorable goal in 1912 when elected to a seat in the Kansas State Senate from the Thirteenth District and to which office he has recently been re-elected, being the first senator to succeed himself from this district, as the counties of Wilson and Masha had rotated the senator.

Senator Paulen was born on a farm in DeWitt County, Illinois, July 14, 1869, and is a son of J. W. and Lucy B. (Johnson) Paulen. His grandfather was Diebold Paulen, who was born at Strassburg, Alsace Lorraine, and after serving in the German regular army emigrated to the United States and settled near Springfield, Sangamon County, Illinois, where he passed the remainder of his life in farming. He was the first of the family to come to the United States, was a pioneer of Sangamon County, and belonged to the sturdy, home-loving type of his race who made good and substantial citizens and whose labors have done much in the settlement and improvement of new sections of the country.

J. W. Paulen, father of Senator Paulen, was born September 8, 1839, on a farm in Sangamon County, Illinois, and was reared and educated in the vicinity of Springfield. He was brought up as a farmer and when ready to enter upon his own career engaged in agricultural pursuits, first in Sangamon and later in DeWitt County. From the latter he came to Kansas in 1869, settling in Wilson County on a farm four miles south of Fredonia. On this tract of 160 acres he resided for five years, at the end of which time he was elected clerk of the District Court and moved into the Town of Fredonia. When his term of five years expired, Mr. Paulen embarked in the banking business at Fredonia and continued therein for three years, but disposed of his interests in that direction to give his full attention to the real estate business, in which he had become interested. In 1879 he also entered mercantile affairs when he opened a hardware establishment, located on the west side of the public square. In 1914 he sold out the hardware stock, and is now engaged in the general mercantile business, in partnership with his son, Ben S. They have built up an excellent trade, which covers the entire city and its surrounding territory. Mr. Paulen is favorably known in business circles, as a shrewd merchant who makes the most of his opportunities, but whose business dealings are always prosecuted in an honorable and straightforward manner. He is a republican in his political views and has long been active and prominent in the ranks of his party, having held a number of minor positions as well as being Mayor of Fredonia for two terms. Fraternally, he is affiliated with Constellation Lodge No. 95, Ancient Free and Accepted Masons; Kilwinning Chapter No. 44, Royal Arch Masons; Abal Del Kader Commandery No. 26, Knights Templar; and Mirza Temple, Ancient Arabic Order of the Noble Mystic Shrine, Pittsburg, Kansas; and to the Ancient Order of United Workmen. While living in Illinois, Mr. Paulen enlisted in the One Hundred and Thirtieth Regiment, Volunteer Infantry, and served two years and eleven months as a Union soldier during the Civil war. He was in the Siege of Vicksburg, took part in many other important engagements, and during Banks' Red River Campaign was made a prisoner at Sabine Cross Roads and held by the enemy for fourteen months at Tyler, Texas, until his exchange could be effected. His war record was an excellent one. Mr. Paulen married Miss Lucy B. Johnson, who was born in 1848, at Frankfort, Kentucky, and to this union there were born six children: Ben S., of this review; Laura E., who resides at Alva, Oklahoma, wife of Fred N. Howell, a teacher in the Oklahoma Normal School; Minnie, the wife of C. E. Burke, bank printer with the Burke Printing Company, a large and well known firm of Fredonia; Mildred, who is the wife of James L. Fitzmorris, a farmer of Fall River, Kansas; Ray, who resides on a farm near Fredonia; and Blanche, who is the wife of Dr. C. A. Thomas, a practicing physician and surgeon of Fredonia.

Ben S. Paulen was thoroughly trained in his youth for his struggle with life, first attending the graded and high schools of Fredonia, from which latter he was graduated in 1887, then going to the Kansas University for one term, and later taking a course in the Saint Louis Business College. In 1889 he entered business with his father, with whom he has continued to be associated to the present time. The store now occupies a floor space 60 by 100 feet, and is stocked with an attractive line of general merchandise, well arranged, tastefully chosen and popularly priced, and the business has grown to be the largest of its kind in Fredonia and this part of the state. As a business man who was progressive, enterprising and energetic, Mr. Paulen began attracting the attention of the people, who soon discovered him possessed of official possibilities. As a member of the city council and as city treasurer of Fredonia he verified these suspicions, and finally was elected mayor, a position which he held for three terms, during which time he did much to advance the civic and material interests of Fredonia. In 1912 he became the candidate of the republican party for the office of state senator from the Thirteenth Senatorial District, and so faithfully and well did he discharge the duties of that office that he received the re-election in 1916. During his first term, Senator Paulen was chairman of the Committee on Printing, and a member of the committees on Cities of the Second Class, Banks and Banking, Oil and Gas, Public Buildings, Municipal Corporations and Engrossed Bills. He was connected with much important legislation, and introduced and championed the bill for cities of the second class to levy special taxes for the purpose of purchasing fire apparatus; the bank check bill which provides a punishment for overdrawing a bank account by check; and the bill for the adoption of the Massachusetts ballot. Senator Paulen is now on the following committees: chairman, Committees and Rules Committee; member Ways and Means, Cities of the Second Class, Banks and Banking, Federal and State Affairs and Gas and Oil committees. He has been appointed by Governor Capper as state inspector of oils for a four year term beginning April 1, 1917.

Senator Paulen belongs to Constellation Lodge No. 95, Ancient Free and Accepted Masons; Kilwinning Chapter No. 44, Royal Arch Masons; Abal Del Lader Commandery No. 26, Knights Templar; and Mirza Temple, Ancient Arabic Order Nobles of the Mystic Shrine, at Pittsburg, Kansas, and is a thirty-second degree Mason, belonging to Consistory No. 1, Wichita. Senator Paulen is a trustee of the Wilson County Hospital. He has been connected with some big business enterprises, and at this time is vice president of the Wilson County Bank and of the Fredonia Ice and Light Company. He resides in his own modern home at No. 415 Eleventh Street, and is the owner of much other property.

On February 14, 1900, Mr. Paulen was married at Holton, Kansas, to Miss Barbara Ellis, daughter of the late E. T. and Thurza Ellis, of Holton, both of whom are now deceased. Mr. Ellis, who was in business at Holton for a number of years and was a Union veteran of the Civil war, was better known as Judge Ellis, because of his many years of service as a justice of the peace.

HON. JOHN T. DENTON. While John T. Denton has been a staid and substantial banker, business man and public spirited citizen of Oneola and Elk County for over thirty years, he has covered a great deal of territory in the course of his earlier experiences, and he came through difficulties and hardships on the road to success. He was left an orphan boy in Kentucky, was reared in the home of relatives, started out to make his own way in the world when sixteen, and has always considered it fortunate that he came to Kansas in the early days of the state, and has found his real destiny in her commonwealth.

Mr. Denton was born at Wyoming, Bath County, Kentucky, March 9, 1850. His ancestors were English people who settled in Virginia in Colonial days. His great-grandfather was born in Virginia, and as a young man crossed the mountains into Kentucky. Mr. Denton's grandfather was William Denton, who spent many years of his life in Kentucky as a farmer, but died at Huntsville, Indiana, in 1850.

Abraham Denton, the father of the Grenola banker, was born in Bath County, Kentucky, and died at Wyoming in that locality in 1855. He spent all his life in Bath County, was a farmer, stockman, merchant and a hotel proprietor. In politics he was a whig, a follower of the great Henry Clay, and was a member of the Christian Church. His wife, Elizabeth Barber, spent her life in Kentucky, dying at Wyoming in 1852. Thus John T. Denton was two years of age when his mother died and five years old when he lost his father. He was the youngest of six children. William, the oldest, a soldier in the Civil war, became a farmer, and died in Lewis County, Kentucky, in 1872. Jane, who now lives at Owensville, Kentucky, is the widow of John Jackson, who was a farmer. James, who died in May, 1915, in Marshall County, Kansas, was a pioneer farmer and stockman in that county, and was a local leader in the republican party, serving as township trustee. Magdaline, who died in Bath County, Kentucky, during the '80s, was the wife of George Jackson, a farmer also deceased. Eliza, who died in Fleming County, Kentucky, in the '80s, married Robert P. Finley, a farmer now deceased.

After the death of his parents John T. Denton was reared by Reuben and Jane Denton in Kentucky. Reuben Denton, who was a double cousin to Abraham Denton, died in 1862, and his wife in 1875. As a boy in their home at Wyoming, Kentucky, John T. Denton attended the public schools, but in 1866 he removed to Hancock County, Illinois, and for a time attended the high school at Hamilton in that county. At the age of sixteen he began working for himself on farms and in other occupations, and in 1870 went west to San Francisco, California. He was employed in a hotel, spent six months in the gold mines of Nevada, and for four years was foreman on a cattle ranch near Portland, Oregon.

In 1875 Mr. Denton returned to Kentucky to visit Jane Denton on her deathbed, the woman who had made a home for him in his childhood and for whom he felt the affection of a son to a mother. In 1876, in Kentucky, Mr. Denton married Miss Leah Elizabeth Havens, daughter of Alfred and Maria (Lloyd) Havens, both of whom are now deceased. Her father was a farmer.

For several years after his marriage Mr. Denton and wife had to struggle for a living. Following his marriage he returned to Hancock County, Illinois, spent one year as a farmer there, and when he came to Kansas in 1877 his principal capital consisted of a horse. This horse he traded for a claim and water hole in Cowley County. This claim was situated sixteen miles west of Grenola. He worked his claim and went through all the hardships of early farming until 1884, and in that time had brought his quarter section to a reasonable degree of improvement and cultivation. In the meantime he had acquired other lands and had developed a large ranch.

Mr. Denton has been a banker at Grenola since 1884. In that year he brought about the organiza-

tion of the Grenola State Bank, and has been its active head for many years. The officers of this institution are: J. E. Denton, president; D. E. Ware, of Grenola, vice president; Alfred A. Denton, cashier; Wellington B. Denton, assistant cashier. The bank has a capital stock of $20,000, surplus and undivided profits of $5,100, and it is a bank which has rendered a splendid service to the community and it has weathered all the financial storms since it was founded. In 1910 the bank erected its modern home on Main Street.

Prosperity seems to attend the efforts of John T. Denton in whatever direction they turn. He has always been one of the prominent farmers and stockmen of this part of Kansas, and he owns farms aggregating 1,500 acres in Elk County. His fine home is situated two blocks north of the bank in Grenola.

Mr. Denton has long been prominent in republican politics in his part of the state. In 1896 he was chairman of the County Central Committee of Elk County, and has served on various other party committees for a number of years. In 1907 he was elected a member of the State Senate, and by re-election continued in that office for eight years, his present term expiring January 1, 1917. In the Senate he has served on the Banks and Banking Committee, the Congressional, Judicial and Legislative Apportionment Committee, the Mines and Mining Committee, the Oil and Gas Committee and the committee on Claims and Accounts. Whenever the Legislature has been in session John T. Denton has been accounted one of the strong and influential men of the Senate.

He rendered an important service to the state at large when in 1915 he was asked to represent the Kansas commissioners on the ground at the Panama Exposition at San Francisco and San Diego. Senator Denton had introduced and had been influential in securing the appropriation by the Kansas Legislature for these expositions, and he remained in California from June 1st until December 4, 1915, looking after the financial and social interests of the state and lending all his expert skill as a business man to the adjustment of the matters entrusted to his care.

Senator Denton is a member of the Kansas State and American Banking associations. His fraternal relations are with Canopy Lodge, No. 248, Ancient Free and Accepted Masons, at Grenola, with Wichita Consistory, No. 2, of the thirty-second degree Scottish Rite, with Midian Temple of the Mystic Shrine at Wichita; with Grenola Lodge No. 86, Ancient Order United Workmen; the Degree of Honor, and the Anti-Horse Thief Association.

Mr. Denton has two sons, both of whom are now associated with him in banking and are able young financiers. Alfred A. is cashier, while Wellington B. is assistant cashier of the Grenola State Bank.

Mr. Denton and his sons are also heavily engaged in the stock business. Mr. Denton has been identified with this vocation for many years and has become recognized as one of the largest stock dealers in Southern Kansas. During the past year he handled 2,000 cattle.

FRANK WILLIAM BOSS. Among the county officials of Cherokee County, one whose previous record, general qualifications for ability and character, gave, at the time of his election, in 1912, every ground for a successful career, and whose discharge of the duties of his office has since vindicated the faith placed in him, is Frank William Boss, county attorney. Mr. Boss has the reputation of being an indefatigable worker, combining scholarship with an active energy and forceful personality, and these qualities have been much esteemed in an office in which the people of the county have endeavored to place men who would lend thorough integrity and practical efficiency to the administration.

Mr. Boss was born at Plymouth, the county seat of Marshall County, Indiana, January 4, 1874, and is a son of John and Mary (Conrad) Boss, and a grandson of a native of the Canton of Berne, Switzerland, who came to the United States and spent his latter years in farming in Kosciusko County, Indiana, where he died. John Boss, the father of Frank W., was born in 1839, in Berne, Switzerland, and was twelve years of age when brought to the United States by his parents. He had commenced his education in his native land, and it was completed in the district schools of Kosciusko County, Indiana, where he was reared to manhood and brought up as a farmer. At the time of his marriage, he engaged in farming on his own account, in Kosciusko County, but some time thereafter removed to Marshall County, Indiana, and located on a farm near Plymouth. He possessed the racial characteristics of industry and honorable dealing, and through persistent and well-directed effort succeeded in the development of a good farm and the founding of a comfortable home. Mr. Boss continued to be engaged in agricultural pursuits until 1900, when, feeling that he had done his share in the world's work, he retired from active affairs and moved to his home at Plymouth, where he now resides. In the several communities in which Mr. Boss has made his home he has shown himself a public-spirited citizen, who has been willing to aid good movements, and as a generous and kindly friend and neighbor. He is a republican, but politics has played but little part in his life, his activities therein being principally confined to the casting of his vote. Mr. Boss married Miss Mary Conrad, who was born in 1842, in Kosciusko County, Indiana, and died at Plymouth, that state, in 1914. They became the parents of the following children: Rose, who married C. W. Wade, a retired farmer of Plymouth, Indiana; Laura, a teacher in the city schools of Plymouth, who makes her home with her father; Ella, who is the wife of F. E. Garn, president of a trust company at Chicago, Illinois; Lizzie, who married W. F. Walter, and resides at Bremen, Indiana, where Mr. Walter is engaged in the mercantile business; Jacob H., a graduate of the Chicago College of Physicians and Surgeons, and now a practicing physician of the Illinois metropolis; Frank William, of this notice; and Carrie, who is a teacher in the city schools of Plymouth, Indiana.

Frank William Boss was brought up on the home farm in Marshall County, Indiana, and secured his primary education in the public schools of that vicinity. Subsequently he pursued a course at the Plymouth High School, from which he was duly graduated in 1894, and immediately thereafter entered the law department of the University of Michigan, at Ann Arbor, where he remained three years. Graduated with the class of 1897 and the degree of Bachelor of Laws, he returned to Plymouth and after some further preparation embarked upon the practice of law in his home community. He remained there for seven years and then secured an appointment to the position of inspector of immigration in the eastern part of the Mexican border, there remaining for three years. In 1910 Mr. Boss located at Scammon, Kansas, where he practiced for two years and served in the capacity of city attorney, and in 1912, upon his election to the office of county attorney, on the republican ticket, came to his present location at Columbus. He has

enforced the law without fear or favor and during his four years of office has shown himself a courageous, energetic and entirely capable official, with a realization of the responsibilities placed in his hands. Mr. Boss' offices are in the Court House, while his residence, which he owns, is at No. 519 Kansas Avenue. Fraternally Mr. Boss is connected with Scammon Lodge No. 351, Ancient Free and Accepted Masons; Fort Scott Consistory No. 6, thirty-second degree, Pittsburg; and Mirza Temple, Ancient Arabic Order Nobles of the Mystic Shrine, and with the Knights of Pythias, of Columbus.

In 1899, at Chicago, Illinois, Mr. Boss was married to Miss Alice Lehr, daughter of H. A. and Eleanor (Carnahan) Lehr, of Bremen, Indiana. Mr. Lehr was for some years county auditor of Marshall County, Indiana, but is now living retired. Mr. and Mrs. Boss are the parents of two children: Marcellus G., born January 24, 1901, who is now a junior in the Cherokee County High School, and Eleanor Mary, born October 12, 1916.

SAMUEL BROWNLEE FISHER of Parsons, consulting engineer of the Missouri, Kansas & Texas Railroad Company, is one of the eminent railway engineers of America. He has had nearly fifty years of active experience and has been identified with the construction of various railway lines in the West and East.

He comes of an old Scotch family of Covenanter stock. On the maternal side his ancestors were the Brownlees, who were Covenanters in Scotland and were exiled because of their religious belief and settled in Pennsylvania. Mr. Fisher's great-great-grandfather in the maternal line, George Wilie, was a soldier in the Revolutionary war, and another member of this same family was Colonel Thompson, an aide to General Washington. Mr. Fisher's maternal grandfather, Samuel Brownlee, was born in Washington, Pennsylvania, in 1792, and spent all his life on a farm in that rugged district of Southwestern Pennsylvania, dying in 1855. He was an active abolitionist in the days before the Civil war and was a member of the Associate Branch of the Presbyterian Church. Samuel Brownlee married Ann Wilie, who was born and died at Washington, Pennsylvania.

The father of Mr. Fisher was Rev. Jacob P. Fisher, who was born in Ohio in 1808, but was reared and married in Washington, Pennsylvania. He was a minister of that branch of Presbyterianism formerly known as the Associate Church. He was also actively identified with the abolition cause. His death occurred in Washington, Pennsylvania, in 1853. Rev. Mr. Fisher married Jane Thompson Brownlee, who was born in Washington, Pennsylvania, in 1820. She died in 1888 while visiting in Montana, her home at that time being in Washington, Pennsylvania. Samuel B. Fisher was the older of the two sons. His brother, George McVey Fisher, is a farmer at Kalispel, Montana, is a graduate of Washington and Jefferson College and is also a Presbyterian minister.

Samuel Brownlee Fisher was born October 24, 1846, while his parents resided at Cherry Fork, Ohio. He grew up in Southwestern Pennsylvania near Washington, attended the district schools there, and in 1868 graduated Bachelor of Science from Washington and Jefferson College at Washington. That splendid old institution has honored him with other degrees because of his prominence in his profession. In 1871 he received the degree master of science, and in 1908 his alma mater conferred upon him the degree of Doctor of Science.

The years 1869-71 Mr. Fisher spent in learning a

trade with the Rogers Locomotive Works at Paterson, New Jersey. From 1873 to 1885 he was in the engineering department of the Pennsylvania lines west of Pittsburg. From 1885 to 1890 he was chief engineer of the Milwaukee & Northern Railway. He was chief engineer of the Soo lines at Minneapolis, Minnesota, from 1890 to 1892. During 1893-94 he was chief engineer of the Everett & Monte Christo Railway in the Puget Sound district of Washington.

Mr. Fisher has been connected with the Missouri, Kansas & Texas Railway Company for the past twenty years. In 1895 he lived in Parsons a few months representing that company, but from 1896 to 1912 was chief engineer with headquarters at St. Louis. Since 1912 he has been chief engineer of construction and was also chairman of the valuation committee. In 1916 he became consulting engineer, and has had his offices in Parsons since 1915. He still owns his home in St. Louis.

Mr. Fisher is a member of the American Society of Civil Engineers, belongs to the Engineers Club of St. Louis, and to the Association of American Railway Engineers. He is a republican and is an elder in the Second Presbyterian Church of St. Louis.

In 1881 in Pittsburg, Pennsylvania, he married Miss Agnes Crooks, daughter of James and Anna Crooks, both now deceased. Her father was a farmer. Mrs. Fisher died at St. Louis in 1906, leaving two children: Brownlee, who completed his education in Washington University at St. Louis, is now secretary of the Van Zandt Gas Appliance Company of St. Louis, and is also a lieutenant in the Naval Reserve. Ann P., who lives with her father, graduated A. B. from Washington University at St. Louis.

CHARLES N. CONVERSE. Identified with banks and banking all through his business life, Charles N. Converse, president of the Citizens State Bank of Altoona, Kansas, is widely known in financial circles where his judgment is deemed sound and accurate, and his reputation has long been that of a forcible, able and efficient business man.

Charles N. Converse was born at Clinton, Illinois, June 22, 1863. His parents were Henry E. and Clara (Weaver) Converse, and his grandfathers were John Converse and Solomon Weaver. Solomon Weaver emigrated from Germany in boyhood and grew up at Clinton, Illinois, in which neighborhood he engaged in farming and there he died in 1883. On the paternal side the family traces its ancestry to France and when the first of the name, two brothers, came together to the American colonies, they spelled it Congiers. The brothers separated, one settling at Boston, Massachusetts, and the other at Philadelphia, Pennsylvania.

John Converse, the paternal grandfather, was born at Woburn, Massachusetts, February 14, 1813, and died at Clinton, Illinois, in June, 1880. He was an early settler in DeWitt County, Illinois, and a pioneer shoemaker at Clinton. He was a member of the Baptist Church and a good and worthy citizen. He married Eurania Nelson, who was born at Sutton, Massachusetts, in 1815, and died at Clinton, Illinois, in 1890. Of their family of children one survives, Frank H., a resident of Decatur, Illinois, a retired contractor and builder. During the Civil war he served as a member of the Eleventh Massachusetts Volunteer Infantry. The grandmother of Charles N. Converse, was a direct descendant of the great British admiral, Lord Horatio Nelson, and belonged also to the same ancestry as did the brave American General Putnam.

Henry E. Converse, father of Charles N. Converse, was born at Woburn, Massachusetts, January 8, 1836, and his death occurred at Burlington, Kansas, January 8, 1909. He was reared at Malden, Massachusetts, until he accompanied his people to Illinois, after which he went into railroad work as an engineer and conductor and during the Civil war served in the latter capacity on the Chicago & Alton Railroad. For a short time afterward he engaged in farming near Clinton, in 1863-4, but returned to railroading and continued until 1907, when he retired, removing then to Burlington, Kansas, where he died January 8, 1909. He belonged to the Masonic fraternity and to the Brotherhood of Locomotive Engineers. In politics he was one of the old-line republicans. He was a broadminded, well informed man with marked sterling traits of character.

Henry E. Converse married Clara Weaver, who was born in 1840, in Union County, Ohio, and died at Clinton, Illinois, in 1898. They were the parents of three children: Clara, who is the wife of A. H. Peck, who is a contractor and builder at Bloomington, Illinois; Charles N., of Altoona; and Frank, who died at Shreveport, Louisiana, when aged forty-seven years. He was a locomotive engineer on the Kansas City & Southern Railroad, running from Shreveport to Port Arthur and New Orleans.

Charles N. Converse enjoyed educational advantages at Clinton, Illinois, and after completing the high school course attended the University of Illinois, at Champaign, and immediately afterward entered the employ of the DeWitt County National Bank at Clinton. After coming to Kansas he was identified for 2½ years with the McPherson Bank, at McPherson, McPherson County, when he retired for a time from the confining cares of business, because of impaired health, seeking out-door exercise as ·a farmer. With this end in view he took up a claim, the third, in Stevens County and laid out the Town of Hugoton, which is now the county seat, and there not only built the first house but hauled all the lumber for its construction a distance of sixty-five miles. He remained one year in Stevens County and then once more gave heed to the call of business problems, for which organizing and executive ability of a high order seem to so well qualify him. After selling his claim he located at Waverly, in Coffey County, where, on February 1, 1902, he organized the First National Bank and served as its cashier until September, 1903, when he went to Burlington, Kansas, where he organized the Farmers National Bank and became at first its cashier and later president of that institution. In October, 1908, he went to Ottawa, Kansas, as vice president of the First National Bank. On March 1, 1911, Mr. Converse came to Altoona as president of the Citizens State Bank.

The Citizens State Bank of Altoona was established as a state bank in 1886. Its present officers are: Charles N. Converse, president; W. H. Hamblin, vice president; and Turner D. Jones, cashier. The capital of the bank is $16,000 and the surplus is $5,900. The bank building, a modern and attractive brick structure on Main Street, was erected in 1908. Under its present management the bank is in a very prosperous condition, great confidence being placed in Mr. Converse both as a very able financier and as a man of the highest personal integrity. He belongs to the Kansas Bankers Association, the Kansas State Bankers Association and the American Bankers Association. During the administration of Governor Bailey, Mr. Converse served by appointment as regent of the Kansas State University.

souri, whence she had been brought by her parents. Dr. Absalom C. and Mary Jane (Hamilton) Sloan were the parents of eight children, as follows: Jeremiah N., born in 1848, in Polk County, Missouri, who followed farming all his life and died in Texas in 1883; Martha M., who died in 1869, at Walnut Grove, Missouri, as the wife of A. P. Routh, deceased, a merchant of that place; Sanford Hamilton, who was a physician and surgeon throughout his career and died in 1901, at Whitesboro, Texas; Dr. E. O., of this notice; Lewis C., who followed farming in the vicinity of Walnut Grove until his death in 1896; Ellen Lincoln, who is the wife of W. G. Miller, a farmer near Walnut Grove; Jacob Samuel, who is also a farmer in that vicinity; and Willard C., a zinc miner near Carthage, Missouri.

E. O. Sloan attended the public schools of Walnut Grove, Missouri, where he secured a high school education. From the time that he was a youth he had held to the resolution that he would one day become a professional man, and chose medicine as that most likely to prove congenial and profitable. Therefore, following his graduation from the high school, he began making plans, and after studying for some time under his father entered the Missouri Medical College of St. Louis, now Washington University, from which he was graduated with the degree of Doctor of Medicine, in 1881. In the meantime, in order to defray his expenses, he was a merchant at Walnut Grove for four years. Doctor Sloan began practice at Walnut Grove immediately after his graduation, but remained there only a short time, in 1882 coming to Kansas and establishing himself in an office at Cherryvale. That city had the benefit of his services for seven years, but in 1890 he changed his scene of activities to Pittsburg, where he has since carried on a general medical and surgical practice. His offices are now located in the Commerce Building. He has an extensive and lucrative practice, holds to high ideals in his professional service, and is justly numbered among the leading professional men of Crawford County, which is distinguished for high rank in the medical profession. Doctor Sloan belongs to the Southeastern Medical Society and to the Crawford County Medical Society, of which he was president for two years, and has been city health officer of Pittsburg for two years. He is intelligently interested in all that pertains to modern progress and improvement, not only along professional, but also material and moral lines, always finding time to study important public questions and ever ready to lend his influence for the betterment of humanity. He is a republican in his political views, belongs to the Christian Church, and is a member of the Masons, in which order he has reached the Knights Templar degree.

On March 30, 1876, at Walnut Grove, Missouri, Doctor Sloan was united in marriage with Miss Lucy Mizener, daughter of E. A. and Cynthia (Sager) Mizener. Mr. Mizener lost his life as a Union soldier at the battle of Chickamauga, during the Civil war, in 1863, but Mrs. Mizener still survives him and resides at Long Beach, California, having reached the remarkable age of ninety-two years. To Doctor and Mrs. Sloan there have been born four children, as follows: Laura Welbber, born December 13, 1877, who died March 19, 1895; Maud S., born February 23, 1880, residing with her parents; Georgia Pauline, born February 22, 1882, and now the wife of Charles W. Osborn, head bookkeeper for the National Bank of Pittsburg; and Edna O., born August 28, 1891, who is the wife of John Winston Hill, employed in the office of the secretary of the Erie Railroad Company, at Kansas City, Missouri.

EARL A. DAVIS, M. D. A native son of Kansas, who is assisting to maintain the prestige of his state in the field of medical achievement, Dr. Earl A. Davis has attained a position of distinction among the physicians and surgeons of Chanute, where he has been engaged in the practice of his calling since 1903. He is the son of a physician, Dr. J. Davis, and was born May 20, 1875, at Ottawa, Franklin County.

The family of which Doctor Davis is a member originated in Wales and came from that country to America during the colonial period, the first members taking up their residence in Pennsylvania. The doctor's grandfather was also a physician and surgeon and for many years practiced in Ohio, where his death occurred. Dr. J. Davis was born in Ohio in 1833, and was there reared and educated. After his preliminary training was completed he enrolled as a student in the Cleveland Medical College, from which he was graduated, and subsequently pursued a course at the Cincinnati Homeopathic College, from which he received his degree. He was married in Ohio and in 1868 came to Kansas, settling as a pioneer physician at Ottawa, where he has continued in practice during a period of nearly a half a century. Doctor Davis is one of the honored members of his profession in Franklin County and has a practice that extends over a wide area of country which has been attracted to him by his thorough knowledge, his technical skill and the natural kindness that goes so far in aiding a practitioner in his humane work. He belongs to the various organizations of the profession, and is a consistent member of the Presbyterian Church. His political support is given to the democratic party. Doctor Davis married Miss Alexina Williamson, who was born in 1840, in Ohio, and who still survives and resides at Ottawa. She belongs to the Society of Colonial Dames, Gen. Edward Hand being the ancestor through whose participation in the struggle of the colonies she derives her membership. A statue to the memory of General Hand, erected by the Daughters of the American Revolution, stands in the new building at Washington, District of Columbia. Mrs. Davis is active in the work and affairs of the Society of Colonial Dames, as she is also in the various movements of the Presbyterian Church, of which she has been a devout member all her life. To Doctor and Mrs. Davis there have been born the following children: Dr. H. W., who is engaged in the practice of dentistry at Salt Lake City, Utah; F. E., who is a postoffice inspector in the service of the United States Government, with headquarters at St. Louis, Missouri; J. D., a graduate of the Ohio Medical College, Cincinnati, Ohio, and now a practicing physician and surgeon of that city; Dr. J. B., also a graduate of that institution and engaged in practice with his father at Salt Lake City, Kansas; E. C., who is a merchant with an establishment at Williamsburg, Kansas; and Dr. Earl A.

The public schools of Ottawa furnished Earl A. Davis with his early education, and after he had attended the high school for several years he began to study medicine under the preceptorship of his father. The son and grandson of physicians, he took naturally and kindly to his calling, but did not enter actively upon its study as a collegian until he had completed a three-year literary course at Ottawa University. He then entered the Ohio Medical College, Cincinnati, where he was graduated with the class of 1902, receiving the degree of Doctor of Medicine. To further prepare himself, he spent the rest of 1902 and a part of 1903 as assistant house surgeon at the Kansas City

General Hospital, and in the latter year came to Chanute. Here he has succeeded well, having built up a liberal and representative practice among the best families. He is not alone a skilled practitioner, but possesses those admirable traits of character which prove such a blessing in the sick room. He maintains offices at No. 114½ East Main Street, while his home, which he owns, is at No. 112 South Highland Avenue. Doctor Davis is a democrat, but has not aspired to political office, his only public service having been in the line of his profession, consisting of two years spent in the capacity of health officer. He holds membership in the Neosho County Medical Society, the Kansas State Medical Society, the Southeastern Medical Society and the American Medical Association. He is likewise widely and favorably known in fraternal circles, being a member of Cedar Lodge No. 103, Ancient Free and Accepted Masons; Chanute Camp No. 852, Modern Woodmen of America; Chanute Lodge No. 96, Ancient Order of United Workmen; Chanute Council No. 420, Fraternal Aid Union; Chanute Lodge No. 806, Benevolent and Protective Order of Elks; and Chanute Aerie No. 521, Fraternal Order of Eagles.

In 1904, at Chanute, Doctor Davis was married to Miss Ethel Southard, daughter of Mr. and Mrs. Whig Southard, the latter of whom is deceased. Mr. Southard, who was a traveling salesman for many years, is now retired from business and makes his home with his son-in-law and daughter. Doctor and Mrs. Davis have no children.

JOHN WILLIAM WALLACE is one of the able and progressive educators in Kansas, now superintendent of schools at Reading. He came to this city from Americus in the fall of 1716. He is a young Kansan by birth and tradition, and has brought to his work as an educator not only thorough training but also a loyal appreciation of this great state and her institutions.

He is of Scotch stock, his great-grandfather having come from Scotland to Massachusetts about the time of the Revolutionary war. Later the family settled in Mohawk Valley of New York. Professor Wallace's father is J. V. Wallace, who was born in Guernsey County, Ohio, in 1862, and is now a farmer and stockman at Waverly in Coffey County, Kansas, where he settled in 1882, when that section of the state was an open range. J. V. Wallace spent the first seven years of his life in his native state, then removed to Iowa, and was married after he came to Coffey County, Kansas. He is a republican who has taken a very active part in county affairs and has served as a member of state conventions. He belongs to the Methodist Church and to the Ancient Order of United Workmen. The maiden name of his wife was Minnie Bazil, who was born in Shelby County, Illinois, in 1868. In the family were fourteen children, mentioned briefly as follows: Mae, wife of Joseph Miller, a retired marble dealer at Burlington, Kansas; John W.; Maggie, who died at the age of fourteen months; Harry, principal of schools at Minneola, Kansas; Howard, who died at the age of two months, and Ethel, who died at the age of six months; Elsie, wife of W. H. Whittington, a farmer in Coffey County; Ray, who died at the age of fourteen months; Ida, Waldo, Opal, Roy and Chester, all of whom reside with their parents and all except Ida are attending school; and Leslie, the youngest, who died at the age of two years.

John William Wallace pursued his studies through the eight grades of the public schools in Coffey County. He grew up on a farm, and had a thorough agricultural training. While teaching he also attended the State Normal School at Emporia and in 1914 was granted a life teacher's certificate by the State of Kansas. After leaving the Normal School he was superintendent of schools at Americus, until he took charge of the schools at Reading in the fall of 1916, where he has done much to organize and introduce efficiency into the curriculum.

Mr. Wallace is a republican, is a member and local preacher in the Methodist Episcopal Church and belongs to the County and State Teachers' Association.

In August, 1914, at Emporia, he married Miss Gracie May Saueressig, daughter of G. E. and Elizabeth Saueressig, who are farmers at Fredonia, Kansas. Mr. and Mrs. Wallace have one child, Vincent Edmund, who was born in October, 1915.

THOMAS E. THOMPSON, a native of Iowa, has lived in Kansas for forty-six years, and is one of the veteran newspaper men of the state, being editor and proprietor of the Howard Courant.

As to his American ancestry, there is record of his Thompson forefathers coming from England and settling in Maine in colonial days. Mr. Thompson's grandfather, Samuel Thompson, was born in Maine in 1781. He took an active part in the pioneer development of the Middle West, lived in Ohio for a number of years, and about 1846 moved to the new State of Iowa, where he was one of the pioneer farmers. He died in Henry County, Iowa, in 1866.

It was in Henry County, Iowa, that Thomas E. Thompson was born, May 23, 1860. His father, Asa Thompson, who was born in Ohio in 1829, was about sixteen years of age when the family removed to Henry County, Iowa, where he grew to maturity and married. He also followed farming, and in 1871 came to Kansas and secured a homestead of 160 acres in Howard County, now Elk County. In 1875 he removed to the Town of Howard, and lived there until his death in 1896. He was a man of much prominence in this section of the state. He served as clerk of the District Court six years, from 1875 to 1881, and in 1887 was elected a representative in the Legislature and also filled a vacancy in the office of probate judge of Elk County. He was a very strong republican. He and his son Thomas were associated in the purchase of the Howard Courant, and he retained a financial interest in the paper until his death. Fraternally he was a member of the Independent Order of Odd Fellows. Asa Thompson married Emma Ables, who was born in Guernsey County, Ohio, in 1829, and died at Howard, Kansas, in 1910. The oldest of their children, a son, died in infancy, and the others were Catherine, Thomas E. and John A. Catherine, who was born in 1852 and died at Howard, Kansas, in 1887, married J. L. Hart, who was one of the early farmers at Grenola, Kansas, and is now deceased. John A. is a photographer living at Eureka, Kansas.

From the time he was eleven years of age Thomas E. Thompson continued his education in the public schools of Elk County. When thirteen he entered a printing office at Boston in Howard County, and completed his apprenticeship by experience in several newspaper plants. He was barely twenty-one years of age when in 1881 he and his father bought the Howard Courant, and its business management and editorial control have been in his hands ever since. The Howard Courant was established in 1874 by Abe Steinberger, and it has always been a republican paper and is still the official organ of Elk County. Mr. Thompson is a very competent newspaper man, and is one of the few journalists in the State of Kansas who have been continuously identified with one paper in one location for so many years. He is the owner of the entire plant, and his well equipped plant is located on Wabash Avenue. The Courant has its circulation and influence all over Elk County and surrounding counties.

Mr. Thompson and family reside in a modern residence which he erected on Pine Street in 1904. He also has another dwelling house on the same street. He has played his part as a citizen in this section of Kansas. In 1891 he was elected mayor of Howard for one term, and from 1899 to 1907 served as postmaster, during the administrations of McKinley and Roosevelt. He is an active republican, is affiliated with Hope Lodge No. 155, Ancient Free and Accepted Masons, at Howard; Howard Chapter No. 49, Royal Arch Masons; Oklahoma Camp No. 935, of the Modern Woodmen of America; Howard Lodge No. 124, Ancient Order United Workmen, and was formerly a member of Emporia Lodge of Elks.

In 1882, at Elk Falls, Kansas, Mr. Thompson married Miss Maude Cummings, daughter of Dr. William M. and Susan (Pike) Cummings. Her mother is now deceased and her father is a retired physician living at San Diego, California. Mr. Thompson takes justifiable pride in the talent shown by his only son, Clad H., who has attained more than local reputation in newspaper circles, and is a member of the staff of the Kansas City Star. He writes the ''Kansas Notes'' and the column of ''Star Beams,'' which are familiar features of that great journal.

ALBERT JAMES HERROD in 1916 was elected judge of the District Court of Wyandotte County for the short term of forty days in Division 3. He has the distinction of being the youngest judge in the state at the present time, and his attainments and ability give promise of a large career of usefulness for the future.

Judge Herrod was born at Newark, England, April 14, 1885. He was the fourth in a family of five children, three boys and two girls, born to Walter and Catherine (Taylor) Herrod. His grandfather John Herrod was a successful English maltster and also owned 160 acres of land. He was the father of thirteen children. After his death in 1885, six of his sons came to America. Three of them, Albert, Allan and Lewis, located in Kansas City, Kansas, bringing letters of introduction to Fowler of the Fowler Packing Company. They secured employment in that old packing firm. Subsequently these three brothers were followed by Harry, Walter and Herbert Edgar. Harry became superintendent of the wholesale department of the old packing house of Sulzberger & Swarzschild now the Wilson Packing Company. Walter took employment as special accountant for the Kingan Packing Company. Herbert Edgar became a timekeeper with Sulzberger & Swarzschild, now Wilson & Company. Of these brothers, Lewis, Harry and Walter are now deceased. Albert and Allan are proprietors of Herrod Brothers, a business founded by them in 1891 at Webb City, Missouri. Albert is now secretary of the Mahoning Valley Employers Association with headquarters at Youngstown, Ohio. He is a lawyer by profession and spent ten years in practice at Chicago.

Walter Herrod remained as an accountant for the Kingan Packing Company for several years, was taken ill, and in spite of all that could be done for him he died in 1897. He left a family of children the oldest of whom was fifteen and the youngest eight. His daughter Florence now lives at Kansas City, Kansas;

John Walter is a resident of Webb City, Missouri; Roby is a representative of the Wilson Packing Company at Buenos Ayres in South America; Judge Herrod was twelve years of age at the time of his father's death; and Constance still lives at Kansas City, Kansas.

Judge Herrod on account of his father's early death had to become self supporting at an early age. He became office boy with the Sulzberger & Swarzschild Packing Company, but all the time was ambitious to gain an education and attended night school and accepted other opportunities to advance his capabilities for usefulness. He later attended the Clark Business College and the Kansas City, Kansas, Business College, and also was a student in the Kansas City School of Law. He was graduated from the latter institution in 1908.

In August, 1903, the family removed to Webb City, Missouri, but Judge Herrod remained there only two years. In 1905 he returned to Kansas City and reentered the employ of Sulzberger & Swarzschild as a hog buyer. He gave the best part of the day to the duties of this position, and spent several hours every night carrying on his studies. In June, 1908, he passed successful examination for membership in the bar.

Besides his work in the Kansas City Law School he read law with John Hale and H. E. Dean and continued in their office for several years after his admission to the bar. In May, 1911, the firm became Hale, Higgins & Herrod. In 1913 Judge Herrod began practice by himself.

He has always manifested an active interest in republican politics. He served as secretary for the Mitchell for Congress Club and of the Wyandotte County Republican Club in 1910-11. He was offered the position of private secretary to Congressman Alexander Mitchell, but declined that honor and subsequently declined an offer to become assistant city attorney. His former partner Judge Higgins has served as city attorney. Judge Herrod has the distinction of having been the first local lawyer to accept a woman on the jury, and he never fails to mention in that connection that he lost his case.

On November 25, 1914, he married Miss Sylvia M. Heider of Kansas City, Missouri. Her father, W. P. Heider, is a building contractor, a large land owner in Kansas City, Missouri, and formerly owned the farm that is now subdivided as Roanoke District around Thirty-ninth and State Line streets.

Judge Herrod is affiliated with the Loyal Order of Moose, having served four years as state deputy supreme dictator. He is a member of the Sons and Daughters of Justice, the Kansas Fraternal Citizens, of the Commercial Club and the Union Club and has served as chairman of the entertainment committee and is now on the legislative committee of the Commercial Club. He and his wife are active in the Episcopal Church. Mrs. Herrod was a delegate to the St. Louis Conference of the Daughters of the King in 1916.

THOMAS F. MORRISON. One of the prominent members of the Neosho County bar is Thomas F. Morrison, who as a practitioner at Chanute since 1903 has been connected with much of the important litigation tried in the courts of this district. He is also a leading member of the democratic party of this portion of the state, where his influence has been widely felt in political as well as professional circles, and has represented his community in the Kansas Legislature, as a member of which body he was the author of some exceedingly beneficial legislation.

Mr. Morrison was born June 19, 1875, in Henry County, Missouri, and is a son of Samuel and Nancy (Phelps) Morrison, and a member of a family which came from Scotland to America during the latter part of the seventeenth century. From the original settlement in Virginia, the family moved to Tennessee, in which state, in 1789, was born the grandfather of Thomas F. Morrison, James Morrison. He passed his entire life in Tennessee, where he was a prominent planter and large slaveholder, and died in 1880 in Greene County. Samuel Morrison, father of Thomas F., was born in Greene County, Tennessee, in 1833, and was there reared, educated and married. He engaged in farming there until 1862, when he enlisted in the Sixth Tennessee Cavalry, for service during the Civil war, and served with that organization throughout the struggle, participating in a number of hard-fought engagements, including the bloody battle of Nashville. On one occasion he was captured by the soldiers of General Forrest, but managed to make his escape. Immediately after the close of the war, he removed with his family to Kentucky, where he was engaged in farming for two years, and then went to Henry County, Missouri, where he continued his agricultural operations. In 1885 he came to Allen County, Kansas, settled on a farm, and devoted himself to the tilling of the soil until his death, which occurred in 1885. He was an industrious farmer, and so directed his affairs that he succeeded in the accumulation of a good property. In politics, Mr. Morrison was a republican, and his religious connection was with the Baptist Church, in the work of which he took an active part, holding a number of the lay offices. Mr. Morrison married Miss Nancy Phelps, who was born in 1833, in Greene County, Tennessee, and died in Woodson County, Kansas, in 1910.

Thomas F. Morrison attended the public schools of Woodson County, Kansas, whence he had been taken by his mother after the death of his father, and subsequently enrolled as a student at the State Normal School, Emporia, Kansas, where he finished the junior year's course. Subsequently, he took a two-year course at the Kansas University, and following this entered the Nebraska State University, at Lincoln, where he was graduated in 1903 with the degree of Bachelor of Laws. In that same year he was admitted to the bar and came to Chanute, where he has since been engaged in a general practice, specializing to some extent in civil and corporation law. His offices are in the Peoples Home State Bank Building. Among others, Mr. Morrison is attorney for the Hydraulic Brick Company of Chanute. He has made a lasting impression upon the bar of the county, both for legal ability of a high order and for the individuality of character which impresses itself upon a community. He possesses broad legal learning, an analytical mind, and a readiness to grasp the points at issue. Earnest effort, close application and the exercise of his native talents have won him prestige as a lawyer in Neosho County. He is a member of the Neosho County Bar Association.

A democrat in politics, Mr. Morrison has long been an influential factor in his party. In 1908 he was elected to the Kansas Legislature, in which body he was an active member, serving on the Judiciary, Oil and Gas and other committees. He was the author of the bill providing that the candidates' names in the primaries should be rotated instead of placed in alphabetical order upon the ballot, and in the session of 1909 introduced the first bank guarantee bill in the House. In 1910 Mr. Morrison was democratic candidate for attorney-general. Fraternally he belongs to Chanute Lodge No. 806, Benevolent and Protective Order of Elks; Chanute Lodge No. 96, Ancient Order of United Workmen; the Fraternal Aid Union, and the

Protected Home Circle. In the management of his property, in the transaction of such matters as daily devolve upon a lawyer, and in the varied duties pertaining to his position as a citizen at large, he finds his time abundantly occupied.

Mr. Morrison was married in 1909, at Chanute, to Miss Suzanne McManus, a native of County Leitrim, Ireland. They have no children.

J. E. ZIMMERMAN. President of the Citizens State Bank of Bronson, Mr. Zimmerman has been a factor in the citizenship of Bourbon County for the past fifteen years, and has been an extensive farmer, stock man and oil producer as well as a banker.

He was born in Ashland County, Ohio, October 10, 1873, descended from a family which as the name indicates came out of Germany and were early settlers in the State of Ohio. D. H. Zimmerman, his father, was born in Ohio in 1838, spent his early life in that state, was married in Ashland County, and did an extensive business in the buying and shipping of live stock. From Ohio he removed to Sheridan County, Missouri, in 1881, and late in life in February, 1915, he came to Bronson, Kansas, where he died in the following April. He was an active member of the Christian Church, was a Mason and a republican voter. D. H. Zimmerman married Annie Dougherty, who was born in Ohio in 1843 and is now living at Bronson, Kansas. There were three children: Grant, who died when twenty-two years of age; Charles, a farmer and stock raiser in the Panhandle of Texas; and J. E. Zimmerman.

J. E. Zimmerman spent most of his early life in Sheridan County, Missouri. He began his education there, and his early training was a mixture of what the public schools could give him and the discipline of the home farm. On leaving home Mr. Zimmerman went south into Texas, and spent four years farming in Harris County near the City of Houston. In 1902 he came to Bourbon County, Kansas, and devoted several years exclusively to the business of farming. He has had his home in Bronson since 1909, and has operated extensively as a stock buyer. He still owns a farm of 160 acres 3½ miles northwest of Bronson, but the land is now all leased for oil operations and Mr. Zimmerman's oil productions contribute largely to his financial prosperity. His home in Bronson is in the northwest part of the town and is surrounded by an extensive tract of thirteen acres of land. In 1912 he remodeled the residence into a modern home. Fraternally Mr. Zimmerman is affiliated with Granite Lodge No. 88 of the Knights of Pythias at Bronson.

He was married in 1895 at Triplett, Missouri, to Miss Abbie Minich, daughter of George and Dulsie (Wolfskill) Minich. Her father was a farmer and is now deceased, and her mother lives at Bronson with Mr. and Mrs. Zimmerman.

OWEN M. THOMAS. The Citizens State Bank of Bronson, of which Owen M. Thomas is vice president, is an institution which has grown rapidly and prospered since it was established less than ten years ago, and its success is largely due to the character of the men entrusted with its executive management.

Mr. Thomas has been actively identified with banking for ten years, both in Oklahoma and in Kansas. Though a young man, his career has apparently been one of rapid accomplishment, and he has achieved as much in ten years as many men do in their entire active life.

Mr. Thomas was born in Oskaloosa, Iowa, February 4, 1883, and spent much of his early youth in

Oklahoma. His grandfather, Owen W. Thomas, was a native of Wales, afterwards became a farmer and property owner at Toulon, Illinois, where he died. Owen W. Thomas, Jr., father of the Bronson banker, was born at Toulon in Stark County, Illinois, in 1851. He grew up in his native county, and spent his brief active career as a farmer. He died at Oskaloosa, Iowa, in March, 1883, a few weeks after the birth of his son, Owen M. The maiden name of his wife was Dora Eisiminger, who was born in Pennsylvania in 1856. By her first husband she had just one child, Owen Mitchell Thomas. She afterwards married E. R. Green, and they participated as settlers on the Cherokee Strip in Oklahoma at the opening in the fall of 1893. Mr. Green made the race for a homestead and secured one of 160 acres on the Tonkawa Indian Reservation. He and his wife lived there and went through all the experiences of developing a farm, and the events of those early times in Oklahoma made a strong impression upon the youthful mind of Owen M. Thomas, who spent part of his youth in that section of Oklahoma. Mrs. Green died at Tonkawa in 1905. Mr. Green is living there a retired farmer. By their marriage they had one child, Lucy M., now living with her father.

Owen Mitchell Thomas was ten years old when the family went to Oklahoma, and much of his early education was acquired in the public schools of Arkansas City, Kansas. He afterwards entered the William Jewell College at Liberty, Missouri, but left college in his junior year in 1901 and returned to the farm of his stepfather at Tonkawa, Oklahoma. He lived on the farm there until the death of his mother in 1905. For a few months of that year he worked as remittance clerk in the Guthrie National Bank at Guthrie, Oklahoma, and then was bookkeeper of the National Bank of Commerce until July, 1907. Another experience that has proved valuable to him in later years was as deputy county treasurer of Kay County, Oklahoma, where he served until February, 1910. For six months or more he was assistant cashier of the Oklahoma Guarantee Bank at Blackwell, Oklahoma, and then became cashier of the First State Bank at Tonkawa. Mr. Thomas sold his interests in the bank at Tonkawa in July, 1913, and coming to Bronson, Kansas, accepted the post of vice president of the Citizens State Bank.

The Citizens State Bank was established under a state charter in 1907. Its modern brick home was erected on Clay Street in the same year. This bank has a capital of $10,000 and surplus of $5,000, and through its conservative financial policies enjoys the complete confidence of its friends and patrons in and around Bronson. Mr. J. E. Zimmerman is president; Mr. Thomas vice president; and F. W. Myer, cashier.

Mr. Thomas has various other business interests. He is a stockholder in the Blackwell Oil & Gas Company of Blackwell, Oklahoma; a stockholder in the Depositors Guarantee and Surety Company of Topeka; a stockholder in the Bronson Co-operative Association, and is owner of a farm comprising 300 acres in Kay County, Oklahoma. His lands are only twelve miles away from one of the most active oil belts in Northern Oklahoma, and the possibility is strong that further development will include his own property.

Mr. Thomas is an independent democrat in political affairs. In Masonry he is affiliated with Bourbon Lodge No. 268, Ancient Free and Accepted Masons at Bronson, of which he was treasurer, belongs to Newkirk Chapter No. 58, Royal Arch Masons, to Fort Scott Consistory No. 4 of the Scottish Rite, and

to Mirza Temple of the Mystic Shrine at Pittsburg, Kansas. He is also a member of Granite Lodge No. 88, Knights of Pythias, Bronson Lodge of Independent Order of Odd Fellows, and Bronson Chapter No. 65 of the Eastern Star.

Mr. Thomas resides on Randolph Street in Bronson. In 1909 at Newkirk, Oklahoma, he married Miss Florence Ford, daughter of S. G. and Catherine (Paine) Ford. Her mother now resides at Dexter, Kansas. Her father after retiring from his farm was elected sheriff of Kay County, Oklahoma, and was killed while performing the duties of his office in March, 1908. Mr. and Mrs. Thomas have one son, Owen Ford, born September 28, 1914.

GEORGE H. GRIMMELL, M. D. One of the first graduates of medicine to set up in practice at Howard, Kansas, was Dr. George H. Grimmell, who rendered his first professional services in that section of Elk County thirty years ago. With the exception of about eight years spent at Onaga, Doctor Grimmell has been continuously in practice at Howard since 1898, and is accounted one of the most competent surgeons in that locality.

The first authentic records of his ancestry is found in the annals of the first crusade of 1096, A. D. There was a Sir John Von Grimmell, who was one of the enthusiastic Germans who joined as followers of the Cross in the endeavor to wrest Jerusalem from the hands of the Moslems. The line of descent from this crusader is traced directly to Dr. George H. Grimmell of Kansas. There is also a coat of arms in the family, and it is a reproduction of Baron Grimmell's insignia as found in the year 1555. The coat consists of shield, quarterings, mantling, helmet, coronet and crest. Those versed in the science of heraldry can find in this coat of arms significant traces of the original Von Grimmell's services as a crusader.

Doctor Grimmell gets his profession naturally, since for several generations the Grimmell family have produced capable medical practitioners. He is a grandson of Henry Charles Augustus Grimmell, who was born in the Kingdom of Hanover, Germany. He was given a liberal education and was learned in all the branches of science then included in the physician and surgeon's arts. He practiced in Germany for some years, and in order to escape the compulsory military service of that country immigrated to America, spending many years in Virginia, but at the close of the Civil war coming North and locating at Des Moines, Iowa, where he died.

The Grimmell family resided for many years in the State of Virginia. Dr. George H. Grimmell himself was born in that state, at Round Hill, on August 20, 1855. His father was George Henry Grimmell, Sr., who was born in Virginia February 5, 1829, and is now living in his eighty-eighth year, at Colorado Springs, Colorado. He is still engaged in the practice of medicine, and is probably the oldest or certainly one of the oldest active members of the profession in America. His career throughout has been one of remarkable virility and service. He was reared and married in Virginia, and went abroad to complete his education, winning his degree Doctor of Medicine from the University of Heidelberg, Germany. For many years he practiced at Round Hill, Virginia, but in 1866 removed to Jefferson, Iowa, and gave more than thirty years of his professional service to that community. In 1908 he moved to Colorado Springs. During the Civil war he was assigned to duties as a surgeon, and had a Government appointment at Harpers Ferry. He is a democrat and a Knight Templar Mason.

Doctor Grimmell, Sr., married Annette McCall, who was born in Tennessee in 1833 and died at Jefferson, Iowa, July 3, 1872. The oldest of their children is Dr. George Henry Grimmell, Jr. Helen Eugenia married David McKelvey, who for many years was a jeweler but is now a retired capitalist living in New York State. Kate May married Adolph Renicker, who was a former United States vice consul at Omsk, Siberia, but they now reside in Florida. Frances married Henry Decker, who for a number of years was superintendent of bridges for the Chicago Northwestern Railway Company and is now an independent contractor for the construction of heavy railroad bridges, living at Des Moines, Iowa. Augusta Josephine was given the degree M. D. by the Iowa State University, being one of the first women graduates in medicine in this country, and she is now the wife of Seldon Whitbeck, a civil engineer, their home being at Syracuse, New York.

Doctor Grimmell was eleven years of age when his parents moved to Iowa, and his literary education was completed in the Dunning Academy at Jefferson, from which he graduated A. B. in 1876. In the meantime he had begun the study of medicine under his father, and on February 13, 1877, he was awarded the degree M. D. by the College of Physicians and Surgeons of Keokuk, Iowa. In 1896 he was given the second degree by the Bonds Medical College of St. Louis, Missouri. He has also taken post-graduate courses in the Chicago Polyclinic and the College of Physicians and Surgeons at New Orleans.

Doctor Grimmell began practice at Jefferson, Iowa, in 1877. In November, 1886, he sought a home in the new Town of Horton, Kansas, remained there four years, and in 1890 went to Onaga, where he was in practice until 1898. Since then he has conducted his general medical and surgical practice at Howard, Kansas, and more and more his time is taken up with his specialty as a general surgeon. He has a large surgical practice in the hospital at Moline, Kansas. His offices are in the Grimmell Building in Howard, a building which was erected by his means on Wabash Avenue. Among other interests Doctor Grimmell has a fine farm of 320 acres in Elk County.

His professional associations are with the County and State Medical societies and the American Medical Association, and for four years he served as health officer of Elk County. He is a democrat, is past master of Hope Lodge No. 155, Ancient Free and Accepted Masons, and is principal sojourner of Howard Chapter No. 49, Royal Arch Masons.

Doctor Grimmell was married July 3, 1916, to Mrs. Ethel (Eggleson) Miles, of Columbus, Kansas.

CLAUDE B. CLEMENTS. Among the men who have won success in the Mid-Continent oil fields, one whose prosperity and present position have been gained solely through hard, unremitting labor and specialized knowledge and ability in this vocation, is Claude B. Clements, of Peru, Kansas. A man of large personal interests, which demand steadfast and undeviating attention, he has managed to reserve a part of his time for public official duties, and at this time is mayor of Peru, an office in which he has gained a reputation that assures him of the confidence and respect of his fellow townsmen.

Mr. Clements was born in Union County, Kentucky, January 27, 1871, being a son of B. J. and Alice (Williams) Clements, and a member of a family which originated in England and whose first American member came to this country during the colonial era and located in Virginia. B. J. Clements was born in 1848, in Union County, Kentucky, and resided there until 1879, when he became a pioneer farmer of Crawford County, Kansas, but in 1884 removed to Chautauqua County, where he engaged in farming until the close of his life. His death occurred at Niotaze, Kansas, November 17, 1885. Mr. Clements was content to devote himself to his agricultural interests, and never sought public position. He was an unassuming man, but energetic and resourceful in his work and had started upon the highroad to success when his early death closed his career. In politics he was a democrat. Mr. Clements married Miss Alice Williams, who was born in Union County, Kentucky, in 1853, and still survives her husband, being a resident of Rupert, Idaho. Seven children were born to their union: Claude B., of this review; Nannie, who is the wife of John Davis, a railroad employe of Manteca, California; Willie, who is engaged in banking and resides at Phoenix, Arizona; Bettie, who died at the age of eight months; Hattie, who married Nat Thomas, a railroad employe of Rupert, Idaho; Aaron, of Hailey, Idaho, sheriff of Blaine County; and Etta B., who is an assistant in the postoffice at Rupert, Idaho.

Claude B. Clements received his education in the public schools of Crawford and Chautauqua counties, Kansas, and attended the high school at Independence. Reared on his father's farm, he was engaged in agricultural pursuits until reaching the age of twenty-three years, at which time he embarked in the oil business in the Mid-Continent field. His start was necessarily a modest one and he was possessed of only limited financial resources, but his hard, intelligent and well-directed labors more than made up for his other lack of advantages and he steadily advanced himself to a leading place among the men in this field. At the present time he has several producing leases in Chautauqua and Montgomery counties, including twelve oil wells in the former and two in the latter, and that these have been very successful is shown in the fact that he was recently offered $100,000 for his interest in one of his leases alone. He owns his own home in the south part of Peru, and is a stockholder in the Eucalatum Company. He has always been a stanch republican, and in the office of mayor of Peru, to which he was elected April 15, 1915, is rendering the city good service. He is fraternally affiliated with Peru Camp No. 1470, Modern Woodmen of America.

Mr. Clements married Miss Effie Floyd, who was born April 25, 1873, in Chautauqua County, Kansas, and to this union there has been born one son: Paul, born April 25, 1896, a graduate of Peru High School, class of 1915, and now a sophomore at Kansas University, Lawrence, Kansas.

Mrs. Clements is of Scotch-Irish descent on her father's side of the family, while her mother is from the same branch of the Arnolds as was Benedict Arnold. Her grandmother on her father's side was a Miss Chaney, who was a cousin to Gen. Winfield Scott. Her father, Dr. William Floyd, was born November 6, 1822, in Somerset County, Kentucky, was reared in Indiana, returned to Kentucky and was married, and became an early settler of Iowa. During the Civil war he gave his services as a surgeon in the pest house at Keokuk, Iowa, when such service meant great hardship, self sacrifice and the greatest danger. In 1870 he came to Chautauqua County, Kansas, as a pioneer physician and surgeon, being a graduate of the Iowa State Medical College, Keokuk, degree of Doctor of Medicine, although .in his younger years he had been a school teacher and instructor in music. He was a man of fine intellectual attainments, a brilliant scholar and a man whose pure and upright life was a powerful influence for good in the community. When he died at Peru, July 25, 1908, the locality lost one of its best and most helpful men. In politics he was a republican, fraternally he belonged to Peru Lodge, No. 106, Independent Order of Odd Fellows, while his religious connection was with the Methodist Episcopal Church. Doctor Floyd married Miss Martha Arnold, who survives him and resides at Peru, born in 1828, in Pulaski County, Kentucky. They became the parents of the following children: Elizabeth, who died at the age of eight years; F. M., who is a retired farmer of Peru, Kansas; Mary, who died at Syracuse, Kansas, March 3, 1908, is the wife of Mr. Dix, who conducts a meat market at Lawton, Oklahoma; W. J., who is engaged in farming in Morton County, Kansas; John, who died in infancy; Martha Ellen, who also died as a child; James, who is a carpenter of Peru, Kansas; Addie M., who married George W. Baker, a farmer of Peru; Emma, who died in infancy; Harriet F., who is the wife of John W. Mertz, an attorney of Sedan, Kansas; and Effie, now Mrs. Clements.

Mrs. Clements graduated from the Peru High School in 1891, following which she attended the Kansas University, at Lawrence, Kansas, for one semester in 1891. She then began teaching school and continued to be so engaged until the time of her marriage. She is one of the best known and most popular ladies of Peru, where she is active in social and religious work, as a member of the Methodist Episcopal Church, the Royal Neighbors and the Women's Relief Corps, the latter of which she attends at Sedan. Mrs. Clements has a fine, clear soprano voice and her services are greatly in demand upon all occasions where a musical programme is offered. She is possessed of much literary ability, and in addition to several papers upon timely subjects, which she has read before clubs and societies, she has written a number of books of poems, and those already published have received high commendation. Among these latter may be mentioned the collection published under the heading of "Home Poems," which included "Father," "Mother," "Husbands," "Paul," "Children," "Winter," "Home," "Blackie," "Temperance," "Arkansas Fruit," "Peru," "Brown," "Christian Church" and "Wild Flowers." The limits to which this review is necessarily confined does not permit of the presentation of these poems, but they all breathe a spirit of lovely thought and of an appreciation of the world's finer things.

ANSEL B. HACKETT. The nation was celebrating the sixtieth anniversary of the signing of the Declaration of Independence when Ansel B. Hackett was born July 4, 1836. His birth occurred at Minot, Cumberland County, Maine. It was in that picturesque district of the Pine Tree State that he spent his early years.

Mr. Hackett, who with his venerable wife, now resides at Carbondale, is one of the true pioneers of Kansas, as is also Mrs. Hackett. Both came here when Kansas was a territory, and they experienced the dangers and hardships of frontier life. It is a matter of special interest that Mrs. Hackett is one of the very few surviving witnesses of the Quantrell raid on Lawrence, in which city she was living at the time. Mr. Hackett has now passed the age of four-score, and nearly sixty of those years have been spent in the State of Kansas. He is one of the honored survivors of the Civil war.

His grandfather Hackett came from Ireland and his grandmother from Scotland, and the Hacketts became identified with America during colonial days. His parents were Barnabas and Abbey Hackett, who had a family of ten children, named: Lucas, Abbey, Ruby, Sarah, Maria, Hattie, Nathan, Daniel, Ansel and Elmer. Ansel and his brother Elmer are the only ones now living.

It was on September 20, 1857, when Ansel B. Hackett arrived in Kansas. He was then twenty-one years of age. His early years had been of circumscribed opportunities, and he came West so that his vigorous youth and ambition might find a new field in which to work out its destiny. He preempted land soon after coming to Kansas, but was employed in various lines of work until the outbreak of the Civil war.

Mr. Hackett spent four years and one month in the service of the Union army. He enlisted August 6, 1861, in the First Kansas Light Artillery, Captain Moonlight, and did not receive his honorable discharge until September 7, 1865. Much of his service was on the frontier, in Kansas, Missouri, and Arkansas, until 1864, when his regiment was transferred east of the Mississippi and took part in the great campaign which the battles of Franklin and Nashville were the culmination. Earlier in the war he fought in the engagements of Cane Hill, Prairie Grove, Dry Wood, near Fort Scott, and throughout the Curtis campaign in Arkansas. After being sent first to Tennessee in 1864 he was in the battle at Johnsonville, and then in those bloody conflicts at Franklin and Nashville. When the resistance of the Confederate arms was broken down by the last named battles, he remained with Thomas' army around Huntsville, and the end of the war found him and his comrades at Chattanooga.

His long service exposed him to countless hardships and dangers, but the only affliction resulting from his honored career was a disease of the eyes, and that has brought him a pension from the United States Government for a number of years.

He was still a member of the army when on May 6, 1863, he married Caroline Evans, of Lawrence. She is a daughter of William and Betsey Evans, who formerly lived at Lynn, Massachusetts. Mrs. Hackett and her mother, Betsey Evans, came to Kansas in the fall of 1856. Thus Mrs. Hackett, who was born October 10, 1829, and is now in her eighty-seventh year, has a vivid recollection of many pioneer events in Kansas Territory during the free-state movement and in subsequent epochs. As already stated, she was living at Lawrence during the Quantrell raid, and in spite of her advanced years has a vivid recollection and can recite in detail many of the incidents of that attack,

After the war Mr. Hackett rejoined his wife at Lawrence, and on either the 5th or 6th of March, 1868, they moved to a farm comprising the southeast quarter of section 21, town 14, range 16. This land lies 2½ miles east of Carbondale. It was the pre-emption claim of Mr. Hackett in 1858, but he had never occupied it for the first ten years, having been employed with other matters in addition to his

A B Hackett

war 'service. On that farm Mr. and Mrs. Hackett lived profitably and comfortably until they retired in 1913 to a pleasant home in Carbondale. Mr. and Mrs. Hackett have no children. In matters of politics Mr. Hackett has voted the republican ticket, and has been affiliated with that organization since the first campaign in 1856. Outside of voting and performing his duties as a good citizen he has had no aspirations for public office.

COL. S. G. ISETT. In the history of the oil industry in Kansas there is no better known figure than Col. S. G. Isett, the man who made Chanute famous. He has been connected with the production and handling of oil since 1902, and has been identified with some of the most famous wells the country has known.

Colonel Isett has had an interesting and spectacular career, featured by incidents and experiences any one of which would have satisfied the ordinary individual's desire for adventure; but while he bears bodily scars as mementos of the thrilling times through which he has passed, his mental capacity remains unimpaired, and today, with faculties sharpened and fully developed, he maintains his position as a leading business man of Chanute, in the midst of the stern competition of the younger generation growing up about him.

Colonel Isett is descended from Green ancestors who operated as merchants on the high seas, and who drifted into England, France and Germany, from which last-named country they came to America prior to the Revolution, first settling in Connecticut, later going to Virginia, then to Pennsylvania. In the Old Dominion State, in 1814, was born James K. Isett, the father of the Colonel. He was reared in Lebanon County, Pennsylvania, from whence he went to Huntingdon County, in the same state, and was there married. As a successful farmer, he was the owner of a large property, and also owned and operated an iron furnace. It is a peculiar fact that he should have died as a result of the Civil war, although not a participant, while his son, who fought in many battles, should have passed safely through. While visiting the battlefield of Gettysburg, he contracted blood-poisoning, from which he died at Marklesburg, Pennsylvania, in 1863. He was a republican. Mr. Isett married Elizabeth Garner, who was born in 1816 at Antietam, Maryland, and on whose grandfather's farm was fought the great battle of Antietam during the Civil war. She died at Marklesburg, Pennsylvania, in 1887. There were eleven children in the family, as follows: John, who died in infancy; Matthew G., who fought as a soldier of the Fifty-third Regiment, Pennsylvania Volunteer Infantry, and was killed at the battle of Gettysburg; Mary, who died in 1895, at Huntingdon, Pennsylvania, as the wife of the late John Stedman, a mine superintendent; George W., who was a retired merchant and died at Marklesburg, Pennsylvania, in 1914, from the effects of an incurable wound received at the battle of Gettysburg, while fighting in the same regiment as his brother Matthew G.; J. M., who is a hardware merchant at Athol, Kansas; Luther, who died in infancy; S. G., of this notice, born in Huntingdon County, Pennsylvania, February 15, 1849; John A., who is a retired farmer of Marklesburg, Pennsylvania; B. F., who for many years was with the Pennsylvania Central Railroad as superintendent of the car shops and is now living retired at Huntingdon, Pennsylvania; H. H., who is in the employ of the United States Mint at Denver, Colorado; and Jennie, who died at Huntingdon, Pennsylvania, as the wife of J. M. Lynn, who at the time of his death was a retired merchant and life insurance agent.

S. G. Isett attended the public schools of Huntingdon County, Pennsylvania, but the war came to interrupt his studies, and to take its toll from his youth. He was but fifteen years and twelve days old when he managed to induce the recruiting officer to accept him as a soldier of the Union, and November 27, 1863, he became a private in the Twenty-second Pennsylvania Cavalry, with which he served until October 27, 1865. With this organization he participated in a number of great engagements, including those at Winchester and Cedar Creek, and fought under such able commanders as Siegel, Hayes and Sheridan, being frequently on staff duty. He was seriously wounded at Fisher's Hill, where a piece of exploded shell struck his left ankle, disabling him for several months; again, at Winchester, September 19, 1864, he was wounded, receiving a sabre cut across the head and at Front Royal he was shot through the left wrist.

At the close of the war the brave young soldier returned to his Huntingdon county home, and was made superintendent and paymaster for R. J. Langdon, at Coal Run, Bedford County, Pennsylvania, positions which he held for two years. He was then transferred to Dunbar, Clearfield County, Pennsylvania, and acted in the same capacities for that firm for one year, when he was made general manager for the Logan Coal Company, at Osceola, Pennsylvania. He was acting in this capacity during the period of the notorious Molly Maguires, a secret society which had been formed in 1877 in the mining districts of Pennsylvania, the members of which sought to effect their purpose by intimidation, carried in some cases to murder. Colonel Isett, always utterly fearless and courageous in face of all threats, seemed to have attracted the animosity of this order, and on one occasion ninety-three buckshot were fired through the window of the room in which he was sleeping, while on another occasion, while riding in a buggy with the president of the company, he was shot at twice. Several members of the Molly Maguires were later arrested, tried and executed, and the organization was broken up and scattered.

On March 21, 1879, Colonel Isett came to Kansas and at Humboldt entered the employ of Curdy & Heed, a firm with which he was connected for four years. In 1883 he was located at Chanute, where he opened up a dry goods, shoe and clothing business, and conducted this for two years. Following this, in 1886 he was appointed assistant land commissioner, an appointment which carried with it a salary of $4,000 per annum, but this he declined, and took in preference a position with Huiskamp Brothers Company, shoe manufacturers of Keokuk, Iowa, for which firm he traveled until January 1, 1902. At that time he began to be an active factor in the oil business at Chanute and drilled the first independent oil well on the famous "Isett Eighty." Subsequently he negotiated a market with the Prairie Oil and Gas Company and put the first barrel of oil in the Standard's pipe line in the Mid-Continent field. Later he opened the famous Isett and Erwin Gas pool, 6½ miles west of Chanute, in which were some of the largest wells ever discovered, running as high as 42,000,000 cubic feet per day. Colonel Isett also opened up the shallow oil pool at Longton and drilled one of the most remarkable freak wells ever opened in an oil field. Having taken up a large block of leases in 1914, he associated himself with Guffy & Gailey, of Pittsburgh, Pennsylvania, and the first well drilled, at 1,500 feet struck the most remarkable oil well in history. This would flow a solid column of oil and sand from 250 to 300 feet through a 6⅝ casing, and these flows would last from twenty minutes to one hour. It would sand up for a distance of eighty feet and then have to be drilled out, and would immediately begin to flow again until sanded up again, and this condition prevailed for thirty days, when the owners inserted a 5½ perforated liner. After flowing for nine hours the well backed in behind the liner, closed the perforation and the well was lost. The company has drilled five other holes surrounding this one and all have come in dry.

Colonel Isett has been widely known in democratic politics. In 1886 he was the democratic candidate for lieutenant-governor, associated with Col. Tom Moonlight, candidate for governor, they being the first two candidates of the democratic party to make a campaign through the state. For three months they proclaimed a baptism ''for a repentence of republican sins,'' but both were defeated. In 1890 Colonel Isett was democratic candidate for secretary of state, with ex-Governor Robinson and the Honored Dave Overmyer on the ticket. In 1890 he was appointed a colonel on the staff of Governor Leedy. Colonel Isett is a charter member of Vicksburg Post No. 72, Grand Army of the Republic, of Humboldt, Kansas. He owns much property in the surrounding territory adjoining Chanute, has his residence in the city, at No. 402 Forest Avenue, and has large oil interests at Longton, Kansas.

Colonel Isett was married in 1873, at Marklesburg, Pennsylvania to Miss Ellen C. Heilig, daughter of the late Rev. J. S. Heilig a minister of the Lutheran Church, and of their children, the following are living: Hal, who is general agent for the Farmers and Bankers Life Insurance Company of Wichita, Kansas, with headquarters at Parsons; Bessie, who resides with her parents; and Frank E., who resides at Longton, Kansas, and is associated with his father in various ventures in the oil business.

B. S. SMITH is one of the oldest business men of Humboldt. He has been a merchant there thirty years. In that time he has built up the largest and most complete dry goods establishment not only in the city but in that part of the state. It is a splendid store, stocked with a varied assortment of all the goods required by a discriminating trade, and has been built up on the foundation of square and honest dealing and a careful and painstaking service. Mr. Smith is also well known in other lines of business and as a public spirited citizen.

He is an example of success attained in spite of early disadvantages and handicaps. Bergen Stelle Smith was born at Quakertown in Hunterdon County, New Jersey, July 27, 1857. His father, Zachariah Smith, was born in the same part of New Jersey in 1832, was a merchant tailor, and died at Quakertown, New Jersey, in 1862 when only thirty years of age. He was a member of the Baptist Church. He married Lydia Ann Johnston, who was born in 1835 and is now living at Paterson, New Jersey. Mr. and Mrs. Zachariah Smith had three children: William Judson, a resident of Humboldt, Kansas; Emma L., at home with her mother at Paterson, New Jersey; and Bergen S. Mrs. Zachariah Smith married for her second husband Nicol Graham. Nicol Graham was born in Newfermland, Scotland, and died at Paterson, New Jersey, in 1901. He entered at an early age the employ of the Rogers Locomotive Works at Paterson, New Jersey, rose to responsibilities in their service, and was finally sent to Australia to supervise the assembling of locomotives sent out by his company. He also served as master mechanic of the Rensselaer & Saratoga Railroad, and at one time

was master mechanic of the Illinois Central Railway. Mr. and Mrs. Graham had two children: Harry D., of Paterson, New Jersey; and Margaret, living at Paterson, the widow of Edward Conley Toie, who was in the insurance business.

B. S. Smith attended the Reading Academy at Flemington, New Jersey, and a private school. He was only thirteen when he left school to make his own way in the world. For a number of years he earned his living as an employe in the office of the Hunterdon County Republican, and acquired considerable knowledge of the newspaper and printing business. In 1877 he left newspaper work to come west, and for a time was in the great department store of Bulleen, Moore & Emery at Kansas City, Missouri, and later became connected with the wholesale house of Tootle-Hanna Dry Goods Company at Kansas City. While with that wholesale firm he learned the dry goods business in many of its details, and the experience has proved invaluable to him in his subsequent career as an independent merchant. Mr. Smith remained with the Tootle-Hanna Company until 1884.

In that year he came to Kansas and located at Cherryvale, where he conducted a clothing and furnishing store for a year and a half. In 1886 he moved to Humboldt, and there established the B. S. Smith dry goods store located on Bridge Street on the north side of the Square. His large stock now fills floor space 50 by 100 feet, and his trade covers a radius of twenty miles east and west of Humboldt and five miles to the north and south of that city.

Mr. Smith has also been vitally connected with the industrial and manufacturing interests of Humboldt, and is a director, stockholder and vice president of the Humboldt Brick Company. He owns considerable business property and land in Morton County, and has recently completed a fine modern home on Osage Street between Eleventh and Twelfth streets. He is treasurer of the Humboldt School Board, an active member of the Board of Trade, and for ten years served as city treasurer of Humboldt. Politically Mr. Smith is a republican and fraternally he is affiliated with Pacific Lodge No. 29, Ancient Free and Accepted Masons, Valley Chapter No. 11, Royal Arch Masons, Chanute Commandery of the Knights Templar, Humboldt Camp No. 987, Modern Woodmen of America, Humboldt Lodge No. 133, Ancient Order of United Workmen, and the Court of Honor. He is a member and elder in the Presbyterian Church.

Mr. Smith was married at Jacksonville, Illinois, in 1903 to Miss Clara D. Nolte, daughter of George H. and Mary (Dunbaugh) Nolte. Her mother now resides at Humboldt, and her father, deceased, was a pork packer in Beardstown and Jacksonville, Illinois. Mrs. Smith died in June, 1904.

GEORGE JAMES SHARP during the thirty odd years he has lived in Elk County has been a farmer, school teacher, county official, abstractor and lawyer, and his friends and associates say that whatever he undertakes he does with all the enthusiasm of his nature and to the limit of his ability. He is an exceedingly useful citizen, and his services have for several years been untilized by the City of Howard through the office of mayor.

Mr. Sharp was born on a farm in Hendricks County, Indiana, December 26, 1862, a son of William P. and Anna T. (Higgins) Sharp. He has a very interesting ancestral record.

The first Americans of the name were Scotch-Irish people who came from the north of Ireland to Virginia in colonial days. Mr. Sharp is descended from revolutionary ancestors on both sides. His great-great-grandfather, James Sharp, participated in the struggle for independence and became a celebrated scout both during that war and afterwards in the western wilderness. This revolutionary patriot was born in Virginia, but after the Revolutionary war he moved across the mountains and settled in Kentucky. In Bath County, Kentucky, is a town named Sharpsburg, where a number of the Sharp family settled in pioneer times. The village was named in honor of Moses Sharp, a relative of the branch of the family now being considered. Moses Sharp was in the Fourth Virginia Continental troops in the Revolutionary war. The great-grandfather of G. J. Sharp was also named James, was a native of Virginia, born in 1784, and was reared at Sharpsburg, Kentucky. He lived there until his marriage, then removed to Bedford County, Tennessee, and died there five years later in 1816. He was a farmer and millwright.

The next individual in the paternal ancestry is the grandfather, also James Sharp, who was born in Bedford County, Tennessee, January 16, 1814. When he was four years of age, in 1818, the family returned to the vicinity of Sharpsburg in Bass County, Kentucky, and he grew up there. Later he moved to New Winchester in Hendrix County, Indiana, and became one of the pioneer farmers and stockmen of that locality. He lived there until his death on January 16, 1872. He married Malinda M. Randall, who was born in Allen County, Kentucky, May 7, 1819, and died at New Winchester, Indiana, in April, 1908.

Of Mr. Sharp's maternal line reference should be made to his great-grandfather, Daniel Higgins, who was born in Augusta County, Virginia, in 1763. He was one of the boyish patriots in the Revolutionary war, and he afterwards drew a pension for his service. Much of this service was done on the western frontier, in fighting the Indians and their British allies. The annals of the Federal Government show a complete record of his various enlistments. He first enlisted in May, 1779, when sixteen years of age, and served one month as a private in Capt. Silas Hardin's company in the Virginia troops. Not long afterward he apparently crossed the mountains into Kentucky, since in April, 1780, he enlisted for a month as a private under Capt. John Cowan, and that service was rendered in Kentucky. In July, 1780, he enlisted, serving six weeks as private under Capt. John Ellison, also in Kentucky, in which state all his remaining enlistments were. In June, 1781, he enlisted and served six months as sergeant under Capt. John Ellison. In March, 1782, he enlisted for six weeks as sergeant under Maj. John Logan. There is record of another enlistment and several weeks of service during 1782 as private under Capt. John Martin. His last enlistment was in October, 1782, and he was a private in the ranks for six months under the noted scout and Indian fighter, Simon Kenton.

William P. Sharp, father of George J., was born on a farm at New Winchester, Indiana, August 5, 1838. He grew up there, married, took up farming, and in 1866 removed to Edgar County, Illinois, where he not only farmed but taught school. From 1871 to 1880 he lived on a farm in Douglas County, Illinois, and in 1880 came to Kansas and located near Waverly in Coffey County. From his farm in that section he removed to Elk County in 1883 and bought the farm which is still owned by his estate. This farm comprises 240 acres and is situated 4½ miles northeast of Longton. That was his home the rest of his

life, but he died during a visit to the scenes of his birth in Hendricks County, Indiana, on July 4, 1904. His body is now at rest at Longton, Kansas. He became one of the early republican voters and exercised his franchise in that direction the rest of his life. Wherever he lived he was an active member of the Christian Church and served for many years as an elder. His only fraternity was the Independent Order of Odd Fellows. His wife, Anna T. Higgins, who was born in April, 1836, at New Winchester, Indiana, is still living, past eighty years of age, at Howard, Kansas. George J. Sharp was the oldest of their children. Dr. E. G. Sharp, a graduate of the Eclectic Medical Institute at Cincinnati, is a physician and surgeon at Guthrie, Oklahoma. Dr. Thomas L., who also graduated from the Eclectic Institute at Cincinnati, is practicing at Orlando, Oklahoma.

George J. Sharp acquired most of his education in Douglas County, Illinois, also attended school in Coffey County, Kansas, and for two years was a student in the Kansas Normal College at Fort Scott. He left that school in 1888, following which he was a teacher in the country districts of Elk County five years, and then put in four years as a farmer. In 1899 Mr. Sharp was elected county clerk of Elk County and gave a creditable administration of that office for five years. In 1904 he opened an office as an abstractor and continues that branch of business to the present time. He is a recognized authority on land titles and descriptions in Elk County and has a very complete set of abstracts. In the intervals of his other business Mr. Sharp carried on the study of law with Mr. Keenan Hurst of Howard, and in January, 1916, was admitted to the Kansas bar.

Mr. Sharp's property includes a half section of farming land five miles northeast of Longton, his residence at Cedar and Monroe streets in Howard, and also the Independent Order of Odd Fellows Building, in which his offices are located.

For eight years up to 1916 he served as justice of the peace, and in April, 1913, was elected for his first term as mayor, being re-elected in 1915. During his administration the City of Howard has advanced municipally by at least two important improvements. One of these was the installation of an electric lighting system, and the other was the establishment of a natural gas plant, both of which are under municipal ownership.

Mr. Sharp is a republican, is an elder in the Christian Church, is past noble grand of Howard Lodge No. 134, Independent Order of Odd Fellows, and a member of Longton Lodge of the Ancient Order of United Workmen.

On August 10, 1902, at Longton, Kansas, he married Miss Ada F. Sutton, daughter of E. R. and Barbara J. (Wenick) Sutton. Her parents reside at Longton, her father being a retired farmer. Two children were born to Mr. and Mrs. Sharp: George H., born August 11, 1903; and William Robert, who died at the age of five years.

CHARLES W. GREEN, a resident of Kansas City, Kansas, since March, 1893, was born in Greene County, New York, July 1, 1868, son of Charles and Avesta (Wright) Green. His father was a farmer and a veteran of the Union army. He was educated in public schools, in Greenville Academy and Eastman's Business College. After some experience as a grocery clerk and in real estate and insurance lines he went west in 1891 to Colorado, was connected two years with a smelting company, and on coming to Argentine, now part of Kansas City, Kansas, had charge of the copper department of the

Consolidated Kansas Smelting and Refining Company until June, 1895. Later he was in the retail business.

In 1907 he became vice president of the First State Bank of Argentine, and since January 1, 1911, has been its president. He has been president of the Clearing House Association of Kansas City, Kansas, and was the founder and until 1910 secretary and treasurer and is now president of the Argentine Building & Loan Association.

Mr. Green served as alderman and mayor of Argentine, afterward represented Argentine as alderman of the seventh ward of Kansas City, Kansas, and was one of the first commissioners under the commission form of government in April, 1910. In 1913 he was elected mayor and re-elected in 1915. Mr. Green was a delegate to the Baltimore Democratic Convention of 1912. He is married and has a wife and one daughter.

ADAM LOCH. The rewards attainable through a life of industry are forcibly illustrated in the career of Adam Loch, one of the leading and successful business men of Chanute and vice president of the Fidelity State Bank. Since early youth he has depended wholly and solely upon his own resources, working out his own success and steadily advancing to success and position along the commercial and financial path. His career should be an incentive for renewed effort by the youth of today who are starting life without friends or fortune to aid them.

Mr. Loch was born at Springfield, Illinois, April 13, 1852, a son of Conrad and Barbara (Hahn) Loch. His father was born in 1825, in the City of Frankfort, Germany, where he learned the trade of shoemaker, and came to the United States as a young man, first locating at Baltimore, Maryland, and after a short time removing to Springfield, Illinois, where he was married. While he was living at Springfield, he became acquainted with Abraham Lincoln, of whom he was always an ardent admirer, although a stanch democrat. He made the shoes which the President wore to Washington. Mr. Loch was a master shoemaker, but did nothing but cut and fit, as he had eighteen men in his employ for the other work. About 1865 he went to Auburn, Illinois, and there his death occurred in 1866. He was a member of the German Lutheran Church, and was fraternally affiliated with the Independent Order of Odd Fellows. Mr. Loch married Barbara Hahn, who was born September 15, 1829, in Bavaria, Germany, and now a resident of Lane, Kansas, and they became the parents of nine children, as follows: William who is a retired merchant of Virden, Illinois; Adam; George, who died when young; Henry, who was a painter and decorator and died at Moberly, Missouri, in 1912; Conrad, who died when young; Charles, who is a tinner and furnace maker of St. Louis, Missouri; George (2), who died when young; John, who is a druggist of Lane, Kansas; and Minnie, who is the wife of John P. Wells, a carpenter and contractor of Lane.

Adam Loch was but fourteen years of age when his father died, and up to that time had attended school at Springfield and Auburn. As a lad he had attended the debates between Lincoln and Douglas, and on one occasion, when introduced to "Honest Abe" informed him that he would not vote for him, as his father was such a strong Douglas Democrat. When but a boy he had shown himself ambitious and industrious as a newsboy, and during the war period often made as high as from $4 to $5 a day. On one occasion, when given a number of drug-

gist's advertisements to peddle, on which there was some matter in regard to the war, he succeeded in selling $1.50 worth of the bills at five cents each, a stroke of business which prophesied a successful commercial career for the lad. When his father died his mother was left with a number of small children, and Adam at once put his shoulder to the wheel and his heart in the work to assist in the family support. The lad of fourteen years proved a good provider, doing a man's work in the field on farms in the vicinity of his home, and whenever he was able attended the district schools during the winter terms. He continued to assist in his mother's support and remained in Illinois until March, 1879, at which time he came to Kansas, feeling that here he could find better opportunities for gaining a fortune. For six months he remained at Wichita, where he worked at any honorable employment that presented itself, and then succeeded, in company with a Mr. Isham, in gathering together a small bunch of cattle which he wintered in Kansas. He then took the herd to Indian Territory, where he handled stock for three years, having a ranch on Red Rock Creek from 1880 until 1883, and in the latter year went to Lane, Kansas, where he established himself in the livery business. For nearly twenty years Mr. Loch continued to conduct this enterprise, of which he made a satisfying success, and during four years of that time, in Cleveland's last administration, served as postmaster of Lane. In 1904 Mr. Loch came to Chanute where he entered the grocery business at No. 1001 North Santa Fe Street, a store which he is still conducting and the business of which he has built up to large proportions. As his interests have increased, he has invested his capital in other enterprises, and at this time is a stockholder in the Dodge City Wholesale Grocery Company and in the Fidelity State Bank of Chanute, of which he is vice president. He owns his own home at Chanute, and is now building a residence at No. 501 North Forest Avenue. Mr. Loch is a democrat in politics, and served for a time as township committeeman of Pottawatomie Township. He joined the Baptist Church at the age of eighteen years, and his fraternal connection is with Chanute Camp No. 852, Modern Woodmen of America.

Mr. Loch was married in 1886, at Ottawa, Kansas, to Miss Sula Meador, daughter of J. A. and Julia (Steel) Meador, both now deceased. Mr. Meador was a merchant of Ottawa and well known in business circles. Three children have been born to Mr. and Mrs. Loch: Zetta, who is the wife of Lester Purdy, of 915 South Lincoln Avenue, stamp and register clerk at the Chanute Postoffice; Marguerite, who is the wife of Carl Lemmert, of 19 North LaFayette Avenue, Chanute, a clerk in the offices of the Atchison Topeka & Santa Fe Railroad; and Esther, a graduate of the Chanute High School, who resides with her parents and is a teacher of music.

JOEL MOORE O'BRIEN is proprietor of the largest department store in Allen County. The present business is the outgrowth of many years of successful experience and gradual development beginning with a single stock of groceries. Mr. O'Brien has proved himself a merchant of unusual sagacity and has been one of the principal factors in recent years in the development and progress of his home city.

The O'Brien family has long been identified with the development of this section of Kansas. Mr. O'Brien's grandfather Daniel Cornelius O'Brien was one of the Kansas pioneers. He was born in Ohio and in 1857 came to Kansas, homesteading 160 acres in Allen County, and keeping his home on the farm until his death in 1872. He died, the same year J. M. O'Brien was born. The latter was born at Humboldt November 10, 1872. The old O'Brien farm on which Grandfather O'Brien lived and died is located three miles north of Humboldt. Daniel C. O'Brien owned the first store ever established in Humboldt. His son, William C. O'Brien, was one of the first mayors of the town, assisted in organizing the municipality, and also conducted the first grist mill and sawmill in this section of the state. Daniel C. O'Brien was first a whig and later a republican.

Isaac N. O'Brien, father of the Humboldt merchant, was born in Pike County, Ohio, in 1835, grew up and married there and at the time of his marriage was serving as clerk of the District Court. Coming to Kansas in 1857, he was one of the early farmers in the district around Humboldt, but in 1887 removed to Chanute, where he conducted the mill, electric light plant and a store for several years. In 1891 he returned to the farm near Humboldt, finally retired in the village, and died there in 1904. During the Civil war Isaac O'Brien enlisted in the Seventh Kansas Regiment of Infantry, took part in some of the guerrilla warfare and also helped repel Price's invasion. He was always a loyal republican. Isaac O'Brien married Maggie P. Moore, who was born in Pike County, Ohio, in 1845, and died at Humboldt, Kansas, in 1905. Their children were: D. C. O'Brien, a dealer in coal and coke at Cincinnati, Ohio; Joel M.; Grace, of Baltimore, Maryland; Harriet, of Kansas City, Missouri; Bertha, wife of L. K. Meek, the leading banker at Mulhall, Oklahoma; Pearl, wife of Chester Squire, their home being on the old Squire farm south of Humboldt; George H., who conducts a meat market at Rawlins, Wyoming.

J. M. O'Brien grew up at Humboldt, attended the public schools of that city, and also at Chanute, where he graduated from high school in 1891. He then spent two years in Baker University, graduating from the Commercial Department. After considerable employment and experience with others he engaged in business for himself on November 1, 1897. On that date he opened a grocery store in Humboldt and having made a success of one line he has added others from time to time until his large store is now completely stocked with nearly everything necessary for the supply of merchandise required in this community. In 1907 he put up a substantial business block in which his store is located at the west side of the Square on Eighth Street and Bridge Street. This store building as much as anything else gives a metropolitan appearance to the business district of Humboldt. The store has three entrances, has a double basement, and the building extends back from the street 140 feet. The trade has been built up on careful and conscientious merchandising principles, and now comes from a country of a radius of fifteen miles around Humboldt. From ten to fifteen clerks are employed in the different departments of the store.

Mr. O'Brien also has considerable farm lands in Allen County, owns two dwelling houses in the city, in addition to his own modern home at 908 Central Avenue. He was organizer and is president of the Humboldt National Oil and Gas Company. Mr. O'Brien is a republican, served two terms as a member of the Humboldt City Council, is active in the Methodist Episcopal Church, being chairman of its board of trustees and chairman of the building committee which is now constructing a handsome

new church edifice. For five years Mr. O'Brien served as superintendent of the Sunday school. Fraternally he belongs to Humboldt Camp No. 987, Modern Woodmen of America, Humboldt Lodge No. 30, Independent Order of Odd Fellows, Fraternal Aid Union, and Knights and Ladies of Security.

On January 7, 1903, at Humboldt he married Miss Adele C. McElroy, daughter of W. T. and Melissa McElroy. Mrs. McElroy is still living at Humboldt, while Mr. McElroy, now deceased, was the pioneer editor of the Humboldt Union. Mrs. O'Brien died at Humboldt December 19, 1903, survived by one child, Max, who was born November 27, 1903. On December 31, 1913, at Erie, Kansas, Mr. O'Brien married Mrs. Austa (Cowan) Van Druff. Her father was the late Doctor Cowan of Valley Falls, Kansas, a prominent pioneer physician of that section.

B. H. ACHTER. In a foremost place on the list of the men who are identified with large business interests at Iola, Kansas, is found the name of B. H. Achter, president of the Iola Wholesale Grocer Company. Mr. Achter is one of the men who have worked their own way to prosperity and prominence, for when he came to this country he was without capital or influence and was compelled to depend alone upon his own resource and ability. His career has been one of marked advancement, and the material rewards which have been his have been fairly and honorably won.

B. H. Achter was born in the Province of Hanover, Germany, March 9, 1850, and is a son of William B. and Angela Achter. His grandfather was Herman H. Achter, who passed his entire life in Hanover as a farmer, and participated in one of the early wars of his country as a teamster. William B. Achter was born in 1804, in Hanover, and early adopted the vocation of a farmer, following that calling throughout a long and active life. He died in his native province in 1876, in the faith of the Roman Catholic Church. He and his wife were the parents of five children: H. H., who still lives in Germany and is engaged in farming; Mary Anna, who died as the wife of Herman Koop, a farmer of Holland, Europe; Frank, who came to the United States and is now engaged in business as a tailor at Cincinnati, Ohio; Teckla, who married Mr. Piper, a general workman of Cincinnati, and died in that city, as did her husband; and B. H.

B. H. Achter was educated in private schools in the vicinity of his native place, and was twenty years of age when he left Germany for the United States. Arriving at Cincinnati, Ohio, in 1870, he secured employment as a private coachman, and continued as such at that city for three years, following this for five years of the same kind of employment at St. Louis, Missouri. Subsequently he removed to Bond County, Illinois, where he invested his savings in a farm and continued as an agriculturist until 1881, when he removed to Humboldt, Kansas, which city has since been his home. On his arrival at Humboldt, he founded a livery business, but subsequently turned his attention toward mercantile lines, being the proprietor of a retail grocery business which after a number of years expanded into a wholesale concern. While he still makes his home at Humboldt, his chief business interests are at Iola, where, since 1910, he has been president of the Iola Wholesale Grocer Company, one of the city's leading firms. He is also vice president of the Dodge City Wholesale Grocery Company. Mr. Achter is well and favorably known in business circles of the several communities where he is interested, and his reputation rests upon many years of honorable and straightforward dealing. The Iola Wholesale Grocer Company has the following officials: president, B. H. Achter; vice president, W. H. Cook; treasurer, H. J. Tholen, Jr.; and secretary, William H. Achter. Mr. Achter maintains an independent stand in political matters. He is a member of the Roman Catholic Church, and is fraternally affiliated with Humboldt Council No. 429, Knights of Columbus; Humboldt Camp, Modern Woodmen of America; and the Catholic Mutual Benefit Association and the Anti Horse Thief Association.

In 1883 Mr. Achter was married at Humboldt, Kansas, to Miss Mary Koppers, daughter of Henry and Johanna Koppers, both now deceased, who were pioneer farming people of Wilson County, Kansas, whence they came in 1872. Mr. and Mrs. Achter have had the following children: William H., who is secretary of the Iola Wholesale Grocer Company; Elizabeth, who is unmarried and resides at Humboldt; B. H., Jr., who is bookkeeper in the Iola Wholesale Grocer Company's branch plant at Fredonia, Kansas; Mary, who is deceased; and Anna and Emilyanna, who are also unmarried and reside with their parents at Humboldt.

HERMON JOHN THOLEN, JR. Prominent among the business men of the younger generation who have won success and prominence in commercial affairs of Iola, Kansas, is Hermon John Tholen, Jr., treasurer of the Iola Wholesale Grocer Company. Mr. Tholen has been connected throughout his business career with this concern, which was founded by his father, and which occupies a place of leadership among the enterprises of its kind in this thriving Kansas City.

Mr. Tholen was born June 26, 1885, at Humboldt, Kansas, and is a son of Hermon John and Ella (Koppers) Tholen. His father was born in 1854, in the Province of Hanover, Germany, and was a young man when he came to the United States, settling at Humboldt, Kansas, in 1878. There he was married to Miss Ella Koppers, who was born in 1856, in Prussia, Germany, and was brought to the United States by her parents when fourteen years of age. Mr. Tholen's first business venture in this country was a dealer in ice, subsequently he embarked in the retail grocery trade, and finally broadened out into wholesale groceries and remained in the latter line at Humboldt until 1900. In that year he changed his location to Iola, where he became the founder of the Iola Wholesale Grocer Company, of which he continued to be present until his death, February 11, 1911. Mr. Tholen was one of the substantial business men of Iola, shrewd, far-seeing and accurate in his judgments, and a man of the strictest integrity and probity. A democrat in politics, he took a wholesome and intelligent interest in public affairs, and for several years served in the capacity of mayor of Humboldt. He was a faithful member of the Roman Catholic Church. Mrs. Tholen, who survives her husband and resides at Iola, has been the mother of the following children: Anna, who died in infancy; May, who makes her home with her mother; Anna (2), who died at the age of twenty-one years, unmarried; Hermon John; and Helene, who is the wife of S. A. Bixby, engaged in the wholesale fruit business at Iola.

Hermon John Tholen, Jr., received his education in the graded and high schools of Humboldt, Kansas, following which he entered Christian Brothers

College, at St. Louis, Missouri, an institution which he attended for one year while taking the commercial course. In 1903 he came to Iola, where he at once became connected with the Iola Wholesale Grocer Company, of which concern he has since acted in the capacity of treasurer. He is a young man of much ability, possessed of modern ideas and progressive spirit, and has the full confidence of his associates who have learned to consult his judgment in matters of importance. The plant of the concern is located at 414 West Madison Avenue, Iola, while a branch department is maintained at Fredonia, and the present officials of the company are: B. H. Achter, president; W. H. Cook, vice president; H. J. Tholen, Jr., treasurer; and William H. Achter, secretary. Mr. Tholen is a democrat, and a member of the Roman Catholic Church. He resides in his country home, which is a beautiful property lying 1½ miles north of Iola.

In 1909 Mr. Tholen was united in marriage with Miss Carrie L. Doggett, of Iola, daughter of R. A. and Sarah Doggett, residents of this city, although Mr. Doggett is connected with a business at Collinsville. Mr. and Mrs. Tholen have no children.

CARL ACKARMAN of Sedan has justified all the predictions and wishes of his friends as to a successful career in the law. He has ability, training, industry and courage, and has handled with exceptional skill every interest entrusted to him since he opened his law office at Sedan. In 1916 he was re-elected for another term as county attorney of Chautauqua County. His first term had given such general satisfaction that he was unopposed by any candidate for re-election.

Born at Moline, Kansas, January 16, 1881, he was reared in Sedan, educated in the public schools, graduating from high school in 1898, and for the following four years gave his time and energy to his father, a well known hardware merchant. He preferred a professional rather than a commercial career, and as soon as he could give up his responsibilities in connection with his father's business he entered the law school of the University of Kansas at Lawrence, where he remained until graduating in 1905 LL. B. Mr. Ackarman made not only a good student record in Lawrence, but also contributed to the athletic prowess of the university team. He played three years on the Kansas University football team, and he contributed to the many victories won by the team in those years. He also excelled in the weight events in the track and field contests. He is a member of the law fraternity Phi Delta Phi.

After completing his course at Lawrence Mr. Ackarman returned to Sedan and has spent ten years in building up a fine practice both in civil and criminal law. His offices are in the First National Bank Building.

Mr. Ackarman likes to do things. Aside from his practice as a lawyer he has found his greatest pleasure in making a home. In 1914 he completed his modern residence on the fair grounds addition to Sedan, and he spent much time in planning and in getting a house to his own liking. He did much of the work himself, and among other modern improvements which he installed is a scientifically constructed septic tank to dispose of the house sewage. He built that himself.

In politics he has affiliated with the republican party For nearly three years he served as city attorney and resigned that office on being elected county attorney in 1914. He served on the Republican County Central Committee in 1912-14. He believes in fraternalism, and is a prominent member of several of the orders represented at Sedan. He served two terms as master of Vesper Lodge No. 136, Ancient Free and Accepted Masons; for one term was high priest and is now secretary of Syroc Chapter No. 42 Royal Arch Masons; is a member of Wichita Consistory No. 2 of the Scottish Rite and of the Mystic Shrine Temple at Wichita. For the past ten years he has been secretary of Sedan Lodge No. 141, Independent Order of Odd Fellows, and has held the position of clerk for six years in Camp No. 40 of the Woodmen of the World at Sedan.

In 1913, at Chickasha, Oklahoma, Mr. Ackarman married Miss Jeannette Surbeck. Her parents were Joseph and Harriet Surbeck, and her father is still living, a retired farmer at Oklahoma City.

Mr. Ackarman is a son of E. C. Ackarman and his wife, Laura (Thornburg) Ackarman, and is a grandson of Andrew Ackarman and a great-grandson of Andrew Ackarman, Sr. His great-grandfather was born in Germany, and settled near Rome City, Indiana, in the very early days, spending his life there as a tanner. Grandfather Andrew Ackarman followed farming near Rome City, where he was born in 1812, and died there in 1890.

E. C. Ackarman was born at Rome, Indiana, August 28, 1847, grew up on a farm, and came to Kansas and settled in Crawford County in 1869. He moved to Howard County in 1871, and a few years later left the farm and engaged in the hardware business at Moline. In 1883 he established a hardware store in Sedan, and conducted that for nearly twenty years, when he finally turned it over to his son, Fred, who is now its proprietor. E. C. Ackarman still lives in Sedan and has long been prominent in local affairs. He has held various offices of trust in his township, was county commissioner three years, was mayor of Sedan two terms, and is a loyal and public spirited citizen. His wife died in Sedan in 1902. Carl Ackarman was the oldest son and the oldest of the children to grow up. His oldest sister, Ethel, died at the age of three years. The next younger in the family is Fred Ackarman, and another brother, Paul, lives at Chautauqua, Kansas. The youngest of the family, Ruth, died at the age of eight years.

CHARLES B. SKIDMORE. To attain success as a member of the Kansas bar requires more than ordinary ability which has been trained along the lines of the legal profession, as well as a vast fund of general information, and keen judgment with regard to men and their motives. In the big and pulsing communities of the Sunflower State there is so much competition, circumstances play such an important part in the shaping of events, and these events crowd each other so closely, that the legist has to be capable of grasping affairs with a competent hand to effect satisfactory results. Among those who have won recognition in this difficult field of endeavor is Charles B. Skidmore, for twenty-five years a Kansas attorney, and for a large part of this time engaged in practice at Columbus, his present location.

Mr. Skidmore was born in Vermilion County, Illinois, February 1, 1871, and is a son of James and Margaret (Ward) Skidmore. The Skidmore family had its founding in Scotland, and the first of the name, of this branch, to come to America settled at an early day in that part of Virginia now included within the borders of West Virginia. James Skidmore, the father of Charles B. Skidmore, was born in 1830 in (West) Virginia, and was there educated and reared to young manhood, when he made his way to Vermilion County, Illinois. A farmer and stock-raiser by vocation, he was so engaged at the outbreak of the Civil war, when he enlisted in the Union army as a private in an Illinois volunteer infantry regiment. With that organization he fought for four years, taking part in numerous bloody and important engagements, but coming through safe to return to his farm. Mr. Skidmore remained in Illinois until 1875, in which year he came to Kansas and settled in Cherokee County, there continuing his agricultural operations until 1884. Since that time he has been a resident of Columbus, where for the first six years he was engaged in the implement business, but is now practically retired. He has led an active, industrious and useful life, and in whatever community he has centered his efforts has been held in high esteem because of the sterling qualities of his character. He has served as justice of the peace, and is active in the work of the Baptist Church, in which he has been a deacon for many years. In politics he is a democrat. Mr. Skidmore married Miss Margaret Ward, who was born in 1840, in New York, and died at Columbus, Kansas, in 1910. They were the parents of two children: Kittie, who married Mr. Cowan, and resides at Mountain Home, Idaho, where Mr. Cowan is engaged in the furniture and undertaking business; and Charles B., of this review. By a former marriage Mr. Skidmore had three children namely: Sallie, of Columbus, Kansas, widow of Mr. Mayhew, who was a farmer and filled the office of constable and other positions; Andrew H., who is a former judge and one of the best known members of the Cherokee County bar; and Mollie, who is the wife of James Radley, a Wyoming farmer and stockman.

Charles B. Skidmore received his education in the public schools of Cherokee County, where he attended high school, and at the age of seventeen years left the schoolroom as a student to re-enter it as a teacher. For several years he acted as educator in the rural districts of Cherokee County, but in the meantime pursued his studies diligently for the legal profession, and for some time read law in the office of his half-brother, Andrew H. Skidmore. In the fall of 1892 he was admitted to the bar of Kansas, and at once began practice at Columbus, where he continued for two years. Next Mr. Skidmore went to Baxter Springs for four years, and then to Galena, where he remained twelve years, finally returning to Columbus, where his broad experience and extensive training at once gained him recognition. He has since built up a large and representative practice which carries him into all of the courts, and is recognized as one of the reliable and thoroughly informed members of his profession practicing at the county seat. His offices are in the Logan Security Building. Among the members of his vocation, Mr. Skidmore is recognized as one who respects the best ethics of the profession, and as a valued associate and a dangerous opponent. He belongs to the various organizations gathered for mutual benefit and an elevation of standards in the profession, and is active in the work of the Commercial Club, of which he is a member. His political beliefs make him a republican, and his religious faith a Methodist.

Mr. Skidmore was married in 1895, at Baxter Springs, Kansas, to Miss Ada Chittenden, daughter of James and Ann (Peckenpaugh) Chittenden, the former of whom, a farmer, is now deceased, while the latter survives and is a resident of Spokane, Washington. Mr. and Mrs. Skidmore have two children: Edward E., born April 3, 1898, a junior in the Cherokee County High School, at Columbus; and James E. born February 17, 1902, a sophomore in the same institution.

man came to the United States, locating at Fort Wayne. There he secured employment as a machinist in the railroad shops, where he worked for five years, and in 1878 came to Kansas as a pioneer farmer, locating in the vicinity of Humboldt. He continued to be engaged as an agriculturist during the remainder of his life, and passed away at the city named in 1901. Mr. Pens saw nine years of service in the United States Navy. He was a democrat in his political views, and belonged to the Lutheran Church. He married a Miss Baker, and they became the parents of four children, namely: William, who is deceased; Henry, who is engaged in farming in the vicinity of Humboldt; Elizabeth, who resides in Montana; and Fred, who is a railroad employe at Huntington, Indiana. Mr. Pens was married the second time to Marie Habbit, who was born in 1842, in Germany, and who survives her husband, being a resident of Missoula, Montana. Eight children, three of whom are deceased, were born to this union: Louis, who is connected with the Armour Packing Company, at Kansas City, Missouri; George W.; Emma, who is the wife of Adam Ziegler, the proprietor of a foundry at Fort Wayne, Indiana; Caroline, who is the wife of Frank Ferguson, a farmer of Coffeyville, Kansas; and Matilda, the wife of Bernard Feil, who occupies an official position at Missoula, Montana.

George W. Pens received a public school education, but the greater part of his schooling has come through experience and coming into contact with his fellowmen. He was but eight years old when he began to work on his father's farm, and resided on the home place until he was twenty-three years of age, when he began to farm for himself. After one year thus spent he became interested in the oil business, in the Mid-Continent fields, and in 1899 came to Chanute as a contractor. He was one of the pioneers in the business here, and has drilled no less than 1,003 wells as a contractor. Mr. Pens is acknowledged to be one of the best informed men in the business in this section, and, from the time of his arrival, his contracts have shown a steady increase, both as to numbers and to size. He has evidenced his faith in the present value and future development of the section by investment in land and property, and at this time owns his own residence at 201 North Evergreen Avenue, a dwelling at No. 207 on the same thoroughfare, another house at 109 North Central Avenue, and a valuable property, devoted to farming and oil development, in Neosho County. He maintains an·independent stand in politics, and takes only a good citizen's interest in public matters.

Mr. Pens was married in 1897, at Iola, Kansas, to Miss Eva Anderson, daughter of J. O. and Matilda Anderson, the latter deceased, and the former a resident of Chanute and a farmer by vocation. Eight children have been born to Mr. and Mrs. Pens: Edna, a graduate of the graded schools; Walter, a sophomore at the Chanute High School; Leota, Maxine and Pauline, who are attending the graded schools; and Kenneth and Marjorie. One child, Mildred, died aged seven months.

JAMES SCOTT CUMMINGS, M. D. A former president of the State Board of Health, a member of the Legislature, and otherwise prominent in local and state affairs, Doctor Cummings is a pioneer physician of Bronson in Bourbon County, and both through his profession and as a citizen he has found many ways in which to make his career count for benefit to his community.

Doctor Cummings represents a pioneer family in Southeastern Kansas. He was born in Parke County, Indiana, June 8, 1851. His Cummings ancestors were emigrants from the North of Ireland to Virginia in colonial times. Doctor Cummings is a grandson of Samuel Cummings, who was born in 1784 in Greenbrier County in that portion of Virginia now the State of West Virginia. He was both a tanner and a farmer. He brought his family west during the '30s and settled in Parke County, Indiana, where he died in 1858, seven years after Doctor Cummings was born. Samuel Cummings married Rachel McClung.

John M. Cummings, father of Doctor Cummings, was born in Rockbridge County, Virginia, September 13, 1820, and spent the first sixteen years of his life in his native locality until his parents moved west to Parke County, Indiana. In Parke County he found employment in his father's tannery until he was thirty years of age, was married at that time in life, and afterwards gave his activities to farming. His attention was early attracted to Kansas. In 1867 he visited in this state in Allen County, and in 1869 came to that county as a permanent settler. He bought a farm in the vicinity of what is now Carlyle, and remained there a prosperous and substantial citizen until his death on April 22, 1876. John M. Cummings was a republican and a very active member and supporter of the Methodist Episcopal Church, serving on its official board for a period of years.

In 1850 John M. Cummings married Catherine Ann Beadle. She was a member of a prominent family. Her brother, Gen. William H. Beadle, who died at San Francisco in 1915, was sent out to the Dakotas in 1867 as surveyor of the territory, and subsequently became author of the school laws of South Dakota, a body of laws especially noteworthy because they assure every child an education. In one of the prominent locations in the City of Pierre, South Dakota, stands a handsome statue to this notable citizen. Mrs. Cummings' brother John H. Beadle was also a man of more than ordinary note. He was author of "The Crimes and Mysteries of Mormonism," "The Danites," and other works, and for many years held the position of editor for the Associated Press in New York City. Catherine Ann Beadle was born in Clark County, Kentucky, in 1832, and died at Bronson, Kansas, in 1898. Dr. James S. Cummings is the oldest of their nine children. Nannie is the wife of William Linebarger, a retired farmer living at Chrisman, Illinois. Laura V., whose home is at Uniontown, Kansas, has been twice a widow, her first husband having been Thomas Jobe, a minister of the Hardshell Baptist Church, and her second was Benson Dark, a farmer. William A. Cummings entered the legal profession and died quite early in his career in 1884 at Iola, Kansas. Lizzie is the wife of C. H. Sater, a retired farmer at Golden City, Missouri. Charles M. is a rancher at Standish, California. Rachel, who lives at Bois D'Arc, Missouri, is the widow of John New, who was a farmer in Linn County, Kansas. Mattie married C. C. Pavey, a real estate and insurance man at Muncie, Indiana. Edmond Beadle Cummings, who was born in Carlyle, Kansas, in 1872 and died at Bronson in 1914, practiced medicine and surgery with notable success for many years and is a graduate of the Kansas Medical College of Topeka.

James Scott Cummings was eighteen years of age when his parents came to Kansas. In the meantime he had made the best of such advantages as were afforded by the public schools of Parke County, Indiana. He also had two years of private instruction under D. M. Smith, later a prominent Kansan. At the age of twenty-one he entered the ranks of the teaching profession, and taught school in the country districts of Allen County until 1879. In the meantime as opportunity offered he had diligently pursued the study of medicine in the office of Dr. G. D. Whittaker of Carlyle, now of Kansas City, Kansas. In 1876 he took his first course in the College of Medicine and Surgery at Cincinnati, Ohio, following which he resumed teaching, and was finally graduated from the Cincinnati institution in 1880 with the degree M. D. Doctor Cummings is as much a student today as he was thirty-five years ago, and keeps in close touch with advanced medical and surgical knowledge. The spring of 1908 he spent in the Chicago Policlinic and the fall of the same year he took a course in the New York Post-Graduate School.

In 1880 Doctor Cummings began practice at what is now called Rocklow in Allen County, but in the spring of 1882 came to Bronson when that townsite was first laid out. The choice of a home and professional location which he made then he has never recalled nor regretted, and he has remained steadily with the community, at first doing largely a country practice and undergoing the hardships of riding and driving in all sorts of weather and over all sorts of roads. In later years the hardships of practice have been largely mitigated by telephones, automobiles, improved highways, and many other facilities which the doctor of thirty-five years ago could not command. In 1882 Doctor Cummings built a home on Randolph Street, but he now owns and occupies another residence on Clay Street, a thoroughly modern home. He has two business buildings on Clay Street and has a well improved farm of 160 acres four miles west of Fort Scott. He is a stockholder and director in the Bank of Bronson.

Doctor Cummings is a member of the County and State Medical societies, the Southeast Kansas Medical Society and the American Medical Association. He has served as health officer of Bronson, was for five years coroner of Bourbon County during the '90s, has been a member of the town council of Bronson, and is now secretary of the Board of Education. In politics he is affiliated with the democrats. In 1912 the Nineteenth District of Bourbon County sent him to the Legislature and during the session of 1913 he was chairman of the health and hygiene committee and a member of the state library and other committees. In 1913 Doctor Cummings was appointed a member of the State Board of Health, and he served in that organization three years, one year as president. With all his many other interests Doctor Cummings does much for church and charitable causes and is a firm believer in the benefits of fraternalism. He is chairman of the board of trustees of the Methodist Episcopal Church and president of the Church Brotherhood. For two terms he filled the office of Master in Bourbon Lodge No. 268, Ancient Free and Accepted Masons at Bronson, belongs to Fort Scott Consistory No. 4 of the Scottish Rite, to Abdallah Temple of the Mystic Shrine at Leavenworth, is past chancellor commander of Granite Lodge No. 88, Knights of Pythias at Bronson, and a member of Bois D'Arc Camp No. 1010, Modern Woodmen of America at Bronson.

Doctor Cummings has an unquestioned reputation as an orator of very effective and persuasive eloquence. As a public speaker his services have been much in demand, particularly for making addresses on public health questions and as a speaker at Masonic reunions and at various gatherings under the auspices of his church. His presence and active part have been considered almost essential to the success of any public occasion in his part of the state for over thirty years. Doctor Cummings is a man of wide travel, and has thus a culture derived not only from books but also from varied associations with men and affairs. He has traveled over the United States from coast to coast, and south to Old Mexico.

On September 22, 1881, the year before he came to Bronson to take up practice, Doctor Cummings was married in Allen County to Miss Libbie Ray. Her parents A. J. and Parmelia (Hovey) Ray are both now deceased. Her father was for a number of years a merchant at Eureka Springs, Arkansas. Doctor and Mrs. Cummings have one child, Mabel. She married G. R. Hughes, a clothing merchant at Fort Scott, where they reside. Mr. and Mrs. Hughes have two children: Elizabeth, born September 28, 1904; and Kathryn, born in 1907.

CHARLES H. APT first came to Kansas in the weeks following the first election of Grover Cleveland for the presidency. He had already been thoroughly trained and for a time had practiced law in Ohio, and deciding upon a location in Kansas, he transferred his professional interests to this state and for more than thirty years has been a successful lawyer, has acquired a large amount of farming interests, and is one of the best known citizens of Iola. He is now head of the law firm of Apt & Apt, having a son in partnership with him.

The Apt family originated in Switzerland. Mr. Apt's grandfather, Henry Apt, was born in Pennsylvania, probably of Swiss parentage, followed the business of carder and wool worker, and died at Basil in Fairfield County, Ohio.

Frederick W. Apt, father of Charles H., was born in Lancaster County, Pennsylvania, in 1824, but when a boy was taken to Fairfield County, Ohio. He grew up and married there, and was a blacksmith by trade. In 1861 he enlisted for service in the Union army, but in a short time was discharged. In 1863 he removed to Indiana and soon afterward again enlisted, this time in the Eighty-seventh Indiana Infantry. He remained in the service until the close of the war, and suffered such hardships and exposure that he was taken seriously ill before being brought home. He was at Washington at the time of the Grand Review, but was not able to march in the procession. He was carried home on August 22, 1865, and died the following September 12. His death occurred at Kewanna, Indiana. He had become a republican during the war, and was a member of the German Reformed Church. Frederick W. Apt married Eliza Lytton, who was born in Northern England in 1834 and died at Kewanna, Indiana, in 1895. Her parents came to this country when she was very young, and her mother settled in Fairfield County, Ohio. Her father died either while at sea or shortly after the arrival in America. Frederick W. Apt and wife had only two children: Charles H. and Elmer E. The latter is a contractor and builder of Pittsburgh, Pennsylvania. Mrs. Frederick W. Apt married for her second husband Abel Graham. He is also deceased. One son by that union was Perry, now a farmer near Kewanna, Indiana .

While his parents were living in Fairfield County, Ohio, Charles H. Apt was born July 15, 1860. He has little recollection of his father, as he was only five years of age at the time of the soldier's death. He began his education in the schools of Kewanna, Indiana, but in 1867 his mother returned to Fairfield County, Ohio, and partly by his own efforts and partly by such means as the family could afford he acquired a liberal education. He attended public school in Ohio, and in 1880 graduated from the Ohio Northern University at Ada, with the degree A. B. He also spent one year in the Ohio State University, taking a course in civil engineering. Mr. Apt had his law course in the Cincinnati Law School, where he was graduated LL. B. in 1884. Admitted to the bar in that year, he began practice at Columbus, Ohio, on July 1, and continued a member of the bar of that city until after the election in November.

On coming to Kansas he visited Topeka, Wichita and Wellington, and in January, 1885, located his professional headquarters at Pratt. From March, 1885, until June 1, 1904, he was successfully engaged in practice at Pratt, and since the latter date has lived in Iola. He still looks after his extensive clientage in the civil and criminal branches of the law, his offices being at 7½ West Madison Avenue.

Mr. Apt has been prospered in a business way and owns some of the best farming land of Pratt County, divided into three different tracts, consisting respectively of 160, 320 and 640 acres, altogether 1,120 acres. He also owns his residence at 222 South Oak Street in Iola, and is on the board of directors of the State Savings Bank of Iola.

Mr. Apt is a democrat. He belongs to the Presbyterian Church, and while at Pratt he assisted in organizing Kilwinning Lodge, No. 265, Ancient Free and Accepted Masons, and still has his membership there. He belongs to Wichita Consistory, No. 2, of the Scottish Rite, to Iola Lodge, No. 43, Knights of Pythias, of which he is past chancellor commander, and has filled all the chairs several times. Other fraternal relations are with Ninnestah Camp, No. 1275, Modern Woodmen of America, at Pratt; with Iola Camp, No. 101, Woodmen of the World; and with the Kansas Fraternal Citizens. Mr. Apt is a member of the Kansas State Bar Association.

On December 26, 1887, at Cincinnati, Ohio, he married Miss Blanche Gazlay, daughter of Carter and Lizzie (Emerson) Gazlay. Both her parents are now deceased, and her father for many years practiced law at Cincinnati, Ohio, and in Indiana. Mr. and Mrs. Apt are the parents of two children: Frederick G. and Elizabeth.

Frederick G. Apt was born at Pratt, Kansas, July 2, 1889, was educated in the public schools at Iola, where he attended high school, and in 1910 finished the law course in the University of Kansas, attaining the degree LL. B. While in university he became affiliated with the Sigma Alpha Epsilon Greek letter fraternity. Admitted to the bar in 1910, he returned to Iola and has carried on a general practice as junior member of the firm of Apt & Apt. He also owns a good farm of eighty acres in Neosho County. Frederick G. Apt is a republican, a member of the Presbyterian Church, of Iola Lodge No. 38, Ancient Free and Accepted Masons, and is a director in the State Savings Bank of Iola. He is unmarried.

WILLIAM TAYLOR WILLIAMS. More than a half century has passed since William T. Williams, one of Sedan's foremost citizens, had his first glimpse of Kansas, of which state, for almost that long, he has been a continuous resident. The marvelous changes which have been wrought in the country through the civilizing industries of men of enterprise, are reflected in some degree, in the advancement of his own fortunes, but none of these developments have come without strenuous effort, persistent energy and never failing courage. This may well be given emphasis in view of the fact that charges have been made in these luxury-loving days, too many American youth appear but too well satisfied with the advantages that have been provided by the manly endurance of an older generation. With leisure and love of ease, they invite weakness instead of seeking strength that comes through courageous bearing of hardships and the stimulation of overcoming obstacles.

William Taylor Williams, vice president of the First National Bank, Sedan, Kansas, was born in Hart County, Kentucky, May 22, 1848. His parents were Ansel and Mary (Gooch) Williams. His grandfather, David Williams, was born in Wythe County, Virginia, in 1801, and died in Grayson County, Kentucky, in 1850. His father was born in Wales and was the founder of the family in America. The grandmother was Jane Jackson, who was born in South Carolina and died in Marion County, Illinois. She was a daughter of a revolutionary soldier.

Ansel Williams, father of William Taylor Williams, was born in 1824, in Green County, Kentucky, and died in 1868, in Crawford County, Kansas. He followed agricultural pursuits all his life. In the spring of 1855, accompanied by his own family and his widowed mother, who lived in Illinois at that time, he removed to Illinois and located on a farm in Marion County, but three years later, in 1858, decided to seek a new home, in Kansas. On reaching Bourbon County he speedily complied with the law governing the securing of homesteads, and on his tract of 160 acres, endeavored to farm profitably, but in 1866 moved into Crawford County and there pre-empted a claim of 160 acres, which proved entirely satisfactory and on that place he remained during the two more years that he lived. In politics he was a democrat. During the Civil war he served as a member of the state militia.

Ansel Williams was twice married. His first wife, Mary Gooch, was born in 1823, in Green County, Kentucky. She died in Grayson County, Kentucky, in 1854. Her father served under General Jackson at New Orleans in 1812. To Ansel and Mary (Gooch) Williams the following children were born: William Taylor; Jane, who is the wife of W. D. Nance, who is a retired farmer residing at Niotaze, Chautauqua County, Kansas; James T., who died in Chautauqua County, in 1894, was a farmer; Ezra, who died at the age of fourteen years, in Crawford County, Kansas; and Sarah, who resides in Crawford County, is the widow of A. D. Nance, who was a well known farmer.

The second wife of Ansel Williams was Mary Frogget, who was born in 1836, in Kentucky, and died in Crawford County, Kansas, in 1886. To this marriage six children were born, as follows: Paul, who died in Crawford County at the age of twenty years; Marvin, who is a farmer residing near Lee Summit, Missouri; Emma, who is the wife of John Brown, a farmer residing near Fort Scott, Kansas; Ida, who is married, lives near Columbus, Ohio; Ora, who is employed in a smelter, near Bartelsville, Oklahoma; and Ansel, who is an employe in a Deaf and Dumb Asylum, at Fulton, Missouri.

William Taylor Williams was seven years old when

MR. AND MRS. W. T. WILLIAMS
NELLIE WILLIAMS   STELLA WILLIAMS WILSON
PERRY WILLIAMS

his father settled in Marion County, Illinois. The public school system had not yet been introduced and he was sent to a subscription school and attended a second subscription school after the family removal to Bourbon County, Kansas, for here was a boy determined to have an education. He assisted his father in Bourbon County and also secured other work, in September, 1863, entering the employ of the Government as a teamster, and during the summer of 1864 helped gather cattle for the Government. In that year he served also as a member of the Third Kansas Militia or Bourbon County Battalion that drove General Price's forces out of the state and he took part in the Battle of Westport, Missouri.

When his father removed to Crawford County, William Taylor accompanied him and worked on the home farm there until the fall of 1867, when he returned to Marion County, Illinois, to attend school, and worked during the summer there and went to the public school in the winter until in December, 1868, when he returned to Crawford County. His father died in that year but he remained on the home farm there until 1870, in the meanwhile, although a man grown by this time, he again took advantage of the opportunity of attending school. In 1870 he moved into Howard County, Kansas, where, in partnership with his brother James T., he took up a claim of 160 acres and resided there and made improvements. In the fall of 1878 he sold that property and removed to a farm already improved in Montgomery County. Two years later he sold that place advantageously, and in 1880 bought a farm of 160 acres situated in Chautauqua County. That was the beginning of Mr. Williams' acquirement of property in this county. Through the exercise of good judgment he has gradually increased his holdings until he now owns 700 acres of exceedingly valuable farm land, lying in Little Caney and Washington townships, Chautauqua County. He devotes his land to general farming. Another of his investments is represented by his handsome, commodious residence which stands on G Street. In the financial field Mr. Williams is recognized as a man of influence and importance and as vice president of the First National Bank at Sedan, and as a director of the Peru State Bank, these institutions have a valuable asset, and an added guarantee of their soundness.

In the fall of 1873, in Crawford County, Kansas, Mr. Williams was married to Miss Caroline Nance. Her parents, now both deceased, were Joshua and Elizabeth (Lucas) Nance. They came to Crawford County late in 1865 and settled on a farm. Mr. and Mrs. Williams have two daughters: Estella, who is the wife of B. D. Wilson, who is the leading merchant at Niotaze, Kansas; and Nellie, who is a graduate of a business college at Wichita, Kansas. Both daughters are graduates of the high school. Perry, the oldest child of Mr. and Mrs. Williams, was born June 26, 1876, and died April 6, 1896.

Mr. Williams has always been a thinker and through reading and study concerning social and economic conditions, has come to the belief that radical changes must be brought about for the benefit of the public at large. Therefore he has identified himself with the political organization termed the Socialist party. He has never been anxious to serve in public offices but consented at one time to accept the office of township trustee for one term in Little Caney Township, and for two terms in Washington Township. He is a member of Camp No. 40, Modern Woodmen of America, at Sedan. He has

had a long, busy and useful life and still continues an important factor in all that concerns his county and city.

HARRY R. HARSHBARGER of Sedan has found varied employment for his energies since he reached manhood, but is now chiefly engaged in the business of oil production, and has some of the most valuable properties of that kind in Chautauqua County. He was born at Vermilion, Edgar County, Illinois, May 28, 1868. His father was John W. Harshbarger, long and favorably known in Kansas. John W. was born in Cabell County, Virginia, in what is now West Virginia, in 1835. His father, John Harshbarger, also a native of Virginia, died in the western part of that state three months before his son, John W., was born. Grandfather John Harshbarger was a blacksmith. His wife was a Miss Doolittle, of a Maryland family, and a sister of United States Senator Doolittle of Maryland. The Harshbargers originated in Switzerland and came to Baltimore in colonial days. John W. Harshbarger was reared in Edgar County, Illinois. He also married there. While a young man he studied medicine and in 1861 he enlisted in Burgess' Sharpshooters and participated in a part of the Missouri campaign and also was in some of the fighting east of the Mississippi, but after the battle of Shiloh was discharged on account of disability. He then re-enlisted as a hospital steward in the regular army and for four years was stationed in that capacity at the Army Hospital in Memphis, Tennessee. He received his honorable discharge in 1866. Returning to Illinois he engaged in the drug business, but still more profitable were his contracts to furnish ties and wood fuel to the Indianapolis and St. Louis Railroad and individually he furnished most of the ties used during the construction of that road. In 1874 John W. Harshbarger moved to Montgomery County, Kansas, buying a farm, was engaged in its cultivation four years, then removed to Cedarvale, where he was proprietor of a hotel two years, and returning to his old home at Vermilion, Illinois, took up the meat business. He again came back to Kansas and conducted a meat market at Chautauqua Springs until he retired in 1909. He died at Chautauqua Springs in 1910. In his early years John W. Harshbarger was a republican, but subsequently became a democrat. An interesting fact in connection with his early career is that during the famous Lincoln-Douglas debates, which more than anything else gave Abraham Lincoln his national reputation and made him available as a candidate for President, Mr. Harshbarger was employed as one of the secretaries for Mr. Lincoln. Fraternally he was a member of the Independent Order of Odd Fellows.

John W. Harshbarger married Amanda Stubbs. She was born in Preble County, Ohio, in 1843, and still resides at Coffeyville, Kansas. Her father, Samuel Stubbs, was a native of Ohio, and died in Edgar County, Illinois, in 1869. He was a pioneer settler there, followed farming and the trade of carpenter, and was a strict Quaker in religion. Samuel Stubbs married a Miss Talbot, who was born in Ohio and died near Vermilion, Illinois, in 1878. The Stubbs family came out of England to Pennsylvania with William Penn. There were three brothers of that name, and from one of these brothers a branch of the family moved into Ohio. Ex-Governor Roscoe Stubbs of Kansas was a third cousin of Mrs. Amanda Stubbs Harshbarger.

The children of Mr. and Mrs. John W. Harshbarger were: Harry R.; Robert Burns, who is a worker in the oil fields and lives at Sperry, Oklahoma; Gay, who lives at Coffeyville and is teaching school, married F. H. Jay; Joseph W. is an attorney practicing at Sperry, Oklahoma; Roscoe is in the dray business at Sperry, Oklahoma.

Harry R. Harshbarger first came to Kansas as a small boy, attended the public schools of Montgomery and Chautauqua counties and received part of his education back in Illinois. At the age of eighteen he left school to become a worker in the business ranks, and for several years was employed in a meat market at Chautauqua Springs and in other places. In 1900 he removed to Holdenville, Oklahoma, where he was proprietor of a meat market and where he married. In the spring of 1902 he came to Sedan, and was engaged in the meat business there until 1910. In that year he moved to a farm, cultivated it three years, and then returned to Sedan. A number of years ago Mr. Harshbarger became interested in the oil business, and is one of the men who have been successful in handling oil leases and in development work. He now has seventeen producing wells near Sedan and is secretary and treasurer of the Deer Creek Oil and Gas Company.

Besides his residence at the corner of Spruce and the county road he owns a business building on Chautauqua Avenue occupied by the National Supply Company and a farm of forty acres adjoining Sedan on the southwest. Mr. Harshbarger is a democrat and has been serving in the city council of Sedan for four years. He is past noble grand of Sedan Lodge No. 141, Independent Order of Odd Fellows; a member of Camp No. 919 of the Modern Woodmen of America; of the Royal Neighbors; the Rebekahs, Lodge No. 33, at Sedan, and takes an active interest in the affairs of the local Commercial Club.

In 1901, at Holdenville, then in Indian Territory, now Oklahoma, he married Miss Clara Whitford. Her father, S. C. Whitford, was born in New York State in 1847 and died in Fayette County, Illinois, in 1882. Mrs. Harshbarger's grandfather Whitford was born in New York State in 1816 and was an early settler on a farm in Fayette County, Illinois, and died there in 1880. The Whitfords came out of England and were early settlers in New York State. S. C. Whitford, who was reared and married in New York State, followed farming, and the year after his marriage moved to Illinois. He was a democrat in politics. He married Frances Babcock, whose ancestors were also of English descent. She was born in New York State in 1844 and now resides at Mount Vernon, Illinois. Mr. and Mrs. Whitford had the following children: Lydia May, who resides at Pacific, Missouri, the widow of James McCasland, who was a cement contractor; Minnie Bell, who died in Chicago in 1896, was the wife of Mr. Wilson, a city mail carrier; Mrs. Harshbarger is the third in age; Catherine married E. O. Hunter, a farmer living at Godfrey, Illinois; Frederick, who died at the age of fifteen.

Mrs. Harshbarger received her early education in the public schools at Farina, Illinois. She is an active member of the Christian Church, a member of Lodge No. 33 of the Rebekahs at Sedan, of the Royal Neighbors and of the Fraternal Aid Union.

ARIO C. MENDENHALL. While the Mendenhall name has been well and honorably known in Kansas for more than a quarter of a century, it is to Pennsylvania that the biographer must turn for the family's earlier history. It has been established that three brothers of that name came to the American colonies from England at the same time that William Penn

headed his party of colonists, and that one of these remained with the great Quaker colonist and peacemaker, and that one crossed the line into Ohio while the third was lost in the far west. The Mendenhalls that Kansas has known descended from the Pennsylvania settler and are yet numerous in the old Keystone State. A worthy representative of this family and bearer of its honorable name, is Ario C. Mendenhall, who, for the past eighteen years has been prominent in the business life of Chanute, Kansas. He was born at Hazleton, Luzerne County, Pennsylvania, December 18, 1870. His parents were Lorenzo Dow and Sarah Jane (Lemon) Mendenhall.

Lorenzo Dow Mendenhall was born in Columbia County, Pennsylvania, October 17, 1827, a son of Eli Mendenhall, who spent his entire life in Columbia County, dying in 1888, at the age of eighty-four years. His wife, who bore the maiden name of Elizabeth Davis, died in 1874 in her native state, at the age of seventy-nine years. They had four children: Carlton, Araminta M., Elizabeth and Lorenzo Dow. Being the eldest son, Lorenzo early became self-supporting, learning the milling business very thoroughly, and also the tanning business, a very important one in those days, which he followed for some years. During the period of the Civil war when General Lee's forces invaded Pennsylvania, he served as a member of the home troops that repelled them. For several years of this time he was also in the employ of the Government as manager of an extensive rice cleaning mill, preparing the grain for the Union army. After he returned to Pennsylvania, Mr. Mendenhall was engaged as manager of the great mills of A. Pardee & Company, situated at Hazleton, and continued to operate these mills for nine years. He then removed to South Bend, Indiana, and there was engaged in the milling business for two years, and for a decade traveled over the country as a dresser of millstones, this being before and when a young man.

In 1880 Mr. Mendenhall removed with his family to Humboldt, Kansas, but did not re-enter the milling business here but turned his attention to agricultural pursuits. He purchased a well located farm of 160 acres, situated in Cottage Grove Township, six miles southeast of Humboldt, and, although entirely without farm experience, succeeded in this enterprise and became a large producer of wheat, corn, oats and flax. He retired from active pursuits in September, 1909, and then came to Chanute, Kansas, where he died December 20 following. On December 31, 1856, he was married to Sarah Jane Lemon, who was born in 1834 at Rohrsburg, Pennsylvania, where she still resides. They became the parents of five children: Lorenzo, who died at the age of eight years; two sons, deceased, one at the age of six years and the other aged eighteen months; Ario C.; and Estella Grace, who is the wife of a Mr. Lackey, a farmer residing near Cement, Oklahoma. Lorenzo Dow Mendenhall was a republican in politics and fraternally he was an Odd Fellow.

Ario C. Mendenhall attended the country schools in Allen County, Kansas, and remained with his father until he was twenty-seven years old, managing the home farm for a number of years. In 1897 he began operating a threshing and also a well drilling outfit and ever since coming to Chanute, September 1, 1898, has made the well drilling business in the various oil fields his main activity, although he also owns a farm of 160 acres in Allen County. Mr. Mendenhall has probably drilled more of the wells in the mid-continent oil and gas fields than any other operator, having worked from Humboldt to Neodesha, in Wilson County, a wide territory, having rigs continually drilling several wells at a time. At present he is interested in seven producing oil leases in Allen County and one gas lease, and has one gas lease in Wilson County. In addition to his large business in this direction, Mr. Mendenhall looks after his farm interests with care and also attends to the management of quite a large amount of real estate that he owns at Chanute, including his handsome residence at No. 601 Highland Avenue. His various interests have brought him into association with all classes of men and their general verdict is that he is a shrewd, far-sighted business man but is one who is honest and upright in all his transactions and rather than take an advantage of anyone, would be more likely to extend a helping hand and financial aid if necessary. Hence he has a wide circle of real friends and well wishers.

In Allen County, in 1896, Mr. Mendenhall was married to Miss Allie Bair, who is a daughter of W. M. and Sarah (Spaulding) Bair. The father of Mrs. Mendenhall was a farmer in Allen County and died there. The mother makes her home with Mr. and Mrs. Mendenhall. They have two children: Roscoe, who was born July 13, 1899, is a student in the Chanute High School; and Ralph, who was born August 16, 1910, who is also in school. In politics Mr. Mendenhall has always been a republican and, in good citizenship is well qualified for public office but he has never consented to serve in any position. He is a member of Chanute Lodge No. 806 Benevolent and Protective Order of Elks.

ALBERT N. CURTIS. One of the most active among the operators in the Mid-Continent oil fields is Albert N. Curtis, an oil man with twenty-two years of experience behind him. Mr. Curtis, who now makes his headquarters at Chanute, came here from Ohio in 1903 and has since occupied a foremost position among producers, having drilled hundreds of wells and being interested at this time in oil and gas wells in four directions from the city. He was born at Monroe, Monroe County, Michigan, January 2, 1864, and is a son of Norman and Minerva (Choate) Curtis, and a member of a family which originated in England and settled in Massachusetts prior to the War of the Revolution.

Norman Curtis was born in 1832, at Dundee, Monroe County, Michigan, and passed his entire life in that state, where he was engaged in successful agricultural operations. In his later years he retired from active affairs and located at Detroit, in which city he passed away in 1906. Mr. Curtis took a leading part in political affairs and civic matters, was a stanch democrat, and served for a time as township supervisor. Fraternally, he was affiliated with the Masonic order. In 1861 he enlisted in a regiment of Michigan Volunteer Infantry, with which he served three years and three months, and then re-enlisted in the hospital corps and continued to act with that branch of the service until the close of the Civil war. He married Minerva Choate, who was born in 1838, at Monroe, Michigan, and they became the parents of four children: Clara, who is the wife of Frank Mulholland, a farmer of Monroe, Michigan; Isie, deceased, who was the wife of the late George Strayer, who was a farmer of Monroe County, Michigan; Albert N.; and Lottie, who died at the age of eighteen years.

Albert N. Curtis was educated in the public schools of his native county, and remained on the home farm until he was twenty-six years of age, at which time he left the parental roof and struck out for himself, renting a farm in the same county, on which

he carried on fairly successful operations for four years. In 1894 he entered the oil business, receiving his introduction thereto in the fields of Ohio, where he became a contractor. He met with success in his enterprises in Sandusky and Wood counties in that state, and in June, 1903, came to Chanute, as a pioneer in the Mid-Continent field, where he has since been engaged in producing and contracting. Mr. Curtis is now producing north, south, east and west from Chanute, being interested in about 100 oil and gas wells, and his furthest property is twelve miles from the city. He has also drilled hundreds of wells and is justly accounted one of the experienced men in this industry, in which he has gained a wide reputation. Mr. Curtis is the owner of a 200-acre farm, located 2½ miles west and one-half mile north of Chanute, and a residence at No. 501 West Fifth Street. His honorable dealing upon all occasions has given him an enviable reputation in business circles. Politically, Mr. Curtis exercises his right of franchise in behalf of the candidates and policies of the democratic party. He fraternizes with Hector Lodge No. 64, Independent Order of Odd Fellows; Chanute Lodge No. 806, Benevolent and Protective Order of Elks; and Chanute Tent No. 56, Knights of the Maccabees. He is also an active member of the Chanute Commercial Club.

Mr. Curtis was first married in 1891, at Monroe, Michigan, to Miss Emma Zoran, who died in December, 1913, at Chanute, leaving three children: Mabel, who resides at Monroe, Michigan; Emerson, who is the proprietor of a wardrobe cleaning business at Chanute; and Emma Thelda, who is attending the Chanute public schools. Mr. Curtis was again married, in March, 1915, at Chanute, to Mrs. Ethel (Scott) Craeg, the widow of Ben Craeg, who was an employe of the Chicago & Alton Railroad.

ALFRED HARRIS HECOX. One of the native sons of Allen County who are now holding official positions in the employ of the United States Government, is Alfred Harris Hecox, who since July, 1914, has served in the capacity of postmaster of the City of Iola. Mr. Hecox has had a diversified and interesting career, in which he has visited various parts of the country and engaged in a number of different occupations which have brought him in close touch with the public and at the same time has given him a broadened experience. These qualities have served him well in the discharge of his official duties and have helped to make him a popular and efficient official.

Mr. Hecox is descended from English ancestors who left their native land and located in the Colony of Connecticut prior to the American War of the Revolution, and from that community the family branched out into other localities to the west and south, the branch of which Mr. Hecox is a member having found settlement in Illinois. He was born on a farm in Allen County, Kansas, October 30, 1869, and is a son of Jeremiah and Sarah (Harris) Hecox. Jeremiah Hecox was born in 1826, in Hancock County, Illinois, and was there reared and married and engaged in farming. He was past middle life when he ventured to take his place among the sturdy farmers of Kansas, and in 1867 located in Allen County, where he homesteaded eighty acres of land six miles northwest of Iola. There he passed the remainder of his life in agricultural pursuits and died in 1883. Mr. Hecox was primarily an agriculturist and had no ambition for a business or financial career or for any position in public life. He was content to till his acres and to realize a modest profit from his labors, and his only share in politics was to vote the democratic ticket. Mrs. Hecox, who was born in 1842, in Hancock County, Illinois, still survives her husband and is a resident of Iola. There are four children in the family: Nancy Jane, who is the wife of Samuel Malcome, employed in the cement plant at Iola; John William, who resides at Haviland, Kansas, and is engaged in farming; Alfred H., of this notice; and Frank Edwards, a farmer of the State of Nebraska.

The rural schools of Allen County furnished Alfred H. Hecox with his educational training, and as a youth he worked on his father's farm. The elder man died when his son was fourteen years of age and he was compelled to contribute his share to the support of the family, continuing to remain on the homestead until he reached the age of nineteen years. At that time he was attracted to the Pacific Coast and started on a trip which finally brought him to Yakima, Washington, where for four years he was variously employed, principally as a general workman. During this time, however, he made some advancement, for he attended the Yakima School of Telegraphy, and, mastering that vocation, became an operator. From Yakima he went to Portland, North Dakota, where he remained for a short time, working as a telegrapher, and in 1894 returned to Kansas and settled in Woodson County. There he found employment in the railroad office at Piqua, as operator, and remained in that capacity three years. In 1899 he came Iola, where he was retained by the Missouri Pacific Railroad as bill clerk in their general offices, and after one year his fidelity and ability had gained him promotion to the position of cashier, of which position he was the incumbent until 1909. He was then made chief clerk of the Missouri, Kansas & Texas Railroad offices at Iola, but after three years of service in this position resigned to become joint station clerk for the Missouri-Kansas Car Service Association, a position which he held until 1914.

Mr. Hecox has been a democrat since reaching his majority, and has been a stalwart supporter of the candidates and policies of his party. In July, 1914, he was appointed by President Wilson as postmaster of Iola, and in this office has continued to the present time. His administration of the affairs of the Iola office has resulted in excellent service for the people of the city, in whose esteem Mr. Hecox has found a well-established place. Fraternally, he belongs to Iola Lodge No. 38, Ancient Free and Accepted Masons; and Iola Lodge No. 21, Independent Order of Odd Fellows, of which he was secretary for two years. Mr. Hecox owns his own comfortable home at No. 812 North Street.

Mr. Hecox was married in 1889, in Woodson County, to Miss Josie Rhodabargar, daughter of Jacob and Abbie (Perry) Rhodabargar, both of whom are now deceased. Mr. Rhodabargar was a pioneer into Kansas, coming to Allen County about 1870 and here spending the balance of his life. Mr. and Mrs. Hecox have been the parents of two children: Harry Milton, who is a traveling salesman and resides at Chanute, Kansas; and Ray, who died at the age of eight months.

ELMER E. GLENN. When Elmer E. Glenn was a young man he learned the blacksmith trade in the railroad shops at Ottawa, Kansas. He spent his early life on a farm near that city. The trade which he learned and worked at for a number of years has been the basis upon which he has built his present successful business at Sedan, where he is proprietor of machine shops specializing in the repair and manufacture of oil well tools.

Though Mr. Glenn has spent most of his life in Kansas he was born at Mattoon, Illinois, November 11, 1874. His ancestors were Scotch-Irish people who emigrated to Pennsylvania in colonial times. His grandfather, Joseph Glenn, who was born in 1800, was an early settler near Mattoon, Illinois, and died there in 1880.

J. R. Glenn, father of the Sedan business man, was born near Mattoon, Illinois, in 1844, was reared and married there, took up the vocation of farmer, and in 1886 removed to Kansas, settling on a farm near Ottawa in Franklin County. That has ever since been his home, though in 1916 he retired, at least temporarily, and has spent his time in Los Angeles, California. J. R. Glenn has always supported the republican party and its candidates, and is an active member of the Methodist Episcopal Church. He is an honored old soldier, having gone out with an Illinois regiment of infantry and seeing much hard service before the close of hostilities. His wife was Catherine Williams. She was born near Mattoon, Illinois, in 1844 and died at Pomona, Kansas, in July, 1893. They became the parents of a large family of children: Joseph, who is a farmer at Fordyce near St. Louis, Missouri; Ella, wife of Harry Huskey, now lives in Los Angeles, California; Elmer E.; Annie, who died in San Bernardino, California, in 1908, was the wife of Charles Johnson, who still resides at that place in California, and is a railroad man; Benjamin is a baker at San Francisco; Madie is the wife of Charles Hughes, a farmer at Pomona, Kansas; William died at the age of twenty-three years.

Elmer E. Glenn received some of his education in his native state and finished it in the public schools near Pomona in Franklin County. Until twenty years of age he lived on his father's farm, and has a practical knowledge of agriculture in all its departments. In the Santa Fe Railway shops at Ottawa he learned the blacksmith's trade, and remained a blacksmith in the employ of that company for nine years. In 1901 he went to Independence, Kansas, and took up the work of his trade with special application to its uses in the oil districts. For the first year he was employed by Mr. Short in the Independence Oil Tool Shops. Coming to Sedan in 1903 Mr. Glenn established the Sedan Machine Shops, at first in company with others, but in 1905 he became sole owner and has since continued this successful business under his immediate management and control. His shop is situated on Main Street, and he has all the equipment and facilities for repairs for the tools used in the oil industry. Mr. Glenn is a republican, is affiliated with Vesper Lodge No. 136, Ancient Free and Accepted Masons, at Sedan; with Sedan Lodge No. 131, Ancient Order of United Workmen, and is a citizen whose support can always be counted upon for any movement affecting the general welfare of his community.

On October 25, 1893, at Pomona, Kansas, he married Miss Laura Wickham, daughter of Morgan and Ellen (Parkison) Wickham. Her father, who was a farmer, is now deceased, and her mother still lives in Pomona. Mr. and Mrs. Glenn are the parents of four children. Audrey, still at home, is a graduate of the Sedan High School and holds a state certificate and is now teaching at St. Charles, Kansas. Ervin is a junior in the high school and Gertrude and Ralph are both in the grade schools.

HON. JOSEPH L. MORRISON. Few men are more prominent or more widely known in the northern part of Neosho County than is Hon. Joseph L. Morrison, mayor of the City of Chanute, who has been an important factor in business affairs and whose success in his undertaking has been so marked that his methods are of interest to the commercial world. He is energetic, prompt and notably reliable, and tireless energy, keen perception, honesty of purpose, and a genius for devising and executing the right thing at the right time are his chief characteristics. As the chief executive of Chanute he is giving the people a clean, progressive and business-like administration.

Mr. Morrison was born on a farm in Stark County, Illinois, July 11, 1867, and is a son of Jacob and Phoebe (Johnson) Morrison. The family originated in Scotland, and it is thought that Mr. Morrison's grandfather, Andrew Morrison, born in 1789, who died in Greene County, Ohio, in 1869, was the first American settler. He was a pioneer into Ohio and passed his long and useful life there engaged in agricultural pursuits. Jacob Morrison, the father of Joseph L., was born on the homestead place in Greene County, Ohio, February 8, 1833, received an ordinary public school education, and as a youth learned the trade of stone mason, which he followed in connection with farming all his life. He was still a young man when he went to Stark County, Illinois, and was there married and for a time carried on operations on a farm, but did not meet with a satisfying measure of success, and accordingly sought a new field of endeavor. Finally deciding on Johnson County, Missouri, as a locality in which to attain prosperity, he settled on a farm there in 1879, but soon moved to Henry County, in the same state, and there made his home for more than thirty years, his death occurring January 8, 1913, when he had nearly reached the age of eighty years. Mr. Morrison was a republican in his political views, but not an office seeker, although he took a lively interest in all that pertained to civic affairs and to the welfare of the locality and its people. His religious connection was with the Methodist Episcopal Church. Mr. Morrison married Miss Phoebe Johnson, who was born March 9, 1839, in Tennessee, a lovable Christian woman who proved a faithful helpmate and whose death occurred in Henry County, Missouri, in 1908. They became the parents of the following children: William, who died at the age of eleven years; Mary, who is the wife of J. E. Ellis, a farmer of North Dakota; Andrew, who died in 1912, in Montana, where he had been engaged in agricultural pursuits; James, of the Gallatin Valley of Montana, a successful farmer and stockman; Joseph L., of this notice; George, who is engaged in farming in Johnson County, Missouri; David, also a tiller of the soil of that county; Albert, who died at the age of one year; John D., who is engaged in farming in Johnson County, Missouri; Ollie, who likewise farms there; and Clarence, who resides on the home farm in Henry County, Missouri.

Joseph L. Morrison was educated in the district schools of Henry County, Missouri, and the high school at Nevada, that state, and grew to manhood in the clean atmosphere of the farm, residing on the home place until he was seventeen years of age. At that time he left the parental roof and embarked upon a career of his own, being engaged in farming in Missouri until his marriage. In 1892 Mr. Morrison came to Wilson County, Kansas, and for six years was engaged in farming, in addition to which for

two years of this time he was connected with the creamery business, and in 1898, in the latter connection, came to Chanute. After three years spent in the same line, Mr. Morrison turned his attention to the livery business, and for four years conducted a boarding and sales stable, and in March, 1906, disposed of his interest therein and became the proprietor of his present store, where he handles dry goods and ladies' ready-to-wear garments. Mr. Morrison is one of the captains of success who have piloted their own ship into the harbor of success. Each step in his career has been a forward one, and in each community in which he has resided he has established a reputation for straightforward and honorable dealing and for success gained with honor and without animosity. In addition to his dry goods business, which is located at No. 30 West Main Street, Mr. Morrison has other interests, being a member of the directing board of the Peoples Home State Bank of Chanute, and president of the firm of Morrison, Martin & Baker Company, of Olathe, Kansas, a dry goods concern. Politically a republican, while in Wilson County Mr. Morrison served for a time as road supervisor. In 1916, the people of Chanute, recognizing the need of a sound business administration, and having had plentiful evidence as to Mr. Morrison's fitness for public office of this character, chose him as the city's executive head for three years, his term commencing in April. During the time that he has been in office he has fully lived up to his pre-election promises and has vindicated the faith reposed in him by the people. Fraternally, Mayor Morrison is identified with Cedar Lodge No. 103, Ancient Free and Accepted Masons of Chanute; Chanute Chapter No. 21, Royal Arch Masons; and Chanute Commandery No. 44, Knight Templars. He is a member of the Methodist Episcopal Church, an active worker therein, and for some time a trustee.

On September 6, 1891, at Vilas, Kansas, Mayor Morrison was united in marriage with Miss Mitta J. Alexander, daughter of B. F. and Almira (Shudder) Alexander, farming people of Wilson County, Kansas, both of whom are now deceased. Mr. and Mrs. Morrison have no children. Like her husband, Mrs. Morrison takes an active and helpful part in church work and her charities are many among the poor and unfortunate.

WILLIAM IRVIN HAMMEL is a young business man at Moran, and since establishing himself in that town has built up a very prosperous enterprise as a grain dealer and owns a half interest in the only elevator in that locality. He has also distinguished himself by a very progressive administration of the local city affairs in the office of mayor.

Mr. Hammel was born in Sangamon County, Illinois, July 30, 1876, but has spent his life since early boyhood in Kansas. His people, the Hammels, came out of Germany and were Pennsylvania settlers in the colonial times. His grandfather, Samuel Hammel, was born in Ohio, moved from there to Sangamon County, Illinois, and died on his farm in that county in 1861.

C. T. Hammel, father of William I., was born in Hancock County near Findlay, Ohio, in 1853. As a child he went to Sangamon County, Illinois, grew up and married there, became a farmer, and in 1884 came to Kansas, locating on a farm seven miles north of Bronson. Subsequently he moved to the Village of Bronson, where for a number of years he was engaged in the grain and livestock business, but is now living practically retired. As a republican he has served as township trustee several terms, and at one time was a candidate for the Legislature. He is a member of the Methodist Church and of the Independent Order of Odd Fellows. C. T. Hammel married Sarah Moomey, who was born in Sangamon County, Illinois, in 1856. They had two children, William I. and Ella. The latter is the wife of J. R. Hall, a hardware merchant at Century, Oklahoma.

William I. Hammel as a boy knew the rural district of Bourbon County, Kansas, attended the country schools there, and in 1894 graduated from high school. He also attended the old Fort Scott Normal School, but gave up his studies there in 1897 and returned to his father's farm. He spent ten years as a farmer and at the same time was associated with his father in the stock business.

When Mr. Hammel came to Moran in 1907 he bought the elevator, the only institution of its kind in the town. It is conveniently located close to the tracks of the Missouri Pacific and the Missouri, Kansas & Texas railways. Mr. Hammel has been a very successful dealer in grain and hay, also handles general feed supplies, and by strict and straightforward business methods has made Moran a popular trading point and market town for a large section of the surrounding agricultural community. He also has an interest in an elevator at Bayard, Kansas. Among other property he has his comfortable residence on Pine Street.

Ever since locating in Moran he has shown a consistent attitude of progressiveness in the matter of public improvements, and he was elected mayor largely by those citizens who believe in a progressive conduct of local affairs. He was first elected in 1910 for a term of two years, and was re-elected in 1912 and 1914. He entered the office April 1, 1911, and his present term expires April 1, 1917. Among other measures which have had his earnest support and leadership was the promotion of the bond issue for the establishment of a municipal water and electric light plant. He has also used the resources of the village for the improvement of streets and sidewalks, and in every way has co-operated with local citizenship in making a better town both commercially and morally.

Mr. Hammel is a republican and has served as precinct committeeman of his party. He belongs to the Kansas Grain Dealers Association and also the National Organization of Grain Dealers, and is member of the Moran Commercial Club. Fraternally he is affiliated with Marmaton Lodge No. 245, Ancient Free and Accepted Masons, of which he was master in 1916 and re-elected for 1917. He has taken eighteen degrees of the Scottish Rite in Fort Scott Consistory No. 4. He also belongs to Moran Lodge No. 459, Independent Order of Odd Fellows, and has held the chair of noble grand several terms.

Mr. Hammel was married in the fall of 1897 at Bronson, Kansas, to Miss Dema Hickson, daughter of James and Kate (Clark) Hickson. Her mother now resides at Moran, and her father, also a farmer and came to Kansas from Indiana in 1882, is now deceased. Mr. and Mrs. Hammel have a family of four children: Mildred, born November 13, 1900, is in the second year of the Moran High School; Marian, born May 21, 1902, is in the first year of the local high school; Catherine was born March 7, 1905; and Clark on February 3, 1909.

PAUL STAFFORD MITCHELL, M. D. Incomplete indeed would be any history of Kansas which did not include distinctive mention of that large body of men who labor in the broad field of medical service. Some have chosen a particular path and some have chosen to work under a particular combination of methods, but all can be justly credited with scientific knowledge and a due regard for the preservation of the public health. To the profession of medicine, Dr. Paul Stafford Mitchell devoted the early years of his manhood, and today, after seventeen years of successful practice, stands as a representative of all that is best and highest in his line of human endeavor, and is justly accounted one of the leading physicians and surgeons of Iola.

Doctor Mitchell was born at Cherry Grove, Rockingham County, Virginia, November 11, 1875, and is a son of Dr. Jacob A. and Emily (Furr) Mitchell. His father, born in 1807, at Londonderry, Ireland, ran away from home while still a lad and emigrated to the United States, and here completed a medical education and began the practice of his calling near Washington, Rappahannock County, Virginia. There he was married and subsequently went to Rockingham County, Virginia. He was successful as a practitioner and was in fairly good circumstances when the Civil war came on, but was an ardent Confederate sympathizer, put all his money into movements for the support of the South, and with the fall of the Lost Cause saw his fortune swept away. Later he practiced in West Virginia and Ohio, but finally returned to Rockingham County, Virginia, and died at Cherry Grove, in 1876. Doctor Mitchell was well and favorably known in his profession, and was an adherent of its highest ethics. While the misfortunes of war caused him to lose his material wealth he held to the last the respect and esteem of his fellow practitioners and of the community at large, and the fact that he did not allow his ill luck to totally discourage him is shown in the fact that he was able to accumulate a property after the war, and left his children 147 acres of land in Rockingham County. He was a democrat all his life and was a stanch adherent of the Baptist Church. Doctor Mitchell had six children by his first wife, Mary, as follows: Ephraim S.; Joseph A.; John A.; Jacob B., who practiced medicine for many years at Manhattan, Kansas, became very wealthy, was president of the Union National Bank of that city, and died at Manhattan in 1903; Benjamin F., who came as a young man to Kansas and subsequently removed to Oklahoma, where he was a minister of the Christian Church; and a son Philip who died in Ohio. All these children are now deceased. Doctor Mitchell took as his second wife Miss Emily Furr, who was born in 1843, in Rockingham County, Virginia, and died in 1910, at Lintner, Illinois, and they had two children: Jennie, who is the wife of H. H. Middleton, a farmer of Renfro, Oklahoma; and Paul Stafford. After the death of her first husband, Mrs. Mitchell married David Traxler, who died in 1909, at Mesa, Arizona, a well-to-do retired farmer. They had two children: Charles A., who is engaged in farming at Lintner, Illinois; and Benjamin J., who was a mail carrier and died at Mesa, Arizona, in 1908.

Paul Stafford Mitchell received his early education in the public school at Hammond, Illinois, following which he spent two years at the Central Normal University, at Danville, Indiana. Next he was engaged in teaching at the rural school at Burrowsville, Illinois, for two years, and in the meantime applied his spare hours to study, this preparing for his entrance at Hering Medical College, where he matriculated in 1895. In 1899 he was graduated from that institu-

tion with the degree of Doctor of Medicine, and in the following year he was granted the same degree by the medical department of the University of Illinois. During this time, Doctor Mitchell had spent his summer vacations doing special work at Northwestern University, where he perfected himself in pathology and bacteriology, and one summer was at the University of Chicago. He began the practice of his calling at Hammond, Illinois, but after one year and four months, seeking a broader field for the display of his abilities, came to Iola, Kansas, where he arrived in the winter of 1901. Here he has been engaged in a general practice of medicine and surgery ever since. Doctor Mitchell took a post-graduate course at the New York Post-Graduate School, in 1903, specializing in surgery. In the summer of 1914 he went to Europe, and during this trip visited hospitals at Paris, France; Bern, Switzerland; Zurich, Switzerland; Munich, Germany; Vienna, Austria; Berlin, Germany; Leipzig, Germany; Heidelberg, Germany; London, England; and Edinburgh, Scotland. He remained in Europe four months after the great war started, and had considerable difficulty in returning to the United States.

Doctor Mitchell's offices are in the Garlinghouse Building. Throughout his career of professional life his duties have been performed with the greatest care and scientific accuracy. In addition to his professional practice in this direction, he is general superintendent and owner of the Physicians and Surgeons Hospital, at 202 East Street, which has accommodations for ten patients, and where Doctor Mitchell performs his own operations. He is never too busy to be courteous and cordial, yet he has never allowed anything to interfere with the careful and honorable conduct of his profession. In its various phases his life is well balanced and makes him highly esteemed in all those circles where true worth is received as the passport into good society. Doctor Mitchell is a republican. He was a member of the school board, and served as president thereof during one year of the eight years in which he was connected with that body. Fraternally, he is a thirty-second degree, Scottish Rite Mason, belonging to Iola Lodge, No. 38, Ancient Free and Accepted Masons; Valley Chapter, No. 8, Royal Arch Masons; Esdraelon Commandery, No. 49, Knights Templar; Fort Scott Consistory, Select Royal Masons; and Mirza Temple, Ancient and Arabic Order Nobles of the Mystic Shrine of Pittsburg. He also belongs to Iola Lodge, No. 569, Benevolent and Protective Order of Elks, and is an ex-member of the Independent Order of Odd Fellows and the Knights of Pythias. Professionally, he is identified with the Allen County Medical Society, the Kansas State Medical Society, of which he has been vice president, the American Medical Association; and the Southeast Kansas Medical Society, of which he was president in 1915.

Doctor Mitchell was married December 25, 1902, at Hammond, Illinois, to Miss Mary G. Jaques, daughter of O. B. and Elizabeth (Farrar) Jaques, residents of Mattoon, Illinois. Doctor and Mrs. Mitchell have no children.

WILLIAM LEE VAUGHAN for a number of years has been one of the foremost business men and merchants of Kansas City, Kansas. Nearly all the residents of that city know his place of business at Eighteenth and Central Avenue, and particularly in that district of Kansas City his influence is recognized as having been one of the chief factors in many lines of development and improvement which have been brought about during the last decade or so.

Mr. Vaughan has an interesting family history. He was born at Sedalia, Missouri, June 29, 1873, but has lived in Kansas for thirty years. He was the only son in seven children born to Richard Clarke and Emma (Sterrett) Vaughan. His father was born in Virginia and his mother in Missouri. Emma Sterrett's father, who was of Pennsylvania-Dutch stock, came overland to Southern Missouri in 1825, locating on a farm of 320 acres in Benton County. He was a man of prominence in that section of Missouri, and added greatly to his holdings until he had a splendid estate. He lived and died there. He was a slave owner and two of his sons fought on the Confederate side during the Civil war. One of these, George, was killed at the battle of Springfield. Augustus, who died at Nevada, Missouri, in 1915, went all through the war and was with Lee at the Appomattox surrender. During the gold rush to California in the early '50s Mr. Sterrett and one of his sons went to the coast, and the son lost his life there, the father subsequently returning to Southern Missouri.

The paternal grandfather of William Lee Vaughan was Dr. William Loving Vaughan. With his family he made the long journey overland from Virginia to Osceola, St. Clair County, Missouri. He was a skillful physician, built up a large practice and became a wealthy man for those days. In the cattle business he was associated with the father of William P. Johnson, now well known through his official connection with the Southwestern National Bank of Kansas City, Missouri. At one time Doctor Vaughan owned the largest part of St. Clair County, and conducted it as a vast cattle ranch. His prosperity continued practically uninterrupted until the time of the war, when, like so many others, his property was dissipated and the family fortunes reduced to a low ebb. During the war fully 1,000 head of cattle were driven off the Vaughan ranch and practically nothing was left but the land. Doctor Vaughan was not only a remarkable business man, but also possessed that integrity which caused people of all classes to repose utmost confidence in him, and it is said that when the war broke out many of the soldiers in going to the front left the entire management of their affairs in his hands. In those troublous times it is not strange that he had some personal enemies in spite of the essential kindliness and generosity of his character. In 1864, while he was riding his horse along the streets of Osceola he was shot down by a personal enemy, and his death was felt as a personal loss and calamity to hundreds of people outside of his own family. He was a devout Presbyterian.

Richard Clarke Vaughan, father of the Kansas City business man, spent his early boyhood days in Missouri, gained an education in the district schools, lived on the farm and later learned the trade of tinsmith. Prior to the war he was in the hardware business and also carried a stock of tinware and other goods in wagons, peddling them over the country districts. He had a genius for business affairs, and like his father enjoyed the complete confidence of all the people with whom he had dealings. He also was exposed to the dangers and hardships of warfare. In the old Town of Osceola his store was burned by a gang of bushwackers, and a little later the Bushwhackers perpetrated another raid upon the town. At the time of the second raid Augustus Sterrett, who had served in the Confederate army, was lying ill at home, but the Federal soldiers expressed a determination to kill him and were only dissuaded from the purpose by his mother, who told him that he was near death.

Following the horrors of war, Richard C. Vaughan resumed the tinning business and followed it largely until his death in 1886. The family fortunes were then in a precarious condition. The mother for several years had supported her family by keeping boarders and by doing sewing, and in 1886 she came with them to Armourdale, now a portion of Kansas City, Kansas. This removal was made in order to give the children better opportunities, and it was largely due to the self-sacrificing love and devotion of the mother that the children had the advantages of good schools. In Armourdale she continued keeping boarders until her children were in a position to do for themselves.

William Lee Vaughan was about thirteen or fourteen years of age when his mother removed to what is now Kansas City, Kansas. Up to that time he had attended the common schools of Missouri, and his first ambition for achievement in life was in the capacity of an undertaker. He soon gave up that design. For one year he worked in the office of Kelley Brothers, coopers, and then found work in the postoffice and filled various grades of responsibility in the Kansas City postoffice for sixteen years. While at work there he turned over in his mind different plans and ambitions for an independent business career, and finally determined to become a druggist. He studied pharmacy at night, also gained all the practical experience he could, and in 1899 he opened his first stock of drugs, on a moderate scale, at Armourdale. He soon had a large business, and was prosperous until his store was practically ruined by the disastrous flood of 1903. It is indicative of his enterprise that he was the first merchant to reopen business after the flood.

He soon determined upon a new location, one on higher ground, and in 1905 he removed his store to the corner of Eighteenth and Central Avenue, where he is now located. He was a pioneer merchant in this district, and the store building which he erected and still occupies was one of the most important business improvements placed in that section. Since then Mr. Vaughan has worked, tirelessly in developing this section of the city. Largely due to his influence Eighteenth Street has been graded and the curves and crooks of the old county road has been straightened out so that Eighteenth Street is now one of the finest avenues in the city.

For one year he was president and was one of the organizers of the Grand View Improvement Company, which is credited with having done more for that section of Kansas City than any other one thing. He was also an effective worker in presenting the petition for the street railway on Eighteenth Street, and was the originator of this plan and of many other plans that have since been carried out and have brought untold benefit to that district. In June, 1911, Mr. Vaughan became one of the organizers of the Security State Bank, and has since served as vice president. He is a member of the Mercantile Club, and has been foremost in every movement in recent years for the improvement and raising of the standards of the public schools of the city. While he is a democrat, he has never been an office seeker.

On June 29, 1898, Mr. Vaughan was married to Miss Ellen N. Buchhalter, of Reading, Pennsylvania, but prior to her marriage she had moved to Kansas.

Mr. and Mrs. Vaughan have four children: Sarah Lee, Charles Clarke, Joseph Harry, William Lee, Jr., all of whom are still at home. Mr. Vaughan is a member of the Ancient Order of United Workmen, the Kansas Fraternal Citizens and belongs to all the Scottish Rite bodies of Masonry and the Mystic Shrine. He and his wife are active in the Presbyterian Church. Besides his store he owns several pieces of valuable real estate in that immediate section.

JAMES HENRY POWELL. Chautauqua County has never had a more popular official than James H. Powell, who is now concluding his second term as sheriff. He has been a farmer, public official and prominent citizen of this section of Kansas for a quarter of a century. A noteworthy fact is that when he was re-elected in the fall of 1914 he was given the largest majority ever given a candidate for any office in Chautauqua County and carried every voting precinct.

One of the valleys of the State of Tennessee has for many years been known as Powell's Valley. The Powell family were the earliest and most influential settlers there, hence the name. It was in that locality that Stephen Powell, father of James H., was born. He was in that section of Tennessee which furnished many soldiers to the Union army during the Civil war. He enlisted himself in the Union army, served until he was taken prisoner, and he endured captivity in the notorious Andersonville prison. He was a farmer by occupation, and after or during the war he had his family removed to Clay County, Kentucky, in order to escape the hostility of the Southern sympathizers in Tennessee. Stephen Powell died in Clay County, Kentucky, in 1867. He married Lavina Stanaford, who was born in Virginia in 1825 and was killed in a railway accident in the winter of 1885.

James Henry Powell was born in Clay County, Kentucky, March 8, 1867, the same year that his father died. He was the youngest of seven children. The other children were: John, a farmer at Elgin, Kansas; William, who was a farmer and died in Clay County, Kentucky, at the age of thirty-five; Nancy, who was killed in an accident in October, 1916, was the wife of George Anderson, a farmer in Chautauqua County, Kansas; Mary, deceased, who was the wife of William Casteel, a farmer in Clay County, Kentucky; Sarah, wife of Henry Cornett, a farmer at Elgin, Kansas; Joseph, a farmer in Chautauqua County.

Mr. Powell due to the early death of his father had to become self supporting and at the age of thirteen left home and found employment with a farmer in Orange County, Indiana. He remained with that employer and had his home there for five years. In the meantime he attended school during the winter terms, and his education was completed at the age of eighteen. He had also attended school in Kentucky.

In 1885 he returned to Clay County, Kentucky, where he married in the following year, and was engaged in farming some Kentucky land until the spring of 1892. That was the date of his coming to Chautauqua County, Kansas. For three years Mr. Powell drove a stage between Elgin, Kansas, and Pawhuska, Oklahoma, and that was an occupation that furnished many risks and incidents. On giving up that work he engaged in the drug business at Elgin from 1895 to 1908, then for two years was in the grocery and meat business, and he sold out his stock of merchandise when elected sheriff in the fall of 1912. His present term expires January 1, 1917. For eighteen years prior to his election as sheriff he was deputy sheriff of Chautauqua County, and also served as constable at Elgin a number of years.

Mr. Powell is a republican, is active in the Christian Church and is affiliated with Olive Lodge No. 350, Ancient Free and Accepted Masons at Elgin, Wichita Consistory No. 2 of the Scottish Rite, Elgin Lodge No. 414 of the Independent Order of Odd Fellows and Elgin Lodge of the Ancient Order of United Workmen.

Mr. Powell was married in Clay County, Kentucky, in 1886, to Miss Margaret Mayfield. Her mother, Mrs. Nancy Mayfield, is still living in Clay County. To their union have been born three children: W. D. Powell, who is a stockman and farmer at Elgin; Oscar, now under sheriff at Sedan; and Samuel, a farmer at Elgin.

HARRY A. MENDENHALL. Though his home is in the largest city of Kansas, Harry A. Mendenhall's business and civic activities have been such as to constitute him one of the best known men of Kansas City, Kansas. For nearly thirty years he has given his best time and energy to the building up of an organization and equipment for the efficient handling of local traffic and freight in the transfer line, he is a former sheriff of Wyandotte County, and is also prominent as a banker.

He was born January 11, 1865, on a farm at the edge of the City of Richmond, Indiana. That section of Indiana was the principal center for the pioneer settlement of a large number of Quaker families in the early days, and the Mendenhalls were also of that religious sect. Mr. Mendenhall is one of four children born to Caleb S. and Rebecca (People's) Mendenhall. Both were natives of Indiana. Caleb S. Mendenhall followed the nursery business for a number of years at Richmond. He served in the Civil war, first as sergeant in Company I of the Eighty-fourth Indiana Volunteer Infantry, and with that command participated in a number of battles until he was wounded when a train was wrecked. After that he was assigned as hospital steward. Following the war he returned home, continued business in eastern Indiana, but finally invested in some lands in Kansas and in order to look after this investment and also acquire better opportunities for himself and his family he came to Topeka in 1869. He was at that time thirty-eight years of age, having been born in 1831. At Topeka he was connected with the engineering corps of the Santa Fe Railway and assisted in laying out various towns along the Arkansas River, including Great Bend. He worked with that company about two years. In 1871 he bought an old time Burr grist mill at Osage City. Osage City then had only twenty houses on its site. As a miller Caleb Mendenhall frequently traded a fifty pound sack of flour for a buffalo ham. He operated a mill for three years, then sold out and bought 320 acres near Osage City, where he engaged as a stock raiser and feeder. For a few years he handled native cattle, and finally brought western cattle to his feeding grounds. He lived there during the grasshopper scourge and the droughts of several years, and in spite of several setbacks he prospered in the main. In 1886 he followed his sons to Kansas City, Kansas, sold his farm, and engaged in the real estate business in association with Mr. Chapman. He continued handling real estate until his death in 1908. His wife died in 1905. Their children were: Orra, now Mrs. Frank Jones of New York; Florence, Mrs. McCloon of Kansas City, Kansas; Lincoln J., who

was for many years actively associated as a business partner with his brother Harry A., and who died in 1907; and Harry A.

Caleb Mendenhall was a prominent man in local affairs in Osage County. He was an active republican, served as a member of the Osage City Council, on the board of education, took a prominent part in the county seat fight there, and he exerted every influence in behalf of better schools and more churches. He was long identified with the Grand Army of the Republic and for one term served as commander of the Post at Kansas City, Kansas. While he adhered throughout his life to the religion in which he was trained as a boy, his wife was active in the Methodist Church.

The public schools of Osage City gave Harry A. Mendenhall his first training and later for one year he attended the Emporia Normal School. He then returned home to assist his father on the farm, and remained there until 1885. In that year he removed to Kansas City, Kansas, and with his brother Lincoln started a lunch counter. He had brought with him from Osage City only $25, and the brothers continued in the business about two years and then in 1888 entered the transfer business, to which Mr. Harry Mendenhall has devoted his best energies ever since. However, from 1901 to 1905, when he filled the office of sheriff of Wyandotte County, he turned over the active management of the transfer business to his brother.

On September 16, 1892, Mr. Mendenhall married Miss Anna Fields of Kansas City, Kansas. Mrs. Mendenhall was born in Missouri. Six children have been born to their marriage: Hal, who is associated in business with his father; Margaret, now Mrs. Eugene Zellars, of Kansas City, Kansas; and Claude, Florence, Samuel and Harriet, all at home. Mrs. Mendenhall takes a very active part in the Episcopal Church.

Always a loyal republican, Mr. Mendenhall has not been active in politics since he retired from the office of sheriff. Prior to that he had served as a member of the city council from 1896 to 1900. In 1905 he became one of the reorganizers of the Home State Bank, and served as its president for nine years. In 1913 he sold his interest in that institution and then bought the Minnesota Avenue State Bank, of which he is now president. Anything that means a bigger and better city has the loyal co-operation of Mr. Mendenhall. He worked consistently in behalf of schools and churches, is a member and trustee of the Mercantile Club and Rotary Club, and is prominent in various fraternities. He belongs to the Scottish Rite bodies of Masonry, also to the Mystic Shrine, was a member of the board for six years and president of the building board of the Masonic Temple. He also belongs to the Ancient Order of United Workmen, the Modern Woodmen of America and the Sons of Veterans.

OSCAR MAXEL YOUNT. The person of this sketch, Oscar Maxel Yount, is perhaps the most wonderful example, everything being taken into consideration, of what a determined will-power can accomplish that the Sunflower State has ever produced. He has been a lawyer and engaged in the active practice of his profession since June 22, 1905. He is a native son of Kansas, and the work he has done in his profession and in civic affairs has brought him a place of special esteem throughout the state and especially in his home community of Galena.

He was not born with a "silver spoon in his mouth," but was handicapped from birth with an extreme case of near-sightedness of vision which is equally as bad, and probably worse, as that of the immortal Blackstone. Mr. Yount never had but little more than 3 per cent of far-sighted vision according to optometrical measurement, his case being one that puzzles the best eye-specialists in this country. He was born on a farm in Cowley County, Kansas, July 28, 1883, and represents one of the early pioneer families of that section. He was started to school at the age of six years under the most trying circumstances, the teacher neglecting to teach him because he was unable to discern the words on the blackboard in the front of the schoolroom and advising his parents to keep him at home until he was twelve or fourteen years old but he was bent on going to school and his parents did not heed the bad advice but continued to send him. To make the situation still worse, he wore glasses and many of the scholars would call him "Grandpa," and he was very sensitive and as a result of this occurrance he had numerous fights which invariably resulted in broken glasses, the sum total being $60 spent by his father during his first term at school for glasses. He was untiring, persevering, industrious, ambitious and extremely methodical from his earliest childhood, and when a small schoolboy it was his determination to make the best of his talents and the most of his resources. After graduating from the high school at Arkansas City, Kansas, in 1901, he spent the summer vacation on the Walnut River fishing and earned enough money from the sale of the fish to purchase Blackstone's Commentaries; subsequently he took up the study of law, first at home, read industriously every authority he could procure for a short time and then entered the office of Hon. John H. Dunn; but the latter soon moved to California, whereupon Mr. Yount entered the office of Norman Barker, where he remained until his admission to the bar June 22, 1905. After his admission to the Kansas Supreme Court he spent a year in the further study of law in Chicago. Mr. Yount is a "self-made man," having educated himself in the law from his own resources. Although his parents were amply able to send him through any law school in America they relied on the erroneous advice of an eminent eye specialist who was of the opinion that the future lawyer was making a mistake when he attempted to study law, and for that reason he did not receive any financial help from them.

But in the course of a few years Oscar Mazel Yount proved the fallacy of the doctor and today feels the stronger for so doing. He has a photographic memory and but few lawyers read more than Mr. Yount. Besides being a hard and constant student of the law he is also a close student of literature and history. He has no such word as "fail" in his vocabulary and his motto is "Go On."

He did his first practice in Arkansas City, Kansas, and while there he was the junior member of the law firm of Long, Beekman & Yount. In April, 1906, he located at Florence, Kansas, where he practiced a few months, locating at Cimarron, Kansas, in August of the same year, where he spent six months. He moved to West Mineral, Kansas, and opened a law office November 17, 1908, where he practiced until June 1, 1909, following which he located at Sharon Springs, Kansas, at which place he practiced law until September 26, 1910, on which date he located permanently in Galena, Cherokee County, Kansas. Since that he has been favored with a growing civil and criminal practice. In 1914 he served as city attorney and made the unusual record of being present at every council meeting

that year. He is now vice president of the Board of Education of Galena. Mrs. Yount has taught the beginners' class in the Methodist Sunday School for the last five years. Nobody in Galena is more interested in general educational matters than the subject of this sketch and his estimable wife are. Mr. Yount owns a comfortable home at No. 809 Joplin Street in Galena. He is a republican, a member of the Methodist Episcopal Church, belongs to the subordinate and Encampment branches of Odd Fellowship, and is a past grand of the Odd Fellows Lodge.

His paternal ancestors, the Younts, came from Germany to South Carolina in colonial days in order to escape the military laws of the Fatherland. Mr. Yount's grandfather, Peter Francis Yount, was born in Washington County, Indiana, in 1830. He served through the Civil war with an Indiana regiment, enlisting from Washington County in 1862. After the war he was a blacksmith and subsequently a farmer, and in 1876 came out to Cowley County, Kansas, and farmed there until he retired to Arkansas City in 1888. He died at Arkansas City March 10, 1889.

John Wesley Yount, father of the Galena lawyer, was born in Washington County, Indiana, September 17, 1855, and was about twenty-one years of age when the family came out to Kansas and settled on the frontier in Cowley County. He worked as a farmer in that section until 1887, and on March 23d of that year took employment with the Santa Fe Railroad and moved to Arkansas City. He has been in the employ of the Santa Fe ever since (now more than thirty years), and is now one of the oldest men in continuous service. He is a democrat in politics, a member of the Christian Church and belongs to the Independent Order of Odd Fellows. John W. Yount married Lovisa Froney Midkiff, who was born in Shelby County, Indiana, August 23, 1863. They had four children: Oscar M., who is the oldest and the subject of this sketch; Louise Ethel, who was born September 15, 1887, and died at the age of twenty-three months; Oral Ray, born August 26, 1890, is employed by the Santa Fe Railway and lives at Arkansas City; Anna Marie, born May 7, 1895, and living at Arkansas City.

Attorney Oscar M. Yount was married at Carthage, Missouri, June 1, 1909, to Miss Pearl Reba Berry, a daughter of Harry Herbert and Agnes E. (Howard) Berry. Her father, who was in the furniture business at Joplin, Missouri, died February 8, 1914. Her mother is living at Seventeenth and Byers Avenue in Joplin. Mr. and Mrs. Yount have two children: Helen Edith was born January 20, 1911, and Kent Eldon was born March 20, 1916, both in Galena, Kansas.

BURTON EMORY CLIFFORD. Chances for success are slight with the lawyer of modern times unless he be a man of sound judgment, possessed of a liberal education and a stern training, combined with a keen insight into human nature and motives. The reason for this lies in the spirit of the age with all its complexities, for modern jurisprudence has become more and more complex because of new laws and conditions. Years of experience and a natural inclination for and inherent ability in his profession are superinduced upon a careful training in the case of Burton Emory Clifford, ex-prosecuting attorney of Allen County and now one of the foremost members of the Iola bar. His career has been characterized by many successful results for his clients, and he has brought to his profession an enthusiasm and belief in its importance which have resulted in his being entrusted with some of the most important cases ever brought to trial in Allen County.

Mr. Clifford was born at Aledo, the county seat of Mercer County, Illinois, May 7, 1872, and is a son of Edward and Gwendoline (Jones) Clifford. His father was born in 1825, in County Cavan, Ireland, and was twenty years of age when he emigrated to the United States, settling first in Harrison County, Ohio, where he was engaged in farming. He spent a number of years there and then removed to Mercer County, Illinois, where in the vicinity of Aledo he passed the remainder of his life, continuing in agricultural pursuits, and died in 1885. He was one of the substantial citizens of his community, a man universally esteemed and respected, and the incumbent of a number of township offices, in which he served efficiently and conscientiously. His politics made him a democrat. Mr. Clifford married Miss Gwendoline Jones, who was born in 1837, in Wales. She was three years of age when brought to the United States by her parents, who became pioneer settlers and agriculturists of Mercer County, Illinois, where both rounded out their lives, and where Mrs. Clifford died August 27, 1916, when nearly eighty years of age. Mr. and Mrs. Clifford were the parents of the following children: John, who passed his life as a farmer in Mercer County, Illinois, and died at Aledo, in 1884; Carl I., who also followed farming and passed away at Aledo; Harry E., who died in infancy at Aledo; Burton E., of this review; Minnie, who is the wife of George P. Graham, the proprietor of a news depot at the Aledo Postoffice; and Roy H., who is engaged in farming near the old homestead.

Burton E. Clifford received his primary and high school training at Aledo, being graduated from the latter with the class of 1890, and then enrolled as a student at the Burlington Institute, Burlington, Iowa, being graduated from that institution in 1892. Following this he spent one year in attendance at the University of Chicago, and in 1894 matriculated at the Kent Law School, Chicago, from which he was graduated with his degree in 1898. In that same year he was admitted to the bar and took up his residence at Iola, where he has since continued in a general practice in civil and criminal law. In 1903 he was elected prosecuting attorney of Allen County, Kansas, a capacity in which he served for two terms, or four years, during which time he displayed fearless courage and established an enviable record. He is equally at home in the various branches of his calling and is accounted an astute, learned and thorough lawyer, a good pleader, a careful counsel and a close student of the intricacies of his difficult calling. He holds membership in the Allen County Bar Association, the Kansas Bar Association and the American Bar Association and has the esteem and friendship of his professional colleagues. Mr. Clifford is a republican. He maintains offices in the McCall Building, on East Madison Street, while his home, which he owns, is at 524 South Buckeye Street. Mr. Clifford is interested in land in Colorado, where he owns a valuable tract of 160 acres, which is under development. Fraternally, Mr. Clifford is affiliated with Iola Lodge No. 38, Ancient Free and Accepted Masons; Valley Chapter, No. 8, Royal Arch Masons, of Iola; Esdraelon Commandery, No. 49, Knights Templar, of Iola; and Mirza Temple, Ancient and Arabic Order Nobles of the Mystic Shrine of Pittsburg, Kansas; Iola Lodge, No. 21, Independent Order of Odd Fellows; and Iola Camp, No. 101, Woodmen of the World.

Mr. Clifford was married at Rock Island, Illinois,

in 1899, to Miss Lucille Miller, daughter of the late G. D. and Sophia (Everett) Miller, who were farming people of Illinois. Mr. and Mrs. Clifford have no children.

JOHN E. KIBLER. Though he did not have the opportunity to attend school regularly after he was thirteen years of age, John E. Kibler found ways and means to acquire a liberal education, and that education has not only sufficed for his own needs but has always made him one of the leading educators in Southeastern Kansas. Mr. Kibler is now county superintendent of schools of Chautauqua County and has been engaged in school work for a long period of years.

He came to Kansas when a small boy, but was born in Fulton County, Illinois, June 11, 1863. His grandfather, Frederick Kibler, was a German farmer, and spent all his life in the old country. His father, Jacob Kibler, who was born near Stuttgart, Wuertemberg, Germany, in 1830, grew up on his father's farm, and about 1851 emigrated to the United States, locating in Fulton County, Illinois. He farmed there a few years, and in 1867 brought his family to Osage County, Kansas, and was one of the pioneers in that section. The Indians had hardly left Osage County, and he pre-empted a claim near Scranton. About 1874 he moved his family to Chautauqua County, and was successfully engaged in farming there until his death in 1880. He was a member of the Lutheran Church. Jacob Kibler married Mary Ellen French, who was born in Lincolnshire, England, in 1843. Her parents came to the United States about 1858, while James Buchanan was president. She met and married Jacob Kibler in Fulton County, Illinois. She died in Chautauqua County, Kansas, in 1885. Her children were: John E.; Caroline, who died in 1877; Charles, a farmer in Chautauqua County; Mary, who lives at Hydro in Caddo County, Oklahoma, the widow of George Benscoter, who was a farmer; and Fred, who is in the livery business at Hydro, Oklahoma.

The regular schooling which John E. Kibler enjoyed as a boy was in Osage and Chautauqua counties. When he left home at the age of thirteen he began earning his own way as a laborer on farms. He continued in that occupation until the death of his father, and in 1881 at the age of eighteen he taught his first term of school in Chautauqua County. He has been a hard student all his life, has mastered many subjects that ordinarily are only taught in the curriculum of higher schools, and is likewise a man of wide experience in the world and in business affairs. Much of his work as an educator was done in the rural schools and it was his high ideals as a teacher and his manifest ability as an executive that caused him to be elected county superintendent in 1912. He was re-elected in 1914, and his present term expires in May, 1917. Mr. Kibler has under his supervision ninety schools in Chautauqua County, 135 teachers, and an enrollment of 3,700 scholars.

Besides his present office, Mr. Kibler served for four years as county surveyor of Chautauqua County. His knowledge of surveying was largely acquired by practical experience and home study. He has used exceptional judgment in managing his business affairs, and at the present time owns several farms aggregating 1,500 acres in Chautauqua County and has considerable city property.

Politically he is a republican. He is a member of the Methodist Episcopal Church, is past noble grand of Sedan Lodge No. 141, Independent Order of Odd Fellows, and is past consul of Woodman Camp. He has long had membership in the Southeast Kansas and the Kansas State Teachers' Association.

In 1890 in Anderson County, Kansas, Mr. Kibler married Miss Elizabeth Gregory, daughter of Asahel and Mary (Wandel) Gregory, both of whom are now deceased. Her father was a farmer. Mr. and Mrs. Kibler have taken great pains to give their own children the best of advantages at home and in school. These children, ten in number, are as follows: Inez is the wife of Mr. Scott, a farmer at Hydro, Oklahoma; J. Emmett, who has had some experience as a teacher is now employed by the Pipe Line Company at Sedan; Mary married Clarence Witt, who is an employe of the Prairie Pipe Line Company at Sedan; Letha, formerly the wife of Archie Parman, is living in Los Angeles, California; Acil lives at home and is a sophomore in the high school; Ray is also in the sophomore class in the Sedan High School; Bessie is in the eighth grade and Harry in the seventh grade of the public schools; and Jesse and Joseph are the youngest members of this large and interesting household.

WILLIAM MANFRED BARBEE. Among the city offices of Chanute, one that has important bearing upon the welfare of the city and its institutions and the duties of which, in their handling, call for more than ordinary ability, is that of commissioner of public utilities. The present incumbent of this office, William Manfred Barbee, has won the confidence of the public through the able and expeditious manner in which he has handled the business of his department and the energy he has displayed in discharging the responsibilities of public service. He is a native son of Neosho County, and was born October 23, 1864, his parents being Sion and Mary Elizabeth (Easley) Barbee.

The Barbee family is of French extraction and its early members in America Colonial settlers of Virginia. From that state the family branched out to Tennessee, where, in 1805, was born the grandfather of William M. Barbee, Joseph Barbee. He was reared on a farm in Wilson County, and there engaged in farming until he was forty years of age, at which time he went to Jefferson County, Illinois, and continued in agricultural pursuits until the time of his death, in 1881. Sion Barbee was born in Wilson County, Tennessee, in 1837, and was eight years of age when taken to Illinois by his parents. There he received his education and was reared to manhood on the home farm, and subsequently went to Sangamon County, Illinois, where he was married. After several years spent in farming, in 1859, he came to Kansas, settling on Big Creek, in Neosho County. Mr. Barbee homesteaded 160 acres and in spite of the many difficulties and hardships which made up a large part of the Kansas farmer's life in that day, succeeded in the accumulation of a valuable property which allowed him to retire to a comfortable home at Chanute in his declining years. Mr. Barbee met his death in a runaway accident on the streets of Chanute, in 1905, when he was thrown from his buggy. When he first came to Kansas, it was as a poor young man whose principal capital was found in his ambition, determination and energy. He subsequently rose to a prominent place in the community, not alone as a successful farmer, but as a man of influence in public affairs. His first presidential vote after coming to Kansas was cast for Abraham Lincoln, and ever thereafter he was actively interested in the welfare of the republican party. He was active in county conventions, did his share of work during campaigns, and served at one time as township trustee of Big Creek

Township. For many years he was an elder of the Cumberland Presbyterian Church. Mr. Barbee joined the Masons at Humboldt, Kansas, when that place was little more than a fort, later demitted to Cedar Lodge No. 103, Ancient Free and Accepted Masons, and also belonged to Council No. 44, Sons and Daughters of Justice, of Chanute. During the Civil war, he was under Captain Newman, in the State Militia, and was stationed at Fort Humboldt. In every way, he was a helpful and public-spirited citizen, and his death was a loss to the community. Mr. Barbee married Miss Mary Elizabeth Easley, who was born in 1847, in Sangamon County, Illinois, and died at Chanute, Kansas, in 1909, and they became the parents of three children: John Thomas, who was engaged in farming near Chanute and died in 1873; William Manfred; and Daniel Curtis, who was a retired farmer and died at Chanute in 1908.

William Manfred Barbee was educated in the district schools of Neosho County, where he was brought up on his father's farm, and in 1883 and 1884 attended the old Kansas Normal School at Fort Scott. At the age of twenty-one years he began to teach school, but after five terms thus spent in Neosho turned his attention to mercantile affairs, entering the hardware store of Davis & Merritt, at Chanute, where he spent five years. He also spent a like period in the employ of the mechanical department of the Atchison, Topeka & Santa Fe Railroad; and was then transferred to the transportation department, where he was employed eleven years, the last six years of which time he was a conductor on the Southern Kansas Division. Mr. Barbee resigned his position January 1, 1911, and engaged in the grocery business at Chanute, but disposed of his interests therein in 1914, when he was elected commissioner of public utilities of Chanute, for a term of three years. As before noted, his duties have been ably and conscientiously discharged, and few city officials hold the public confidence in greater degree. Mr. Barbee is a republican. His offices are in the City Hall, while his home, one of the most attractive and modern bungalows of Chanute, is situated at No. 610 South Evergreen Avenue. He is secretary of the Old Settlers Association, in the work of which he takes a great interest and among the members of which he is very popular. He stands high in Masonry, belonging to Cedar Lodge No. 103, Ancient Free and Accepted Masons; Iola Council No. 8, Royal and Select Masters; Chanute Chapter No. 21, Royal Arch Masons; Temple Commandery No. 44, Knight Templars; belongs also to Chanute Council No. 44, Sons and Daughters of Justice; and is also an active member of the Chanute Commercial Club.

In 1885 Mr. Barbee was married in Neosho County to Miss Anna Englis, daughter of Elias and Martha (Lee) Englis, both now deceased. Mr. Englis was a lifelong farmer and during the latter part of his life carried on operations in Neosho County. Mrs. Englis was a relative of Gen. Robert E. Lee. To Mr. and Mrs. Barbee the following children have been born: Ola, who died in infancy; twin boys, one of whom also died in infancy and Talmage, the other twin, who died aged nineteen years, in 1909; and William Marcus, born February 13, 1891, who resides with his parents. William M. Barbee, Jr., is one of the enterprising and energetic young business men of Chanute, a graduate of the Chanute High School, and now bookkeeper and secretary of the Commonwealth Oil Company. He is a member of the Chanute Band, and belongs to Cedar Lodge No. 103, Ancient Free and Accepted Masons; and to Chanute Lodge No. 806, Benevolent and Protective Order of Elks, and is one of the most popular young men in the city.

SAMUEL C. VARNER, a retired banker and merchant at Moran, is a veteran of the Civil war, and was one of the earliest business men to locate in Moran.

His paternal ancestors came out of Germany and were colonial settlers in Pennsylvania. Samuel C. Varner was born in Pennsylvania at Monongahela on December 10, 1845. His grandfather, John Varner, was born in the eastern part of that state at Lancaster, was a cabinet maker by trade, was a soldier in the War of 1812, and spent most of his years at Monongahela City and at Pittsburg. He married Elizabeth McKnight, of Maysville, Kentucky. She died at Pittsburg, Pennsylvania.

John McKnight Varner, father of Samuel C., was born at Pittsburg, Pennsylvania, March 26, 1817. He spent his early life at Pittsburg, was married at Elizabethtown, Pennsylvania, and then lived for a number of years at Monongahela City. In early life he was a glass blower by trade, subsequently became a merchant, and in March, 1857, he came west and located at Canton in Fulton County, Illinois. After coming to Illinois he followed the trade of painter. In 1867 he went to Bushnell, Illinois, and that city was his home the rest of his life. However, he died while on a visit to Moran, Kansas, in October, 1895. He was laid to rest at his old home in Bushnell. Though quite an old man at the time he did a gallant service as a soldier in the Union army during the Civil war. He enlisted in 1862 in the One Hundred and Third Illinois Infantry and was in service three years, three months. He was with his regiment in the hard fought battles of Missionary Ridge, Lookout Mountain, Chickamauga and Kenesaw Mountain and was present for duty at all times with his regiment until detailed to take charge of a hospital in Chattanooga. This service prevented him from marching with Sherman to the sea. He was a loyal republican, in early life belonged to the Methodist Church, and was affiliated with the Independent Order of Odd Fellows. John M. Varner married Lucinda Collins. She was of Welsh ancestry, the family having located in Virginia in colonial times. She was born August 27, 1819, and died in Bushnell, Illinois, November 10, 1901. The children of these parents were: William Hughs, who died in infancy; Elizabeth Frances, who lives at Freeport, Illinois, is twice a widow, her first husband, Henry Shoup, having been a merchant, and her second husband, Jacob Weaver, was a farmer and later served as city marshal, and game warden at Bushnell, Illinois. Wilson Thompson, who died at Bushnell, Illinois, was a veteran of the Civil war and afterwards a coal mine owner and operator. Samuel C., who was the fourth in age; Melissa, who died in 1915, wife of W. T. Bell, a carriage maker living at Canton, Illinois; Edward, a painter and merchant, who died at Colony, Kansas; Thomas, who died in infancy; John J., a merchant and now serving as mayor of Iola, Kansas; Anna Virginia, wife of George Seldomridge, a merchant at Seattle, Washington; Homer M., who has a restaurant at Moran, Kansas; and Olive June, wife of William Morgan, a painter living at Wichita, Kansas.

Samuel C. Varner lived in his native city of Monongahela City, Pennsylvania, until he was about twelve years of age. He began his education in the public schools there. After that he lived in Canton, Illinois, until he enlisted in May, 1862, in the Sixty-seventh Regiment of Illinois Infantry. During that enlistment he served four months and was mustered out. In 1864 he returned to the army, this time as first lieutenant of Company B, One Hundred and Forty-eighth Illinois Infantry. He then remained in the service until finally mustered out September 5, 1865.

After the war Mr. Varner became a merchant at Kirkwood, Illinois, and in 1867 removed to Bushnell, where he continued merchandising for one year. He spent three years as a merchant at Des Moines, Iowa, was a farmer in Adair County in that state five years, and returning to Illinois continued farming in McLean County for about five years.

Mr. Varner came to Kansas and located at Colony in April, 1880. He was in the lumber and hardware business there until 1883 and since the latter year his home has been at Moran. He established himself in the lumber and hardware business, built up a large trade, and his successful efforts as a merchant brought him many close connections with the business and civic life of the community. He established and owned the People's State Bank, served as its president, but retired from that office in 1912. Mr. Varner owns his home at the corner of Cedar and Third streets, and is now enjoying a well-earned leisure.

He is a member of the Christian Church. He has always taken much interest in Masonry, and organized the Marmaton Lodge No. 245 and the Colony Lodge, and was the first master of each of these bodies. He also belongs to Zion Chapter No. 24, Royal Arch Masons, at Garnett, Kansas, and to Esdraelon Commandery No. 49, Knights Templar. Another fraternal relationship is with Moran Lodge No. 240, Ancient Order of United Workmen.

In the intervals of his service in the Union army, on September 27, 1863, at Farmington, Illinois, Mr. Varner married Miss Annie McCord, daughter of Thomas Jefferson and Mary (Layton) McCord. Her father was a farmer in Knox County, Illinois.

LOUIS L. MARCELL. The discovery of oil and gas and its development in Neosho and the surrounding counties has not only added to the wealth and prosperity of this section of the state but has also brought forward a new type of business man: the oil producer and refiner.

Today one of the leading representatives of the oil industry in the Mid-Continent field is Louis L. Marcell of Chanute, Kansas, who became interested when the business was in its infancy and has been a factor in making it one of the largest industries of the state.

Mr. Marcell was born in Highland, Doniphan County, Kansas. He is the son of Charles Louis and Mattie J. Birchfield Marcell. Though a Kansan by birth, his family had its origin in France. It was from the Canton of Lucerne, Switzerland, that Peter Marcell, the first American ancestor and the great grandfather of Louis L. Marcell came to this country settling in New York City. His son Charles M. Marcell removed from New York to Frankfort, Kentucky, coming to Kansas in 1857 and settling on a farm in Doniphan County. Charles L. Marcell was then ten years of age. At sixteen years of age he enlisted with the National Guards of Kansas toward the close of the Civil war. Mr. Marcell still owns the farm settled by his father. Charles L. Marcell is one of the oldest members of the Independent Order of Odd Fellows in Kansas.

Louis L. Marcell acquired a good education in the public schools and later attending Campbell University at Holten, Kansas. In 1895 he accepted a position with the Bank of Highland which he retained until 1903. Having become interested in the development of the oil business, he became a pioneer in that industry and removed to Chanute which was then the center of the oil and gas activities. His choice proved an exceptionally fortunate one and speaks much for his foresight and judgment as well as for his faith in the future of the business and his confidence in his own ability. He became manager of three of the largest companies of the field, and after having spent three years in the producing of oil and gas, he early saw the need of refining their own production and placing it directly upon the market. In 1905 there was an overproduction of crude oil and the Standard Oil Company refused to take the oil from the producers, so it became almost necessary for the oil producer to own his own refinery in order to market his own oil.

During the year 1906 The Chanute Refining Company was organized with a capitalization of $50,000, and a refinery was built in Chanute which grew beyond the production of this field and crude oil was shipped from Cushing, Oklahoma, where later they built another refinery with double the capacity of the Chanute plant, this making the Chanute Refining Company one of the largest independent refineries in the Mid-Continent field. Mr. Marcell was manager of this company until the year 1916 when they sold their interests to the Sinclair Refining Company.

Mr. Marcell has large interests as a producer and refiner in both Kansas and Oklahoma, and is recognized as a business man of ability and sound judgment, a man of strong character, honest, ambitious, alert, energetic, decisive, calling into action without delay all the qualities of a resourceful nature, and yet few men in business life display as much consideration for the courtesies and amenities which go far toward establishing just and equitable relations between man and his fellow men.

Mr. Marcell is an independent voter, having taken little part in political affairs. He is a member of the First Presbyterian Church in which he has served for some years as an elder, and has always taken an interest in all matters of a public nature dealing with the welfare and prosperity of the community.

Mr. Marcell was married in 1899 to Miss Virginia Overlander, daughter of G. W. and Sarah E. Overlander of Highland, Kansas. They have one daughter, Miss Genevieve, a student in the Chanute High School.

EDGAR M. FORDE is now grand recorder for Kansas of the Ancient Order of United Workmen, having succeeded his honored father in that office when the late Edgar M. Forde, Sr., died in August, 1912.

The official headquarters of this great fraternal order in Kansas are at 417-419 Commercial Street in Emporia. In the year 1916 the Ancient Order of United Workmen had 40,000 members in Kansas, 400 lodges, and there are two lodges in Emporia, Lodge No. 2 and Lodge No. 184.

Mr. Forde was born in Emporia September 4, 1885, a son of Edgar M. Forde, who was born in Buffalo, New York, February 6, 1851. His parents were Matthew and Jessie (Edgar) Forde. Matthew Forde, though born in Ireland, was of English parentage, and he was married in Scotland in 1850 to Miss Jessie Edgar, a native of Scotland. In the same year of their marriage they set out for America, locating in Buffalo, New York, where Matthew Forde was connected with railroad service until his death January 12, 1881. Matthew Forde and wife had twin sons, Edwin J. and Edgar M. Edwin made his home in Buffalo and died there June 24, 1879.

The late Edgar M. Forde grew up in Buffalo, his native city, graduated from the high school in 1868, and for three years prepared for the profession of law in an office at Buffalo. He came as one of the pioneers of Emporia, where he located in 1871. He was admitted to the bar March 4, 1872, being at that time twenty-one years of age. From that time until 1875 he was in practice in the office of the late Senator Preston B. Plumb, and after leaving the office of that great Kansan formed a partnership with Almerin Gillett, which was maintained until 1880.

It was in 1880 that the late Mr. Forde was elected Grand Master Workman of the Ancient Order of United Workmen, and the following year was elected grand recorder, an office he held until his death more than thirty years later. He was the official who more than any other made the Ancient Order of United Workmen, one of the greatest fraternal organizations in Kansas. He held all the offices in the order, and was past grand chief of honor in the Degree of Honor in the same organization.

He was also a successful business man and acquired some valuable property in Emporia. From 1874 to 1888 he was Emporia's city clerk. In other fraternities he attained the thirty-second degree of Scottish Rite in Masonry and was also a Knight Templar, was a member of the Modern Woodmen of America, the Select Knights, the Fraternal Aid Association and the Royal Arcanum. On September 1, 1875, Edgar M. Forde, Sr., married Miss Louisa Tillottson, a daughter of Samuel Tillottson, who was a merchant and came to Kansas from Ohio and later moved to Illinois, where she died. Mrs. Louisa Forde died in December, 1882, leaving a daughter, Jessie L., who graduated from the State Normal School at Emporia and is a teacher in the State Normal School at Charleston, Illinois. On June 12, 1882, the senior Mr. Forde married Miss Mary J. Ingram, a daughter of William H. Ingram of Buffalo, New York, where she was born in 1861. She survived her honored husband and still makes her home in Emporia. Her children are: Edgar M., Jr.; Margaret, wife of Elmer Sigler, a mechanical engineer in Kansas City, Missouri; W. I., who has made a name for himself in vaudeville circles and resides in New York City; and Mary E., who is now a senior in the State Normal School at Emporia. The late Mr. Forde was a member of the Presbyterian Church and politically was a republican.

Edgar M. Forde, Jr., grew up in Emporia, attended the public schools, and for two years was a student in the Presbyterian College in that city. He then entered the Kansas State University where he graduated LL. B. with the class of 1910. He was very prominent in college affairs, made the University football team, was a member of the Glee Club, which he managed for two years, and also belonged to the college dramatic organization, the Masque Club. He is a Beta Theta Pi.

After leaving law school in 1910, instead of taking up active practice, he entered the office of the Ancient Order of United Workmen to assist his father, and succeeded him as grand recorder of the organization.

He is a member of Lodge No. 2, Ancient Order of United Workmen, and is also affiliated with Emporia Lodge No. 12, Ancient Free and Accepted Masons; Emporia Chapter No. 12, Royal Arch Masons; Emporia Commandery No. 8, Knight Templars; and Emporia Lodge No. 633, Benevolent Protective Order of Elks, and Emporia Camp No.

615, Modern Woodmen of America. He is active in the Emporia Commercial Club and politically is a republican.

On October 1, 1913, at Clay Center, Kansas, Mr. Forde married Miss Hazel Allison, a daughter of S. T. and Lettie Allison, her father being a traveling salesman with home at Clay Center. Mrs. Forde is also a graduate of the University of Kansas, where she took her A. B. degree in 1910, the same year her husband graduated from the law department. She is a member of the Kappa Alpha Theta Sorority, and at the present time is grand vice president for the United States.

ROY L. FRUIT, one of the progressive newspaper men of the state, is publisher and proprietor of the Sedan Times-Star, one of the oldest republican journals in the southeastern quarter of the state.

The Times-Star inherits the history of half a dozen or more papers which have had their share in the newspaper history of Chautauqua County. The Chautauqua Journal was founded at Sedan in 1875 by H. B. Kelley and R. S. Turner. It was consolidated with the Sedan Times in 1885. The Cedarvale Times, founded in 1878, was removed to Sedan the same year and the name changed to the Chautauqua County Times with P. H. Albright editor and publisher. Another change of name occurred in 1901 after which it was the Sedan Times, with A. D. Dunn as publisher. As already stated it was consolidated in 1885 with the Chautauqua Journal under the name Sedan Times-Journal and with R. G. Ward editor and publisher. The Cedarvale Star was founded in 1884 by I. D. McKeehan and was consolidated with the Times-Journal at Sedan in 1894 and the name of the consolidated paper became the Weekly Times-Star. Adrian Reynolds and F. G. Kenesson were editors and publishers. Freeman's Lance, founded in Peru in 1891 by W. A. Tanksley, was moved to Sedan in 1892, was known as the Sedan Lance, and A. S. Koonce was its editor and D. E. Shartell publisher. This was consolidated with the Times-Star in 1909. The Sedan Republican, founded in 1890 by T. B. Ferguson, was sold to the Lance in 1892. The Chautauqua County Democrat and the Chautauqua County Journal were two other constituents papers of the Times-Star early history. The first was absorbed by the Times-Star in 1894 and the latter in 1912.

Mr. Fruit has done a great deal to maintain the best standards in the management of the Times-Star and has also secured a mechanical equipment equal to the best. The plant is situated on Chautauqua Street and it has a full equipment of a modern linotype, power presses and other facilities.

Roy Lee Fruit has been in the newspaper business for nearly ten years. He was born at Wapella, Illinois, February 20, 1888. His paternal ancestors came from Wales to Virginia about 1750. His grandfather William Porter Fruit was born in Kentucky in 1811, was one of the early settlers in DeWitt County, Illinois, and in 1871 removed to Montgomery County, Kansas, where he was a pioneer farmer. He died at Cherryvale, Kansas, in 1896.

William P. Fruit, father of the Sedan editor, was born near Wapella, Illinois, May 10, 1862. He was reared and married in that locality, became a farmer, and in 1897 removed to Table Grove, Illinois, where he was in the mercantile business for about a year and in May, 1898, came to Cherryvale, Kansas, where he has followed the business of carpenter and builder. He is still a resident of Cherryvale. From 1890 to 1894 he served as deputy sheriff of DeWitt County,

Illinois. He is a republican and a member of the Knights of Pythias. William P. Fruit married Josephine Jones, who was born in Peoria County, Illinois, in February, 1864.

The only child of his parents, Roy Lee Fruit was educated in the public schools of DeWitt County, Illinois, continued his education after coming to Cherryvale, Kansas, was graduated from the high school there in 1905, and during the year 1906-07 was a student in the University of Kansas at Lawrence. His first business experience was in a drug store with Charles L. McAdams, with whom he remained a year, and he then entered the newspaper work at Sapulpa, Oklahoma, being connected with the Sapulpa Democrat, associated with Senator H. W. Davis. After two years at Sapulpa he removed to Joplin, Missouri, where he was in the newspaper work a year, then spent twenty months with the Cherryvale Republican and in April, 1913, bought the plant of the Sedan Times-Star from H. G. James.

Mr. Fruit is a republican in his personal political convictions and is an active member of the Third District Republican Editors' Association, a member of the State Editorial Association and is affiliated with Vesper Lodge No. 136, Ancient, Free and Accepted Masons, at Sedan and Camp No. 919 of the Modern Woodmen of America at Sedan.

July 20, 1913, at Cherryvale he married Miss Yolande Dobson. Her mother, Mrs. F. N. (Dobson) Michener is still living at Cherryvale. Mr. and Mrs. Fruit have one child, Jeannette Frances, born May 24, 1916.

WILLIAM H. SMITH. It is almost a half century that has crept around on the world's clock since William H. Smith, one of Chanute's substantial and respected citizens, came to Kansas, locating in Neosho County, where at present he is held in high esteem with the Old Settlers' Association, of which he is president. With interest he has watched this section develop and has assisted very materially, ever lending his influence to law and order, encouraging the investment of capital, and setting an industrious example that might very profitably be emulated. William H. Smith was born January 25, 1846, in Warren County, Ohio. His parents were Samuel M. and Phebe (Wharton) Smith.

The early records of the Smith family show that in colonial times there were pioneering members who dared the dangers of the deep and crossed the Atlantic Ocean from England to America, finding harbor in New Jersey, and from these descended Abram C. Smith, who was the grandfather of William H. Smith of Chanute, Kansas. He was born in New Jersey in 1781, was a quiet, peaceful farmer who removed with his family to Warren County, Ohio, in 1835 and died there in 1867. The family were Quakers.

Samuel M. Smith, father of William H., was born near Camden, New Jersey, in 1817, and died at the latter's home at Chanute, in February, 1902. He came to Kansas in the fall of 1884 and lived practically retired until his death. In politics he was a republican and fraternally was an Odd Fellow, being past noble grand in that order. He was married to Phebe Wharton, who was born in Ohio in 1820 and died in Warren County, that state, in 1847. They had three children: John, who was a soldier in the Thirty-fourth Ohio, a Zouave regiment, during the Civil war, met a soldier's death at Wytheville, Virginia; Jane, who was the wife of Harvey Beach, a farmer, now deceased, died in Indiana in 1898; and William H.

William H. Smith was reared on his father's farm and remained at home until he was nineteen years of age, in the meanwhile attending school in Warren County. He then went to Indiana and for four years engaged in farming and teaming near South Bend, but in 1869 he came farther west and located at Osage City in Neosho County, Kansas, and worked in the livestock business with his uncle, B. M. Smith, until the fall of 1870. At that time the present thriving City of Chanute was a village bearing the name of Tioga, and there Mr. Smith went into the livery business, in which he continued for two years and then followed farming for a year in this county.

In the meanwhile travel increased, new settlers kept coming in and the population of Chanute greatly increased, and when Mr. Smith, taking advantage of a business opportunity, opened a cafe, it was a very popular venture and he conducted it until 1878. Because of his business enterprise and personal qualities he became a man of public importance and served both as street commissioner and as city marshal. In 1884 Mr. Smith turned his attention again to farming, having eighty acres of excellent land situated five miles east of Chanute, and continued to conduct this farm until 1901, when he traded it for forty acres nearer Chanute, just north of the present city limits, the present site of the Ashgrove Lime and Portland Cement plant. On that land Mr. Smith engaged in farming and fruit growing for two years, when, having an excellent offer, he sold the place and moved into Chanute, erecting his comfortable residence at No. 313 North Highland Avenue. Other property owned by Mr. Smith as the result of his industry and good judgment includes: a dwelling at No. 707 North Santa Fe Avenue; another at No. 330 West Third Street, and a third at No. 1302 South Edith Avenue; a lot on North Grant Avenue; and a farm of 160 acres located five miles east of Chanute.

Active all his life, Mr. Smith could not be contentedly idle, after coming to Chanute, and he entered the employ of Bloomheart Brothers as a clerk in their grocery store and remained with that firm for ten years. Since Hector Lodge No. 64 was organized at Chanute in 1894 he has been secretary, and is past noble grand, and also is secretary of Evergreen Encampment No. 27, and since 1914 has acted as janitor and caretaker of the lodge rooms. He belongs also to the Chanute Lodge No. 158, Rebekahs, and to the Sons and Daughters of Justice.

At Caldwell, Kansas, in 1877, Mr. Smith was married to Miss Lizzie W. Wendell, whose parents, both now deceased, were J. H. and Catherine Wendell. The father of Mrs. Smith was proprietor of a hotel at Caldwell. Mr. and Mrs. Smith have two children: Walter L., who is a druggist and resides at Kansas City, Missouri; and Katy L., who is the wife of Morris Montague, who is in the implement business with his brother, F. W. Montague. Mr. and Mrs. Montague reside at No. 518 North Highland Avenue, Chanute.

In political sentiment Mr. Smith has always been a democrat and on numerous occasions his fellow citizens have elected him to office. He served many years as trustee of Big Creek and Tioga townships, Neosho County. In 1890 he was his party's candidate for sheriff and his popularity was shown when, in a normally republican county he lacked only fourteen votes of election.

JAMES A. VAUGHAN, M. D. During his long and active career as a physician Doctor Vaughan has spent his most useful and profitable years in the State of Kansas. For more than ten years he has practiced successfully in Mound Valley in Labette County.

Though most of his early years were spent in Southwest Missouri, Doctor Vaughan was born in Benton County, Arkansas, October 21, 1868. He is of English stock, and his great-grandfather came over from England and settled in Tennessee in the early days. His father, G. W. Vaughan, was born in Illinois in 1843, was reared in Arkansas, where his parents had located in Benton County as early as 1845. G. W. Vaughan after the Civil war broke out entered the service of the Confederate army and served for three years, reaching the rank of lieutenant. He was in many battles and campaigns, fought at Pea Ridge, Arkansas, and was one of the gallant defenders of the Mississippi stronghold at Vicksburg until its fall. Since the war he has followed farming all his life, and in the year that R. B. Hayes was elected President of the United States, in 1876, he moved to Creighton in Cass County, Missouri, where he still resides, being now retired. He is a democrat and a member of the Baptist Church. G. W. Vaughan married Louise Neil, who was born in Tennessee in 1844. Their children are: Dr. James A.; William, who is a physician by training but spends his time in travel; Leona, who resides at Boulder, Colorado, the widow of John Coe, who was a dentist; John, a mail carrier at Creighton, Missouri; and Mrs. Dollie Samuels, who lives in Kansas City, Missouri, where her husband is on the police force.

Doctor Vaughan was reared on his father's farm in Southwest Missouri. He attended the public schools of that state, and secured his medical education in Kansas City. For one year he was in the medical department of the Kansas University, and then two years in the Kansas City Medical College. He graduated M. D. in 1892, and the subsequent quarter of a century has been spent in active practice. For two months he was located at Dayton, Missouri, for a similar time at Seligman, Missouri, and then came to Kansas. For seven years Doctor Vaughan practiced at Neodesha, one year at Cherryvale, at Angola four years, and since 1905 has been successfully located at Mound Valley. He has a general medical and surgical practice, and has offices on Commercial Street. He is now serving as county health officer of that county, and is United States pension examining physician. He is prominent in medical circles in that part of Kansas, is now vice president of the Labette County Medical Society, and also belongs to the State and Southwestern Medical societies.

Doctor Vaughan is a democrat in politics. He owns a residence on Hickory Street in Mound Valley. April 20, 1899, at Cherryvale he married Miss Artie Inman, who came from Indiana. They are the parents of three children. Christine, who was born March 25, 1900, and is now a sophomore in the Parsons High School; Leona, born June 2, 1911; and Delma Aldis, born July 28, 1915.

ROBERT N. MCMILLEN, M. D. Doctor McMillen began the practice of medicine in Kansas thirty-five years ago, and was among the first physicians in Pratt County. Much of his early practice was among the pioneer homes of that section. For seventeen years his home and offices have been at Iola, and he still carries the burden of a heavy practice at that city.

Doctor McMillen represents Scotch ancestry, who came to America many years ago and were pioneers in the State of Kentucky. His grandfather Robert McMillen was a native of Kentucky, was a farmer there, and met his death as a result of accident.

Isaac McMillen, the father of Doctor McMillen, was born near Lexington, Kentucky, in 1826. He grew up in that state, and was early attracted into a profession which engaged the services of many men in the early half of the last century just as railroading does today. He became a steamboat captain, piloting boats up and down the Ohio and Mississippi rivers from St. Louis to New Orleans and also from Pittsburg to St. Louis. For a number of years he had his home at Bellaire, Ohio, in Belmont County. He married there, and his death occurred at Bellaire March 23, 1857. The cause of his death was smallpox. In politics he was a democrat. Captain McMillen married Margaret J. Davis, who was born at Bellaire, Ohio, in 1836. By her marriage to Captain McMillen she had three children: Doctor McMillen; Jacob, who is a plasterer living at Preston in Pratt County, Kansas; and Charles Vincent, who died in 1857, at the age of six months, of smallpox, dying at the same time as the father. After the death of her husband Mrs. McMillen married Dr. J. C. Beam, who was born in Westmoreland, Pennsylvania, and for many years practiced his profession in Somerset and Cambria County, Pennsylvania. He died in January, 1914. During the Civil war Mrs. J. C. Beam removed from Eastern Ohio to Johnstown, Pennsylvania. She lived there for a number of years, but finally went to San Diego, California. The great flood at Johnstown, Pennsylvania, occurred on May 31, 1889, and when the news of the disaster reached Mrs. Beam the shock was such as to prove the immediate cause of her death. She died June 7, 1889.

Dr. Robert N. McMillen was born at Bellaire in Belmont County, Ohio, March 4, 1850. Bellaire is a city on the west bank of the Ohio River near Wheeling, West Virginia, and its chief importance when Doctor McMillen was a boy was due to the fact that it was a river port and also the point at which the pioneer railway over the Alleghenies crossed the river. Doctor McMillen grew up in that river town, attended the public schools, including high school, and also lived for a time in Western Pennsylvania. He pursued his medical studies in the Louisville Medical College of Kentucky, where he was graduated Doctor of Medicine in 1875. His early professional experience was in the ill fated City of Johnstown, Pennsylvania, where he practiced until 1882. He then came out to Kansas, locating in Pratt County, and remained there giving his service to the early settlers for thirteen years. In 1895 Doctor McMillen moved to Marceline, Missouri, but in 1900 returned to Kansas and located in January of that year at Iola. He is an active member of the Allen County and State Medical societies, the Southeast Kansas Medical Society and the American Medical Association. His offices are at 10 South Washington Avenue, and his home, which he owns, at 309 West Madison Avenue.

Doctor McMillen has served as county coroner of Allen County. He is a progressive republican, was formerly a member of the Independent Order of Odd Fellows, and is affiliated with Iola Camp, No. 101, Woodmen of the World.

On October 5, 1876, soon after he began practice, he was married at Johnstown, Pennsylvania, to Miss Harriet A. White, daughter of Thomas and Harriet (Simpson) White, both now deceased. Her father was a farmer. Doctor and Mrs. McMillen are the parents of five children. Margaret M. married C. B.

Crick, mailing clerk in the postoffice at Iola. Robert N., Jr., is a successful young attorney practicing at McAlester, Oklahoma, and completed his law studies in the University of Missouri. Walter White, a mining and civil engineer, and a graduate of the School of Mines at Rolla, Missouri, is now practicing his profession at Morenci, Arizona. Gertrude E. is still at home with her parents. Harriet Stewart is the wife of William P. Harriss, professor of physics and civics in the high school of Kansas City, Kansas.

WILLIAM L. McNAUGHTEN, M. D., has been long and favorably known as a capable physician and surgeon in Chautauqua County, and now controls a large practice at Sedan. In his younger days he met and overcame obstacles and had to work for every step of his advancement while gaining his education and preparing himself for his profession.

When nineteen years of age his education in the common schools was completed, and he then began working on a farm and learning the carpenter's trade. As a carpenter he worked in Missouri and in 1883 moved to Kansas, locating in Montgomery County. For nine years he was one of the force of carpenters employed by the Missouri Pacific Railroad Company. He had long felt that his real sphere was in the profession of medicine, but having a family to care for there were some weighty reasons why he should continue working at his mechanical trade. All the leisure time he had be applied to the study of medicine and he followed that with a course in the Kansas City College of Physicians and Surgeons and in 1897 entered the Columbian Medical College for one year. As an undergraduate he practiced for a year in Cedar County, Missouri, and in 1901 was given his degree M. D. In the meantime Doctor McNaughten had located in Chautauqua County in 1898 and was in practice at Elgin for eleven years. In 1909 he removed to Sedan and now looks after a very general practice both in medicine and surgery. His offices are over the White Front drug store on Main Street. He is the present county health officer and coroner of Chautauqua County.

Doctor McNaughten's ancestors came from Scotland to the United States in colonial times. His grandfather Alexander McNaughten was born in 1789, was one of the early settlers in Henry County, Illinois, where he followed farming and died in that county in 1863.

It was in Henry County, Illinois, that Doctor McNaughten was born May 19, 1861. His father, William N. McNaughten, was born in Knox County, Illinois, in 1832, was reared in that locality and was married near Moline in Rock Island County. By trade he was a miller. He followed that occupation and reared his family in Henry County, Illinois, subsequently moving to Stuart in Guthrie County, Iowa, where he helped to build the first flour mill. From there he went to Dallas County, Iowa, and later to Davenport, where he died in 1906. He was a republican in politics, a member of the Baptist Church, and was affiliated with the Independent Order of Odd Fellows. He married Miss Martha Harris, who was born in Ohio in 1842 and died at Davenport, Iowa, in 1896. A record of their children is briefly as follows: Helen, who died at the age of three years; Isabelle, wife of Robert Atwater, a real estate and insurance man living at Superior, Nebraska; Dr. William L.; Carrie, wife of Patrick Nagle, engineer of the city waterworks plant at Davenport, Iowa; Lottie, who died at the age of seven years; Arthur B., a baker by trade, living at Salt Lake City, Utah.

Doctor McNaughten received his early education while living with his parents in Henry County, Illinois. He has not only gained an enviable place in his profession, but has prospered in a business way and has also exercised his influence to the good of the various communities where he has made his home. He owns his residence on Montgomery Street in Chautauqua and also has some business property in Elgin. Politically he is a republican, has served on the school board at Elgin and is a worker for anything that will benefit his community. He is treasurer and chairman of the Board of Trustees of the Baptist Church at Sedan, is a member of the Chautauqua County and State Medical Societies and the American Medical Association, and is affiliated with Vesper Lodge No. 136 Ancient, Free and Accepted Masons; Sedan Chapter of the Order of Eastern Star, Sedan Lodge No. 141 Independent Order of Odd Fellows, Camp No. 40 of the Woodmen of the World at Sedan, the lodge of the Ancient Order of United Workmen at Elgin, the Woodmen Circle at Sedan.

On September 9, 1883, at Winterset, Iowa, Doctor McNaughten married Miss Lucina Young, daughter of G. W. and Mollie (Custer) Young. Her father is a farmer and both her parents now reside in Cedar County, Missouri. After their marriage Doctor and Mrs. McNaughten started out to establish a home and do all they could for the rearing and training of their children to lives of usefulness and honor, and the outcome of these efforts is a matter of pride to them both. Five children were born to them: Roy and Kittie, both of whom died in infancy; Jesse N., who is a furniture merchant at Sedan, Kansas; Nona, who died at the age of eighteen months; and Ivan, who lives with his parents but is a student of music in New York City.

SETH J. BAILEY. The gratifying success which has crowned the efforts of Seth J. Bailey, of Chanute, clearly and emphatically evidence the business skill, perseverance and enterprise of this individual, who has been engaged in business here since the fall of 1900. This is a utilitarian age, one in which advancement and progress come through activity in the industrial and commercial interests of life. There is nothing to which America owes her pre-eminence among the nations of the earth so much as to her inventions, and each year sees additions to the list which bear marked impress upon the world of trade. It is not as an inventor, however, but as a manufacturer of inventions that Mr. Bailey is known. He had the foresight to see the possibilities of a certain appliance and the courage to back his judgment, and the result has been the building up of one of Chanute's prominent and substantial business concerns, the Sunshine Mantle Company, manufacturers of incandescent gas mantles.

Mr. Bailey is a native son of Kansas, born in the City of Topeka, May 2, 1868, his parents being Dr. M. and Laura A. (Jarboe) Bailey. The family is of English origin, and was founded in Pennsylvania prior to the War of the Revolution. William Bailey, the grandfather of Seth J. Bailey, was born in either Pennsylvania or Ohio; at least it is known that he was in the latter state in pioneer days and there was engaged in farming and died before the birth of his grandson. He was of Quaker stock and married a Miss Garretson. Dr. M. Bailey, the father of Seth J. Bailey, was born near the City of Salem, Ohio, in 1835, and was there reared and educated. As a young man he went to Muscatine, Iowa, in which city he was married, and about the year 1857 came to Kansas and for a time practiced medicine at Emporia, where one of his intimate friends was the late Senator P. B.

Plumb. When the Civil war came on he became assistant surgeon of the First Kansas Volunteers, and later was made surgeon of that regiment, remaining with it throughout its various campaigns. Near the close of the war he was in Iowa, and after peace had been declared took up his residence at Topeka. He remained there, however, only until 1868, when he went to Fort Sill, Indian Territory, as surgeon of the Nineteenth Kansas Regiment, and continued in that capacity for six months, after which he returned to Topeka and again took up the practice of his profession. In 1871 he came to Chanute, and while he continued to practice his calling at various times from that year on, the greater part of his attention was given to a private banking business, conducted under the style of M. Bailey & Company. His medical degree was secured from the St. Louis Medical College and he was a man of skill and learning in his profession, but possessed various other talents as well. He was widely known for his personal integrity and public spirit, and during the two terms that he served as mayor of Chanute gave the city excellent service. He always supported the policies of the republican party. He was a member of the school board and did much to advance the cause of education. Doctor Bailey married Miss Laura A. Jarboe, who was born in 1839, in Illinois, and died at Chanute, in 1914, having survived the Doctor twenty-one years. Their children were as follows: L. L., who as a miner and mining expert visited Asia and other parts of the world and died at Chanute, in May, 1916; Seth J., of this notice; William J., who is a hardware merchant of Tacoma, Washington; Mabel B., who married Fred Grubb and is a resident of Chanute, Kansas; and Marc, who is superintendent of a copper mine at Bisbee, Arizona.

Seth J. Bailey attended the public schools of Chanute and was graduated from the high school here in 1886, following which he spent two years at the Kansas University, at Lawrence, where he had as a classmate William Morgan. He then spent two years in the bank of M. Bailey & Company, with his father, and for the following two years was variously employed, during which time he took trips to Maine and Colorado. Mr. Bailey then went to the Malay Peninsula, Asia, where he was associated with his brother, L. L., in gold mining, being identified with a British company which had a large concession there. After 1½ years he returned to Chanute and engaged in the mantle manufacturing business. The Sunshine Mantle Company was established in the fall of 1900, with a capital stock of $100, a modest start from which has grown the present great business. The factory, located at 208-210-212 East First Street, is 50 by 65 feet, two stories in height and including a basement, and is fitted out with the latest and most highly improved equipment for the manufacture of incandescent gas mantles, commonly known as Welsbach mantles. The trade has grown steadily, particularly during recent years, and now covers the entire mid-continent gas field, including the states of Pennsylvania, Ohio, Kentucky, West Virginia, Texas, Louisiana, Arkansas, Oklahoma, Missouri and Kansas. This great growth of business may be accredited to the efforts and abilities of Mr. Bailey, who is accounted one of the progressive and energetic business men of the city. Mr. Bailey is a director in the Chanute Building and Loan Association and belongs to the Commercial Club, of which he was president for one year.

In political affairs Mr. Bailey is a stanch republican, and has served as a member of the Chanute City Council. He has also been a member of the library board and in various ways has aided in his city's growth and development. His religious connection is with the Episcopal Church, of which he is senior warden. Fraternally he is affiliated with Cedar Lodge No. 103, Ancient, Free and Accepted Masons; Chanute Chapter No. 21, Royal Arch Masons; and Chanute Commandery No. 44, Knights Templar; Chanute Lodge No. 806, Benevolent and Protective Order of Elks; and (by inheritance) the Loyal Legion. He owns his own comfortable home at No. 946 South Highland Avenue and is interested in other realty holdings at and adjacent to Chanute.

In 1891, at Pittsburg, Kansas, Mr. Bailey was united in marriage with Miss Edna Sawyer, daughter of Hudson and Frances (Crane) Sawyer, the former of whom, now deceased, was a minister of the Episcopal Church, while the latter survives and resides with her son-in-law and daughter. Mr. and Mrs. Bailey are the parents of one daughter: Lael B., who is the wife of W. M. Gray, Jr., of Chanute, secretary of the Sunshine Mantle Company and general superintendent of the factory of this concern.

J. M. MASSEY. One of the live and prosperous communities of Southeastern Kansas which is offering unsurpassed opportunities for the development of men and large business interests is the growing City of Chanute. In this locality may be found many of the raw materials, or they can be easily obtained through railroad shipments. Here is an immense local market, and here are the men, solid, reliable and aggressive, ready and willing to push ahead to the ultimate end whatever enterprise they connect themselves with. Once an individual establishes himself in the line for which he is best fitted, if he possess business sense and acumen, it is certain that success of one or another kind will reward his efforts. One of the men of Chanute who has admirably proven his own worth and increased his value as a citizen by developing large interests, is J. M. Massey, junior member of the large clothing firm of Garvin & Massey, and vice president of the First National Bank. He has been a resident of Chanute since 1896 and during this time has steadily risen to a place of prominence through a recognition and ready grasp of the opportunities which have presented themselves.

Mr. Massey was born at Lock Haven, Clinton County, Pennsylvania, May 25, 1843, and is a son of Dr. A. B. and Ann R. (McMeen) Massey, and a member of a family which, originating in England, came to America and located in Maryland during the days of Lord Baltimore. His great-grandfather was Aquilla Massey, a planter and slaveholder of Maryland, and that name was also borne by his grandfather, who was born in Maryland in 1741. The latter was a farmer, owned a large plantation and many slaves, and attained a great age, being past his ninety-ninth birthday when he died at Darlington, Maryland, in 1851.

A. B. Massey was born in 1808 at Darlington, Hartford County, Maryland, received his education at Annapolis, and became a physician and surgeon. He was reared in his native place, but as a young man went to Lock Haven, Pennsylvania, where he was married, and where he practiced until the year 1857, when he came to Kansas. After a short stay at Kansas City, he went to Paola, but spent only two months at the latter place, then moving on to Trading Post, Linn County. There he opened a store and continued as a physician and merchant until the outbreak of the Civil war, when he became surgeon of the Second Kansas Infantry. He was with his command at Wilson Creek, with Gen. R.

B. Mitchell in Tennessee, and in numerous engagements, and the rigors of the war probably were more than his constitution could stand, for in the fall of 1865 he passed away at Leavenworth, Kansas. Doctor Massey came of peaceful Quaker stock, which had never believed in war, but he was ready to assist his country when his services were needed. He was a republican in politics. Mrs. Massey was born in 1822, in Pennsylvania, and died at Leavenworth, Kansas, in March, 1909. There were two children in the family: J. M.; and Annie, who is a resident of Leavenworth, Kansas, and widow of Dr. J. McCormick, who was for fifty years engaged in the practice of medicine at that place.

J. M. Massey received his education in the public schools of Lock Haven, Pennsylvania, and academy at Williamsport, Pennsylvania. In 1857 he came to Kansas, and after a short stay moved on from Kansas City to Trading Post, Linn County, where he arrived in the spring of 1858. There he assisted his father in the store until the outbreak of the Civil war, at which time he moved to Leavenworth and joined the hospital service, later enlisting in the Seventh Regiment, Missouri Volunteer Infantry, with which he fought for nine months, being in the battles of Hickman's Mills, Westport, Independence and Mine Creek, during Price's raid. Following his military service, he went from Leavenworth to Benton, Montana, and following this spent five years in Texas, Arizona and New Mexico, later engaging in the wholesale merchandise business at Leavenworth and Chicago and in Michigan. Returning to Kansas in 1876, he located at Wichita, where for one year he was employed in the New York Store, conducted by Kohn Brothers. Later he went to Sedgwick, Kansas, where for a number of years he conducted a business of his own as a merchant, and January 1, 1896, came to Chanute and entered business in association with Mr. Garvin, whose partner's interest he purchased. They have since continued in business as clothing dealers, under the firm style of Garvin & Massey, with an establishment at No. 3 East Main Street, one of the substantial business houses of Chanute, with a large and constantly growing patronage. Mr. Massey enjoys an excellent reputation in business circles of Chanute and is vice president of the First National Bank and a stockholder therein. He possesses the qualities so necessary to success in commercial circles, shrewdness, acumen, foresight, aggressiveness and modern progressiveness, and the fact that his integrity has never been questioned is an asset to his business the worth of which cannot be properly estimated. He is the owner of his residence at No. 101 South Kansas Avenue, and other real estate at Chanute, and is interested in several farms in Neosho County. Politically a republican, Mr. Massey's only public service has been as a member of the school board. He is fraternally affiliated with Cedar Lodge No. 103, A. F. & A. M., and also belongs to Chanute Post of the Grand Army of the Republic, is past commander of the Grand Army Post at Conway Springs, Kansas, and is a member of the Loyal Legion.

Mr. Massey was married in 1878, at Sedgwick, Kansas, to Miss Alice Fuller, daughter of Mr. and Mrs. Stephen Fuller, both of whom are now deceased. Mr. Fuller was a carriage manufacturer of Potsdam, New York, and later came to Kansas. Two children have been born to Mr. and Mrs. Massey: Aquilla B., who is a resident of Fresno, California; and Mark F., who holds a position in the Government employ in the Army and Navy Building, at Washington, D. C.

H. L. KINNAMAN. The present county treasurer of Chautauqua County is one of the oldest residents of that section of the state. More than forty years ago he began farming on some of the virgin acres of this county, and the careful study and energy he gave to the business brought him an ample competence besides providing liberally for his growing family. He is now a resident of the City of Sedan and has recently been chosen for a second term to the responsibilities of the county treasuryship.

Mr. Kinnaman represents old American stock. His Kinnaman ancestors were German people and colonial settlers in North Carolina. Mr. H. L. Kinnaman was born in Madison County, Indiana, February 1, 1852. His father, H. L. Kinneman, Sr., was born in North Carolina January 2, 1809, a son of Walter Kinnaman, a native of the same state. In 1818 Walter Kinnaman and family came from North Carolina to the State of Ohio, and Walter subsequently lived in Indiana and Illinois, and died on his farm in the latter state. H. L. Kinnaman, Sr., grew up in Ohio, and in 1830 moved to Madison County, Indiana, where he married. He was one of the pioneers in that rich and picturesque section of Eastern Indiana, and prosperity came to him in generous measure. He was both a farmer and stock raiser. After the organization of the republican party he found a place in its ranks, and always loyally supported its candidates. For a number of years he served on the school board of his home district. H. L. Kinnaman, Sr., died in Carroll County, Missouri, in 1896 when eighty-eight years of age. He was a member of the Christian Church. His wife was Cassandra Crossley, who was born in Madison County, Indiana, in 1813. The Crossleys were among the first white people to locate in that county, and that was when Indiana was still a territory and only a short time after the Indians had been driven away from these hunting grounds. She died in Madison County in 1870. Her children were: David, who died in California, in 1855, having gone out to the Pacific coast during the days of the gold excitement; Conrad, who was a farmer and died in Madison County, Indiana; Walter, who is a retired farmer living at Tillamook, Oregon; Henry, a farmer who died in Madison County, Indiana; Hannah Jane, who lives at Pendleton, Madison County, widow of William Smith, who at the time of his death was a retired farmer; Emeline, who died in Madison County, the wife of Ransom Smith, who is now a retired farmer at Pendleton; Madison Marion, who was a farmer and died in Carroll County, Missouri; Sarah, who died in Carroll County, Missouri, the wife of Edward Purdy, who is a farmer still living there; Margaret, who died at the age of four years; H. L. Kinnaman, Jr.; William A., who also came to Chautauqua County, Kansas, became a farmer and died in 1886; Richard, who died on his farm in Chautauqua County.

Mr. Kinnaman grew up and received his early education in the public schools of Madison County, Indiana. When he left his father's farm at the age of twenty-one, he came out to Chautauqua County in 1874, and joined his efforts to the comparatively few people who were at that time struggling to win a livelihood from the resources of the soil and climate. He stuck to his post during the many vicissitudes which beset Kansas farming in the early years, and kept up the work actively until 1915. Mr. Kinnaman still owns a fine place of 400 acres in Jefferson Town-

ship, six miles east of Cedarvale. He also owns his comfortable residence on Osage Street in Sedan.

Mr. Kinnaman has been voting the republican ticket since the days when Grant, Colfax, Hayes and other distinguished figures were in the ascendancy. After coming to Kansas his first important office was county commissioner, which he held from 1884 to 1887. He was also township treasurer of Jefferson Township four years, and was continuously clerk of the local school board for twenty-eight years. In 1914 he was elected for his first term as county treasurer but did not take office until October, 1915. In November, 1916, he was re-elected for another term of two years. Mr. Kinnaman is past noble grand of Wannetta Lodge, No. 241, Independent Order of Odd Fellows, was formerly identified with the Encampment of that order, is also a member of the Anti-Horse Thief Association, and belongs to Lodge No. 131 of the Ancient Order of United Workmen at Sedan.

On March 26, 1874, in Indianapolis, Indiana, he married Miss Laura Wiley. Almost immediately after his marriage he brought his bride to Chautauqua County and they started to make a home in this new country. Mrs. Kinnaman died January 8, 1917, aged sixty years, her death occurring on her birthday. She was a daughter of Jacob and Margaret Ringer Wiley, both of whom are deceased. Her father was an Indiana farmer. Mr. and Mrs. Kinnaman had four children: Lillie, who died at the age of twenty-two in Chautauqua County, was the wife of J. W. Leonard, who lives on a farm in Jefferson Township of Chautauqua County. Arminta married I. H. Johnson and they live near Elgin, Kansas, but on a farm just over the line in the State of Oklahoma; Alta died in infancy; Harry R. is one his farm adjoining that of his father in Jefferson Township.

REV. AUGUSTINE P. HEIMANN is the beloved priest and rector of St. Martin's Catholic Church at Piqua, Kansas. He is a veteran in the service of the church in Kansas. He came to the state more than a quarter of a century ago, soon after his ordination as a priest, and for years has devoted himself to the constructive as well as the spiritual administration of several important parishes in different counties.

Father Heimann was born in Lafayette, Indiana, February 15, 1866. His father, August Heimann, was born in Silesia, Prussia, in 1834. When eighteen years of age he came to America, locating at Lafayette, Indiana, and spent many years in the railroad service. He finally retired and came to Kansas to live with his son, Father Heimann, and died at Odin in this state in 1910. August Heimann married Louisa Miller. She was born in 1836, at Dunningen in Wuertemberg, Germany, and her parents came to this country in 1850, locating in Covington, Indiana. August Heimann and wife had the following family: Albert, who died at the age of four years; Mary, who died when three years old; Augustine P.; and Emma, who became a member of the Sisterhood of the Precious Blood and died in 1912.

Father Heimann was educated in the parochial schools of Lafayette, Indiana. He was early destined for the priesthood, and for five years pursued the classical course in St. Lawrence College at Mount Calvary in Fond du Lac County, Wisconsin. This was followed by three years of study of philosophy and theology at St. Francis Seminary near Milwaukee, and he took his last course in the-

Aug. P. Heimann.

ology at Mount St. Mary's in Cincinnati. He was ordained at Cincinnati June 29, 1889.

He was at once sent out to Kansas, and his first service was at Colby in Thomas County. There he put in three years of strenuous missionary work, having charge of twenty-three missions in six different counties. In 1892 he became pastor of the Catholic Church at Beloit, Kansas, remaining one year, then was rector of the church at Herndon, and for fourteen years had the administration of the church at Odin. Following that was several months at Garden City, and one year at Kinsley, and in 1912 he became rector of St. Martin's Church of Piqua.

St. Martin's Parish was established in 1886. Its founder was Father Buechler. It is a large parish, extending north of Piqua six miles, south the same distance, and easterly it includes the Owl Creek and Yates Center Missions, under Father Heimann, and to the west it extends four miles. The parish has seventy families at Piqua, thirty families at Owl Creek and twenty families at Yates Center.

Recently fifteen acres of land were donated to the parish by Herman Wille whose place adjoins Piqua on the southwest. An extensive program of building on the new site has been undertaken, including a new rectory, a new school, a new Sisters' residence, parish hall and church. All these buildings will be successively undertaken; the rectory will be finished in May of 1917. During Father Heimann's career in the priesthood and under his direction twelve ecclesiastical buildings were erected, exclusive of those proposed at Piqua.

Father Heimann is a member of the Knights of Columbus, the Catholic Mutual Benefit Association, the Catholic Federation and the "Central-Verein."

NORMAN L. HAY. When a group of really progressive, enterprising and public-spirited men get in control of a local government, it matters little what special form of charter or municipal organization they operate under, they do things and an entire community feels an uplift. This is well illustrated in the case of the City of Sedan, where Norman L. Hay has been mayor since 1912, and in close co-operation with the city council dominated by similar ideas as to the public good, he has brought about results which justify unusual pride in the part of Sedan in its civic and municipal efficiency.

Mr. Hay had served on the city council three years before he was elected mayor. When he took charge of the city government there was a municipal debt of $8,000. Under the old regime this debt was almost stationary, but during the first two years of the Hay administration, with the aid of the council, old debts to the extent of $3,500 were paid, expenses were kept rigidly within the budget of allowances, no new debts were contracted, and the city now has the pleasant anticipation of retiring all its bonds, except the waterworks bonds, in April, 1917.

At the same time the municipal administration has been exceedingly progressive. An electric lighting system was installed, and a franchise was granted to the Sedan Electric Light Company, and an unusual feature of this grant is that the city is paid 1 per cent of the gross receipts. The old custom was to grant franchises without any return to the city, and the action of Sedan is an illustration of the experience that franchises have real value. During the present administration a stone crusher was bought by the city government, and it has been possible to deliver crushed stone on the streets for paving and

other purposes at 95 cents a ton. New equipment has been bought for the fire department, including a modern motor truck, and the standards of efficiency have been raised.

The weak spot in municipal government too often has been the accounting system. No one, not even the city officials, have had a real knowledge of where the money comes from, how it is paid out, or the proportion between income and expenditures. Perhaps the most notable accomplishment of Mayor Hay's administration has been the installation of a complete financial accounting system. By this system the revenues of the city are so classified, the bonded and the current debts are so discriminated, and the financial condition of every department of the city government is so concisely stated, that any citizen can tell almost at a glance the general fiscal condition. These financial reports of the city are a model, and they would go further than any other one thing toward the introduction of real business methods into the management of a municipality.

Norman L. Hay, apart from his official relation with Sedan is best known as a successful oil producer. He was born at Tracy, LaPorte, Indiana, January 6, 1861. His ancestors were Scotch people who came to New York in colonial times. His grandfather, James Hay, was born in New York in 1785 and died in Schoharie County of the same state in 1865. His life was spent as a farmer.

Samuel S. Hay, father of Mayor Hay, was born in Schoharie County, New York, in 1829, and died at LaPorte, Indiana, in 1910. He was reared and married in his native county, and soon after his marriage removed to LaPorte County, Indiana. He was one of the early settlers there, developed a farm from the wilderness, and the prosperity that rewarded his strenuous efforts enabled him eventually to retire into the City of LaPorte, where he spent his last days. When he began voting he supported the whig ticket, later became a republican, and was very much interested in local affairs, serving as township trustee of Union Township in Laporte County. He was one of the founders of the Methodist Protestant Church at Tracy, Indiana, and served as trustee of that organization. Samuel S. Hay married Emma J. Richtmeyer, who was born in New York State in 1835, and died in LaPorte, Indiana, in August, 1913. They had two children. The older is Eva E., wife of August Kregle, and as retired farmers they now make their home in LaPorte.

Norman L. Hay grew up on a farm, attended the public schools of LaPorte County, spent two years in Valparaiso University, and in 1881 entered upon a career as a teacher. He was long identified with educational work and put in fifty-five months of teaching in Laporte County.

On leaving Indiana Mr. Hay went to Minneapolis, Minnesota, and became connected with the S. H. Hall & Company, potato dealers. This company had four plants for the making of potato flour. Mr. Hay was employed as a traveling salesman and placed large quantities of this flour all over the East, in Philadelphia, Baltimore and other cities.

Coming to Sedan, Kansas, in 1903, Mr. Hay began buying oil properties for Mr. S. H. Hall, Ernest F. Smith and E. C. Best of Minneapolis. This brought him into intimate touch with the oil industry of Southern Kansas, and in 1906 he took up independent production. His scope of efforts has been largely in Chautauqua County and he now has interests in eighty-one oil wells. He bought a home on Douglas Street, and in 1912 extensively remodeled it so that it is perfectly adapted both for summer and winter residence.

In matters of politics Mr. Hay has exercised an independent choice among the candidates and policies which have corresponded to his convictions. He is a member of the Modern Woodmen of America at Sedan, and takes a very active part in the Baptist Church, being a trustee of the church and sings his part in the choir.

In 1885 at Waupaca, Wisconsin, Mr. Hay married Miss Grace E. Hall, daughter of Henry H. and Henrietta (Woodard) Hall, both of whom are now deceased. Her father died at the venerable age of ninety-six years, at Waupaca, Wisconsin. He spent most of his active life as a farmer. Mr. and Mrs. Hay have two children. Elvie Mae died at the age of eight months. Cressy J., who was born August 23, 1888, and still makes her home with her parents at Sedan, is a graduate in the expression department of Ottawa University, at Ottawa, Kansas, and also studied expression in Curry's School of Expression at Boston, Massachusetts. She is a very cultured young woman.

CHARLES P. BEEBE. Among the well known newspaper men of Wilson County, one who has had broad experience in his vocation is Charles P. Beebe, who during the past three years has been managing editor of the Neodesha Daily Sun. Mr. Beebe learned the newspaper business at the case, and has worked his way up through the various departments of the business so that he has a thorough knowledge of all its details. Under his editorial management this publication has become one of the best daily papers of Wilson County and wields a wide influence all over this section.

Mr. Beebe was born March 31, 1879, in the City of Salina, Kansas, and is a son of David and Mary Baldi (Moore) Beebe. He comes of colonial stock, the founder of the family having come from England to New York prior to the Revolution and is a grandson of Ambrose Beebe, a native of the Empire State, who died in Cleveland, Ohio. David Beebe, the father of Charles P. Beebe, was born in 1832, at Norwalk, Ohio, and was there reared and educated. At the outbreak of the Civil war he enlisted in a Nebraska regiment of volunteer infantry, with which he fought during the entire period of the struggle, and not long after the close thereof, in 1867, located as a pioneer in Saline County, Kansas. The homestead upon which he located is now included in the south part of the City of Salina, and when that city was established he took up his residence there. In 1875 he established the first daily newspaper, The Farmers Advocate, which he conducted for some years, but finally retired from active life and died at Salina, April 12, 1890. Mr. Beebe was a republican in politics and very active in civic affairs. He served as county clerk for a period of sixteen years, and also held various other offices, including those of city clerk and township trustee. He was a faithful member of the Methodist Episcopal Church. Mr. Beebe married Mary Baldi Moore, who was born in 1848, in Rockcastle County, Kentucky, and died December 9, 1914, at Neodesha, Kansas, and three children were born to this union: Charles P.; Mamie, who is the wife of G. H. Wiley, a clerk for the St. Louis and San Francisco Railway at Kansas City, Missouri; and Ray, a traveling salesman who died at Neodesha in 1915 and is buried at Salina.

Charles P. Beebe attended the public schools of Salina, Kansas, but is practically self-educated, for at the age of eleven years he left school and began to serve his apprenticeship to the printing business in the office of the Salina Sun, of which W. H. Johnson was editor and proprietor. Subsequently he became a reporter on the staff of the Salina Union, of which N. H. Gaines was the proprietor, and later was made city editor of that paper. He held a like position with the Salina Republican, but in 1904 went to Monett, Missouri, where he purchased the Monett Star, a paper with which he was connected for ten years. In 1914, at the solicitation of C. E. Cowdery, proprietor, he came to Neodesha to accept the position of managing editor of the Neodesha Daily Sun, which printed its first issue September 21, 1898. The Daily Derrick was the first daily paper published at Neodesha. On May 14, 1896, that paper was started with Robert Akin and Mrs. Lizzie Jones as the publishers. Mr. Akin, a very bright young man, a good printer and a hard worker, had for a number of years been foreman of the Neodesha Register, published by J. Kansas Morgan, who about that time was also publishing the Railroad Register, a paper for railroad men. This he moved to Topeka about 1893 or 1894 and went to that city himself, leaving Mr. Akin to conduct the Register. The railroad paper eventually failed and Mr. Morgan came back, but, while Mr. Akin was retained on the Register he had had a taste of the "front" work on a paper, and decided to start a job printing office. About that time the oil fields in the vicinity of Neodesha commenced to boom and Mr. Akin and Mrs. Jones started the Daily Derrick, as above noted. It was a four-column folio, just the size of the High School Booster, with patent insides, and for a time flourished. Then the Register started a daily and a warm fight was started between the two which continued until some time during the summer of 1898, when Mr. Akin sold his subscription list, about 150 subscribers, to the Wilson County Sun for $12. The plant was moved to Cherryvale. The Sun continued to publish the Derrick the same size, but with home print, until September 21, 1898, when it was changed to the Neodesha Daily Sun and enlarged to a five-column folio, with patent insides. Soon after the Daily Sun was founded, at the solicitation of Mr. Morgan and by agreement, both daily editions of the Sun and Register were discontinued. For about two years Neodesha was without a daily paper, and then, in November, 1900, the Daily Sun and Daily Register started simultaneously and the Sun has not missed an issue since. On November 10, 1905, at the suggestion of some of the business men that two dailies and two weeklies were too many, Paul Wiley then being publisher of the Register, the Daily Register and Weekly Sun were discontinued. C. E. Cowdery, continued with the Sun, during both its daily and weekly existence from April, 1894, until his death on February 15, 1917, and the paper is now being published by his estate, with Mr. Beebe as editor and manager.

Mr. Beebe is one of the skilled men of his craft. He is presenting the readers of the paper with a neat, well-printed and well-edited publication, clean and reliable, and accurate and conservative in the handling of news. Its added subscription list of recent years makes it a valuable advertising medium, and it is receiving the support of the most representative people of the field in which it operates. As a live and progressive citizen Mr. Beebe takes part in civic matters and at the present time is the hardworking and energetic secretary of the Neodesha Commercial Club. He is a republican, belongs to the Christian Church, and is a member of Monett Lodge of Elks. He is unmarried.

WALTER L. PAYNE, a native son of Kansas, has been closely identified with a number of its business and public activities for a number of years, and is vice-president of the Pioneer State Bank of Burlingame. The Payne family have had a part in the making of Kansas for fully sixty years.

It was Mr. Payne's grandparents, Lorenzo Dow and Mary Ann (Wildman) Payne, who were the pioneers of the family in Kansas. They located at Trading Post in Miami County, where Lorenzo D., who was a physician by profession, practiced for two years until the border ruffians drove him across the line into Douglas County. In that county he continued his practice until his death in 1875. Doctor Payne and family had come to Kansas overland in the usual custom of the early settlers, and made the journey in a prairie schooner. He was a man of splendid influence as well as a successful physician and did much to build up his community. It was the exposure incident to a hard and continuous practice in a new country, involving long and arduous riding and driving from place to place, that eventually brought about his death.

This branch of the Payne family is descended from one of five brothers who came from England to America in the early days. Merton Anson Payne, father of the Burlingame banker, was born December 25, 1837, in the State of Ohio. He was educated in common schools and had the advantages of an academy at Wolcott, Indiana. For several years he was associated with his uncle in a bank in Indiana, and in 1859 followed his parents to Kansas. He made the journey by way of railroad as far as Kansas City, thence took a steamboat up the Missouri River to Leavenworth, and from there by stage to Lawrence. His destination was the settlement called Clinton, ten miles southwest of Lawrence. Merton A. Payne had hardly become established in Kansas before the war broke out. He enlisted in the Fourteenth Kansas Infantry, served as a sergeant, and when that regiment was reorganized he became first lieutenant of the Fourth Arkansas Volunteer Infantry. He was in many of the hard fought campaigns in the Trans-Mississippi region, and continued with the army until discharged in 1864. Returning to Clinton, Kansas, he was married in October, 1865, to Catherine McCoach. She was a daughter of John and Mary (Hazeltino) McCoach, both of whom were born in County Donegal in Northern Ireland. John McCoach when nine years of age was a stowaway on a sailing vessel and landed in Philadelphia. By hard work he saved enough money to bring over his three sisters. He became a prominent coal merchant in Philadelphia, but eventually on account of the ill health of some of his family moved to Armstrong County, Pennsylvania, and in 1857 came overland and took up a claim southwest of Lawrence, Kansas. Two years later he brought his family to the west and he was identified with the State of Kansas the rest of his years. John McCoach died in 1896, and his wife in 1876. There were eight children in the McCoach family. One daughter, Mary, is now deceased. George McCoach was a Union soldier in a regiment of Illinois Infantry, was in the famous march to the sea, spent eleven months in Andersonville prison and afterwards died in Ohio from wounds he had received while attempting an escape from that notorious stockade prison. While attempting his escape he was shot in the neck by buckshot and was also bitten by hounds. The son, John McCoach, was a member of the First Kansas Volunteers and served throughout the entire war, participating in Wilson Creek as his first battle, held the rank of second

lieutenant and is now living in Colorado Springs. James McCoach at the age of seventeen went to Leavenworth and in 1865 started across the plains with a freight train and was never afterwards heard of. William McCoach at the age of fifteen crossed the plains and located in Helena, Montana. Thomas McCoach is now living in Colorado.

After his marriage Merton A. Payne with his father, Doctor Payne, bought a building and store that had been erected by John Beam in 1856. This was a landmark in that section of Kansas, and stood until it was burned in 1904. Its sills had been hewed with a hand ax, and the floor was of 12 by 2 inch planking. From that time forward until his death on January 19, 1883, Merton Anson Payne was an active and successful merchant. He was a republican, though never in any sense a politician. He was considered one of the leading men of his community, lived an upright and temperate life, and was a member of the Masons and Odd Fellows. He and his wife were active Methodists, and his widow has always maintained a very close association with church affairs. Mrs. Payne now lives on the old homestead at Clinton, Kansas.

Walter L. Payne, who was born on the home farm in Douglas County, Kansas, April 13, 1867, is the oldest of three brothers. His brother, Edgar A., is connected with the Standard Oil Company at Lawrence. Rolla Merton, the youngest, died in 1873.

A substantial education trained Walter L. Payne for his active business career. He attended the public schools of Clinton and also Baker University. For two years he was a cowboy in Meade County, and then returned to Clinton and took up a career as a general merchant. He successfully managed the store there until 1896, and during that time from 1890 to 1895 was postmaster.

On May 24, 1894, Mr. Payne married Miss Vienna C. Chilcott. Mrs. Payne was born in Iowa, was brought to Kansas and lived first in Jefferson County and then in Douglas County on a farm. She was liberally educated, having studied in Baker University and having pursued post-graduate work in Kansas University. For four years before her marriage she taught school. After their marriage Mr. and Mrs. Payne lived on a farm in Douglas County and his younger brother was on the homestead at the time. Mr. and Mrs. Payne are the parents of two children: Roland Dow, who is assistant attorney general to S. M. Brewster at Topeka; and LaVergne, who is assistant cashier in the Pioneer State Bank at Burlingame.

In 1896 Mr. Payne removed to Lawrence, where he was a prosperous clothing merchant until 1900. In that year he was appointed deputy county clerk, an office he filled until January, 1903. Then for four years he was assistant state treasurer under T. T. Kelly, and for six years filled a similar appointment under the late Mark Tulley. Thus, for ten years Mr. Payne came into close touch with the state official life at Topeka, and is one of the most widely known men in Kansas.

In January, 1913, he came to Burlingame and has since given most of his time and attention to his duties as vice president of the Pioneer Bank. In 1912 he was republican candidate for the office of state treasurer, having been defeated by a very narrow margin. In 1916 he again became a candidate for this office, was elected November 7, 1916, and is now serving as treasurer of Kansas. Mr. Payne is one of the men of leadership and influence in his home city, and since 1915 has been president of the city council and for two years in 1914-15 was president of the Commercial Club. He is a thirty-second degree Scottish Rite Mason, being a member of Consistory No. 1 at Topeka, has been prominent in Scottish Rite work for the past ten years, and belongs to the Royal Arch Chapter at Burlingame, to the Knights of Pythias, the Modern Woodmen of America, the Fraternal Aid Union and the Knights and Ladies of Security.

Both Mr. and Mrs. Payne have a deep and active interest in the First Presbyterian Church at Burlingame, in which Mr. Payne is an elder. Mrs. Payne gives much of her time to church affairs, is a member of the Ladies Guild, and also belongs to the Saturday Afternoon Club and other ladies' organizations in that city. While little is known of the fact, Mrs. Payne has dispensed a broad charity for a number of years, and during her residence in Topeka was a working member in several charitable organizations.

ARMOUR & CO. In the year 1870 Plankinton and Armour erected their first packing house in Kansas

products to every habitable portion of the globe. Its splendid plant represents a lavish expenditure of effort, time and money. Cleanliness and sanitation prevail; efficiency is multiplied; the health, welfare and safety of employes is protected. The aim of Armour & Co. in producing food products is toward perfection.

FRED ACKARMAN lost no time after graduating from the high school at Sedan with the class of 1902 before finding his real and permanent vocation in life. For the past thirty-five years an old and widely patronized hardware store at Sedan has been conducted under the Ackarman name, and on leaving high school Fred Ackarman entered the store to give his father his active assistance and in 1903, when his father retired from business, the son was thoroughly competent to handle the business and maintain the prestige of the establishment over Chautauqua County.

Born at Sedan, September 1, 1882, Fred Ackarman is a son of Mr. E. C. Ackarman, who is still living at Sedan, now retired. E. C. Ackarman was born at Rome City, Indiana, August 28, 1847. The

PLANT OF ARMOUR & CO., PACKERS, KANSAS CITY, KANSAS

City, Kansas. It was in charge of Simeon B. Armour. In October, 1884, the Armours purchased the interests of Plankinton and the firm was changed to Armour Packing Company.

From this small plant, with its crude manner of handling meat products and where slaughtering was only done in the winter time on account of no refrigeration and a mere handful of men were employed, it has grown under the guiding hand of S. B. Armour from its beginning until 1889, under Kirkland B. Armour, eldest son of A. W. Armour, from 1899 to 1901, and from that date in charge of Charles W. Armour, who is its present head, until today this organization employs 4,000 men, with an average yearly pay roll of $2,750,000, and an average yearly expenditure for livestock of $40,550,000.

In January, 1911, the style of this firm was changed to Armour & Co., and it became part of the great house of Armour & Co. with its fifteen meat-packing plants located in the United States. It sends food

family history of the Ackarmans in America largely centers around that old Indiana town. Fred Ackarman's great-grandfather, Andrew Ackarman, came from Germany and was one of the first settlers in the vicinity of Rome, Indiana. He followed his trade as tanner there until his death. The grandfather, whose name was also Andrew Ackarman, was born near Rome, Indiana, in 1812, and died there in 1890. His life was spent as a farmer. He was active in the Masonic fraternity and the Methodist Church. He married Ruth Carr, who was born in Kentucky, in 1820, and died on the old homestead near Rome in 1894. The record of their children is as follows: Hiram, who died on a farm near Rome, Indiana, in 1876; E. C. Ackarman; Andrew J., who was also a farmer and died near Rome in 1908; Henry, who is a doctor and resides at Evansville, Indiana; Hugh, a farmer, who died near Rome, Indiana, in 1896; Annie, deceased, whose husband, Mr. Cunningham is a traveling salesman living in New York State; Mary, who died in Kansas City, Missouri, married Flint DeWeese, a practicing attorney at Kansas City.

Mr. E. C. Ackarman was reared on the old Indiana farm, but in 1868, at the age of twenty-one, left home and moved to Butler in Bates County, Missouri, and in 1869 came across the Kansas line to Crawford County. In 1871 he located in Howard County, was a farmer there, and first engaged in the mercantile business by opening a stock of hardware at Moline. In 1876 he removed to Sedan, and in 1883 established the hardware business which is now owned and conducted by his son, Fred. This store is situated on Lot 2, Block 15, on Main Street. It is a store where everything in the hardware and general implement line may be found, and it is also a local agency for several of the best makes of automobiles. As a business that has been in successful operation over thirty years its trade is naturally widely extended, and there are regular patrons of the store who reside at least twenty-five miles away from Sedan. Mr. E. C. Ackarman has always been a stanch advocate of the republican party and principles. He has been again and again entrusted with local offices, having served as township trustee of Center Township, township treasurer of Sedan Township, was county commissioner of Chautauqua County three years, from 1886 to 1889, and was mayor of Sedan two terms. His church is the Universalist. Mr. E. C. Ackarman married Laura Thornburg. She was born in Missouri in 1851 and died in Sedan, Kansas, in 1902. Ethel, the oldest of their children, died when three years of age. Carl, the second, is a successful lawyer at Sedan and is now county attorney of Chautauqua County. The third in age is Fred Ackarman. Paul is a worker in the oil fields and lives at Chautauqua. Ruth, the youngest, died at the age of eight years.

Fred Ackarman grew up in his native town, graduated from the high school in 1902, and immediately entered his father's store. He is a young business man who can be counted upon to lend his aid to every public enterprise. He has served as clerk of Sedan Township, is a republican, a member of the Christian Church and a deacon in the same, and is affiliated with Camp No. 919 of the Modern Woodmen of America and Camp No. 40 of the Woodmen of the World at Sedan. He owns a comfortable home in the northwest part of town.

In 1903, at Sedan, he married Miss Inez Park, daughter of Sam and Ida (Gilman) Park. Her parents both reside at Sedan, and her father is in the produce and feed business. Two daughters have been born to Mr. and Mrs. Ackarman: Beth, born March 9, 1911, and Mona, born April 30, 1915.

HON. G. K. SIPPLE. During 1910 the retired colony of Neodesha was augmented by the arrival of G. K. Sipple, whose activities have been centered in Wilson County since the year 1881, and whose career is expressive of the possibilities of country life when directed by a well-trained mind, an earnest purpose and a keen appreciation of its benefits and prerogatives. Mr. Sipple is a Union veteran of the Civil war, and a citizen who has contributed to his community's welfare. That his worth has been appreciated is evidenced by the positions of public trust which he has filled, his public service culminating in his election as a representative to the Kansas Legislature.

G. K. Sipple was born in Grant County, Kentucky, March 12, 1844, and is a son of Rev. W. H. and Nancy (Ashcraft) Sipple. The original member of the family in this country was Caleb Sipple, who took part in the settlement of Delaware with Lord Delaware's party. John Sipple, the grandfather of G. K. Sipple, was born in 1780, in Delaware, where as a young man he engaged in schoolteaching, and subsequently turned his attention to farming. He went as a pioneer farmer to Harrison County, Kentucky, and in 1862 removed to Tuscola, Illinois, where his death occurred two years later.

Rev. W. H. Sipple was born in 1813, in Harrison County, Kentucky, where he was reared and educated, and as a young man joined the ministry of the Methodist Episcopal Church, in which he labored for many years as a circuit-rider. He was married in Grant County, Kentucky, and in 1857 removed to Tuscola, Douglas County, Illinois, where he became one of the prominent men of his community, serving as superintendent of public instruction for two years and as county judge for several terms. He was a stanch democrat in politics and a member of the Masonic fraternity. In 1868 he removed to near Fulton, Calloway County, Missouri, retired from active life, and there died August 6, 1873. Reverend Sipple married Nancy Ashcraft, who was born at Williamstown, Kentucky, in 1815, and died in Grant County, Kentucky, August 26, 1855, and they were the parents of the following children: Amelia Elizabeth, deceased, who was the wife of the late William Beverly, who was a farmer of Grant County, Kentucky, where both passed away; Martha Ann, who died in 1914, near Williamstown, Kentucky, as the widow of the late W. A. Ashcraft, a farmer of Grant County; Caleb Walker, who died at the age of thirteen years; William H., who was a merchant of Neodesha, Kansas, until October, 1893, since which time no record has been kept of his movements; John I., who is a retired merchant of Parsons, Kansas; G. K.; Mary Beverly, who died at the age of six years; Sarah Jane, who is the widow of Reverend Barnett, late of the St. Louis Conference of the Methodist Episcopal Church, and resides at Gillam, Saline County, Missouri; and Lewis Harper, who is engaged in farming in the vicinity of Fayette, Missouri.

G. K. Sipple was educated in the public schools of Grant County, Kentucky, and Tuscola, Illinois, and left school and home at the age of seventeen years to become a soldier of the Union. He enlisted in 1861, in Company D, Twenty-first Regiment, Illinois Volunteer Infantry, was mustered out at San Antonio, Texas, in 1865, and received his honorable discharge at Springfield, Illinois. During his long period of service Mr. Sipple participated in numerous hard-fought engagements, the Twenty-first always being in the thick of the fight. Among his more important battles were Shiloh, Perryville, Stone River, Chickamauga and Missionary Ridge, following which he was with the troops of General Sherman on the famous campaign from Dalton, Georgia, to Atlanta, and he then took part in the bloody battles of Franklin and Nashville, Tennessee. He at all times bore himself bravely and courageously and established a record as a faithful soldier, deserving of the honor of wearing his country's uniform.

When his military service was completed, Mr. Sipple returned to Douglas County, Illinois, and engaged in farming, but in the spring of 1872 came to Labette County, Kansas, and took up a claim of 160 acres, which he deeded. He remained on that property until 1881, when he came to Wilson County, and here followed farming and stockraising successfully until 1910, when he retired from active life and moved to Neodesha, where he has a comfortable home at No.

207 South Fifth Avenue. He is still the owner of 120 acres of good land four miles east of Neodesha. Mr. Sipple made a success of his agricultural operations through industry and good management and the period of rest which he is now taking has been fairly and deservedly earned.

Mr. Sipple is a democrat. He has been prominent in public affairs for a number of years, and while residing in Labette County served as township trustee of Liberty Township. In Neodesha Township he acted as township treasurer, and in 1907 was sent as the representative of his district to the Kansas Legislature, in which he served his constituents faithfully and well. In that body he was a member of the committee on judiciary; introduced and had passed a bill compelling traveling druggists to pay an annual license of $50; and another to provide for the examination of veterinary surgeons before allowing them to practice, and had a hand in much legislation affecting the interests of his community and its people. His record in the legislative body was an excellent one. Mr. Sipple is a member of the Methodist Episcopal Church, in which he is steward and class leader. He is a popular comrade of Neodesha Post, Grand Army of the Republic.

On January 3, 1871, at Tuscola, Illinois, Mr. Sipple was married to Miss Molly Brady, daughter of the late Henry and Carrie Brady, farming people. To this union there were born four children: Ida B., who is the wife of W. A. Rankin, a farmer of the vicinity of Neodesha; Elmer W., who died at the age of three years; Hulbert L., who is identified with the Prudential Life Insurance Company, at Portland, Oregon; and Clarence E., who is an employe of a railroad and resides in Oakland, California.

·RALPH RANDOLPH HIBBEN. Parsons is the home and headquarters of a number of men who have given many years of faithful service to the Missouri, Kansas & Texas Railway Company. One of these is Ralph Randolph Hibben, Assistant Fuel Agent for this road, and for, almost a quarter of a century has been continuously identified with the Coal Department of this company. He is also a member of the Board of Directors of the International Railway Fuel Association of America. He is of English, Irish stock originally, his ancestors on his mother's side coming to America with William Penn, and settled in Pennsylvania. His ancestors on his father's side were from Ireland and they also settled in Pennsylvania, prior to the Revolutionary war.

Mr. Hibben is a native of Kansas and son of a distinguished pioneer physician, Dr. W. W. Hibben. Doctor Hibben settled in Emporia October 31, 1867, and was engaged in the practice of medicine from that time until his death, October, 1883. In addition to his regular practice, he was associated with one Doctor Jacobs in the drug business. He was a member of the City Council for two terms and held the office of coroner for one term. He was also examining surgeon for Board of Pensions at Emporia for nine years and was the president of this board from its incipiency to his death. He was a member of the County and State Medical societies, was also member of Lodge No. 12, Ancient Free and Accepted Masons, and of Chapter No. 12, Royal Arch Masons, and was a charter member of the Emporia Commandery No. 8, Knights Templar.

Doctor Hibben was born in Uniontown, Fayette County, Pennsylvania, April 7, 1825, moved to James-town, Green County, Ohio, with his parents in 1832, remaining there until he moved to Kansas. He received his medical education in the Ohio Medical College, and in the Cincinnati College of Medicine and Surgery, from which he was graduated in 1854. He commenced to practice in Jamestown, Green County, Ohio, but after a short time removed to Paintersville, and one year later to Lumberton, Clinton County, Ohio. He was one of the first medical practitioners at Emporia, and practiced there with much success until his death in 1883. For a number of years he was surgeon for the Atchison, Topeka & Santa Fe Railway Company. He was an old line republican, having been identified with that party from its origin. He was a member of the Methodist Episcopal Church.

Doctor Hibben was married in Paintersville, Ohio, February 9, 1854, to Euphemia A. Watson, a native of Quakertown, Bucks County, Pennsylvania, she being born in Quakertown in the year 1832, and died in Los Angeles, California, in the year 1912. Their children were J. H., who is superintendent of the Coal Department of the Missouri, Kansas & Texas Railway, at Parsons; Charles H., connected with the Hooker Pipe Company, at Los Angeles, California; George, a farmer living at Los Angeles; William, twin brother of George, who is connected with the Wells Fargo & Company Express, at Kansas City, Missouri; Mayme, wife of G. Gillelan, a retired loan and real estate dealer, living at Los Angeles; Ralph R.; and Jennie, wife of Charles E. Jarvis, who is secretary to the Board of Directors of the First Church of Christ Scientists, Boston, Massachusetts.

Ralph Randolph Hibben was born at Emporia, Kansas, October 28, 1872, and lived in that city during his youth. He attended the public schools, and nearly completed his senior year in the high school. On leaving high school in 1890, he began working for the Wells Fargo & Company Express, and was there employed until April, 1892. On June 1, 1892, Mr. Hibben entered the service of the Missouri, Kansas & Texas Railway Company in the Fuel Department. His first position was that of fuel foreman, and he has been steadily at work in that department ever since, and is now assistant fuel agent for this great corporation with offices in the general headquarters at Parsons.

Mr. Hibben is independent in politics and a member of the Christian Science Church. He belongs to the Parsons Commercial Club, and fraternally is affiliated with Parsons Lodge No. 117, Ancient Free and Accepted Masons, and Parsons Chapter No. 39, Royal Arch Masons and Coeur De Leon Commandery No. 17, Knights Templar at Parsons.

Mr. Hibben owns an attractive residence at No. 1404 Broadway. On March 4, 1912, at Parsons, he married Miss Harriett Kiser, daughter of J. Q. Kiser, now deceased, who was a farmer and stock raiser near Emporia.

DENTON & LIMBOCKER. More of the business of the town of South Mound in Neosho County, is handled through the firm of Denton & Limbocker than any other one commercial organization. They are grain dealers, merchants, farmers, bankers, and both partners also have an important part in public affairs, Mr. Denton being postmaster of South Mound, while Mr. Limbocker is a county commissioner.

John F. Denton was born in Pulaski County, Missouri, September 9, 1878. His ancestors were Scotch-Irish people who were early settlers in Kentucky.

Samuel Holmes
Elizabeth Holmes

His grandfather, Thomas Denton, was born in Kentucky, moved into Missouri, and died in Hancock County of that state in 1896.

F. M. Denton, father of John F., was born in Kentucky, in 1851, but was reared and married in Pulaski County, Missouri. After farming for a few years he engaged in merchandising at Hancock in Pulaski County, and in June, 1889, came to Kansas. After a month at St. Paul he removed to South Mound, and there took up merchandising and the grain business, which he followed until his death, in May, 1915. He was always a loyal democrat, and was an active supporter of the Methodist Episcopal Church, serving as trustee of the church at South Mound. Fraternally he was affiliated with the Masonic Order and the Independent Order of Odd Fellows. F. M. Denton married Mollie J. Decker, who was born in Illinois, in 1853, and is now living at South Mound. Their children were: C. A. Denton, who was a boilermaker at Parsons, Kansas; John F.; Mollie, wife of F. H. Hoover, a farmer at South Mound; Hattie V., wife of Mr. Glenn Limbocker, partner of John F. Denton; E. E. Denton, who is a railroad engineer with the Missouri, Kansas & Texas Railway, living at Parsons; the sixth child, a daughter, died in infancy; A. A. Denton is a boilermaker at Springfield, Missouri; and Ethel E., wife of Roy E. Burt, a minister of the Methodist Episcopal Church, living at Lawrence, Kansas.

John F. Denton received his early training in the public schools of South Mound, and afterward took a course in the business college at Sedalia, Missouri. While he has had a most successful career, he is one of those men who do well in various occupations. He was a farmer for three years at South Mound, and then for eight years was a railroad man, being employed in the general offices and shops at Springfield, Missouri. Returning to South Mound, he engaged in the mercantile business, and the firm of Denton & Limbocker now have an immense trade, extending all over the country around South Mound. They also conduct a grain elevator, this elevator being situated on the Missouri, Kansas & Texas tracks, while the store is on Main Street. Mr. Denton also has a good residence on Main Street. The firm owns and uses as an adjunct to their business a farm of 110 acres in South Mound.

Mr. Denton was reared a democrat, and has always been active in that party. In April, 1915, he was appointed by President Wilson as postmaster at South Mound. At one time he served a term as township treasurer. He is a member and trustee of the Methodist Episcopal Church, is affiliated with Lodge No. 53, Independent Order of Odd Fellows, at Osage Mission, with Parsons Lodge of Masons, with South Mound Camp No. 8036, Modern Woodmen of America. Much of his time Mr. Denton gives to his office as president of the South Mound State Bank. In 1903 at South Mound he married Miss Lettie P. Limbocker, a sister of his business partner. Her parents, J. G. and Jennie (McKee) Limbocker, reside at South Mound, her father being a farmer.

Glenn Limbocker, of the firm of Denton & Limbocker, and present county commissioner of Neosho County, was born at South Mound, Kansas, on a farm, September 15, 1877. His ancestors came from Germany, the family having lived in America for several generations. His father, Joseph Gilbert Limbocker, who lives on a farm 2½ miles east of South Mound, was born in Iowa in 1854, spent the first sixteen years of his life there, and about 1870

came to Neosho County, Kansas, and established his home within half a mile of the farm where he now resides. He has been a successful man and has a highly-improved place of eighty acres. In politics he is a republican, and has served two terms as township trustee in Neosho County. His church is the Methodist. He married Jennie McKee, who was born in Indiana in 1852. The oldest of their children is Mr. Glenn Limbocker. Earl, who died in 1904, at Van Buren, Arkansas, had made a balloon ascension and was drowned after his descent. Lettie Pearl has been mentioned above as the wife of John F. Denton. Lettie's twin sister died in infancy.

Glenn Limbocker acquired an education in the common schools of South Mound and lived on his father's farm until the age of twenty-two. After that he was farming for himself until 1907, and then moved to South Mound and was a general merchant for two years, at the end of which time the present firm of Denton & Limbocker was established. Mr. Limbocker owns a good residence on Main Street and is a stockholder in the South Mound State Bank.

While his partner is a loyal democrat, Mr. Limbocker is equally firm in his allegiance to the republican organization. In 1914 he was elected to the office of county commissioner, and has filled that office since January, 1915, his term expiring December 31, 1918. Some years ago he was elected constable and served two years, and he was the republican postmaster of South Mound under President Roosevelt and President Taft, serving for eight years. He is a member and steward in the Methodist Episcopal Church.

December 7, 1899, at South Mound, he married Miss Hattie D. Denton, sister of his business partner, John F. Denton. Three children were born to their marriage: A son that died in infancy; Paul L., born September 15, 1902; and Hazel C., born April 19, 1905.

SAMUEL HOLMES has shown an ability amounting to genius for the successful handling of business affairs, especially landed transactions, and during his long residence in Kansas has accumulated some of the finest sections of farming land in Greenwood and surrounding counties. Mr. Holmes learned the value of industry when a boy, also the principles of straightforward integrity, and it may be said that in consequence he has always been a successful man. He is now eighty-three years of age and lives practically retired at Eureka. One of the connections he still retains is as vice president of the Home National Bank. Mr. Holmes is an honored veteran of the Civil war, in which he fought on the Union side.

He was born in Carroll County, Ohio, December 8, 1834, and lived on his father's farm there until 1853. In the meantime he attended the rural schools. Most of the schools at that time were supported on the subscription plan, and their advantages were correspondingly meager. In the spring of 1853 he moved out to Wayne County, Illinois, where his father followed him in the fall of the same year. Mr. Holmes laid the foundation of his success as a farmer in Illinois, and from that state brought considerable capital as well as experience to Kansas in the spring of 1870. Locating in Greenwood County, he pre-empted a claim and paid $1.25 per acre. This land was in the Osage reservation near Climax. On his quarter section there he lived until 1886, and in the meantime invested his surplus capital in various other quarter sections. He still owns the old homestead, but for the past thirty years has lived in Eureka. His individual ownership now includes 182 acres. But in the meantime he has given away 1,040 acres to his children. Each of his seven children received 160 acres except his daughter Ida, who accepted eighty acres and the equivalent of the other eighty acres she took in bank stocks. Mr. Holmes has done a magnificent part by his children, and they are all prosperous and have done their individual share of the world's work. Mr. Holmes also owns a comfortable residence on Mulberry Street in Eureka.

The beginning of his military service came in August, 1862, when he enlisted in Company D of the Eighty-seventh Illinois Infantry. He was in active service until the close of the war. His first important campaign was the siege of Vicksburg, and during the progress of operations against that city he participated in the severely fought battle at Jackson, Mississippi. Later his regiment was mounted and participated in Banks campaign up the Red River, and from that time until the end of the war he was engaged in scouting up and down the Mississippi River. He had numerous escapes from danger, and put in nearly three years of hard fighting for the preservation of the Union.

Mr. Holmes is a democrat, and for three years held the office of county commissioner of Greenwood County. He is a past master of Twin Falls Lodge of Masons and now has membership in Fidelity Lodge No. 106 Ancient Free and Accepted Masons.

Mr. Holmes comes of long lived and rugged stock, and both he and his ancestors have shown great vitality. The family record is noteworthy in several ways. Mr. Holmes was one of the eighteen children borne by his mother, while his father had fully twenty-six children by his three marriages.

The Holmes ancestors came from Scotland and were early settlers in Westmoreland County, Pennsylvania. Mr. Holmes' great-grandfather was a soldier in the Revolutionary war. His name was Joel Holmes, and he was the founder of the family on this side of the Atlantic. The grandfather was John Holmes, who was born in Pennsylvania, took part as a soldier in the War of 1812, developed a pioneer farm in the wilds of Ohio and died in Seneca County of that state. Thus there has been members of this family participants in every great war in which this country has engaged.

William Holmes, father of Samuel, was born at Tuscarora, Pennsylvania, in 1801. He was reared and married in his native state, followed farming there, later removed to Carroll County, Ohio, a few years before Samuel was born, and developed one of the best farms in that county. He also became a man of prominence in local affairs, serving four years as auditor of Carroll County and four years as county treasurer. In 1853 he removed to Wayne County, Illinois, and afterwards retired from farming and spent the rest of his years there. His death occurred in 1887, when eighty-six years of age. He was a democrat in politics.

William Holmes' first wife was a Miss Joseph. Her four children, all now deceased, were Mary, Elizabeth, William and John. For his second wife William Holmes married Eliza Davis, the mother of Samuel Holmes. She was born at Tuscarora, Pennsylvania, in 1807, and died in Carroll County, Ohio, in 1849. A brief record of her large family of children is as follows: Isaac, who was a farmer in Putnam County, Ohio, and died in 1915; Catherine,

who died in Carroll County, Ohio; Martha, who died in Carroll County; Jonathan, who was killed when a young man in Carroll County by a tree falling upon him; James, who was a physician and went to the Civil war as a Union soldier having charge of a Government hospital, and was never heard of afterwards; Miriam, who died in Wayne County, Illinois, in the summer of 1916; Samuel, who was the seventh of his mother's children; Eliza, who died in Wayne County, Illinois, in 1914; David, a veteran of the Civil war, afterwards a farmer, and died in Wayne County in 1914; Oliver, who died in Wayne County, was a farmer, served as county clerk four years, and as county treasurer the same length of time; Martin and Daniel, both of whom died in childhood; Milton, who is a farmer in Wayne County, Illinois; Sarah, who died at Madison, Kansas, in 1908; Eleanor, who died in Wayne County in 1904; Samantha, wife of Jesse Robinson, a retired veteran of the Civil war, her home being in Edwards County, Illinois; Calvin, a retired land owner at Mulberry, Arkansas; and the eighteenth and youngest was a son that died in infancy, his mother passing away at the same time. William Holmes married for his third wife Martha Wiseman. She was born at Massillon, Ohio, and died in Wayne County, Illinois, in 1870. She became the mother of four children: Eli, who was a physician and surgeon and died at St. Louis, Missouri; Malissa, who resides at Glenwood Springs, Colorado, widow of Caney Staton, who was a farmer; George, who is a farmer on the Roaring Fork of the Rio Grande in Colorado; and Mary, wife of William Westfall, employed in the steel factory at Pueblo, Colorado.

Mr. Samuel Holmes was married in Wayne County, Illinois, in 1856, to Miss Elizabeth Porterfield, a daughter of John and Elizabeth (Thompson) Porterfield. Her father was a farmer and both parents are now deceased. Mrs. Holmes died at Eureka, February 14, 1911, about five years after they had celebrated their golden wedding anniversary. It is the privilege of few couples to travel such a long part of the journey of life together as was the lot of Mr. and Mrs. Samuel Holmes. Of their children the oldest is Elsina, wife of Marshall Moore, a farmer on Honey Creek in Greenwood County; Elmer, has been a farmer but is now living retired at Severy, Kansas; Alvin, whose home is on a farm at Climax, has completed one term of four years as county commissioner of Greenwood County and in 1916 was re-elected for another similar term; Mariett, is the wife of E. B. Powers, a farmer at Climax, Kansas; Arizona, who lives with her father in Eureka, is the widow of Harry Wyant, who was a farmer; Ida has always lived with her father and is unmarried; Murray, the youngest of the children, is cashier of the Home National Bank of Eureka. He was born in Greenwood County in April, 1882, was educated in the public schools of Eureka, graduating from high school in 1900, and also had a course in the Kansas City Business College at Kansas City, Missouri. On completing his education he became bookkeeper in the Citizens National Bank of Eureka, and in 1904, when the Home National Bank was organized he took the post of assistant cashier and bookkeeper and was advanced to cashier in 1912. He is an active democrat, is treasurer of the Board of Education of Eureka, and is one of the vigorous and progressive younger citizens of Greenwood County. Besides his home on Elm Street, he owns a 160-acre farm, given him by his father, in Greenwood County. Murray Holmes was married May 16, 1906, to Miss Jo Burris, daughter of A. P. and Lydia (McGanan) Burris, who reside on a farm at Virgil, Kansas. Mr. and Mrs. Murray Holmes have two children: Burris, born August 11, 1907, and Horace, born January 8, 1909.

OLIVER W. SPARKS. In a greater degree than is true of most towns the City of Galena is the result of the enterprise of a comparatively small group of men. Oliver W. Sparks came along and discovered zinc and lead on the Schermerhorn farm. That marked the opening chapter in the industrial history of one of the most progressive mining towns of Southeastern Kansas. After his first strike Mr. Sparks opened up other mineral deposits on the Maston land, later on the Bunco farm, and now for many years he has been continuously operating in that vicinity. Today he is the largest mine operator in the Galena district, and there is no question that Galena has become a city largely as a result of his and a few other men's operations and the results that have grown from his enterprise.

Both he and his father were among the pioneers in this mining district. His father, the late Samuel Sparks, who died at Galena, in 1907, came to the Stanley diggings in Cherokee County in 1877. Oliver W. Sparks was at that time seventeen years of age and he gained his first experience in Cherokee County with his father. In 1879 father and son went to Leadville, Colorado, remaining there three years, but then returned to Galena, where Samuel Sparks continued his business as a zinc and lead miner until his death in 1907.

Samuel Sparks was born in Louisville, Kentucky, in 1835. His ancestors came from Ireland, were early settlers in Kentucky, and his father, Henry Sparks, was born in Kentucky, was reared and married there and became a pioneer farmer at Shelbina, Missouri, where he died in 1873. Samuel Sparks spent most of his early life at Shelbina, and was reared and married on a farm at the edge of that town. His early experience was all connected with farming, but in 1873 he removed to Joplin, Missouri, and took up lead and zinc mining. During the Civil war he was a captain in the Confederate army and was in active service from the beginning to the end of the struggle. In a fight at Granby, Missouri, he was wounded, but otherwise escaped any serious injury. Politically he was always a democratic voter. Samuel Sparks married four times. His first wife was Lydia Lewis, who was born in Shelbina, Missouri, in 1839 and died September, 1862. Her children were: Mary Ellen, who married Baptist Patton, a school teacher, and both are now deceased; Jennie, who died in infancy; and Oliver W., who was born August 5, 1862, at Shelbina, Missouri, only a few days before his mother's death. His father married for his second wife Catherine Adams, who died in Joplin, Missouri. She had two children: Ed, who is a farmer at Klondyke, in Cherokee County; and Lulie, who lives with her half-brother, Oliver, and is the widow of Lafayette Rowe, who was a mine operator and for a number of years served as deputy sheriff of Cherokee County. The third wife of Samuel Sparks was Nancy Stanley, who died at Galena, without children. His fourth wife, Maggie Stoopes, now lives at Empire City, Kansas.

Oliver W. Sparks is an illustration of the fact that the ambitious and energetic man is not dependent upon schools and liberal advantages either for his education or his success in life. Altogether he spent only about one year in public school and

that was in Joplin, Missouri. Nevertheless, he is a well-informed man. Thus he has acquired, partly by experience and partly by reading and study, a habit early acquired, of turning every experience to his advantage as an asset for future action. He was with his father up to the age of nineteen, and as already stated, came with the elder Sparks to Cherokee County, in 1877, and two years later went to Leadville, Colorado. At the age of nineteen he began mining on his own account, and now has been in that business continuously for about thirty-five years. As already mentioned he was one of the first operators in and around Galena.

At the present time Mr. Sparks is general manager and treasurer of a group of mining companies, whose properties are located in Jasper County, Missouri, as follows: The Sparkler Mining Company, of which he is owner; the Dick Turpin mine, the Yellow Pup mine, the Lock mine, and the Alpha mine. He also owns an interest in and is manager of the Allsparks mine at Miami, Oklahoma.

He is individually owner of a large amount of mineral lands, including 314 acres in Spring River, Cherokee County; 270 acres adjacent to Galena; 119 acres where the Yellow Pup mine is located; and 400 acres at Clinton, Oklahoma.

With all his strenuous participation in business affairs Mr. Sparks has not neglected the public welfare. He spent two terms as mayor of Galena, was also on the city council two terms, and from 1907 to 1912, five years, was sheriff of Cherokee County. While he was sheriff a law was passed requiring a uniform term of office throughout the state. In his individual case Mr. Sparks resisted the application of this law, defeated the suit brought against him, and therefore served the extra year until his successor was elected at the next general election. A few years ago he was candidate for representative to the legislature against C. S. Westcott, republican. Mr. Sparks is an active democrat and has many times represented his party in county and state conventions. Mr. Sparks was elected a member of the state legislature for the sessions 1917-18, and is a member of the judiciary committee, utilities commission, mines and miners' committee and labor committee of cities of the second class. He is also father of the segregation bill, separating the white from the colored children in the public schools.

Fraternally he is affiliated with Galena Lodge No. 677, Benevolent and Protective Order of Elks, Aerie No. 266, Fraternal Order of Eagles, and was formerly a member of the Independent Order of Odd Fellows and Knights of Pythias.

In 1888 at Galena he married Miss Ida Keller, who died in 1899. There are three children: Dorothy, wife of Peter Demertin, a mine operator at Galena; Una, still at home; and Warren, who is assisting his father in business. In 1903 at Columbus, Kansas, Mr. Sparks married for his present wife Ambrosia Newton, daughter of Mr. and Mrs. Wallace Newton. Mr. and Mrs. Sparks have one son, Oliver Wallace.

MAX J. KENNEDY. An enterprise which, founded in 1904, has grown to large and important proportions is that of the Kennedy Printing Company, of Fredonia. In an era of specialization, the proprietor of this business, Max J. Kennedy, has confined the activities of his establishment to the printing of matter for banking houses, a field in which he has not only had phenomenal success in the immediate locality in which his business is located, but in towns and cities far distant, one of the most important branches of his house being that which handles the mail orders. Mr. Kennedy is one of the most progressive and enterprising of Fredonia's young business men, and is also a leader in politics in this locality, being at this time chairman of the Democratic County Central Committee of Wilson County.

Max J. Kennedy was born at Fredonia, Kansas, December 27, 1883, and is a son of James M. and Elizabeth (Stivers) (Jordan) Kennedy. His grandfather, Patrick Kennedy, was born in County Tipperary, Ireland, in 1832, came to the United States as a young man, resided at Indianapolis, Indiana, and near Fond du Lac, Wisconsin, and fought as a Union soldier in an Illinois regiment of volunteer infantry during the Civil war. In 1869 he came to Kansas and took up a claim of 160 acres in Wilson County, and resided thereon until his retirement, in 1902, when he removed to the City of Fredonia, and died there in 1912. He married Alice Moore, who was born in 1835, also in County Tipperary, Ireland, and died in Wilson County, in 1896, and they became the parents of four children: John L., who was one of the appointees of President McKinley to a position on the Industrial Commission and is now a printer of Washington, District of Columbia; Mary, who is the owner of the family homestead in Wilson County and of real estate at Fredonia; James M.; and William T., a ranchman and county commissioner of Colorado Springs, Colorado.

James M. Kennedy, the father of Max J. Kennedy, was born near Fond du Lac, Wisconsin, November 11, 1857, and was twelve years old when brought to Kansas. Here he attended the rural schools of Wilson County for two years, and then began working among the farmers of the locality. While thus engaged he managed to secure an education through home study, and when twenty years old started teaching in the Wilson County country schools. He was later superintendent of schools for Fredonia for four years and a teacher in the summer normal schools for eight years, and in the meantime applied himself assiduously to the study of law, so that after a period spent in the office of S. S. Kirkpatrick, a Fredonia lawyer, and a short experience in the farm loan business he was admitted to the bar in 1890. He has since been engaged in practice and is one of the leading members of the profession at Fredonia. He is also an extensive property owner and a well-known business man, being president of the Excelsior Brick Company, the largest of its kind west of the Mississippi. He is a Mason, is independent in politics, and served two terms as county attorney. James M. Kennedy was married in 1882 to Mrs. Elizabeth (Stivers) Jordan, daughter of Hon. William and Matilda (Young) Stivers, both now deceased. Judge Stivers was auditor of Tipton County, Indiana, for eight years, and for twelve years was judge of the Probate Court of Wilson County, Kansas. Three children were born to Mr. and Mrs. Kennedy: William R., Kansas University, LL. B., and a practicing attorney of Greenville, Missouri, married Edith Van Duser and has three children, Hugh, James Randall and Gilbert; Max J., of this review; and Madge, a graduate of Kansas University and now the wife of Frederick Cambern, cashier of the State Bank of Fredonia, and has one daughter, Elizabeth.

Max J. Kennedy was educated in the public schools of Fredonia, and after he finished his studies in the high school entered the printing business. He had a natural aptitude for this vocation, and, as is usual with young men in this business, had ambitions to enter the newspaper field. Before he was twenty years of age he published the first issue of the Daily Herald, of which he was the proprietor until 1906, in which year he sold out. In the meantime, in 1904, he had established the Kennedy Printing Company, the business of which grew to such an extent that his entire attention was needed for its handling, which was the real reason for his retirement from the field of journalism. The Kennedy Printing Company, as noted, devotes itself exclusively to bank printing, and orders for this kind of work come from all over the United States. Mr. Kennedy has made a keen study of this branch of printing, and his ideas, workmanship and knowledge of bank printing have combined to give him a prominent place in this particular field. His plant is equipped wth the most up-to-date machinery of all kinds for the proper handling of every kind of bank work, and the Kennedy workmanship bears a distinctiveness that makes it known anywhere. In addition to his printing business, Mr. Kennedy has interested himself in farming. He is the owner of a handsome property of 440 acres, lying two miles northeast of Fredonia, with modern buildings of all kinds, including dairy barns and silos, and there he has particularly interested himself in the breeding of registered Holstein-Friesian cattle, of which he has a magnificent herd. For several years his activities in the political field have made him one of the best known democrats in Wilson County, and at this time he is doing much for the success of his party as chairman of the Democratic County Central Committee. He is well, prominently and popularly known in fraternal circles, being a member of the Knights of Pythias, the Modern Woodmen of America; Cherryvale Lodge No. 929, Benevolent and Protective Order of Elks; Constellation Lodge No. 95, Ancient Free and Accepted Masons; Kilwinning Chapter No. 44, Royal Arch Masons, and Ab-Del-Kader Commandery Knights Templar, all of Fredonia; and Mirza Temple, Ancient Arabic Order Nobles of the Mystic Shrine, of Pittsburg, Kansas. In addition to his farm, Mr. Kennedy is the owner of his own home, at No. 310 North Seventh Street; and an office building on the north side of the Square.

Mr. Kennedy was married in 1904, at Excelsior Springs, Missouri, to Miss Bessie F. Wolever, daughter of Mr. and Mrs. John H. Wolever, the latter a resident of Fredonia. Mr. Wolever, who was a veteran of the Civil war, became a pioneer contractor of Fredonia, where his death occurred. To Mr. and Mrs. Kennedy two children have been born: Kenneth, November 25, 1905; and Conrad Max, August 13, 1907.

JAMES M. CAVANESS. The name Cavaness belongs to both the pioneer and modern era of Kansas. Anywhere in the southeastern part of the state the name is most closely associated with the newspaper business, and two generations are still active in that work, James M. Cavaness and two of his sons, Herbert and Wilfrid, all of whom are connected in some official capacity with the Chanute Tribune.

The origin of the Cavaness family was undoubtedly in Ireland, but the first of the name came to America in the colonial period and settled in North Carolina.

Urban C. Cavaness, father of James M. Cavaness, was born May 10, 1810, in Randolph County, North Carolina. He was reared and married in his native state, and his first child was born in Randolph County. In 1834 he removed to Indiana and was the pioneer shoemaker at Monrovia in that state. Later he became a hotel proprietor. In 1856 Urban C. Cavaness arrived at Lawrence, Kansas. Later he moved to Baldwin, where he kept one of the first houses of public entertainment in that college town, and he also had a hack for the conveyance of mail and passengers. He was identified with the movement to make Kansas a free state, and during the war saw some active service in helping to repel Price's raid. Though he was a democrat by inheritance he later became a republican. He was a member of the Methodist Episcopal Church and of the Masonic fraternity. His death occurred at Baldwin, Kansas, January 11, 1899, when nearly ninety years old. In November, 1832, he married Miss Mary Amick, who was born in North Carolina in 1806 and died at Baldwin, Kansas, December 27, 1898, at the age of ninety-two. Their children were: Francis M., who died at the age of twenty-one; William F., who died when three years old; Alpheus A. B., who was a carpenter early in life, saw active service in the Union army during the Civil war, and was severely wounded, and on account of this injury subsequently conducted a book store at Baldwin, Kansas, where he died April 18, 1816; James M.; Sarah C., who lives at Baldwin, the widow of S. L. Clayton, who was a carpenter and farmer; Mary C., who died at Kansas City, Missouri, in 1914, and her husband, E. E. Gaddis, also deceased, was in the real estate business and also a weigher in a packing house at Kansas City; Alvira, who died in infancy.

James M. Cavaness was born at Monrovia, Indiana, March 29, 1842, and was a boy of about fourteen when his parents came to Kansas. In 1866 he was a member of the first graduating class from Baker University. He received the degree A. B. and spent the two succeeding years in work as principal of schools at Butler, Missouri, and Paola, Kansas. Since the fall of 1869, when he entered the Advance office at Chetopa, his work and interests have been constantly in the newspaper field. He was connected with the Chetopa Advance for thirty years, and twenty-five years as manager and editor. In 1899 he removed to Chanute and acquired the Tribune, and is still helping to run that paper. His political influence has always been given the republican party. For nearly eleven years he served as postmaster at Chetopa, and while in college served as postmaster at Baldwin, having been appointed to that office by President Lincoln. He is a member of the Methodist Episcopal Church, and was formerly affiliated with the Independent Order of Odd Fellows and Knights of Pythias.

In 1873 at Garnett, Kansas, James M. Cavaness married Mary I. Swallow, who was born in Ohio in 1853. Their children are: Ethel, wife of J. Luther Taylor, who is an attorney and also in the real estate and loan business at Pittsburg, Kansas; Wilfrid and Herbert, both mentioned in succeeding paragraphs.

James M. Cavaness is a well-known member of the Kansas Authors Club of Topeka, and of the Quill Club of Kansas City. His literary efforts have mainly been in the field of poetry. His brother, the late A. A. B. Cavaness, was a graceful writer of verse, and in 1896 he and James M. Cavaness published a book entitled "Poems by Two Brothers." Later J. M. Cavaness published a book entitled "Jay Hawker Juleps." This book is now in its third edition. Another product of his pen is "Rythmic Studies of the World," published in 1911, a second volume in 1916. A. A. B. Cavaness in 1906 published "Rubaiyat of Hope."

Wilfrid Cavaness, who has been a Kansas newspaper man for over twenty years, was born at Chetopa November 24, 1875. He attended the public schools there, graduating from high school in 1892, and for two years was a student in Baker University. In 1895 he became connected with the Chetopa Advance under his father, and remained there until 1899. For the following two years he was with the Columbus Courier, and in 1901 came to Chanute and is now treasurer and manager of the Chanute Tribune.

The Chanute Tribune was established April 8, 1892, by George M. Dewey. It has always been published as a republican paper, and is now both a daily and weekly and has a large circulation and influence over Neosho and surrounding counties. The officers of the Tribune Company are: Herbert Cavaness, president; Wilfrid Cavaness, treasurer and manager; George L. Barcus, vice president; and Fletcher Maclary secretary. The Tribune plant is thoroughly equipped with all the modern machinery for printing and typesetting, and it is a very successful newspaper. The plant and offices are located at 14 North Lincoln Avenue, and Cavaness Brothers own the building.

Wilfrid Cavaness is a republican, is affiliated with Cedar Lodge No. 103, Ancient, Free and Accepted Masons, Cedar Chapter No. 21, Royal Arch Masons, Cedar Commandery No. 44, Knights Templar, Mirza Temple of the Mystic Shrine at Pittsburg, Fort Scott Consistory No. 4 of the Scottish Rite, Chanute Lodge No. 806, Benevolent and Protective Order of Elks, and also the Ancient Order of United Workmen, the Modern Woodmen of America and the Commercial Club. Mr. Cavaness is vice president of the People's Amusement Company of Chanute and has some interests in the oil fields in Kansas and Oklahoma.

In 1908 at St. Joseph, Missouri, he married Miss Wynona L. Stewart, daughter of Mr. and Mrs. J. L. Stewart, who now resides at Chanute, where Mr. Stewart is locomotive engineer on the Santa Fe Road.

Herbert Cavaness, president of the Tribune Company at Chanute, was born at Chetopa August 23, 1877. He was graduated from the Chetopa High School in 1893, and took the full literary course in Baker University, where he was graduated A. B. in 1899. While in university he was a member of the Kappa Sigma fraternity and the Athenian Literary Society. There was hardly a break between his college career and his work as a newspaper man, which he has followed with great enthusiasm and success. In September, 1899, he went to work on the Chanute Tribune, and gives practically all his time to his office as president and editor. At the February, 1916, meeting of the Kansas State Editorial Association, he was elected president and on February 24, 1917, was elected a member of the Topeka Press Club. For eight years he served as postmaster at Chanute, having been appointed in 1906 by President Roosevelt and re-appointed under President Taft. He is an active republican, a member of Cedar Lodge No. 103, Ancient, Free and Accepted Masons, Fort Scott Consistory No. 4 of the Scottish Rite, Chanute Chapter No. 21, Royal Arch Masons, Chanute Commandery No. 44 Knights Templar, and Mirza Temple of the Mystic Shrine at Pittsburg. He also belongs to Hilda Parker Chapter No. 385 of the Eastern Star, and Lodge No. 806 of the Benevolent and Protective Order of Elks and Chanute Lodge No. 96 Ancient Order of United Workmen. He is an active member of the Chanute Commercial Club.

Mr. Cavaness was married to Miss Ora Allen, November 24, 1916, the only daughter of the late R. N. Allen, one of the oldest residents of Chanute.

JAMES M. KENNEDY, who has lived in Kansas since 1869, was formerly a teacher, but since 1890 has been an active member of the Fredonia bar.

He was born near the City of Fond du Lac, Wisconsin, November 11, 1867. His father, Patrick Kennedy, was born in 1832 in County Tipperary, Ireland, came when a young unmarried man to the United States, first locating on a farm near Indianapolis, Indiana, and subsequently removing to Wisconsin, where he was a farmer near Fond du Lac. Just prior to the Civil war he returned to Indianapolis. In 1861 he enlisted in the Eighth Regiment, Illinois Volunteer Infantry, Colonel Oglesby's regiment. His service as a Union soldier continued for three years and eight months. He fought at Shiloh, Lookout Mountain, and all the battles fought by the army of General Grant in the West. After his honorable discharge from the ranks he returned to Hancock County, Indiana, bought a farm, but in 1869 came to the newer west and took up a claim of 160 acres, twelve miles east of Fredonia, in Wilson County. This land, which he acquired in its virgin state, he developed by many years of labor into a valuable property, and it is now owned by his daughter, Mary. In 1902 he left the farm and lived in Fredonia until his death in 1912. Though a republican, a warm admiration for William Jennings Bryan caused him to support that Nebraskan for the presidency. He was also affiliated with the Grand Army of the Republic. His wife, Alice Moore, was born in County Tipperary, Ireland, in 1833, and died on the Wilson County farm in 1896. There were four children: John L., who was appointed by President McKinley to membership on the Industrial Commission and is now a printer in Washington, D. C.; Mary, who owns the old homestead in Wilson County and other real estate at Fredonia where she makes her home; James M.; and William T., a rancher at Colorado Springs, Colorado, and for several years a member of the Board of County Commissioners of El Paso County.

James M. Kennedy received most of his early training in the public schools of Indiana, and for two years was a student in the rural schools of Wilson County. At the age of fourteen he began working out among the farmers of his locality and earned his living in that way until he was twenty. He had improved his leisure time by the study of books, and thus qualified himself as a teacher. He taught in the country schools of Wilson County twelve years, became superintendent of schools at Fredonia, for four years, and established almost a record by eight years of teaching in the Teachers Summer Normal School of the county.

He gave up teaching to enter the farm loan business at Fredonia. His earliest ambition had been for a career as a lawyer. As he had qualified himself for teaching by study while a farm hand, so also he pursued his studies of the law in the intervals of other occupations, completing these studies with S. S. Kirkpatrick at Fredonia. In 1890 he was admitted to the bar and for over a quarter of a century has handled a civil and criminal practice at Fredonia. Long experience, sound knowledge and hard work have given him an undoubted place of leadership in the Wilson County bar. His offices are in the Kennedy Building, on the west side of the square. He is independent in politics, has never been a seeker for office, although for two terms he served as county attorney. Mr. Kennedy owns the office building above mentioned, also his home at 321 Eighth Street, another business building on the west side of the square, and 200 acres of farming land south of the city. Mr. Kennedy is president of the Excelsior Brick Company, the largest brick manufacturing plant west of the Mississippi River. Other associates in that business are Dr. A. C. Flack, S. J. Hess, J. D. Lingenfelter, Mrs. W. B. Hess, and W. B. Kennedy. W. B. Kennedy is a son of Mr. Kennedy and is also a lawyer, being a partner in the law firm of Kennedy & Kennedy. Aside from the organizations of his profession Mr. Kennedy belongs only to Constellation Lodge No. 95, Ancient Free and Accepted Masons.

In 1882, at Fredonia, he married Mrs. Elizabeth (Stivers) Jordan, daughter of Hon. William and Matilda (Young) Stivers, both deceased. Judge Stivers was auditor of Tipton County, Indiana, for eight years and for twelve years was judge of the Probate Court of Wilson County, Kansas. Mr. and Mrs. Kennedy have three children. William B., a graduate of the Fredonia High School and of the University of Kansas with the degree of Bachelor of Laws, is now in active practice at Fredonia; he married Edith Van Duser of Fredonia and their three children are: Hugh, born July 18, 1913, and James Randall and Gilbert, twins, born February 25, 1916. Max, a graduate of the Fredonia High School, is now sole proprietor of the Kennedy Printing Company of Fredonia; he married Bessie F. Wolever of Fredonia and has two children: Kenneth, born November 25, 1905; and Conrad Max, born August 13, 1907. Madge, the youngest child, is a graduate of the high school and of the University of Kansas and is the wife of Frederick Cambern, cashier of the State Bank of Fredonia. They have one daughter, Elizabeth, born February 18, 1911.

PROF. GEORGE A. GEMMELL. It is doubtful if there is any other profession which demands so much judgment, tact, specialized knowledge, patient and natural executive ability as that of the educator, and the individual selecting it as his calling must be prepared to make many personal sacrifices, to endure many disappointments, to often spend himself for others without apparent gratitude in return, and to give the best years of his life without the material emoluments that equal effort would surely bring in any other profession. It is a profession for which there is no established table of weights and measures, but it is one which affords the man who would serve the race an opportunity than which there are none greater. Of the educators of Kansas who are engaged in a good and helpful work, one who has not allowed himself to be tied down by old methods or ancient dogmas is Prof. George A. Gemmell, principal of the Crawford County High School, at Cherokee. Mr. Gemmell has made teaching his life work, and in going beyond prescribed limits has shown himself one who is an educator in the best sense and whose practical instruction will be of lasting benefit to those who come under his charge.

George A. Gemmell was born July 29, 1882, in Crawford County, Kansas, and is a son of A. J. C. and Cora I. (Clay) Gemmell. His grandfather, Alexander Gemmell, was born near the City of Glasgow, Scotland, and in 1855, with his wife and eldest child, made the trip across the Atlantic to America, locating first for a short time in Canada, and then going to Illinois. For a number of years he was engaged in agricultural pursuits near Centralia, that state, but in 1882 came to Kansas and located in Crawford County, one mile south of Girard, to which city he removed at the time of his retirement. Not long thereafter his death occurred, in

1910, when he was eighty-three years of age. Mr. Gemmell was a sturdy Scotch farmer, who combined in his character all the sterling qualities of his race, and who took to each new community an influence for industry and good citizenship. He was married in his native land to Sarah Anderson, who was born in 1831, also near Glasgow, and they became the parents of the following children: John, who was for many years engaged in farming in Crawford County, but now a retired and well-to-do resident of Pomona, California, whence he went for the health of his family; A. J. C.; Alex, who is the owner of a fruit ranch at Claremont, California; Margaret, who is the wife of Alexander Cuthbertson, and lives on a farm seven miles southwest of Girard; William, who was engaged in farming and died in August, 1916, in the State of Washington; Sarah, who is the wife of Albert Cuthbertson and lives on a farm 5½ miles southwest of Girard; Mary, who married J. T. Lindsay, a retired farmer of Emporia, Kansas; Miss Martha, who resides at Girard; and Nellie, who is the wife of Charles Thompson and lives six miles north of McCune, on a farm.

A. J. C. Gemmell was born September 1, 1855, in Canada, not long after his parents' arrival in America, and was still an infant when brought to the United States, his boyhood, youth and early manhood being passed in Illinois, where he was reared on a farm and educated in the public schools. He was married in that state and engaged in farming until 1880, when he came to Crawford County, Kansas, and here has since continued to be engaged in general farming and stock raising, owning a valuable tract of land eight miles north of McCune. He is one of the substantial men of his community, is known as a practical and thorough agriculturist, and has served as census enumerator and township clerk. He is active in the work of the Presbyterian Church, and is now serving in the capacity of elder. Politically he supports republican policies and candidates. Mr. Gemmell was married in Illinois to Miss Cora I. Clay, who was born in that state, August 21, 1861, and to them there have been born four children: George A.; Alvin J.; who was a homesteader at Holly, Colorado, and died there at the age of twenty years; William, who served for five years in the United States army, and is now a farmer in Crawford County; and Ralph, who is carrying on operations on the old homestead place in Crawford County.

George A. Gemmell was reared on his father's farm, on which he resided until he was twenty-one years of age, in the meantime securing a good education in the district schools of Crawford County and the State Normal School, at Emporia, which he attended for one year. This was later supplemented by attendance at the State Manual Training Normal School, where he was a student for four years, all told, and from which he received a teacher's life certificate at the time of his graduation, in 1913. Long before this he had entered upon his career as an educator, having taught in the district schools of the county for six years, and in 1905 was appointed county superintendent of schools by the board of county commissioners, an office in which he served for five years. Following this he was made principal of schools of Arcadia, where he remained one year, and in 1912 came to Cherokee to become teacher of science and mathematics in the Crawford County High School. After three years in this chair, in 1915, Professor Gemmell was made principal. He now has ten teachers and 220 pupils in his charge.

Owing to the fact that his pupils come principally from farming districts, Mr. Gemmell is carrying out a plan which he firmly believes is just as important an item in their education as that which trains them in book knowledge. In accordance with this project, he has induced the school to buy a ten-acre tract of land, a team of pure-bred Percheron mares, a pure-bred Jersey cow, four registered pigs, a wagon, harness, implements, etc., and has established a miniature farm, on which the boys of the school connected with the woodworking department recently erected a barn. Here, largely under the supervision of the Manhattan State Agricultural College, the boys are trained in agricultural work, not merely through propaganda, but through actual participation in the occupations which make up the daily routine of farm life. The newest methods are taught and the use of improved machinery is shown, and, in as far as possible, the youths are taught to be skilled in every department that makes for successful farming and stock breeding. This is a worthy object, and, as its author, Professor Gemmell deserves the gratitude of the agriculturists and of the people at large.

Professor Gemmell is a member of the Kansas State Teachers' Association, the Crawford County Teachers' Association and the Southeastern Teachers' Association. He began voting the republican ticket at the age of twenty-one years, at which time he was elected as a member of the board of township trustees. With his family, he belongs to the Methodist Episcopal Church, and his fraternal affiliation is with the Girard Lodge of the Knights of Pythias, and McCune Lodge, Ancient Free and Accepted Masons.

In 1906, in Crawford County, Professor Gemmell was married to Miss Mary V. Smith, daughter of John W. and Nannie (Meek) Smith, who reside on their farm five miles southwest of Girard. To this union there has come one son, Lee, born October 8, 1910.

ALEXANDER C. FLACK, M. D. Thirty-one years of practice at Fredonia entitles Dr. Alexander C. Flack to recognition as the second oldest physician and surgeon of the city, whence he came in 1885 shortly after receiving his diploma. He has since been one of the reliable members of the medical fraternity here and a citizen who has done his share in aiding in the city's progress and prosperity. Doctor Flack is a native of the Buckeye state, born at East Liberty, Logan County, Ohio, May 2, 1858, a son of Thomas H. and Agnes (Bell) Flack.

Hugh Flack, the grandfather of Doctor Flack, was born at Bailieborough, County Cavan, Ireland, and was a grandson of people on the paternal side who were born in Scotland. His mother, Christine Linster, was born in Ireland of Scotch descent. Hugh Flack passed his entire life as a farmer and never left the shores of his native Erin, passing away in County Cavan. He was the father of twin sons: Thomas H.; and Patrick, the latter of whom died near East Liberty, Ohio, after a career passed in agricultural pursuits. Walter Bell, the maternal grandfather of Doctor Flack, was born in Ireland, but his parents came from England, while his wife, who bore the maiden name of Nancy Parker, was born in Ireland, but of Scotch parentage.

Thomas H. Flack was born at Bailieborough, County Cavan, Ireland, in 1818, and was twenty-two years of age when he emigrated to the United States. He first located in New York City, where he secured employment in a wholesale house, and worked therein for four years and four months. In his native land he had been reared on a farm, and he finally answered the call of the soil, going to East Liberty, Ohio, where he settled on a farm. On that property he continued to be engaged in operations during the remainder of his life, and died in 1912, at the remarkable age of ninety-four years. He was a good citizen and an honorable man of business and won the respect and esteem of those with whom he came into contact. In his political views he was a democrat, but politics played only a small part in his life, and he never sought personal preferment at the hands of his party or of his fellow-citizens. His religious faith was that of the Presbyterian Church, and he lived his faith daily. Mr. Flack married Miss Agnes Bell, who was born February 10, 1827, near the Town of Bailieborough, and died at East Liberty in 1909. They became the parents of the following children: Walter, born June 2, 1849, who died in infancy in New York City; William Henry, born June 11, 1851, who was a prosperous retired farmer and schoolteacher of East Liberty, Ohio, until his death October 19, 1916; Thomas, born June 15, 1853, who died at the age of twelve years; Tillie Jane, born December 9, 1855, who is the wife of J. R. Lynch, of Muncie, Indiana, a machinist and specialist in the work of making special parts in an automobile factory; Dr. Alexander C., of this notice; Lida, born October 3, 1861, who died August 16, 1866; Lillie Fay, born December 14, 1863, who married Oscar Alexander, a farmer, and resides in one of the most beautiful and modern homes in the country, at Bellefontaine, Ohio; Dr. Orra M., born June 24, 1886, a graduate of the Medical College of Ohio, at Cincinnati, and now a successful practicing physician and surgeon of Boswell, Indiana; and Anna Belle, born December 7, 1868, who is the wife of Pearl J. Humphreys, a lumber merchant and farmer of East Liberty, Ohio.

Alexander C. Flack received his early education in the rural schools near East Liberty, Ohio, and subsequently attended the National Normal University at Lebanon, Ohio, from which he was graduated with the degree of Bachelor of Science in 1881. In the meantime he had taught school for three years in the country and two years at Copley, Ohio, where he was principal of schools, and during this time also studied medicine whenever he could get the leisure. Doctor Flack pursued his medical studies at the Medical College of Ohio, at Cincinnati, from which he was graduated in 1885, with the degree of Doctor of Medicine, and almost immediately thereafter came to Fredonia, where he has continued in a general medical and surgical practice. In point of practice he is the second oldest physician now living at Fredonia. Doctor Flack maintains well appointed offices at No. 520 Madison Street, where he has a large and comprehensive medical library and all instruments and appliances for the practice of his calling. In addition to his own modern residence, at No. 303 Eighth Street, he owns 226 acres of fine land on the Verdigris River bottoms in Wilson County.

Doctor Flack is local surgeon for the Atchison, Topeka & Santa Fe Railroad. He belongs to the Wilson County Medical Society, the Kansas State Medical Society and the American Medical Association, and is a respecter of the highest ethics of his profession, among the members of which he bears an excellent reputation. A democrat in politics, he has long taken an active part in civic matters, but is apt to maintain an independent stand in local affairs. He is a member of the school board of Fredonia, and has been for some years, was formerly a member of the city council, and on one occasion was candidate for the office of mayor. Aside from his profession, he has a number of interests, being vice president and a director of the Citizens State Bank, of which he was formerly president for 1½ years; a stockholder in the Fredonia Portland Cement Company; and treasurer, a director, and one of the stockholders of the Excelsior Brick Company, one of the largest concerns of its kind in Kansas, which is manufacturing 27,000,000 brick annually. He has been identified with many movements that have added to Fredonia's prestige as one of the thriving and growing cities of southeastern Kansas.

Doctor Flack was married first in 1886 to Miss Hattie J. Wells, who died November 18, 1890. The doctor was again married, in the fall of 1892, to Anna Herron, who is also deceased. In 1914 he married his present wife, who was Lena M. Koch. She was for a number of years a teacher in the Fredonia public schools. Doctor Flack has three children: Mary Agnes, who is the wife of Mark O. Wiley, cashier of the Citizens State Bank of Fredonia; Wilma, who took two years of study at Emporia College and now is a junior at the University of Michigan, Ann Arbor; and Herron, who is a member of the senior class at the Fredonia High School.

WARNER E. WILLIAMS. While now one of the great trunk railway systems of the country, the Missouri, Kansas & Texas Railroad was largely developed as a Kansas corporation. The main offices of the company at Kansas are at Parsons, where 2,200 of its employes reside. The different lines of the road converge and diverge from that point in six directions: To Hannibal and St. Louis, Missouri; to Kansas City, Missouri; to Junction City, Kansas; to Joplin, Missouri, to Denison, Texas; and to Oklahoma City, Oklahoma.

For several years the general manager of the system with headquarters at Parsons was Warner E. Williams, who has recently been transferred to Dallas, Texas, where he began his career as a railroad man and where he is now general manager of the Missouri, Kansas & Texas Railway of Texas.

Mr. Williams was born at Houston, Texas, May 29, 1864, attended the public schools at Houston, and as a boy worked as a messenger in a law office. He was similarly employed in a wholesale grocery house at Houston, but in 1881 at the age of seventeen he became check clerk at the freight house of the International and Great Northern Railroad at Taylor, Texas. During his thirty-five years of experience he has been steadily promoted in the scale of responsibility. At Palestine, Texas, he was roadmaster's clerk, filled other places in the transportation office, was chief clerk in the superintendent's office, secretary to the general manager and secretary of the receivers' department. He was then promoted to purchasing agent and general store keeper, but in 1897 he left the International & Great Northern and became chief clerk to the general superintendent of the Missouri, Kansas & Texas at Dallas. He was promoted to car accountant and in 1901 was transferred to Greenville, Texas, as trainmaster. In 1902 he became superintendent at Greenville and in 1905 superintendent at Denison, Texas. He was subsequently assigned as superintendent at Sedalia, Missouri, and at St. Louis, but in 1911 was made general superintendent of the Missouri, Kansas and Texas Railway and in 1912 located at Parsons. Mr. Williams was a resident of Parsons for several years and in February, 1915, was made general manager, a post he held until recently when he returned to Dallas.

BOBBIE J. DUNNING

THOMAS GRAY is one of the largest stock raisers in Osage County. His fortunes have been identified with this state since early manhood, and though he had to start out with only an ordinary equipment of training and capital, he has made prosperity by sheer force of ability and constant exercise of good judgment and hard work.

He was born on a farm at Crows Hill, New York, March 9, 1854. Of the eight children born to Joshua and Elizabeth (Foxley) Gray he is the only one now living. His parents were English people and on account of the crowded conditions socially and economically in that country they emigrated to the New World. From New York they came west to Illinois, in the early '50s, and spent about twenty years in Coles County. Then on account of ill health they traded their farm for one in Osage County, Kansas. This Kansas farm contained 160 acres and Joshua Gray devoted the rest of his life to general farming and stock raising. While in England he had learned the trade of stone mason and plasterer. He had only such education as was given in English schools in the early part of the last century. He possessed very keen business judgment, and in every community where he resided enjoyed the highest respect. After becoming a naturalized American he voted the republican ticket but was not interested in the holding of office. He was a member of the United Brethren Church. Joshua Gray died in February and his wife in December of 1889.

His parents removing to Illinois during his infancy, Thomas Gray spent his early life in that state, attended the local schools and was about grown when his parents removed to Kansas.

On January 13, 1881, he married Olive J. Lamond. Mrs. Gray was born February 17, 1856, in Putnam County, Ohio, on a farm, a daughter of Henry Nelson and Sarah Ann (Kendall) Lamond. Her parents were both natives of Ohio, and in 1868 they brought their family from Ohio to Kansas, making the entire journey with wagons and teams, and being five weeks on the road. Mr. Lamond died in 1900 and his wife in 1899.

After his marriage Mr. Gray lived with his parents and rented a farm, and he then bought 120 acres. He proceeded rapidly and energetically in the development of that land, from time to time has increased his holdings until he now owns and operates 400 acres in Sections 5, 6 and 7 of Valley Brook Township, Osage County. He has made special success in the raising of stock, and he specializes in the Poland China hogs and Shorthorn cattle. When he and his wife began housekeeping they lived in a small two-room house. A visible evidence of their prosperity is found in their fine modern home, with a complete light, heating and water plant and with all the conveniences.

Mr. and Mrs. Gray had born to them six children: William J., who died in 1903; Thomas R.; Henry G.; Dean L.; Albert W.; and George C., who died in 1900.

Mr. Gray is a republican in politics, has given his own children good educational advantages and has done much in his community towards the building of churches and the establishment of good schools. He favors prohibition, and wherever possible has exerted his influence in behalf of good roads. Fraternally he is affiliated with the Knights of Pythias. Mr. Gray's brother John enlisted for service in the Union army, but was soon afterwards taken sick and died in a hospital.

BOBBIE J. DUNNING. Some men in the course of their careers gain wealth, others high public position, but probably the greatest good fortune that comes to any one is a wealth of esteem and true-hearted friendship such as surrounded the late Bobbie J. Dunning of Kansas City, Kansas. He was one of the widest known Masons in the state, and had pre-eminently the faculty of making and retaining friends. He was by no means unsuccessful in business, and started in a small way, and though still a young man at the time of his death, he built up one of the most complete jewelry stores in Kansas City, Kansas.

His life was a continuation of the careers of pioneer families in this section of the state. Mr. Dunning was born in Kansas City, Kansas, November 29, 1868, and died there February 2, 1911, at the comparatively early age of forty-three. He was one of the three children of Robert and Alvira (Bebee) Dunning, the former a native of Philadelphia and the latter of Council Bluffs, Iowa. Alvira Bebee was a granddaughter of one of the first white men to come into the Indian reservations of the West, being sent by the Government long before white settlers had chosen the country west of the Missouri River as homes. Robert Dunning was a painter and decorator by trade, and coming west at an early age lived for a time at Council Bluffs, Iowa, where he married and in 1854 he brought his family to Kansas, locating at Old Wyandotte. He was one of the pioneers in what is now Kansas City, Kansas, and for many years was employed as an interior decorator and also as a builder. He founded and built the old Dunning Opera House, the first theater in either Kansas City, Kansas, or Kansas City, Missouri. It was located at the corner of Fourth and State streets and was a famous show place in its time. It was the first place in Kansas City, Kansas, used to hold city and county conventions. Practically every leading troupe or theatrical played in the house, and those who can look back in their careers fifty or sixty years have many interesting recollections of the old play house. Robert Dunning operated this house until his death, about 1891. He was prominent in the Masonic Order and gave his time and means liberally for the good of the community. His wife was well known socially and active in the Congregational Church. Robert Dunning was a republican without political aspirations, and became a very successful man, though he had begun life with very little school education.

B. J. Dunning grew up in Kansas City, Kansas, attended the public schools and was a graduate of the Palmer's Academy. He was still a boy when he entered the jewelry store established by his brother Edwin, and learned the trade of jeweler. At the age of eighteen he was active in business and gradually built up a large trade. He was one of the first opticians in Kansas City, and the practice of that profession was a large factor in his success. At the time of his death he had one of the largest stores in Kansas City, Kansas, and also owned considerable real estate. Public spirit went hand in hand with business success, and he was ever ready to give time and thought to the consideration of a movement for the general benefit, and found the greatest delight in aiding and working with his friends. He was also a factor in democratic politics and was at various times mentioned for public office, though he steadfastly refused to consider any such proffers.

On November 28, 1889, Mr. Dunning married Miss Minnie Banbury, who was born at Ingersoll, Province of Ontario, Canada. Her parents, Charles and Almira (Waggoner) Banbury, were natives, respectively, of England and Canada. Jesse F. Woodward, a grandfather of Mrs. Banbury, was a private in the War of 1812, serving throughout that struggle and being given a grant of land for his services in Wisconsin. His father, Caleb Woodward, was a Revolutionary soldier and captain of a company. The Waggoner family originated in Germany, and in coming to America the ship on which they were passengers was captured by pirates and they were held for some time as prisoners. The Waggoners came west from New York.

The late B. J. Dunning attended worship in the Congregational Church. He found the best expression of his social spirit through the Masonic Order. He was a member of Wyandotte Lodge No. 272, Ancient, Free and Accepted Masons, but was especially active in the Scottish Rite bodies. He was secretary of the building committee and one of the organizers of the Masonic Temple of Kansas City, Kansas, and on account of his important services was given the supreme honorary thirty-third degree in the Scottish Rite. He was also a member of the Abdallah Temple of the Mystic Shrine at Leavenworth and was frequently a delegate to national conventions. Both he and his wife are members of the Eastern Star. Mrs. Dunning since her husband's death has shown great capability in the management of the business, in which she is actively assisted by Mr. Dunning's brother Edwin. Mrs. Dunning is an active member of the Presbyterian Church. She has one son, Robert, who is now a student in the Kansas City (Kansas) High School.

WALTER CHARLES ISERN, a young and progressive business man of Kansas, is the responsible head of the chief mercantile enterprise of Alden. Mr. Isern grew up in the atmosphere of a store and has developed his talents for business by careful and painstaking work since he left school.

Mr. Isern was born at Ellinwood, Kansas, October 18, 1887. He is of German ancestry. His grandfather, Frederick Isern, came from Germany more than seventy years ago, after serving his time in the regular German army. He located at New Bremen, Ohio, where he was a farmer and carpenter until his death.

Adolph Isern, father of the Alden merchant, was born at New Bremen, Ohio, in 1845. He grew up and married there and spent his active career as a farmer. Coming to Kansas in 1878, he located at Ellinwood, where he was prosperously engaged in the management of a farm until his death in 1897. He was a democrat of the old school and an active member of the Lutheran Church. Adolph Isern married Minnie Nordman. She was born in Germany, near Bremen, in 1855 and is still living at Ellinwood. They had three children: Alvin, a farmer at Ellinwood; Alfred, also a farmer in that vicinity; and Walter C.

Walter C. Isern acquired his education chiefly at Ellinwood, leaving the high school there at the age of sixteen. After a course in the business college at Salina during 1904 he became clerk in the store at Ellinwood of the Stephan & Isern Mercantile Company. This is a large and prosperous organization, with stores both at Ellinwood and Alden. In April, 1914, Mr. Isern came to Alden as manager of the store, which is a completely stocked department business, occupying floor space seventy-five by seventy-five feet. The store is on Main Street, and the patronage comes from all the surrounding country for a radius of twelve miles. It is the largest

store in Alden and the only department store. Mr. Isern is both a stockholder and director in the company besides being manager of the business at Alden.

Politically he is a democrat and has served as clerk of Valley Township in Rice County. He is an active member and a steward in the Methodist Episcopal Church.

In March, 1911, at Aledo, Illinois, Mr. Isern married Phoebe Scannell, daughter of John and Mary (Durning) Scannell. Her mother is deceased and her father is a retired resident of Aledo. Mr. and Mrs. Isern have one child, Mary Gretchen, born April 5, 1916.

WILLIAM C. SUTTLE. Under modern conditions the water works of any thriving and prosperous community is one of the most important branches of the civic service, and its management requires abilities far beyond the ordinary. Fredonia boasts of one of the best water systems in Southeastern Kansas, and much of the credit for the present excellent conditions existing in this enterprising city is due to the capable and experienced work of the superintendent of the water works, William C. Suttle, who has been connected with this department for about eleven years and has been in his present position since 1913.

Mr. Suttle is a native son of Kansas, and was born on a farm in Johnson County, July 27, 1870, his parents being Benjamin O. and Abigail (Hazelett) Suttle. The family is of English origin and has resided in America since colonial days when the original emigrant located in Virginia. Benjamin O. Suttle was born in 1821, in Virginia, and was reared and educated in the Old Dominion state, from whence he went to Kentucky as a young man and engaged in farming in the vicinity of Franklin. He was married in that state and in 1870 migrated to Kansas, settling in Johnson County, where he farmed for two years. He then changed his residence to Coffey County, settled on a farm, and continued to be engaged in agricultural pursuits until his death in 1881. He supported the republican ticket as a voter, and was a strong member of the Baptist Church, in which he served as a deacon. Mr. Suttle was married to Miss Abigail Hazelett, in Kentucky, in which state she was born in 1832. She died at Fredonia, Kansas, in 1913, having been the mother of four children, as follows: Katherine, who is the wife of Charles Best and resides in Kentucky; Maggie, who is the widow of John Adair, a farmer, and lives at Pasadena, California; R. M., who is engaged in farming and makes his home at San Diego, California; and William C.

William C. Suttle received his education in the rural schools of Coffey County and at the Burlington (Kansas) High School, from which he was graduated in 1889. He then gave his attention to the machinist's trade, for which he early showed a predilection, and worked in that capacity with railroads and mills until 1899, when he entered the employ of the water works department of Arkansas City, Kansas. After 2½ years he went to Great Bend, Kansas, where he worked in a similar capacity, and in 1905 came to Fredonia. Entering the water works in a minor position he steadily worked his way up to the superintendency, to which he was appointed in 1913. He has proven an excellent official, careful, energetic and capable, and under his management the department is giving the city very satisfactory service. He maintains offices in the City Hall Building. The City of Fredonia has a gravity water plant, with a reservoir of 2,500,000 gallons capacity, and sixty-five pounds maximum pressure, and a direct pressure can be attained if necessary, although this is reserved for use during a serious conflagration. The plant has steam, water and electric power, is equipped with the most modern machinery throughout, and secured its water from Fall River.

Mr. Suttle is a republican. He belongs to the Methodist Episcopal Church, in which he is a steward, and is fraternally affiliated with Constellation Lodge No. 18, Ancient Free and Accepted Masons, of Ottawa, Kansas. He is a stockholder in a furniture factory at Ottawa, Kansas, where he also owns a business block, and has his own residence at No. 112 South Seventh Street, Fredonia. His career has been a successful one, and the position which he occupies has been gained solely through his own effort and ability.

Mr. Suttle was married in 1888, at Burlington, Kansas, to Miss Josie Baldwin, a daughter of the late James M. and Hannah (Baldwin) Baldwin, who were farming people of the vicinity of Burlington. Mr. and Mrs. Suttle have no children.

REV. PETER WELLING, O. F. M., has for many years been a constructive factor in the upbuilding of the Catholic Church and its institutions in Kansas, and his name and career are especially associated with the town of Olpe in Lyon County, where he is pastor of St. Joseph's Catholic Church. The first Catholic services in that locality were held about 1884, when the mission was attended by priests from Emporia. The fine new modern church, situated in the northeastern part of the village on Main Street, was erected in 1910 during the pastorate of Father Welling, O. F. M. It has seating capacity for 700, and the church edifice is one of a group of buildings comprising also the parsonage, the parochial school and the Sister's residence. The parochial school has an enrollment of 135 scholars. In thirty years the parish has grown from small beginnings and has especially prospered under Father Welling's direction, and it is still vigorously growing. The parish extends from Olpe to one-half the distance to Emporia, eleven miles away, its southern boundary is to one-half the distance to Eagle Creek, five miles, while it extends an indefinite distance to the east and west.

Father Peter Welling is a member of the Franciscan Order. He was born at Oldenburg, Indiana, May 11, 1857, and attended the parochial schools of Cincinnati and the preparatory college of St. Francis in that city, and finished his courses in theology and philosophy at St. Boniface Seminary in Louisville, Kentucky, in December, 1885. He was then ordained a priest, and his first charge was at Lafayette, Indiana, from which point he visited the missions at Reynolds, Frankfort and Medaryville for two and a half years. Then he was stationed at Streeter, Illinois, for two years, and visited the missions of Benson and Washington. Then followed pastorates at Havelock, Nebraska, two years; Calumet, Michigan, in the copper regions, six years, and three years at Mount Airy, Cincinnati. He was then stationed at St. Bernard, Cincinnati, where he attended the city infirmary, Longview, and the county infirmary. From 1903 Father Welling was pastor of the Holy Family Church in Leads, Missouri, for three years, then was stationed a year and a half at Osceola, and since 1909 has had full charge of St. Joseph's Church at Olpe.

His father was Henry Welling, who was born in 1805 in Linge, Germany. He came to America when a young man, was a general workman, and lived in Cincinnati for some years, where he married. About 1854 he removed to Oldenburg, Indiana, and later to Hamburg, Indiana, where he died in 1885. He was a democrat and a member of the Catholic Church. Before leaving Germany he served as a soldier in the army. He married Catherine Nieman, who was born in 1816 at Dinklage, Germany, came to Cincinnati when a young girl, and died at Hamburg, Indiana, in 1897. Her four children were: Vincent, who was a teacher and died in Hamburg, Indiana, at the age of fifty-six; Josephine, who died in Dayton, Kentucky, in 1902, as the wife of Joseph Kuhling, who is also deceased; Carrie, who lives at Hamburg, Indiana; and Father Peter Welling.

WILLIAM S. TYNER was one of the early settlers of Kansas, though he lived in the state only a few years, but founded a family which has become especially well known and prominent in Osage County.

The Tyners were an old and prominent family of Indiana. William S. Tyner was one of seven sons and was born on a farm in Rush County, Indiana, September 20, 1820. His parents were John and Nancy (Sailors) Tyner, both Indiana people. William S. Tyner was a cousin of James N. Tyner, who served as postmaster-general under President Hayes.

The early education of William S. Tyner was acquired in the district school of Rush County. When he was nineteen years of age his family removed to Wabash County in that state. In 1842 William Hyner married Mary Washburn of Indiana. Six children were born to their union: Milton, deceased; Helen, Mrs. Hiza Wilson of Michigan Valley, Kansas; Jonas of California; Willis H. of Lyndon; Arminda, who lives on the old homestead in Indiana; Edgar, deceased; and Melvin of Arcadia, Tennessee.

The Indiana home of William S. Tyner for many years was a 160-acre farm. There he and his wife reared their family. In 1869 he followed two of his older sons, Milton and Jonas, to Kansas, located on a farm of a quarter section in Douglas County. In Douglas County he became prominent as a citizen and did much to build up that country in the years following the war. He was very active on the farm and in community affairs until the death of his wife in 1884. He then returned to Wabash, Indiana, and lived retired until his death. William S. Tyner was always favorably impressed and an enthusiastic advocate of the advantages and opportunities of the great State of Kansas. This was true despite the fact that he had weathered the storms and vicissitudes of early Kansas farming. He endured the troubles of the grasshopper year, the drought, and practically all the other hardships which the people of that time had to endure. Though a loyal republican, William S. Tyner was no politician and never held an office. He was an active member of the Grange and both he and his wife were devout Baptists and active in church work. During his residence in Kansas he identified himself with the upbuilding of schools and churches and lent a helping hand to everything for community good.

Willis H. Tyner, a son of this old time settler, is one of the foremost citizens of Lyndon in Osage County. He was born on a farm near Wabash, Indiana, January 14, 1852. He attended school there and worked on a farm and was about seventeen years of age when he came with his parents to Kansas. After several years in this state he returned to Indiana. Mr. Tyner married Rebecca Moore of

Baldwin, Kansas, but a native of Illinois. Her parents were Leroy and Sarah (Eliott) Moore, who on coming to Kansas located at Ottawa. Leroy Moore was deputy sheriff of Franklin County two terms and had also served as sheriff for two terms in Mercer County, Illinois.

When the plague of grasshoppers swept Kansas during the '70s, Mr. and Mrs. Willis H. Tyner went back to Indiana, where he rented a farm of 160 acres. Later he rented 300 acres near Wabash, and lived there for twelve years, enjoying a steadily increasing prosperity. In the meantime he had not forgotten Kansas, and his admiration for the state grew apace and finally brought him back within its limits. Mr. Tyner bought eighty acres in Junction Township of Osage County on One Hundred Ten Creek, and when he retired he had 117 acres of fine farming land which he sold. In 1903 he bought 160 acres near Lyndon, and lived on and managed that place until 1909. After renting his farm he moved into the city of Lyndon, and became the active business partner of L. T. Hussey, now state fire marshal. They were engaged in the real estate and insurance business under the name of Hussey & Tyner, and they were also closely associated in much public-spirited and welfare work. Mr. Tyner served as township trustee of Valley Brook Township for two years, in 1909-10, and was a member of the town council of Lyndon from 1909 to 1915. While township trustee he and Mr. Hussey, who was then mayor of Lyndon, did much to acquire a Carnegie library for the city. While in the council Mr. Tyner was interested in the adoption of the light, water and sewer system, and he also helped to extend the lines of the electric light plant to Quenemo and Malvern, two towns now lighted from the municipal plant of Lyndon.

Mr. Tyner is an active republican, served for nine years as trustee of the Independent Order of Odd Fellows Lodge and is a member of the Ancient Order of United Workmen. He and his wife are members of the Christian Church. To their marriage were born two children: Cora Belle is now Mrs. S. B. Reed of Barton County, Kansas; Nora May, now deceased, was formerly Mrs. Calvin Leonard, of Quenemo, Kansas. Mrs. Leonard is survived by two daughters, Cora and Ruth.

GEORGE PIERSON MOREHOUSE has a place among the prominent and well known public men of Kansas due to an exceptional range of interests and activities. His life has touched agricultural and business affairs, and has had its influence in the political, legal and literary life of the West. For many years he lived at Diamond Springs or Council Grove in Morris County, but at present resides in Topeka, though he still spends considerable time upon the large stock farm known as the old "Morehouse Ranche" at Diamond Springs, which he owns and upon which the family settled nearly fifty years ago.

At that time, the Kansa or Kaw Indians were on their reservation nearby, and going back and forth to the great buffalo ranges only two days drive to the westward. Large herds of long-horned cattle were driven along the old Santa Fe trail and the Kaw Indian trail, guarded by the then simon-pure festive cow-boy; the only settlers were few, scattered and located along the watered and wooded streams; and the vast sea of luxuriant prairie grass between the water courses died unused and became the dangerous food for the conflagrations which annually swept over that region. Game also was very plentiful.

Inured to the many rigors of frontier life of that period, George P. Morehouse grew to manhood and became expert as a hunter and horseman. Money procured from the sale of furs, skins and wolf pelts bought clothes, school books and other luxuries. The terms of the district school on Diamond Valley at that time were short and primitive, but with the required preparation, principally by self-study, he entered the Albion Academy in New York, where he graduated in 1884, and also became an academic graduate of the University of New York before returning to Kansas. Apparently he adapted himself to the change from the crudeness of Kansas ranch life to the refinements of eastern schools; for, before he returned to his western home he was elected president and orator of his class and won three prizes—the Bailey prize in anatomy and physiology; the Coann prize in oratory; and the Inter-Academic rhetorical prize.

While in the East he began the study of law but came home and engaged in the management of the cattle ranch for two or three years. During this time he was chosen trustee and assessor of Diamond Valley Township, which was at that time about four times its present size. He became active in public development in the community; helped locate the present line of the Atchison, Topeka and Santa Fe Railway through Morris County; and personally secured the two stations of Burdick and Diamond Springs in the then Diamond Valley Township, when the railway was determined, according to their policy, to give the township but one station.

Mr. Morehouse afterwards finished his legal education at Council Grove and was admitted to the bar of Morris County in 1889. Within a short time he was appointed city attorney of Council Grove and served in that position for nearly six years. Afterwards he was appointed to fill a vacancy in the office of county attorney of Morris County, and at the end was elected for a full term to that office and prosecuted the violators of the prohibition cause with unusual vigor. When a mere boy he received a commission as United States census enumerator for the southwestern part of Morris County and before he was old enough to vote was a frequent speaker and debater upon early railway matters and politics. During his long residence at Council Grove he became active and widely known in the organization of the republican party and often served as secretary of the county central committee, secretary and chairman of the congressional committee, and also as a member of the Republican State Central Committee.

The only partner Mr. Morehouse ever had in his legal practice was his young friend, the late Clarence A. Crowley, who also served several terms as county attorney.

In the campaign of 1900 Mr. Morehouse was a candidate for state senator of the Twenty-third District (Morris, Marion and Chase counties) and was elected by over 1,000 majority, serving through three sessions during the four years. He took an active part in the legislation of that strenuous political period, serving as chairman of the Congressional Apportionment Committee and as a member of the Judiciary, Elections, Education and Public Health committees. During the session as member of the Election Committee he tried four important contest cases—three senatorial and one judicial—winning favorable comment for his judicial thoroughness and fairness.

He was the author of the first automobile legislation in the West, and at a time when much ridicule was cast upon such then advanced legislation. This measure, which provided how automobiles should be equipped with safety devices, their rate of speed in city and country, and how they should be operated when meeting frightened horses, etc., caused much comment and was the foundation of legislation along that line which all now admit is proper.

It was his measure that legally recognized the sunflower as the state flower and floral emblem of Kansas and advertised it as the "Sunflower State" of the nation.

When the Soldier's Monument Bill was before the Senate and drew out a spirited debate, the Topeka Capital in mentioning the occasion and in publishing most of his remarks, said: "One of the best speeches in the senate in favor of the bill to provide a monument for the soldiers of Kansas was made by Senator George P. Morehouse. He is one of the most forceful speakers in the senate and his address on this occasion was one of the best efforts of the session."

When the new manual training and industrial educational bill was before the Legislature and such an institution was established at Pittsburgh, Senator Morehouse was leading advocate in the Senate and his speech on that new departure in educational methods was published and widely circulated.

In the Senate and upon the stump he was a pioneer advocate of equal rights and suffrage for the women of Kansas. As early as 1901 he introduced and secured the passage by the Senate of "an act relating to suffrage, being an act to give women the right to vote for presidential electors." Had it become a law, Kansas women would have taken part in three presidential elections prior to their first experience in 1916 under the general suffrage amendment clause.

While he was a member of the Kansas Senate the Council Grove Republican had this to say: "The Senate of Kansas has always been a body of bright men—able lawyers or individuals of more than local influence and reputation. To maintain a standing among them, one must possess a high grade of tact and ability. Among the present leaders and influential members of that body is Senator George P. Morehouse. He has lived in this county most of his life and has taken such an important part in all public affairs, even since before he was a voter, that he is known by everybody. . . . While Senator Morehouse does not shun the rough and tumble of a political campaign and is an effective public speaker and popular 'political mixer' yet his tastes are of a scholarly character and have been more or less broadened by travel and as a student of the best books, with which his private library is filled. He is active in literary and educational work such as the Shakespeare Club and Library Association and prominent in the work of the Presbyterian Church.

"His political convictions along republican lines are such that no one ever doubts where he stands upon public questions. In the senate last winter he was placed on six of the leading committees and was one of the hardest worked members of that body. As a member of the elections committee he helped frame that new ballot law upon which fusion has been broken, and was an able advocate of the stringent temperance law—the Hurrell bill—and frequently defended it against the attacks of the whiskey power.

"Senator Morehouse by his presence in the senate lent an odor of clean politics to the surroundings of

that prominent body and whenever he arose to cast a vote or express a view upon any matter, he commanded the respect and attention of both the members and the visitors present. His every act and word were for the interest of his constituents and the state at large, and won for him many kind words from the press and public men. There is hardly a paper in the state that has not commented favorably upon his work and felt proud that he was a member of the senate. We may well feel proud that we possess such a good citizen and able representative in the senate."

During the latter part of his senatorial term Mr. Morehouse was chosen as president of the Kansas State Republican League—often termed the "Boss Busters" —the pioneer organization which did so much to reform Kansas politics from its "skull and cross bones" tendency, and which started the movement for the election of United States senators by popular vote.

As the historian and genealogist of the Morehouse Family Association of America, Mr. Morehouse has gathered the largest collection of the history of that family in existence. This history will probably be published. It has always been a matter of Morehouse family pride that its ancestors were among the early pioneer settlers of America. Some of them came prior to 1640 and were active in the founding of early New England towns and in the formation of the colonial governments.

The family is of Scotch-English origin, the name first appearing soon after the year 1000 in North England, where it was originally Moorhouse, from having built their "houses-upon-the-moors" or "Moorhouses" as it is still used in Scotland and Yorkshire.

Thomas Morehouse, recognized as the emigrant ancestor of most of the American Morehouse families, was in Watertown, Massachusetts, about 1635; at Wethersfield, Connecticut, 1640; at Stamford, Connecticut, in 1641, where he was one of the original settlers who purchased the townsite from the Indians for one hundred bushels of corn. He came from Yorkshire, England, with the migration of Puritans conducted by Sir Richard Saltonstall. He settled permanently at Fairfield, Connecticut, prior to 1653 and became prominent in its development—owning the tide-water mill and being sent as a member to the General Court (Legislature) at Hartford. He left four sons—Samuel, Thomas, Jonathan and John—who at an early date became the heads of the numerous branches and descendants which settled in New York, New Jersey, Ohio and the West. Thomas Morehouse, the first, died at Fairfield in 1658, leaving a will. It is estimated that over two hundred of his descendants served in the Revolutionary war.

His son John settled at Southampton, Long Island; was an ensign in King Phillip's war in 1676 and was the ancestor of George P. Morehouse, who is of the eighth generation from Thomas the immigrant.

The history of the family is one of honorable achievement from the time its heroic members took part in the Crusades to the Holy Land and received the honorable decoration of the large Saltire or St. Andrew's Cross, down to the present, whether in the public or private walks of life.

Horace Morehouse, father of George P., was a native of Tompkins County, New York. In the early '50s he removed to Decatur, Illinois, before a railroad had reached that place, and established the well known hardware firm of Morehouse-Wells Company, as afterwards known under the management of his younger brother George E. Morehouse, to whose estate it still belongs. Horace Morehouse was one of the founders of the republican party in the west and active in securing the nomination of Abraham Lincoln for the presidency in 1860. He helped build the noted "Wigwam" at Decatur, in which was held the first republican state convention, where the noted Lincoln rails were presented and where Lincoln was first mentioned at the "rail splitter candidate."

In 1871, with others, Horace Morehouse drove overland in covered wagons to Diamond Springs, Morris County, Kansas, where he opened up the stock farm still known as the old "Morehouse Ranche," as above mentioned. Horace Morehouse like many of his ancestors was an elder in the Presbyterian Church and active in its work, being one of the founders of the Presbyterian Church at Council Grove, where for several years he was engaged in the mercantile business. He died in the City of Topeka in 1915 in his ninetieth year.

George P. Morehouse was born at Decatur, Illinois, July 28, 1859. Besides him there are four living brothers: Charles H. of Salt Lake City, Utah; Robert H. of Topeka; James H. and Maxey M. of Twin Falls, Idaho.

The mother was Lavinia F. Strong, a native of Auburn, New York, who died at Diamond Springs, Kansas, in 1885. She was a woman of scholarly tastes, a clever writer of prose and poetry, and her influence encouraged Senator Morehouse along the same line and fired his ambition to seek a more liberal education than was possible at frontier district schools. She was the only daughter of Rev. Noble Davies Strong M. A., a Presbyterian minister, an early graduate of Middlebury College, Vermont, author and educator and for years at the head of academies at Auburn and Cortland, New York. He was a descendant of "Elder John Strong" one of the founders of Northampton, Massachusetts, who came with the Puritans in 1630, and was the father of the numerous and noted Strong family in America, which has produced so many educators, authors, jurists and divines.

April 23, 1906, George P. Morehouse married Mrs. Louise Thorne Hull at Los Angeles, California. She is a native of Morgantown, West Virginia, a daughter of Captain Amaltha and Anna (Berkshire) Thorne, late of Piqua, Ohio, and through them a descendant of prominent Virginia families. Her grandfather, Col. Ralph Berkshire, was a colonel of Virginia troops and served several terms in the Virginia Legislature. In 1834 he became a pioneer to Henry County, Indiana, where he was also a state legislature and probate judge for many years. Her cousin Judge Ralph L. Berkshire of Morgantown was one of the early circuit judges of the new State of West Virginia, and also presiding judge of the Supreme Court for six years. He was prominent in the formation of the new state and a member of the committee at Morgantown, which on April 17, 1861, drafted the first resolution, widely published, and known as "The First Loyal Voice from West Virginia."

Mrs. Morehouse has been a resident of Topeka since 1881, coming in that year from Piqua, Ohio, with her younger sister Emma (Mrs. C. H. Morgan). A recent Kansas publication has said: "Mrs. Morehouse is a lady of education and refinement, personally popular and widely known for her business ability and her substantial support to educational and moral institutions. The Morehouse home, opposite the State Capitol, is noted for its informal and generous hospitality. For several years past it has been the frequent meeting place for the sessions of the Kansas Authors Club and the 'rest haven' where Kansas writers and literary people have passed many pleasant hours. For a number of years Mr. Morehouse has been active in the affairs of the Kansas Authors Club, serving two terms as its president. For six years past he has acted as its secretary, during which time it has been incorporated and become the leading literary organization in the state, its annual state meetings and banquets being noted events."

For many years Mr. Morehouse has been a director and life member of the Kansas State Historical Society; and at the present time is also first vice president and in line for its president next year. He has been devoted to its work and interests; serves as the chairman of its archæological department and has contributed numerous historical articles for the society's publications. He was probably the first person to suggest the movement to permanently mark the old Santa Fe Trail and other famous overland highways and helped the Historical Society and the Daughters of the American Revolution in that worthy undertaking, making many historical addresses at the celebrations incident to the dedication of the Santa Fe Trail monuments across Kansas.

Many years ago he commenced the preservation of original data concerning this pioneer highway of old time Kansas (which passed his early home) and has also saved a large fund of the language, legends and traditional lore of the Kansa or Kaw Indians and has contributed numerous articles along those lines for newspapers and magazines. In recognition of this, and especially for having written a history of the tribe, he was chosen its official historian at one of the last council meetings it ever held; he possesses some of their ancient sacred charts and data, which is being prepared for publication. Mr. Morehouse is the author of several widely published articles, addresses, poems and pamphlets upon ancient western highways, early Spanish and French explorations, archæology, Indian life and legends. He discovered the correct meaning and derivation of the word Kansas and shows that it is of neither Indian nor French origin—as usually claimed—but that it comes from the Spanish verb "cansar" which means to molest, stir up and harass, and the noun "cansado" a disturber and troublesome fellow; and was first used by the Spanish explorers with Onate about 1601, when they called those Indians which bothered them "Escansaques." From this came the names Cansa, Cansez, Kansa, Kansas and one hundred and fifty other variations applied to this tribe, of which Mr. Morehouse has found historical record.

He is a working member of the International Society of Archæologists and as a student of aboriginal, Spanish and French matters of early Kansas has made some important discoveries not heretofore mentioned by Kansas historians. Some time ago he recovered from the Indians an ancient Aztec historical chart. It is a remarkable document 18 feet long by 8 inches wide and one of the largest ever found. Its hundreds of signs, symbols, pictures and hieroglyphics give, according to competent authority, 200 years of the history of the Aztec Nation after they left Aztlan and came to Mexico.

Mr. Morehouse is a Knight of Pythias and once served as chancellor commander of the order at Council Grove and deputy grand chancellor of the state jurisdiction. He was also an officer of the Modern Woodmen of America. He is a member of the Presbyterian Church and for many years was superintendent of its Sunday school at Council Grove. He was one of the incorporators of the Council Grove Library Association and acted as its treasurer for a long time.

His great-grandfather having been a commissioned officer in the Revolutionary war, Mr. Morehouse is a

Son of the American Revolution. At one time he contemplated a military career; but his only experience along that line was being commissioned a lieutenant and recruiting officer in the Kansas National Guard. He is a working member of the Kansas State Bar Association and at present chairman of its memorial committee.

In his library Mr. Morehouse has collected much rare Americana, also many ancient legal, literary, scientific and religious works, many in Latin, some of which are the oldest in this country, having been published in the Old World over 400 years ago. The Morehouse home in Topeka is on Capitol Square, at 216 West Eighth Street.

BURRITT H. HILL. Men of force are found in every prosperous community who by reason of their natural ability, by their capacity for handling large enterprises, by the use of their brains and the soundness of their judgment, attain distinction and acquire authority. Working industriously toward a given goal, in helping themselves these men add to the welfare and prosperity of their city, and their efforts not only bring into being the substantial industries that support commerce, but conduct them along the safe and sane channels which assure public progress and general contentment. In Wilson County one of the men of this class is found in the person of Burritt H. Hill. Mr. Hill is a successful business man and vice president of the First National Bank of Neodesha, but also he is one of the public-spirited citizens who have helped the community to grow and develop, having merged the two characters of business man and citizen into a fine combination that is well worthy of emulation.

Burritt H. Hill was born at Neodesha, Wilson County, Kansas, July 10, 1873, and is a son of William and Ellen Clark (Maxwell) Hill. His grandfather, James Hill, was born in 1810, near Glasgow, Scotland, emigrated to the United States in 1844, became a pioneer of Ohio and Wisconsin, where he engaged in farming and as a millwright, and died at Baraboo, in the latter state, in 1893. William Hill was born October 18, 1831, near Glasgow, Scotland, and was about eleven years of age when brought by his parents to the United States. The family first settled at what was known as New Philadelphia, in Ashtabula County, Ohio, where young William was apprenticed to a merchant, but two years later removed to Sauk County, Wisconsin. There the youth learned the trade of printer, which he followed for some years in Wisconsin and at other points, and in 1861, when the Civil war came on, was working in Missouri. He enlisted in Company B, Eighth Regiment, Missouri Volunteer Infantry, with which organization he fought throughout the period of the war, participating in numerous engagements, including Forts Henry and Donelson, Pittsburg Landing, Siege of Vicksburg and Lookout Mountain. When the war was over he returned to Wisconsin, and was married in Sauk County to Miss Ellen Clark Maxwell, who was born May 10, 1845, in Wisconsin. In that state he entered the newspaper business and became editor of the Baraboo Republic, with which he was identified until he came to Kansas, in 1873, in April of which year he embarked in the banking business. He has since that time been the directing head of the First National Bank of Neodesha. He is also interested in 1,900 acres of farm lands in Wilson County and has various other holdings. Mr. Hill is independent in politics, and a member of the Kansas State Bankers Association and the National Bankers Association. He resides at No. 416 North Eighth Street, and is one of Neodesha's most prominent and substantial men.

Mr. and Mrs. Hill have had the following children: A.; L., who is a lumber dealer of Medford, Oregon; Aeo, who died in 1893, at Oswego, Kansas, as the wife of Samuel Carpenter, a merchant of that city; H. M., who is a stockman and farmer of Lafontaine, Kansas; Burritt H.; and Irving, who resides at Lawrence, Kansas, as manager of the Corrugated Paper Mills.

Burritt H. Hill acquired his preliminary education in the public schools of Neodesha, being graduated from the high school in the class of 1890, and following this entered Kansas University, where he was a member of the exclusive honorary scientific Greek letter society of Sigma Psi. Graduating with the degree of Bachelor of Arts, in 1894, he at once entered the banking business with the First National Bank of Neodesha, as bookkeeper. He was successively advanced to assistant cashier and cashier, and in 1914 was made vice president of the concern, a business relation which still obtains. The First National Bank of Neodesha was established in 1872, as a state bank, and was known as the Neodesha Savings Bank, its officers at that time being J. V. Pierce, president; John Gray, vice president; and Charles Henderson, cashier. Its capital was $10,000. The bank was nationalized in 1903, with D. Stewart as president; A. L. Hill, as vice president; and William Hill as cashier. Its present officers are: William Hill, president; B. H. Hill, vice president; and H. H. Woodring, cashier, and its capital is now $50,000, its surplus, $20,000, and its undivided profits, $5,000. The modern new brick banking house was erected in June, 1915, at the corner of Sixth and Main streets, with the bank's quarters on the first floor and offices on the second. The bank is one of the oldest and most substantial in Wilson County, and its influence is wide and its results far reaching. Its policies governed and directed by men of acknowledged ability and integrity it shares in no small degree the confidence of the people of the locality, and its depositors come from all over this part of the county.

B. H. Hill has various interests in addition to those connected with the bank, being secretary of the Neodesha Building and Loan Association; of the V. V. V. Brick and Tile Company, the plant of which is the largest hand plant west of the Mississippi River; and the Neodesha Crystal Ice Company. He also owns much real estate in the city and several farms. Like his father, he maintains an independent stand upon political questions, preferring to use his own judgment in his selection of candidates worthy of his vote rather than to be guided by party lines and therefore restricted. His own public service is confined to fourteen years of occupancy of the office of city treasurer of Neodesha, on two occasions. Mr. Hill takes a lively interest in civic affairs and is a member of the Neodesha Commercial Club and the Anti-Horse Thief Association. As a fraternalist he belongs to Harmony Lodge No. 94, Ancient Free and Accepted Masons, of which he is past master; Orient Chapter No. 72, Royal Arch Masons, of which he is past high priest; Ab-Del-Kader Commandery No. 27, Knights Templar; Topeka Council, Scottish Rite Masons; Wichita Consistory No. 2, of the thirty-second degree; and Abdullah Temple, Ancient Arabic Order Nobles of the Mystic Shrine, at Leavenworth.

Mr. Hill was married in 1898, at Neodesha, to Miss Essie Eson, daughter of Mrs. Laura Esson. Mrs. Hill died in 1899, at Neodesha, having been the mother of one daughter: Aeo, born July 27, 1899.

CHARLES SOUTH. The oil industry in the Mid-Continent field of Kansas has an able representative in the person of Charles South, of Chanute, who has been producing in this field since 1903. Like many of the men interested in the business here, Mr. South had his introduction to oil production in the Pennsylvania fields, and when he arrived in Kansas had a number of years of experience back of him to assist him in his enterprises.

Mr. South was born near the City of Pittsburgh, Pennsylvania, April 26, 1864, and is a son of John and Vilinda (Everly) South. He belongs to a family which traces its ancestry back to Cromwell's time in England, when the family sided with King Charles, and which was founded in America during the days previous to the outbreak of the War of the American Revolution. Benjamin South, the great-grandfather of Charles South, was born in New Jersey, and went with his son Enoch to Greene County, Pennsylvania, where his death occurred. Enoch South, grandfather of Charles, was born in 1787, in New Jersey, subsequently became a pioneer of Western Pennsylvania, where he was an extensive land owner, and died in Greene County, that state, in 1863. The family has a fine Revolutionary record, the eight sons of the original emigrant (who was the great-great-great-grandfather of Charles South) having fought as soldiers of the Continental line, enlisting from the colony of New Jersey.

John South was born in 1822, in Greene County, Pennsylvania. He was reared to manhood and educated in Greene County, and like his father became an extensive landholder, also building up a large business as a raiser of and dealer in live stock. Through an industrious life, in which his business affairs were ably managed, he accumulated a handsome property. He died in his native county in 1902. Mr. South was prominent in democratic politics and civic affairs, and at one time served as county treasurer of Greene County. He came of Quaker stock, but never affiliated with any church. Mr. South married Miss Vilinda Everly, who was born in 1837, in Greene County, and passed her entire life there, dying in 1911. They became the parents of fourteen children. Those who grew to manhood and womanhood were as follows: Furman, who was a manufacturer and died at Pittsburgh, Pennsylvania, in January, 1914; Gilpin, who is a land owner and stock raiser of Greene County, Pennsylvania; Sarah, who is unmarried and resides at Waynesburg, Pennsylvania; Everly, who is a retired investor and lives at Bridgeport, Ohio; Charles, of this review; Taylor, who is an oil producer of Chanute, Kansas; Malinda, who is the wife of J. B. F. Rhinehart, a manufacturer of Waynesburg, Pennsylvania; Laura, who is the wife of Clarence Wilson, a merchant of Waynesburg; Retta, who is unmarried and resides at Waynesburg, Pennsylvania; and Dora, who died at Waynesburg, as the wife of Fred Kelsey, auditor for the Gulf Pipe Line Company, at Pittsburgh, Pennsylvania.

Charles South received his education in the public schools of his native county and at Waynesburg College, which institution he left in 1884 to become connected with the oil business. His first experience was gained in the fields of Washington, Pennsylvania, following which he went to the Sisterville, West Virginia fields, and those of Kentucky. For a short time he gave up the oil business to engage in mining in the zinc fields of Joplin, Missouri, but in 1903 returned to the business when he came to Chanute. At this time Mr. South has extensive oil producing interests near Chanute, as well as other interests, and is considered one of the successful operators of the Mid-Continent field. He devotes his entire time to

his business, and his only activity in politics is in the casting of his vote for the candidates of the democratic party. Mr. South is unmarried.

HON. ISAAC M. HINDS. Mound Valley and Labette County have for many years been the scene of the extensive business and public activities of Isaac M. Hinds. Some years ago that district sent Mr. Hinds to represent its interests in the State Senate, and he is still a member of the upper house of the State Legislature.

Though he has spent nearly all his years in Kansas, Senator Hinds was born in Cole County, Missouri, December 30, 1862. He was brought to this state when an infant. Going back several generations his Hinds ancestors were Germans who came to America and were early settlers about Bowling Green, Kentucky. The grandfather of Senator Hinds was Benjamin, a native of Kentucky. He went to Missouri and became a pioneer in Cole County, where he died before Senator Hinds was born.

Isaac Hinds, father of Senator Hinds, was born in Kentucky in 1833, was reared and married in Missouri, and followed farming as his life's vocation. He died in Cole County in February, 1863. The maiden name of his wife was Cordelia A. Stephens. She was born in Cole County, Missouri, August 4, 1833, and is still living at the age of eighty-three, making her home with her son, Senator Hinds. She married for her second husband James M. Richardson, who died in Mound Valley, Kansas, where he was a retired farmer. Isaac Hinds and wife had the following children: Benjamin F., who is a mechanic living at Kansas City, Missouri; William M., who died in young manhood at Mound Valley in 1876; Joseph, who died at Mound Valley in 1874; Jennie, wife of L. W. Wilmoth of San Diego, California; and Isaac M.

While the Civil war was still in progress Mr. Hinds' mother brought her family to Kansas and located on a farm three miles southwest of Mound Valley. In that locality Isaac M. Hinds spent his early youth and childhood. He attended the district schools of Labette County, and in 1882 completed the teachers' course in the Fort Scott Normal College. Following that came two years of teaching in Montgomery County. A desire to see the world then seized him, and he made a trip not unaccompanied by hardships and hard work through Arizona, New Mexico, California, Oregon and Washington, going as far as Seattle. The winter of 1883-84 he spent in the hazardous occupation of logging in the State of Washington.

On returning to Kansas Mr. Hinds, in the fall of 1884, engaged in the drug business at Mound Valley. After about a year he sold his store and then took a course in the St. Louis College of Pharmacy. He received his certificate as a registered pharmacist from the State Board of Pharmacy, in 1887, and though he has not been in the drug business for a number of years he still keeps his certificate up-to-date as a registered druggist. Mr. Hinds had the leading drugstore at Mound Valley until 1905. In that year his business interests became more widely extended. He began buying land near Brownsville, in the extreme southern end of Texas, and since then has bought and sold land not only in Texas but in Kansas and Oklahoma. He deals entirely in his own properties and has done a great deal to develop some of the newer localities of the Southwest.

For four years Mr. Hinds was vice president of

Chas. S. Walker

the Mound Valley State Bank. He has long been prominent in the councils of the democratic party. He served as councilman a number of terms at Mound Valley, was mayor two years, assessor one year, and in 1912 was elected for his first term in the State Senate. That term expires in January, 1917, and at this writing he is a candidate for re-election.

Senator Hinds has the distinction of being the only senator who is chairman of two committees. These two committees are: Employees Committee and Temperance and Hygiene Committee. He is also a member of the Banks and Banking Committee, the Federal and State Affairs Committee, Mines and Mining, Oil and Gas, and the Ways and Means committees.

Senator Hinds has been a conspicuous figure in the county and state conventions of his party for many years. In 1904 he was nominated as a delegate to the National Convention, and in 1912 attended the convention at Baltimore as a delegate. During Cleveland's second administration he served as postmaster of Mound Valley from January 1, 1893, to January 1, 1897. He was president of the Mound Valley Commerical Club when that organization was in flourishing existence. Fraternally he is past master of Mound Valley Lodge No. 218, Ancient Free and Accepted Masons, and is affiliated with Lodge No. 211, Independent Order of Odd Fellows, Lodge No. 61, Ancient Order United Workmen, and the Modern Woodmen of America at Mound Valley.

Senator Hinds is the owner of over 700 acres of land in Kansas and Oklahoma. At Mound Valley he owns the postoffice building on Hickory Street, and has his own home at the corner of Commercial and Hickory streets, and another dwelling on Hickory Street. His offices are on Main Street. During the disastrous fire of 1907 he lost a hotel and four other business buildings.

In 1887 at Mound Valley Mr. Hinds married Miss Zenora Gandy. Mrs. Hinds was born in Iowa in 1869, a daughter of R. W. and Mary Gandy, both of whom are now deceased. Her father was a merchant. To their marriage have been born two children, Cecil L. and Thelma A. The daughter, who was born October 15, 1899, is now a senior in the high school at Mound Valley. The son, Cecil, who was born at Mound Valley, November 15, 1889, was educated in the public schools, graduating from high school in 1906, and had his early business experience in his father's drugstore. For a year he conducted a flour and feed mill, for another year ran a store at Preston, Nebraska, and then for five years was assistant cashier of the Mound Valley State Bank. September 10, 1915, Cecil L. Hinds became postmaster at Mound Valley under the administration of President Wilson. He is thus filling an office which his father served in with commendable credit twenty years ago. Cecil Hinds is an active democrat, is affiliated with Lodge No. 61, Ancient Order United Workmen, at Mound Valley, and Mound Valley Lodge No. 218, Ancient Free and Accepted Masons. In 1912 at Mound Valley he married Miss Alice Morris, daughter of A. W. and Paralee Morris. Her parents reside at Shelbina in Shelby County, Missouri.

THE FARMERS UNION OF KANSAS is a branch of the great national organization known as The Farmers Educational and Co-operative Union, with business headquarters at Atlanta, Georgia. C. S. Barrett is president of the national organization. This organ-ization has a membership of 2,500,000, located in thirty-one different states. The head office of the Kansas organization is at Saline, and the president of The State Farmers Union is Maurice McAuliffe, while the manager, with headquarters at Kansas City, Kansas, is Mr. Charles S. Walker.

The Kansas Union has 50,000 members, and has undoubtedly been the greatest single factor in creating a stability of values, an equalization of opportunities; and a general strengthening of the agricultural interests in competition with so many other organizations which now dominate the field of industry and commerce. The Farmers Union of Kansas had its birth about 1907. Out of this has grown the Kansas Jobbing Association, organized about 1912. This association operates 200 elevators and has fifty-seven co-operative stores and about fifty produce stations, and through this association direct benefits of higher prices and better marketing conditions are brought to Kansas farmers, as similar organizations in the Far West have benefitted the orange growers and other producers. In 1916 the total volume of business transacted through the Jobbing Association amounted to a hundred million dollars. The organization is made up of progressive farmers and through its work the agricultural interests are rapidly learning the principle that in union there is strength.

Mr. Charles S. Walker, manager of the union, is himself a practical and successful Kansas farmer. He was born on a farm in Morris County, Kansas, September 12, 1875. He was one of nine children, five of whom are still living. His parents, Joseph and Emma (Peck) Walker, were natives, respectively, of England and New York State. Joseph Walker came from England in 1871 with a colony of English people to locate in Kansas. He was a son of Samuel and Mary Walker, who came at the same time. Joseph was the last survivor of their twelve children. Samuel Walker bought a farm in Morris County and was one of the early settlers, and before his death some seven or eight years later had eighty acres of his land broken up and in cultivation. Joseph Walker married Emma Peck in Kansas. She had come with her parents, and they all became farmers in Morris County. Joseph Walker was a republican and a quite active factor in his community, though never holding office. He did much to build up and support schools, churches and other enterprises, and he and his family were Methodists.

Charles S. Walker grew up on the farm, attended district schools and the schools at Parkersville, and later the Council Grove High School. He worked his way through high school, paying for his board by doing chores at morning and night. He also taught school for a time, but did not find this a very remunerative undertaking. He completed his education during the intervals of farm work continued for about seven years. It was his ambition to complete a course in the University of Kansas, but lack of finances compelled him to abandon this. For a time he rented a farm and gradually got ahead in the world and reached a point where he was able to buy 160 acres for himself. He did not stop there, and in time he had a complete section of land, but subsequently sold this.

In 1907 he became identified with The Farmers Union of Kansas at the time of its organization, and has been a prime mover in its work ever since. At the same time he continued his farming operations until 1912, when he left the farm to give all his time to the work of the organization. He has been a delegate to all the state conventions of The Farmers Union since it was organized and has held the offices

He attended the Wolcott High School in 1896, and at that time learned the trade of glass cutting, a vocation which he followed at Covington, Pennsylvania; and at Mount Jewett, Kane, Hazelhurst and Bradford, in that state. He became a resident of Kansas in 1902, in which year he settled at Fredonia, where he was made superintendent of the cutting department of the Fredonia Window Glass Company. In 1907 he engaged in the general builders' supply business, at Oklahoma City, Oklahoma, and continued there until 1914, at that time going to Rochester, New York, where he carried on the weather-stripping business. In 1915 he returned to Fredonia, and here again accepted the superintendency of the cutting department of the Fredonia Window Glass Company, a position which he now holds. He is a stanch republican, a member of the Presbyterian Church, and a Mason and Modern Woodman as to fraternal connection. In 1900, at Red Creek, New York, he was married to Grace Warner, daughter of Truman and Francena (Howell) Warner, residents of Red Creek, where Mr. Warner is engaged in farming. Mr. and Mrs. Lutes have one daughter—Geraldine, born August 5, 1911. After the death of his first wife, F. W. Lutes was married to Miss Maria Griffin, who survives him and resides at Wolcott, New York. To this union there were born three children, as follows: Harry, who is a glasscutter and resides at Fredonia; Florence, who is the wife of Lemon Olmstead, a merchant of Fredonia; and Fred, who is a glasscutter by occupation and now a resident of Fredonia.

C. F. Lutes was educated in the public schools of Clyde, New York, and was only fifteen years of age when he began to learn the trade of glass making. He learned the trade from his father and brother who were also in the glass business, and was obliged to serve a three years' apprenticeship without pay. That apprenticeship was in learning the first step in the business. This is described technically as "gathering," it being very necessary that the workman shall learn to gather before he learns to blow. Two years later Mr. Lutes learned to blow, and worked at Clyde, New York, and Wellsboro and Smithport, Pennsylvania, and in the year 1892 went into business as a manufacturer at Covington, Pennsylvania.

Window glass workmen are very strongly organized, and have been for many years. The organization is so strictly maintained that outsiders are practically unable to learn the trade. The only ones allowed to learn are very strictly limited. Thus a father can teach a son or a brother teach a brother, and this tends to keep the followers of the trade largely in family line, as was true of some of the ancient workmen's guilds. Mr. Lutes' ancestors were in the glass business as far back as he has any record. It is also a matter that many people will learn with surprise that window glass blowers are the highest paid skilled labor in the United States. Their wages will average about $12 per day and some have been known to make as high as $600 or $700 per month.

Mr. Lutes came to Kansas in 1904 as president and general manager of the Fredonia Window Glass Company. As this is the largest concern of its kind in Kansas, some of the more important facts concerning the industry may appropriately be considered in this sketch.

Ground was broken for the glass plant at Fredonia on July 0, 1904. The first window glass was made December 24, 1904. The Caney plant started a couple of years later. The Fredonia plant is described as a 48-blower capacity, employing 48 blowers, 48 gatherers, 48 snappers, 12 flatteners and 16 cutters, these with other employes making about 300 men. The production of this plant is over 5,000 boxes of window glass per week, each mercantile box containing fifty square feet. The Caney plant is what is termed as a 30-blower capacity, requiring 30 blowers, 30 gatherers, 30 snappers, 10 cutters and 9 flatteners.

In the making of window glass a large furnace or tank is required. The materials used in the building of such a furnace include the very best fire clay to be had, most of which is imported from Germany. During the last few years the Fredonia Company has been mixing this German clay with a clay obtained in Missouri. The walls of the furnace are sixteen inches thick. That is, the size of the blocks used in building up the walls is each 12 by 16 by 24 inches. The tops of the furnace are made of silica brick, each brick 2 by 16 by 12. After the furnace is constructed it is filled with large quantities of broken glass, called by the trade name "cullet." It requires 700 tons to fill such a furnace as that at Fredonia. This broken glass is fused by intense heat. This step is necessary in order to preserve the fire clay blocks, the molten glass forms a glazing over the blocks and preserves them, whereas had raw material been introduced at first the molten mass would have eaten into the fire clay and honeycombed them so they would last only two or three weeks.

The raw materials used in making window glass consists of sand, crushed limestone, sulphate of soda, commonly known as salt cake, soda ash and carbon. The proportions vary some under different atmospheres. For the blowing of the large glass natural gas is used for fuel. In a plant of the size of that at Fredonia about 1,500,000 cubic feet per day are required. All window glass is first made into a cylinder, then being cracked open from end to end. Each cylinder then reheated in what is termed as a flattening oven and flattened out on large flat fire clay stones. While the heat required for the melting of the raw material is between 2,800° and 3,200° Fahrenheit, the heat required in the flattening process is from 1,400° to 1,600° Fahrenheit. After the glass is flattened it goes through annealing lehrs then comes out into the cutting room, where it is assorted and cut with a diamond.

Mr. Lutes is authority for the statement that the first glass made west of the Mississippi River was at Fort Scott, Kansas, in the year 1888-89. That plant, which was financed by local capital, existed a very short time, only part of one year. Mr. Lutes has been very successful in the glass business in Kansas, and it is no small tribute to his energy and experience that the Fredonia plant has been making money while many other similar plants have failed. In 1911 there were eleven window glass plants in Kansas. At the present time there are only three. Some of them failed completely, and others were obliged to move away on account of the fuel situation. Besides the plants at Fredonia and Caney there was a third plant, of which Mr. Lutes was president and general manager until 1914, located at Okmulgee, Oklahoma. This was a machine plant with 150-blower capacity.

Mr. Lutes is a republican in his political views, and while he has not cared for public office has always capably and faithfully performed the duties pertaining to good citizenship. He is fraternally affiliated with Constellation Lodge No. 95, Ancient Free and Accepted Masons, the Benevolent and Protective Order of Elks and the Commercial Club. He holds stock in the Wilson County Bank of Fredonia, and is generally recognized as one of the substantial men of the city. As a realty holder he owns a number of valuable properties at and about Fredonia, which include a residence one mile south of the town, an eighty-acre farm 1¼ miles south of the city limits and four dwellings at Fredonia, one of which is situated at the corner of Washington and Eighth streets, one at the corner of Eighth and Madison streets, one on Fifteenth Street and one on Eighth Street. In business and social circles Mr. Lutes possesses an excellent reputation. His career is one worthy of emulation, since he won his way to the front through the medium of his own effort and through honorable and straightforward dealing with his fellow men.

In passing something should be said of his fine rural or suburban residence at Fredonia. It is one mile south of the town on what is called the Cement Road. It comprises a twenty-five acre farm with all modern improvements. Mr. Lutes has found no greater pleasure in business success than in using his profits for the development of this home. He has installed an individual electric plant, consisting of storage batteries, and capable of furnishing sixty lights per night. In digging a well he was fortunate in striking an abundance of water, which is pumped into a large tank and is sufficient to irrigate the entire place. There is a complete water system in the house, a vacuum and sweeping system has been installed, and the home also has its own sewerage system with septic tank. About five acres of the land is developed to orchard and grapes. As a small farm it is operated with the last word of efficiency. Mr. Lutes keeps fine grade horses, cows, hogs and chickens, and he uses a tractor for his plowing. Mention has already been made of the well which supplies an abundance of water for all purposes. In digging this well the bore penetrated a stratum of pure glass sand or silica, and seventeen carloads were taken from that stratum for the manufacture of glass.

Mr. Lutes' family consists of one daughter, Clara, who was born March 7, 1899, to his first marriage; and his wife and step-son, Donald Ritchie. Mr. Lutes was married in April, 1915, to Mrs. Catherine (Llewellyn) Ritchie of Fredonia. They were married at Wichita. Mrs. Lutes takes as much pride as her husband in their beautifully appointed home and assumes many of the practical details connected with the management of the farm.

FRED L. STONE. One of the first men to strike a pick into the mineral deposits around the present City of Galena in Cherokee County was the late Joseph T. Stone, whose experiences in that new mining field began nearly forty years ago. His son Fred L. Stone has spent the greater part of his active career in and around mines, beginning as a miner and later developing a business of his own, and is now one of the leading mine operators and business men of Galena.

This is a family that has been in America since colonial days. The Stones were English people who came to America and settled in New Jersey. Fred Stone's grandfather, Lewis Stone, was born in New Jersey, went to Kentucky early in life, where he was a farmer and blacksmith, and he enlisted from that state and saw service throughout the period of the Mexican War during the '40s. His death occurred in Barren County, Kentucky. before Fred Stone was born.

Joseph T. Stone, above mentioned, was born in Barren County, Kentucky, in 1847, and in 1852 he was taken by his parents to Southern Missouri. Though a small boy at the time he enlisted in 1862 at Springfield, Missouri, in the Eighth Missouri Volunteer Cavalry, and was in service three years,

twenty-one days. He was in the campaigns at Wilson Creek, Neosho, Springfield, Missouri, on Bear Creek, was taken a prisoner of war, and escaped from Baxter Springs, Kansas, just a few hours before Blount's Guard arrived at Fort Baxter. For a year or so after the war Joseph Stone made his living chiefly by hauling corn meal from Fort Baxter to Granby, Missouri, with an ox team. He then became a miner and followed that occupation the rest of his life. As already mentioned he was one of the first miners at Galena, arriving there and beginning work in the fall of 1878. He died at Galena May 12, 1892. He was a republican and a member of the Baptist Church. His wife, Emma E. Williams, was born in Kentucky in 1846 and died in Galena in 1894. Their four children were: Fred L. Stone, who was born at Granby, Missouri, May 14, 1867; Lula, wife of S. P. Anthony, a contractor at Webb City, Missouri; Oliver R., a blacksmith at Galena; and Bettie D., who is unmarried and lives at Aurora, Missouri.

Fred L. Stone has lived in Galena since he was ten or eleven years of age. He attended the local schools, but left his books and studies at the age of seventeen to find regular employment in the mines. He also learned the trade of machinist, and is now head of the firm of Stone & Pinson, operating a general machine shop at 203-205 East Seventh Street in Galena.

In 1901 Mr. Stone became an independent mine operator, and is now operating a mine a mile out of Galena on West Seventh Street. He is also sole owner and proprietor of the Black Hill Mining Company, engaged in the production of lead and zinc. Besides the ownership of considerable mineral lands, Mr. Stone has an attractive residence at 617 East Seventh Street.

He is a republican, has served on the city council two years, is affiliated with Galena Lodge No. 195 Independent Order of Odd Fellows; Galena Camp No. 804, Modern Woodmen of America, and the Sons and Daughters of Justice. He is a member of the Methodist Episcopal Church and of the Community Club at Galena.

On June 25, 1890, at Galena, he married Miss Mary A. Dickey, daughter of George W. and Mahala (Fisk) Dickey. Her parents came from Indiana, both are now deceased, her father having been a farmer. Mr. and Mrs. Stone have two children: Fred T., who is a graduate of the Galena High School, spent one year in Baker University, and is now a mail carrier living at home with his parents; and Martha L., who is still pursuing her education in the schools of Galena.

JOSEPH C. MERRITT, chairman of the board of directors of the First National Bank of Chanute, the largest financial institution in Neosho County, is a pioneer Kansan. He came to Iola in 1871, and for a number of years was engaged in the cattle business.

His home has been in Chanute since 1878. For more than thirty years, until he sold out in 1909, Mr. Merritt conducted a hardware store at the corner of East Main and Harlan Avenue. As successful merchant, it was only natural that he should participate in other business affairs in the city, and he early became identified as a director with the First National Bank, served as its president five years, and since 1912 has been president of its board of directors. The other officers of this bank are: A. N. Allen, president; D. N. Kennedy, vice president; W. F. Allen, cashier. The bank has a capital of $100,000 and a surplus of $20,000. For twenty-five years the modern bank building has stood at the corner of East Main Street and Lincoln Avenue.

The Merritt family from which Joseph C. Merritt is descended came over from England to New York in Colonial days. His father, Joseph Merritt, was born in New York State, in 1784, spent most of his life on a farm in Putnam County, New York, and died at Patterson in that county in 1854. He was a member of the Presbyterian faith. He married Esther Dean, who was born in New York State in 1818 and died at Patterson, New York, in 1896. Joseph C. is one of the two children living, his brother, James A., still occupying the old homestead in Putnam County, New York, where he was born and reared.

Joseph C. Merritt was born in Dutchess County, New York, January 22, 1839, was educated in the public schools of Putnam County, and spent the first twenty-two years of his life on his father's farm. He left the farm to engage in the lumber and coal business, and also branched out as a dealer in feed and grain. These lines occupied him in his home state until 1871, when he came to Kansas.

Outside of business he has given considerable time to the public welfare of Chanute. Politically he is classed as an independent. He has sat in the city council and also as mayor of the city, and during his term as mayor the municipal government was changed from a third to a second-class city. He is affiliated with Cedar Lodge No. 103, Ancient Free and Accepted Masons, Chanute Chapter No. 21, Royal Arch Masons, the Ancient Order of United Workmen, and the Modern Woodmen of America. His home is at 427 South Highland avenue.

December 3, 1863, in Putnam County, New York, Mr. Merritt married Miss Caroline L. Holmes. She died in August, 1869, leaving one child, Grace L., wife of George T. Davis, who is a hardware merchant at Chanute. On July 1, 1875, at Iola, Kansas, Mr. Merritt married Mary E. Davis, daughter of H. W. Davis, now deceased, who was a hardware merchant.

WILLIAM GEORGE JACK, M. D. Though born and reared on a farm and spending most of his early years in the vicinity of Chautauqua, William G. Jack had an early ambition for a professional career and gratified it after a thorough course in colleges and clinics and for the past fifteen years has successfully practiced as a physician and surgeon at Chautauqua. He is regarded as one of the best informed physicians and most skillful surgeons in this section of the state.

A resident of Chautauqua County since he was nine years of age, William George Jack was born in Des Moines, Iowa, July 24, 1874. His father A. J. Jack was born in Scotland in 1831, and in 1833 was brought to America by his parents who settled near Coshocton, Ohio. In that Ohio community he grew up and married, and becoming a carpenter and builder followed that trade in both Ohio and Iowa. In 1883 he came to Kansas and was one of the earliest contractors and builders in the Town of Chautauqua. For a number of years he also conducted a lumber yard and hardware business in that town, but giving up his commercial activities he retired in 1903 to his farm a mile northwest of Chautauqua, where he now lives. He is eighty-five years of age and has had a long and useful career. During the Civil war he served as a member of the Iowa State Guards. He is a republican, having become affiliated with that party when it was first organized. His church is the Presbyterian. The

maiden name of his wife was Julia A. Young, and she was born in Ohio in 1843 and is now seventy-three years of age. Their children were: Dora M., who died at El Reno, Oklahoma, at the age of forty-five and was at that time president of the Women's Christian Temperance Union of Oklahoma; she married C. A. Cleveland, who was a merchant at Anadarko, Oklahoma. Sadie B. is the wife of J. M. Chittenden, and they reside on their farm on Coon Creek 2½ miles west of Chautauqua. Belle is an invalid and lives with her parents. A. J. Jack, Jr., is a farmer a half mile north of Chautauqua.

Doctor Jack, the youngest of his parents' children, attended the public schools of Chautauqua, and gained the equivalent of a modern high school education. At the age of nineteen he left school and for a time was employed in his father's lumber business. He studied medicine in the Kansas City Medical College at Kansas City, Missouri, and was graduated from there with the class of 1900 and the degree M. D. He has since taken much post graduate work in the clinics and hospitals of Kansas City, at the hospitals in Chicago, at the Chicago Policlinic and has also attended the Surgical Congress in Chicago.

In 1899, the year before his graduation, he was licensed to practice and opened his office in Chautauqua, where he has since centered his practice with the exception of one year spent at Sedan. His offices are on Main Street, and he owns the building in which his office is located, and he also has a comfortable residence in the west central part of town.

Doctor Jack served one year as health officer of Chautauqua County, as coroner four years, and is now a member of the school board. He is a live and energetic citizen and has always made the best interests of the town his own. He is a member of the County and State Medical societies, the Medical Association of the Southwest and the American Medical Association. Politically he is a republican. Doctor Jack takes much interest in Masonry, being affiliated with Vesper Lodge No. 136 Ancient Free and Accepted Masons at Sedan, with Wichita Consistory No. 2 of the Scottish Rite, and with Midian Temple of the Mystic Shrine at Wichita. Among other interests he is a member of the Chautauqua State Bank.

On November 5, 1906, at Kansas City, Missouri, Doctor Jack married Miss Ermie L. Lemmon, daughter of W. F. and Mattie (Crockett) Lemmon, who are now living near Peru, Kansas. Her father is an oil producer. Doctor and Mrs. Jack have two children: George, born August 31, 1908; and Pauline, born March 5, 1910.

WILLIAM GEISER. An impressive illustration of what may be accomplished through industry, sobriety and persistent endeavor is furnished in the career of William Geiser, one of the well known oil producers of the Mid-Continent field and the directing head of the Geiser & Bogue Machine Shops at Neodesha. Without aid and relying solely upon his own inherent energy, perseverance and sound judgment, he has worked his way upward from the very bottom of the ladder, and has built up a business that is highly creditable to himself and the community of which he is a worthy member. While he has been so doing, Mr. Geiser has not been unmindful of the needs of the community, for on various occasions he has contributed cheerfully of his time and abilities to the furtherance of civic welfare movements, and in positions of trust has rendered services to the city of his adoption that have been of incalculable value.

Mr. Geiser was born at Sasbachwalden, Baden,

Germany, May 23, 1847. His father died when he was still a small child, and when he was seven years old he was brought to the United States by his mother, Mrs. Helena Geiser, who was born in Germany and died at York, Pennsylvania, in 1886. William was the youngest of three children, the others being: Mary, deceased, who was the wife of the late Henry Schum of York, Pennsylvania; and Anthony, who still resides in that city and is now retired from active pursuits.

The family was in very modest circumstances, but the mother bravely endeavored to give her children the advantages of an education, and William was first sent to the public schools of Baltimore, Maryland, where the family settled on its arrival, and later to the York, Pennsylvania, schools. He was still little more than a lad, just entering upon his "teens" when the Civil war broke out, and he at once began importuning his mother to allow him to enlist. She would not listen to his appeals, and when he was only between fourteen and fifteen years of age he ran away from home, left his studies, and, being large for his age, succeeded in being accepted as a soldier of the Third Regiment, Maryland Volunteer Infantry, March 30, 1862. With this organization the youth bravely withstood the rigors of army life, army discipline and army experience. With it he took part in the long and dreary marches, the innumerable skirmishes, the patrols and sentry duty, and the thousand things that try the body and mind of the soldier. His battles were numerous and included some of the most important fought during the entire war, on the list appearing such formidable and sinister names as Wilderness, Spottsylvania Court House, Cedar Mountain, Cold Harbor, North Anna, Weldon Railroad and Poplar Grove Church. He was present at the siege of Petersburg, and one of those who took part in the charge when the beleaguered city's fortifications were blown up, July 30, 1864, and in all his engagements was always at his post of duty and gave a good account of himself as a brave and valiant soldier. He was mustered out of the service July 31, 1865.

Mr. Geiser, leaving home a boy, returned a man, hardened, experienced and with a spirit of self-reliance gained on many fields of battle where he had been compelled to test his strength against that of those who faced him. In search for employment he accepted a position with a railroad at York, Pennsylvania, but soon decided that this was not the field for him to win success in, and after nine days left and went to the oil fields. Necessarily he began life in this business in the humblest capacity, but as he learned more and more of the business he received succeeding promotions, and finally became a contractor and later a producer. He followed the industry in the Venango and Clarion County fields in Pennsylvania until 1895, when he came to Neodesha, Kansas, and here he has since been engaged, being known as one of the most prominent operators and producers here. Mr. Geiser sold the first oil to the Standard Oil Company from this field, to the fuel department of Chicago, that went to the Bolt and Nut Works, Kansas City, Missouri, this being sold by the William Geiser Oil Company, of which he was the sole owner. He now has productions north of Neodesha. Formerly Mr. Geiser was interested in the State Oil and Gas Company, the Union Oil Company, Ewers & Company, Geiser Oil Company (sole owner), Almeda Oil Company and Pen-Mar Oil Company, having been the organizer of all of these companies with the exception of the Almeda. Mr. Geiser disposed of all his interests in these companies in 1913. In 1910 he established the Geiser & Bogue Machine Shops, situated on Main and

Ninth streets, Neodesha, in which he owns a three-quarters interest, in addition to being the owner of the adjoining property. This concern manufactures a patent oil barrel for the oil fields, known as the "Geiser Working Barrel," which has a large sale in the Mid-Continent and other fields. The business has grown extensively during recent years, and the company has a recognized place among business establishments of Neodesha.

Mr. Geiser is a republican and has long been prominent in the councils of his party. At various times he has been called upon to fill offices of public trust, and while a resident of Peru, Kansas, served as mayor of that city for two terms. In 1909 he was elected mayor of Neodesha, and his first term was so acceptable to the people that he received an unanimous nomination for a second term and was duly elected. After five years of worthy service, in 1914 he resigned, his business interests demanding his undivided attention. When Mr. Geiser first took up the reins of office the city, through poor administration of its affairs, was heavily in debt. His business acumen and energy not only enabled him to liquidate this indebtedness, but to secure funds for the installation of numerous improvements, in the way of paving, lighting, new schools, etc. His interest in his community has been steadfast and has been substantial in form. Mr. Geiser is a member of the Roman Catholic Church. He is the owner of a residence at Indiana and Eighth Street, but makes his home at the Brown Hotel.

In 1872, at Oil City, Pennsylvania, Mr. Geiser was married to Miss Kate Wilson, who died in 1905, at Columbus, Ohio. In 1905 Mr. Geiser was again married, at Neodesha, Kansas, to Miss Vada Harrison of this city. They have no children.

ANDREW C. JOBES. Though vice president of the First National Bank of Kansas City, Missouri, Mr. Jobes still has his home in Kansas and has been a resident of the state for thirty-two years. Throughout that time he has been an active factor in banking, and made his reputation which preceded him to the metropolitan district of Kansas City at Wichita, where he assisted in building up one of the largest and strongest banks of Southern Kansas.

Like many men who have gained prominence in the financial world Mr. Jobes was born in a home of comparative poverty, and was reared close to the simple realities of life, finding some encouragement outside and much more within himself to make the best of his opportunities. He was born at Damascus in Mahoning County, Ohio, April 21, 1857, youngest of the four children of Andrew and Mary (French) Jobes. Both parents were natives of Ohio, and the grandfather, Louis Jobes, was a native of New York State, his wife having come from Ireland about 1801. Andrew Jobes, Sr., was a cabinet maker by trade. He died just sixty days after the birth of his youngest son Andrew. That left the widowed mother and four children. The two oldest sons, William and Charles, were respectively eight and four years of age. The town where Mr. Jobes was born was the center of a Quaker community and a Quaker Academy was maintained there. In order to support her little family the widowed mother for some years boarded the students in the academy. The sons as they attained sufficient age and strength did their share by working on farms in the community and attending school in town as opportunity offered. By much self sacrifice and hard work they finished the course of the Quaker Academy and Andrew C. Jobes graduated there.

He went to Philadelphia in 1876, when nineteen years of age. The great Centennial Exhibition was being held at Philadelphia that year. Through the influence of his uncle, O. C. French, of Mississippi he secured a position in the transportation department of the Centennial, and while there he learned telegraphy. As a telegraph operator he worked with the Pennsylvania Railway at Philadelphia from November, 1876, to November, 1878. In the meantime his brother, Charles S., had gone south and for four years had conducted a private bank at Kosciusko, Mississippi. Andrew joined him there late in 1878 and became the cashier of the bank.

On June 22. 1881, he married Miss Florence Coleman, of Kosciusko, Mississippi, but a native of Charleston, South Carolina. After his marriage Mr. Jobes bought the private bank from his brother and continued its operation under his control until 1885. In the meantime he also organized and built a telegraph line extending from Kosciusko to Lexington, Mississippi. He sold these business interests in the fall of 1884.

Acting on the advice of the late Frank Hammond Mr. Jobes came to Kansas. At that time the town of Attica in Harper County was the terminus of the Southern Kansas Division of the Santa Fe. Locating there Mr. Jobes organized and managed until 1887 the Attica State Bank. He left that to become vice president of the Kansas National Bank of Wichita, subsequently acquired a controlling interest and was the chief factor in its management until he sold out in 1895. In June, 1896, Mr. Jobes organized the Bank of Commerce in Wichita. In January, 1889, this was made the National Bank of Commerce, and for a number of years has ranked as one of the largest and strongest banking houses of Wichita and in that section of the state. Mr. Jobes continued as president of the National Bank of Commerce until January, 1908, when he severed his connection to remove to Kansas City, Missouri, and became vice president of the First National Bank.

In August, 1898, Mr. Jobes was elected a director of the Santa Fe Railway Company to succeed the late Governor Osborn, and has been a director in the Santa Fe ever since. He is a director of the Citizens National Bank of Fort Scott, has been a shareholder in the Farmers State Bank of Wellington since its organization in 1891; in 1913 organized the Satanta State Bank of Satanta, Kansas, and in 1915 organized the Elkhart State Bank of Elkhart, Kansas, of which he is vice president. Mr. Jobes is financially interested in Kansas agriculture as the owner of lands in the western part of the state and a large farm of 634 acres south of Lawrence.

After his removal to Kansas City, Missouri, he bought 5½ acres in Mission Township of Johnson County, Kansas. He has developed that as a beautiful country home, with a modern dwelling, and it is located at what is known as Mission Hills, one of the most attractive residence suburbs around Kansas City, Missouri. Mr. Jobes is a stanch republican and has remained loyal to the party through all the various influences which have sought to disrupt its organization. Office has never attracted him.

He is also a director of the Southwestern Bell Telephone Company, and is a Scottish Rite Mason, a member of the Consistory No. 2 at Wichita, is a Knight of Pythias, belongs to the Kansas City Country Club, the Blue Hills Golf Club, the Kansas City Club, the Wichita Commercial Club and the Chamber of Commerce of Kansas City, Missouri. He has given liberally to church and charity and his wife is a Presbyterian and his children are members of the Episcopal Church. Mr. and Mrs. Jobes have three daughters. Iley is the wife of Walter S. Hoyt, an oil and gas operator at Wichita. Mr. and Mrs. Hoyt have two children, Walter Stiles and Andrew Jobes. Alice Camilla Jobes, the second daughter, has developed rare talent as a violinist. Frances M. Jobes is now a student in the Kansas University.

JAMES S. ADAM has been a prominent factor in business affairs at Dunlap for the past fifteen years, and is regarded as the banker of the village.

He was born in Kirkentelloch, Scotland, March 12, 1870, a son of William and Mary Adam. The father was born in Glasgow, Scotland, in 1832, and brought his family to America in 1880, settling in White City, Kansas. From there he removed to Parkerville, in 1894, and lived there until his death, in 1896. He was a farmer and stockman. Ten years old when brought to this country, James S. Adam had his early training in the schools of Scotland, and then grew up on his father's farm in Kansas until he was about eighteen. His first ambition was for railroad work, and becoming an operator he was stationed at various points along the line of the Missouri, Kansas & Texas Railway, both in Oklahoma and Kansas. Since 1902 his home has been at Dunlap, where at first he was active as a merchant and is still largely interested in the leading general store. In 1905 he took the executive post of cashier in the Dunlap Farmers Bank and has since successfully managed the affairs of this institution. Mr. Adam is a democrat and is affiliated with the Independent Order of Odd Fellows, the Knights of Pythias, the Modern Woodmen of America, the Ancient Order of United Workmen, and belongs to the Kansas State Bankers' Associations and the American Bankers' Association. He is a trustee and steward in the Methodist Church.

In 1894, In Council Grove, Kansas, Mr. Adam married Miss Annie Farmer. Mrs. J. S. Adam is a leader in church and social affairs at Dunlap, is a member of the Twentieth Century Club and of the Fraternal Aid, and is active in the Sunday school of the Methodist Church, in which Mr. Adam teaches the Young Men's Bible Class.

Mrs. Adam was born in White City, Kansas, and attended the grammar and high schools there and prior to her marriage spent one year as a teacher. Her father, R. M. Farmer, was born in Devonshire, England, in 1850, and came to White City, Kansas, in 1870, being one of the early settlers in that community. After farming for a number of years he became a merchant, and now lives retired in White City. He is a prohibitionist and a member of the Congregational Church. R. M. Farmer married Eliza Wallis, who was born in Devonshire in 1851. Their children are: Mary, widow of H. S. Baer who was a druggist, and she now resides at White City; Mrs. J. S. Adam; George, a traveling salesman with home at White City; Samuel, also a traveling salesman at Belleville, Kansas.

Mr. and Mrs. Adam have some extensive farming and ranching interests in Lyon County, owning three farms aggregating about 1,400 acres, besides their residence at Dunlap and their interest in the general store. On their farms they have raised considerable blooded stock.

Their children are six in number: Mary Edna, who has finished the course in the high school at Dunlap

and has also taken courses in music and still lives at home; Robert Edward, assistant cashier in the Farmers Bank; James Dale, a sophomore in the Dunlap High School; Marjorie Maude a freshman in the high school; Wallace William, in the seventh grade, and Frank Farmer, in the sixth grade.

WILLIAM W. ROSE has been practicing his profession as architect in the metropolitan district of Kansas City for thirty years. Without question he ranks as one of the ablest men both in the artistic and practical branches of his profession. Mr. Rose has also been prominently identified with civic affairs, and is well remembered as mayor of Kansas City, Kansas, during a very critical period of municipal affairs. He is now head of the architectural firm of Rose & Peterson, with offices in the Barker Building.

He was born at Oyster Bay, Long Island, New York, March 12, 1864, second of the three children of George Bruce and Charlotte N. (Warren) Rose. His father was a native of Jefferson County and his mother of St. Lawrence County, New York, the former born August 24, 1827, and the latter July 9, 1830. George B. Rose was of Scotch descent and spent forty years in the milling business, chiefly at Ogdensburg, New York. He died in 1887 and his wife in 1904. He was a republican, a member of the Masonic Order, and he and his wife were active in the Congregational Church.

William W. Rose had a good home environment as a boy and attended the common schools and the Ogdensburg University. His inclinations and early talents were in the direction of architecture, and he gained his first training with G. A. Schellinger at Ogdensburg. He afterwards went with Mr. Schellinger to New York City and remained in his office for about five years. With this thorough experience Mr. Rose entered independent practice in 1885 at Birmingham, Alabama, where he soon won three contracts in competition with leading architects of the state. Though this was a promising beginning, he was not entirely satisfied with the South as a professional location, and in 1886 came to Kansas City, Missouri, and for ten years was associated in practice with James Oliver Hogg. They maintained offices both in Kansas City, Missouri, and Kansas City, Kansas. In 1896 Mr. Rose withdrew from the firm, and since then has concentrated his time and attention on the business in Kansas City, Kansas. Since December, 1909, he has been associated in practice with David B. Peterson under the name Rose & Peterson.

In Kansas City and elsewhere many splendid buildings attest the architectural skill of Mr. Rose. He was architect of the City Hall, the Carnegie Library, the High School Building, the Masonic Temple and many of the finest homes of Kansas City, and has also drawn the plans for and supervised the construction of various public and private structures throughout the country.

Outside of his profession Mr. Rose has shown a practical energy and a common sense attitude towards public affairs which have won him a large and loyal following and has made him a leader properly credited with much of the material advancement of Kansas City, Kansas. In 1897 he was democratic nominee for the office of mayor. In the spring of 1905 he was elected mayor of the city by more than 800 votes over his opponent. While mayor Mr. Rose took practical steps in the campaign which eventually brought both the city waterworks and the city lighting plant under municipal ownership and operation. But the main feature of his administration was the problem of enforcing the state laws with regard to the restriction of the liquor traffic. These state laws had been practically violated in all preceding years. Kansas City, Kansas, had a "wide open town" in spite of the Kansas prohibitory laws. Mayor Rose's contribution to the problem was his refusal to accept an office on the ambiguous and hypocritical principles of quietly conniving at conditions which he felt powerless to prevent. At the beginning of his term he announced his open decision not to attempt the enforcement of the law which if carried out would deprive the city of a large part of its revenues and at best effect only a partial restriction of the liquor traffic. The Kansas Supreme Court soon afterwards issued an injunction prohibiting Mr. Rose from serving as mayor. Three days before the injunction was served Mr. Rose resigned. He at once became a candidate for re-election despite the injunction. That he had the support of the majority of the citizens is proved by the fact that he was given 1,600 plurality over opposing candidates. Again he was enjoined by the Kansas Supreme Court from administering the office of mayor, but he presided over the city council and was fined $1,000 seemingly for having been re-elected. After serving as mayor, during 1906 and nine months in 1907, he resigned. A few months later he again became a candidate, but was defeated by less than 600 votes, due to the power and influence of the water company. Thus he was a candidate for the office three times himself and once by proxy in less than two years, and it is said for a parallel to his case it is necessary to go back more than 100 years to Edward Wright, a member of Parliament in England.

Mr. Rose was also nominated in a democratic convention at Lawrence as congressman for the Second District, but declined to make the race. He was unsuccessful candidate for state senator in 1916.

Mr. Rose and his firm have been architects for the Kansas City, Kansas, school board for many years. Throughout his career his course has been characterized by an ability to fight hard for whatever he believes to be right and for the best interests of the community. Fraternally he is a Scottish Rite Mason and a Shriner, is past master of Wyandotte Lodge No. 3. Ancient, Free and Accepted Masons, and belongs to Kansas City Lodge No. 440, Benevolent and Protective Order of Elks. In the Scottish Rite he was venerable master of the Lodge of Perfection. In 1912 Mr. Rose served as president and director of the Mercantile Club and has also been director of the Rotary Club.

He was married November 14, 1888, to Miss Clara D. Grandy. Mrs. Rose was born in St. Lawrence County, New York, daughter of John L and Arvilla (Gibbs) Grandy. Mr. and Mrs. Rose have two children: Pauline, now Mrs. H. S. Gille, Jr., of Kansas City, Kansas; and Spencer G., who is pursuing architectural studies in Washington University at St. Louis.

FLOYD C. FLORY is postmaster of Grenola. He is also widely known among the newspaper profession in Kansas, and gave up his duties as editor of the Grenola Leader to accept his present office.

Mr. Flory is a native of Kansas, and the family have lived in this state for many years.

Fred C. Flory, a well known citizen of Howard, Kansas, and father of the Grenola postmaster, was born in Iowa in December, 1858. He grew up in that state, came to Kansas when a young man, his first home being at Independence, and he soon afterward became editor of the paper at Longton. He was married near Independence, and then removed to Greeley

County, Kansas, taking up a homestead of 160 acres. While living in Greeley County he served as postmaster. He afterward resumed the newspaper and job printing business at Pueblo, Colorado, but in 1895 located at Howard, Kansas, where he has since been editor of the Elk County Citizen. He is an active democrat, is a member and elder in the Presbyterian Church, and has served on both the democratic state and county central committees. Fred C. Flory married Julia A. White, who was born in Illinois in 1861. Their children are: Tom, who is editor of the Gridley Light, at Gridley, Kansas; Floyd C.; Mabel, wife of Carl Zeller of Kansas City, Missouri; Ruth, who lives with her parents and is teacher of domestic science in the Howard public schools; Allen, who assists his father in the newspaper business; and Ebbert, a farmer at Howard, Kansas; Frank, now a junior in the high school at Howard.

Floyd C. Flory was born on a farm near Horace in Greeley County, Kansas, October 30, 1887. His early training came from the public schools of Howard, and he graduated from the high school in 1907. He had considerable experience in various branches of newspaper work and printing in his father's office, and subsequently was employed on the Emporia Gazette, and on the Burlington Democrat at Burlington, Kansas. Mr. Flory has been a resident of Grenola since November 11, 1909. At that date he bought the Grenola Leader, and continued as its editor until June, 1914. In February, 1914, he was appointed postmaster of Grenola by President Wilson, and has filled that office with credit to the present time.

Mr. Flory is a democrat, is a member of Canopy Lodge, No. 248, Ancient Free and Accepted Masons, at Grenola, and of Camp No. 365, Modern Woodmen of America, at Grenola. He is the owner of a comfortable home in the northwest part of town.

On November 30, 1911, Mr. Flory married Miss Mollie Logston, daughter of George T. and Rena (Riddle) Logston. Her parents reside at Grenola, Mr. Logston being a carpenter and contractor.

EDWARD P. MOULTON. In making a study of the lives and characters of men who have risen to acknowledged position in business, in the professions or in public life, it is but natural to inquire into the secret of their success and the motives that have prompted their actions. Real success comes to but a comparatively few, and a study of the careers of those who occupy places of prominence proves that in nearly every case those who have perseveringly followed one line of procedure have gradually but surely risen. Self-reliance, honesty, energy and conscientiousness are characteristics that appear to have accomplished the best results, and to these we may attribute much of the success that has rewarded the efforts of Edward P. Moulton, proprietor of the leading hardware establishment of Neodesha, and a sound and substantial citizen.

Mr. Moulton is a native son of Wilson County, and like a number of men who have found prosperity in the business world here is a product of the soil. He was born on the home farm of his father, near Neodesha, August 27, 1872, his parents being John H. and Susan (Jones) Moulton, and his ancestry in America dates back to colonial Massachusetts, when the first bearing the name of this branch of the family emigrated to America from England. Samuel Moulton, the grandfather of Edward P., was born in 1800, in Vermont, and when still a young man was sent as a missionary to the Choctaw Indians in Mississippi. Later he spent some years in the same labor in Arkansas, and finally settled at Waverly, Illinois, where his death occurred in 1881, when he was eighty-one years of age. He was one of the courageous, sturdy men of New England, who not only lived his faith as he saw it, but who battled against great odds in an effort to spread the Word of his Master.

John H. Moulton was born in 1835, in Arkansas, and when still a youth was taken by his parents to Illinois, where, at Waverly, he received his education, was reared to manhood, and married. In 1866 he came to Kansas, settling as a pioneer in Wilson County, where he homesteaded 160 acres of land near Neodesha. He was an industrious workman, who was anxious to develop a good property and to make a home for his family, but did not live to realize in full his ambitions, as his death occurred in 1877, when he was only forty-two years of age. No doubt his demise was hastened by the hardships which he underwent while a soldier of the Union during the Civil war, through which he fought as a member of the Thirty-third Regiment, Illinois Volunteer Infantry. He was a stanch republican in politics, and an active member of the Congregational Church, to which Mrs. Moulton also belongs. She was born in Morgan County, Illinois, in 1847, and now resides at Neodesha, one of the highly esteemed and respected ladies of the city. Three children were born to Mr. and Mrs. Moulton: Edward P.; Frederick C., who is carrying on operations on the home farm three miles from Neodesha; and Carrie J., who is the wife of H. W. Kimball and lives on a farm in the vicinity of Neodesha.

Edward P. Moulton was only five years of age when his father died, but his mother managed to give him good educational advantages and he passed through the graded and high school courses, graduating from the Neodesha High School with the class of 1892. He had been brought up as a farmer, and for four years remained on the home property, but felt that better opportunities awaited him in the business world and accordingly, to fit himself, attended the Quincy (Illinois) Commercial College for one year. At the end of that time he received his introduction to business methods in a hardware store at Anaconda, Montana, where he pleased his employer to the extent that he remained for four years, but then resigned and returned to Neodesha, where he entered the Neodesha National Bank, in the capacity of assistant cashier. This position he held for six years, but in the meantime, in 1903, he had purchased the hardware business of Marion Cross, and when he left the banking institution began to give his entire attention to building up his new enterprise. That he has been successful in his undertaking is shown in the fact that he now has the largest hardware store at Neodesha and a trade that not only covers the immediate locality but extends far out into the country on all sides. He carries a full and up-to-date stock of shelf and heavy hardware, stoves, agricultural machinery, tools and implements, and kindred articles, attractively arranged and popularly priced. The store is situated at No. 511 Main Street and compares favorably with the establishments of the larger cities. Mr. Moulton has proved himself an excellent man of business, who has established a reputation for fidelity and integrity that has helped his enterprise immeasurably. As a property holder he is the owner of his own home at No. 611 North Eighth Street, as well as a farm situated five miles northwest of Neodesha, and all that he owns today has been obtained through the medium of his own efforts. In politics he is a republican. He has always been ready to serve his community, and in an official way has done much to help Neodesha, having been a member of the school board and the city council and also having acted in the capacity of city clerk. He takes an active part in the work of the Neodesha Commercial Club, and is a director in the Neodesha National Bank. Fraternally Mr. Moulton is affiliated with Harmony Lodge No. 94, Ancient Free and Accepted Masons, and Fort Scott Consistory No. 4, thirty-second degree, and with Neodesha Lodge, Independent Order of Odd Fellows.

While a resident of Anaconda, Montana, Mr. Moulton was married, in 1898, to Miss Belle Burkett, a daughter of Joel and Nancy Burkett, the former of whom died in Montana after many years spent in agricultural pursuits, while the latter still survives and is a resident of Neodesha. Mr. and Mrs. Moulton are the parents of three children: Howard, born September 12, 1899, who is a member of the junior class of the Neodesha High School; Owen, born in October, 1901, who belongs to the same class as his brother; and Leo, born January 9, 1910, who has just started to attend the graded school.

PARIS TILGHMAN ELLIS, of Pittsburg, dealer in insurance, real estate, loans and rentals, is a native Kansan, and since entering business for himself has enjoyed a satisfactory success and at the same time has proved his worth and public spirit as a citizen.

Mr. Ellis was born on a farm in Montgomery County, Kansas, June 17, 1878, a son of C. R. and Martha A. (Ferguson) Ellis. In early Colonial days three sailor brothers left England and immigrated to America, locating in the colony of Virginia. From there the family went across the mountains into Kentucky. Mr. Ellis' grandfather, R. R. Ellis, was born in Kentucky in 1807, and later went as a pioneer into Crawford County, Indiana. There he cleared a farm from the wilderness, engaged in agricultural pursuits, and spent the rest of his life as a farmer. He was one of his community's most highly respected citizens when he died in 1884 at Hardinsburg.

C. R. Ellis was born in 1854, in Crawford County, Indiana, was educated there in the public schools and was reared on his father's farm. Not long after his marriage he left his native community to seek the greater opportunities of the open West. Thus in 1875 he arrived in Montgomery County, Kansas, and was identified with the early settlement and development of that section. From farming he finally turned his attention to railroad work as a construction hand. At that time the Santa Fe was building its lines through Montgomery County, and C. R. Ellis after the construction work was completed continued with the railroad company for many years. He was promoted from time to time, and in 1906 was made road master for the Joplin & Pittsburg Railroad. He was active in the duties of that position until the time of his death March 12, 1916, at Pittsburg. Among his associates he was known as a steady, reliable workman, and at the same time won and retained the confidence of his employers. He was a life long democrat in his political views, and fraternally was identified with the Independent Order of Odd Fellows and the Ancient Order of United Workmen. While he held no positions in public affairs, he rendered service to his community as a supporter of good men and beneficial measures. C. R. Ellis married Miss Martha A. Ferguson. She was born in Crawford County, Indiana, in 1854, and is now living at Pittsburg. They were the parents of four children: Paris Tilghman; B. F., a locomotive engineer living at Monette, Missouri; Emma, wife of Thomas Mawson, Jr., a machinist at Pittsburg, Kansas; and R. H., a machinist at Monette, Missouri.

Paris Tilghman Ellis was educated in the public schools of Pittsburg, graduating from high school in 1900, and in the following year was a student in Baker University. While a student in the high school he assisted in organizing the first inter high school athletic association in Southeastern Kansas; was a leader in athletics, carrying off first honors, and his work as an organizer, debater and orator also won many honors for the school. His last good work while in school was to promote and edit the High School Purple and White Journal, which is still the chief paper read and kept by all students. He left college because of failure of his eyes from over-study and entered the ranks of wage earners, being employed by Wells Fargo & Company's Express. He traveled through various points in Kansas, and for a few years was located at Topeka.

In this work he gained business experience and also saw the opportunity which in 1908 caused him to resign from the express company and engage in the insurance, real estate, loan and rental business at Pittsburg. He is associated with Mr. O. L. Stamm under the firm name of Ellis & Stamm. Through energy, industry and business ability Mr. Ellis has made himself a factor in the business life of this city and has contracted some of the large insurance and realty deals. With a fine knowledge of land values, he is regarded as one of the best qualified men in his line in Crawford County.

His interest has always been keen in the welfare of his home city, participating enthusiastically in all public matters. A republican in politics, he acted for several years as city auditor, was appointed city treasurer, and is now filling that office. He is also treasurer of the school board, has been treasurer of the Chamber of Commerce and is a member of the official board of the latter organization and now its president. He is also president of the Federated Council of Churches and member of the board of directors of the Young Men's Christian Association. Besides his home at 512 West Second Street, Mr. Ellis owns several residences in Pittsburg, and is secretary and treasurer of the Mutual Investment Company of that city. He is affiliated with Pittsburg Lodge No. 196, Independent Order of Odd Fellows, and with Smelter Camp No. 691, Modern Woodmen of America and Pittsburg Lodge 187, Ancient, Free and Accepted Masons. With the members of his family he belongs to the United Presbyterian Church, is chairman of its board of trustees, and has been superintendent of its Sabbath School for about seven years. Mr. Ellis was married at Pittsburg in 1906, to Miss Vernia A. Ralston. Her parents, J. H. and Susan (Onstadt) Ralston, are retired residents of Pittsburg. Mr. and Mrs. Ellis have one son, Paul Thomas, born July 27, 1913.

BENJAMIN E. LEWIS. It is invariably found in tracing the influences which make for good citizenship, integrity and morality that the fundamental of these qualities lies in education. Therein is found the basis of intelligence, of judgment according to the value, of comprehension, and, equipped with these, youth may enter upon the struggle of life well prepared to fight its battles. Southeastern Kansas has no reason to feel ashamed of its educational system, or of the men who direct it. The individuals chosen to manage and to discipline have been carefully selected, and in their ranks are found men of broad and comprehensive learning, who have had their training in some of the most distinguished educational institutions in the country. In this latter class is found Prof. Benjamin E. Lewis, superintendent of city schools of Iola, Kansas, and a man who has devoted his life to the educational profession.

Benjamin E. Lewis, was born at Lecompton, Douglas County, Kansas, April 10, 1869, and is a son of Dr. P. M. and Martha Jane (Baird) Lewis. The family to which he belongs originated in Wales, from which country, during Colonial times, it emigrated to America, the early members settling in New Jersey and Pennsylvania and their descendants becoming pioneers of North Carolina and Tennessee. It was in the latter state, in 1809, that the grandfather of Professor Lewis, Ephraim Lewis, was born. He later moved with his parents to Indiana. He was reared as an agriculturist and became the pioneer of the family into Kansas, settling in 1857 in Linn County. It was during those days that the border troubles came to a head and bloodshed became a common occurrence, and, being a Free State man, and outspoken in his sentiments, Mr. Lewis, fearing more for the safety of his family than for his own, moved into Marshall County, where he took up his residence in 1858. There he passed the remainder of his life in agricultural pursuits, being an influential citizen and serving several terms as county commissioner. He died at Frankfort, Marshall County, in 1893. He was related to the famous trapper and frontiersman, Daniel Boone. Mr. Lewis married a Miss Johnson, who also died in Marshall County.

Dr. P. M. Lewis was born February 20, 1841, in Delaware County, Indiana, where he received his early education and was sixteen years of age when he made the journey overland with his parents to the frontier of Kansas, settling in Linn County. There he secured such education as the pioneer schools of the day and locality afforded, and one year later went to Marshall County, where he completed his literary education. Adopting medicine as his life work, he fitted himself for that profession, and began his practice in Iowa, where he continued his professional labors for some years. During this time he was married at St. Charles, that state. He later attended Rush Medical College, Chicago, finally receiving the honors of graduation from the Kansas City Medical College, Kansas City, Missouri. Doctor Lewis removed to Lecompton, Douglas County, Kansas, in 1867, and became the pioneer physician at that place, where he remained in continuous practice for a period of forty years, at the end of that time retiring and spending the rest of his life in the comforts which he had gained through his well-directed and useful labors. He died at Lecompton, December 5, 1916. Doctor Lewis was one of the old-time physicians who won the love and reverence of the people and who gave the best of themselves to their profession and to the alleviation of the ills of humanity. He was a republican in his political views, and for a number of years served as mayor and councilman of Lecompton. During a period of a half a century he belonged to the United Brethren Church, the faith of which he lived every day, and his only fraternal connection was with the Independent Order of Odd Fellows. He was married at St. Charles, Iowa, to Miss Martha Jane Baird, who was born in Ohio, January 7, 1846, later moving to Iowa with her parents. She still survives and resides at Lecompton. They became the parents of three children, two of whom are now living: Benjamin E.; and Margaret, who is the wife of Dr. H. L. Chambers, a practicing physician and surgeon of Lawrence, Kansas.

Benjamin E. Lewis received excellent educational advantages in his youth. He received his early instruction in the graded and high schools of Lecomp-

ton, following which he entered the academic department of Lane University, Lecompton, and graduated with the class of 1894, receiving the degree of Bachelor of Science. In the fall of that year he began teaching school in Nemaha County, and remained at Centralia until 1899, when he entered Kansas University. He was graduated from that institution in 1901, with the degree of Bachelor of Arts, and in 1902 took post-graduate work and received the degree of Master of Arts. At that time Mr. Lewis became superintendent of schools of Eureka, Kansas, a position which he held until 1908, then resigning to begin post-graduate work at Yale University, which he attended during 1908 and 1909, in the latter year receiving the degree of Master of Arts from that famous institution of learning. Returning to Kansas, in 1909, he became superintendent of schools of Anthony, Kansas, and in the fall of the year 1915 came to Iola as superintendent of schools. Under his supervision are eight schools, sixty-seven teachers and 2,700 scholars. Professor Lewis has worked untiringly to elevate the standard of education at Iola. He is a man of extensive learning and withal is possessed of the executive ability so necessary in the handling of organized work. His intelligent interest in modern affairs, combined with his exhaustive knowledge of those topics which have interested scholars throughout the ages, well fit him to lead others and to implant in the minds of his pupils during their formative period a love for pure ideals, high standards of living, and thoroughness of action along any line of endeavor, which cannot help but work out for the development of the best type of citizenship. Professor Lewis belongs to the Kansas State Teachers' Association and the Southeast Kansas Teachers' Association, and is a republican in politics. He makes his home at No. 119 South First Street.

In 1896, at Lecompton, Kansas, Professor Lewis was married to Miss Hattie S. Snyder, daughter of J. H. and Lou (Lee) Snyder, who reside at Stuart, Florida, Mr. Snyder being a retired minister of the United Brethren Church. Mr. and Mrs. Lewis are the parents of two children: Erma E., born September 28, 1901; and Philip Henry, born June 16, 1907.

CHARLES F. OSBORN. While the continued residence of Mr. Osborn at Howard for thirty-five years is a noteworthy fact, still more important is the service he has rendered during this long period of citizenship. Everywhere in that section of Kansas he is esteemed as one of the foremost men, and if he had done nothing else, his connection with permanent improvements and good roads in Elk County would entitle him to mention among the representative men of Kansas.

He came to Howard in March, 1881. He was associated with his brother Frank Osborn in the loan business, and they also owned a large ranch devoted to the cattle industry until 1887. From 1888 to 1895 Mr. Charles Osborn was secretary and treasurer of the Howard Investment Company. After that he was interested in a loan and real estate business under the firm name of Reid and Osborn until 1900.

During all these years, when he was piling up a success that would have been sufficient to gratify the ambitions of most men, his keenest desires were for work as a civil engineer, a profession that had always fascinated him. He had never let slip an opportunity to gain practical experience and knowledge of all the details of the profession, and he was well qualified for its practice long before he was given his first official opportunity to demonstrate his skill therein. In 1900 he was appointed county surveyor of Elk

County, and in 1902 was elected to the office. Since then every two years he has been reelected, and in 1916 he was given the largest vote he had ever received. Since 1910 Mr. Osborn has also been county engineer, having been one of the first appointees under the new state law.

It was due to Mr. Osborn's influence that the first permanent stone bridge was built in Elk County. At the present time the county has about 900 permanent bridges and culverts, all of which were built either directly or indirectly from plans originating on Mr. Osborn's draughting board. He has been officially or personally identified with every such permanent improvement in the county and that is a record such as no other engineer in the state can claim.

The years of his life before he came to Kansas Mr. Osborn spent in Northern Ohio. He was born at North Fairfield in Huron County of that state, August 28, 1861. His father W. M. Osborn was of an old Connecticut family, a state which sent so many emigrants in the early days to Northern Ohio, particularly the Western Reserve. W. M. Osborn was born between Norwalk and South Fairfield, Connecticut, in 1812. During his boyhood the most beautiful of public improvement in the United States if not in the world was the construction of the great Erie Canal from the Great Lakes at Buffalo to the Hudson River at Albany. This great waterway was open to traffic in 1825, and in the preceding year W. M. Osborn, then a boy of twelve, was employed in work fitting his age and strength on the canal. In 1884 he was married at Trumansburg, New York, to Harriet Pease, who was born in that town in 1824. She represented a family of French Huguenots that after being expelled from France came to New York. Her father Simeon Pease was born in New York State in 1779 and died at Trumansburg in 1867. He was a farmer, and at one time owned 400 acres near Ithaca, New York.

Soon after his marriage W. M. Osborn started for Ohio, traveling by the canal and the Great Lakes, and settling in the midst of the woods where the Village of North Fairfield was afterwards built. He literally hewed a farm out of those woods, and became quite a prominent man in his section. He was a drover and stock buyer, and drove a great many horses and cattle to market at Buffalo, New York, and places between. His death occurred at the county seat of Huron County, Norwalk, in 1887. As a young man he became an ardent supporter of the old whig party and thus became a lineal convert to the doctrines of the republican party when it was organized in the '50s. He was given the honor of various township offices. For a number of years in Northern Ohio he kept a tavern and had a set of scales for weighing stock. One of the frequent guests at the Osborn Tavern was Gen. John C. Fremont, who in 1856 was given the distinction of the first nomination of the republican party for president. The name of that pioneer republican standard bearer is now the middle name of Charles F. Osborn of Howard. His father was a member of the Baptist Church and was a Mason. In the early days he belonged to the military organization known as the Squirrel Hunters. This organization was called into active service by Governor David Tod of Ohio to repel Morgan's raid through the southern counties of Ohio in the Civil war. W. M. Osborn was given his honorable discharge in September, 1862. His wife died at Norwalk, Ohio, in 1897. Mr. Charles F. Osborn was the youngest of three children. His older brother Frank, who now resides retired at Howard, Kansas, was for many years associated with his brother Charles in the loan and insurance business, and for eight years served as assistant state bank examiner under John Breidenthal. In later years he became in-

terested in Colorado mining affairs, and still has interests there. The only daughter, Sarah, married H. H. Hanford, and in 1881 they took up their residence at Duluth, Minnesota, where Mr. Hanford was in the lumber business until his death in 1914, Mrs. Hanford still making her home in that city.

Charles F. Osborn gained his early training in the public schools of Norwalk, Ohio. When fifteen years of age he began earning his own way as clerk in a shoe store at Norwalk. He was not yet twenty years of age when he came to Howard, Kansas, and entered upon the active career which has already been briefly sketched.

No reference as yet has been made to Mr. Osborn's important service during the past eight years as a member of the State Good Roads Association. He was assistant secretary and treasurer for two terms, was on the executive committee four years, and in 1916 became one of the three members of the legislative committee. There is perhaps no man in Kansas better informed on all the details and the technique of good roads, and he has been in a position to render a splendid service in behalf of the state road movement which has taken so firm a hold in Kansas.

Mr. Osborn is a republican, is an elder in the Presbyterian Church, and is affiliated with Hope Lodge No. 155, Ancient Free and Accepted Masons at Howard, Howard Chapter No. 49 Royal Arch Masons, and Ab-Del-Kader Commandery of the Knights Templar at Fredonia. Mr. Osborn has been very successful in business affairs and is the owner of four different farms, aggregating 960 acres in Elk County. He also owns his modern residence on Washington Street at the corner of Penn Avenue. His offices are in the courthouse.

In 1886 at Howard, Mr. Osborn married Miss Mattie E. Cook, daughter of J. H. and Sophia (Shellenberger) Cook. Her parents, who are now deceased, were Kansas pioneers, having come overland with wagon and ox team from Michigan in 1857 and locating near Lawrence. In 1883 they came to Howard, and Mr. Cook was proprietor of the Windsor Hotel. Fred P. Osborn, only son and child of Mr. Osborn, was born April 30, 1888. He was educated in the public schools at Howard, graduating from high school, and for two years pursued the engineering course in the University of Kansas. He still makes his home at Howard, but is employed by an oil company working with the geologists in Eastern Kansas. Fred P. Osborn married Miss Hazel Keifer.

ANDERSON M. SHARP. Widely known in the financial field of Kansas and prominent in business and public life at Neodesha, is Anderson M. Sharp, president of the Neodesha National Bank, who has been officially identified with this institution since it was organized as the Bank of Neodesha, in the spring of 1899. For thirty-three years Mr. Sharp has been a resident of Wilson County, early proving his stable character as a business man and his public spirit as an earnest citizen. He was born July 28, 1859, in Calloway County, Missouri. His parents were William and Mary (Maupin) Sharp.

The Sharp family is of Scotch and English extraction and it may yet be numerously found in Virginia, to which state, in colonial days, the Sharps came from across the Atlantic Ocean. On down to the present the name has been honorably borne in business, professional and public life. Apparently the first pioneer of the family westward was the grandfather of Anderson M. Sharp, a minister in the Methodist Episcopal Church, who settled very early in Monroe County, Missouri, and his life and labors ended there before his grandson was born.

William Sharp, father of Anderson M. Sharp, was born in 1805, in Albemarle County, Virginia, and died in 1881, in Calloway County, Missouri. As his father for some years was a traveling evangelist, the family home, during his boyhood, was in Kentucky, and from there, in 1826, he moved to Monroe County, Missouri. He followed agricultural pursuits during his entire life and accumulated wealth, but he was more than a farmer and occupied a prominent position in public affairs and was a man of influence in every section in which he lived. All his life a staunch democrat he filled many local offices in the gift of his party and with distinction served one term in the State Legislature, representing Monroe County. He was less active in political life after removing to Calloway County, but he continued a leader in Methodist Church affairs and held every lay office in the local body. During the mustering days he was placed in charge of the state militia and for that reason was subsequently addressed as General Sharp. He was a Knight Templar Mason for many years.

William Sharp was married, first, in early manhood, in Kentucky, and thereby became the father of three children: Jane, who became the wife of John Moore, is now deceased as is her husband; Robert, who was a soldier during the Civil war and lost his life at the siege of Vicksburg; and R. V., who is a farmer residing in Pike County, Missouri. To a second marriage one son was born, James P., who was a retired farmer when his death occurred at Mexico, Missouri. Mr. Sharp's third wife was survived by one daughter, Mary, who is a resident of Moberly, Missouri, and is the widow of William Barker, an insurance agent, who died at Baltimore, Maryland.

William Sharp's last marriage was to Mary Maupin, who was born at Staunton, Virginia, in 1818, and died in 1884, in Audrain County, Missouri. Seven children were born to them, as follows: Annie, who died at Moberly, Missouri, in 1914, was the widow of John Furnish, who had been a retired farmer; John T., who was a dental practitioner, died in 1883, at Vandalia, Missouri; Kate, who is the wife of T. N. Furnish, a retired farmer, resides at Shelbina, Missouri; William A., who is in the real estate business at Mexico, Missouri; Anderson M., who is president of the Neodesha National Bank; Fannie, who was the wife of the late W. A. Edmonston, an attorney, died in 1897, at Mexico, Missouri; and J. B., who is a resident of Fulton, Missouri, is assistant cashier of the Southern Bank at that place.

Anderson M. Sharp attended the public schools in Calloway County, and then entered Fayette College, at Fayette, Missouri, where he remained a student until September, 1881, completing his junior year. Impaired health then made it almost a matter of necessity that he should put aside his books for a time, therefore for the next year he traveled, visiting Colorado, New Mexico and Arizona before returning to Calloway County. From there, in the spring of 1883, he came to Neodesha, establishing himself near the city on a farm and becoming interested in the business of handling stock. He also taught school and additionally, for two years, served as clerk of the District Court at Fredonia.

The spring of 1899 found Mr. Sharp with health restored and ready to enter actively into business and accepted the position of assistant cashier of the Bank of Neodesha, in April, 1899, becoming cashier and continuing until 1903, when the bank was reorganized as the Neodesha National Bank, of which he became president on January 1, 1916.

The Neodesha National Bank has a working capital of $50,000, with a surplus of $11,000. The first officers after its organization as a national bank were:

C. M. Condon, of Oswego, president; W. H. Condon, of Oswego, vice president, and Anderson M. Sharp, of Neodesha, cashier. The present officers are: Anderson M. Sharp, president; W. H. Condon, vice president; and G. C. Pitney, cashier. The bank is housed in a handsome, modern brick building, erected in 1903, the bank occupying the first floor and the second floor rented as offices. It is located in the business district, on the corner of Main and Fifth streets. As president Mr. Sharp manages the business with a careful conservatism that is reassuring to both the business interests of the city and to the individual depositor, and his name stands for soundness and integrity in every enterprise with which it is connected.

Politically reared in the democratic party, Mr. Sharp still upholds the principles of that organization but has no desire for public office, although he is active as a member of the school board, and, during one term, as mayor, gave the city one of the best business administrations it has ever had. At different times he has served on boards and committees of importance and at present is a member of the board of trustees and is secretary of the Wilson County Hospital. While not always, because of lack of time, accepting official position in the various benevolent organizations of the city, Mr. Sharp is a generous contributor to their maintenance, as he also is to all charitable movements of worth that are brought to his attention.

In 1888, in this city, Mr. Sharp was married to Miss Hattie Kimball, who was born in Indiana and is a daughter of H. H. and Jane (Tanquary) Kimball. The mother of Mrs. Sharp is deceased, but the father, who is a retired farmer and a bank director, resides in this city. Mr. and Mrs. Sharp have three children: Jessie, Frances M. and Lowell. Miss Jessie Sharp is a popular teacher in the Neodesha High School. She was graduated from Lexington College, Lexington, Missouri, with the degree of A. B. Frances M., the second daughter, is a member of the freshman class in the Kansas State University, while Lowell, the only son, is completing the high school course at Neodesha preparatory to entering college. The handsome family residence is situated at No. 222 Main Street, and Mr. Sharp owns also a half interest in a farm of 180 acres, located three miles south of Neodesha.

As a Mason Mr. Sharp is identified with Harmony Lodge No. 94, Free and Accepted Masons; Fort Scott Consistory No. 4, and Mirza Temple, Mystic Shrine, at Pittsburg, Kansas. He is a valued member of the Kansas Bankers', the American Bankers' and the Wilson County Bankers' associations, and is an important factor in the Commercial Club at Neodesha.

EDGAR FENTON BROOMHALL is secretary of the Missouri, Kansas & Texas Railway Company with headquarters and home at Parsons. Native ability and long experience in railroading have given Mr. Broomhall unusual qualifications for the large responsibilities he now enjoys.

He was born in Chicago August 18, 1877, and from that date it will be seen that he is still a young man. His father, Charles W. Broomhall, was born in Wilmington, Ohio, August 9, 1850, grew up and married in his native state, and in early life learned telegraphy and was an operator until 1888. For several years he was a clerk in the offices of the Missouri Pacific Railway Company, but for the past twenty-five years has been employed by the St. Louis Transfer Company, and resides at St. Louis. He is a republican and a member of the Methodist Episcopal Church. Charles W. Broomhall married Lodema Jane Nitchman, who was born in Ohio February 3, 1855. Their children are: Edith May, widow of August Busch, who was a painter at St. Louis;

Edgar F.; and Florence, wife of Bruce Cameron, who is superintendent of transportation of the United Railways at St. Louis, Mrs. Cameron having taught school six years before her marriage.

Edgar F. Broomhall received his early education in the public schools of Chicago and St. Louis. He had one year in the St. Louis High School, and in 1892 gave up his books and studies to find place as a practical worker in the world. He started as a messenger and continued that occupation about five months. For four years he was employed by the St. Louis Transfer Company. In 1897 he became clerk in the offices of the Missouri Pacific Railway. He was promoted to station accountant, and resigned that in 1903 to enter the service of the Missouri, Kansas & Texas Railway Company, where many subsequent promotions have brought him to his office as secretary. For a time he was traveling auditor with headquarters at Muskogee, Oklahoma. After three years he was promoted to general bookkeeper in the offices at St. Louis, and filled that position three years. He was then made auditor of disbursement of The Missouri, Kansas & Texas Railway Co., of Texas, at Dallas, Texas. Resigning after one year he returned to Kansas and was traveling auditor for about one year, and then took a position in the home offices representing the comptroller and auditor in matters of disbursements. He filled that place for two years until 1914. Since then he has been accountant of the Valuation Committee, and on September 15, 1915, also assumed the duties of secretary of the Missouri, Kansas & Texas Railway Company.

Since July 1, 1915, Mr. Broomhall has had his home in Parsons, at 619 S. Fifteenth St. He is a republican, a member of the Presbyterian Church, belongs to Cornerstone Lodge No. 323, Ancient Free and Accepted Masons at St. Louis, and in Scottish Rite affiliation belongs to Indian Consistory No. 2 at McAlester, Oklahoma.

On June 12, 1909, at St. Louis he married Miss Tillie M. Rauschkolb, daughter of Louis and Minnie Rauschkolb. Her father, now deceased, was a painter by trade. Her mother is still living in St. Louis. Mr. and Mrs. Broomhall have two children: Mary, born May 14, 1910; and Russell, born October 11, 1914. Mr. Broomhall is of English ancestors, various members of the family having come from England to Pennsylvania in colonial times. His grandfather Webb Broomhall, was a resident of Ohio where he died.

JOHN FRANCIS HUGHS. During the past five years Prof. John Francis Hughs has been superintendent of the city schools of Chanute, and in this time has gained a strong and lasting place in the confidence of the people of the community. His interest in his work has been deep, sincere and unabating, and the splendid school system of the city at the present time may be largely accredited to his efforts. His labors have been progressive and practical in character and have proved of the greatest benefit to Chanute.

Professor Hughs was born at Fort Scott, Bourbon County, Kansas, August 16, 1881, and is a son of William and Elizabeth (Hopkin) Hughs, natives of South Wales, England. His father was born in 1838 and received an ordinary education in his native land, where, as a young man he engaged in farming in a small way. He was married in his native land and there continued to be engaged in agricultural pursuits for some years, but did not advance as rapidly as he desired and felt that his fortunes might be bettered in America. He accordingly came to this country in 1873, and after a brief stop at Paola,

Kansas, located among the pioneers of Bourbon County, where he had a homestead in the vicinity of Fort Scott. There Mr. Hughs passed the remainder of his life, his death occurring at Fort Scott in 1898, when he was sixty years of age. He was an industrious and practical farmer and desired no further honors, for he never sought office nor took any more than a good citizen's interest in public affairs. He voted the republican ticket in national affairs, while in local matters he was inclined to favor the man whom he deemed best fitted for the office, although, all else being equal, he gave his ballot to the representative of the Grand Old Party. A lifelong member of the Congregational Church, he lived his religion and took an active part in the work of the church, in which he acted as deacon for a number of years. Mr. Hughs was married in his native land to Elizabeth Hopkin, who was born in 1846, in South Wales, and who survives him and resides at Fort Scott. Mrs. Hughs is a member of the Congregational Church, and a woman of strong character and kindly heart. They became the parents of seven children, as follows: Mary, who is the wife of N. W. Bass and resides at Eldorado, Kansas, where Mr. Bass is a mail clerk; G. R., ex-postmaster of Fort Scott, where he is the proprietor of a successful mercantile business; Lizzie, unmarried, one of the well known educators of Bourbon County, and now principal of the Main Street School, Fort Scott; W. G., who is a farmer in Bourbon County, conducting operations on the old homestead place south of Fort Scott; Dollie, who is the wife of R. H. Hubbard, chief despatcher for the Frisco Railroad, at Fort Scott; John Francis, of this review; and Reese, who is a teacher in the Fort Scott High School.

John Francis Hughs was brought up in an agricultural atmosphere and trained to the duties of the home farm, but his inclinations and talents lay in another direction and he early evidenced a desire to enter the educator's profession. During the winter terms he attended the district schools of Bourbon County, and subsequently pursued a course at the old Kansas Normal School, at Fort Scott, from which he was graduated. His studies were further prosecuted at Washburn College, where he was graduated with the class of 1909, and given the degree of Bachelor of Arts, and in the summer of 1916 he attended Kansas University for post-graduate work. During the summers of 1907 and 1908 he also attended the University of Chicago.

In the meantime Professor Hughs had been teaching since his eighteenth year. In 1899 and 1900 he had his initiation in his profession in the country schools of Bourbon County, and again in 1902 and 1903 he taught there. With this preparation, he went to Fort Scott, in the spring of 1906 and began teaching in the schools of that city, where he was principal of the Fort Scott High School for two years, then principal of the Central School for two years, and again principal of the high school for a like period. His reputation as an educator was by this time established, and in the fall of 1911 he was induced to come to Chanute, where he has since been superintendent of city schools. Under his supervision are six schools, sixty teachers and 2,200 scholars. The cause of education has indeed found in Professor Hughs a true friend. With a just appreciation of its value as a preparation for life's responsibilities, he has made it his constant aim to so improve the schools that the instruction will be of the greatest possible benefit to the young. He has continually promoted the standard of the schools until Chanute has every reason to be proud of its system, which is most thorough, practical and beneficial. Professor Hughs is a member of the Kansas State Teachers' Association and of the Southeastern Kansas Teachers' Association, and the high esteem in which he is held by his fellow-educators is shown in the fact that he is chairman of the executive committee of the latter organization. He maintains offices in the Senior High School Building, and resides at No. 503 South Steuben Street. In politics he is a republican, but has not desired to shine in the public light. His religious connection is with the Presbyterion Church, in which he is an elder and superintendent of the Sunday school, and fraternally he is affiliated with Cedar Lodge No. 103, Ancient Free and Accepted Masons, and Chanute Camp No. 852, Modern Woodmen of America, in both of which orders he has numerous friends.

Professor Hughs was married in 1909, at Topeka, Kansas, to Miss Ione Hill White, daughter of O. H. and Carrie (Hill) White, residents of Topeka, where Mr. White is president of the Topeka Transfer and Storage Company, one of that city's large business houses. Three children have been born to Mr. and Mrs. Hughs, namely: Carroll, born May 23, 1910, and now attending school; Helen, born January 25, 1914; and Jeannette, born May 26, 1916.

JACOB RUMBAUGH was for twenty-eight years one of the most widely known citizens of Fort Scott. He had come to that section of Kansas and established a home on lands just across the state line in Missouri in 1870. He endured all the trials and vicissitudes that beset the average farmer of his day. But he was not himself an average man. He had a resourcefulness, a faculty for hard work, that often made him prosper while others were blaming fate for hard times and misfortunes. He was optimistic. As long as he lived he was sustained by hope. It has been well said that when a man ceases to hope he is spiritually dead. Hope is only another word for faith. It was faith that took Jacob Rumbaugh through every trial of life. It was faith that sustained him during the 15 years he spent as an invalid prior to his death on December 1, 1910. As a citizen he was liberal minded, always ready to do his share or more than his share in any undertaking for the public benefit. He was a generous neighbor and friend, and in spite of the sufferings that burdened his later years he was never heard to complain.

Apart from his experiences, his achievements, his useful life in the state and among his family and neighbors, he rendered an especially noteworthy service when in his declining years he put down on paper the words which were published in the year of his death under the title "Reminiscences of Jacob Rumbaugh." These reminiscences were written and dedicated to his children and grandchildren, but they have a wider appeal and an interest to all who would know the individual part played by men in the making of modern Kansas. The reminiscences make a small book that is a rare privilege to read, and it is one that should be part of the permanent literature of Kansas.

The keynote of the book is happily stated in his concluding words: "As fathers before me have told their sons and daughters the story of their ancestors that the children of their children might profit by the experience of past generations, so I have told mine, with the hope that their knowing of the days gone by may strengthen them for the days to come and may make their thoughts coextensive with the life of the race. For what is history but truth clad in a living personality and acted out anew in each generation."

Much condensation is necessary that the life of Jacob Rumbaugh told in his own words may be reduced to the limits assigned this article in the History of Kansas.

Jacob Rumbaugh was born in Seneca County, Ohio, July 26, 1839. His grandfather, John Rumbaugh, at the close of the Revolutionary war, in which he had participated as a soldier, settled in Virginia, where he owned a sawmill and also had a number of teams with which he did freighting. His wife lived to be eighty-five years of age. There were eight children, five sons and three daughters. The sons were George, Christopher, Nicholas, John and William.

William Rumbaugh, father of Jacob, was born in 1799. When he was thirteen years of age the War of 1812 broke out, and his older brothers went into the service, while he remained at home and assumed double responsibilities. The old homestead was located near Harpers Ferry, Virginia. At the age of twenty-two, in 1821, William Rumbaugh married Polly Musceteer, daughter of a prosperous planter and one of thirteen children. Mr. Jacob Rumbaugh pays some beautiful tributes to his mother, who died March 8, 1847, when he was eight years of age. She was a woman of great industry, proficient in all the household arts, well fitted for bearing pioneer burdens, and was kind, generous and lovable.

After his marriage William Rumbaugh moved to Ohio and located in Seneca County on a land warrant given to John Rumbaugh and his sons for their services during the Revolutionary war. This land comprised 320 acres, situated in the midst of the forest. On one 80-acre tract William built a log cabin 20x22 feet, and moved his family into it in 1826. While he worked in a nearby sawmill and in the intervals did what he could in clearing and cultivating a small tract of land, his wife remained at home carding, spinning, weaving and making the clothes for the family. William and Polly had three children when they moved to Seneca County, Ann, John and Susan. Five others were born in the pioneer home, George, William, Christopher, Mary and James, and then in 1839 was born Jacob. In the spring of 1843 the family moved to another farm in a community where the neighbors had organized a school district and had put up a schoolhouse out of logs. There Jacob Rumbaugh received his first schooling. After three years the family returned to the old homestead, another child having been born in the meantime, named Rufus. It was not long after the return to the old homestead that the mother was taken ill with the measles and died. William Rumbaugh never recovered from the shock of his wife's death and spent his last years as an invalid, carefully looked after by his sons.

"When I was twelve years old," wrote Mr. Rumbaugh, "brother James and I took entire charge of the farm and my school days were over. All counted, the number of days I spent at school were less than the number of days in one year; but in that time I finished an old English reader, Gray's arithmetic (to part third), a curious looking geography, and the elementary spelling book. The only book to read in my house consisted of a common sized Bible, bound in smooth leather and printed in small type, and a prayer book about the same size, which was printed in larger type. There were no newspapers until the time of the Kansas border troubles, and then we took a county paper. There were no magazines and I never saw my mother with a book of any kind in her hands. My parents were good Christian people and very strict in many ways, especially in observing the Sabbath day. In after years there was a Sunday school organized at the schoolhouse, and then a New Testament was purchased, and father was very proud of it, and it was lighter than the old family Bible and easier for him to hold. Then, too, he enjoyed the small story book circulated to the people from this private Sunday school library. If I was more innocent of books, I was rich in the lore of Nature's works. I lived so near to Nature's breast that I knew her voices well; the signs of the moon, the names of every tree that grew, hundreds of different animals, birds and fishes, all these and more. I was always industrious and frugal. I loved to work and never wanted to idle away any time.''

When Jacob Rumbaugh became twenty-one years of age, in July, 1860, he applied himself to reading and discussing the various platforms of the political parties. His father was a whig, two of his brothers were republicans, and two brothers and two brothers-in-law and a stanch friend were democrats and admirers of Stephen A. Douglas. Jacob thought he was a democrat, but when the republican party issued its platform he was strongly impressed with its plank against the extension of slavery, and in the following fall he voted for Abraham Lincoln and the republican ticket, and thereby as he says became a republican for life.

About that time he left home and ventured into business for himself. He sold books in the vicinity around Saginaw Bay, Michigan, and by work all the winter earned a large commission and was pronounced a first-class salesman.

In nearly every career there is a point where a man's destiny seems to come upon him suddenly and transform all the future. This point in Mr. Rumbaugh's career was the Easter Sabbath of 1861. He attended church at Bettsville. Church was held in a very rude and unpretentious building, with the old slab benches which have been made familiar by the recollections of school children of that and earlier years. Before the service began four young ladies from the town of Tiffin, Ohio, came in and took seats immediately opposite him. By one in particular he was attracted, and he thought ''there never was such perfection of womanly grace and loveliness.'' He found it impossible to fix his attention on the preacher, and before the service concluded he realized that he was ''head over heels in love.'' That was the beginning of his life's great romance, and less than a year and a half later he was married.

In the meantime he and his brother James had rented a farm and were busy with the preparations for a crop. War came on, and James Rumbaugh turned over the farm to Jacob and enlisted in the Fifty-fifth Ohio Regiment. He continued with the management of the farm and the crop and was also pressing his courtship to Miss Isabel Holt. On August 6, 1862, at her Uncle William Holt's home in Tiffin they were married. He was then twenty-three and she in her eighteenth year.

Very soon after the war began Lincoln's call for 600,000 more soldiers started him from his fireside and caused him to enlist in the Forty-ninth Ohio Infantry. He sold his team of horses and farming implements at a sacrifice, left his crops with his brother-in-law, and while Mrs. Rumbaugh prepared to teach school during his absence he marched away to the front. He had hardly arrived at Camp Chase when he was taken ill with fever and quinsy, and he remained in the hospital for some days. The first news he read in the paper after getting out of the hospital was about the battle of Chancellorsville, and midway in the list of dead was the name of his brother James. The war went on, many battles were fought and many lives were lost. Then came the surrender of Lee, and Mr. Rumbaugh was back at home, overjoyed to be again in the presence of his wife, but finding that the management of the farm had not prospered during his absence.

About that time he worked out the plans for an improved cider press and was getting ready to have his invention patented, when the perfected form of an invention came along so similar to his that he abandoned the idea of getting a patent. He originated several other devices, but never applied for any patents. For several years after the war he engaged in buying stock, and was one of the pioneer dealers in poultry in that section of Ohio, and made considerable money as a dealer. He made money, and also lost some, and both the good and bad were mixed in his fortunes then as also during the early years he spent in Kansas. From Ohio he moved with his family to the vicinity of Kendallville, Indiana, and occupied a one-room log cabin, which his wife made exceedingly attractive and homelike by her industry and domestic tastes. They enjoyed two prosperous years in Indiana. While living in Ohio their first child was born, Lura, and in Indiana Minnie Bell was born February 26, 1869.

Several times Mr. Rumbaugh had been stricken with an attack of ''Kansas fever,'' and late in the fall of 1869 he again determined to move to Kansas. After selling everything except his wheat crop he found himself possessed of about $800. His household goods were shipped by rail to Kansas City, and after a final visit among relatives and friends in Indiana and Ohio, Mr. Rumbaugh and his wife and children arrived at Olathe, then the terminus of the railroad, in January, 1870. It was a very expensive removal Mr. Rumbaugh found. He paid really exorbitant prices for the miserable hotel accommodations afforded them, and it cost $5 a hundred weight to get his goods freighted from Kansas City to his destination. In his reminiscences he recalls that flour sold for $7 a sack, meat for 25 cents a pound, corn and potatoes $2.50 a bushel, butter 50 cents a pound, while a dollar's worth of sugar or coffee could easily be carried in a man's coat pocket. Mr. Rumbaugh spent many days riding over the country on horseback, and finally determined to buy land in the hilly region to be above the damp, and chills and fever from which they had suffered back in Indiana. Thus he finally arrived in the country around Fort Scott. Mr. Rumbaugh assigns several reasons for choosing land across the line in Missouri rather than in Kansas. In the first place he found it difficult to accustom himself to the idea of negro and white children attending the same school, as was done in Kansas. Then again, the laws in Kansas were very liberal in exemptions. While in Ohio he had had a rather unpleasant experience with a partner who had gone to Michigan and by the laws of that state had been exempted from his responsibility for debt left behind in Ohio and which Mr. Rumbaugh had to assume. After some investigation he found that in Missouri there was no exemption law; that a man, rich or poor, was subject to his debts, and this was more and more in accordance with his way of thinking. ''I wanted to pay my taxes and have the protection of a citizen of America and the benefit of all its laws. I was willing to be sold out if I did not pay my debts, provided that I had the right to sell out others who refused to pay me.''

Thus in the spring of 1870 Mr. Rumbaugh bought, paying part of the purchase price in cash, 120 acres of land in Vernon County, Missouri. "I bought cabin logs for $20, lumber for $23, walnut shingles for $15, and did all the work myself, even to the chinking and mortaring, and had the house finished and my family moved into it before the holidays." The distinctive part about the career of Jacob Rumbaugh, and an important lesson that may be gleaned from his reminiscences, is that when he was halted by an obstacle in one direction, he was so resourceful that he was not long in discovering a way out of any financial difficulty. Thus when a mortgage was overhanging his farm in Vernon County and no immediate prospect of his crops giving him sufficient money to pay it, he recognized a general demand all over that section for fruit trees, and he bought a stock of apple trees and begun selling them at a good profit, buying and selling some 7,000 trees in one winter. Later other nursery men came in from a distance and reduced the price, but in the meantime he had effected his purpose and he was ready to give up selling trees.

On April 29, 1872, another child was born, Nellie Blanche. This child was a constant source of joy and delight to her father, and her death in August, 1873, was the hardest blow he ever sustained.

The experiences of several following years are best told in Mr. Rumbaugh's own words: "In 1874 there was a great drought throughout all the country; many people did not raise any corn, but I had plenty for our needs and a little to sell. In 1875 the grasshoppers took possession of the country; they came in such clouds that the sun could be but dimly seen behind them, and when they settled they left the country brown. Everything green, from a stalk of corn to a young tree was destroyed. They were so thick on the ground that one could not step without walking on them. They would hop into the houses and on the beds unless the doors and windows were kept closed. There was a great financial panic among the people; some were frightened into 'greenbackism,' 'beggingism' and 'pauperism.' But strange to say, I never raised a better crop of corn, and I also sold my first three head of fat cattle.

"In 1881 Lura graduated from the Kansas Normal College and taught the summer and winter terms of school at Lone Oak.

"Our prosperity continued without a break and in 1882 we commenced to build us a beautiful home, with pillared porches, great bay windows, octagonal fronts, and long, wide halls with curly birch and walnut finish on all the doors and window facings; there were dainty boudoirs, a bathroom with all the modern conveniences, dens, a music room and a library with good books and magazines; the basement extended under all, and was partitioned into rooms for milk and cheese, for potatoes, apples, and all kinds of fruit and vegetables. In 1883 it was finished, painted and decorated at a cost of $4,600. This year I was even more prosperous and I bought a carriage for $350, to which I harnessed a 'fine team. I had dozens of horses now. Then, too, the girls needed a new piano; so one day Isabel and I drove to Nevada, Missouri, and purchased a handsome square piano for $450.

"In 1884 I raised 12,000 bushels of corn and 100 tons of German millet hay, and sold hogs to the amount of $2,000 and cattle amounting to $7,500. Our personal property was estimated at $30,000, and we were exceedingly prosperous. In the early spring of this year Isabel visited in Ohio. On April 5th Minnie graduated from the Kansas Normal College and went to Nevada, Missouri, for the teachers' examination, from which she received a first-class cer-

tificate, and taught a summer term of three months at the Lone Oak School."

Those conditions that surrounded country life in America twenty-five or thirty years ago were such that material prosperity did not bring with it all those things which people of essential culture and broad intelligence demanded as a normal part of their lives. In that more than anything else can be found the real cause for the movement from country to town, which was the dominating feature of America's industrial and social life in the last quarter of the last century. The Rumbaugh family having reached a status of prosperity, found that money would not bring to their country home the advantages, the cultured association, the environment of music and art, which in order to enjoy they must live in town. Though farm management was as congenial as it was profitable to Mr. Rumbaugh, he felt his duty to his family obliged him to part, from his business, and consequently he moved to Fort Scott, and lived for a time in a rented house. Later he bought a homesite at 720 National Avenue, and proceeded to erect the first Queen Anne house in the city, which his widow still owns. As he says, "it created much comment, and a mention of it was made in the daily papers from time to time as it progressed." It was a modern home, and when the family occupied it in 1886 its cost aggregated $6,700.

In the meantime Mr. Rumbaugh had experienced much difficulty in getting capable managers for his farm, and he also had to contend with poor markets, some of his cattle selling for only $1.50 a hundred weight and wheat for 42 cents a bushel. His early business experiences in Fort Scott was not profitable. When he went to the city there was a real estate boom. He was influenced into buying property at enormously inflated prices, and while he recognized the end before it came, he was unable to get out without the loss of much money. He also became identified with a manufacturing company and lost money in that.

One compensation was the happiness and the fine progress made by his daughters in their respective studies of art and music. On October 11, 1887, the daughter Minnie married Mr. Curt Myers of Fort Scott. Then, on January 5, 1888, another wedding occurred in their home at Fort Scott, when the daughter Lura married Mr. Greene, a wealthy and influential citizen of Wichita. The loneliness of the home without these daughters was greatly accentuated by other business losses and reverses which had followed closely in a train. It was characteristic of Mr. Rumbaugh that he gave no hint of these various troubles to the daughters who were then enjoying the happiness of marriage, but when both the daughters were gone he found himself in debt a number of thousand dollars. Again and again he secured tenants for his farm, and again and again each one disappointed him by shiftlessness or by unscrupulous business methods. Finally in 1891 he took complete charge of the old farm, and the 800 acres which he had acquired soon felt the impulse of his management and returned to him a prosperity sufficient to satisfy all his creditors and leave him much besides. He continued more or less actively identified with his farm and other properties until 1898, when his health finally broke down and reduced him to that stage of invalidism in which he spent fifteen or more years before his death.

And then, only a few weeks before the end came, he was able to write the following words which have in them nothing of vaunt and breathe only a humble

Isabel Holt Rumbaugh

gratefulness for the fortunes that had followed him through his lifetime:

"And now having emerged from the poverty and the obscurity in which I was born and bred to a state of affluence and some degree of reputation in the world, I look back to the pioneer days of the wilderness and see where the stump-dotted clearings have expanded into vast stretches of fertile farm lands. I see small towns or cities where log cabins once stood. All civilization has changed and developed with extraordinary rapidity, and I find myself comfortably situated, my debts all paid, and with abundance of money and worldly goods. I see my farm advanced from $5, $10 and $15 to $75 and $80 an acre, and bringing in a liberal income. And though shut in from all the world without, I sit by the side of Isabel in our home at Fort Scott, content to let the cold winds roar, while the perforated rough-barked, firebrick logs lie between the andirons and support the flaky asbestos which reddens with a glow that comes from the lighted gas. No more we do fourteen hours a day of hard work to earn money and then drive long miles to spend it: but rather, we turn by our glowing fire of gas and telephone our needs, and forthwith every want is gratified."

Some time before his death he was sitting by the window. When his chair was wheeled back to bed, a paper was picked up from beneath it. He had penned the following words: "The sunset of life approaches and soon the pleasures, desires and struggles, fears, hopes and mysteries will be over, and soon I will cross the river of destiny to meet the angel of destiny for weal or woe. Now, when the pleasant, happy and beautiful pilgrimage of life with me is over, then may my spirit be transformed into love and abide with the angels of the resurrection." An invalid fifteen years, and awaiting the sunset, he realized the passing as those around him could not.

ISABEL HOLT RUMBAUGH, widow of the late Jacob Rumbaugh of Fort Scott, Kansas, has for years stood among the foremost club women of Kansas, and if there is any one who can speak with the authority born of actual experience concerning woman's lot, especially in the country and rural districts of America during the last half century, it is Mrs. Rumbaugh. In the years when the door of aspirations was shut in almost every woman's face, Mrs. Rumbaugh was loyally, faithfully, self-sacrificingly playing her part, often of drudgery and with none of the influences and associations that tend to enlighten and cheer the existence of human life. When her own duties as a home maker and a mother were fulfilled and after her daughters had left home, she began seeking those advantages which a cultured woman craves. At the same time she commenced to bend every effort toward the betterment of the lot of her sisters, not so much in material welfare as in those things which count a great deal more and which the mere possession of money cannot satisfy. Since then, for many years she has worked alongside other prominent leaders in the woman's movement, not only in Kansas, but in the nation.

While many of the facts of her experience have been told in the article upon the career of her husband, Jacob Rumbaugh, it will serve the better to indicate her point of view and attitude toward some of the issues of life, if many of her early and later experiences can be set down, practically in the words which she herself has used in describing these experiences.

"At the age of fifteen," she says, "a stepmother requested that I leave high school and earn my own living. I was proud and ambitious. The professor of the high school urged me to try for a school. I passed the examination, receiving a certificate for six months. I do not believe the average girl of fifteen has the nerve or bluff that I possessed at that age. I remember well the day that I started off to be a school mar'm and my father, driving a two-horse covered carriage over a plank toll road just after a rain, fourteen miles to a village named Bettsville, Ohio. I was but a small girl, with my braided hair hanging down my back. I took up my duties at once and enrolled seventy-five names. When I looked into the faces of young men, eighteen and nineteen years old and recalled what the directors had told me, that these same boys had caused the school to be closed that winter, I could not help but wonder how I should come through the summer. But one thing I knew, that as soon as these boys could plow they would not be in school. My only trouble during the term was with a woman who came to the school one day and told me what she thought of me for forbidding her children to chew gum in school. The pay was not munificent then. For the summer school I received $6 a month and boarded around at the homes of the scholars, and for the winter term I was paid $10 per month. That amount was as much as the experienced teachers, both men and women, received as compensation. I taught two years. On August 6, 1862, at the age of eighteen, I was married at Tiffin, Ohio, but I continued to teach while Mr. Rumbaugh was in the army.

"When we commenced keeping house it was the money that I had earned by my teaching that furnished our home in a simple but useful fashion. How pleased I was with my first rag carpet can be imagined. That was during the Civil war, and I often live through again some of those exciting times. To my notion the war songs had more music in them than any that have ever been composed since. How proud we were of our president, Abraham Lincoln, and how every head was bowed in grief when he was assassinated.

"We were so very poor and worked so hard. Life was so different then. Everybody worked; some had more than others, but all worked, and the wisest counted it a blessing. In the course of time my husband, like many others, got the Kansas fever, and talked of going West. At last he secured my consent to make the move, though I must confess that I was not eager to go. The tiresome trip was made with our main destination as Kansas City, in 1870. Having located on a farm near Stotesberry, I found myself with my two little girls so lonesome as no one can ever know. Everything was strange. Our home was a two-room log cabin built on a hill. Visitors were a rarity. I shall never forget the prairie fires. Every time I would see the blaze shooting up to the sky I thought we were surely in the line of destruction. There was not a neighbor near; the prairie grass was as high as the horses' backs, and it was sixteen miles to the postoffice at Fort Scott. There was no fruit and I would get so hungry for apples. Taking my butter and eggs to Fort Scott, I would sell them for just enough to secure some necessary things for the children, while I looked longingly at the apples, which were such a luxury to me. and came near taking one.

"About that time a schoolhouse was built in the district and I boarded the teacher. The first money she paid me was invested in calves, which was the beginning of a prosperous era for us. The teacher furnished companionship, and life became more interesting. Yet I was not content. We added to our land holdings each year until we had eight hundred acres. The curious ox teams used for plowing began to be replaced by horses, just as in this day that noble animal is being supplanted by the steam tractors. Every year I cooked for ten or twelve men. How the loaves of bread, pies and cakes would disappear! I was so hungry for knowledge and so dissatisfied, yet kept it to myself, for no one was near to be in sympathy with me. I could not make others understand what I craved.

"But the time came when I realized my ideals in an unexpected way. The Normal College was opened in Fort Scott. Professor Sanders came out soliciting for pupils. I was happy that I could see my way clear to giving my girls what I had craved for myself. They were enrolled. The older daughter graduated in the business course and the younger in the teacher's course. I drove a team of young horses hitched to a spring wagon to Fort Scott every week for three years to look after the girls. I shall never forget the fright I had one evening on one of these trips. After eating dinner at the school with the girls, I went to the bank to deposit four hundred dollars which Mr. Rumbaugh had given me. I noticed a man watching me count the money at the window. I can see him yet—dirty and wearing a slouch hat. And I looked right in his eye. I started home about half past three o'clock. It was almost a prairie, with the exception of a long stretch of hedge on either side of the road, which obstructed the view. I was half way through the hedge, when this man I had observed in the bank came through the hedge and almost took the bridle in his hand. He probably thought I had withdrawn the money and had it on my person. He was quick, but I was quicker. I struck the horse next to him with all my strength; the animal lunged and started at a gallop, taking her companion with her. We were five miles from home and the horses' hoofs hardly touched the ground until we arrived there. Never after that did we carry any money, but transacted our business by checks.

"When the girls had graduated they decided to follow in their mother's footsteps, and they taught country schools. Later we moved to Fort Scott, where we were not long in receiving those social advantages which we had so long looked forward to. The farm was not a success after we left it, but the best part of my life was spent on the farm in hard work. At this time the clubs being organized had as their object self culture, that which I desired. But I look back now, as through a mist, and see how little we really accomplished. What a small beginning. How often I have thanked God for the calling I could not resist —to go out into the world to the work that helps to bring people together for the noble things of life, the uplift, the broadening and reaching out of a helping hand to others. Even yet I am a farmer, with eight hundred acres of land, shipping my own hay and corn, and I love the farm also.'' In later years Mrs. Rumbaugh was an advocate for a rest room for farmers' wives, which she helped to start in a humble way. It proved a great comfort to weary mothers and shoppers in Fort Scott.

Mrs. Rumbaugh has always been a woman of boundless energy, and aside from her club life gave much time to church and civic affairs. She was president of St. Andrew's Episcopal Guild in 1903, at that period when funds were being raised for the erection of a beautiful new church edifice. She did her part when plans were first suggested for a new Railroad Young Men's Christian Association Building, erected in 1907. Mrs. Rumbaugh put forth every effort as president of the Ladies' Auxiliary of the Young Men's Christian Association to make money, which was used for equipment and furnishing of the linen and silver chests. At this time the ladies also assisted by serving suppers at the men's weekly meetings. When the need of larger quarters became apparent for the Epworth Home for Orphan Children, Mrs. Rumbaugh was chairman of the committee of ladies who gave a rummage sale, which realized a large sum with which it was intended to buy a permanent home. The seed then sown afterwards bore fruit, when the home was enlarged and became the Goodlander Home for Homeless Children. She was also a valuable worker in the Bourbon County Historical Society.

Mrs. Rumbaugh became a member of the first club organized in Fort Scott, the Castilian Club, organized in 1882, with Mrs. C. H. Haynes as the first president. The next club joined was the Social Science Club of Kansas and Missouri, which was organized in 1881, joining the General Federation in 1890. It became the Kansas Social Science Federation in 1895, and afterwards the Kansas Federation of Women's Clubs in 1904.

A number of years ago Mrs. Rumbaugh accomplished what was considered almost the impossible, when she called all the clubs of Fort Scott together at her home and brought about the organization of the City Federation, on March 25, 1906. In 1912 she took the initiative in organizing the Women's Athenaeum, which in turn organized the Women's Current Topic Club with seventy-five members.

Mrs. Rumbaugh has attended as a delegate some of the greatest conventions of women in the country within recent years. In 1915 she was state delegate from Kansas to the Mid-Biennial Council, General Federation of Women's Clubs, at Washington, D. C., when 2,000 women were in attendance and when the White House was opened for their reception by President Woodrow Wilson and the first Mrs. Wilson. Mrs. Rumbaugh was also a delegate to the Eleventh Annual Conference on Child Labor, which opened on May 28, 1915, at San Francisco, California, having received her appointment from Governor Capper of Kansas. She was also state delegate to the Ninth National Biennial of Women's Clubs at Boston in 1908; to the Twelfth Biennial at Chicago in June, 1914; to the Thirteenth Biennial at New York City in June, 1916. Mrs. Rumbaugh also received the appointment as state delegate to the World's Court Congress, held in May, 1916, from Mrs. J. M. Miller, president of the Kansas Federated Clubs. In June, 1915, the Athenaeum Club elected her as delegate to the Biennial Council Meeting of General Federation of Clubs at Portland, Oregon.

Among the conventions of her own state which Mrs. Rumbaugh has attended was that held at Manhattan in May, 1908, when she was the president of the Current Literature Club, which was organized in 1905. She was sent by the City Federation of Fort Scott as their delegate to the nineteenth annual convention held in Wichita in 1914. She was the delegate of the Athenaeum Club at Iola in 1916 and delegate of the Women's Christian Temperance Union at Pittsburg, Kansas, in 1917. She represented her district at the Anti-Saloon League at Topeka in June, 1917. On January 29, 1914, Mrs. Rumbaugh was elected president of the Second District of the Kansas Day Club, which meets annually in Topeka, on Kansas Day. Her latest appointment was received from Governor Arthur Capper as delegate to the Thirteenth National Conference on Child Labor, which opened in Baltimore, Maryland, on March 23, 1917. After the return from that meeting Governor Capper wrote expressing his appreciation of the genuine service she had rendered both the cause and the State of Kansas. One of the most inspiring meetings she ever attended was as a delegate to the tenth biennial convention of the General Federation of Women's Clubs at Cincinnati in May, 1910.

Mrs. Rumbaugh has lived during two great national crisis, the Civil war and the World war, and she was one to assist nobly with Red Cross work. The high food prices caused much hardship among the working people, Mrs. Rumbaugh, as a farmer, particularly noticed the price of prairie hay at $22.00 per ton, corn at $1.60 per bushel, wheat at $3.50 per bushel, potatoes at $3.50 per bushel and other products accordingly.

Thus for a number of years Mrs. Rumbaugh has accepted the opportunities, privileges and responsibilities of commingling in a spirit of co-operation with those organized movements which have put forward the individual and collective welfare, not only of women, but of families and society at large, to a greater degree within the past quarter of a century than has been accomplished in any preceding century. Mrs. Rumbaugh is a woman of broad culture, has traveled extensively, making many trips with her husband. Her home at Fort Scott for years has been a center from which has radiated high ideals, and some of the impulses which make an entire community better and more enlightened.

JAMES HOWARD BEEGLE. While the development of oil properties has not been, perhaps, so spectacular in Kansas as in some other states, it has been a steady, remunerative business since the beginning and the work has enlisted the interest and services of some of the most farsighted men of the state after they have had experiences in the same line in other and older sections. One of these keen business men is James Howard Beegle, oil well contractor and producer and owner of numerous profitable producing wells, in the neighborhood of Neodesha, Kansas, which has been his home since 1903.

James Howard Beegle was born at Bedford, Pennsylvania, December 13, 1867. His parents were Frederick J. and Rebecca (Shoemaker) Beegle. It was the great-great-grandfather, Frederick Beegle, who was born in Germany, who was the first of the name to come to America. He settled in Pennsylvania and there he and his descendants for the most part, became farmers and prospered greatly. Joseph F. Beegle, the grandfather of James Howard Beegle, was born on his father's farm near Bedford, Pennsylvania, in 1815, spent his life there and died in 1897.

Frederick J. Beegle, father of James H., was born on his father's farm near Bedford in 1841 and he also passed his entire life there, dying in 1915, respected by all who knew him. He was a democrat in his political views and for many years was a member of the Order of Odd Fellows. He was reared in the Lutheran faith and was a liberal supporter of the church. He married Rebecca Shoemaker, who was born near Bedford, Pennsylvania in 1843 and died there in 1908. They were the parents of the following children: Daniel C, who is an oil operator, residing at Coalinga, California; James Howard; Emma Laura, who is the wife of J. T. Rogers, who is in the real estate business at Everett, Washington; Louisa Virginia, who is the wife of Elmer Killinger, who is in the employ of the Westinghouse Company at Wilkinsburg, Pennsylvania; Elizabeth Sophia, who is the wife of Scott Fetter, who is a farmer living near Bedford; and Charles, who remains on the old homestead.

James Howard Beegle was reared on his father's farm and followed agricultural pursuits there until he was twenty-five years of age, in the meanwhile obtaining a good common school education. He was less interested in farming or, perhaps was more ambitious than some of his kindred, for he gave heed to the stories told of fortunes being made in the oil fields and finally started out to investigate for himself. Like many others Mr. Beegle probably had many disappointments as he followed the oil business in Ohio, in Indiana and in Wyoming, but he has had a life filled with experiences and has prospered to a much larger extent than he could have hoped to do even with a valuable Bedford County farm. His producing wells east, south and north of Neodesha are substantial properties. He is well known all through the Kansas oil fields and has drilled hundreds of wells here and at other points. He is considered an authority on the oil industry here, knows its past and is frequently consulted as to its probable future.

In April, 1914, Mr. Beegle was married to Mrs. Elsie (Nichols) Cowdery, who is a daughter of H. A. and Lucinda (Milliron) Nichols. Mr. Beegle owns his comfortable residence at No. 202 East Main Street, Neodesha, has other city interests and also has an interest in the old home farm in Bedford County.

In politics Mr. Beegle has always been a democrat. He is serving as commissioner of public utilities at Neodesha. He is a valued and useful member of the Commercial Club. His fraternal connections are with the Knights of Pythias, the Benevolent and Protective Order of Elks, and the Masons. He belongs to Harmony Lodge No. 94, Ancient Free and Accepted Masons; Orient Chapter, No. 72, Royal Arch Masons; Ab-Del-Kader Commandery, No. 27, Knights Templar; Mirza Temple, Mystic Shrine, at Pittsburg, Kansas; Fort Scott Consistory thirty-second degree, and to Wichita Council, Wichita, Kansas.

GEORGE O. LINES. The real estate and insurance business established by George O. Lines in 1911 has gone hand in hand with the development of Neodesha during the past five years, and undoubtedly has contributed as largely during this time toward the advantageous disposal of property and the honorable placing of insurance as any concern of its kind in Wilson County. Mr. Lines is one of Neodesha's foremost and most substantial citizens, and while his name necessarily is associated with one of the early and influential families of the county, his success has been self-attained, and in its usefulness and scope attracts attention to qualities of business integrity, perseverance and ability and high regard for the welfare of the community. He was born on a farm in Wilson County, Kansas, January 3, 1874, and is a son of S. N. and Sarah (Livezey) Lines.

The family of which Mr. Lines is a member originated in Ireland, and the first of the name to come to America located in Connecticut prior to the Revolutionary war. Thomas Lines, the great-grandfather of George O. Lines, was born in 1810, in Indiana, and in addition to being a farmer was a minister of the Baptist Church and preached in that faith in Indiana for approximately fifty years. His death occurred in Henry County, Indiana, in 1901, when he had reached the advanced age of ninety-one years. Elijah Lines, the grandfather of George O. Lines, was born in 1830, in Indiana, and as a young man took up farming as his life work. His career, however, was interrupted by the outbreak of the Civil war, and in 1862 he enlisted in Company C, Fifth Indiana Cavalry. While serving as a dispatch bearer, in Tennessee, in 1863, he received a severe wound, and while he lived long enough to reach home, he could not recover, and soon passed away. Mr. Lines married Elizabeth Beaubout, who was born in Indiana, in 1832, and died near Greencastle, that state, in 1910, and seven children were born to their union: S. N., the father of George O.; Margaret, who is the widow of James Feezer and resides at Richmond, Indiana; Thomas, who is a retired farmer of Mooreland, Indiana; Sarah, who is the widow of William Alexander, a farmer, and resides at Indianapolis; Erastus, who is a farmer of Messick, Indiana; Ella, who is the wife of Charles Sudworth, a Government printer, who has retained his position at Washington, District of Columbia, since his appointment by President Cleveland; and Amanda, who died at the age of thirteen years.

S. N. Lines, father of George O. Lines, was born November 26, 1849, in Henry County, Indiana, and was there reared and educated, became married, and engaged in farming. In 1868 he removed with Mrs. Lines to Brown County, Kansas, where he became a pioneer agriculturist, but remained there only two years, at the end of which time he came to Wilson County, Kansas, and homesteaded 160 acres. This property he cultivated until 1882, when he went to Newcastle and lived there until 1887, when he returned to Wilson County and again took up farming on his homestead. In 1898 he returned to Indiana and engaged in farming at Messick, but has since turned his attention to commercial pursuits, and at this time is one of the leading merchants of that place. He is a republican in politics, and while a resident of Wilson County, Kansas, served in the capacity of justice of the people. Mr. Lines married Miss Sarah Livezey, who was born in 1842, in Indiana, and to this union there were born seven children: W. C., who is engaged in the hardware business at Neodesha; Cordelia, who is the wife of W. J. Welty, employed in the Neodesha postoffice; George O.; Edith, who is the wife of F. E. Howerton, an employe of a refinery at Chanute, Kansas; Thomas O., who is engaged in the hardware business at Neodesha; Gertrude, who is the wife of Oscar Bond, an oil well shooter at Sapulpa, Oklahoma; and Mary, who is the wife of J. R. Heath, engaged in the grocery business at Neodesha.

George O. Lines received a good education, attending the public schools of Wilson County, Kansas, and Newcastle, Indiana, and the State Normal School at Emporia, Kansas, during the summer seasons. While attending the latter he taught during the winter months, and continued as an educator after his own education was completed, his career as an instructor covering a period of ten years, six years of which were in the Neodesha schools. In 1902 he was made assistant postmaster of Neodesha, a position which he held for two years, and when his term was expired embarked in the hardware and implement business, to which he gave his entire attention for seven years. In the meantime he had become interested in realty values at Neodesha, and finally, in 1911, entered the real estate and insurance business here, which has since occupied the greater part of his time and energies. His worth while and reliable qualities as a business man have given him an excellent standing in commercial and financial circles, in addition to having assisted him in the building up of a large and important business enterprise. He is the owner of his own residence, at No. 223 North Fourth Street, and the Postoffice Building, at the corner of North Seventh and Main streets. Politically he is a republican, and he and his family are members of the Methodist Episcopal Church. He belongs to the Anti-Horse Thief Association, and joined the Sons of Veterans at Rest, Kansas.

In 1903, at Neodesha, Mr. Lines was married to Miss Mildred Andrews, who was born in Illinois, but reared at Neodesha. They have two children: Howard, born November 8, 1904; and Lois, born September 22, 1908.

W. C. Lines, the eldest son of S. N. and Sarah (Livezey) Lines, was born February 23, 1869, in Brown County, Kansas, and received his education in the public schools of Wilson County, Kansas; Newcastle, Indiana, and Chanute, Kansas, graduating from the high school at the latter place in 1889. For thirteen years thereafter he was engaged in teaching school in Wilson County; but in June, 1902, gave up teaching to become a railway postal clerk, but resigned his position in October of the same year and became stillman for the Standard Oil Company. In 1904 he turned his attention to the hardware business, and is now assisting his brother, Thomas O., in the conduct of the modern establishment at No. 706 Main Street, Neodesha. He owns his home at No. 702 Illinois Street. Mr. Lines is a republican, and is fraternally affiliated with Neodesha Camp No. 1532, Modern Woodmen of America. On September 14, 1894, in Wilson County, Mr. Lines was married to Miss Rosa Reeves, daughter of Mr. and Mrs. G. A. Reeves, the latter deceased, and the former a retired farmer of Neodesha. To this union there have been born two children: Jessie, born July 26, 1895, and now residing with her parents; and Vida, born January 21, 1897, the wife of Addis O'Hara, of 704 Illinois Street, Neodesha, foreman for the Standard Oil Company.

Thomas O. Lines, the youngest son of S. N. and Sarah (Livezey) Lines, was born January 15, 1880, in Wilson County, and received his education in the public schools of Newcastle, Indiana, and Wilson County, Kansas. He left school at the age of sixteen years and began teaching school in Wilson County, a vocation which he followed for four years. In 1901 he had his first business experience as a clerk in a hardware store at Neodesha, and four years later became associated with his brother, George O., in the management of the hardware business now carried on in Neodesha. He is a republican in politics and resides at No. 620 Indiana Street. Mr. Lines was married April 10, 1901, at Fredonia, Kansas, to Miss Rosa Brown, daughter of Robert and Frances (Keller) Brown, both of whom are deceased, Mr. Brown having been a farmer and sawmill proprietor. Mr. and Mrs. Lines have three children: Marion, born January 26, 1902; Harold, born July 13, 1910; and Robert, born November 8, 1912.

WALTER A. WOODS was elected sheriff of Greenwood County in 1914. That his record during the first term was thoroughly appreciated by his fellow citizens is amply vouched for in the fact that on November 7, 1916, he was re-elected for another term by the significant majority of 1,826. Mr. Woods is as capable in public office as he has been in his private business affairs, and is one of the most thoroughly trusted and popular citizens of the county.

Though most of his life has been spent in Kansas Mr. Woods was born in Barton County, Missouri, July 3, 1874. He is of Scotch-Irish ancestry, and his forefathers came to America in colonial days. His grandfather was Dow Woods, who was born in Ohio in 1809. Though quite old at the time he took part as a soldier in the Civil war, spent his active career as a farmer in Ohio and died at the Soldiers Home at Dayton, Ohio, in 1895.

The father of Sheriff Woods was Hanson L. Woods, an early settler of Greenwood County, Kansas. He was born in Ohio in 1837, grew up in that state, and when a young man removed to Sidney, Iowa. He had previously served four years three months as a Union soldier in the Civil war. He enlisted in 1861 in an Ohio regiment of infantry, and participated in some of the most bitterly fought campaigns and battles of the war. He was in the battles of Shiloh, Stone River, Chickamauga, Missionary Ridge and many other engagements, and subsequently joined Sherman's great army which advanced upon and captured Atlanta and thence marched through Georgia to the sea. From Iowa he moved to Barton County, Missouri, in 1870, followed farming there as he had in Iowa, and in 1879 moved to LaBette County, Kansas. In 1881 he transferred his residence to Greenwood County, and was a farmer there until his death in 1888. He was a loyal republican in politics, served a term as justice of the peace, and was very active in the Presbyterian Church, which he served as an elder. He also belonged to the Masonic fraternity. His first wife was a Miss Fort, but there were no children of that union. For his second wife he married Mary E. Hodges (Goode). She was born in Iowa in 1845, and died in Greenwood County, Kansas, in 1887. The children of their marriage were: Frank, a farmer in Greenwood County; Walter A.; Allie, wife of J. G. Smith, a farmer in Greenwood County; Essie, wife of James Piatt, a farmer at Hamilton, Kansas. The mother of these children by her first marriage had two daughters: Emma, who died at the age of sixteen; and Dallie, who now lives in McPherson County, Kansas.

The first sixteen years of his life Walter A. Woods spent on his father's farm in Barton County, Missouri, and in LaBette and Greenwood counties, Kansas. In the meantime he received his education from the Greenwood county schools and when he left school and the home farm he went to the Northwest, spending four years as a farm hand near Walla Walla, Washington. On returning to Greenwood County he took up farming as an independent vocation, and has proved unusually successful as a stock raiser and as a stock dealer. Though he sold his fine farm in February, 1914, he is still handling stock and is one of the chief cattle dealers of the county.

Mr. Woods has always been an active member of the republican party. When his home was on a farm in Madison Township he served as township trustee. Fraternally he is affiliated with Fidelity Lodge No. 106, Ancient, Free and Accepted Masons, at Eureka, and with Ossiam Lodge No. 58 of the Knights of Pythias in the same place.

Sheriff Woods was married in Greenwood County in 1901 to Miss Mollie Laird, daughter of J. E. and Annie Laird, who reside on their farm in Greenwood County. Mr. and Mrs. Woods have three children, Irene, born May 26, 1905; Mabel, born May 24, 1907; and Edna May, born July 26, 1913.

JOSEPH A. FULLER is clerk of the district court of Greenwood County, with home and offices at Eureka. For a man not yet thirty years of age he has had a great variety of experience, has been a successful teacher, and has also been a participant in the farming and stock raising activities of his home county.

*His Fuller ancestors came to the colonies in the Mayflower. His grandfather was Joseph Allen Fuller, for whom he was named. The grandfather was born in Illinois, and in 1860 came out to Kansas and was one of the early settlers at Emporia. He served as a soldier in the Civil war, being with an Illinois regiment for a time and afterwards joined

Vol. IV—88

a Kansas regiment in assisting to repel Price's invasion. During that campaign he received a gunshot wound, and that hastened his death. He served as deputy sheriff at Emporia, and died there a number of years before his grandson was born.

Joseph Allen Fuller, of Eureka, was born near Madison, Kansas, March 11, 1888. His father, Robert Allen Fuller, who resides on the old farm at Madison, was born in Emporia in 1860, grew up in that town and when a young man came to Greenwood County where he married. He bought a farm near Madison, and has been very successful in diversified agriculture and stock raising. He now has 320 acres. At one time he enjoyed more than a local reputation as a breeder of Shorthorn cattle. He is a republican, an active supporter of the Methodist Church, belongs to the Kansas State Grange, and is a member of the Anti-Horse Thief Association. He married Viola Josephine Huntington, who was born in Illinois in 1861. Their children are: O. K. Fuller, who is district manager with the Cudahy Oil Company and with home at Emporia; the second child died in infancy; Joseph A., is the third in order of birth; John W. is a farmer at Madison; Mildred A., is the wife of Erie Honeyman, a farmer near Madison, Kansas; Frank Alva is a student in the Eureka High School.

Joseph Allen Fuller gained his early education in the rural schools of Greenwood County. His local school was three and a half miles from home and he walked back and forth every day. Afterwards he had the advantages of the Kansas State Normal School at Emporia for two and a half years and with that preparation he became a teacher. He taught ten winter terms in Greenwood County, the alternate summers being spent in farming. He also had some courses in the State Agricultural College at Manhattan. He continued as a farmer until he was elected clerk of the District Court in 1914. In 1916 his previous term was given approval by a large majority, and he is now on his second term. Mr. Fuller owns his home on West Third Street. He is a member of the Methodist Church and a teacher in its Sunday School. In 1911 at Eureka, Kansas, he married Miss C. Shell Swenney, daughter of William and Carrie (Thompson) Swenney. William Swenney resides with Mr. and Mrs. Fuller, being a retired farmer, and her mother is now deceased. Mr. and Mrs. Fuller have one daughter, Ruth Mildred, born November 10, 1913.

CHARLES F. MILLER. In making mention of some of the business firms of Fort Scott the name of C. F. Miller stands as a representative of an established business in the implement, vehicle and automobile line. Mr. Miller has virtually grown up with the business, which through the years has gradually expanded and grown and now occupies an important place among the city's commercial institutions.

Mr. Miller was born and reared in Fort Scott, his parents being among the early settlers, having come to Kansas in 1859. Mr. Miller comes of English, German and Scotch ancestry, and is also a descendant of the historic character of New England, Hannah Dustin. His father, the late Dr. Jonathan G. Miller, was a native of Morgantown, West Virginia, where he was born in 1826. He practiced medicine at Newcastle, Indiana, before coming to Kansas. Doctor Miller invested in land and built the Miller Block at Fort Scott in 1863. This block stands at the corner of Main and Wall streets.

When twenty years of age Charles F. Miller became assistant bookkeeper for the Durkee & Stout

Implement & Grain Company. Afterwards he became bookkeeper and assistant manager for H. L. Page in the same line. Starting at the bottom of the ladder he learned the business in every detail. He soon bought an interest in the concern which became known as the Page & Miller Implement Company. After some years Mr. Page retired and Mr. Miller became sole owner. From 1902 to 1915 he continued to operate the concern, adding automobiles and specializing on the Ford car. In the latter year he bought the implement business of the Fort Scott Grain and Implement Company. His business now occupies a modern display room and office which would do credit to similar establishments in the largest cities of the country. His activities in the sale of automobiles, agricultural implements, harness and seeds extend over the larger part of Bourbon County and require the service of a number of employes. These operations have entitled him to be known as one of the largest dealers in his line in Southeastern Kansas.

Besides being interested in the business life of Fort Scott Mr. Miller has taken a deep interest in the community welfare, especially along the line of improved agriculture. Scientific agriculture is one of his chief hobbies. He was one of the organizers of the Bourbon County Farmers' Institute of which he was secretary for many years. His work has been carried along in connection with the Agricultural College and with other citizens he assisted in organizing and maintaining farmers' institutes and extension schools. He is also devoting a great deal of time and energy to the good roads movement. He helped organize the first Kansas State Good Roads Association and also the Bourbon County Good Roads Association, and was president of the former in 1905 and has been president of the county association. Largely through his efforts a state highway engineer was secured. Although not a politician Mr. Miller served two years in the city council and worked energetically for sound finance, civic improvements and the best sanitary conditions. He is a member of the Chamber of Commerce and co-operates with other citizens in that body toward the promotion of Fort Scott's commercial interests. He belongs to the Masonic Order, including the Scottish Rite Consistory, is also an Elk and for many years has been a trustee of the Presbyterian Church.

Mr. Miller was married at Fort Scott in 1910 to Miss Rosalind I. Bell, daughter of John S. and Nancy (Groves) Bell. Mrs. Miller is a post-graduate of the Fort Scott High School and is well known in club circles. She is especially active as a member of the Pierian Club and as vice president of the Federation of Women's Clubs of this district and president of the City Federation. She is also vice regent of the Daughters of the American Revolution.

HON. WILLIAM M. PRICE, a resident of Kansas for fifteen years, is a successful banker, being now president of the Lyon County State Bank at Emporia, but over the state at large is best known through his services as a member of the State Senate.

Senator Price was elected to the Senate in 1912, his present term expiring January 1, 1917. He represents the senatorial district comprising Greenwood and Lyon counties. He has the distinction of having been the chief supporter of the measure now on the Kansas statute books providing pensions for mothers. The Mothers' Pension Bill as he introduced it in the Senate was drawn up along the lines endorsed by the courts and the various woman's organizations, and though not adopted in that form he ardently championed it

and deserves much credit for the passage of the modified measure as it now stands.

During the legislative session of 1915 Senator Price was chairman of the banking committee and a member of the assessment and taxation committee, public utilities committee, election committee, and cities of second class committee. He is regarded as one of the most progressive leaders in his section of the state.

William M. Price was born in San Antonio, Texas, July 31, 1870, a son of H. F. and Rebecca M. (Chilcutt) Price, and in the paternal line is of Scotch-Welsh ancestors and German on his mother's side. H. F. Price was born in Tennessee in 1824, grew up and married in that state, and in 1850 went to Texas, becoming a pioneer settler on a ranch near the Medina River west of San Antonio. That district was very sparsely settled at that time, since the troublous conditions prevailing during the era from 1836 to the close of the Mexican war had not yet subsided. He continued to reside there until several years after the Civil war, when he removed to San Antonio and was a merchant in that city at the time of his death in 1874. During the war, too old for active service, he served as a shoemaker for the Confederacy. He was a democrat and he and his wife active members of the Methodist Episcopal Church. His wife was born in Tennessee in 1836 and after the death of her husband lived with a daughter at Dallas, Texas, until her death. She was the heroine of an interesting incident during the war. In 1863, when negro slaves who had escaped from their masters were running at large in all sections of Texas, one of the fugitives, a large burly negro, appeared at the Price Ranch in a famished condition and applied for food. The husband was away at the time and Mrs. Price was the only person in the house. Fully realizing her unprotected condition, she hastily devised means of capturing the intruder. Concealing the anxiety which she felt, she invited the man into the kitchen, where she had food prepared, and while he was devouring it, she slipped from the room and secured her husband's shot gun, and then returning aimed the weapon directly at the negro's head, forced him to throw up his hands, and then marched him to the home of a neighbor where her prisoner was turned over to the man of the house. Mrs. Price was presented with the horse that the negro was riding. Of the children of this couple now living mention is made as follows: H. F., who is a merchant at San Diego, California; Elizabeth, wife of H. P. Berry, also at San Diego; Senator Price; J. F., for a number of years was a mining engineer in Mexico, but due to the revolution in that country has recently kept his residence in Texas; Effie, wife of F. Carter, who is connected with a mining company of Oxnard, California.

Senator Price spent his early boyhood in San Antonio, where he attended the public schools, and at the age of sixteen went out to El Paso, Texas, for seven years worked as a clerk, and then engaged in the mercantile business for himself until 1902. Since that year his home has been in Kansas and in August, 1902, he located in Greenwood County where he became actively identified with banking as cashier of the First National Bank, and eleven years later, in 1913, moved to Emporia and organized the Lyon County State Bank, of which he has been president. The other officers are: C. M. Wilson, vice president; and W. T. Ball, cashier. This is one of the strong and flourishing younger banks of that section of Kansas, has a capital of $50,000 and earned surplus of $5,000. The bank is located at 508 Commercial Street.

Senator Price is a democrat, and on that ticket was elected to the Senate in 1912. He is active in the

Commercial Club, and is well known in fraternal circles, being especially prominent in Masonry. He affiliates with El Paso Lodge No. 130, Ancient Free and Accepted Masons; Emporia Chapter No. 12, Royal Arch Masons; Emporia Commandery No. 8, Knight Templars; and Wichita Consistory of the thirty-second degree Scottish Rite. He is also a member of Union Lodge No. 15, Independent Order of Odd Fellows at Emporia, Camp No. 184 of the Ancient Order of United Workmen at Emporia; and Emporia Camp of the Modern Woodmen of America and the local organization of the Loyal Order of Moose.

He is a vestryman in St. Andrew's Episcopal Church and his wife and two sons are also members of that church. In 1898 at Elk City, Montgomery County, Kansas, Senator Price married Miss Chandler Berryman. Her father was the late Dr. G. Q. Berryman, a physician and surgeon of Elk City. They have two children: William Gerard a sophomore in the Emporia High School, and Lloyd Berryman, who is attending the State Normal School at Emporia.

HARRY PRAY STUDY, A. B., A. M. Among the learned callings there is none, perhaps, that demands a greater degree of patience, tact, specialized knowledge, judgment and natural executive ability than that of the educator, and the individual who enters into this important field, selecting it as a calling, is called upon to make many personal sacrifices and to give many of the best years of his life unreservedly to its demands, often without the emoluments that would be attached to an equal amount of labor expended in another direction. However, there are many satisfying rewards which come to the successful teacher, and some of the best of these have come to Prof. Harry Pray Study, superintendent of schools of Neodesha, Kansas, and an educator of high talents, broad knowledge and extensive experience.

Professor Study was born at Fountain City, Indiana, January 7, 1879, and is a son of William H. and Louisa (Cranor) Study. The family originated in Baden, Baden, Germany, and it is thought that the great-grandfather, who was a homesteader into Indiana, was the original emigrant to America, his first residence being in Maryland. In one of these two states, in 1817, was born Isaac Study, the grandfather of Professor Study. He engaged in farming during the greater part of his life, in Indiana, and died at Williamsburg, that state, in 1861. William H. Study was born at or near Williamsburg, Indiana, in 1841, and was there reared and educated. In 1861, at the outbreak of the Civil war, he enlisted for service in the Union army, joining the Eighth Regiment, Indiana Volunteer Infantry, with which organization he served throughout the struggle, participating in all the engagements of his regiment, including Cedar Creek and Pea Ridge, rising to the rank of lieutenant, and being wounded in one of the engagements that took place in front of Vicksburg during the siege of that city. On his return from the war, with an honorable record for courage and fidelity, he was made deputy sheriff of Wayne County, Indiana, and after acting in that capacity for two years was elected sheriff and held that office four years. On his retirement from the shrievalty he turned his attention to mercantile pursuits, and for a number of years was a merchant at Fountain City, Indiana, but in 1884 came to Kansas and secured a ranch 4½ miles southeast of Cedarvale, in Chautauqua County. He lived on that property and in the vicinity for fourteen years, when, upon his election to the office of probate judge of Chautauqua County he took up his residence at Sedan, Kansas, and when his four-

year term was completed remained in the office and assisted in the duties of his successor. Judge Study then retired from active life, but was recalled to public affairs as police judge of Sedan, and was acting in that capacity at the time of his death, which occurred July 7, 1911. He was a republican in politics, a member of the Methodist Episcopal Church, and belonged to the Independent Order of Odd Fellows. In all the relations of life he was a man who conducted his dealings in a strictly honorable manner, and in each community in which he resided gained and retained the confidence, respect and friendship of his fellow-men. Judge Study married Miss Louisa Cranor, who was born November 6, 1843, in Indiana, and died January 1, 1916, at Sedan, Kansas, and they became the parents of five children: Bert C., who was a traveling salesman and died at Denver, Colorado, in 1914; Clarence M., who is a scaler in lumber camps and resides at Fullerton, Louisiana; Lorena, who died at the age of five years; Kizzie, who died when four years of age; and Harry Pray.

Harry P. Study received his early education in the rural schools of Chautauqua County, Kansas, and was graduated from the Cedar Vale High School in 1897. Following this he entered Baker University, Baldwin, Kansas, from which he was graduated with the class of 1903, and the degree of Bachelor of Arts, and while attending that institution joined the exclusive Delta Tau Delta fraternity, of which he is still a member. On leaving the university Professor Study became principal of the Eureka (Kansas) High School, a position which he filled during the school year of 1903-4, and then went, in the same capacity, to Ottawa, Kansas, where he remained during the school years of 1904-5 and 1905-6. In order to further his studies he then attended Boston University, following which he took a European trip, visiting England, Germany and France, in 1907-8, and attending lectures in all these countries. In 1911 he received the degree of Master of Art from Boston University. In 1908, on his return to the United States, Professor Study became head of the history department of Tome School for Boys, at Port Deposit, Maryland, where he also discharged the duties of dormitory master, and remained for two years. In the year 1910-11 he was head of the history department of the Horace Mann School, New York City, and then returned to Sedan to look after his father, who had had an attack of illness. There Professor Study was superintendent of schools for the year 1911-12, and in the latter year came to Neodesha to act in a like capacity, now having under his superintendency four schools, forty teachers and 1,250 scholars. From the start Professor Study has sought to better conditions in every way and to advance the educational standard, and in both these directions has been successful. A thorough student of the science of education and possessed of a natural instinct for child psychology, he has made his schools living, growing organisms responsive to the best in teacher and pupil. Professor Study is a member of the Kansas State Teachers' Association and the Schoolmasters' Club. As a fraternalist he holds membership in Little Bear Lodge, Ancient Free and Accepted Masons; Neodesha Chapter, Royal Arch Masons; and Ab-Del-Kader Commandery, Knights Templar, of Fredonia. His residence is at No. 806 Iowa Street.

In 1911 Professor Study was married, at Meadville, Pennsylvania, to Miss Clara Louise Lord, daughter of L. L. and Mary (Welch) Lord, who live at No. 730 North Main Street, Meadville, Mr. Lord being engaged in the plumbing contracting business. Professor and Mrs. Study have one child, Mary Lord, born November 2, 1916.

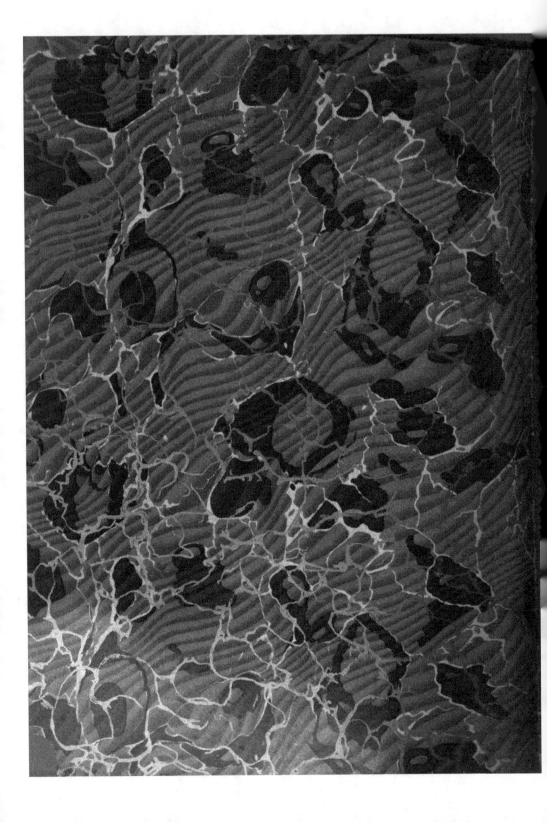